# U.S. ADMINISTRATIVE LAW:
# A CASEBOOK

Third Edition

Jud Mathews

# U.S. Administrative Law: A Casebook

*About the cover image:*

*The cover depicts a battery for hatching whitefish and was included in a Report of the Commissioner of the United States Commission of Fish and Fisheries from 1896/1897. Whitefish figure prominently in the case* United States v. Nova Scotia Food Products Corporation, *which concerns a challenge to a regulation of the Food and Drug Administration.*

*This public domain image comes from the Freshwater and Marine Image Bank at the University of Washington.*

# INTRODUCTION

Welcome to the other 99% of law!

These were the words, more or less, with which my administrative law professor opened his course many years ago. His point: although most of law school is spent on cases and statutes, most of the law people encounter out in the world is administrative law. By almost any measure you choose—raw numbers of rules, impact on the economy, volume of text—the amount of law made by federal agencies in a given year, in the form of regulations, far outstrips the legislative output of Congress. And the number of individual cases decided in a given year by agencies—immigration proceedings; social security disability determinations; permit applications for discharges into federal wetlands, et cetera, et cetera—dwarfs the number of cases decided by all federal courts.

This is a class about how administrative law is made. It is an introduction to the constitutional, statutory and judge-made rules governing what agencies may do, the procedures they must follow, and how they can be held to account.

If you have just enrolled in administrative law and are cracking open this book for the first time, you might be resigning yourself to a course that is a little . . . dry. Certainly the title "Administrative Law" does not set the heart aflutter. And it is true, as you will see, that some of the cases involve technical legal questions and rather bloodless facts. But at the same time, administrative law is as dynamic, important, and intellectually engaging a field of law as you will find.

A lot is at stake in administrative law. The decisions that agencies make affect all of us profoundly. And administrative law has become the site for some of the fiercest and most momentous conflicts in American law today. The centrality of agencies to governance in the United States, long accepted by mainstream administrative law doctrine, is increasingly coming in for challenge from U.S. courts, including the U.S. Supreme Court. Behind the narrower doctrinal questions that embody this challenge loom deeper questions about how to interpret the Constitution and statutes, about the proper role for government in America, and even about the nature of law itself. The materials in this book should help you to understand the contours of these debates and form your own judgments.

There are many different administrative law casebooks on the market. Part of the reason behind this, I think, is that administrative law is a hard subject to throw your arms around, and different law professors have tried lots of different strategies. There are different views about what even counts as administrative law, and how much emphasis different topics deserve.

My basic strategy is (1) to include only a reasonable number of cases, the ones I think of as being really important or revealing, (2) to give you fairly lengthy edits of them, and (3) to keep the notes to a bare minimum. I have heard it suggested that you could teach someone the essentials of administrative law using twelve cases. I'm not going that far—don't get excited—but I do think that, for a number of the core concepts, taking a deep dive into a few central cases is worth more than shallow swims in each of ten, all pointing in different directions. My own teaching strategy is to use the facts of some other cases as the basis for problems that we can discuss in class.

I want the book to reflect the present state of the law, of course, but I also include some "oldies but goodies" from the early years of American administrative law that many contemporary casebooks cut. I do this for a couple of reasons. One, I think some of the old cases are great for laying out core concepts. Two, as described above, we live in an age where much of contemporary doctrine is up for challenge. Many of the challenges are rooted in the past: in arguments about historical practices and precedents. Students whose knowledge of caselaw only goes back a couple of decades will be ill-equipped to make or parry arguments rooted in older legal developments.

Inevitably, this book omits some topics that some other texts will cover. Three come to mind. First, this book is exclusively focused on federal administrative law. (In this respect, it is similar to most other books on the market.) The states have administrative law too, and most states' statutes are modeled on the federal Administrative Procedure Act, so many of the doctrines and principles found in this book have some application to the states. Second, this book contains nothing on the Freedom of Information Act, an amendment to the Administrative Procedure Act creating a right to information possessed by agencies (subject to exceptions). Third, this book omits materials on the government's liability to citizens for torts committed by agencies, under the Federal Tort Claims Act. If you are looking to get information or money damages out of Uncle Sam, you will need to look elsewhere for guidance.

Another feature or bug of this book, depending on your point of view: it is emphatically a *case*book. Almost everything between the covers is a judicial opinion. You're probably heard the joke about the man who looked for his keys under the streetlight—not because that was where he lost them, but because that's where the light was better. (It's a funnier joke when someone other than a law professor tells it.) In law school courses, we sometimes tend to look for the law in cases, because that is where we have the most experience looking. But there is lots of "law" in administrative law that never finds its way into a courtroom. For instance: over the past four decades, a series of Executive Orders have required agencies to demonstrate to the White House's satisfaction that the benefits of significant regulations justify the costs before publishing proposed and final rules. This presidential rulemaking review can profoundly shape agency regulatory behavior, but in ways that evade judicial review almost entirely. More generally, it is worth noting that most agency actions are never challenged in court. Those actions that *are* challenged in court are, by definition, outliers. Learning administrative law through an exclusive diet of cases could yield a distorted sense of what "normal" administrative law is like.

Still, there are good reasons to focus heavily on caselaw, as this book does. Lawyers do many different things, but perhaps the most distinctively lawyerly work, at least in the U.S., is the work we do with cases: making sense of them, synthesizing them into a doctrinal framework, and building arguments that are persuasive within the terms of that framework. This casebook focuses on that kind of work.

For the sake of readability, I have cut footnotes and citations freely, except when they support quotations or make connections within caselaw that I think are noteworthy; all other textual omissions are marked * * *. My research assistants provided invaluable help putting this book together: thanks to Abigail Aumen, James Burns, Yong Cui, Bhargavi Kannan, and Derek Savko.

I'll stop here. I hope you enjoy your course in administrative law.

Jud Mathews

# CHAPTER 1: AGENCIES AND THE CONSTITUTION

## A. Agencies and the Legislative Power

Article I of the Constitution is Article I of the Constitution for a reason: as far as the Framers were concerned, the legislative branch was, in many respects, the most important organ of a republic. But one of the realities that all contemporary states face is that the demand for rules in a modern industrialized society far outstrips the supply that a single legislative body can produce, at least if we expect its members to consider their content carefully and deliberately. In the United States, the basic solution is that the legislative branch enlists administrative agencies to come up with some of the rules. And so they do, chiefly in the form of regulations that have the effect of law. But this state of affairs raises some questions, two of which we address in this section of the course. The first is, if the Constitution vests the legislative power in Congress, what limits are there on Congress's ability to delegate power to agencies to come up with rules that function like laws? The second is, if Congress is going to give some power to agencies, can Congress innovate new procedures to keep better tabs on what agencies do with it?

### 1. The Non-delegation Doctrine

Article I, section 1 of the Constitution provides that "the legislative powers herein granted shall be vested in a Congress of the United States, which shall consist of a Senate and House of Representatives." Article I goes on to specify the process Congress must follow when it uses the legislative power, and also the subjects on which Congress is entitled to legislate.

The core idea behind the "Nondelegation Doctrine" is that the power to legislate belongs to Congress, and Congress cannot give it to others: cannot, in other words, *delegate* legislative powers. That sounds good, but what does it really mean? We would probably all agree that Congress couldn't declare that the President of the United States, or for that matter, the Sacramento City Council or the executive board of Alpha Gamma Rho fraternity shall henceforth have the power to enact federal statutes. But what about when Congress grants a federal agency the power to issue regulations that      set maximum permissible exposure levels for toxic chemicals and have the force of law? As we will see in this course, Congress grants agencies powers like that all the time, and the courts have sustained these grants of power. There are clear reasons for Congress to do so: the demand for legal norms in a complex, industrialized society like ours far outstrips Congress's capacity to supply them by itself. But how do we reconcile this reality with the constitutional commitment of the lawmaking power to Congress? What are the limits to how Congress can empower other actors and institutions to make norms with the force of law?

1 In this section, we will see how the Supreme Court has answered these questions.
2 Nearly a century ago, Chief Justice William Howard Taft declared that Congress
3 must "lay down by legislative act an intelligible principle to which the person or
4 body authorized to [act] is directed to conform." Applying this "intelligible
5 principle test," the Supreme Court has blessed extensive delegations of power to
6 agencies. But in 2019, only a plurality of the Court endorsed this approach in
7 *United States v. Gundy*. Are we standing on the verge of a doctrinal revolution?

8 This section also explores the question of **subdelegation**: under what
9 circumstances can agency officials vested with decision-making authority by
10 Congress pass that power on to others?

11

## U.S. Constitution, Article I, section 1

13 All legislative powers herein granted shall be vested in a Congress of the United
14 States, which shall consist of a Senate and House of Representatives.

15

## Panama Refining Co. v. Ryan

17 293 U.S. 388 (1935)

18 January 7, 1935

19 MR. CHIEF JUSTICE HUGHES delivered the opinion of the Court.

20 On July 11, 1933, the President, by Executive Order, prohibited "the transportation
21 in interstate and foreign commerce of petroleum and the products thereof
22 produced or withdrawn from storage in excess of the amount permitted to be
23 produced or withdrawn from storage by any State law or valid regulation or order
24 prescribed thereunder, by any board, commission, officer, or other duly authorized
25 agency of a State."

26 This action was based on § 9(c) of title 1 of the National Industrial Recovery Act of
27 June 16, 1933, 48 Stat. 195, 200, 15 U.S.C. Tit. 1, § 709(c). That section provides:

28 "Sec. 9 (c) The President is authorized to prohibit the transportation in
29 interstate and foreign commerce of petroleum and the products thereof
30 produced or withdrawn from storage in excess of the amount permitted to
31 be produced or withdrawn from storage by any State law or valid regulation
32 or order prescribed thereunder, by any board, commission, officer, or other
33 duly authorized agency of a State. Any violation of any order of the
34 President issued under the provisions of this subsection shall be punishable
35 by fine of not to exceed $1,000, or imprisonment for not to exceed six
36 months, or both."

37 * * *

2

1    * * * Section 9(c) is assailed upon the ground that it is an unconstitutional
2    delegation of legislative power. The section purports to authorize the President to
3    pass a prohibitory law. * * *

4    Assuming for the present purpose, without deciding, that the Congress has power
5    to interdict the transportation of that excess in interstate and foreign commerce,
6    the question whether that transportation shall be prohibited by law is obviously
7    one of legislative policy. Accordingly, we look to the statute to see whether the
8    Congress has declared a policy with respect to that subject; whether the Congress
9    has set up a standard for the President's action; whether the Congress has required
10   any finding by the President in the exercise of the authority to enact the
11   prohibition.

12   Section 9(c) is brief and unambiguous. It does not attempt to control the
13   production of petroleum and petroleum products within a state. It does not seek to
14   lay down rules for the guidance of state Legislatures or state officers. It leaves to
15   the states and to their constituted authorities the determination of what
16   production shall be permitted. It does not qualify the President's authority by
17   reference to the basis or extent of the state's limitation of production. Section 9(c)
18   does not state whether or in what circumstances or under what conditions the
19   President is to prohibit the transportation of the amount of petroleum or
20   petroleum products produced in excess of the state's permission. It establishes no
21   criteria to govern the President's course. It does not require any finding by the
22   President as a condition of his action. The Congress in § 9(c) thus declares no policy
23   as to the transportation of the excess production. So far as this section is
24   concerned, it gives to the President an unlimited authority to determine the policy
25   and to lay down the prohibition, or not to lay it down, as he may see fit. And
26   disobedience to his order is made a crime punishable by fine and imprisonment.

27                                        * * *

28   * * * The question whether such a delegation of legislative power is permitted by
29   the Constitution is not answered by the argument that it should be assumed that
30   the President has acted, and will act, for what he believes to be the public good.
31   The point is not one of motives, but of constitutional authority, for which the best
32   of motives is not a substitute. While the present controversy relates to a delegation
33   to the President, the basic question has a much wider application. If the Congress
34   can make a grant of legislative authority of the sort attempted by § 9(c), we find
35   nothing in the Constitution which restricts the Congress to the selection of the
36   President as grantee. The Congress may vest the power in the officer of its choice
37   or in a board or commission such as it may select or create for the purpose. * * *
38   The Constitution provides that

39       "All legislative Powers herein granted shall be vested in a Congress of the
40       United States, which shall consist of a Senate and House of
41       Representatives."

1    Article I, § 1. And the Congress is empowered "To make all Laws which shall be
2    necessary and proper for carrying into Execution" its general powers. Article I, § 8,
3    par. 18. The Congress manifestly is not permitted to abdicate or to transfer to
4    others the essential legislative functions with which it is thus vested. * * *

5    We cannot regard the President as immune from the application of these
6    constitutional principles. When the President is invested with legislative authority
7    as the delegate of Congress in carrying out a declared policy, he necessarily acts
8    under the constitutional restriction applicable to such a delegation.

9    We see no escape from the conclusion that the Executive Orders of July 11, 1933,
10    and July 14, 1933, and the regulations issued by the Secretary of the Interior
11    thereunder, are without constitutional authority.

12                                      * * *

13    MR. JUSTICE CARDOZO, dissenting.

14                                       * * *

15    I am unable to assent to the conclusion that § 9(c) of the National Recovery Act, a
16    section delegating to the President a very different power from any that is involved
17    in the regulation of production or in the promulgation of a code, is to be nullified
18    upon the ground that his discretion is too broad or for any other reason. * * *

19                                       * * *

20    * * * If we look to the whole structure of the statute, the test is plainly this, that the
21    President is to forbid the transportation of the oil when he believes, in the light of
22    the conditions of the industry as disclosed from time to time, that the prohibition
23    will tend to effectuate the declared policies of the act—not merely his own
24    conception of its policies, undirected by any extrinsic guide, but the policies
25    announced by § 1 in the forefront of the statute as an index to the meaning of
26    everything that follows.[1]

---

[1] "Section 1. . . . It is hereby declared to be the policy of Congress to remove obstructions to the free flow of interstate and foreign commerce which tend to diminish the amount thereof; and to provide for the general welfare by promoting the organization of industry for the purpose of cooperative action among trade groups, to induce and maintain united action of labor and management under adequate governmental sanctions and supervision, to eliminate unfair competitive practices, to promote the fullest possible utilization of the present productive capacity of industries, to avoid undue restriction of production (except as may be temporarily required), to increase the consumption of industrial and agricultural products by increasing purchasing power, to reduce and relieve unemployment, to improve standards of labor, and otherwise to rehabilitate industry and to conserve natural resources."

Oil produced or transported in excess of a statutory quota is known in the industry as "hot oil," and the record is replete with evidence as to the effect of such production and transportation upon the economic situation and upon national recovery. A declared policy of Congress in the adoption of the act is "to eliminate unfair competitive practices." Beyond question, an unfair competitive practice exists when "hot oil" is transported in interstate commerce with the result that law-abiding dealers must compete with lawbreakers. Here is one of the standards set up in the act to guide the President's discretion. Another declared policy of Congress is "to conserve natural resources." Beyond question, the disregard of statutory quotas is wasting the oil fields in Texas and other states and putting in jeopardy of exhaustion one of the treasures of the nation. All this is developed in the record and in the arguments of counsel for the government with a wealth of illustration. * * *

* * *

I am persuaded that a reference, express or implied, to the policy of Congress as declared in § 1, is a sufficient definition of a standard to make the statute valid. Discretion is not unconfined and vagrant. It is canalized within banks that keep it from overflowing. * * *

## A. L. A. Schechter Poultry Corp. v. United States

295 U.S. 495 (1935)

May 27, 1935

MR. CHIEF JUSTICE HUGHES delivered the opinion of the Court.

Petitioners were convicted in the District Court of the United States for the Eastern District of New York on eighteen count of an indictment charging violations of what is known as the "Live Poultry Code," and on an additional count for conspiracy to commit such violations. By demurrer to the indictment and appropriate motions on the trial, the defendants contended (1) that the Code had been adopted pursuant to an unconstitutional delegation by Congress of legislative power * * *.

* * *

The "Live Poultry Code" was promulgated under § 3 of the National Industrial Recovery Act. That section—the pertinent provisions of which are set forth in the margin—authorizes the President to approve "codes of fair competition." Such a code may be approved for a trade or industry, upon application by one or more

---

* * *

trade or industrial associations or groups, if the President finds (1) that such associations or groups "impose no inequitable restrictions on admission to membership therein and are truly representative," and (2) that such codes are not designed "to promote monopolies or to eliminate or oppress small enterprises and will not operate to discriminate against them, and will tend to effectuate the policy" of Title I of the Act. Such codes "shall not permit monopolies or monopolistic practices." As a condition of his approval, the President may "impose such conditions (including requirements for the making of reports and the keeping of accounts) for the protection of consumers, competitors, employees, and others, and in furtherance of the public interest, and may provide such exceptions to and exemptions from the provisions of such code, as the President in his discretion deems necessary to effectuate the policy herein declared." Where such a code has not been approved, the President may prescribe one, either on his own motion or on complaint. Violation of any provision of a code (so approved or prescribed) "in any transaction in or affecting interstate or foreign commerce" is made a misdemeanor punishable by a fine of not more than $500 for each offense, and each day the violation continues is to be deemed a separate offense.

\* \* \*

Under § 3, whatever "may tend to effectuate" these general purposes may be included in the "codes of fair competition." We think the conclusion is inescapable that the authority sought to be conferred by § 3 was not merely to deal with "unfair competitive practices" which offend against existing law, and could be the subject of judicial condemnation without further legislation, or to create administrative machinery for the application of established principles of law to particular instances of violation. Rather, the purpose is clearly disclosed to authorize new and controlling prohibitions through codes of laws which would embrace what the formulators would propose, and what the President would approve, or prescribe, as wise and beneficient measures for the government of trades and industries in order to bring about their rehabilitation, correction and development, according to the general declaration of policy in section one. Codes of laws of this sort are styled "codes of fair competition." \* \* \*

\* \* \*

The Government urges that the codes will "consist of rules of competition deemed fair for each industry by representative members of that industry—by the persons most vitally concerned and most familiar with its problems." Instances are cited in which Congress has availed itself of such assistance; as, e.g., in the exercise of its authority over the public domain with respect to the recognition of local customs or rules of miners as to mining claims, or, in matters of a more or less technical nature, as in designating the standard height of drawbar. But would it be seriously contended that Congress could delegate its legislative authority to trade or industrial associations or groups so as to empower them to enact the laws they deem to be wise and beneficent for the rehabilitation and expansion of their trade or industries? Could trade or industrial associations or groups be constituted

6

legislative bodies for that purpose because such associations or groups are familiar with the problems of their enterprises? And, could an effort of that sort be made valid by such a preface of generalities as to permissible aims as we find in section 1 of title I? The answer is obvious. Such a delegation of legislative power is unknown to our law, and is utterly inconsistent with the constitutional prerogatives and duties of Congress.

The question, then, turns upon the authority which § 3 of the Recovery Act vests in the President to approve or prescribe. If the codes have standing as penal statutes, this must be due to the effect of the executive action. But Congress cannot delegate legislative power to the President to exercise an unfettered discretion to make whatever laws he thinks may be needed or advisable for the rehabilitation and expansion of trade or industry.

Accordingly, we turn to the Recovery Act to ascertain what limits have been set to the exercise of the President's discretion. * * * [T]he President is required to find that the code is not "designed to promote monopolies or to eliminate or oppress small enterprises, and will not operate to discriminate against them." And to this is added a proviso that the code "shall not permit monopolies or monopolistic practices." But these restrictions leave virtually untouched the field of policy envisaged by section one, and, in that wide field of legislative possibilities, the proponents of a code, refraining from monopolistic designs, may roam at will, and the President may approve or disapprove their proposals as he may see fit. That is the precise effect of the further finding that the President is to make—that the code "will tend to effectuate the policy of this title." While this is called a finding, it is really but a statement of an opinion as to the general effect upon the promotion of trade or industry of a scheme of laws. These are the only findings which Congress has made essential in order to put into operation a legislative code having the aims described in the "Declaration of Policy."

\* \* \*

To summarize and conclude upon this point: Section 3 of the Recovery Act is without precedent. It supplies no standards for any trade, industry or activity. It does not undertake to prescribe rules of conduct to be applied to particular states of fact determined by appropriate administrative procedure. Instead of prescribing rules of conduct, it authorizes the making of codes to prescribe them. For that legislative undertaking, § 3 sets up no standards, aside from the statement of the general aims of rehabilitation, correction and expansion described in section one. In view of the scope of that broad declaration, and of the nature of the few restrictions that are imposed, the discretion of the President in approving or prescribing codes, and thus enacting laws for the government of trade and industry throughout the country, is virtually unfettered. We think that the code-making authority this conferred is an unconstitutional delegation of legislative power.

\* \* \*

MR. JUSTICE CARDOZO, concurring.

The delegated power of legislation which has found expression in this code is not canalized within banks that keep it from overflowing. It is unconfined and vagrant, if I may borrow my own words in an earlier opinion. *Panama Refining Co. v. Ryan.*

\* \* \*

## Mistretta v. United States

488 U.S. 361 (1989)

January 18, 1989

JUSTICE BLACKMUN delivered the opinion of the Court.

\* \* \*

I

*A. Background*

For almost a century, the Federal Government employed in criminal cases a system of indeterminate sentencing. Statutes specified the penalties for crimes, but nearly always gave the sentencing judge wide discretion to decide whether the offender should be incarcerated and for how long, whether restraint, such as probation, should be imposed instead of imprisonment or fine. This indeterminate sentencing system was supplemented by the utilization of parole, by which an offender was returned to society under the "guidance and control" of a parole officer.

\* \* \*

Historically, federal sentencing—the function of determining the scope and extent of punishment—never has been thought to be assigned by the Constitution to the exclusive jurisdiction of any one of the three Branches of Government. \* \* \* Congress early abandoned fixed sentence rigidity, however, and put in place a system of ranges within which the sentencer could choose the precise punishment. Congress delegated almost unfettered discretion to the sentencing judge to determine what the sentence should be within the customarily wide range so selected. This broad discretion was further enhanced by the power later granted the judge to suspend the sentence and by the resulting growth of an elaborate probation system. Also, with the advent of parole, Congress moved toward a "three-way sharing" of sentencing responsibility by granting corrections personnel in the Executive Branch the discretion to release a prisoner before the expiration of the sentence imposed by the judge. Thus, under the indeterminate sentence system, Congress defined the maximum, the judge imposed a sentence within the statutory range (which he usually could replace with probation), and the Executive Branch's parole official eventually determined the actual duration of imprisonment.

1 * * *

2 * * * Fundamental and widespread dissatisfaction with the uncertainties and the
3 disparities continued to be expressed. Congress had wrestled with the problem for
4 more than a decade when, in 1984, it enacted the sweeping reforms that are at issue
5 here.

6 * * *

7 *B. The Act*

8 The Act, as adopted, revises the old sentencing process in several ways:

9 1. It rejects imprisonment as a means of promoting rehabilitation, 28 U.S.C. §
10 994(k), and it states that punishment should serve retributive, educational,
11 deterrent, and incapacitative goals, 18 U.S.C. § 3553(a)(2).

12 2. It consolidates the power that had been exercised by the sentencing judge and
13 the Parole Commission to decide what punishment an offender should suffer. This
14 is done by creating the United States Sentencing Commission, directing that
15 Commission to devise guidelines to be used for sentencing, and prospectively
16 abolishing the Parole Commission. 28 U.S.C. §§ 991, 994, and 995(a)(1).

17 3. It makes all sentences basically determinate. A prisoner is to be released at the
18 completion of his sentence reduced only by any credit earned by good behavior
19 while in custody. 18 U.S.C. §§ 3624(a) and (b).

20 4. It makes the Sentencing Commission's guidelines binding on the courts,
21 although it preserves for the judge the discretion to depart from the guideline
22 applicable to a particular case if the judge finds an aggravating or mitigating factor
23 present that the Commission did not adequately consider when formulating
24 guidelines. §§ 3553(a) and (b). The Act also requires the court to state its reasons
25 for the sentence imposed, and to give "the specific reason" for imposing a sentence
26 different from that described in the guideline. § 3553(c).

27 * * *

28 *C. The Sentencing Commission*

29 The Commission is established "as an independent commission in the judicial
30 branch of the United States." § 991(a). It has seven voting members (one of whom
31 is the Chairman) appointed by the President "by and with the advice and consent
32 of the Senate."

33 "At least three of the members shall be Federal judges selected after considering a
34 list of six judges recommended to the President by the Judicial Conference of the
35 United States."

36 *Ibid.* No more than four members of the Commission shall be members of the same
37 political party. The Attorney General, or his designee, is an *ex officio* nonvoting

member. The Chairman and other members of the Commission are subject to removal by the President "only for neglect of duty or malfeasance in office or for other good cause shown." *Ibid.* Except for initial staggering of terms, a voting member serves for six years, and may not serve more than two full terms.

\* \* \*

## II. *This Litigation*

On December 10, 1987, John M. Mistretta (petitioner) and another were indicted in the United States District Court for the Western District of Missouri on three counts centering in a cocaine sale. Mistretta moved to have the promulgated Guidelines ruled unconstitutional on the grounds that the Sentencing Commission was constituted in violation of the established doctrine of separation of powers, and that Congress delegated excessive authority to the Commission to structure the Guidelines. As has been noted, the District Court was not persuaded by these contentions.

\* \* \*

## III. *Delegation of Power*

Petitioner argues that, in delegating the power to promulgate sentencing guidelines for every federal criminal offense to an independent Sentencing Commission, Congress has granted the Commission excessive legislative discretion in violation of the constitutionally based nondelegation doctrine. We do not agree.

The nondelegation doctrine is rooted in the principle of separation of powers that underlies our tripartite system of Government. The Constitution provides that "[a]ll legislative Powers herein granted shall be vested in a Congress of the United States," U.S. Const., Art. I, § 1, and we long have insisted that "the integrity and maintenance of the system of government ordained by the Constitution" mandate that Congress generally cannot delegate its legislative power to another Branch. We also have recognized, however, that the separation of powers principle, and the nondelegation doctrine in particular, do not prevent Congress from obtaining the assistance of its coordinate Branches. In a passage now enshrined in our jurisprudence, Chief Justice Taft, writing for the Court, explained our approach to such cooperative ventures: "In determining what [Congress] may do in seeking assistance from another branch, the extent and character of that assistance must be fixed according to common sense and the inherent necessities of the government coordination." *J. W. Hampton, Jr., & Co. v. United States*, 276 U.S. 394, 406 (1928). So long as Congress "shall lay down by legislative act an intelligible principle to which the person or body authorized to [exercise the delegated authority] is directed to conform, such legislative action is not a forbidden delegation of legislative power."

10

1   Applying this "intelligible principle" test to congressional delegations, our
2   jurisprudence has been driven by a practical understanding that, in our
3   increasingly complex society, replete with ever-changing and more technical
4   problems, Congress simply cannot do its job absent an ability to delegate power
5   under broad general directives. * * * Accordingly, this Court has deemed it
6   "constitutionally sufficient if Congress clearly delineates the general policy, the
7   public agency which is to apply it, and the boundaries of this delegated authority."
8   *American Power & Light Co. v. SEC,* 329 U.S. 90, 105 (1946). Until 1935, this Court
9   never struck down a challenged statute on delegation grounds.

10  In light of our approval of these broad delegations, we harbor no doubt that
11  Congress' delegation of authority to the Sentencing Commission is sufficiently
12  specific and detailed to meet constitutional requirements. Congress charged the
13  Commission with three goals: to "assure the meeting of the purposes of sentencing
14  as set forth" in the Act; to "provide certainty and fairness in meeting the purposes
15  of sentencing, avoiding unwarranted sentencing disparities among defendants
16  with similar records ... while maintaining sufficient flexibility to permit
17  individualized sentences," where appropriate; and to "reflect, to the extent
18  practicable, advancement in knowledge of human behavior as it relates to the
19  criminal justice process." 28 U.S.C. § 991(b)(1). Congress further specified four
20  "purposes" of sentencing that the Commission must pursue in carrying out its
21  mandate: "to reflect the seriousness of the offense, to promote respect for the law,
22  and to provide just punishment for the offense"; "to afford adequate deterrence to
23  criminal conduct"; "to protect the public from further crimes of the defendant";
24  and "to provide the defendant with needed . . . correctional treatment." 18 U.S.C. §
25  3553(a)(2).

26  In addition, Congress prescribed the specific tool—the guidelines system—for the
27  Commission to use in regulating sentencing. More particularly, Congress directed
28  the Commission to develop a system of "sentencing ranges" applicable "for each
29  category of offense involving each category of defendant." 28 U.S.C. § 994(b).
30  Congress instructed the Commission that these sentencing ranges must be
31  consistent with pertinent provisions of Title 18 of the United States Code, and
32  could not include sentences in excess of the statutory maxima. Congress also
33  required that, for sentences of imprisonment, "the maximum of the range
34  established for such a term shall not exceed the minimum of that range by more
35  than the greater of 25 percent or 6 months, except that, if the minimum term of
36  the range is 30 years or more, the maximum may be life imprisonment." §
37  994(b)(2). * * * To guide the Commission in its formulation of offense categories,
38  Congress directed it to consider seven factors: the grade of the offense; the
39  aggravating and mitigating circumstances of the crime; the nature and degree of
40  the harm caused by the crime; the community view of the gravity of the offense;
41  the public concern generated by the crime; the deterrent effect that a particular
42  sentence may have on others; and the current incidence of the offense. Congress
43  set forth 11 factors for the Commission to consider in establishing categories of
44  defendants. These include the offender's age, education, vocational skills, mental

1 and emotional condition, physical condition (including drug dependence),
2 previous employment record, family ties and responsibilities, community ties, role
3 in the offense, criminal history, and degree of dependence upon crime for a
4 livelihood. § 994(d)(1)-(11). Congress also prohibited the Commission from
5 considering the "race, sex, national origin, creed, and socioeconomic status of
6 offenders," § 994(d), and instructed that the guidelines should reflect the "general
7 inappropriateness" of considering certain other factors, such as current
8 unemployment, that might serve as proxies for forbidden factors. In addition to
9 these overarching constraints, Congress provided even more detailed guidance to
10 the Commission about categories of offenses and offender characteristics. * * *

11                                          * * *

12 * * * In other words, although Congress granted the Commission substantial
13 discretion in formulating guidelines, in actuality it legislated a full hierarchy of
14 punishment—from near maximum imprisonment, to substantial imprisonment, to
15 some imprisonment, to alternatives—and stipulated the most important offense
16 and offender characteristics to place defendants within these categories.

17 We cannot dispute petitioner's contention that the Commission enjoys significant
18 discretion in formulating guidelines. * * * But our cases do not at all suggest that
19 delegations of this type may not carry with them the need to exercise judgment on
20 matters of policy. In *Yakus v. United States,* 321 U.S. 414, 420 (1944), the Court
21 upheld a delegation to the Price Administrator to fix commodity prices that "in his
22 judgment will be generally fair and equitable and will effectuate the purposes of
23 this Act" to stabilize prices and avert speculation. In *National Broadcasting Co. v.*
24 *United States,* 319 U.S. 190 (1943), we upheld a delegation to the Federal
25 Communications Commission granting it the authority to promulgate regulations
26 in accordance with its view of the "public interest." In *Yakus,* the Court laid down
27 the applicable principle:

28          "It is no objection that the determination of facts and the inferences to be
29          drawn from them in the light of the statutory standards and declaration of
30          policy call for the exercise of judgment, and for the formulation of
31          subsidiary administrative policy within the prescribed statutory
32          framework. . . .

33          ". . . Only if we could say that there is an absence of standards for the
34          guidance of the Administrator's action, so that it would be impossible in a
35          proper proceeding to ascertain whether the will of Congress has been
36          obeyed, would we be justified in overriding its choice of means for effecting
37          its declared purpose. . . ." 321 U.S., at 425, 426.

38 Congress has met that standard here. The Act sets forth more than merely an
39 "intelligible principle" or minimal standards. * * *

40 Developing proportionate penalties for hundreds of different crimes by a virtually
41 limitless array of offenders is precisely the sort of intricate, labor-intensive task for

which delegation to an expert body is especially appropriate. Although Congress has delegated significant discretion to the Commission to draw judgments from its analysis of existing sentencing practice and alternative sentencing models," Congress is not confined to that method of executing its policy which involves the least possible delegation of discretion to administrative officers. *Yakus v. United States,* 321 U.S., at 425, 426. We have no doubt that, in the hands of the Commission, "the criteria which Congress has supplied are wholly adequate for carrying out the general policy and purpose" of the Act. *Sunshine Coal Co. v. Adkins,* 310 U.S. 381, 398 (1940).

* * *

JUSTICE SCALIA, dissenting.

While the products of the Sentencing Commission's labors have been given the modest name "Guidelines," *see* 28 U.S.C. § 994(a)(1) (1982 ed., Supp. IV); United States Sentencing Commission Guidelines Manual (June 15, 1988), they have the force and effect of laws, prescribing the sentences criminal defendants are to receive. * * *

* * *

It should be apparent from the above that the decisions made by the Commission are far from technical, but are heavily laden (or ought to be) with value judgments and policy assessments. This fact is sharply reflected in the Commission's product * * * .

* * *

Petitioner's most fundamental and far-reaching challenge to the Commission is that Congress' commitment of such broad policy responsibility to any institution is an unconstitutional delegation of legislative power. It is difficult to imagine a principle more essential to democratic government than that upon which the doctrine of unconstitutional delegation is founded: except in a few areas constitutionally committed to the Executive Branch, the basic policy decisions governing society are to be made by the Legislature. Our Members of Congress could not, even if they wished, vote all power to the President and adjourn *sine die.*

But while the doctrine of unconstitutional delegation is unquestionably a fundamental element of our constitutional system, it is not an element readily enforceable by the courts. Once it is conceded, as it must be, that no statute can be entirely precise, and that some judgments, even some judgments involving policy considerations, must be left to the officers executing the law and to the judges applying it, the debate over unconstitutional delegation becomes a debate not over a point of principle, but over a question of degree. * * *

In short, I fully agree with the Court's rejection of petitioner's contention that the doctrine of unconstitutional delegation of legislative authority has been violated because of the lack of intelligible, congressionally prescribed standards to guide the Commission.

Precisely because the scope of delegation is largely uncontrollable by the courts, we must be particularly rigorous in preserving the Constitution's structural restrictions that deter excessive delegation. The major one, it seems to me, is that the power to make law cannot be exercised by anyone other than Congress, except in conjunction with the lawful exercise of executive or judicial power.

The whole theory of *lawful* congressional "delegation" is not that Congress is sometimes too busy or too divided, and can therefore assign its responsibility of making law to someone else, but rather that a certain degree of discretion, and thus of lawmaking, *inheres* in most executive or judicial action, and it is up to Congress, by the relative specificity or generality of its statutory commands, to determine— up to a point—how small or how large that degree shall be. Thus, the courts could be given the power to say precisely what constitutes a "restraint of trade," *see Standard Oil Co. of New Jersey v. United States,* 221 U.S. 1 (1911), or to adopt rules of procedure, *see Sibbach v. Wilson & Co.,* 312 U.S. 1, 22 (1941), or to prescribe by rule the manner in which their officers shall execute their judgments, *Wayman v. Southard,* 23 U.S. 45 (1825), because that "lawmaking" was ancillary to their exercise of judicial powers. And the Executive could be given the power to adopt policies and rules specifying in detail what radio and television licenses will be in the "public interest, convenience or necessity," because that was ancillary to the exercise of its executive powers in granting and policing licenses and making a "fair and equitable allocation" of the electromagnetic spectrum. *See Federal Radio Comm'n v. Nelson Brothers Bond & Mortgage Co.,* 289 U.S. 266, 285 (1933). Or, to take examples closer to the case before us: Trial judges could be given the power to determine what factors justify a greater or lesser sentence within the statutorily prescribed limits, because that was ancillary to their exercise of the judicial power of pronouncing sentence upon individual defendants. And the President, through the Parole Commission subject to his appointment and removal, could be given the power to issue Guidelines specifying when parole would be available, because that was ancillary to the President's exercise of the executive power to hold and release federal prisoners.

\* \* \*

In *United States v. Grimaud,* 220 U.S. 506, 517 (1911), which upheld a statutory grant of authority to the Secretary of Agriculture to make rules and regulations governing use of the public forests he was charged with managing, the Court said:

> "From the beginning of the Government, various acts have been passed conferring upon executive officers power to make rules and regulations— not for the government of their departments, *but for administering the laws which did govern.* None of these statutes could confer legislative power."

14

1 (Emphasis added.) * * * The focus of controversy, in the long line of our so-called
2 excessive delegation cases, has been whether the *degree* of generality contained in
3 the authorization for exercise of executive or judicial powers in a particular field is
4 so unacceptably high as to *amount* to a delegation of legislative powers. I say "so-
5 called excessive delegation" because, although that convenient terminology is
6 often used, what is really at issue is whether there has been *any* delegation of
7 legislative power, which occurs (rarely) when Congress authorizes the exercise of
8 executive or judicial power without adequate standards. Strictly speaking, there is
9 *no* acceptable delegation of legislative power * * * In the present case, however, a
10 pure delegation of legislative power is precisely what we have before us. It is
11 irrelevant whether the standards are adequate, because they are not standards
12 related to the exercise of executive or judicial powers; they are, plainly and simply,
13 standards for further legislation.

14 The lawmaking function of the Sentencing Commission is completely divorced
15 from any responsibility for execution of the law or adjudication of private rights
16 under the law. It is divorced from responsibility for execution of the law not only
17 because the Commission is not said to be "located in the Executive Branch" (as I
18 shall discuss presently, I doubt whether Congress can "locate" an entity within one
19 Branch or another for constitutional purposes by merely saying so); but, more
20 importantly, because the Commission neither exercises any executive power on its
21 own, nor is subject to the control of the President, who does. The only functions it
22 performs, apart from prescribing the law, conducting the investigations useful and
23 necessary for prescribing the law, and clarifying the intended application of the law
24 that it prescribes, are data collection and intragovernmental advice-giving and
25 education. These latter activities—similar to functions performed by congressional
26 agencies and even congressional staff—neither determine nor affect private rights,
27 and do not constitute an exercise of governmental power. *See Humphrey's*
28 *Executor v. United States.* And the Commission's lawmaking is completely
29 divorced from the exercise of judicial powers since, not being a court, it has no
30 judicial powers itself, nor is it subject to the control of any other body with judicial
31 powers. The power to make law at issue here, in other words, is not ancillary, but
32 quite naked. The situation is no different in principle from what would exist if
33 Congress gave the same power of writing sentencing laws to a congressional agency
34 such as the General Accounting Office, or to members of its staff.

35 The delegation of lawmaking authority to the Commission is, in short,
36 unsupported by any legitimating theory to explain why it is not a delegation of
37 legislative power. * * *

38 Today's decision follows the regrettable tendency of our recent separation of
39 powers jurisprudence, *see Morrison,* to treat the Constitution as though it were no
40 more than a generalized prescription that the functions of the Branches should not
41 be commingled too much—how much is too much to be determined, case-by-case,
42 by this Court. The Constitution is not that. Rather, as its name suggests, it is a
43 prescribed structure, a framework, for the conduct of Government. In designing
44 that structure, the Framers *themselves* considered how much commingling was, in

the generality of things, acceptable, and set forth their conclusions in the document. * * *

I think the Court errs, in other words, not so much because it mistakes the degree of commingling, but because it fails to recognize that this case is not about commingling, but about the creation of a new Branch altogether, a sort of junior varsity Congress. It may well be that, in some circumstances, such a Branch would be desirable; perhaps the agency before us here will prove to be so. But there are many desirable dispositions that do not accord with the constitutional structure we live under. And, in the long run, the improvisation of a constitutional structure on the basis of currently perceived utility will be disastrous.

## Whitman v. American Trucking Associations, Inc.

531 U.S. 457 (2001)

February 27, 2001

JUSTICE SCALIA delivered the opinion of the Court.

These cases present the following questions: (1) Whether § 109(b)(1) of the Clean Air Act (CAA) delegates legislative power to the Administrator of the Environmental Protection Agency (EPA). * * *

I

Section 109(a) of the CAA requires the Administrator of the EPA to promulgate NAAQS for each air pollutant for which "air quality criteria" have been issued under § 108, 42 U.S.C. § 7408. Once a NAAQS has been promulgated, the Administrator must review the standard (and the criteria on which it is based) "at five-year intervals" and make "such revisions . . . as may be appropriate." CAA § 109(d)(1), 42 U.S.C. § 7409(d)(1). These cases arose when, on July 18, 1997, the Administrator revised the NAAQS for particulate matter and ozone. American Trucking Associations, Inc. * * * challenged the new standards in the Court of Appeals for the District of Columbia Circuit, pursuant to 42 U.S.C. § 7607(b)(1).

The District of Columbia Circuit accepted some of the challenges and rejected others. It agreed with the No. 99-1257 respondents (hereinafter respondents) that § 109(b)(1) delegated legislative power to the Administrator in contravention of the United States Constitution, Art. I, § 1, because it found that the EPA had interpreted the statute to provide no "intelligible principle" to guide the agency's exercise of authority. The court thought, however, that the EPA could perhaps avoid the unconstitutional delegation by adopting a restrictive construction of § 109(b)(1), so instead of declaring the section unconstitutional the court remanded the NAAQS to the agency. * * *

* * *

### III

Section 109(b)(1) of the CAA instructs the EPA to set "ambient air quality standards the attainment and maintenance of which in the judgment of the Administrator, based on [the] criteria [documents of § 108] and allowing an adequate margin of safety, are requisite to protect the public health." The Court of Appeals held that this section as interpreted by the Administrator did not provide an "intelligible principle" to guide the EPA's exercise of authority in setting NAAQS. "[The] EPA," it said, "lack[ed] any determinate criteria for drawing lines. It has failed to state intelligibly how much is too much." The court hence found that the EPA's interpretation (but not the statute itself) violated the nondelegation doctrine. We disagree.

In a delegation challenge, the constitutional question is whether the statute has delegated legislative power to the agency. Article I, § 1, of the Constitution vests "[a]ll legislative Powers herein granted . . . in a Congress of the United States." This text permits no delegation of those powers, and so we repeatedly have said that when Congress confers decisionmaking authority upon agencies *Congress* must "lay down by legislative act an intelligible principle to which the person or body authorized to [act] is directed to conform." *J. W Hampton, Jr., & Co.* We have never suggested that an agency can cure an unlawful delegation of legislative power by adopting in its discretion a limiting construction of the statute. * * * The idea that an agency can cure an unconstitutionally standardless delegation of power by declining to exercise some of that power seems to us internally contradictory. The very choice of which portion of the power to exercise—that is to say, the prescription of the standard that Congress had omitted—would itself be an exercise of the forbidden legislative authority. Whether the statute delegates legislative power is a question for the courts, and an agency's voluntary self-denial has no bearing upon the answer.

We agree with the Solicitor General that the text of § 109(b)(1) of the CAA at a minimum requires that "[f]or a discrete set of pollutants and based on published air quality criteria that reflect the latest scientific knowledge, [the] EPA must establish uniform national standards at a level that is requisite to protect public health from the adverse effects of the pollutant in the ambient air." Requisite, in turn, "mean[s] sufficient, but not more than necessary." These limits on the EPA's discretion are strikingly similar to the ones we approved in *Touby v. United States*, 500 U.S. 160 (1991), which permitted the Attorney General to designate a drug as a controlled substance for purposes of criminal drug enforcement if doing so was "'necessary to avoid an imminent hazard to the public safety.'" They also resemble the Occupational Safety and Health Act of 1970 provision requiring the agency to "'set the standard which most adequately assures, to the extent feasible, on the basis of the best available evidence, that no employee will suffer any impairment of health'"—which the Court upheld in *Industrial Union Dept., AFL-CIO v. American Petroleum Institute*, 448 U.S. 607, 646 (1980). * * *

1    The scope of discretion § 109(b)(1) allows is in fact well within the outer limits of
2    our nondelegation precedents. In the history of the Court we have found the
3    requisite "intelligible principle" lacking in only two statutes, one of which provided
4    literally no guidance for the exercise of discretion, and the other of which conferred
5    authority to regulate the entire economy on the basis of no more precise a standard
6    than stimulating the economy by assuring "fair competition." *See Panama*
7    *Refining Co. v. Ryan*, 293 U.S. 388 (1935); *A. L. A. Schechter Poultry Corp. v.*
8    *United States*, 295 U.S. 495 (1935). We have, on the other hand, upheld the validity
9    of § 11(b)(2) of the Public Utility Holding Company Act of 1935, which gave the
10   Securities and Exchange Commission authority to modify the structure of holding
11   company systems so as to ensure that they are not "unduly or unnecessarily
12   complicate[d]" and do not "unfairly or inequitably distribute voting power among
13   security holders." *American Power & Light Co. v. SEC*, 329 U.S. 90, 104 (1946).
14   We have approved the wartime conferral of agency power to fix the prices of
15   commodities at a level that "'will be generally fair and equitable and will effectuate
16   the [in some respects conflicting] purposes of the Act.'" *Yakus v. United States*, 321
17   U.S. 414, 420, 423-426 (1944). And we have found an "intelligible principle" in
18   various statutes authorizing regulation in the "public interest." *See, e.g., National*
19   *Broadcasting Co. v. United States*, 319 U.S. 190, 225, 226 (1943) (Federal
20   Communications Commission's power to regulate airwaves); *New York Central*
21   *Securities Corp. v. United States*, 287 U.S. 12, 24, 25 (1932) (Interstate Commerce
22   Commission's power to approve railroad consolidations). In short, we have
23   "almost never felt qualified to second-guess Congress regarding the permissible
24   degree of policy judgment that can be left to those executing or applying the law."
25   *Mistretta v. United States*, 488 U.S. 361, 416 (1989) (SCALIA, J., dissenting); *see*
26   *id.*, at 373 (majority opinion).

27   It is true enough that the degree of agency discretion that is acceptable varies
28   according to the scope of the power congressionally conferred. While Congress
29   need not provide any direction to the EPA regarding the manner in which it is to
30   define "country elevators," which are to be exempt from new-stationary-source
31   regulations governing grain elevators, it must provide substantial guidance on
32   setting air standards that affect the entire national economy. But even in sweeping
33   regulatory schemes we have never demanded, as the Court of Appeals did here,
34   that statutes provide a "determinate criterion" for saying "how much [of the
35   regulated harm] is too much." In *Touby*, for example, we did not require the statute
36   to decree how "imminent" was too imminent, or how "necessary" was necessary
37   enough, or even—most relevant here–how "hazardous" was too hazardous. 500
38   U.S., at 165-167. Similarly, the statute at issue in *Lichter* authorized agencies to
39   recoup "excess profits" paid under wartime Government contracts, yet we did not
40   insist that Congress specify how much profit was too much. 334 U.S., at 783-786.
41   It is therefore not conclusive for delegation purposes that, as respondents argue,
42   ozone and particulate matter are "nonthreshold" pollutants that inflict a
43   continuum of adverse health effects at any airborne concentration greater than
44   zero, and hence require the EPA to make judgments of degree. "A certain degree of
45   discretion, and thus of lawmaking, inheres in most executive or judicial action."

*Mistretta v. United States, supra,* at 417 (SCALIA, J., dissenting) (emphasis deleted); *see* 488 U.S., at 378-379 (majority opinion). Section 109(b)(1) of the CAA, which to repeat we interpret as requiring the EPA to set air quality standards at the level that is "requisite"—that is, not lower or higher than is necessary—to protect the public health with an adequate margin of safety, fits comfortably within the scope of discretion permitted by our precedent.

We therefore reverse the judgment of the Court of Appeals remanding for reinterpretation that would avoid a supposed delegation of legislative power. It will remain for the Court of Appeals-on the remand that we direct for other reasons-to dispose of any other preserved challenge to the NAAQS under the judicial-review provisions contained in 42 U.S.C. § 7607(d)(9).

* * *

JUSTICE THOMAS, concurring.

I agree with the majority that § 109's directive to the agency is no less an "intelligible principle" than a host of other directives that we have approved. I also agree that the Court of Appeals' remand to the agency to make its own corrective interpretation does not accord with our understanding of the delegation issue. I write separately, however, to express my concern that there may nevertheless be a genuine constitutional problem with § 109, a problem which the parties did not address.

The parties to these cases who briefed the constitutional issue wrangled over constitutional doctrine with barely a nod to the text of the Constitution. Although this Court since 1928 has treated the "intelligible principle" requirement as the only constitutional limit on congressional grants of power to administrative agencies, *see J. W Hampton, Jr., & Co. v. United States*, 276 U.S. 394, 409 (1928), the Constitution does not speak of "intelligible principles." Rather, it speaks in much simpler terms: "*All* legislative Powers herein granted shall be vested in a Congress." U.S. Const., Art. 1, § 1 (emphasis added). I am not convinced that the intelligible principle doctrine serves to prevent all cessions of legislative power. I believe that there are cases in which the principle is intelligible and yet the significance of the delegated decision is simply too great for the decision to be called anything other than "legislative."

As it is, none of the parties to these cases has examined the text of the Constitution or asked us to reconsider our precedents on cessions of legislative power. On a future day, however, I would be willing to address the question whether our delegation jurisprudence has strayed too far from our Founders' understanding of separation of powers.

JUSTICE STEVENS, with whom JUSTICE SOUTER joins, concurring in part and concurring in the judgment.

1 \* \* \* [T]he Court convincingly explains why the Court of Appeals erred when it
2 concluded that § 109 effected "an unconstitutional delegation of legislative power."
3 *American Trucking Assns., Inc. v. EPA*, 175 F.3d 1027, 1033 (CADC 1999) (*per*
4 *curiam*). I wholeheartedly endorse the Court's result and endorse its explanation
5 of its reasons, albeit with the following caveat.

6 The Court has two choices. We could choose to articulate our ultimate disposition
7 of this issue by frankly acknowledging that the power delegated to the EPA is
8 "legislative" but nevertheless conclude that the delegation is constitutional because
9 adequately limited by the terms of the authorizing statute. Alternatively, we could
10 pretend, as the Court does, that the authority delegated to the EPA is somehow not
11 "legislative power." Despite the fact that there is language in our opinions that
12 supports the Court's articulation of our holding, I am persuaded that it would be
13 both wiser and more faithful to what we have actually done in delegation cases to
14 admit that agency rulemaking authority is "legislative power."

15 The proper characterization of governmental power should generally depend on
16 the nature of the power, not on the identity of the person exercising it. *See* Black's
17 Law Dictionary 899 (6th ed. 1990) (defining "legislation" as, inter alia,
18 "[f]ormulation of rule[s] for the future"); 1 K. Davis & R. Pierce, Administrative
19 Law Treatise § 2.3, p. 37 (3d ed. 1994) ("If legislative power means the power to
20 make rules of conduct that bind everyone based on resolution of major policy
21 issues, scores of agencies exercise legislative power routinely by promulgating
22 what are candidly called 'legislative rules' "). If the NAAQS that the EPA
23 promulgated had been prescribed by Congress, everyone would agree that those
24 rules would be the product of an exercise of "legislative power." The same
25 characterization is appropriate when an agency exercises rulemaking authority
26 pursuant to a permissible delegation from Congress.

27 My view is not only more faithful to normal English usage, but is also fully
28 consistent with the text of the Constitution. In Article I, the Framers vested "All
29 legislative Powers" in the Congress, Art. I, § 1, just as in Article II they vested the
30 "executive Power" in the President, Art. II, § 1. Those provisions do not purport to
31 limit the authority of either recipient of power to delegate authority to others. *See*
32 *Bowsher v. Synar*, 478 U.S. 714, 752 (1986) (STEVENS, J., concurring in
33 judgment) ("Despite the statement in Article I of the Constitution that 'All
34 legislative powers herein granted shall be vested in a Congress of the United
35 States,' it is far from novel to acknowledge that independent agencies do indeed
36 exercise legislative powers"); *INS v. Chadha*, 462 U.S. 919, 985, 986 (1983)
37 (WHITE, J., dissenting) ("[L]egislative power can be exercised by independent
38 agencies and Executive departments ... "). Surely the authority granted to
39 members of the Cabinet and federal law enforcement agents is properly
40 characterized as "Executive" even though not exercised by the President.

41 It seems clear that an executive agency's exercise of rulemaking authority pursuant
42 to a valid delegation from Congress is "legislative." As long as the delegation
43 provides a sufficiently intelligible principle, there is nothing inherently

1  unconstitutional about it. Accordingly, * * * I would hold that when Congress
2  enacted § 109, it effected a constitutional delegation of legislative power to the
3  EPA.

4  JUSTICE BREYER, concurring in part and concurring in the judgment. [Omitted.]

5

6  **Gundy v. United States**

7  139 S. Ct. 2116 (2019)

8  June 20, 2019

9  JUSTICE KAGAN announced the judgment of the Court and delivered an opinion,
10  in which JUSTICE GINSBURG, JUSTICE BREYER, and JUSTICE SOTOMAYOR
11  join.

12  The nondelegation doctrine bars Congress from transferring its legislative power
13  to another branch of Government. This case requires us to decide whether 34
14  U.S.C. §20913(d), enacted as part of the Sex Offender Registration and Notification
15  Act (SORNA), violates that doctrine. We hold it does not. Under §20913(d), the
16  Attorney General must apply SORNA's registration requirements as soon as
17  feasible to offenders convicted before the statute's enactment. That delegation
18  easily passes constitutional muster.

19                                        I

20  Congress has sought, for the past quarter century, to combat sex crimes and crimes
21  against children through sex-offender registration schemes. * * *

22                                      * * *

23  The basic registration scheme works as follows. A "sex offender" is defined as "an
24  individual who was convicted of" specified criminal offenses: all offenses
25  "involving a sexual act or sexual contact" and additional offenses "against a minor."
26  Such an individual must register—provide his name, address, and certain other
27  information—in every State where he resides, works, or studies. And he must keep
28  the registration current, and periodically report in person to a law enforcement
29  office, for a period of between fifteen years and life (depending on the severity of
30  his crime and his history of recidivism). Section 20913—the disputed provision
31  here—elaborates the "[i]nitial registration" requirements for sex offenders.
32  §§20913(b), (d). Subsection (b) sets out the general rule: An offender must register
33  "before completing a sentence of imprisonment with respect to the offense giving
34  rise to the registration requirement" (or, if the offender is not sentenced to prison,
35  "not later than [three] business days after being sentenced"). Two provisions down,
36  subsection (d) addresses (in its title's words) the "[i]nitial registration of sex
37  offenders unable to comply with subsection (b)." The provision states:

> "The Attorney General shall have the authority to specify the applicability of the requirements of this subchapter to sex offenders convicted before the enactment of this chapter . . . and to prescribe rules for the registration of any such sex offenders and for other categories of sex offenders who are unable to comply with subsection (b)."

Subsection (d), in other words, focuses on individuals convicted of a sex offense before SORNA's enactment—a group we will call pre-Act offenders. Many of these individuals were unregistered at the time of SORNA's enactment, either because pre-existing law did not cover them or because they had successfully evaded that law (so were "lost" to the system). And of those potential new registrants, many or most could not comply with subsection (b)'s registration rule because they had already completed their prison sentences. For the entire group of pre-Act offenders, once again, the Attorney General "shall have the authority" to "specify the applicability" of SORNA's registration requirements and "to prescribe rules for [their] registration."

Under that delegated authority, the Attorney General issued an interim rule in February 2007, specifying that SORNA's registration requirements apply in full to "sex offenders convicted of the offense for which registration is required prior to the enactment of that Act." The final rule, issued in December 2010, reiterated that SORNA applies to all pre-Act offenders. That rule has remained the same to this day.

Petitioner Herman Gundy is a pre-Act offender. The year before SORNA's enactment, he pleaded guilty under Maryland law for sexually assaulting a minor. After his release from prison in 2012, Gundy came to live in New York. But he never registered there as a sex offender. A few years later, he was convicted for failing to register, in violation of §2250. He argued below (among other things) that Congress unconstitutionally delegated legislative power when it authorized the Attorney General to "specify the applicability" of SORNA's registration requirements to pre-Act offenders. §20913(d). The District Court and Court of Appeals for the Second Circuit rejected that claim, as had every other court (including eleven Courts of Appeals) to consider the issue. We nonetheless granted certiorari. Today, we join the consensus and affirm.

II

Article I of the Constitution provides that "[a]ll legislative Powers herein granted shall be vested in a Congress of the United States." §1. Accompanying that assignment of power to Congress is a bar on its further delegation. Congress, this Court explained early on, may not transfer to another branch "powers which are strictly and exclusively legislative." *Wayman v. Southard*, 23 U.S. 1, 42–43 (1825). But the Constitution does not "deny[ ] to the Congress the necessary resources of flexibility and practicality [that enable it] to perform its function[s]." *Yakus v. United States*, 321 U.S. 414, 425 (1944) (internal quotation marks omitted). Congress may "obtain[ ] the assistance of its coordinate Branches"—and in particular, may confer substantial discretion on executive agencies to implement and enforce the laws. *Mistretta v. United States*, 488 U.S. 361, 372 (1989). "[I]n our increasingly complex society, replete with ever changing and more technical problems," this Court has understood that "Congress simply cannot do its job absent an ability to delegate power under broad general directives." *Ibid.* So we have held, time and again, that a statutory delegation is constitutional as long as Congress "lay[s] down by legislative act an intelligible principle to which the person or body authorized to [exercise the delegated authority] is directed to conform." *Ibid.* (quoting *J. W. Hampton, Jr., & Co. v. United States*, 276 U.S. 394, 409 (1928); brackets in original).

Given that standard, a nondelegation inquiry always begins (and often almost ends) with statutory interpretation. The constitutional question is whether Congress has supplied an intelligible principle to guide the delegee's use of discretion. So the answer requires construing the challenged statute to figure out what task it delegates and what instructions it provides. See, *e.g., Whitman v. American Trucking Assns., Inc.*, 531 U.S. 457, 473 (2001) (construing the text of a delegation to place constitutionally adequate "limits on the EPA's discretion"); *American Power & Light Co. v. SEC*, 329 U.S. 90, 104–105 (1946) (interpreting a statutory delegation, in light of its "purpose[,] factual background[, and] context," to provide sufficiently "definite" standards). Only after a court has determined a challenged statute's meaning can it decide whether the law sufficiently guides executive discretion to accord with Article I. And indeed, once a court interprets the statute, it may find that the constitutional question all but answers itself.

That is the case here, because §20913(d) does not give the Attorney General anything like the "unguided" and "unchecked" authority that Gundy says. The provision, in Gundy's view, "grants the Attorney General plenary power to determine SORNA's applicability to pre-Act offenders—to require them to register, or not, as she sees fit, and to change her policy for any reason and at any time." If that were so, we would face a nondelegation question. But it is not. This Court has already interpreted §20913(d) to say something different—to require the Attorney General to apply SORNA to all pre-Act offenders as soon as feasible. See *Reynolds v. United States*, 565 U.S. 432, 442-443 (2012). And revisiting that issue yet more fully today, we reach the same conclusion. The text, considered alongside its context, purpose, and history, makes clear that the Attorney General's discretion extends only to considering and addressing feasibility issues. Given that statutory meaning, Gundy's constitutional claim must fail. Section 20913(d)'s delegation falls well within permissible bounds.

A

This is not the first time this Court has had to interpret §20913(d). In *Reynolds*, the Court considered whether SORNA's registration requirements applied of their own force to pre-Act offenders or instead applied only once the Attorney General said they did. We read the statute as adopting the latter approach. But even as we

1  did so, we made clear how far SORNA limited the Attorney General's authority.
2  And in that way, we effectively resolved the case now before us.

3                                   * * *

4  * * * At the moment of SORNA's enactment, many pre-Act offenders were "unable
5  to comply" with the Act's initial registration requirements. §20913(d); *Reynolds*,
6  565 U.S., at 440. That was because, once again, the requirements assumed that
7  offenders would be in prison, whereas many pre-Act offenders were on the streets.
8  In identifying that issue, §20913(d) itself reveals the nature of the delegation to the
9  Attorney General. It was to give him the time needed (if any) to address the various
10 implementation issues involved in getting pre-Act offenders into the registration
11 system. "Specify the applicability" thus does not mean "specify *whether* to apply
12 SORNA" to pre-Act offenders at all, even though everything else in the Act
13 commands their coverage. The phrase instead means "specify *how* to apply
14 SORNA" to pre-Act offenders if transitional difficulties require some delay. In that
15 way, the whole of §20913(d) joins the rest of SORNA in giving the Attorney General
16 only time-limited latitude to excuse pre-Act offenders from the statute's
17 requirements. Under the law, he had to order their registration as soon as feasible.

18                                  * * *

19                                   C

20 Now that we have determined what §20913(d) means, we can consider whether it
21 violates the Constitution. The question becomes: Did Congress make an
22 impermissible delegation when it instructed the Attorney General to apply
23 SORNA's registration requirements to pre-Act offenders as soon as feasible?
24 Under this Court's long-established law, that question is easy. Its answer is no.

25 As noted earlier, this Court has held that a delegation is constitutional so long as
26 Congress has set out an "intelligible principle" to guide the delegee's exercise of
27 authority. *J. W. Hampton, Jr., & Co.*, 276 U.S., at 409. Or in a related formulation,
28 the Court has stated that a delegation is permissible if Congress has made clear to
29 the delegee "the general policy" he must pursue and the "boundaries of [his]
30 authority." *American Power & Light*, 329 U.S., at 105. Those standards, the Court
31 has made clear, are not demanding. "[W]e have 'almost never felt qualified to
32 second-guess Congress regarding the permissible degree of policy judgment that
33 can be left to those executing or applying the law.'" *Whitman*, 531 U.S., at 474–475
34 (quoting *Mistretta*, 488 U.S., at 416 (SCALIA, J., dissenting)). Only twice in this
35 country's history (and that in a single year) have we found a delegation excessive—
36 in each case because "Congress had failed to articulate *any* policy or standard" to
37 confine discretion. *Mistretta*, 488 U.S., at 373, n. 7 (emphasis added); see *A. L. A.
38 Schechter Poultry Corp. v. United States*, 295 U.S. 495 (1935); *Panama Refining
39 Co. v. Ryan*, 293 U.S. 388 (1935). By contrast, we have over and over upheld even
40 very broad delegations. Here is a sample: We have approved delegations to various
41 agencies to regulate in the "public interest." See, *e.g., National Broadcasting Co.*,
42 319 U.S., at 216. We have sustained authorizations for agencies to set "fair and
   24

equitable" prices and "just and reasonable" rates. *Yakus*, 321 U.S., at 422, 427; *FPC v. Hope Natural Gas Co.*, 320 U.S. 591 (1944). We more recently affirmed a delegation to an agency to issue whatever air quality standards are "requisite to protect the public health." *Whitman*, 531 U.S., at 472 (quoting 42 U.S.C. §7409(b)(1)). And so forth.

In that context, the delegation in SORNA easily passes muster (as all eleven circuit courts to have considered the question found). The statute conveyed Congress's policy that the Attorney General require pre-Act offenders to register as soon as feasible. Under the law, the feasibility issues he could address were administrative—and, more specifically, transitional—in nature. Those issues arose, as *Reynolds* explained, from the need to "newly register[ ] or reregister[ ] 'a large number' of pre-Act offenders" not then in the system. 565 U.S., at 440; see *supra*. And they arose, more technically, from the gap between an initial registration requirement hinged on imprisonment and a set of pre-Act offenders long since released. Even for those limited matters, the Act informed the Attorney General that he did not have forever to work things out. By stating its demand for a "comprehensive" registration system and by defining the "sex offenders" required to register to include pre-Act offenders, Congress conveyed that the Attorney General had only temporary authority. Or again, in the words of *Reynolds*, that he could prevent "*instantaneous* registration" and impose some "implementation delay." 565 U.S., at 443. That statutory authority, as compared to the delegations we have upheld in the past, is distinctly small-bore. It falls well within constitutional bounds.

Indeed, if SORNA's delegation is unconstitutional, then most of Government is unconstitutional—dependent as Congress is on the need to give discretion to executive officials to implement its programs. Consider again this Court's long-time recognition: "Congress simply cannot do its job absent an ability to delegate power under broad general directives." *Mistretta*, 488 U.S., at 372. Or as the dissent in that case agreed: "[S]ome judgments . . . must be left to the officers executing the law." 488 U.S., at 415 (opinion of SCALIA, J.); see *Whitman*, 531 U.S., at 475 ("[A] certain degree of discretion[ ] inheres in most executive" action (internal quotation marks omitted)). Among the judgments often left to executive officials are ones involving feasibility. In fact, standards of that kind are ubiquitous in the U.S. Code. See, *e.g.*, 12 U.S.C. §1701z–2(a) (providing that the Secretary of Housing and Urban Development "shall require, to the greatest extent feasible, the employment of new and improved technologies, methods, and materials in housing construction[ ] under [HUD] programs"); 47 U.S.C. §903(d)(1) (providing that "the Secretary of Commerce shall promote efficient and cost-effective use of the spectrum to the maximum extent feasible" in "assigning frequencies for mobile radio services"). In those delegations, Congress gives its delegee the flexibility to deal with real-world constraints in carrying out his charge. So too in SORNA.

It is wisdom and humility alike that this Court has always upheld such "necessities of government." *Mistretta*, 488 U.S., at 416 (SCALIA, J., dissenting) (internal quotation marks omitted); see *ibid.* ("Since Congress is no less endowed with

25

common sense than we are, and better equipped to inform itself of the 'necessities' of government; and since the factors bearing upon those necessities are both multifarious and (in the nonpartisan sense) highly political . . . it is small wonder that we have almost never felt qualified to second-guess Congress regarding the permissible degree of policy judgment that can be left to those executing or applying the law"). We therefore affirm the judgment of the Court of Appeals.

It is so ordered.

JUSTICE KAVANAUGH took no part in the consideration or decision of this case.

JUSTICE ALITO, concurring in the judgment.

The Constitution confers on Congress certain "legislative [p]owers," Art. I, §1, and does not permit Congress to delegate them to another branch of the Government. See *Whitman v. American Trucking Assns., Inc.*, 531 U.S. 457, 472 (2001). Nevertheless, since 1935, the Court has uniformly rejected nondelegation arguments and has upheld provisions that authorized agencies to adopt important rules pursuant to extraordinarily capacious standards. See *ibid*.

If a majority of this Court were willing to reconsider the approach we have taken for the past 84 years, I would support that effort. But because a majority is not willing to do that, it would be freakish to single out the provision at issue here for special treatment.

Because I cannot say that the statute lacks a discernable standard that is adequate under the approach this Court has taken for many years, I vote to affirm.

JUSTICE GORSUCH, with whom THE CHIEF JUSTICE and JUSTICE THOMAS join, dissenting.

The Constitution promises that only the people's elected representatives may adopt new federal laws restricting liberty. Yet the statute before us scrambles that design. It purports to endow the nation's chief prosecutor with the power to write his own criminal code governing the lives of a half-million citizens. Yes, those affected are some of the least popular among us. But if a single executive branch official can write laws restricting the liberty of this group of persons, what does that mean for the next?

Today, a plurality of an eight-member Court endorses this extraconstitutional arrangement but resolves nothing. Working from an understanding of the Constitution at war with its text and history, the plurality reimagines the terms of the statute before us and insists there is nothing wrong with Congress handing off so much power to the Attorney General. But JUSTICE ALITO supplies the fifth vote for today's judgment and he does not join either the plurality's constitutional or statutory analysis, indicating instead that he remains willing, in a future case with a full Court, to revisit these matters. Respectfully, I would not wait.

I

For individuals convicted of sex offenses *after* Congress adopted the Sex Offender Registration and Notification Act (SORNA) in 2006, the statute offers detailed instructions. * * *

But what about those convicted of sex offenses *before* the Act's adoption? At the time of SORNA's enactment, the nation's population of sex offenders exceeded 500,000, and Congress concluded that something had to be done about these "pre-Act" offenders too. But it seems Congress couldn't agree what that should be. The treatment of pre-Act offenders proved a "controversial issue with major policy significance and practical ramifications for states." * * * So Congress simply passed the problem to the Attorney General. For all half-million pre-Act offenders, the law says only this, in 34 U.S.C. §20913(d):

> "The Attorney General shall have the authority to specify the applicability of the requirements of this subchapter to sex offenders convicted before the enactment of this chapter . . . and to prescribe rules for the registration of any such sex offender."

Yes, that's it. The breadth of the authority Congress granted to the Attorney General in these few words can only be described as vast. As the Department of Justice itself has acknowledged, SORNA "does not require the Attorney General" to impose registration requirements on pre-Act offenders "within a certain time frame or by a date certain; it does not require him to act at all."[8] If the Attorney General does choose to act, he can require all pre-Act offenders to register, or he can "require some but not all to register."[9] For those he requires to register, the Attorney General may impose "some but not all of [SORNA's] registration requirements," as he pleases.[10] And he is free to change his mind on any of these matters "at any given time or over the course of different [political] administrations."[11] * * *

Unsurprisingly, different Attorneys General have exercised their discretion in different ways. For six months after SORNA's enactment, Attorney General Gonzales left past offenders alone. Then the pendulum swung the other direction when the Department of Justice issued an interim rule requiring pre-Act offenders to follow all the same rules as post-Act offenders. A year later, Attorney General Mukasey issued more new guidelines, this time directing the States to register some but not all past offenders Three years after that, Attorney General Holder required the States to register only those pre-Act offenders convicted of a new felony after SORNA's enactment. Various Attorneys General have also taken

---

[8] Brief for United States in Reynolds v. United States, O. T. 2011, No. 106549, p. 23.
[9] *Id.*, at 24.
[10] *Ibid.*
[11] *Ibid.*

1  different positions on whether pre-Act offenders might be entitled to credit for
2  time spent in the community before SORNA was enacted.

3  These unbounded policy choices have profound consequences for the people they
4  affect. Take our case. Before SORNA's enactment, Herman Gundy pleaded guilty
5  in 2005 to a sexual offense. After his release from prison five years later, he was
6  arrested again, this time for failing to register as a sex offender according to the
7  rules the Attorney General had then prescribed for pre-Act offenders. As a result,
8  Mr. Gundy faced an additional 10-year prison term—10 years more than if the
9  Attorney General had, in his discretion, chosen to write the rules differently.

10                                    II

11                                    A

12  Our founding document begins by declaring that "We the People . . . ordain and
13  establish this Constitution." At the time, that was a radical claim, an assertion that
14  sovereignty belongs not to a person or institution or class but to the whole of the
15  people. From that premise, the Constitution proceeded to vest the authority to
16  exercise different aspects of the people's sovereign power in distinct entities. In
17  Article I, the Constitution entrusted all of the federal government's legislative
18  power to Congress. In Article II, it assigned the executive power to the President.
19  And in Article III, it gave independent judges the task of applying the laws to cases
20  and controversies.

21  To the framers, each of these vested powers had a distinct content. When it came
22  to the legislative power, the framers understood it to mean the power to adopt
23  generally applicable rules of conduct governing future actions by private persons—
24  the power to "prescrib[e] the rules by which the duties and rights of every citizen
25  are to be regulated," or the power to "prescribe general rules for the government of
26  society."

27  The framers understood, too, that it would frustrate "the system of government
28  ordained by the Constitution" if Congress could merely announce vague
29  aspirations and then assign others the responsibility of adopting legislation to
30  realize its goals. Through the Constitution, after all, the people had vested the
31  power to prescribe rules limiting their liberties in Congress alone. No one, not even
32  Congress, had the right to alter that arrangement. As CHIEF JUSTICE
33  MARSHALL explained, Congress may not "delegate . . . powers which are strictly
34  and exclusively legislative." * * *

35  Why did the framers insist on this particular arrangement? They believed the new
36  federal government's most dangerous power was the power to enact laws
37  restricting the people's liberty. An "excess of law-making" was, in their words, one
38  of "the diseases to which our governments are most liable." To address that
39  tendency, the framers went to great lengths to make lawmaking difficult. In Article
40  I, by far the longest part of the Constitution, the framers insisted that any proposed
41  law must win the approval of two Houses of Congress—elected at different times,

28

by different constituencies, and for different terms in office—and either secure the President's approval or obtain enough support to override his veto. Some occasionally complain about Article I's detailed and arduous processes for new legislation, but to the framers these were bulwarks of liberty.

* * *

* * * As Madison explained, "'[t]here can be no liberty where the legislative and executive powers are united in the same person, or body of magistrates.'" The framers knew, too, that the job of keeping the legislative power confined to the legislative branch couldn't be trusted to self-policing by Congress; often enough, legislators will face rational incentives to pass problems to the executive branch. Besides, enforcing the separation of powers isn't about protecting institutional prerogatives or governmental turf. It's about respecting the people's sovereign choice to vest the legislative power in Congress alone. And it's about safeguarding a structure designed to protect their liberties, minority rights, fair notice, and the rule of law. So when a case or controversy comes within the judicial competence, the Constitution does not permit judges to look the other way; we must call foul when the constitutional lines are crossed. * * *

B

Accepting, then, that we have an obligation to decide whether Congress has unconstitutionally divested itself of its legislative responsibilities, the question follows: What's the test? Madison acknowledged that "no skill in the science of government has yet been able to discriminate and define, with sufficient certainty, its three great provinces—the legislative, executive, and judiciary." Chief Justice Marshall agreed that policing the separation of powers "is a subject of delicate and difficult inquiry." Still, the framers took this responsibility seriously and offered us important guiding principles.

First, we know that as long as Congress makes the policy decisions when regulating private conduct, it may authorize another branch to "fill up the details." In *Wayman v. Southard*, this Court upheld a statute that instructed the federal courts to borrow state-court procedural rules but allowed them to make certain "alterations and additions." Writing for the Court, Chief Justice Marshall distinguished between those "important subjects, which must be entirely regulated by the legislature itself," and "those of less interest, in which a general provision may be made, and power given to those who are to act . . . to fill up the details." The Court upheld the statute before it because Congress had announced the controlling general policy when it ordered federal courts to follow state procedures, and the residual authority to make "alterations and additions" did no more than permit courts to fill up the details.

* * *

Second, once Congress prescribes the rule governing private conduct, it may make the application of that rule depend on executive fact-finding. Here, too, the power extended to the executive may prove highly consequential. During the Napoleonic Wars, for example, Britain and France each tried to block the United States from trading with the other. Congress responded with a statute instructing that, if the President found that either Great Britain or France stopped interfering with American trade, a trade embargo would be imposed against the other country. In *Cargo of Brig Aurora v. United States*, this Court explained that it could "see no sufficient reason, why the legislature should not exercise its discretion [to impose an embargo] either expressly or *conditionally*, as their judgment should direct." Half a century later, Congress likewise made the construction of the Brooklyn Bridge depend on a finding by the Secretary of War that the bridge wouldn't interfere with navigation of the East River. The Court held that Congress "did not abdicate any of its authority" but "simply declared that, upon a certain fact being established, the bridge should be deemed a lawful structure, and employed the secretary of war as an agent to ascertain that fact."

Third, Congress may assign the executive and judicial branches certain non-legislative responsibilities. While the Constitution vests all federal legislative power in Congress alone, Congress's legislative authority sometimes overlaps with authority the Constitution separately vests in another branch. So, for example, when a congressional statute confers wide discretion to the executive, no separation-of-powers problem may arise if "the discretion is to be exercised over matters already within the scope of executive power." Though the case was decided on different grounds, the foreign-affairs-related statute in *Cargo of the Brig Aurora* may be an example of this kind of permissible lawmaking, given that many foreign affairs powers are constitutionally vested in the president under Article II. *Wayman* itself might be explained by the same principle as applied to the judiciary: Even in the absence of any statute, courts have the power under Article III "to regulate their practice."

C

Before the 1930s, federal statutes granting authority to the executive were comparatively modest and usually easily upheld. But then the federal government began to grow explosively. And with the proliferation of new executive programs came new questions about the scope of congressional delegations. Twice the Court responded by striking down statutes for violating the separation of powers.

* * *

After *Schechter Poultry* and *Panama Refining*, Congress responded by writing a second wave of New Deal legislation more "[c]arefully crafted" to avoid the kind of problems that sank these early statutes. And since that time the Court hasn't held another statute to violate the separation of powers in the same way. * * * [M]aybe the most likely explanation of all lies in the story of the evolving "intelligible principle" doctrine.

This Court first used that phrase in 1928 in *J. W. Hampton, Jr., & Co. v. United States*, where it remarked that a statute "lay[ing] down by legislative act an

30

1  intelligible principle to which the [executive official] is directed to conform"
2  satisfies the separation of powers. No one at the time thought the phrase meant to
3  effect some revolution in this Court's understanding of the Constitution. While the
4  exact line between policy and details, lawmaking and fact-finding, and legislative
5  and non-legislative functions had sometimes invited reasonable debate, everyone
6  agreed these were the relevant inquiries. And when Chief Justice Taft wrote of an
7  "intelligible principle," it seems plain enough that he sought only to explain the
8  operation of these traditional tests; he gave no hint of a wish to overrule or revise
9  them. * * *

10                                     * * *

11  Still, it's undeniable that the "intelligible principle" remark eventually began to
12  take on a life of its own. * * * For two decades, no one thought to invoke the
13  "intelligible principle" comment as a basis to uphold a statute that would have
14  failed more traditional separation-of-powers tests. In fact, the phrase sat more or
15  less silently entombed until the late 1940s. Only then did lawyers begin digging it
16  up in earnest and arguing to this Court that it had somehow displaced (*sub silentio*
17  of course) all prior teachings in this area.

18  This mutated version of the "intelligible principle" remark has no basis in the
19  original meaning of the Constitution, in history, or even in the decision from which
20  it was plucked. Judges and scholars representing a wide and diverse range of views
21  have condemned it as resting on "misunderst[ood] historical foundations." They
22  have explained, too, that it has been abused to permit delegations of legislative
23  power that on any other conceivable account should be held unconstitutional.
24  Indeed, where some have claimed to see "intelligible principles" many "less
25  discerning readers [have been able only to] find gibberish." Even JUSTICE
26  DOUGLAS, one of the fathers of the administrative state, came to criticize
27  excessive congressional delegations in the period when the intelligible principle
28  "test" began to take hold.

29                                     * * *

30                                      III

31                                       A

32  Returning to SORNA with this understanding of our charge in hand, problems
33  quickly emerge. Start with this one: It's hard to see how SORNA leaves the Attorney
34  General with only details to fill up. Of course, what qualifies as a detail can
35  sometimes be difficult to discern and, as we've seen, this Court has upheld statutes
36  that allow federal agencies to resolve even highly consequential details so long as
37  Congress prescribes the rule governing private conduct. But it's hard to see how
38  the statute before us could be described as leaving the Attorney General with only
39  details to dispatch. As the government itself admitted in *Reynolds*, SORNA leaves
40  the Attorney General free to impose on 500,000 pre-Act offenders all of the
41  statute's requirements, some of them, or none of them. The Attorney General may

1   choose which pre-Act offenders to subject to the Act. And he is free to change his
2   mind at any point or over the course of different political administrations. In the
3   end, there isn't a single policy decision concerning pre-Act offenders on which
4   Congress even tried to speak, and not a single other case where we have upheld
5   executive authority over matters like these on the ground they constitute mere
6   "details." This much appears to have been deliberate, too. Because members of
7   Congress could not reach consensus on the treatment of pre-Act offenders, it seems
8   this was one of those situations where they found it expedient to hand off the job
9   to the executive and direct there the blame for any later problems that might
10  emerge.

11  Nor can SORNA be described as an example of conditional legislation subject to
12  executive fact-finding. * * *

13                                  * * *

14  Finally, SORNA does not involve an area of overlapping authority with the
15  executive. * * *

16                                  * * *

17                                    B

18  What do the government and the plurality have to say about the constitutional
19  concerns SORNA poses? Most everyone, the plurality included, concedes that if
20  SORNA allows the Attorney General as much authority as we have outlined, it
21  would present "a nondelegation question." So the only remaining available tactic
22  is to try to make this big case "small-bore" by recasting the statute in a way that
23  might satisfy any plausible separation-of-powers test. So, yes, just a few years ago
24  in *Reynolds* the government represented to this Court that SORNA granted the
25  Attorney General nearly boundless discretion with respect to pre-Act offenders.
26  But *now*, faced with a constitutional challenge, the government speaks out of the
27  other side of its mouth and invites us to reimagine SORNA as compelling the
28  Attorney General to register pre-Act offenders "to the maximum extent feasible."
29  And, as thus reinvented, the government insists, the statute supplies a clear
30  statement of legislative policy, with only details for the Attorney General to clean
31  up.

32  But even this new dream of a statute wouldn't be free from doubt. A statute
33  directing an agency to regulate private conduct to the extent "feasible" can have
34  many possible meanings: It might refer to "technological" feasibility, "economic"
35  feasibility, "administrative" feasibility, or even "political" feasibility. Such an
36  "evasive standard" could threaten the separation of powers if it effectively allowed
37  the agency to make the "important policy choices" that belong to Congress while
38  frustrating "meaningful judicial review." And that seems exactly the case here,
39  where the Attorney General is left free to make all the important policy decisions
40  and it is difficult to see what standard a court might later use to judge whether he
41  exceeded the bounds of the authority given to him.

1 * * *

2 Nothing found here can come as a surprise. In *Reynolds*, the government told this
3 Court that SORNA supplies no standards regulating the Attorney General's
4 treatment of pre-Act offenders. This Court agreed, and everyone proceeded with
5 eyes open about the potential constitutional consequences; in fact, the dissent
6 expressly warned that adopting such a broad construction of the statute would
7 yield the separation-of-powers challenge we face today. Now, when the statute
8 faces the chopping block, the government asks us to ignore its earlier arguments
9 and reimagine (really, rewrite) the statute in a new and narrower way to avoid its
10 long-predicted fate. No wonder some of us are not inclined to play along.

11 The only real surprise is that the Court fails to make good on the consequences the
12 government invited, resolving nothing and deferring everything. In a future case
13 with a full panel, I remain hopeful that the Court may yet recognize that, while
14 Congress can enlist considerable assistance from the executive branch in filling up
15 details and finding facts, it may never hand off to the nation's chief prosecutor the
16 power to write his own criminal code. That "is delegation running riot."

17

18 ## 2. Subdelegation

19 **United States Telecom Association v. Federal Communications**
20 **Commission**

21 359 F.3d 554 (D.C. Cir. 2004)

22 March 2, 2004

23 WILLIAMS, Senior Circuit Judge:

24 The Telecommunications Act of 1996 (the "Act") sought to foster a competitive
25 market in telecommunications. To enable new firms to enter the field despite the
26 advantages of the incumbent local exchange carriers ("ILECs"), the Act gave the
27 Federal Communications Commission broad powers to require ILECs to make
28 "network elements" available to other telecommunications carriers, *id.* §§ 251(c)
29 (3), (d), most importantly the competitive local exchange carriers ("CLECs"). The
30 most obvious candidates for such obligatory provision were the copper wire loops
31 historically used to carry telephone service over the "last mile" into users' homes.
32 But Congress left to the Commission the choice of elements to be "unbundled,"
33 specifying that in doing so it was to consider, at a minimum, whether * * * the
34 failure to provide access to such network elements would *impair* the ability of the
35 telecommunications carrier seeking access to provide the services that it seeks to
36 offer. *Id.* § 251(d) (2) (emphasis added).

37 The Act became effective on February 8, 1996, a little more than eight years ago.
38 Twice since then the courts have faulted the Commission's efforts to identify the
39 elements to be unbundled. The Supreme Court invalidated the first effort in *AT&T*

33

*Corp. v. Iowa Utilities Board*, 525 U.S. 366, 389-90 (1999) ("*AT&T*"). We invalidated much of the second effort (including separately adopted "line-sharing" rules) in *United States Telecom Association v. FCC*, 290 F.3d 415 (D.C. Cir. 2002) ("USTA I"). The Commission consolidated our remand in that case with its "triennial review" of the scope of obligatory unbundling and issued the Order on review here. Again, regrettably, much of the resulting work is unlawful.

* * *

Section 251(c)(3) of the Act imposes on each ILEC the duty to provide any requesting telecommunications carrier with access to network elements on an unbundled basis at any technically feasible point on rates, terms, and conditions that are just, reasonable, and nondiscriminatory in accordance with * * * the requirements of this section and section 252 of this title.

* * *

The Commission made a nationwide finding that CLECs are impaired without unbundled access to ILEC switches for the "mass market," consisting of residential and relatively small business users. * * * But the Commission, apparently concerned that a blanket nationwide impairment determination might be unlawfully overbroad in light of the record evidence of substantial market-by-market variation in hot cut costs, delegated authority to state commissions to make more "nuanced" and "granular" impairment determinations.

First, the Commission directed the state commissions to eliminate unbundling if a market contained at least three competitors in addition to the ILEC, or at least two non-ILEC third parties that offered access to their own switches on a wholesale basis. For purposes of this exercise the Commission gave the states virtually unlimited discretion over the definition of the relevant market. Second, where these "competitive triggers" are not met, the Commission instructed the states to consider whether, despite the many economic and operational entry barriers deemed relevant by the Commission, competitive supply of mass market switching was nevertheless feasible. The Commission also instructed the states to explore specific mechanisms to ameliorate or eliminate the costs of the "hot cut" process. * * * If a state failed to perform the requisite analysis within nine months, the Commission would step into the position of the state commission and do the analysis itself. Finally, the Order provided that a party "aggrieved" by a state commission decision could seek a declaratory ruling from the Commission, though with no assurance when, or even whether, the Commission might respond.

We consider first whether the Commission's subdelegation of authority to the state commissions is lawful. We conclude that it is not. * * *

The FCC acknowledges that § 251(d)(2) instructs "the Commission" to "determine[]" which network elements shall be made available to CLECs on an unbundled basis. But it claims that agencies have the presumptive power to subdelegate to state commissions, so long as the statute authorizing agency action refrains from foreclosing such a power. Given the absence of any express foreclosure, the Commission argues that its interpretation of the statute on the matter of subdelegation is entitled to deference under *Chevron U.S.A. v. Natural Resources Defense Council*, 467 U.S. 837 (1984). And it claims that its interpretation is reasonable given the state commissions' independent jurisdiction over the general subject matter, the magnitude of the regulatory task, and the need for close cooperation between state and federal regulators in this area.

The Commission's position is based on a fundamental misreading of the relevant case law. When a statute delegates authority to a federal officer or agency, subdelegation to a subordinate federal officer or agency is presumptively permissible absent affirmative evidence of a contrary congressional intent. *See United States v. Giordano*, 416 U.S. 505 (1974); *Fleming v. Mohawk Wrecking & Lumber Co.*, 331 U.S. 111 (1947). But the cases recognize an important distinction between subdelegation to a subordinate and subdelegation to an outside party. The presumption that subdelegations are valid absent a showing of contrary congressional intent applies only to the former. There is no such presumption covering subdelegations to outside parties. Indeed, if anything, the case law strongly suggests that subdelegations to outside parties are assumed to be improper absent an affirmative showing of congressional authorization. * * *

This distinction is entirely sensible. When an agency delegates authority to its subordinate, responsibility—and thus accountability—clearly remain with the federal agency. But when an agency delegates power to outside parties, lines of accountability may blur, undermining an important democratic check on government decision-making. Also, delegation to outside entities increases the risk that these parties will not share the agency's "national vision and perspective," and thus may pursue goals inconsistent with those of the agency and the underlying statutory scheme. In short, subdelegation to outside entities aggravates the risk of policy drift inherent in any principal-agent relationship.

The fact that the subdelegation in this case is to state commissions rather than private organizations does not alter the analysis. Although *United States v. Mazurie*, 419 U.S. 544 (1975), noted that "limits on the authority of *Congress* to delegate its legislative power . . . are [] less stringent in cases where the entity exercising the delegated authority itself possesses independent authority over the subject matter," that decision has no application here: it involved a constitutional challenge to an express congressional delegation, rather than an administrative subdelegation, and the point of the discussion was to distinguish the still somewhat suspect case of congressional delegation to purely private organizations.

* * *

We therefore hold that, while federal agency officials may subdelegate their decision-making authority to subordinates absent evidence of contrary congressional intent, they may not subdelegate to outside entities—private or sovereign—absent affirmative evidence of authority to do so.

1             * * *

2 The FCC invokes a number of other cases in support of its idea of a presumptive
3 authority to subdelegate to entities other than subordinates. These are inapposite
4 because they do not involve subdelegation of decision-making authority. They
5 merely recognize three specific types of legitimate outside party input into agency
6 decision-making processes: (1) establishing a reasonable condition for granting
7 federal approval; (2) fact gathering; and (3) advice giving. The scheme established
8 in the Order fits none of these models.

9             * * *

10 We therefore vacate, as an unlawful subdelegation of the Commission's § 251(d)(2)
11 responsibilities, those portions of the Order that delegate to state commissions the
12 authority to determine whether CLECs are impaired without access to network
13 elements, and in particular we vacate the Commission's scheme for subdelegating
14 mass market switching determinations. * * *

15

## 3. The Legislative Veto

16

17 *INS v. Chadha* takes up the issue of the so-called legislative veto: a statutory
18 provision by which Congress reserves to itself (or some part of itself: a single
19 chamber; a committee) the power to reverse an administrative decision with the
20 force of law. Congress inserted hundreds of these provisions into statutes in the
21 years leading up to *Chadha*. One can think of legislative vetoes as an insurance
22 policy on Congress's part: even as Congress delegates enormous amounts of power
23 to agencies, it reserves the right to tell agencies no, without resorting to the
24 prohibitively time-consuming and difficult process of passing a statute. But is this
25 constitutional?

26

## U.S. Constitution, Article I, section 7, clause 2

27

28 Every bill which shall have passed the House of Representatives and the Senate,
29 shall, before it become a law, be presented to the President of the United States; if
30 he approve he shall sign it, but if not he shall return it, with his objections to that
31 House in which it shall have originated, who shall enter the objections at large on
32 their journal, and proceed to reconsider it. If after such reconsideration two thirds
33 of that House shall agree to pass the bill, it shall be sent, together with the
34 objections, to the other House, by which it shall likewise be reconsidered, and if
35 approved by two thirds of that House, it shall become a law. But in all such cases
36 the votes of both Houses shall be determined by yeas and nays, and the names of
37 the persons voting for and against the bill shall be entered on the journal of each
38 House respectively. If any bill shall not be returned by the President within ten
39 days (Sundays excepted) after it shall have been presented to him, the same shall

1  be a law, in like manner as if he had signed it, unless the Congress by their
2  adjournment prevent its return, in which case it shall not be a law.

3

4  **Immigration and Naturalization Service v. Chadha**

5  462 U.S. 919 (1983)

6  June 23, 1983

7  CHIEF JUSTICE BURGER delivered the opinion of the Court.

8  * * *

9  I

10  Chadha is an East Indian who was born in Kenya and holds a British passport. He
11  was lawfully admitted to the United States in 1966 on a nonimmigrant student visa.
12  His visa expired on June 30, 1972. On October 11, 1973, the District Director of the
13  Immigration and Naturalization Service ordered Chadha to show cause why he
14  should not be deported for having "remained in the United States for a longer time
15  than permitted." Pursuant to § 242(b) of the Immigration and Nationality Act
16  (Act), 8 U.S.C. § 1252(b), a deportation hearing was held before an Immigration
17  Judge on January 11, 1974. Chadha conceded that he was deportable for
18  overstaying his visa, and the hearing was adjourned to enable him to file an
19  application for suspension of deportation under § 244(a)(1) of the Act. Section
20  244(a)(1), at the time in question, provided:

21     "As hereinafter prescribed in this section, the Attorney General may, in his
22     discretion, suspend deportation and adjust the status to that of an alien
23     lawfully admitted for permanent residence, in the case of an alien who
24     applies to the Attorney General for suspension of deportation and —

25     "(1) is deportable under any law of the United States except the provisions
26     specified in paragraph (2) of this subsection; has been physically present in
27     the United States for a continuous period of not less than seven years
28     immediately preceding the date of such application, and proves that during
29     all of such period he was and is a person of good moral character; and is a
30     person whose deportation would, in the opinion of the Attorney General,
31     result in extreme hardship to the alien or to his spouse, parent, or child,
32     who is a citizen of the United States or an alien lawfully admitted for
33     permanent residence."

34  After Chadha submitted his application for suspension of deportation, the
35  deportation hearing was resumed on February 7, 1974. On the basis of evidence
36  adduced at the hearing, affidavits submitted with the application, and the results
37  of a character investigation conducted by the INS, the Immigration Judge, on June

25, 1974, ordered that Chadha's deportation be suspended. The Immigration Judge found that Chadha met the requirements of § 244(a)(1): he had resided continuously in the United States for over seven years, was of good moral character, and would suffer "extreme hardship" if deported.

Pursuant to § 244(c)(1) of the Act, 8 U.S.C. § 1254(c)(1), the Immigration Judge suspended Chadha's deportation and a report of the suspension was transmitted to Congress. Section 244(c)(1) provides:

> "Upon application by any alien who is found by the Attorney General to meet the requirements of subsection (a) of this section the Attorney General may in his discretion suspend deportation of such alien. If the deportation of any alien is suspended under the provisions of this subsection, a complete and detailed statement of the facts and pertinent provisions of law in the case shall be reported to the Congress with the reasons for such suspension. Such reports shall be submitted on the first day of each calendar month in which Congress is in session."

Once the Attorney General's recommendation for suspension of Chadha's deportation was conveyed to Congress, Congress had the power under § 244(c)(2) of the Act, 8 U.S.C. § 1254(c)(2), to veto the Attorney General's determination that Chadha should not be deported. Section 244(c)(2) provides:

> "(2) In the case of an alien specified in paragraph (1) of subsection (a) of this subsection —

> "if during the session of the Congress at which a case is reported, or prior to the close of the session of the Congress next following the session at which a case is reported, either the Senate or the House of Representatives passes a resolution stating in substance that it does not favor the suspension of such deportation, the Attorney General shall thereupon deport such alien or authorize the alien's voluntary departure at his own expense under the order of deportation in the manner provided by law. If, within the time above specified, neither the Senate nor the House of Representatives shall pass such a resolution, the Attorney General shall cancel deportation proceedings."

The June 25, 1974, order of the Immigration Judge suspending Chadha's deportation remained outstanding as a valid order for a year and a half. For reasons not disclosed by the record, Congress did not exercise the veto authority reserved to it under § 244(c)(2) until the first session of the 94th Congress. This was the final session in which Congress, pursuant to § 244(c)(2), could act to veto the Attorney General's determination that Chadha should not be deported. The session ended on December 19. Absent congressional action, Chadha's deportation proceedings would have been canceled after this date and his status adjusted to that of a permanent resident alien.

38

1   On December 12, 1975, Representative Eilberg, Chairman of the Judiciary
2   Subcommittee on Immigration, Citizenship, and International Law, introduced a
3   resolution opposing "the granting of permanent residence in the United States to
4   [six] aliens," including Chadha. * * * So far as the record before us shows, the
5   House consideration of the resolution was based on Representative Eilberg's
6   statement from the floor that

7       "[it] was the feeling of the committee, after reviewing 340 cases, that the
8       aliens contained in the resolution [Chadha and five others] did not meet
9       these statutory requirements, particularly as it relates to hardship; and it is
10      the opinion of the committee that their deportation should not be
11      suspended." 121 Cong. Rec. 40800

12  The resolution was passed without debate or recorded vote. Since the House action
13  was pursuant to § 244(c)(2), the resolution was not treated as an Art. I legislative
14  act; it was not submitted to the Senate or presented to the President for his action.

15  After the House veto of the Attorney General's decision to allow Chadha to remain
16  in the United States, the Immigration Judge reopened the deportation proceedings
17  to implement the House order deporting Chadha. Chadha moved to terminate the
18  proceedings on the ground that § 244(c)(2) is unconstitutional. The Immigration
19  Judge held that he had no authority to rule on the constitutional validity of §
20  244(c)(2). On November 8, 1976, Chadha was ordered deported pursuant to the
21  House action.

22                                        * * *

23  * * * [T]he [Ninth Circuit] Court of Appeals held that the House was without
24  constitutional authority to order Chadha's deportation; accordingly it directed the
25  Attorney General "to cease and desist from taking any steps to deport this alien
26  based upon the resolution enacted by the House of Representatives." The essence
27  of its holding was that § 244(c)(2) violates the constitutional doctrine of separation
28  of powers.

29  We granted certiorari * * *, and we now affirm.

30                                        * * *

31                                         III

32                                          A

33  We turn now to the question whether action of one House of Congress under §
34  244(c)(2) violates strictures of the Constitution. We begin, of course, with the
35  presumption that the challenged statute is valid. Its wisdom is not the concern of
36  the courts; if a challenged action does not violate the Constitution, it must be
37  sustained:

1 "Once the meaning of an enactment is discerned and its constitutionality
2 determined, the judicial process comes to an end. We do not sit as a committee of
3 review, nor are we vested with the power of veto." *TVA v. Hill*, 437 U.S. 153, 194-
4 195 (1978).

5 By the same token, the fact that a given law or procedure is efficient, convenient,
6 and useful in facilitating functions of government, standing alone, will not save it
7 if it is contrary to the Constitution. Convenience and efficiency are not the primary
8 objectives—or the hallmarks—of democratic government, and our inquiry is
9 sharpened, rather than blunted, by the fact that congressional veto provisions are
10 appearing with increasing frequency in statutes which delegate authority to
11 executive and independent agencies:

12 "Since 1932, when the first veto provision was enacted into law, 295
13 congressional veto-type procedures have been inserted in 196 different
14 statutes as follows: from 1932 to 1939, five statutes were affected; from
15 1940-49, nineteen statutes; between 1950-59, thirty-four statutes; and
16 from 1960-69, forty-nine. From the year 1970 through 1975, at least one
17 hundred sixty-three such provisions were included in eighty-nine laws."

18 JUSTICE WHITE undertakes to make a case for the proposition that the one-
19 House veto is a useful "political invention," and we need not challenge that
20 assertion. We can even concede this utilitarian argument, although the long-range
21 political wisdom of this "invention" is arguable. It has been vigorously debated,
22 and it is instructive to compare the views of the protagonists. But policy arguments
23 supporting even useful "political inventions" are subject to the demands of the
24 Constitution, which defines powers and, with respect to this subject, sets out just
25 how those powers are to be exercised.

26 Explicit and unambiguous provisions of the Constitution prescribe and define the
27 respective functions of the Congress and of the Executive in the legislative process.
28 Since the precise terms of those familiar provisions are critical to the resolution of
29 these cases, we set them out verbatim. Article I provides:

30 "All legislative Powers herein granted shall be vested in a Congress of the
31 United States, which shall consist of a Senate *and* House of
32 Representatives."

33 Art. I, § 1. (Emphasis added.)

34 "Every Bill which shall have passed the House of Representatives *and* the
35 Senate, *shall*, before it becomes a law, be presented to the President of the
36 United States...."

37 Art. I, § 7, cl. 2. (Emphasis added.)

38 *"Every* Order, Resolution, or Vote to which the Concurrence of the Senate
39 and House of Representatives may be necessary (except on a question of

1     Adjournment) *shall be* presented to the President of the United States; and
2     before the Same shall take Effect, *shall be* approved by him, or being
3     disapproved by him, *shall be* repassed by two thirds of the Senate and
4     House of Representatives, according to the Rules and Limitations
5     prescribed in the Case of a Bill."

6     Art. I, § 7, cl. 3. (Emphasis added.)

7     These provisions of Art. I are integral parts of the constitutional design for the
8     separation of powers. We have recently noted that "[t]he principle of separation of
9     powers was not simply an abstract generalization in the minds of the Framers: it
10    was woven into the document that they drafted in Philadelphia in the summer of
11    1787." *Buckley v. Valeo*, 424 U.S., at 124 (1976). Just as we relied on the textual
12    provision of Art. II, § 2, cl. 2, to vindicate the principle of separation of powers in
13    *Buckley*, we see that the purposes underlying the Presentment Clauses, Art. I, § 7,
14    cls. 2, 3, and the bicameral requirement of Art. I, § 1, and § 7, cl. 2, guide our
15    resolution of the important question presented in these cases. The very structure
16    of the Articles delegating and separating powers under Arts. I, II, and III
17    exemplifies the concept of separation of powers, and we now turn to Art. I.

18    B

19    *The Presentment Clauses*

20    The records of the Constitutional Convention reveal that the requirement that all
21    legislation be presented to the President before becoming law was uniformly
22    accepted by the Framers. Presentment to the President and the Presidential veto
23    were considered so imperative that the draftsmen took special pains to assure that
24    these requirements could not be circumvented. During the final debate on Art. I, §
25    7, cl. 2, James Madison expressed concern that it might easily be evaded by the
26    simple expedient of calling a proposed law a "resolution" or "vote," rather than a
27    "bill." As a consequence, Art. I, § 7, cl. 3 was added.

28    The decision to provide the President with a limited and qualified power to nullify
29    proposed legislation by veto was based on the profound conviction of the Framers
30    that the powers conferred on Congress were the powers to be most carefully
31    circumscribed. It is beyond doubt that lawmaking was a power to be shared by both
32    Houses and the President. In The Federalist No. 73, Hamilton focused on the
33    President's role in making laws:

34    "If even no propensity had ever discovered itself in the legislative body to
35    invade the rights of the Executive, the rules of just reasoning and theoretic
36    propriety would of themselves teach us that the one ought not to be left to
37    the mercy of the other, but ought to possess a constitutional and effectual
38    power of self-defence." [sic]

39    * * *

1 The Court also has observed that the Presentment Clauses serve the important
2 purpose of assuring that a "national" perspective is grafted on the legislative
3 process:

4 "The President is a representative of the people just as the members of the Senate
5 and of the House are, and it may be, at some times, on some subjects, that the
6 President elected by all the people is rather more representative of them all than
7 are the members of either body of the Legislature, whose constituencies are local
8 and not countrywide. . . ." *Myers v. United States*, 272 U.S. 52, 123 (1926).

9 C

10 *Bicameralism*

11 The bicameral requirement of Art. I, §§ 1, 7, was of scarcely less concern to the
12 Framers than was the Presidential veto, and indeed the two concepts are
13 interdependent. By providing that no law could take effect without the concurrence
14 of the prescribed majority of the Members of both Houses, the Framers
15 reemphasized their belief, already remarked upon in connection with the
16 Presentment Clauses, that legislation should not be enacted unless it has been
17 carefully and fully considered by the Nation's elected officials. In the Constitutional
18 Convention debates on the need for a bicameral legislature, James Wilson, later to
19 become a Justice of this Court, commented:

20 "Despotism comes on mankind in different shapes, sometimes in an Executive,
21 sometimes in a military, one. Is there danger of a Legislative despotism? Theory &
22 practice both proclaim it. If the Legislative authority be not restrained, there can
23 be neither liberty nor stability; and it can only be restrained by dividing it within
24 itself, into distinct and independent branches. In a single house there is no check
25 but the inadequate one of the virtue & good sense of those who compose it." 1
26 Farrand 254.

27 Hamilton argued that a Congress comprised of a single House was antithetical to
28 the very purposes of the Constitution. Were the Nation to adopt a Constitution
29 providing for only one legislative organ, he warned:

30 "[We] shall finally accumulate, in a single body, all the most important
31 prerogatives of sovereignty, and thus entail upon our posterity one of the most
32 execrable forms of government that human infatuation ever contrived. Thus we
33 should create in reality that very tyranny which the adversaries of the new
34 Constitution either are, or affect to be, solicitous to avert." The Federalist No. 22.

35 * * *

36 However familiar, it is useful to recall that, apart from their fear that special
37 interests could be favored at the expense of public needs, the Framers were also
38 concerned, although not of one mind, over the apprehensions of the smaller states.
39 Those states feared a commonality of interest among the larger states would work
40 to their disadvantage; representatives of the larger states, on the other hand, were

42

1   skeptical of a legislature that could pass laws favoring a minority of the people. It
2   need hardly be repeated here that the Great Compromise, under which one House
3   was viewed as representing the people and the other the states, allayed the fears of
4   both the large and small states.

5   We see therefore that the Framers were acutely conscious that the bicameral
6   requirement and the Presentment Clauses would serve essential constitutional
7   functions. The President's participation in the legislative process was to protect the
8   Executive Branch from Congress and to protect the whole people from improvident
9   laws. The division of the Congress into two distinctive bodies assures that the
10  legislative power would be exercised only after opportunity for full study and
11  debate in separate settings. The President's unilateral veto power, in turn, was
12  limited by the power of two-thirds of both Houses of Congress to overrule a veto,
13  thereby precluding final arbitrary action of one person. It emerges clearly that the
14  prescription for legislative action in Art. I, §§ 1, 7, represents the Framers' decision
15  that the legislative power of the Federal Government be exercised in accord with a
16  single, finely wrought and exhaustively considered, procedure.

17                                      IV

18  The Constitution sought to divide the delegated powers of the new Federal
19  Government into three defined categories, Legislative, Executive, and Judicial, to
20  assure, as nearly as possible, that each branch of government would confine itself
21  to its assigned responsibility. The hydraulic pressure inherent within each of the
22  separate Branches to exceed the outer limits of its power, even to accomplish
23  desirable objectives, must be resisted.

24  Although not "hermetically" sealed from one another, *Buckley v. Valeo*, 424 U.S.,
25  at 121, the powers delegated to the three Branches are functionally identifiable.
26  When any Branch acts, it is presumptively exercising the power the Constitution
27  has delegated to it. *See J. W. Hampton & Co. v. United States*, 276 U.S. 394, 406
28  (1928). When the Executive acts, he presumptively acts in an executive or
29  administrative capacity as defined in Art. II. And when, as here, one House of
30  Congress purports to act, it is presumptively acting within its assigned sphere.

31  Beginning with this presumption, we must nevertheless establish that the
32  challenged action under § 244(c)(2) is of the kind to which the procedural
33  requirements of Art. I, § 7, apply. Not every action taken by either House is subject
34  to the bicameralism and presentment requirements of Art. I. Whether actions
35  taken by either House are, in law and fact, an exercise of legislative power depends
36  not on their form, but upon "whether they contain matter which is properly to be
37  regarded as legislative in its character and effect."

38  Examination of the action taken here by one House pursuant to § 244(c)(2) reveals
39  that it was essentially legislative in purpose and effect. In purporting to exercise
40  power defined in Art. I, § 8, cl. 4, to "establish an uniform Rule of Naturalization,"
41  the House took action that had the purpose and effect of altering the legal rights,
42  duties, and relations of persons, including the Attorney General, Executive Branch

officials and Chadha, all outside the Legislative Branch. Section 244(c)(2) purports to authorize one House of Congress to require the Attorney General to deport an individual alien whose deportation otherwise would be canceled under § 244. The one-House veto operated in these cases to overrule the Attorney General and mandate Chadha's deportation; absent the House action, Chadha would remain in the United States. Congress has acted, and its action has altered Chadha's status.

The legislative character of the one-House veto in these cases is confirmed by the character of the congressional action it supplants. Neither the House of Representatives nor the Senate contends that, absent the veto provision in § 244(c)(2), either of them, or both of them acting together, could effectively require the Attorney General to deport an alien once the Attorney General, in the exercise of legislatively delegated authority, had determined the alien should remain in the United States. Without the challenged provision in § 244(c)(2), this could have been achieved, if at all, only by legislation requiring deportation. Similarly, a veto by one House of Congress under § 244(c)(2) cannot be justified as an attempt at amending the standards set out in § 244(a)(1), or as a repeal of § 244 as applied to Chadha. Amendment and repeal of statutes, no less than enactment, must conform with Art. I.

The nature of the decision implemented by the one-House veto in these cases further manifests its legislative character. After long experience with the clumsy, time-consuming private bill procedure, Congress made a deliberate choice to delegate to the Executive Branch, and specifically to the Attorney General, the authority to allow deportable aliens to remain in this country in certain specified circumstances. It is not disputed that this choice to delegate authority is precisely the kind of decision that can be implemented only in accordance with the procedures set out in Art. I. Disagreement with the Attorney General's decision on Chadha's deportation—that is, Congress' decision to deport Chadha—no less than Congress' original choice to delegate to the Attorney General the authority to make that decision, involves determinations of policy that Congress can implement in only one way; bicameral passage followed by presentment to the President. Congress must abide by its delegation of authority until that delegation is legislatively altered or revoked.

Finally, we see that, when the Framers intended to authorize either House of Congress to act alone and outside of its prescribed bicameral legislative role, they narrowly and precisely defined the procedure for such action. There are four provisions in the Constitution, explicit and unambiguous, by which one House may act alone with the unreviewable force of law, not subject to the President's veto:

> (a) The House of Representatives alone was given the power to initiate impeachments. Art. I, § 2, cl. 5;

> (b) The Senate alone was given the power to conduct trials following impeachment on charges initiated by the House, and to convict following trial. Art. I, § 3, cl. 6;

44

1         (c) The Senate alone was given final unreviewable power to approve or to
2         disapprove Presidential appointments. Art. II, § 2, cl. 2;

3         (d) The Senate alone was given unreviewable power to ratify treaties
4         negotiated by the President. Art. II, 2, cl. 2.

5    Clearly, when the Draftsmen sought to confer special powers on one House,
6    independent of the other House, or of the President, they did so in explicit,
7    unambiguous terms. * * *

8    Since it is clear that the action by the House under § 244(c)(2) was not within any
9    of the express constitutional exceptions authorizing one House to act alone, and
10   equally clear that it was an exercise of legislative power, that action was subject to
11   the standards prescribed in Art. I. The bicameral requirement, the Presentment
12   Clauses, the President's veto, and Congress' power to override a veto were intended
13   to erect enduring checks on each Branch and to protect the people from the
14   improvident exercise of power by mandating certain prescribed steps. To preserve
15   those checks, and maintain the separation of powers, the carefully defined limits
16   on the power of each Branch must not be eroded. To accomplish what has been
17   attempted by one House of Congress in this case requires action in conformity with
18   the express procedures of the Constitution's prescription for legislative action:
19   passage by a majority of both Houses and presentment to the President.

20   JUSTICE POWELL, concurring in the judgment.

21   The Court's decision, based on the Presentment Clauses, Art. I, § 7, cls. 2 and 3,
22   apparently will invalidate every use of the legislative veto. The breadth of this
23   holding gives one pause. Congress has included the veto in literally hundreds of
24   statutes, dating back to the 1930's. Congress clearly views this procedure as
25   essential to controlling the delegation of power to administrative agencies. One
26   reasonably may disagree with Congress' assessment of the veto's utility, but the
27   respect due its judgment as a coordinate branch of Government cautions that our
28   holding should be no more extensive than necessary to decide these cases. In my
29   view, the cases may be decided on a narrower ground. When Congress finds that a
30   particular person does not satisfy the statutory criteria for permanent residence in
31   this country, it has assumed a judicial function in violation of the principle of
32   separation of powers. Accordingly, I concur only in the judgment.

33                       * * *

34                       I

35                       * * *

36                       B

37   The Constitution does not establish three branches with precisely defined
38   boundaries. See *Buckley v. Valeo*, 424 U.S. 1, 121 (1976) (*per curiam*). Rather, as
39   JUSTICE JACKSON wrote: "While the Constitution diffuses power the better to

1   secure liberty, it also contemplates that practice will integrate the dispersed powers
2   into a workable government. It enjoins upon its branches separateness but
3   interdependence, autonomy but reciprocity." *Youngstown Sheet & Tube Co. v.*
4   *Sawyer*, 343 U.S. 579, 635 (1952) (concurring in judgment). The Court thus has
5   been mindful that the boundaries between each branch should be fixed "according
6   to common sense and the inherent necessities of the governmental coordination."
7   *J. W. Hampton & Co. v. United States*, 276 U.S. 394, 406 (1928). But where one
8   branch has impaired or sought to assume a power central to another branch, the
9   Court has not hesitated to enforce the doctrine.

10   Functionally, the doctrine may be violated in two ways. One branch may interfere
11   impermissibly with the other's performance of its constitutionally assigned
12   function. See *Nixon v. Administrator of General Services*, 433 U.S. 425, 433
13   (1977); *United States v. Nixon*, 418 U.S. 683 (1974). Alternatively, the doctrine may
14   be violated when one branch assumes a function that more properly is entrusted
15   to another. See *Youngstown Sheet & Tube Co. v. Sawyer, supra*, at 343 U.S. 587;
16   *Springer v. Philippine Islands*, 277 U.S. 189, 203 (1928). These cases present the
17   latter situation.

18   II

19   * * *

20   On its face, the House's action appears clearly adjudicatory. The House did not
21   enact a general rule; rather, it made its own determination that six specific persons
22   did not comply with certain statutory criteria. It thus undertook the type of
23   decision that traditionally has been left to other branches. Even if the House did
24   not make a *de novo* determination, but simply reviewed the Immigration and
25   Naturalization Service's findings, it still assumed a function ordinarily entrusted
26   to the federal courts. * * *

27   The impropriety of the House's assumption of this function is confirmed by the fact
28   that its action raises the very danger the Framers sought to avoid—the exercise of
29   unchecked power. In deciding whether Chadha deserves to be deported, Congress
30   is not subject to any internal constraints that prevent it from arbitrarily depriving
31   him of the right to remain in this country. Unlike the judiciary or an administrative
32   agency, Congress is not bound by established substantive rules. Nor is it subject to
33   the procedural safeguards, such as the right to counsel and a hearing before an
34   impartial tribunal, that are present when a court or an agency adjudicates
35   individual rights. The only effective constraint on Congress' power is political, but
36   Congress is most accountable politically when it prescribes rules of general
37   applicability. When it decides rights of specific persons, those rights are subject to
38   "the tyranny of a shifting majority."

39   * * *

40   JUSTICE WHITE, dissenting.

Today the Court not only invalidates § 244(c)(2) of the Immigration and Nationality Act, but also sounds the death knell for nearly 200 other statutory provisions in which Congress has reserved a "legislative veto." For this reason, the Court's decision is of surpassing importance. And it is for this reason that the Court would have been well advised to decide the cases, if possible, on the narrower grounds of separation of powers, leaving for full consideration the constitutionality of other congressional review statutes operating on such varied matters as war powers and agency rulemaking, some of which concern the independent regulatory agencies.

The prominence of the legislative veto mechanism in our contemporary political system and its importance to Congress can hardly be overstated. It has become a central means by which Congress secures the accountability of executive and independent agencies. Without the legislative veto, Congress is faced with a Hobson's choice: either to refrain from delegating the necessary authority, leaving itself with a hopeless task of writing laws with the requisite specificity to cover endless special circumstances across the entire policy landscape, or, in the alternative, to abdicate its lawmaking function to the Executive Branch and independent agencies. To choose the former leaves major national problems unresolved; to opt for the latter risks unaccountable policymaking by those not elected to fill that role. * * *

* * *

* * * The Court's holding today that all legislative-type action must be enacted through the lawmaking process ignores that legislative authority is routinely delegated to the Executive Branch, to the independent regulatory agencies, and to private individuals and groups.

* * *

This Court's decisions sanctioning such delegations make clear that Art. I does not require all action with the effect of legislation to be passed as a law.

* * *

The wisdom and the constitutionality of these broad delegations are matters that still have not been put to rest. But for present purposes, these cases establish that, by virtue of congressional delegation, legislative power can be exercised by independent agencies and Executive departments without the passage of new legislation. For some time, the sheer amount of law—the substantive rules that regulate private conduct and direct the operation of government—made by the agencies has far outnumbered the lawmaking engaged in by Congress through the traditional process. There is no question but that agency rulemaking is lawmaking in any functional or realistic sense of the term. * * * When agencies are authorized to prescribe law through substantive rulemaking, the administrator's * * * regulations bind courts and officers of the Federal Government, may preempt state

1  law and grant rights to and impose obligations on the public. In sum, they have the
2  force of law.

3  If Congress may delegate lawmaking power to independent and Executive
4  agencies, it is most difficult to understand Art. I as prohibiting Congress from also
5  reserving a check on legislative power for itself. Absent the veto, the agencies
6  receiving delegations of legislative or quasi-legislative power may issue regulations
7  having the force of law without bicameral approval and without the President's
8  signature. It is thus not apparent why the reservation of a veto over the exercise of
9  that legislative power must be subject to a more exacting test. In both cases, it is
10  enough that the initial statutory authorizations comply with the Art. I
11  requirements.

12                                    * * *

13  The central concern of the presentment and bicameralism requirements of Art. I is
14  that, when a departure from the legal status quo is undertaken, it is done with the
15  approval of the President and both Houses of Congress—or, in the event of a
16  Presidential veto, a two-thirds majority in both Houses. This interest is fully
17  satisfied by the operation of § 244(c)(2). The President's approval is found in the
18  Attorney General's action in recommending to Congress that the deportation order
19  for a given alien be suspended. The House and the Senate indicate their approval
20  of the Executive's action by not passing a resolution of disapproval within the
21  statutory period. Thus, a change in the legal status quo—the deportability of the
22  alien—is consummated only with the approval of each of the three relevant actors.
23  The disagreement of any one of the three maintains the alien's preexisting status:
24  the Executive may choose not to recommend suspension; the House and Senate
25  may each veto the recommendation. The effect on the rights and obligations of the
26  affected individuals and upon the legislative system is precisely the same as if a
27  private bill were introduced but failed to receive the necessary approval. "The
28  President and the two Houses enjoy exactly the same say in what the law is to be
29  as would have been true for each without the presence of the one-House veto, and
30  nothing in the law is changed absent the concurrence of the President and a
31  majority in each House." *Atkins v. United States*, 556 F.2d 1028, 1064 (1977).

32                                    * * *

33  JUSTICE REHNQUIST, with whom JUSTICE WHITE joins, dissenting.

34  A severability clause creates a presumption that Congress intended the valid
35  portion of the statute to remain in force when one part is found to be invalid. A
36  severability clause does not, however, conclusively resolve the issue. "[T]he
37  determination, in the end, is reached by" asking "[w]hat was the intent of the
38  lawmakers,", and "will rarely turn on the presence or absence of such a clause."
39  Because I believe that Congress did not intend the one-House veto provision of §
40  244(c)(2) to be severable, I dissent.

Section 244(c)(2) is an exception to the general rule that an alien's deportation shall be suspended when the Attorney General finds that statutory criteria are met. It is severable only if Congress would have intended to permit the Attorney General to suspend deportations without it. This Court has held several times over the years that exceptions such as this are not severable because, "by rejecting the exceptions intended by the legislature . . . the statute is made to enact what confessedly the legislature never meant. It confers upon the statute a positive operation beyond the legislative intent, and beyond what anyone can say it would have enacted in view of the illegality of the exceptions." *Spraigue v. Thompson*, 118 U.S. 90, 95 (1886).

\* \* \*

The Court finds that the legislative history of § 244 shows that Congress intended § 244(C)(2) to be severable because Congress wanted to relieve itself of the burden of private bills. But the history elucidated by the Court shows that Congress was unwilling to give the Executive Branch permission to suspend deportation on its own. Over the years, Congress consistently rejected requests from the Executive for complete discretion in this area. Congress always insisted on retaining ultimate control, whether by concurrent resolution, as in the 1948 Act, or by one-House veto, as in the present Act. Congress has never indicated that it would be willing to permit suspensions of deportation unless it could retain some sort of veto.

It is doubtless true that Congress has the power to provide for suspensions of deportation without a one-House veto. But the Court has failed to identify any evidence that Congress intended to exercise that power. On the contrary, Congress' continued insistence on retaining control of the suspension process indicates that it has never been disposed to give the Executive Branch a free hand. By severing § 244(c)(2), the Court has "'confounded'" Congress' "'intention'" to permit suspensions of deportation "'with their power to carry that intention into effect.'"

Because I do not believe that § 244(c)(2) is severable, I would reverse the judgment of the Court of Appeals.

## B. Agencies and the Executive Power

The President is the head of the executive branch, vested by Article II of the Constitution with the power and responsibility to "take care that the laws be faithfully executed." Of course, as a practical matter, it is agencies that are on the front lines of executing the law. How do we reconcile the grant of executive responsibilities to the President with the reality that lower-level officials–agency personnel–actually carry out the law (and have since the beginning)? What does Article II of the Constitution say (or imply) about the President's relation to those officials?

1 The relevant caselaw is concerned mostly with two issues: the rules that govern the
2 appointing of officers of the United States, and the President's power to remove
3 officials. The first two units of this section address these topics, respectively.

4 Appointment and removal of officers are by no means the only, or necessarily the
5 most important, tools the President has to shape the operation of the
6 administrative state. Later we will address a series of moves Presidents have made,
7 going back four decades, to exert more control over agency policymaking, and
8 specifically over agencies' production of regulations.

9

## 1. Appointment of Officers

11 The Constitution provides fairly detailed instructions, in Article II, section 2,
12 clause 2, for the appointment of "Officers of the United States." There is one
13 procedure that must be followed for the appointment of principal officers
14 (nominated by the President, confirmed by the Senate) and three additional
15 options available for the appointment of inferior officers (appointment vested in
16 President alone, or heads of department, or courts of law).

17 So far so good. Still, to know what appointment procedures govern in a specific
18 instance, we need answers to two further questions: (1) Who is an officer of the
19 United States? (2) What is the difference between a principal officer and an inferior
20 officer?

21 The cases that follow address these questions.

22 As the number of cases in this section reflects, the Supreme Court has devoted
23 substantial attention to these questions in recent years. How close are we to having
24 workable answers? Are the Court's doctrines clear enough that we can apply them
25 to the diverse array of agency structures we find "in the wild" with predictable
26 results? Do they lead to results that work well for the government of a large and
27 complex country in the twenty-first century?

28 In the 1988 case *Morrison v. Olson*, the Supreme Court adopted a functionalist
29 approach to appointment and removal issues, in which an important consideration
30 was how given arrangements impacted how the branches performed their
31 constitutional functions. The Court appears to move away from this approach in
32 its more recent cases, a move that Justice Breyer laments when he writes separately
33 in *Arthrex*. The majority in *Arthrex* takes a more formalist approach, making the
34 cases' outcome hinge on a bright-line rule, albeit a rule for which four Justices find
35 no basis in the Constitution. Based on your reading of these cases, does a formalist
36 or a functionalist approach come out looking better?

37 The 1991 case *Freytag v. Commissioner* also raises an appointments issue, and is
38 discussed at length in one of the Supreme Court's most recent pronouncement on
39 appointments, *Lucia v. SEC*. But because *Freytag* raises a question about how

1    agencies relate to the judicial branch as well, it is included in the unit on agencies
2    and the judicial branch.

3

## 4   U.S. Constitution, art. II, § 2, cl. 2

5    [The President] shall have Power, by and with the Advice and Consent of the
6    Senate, to make Treaties, provided two thirds of the Senators present concur; and
7    he shall nominate, and by and with the Advice and Consent of the Senate, shall
8    appoint Ambassadors, other public Ministers and Consuls, Judges of the supreme
9    Court, and all other Officers of the United States, whose Appointments are not
10   herein otherwise provided for, and which shall be established by Law: but the
11   Congress may by Law vest the Appointment of such inferior Officers, as they think
12   proper, in the President alone, in the Courts of Law, or in the Heads of
13   Departments.

14

## 15   Buckley v. Valeo

16   424 U.S. 1 (1976)

17   January 30, 1976

18   PER CURIAM.

19   These appeals present constitutional challenges to the key provisions of the
20   Federal Election Campaign Act of 1971 (Act), and related provisions of the Internal
21   Revenue Code of 1954, all as amended in 1974.

22   The Court of Appeals, in sustaining the legislation in large part against various
23   constitutional challenges, viewed it as "by far the most comprehensive reform
24   legislation [ever] passed by Congress concerning the election of the President,
25   Vice-President, and members of Congress." The statutes at issue, summarized in
26   broad terms, contain the following provisions: (a) individual political
27   contributions are limited to $1,000 to any single candidate per election, with an
28   over-all annual limitation of $25,000 by any contributor; independent
29   expenditures by individuals and groups "relative to a clearly identified candidate"
30   are limited to $1,000 a year; campaign spending by candidates for various federal
31   offices and spending for national conventions by political parties are subject to
32   prescribed limits; (b) contributions and expenditures above certain threshold
33   levels must be reported and publicly disclosed; (c) a system for public funding of
34   Presidential campaign activities is established by Subtitle H of the Internal
35   Revenue Code; and (d) a Federal Election Commission is established to administer
36   and enforce the legislation.

37   This suit was originally filed by appellants in the United States District Court for
38   the District of Columbia. Plaintiffs included a candidate for the Presidency of the

United States, a United States Senator who is a candidate for reelection, a potential contributor, the Committee for a Constitutional Presidency—McCarthy '76, the Conservative Party of the State of New York, the Mississippi Republican Party, the Libertarian Party, the New York Civil Liberties Union, Inc., the American Conservative Union, the Conservative Victory Fund, and Human Events, Inc. The defendants included the Secretary of the United States Senate and the Clerk of the United States House of Representatives, both in their official capacities and as ex officio members of the Federal Election Commission. The Commission itself was named as a defendant. Also named were the Attorney General of the United States and the Comptroller General of the United States.

* * * The complaint sought both a declaratory judgment that the major provisions of the Act were unconstitutional and an injunction against enforcement of those provisions.

* * *

## IV. THE FEDERAL ELECTION COMMISSION

The 1974 amendments to the Act create an eight-member Federal Election Commission (Commission) and vest in it primary and substantial responsibility for administering and enforcing the Act. The question that we address in this portion of the opinion is whether, in view of the manner in which a majority of its members are appointed, the Commission may, under the Constitution, exercise the powers conferred upon it. * * *

Chapter 14 of Title 2 makes the Commission the principal repository of the numerous reports and statements which are required by that chapter to be filed by those engaging in the regulated political activities. Its duties under § 438(a) with respect to these reports and statements include filing and indexing, making them available for public inspection, preservation, and auditing and field investigations. It is directed to "serve as a national clearinghouse for information in respect to the administration of elections." § 438(b).

Beyond these recordkeeping, disclosure, and investigative functions, however, the Commission is given extensive rulemaking and adjudicative powers. Its duty under § 438(a)(10) is "to prescribe suitable rules and regulations to carry out the provisions of . . . chapter [14]." Under § 437d(a)(8), the Commission is empowered to make such rules "as are necessary to carry out the provisions of this Act." Section 437d(a)(9) authorizes it to "formulate general policy with respect to the administration of this Act" and enumerated sections of Title 18's Criminal Code, as to all of which provisions the Commission "has primary jurisdiction with respect to [their] civil enforcement." § 437c(b). The Commission is authorized under § 437f(a) to render advisory opinions with respect to activities possibly violating the Act, the Title 18 sections, or the campaign funding provisions of Title 26, the effect of which is that, "[n]otwithstanding any other provision of law, any person with respect to whom an advisory opinion is rendered . . . who acts in good faith in accordance with the provisions and findings [thereof] shall be presumed to be in compliance with the [statutory provision] with respect to which such advisory opinion is rendered." § 437f(b). In the course of administering the provisions for Presidential campaign financing, the Commission may authorize convention expenditures which exceed the statutory limits.

The Commission's enforcement power is both direct and wide-ranging. It may institute a civil action for (i) injunctive or other relief against "any acts or practices which constitute or will constitute a violation of this Act," § 437g(a)(5); (ii) declaratory or injunctive relief "as may be appropriate to implement or cons[true] any provisions" of Chapter 95 of Title 26, governing administration of funds for Presidential election campaigns and national party conventions; and (iii) "such injunctive relief as is appropriate to implement any provision" of Chapter 96 of Title 26, governing the payment of matching funds for Presidential primary campaigns. If, after the Commission's post-disbursement audit of candidates receiving payments under Chapter 95 or 96, it finds an overpayment, it is empowered to seek repayment of all funds due the Secretary of the Treasury. In no respect do the foregoing civil actions require the concurrence of or participation by the Attorney General; conversely, the decision not to seek judicial relief in the above respects would appear to rest solely with the Commission. With respect to the referenced Title 18 sections, § 437g(a)(7) provides that, if, after notice and opportunity for a hearing before it, the Commission finds an actual or threatened criminal violation, the Attorney General, "upon request by the Commission . . . , shall institute a civil action for relief." Finally, as "[a]dditional enforcement authority," § 456(a) authorizes the Commission, after notice and opportunity for hearing, to make "a finding that a person . . . while a candidate for Federal office, failed to file" a required report of contributions or expenditures. If that finding is made within the applicable limitations period for prosecutions, the candidate is thereby "disqualified from becoming a candidate in any future election for Federal office for a period of time beginning on the date of such finding and ending one year after the expiration of the term of the Federal office for which such person was a candidate."

The body in which this authority is reposed consists of eight members. The Secretary of the Senate and the Clerk of the House of Representatives are *ex officio* members of the Commission without the right to vote. Two members are appointed by the President pro tempore of the Senate "upon the recommendations of the majority leader of the Senate and the minority leader of the Senate." Two more are to be appointed by the Speaker of the House of Representatives, likewise upon the recommendations of its respective majority and minority leaders. The remaining two members are appointed by the President. Each of the six voting members of the Commission must be confirmed by the majority of both Houses of Congress, and each of the three appointing authorities is forbidden to choose both of their appointees from the same political party.

\* \* \*

## B. The Merits

1   Appellants urge that, since Congress has given the Commission wide-ranging
2   rulemaking and enforcement powers with respect to the substantive provisions of
3   the Act, Congress is precluded under the principle of separation of powers from
4   vesting in itself the authority to appoint those who will exercise such authority.
5   Their argument is based on the language of Art. II, § 2, cl. 2, of the Constitution,
6   which provides in pertinent part as follows:

7   "[The President] shall nominate, and by and with the Advice and Consent
8   of the Senate, shall appoint . . . all other Officers of the United States, whose
9   Appointments are not herein otherwise provided for, and which shall be
10  established by Law: but the Congress may by Law vest the Appointment of
11  such inferior Officers, as they think proper, in the President alone, in the
12  Courts of Law, or in the Heads of Departments."

13  Appellants' argument is that this provision is the exclusive method by which those
14  charged with executing the laws of the United States may be chosen. Congress, they
15  assert, cannot have it both ways. If the Legislature wishes the Commission to
16  exercise all of the conferred powers, then its members are, in fact, "Officers of the
17  United States," and must be appointed under the Appointments Clause. But if
18  Congress insists upon retaining the power to appoint, then the members of the
19  Commission may not discharge those many functions of the Commission which
20  can be performed only by "Officers of the United States," as that term must be
21  construed within the doctrine of separation of powers.

22  Appellee Commission and amici in support of the Commission urge that the
23  Framers of the Constitution, while mindful of the need for checks and balances
24  among the three branches of the National Government, had no intention of
25  denying to the Legislative Branch authority to appoint its own officers. Congress,
26  either under the Appointments Clause or under its grants of substantive legislative
27  authority and the Necessary and Proper Clause in Art. I, is, in their view,
28  empowered to provide for the appointment to the Commission in the manner
29  which it did because the Commission is performing "appropriate legislative
30  functions."

31  The majority of the Court of Appeals * * * described appellants' argument based
32  upon Art. II, § 2, cl. 2 as "strikingly syllogistic," and concluded that Congress had
33  sufficient authority under the Necessary and Proper Clause of Art. I of the
34  Constitution not only to establish the Commission but to appoint the
35  Commission's members.

36                                      * * *

37  We do not think appellants' arguments based upon Art. II, § 2, cl. 2, of the
38  Constitution may be so easily dismissed as did the majority of the Court of Appeals.
39  * * *

40                                      * * *

54

The Appointments Clause could, of course, be read as merely dealing with etiquette or protocol in describing "Officers of the United States," but the drafters had a less frivolous purpose in mind. * * *

* * *

We think that the term "Officers of the United States," as used in Art. II, * * * is a term intended to have substantive meaning. We think its fair import is that any appointee exercising significant authority pursuant to the laws of the United States is an "Officer of the United States," and must, therefore, be appointed in the manner prescribed by § 2, cl. 2, of that Article.

* * * If a postmaster first class, *Myers v. United States*, 272 U.S. 52 (1926), and the clerk of a district court, *Ex parte Hennen*, 13 Pet. 230 (1839), are inferior officers of the United States within the meaning of the Appointments Clause, as they are, surely the Commissioners before us are, at the very least, such "inferior Officers" within the meaning of that Clause.

Although two members of the Commission are initially selected by the President, his nominations are subject to confirmation not merely by the Senate, but by the House of Representatives as well. The remaining four voting members of the Commission are appointed by the President pro tempore of the Senate and by the Speaker of the House. While the second part of the Clause authorizes Congress to vest the appointment of the officers described in that part in "the Courts of Law, or in the Heads of Departments," neither the Speaker of the House nor the President pro tempore of the Senate comes within this language.

The phrase "Heads of Departments," used as it is in conjunction with the phrase "Courts of Law," suggests that the Departments referred to are themselves in the Executive Branch or at least have some connection with that branch. While the Clause expressly authorizes Congress to vest the appointment of certain officers in the "Courts of Law," the absence of similar language to include Congress must mean that neither Congress nor its officers were included within the language "Heads of Departments" in this part of cl. 2.

Thus, with respect to four of the six voting members of the Commission, neither the President, the head of any department, nor the Judiciary has any voice in their selection.

The Appointments Clause specifies the method of appointment only for "Officers of the United States" whose appointment is not "otherwise provided for" in the Constitution. But there is no provision of the Constitution remotely providing any alternative means for the selection of the members of the Commission or for anybody like them. * * *

* * *

Appellee Commission and amici urge that, because of what they conceive to be the extraordinary authority reposed in Congress to regulate elections, this case stands

1   on a different footing than if Congress had exercised its legislative authority in
2   another field. There is, of course, no doubt that Congress has express authority to
3   regulate congressional elections * * * . But Congress has plenary authority in all
4   areas in which it has substantive legislative jurisdiction, *M'Culloch v. Maryland*,
5   17 U.S. 316 (1819), so long as the exercise of that authority does not offend some
6   other constitutional restriction. We see no reason to believe that the authority of
7   Congress over federal election practices is of such a wholly different nature from
8   the other grants of authority to Congress that it may be employed in such a manner
9   as to offend well established constitutional restrictions stemming from the
10  separation of powers.

11  The position that, because Congress has been given explicit and plenary authority
12  to regulate a field of activity, it must therefore have the power to appoint those who
13  are to administer the regulatory statute is both novel and contrary to the language
14  of the Appointments Clause. Unless their selection is elsewhere provided for, *all*
15  officers of the United States are to be appointed in accordance with the Clause.
16  Principal officers are selected by the President with the advice and consent of the
17  Senate. Inferior officers Congress may allow to be appointed by the President
18  alone, by the heads of departments, or by the Judiciary. No class or type of officer
19  is excluded because of its special functions. * * *

20                                  * * *

21  We are also told by appellees and amici that Congress had good reason for not
22  vesting in a Commission composed wholly of Presidential appointees the authority
23  to administer the Act, since the administration of the Act would undoubtedly have
24  a bearing on any incumbent President's campaign for reelection. While one cannot
25  dispute the basis for this sentiment as a practical matter, it would seem that those
26  who sought to challenge incumbent Congressmen might have equally good reason
27  to fear a Commission which was unduly responsive to members of Congress whom
28  they were seeking to unseat. But such fears, however rational, do not, by
29  themselves, warrant a distortion of the Framers' work.

30  Appellee Commission and amici finally contend, and the majority of the Court of
31  Appeals agreed with them, that, whatever shortcomings the provisions for the
32  appointment of members of the Commission might have under Art. II, Congress
33  had ample authority under the Necessary and Proper Clause of Art. I to effectuate
34  this result. We do not agree. The proper inquiry when considering the Necessary
35  and Proper Clause is not the authority of Congress to create an office or a
36  commission, which is broad indeed, but rather its authority to provide that its own
37  officers may make appointments to such office or commission.

38  So framed, the claim that Congress may provide for this manner of appointment
39  under the Necessary and Proper Clause of Art. I stands on no better footing than
40  the claim that it may provide for such manner of appointment because of its
41  substantive authority to regulate federal elections. Congress could not, merely
42  because it concluded that such a measure was "necessary and proper" to the

discharge of its substantive legislative authority, pass a bill of attainder or ex post facto law contrary to the prohibitions contained in § 9 of Art. I. No more may it vest in itself, or in its officers, the authority to appoint officers of the United States when the Appointments Clause, by clear implication, prohibits it from doing so.

\* \* \*

### 3. The Commission's Powers

Thus, on the assumption that all of the powers granted in the statute may be exercised by an agency whose members have been appointed in accordance with the Appointments Clause, the ultimate question is which, if any, of those powers may be exercised by the present voting Commissioners, none of whom was appointed as provided by that Clause. \* \* \* [T]he Commission's powers fall generally into three categories: functions relating to the flow of necessary information—receipt, dissemination, and investigation; functions with respect to the Commission's task of fleshing out the statute—rulemaking and advisory opinions; and functions necessary to ensure compliance with the statute and rules—informal procedures, administrative determinations and hearings, and civil suits.

Insofar as the powers confided in the Commission are essentially of an investigative and informative nature, falling in the same general category as those powers which Congress might delegate to one of its own committees, there can be no question that the Commission as presently constituted may exercise them.

\* \* \*

But when we go beyond this type of authority to the more substantial powers exercised by the Commission, we reach a different result. The Commission's enforcement power, exemplified by its discretionary power to seek judicial relief, is authority that cannot possibly be regarded as merely in aid of the legislative function of Congress. A lawsuit is the ultimate remedy for a breach of the law, and it is to the President, and not to the Congress, that the Constitution entrusts the responsibility to "take Care that the Laws be faithfully executed." Art. II, § 3

Congress may undoubtedly under the Necessary and Proper Clause create "offices" in the generic sense and provide such method of appointment to those "offices" as it chooses. But Congress' power under that Clause is inevitably bounded by the express language of Art. II, § 2, cl. 2, and, unless the method it provides comports with the latter, the holders of those offices will not be "Officers of the United States." They may, therefore, properly perform duties only in aid of those functions that Congress may carry out by itself, or in an area sufficiently removed from the administration and enforcement of the public law as to permit their being performed by persons not "Officers of the United States."

\* \* \*

We hold that these provisions of the Act, vesting in the Commission primary responsibility for conducting civil litigation in the courts of the United States for vindicating public rights, violate Art. II, § 2, cl. 2, of the Constitution. Such functions may be discharged only by persons who are "Officers of the United States" within the language of that section.

All aspects of the Act are brought within the Commission's broad administrative powers: rulemaking, advisory opinions, and determinations of eligibility for funds and even for federal elective office itself. These functions, exercised free from day-to-day supervision of either Congress or the Executive Branch, are more legislative and judicial in nature than are the Commission's enforcement powers, and are of kinds usually performed by independent regulatory agencies or by some department in the Executive Branch under the direction of an Act of Congress. Congress viewed these broad powers as essential to effective and impartial administration of the entire substantive framework of the Act. Yet each of these functions also represents the performance of a significant governmental duty exercised pursuant to a public law. While the President may not insist that such functions be delegated to an appointee of his removable at will, *Humphrey's Executor v. United States*, 295 U.S. 602 (1935), none of them operates merely in aid of congressional authority to legislate or is sufficiently removed from the administration and enforcement of public law to allow it to be performed by the present Commission. These administrative functions may therefore be exercised only by persons who are "Officers of the United States."

* * *

MR. CHIEF JUSTICE BURGER, concurring in part and dissenting in part. [Omitted.]

MR. JUSTICE WHITE, concurring in part and dissenting in part. [Omitted.]

MR. JUSTICE MARSHALL, concurring in part and dissenting in part. [Omitted.]

MR. JUSTICE BLACKMUN, concurring in part and dissenting in part. [Omitted.]

MR. JUSTICE REHNQUIST, concurring in part and dissenting in part. [Omitted.]

❧

*Morrison v. Olson*, from 1988, involved two constitutional challenges to the Ethics in Government Act, the statute authorizing the appointment of an independent counsel to investigate executive branch personnel: one with respect to how the independent counsel is appointed, and the other with respect to the restrictions on the independent counsel's removal. The portion of the case addressing the appointments issue is addressed here, and the portion addressing the removal issue is presented below.

1    **Morrison v. Olson**

2    487 U.S. 654 (1988)

3    June 29, 1988

4    CHIEF JUSTICE REHNQUIST delivered the opinion of the Court.

5    This case presents us with a challenge to the independent counsel provisions of the
6    Ethics in Government Act of 1978, 28 U.S.C. §§ 49, 591 *et seq.* (1982 ed., Supp. V).
7    We hold today that these provisions of the Act do not violate the Appointments
8    Clause of the Constitution, Art. II, § 2, cl. 2[.] * * *

9                                                    I

10   Briefly stated, Title VI of the Ethics in Government Act (Title VI or the Act), 28
11   U.S.C. §§ 591-599 (1982 ed., Supp. V), allows for the appointment of an
12   "independent counsel" to investigate and, if appropriate, prosecute certain high-
13   ranking Government officials for violations of federal criminal laws. The Act
14   requires the Attorney General, upon receipt of information that he determines is
15   "sufficient to constitute grounds to investigate whether any person [covered by the
16   Act] may have violated any Federal criminal law," to conduct a preliminary
17   investigation of the matter. When the Attorney General has completed this
18   investigation, or 90 days has elapsed, he is required to report to a special court (the
19   Special Division) created by the Act "for the purpose of appointing independent
20   counsels." If the Attorney General determines that "there are no reasonable
21   grounds to believe that further investigation is warranted," then he must notify the
22   Special Division of this result. In such a case, "the division of the court shall have
23   no power to appoint an independent counsel." § 592(b)(1). If, however, the
24   Attorney General has determined that there are "reasonable grounds to believe
25   that further investigation or prosecution is warranted," then he "shall apply to the
26   division of the court for the appointment of an independent counsel." The Attorney
27   General's application to the court "shall contain sufficient information to assist the
28   [court] in selecting an independent counsel and in defining that independent
29   counsel's prosecutorial jurisdiction." § 592(d). Upon receiving this application, the
30   Special Division "shall appoint an appropriate independent counsel and shall
31   define that independent counsel's prosecutorial jurisdiction." § 593(b).

32   With respect to all matters within the independent counsel's jurisdiction, the Act
33   grants the counsel "full power and independent authority to exercise all
34   investigative and prosecutorial functions and powers of the Department of Justice,
35   the Attorney General, and any other officer or employee of the Department of
36   Justice." § 594(a). The functions of the independent counsel include conducting
37   grand jury proceedings and other investigations, participating in civil and criminal
38   court proceedings and litigation, and appealing any decision in any case in which
39   the counsel participates in an official capacity. §§ 594(a)(1)-(3). Under § 594(a)(9),
40   the counsel's powers include "initiating and conducting prosecutions in any court
41   of competent jurisdiction, framing and signing indictments, filing informations,

1   and handling all aspects of any case, in the name of the United States." The counsel
2   may appoint employees, § 594(c), may request and obtain assistance from the
3   Department of Justice, § 594(d), and may accept referral of matters from the
4   Attorney General if the matter falls within the counsel's jurisdiction as defined by
5   the Special Division, § 594(e). The Act also states that an independent counsel
6   "shall, except where not possible, comply with the written or other established
7   policies of the Department of Justice respecting enforcement of the criminal laws."
8   § 594(f). In addition, whenever a matter has been referred to an independent
9   counsel under the Act, the Attorney General and the Justice Department are
10  required to suspend all investigations and proceedings regarding the matter. §
11  597(a). An independent counsel has "full authority to dismiss matters within [his
12  or her] prosecutorial jurisdiction without conducting an investigation or at any
13  subsequent time before prosecution, if to do so would be consistent" with
14  Department of Justice policy. § 594(g).

15  Two statutory provisions govern the length of an independent counsel's tenure in
16  office. The first defines the procedure for removing an independent counsel.
17  Section 596(a)(1) provides:

18      "An independent counsel appointed under this chapter may be removed
19      from office, other than by impeachment and conviction, only by the
20      personal action of the Attorney General and only for good cause, physical
21      disability, mental incapacity, or any other condition that substantially
22      impairs the performance of such independent counsel's duties."

23                                    * * *

24  The other provision governing the tenure of the independent counsel defines the
25  procedures for "terminating" the counsel's office. Under § 596(b)(1), the office of
26  an independent counsel terminates when he or she notifies the Attorney General
27  that he or she has completed or substantially completed any investigations or
28  prosecutions undertaken pursuant to the Act. In addition, the Special Division,
29  acting either on its own or on the suggestion of the Attorney General, may
30  terminate the office of an independent counsel at any time if it finds that "the
31  investigation of all matters within the prosecutorial jurisdiction of such
32  independent counsel . . . have been completed or so substantially completed that it
33  would be appropriate for the Department of Justice to complete such
34  investigations and prosecutions." § 596(b)(2).

35  Finally, the Act provides for congressional oversight of the activities of
36  independent counsel. An independent counsel may from time to time send
37  Congress statements or reports on his or her activities. § 595(a)(2). The
38  "appropriate committees of the Congress" are given oversight jurisdiction in
39  regard to the official conduct of an independent counsel, and the counsel is
40  required by the Act to cooperate with Congress in the exercise of this jurisdiction.
41  § 595(a)(1). The counsel is required to inform the House of Representatives of
42  "substantial and credible information which [the counsel] receives . . . that may

1  constitute grounds for an impeachment." § 595(c). In addition, the Act gives
2  certain congressional committee members the power to "request in writing that
3  the Attorney General apply for the appointment of an independent counsel." §
4  592(g)(1). The Attorney General is required to respond to this request within a
5  specified time, but is not required to accede to the request. § 592(g)(2).

6  The proceedings in this case provide an example of how the Act works in practice.
7  In 1982, two Subcommittees of the House of Representatives issued subpoenas
8  directing the Environmental Protection Agency (EPA) to produce certain
9  documents relating to the efforts of the EPA and the Land and Natural Resources
10 Division of the Justice Department to enforce the "Superfund Law." At that time,
11 appellee Olson was the Assistant Attorney General for the Office of Legal Counsel
12 (OLC), appellee Schmults was Deputy Attorney General, and appellee Dinkins was
13 the Assistant Attorney General for the Land and Natural Resources Division.
14 Acting on the advice of the Justice Department, the President ordered the
15 Administrator of EPA to invoke executive privilege to withhold certain of the
16 documents on the ground that they contained "enforcement-sensitive
17 information." The Administrator obeyed this order and withheld the documents.
18 In response, the House voted to hold the Administrator in contempt, after which
19 the Administrator and the United States together filed a lawsuit against the House.
20 The conflict abated in March, 1983, when the administration agreed to give the
21 House Committees limited access to the documents.

22 The following year, the House Judiciary Committee began an investigation into the
23 Justice Department's role in the controversy over the EPA documents. During this
24 investigation, appellee Olson testified before a House Subcommittee on March 10,
25 1983. Both before and after that testimony, the Department complied with several
26 Committee requests to produce certain documents. Other documents were at first
27 withheld, although these documents were eventually disclosed by the Department
28 after the Committee learned of their existence. In 1985, the majority members of
29 the Judiciary Committee published a lengthy report on the Committee's
30 investigation. Report on Investigation of the Role of the Department of Justice in
31 the Withholding of Environmental Protection Agency Documents from Congress
32 in 1982-83, H.R.Rep. No. 99-435 (1985). The report not only criticized various
33 officials in the Department of Justice for their role in the EPA executive privilege
34 dispute, but it also suggested that appellee Olson had given false and misleading
35 testimony to the Subcommittee on March 10, 1983, and that appellees Schmults
36 and Dinkins had wrongfully withheld certain documents from the Committee, thus
37 obstructing the Committee's investigation. The Chairman of the Judiciary
38 Committee forwarded a copy of the report to the Attorney General with a request,
39 pursuant to 28 U.S.C. § 592(c), that he seek the appointment of an independent
40 counsel to investigate the allegations against Olson, Schmults, and Dinkins.

41 The Attorney General directed the Public Integrity Section of the Criminal Division
42 to conduct a preliminary investigation. The Section's report concluded that the
43 appointment of an independent counsel was warranted to investigate the
44 Committee's allegations with respect to all three appellees. After consulting with

other Department officials, however, the Attorney General chose to apply to the Special Division for the appointment of an independent counsel solely with respect to appellee Olson. The Attorney General accordingly requested appointment of an independent counsel to investigate whether Olson's March 10, 1983, testimony

> "regarding the completeness of [OLC's] response to the Judiciary Committee's request for OLC documents, and regarding his knowledge of EPA's willingness to turn over certain disputed documents to Congress, violated 18 U.S.C. § 1505, § 1001, or any other provision of federal criminal law."

The Attorney General also requested that the independent counsel have authority to investigate "any other matter related to that allegation."

On April 23, 1986, the Special Division appointed James C. McKay as independent counsel to investigate

> "whether the testimony of . . . Olson and his revision of such testimony on March 10, 1983, violated either 18 U.S.C. § 1505 or § 1001, or any other provision of federal law."

The court also ordered that the independent counsel

> "shall have jurisdiction to investigate any other allegation of evidence of violation of any Federal criminal law by Theodore Olson developed during investigations, by the Independent Counsel, referred to above, and connected with or arising out of that investigation, and Independent Counsel shall have jurisdiction to prosecute for any such violation."

McKay later resigned as independent counsel, and on May 29, 1986, the Division appointed appellant Morrison as his replacement, with the same jurisdiction.

\* \* \*

III

\* \* \*

The parties do not dispute that "[t]he Constitution for purposes of appointment . . . divides all its officers into two classes." *United States v. Germaine*, 99 U.S. 508, 509 (1879). As we stated in *Buckley v. Valeo*, 424 U.S. 1, 132 (1976): "Principal officers are selected by the President with the advice and consent of the Senate. Inferior officers Congress may allow to be appointed by the President alone, by the heads of departments, or by the Judiciary." The initial question is, accordingly, whether appellant is an "inferior" or a "principal" officer. If she is the latter, as the Court of Appeals concluded, then the Act is in violation of the Appointments Clause.

1   The line between "inferior" and "principal" officers is one that is far from clear, and
2   the Framers provided little guidance into where it should be drawn. *See*, e.g., 2 J.
3   Story, Commentaries on the Constitution § 1536, pp. 397, 398 (3d ed. 1858) ("In
4   the practical course of the government, there does not seem to have been any exact
5   line drawn, who are and who are not to be deemed inferior officers, in the sense of
6   the constitution, whose appointment does not necessarily require the concurrence
7   of the senate"). We need not attempt here to decide exactly where the line falls
8   between the two types of officers, because, in our view, appellant clearly falls on
9   the "inferior officer" side of that line. Several factors lead to this conclusion.

10  First, appellant is subject to removal by a higher Executive Branch official.
11  Although appellant may not be "subordinate" to the Attorney General (and the
12  President) insofar as she possesses a degree of independent discretion to exercise
13  the powers delegated to her under the Act, the fact that she can be removed by the
14  Attorney General indicates that she is, to some degree, "inferior" in rank and
15  authority. Second, appellant is empowered by the Act to perform only certain,
16  limited duties. An independent counsel's role is restricted primarily to
17  investigation and, if appropriate, prosecution for certain federal crimes.
18  Admittedly, the Act delegates to appellant "full power and independent authority
19  to exercise all investigative and prosecutorial functions and powers of the
20  Department of Justice," § 594(a), but this grant of authority does not include any
21  authority to formulate policy for the Government or the Executive Branch, nor
22  does it give appellant any administrative duties outside of those necessary to
23  operate her office. The Act specifically provides that, in policy matters, appellant is
24  to comply to the extent possible with the policies of the Department. § 594(f).

25  Third, appellant's office is limited in jurisdiction. Not only is the Act itself
26  restricted in applicability to certain federal officials suspected of certain serious
27  federal crimes, but an independent counsel can only act within the scope of the
28  jurisdiction that has been granted by the Special Division pursuant to a request by
29  the Attorney General. Finally, appellant's office is limited in tenure. There is
30  concededly no time limit on the appointment of a particular counsel. Nonetheless,
31  the office of independent counsel is "temporary" in the sense that an independent
32  counsel is appointed essentially to accomplish a single task, and when that task is
33  over, the office is terminated, either by the counsel herself or by action of the
34  Special Division. Unlike other prosecutors, appellant has no ongoing
35  responsibilities that extend beyond the accomplishment of the mission that she
36  was appointed for and authorized by the Special Division to undertake. In our view,
37  these factors relating to the "ideas of tenure, duration . . . and duties" of the
38  independent counsel, *Germaine, supra,* 99 U.S., at 511, are sufficient to establish
39  that appellant is an "inferior" officer in the constitutional sense.

40                                        * * *

41  This does not, however, end our inquiry under the Appointments Clause. Appellees
42  argue that, even if appellant is an "inferior" officer, the Clause does not empower
43  Congress to place the power to appoint such an officer outside the Executive

1 Branch. They contend that the Clause does not contemplate congressional
2 authorization of "interbranch appointments," in which an officer of one branch is
3 appointed by officers of another branch. The relevant language of the
4 Appointments Clause is worth repeating. It reads: ". . . but the Congress may by
5 Law vest the Appointment of such inferior Officers, as they think proper, in the
6 President alone, in the courts of Law, or in the Heads of Departments." On its face,
7 the language of this "excepting clause" admits of no limitation on interbranch
8 appointments. Indeed, the inclusion of "as they think proper" seems clearly to give
9 Congress significant discretion to determine whether it is "proper" to vest the
10 appointment of, for example, executive officials in the "courts of Law." * * *

11                                          * * *

12 We do not mean to say that Congress' power to provide for interbranch
13 appointments of "inferior officers" is unlimited. In addition to separation of
14 powers concerns, which would arise if such provisions for appointment had the
15 potential to impair the constitutional functions assigned to one of the branches,
16 *Siebold* itself suggested that Congress' decision to vest the appointment power in
17 the courts would be improper if there was some "incongruity" between the
18 functions normally performed by the courts and the performance of their duty to
19 appoint. *Ex parte Siebold*, 100 U.S., at 398 (1880) ("[T]he duty to appoint inferior
20 officers, when required thereto by law, is a constitutional duty of the courts; and in
21 the present case, there is no such incongruity in the duty required as to excuse the
22 courts from its performance, or to render their acts void"). In this case, however,
23 we do not think it impermissible for Congress to vest the power to appoint
24 independent counsel in a specially created federal court. * * *

25                                          * * *

26 JUSTICE SCALIA, dissenting.

27                                          * * *

28 Article II, § 2, cl. 2, of the Constitution provides as follows:

29      "[The President] shall nominate, and by and with the Advice and Consent
30      of the Senate, shall appoint Ambassadors, other public Ministers and
31      Consuls, Judges of the supreme Court, and all other Officers of the United
32      States, whose Appointments are not herein otherwise provided for, and
33      which shall be established by Law: but the Congress may by Law vest the
34      Appointment of such inferior Officers, as they think proper, in the
35      President alone, in the Courts of Law, or in the Heads of Departments."

36 Because appellant (who all parties and the Court agree is an officer of the United
37 States) was not appointed by the President with the advice and consent of the
38 Senate, but rather by the Special Division of the United States Court of Appeals,
39 her appointment is constitutional only if (1) she is an "inferior" officer within the

1  meaning of the above Clause, and (2) Congress may vest her appointment in a court
2  of law.

3  As to the first of these inquiries, the Court does not attempt to "decide exactly"
4  what establishes the line between principal and "inferior" officers, but is confident
5  that, whatever the line may be, appellant "clearly falls on the inferior officer' side"
6  of it. The Court gives three reasons: *First*, she "is subject to removal by a higher
7  Executive Branch official," namely, the Attorney General. *Second*, she is
8  "empowered by the Act to perform only certain, limited duties." *Third*, her office
9  is "limited in jurisdiction" and "limited in tenure."

10  The first of these lends no support to the view that appellant is an inferior officer.
11  Appellant is removable only for "good cause" or physical or mental incapacity. By
12  contrast, most (if not all) *principal* officers in the Executive Branch may be
13  removed by the President *at will*. I fail to see how the fact that appellant is more
14  difficult to remove than most principal officers helps to establish that she is an
15  inferior officer. And I do not see how it could possibly make any difference to her
16  superior or inferior status that the President's limited power to remove her must
17  be exercised through the Attorney General. If she were removable at will by the
18  Attorney General, then she would be subordinate to him, and thus properly
19  designated as inferior; but the Court essentially admits that she is not subordinate.
20  If it were common usage to refer to someone as "inferior" who is subject to removal
21  for cause by another, then one would say that the President is "inferior" to
22  Congress.

23  The second reason offered by the Court—that appellant performs only certain,
24  limited duties—may be relevant to whether she is an inferior officer, but it
25  mischaracterizes the extent of her powers. As the Court states: "Admittedly, the
26  Act delegates to appellant [the] *full power and independent authority to exercise*
27  *all investigative and prosecutorial functions and powers of the Department of*
28  *Justice.*'" (emphasis added). Moreover, in addition to this general grant of power,
29  she is given a broad range of specifically enumerated powers, including a power
30  not even the Attorney General possesses: to "contes[t] in court . . . any claim of
31  privilege or attempt to withhold evidence on grounds of national security." §
32  594(a)(6). Once all of this is "admitted," it seems to me impossible to maintain that
33  appellant's authority is so "limited" as to render her an inferior officer. The Court
34  seeks to brush this away by asserting that the independent counsel's power does
35  not include any authority to "formulate policy for the Government or the Executive
36  Branch." But the same could be said for all officers of the Government, with the
37  single exception of the President. All of them only formulate policy within their
38  respective spheres of responsibility—as does the independent counsel, who must
39  comply with the policies of the Department of Justice only to the extent possible. §
40  594(f).

41  The final set of reasons given by the Court for why the independent counsel clearly
42  is an inferior officer emphasizes the limited nature of her jurisdiction and tenure.
43  Taking the latter first, I find nothing unusually limited about the independent

counsel's tenure. To the contrary, unlike most high ranking Executive Branch officials, she continues to serve until she (or the Special Division) decides that her work is substantially completed. This particular independent prosecutor has already served more than two years, which is at least as long as many Cabinet officials. As to the scope of her jurisdiction, there can be no doubt that is small (though far from unimportant). But within it, she exercises more than the full power of the Attorney General. The Ambassador to Luxembourg is not anything less than a principal officer simply because Luxembourg is small. And the federal judge who sits in a small district is not for that reason "inferior in rank and authority." If the mere fragmentation of executive responsibilities into small compartments suffices to render the heads of each of those compartments inferior officers, then Congress could deprive the President of the right to appoint his chief law enforcement officer by dividing up the Attorney General's responsibilities among a number of "lesser" functionaries.

More fundamentally, however, it is not clear from the Court's opinion why the factors it discusses—even if applied correctly to the facts of this case—are determinative of the question of inferior officer status. The apparent source of these factors is a statement in *United States v. Germaine*, 99 U.S. 508, 511 (1879) (discussing *United States v. Hartwell*, 73 U.S. 393 (1868)), that "the term [officer] embraces the ideas of tenure, duration, emolument, and duties." Besides the fact that this was dictum, it was dictum in a case where the distinguishing characteristics of inferior officers versus superior officers were in no way relevant, but rather only the distinguishing characteristics of an "officer of the United States" (to which the criminal statute at issue applied), as opposed to a mere employee. Rather than erect a theory of who is an inferior officer on the foundation of such an irrelevancy, I think it preferable to look to the text of the Constitution and the division of power that it establishes. These demonstrate, I think, that the independent counsel is not an inferior officer, because she is not subordinate to any officer in the Executive Branch (indeed, not even to the President). Dictionaries in use at the time of the Constitutional Convention gave the word "inferiour" two meanings which it still bears today: (1) "[l]ower in place, . . . station, . . . rank of life, . . . value or excellency," and (2) "[s]ubordinate." S. Johnson, Dictionary of the English Language (6th ed. 1785). In a document dealing with the structure (the constitution) of a government, one would naturally expect the word to bear the latter meaning—indeed, in such a context, it would be unpardonably careless to use the word unless a relationship of subordination was intended. If what was meant was merely "lower in station or rank," one would use instead a term such as "lesser officers." At the only other point in the Constitution at which the word "inferior" appears, it plainly connotes a relationship of subordination. Article III vests the judicial Power of the United States in "one supreme Court, and in such *inferior* Courts as the Congress may from time to time ordain and establish." U.S. Const., Art. III, § 1 (emphasis added). In Federalist No. 81, Hamilton pauses to describe the "inferior" courts authorized by Article III as inferior in the sense that they are "subordinate" to the Supreme Court.

* * *

To be sure, it is not a *sufficient* condition for "inferior" officer status that one be subordinate to a principal officer. Even an officer who is subordinate to a department head can be a principal officer. * * * But it is surely a *necessary* condition for inferior officer status that the officer be subordinate to another officer.

The independent counsel is not even subordinate to the President. The Court essentially admits as much * * * .

* * *

Because appellant is not subordinate to another officer, she is not an "inferior" officer, and her appointment other than by the President with the advice and consent of the Senate is unconstitutional.

* * *

## Edmond v. United States

520 U.S. 651 (1997)

May 19, 1997

JUSTICE SCALIA delivered the opinion of the Court.

We must determine in this case whether Congress has authorized the Secretary of Transportation to appoint civilian members of the Coast Guard Court of Criminal Appeals, and if so, whether this authorization is constitutional under the Appointments Clause of Article II.

I

The Coast Guard Court of Criminal Appeals (formerly known as the Coast Guard Court of Military Review) is an intermediate court within the military justice system. It is one of four military Courts of Criminal Appeals; others exist for the Army, the Air Force, and the Navy-Marine Corps. The Coast Guard Court of Criminal Appeals hears appeals from the decisions of courts-martial, and its decisions are subject to review by the United States Court of Appeals for the Armed Forces (formerly known as the United States Court of Military Appeals).

Appellate military judges who are assigned to a Court of Criminal Appeals must be members of the bar, but may be commissioned officers or civilians. Art. 66(a), Uniform Code of Military Justice (UCMJ), 10 U.S.C. § 866(a). During the times relevant to this case, the Coast Guard Court of Criminal Appeals has had two civilian members, Chief Judge Joseph H. Baum and Associate Judge Alfred F. Bridgman, Jr. These judges were originally assigned to serve on the court by the General Counsel of the Department of Transportation, who is, ex officio, the Judge Advocate General of the Coast Guard. * * *

67

1                         \* \* \*

2   \* \* \* On January 15, 1993, the Secretary of Transportation issued a memorandum
3   "adopting" the General Counsel's assignments to the Coast Guard Court of Military
4   Review "as judicial appointments of my own." The memorandum then listed the
5   names of "those judges presently assigned and appointed by me," including Chief
6   Judge Baum and Judge Bridgman.

7                         \* \* \*

8                         III

9                         \* \* \*

10   The prescribed manner of appointment for principal officers is also the default
11   manner of appointment for inferior officers. "[B]ut," the Appointments Clause
12   continues, "the Congress may by Law vest the Appointment of such inferior
13   Officers, as they think proper, in the President alone, in the Courts of Law, or in
14   the Heads of Departments." \* \* \* Section 323(a), which confers appointment
15   power upon the Secretary of Transportation, can constitutionally be applied to the
16   appointment of Court of Criminal Appeals judges only if those judges are "inferior
17   Officers."

18   Our cases have not set forth an exclusive criterion for distinguishing between
19   principal and inferior officers for Appointments Clause purposes. Among the
20   offices that we have found to be inferior are that of a district court clerk, *Ex parte*
21   *Hennen,* 13 Pet. 225, 258 (1839), an election supervisor, *Ex parte Siebold,* 100 U.S.
22   371, 397-398 (1880), a vice consul charged temporarily with the duties of the
23   consul, *United States v. Eaton,* 169 U.S. 331, 343 (1898), and a "United States
24   commissioner" in district court proceedings, *Go-Bart Importing Co. v. United*
25   *States,* 282 U.S. 344, 352-354 (1931). Most recently, in *Morrison v. Olson,* 487 U.S.
26   654 (1988), we held that the independent counsel created by provisions of the
27   Ethics in Government Act of 1978 was an inferior officer. In reaching that
28   conclusion, we relied on several factors: that the independent counsel was subject
29   to removal by a higher officer (the Attorney General), that she performed only
30   limited duties, that her jurisdiction was narrow, and that her tenure was limited.
31   487 U.S., at 671-672.

32   Petitioners are quite correct that the last two of these conclusions do not hold with
33   regard to the office of military judge at issue here. It is not "limited in tenure," as
34   that phrase was used in *Morrison* to describe "appoint[ment] essentially to
35   accomplish a single task [at the end of which] the office is terminated." *Id.,* at 672.
36   Nor are military judges "limited in jurisdiction," as used in *Morrison* to refer to the
37   fact that an independent counsel may investigate and prosecute only those
38   individuals, and for only those crimes, that are within the scope of jurisdiction
39   granted by the special three-judge appointing panel. *See Weiss,* 510 U.S., at 192
40   (SOUTER, J., concurring). However, *Morrison* did not purport to set forth a
41   definitive test for whether an office is "inferior" under the Appointments Clause.

To the contrary, it explicitly stated: "We need not attempt here to decide exactly where the line falls between the two types of officers, because in our view [the independent counsel] clearly falls on the 'inferior officer' side of that line." 487 U.S., at 671.

To support principal-officer status, petitioners emphasize the importance of the responsibilities that Court of Criminal Appeals judges bear. They review those court-martial proceedings that result in the most serious sentences, including those "in which the sentence, as approved, extends to death, dismissal . . . , dishonorable or bad-conduct discharge, or confinement for one year or more." Art. 66(b)(1), UCMJ, 10 U.S.C. § 866(b)(1). They must ensure that the court-martial's finding of guilt and its sentence are "correct in law and fact," *id.*, Art. 66(c), § 866(c), which includes resolution of constitutional challenges. And finally, unlike most appellate judges, Court of Criminal Appeals judges are not required to defer to the trial court's factual findings, but may independently "weigh the evidence, judge the credibility of witnesses, and determine controverted questions of fact, recognizing that the trial court saw and heard the witnesses." *Ibid.* We do not dispute that military appellate judges are charged with exercising significant authority on behalf of the United States. This, however, is also true of offices that we have held were "inferior" within the meaning of the Appointments Clause. *See, e. g., Freytag v. Commissioner*, 501 U.S., at 881-882 (special trial judges having "significan[t] . . . duties and discretion" are inferior officers). The exercise of "significant authority pursuant to the laws of the United States" marks, not the line between principal and inferior officer for Appointments Clause purposes, but rather, as we said in *Buckley*, the line between officer and nonofficer. 424 U.S., at 126.

Generally speaking, the term "inferior officer" connotes a relationship with some higher-ranking officer or officers below the President: whether one is an "inferior" officer depends on whether he has a superior. It is not enough that other officers may be identified who formally maintain a higher rank, or possess responsibilities of a greater magnitude. If that were the intention, the Constitution might have used the phrase "lesser officer." Rather, in the context of a Clause designed to preserve political accountability relative to important Government assignments, we think it evident that "inferior officers" are officers whose work is directed and supervised at some level by others who were appointed by Presidential nomination with the advice and consent of the Senate.

\* \* \*

Supervision of the work of Court of Criminal Appeals judges is divided between the Judge Advocate General (who in the Coast Guard is subordinate to the Secretary of Transportation) and the Court of Appeals for the Armed Forces. The Judge Advocate General exercises administrative oversight over the Court of Criminal Appeals. He is charged with the responsibility to "prescribe uniform rules of procedure" for the court, and must "meet periodically [with other Judge Advocates General] to formulate policies and procedure in regard to review of court-martial cases." It is conceded by the parties that the Judge Advocate General may also remove a Court of Criminal Appeals judge from his judicial assignment without cause. The power to remove officers, we have recognized, is a powerful tool for control. *Bowsher v. Synar,* 478 U.S. 714, 727 (1986); *Myers v. United States,* 272 U.S. 52 (1926).

The Judge Advocate General's control over Court of Criminal Appeals judges is, to be sure, not complete. He may not attempt to influence (by threat of removal or otherwise) the outcome of individual proceedings, and has no power to reverse decisions of the court. This latter power does reside, however, in another Executive Branch entity, the Court of Appeals for the Armed Forces. That court reviews every decision of the Courts of Criminal Appeals in which: (a) the sentence extends to death; (b) the Judge Advocate General orders such review; or (c) the court itself grants review upon petition of the accused. The scope of review is narrower than that exercised by the Court of Criminal Appeals: so long as there is some competent evidence in the record to establish each element of the offense beyond a reasonable doubt, the Court of Appeals for the Armed Forces will not reevaluate the facts. This limitation upon review does not in our opinion render the judges of the Court of Criminal Appeals principal officers. What is significant is that the judges of the Court of Criminal Appeals have no power to render a final decision on behalf of the United States unless permitted to do so by other Executive officers.

Finally, petitioners argue that *Freytag v. Commissioner,* 501 U.S. 868 (1991), which held that special trial judges charged with assisting Tax Court judges were inferior officers and could be appointed by the Chief Judge of the Tax Court, suggests that Court of Criminal Appeals judges are principal officers. Petitioners contend that Court of Criminal Appeals judges more closely resemble Tax Court judges—who we implied (according to petitioners) were principal officers—than they do special trial judges. We note initially that *Freytag* does not hold that Tax Court judges are principal officers; only the appointment of special trial judges was at issue in that case. Moreover, there are two significant distinctions between Tax Court judges and Court of Criminal Appeals judges. First, there is no Executive Branch tribunal comparable to the Court of Appeals for the Armed Forces that reviews the work of the Tax Court; its decisions are appealable only to courts of the Third Branch. And second, there is no officer comparable to a Judge Advocate General who supervises the work of the Tax Court, with power to determine its procedural rules, to remove any judge without cause, and to order any decision submitted for review. *Freytag* does not control our decision here.

We conclude that 49 U.S.C. § 323(a) authorizes the Secretary of Transportation to appoint judges of the Coast Guard Court of Criminal Appeals; and that such appointment is in conformity with the Appointments Clause of the Constitution, since those judges are "inferior Officers" within the meaning of that provision, by reason of the supervision over their work exercised by the General Counsel of the Department of Transportation in his capacity as Judge Advocate General and the Court of Appeals for the Armed Forces. The judicial appointments at issue in this case are therefore valid.

* * *

JUSTICE SOUTER, concurring in part and concurring in the judgment.

* * *

Because the term "inferior officer" implies an official superior, one who has no superior is not an inferior officer. This unexceptionable maxim will in some instances be dispositive of status; it might, for example, lead to the conclusion that United States district judges cannot be inferior officers, since the power of appellate review does not extend to them personally, but is limited to their judgments.

It does not follow, however, that if one is subject to some supervision and control, one is an inferior officer. Having a superior officer is necessary for inferior officer status, but not sufficient to establish it. *See, e. g., Morrison v. Olson,* 487 U.S. at 654, 722 ("To be sure, it is not a *sufficient* condition for 'inferior' officer status that one be subordinate to a principal officer. Even an officer who is subordinate to a department head can be a principal officer") (SCALIA, J., dissenting). Accordingly, in *Morrison,* the Court's determination that the independent counsel was "to some degree 'inferior'" to the Attorney General, see *id.* at 671, did not end the enquiry. The Court went on to weigh the duties, jurisdiction, and tenure associated with the office before concluding that the independent counsel was an inferior officer. Thus, under *Morrison,* the Solicitor General of the United States, for example, may well be a principal officer, despite his statutory "inferiority" to the Attorney General. The mere existence of a "superior" officer is not dispositive.

* * *

In having to go beyond the Court's opinion to decide that the criminal appeals judges are inferior officers, I do not claim the convenience of a single sufficient condition, and, indeed, at this stage of the Court's thinking on the matter, I would not try to derive a single rule of sufficiency. What is needed, instead, is a detailed look at the powers and duties of these judges to see whether reasons favoring their inferior officer status within the constitutional scheme weigh more heavily than those to the contrary. Having tried to do this in a concurring opinion in *Weiss v. United States,* 510 U.S. 163, 182 (1994), I will not repeat the essay. *See id.* at 192-194 (reviewing the *Morrison* factors, including tenure, jurisdiction, duties, and removal; concluding that because it is "hard to say with any certainty" whether Courts of Military Review judges should be considered principal or inferior officers, deference to the political branches' judgment is appropriate). Here it is enough to add that after the passage of three Terms since writing in *Weiss,* I am unrepentant. I therefore join not only in the Court's conclusion that the necessary supervisory condition for inferior officer status is satisfied here, but in the Court's ultimate holding that the judges of the Coast Guard Court of Criminal Appeals are inferior officers within the meaning of the Appointments Clause.

# 1 Lucia v. Securities and Exchange Commission

2 138 S. Ct. 2044 (2018)

3 June 28, 2018

4 Justice KAGAN delivered the opinion of the Court.

5 The Appointments Clause of the Constitution lays out the permissible methods of
6 appointing "Officers of the United States," a class of government officials distinct
7 from mere employees. Art. II, § 2, cl. 2. This case requires us to decide whether
8 administrative law judges (ALJs) of the Securities and Exchange Commission (SEC
9 or Commission) qualify as such "Officers." In keeping with *Freytag v.*
10 *Commissioner*, 501 U.S. 868 (1991), we hold that they do.

11 I

12 The SEC has statutory authority to enforce the nation's securities laws. One way it
13 can do so is by instituting an administrative proceeding against an alleged
14 wrongdoer. By law, the Commission may itself preside over such a proceeding. But
15 the Commission also may, and typically does, delegate that task to an ALJ. The
16 SEC currently has five ALJs. Other staff members, rather than the Commission
17 proper, selected them all.

18 An ALJ assigned to hear an SEC enforcement action has extensive powers—the
19 "authority to do all things necessary and appropriate to discharge his or her duties"
20 and ensure a "fair and orderly" adversarial proceeding. Those powers "include, but
21 are not limited to," supervising discovery; issuing, revoking, or modifying
22 subpoenas; deciding motions; ruling on the admissibility of evidence;
23 administering oaths; hearing and examining witnesses; generally "[r]egulating the
24 course of" the proceeding and the "conduct of the parties and their counsel"; and
25 imposing sanctions for "[c]ontemptuous conduct" or violations of procedural
26 requirements. As that list suggests, an SEC ALJ exercises authority "comparable
27 to" that of a federal district judge conducting a bench trial.

28 After a hearing ends, the ALJ issues an "initial decision." That decision must set
29 out "findings and conclusions" about all "material issues of fact [and] law"; it also
30 must include the "appropriate order, sanction, relief, or denial thereof." The
31 Commission can then review the ALJ's decision, either upon request or *sua sponte*.
32 But if it opts against review, the Commission "issue[s] an order that the [ALJ's]
33 decision has become final." At that point, the initial decision is "deemed the action
34 of the Commission."

35 This case began when the SEC instituted an administrative proceeding against
36 petitioner Raymond Lucia and his investment company. Lucia marketed a
37 retirement savings strategy called "Buckets of Money." In the SEC's view, Lucia
38 used misleading slideshow presentations to deceive prospective clients. The SEC
39 charged Lucia under the Investment Advisers Act, § 80b-1 et seq., and assigned
40 ALJ Cameron Elliot to adjudicate the case. * * * [ALJ Elliot concluded, after that

72

administrative proceedings, that Lucia violated the Act. The ALJ imposed as sanctions a $300,000 fine and a lifetime bar from the investment industry.]

On appeal to the SEC, Lucia argued that the administrative proceeding was invalid because Judge Elliot had not been constitutionally appointed. * * * [The commission concluded that its ALJs are not "Officers of the United States" but "mere employees"— officials who fall outside the Appointments Clause. Lucia petitioned for review of the Commission's order. A three-judge panel of the D.C. Circuit rejected Lucia's Appointments Clause argument. On rehearing en banc, the court divided 5-5 on the validity of the ALJ's appointment, leaving the panel's judgment in place.] That decision conflicted with one from the Court of Appeals for the Tenth Circuit. *See Bandimere v. SEC*, 844 F. 3d 1168, 1179 (2016).

Lucia asked us to resolve the split by deciding whether the Commission's ALJs are "Officers of the United States within the meaning of the Appointments Clause." Up to that point, the Federal Government (as represented by the Department of Justice) had defended the Commission's position that SEC ALJs are employees, not officers. But in responding to Lucia's petition, the Government switched sides.[1] So when we granted the petition, we also appointed an amicus curiae to defend the judgment below. We now reverse.

## II

The sole question here is whether the Commission's ALJs are "Officers of the United States" or simply employees of the Federal Government. The Appointments Clause prescribes the exclusive means of appointing "Officers." * * * Two decisions set out this Court's basic framework for distinguishing between officers and employees. *United States v. Germaine* 99 U.S. 508, 510 (1879), held that "civil surgeons" (doctors hired to perform various physical exams) were mere employees because their duties were "occasional or temporary" rather than "continuing and permanent." Stressing "ideas of tenure [and] duration," the Court there made clear that an individual must occupy a "continuing" position established by law to qualify as an officer. *Buckley v. Valeo*, 424 U.S. 1 (1976) (per curiam) then set out another requirement, central to this case. It determined that members of a federal commission were officers only after finding that they "exercis[ed] significant authority pursuant to the laws of the United States." The inquiry thus focused on the extent of power an individual wields in carrying out his assigned functions.

---

[1] In the same certiorari-stage brief, the Government asked us to add a second question presented: whether the statutory restrictions on removing the Commission's ALJs are constitutional. When we granted certiorari, we chose not to take that step. The Government's merits brief now asks us again to address the removal issue. We once more decline. No court has addressed that question, and we ordinarily await "thorough lower court opinions to guide our analysis of the merits."

1   Both the amicus and the Government urge us to elaborate on *Buckley*'s "significant
2   authority" test, but another of our precedents makes that project unnecessary. * * *
3   [I]n *Freytag v. Commissioner*, 501 U.S. 868 (1991), we applied the unadorned
4   "significant authority" test to adjudicative officials who are near-carbon copies of
5   the Commission's ALJs. * * * The officials at issue in *Freytag* were the "special trial
6   judges" (STJs) of the United States Tax Court. * * * This Court held that the Tax
7   Court's STJs are officers, not mere employees. * * *

8                                            * * *

9   *Freytag* says everything necessary to decide this case. To begin, the Commission's
10  ALJs, like the Tax Court's STJs, hold a continuing office established by law. * * *
11  And that appointment is to a position created by statute, down to its "duties, salary,
12  and means of appointment." *Freytag*, 501 U.S., at 881; see 5 U.S.C. §§ 556-557,
13  5372, 3105.

14  Still more, the Commission's ALJs exercise the same "significant discretion" when
15  carrying out the same "important functions" as STJs do. Both sets of officials have
16  all the authority needed to ensure fair and orderly adversarial hearings—indeed,
17  nearly all the tools of federal trial judges. Consider in order the four specific (if
18  overlapping) powers *Freytag* mentioned. First, the Commission's ALJs (like the
19  Tax Court's STJs) "take testimony." More precisely, they "[r]eceiv[e] evidence" and
20  "[e]xamine witnesses" at hearings, and may also take pre-hearing depositions.
21  Second, the ALJs (like STJs) "conduct trials." As detailed earlier, they administer
22  oaths, rule on motions, and generally "regulat[e] the course of" a hearing, as well
23  as the conduct of parties and counsel. Third, the ALJs (like STJs) "rule on the
24  admissibility of evidence." They thus critically shape the administrative record (as
25  they also do when issuing document subpoenas). And fourth, the ALJs (like STJs)
26  "have the power to enforce compliance with discovery orders." In particular, they
27  may punish all "[c]ontemptuous conduct," including violations of those orders, by
28  means as severe as excluding the offender from the hearing. So point for point—
29  straight from *Freytag*'s list—the Commission's ALJs have equivalent duties and
30  powers as STJs in conducting adversarial inquiries.

31  And at the close of those proceedings, ALJs issue decisions much like that in
32  *Freytag*—except with potentially more independent effect. As the *Freytag* Court
33  recounted, STJs "prepare proposed findings and an opinion" adjudicating charges
34  and assessing tax liabilities. Similarly, the Commission's ALJs issue decisions
35  containing factual findings, legal conclusions, and appropriate remedies. And what
36  happens next reveals that the ALJ can play the more autonomous role. In a major
37  case like *Freytag*, a regular Tax Court judge must always review an STJ's opinion.
38  And that opinion counts for nothing unless the regular judge adopts it as his own.
39  By contrast, the SEC can decide against reviewing an ALJ decision at all. And when
40  the SEC declines review (and issues an order saying so), the ALJ's decision itself
41  "becomes final" and is "deemed the action of the Commission." That last-word
42  capacity makes this an a fortiori case: If the Tax Court's STJs are officers, as
43  *Freytag* held, then the Commission's ALJs must be too.

74

* * *

The only issue left is remedial. For all the reasons we have given, and all those *Freytag* gave before, the Commission's ALJs are "Officers of the United States," subject to the Appointments Clause. And as noted earlier, Judge Elliot heard and decided Lucia's case without the kind of appointment the Clause requires. This Court has held that "one who makes a timely challenge to the constitutional validity of the appointment of an officer who adjudicates his case" is entitled to relief. *Ryder v. United States*, 515 U.S. 177, 182, 183 (1995). Lucia made just such a timely challenge: He contested the validity of Judge Elliot's appointment before the Commission, and continued pressing that claim in the Court of Appeals and this Court. So what relief follows? This Court has also held that the "appropriate" remedy for an adjudication tainted with an appointments violation is a new "hearing before a properly appointed" official. [*Ryder v. United States*, 515 U.S. 177, 188 (1995).] And we add today one thing more. That official cannot be Judge Elliot, even if he has by now received (or receives sometime in the future) a constitutional appointment.

Judge Elliot has already both heard Lucia's case and issued an initial decision on the merits. He cannot be expected to consider the matter as though he had not adjudicated it before. To cure the constitutional error, another ALJ (or the Commission itself) must hold the new hearing to which Lucia is entitled.[6]

We accordingly reverse the judgment of the Court of Appeals and remand the case for further proceedings consistent with this opinion.

JUSTICE THOMAS, with whom JUSTICE GORSUCH joins, concurring.

I agree with the Court that this case is indistinguishable from *Freytag v. Commissioner*, 501 U.S. 868 (1991). * * * While precedents like *Freytag* discuss what is *sufficient* to make someone an officer of the United States, our precedents have never clearly defined what is *necessary*. I would resolve that question based on the original public meaning of "Officers of the United States." To the Founders, this term encompassed all federal civil officials "with responsibility for an ongoing statutory duty." For federal officers, that duty is "established by Law"—that is, by statute. Art. II, §2, cl. 2. The Founders considered individuals to be officers even if they performed only ministerial statutory duties—including recordkeepers, clerks, and tidewaiters (individuals who watched goods land at a customhouse). With

---

[6] While this case was on judicial review, the SEC issued an order "ratif[ying]" the prior appointments of its ALJs. Lucia argues that the order is invalid. We see no reason to address that issue. The Commission has not suggested that it intends to assign Lucia's case on remand to an ALJ whose claim to authority rests on the ratification order. The SEC may decide to conduct Lucia's rehearing itself. Or it may assign the hearing to an ALJ who has received a constitutional appointment independent of the ratification.

1 exceptions not relevant here, Congress required all federal officials with ongoing
2 statutory duties to be appointed in compliance with the Appointments Clause.

3                                   * * *

4 JUSTICE BREYER, with whom JUSTICE GINSBURG and JUSTICE
5 SOTOMAYOR join as to Part III, concurring in the judgment in part and dissenting
6 in part.

7 I agree with the Court that the Securities and Exchange Commission did not
8 properly appoint the Administrative Law Judge who presided over petitioner
9 Lucia's hearing. But I disagree with the majority in respect to two matters. First, I
10 would rest our conclusion upon statutory, not constitutional, grounds. I believe it
11 important to do so because I cannot answer the constitutional question that the
12 majority answers without knowing the answer to a different, embedded
13 constitutional question, which the Solicitor General urged us to answer in this case:
14 the constitutionality of the statutory "for cause" removal protections that Congress
15 provided for administrative law judges. Cf. *Free Enterprise Fund v. Public
16 Company Accounting Oversight Bd.*, 561 U.S. 477 (2010). Second, I disagree with
17 the Court in respect to the proper remedy.

18                                    I

19 The relevant statute here is the Administrative Procedure Act. That Act governs
20 the appointment of administrative law judges. It provides (as it has, in substance,
21 since its enactment in 1946) that "[e]ach agency shall appoint as many
22 administrative law judges as are necessary for" hearings governed by the
23 Administrative Procedure Act. In the case of the Securities and Exchange Com-
24 mission, the relevant "agency" is the Commission itself. But the Commission did
25 not appoint the Administrative Law Judge who presided over Lucia's hearing.
26 Rather, the Commission's staff appointed that Administrative Law Judge, without
27 the approval of the Commissioners themselves.

28 I do not believe that the Administrative Procedure Act permits the Commission to
29 delegate its power to appoint its administrative law judges to its staff. * * *

30                                   * * *

31                                    II

32 The reason why it is important to go no further arises from the holding in a case
33 this Court decided eight years ago, *Free Enterprise Fund*. The case concerned
34 statutory provisions protecting members of the Public Company Accounting
35 Oversight Board from removal without cause. The Court held in that case that the
36 Executive Vesting Clause of the Constitution, Art. II, § 1, forbade Congress from
37 providing members of the Board with "multilevel protection from removal" by the
38 President. Because, in the Court's view, the relevant statutes (1) granted the
39 Securities and Exchange Commissioners protection from removal without cause,
40 (2) gave the Commissioners sole authority to remove Board members, and (3)

protected Board members from removal without cause, the statutes provided Board members with two levels of protection from removal and consequently violated the Constitution.

In addressing the constitutionality of the Board members' removal protections, the Court emphasized that the Board members were "executive officers"—more specifically, "inferior officers" for purposes of the Appointments Clause. * * *

* * *

The Administrative Procedure Act * * * allows administrative law judges to be removed only "for good cause" found by the Merit Systems Protection Board. § 7521(a). And the President may, in turn, remove members of the Merit Systems Protection Board only for "inefficiency, neglect of duty, or malfeasance in office." § 1202(d). Thus, Congress seems to have provided administrative law judges with two levels of protection from removal without cause—just what *Free Enterprise Fund* interpreted the Constitution to forbid in the case of the Board members.

The substantial independence that the Administrative Procedure Act's removal protections provide to administrative law judges is a central part of the Act's overall scheme. Before the Administrative Procedure Act, hearing examiners "were in a dependent status" to their employing agency, with their classification, compensation, and promotion all dependent on how the agency they worked for rated them. As a result of that dependence, "[m]any complaints were voiced against the actions of the hearing examiners, it being charged that they were mere tools of the agency concerned and subservient to the agency heads in making their proposed findings of fact and recommendations." The Administrative Procedure Act responded to those complaints by giving administrative law judges "independence and tenure within the existing Civil Service system." *Ramspeck v. Federal Trial Examiners Conference*, 345 U.S. 128, 130, 132 (1953). If the *Free Enterprise Fund* Court's holding applies equally to the administrative law judges— and I stress the "if"—then to hold that the administrative law judges are "Officers of the United States" is, perhaps, to hold that their removal protections are unconstitutional. * * *

* * *

The *Free Enterprise Fund* Court gave three reasons why administrative law judges were distinguishable from the Board members at issue in that case. First, the Court said that "[w]hether administrative law judges are necessarily 'Officers of the United States' is disputed." Second, the Court said that "unlike members of the Board, many administrative law judges of course perform adjudicative rather than enforcement or policymaking functions, see [5 U.S.C.] §§ 554(d), 3105, or possess purely recommendatory powers." And, third, the Court pointed out that the civil service "employees" and administrative law judges to whom I referred in my dissent do not "enjoy the same significant and unusual protections from Presidential oversight as members of the Board." The Court added that the kind of

1  "for cause" protection the statutes provided for Board members was "unusually
2  high."

3  The majority here removes the first distinction, for it holds that the Commission's
4  administrative law judges are inferior "Officers of the United States." The other
5  two distinctions remain. See, e.g., *Wiener v. United States*, 357 U.S. 349, 355-356
6  (1958) (holding that Congress is free to protect bodies tasked with "'adjudicat[ing]
7  according to law' . . . 'from the control or coercive influence, direct or indirect,' . . .
8  of either the Executive or Congress") (quoting *Humphrey's Executor v. United
9  States*, 295 U.S. 602, 629 (1935)). But the Solicitor General has nevertheless
10  argued strongly that we should now decide the constitutionality of the
11  administrative law judges' removal protections as well as their means of
12  appointment. And in his view, the administrative law judges' statutory removal
13  protections violate the Constitution (as interpreted in Free Enterprise Fund),
14  unless we construe those protections as giving the Commission substantially
15  greater power to remove administrative law judges than it presently has.

16                              * * *

17  And now it should be clear why the application of *Free Enterprise Fund* to
18  administrative law judges is important. If that decision does not limit or forbid
19  Congress' statutory "for cause" protections, then a holding that the administrative
20  law judges are "inferior Officers" does not conflict with Congress' intent as revealed
21  in the statute. But, if the holding is to the contrary, and more particularly if a
22  holding that administrative law judges are "inferior Officers" brings with it
23  application of *Free Enterprise Fund*'s limitation on "for cause" protections from
24  removal, then a determination that administrative law judges are, constitutionally
25  speaking, "inferior Officers" would directly conflict with Congress' intent, as
26  revealed in the statute. * * *

27  [In Part III of his concurrence, Justice BREYER argues that there is no reason to
28  remand the case to an ALJ other than Judge Elliot.]

29  Justice SOTOMAYOR, with whom JUSTICE GINSBURG joins, dissenting.

30  The Court today and scholars acknowledge that this Court's Appointments Clause
31  jurisprudence offers little guidance on who qualifies as an "Officer of the United
32  States." * * * As the majority notes, this Court's decisions currently set forth at least
33  two prerequisites to officer status: (1) an individual must hold a "continuing" office
34  established by law, *United States v. Germaine*, 99 U.S. 508, 511, 512 (1879), and
35  (2) an individual must wield "significant authority," *Buckley v. Valeo*, 424 U.S. 1,
36  126 (1976) (*per curiam*). * * *

37  To provide guidance to Congress and the Executive Branch, I would hold that one
38  requisite component of "significant authority" is the ability to make final, binding
39  decisions on behalf of the Government. Accordingly, a person who merely advises
40  and provides recommendations to an officer would not herself qualify as an officer.

* * *

* * * Commission ALJs are not officers because they lack final decisionmaking authority. As the Commission explained below, the Commission retains "'plenary authority over the course of [its] administrative proceedings and the rulings of [its] law judges.'" Commission ALJs can issue only "initial" decisions. The Commission can review any initial decision upon petition or on its own initiative. The Commission's review of an ALJ's initial decision is *de novo*. It can "make any findings or conclusions that in its judgment are proper and on the basis of the record." 17 CFR § 201.411(a) (2017). The Commission is also in no way confined by the record initially developed by an ALJ. The Commission can accept evidence itself or refer a matter to an ALJ to take additional evidence that the Commission deems relevant or necessary. In recent years, the Commission has accepted review in every case in which it was sought. Even where the Commission does not review an ALJ's initial decision, as in cases in which no party petitions for review and the Commission does not act *sua sponte*, the initial decision still only becomes final when the Commission enters a finality order. And by operation of law, every action taken by an ALJ "shall, for all purposes, . . . be deemed the action of the Commission." 15 U.S.C. § 78d-1(c) (emphasis added). In other words, Commission ALJs do not exercise significant authority because they do not, and cannot, enter final, binding decisions against the Government or third parties.

The majority concludes that this case is controlled by *Freytag v. Commissioner*, 501 U.S. 868 (1991). In *Freytag*, the Court suggested that the Tax Court's special trial judges (STJs) acted as constitutional officers even in cases where they could not enter final, binding decisions. In such cases, the Court noted, the STJs presided over adversarial proceedings in which they exercised "significant discretion" with respect to "important functions," such as ruling on the admissibility of evidence and hearing and examining witnesses. That part of the opinion, however, was unnecessary to the result. The Court went on to conclude that even if the STJs' duties in such cases were "not as significant as [the Court] found them to be," its conclusion "would be unchanged." The Court noted that STJs could enter final decisions in certain types of cases, and that the Government had conceded that the STJs acted as officers with respect to those proceedings. Because STJs could not be "officers for purposes of some of their duties . . . , but mere employees with respect to other[s]," the Court held they were officers in all respects. *Freytag* is, therefore, consistent with a rule that a prerequisite to officer status is the authority, in at least some instances, to issue final decisions that bind the Government or third parties.

* * *

## United States v. Arthrex

141 S. Ct. 1970 (2021)

1    June 21, 2021

2    CHIEF JUSTICE ROBERTS delivered the opinion of the Court with respect to
3    Parts I and II.

4                                    * * *

5                                     I

6                                     A

7                                    * * *

8    This suit centers on the Patent Trial and Appeal Board (PTAB), an executive
9    adjudicatory body within the PTO established by the Leahy-Smith America Invents
10   Act of 2011. 125 Stat. 313. The PTAB sits in panels of at least three members drawn
11   from the Director, the Deputy Director, the Commissioner for Patents, the
12   Commissioner for Trademarks, and more than 200 Administrative Patent Judges
13   (APJs). 35 U.S.C. §§6(a), (c). The Secretary of Commerce appoints the members of
14   the PTAB (except for the Director), including the APJs at issue in this dispute. . . .
15   [T]he modern Board decides whether an invention satisfies the standards for
16   patentability on review of decisions by primary examiners. §§6(b)(1), 134(a).

17   Through a variety of procedures, the PTAB can also take a second look at patents
18   previously issued by the PTO. §§6(b)(2)–(4). One such procedure is inter partes
19   review. Established in 2011, inter partes review is an adversarial process by which
20   members of the PTAB reconsider whether existing patents satisfy the novelty and
21   nonobviousness requirements for inventions. Any person—other than the patent
22   owner himself—can file a petition to institute inter partes review of a patent. 35
23   U.S.C. §311(a). The Director can institute review only if, among other
24   requirements, he determines that the petitioner is reasonably likely to prevail on
25   at least one challenged patent claim. §314(a). Congress has committed the decision
26   to institute inter partes review to the Director's unreviewable discretion. By
27   regulation, the Director has delegated this authority to the PTAB itself. 37 CFR
28   §42.4(a) (2020).

29   The Director designates at least three members of the PTAB (typically three APJs)
30   to conduct an inter partes proceeding. 35 U.S.C. §6(c). The PTAB then assumes
31   control of the process, which resembles civil litigation in many respects. * * * A
32   party who disagrees with a decision may request rehearing by the PTAB. 35 U.S.C.
33   §6(c); 37 CFR §42.71(d).

34   The PTAB is the last stop for review within the Executive Branch. A party
35   dissatisfied with the final decision may seek judicial review in the Court of Appeals
36   for the Federal Circuit. 35 U.S.C. § 319. At this stage, the Director can intervene
37   before the court to defend or disavow the Board's decision. §143. The Federal

1   Circuit reviews the PTAB's application of patentability standards de novo and its
2   underlying factual determinations for substantial evidence. * * *

3                                           B

4   Arthrex, Inc. develops medical devices and procedures for orthopedic surgery. In
5   2015, it secured a patent on a surgical device for reattaching soft tissue to bone
6   without tying a knot, U.S. Patent No. 9,179,907 ('907 patent). Arthrex soon claimed
7   that Smith & Nephew, Inc. and ArthroCare Corp. (collectively, Smith & Nephew)
8   had infringed the '907 patent, and the dispute eventually made its way to inter
9   partes review in the PTO. Three APJs formed the PTAB panel that conducted the
10  proceeding and ultimately concluded that a prior patent application "anticipated"
11  the invention claimed by the '907 patent, so that Arthrex's patent was invalid.

12  On appeal to the Federal Circuit, Arthrex raised for the first time an argument
13  premised on the Appointments Clause of the Constitution. * * * Arthrex argued
14  that the APJs were principal officers and therefore that their appointment by the
15  Secretary of Commerce was unconstitutional. The Government intervened to
16  defend the appointment procedure.

17  The Federal Circuit agreed with Arthrex that APJs were principal officers. 941 F.
18  3d 1320, 1335 (2019). Neither the Secretary nor Director had the authority to
19  review their decisions or to remove them at will. The Federal Circuit held that these
20  restrictions meant that APJs were themselves principal officers, not inferior
21  officers under the direction of the Secretary or Director.

22  To fix this constitutional violation, the Federal Circuit invalidated the tenure
23  protections for APJs. Making APJs removable at will by the Secretary, the panel
24  held, prospectively "renders them inferior rather than principal officers." *Id.*, at
25  1338. The Federal Circuit vacated the PTAB's decision and remanded for a fresh
26  hearing before a new panel of APJs, who would no longer enjoy protection against
27  removal.

28  This satisfied no one. The Government, Smith & Nephew, and Arthrex each
29  requested rehearing en banc, which the Court of Appeals denied. The parties then
30  requested review of different aspects of the panel's decision in three petitions for
31  certiorari.

32  We granted those petitions to consider whether the PTAB's structure is consistent
33  with the Appointments Clause, and the appropriate remedy if it is not.

34                                          II

35                                          A

36                                        * * *

1                                  B

2 Congress provided that APJs would be appointed as inferior officers, by the
3 Secretary of Commerce as head of a department. The question presented is
4 whether the nature of their responsibilities is consistent with their method of
5 appointment. As an initial matter, no party disputes that APJs are officers—not
6 "lesser functionaries" such as employees or contractors—because they "exercis[e]
7 significant authority pursuant to the laws of the United States." *Buckley v. Valeo*,
8 424 U.S. 1, 126, and n. 162 (1976) (per curiam); see *Lucia v. SEC*, 585 U.S. \_\_\_\_,
9 \_\_\_\_–\_\_\_\_ (2018) (slip op., at 8–9). APJs do so when reconsidering an issued
10 patent, a power that (the Court has held) involves the adjudication of public rights
11 that Congress may appropriately assign to executive officers rather than to the
12 Judiciary.

13 The starting point for each party's analysis is our opinion in *Edmond*. There we
14 explained that "[w]hether one is an 'inferior' officer depends on whether he has a
15 superior" other than the President. 520 U.S., at 662. An inferior officer must be
16 "directed and supervised at some level by others who were appointed by
17 Presidential nomination with the advice and consent of the Senate." *Id.*, at 663.

18 In *Edmond*, * * * [w]e held that the judges were inferior officers because they were
19 effectively supervised by a combination of Presidentially nominated and Senate
20 confirmed officers in the Executive Branch: first, the Judge Advocate General, who
21 "exercise[d] administrative oversight over the Court of Criminal Appeals" by
22 prescribing rules of procedure and formulating policies for court-martial cases,
23 and could also "remove a Court of Criminal Appeals judge from his judicial
24 assignment without cause"; and second, the Court of Appeals for the Armed
25 Forces, an executive tribunal that could review the judges' decisions under a de
26 novo standard for legal issues and a deferential standard for factual issues. *Id.*, at
27 664–665. "What is significant," we concluded, "is that the judges of the Court of
28 Criminal Appeals have no power to render a final decision on behalf of the United
29 States unless permitted to do so by other Executive officers." *Id.*, at 665.

30 Congress structured the PTAB differently, providing only half of the "divided"
31 supervision to which judges of the Court of Criminal Appeals were subject. *Id.*, at
32 664. Like the Judge Advocate General, the PTO Director possesses powers of
33 "administrative oversight." *Ibid.* The Director fixes the rate of pay for APJs,
34 controls the decision whether to institute inter partes review . . . selects the APJs
35 to reconsider the validity of the patent. . . . promulgates regulations governing inter
36 partes review, issues prospective guidance on patentability issues, and designates
37 past PTAB decisions as "precedential" for future panels. . . . He is the boss, except
38 when it comes to the one thing that makes the APJs officers exercising "significant
39 authority" in the first place—their power to issue decisions on patentability.
40 *Buckley*, 424 U.S., at 126. In contrast to the scheme approved by *Edmond*, no

principal officer at any level within the Executive Branch "direct[s] and supervise[s]" the work of APJs in that regard. 520 U.S., at 663.

What was "significant" to the outcome [in *Edmond*]—review by a superior executive officer—is absent here: APJs have the "power to render a final decision on behalf of the United States" without any such review by their nominal superior or any other principal officer in the Executive Branch. *Id.*, at 665. The only possibility of review is a petition for rehearing, but Congress unambiguously specified that "[o]nly the Patent and Trial Appeal Board may grant rehearings." §6(c). Such review simply repeats the arrangement challenged as unconstitutional in this suit.

This "diffusion of power carries with it a diffusion of accountability." *Free Enterprise Fund*, 561 U.S., at 497. The restrictions on review relieve the Director of responsibility for the final decisions rendered by APJs purportedly under his charge. * * * The Government and Smith & Nephew assemble a catalog of steps the Director might take to affect the decision-making process of the PTAB, despite his lack of any statutory authority to review its decisions. The Government reminds us that it is the Director who decides whether to initiate inter partes review. The Director can also designate the APJs who will decide a particular case and can pick ones predisposed to his views. And the Director, the Government asserts, can even vacate his institution decision if he catches wind of an unfavorable ruling on the way. The "proceeding will have no legal consequences" so long as the Director jumps in before the Board issues its final decision. Brief for United States 31.

If all else fails, the Government says, the Director can intervene in the rehearing process to reverse Board decisions. The Government acknowledges that only the PTAB can grant rehearing under §6(c). But the Director, according to the Government, could manipulate the composition of the PTAB panel that acts on the rehearing petition * * * "stack[ing]" the original panel to rehear the case with additional APJs assumed to be more amenable to his preferences. * * * The Government insists that the Director, by handpicking (and, if necessary, repicking) Board members, can indirectly influence the course of inter partes review.

That is not the solution. It is the problem. The Government proposes (and the dissents embrace) a roadmap for the Director to evade a statutory prohibition on review without having him take responsibility for the ultimate decision. Even if the Director succeeds in procuring his preferred outcome, such machinations blur the lines of accountability demanded by the Appointments Clause. * * *

* * *

Review outside Article II—here, an appeal to the Federal Circuit—cannot provide the necessary supervision. While the duties of APJs "partake of a Judiciary quality as well as Executive," APJs are still exercising executive power and must remain

1    "dependent upon the President." 1 Annals of Cong., at 611–612 (J. Madison); see
2    *Oil States Energy Services, LLC v. Greene's Energy Group, LLC*, 584 U.S. \_\_\_,
3    \_\_\_ (2018) (slip op., at 8). The activities of executive officers may "take 'legislative'
4    and 'judicial' forms, but they are exercises of—indeed, under our constitutional
5    structure they must be exercises of—the 'executive Power,'" for which the President
6    is ultimately responsible. *Arlington v. FCC*, 569 U.S. 290, 305, n. 4 (2013) (quoting
7    Art. II, §1, cl. 1).

8    Given the insulation of PTAB decisions from any executive review, the President
9    can neither oversee the PTAB himself nor "attribute the Board's failings to those
10   whom he can oversee." *Free Enterprise Fund*, 561 U.S., at 496. APJs accordingly
11   exercise power that conflicts with the design of the Appointments Clause "to
12   preserve political accountability." *Edmond*, 520 U.S., at 663.

13                                                    C

14                                                 * * *

15   We hold that the unreviewable authority wielded by APJs during inter partes
16   review is incompatible with their appointment by the Secretary to an inferior office
17   . * * * Only an officer properly appointed to a principal office may issue a final
18   decision binding the Executive Branch in the proceeding before us.

19   In reaching this conclusion, we do not attempt to "set forth an exclusive criterion
20   for distinguishing between principal and inferior officers for Appointments Clause
21   purposes." *Edmond*, 520 U.S., at 661. Many decisions by inferior officers do not
22   bind the Executive Branch to exercise executive power in a particular manner, and
23   we do not address supervision outside the context of adjudication. Here, however,
24   Congress has assigned APJs "significant authority" in adjudicating the public
25   rights of private parties, while also insulating their decisions from review and their
26   offices from removal. *Buckley*, 424 U.S., at 126.

27                                                   III

28   We turn now to the appropriate way to resolve this dispute given this violation of
29   the Appointments Clause. In general, "when confronting a constitutional flaw in a
30   statute, we try to limit the solution to the problem" by disregarding the
31   "problematic portions while leaving the remainder intact." *Ayotte v. Planned*
32   *Parenthood of Northern New Eng.*, 546 U.S. 320, 328–329 (2006).* * *

33                                                 * * *

34   We conclude that a tailored approach is the appropriate one: Section 6(c) cannot
35   constitutionally be enforced to the extent that its requirements prevent the
36   Director from reviewing final decisions rendered by APJs. Because Congress has
37   vested the Director with the "power and duties" of the PTO, §3(a)(1), the Director

has the authority to provide for a means of reviewing PTAB decisions. See also §§3(a)(2)(A), 316(a)(4). The Director accordingly may review final PTAB decisions and, upon review, may issue decisions himself on behalf of the Board. Section 6(c) otherwise remains operative as to the other members of the PTAB.

\* \* \*

We also conclude that the appropriate remedy is a remand to the Acting Director for him to decide whether to rehear the petition filed by Smith & Nephew. Although the APJs' appointment by the Secretary allowed them to lawfully adjudicate the petition in the first instance, see *Freytag*, 501 U.S., at 881–882, they lacked the power under the Constitution to finally resolve the matter within the Executive Branch. Under these circumstances, a limited remand to the Director provides an adequate opportunity for review by a principal officer. Because the source of the constitutional violation is the restraint on the review authority of the Director, rather than the appointment of APJs by the Secretary, Arthrex is not entitled to a hearing before a new panel of APJs. Cf. *Lucia*, 585 U.S., at \_\_\_–\_\_\_ (slip op., at 12–13)

\* \* \*

Today, we reaffirm and apply the rule from *Edmond* that the exercise of executive power by inferior officers must at some level be subject to the direction and supervision of an officer nominated by the President and confirmed by the Senate. The Constitution therefore forbids the enforcement of statutory restrictions on the Director that insulate the decisions of APJs from his direction and supervision. To be clear, the Director need not review every decision of the PTAB. What matters is that the Director have the discretion to review decisions rendered by APJs. In this way, the President remains responsible for the exercise of executive power—and through him, the exercise of executive power remains accountable to the people.

The judgment of the United States Court of Appeals for the Federal Circuit is vacated, and the cases are remanded for further proceedings consistent with this opinion.

It is so ordered.

JUSTICE GORSUCH, concurring in part and dissenting in part. [omitted]

[Justice Gorsuch agreed with the majority's analysis in Parts I and II but dissented with respect to the remedy. Finding that the APJs' principal officer status was a function of multiple statutory provisions, Justice Gorsuch would have simply vacated the PTAB's decision rather than engaging in a "legislative scéance[]" to fix the problem by rewriting the law.]

1

JUSTICE BREYER, with whom JUSTICE SOTOMAYOR and JUSTICE KAGAN join, concurring in the judgment in part and dissenting in part.

I

I agree with JUSTICE THOMAS' discussion on the merits and I join Parts I and II of his dissent. Two related considerations also persuade me that his conclusion is correct.

First, in my view, the Court should interpret the Appointments Clause as granting Congress a degree of leeway to establish and empower federal offices. Neither that Clause nor anything else in the Constitution describes the degree of control that a superior officer must exercise over the decisions of an inferior officer. To the contrary, the Constitution says only that "Congress may by Law vest the Appointment of such inferior Officers, as they think proper, . . . in the Heads of Departments." Art. II, §2, cl. 2. The words "by Law . . . as they think proper" strongly suggest that Congress has considerable freedom to determine the nature of an inferior officer's job, and that courts ought to respect that judgment. See *Lucia* v. SEC, 585 U.S. ___, ___–___ (2018) (BREYER, J., concurring in judgment in part and dissenting in part) (slip op., at 9–10). * * *

* * *

Second, I believe the Court, when deciding cases such as these, should conduct a functional examination of the offices and duties in question rather than a formalist, judicial-rules-based approach. In advocating for a "functional approach," I mean an approach that would take account of, and place weight on, why Congress enacted a particular statutory limitation. It would also consider the practical consequences that are likely to follow from Congress' chosen scheme.

* * *

In this suit, a functional approach, which considers purposes and consequences, undermines the Court's result. Most agencies (and courts for that matter) have the power to reconsider an earlier decision, changing the initial result if appropriate. Congress believed that the PTO should have that same power and accordingly created procedures for reconsidering issued patents. Congress also believed it important to strengthen the reconsideration power with procedural safeguards that would often help those whom the PTO's initial decision had favored, such as the requirement that review be available only when there is a "reasonable likelihood" that the patent will be invalid. 35 U.S.C. §314(a). Given the technical nature of patents, the need for expertise, and the importance of avoiding political interference, Congress chose to grant the APJs a degree of independence. These considerations set forth a reasonable legislative objective sufficient to justify the restriction upon the Director's authority that Congress imposed. * * *

More broadly, I see the Court's decision as one part of a larger shift in our separation-of-powers jurisprudence. The Court applied a similarly formal approach in *Free Enterprise Fund v. Public Company Accounting Oversight Bd.*, 561 U.S. 477 (2010), where it considered the constitutional status of the members of an accounting board appointed by the Securities and Exchange Commission. * * * The Court also applied a formalist approach in *Seila Law LLC v. Consumer Financial Protection Bureau*, 591 U.S. ___ (2020) * * *. My dissent in the first case and JUSTICE KAGAN's dissent in the second explain in greater detail why we believed that this shift toward formalism was a mistake.

I continue to believe that a more functional approach to constitutional interpretation in this area is superior. As for this particular suit, the consequences of the majority's rule are clear. The nature of the PTAB calls for technically correct adjudicatory decisions. And * * * that fact calls for greater, not less, independence from those potentially influenced by political factors. The Court's decision prevents Congress from establishing a patent scheme consistent with that idea.

* * *

## II

In my view, today's decision is both unprecedented and unnecessary, and risks pushing the Judiciary further into areas where we lack both the authority to act and the capacity to act wisely. I respectfully dissent.

JUSTICE THOMAS, with whom JUSTICE BREYER, JUSTICE SOTOMAYOR, and JUSTICE KAGAN join as to Parts I and II, dissenting.

For the very first time, this Court holds that Congress violated the Constitution by vesting the appointment of a federal officer in the head of a department. Just who are these "principal" officers that Congress unsuccessfully sought to smuggle into the Executive Branch without Senate confirmation? About 250 administrative patent judges who sit at the bottom of an organizational chart, nestled under at least two levels of authority. Neither our precedent nor the original understanding of the Appointments Clause requires Senate confirmation of officers inferior to not one, but two officers below the President.

## I

The Executive Branch is large, and the hierarchical path from President to administrative patent judge is long. At the top sits the President, in whom the

1   executive power is vested. Below him is the Secretary of Commerce, who oversees
2   the Department of Commerce and its work force of about 46,000. Within that
3   Department is the United States Patent and Trademark Office led by a Director..
4   In the Patent and Trademark Office is the Patent Trial and Appeal Board. Serving
5   on this Board are administrative patent judges.

6                           \* \* \*

7                           II

8                           A

9                           \* \* \*

10  There can be no dispute that administrative patent judges are, in fact, inferior:
11  They are lower in rank to at least two different officers. As part of the Board, they
12  serve in the Patent and Trademark Office, run by a Director "responsible for
13  providing policy direction and management supervision for the Office and for the
14  issuance of patents and the registration of trademarks." 35 U.S.C. §3(a)(2)(A). That
15  Office, in turn, is "[w]ithin the Department of Commerce" and "subject to the
16  policy direction of the Secretary of Commerce." §1(a). The Secretary, in
17  consultation with the Director, appoints administrative patent judges. §6(a).

18  As a comparison to the facts in *Edmond* illustrates, the Director and Secretary are
19  also functionally superior because they supervise and direct the work
20  administrative patent judges perform. \* \* \*

21                         \* \* \*

22  To be sure, the Director's power over administrative patent judges is not complete.
23  He cannot singlehandedly reverse decisions. Still, he has two powerful checks on
24  Board decisions not found in *Edmond*.

25  Unlike the Judge Advocate General and CAAF in *Edmond*, the Director may
26  influence individual proceedings. The Director decides in the first instance
27  whether to institute, refuse to institute, or de-institute particular reviews, a
28  decision that is "final and nonappealable." 35 U.S.C. §314(d); see also §314(a). If
29  the Director institutes review, he then may select which administrative patent
30  judges will hear the challenge. §6(c). Alternatively, he can avoid assigning any
31  administrative patent judge to a specific dispute and instead designate himself, his
32  Deputy Director, and the Commissioner of Patents. In addition, the Director
33  decides which of the thousands of decisions issued each year bind other panels as
34  precedent. No statute bars the Director from taking an active role to ensure the
35  Board's decisions conform to his policy direction.

1 But, that is not all. If the administrative patent judges "(somehow) reach a result
2 he does not like, the Director can add more members to the panel—including
3 himself—and order the case reheard." *Oil States Energy Services, LLC v. Greene's*
4 *Energy Group, LLC*, 584 U.S. ___, ___ (2018) (GORSUCH, J., dissenting) (slip
5 op., at 3). * * *This broad oversight ensures that administrative patent judges "have
6 no power to render a final decision on behalf of the United States unless permitted
7 to do so by other Executive officers." *Edmond*, 520 U.S., at 665.

8 B

9 The Court today appears largely to agree with all of this. "In every respect" save
10 one, the plurality says, "[administrative patent judges] appear to be inferior
11 officers." Ante, at 20–21. But * * * the majority suggests most of *Edmond* is
12 superfluous: All that matters is whether the Director has the statutory authority to
13 individually reverse Board decisions.

14 The problem with that theory is that there is no precedential basis (or historical
15 support) for boiling down "inferior officer" status to the way Congress structured
16 a particular agency's process for reviewing decisions. * * *

17 Perhaps the better way to understand the Court's opinion today is as creating a
18 new form of intrabranch separation of-powers law. Traditionally, the Court's task
19 when resolving Appointments Clause challenges has been to discern whether the
20 challenged official qualifies as a specific sort of officer and whether his
21 appointment complies with the Constitution. See *Lucia v. SEC*, 585 U.S. ___, ___
22 (2018) (slip op., at 1) ("This case requires us to decide whether administrative law
23 judges . . . qualify as [officers of the United States]"). If the official's appointment
24 is inconsistent with the constitutional appointment process for the position he
25 holds, then the Court provides a remedy. Otherwise, the Court must conclude that
26 the "appointments at issue in th[e] case are . . . valid." *Edmond*, 520 U.S., at 666.

27 Today's majority leaves that tried-and-true approach behind. It never expressly
28 tells us whether administrative patent judges are inferior officers or principal. And
29 the Court never tells us whether the appointment process complies with the
30 Constitution. The closest the Court comes is to say that "the source of the
31 constitutional violation" is not "the appointment of [administrative patent judges]
32 by the Secretary." Under our precedent and the Constitution's text, that should
33 resolve the suit. If the appointment process for administrative patent judges—
34 appointment by the Secretary—does not violate the Constitution, then
35 administrative patent judges must be inferior officers. See Art. II, §2, cl. 2. And if
36 administrative patent judges are inferior officers and have been properly
37 appointed as such, then the Appointments Clause challenge fails. After all, the
38 Constitution provides that "Congress may by Law vest the Appointment of . . .
39 inferior Officers . . . in the Heads of Departments." *Ibid.*

The majority's new Appointments Clause doctrine, though, has nothing to do with the validity of an officer's appointment. Instead, it polices the dispersion of executive power among officers. Echoing our doctrine that Congress may not mix duties and powers from different branches into one actor, the Court finds that the constitutional problem here is that Congress has given a specific power—the authority to finally adjudicate inter partes review disputes—to one type of executive officer that the Constitution gives to another. See ante, at 21 (plurality opinion); see also, e.g., *Stern v. Marshall*, 564 U.S. 462, 503 (2011) (assignment of Article III power to Bankruptcy Judge); *Bowsher v. Synar*, 478 U.S. 714, 728–735 (1986) (assignment of executive power to a legislative officer). That analysis is doubly flawed.

For one thing, our separation-of-powers analysis does not fit. The Constitution recognizes executive, legislative, and judicial power, and it vests those powers in specific branches. Nowhere does the Constitution acknowledge any such thing as "inferior-officer power" or "principal-officer power." And it certainly does not distinguish between these sorts of powers in the Appointments Clause.

* * *

More broadly, interpreting the Appointments Clause to bar any nonprincipal officer from taking "final" action poses serious line-drawing problems. The majority assures that not every decision by an inferior officer must be reviewable by a superior officer. But this sparks more questions than it answers. Can a line prosecutor offer a plea deal without sign off from a principal officer? If faced with a life-threatening scenario, can an FBI agent use deadly force to subdue a suspect? Or if an inferior officer temporarily fills a vacant office tasked with making final decisions, do those decisions violate the Appointments Clause? And are courts around the country supposed to sort through lists of each officer's (or employee's) duties, categorize each one as principal or inferior, and then excise any that look problematic?

Beyond those questions, the majority's nebulous approach also leaves open the question of how much "principal officer power" someone must wield before he becomes a principal officer. What happens if an officer typically engages in normal inferior-officer work but also has several principal-officer duties? Is he a hybrid officer, properly appointed for four days a week and improperly appointed for the fifth? And whatever test the Court ultimately comes up with to sort through these difficult questions, are we sure it is encapsulated in the two words "inferior officer"?

* * *

The Court today draws a new line dividing inferior officers from principal ones. The fact that this line places administrative patent judges on the side of

90

Ambassadors, Supreme Court Justices, and department heads suggests that something is not quite right. At some point, we should take stock of our precedent to see if it aligns with the Appointments Clause's original meaning. But, for now, we must apply the test we have. And, under that test, administrative patent judges are both formally and functionally inferior to the Director and to the Secretary. I respectfully dissent.

## 2. Presidential Removal Power

As we saw in the previous section, the Constitution lays down some rules governing the appointment of officers. Here's what the Constitution has to say about the removal of officers:

That's right. Literally nothing.

What are we to make of the Constitution's silence about removal?

Should removal mirror appointment: for instance, if the President wants to remove a principal officer, should the Senate be required to sign off? Should the President have the power to remove officers at will? Should Congress be able to place whatever restrictions it wishes on the removal of officers (after all, it is Congress that creates the offices in the first place)?

At least some questions were resolved early in our history. In what is known as the Decision of 1789, the first Congress decided that the Constitution's silence on a removal process, in contrast to its detailed regulation of appointment, meant that, by default, the President enjoyed the power to remove officers at will. But important questions remained open. In particular: could Congress change that default rule, by limiting the President's removal power through statute?

The Court only addressed this question squarely in the twentieth century, in *Myers v. United States*. In a very thorough opinion authored by Chief Justice Taft, the Court seemed to answer decisively: no. But be forewarned: as more cases came down the pike over the years, the Court's position became less unequivocal, and more complex. Reading through the cases in this unit, how would you articulate the current state of the law on the President's removal power?

**Myers v. United States**

272 U.S. 52 (1926)

October 25, 1926

MR. CHIEF JUSTICE TAFT delivered the opinion of the Court.

1 This case presents the question whether, under the Constitution, the President has
2 the exclusive power of removing executive officers of the United States whom he
3 has appointed by and with the advice and consent of the Senate.

4 Myers, appellant's intestate, was, on July 21, 1917, appointed by the President, by
5 and with the advice and consent of the Senate, to be a postmaster of the first class
6 at Portland, Oregon, for a term of four years. On January 20, 1920, Myers'
7 resignation was demanded. He refused the demand. On February 2, 1920, he was
8 removed from office by order of the Postmaster General, acting by direction of the
9 President. February 10th, Myers sent a petition to the President and another to the
10 Senate Committee on Post Offices, asking to be heard if any charges were filed. He
11 protested to the Department against his removal, and continued to do so until the
12 end of his term. He pursued no other occupation, and drew compensation for no
13 other service during the interval. On April 21, 1921, he brought this suit in the Court
14 of Claims for his salary from the date of his removal, which, as claimed by
15 supplemental petition filed after July 21, 1921, the end of his term, amounted to
16 $8,838.71. In August, 1920, the President made a recess appointment of one Jones,
17 who took office September 19, 1920.

18 * * *

19 By the 6th section of the Act of Congress of July 12, 1876, 19 Stat. 80, 81, c. 179,
20 under which Myers was appointed with the advice and consent of the Senate as a
21 first-class postmaster, it is provided that:

22 "Postmasters of the first, second and third classes shall be appointed and
23 may be removed by the President by and with the advice and consent of the
24 Senate and shall hold their offices for four years unless sooner removed or
25 suspended according to law."

26 The Senate did not consent to the President's removal of Myers during his term. If
27 this statute, in its requirement that his term should be four years unless sooner
28 removed by the President by and with the consent of the Senate, is valid, the
29 appellant, Myers' administratrix, is entitled to recover his unpaid salary for his full
30 term, and the judgment of the Court of Claims must be reversed. The Government
31 maintains that the requirement is invalid for the reason that, under Article II of
32 the Constitution the President's power of removal of executive officers appointed
33 by him with the advice and consent of the Senate is full and complete without
34 consent of the Senate. If this view is sound, the removal of Myers by the President
35 without the Senate's consent was legal, and the judgment of the Court of Claims
36 against the appellant was correct, and must be affirmed, though for a different
37 reason from that given by that court. We are therefore confronted by the
38 constitutional question, and cannot avoid it.

39 * * *

40 The question where the power of removal of executive officers appointed by the
41 President by and with the advice and consent of the Senate was vested was

1 presented early in the first session of the First Congress. There is no express
2 provision respecting removals in the Constitution, except as Section 4 of Article II
3 * * * provides for removal from office by impeachment. The subject was not
4 discussed in the Constitutional Convention. Under the Articles of Confederation,
5 Congress was given the power of appointing certain executive officers of the
6 Confederation, and, during the Revolution and while the Articles were given effect,
7 Congress exercised the power of removal.

8                                                     * * *

9 The vesting of the executive power in the President was essentially a grant of the
10 power to execute the laws. But the President, alone and unaided, could not execute
11 the laws. He must execute them by the assistance of subordinates. This view has
12 since been repeatedly affirmed by this Court. As he is charged specifically to take
13 care that they be faithfully executed, the reasonable implication, even in the
14 absence of express words, was that, as part of his executive power, he should select
15 those who were to act for him under his direction in the execution of the laws. The
16 further implication must be, in the absence of any express limitation respecting
17 removals, that, as his selection of administrative officers is essential to the
18 execution of the laws by him, so must be his power of removing those for whom he
19 cannot continue to be responsible. It was urged that the natural meaning of the
20 term "executive power" granted the President included the appointment and
21 removal of executive subordinates. If such appointments and removals were not
22 an exercise of the executive power, what were they? They certainly were not the
23 exercise of legislative or judicial power in government as usually understood.

24 It is quite true that, in state and colonial governments at the time of the
25 Constitutional Convention, power to make appointments and removals had
26 sometimes been lodged in the legislatures or in the courts, but such a disposition
27 of it was really vesting part of the executive power in another branch of the
28 Government. * * *

29                                                     * * *

30 * * * The view of Mr. Madison and his associates was that not only did the grant of
31 executive power to the President in the first section of Article II carry with it the
32 power of removal, but the express recognition of the power of appointment in the
33 second section enforced this view on the well approved principle of constitutional
34 and statutory construction that the power of removal of executive officers was
35 incident to the power of appointment. * * *

36                                                     * * *

37 It was pointed out in this great debate that the power of removal, though equally
38 essential to the executive power, is different in its nature from that of appointment.
39 A veto by the Senate—a part of the legislative branch of the Government—upon
40 removals is a much greater limitation upon the executive branch and a much more
41 serious blending of the legislative with the executive than a rejection of a proposed

appointment. It is not to be implied. The rejection of a nominee of the President for a particular office does not greatly embarrass him in the conscientious discharge of his high duties in the selection of those who are to aid him, because the President usually has an ample field from which to select for office, according to his preference, competent and capable men. The Senate has full power to reject newly proposed appointees whenever the President shall remove the incumbents. Such a check enables the Senate to prevent the filling of offices with bad or incompetent men or with those against whom there is tenable objection.

The power to prevent the removal of an officer who has served under the President is different from the authority to consent to or reject his appointment. When a nomination is made, it may be presumed that the Senate is, or may become, as well advised as to the fitness of the nominee as the President, but, in the nature of things, the defects in ability or intelligence or loyalty in the administration of the laws of one who has served as an officer under the President are facts as to which the President, or his trusted subordinates, must be better informed than the Senate, and the power to remove him may, therefore, be regarded as confined, for very sound and practical reasons, to the governmental authority which has administrative control. The power of removal is incident to the power of appointment, not to the power of advising and consenting to appointment, and when the grant of the executive power is enforced by the express mandate to take care that the laws be faithfully executed, it emphasizes the necessity for including within the executive power as conferred the exclusive power of removal.

* * *

Made responsible under the Constitution for the effective enforcement of the law, the President needs as an indispensable aid to meet it the disciplinary influence upon those who act under him of a reserve power of removal. But it is contended that executive officers appointed by the President with the consent of the Senate are bound by the statutory law, and are not his servants to do his will, and that his obligation to care for the faithful execution of the laws does not authorize him to treat them as such. The degree of guidance in the discharge of their duties that the President may exercise over executive officers varies with the character of their service as prescribed in the law under which they act. The highest and most important duties which his subordinates perform are those in which they act for him. In such cases, they are exercising not their own, but his, discretion. This field is a very large one. It is sometimes described as political. Each head of a department is and must be the President's alter ego in the matters of that department where the President is required by law to exercise authority.

* * *

In all such cases, the discretion to be exercised is that of the President in determining the national public interest and in directing the action to be taken by his executive subordinates to protect it. In this field, his cabinet officers must do his will. He must place in each member of his official family, and his chief executive subordinates, implicit faith. The moment that he loses confidence in the intelligence, ability, judgment or loyalty of anyone of them, he must have the power to remove him without delay. To require him to file charges and submit them to the consideration of the Senate might make impossible that unity and coordination in executive administration essential to effective action.

The duties of the heads of departments and bureaus in which the discretion of the President is exercised and which we have described are the most important in the whole field of executive action of the Government. There is nothing in the Constitution which permits a distinction between the removal of the head of a department or a bureau, when he discharges a political duty of the President or exercises his discretion, and the removal of executive officers engaged in the discharge of their other normal duties. The imperative reasons requiring an unrestricted power to remove the most important of his subordinates in their most important duties must, therefore, control the interpretation of the Constitution as to all appointed by him.

But this is not to say that there are not strong reasons why the President should have a like power to remove his appointees charged with other duties than those above described. The ordinary duties of officers prescribed by statute come under the general administrative control of the President by virtue of the general grant to him of the executive power, and he may properly supervise and guide their construction of the statutes under which they act in order to secure that unitary and uniform execution of the laws which Article II of the Constitution evidently contemplated in vesting general executive power in the President alone. Laws are often passed with specific provision for the adoption of regulations by a department or bureau head to make the law workable and effective. The ability and judgment manifested by the official thus empowered, as well as his energy and stimulation of his subordinates, are subjects which the President must consider and supervise in his administrative control. Finding such officers to be negligent and inefficient, the President should have the power to remove them. Of course, there may be duties so peculiarly and specifically committed to the discretion of a particular officer as to raise a question whether the President may overrule or revise the officer's interpretation of his statutory duty in a particular instance. Then there may be duties of a quasi-judicial character imposed on executive officers and members of executive tribunals whose decisions after hearing affect interests of individuals, the discharge of which the President cannot in a particular case properly influence or control. But even in such a case, he may consider the decision after its rendition as a reason for removing the officer, on the ground that the discretion regularly entrusted to that officer by statute has not been, on the whole, intelligently or wisely exercised. Otherwise, he does not discharge his own constitutional duty of seeing that the laws be faithfully executed.

* * *

MR. JUSTICE HOLMES, dissenting. [Omitted.]

1　MR. JUSTICE BRANDEIS, dissenting.

2　In 1833, MR. JUSTICE STORY, after discussing in §§ 1537-1543 of his
3　Commentaries on the Constitution the much debated question concerning the
4　President's power of removal, said in § 1544:

5　　"If there has been any aberration from the true constitutional exposition of
6　　the power of removal (which the reader must decide for himself), it will be
7　　difficult, and perhaps impracticable, after forty years' experience, to recall
8　　the practice to the correct theory. But, at all events, it will be a consolation
9　　to those who love the Union and honor a devotion to the patriotic discharge
10　　of duty that, in regard to 'inferior officers' (which appellation probably
11　　includes ninety-nine out of a hundred of the lucrative offices in the
12　　government), the remedy for any permanent abuse is still within the power
13　　of Congress by the simple expedient of requiring the consent of the Senate
14　　to removals in such cases."

15　Postmasters are inferior officers. Congress might have vested their appointment in
16　the head of the department. The Act of July 12, 1876, c. 17, § 6, 19 Stat. 78, 80,
17　reenacting earlier legislation, provided that "postmasters of the first, second, and
18　third classes shall be appointed and may be removed by the President by and with
19　the advice and consent of the Senate, and shall hold their offices for four years
20　unless sooner removed or suspended according to law." That statute has been in
21　force unmodified for half a century. Throughout the period, it has governed a large
22　majority of all civil offices to which appointments are made by and with the advice
23　and consent of the Senate. May the President, having acted under the statute
24　insofar as it creates the office and authorizes the appointment, ignore, while the
25　Senate is in session, the provision which prescribes the condition under which a
26　removal may take place?

27　It is this narrow question, and this only, which we are required to decide. We need
28　not consider what power the President, being Commander in Chief, has over
29　officers in the Army and the Navy. We need not determine whether the President,
30　acting alone, may remove high political officers. We need not even determine
31　whether, acting alone, he may remove inferior civil officers when the Senate is not
32　in session. * * *

33　　　　　　　　　　　　　　　　　　　* * *

34　To imply a grant to the President of the uncontrollable power of removal from
35　statutory inferior executive offices involves an unnecessary and indefensible
36　limitation upon the constitutional power of Congress to fix the tenure of inferior
37　statutory offices. That such a limitation cannot be justified on the ground of
38　necessity is demonstrated by the practice of our governments, state and national.
39　In none of the original thirteen States did the chief executive possess such power
40　at the time of the adoption of the Federal Constitution. In none of the forty-eight

1  States has such power been conferred at any time since by a state constitution, with
2  a single possible exception. * * *

3  Over removal from inferior civil offices, Congress has, from the foundation of our
4  Government, exercised continuously some measure of control by legislation. The
5  instances of such laws are many. Some of the statutes were directory in character.
6  Usually, they were mandatory. Some of them, comprehensive in scope, have
7  endured for generations. * * *

8                                                    * * *

9  The assertion that the mere grant by the Constitution of executive power confers
10 upon the President as a prerogative the unrestricted power of appointment and of
11 removal from executive offices, except so far as otherwise expressly provided by
12 the Constitution, is clearly inconsistent also with those statutes which restrict the
13 exercise by the President of the power of nomination. There is not a word in the
14 Constitution which, in terms, authorizes Congress to limit the President's freedom
15 of choice in making nominations for executive offices. It is to appointment, as
16 distinguished from nomination, that the Constitution imposes in terms the
17 requirement of Senatorial consent. But a multitude of laws have been enacted
18 which limit the President's power to make nominations, and which, through the
19 restrictions imposed, may prevent the selection of the person deemed by him best
20 fitted. Such restriction upon the power to nominate has been exercised by Congress
21 continuously since the foundation of the Government. Every President has
22 approved one or more of such acts. Every President has consistently observed
23 them. This is true of those offices to which he makes appointments without the
24 advice and consent of the Senate, as well as of those for which its consent is
25 required.

26                                                   * * *

27 Checks and balances were established in order that this should be "a government
28 of laws, and not of men." As White said in the House in 1789, an uncontrollable
29 power of removal in the Chief Executive "is a doctrine not to be learned in
30 American governments." Such power had been denied in Colonial Charters, and
31 even under Proprietary Grants and Royal Commissions. It had been denied in the
32 thirteen States before the framing of the Federal Constitution. The doctrine of the
33 separation of powers was adopted by the convention of 1787 not to promote
34 efficiency, but to preclude the exercise of arbitrary power. The purpose was not to
35 avoid friction but, by means of the inevitable friction incident to the distribution of
36 the governmental powers among three departments, to save the people from
37 autocracy. In order to prevent arbitrary executive action, the Constitution provided
38 in terms that presidential appointments be made with the consent of the Senate,
39 unless Congress should otherwise provide, and this clause was construed by
40 Alexander Hamilton in The Federalist, No. 77, as requiring like consent to
41 removals. Limiting further executive prerogatives customary in monarchies, the
42 Constitution empowered Congress to vest the appointment of inferior officers, "as

1 they think proper, in the President alone, in the Courts of Law, or in the Heads of
2 Departments." Nothing in support of the claim of uncontrollable power can be
3 inferred from the silence of the Convention of 1787 on the subject of removal. For
4 the outstanding fact remains that every specific proposal to confer such
5 uncontrollable power upon the President was rejected. In America, as in England,
6 the conviction prevailed then that the people must look to representative
7 assemblies for the protection of their liberties. And protection of the individual,
8 even if he be an official, from the arbitrary or capricious exercise of power was then
9 believed to be an essential of free government.

10

## Humphrey's Executor v. United States

12 295 U.S. 602 (1935)

13 May 27, 1935

14 MR. JUSTICE SUTHERLAND delivered the opinion of the Court.

15 Plaintiff brought suit in the Court of Claims against the United States to recover a
16 sum of money alleged to be due the deceased for salary as a Federal Trade
17 Commissioner from October 8, 1933, when the President undertook to remove him
18 from office, to the time of his death on February 14, 1934. The court below has
19 certified to this court two questions in respect of the power of the President to make
20 the removal. The material facts which give rise to the questions are as follows:

21 William E. Humphrey, the decedent, on December 10, 1931, was nominated by
22 President Hoover to succeed himself as a member of the Federal Trade
23 Commission, and was confirmed by the United States Senate. He was duly
24 commissioned for a term of seven years expiring September 25, 1938; and, after
25 taking the required oath of office, entered upon his duties. On July 25, 1933,
26 President Roosevelt addressed a letter to the commissioner asking for his
27 resignation, on the ground "that the aims and purposes of the Administration with
28 respect to the work of the Commission can be carried out most effectively with
29 personnel of my own selection," but disclaiming any reflection upon the
30 commissioner personally or upon his services. The commissioner replied, asking
31 time to consult his friends. After some further correspondence upon the subject,
32 the President, on August 31, 1933, wrote the commissioner expressing the hope
33 that the resignation would be forthcoming, and saying: "You will, I know, realize
34 that I do not feel that your mind and my mind go along together on either the
35 policies or the administering of the Federal Trade Commission, and, frankly, I
36 think it is best for the people of this country that I should have a full confidence."

37 The commissioner declined to resign, and on October 7, 1933, the President wrote
38 him: "Effective as of this date, you are hereby removed from the office of
39 Commissioner of the Federal Trade Commission."

1     Humphrey never acquiesced in this action, but continued thereafter to insist that
2     he was still a member of the commission, entitled to perform its duties and receive
3     the compensation provided by law at the rate of $10,000 per annum. * * *

4     * * *

5     The Federal Trade Commission Act creates a commission of five members to be
6     appointed by the President by and with the advice and consent of the Senate, and
7     § 1 provides:

8     "Not more than three of the commissioners shall be members of the same
9     political party. The first commissioners appointed shall continue in office
10     for terms of three, four, five, six, and seven years, respectively, from the
11     date of the taking effect of this Act, the term of each to be designated by the
12     President, but their successors shall be appointed for terms of seven years,
13     except that any person chosen to fill a vacancy shall be appointed only for
14     the unexpired term of the commissioner whom he shall succeed. The
15     commission shall choose a chairman from its own membership. No
16     commissioner shall engage in any other business, vocation, or
17     employment. Any commissioner may be removed by the President for
18     inefficiency, neglect of duty, or malfeasance in office. . . ."

19     * * *

20     * * * To support its contention that the removal provision of § 1, as we have just
21     construed it, is an unconstitutional interference with the executive power of the
22     President, the government's chief reliance is *Myers v. United States*, 272 U.S. 52
23     (1926). * * * [T]he narrow point actually decided was only that the President had
24     power to remove a postmaster of the first class without the advice and consent of
25     the Senate as required by act of Congress. In the course of the opinion of the court,
26     expressions occur which tend to sustain the government's contention, but these
27     are beyond the point involved, and, therefore do not come within the rule of stare
28     decisis. In so far as they are out of harmony with the views here set forth, these
29     expressions are disapproved. * * *

30     * * *

31     The office of a postmaster is so essentially unlike the office now involved that the
32     decision in the Myers case cannot be accepted as controlling our decision here. A
33     postmaster is an executive officer restricted to the performance of executive
34     functions. He is charged with no duty at all related to either the legislative or
35     judicial power. The actual decision in the *Myers* case finds support in the theory
36     that such an officer is merely one of the units in the executive department, and,
37     hence, inherently subject to the exclusive and illimitable power of removal by the
38     Chief Executive, whose subordinate and aid he is. Putting aside dicta, which may
39     be followed if sufficiently persuasive but which are not controlling, the necessary
40     reach of the decision goes far enough to include all purely executive officers. It goes
41     no farther; much less does it include an officer who occupies no place in the

1  executive department, and who exercises no part of the executive power vested by
2  the Constitution in the President.

3  The Federal Trade Commission is an administrative body created by Congress to
4  carry into effect legislative policies embodied in the statute in accordance with the
5  legislative standard therein prescribed, and to perform other specified duties as a
6  legislative or as a judicial aid. Such a body cannot in any proper sense be
7  characterized as an arm or an eye of the executive. Its duties are performed without
8  executive leave, and, in the contemplation of the statute, must be free from
9  executive control. In administering the provisions of the statute in respect of
10 "unfair methods of competition"—that is to say, in filling in and administering the
11 details embodied by that general standard—the commission acts in part quasi-
12 legislatively and in part quasi-judicially. In making investigations and reports
13 thereon for the information of Congress under § 6, in aid of the legislative power,
14 it acts as a legislative agency. Under § 7, which authorizes the commission to act as
15 a master in chancery under rules prescribed by the court, it acts as an agency of the
16 judiciary. To the extent that it exercises any executive function—as distinguished
17 from executive power in the constitutional sense—it does so in the discharge and
18 effectuation of its quasi-legislative or quasi-judicial powers, or as an agency of the
19 legislative or judicial departments of the government.

20                                    * * *

21 We think it plain under the Constitution that illimitable power of removal is not
22 possessed by the President in respect of officers of the character of those just
23 named. The authority of Congress, in creating quasi-legislative or quasi-judicial
24 agencies, to require them to act in discharge of their duties independently of
25 executive control cannot well be doubted; and that authority includes, as an
26 appropriate incident, power to fix the period during which they shall continue in
27 office, and to forbid their removal except for cause in the meantime. For it is quite
28 evident that one who holds his office only during the pleasure of another cannot be
29 depended upon to maintain an attitude of independence against the latter's will.

30 The fundamental necessity of maintaining each of the three general departments
31 of government entirely free from the control or coercive influence, direct or
32 indirect, of either of the others has often been stressed, and is hardly open to
33 serious question. So much is implied in the very fact of the separation of the powers
34 of these departments by the Constitution, and in the rule which recognizes their
35 essential coequality. The sound application of a principle that makes one master in
36 his own house precludes him from imposing his control in the house of another
37 who is master there. * * *

38 The power of removal here claimed for the President falls within this principle,
39 since its coercive influence threatens the independence of a commission which is
40 not only wholly disconnected from the executive department, but which, as already
41 fully appears, was created by Congress as a means of carrying into operation

legislative and judicial powers, and as an agency of the legislative and judicial departments.

\* \* \*

The result of what we now have said is this: whether the power of the President to remove an officer shall prevail over the authority of Congress to condition the power by fixing a definite term and precluding a removal except for cause will depend upon the character of the office; the *Myers* decision, affirming the power of the President alone to make the removal, is confined to purely executive officers, and, as to officers of the kind here under consideration, we hold that no removal can be made during the prescribed term for which the officer is appointed except for one or more of the causes named in the applicable statute. \* \* \*

\* \* \*

## Bowsher v. Synar

478 U.S. 714 (1986)

July 7, 1986

CHIEF JUSTICE BURGER delivered the opinion of the Court.

The question presented by these appeals is whether the assignment by Congress to the Comptroller General of the United States of certain functions under the Balanced Budget and Emergency Deficit Control Act of 1985 violates the doctrine of separation of powers.

I

A

On December 12, 1985, the President signed into law the Balanced Budget and Emergency Deficit Control Act of 1985, popularly known as the "Gramm-Rudman-Hollings Act." The purpose of the Act is to eliminate the federal budget deficit. To that end, the Act sets a "maximum deficit amount" for federal spending for each of fiscal years 1986 through 1991. The size of that maximum deficit amount progressively reduces to zero in fiscal year 1991. If in any fiscal year the federal budget deficit exceeds the maximum deficit amount by more than a specified sum, the Act requires across-the-board cuts in federal spending to reach the targeted deficit level, with half of the cuts made to defense programs and the other half made to nondefense programs. The Act exempts certain priority programs from these cuts.

These "automatic" reductions are accomplished through a rather complicated procedure, spelled out in § 251, the so-called "reporting provisions" of the Act. Each year, the Directors of the Office of Management and Budget (OMB) and the

Congressional Budget Office (CBO) independently estimate the amount of the federal budget deficit for the upcoming fiscal year. If that deficit exceeds the maximum targeted deficit amount for that fiscal year by more than a specified amount, the Directors of OMB and CBO independently calculate, on a program-by-program basis, the budget reductions necessary to ensure that the deficit does not exceed the maximum deficit amount. The Act then requires the Directors to report jointly their deficit estimates and budget reduction calculations to the Comptroller General.

The Comptroller General, after reviewing the Directors' reports, then reports his conclusions to the President. § 251(b). The President, in turn, must issue a "sequestration" order mandating the spending reductions specified by the Comptroller General. § 252. There follows a period during which Congress may by legislation reduce spending to obviate, in whole or in part, the need for the sequestration order. If such reductions are not enacted, the sequestration order becomes effective and the spending reductions included in that order are made.

* * *

B

* * *

A three-judge District Court, appointed pursuant to 2 U.S.C. § 922(a)(5) invalidated the reporting provisions. * * *

* * *

Although the District Court concluded that the Act survived a delegation doctrine challenge, it held that the role of the Comptroller General in the deficit reduction process violated the constitutionally imposed separation of powers. The court first explained that the Comptroller General exercises executive functions under the Act. However, the Comptroller General, while appointed by the President with the advice and consent of the Senate, is removable not by the President but only by a joint resolution of Congress or by impeachment. The District Court reasoned that this arrangement could not be sustained under this Court's decisions in *Myers v. United States*, 272 U.S. 52 (1926), and *Humphrey's Executor v. United States*, 295 U.S. 602 (1935). Under the separation of powers established by the Framers of the Constitution, the court concluded, Congress may not retain the power of removal over an officer performing executive functions. The congressional removal power created a "here-and-now subservience" of the Comptroller General to Congress. The District Court therefore held that,

> "since the powers conferred upon the Comptroller General as part of the automatic deficit reduction process are executive powers, which cannot constitutionally be exercised by an officer removable by Congress, those powers cannot be exercised, and therefore the automatic deficit reduction process to which they are central cannot be implemented."

1  Appeals were taken directly to this Court pursuant to § 274(b) of the Act. We noted
2  probable jurisdiction and expedited consideration of the appeals. We affirm.

3                                    * * *

4                                    III

5                                    * * *

6  The Constitution does not contemplate an active role for Congress in the
7  supervision of officers charged with the execution of the laws it enacts. The
8  President appoints "Officers of the United States" with the "Advice and Consent of
9  the Senate. . . ." Art. II, § 2. Once the appointment has been made and confirmed,
10 however, the Constitution explicitly provides for removal of Officers of the United
11 States by Congress only upon impeachment by the House of Representatives and
12 conviction by the Senate. An impeachment by the House and trial by the Senate
13 can rest only on "Treason, Bribery or other high Crimes and Misdemeanors." Art.
14 II, § 4. A direct congressional role in the removal of officers charged with the
15 execution of the laws beyond this limited one is inconsistent with separation of
16 powers.

17                                   * * *

18 [The Court discussed a number of its removal power precedents.]

19 In light of these precedents, we conclude that Congress cannot reserve for itself the
20 power of removal of an officer charged with the execution of the laws except by
21 impeachment. To permit the execution of the laws to be vested in an officer
22 answerable only to Congress would, in practical terms, reserve in Congress control
23 over the execution of the laws. As the District Court observed: "Once an officer is
24 appointed, it is only the authority that can remove him, and not the authority that
25 appointed him, that he must fear and, in the performance of his functions, obey."
26 The structure of the Constitution does not permit Congress to execute the laws; it
27 follows that Congress cannot grant to an officer under its control what it does not
28 possess.

29                                   * * *

30                                   IV

31 Appellants urge that the Comptroller General performs his duties independently
32 and is not subservient to Congress. We agree with the District Court that this
33 contention does not bear close scrutiny.

34 The critical factor lies in the provisions of the statute defining the Comptroller
35 General's office relating to removability. Although the Comptroller General is
36 nominated by the President from a list of three individuals recommended by the
37 Speaker of the House of Representatives and the President pro tempore of the
38 Senate, and confirmed by the Senate, he is removable only at the initiative of

1 Congress. He may be removed not only by impeachment, but also by joint
2 resolution of Congress "at any time" resting on any one of the following bases:

3     (i) permanent disability;

4     (ii) inefficiency;

5     (iii) neglect of duty;

6     (iv) malfeasance; or

7     (v) a felony or conduct involving moral turpitude.

8           \* \* \*

9           V

10           \* \* \*

11 Appellants suggest that the duties assigned to the Comptroller General in the Act
12 are essentially ministerial and mechanical, so that their performance does not
13 constitute "execution of the law" in a meaningful sense. On the contrary, we view
14 these functions as plainly entailing execution of the law in constitutional terms.
15 Interpreting a law enacted by Congress to implement the legislative mandate is the
16 very essence of "execution" of the law. Under § 251, the Comptroller General must
17 exercise judgment concerning facts that affect the application of the Act. He must
18 also interpret the provisions of the Act to determine precisely what budgetary
19 calculations are required. Decisions of that kind are typically made by officers
20 charged with executing a statute.

21 The executive nature of the Comptroller General's functions under the Act is
22 revealed in § 252(a)(3), which gives the Comptroller General the ultimate authority
23 to determine the budget cuts to be made. Indeed, the Comptroller General
24 commands the President himself to carry out, without the slightest variation (with
25 exceptions not relevant to the constitutional issues presented), the directive of the
26 Comptroller General as to the budget reductions \* \* \* .

27           \* \* \*

28 JUSTICE STEVENS, with whom JUSTICE MARSHALL joins, concurring in the
29 judgment.

30           \* \* \*

31 Everyone agrees that the powers assigned to the Comptroller General by § 251(b)
32 and § 251(c)(2) of the Gramm-Rudman-Hollings Act are extremely important.
33 They require him to exercise sophisticated economic judgment concerning
34 anticipated trends in the Nation's economy, projected levels of unemployment,
35 interest rates, and the special problems that may be confronted by the many
36 components of a vast federal bureaucracy. His duties are anything but

ministerial—he is not merely a clerk wearing a "green eyeshade" as he undertakes these tasks. Rather, he is vested with the kind of responsibilities that Congress has elected to discharge itself under the fallback provision that will become effective if and when § 251(b) and § 251(c)(2) are held invalid. Unless we make the naive assumption that the economic destiny of the Nation could be safely entrusted to a mindless bank of computers, the powers that this Act vests in the Comptroller General must be recognized as having transcendent importance.

The Court concludes that the Gramm-Rudman-Hollings Act impermissibly assigns the Comptroller General "executive powers." JUSTICE WHITE's dissent agrees that "the powers exercised by the Comptroller under the Act may be characterized as 'executive' in that they involve the interpretation and carrying out of the Act's mandate." This conclusion is not only far from obvious, but also rests on the unstated and unsound premise that there is a definite line that distinguishes executive power from legislative power.

\* \* \*

One reason that the exercise of legislative, executive, and judicial powers cannot be categorically distributed among three mutually exclusive branches of Government is that governmental power cannot always be readily characterized with only one of those three labels. On the contrary, as our cases demonstrate, a particular function, like a chameleon, will often take on the aspect of the office to which it is assigned. For this reason, "[w]hen any Branch acts, it is presumptively exercising the power the Constitution has delegated to it." *INS v. Chadha*, 462 U.S., at 951.

The *Chadha* case itself illustrates this basic point. The governmental decision that was being made was whether a resident alien who had overstayed his student visa should be deported. From the point of view of the Administrative Law Judge who conducted a hearing on the issue—or, as JUSTICE POWELL saw the issue in his concurrence—the decision took on a judicial coloring. From the point of view of the Attorney General of the United States, to whom Congress had delegated the authority to suspend deportation of certain aliens, the decision appeared to have an executive character. But, as the Court held, when the House of Representatives finally decided that Chadha must be deported, its action "was essentially legislative in purpose and effect." *Id.* at 952.

The powers delegated to the Comptroller General by § 251 of the Act before us today have a similar chameleon-like quality. The District Court persuasively explained why they may be appropriately characterized as executive powers. But, when that delegation is held invalid, the "fallback provision" provides that the report that would otherwise be issued by the Comptroller General shall be issued by Congress itself. In the event that the resolution is enacted, the congressional report will have the same legal consequences as if it had been issued by the Comptroller General. In that event, moreover, surely no one would suggest that Congress had acted in any capacity other than "legislative." \* \* \* Under the District

Court's analysis, and the analysis adopted by the majority today, it would therefore appear that the function at issue is "executive" if performed by the Comptroller General, but "legislative" if performed by the Congress. In my view, however, the function may appropriately be labeled "legislative" even if performed by the Comptroller General or by an executive agency.

Despite the statement in Article I of the Constitution that "All legislative Powers herein granted shall be vested in a Congress of the United States," it is far from novel to acknowledge that independent agencies do indeed exercise legislative powers. * * *

* * *

Thus, I do not agree that the Comptroller General's responsibilities under the Gramm-Rudman-Hollings Act must be termed "executive powers," or even that our inquiry is much advanced by using that term. For, whatever the label given the functions to be performed by the Comptroller General under § 251—or by the Congress under § 274—the District Court had no difficulty in concluding that Congress could delegate the performance of those functions to another branch of the Government. If the delegation to a stranger is permissible, why may not Congress delegate the same responsibilities to one of its own agents? That is the central question before us today.

Congress regularly delegates responsibility to a number of agents who provide important support for its legislative activities. * * *

The Gramm-Rudman-Hollings Act assigns to the Comptroller General the duty to make policy decisions that have the force of law. The Comptroller General's report is, in the current statute, the engine that gives life to the ambitious budget reduction process. It is the Comptroller General's report that "provide[s] for the determination of reductions" and that "contain[s] estimates, determinations, and specifications for all of the items contained in the report" submitted by the Office of Management and Budget and the Congressional Budget Office. § 251(b). It is the Comptroller General's report that the President must follow and that will have conclusive effect. § 252. It is, in short, the Comptroller General's report that will have a profound, dramatic, and immediate impact on the Government and on the Nation at large.

Article I of the Constitution specifies the procedures that Congress must follow when it makes policy that binds the Nation: its legislation must be approved by both of its Houses and presented to the President. In holding that an attempt to legislate by means of a "one-House veto" violated the procedural mandate in Article I, we explained:

> "We see therefore that the Framers were acutely conscious that the bicameral requirement and the Presentment Clauses would serve essential constitutional functions. The President's participation in the legislative process was to protect the Executive Branch from Congress and to protect

the whole people from improvident laws. The division of the Congress into two distinctive bodies assures that the legislative power would be exercised only after opportunity for full study and debate in separate settings. The President's unilateral veto power, in turn, was limited by the power of two-thirds of both Houses of Congress to overrule a veto, thereby precluding final arbitrary action of one person. It emerges clearly that the prescription for legislative action in Art. I, §§ 1, 7, represents the Framers' decision that the legislative power of the Federal Government be exercised in accord with a single, finely wrought and exhaustively considered, procedure." *INS v. Chadha*, 462 U.S., at 951.

If Congress were free to delegate its policymaking authority to one of its components, or to one of its agents, it would be able to evade "the carefully crafted restraints spelled out in the Constitution." *Id.* at 959. That danger—congressional action that evades constitutional restraints—is not present when Congress delegates lawmaking power to the executive or to an independent agency.

\* \* \*

As a result, to decide this case, there is no need to consider the Decision of 1789, the President's removal power, or the abstract nature of "executive powers." Once it is clear that the Comptroller General, whose statutory duties define him as an agent of Congress, has been assigned the task of making policy determinations that will bind the Nation, the question is simply one of congressional process. There can be no doubt that the Comptroller General's statutory duties under Gramm-Rudman-Hollings do not follow the constitutionally prescribed procedures for congressional lawmaking.

In short, even though it is well settled that Congress may delegate legislative power to independent agencies or to the Executive, and thereby divest itself of a portion of its lawmaking power, when it elects to exercise such power itself, it may not authorize a lesser representative of the Legislative Branch to act on its behalf. It is for this reason that I believe § 251(b) and § 251(c)(2) of the Act are unconstitutional.

\* \* \*

JUSTICE WHITE, dissenting. [Omitted.]

JUSTICE BLACKMUN, dissenting. [Omitted.]

## Morrison v. Olson

487 U.S. 654 (1988)

June 29, 1988

1    CHIEF JUSTICE REHNQUIST delivered the opinion of the Court.

2    [Refer to the excerpt of this case in the Appointments Power materials for more
3    information on the statute at issue and the legal challenges posed to it.]

4                                    * * *

5                                     V

6    We now turn to consider whether the Act is invalid under the constitutional
7    principle of separation of powers. Two related issues must be addressed: the first
8    is whether the provision of the Act restricting the Attorney General's power to
9    remove the independent counsel to only those instances in which he can show
10   "good cause," taken by itself, impermissibly interferes with the President's exercise
11   of his constitutionally appointed functions. The second is whether, taken as a
12   whole, the Act violates the separation of powers by reducing the President's ability
13   to control the prosecutorial powers wielded by the independent counsel.

14                                    A

15                                   * * *

16   Unlike both *Bowsher* and *Myers*, this case does not involve an attempt by Congress
17   itself to gain a role in the removal of executive officials other than its established
18   powers of impeachment and conviction. The Act instead puts the removal power
19   squarely in the hands of the Executive Branch; an independent counsel may be
20   removed from office, "only by the personal action of the Attorney General, and only
21   for good cause." § 596(a)(1). There is no requirement of congressional approval of
22   the Attorney General's removal decision, though the decision is subject to judicial
23   review. § 596(a)(3). In our view, the removal provisions of the Act make this case
24   more analogous to *Humphrey's Executor v. United States*, 295 U.S. 602 (1935),
25   and *Wiener v. United States*, 357 U.S. 349 (1958), than to *Myers* or *Bowsher*.

26   In *Humphrey's Executor*, we found it "plain" that the Constitution did not give the
27   President "illimitable power of removal" over the officers of independent agencies.
28   Were the President to have the power to remove FTC commissioners at will, the
29   "coercive influence" of the removal power would "threate[n] the independence of
30   [the] commission."

31                                   * * *

32   Appellees contend that *Humphrey's Executor* and *Wiener* are distinguishable
33   from this case because they did not involve officials who performed a "core
34   executive function." They argue that our decision in *Humphrey's Executor* rests on
35   a distinction between "purely executive" officials and officials who exercise "quasi-
36   legislative" and "quasi-judicial" powers. In their view, when a "purely executive"
37   official is involved, the governing precedent is *Myers*, not *Humphrey's Executor*.
38   *See Humphrey's Executor*, at 295 U.S. 628. And, under *Myers*, the President must

1     have absolute discretion to discharge "purely" executive officials at will. *See Myers*,
2     272 U.S., at 132-134.

3     We undoubtedly did rely on the terms "quasi-legislative" and "quasi-judicial" to
4     distinguish the officials involved in *Humphry's Executor* and *Wiener* from those
5     in *Myers*, but our present considered view is that the determination of whether the
6     Constitution allows Congress to impose a "good cause"-type restriction on the
7     President's power to remove an official cannot be made to turn on whether or not
8     that official is classified as "purely executive." The analysis contained in our
9     removal cases is designed not to define rigid categories of those officials who may
10    or may not be removed at will by the President, but to ensure that Congress does
11    not interfere with the President's exercise of the "executive power" and his
12    constitutionally appointed duty to "take care that the laws be faithfully executed"
13    under Article II. *Myers* was undoubtedly correct in its holding, and in its broader
14    suggestion that there are some "purely executive" officials who must be removable
15    by the President at will if he is to be able to accomplish his constitutional role. * * *

16                                       * * *

17    * * * We do not mean to suggest that an analysis of the functions served by the
18    officials at issue is irrelevant. But the real question is whether the removal
19    restrictions are of such a nature that they impede the President's ability to perform
20    his constitutional duty, and the functions of the officials in question must be
21    analyzed in that light.

22    Considering for the moment the "good cause" removal provision in isolation from
23    the other parts of the Act at issue in this case, we cannot say that the imposition of
24    a "good cause" standard for removal by itself unduly trammels on executive
25    authority. There is no real dispute that the functions performed by the independent
26    counsel are "executive" in the sense that they are law enforcement functions that
27    typically have been undertaken by officials within the Executive Branch. As we
28    noted above, however, the independent counsel is an inferior officer under the
29    Appointments Clause, with limited jurisdiction and tenure and lacking
30    policymaking or significant administrative authority. Although the counsel
31    exercises no small amount of discretion and judgment in deciding how to carry out
32    his or her duties under the Act, we simply do not see how the President's need to
33    control the exercise of that discretion is so central to the functioning of the
34    Executive Branch as to require as a matter of constitutional law that the counsel be
35    terminable at will by the President.

36    Nor do we think that the "good cause" removal provision at issue here
37    impermissibly burdens the President's power to control or supervise the
38    independent counsel, as an executive official, in the execution of his or her duties
39    under the Act. This is not a case in which the power to remove an executive official
40    has been completely stripped from the President, thus providing no means for the
41    President to ensure the "faithful execution" of the laws. Rather, because the
42    independent counsel may be terminated for "good cause," the Executive, through

the Attorney General, retains ample authority to assure that the counsel is competently performing his or her statutory responsibilities in a manner that comports with the provisions of the Act. Although we need not decide in this case exactly what is encompassed within the term "good cause" under the Act, the legislative history of the removal provision also makes clear that the Attorney General may remove an independent counsel for "misconduct." Here, as with the provision of the Act conferring the appointment authority of the independent counsel on the special court, the congressional determination to limit the removal power of the Attorney General was essential, in the view of Congress, to establish the necessary independence of the office. We do not think that this limitation as it presently stands sufficiently deprives the President of control over the independent counsel to interfere impermissibly with his constitutional obligation to ensure the faithful execution of the laws.

B

The final question to be addressed is whether the Act, taken as a whole, violates the principle of separation of powers by unduly interfering with the role of the Executive Branch. Time and again we have reaffirmed the importance in our constitutional scheme of the separation of governmental powers into the three coordinate branches. * * * On the other hand, we have never held that the Constitution requires that the three branches of Government "operate with absolute independence." *United States v. Nixon*, 418 U.S., at 707; In the often-quoted words of JUSTICE JACKSON:

> "While the Constitution diffuses power the better to secure liberty, it also contemplates that practice will integrate the dispersed powers into a workable government. It enjoins upon its branches separateness but interdependence, autonomy but reciprocity."

*Youngstown Sheet & Tube Co. v. Sawyer*, 343 U.S. 579, 635 (1952) (concurring opinion).

We observe first that this case does not involve an attempt by Congress to increase its own powers at the expense of the Executive Branch. *Cf. Commodity Futures Trading Comm'n v. Schor*, 478 U.S., at 856. Unlike some of our previous cases, most recently *Bowsher v. Synar*, this case simply does not pose a "dange[r] of congressional usurpation of Executive Branch functions." *see also INS v. Chadha*, 462 U.S. 919, 958 (1983). * * *

* * *

* * * It is undeniable that the Act reduces the amount of control or supervision that the Attorney General and, through him, the President exercises over the investigation and prosecution of a certain class of alleged criminal activity. The Attorney General is not allowed to appoint the individual of his choice; he does not determine the counsel's jurisdiction; and his power to remove a counsel is limited. Nonetheless, the Act does give the Attorney General several means of supervising

110

or controlling the prosecutorial powers that may be wielded by an independent counsel. Most importantly, the Attorney General retains the power to remove the counsel for "good cause," a power that we have already concluded provides the Executive with substantial ability to ensure that the laws are "faithfully executed" by an independent counsel. No independent counsel may be appointed without a specific request by the Attorney General, and the Attorney General's decision not to request appointment if he finds "no reasonable grounds to believe that further investigation is warranted" is committed to his unreviewable discretion. The Act thus gives the Executive a degree of control over the power to initiate an investigation by the independent counsel. In addition, the jurisdiction of the independent counsel is defined with reference to the facts submitted by the Attorney General, and once a counsel is appointed, the Act requires that the counsel abide by Justice Department policy unless it is not "possible" to do so. Notwithstanding the fact that the counsel is to some degree "independent" and free from Executive supervision to a greater extent than other federal prosecutors, in our view, these features of the Act give the Executive Branch sufficient control over the independent counsel to ensure that the President is able to perform his constitutionally assigned duties.

\* \* \*

JUSTICE SCALIA, dissenting.

It is the proud boast of our democracy that we have "a government of laws, and not of men." Many Americans are familiar with that phrase; not many know its derivation. It comes from Part the First, Article XXX, of the Massachusetts Constitution of 1780, which reads in full as follows:

> "In the government of this Commonwealth, the legislative department shall never exercise the executive and judicial powers, or either of them: The executive shall never exercise the legislative and judicial powers, or either of them: The judicial shall never exercise the legislative and executive powers, or either of them: to the end it may be a government of laws, and not of men."

The Framers of the Federal Constitution similarly viewed the principle of separation of powers as the absolutely central guarantee of a just government. \* \* \* Without a secure structure of separated powers, our Bill of Rights would be worthless, as are the bills of rights of many nations of the world that have adopted, or even improved upon, the mere words of ours.

\* \* \*

II

If to describe this case is not to decide it, the concept of a government of separate and coordinate powers no longer has meaning. The Court devotes most of its attention to such relatively technical details as the Appointments Clause and the

1 removal power, addressing briefly and only at the end of its opinion the separation
2 of powers. As my prologue suggests, I think that has it backwards. Our opinions
3 are full of the recognition that it is the principle of separation of powers, and the
4 inseparable corollary that each department's "defense must ... be made
5 commensurate to the danger of attack," Federalist No. 51 (J. Madison), which gives
6 comprehensible content to the Appointments Clause, and determines the
7 appropriate scope of the removal power. Thus, while I will subsequently discuss
8 why our appointments and removal jurisprudence does not support today's
9 holding, I begin with a consideration of the fountainhead of that jurisprudence, the
10 separation and equilibration of powers.

11 * * *

12 To repeat, Article II, § 1, cl. 1, of the Constitution provides:

13 "The executive Power shall be vested in a President of the United States."

14 As I described at the outset of this opinion, this does not mean some of the
15 executive power, but *all* of the executive power. It seems to me, therefore, that the
16 decision of the Court of Appeals invalidating the present statute must be upheld on
17 fundamental separation of powers principles if the following two questions are
18 answered affirmatively: (1) Is the conduct of a criminal prosecution (and of an
19 investigation to decide whether to prosecute) the exercise of purely executive
20 power? (2) Does the statute deprive the President of the United States of exclusive
21 control over the exercise of that power? Surprising to say, the Court appears to
22 concede an affirmative answer to both questions, but seeks to avoid the inevitable
23 conclusion that, since the statute vests some purely executive power in a person
24 who is not the President of the United States, it is void.

25 The Court concedes that "[t]here is no real dispute that the functions performed
26 by the independent counsel are executive" * * * . There is no possible doubt that
27 the independent counsel's functions fit this description. She is vested with the "full
28 power and independent authority to exercise all *investigative* and *prosecutorial*
29 functions and powers of the Department of Justice [and] the Attorney General."
30 * * *

31 As for the second question, whether the statute before us deprives the President of
32 exclusive control over that quintessentially executive activity: the Court does not,
33 and could not possibly, assert that it does not. That is indeed the whole object of
34 the statute. Instead, the Court points out that the President, through his Attorney
35 General, has at least some control. That concession is alone enough to invalidate
36 the statute, but I cannot refrain from pointing out that the Court greatly
37 exaggerates the extent of that "some" Presidential control. "Most importan[t]"
38 among these controls, the Court asserts, is the Attorney General's "power to
39 remove the counsel for good cause.'" This is somewhat like referring to shackles as
40 an effective means of locomotion. As we recognized in *Humphrey's Executor v.*
41 *United States*, 295 U.S. 602 (1935)—indeed, what Humphrey's Executor was all

1  about—limiting removal power to "good cause" is an impediment to, not an
2  effective grant of, Presidential control. * * *

3  * * * Finally, the Court points out that the Act directs the independent counsel to
4  abide by general Justice Department policy, except when not "possible." *See* 28
5  U.S.C. § 594(f) (1982 ed., Supp. V). The exception alone shows this to be an empty
6  promise. Even without that, however, one would be hard put to come up with many
7  investigative or prosecutorial "policies" (other than those imposed by the
8  Constitution or by Congress through law) that are absolute. Almost all investigative
9  and prosecutorial decisions—including the ultimate decision whether, after a
10  technical violation of the law has been found, prosecution is warranted—involve
11  the balancing of innumerable legal and practical considerations. Indeed, even
12  political considerations (in the nonpartisan sense) must be considered, as
13  exemplified by the recent decision of an independent counsel to subpoena the
14  former Ambassador of Canada, producing considerable tension in our relations
15  with that country. Another preeminently political decision is whether getting a
16  conviction in a particular case is worth the disclosure of national security
17  information that would be necessary. The Justice Department and our intelligence
18  agencies are often in disagreement on this point, and the Justice Department does
19  not always win. The present Act even goes so far as specifically to take the
20  resolution of that dispute away from the President and give it to the independent
21  counsel. 28 U.S.C. § 594(a)(6) (1982 ed., Supp. V). In sum, the balancing of various
22  legal, practical, and political considerations, none of which is absolute, is the very
23  essence of prosecutorial discretion. To take this away is to remove the core of the
24  prosecutorial function, and not merely "some" Presidential control.

25  As I have said, however, it is ultimately irrelevant *how much* the statute reduces
26  Presidential control. The case is over when the Court acknowledges, as it must, that
27  "[i]t is undeniable that the Act reduces the amount of control or supervision that
28  the Attorney General and, through him, the President exercises over the
29  investigation and prosecution of a certain class of alleged criminal activity." * * * It
30  is not for us to determine, and we have never presumed to determine, how much
31  of the purely executive powers of government must be within the full control of the
32  President. The Constitution prescribes that they *all* are.

33  * * *

34  Is it unthinkable that the President should have such exclusive power, even when
35  alleged crimes by him or his close associates are at issue? No more so than that
36  Congress should have the exclusive power of legislation, even when what is at issue
37  is its own exemption from the burdens of certain laws. *See* Civil Rights Act of 1964,
38  Title VII, 42 U.S.C. § 2000e et seq. (prohibiting "employers," not defined to include
39  the United States, from discriminating on the basis of race, color, religion, sex, or
40  national origin). No more so than that this Court should have the exclusive power
41  to pronounce the final decision on justiciable cases and controversies, even those
42  pertaining to the constitutionality of a statute reducing the salaries of the Justices.
43  *See United States v. Will*, 449 U.S. 200, 211-217 (1980). A system of separate and

1    coordinate powers necessarily involves an acceptance of exclusive power that can
2    theoretically be abused. As we reiterate this very day, "[i]t is a truism that
3    constitutional protections have costs." *Coy v. Iowa*, 487 U.S., at 1020. While the
4    separation of powers may prevent us from righting every wrong, it does so in order
5    to ensure that we do not lose liberty. The checks against any branch's abuse of its
6    exclusive powers are twofold: first, retaliation by one of the other branch's use of
7    its exclusive powers: Congress, for example, can impeach the executive who
8    willfully fails to enforce the laws; the executive can decline to prosecute under
9    unconstitutional statutes, *cf. United States v. Lovett*, 328 U.S. 303 (1946); and the
10   courts can dismiss malicious prosecutions. Second, and ultimately, there is the
11   political check that the people will replace those in the political branches (the
12   branches more "dangerous to the political rights of the Constitution," Federalist
13   No. 78) who are guilty of abuse. Political pressures produced special prosecutors—
14   for Teapot Dome and for Watergate, for example—long before this statute created
15   the independent counsel.

16   The Court has, nonetheless, replaced the clear constitutional prescription that the
17   executive power belongs to the President with a "balancing test." What are the
18   standards to determine how the balance is to be struck, that is, how much removal
19   of Presidential power is too much? Many countries of the world get along with an
20   executive that is much weaker than ours—in fact, entirely dependent upon the
21   continued support of the legislature. Once we depart from the text of the
22   Constitution, just where short of that do we stop? The most amazing feature of the
23   Court's opinion is that it does not even purport to give an answer. It simply
24   announces, with no analysis, that the ability to control the decision whether to
25   investigate and prosecute the President's closest advisers, and indeed the
26   President himself, is not "so central to the functioning of the Executive Branch" as
27   to be constitutionally required to be within the President's control. Apparently that
28   is so because we say it is so. * * *

29                                      * * *

30   Besides weakening the Presidency by reducing the zeal of his staff, it must also be
31   obvious that the institution of the independent counsel enfeebles him more
32   directly in his constant confrontations with Congress, by eroding his public
33   support. Nothing is so politically effective as the ability to charge that one's
34   opponent and his associates are not merely wrongheaded, naive, ineffective, but,
35   in all probability, "crooks." And nothing so effectively gives an appearance of
36   validity to such charges as a Justice Department investigation and, even better,
37   prosecution. The present statute provides ample means for that sort of attack,
38   assuring that massive and lengthy investigations will occur, not merely when the
39   Justice Department in the application of its usual standards believes they are called
40   for, but whenever it cannot be said that there are "no reasonable grounds to
41   believe" they are called for. * * *

42                                      * * *

114

IV

I will not discuss at any length why the restrictions upon the removal of the independent counsel also violate our established precedent dealing with that specific subject. * * * I cannot avoid commenting, however, about the essence of what the Court has done to our removal jurisprudence today.

* * *

Since our 1935 decision in *Humphrey's Executor v. United States*, 295 U.S. 602—which was considered by many at the time the product of an activist, anti-New Deal Court bent on reducing the power of President Franklin Roosevelt—it has been established that the line of permissible restriction upon removal of principal officers lies at the point at which the powers exercised by those officers are no longer purely executive. Thus, removal restrictions have been generally regarded as lawful for so-called "independent regulatory agencies," such as the Federal Trade Commission, the Interstate Commerce Commission, and the Consumer Product Safety Commission, which engage substantially in what has been called the "quasi-legislative activity" of rulemaking, and for members of Article I courts, such as the Court of Military Appeals, who engage in the "quasi-judicial" function of adjudication. It has often been observed, correctly in my view, that the line between "purely executive" functions and "quasi-legislative" or "quasi-judicial" functions is not a clear one, or even a rational one. *Bowsher v. Synar*, 478 U.S. 714, 761, n. 3 (1986) (WHITE, J., dissenting); *FTC v. Ruberoid Co.*, 343 U.S. 470, 487, 488 (1952) (JACKSON, J., dissenting). But at least it permitted the identification of certain officers, and certain agencies, whose functions were entirely within the control of the President. Congress had to be aware of that restriction in its legislation. Today, however, *Humphrey's Executor* is swept into the dustbin of repudiated constitutional principles. "[O]ur present considered view," the Court says, "is that the determination of whether the Constitution allows Congress to impose a 'good cause'-type restriction on the President's power to remove an official cannot be made to turn on whether or not that official is classified as 'purely executive.'"

What *Humphrey's Executor* (and presumably *Myers*) really means, we are now told, is not that there are any "rigid categories of those officials who may or may not be removed at will by the President," but simply that Congress cannot "interfere with the President's exercise of the 'executive power' and his constitutionally appointed duty to 'take care that the laws be faithfully executed.'"

One can hardly grieve for the shoddy treatment given today to *Humphrey's Executor*, which, after all, accorded the same indignity (with much less justification) to CHIEF JUSTICE TAFT's opinion 10 years earlier in *Myers v. United States*, 272 U.S. 52 (1926)—gutting, in six quick pages devoid of textual or historical precedent for the novel principle it set forth, a carefully researched and reasoned 70-page opinion. It is in fact comforting to witness the reality that he who lives by the *ipse dixit* dies by the *ipse dixit*. But one must grieve for the

Constitution. *Humphrey's Executor* at least had the decency formally to observe the constitutional principle that the President had to be the repository of all executive power, *see* 295 U.S. 627, 628, which, as *Myers* carefully explained, necessarily means that he must be able to discharge those who do not perform executive functions according to his liking. * * * By contrast, "our present considered view" is simply that *any* executive officer's removal can be restricted, so long as the President remains "able to accomplish his constitutional role." There are now no lines. If the removal of a prosecutor, the virtual embodiment of the power to "take care that the laws be faithfully executed," can be restricted, what officer's removal cannot? This is an open invitation for Congress to experiment. What about a special Assistant Secretary of State, with responsibility for one very narrow area of foreign policy, who would not only have to be confirmed by the Senate but could also be removed only pursuant to certain carefully designed restrictions? Could this possibly render the President "[un]able to accomplish his constitutional role"? Or a special Assistant Secretary of Defense for Procurement? The possibilities are endless, and the Court does not understand what the separation of powers, what "[a]mbition . . . counteract[ing] ambition," Federalist No. 51 (Madison), is all about if it does not expect Congress to try them. As far as I can discern from the Court's opinion, it is now open season upon the President's removal power for all executive officers, with not even the superficially principled restriction of *Humphrey's Executor* as cover. The Court essentially says to the President: "Trust us. We will make sure that you are able to accomplish your constitutional role." I think the Constitution gives the President—and the people— more protection than that.

* * *


## Free Enterprise Fund v. Public Company Oversight Board

561 U.S. 477 (2010)

June 28, 2010

CHIEF JUSTICE ROBERTS delivered the opinion of the Court.

Our Constitution divided the "powers of the new Federal Government into three defined categories, Legislative, Executive, and Judicial." *INS v. Chadha*, 462 U.S. 919, 951 (1983). Article II vests "[t]he executive Power . . . in a President of the United States of America," who must "take Care that the Laws be faithfully executed." Art. II, §1, cl. 1; §3. In light of "[t]he impossibility that one man should be able to perform all the great business of the State," the Constitution provides for executive officers to "assist the supreme Magistrate in discharging the duties of his trust." 30 Writings of George Washington 334 (J. Fitzpatrick ed. 1939).

Since 1789, the Constitution has been understood to empower the President to keep these officers accountable—by removing them from office, if necessary. *See*

1    *generally Myers v. United States*, 272 U.S. 52 (1926). This Court has determined,
2    however, that this authority is not without limit. In *Humphrey's Executor v.*
3    *United States*, 295 U.S. 602 (1935), we held that Congress can, under certain
4    circumstances, create independent agencies run by principal officers appointed by
5    the President, whom the President may not remove at will but only for good cause.
6    Likewise, in *United States v. Perkins*, 116 U.S. 483 (1886), and *Morrison v. Olson*,
7    487 U.S. 654 (1988), the Court sustained similar restrictions on the power of
8    principal executive officers—themselves responsible to the President—to remove
9    their own inferiors. The parties do not ask us to reexamine any of these precedents,
10   and we do not do so.

11   We are asked, however, to consider a new situation not yet encountered by the
12   Court. The question is whether these separate layers of protection may be
13   combined. May the President be restricted in his ability to remove a principal
14   officer, who is in turn restricted in his ability to remove an inferior officer, even
15   though that inferior officer determines the policy and enforces the laws of the
16   United States?

17   We hold that such multilevel protection from removal is contrary to Article II's
18   vesting of the executive power in the President. The President cannot "take Care
19   that the Laws be faithfully executed" if he cannot oversee the faithfulness of the
20   officers who execute them. Here the President cannot remove an officer who enjoys
21   more than one level of good-cause protection, even if the President determines that
22   the officer is neglecting his duties or discharging them improperly. That judgment
23   is instead committed to another officer, who may or may not agree with the
24   President's determination, and whom the President cannot remove simply because
25   that officer disagrees with him. This contravenes the President's "constitutional
26   obligation to ensure the faithful execution of the laws."

27                                I

28                                A

29   After a series of celebrated accounting debacles, Congress enacted the Sarbanes-
30   Oxley Act of 2002 (or Act), 116 Stat. 745. Among other measures, the Act
31   introduced tighter regulation of the accounting industry under a new Public
32   Company Accounting Oversight Board. The Board is composed of five members,
33   appointed to staggered 5-year terms by the Securities and Exchange Commission.
34   It was modeled on private self-regulatory organizations in the securities industry—
35   such as the New York Stock Exchange—that investigate and discipline their own
36   members subject to Commission oversight. Congress created the Board as a private
37   "nonprofit corporation," and Board members and employees are not considered
38   Government "officer[s] or employee[s]" for statutory purposes. The Board can thus
39   recruit its members and employees from the private sector by paying salaries far
40   above the standard Government pay scale.

41   Unlike the self-regulatory organizations, however, the Board is a Government-
42   created, Government-appointed entity, with expansive powers to govern an entire

industry. Every accounting firm—both foreign and domestic—that participates in auditing public companies under the securities laws must register with the Board, pay it an annual fee, and comply with its rules and oversight. The Board is charged with enforcing the Sarbanes-Oxley Act, the securities laws, the Commission's rules, its own rules, and professional accounting standards. To this end, the Board may regulate every detail of an accounting firm's practice, including hiring and professional development, promotion, supervision of audit work, the acceptance of new business and the continuation of old, internal inspection procedures, professional ethics rules, and "such other requirements as the Board may prescribe." § 7213(a)(2)(B).

The Board promulgates auditing and ethics standards, performs routine inspections of all accounting firms, demands documents and testimony, and initiates formal investigations and disciplinary proceedings. The willful violation of any Board rule is treated as a willful violation of the Securities Exchange Act of 1934—a federal crime punishable by up to 20 years' imprisonment or $25 million in fines ($5 million for a natural person). And the Board itself can issue severe sanctions in its disciplinary proceedings, up to and including the permanent revocation of a firm's registration, a permanent ban on a person's associating with any registered firm, and money penalties of $15 million ($750,000 for a natural person). Despite the provisions specifying that Board members are not Government officials for statutory purposes, the parties agree that the Board is "part of the Government" for constitutional purposes, *Lebron v. National Railroad Passenger Corporation*, 513 U.S. 374, 397 (1995), and that its members are "'Officers of the United States'" who "exercis[e] significant authority pursuant to the laws of the United States," *Buckley v. Valeo*, 424 U.S. 1, 125, 126 (1976) (per curiam) (quoting Art. II, §2, cl. 2).

The Act places the Board under the SEC's oversight, particularly with respect to the issuance of rules or the imposition of sanctions (both of which are subject to Commission approval and alteration). But the individual members of the Board— like the officers and directors of the self-regulatory organizations—are substantially insulated from the Commission's control. The Commission cannot remove Board members at will, but only "for good cause shown," "in accordance with" certain procedures. § 7211(e)(6).

Those procedures require a Commission finding, "on the record" and "after notice and opportunity for a hearing," that the Board member

"(A) has willfully violated any provision of th[e] Act, the rules of the Board, or the securities laws;

"(B) has willfully abused the authority of that member; or

"(C) without reasonable justification or excuse, has failed to enforce compliance with any such provision or rule, or any professional standard by any registered public accounting firm or any associated person thereof." §7217(d)(3).

1  Removal of a Board member requires a formal Commission order and is subject to
2  judicial review. * * * The parties agree that the Commissioners cannot themselves
3  be removed by the President except under the *Humphrey's Executor* standard of
4  "inefficiency, neglect of duty, or malfeasance in office," 295 U.S., at 620 (internal
5  quotation marks omitted), and we decide the case with that understanding.

6                                       * * *

7                                        III

8  We hold that the dual for-cause limitations on the removal of Board members
9  contravene the Constitution's separation of powers.

10                                      * * *

11                                        B

12  As explained, we have previously upheld limited restrictions on the President's
13  removal power. In those cases, however, only one level of protected tenure
14  separated the President from an officer exercising executive power. It was the
15  President—or a subordinate he could remove at will—who decided whether the
16  officer's conduct merited removal under the good-cause standard.

17  The Act before us does something quite different. It not only protects Board
18  members from removal except for good cause, but withdraws from the President
19  any decision on whether that good cause exists. That decision is vested instead in
20  other tenured officers—the Commissioners—none of whom is subject to the
21  President's direct control. The result is a Board that is not accountable to the
22  President, and a President who is not responsible for the Board.

23  The added layer of tenure protection makes a difference. Without a layer of
24  insulation between the Commission and the Board, the Commission could remove
25  a Board member at any time, and therefore would be fully responsible for what the
26  Board does. The President could then hold the Commission to account for its
27  supervision of the Board, to the same extent that he may hold the Commission to
28  account for everything else it does.

29  A second level of tenure protection changes the nature of the President's review.
30  Now the Commission cannot remove a Board member at will. The President
31  therefore cannot hold the Commission fully accountable for the Board's conduct,
32  to the same extent that he may hold the Commission accountable for everything
33  else that it does. The Commissioners are not responsible for the Board's actions.
34  They are only responsible for their own determination of whether the Act's
35  rigorous good-cause standard is met. And even if the President disagrees with their
36  determination, he is powerless to intervene—unless that determination is so
37  unreasonable as to constitute "inefficiency, neglect of duty, or malfeasance in
38  office." *Humphrey's Executor*, 295 U.S., at 620 (internal quotation marks
39  omitted).

This novel structure does not merely add to the Board's independence, but transforms it. Neither the President, nor anyone directly responsible to him, nor even an officer whose conduct he may review only for good cause, has full control over the Board. The President is stripped of the power our precedents have preserved, and his ability to execute the laws—by holding his subordinates accountable for their conduct—is impaired.

That arrangement is contrary to Article II's vesting of the executive power in the President. Without the ability to oversee the Board, or to attribute the Board's failings to those whom he can oversee, the President is no longer the judge of the Board's conduct. He is not the one who decides whether Board members are abusing their offices or neglecting their duties. He can neither ensure that the laws are faithfully executed, nor be held responsible for a Board member's breach of faith. This violates the basic principle that the President "cannot delegate ultimate responsibility or the active obligation to supervise that goes with it," because Article II "makes a single President responsible for the actions of the Executive Branch." *Clinton v. Jones*, 520 U.S. 681, 712, 713 (1997) (BREYER, J., concurring in judgment).

Indeed, if allowed to stand, this dispersion of responsibility could be multiplied. If Congress can shelter the bureaucracy behind two layers of good-cause tenure, why not a third? At oral argument, the Government was unwilling to concede that even *five* layers between the President and the Board would be too many. The officers of such an agency—safely encased within a Matryoshka doll of tenure protections— would be immune from Presidential oversight, even as they exercised power in the people's name.

\* \* \*

The diffusion of power carries with it a diffusion of accountability. The people do not vote for the "Officers of the United States." Art. II, §2, cl. 2. They instead look to the President to guide the "assistants or deputies ... subject to his superintendence." The Federalist No. 72 (A. Hamilton). Without a clear and effective chain of command, the public cannot "determine on whom the blame or the punishment of a pernicious measure, or series of pernicious measures ought really to fall." *Id.* No. 70. That is why the Framers sought to ensure that "those who are employed in the execution of the law will be in their proper situation, and the chain of dependence be preserved; the lowest officers, the middle grade, and the highest, will depend, as they ought, on the President, and the President on the community." 1 Annals of Cong., at 499 (J. Madison).

By granting the Board executive power without the Executive's oversight, this Act subverts the President's ability to ensure that the laws are faithfully executed—as well as the public's ability to pass judgment on his efforts. The Act's restrictions are incompatible with the Constitution's separation of powers.

C

1     Respondents and the dissent resist this conclusion, portraying the Board as "the
2     kind of practical accommodation between the Legislature and the Executive that
3     should be permitted in a 'workable government.'" *Metropolitan Washington*
4     *Airports Authority v. Citizens for Abatement of Aircraft Noise, Inc.*, 501 U.S. 252,
5     276 (1991) (*quoting Youngstown Sheet & Tube Co. v. Sawyer*, 343 U.S. 579, 635
6     (1952) (JACKSON, J., concurring)). According to the dissent, Congress may
7     impose multiple levels of for-cause tenure between the President and his
8     subordinates when it "rests agency independence upon the need for technical
9     expertise." The Board's mission is said to demand both "technical competence" and
10    "apolitical expertise," and its powers may only be exercised by "technical
11    professional experts." * * *

12    No one doubts Congress's power to create a vast and varied federal bureaucracy.
13    But where, in all this, is the role for oversight by an elected President? The
14    Constitution requires that a President chosen by the entire Nation oversee the
15    execution of the laws. And the "'fact that a given law or procedure is efficient,
16    convenient, and useful in facilitating functions of government, standing alone, will
17    not save it if it is contrary to the Constitution,'" for "'[c]onvenience and efficiency
18    are not the primary objectives—or the hallmarks—of democratic government.'"
19    *Bowsher*, 478 U.S., at 736 (*quoting Chadha*, 462 U.S., at 944).

20    One can have a government that functions without being ruled by functionaries,
21    and a government that benefits from expertise without being ruled by experts. Our
22    Constitution was adopted to enable the people to govern themselves, through their
23    elected leaders. The growth of the Executive Branch, which now wields vast power
24    and touches almost every aspect of daily life, heightens the concern that it may slip
25    from the Executive's control, and thus from that of the people. This concern is
26    largely absent from the dissent's paean to the administrative state.

27                                  * * *

28    * * * [R]espondents portray the Act's limitations on removal as irrelevant,
29    because—as the Court of Appeals held—the Commission wields "at-will removal
30    power over Board *functions* if not Board members." The Commission's general
31    "oversight and enforcement authority over the Board," §7217(a), is said to "blun[t]
32    the constitutional impact of for-cause removal," and to leave the President no
33    worse off than "if Congress had lodged the Board's functions in the SEC's own
34    staff."

35    Broad power over Board functions is not equivalent to the power to remove Board
36    members. . . . The Commission may, for example, approve the Board's budget,
37    issue binding regulations, relieve the Board of authority, amend Board sanctions,
38    or enforce Board rules on its own. But altering the budget or powers of an agency
39    as a whole is a problematic way to control an inferior officer. The Commission
40    cannot wield a free hand to supervise individual members if it must destroy the
41    Board in order to fix it.

42                                  * * *

1 JUSTICE BREYER, with whom JUSTICE STEVENS, JUSTICE GINSBURG, and
2 JUSTICE SOTOMAYOR join, dissenting.

3 The Court holds unconstitutional a statute providing that the Securities and
4 Exchange Commission can remove members of the Public Company Accounting
5 Oversight Board from office only for cause. It argues that granting the "inferior
6 officer[s]" on the Accounting Board "more than one level of good-cause protection
7 . . . contravenes the President's 'constitutional obligation to ensure the faithful
8 execution of the laws.'" I agree that the Accounting Board members are inferior
9 officers. But in my view the statute does not significantly interfere with the
10 President's "executive Power." Art. II, §1. It violates no separation-of-powers
11 principle. And the Court's contrary holding threatens to disrupt severely the fair
12 and efficient administration of the laws. I consequently dissent.

13 I

14 A

15 The legal question before us arises at the intersection of two general constitutional
16 principles. On the one hand, Congress has broad power to enact statutes
17 "necessary and proper" to the exercise of its specifically enumerated constitutional
18 authority. * * *

19 On the other hand, the opening sections of Articles I, II, and III of the Constitution
20 separately and respectively vest "all legislative Powers" in Congress, the "executive
21 Power" in the President, and the "judicial Power" in the Supreme Court (and such
22 "inferior Courts as Congress may from time to time ordain and establish"). In doing
23 so, these provisions imply a structural separation-of-powers principle. * * *
24 Indeed, this Court has held that the separation-of-powers principle guarantees the
25 President the authority to dismiss certain Executive Branch officials at will. *Myers*
26 *v. United States*, 272 U.S. 52 (1926).

27 But neither of these two principles is absolute in its application to removal cases.
28 The Necessary and Proper Clause does not grant Congress power to free *all*
29 Executive Branch officials from dismissal at the will of the President. Nor does the
30 separation-of-powers principle grant the President an absolute authority to
31 remove *any* and *all* Executive Branch officials at will. Rather, depending on, say,
32 the nature of the office, its function, or its subject matter, Congress sometimes
33 may, consistent with the Constitution, limit the President's authority to remove an
34 officer from his post. *See Humphrey's Executor v. United States*, 295 U.S. 602
35 (1935), overruling in part *Myers*, *supra*; *Morrison v. Olson*, 487 U.S. 654 (1988).
36 And we must here decide whether the circumstances surrounding the statute at
37 issue justify such a limitation.

38 * * *

39 B

When previously deciding this kind of nontextual question, the Court has emphasized the importance of examining how a particular provision, taken in context, is likely to function. * * * The Court has thereby written into law Justice Jackson's wise perception that "the Constitution . . . contemplates that practice will integrate the dispersed powers into *a workable government.*" *Youngstown Sheet & Tube Co. v. Sawyer*, 343 U.S. 579, 635 (1952) (opinion concurring in judgment) (emphasis added).

It is not surprising that the Court in these circumstances has looked to function and context, and not to bright-line rules. For one thing, that approach embodies the intent of the Framers. As CHIEF JUSTICE MARSHALL long ago observed, our Constitution is fashioned so as to allow the three coordinate branches, including this Court, to exercise practical judgment in response to changing conditions and "exigencies," which at the time of the founding could be seen only "dimly," and perhaps not at all. *McCulloch*, 17 U.S. 316 [(1819)].

For another, a functional approach permits Congress and the President the flexibility needed to adapt statutory law to changing circumstances. That is why the "powers conferred upon the Federal Government by the Constitution were phrased in language broad enough to allow for the expansion of the Federal Government's role" over time. *New York v. United States*, 505 U.S. 144, 157 (1992) . Indeed, the Federal Government at the time of the founding consisted of about 2,000 employees and served a population of about 4 million. Today, however, the Federal Government employs about 4.4 million workers who serve a Nation of more than 310 million people living in a society characterized by rapid technological, economic, and social change.

* * *

The upshot is that today vast numbers of statutes governing vast numbers of subjects, concerned with vast numbers of different problems, provide for, or foresee, their execution or administration through the work of administrators organized within many different kinds of administrative structures, exercising different kinds of administrative authority, to achieve their legislatively mandated objectives. And, given the nature of the Government's work, it is not surprising that administrative units come in many different shapes and sizes.

The functional approach required by our precedents recognizes this administrative complexity and, more importantly, recognizes the various ways presidential power operates within this context—and the various ways in which a removal provision might affect that power. As human beings have known ever since Ulysses tied himself to the mast so as safely to hear the Sirens' song, sometimes it is necessary to disable oneself in order to achieve a broader objective. Thus, legally enforceable commitments—such as contracts, statutes that cannot instantly be changed, and, as in the case before us, the establishment of independent administrative institutions—hold the potential to empower precisely because of their ability to constrain. If the President seeks to regulate through impartial adjudication, then

1    insulation of the adjudicator from removal at will can help him achieve that goal.
2    And to free a technical decisionmaker from the fear of removal without cause can
3    similarly help create legitimacy with respect to that official's regulatory actions by
4    helping to insulate his technical decisions from nontechnical political pressure.

5    Neither is power always susceptible to the equations of elementary arithmetic. A
6    rule that takes power from a President's friends and allies may weaken him. But a
7    rule that takes power from the President's opponents may strengthen him. And
8    what if the rule takes power from a functionally neutral independent authority? In
9    that case, it is difficult to predict how the President's power is affected in the
10   abstract.

11   These practical reasons not only support our precedents' determination that cases
12   such as this should examine the specific functions and context at issue; they also
13   indicate that judges should hesitate before second-guessing a "for cause" decision
14   made by the other branches. *See, e.g.,* *Chadha*, 462 U.S., at 944 (applying a
15   "presumption that the challenged statute is valid"); *Bowsher*, 478 U.S., at 736
16   (STEVENS, J., concurring in judgment). Compared to Congress and the President,
17   the Judiciary possesses an inferior understanding of the realities of
18   administration, and the manner in which power, including and most especially
19   political power, operates in context.

20                                   \* \* \*

21   Thus, here, as in similar cases, we should decide the constitutional question in light
22   of the provision's practical functioning in context. And our decision should take
23   account of the Judiciary's comparative lack of institutional expertise.

24                                   II

25                                   A

26   To what extent then is the Act's "for cause" provision likely, as a practical matter,
27   to limit the President's exercise of executive authority? In practical terms no "for
28   cause" provision can, in isolation, define the full measure of executive power. This
29   is because a legislative decision to place ultimate administrative authority in, say,
30   the Secretary of Agriculture rather than the President, the way in which the statute
31   defines the scope of the power the relevant administrator can exercise, the decision
32   as to who controls the agency's budget requests and funding, the relationships
33   between one agency or department and another, as well as more purely political
34   factors (including Congress' ability to assert influence) are more likely to affect the
35   President's power to get something done. That is why President Truman
36   complained that "'the powers of the President amount to'" bringing "'people in and
37   try[ing] to persuade them to do what they ought to do without persuasion.'" And
38   that is why scholars have written that the President "is neither dominant nor
39   powerless" in his relationships with many Government entities, "whether
40   denominated executive or independent." Those entities "are *all* subject to

presidential direction in significant aspects of their functioning, and [are each] able to resist presidential direction in others." (emphasis added).

Indeed, notwithstanding the majority's assertion that the removal authority is "*the key*" mechanism by which the President oversees inferior officers in the independent agencies, it appears that no President has ever actually sought to exercise that power by testing the scope of a "for cause" provision.

But even if we put all these other matters to the side, we should still conclude that the "for cause" restriction before us will not restrict presidential power significantly. For one thing, the restriction directly limits, not the President's power, but the power of an already independent agency. The Court seems to have forgotten that fact when it identifies its central constitutional problem: According to the Court, the President "is powerless to intervene" if he has determined that the Board members' "conduct merit[s] removal" because "[t]hat decision is vested instead in other tenured officers—the Commissioners—none of whom is subject to the President's direct control." But so long as the President is *legitimately* foreclosed from removing the Commissioners except for cause (as the majority assumes), nullifying the Commission's power to remove Board members only for cause will not resolve the problem the Court has identified: The President will still be "powerless to intervene" by removing the Board members if the Commission reasonably decides not to do so.

\* \* \*

## B

At the same time, Congress and the President had good reason for enacting the challenged "for cause" provision. First and foremost, the Board adjudicates cases. This Court has long recognized the appropriateness of using "for cause" provisions to protect the personal independence of those who even only sometimes engage in adjudicatory functions. *Humphrey's Executor, supra*, at 623–628; *Morrison*, 487 U.S., at 690–691, and n. 30; *McAllister v. United States*, 141 U.S. 174, 191–201 (1891) (FIELD, J., dissenting). Indeed, as early as 1789 James Madison stated that "there may be strong reasons why an" executive "officer" such as the Comptroller of the United States "should not hold his office at the pleasure of the Executive branch" if one of his "principal dut[ies]" "partakes strongly of the judicial character." 1 Annals of Congress 611–612; *cf. ante*, at 500, n. 6 (noting that the statute Congress ultimately enacted limited Presidential control over the Comptroller in a different fashion). The Court, however, all but ignores the Board's adjudicatory functions when conducting its analysis. And when it finally does address that central function (in a footnote), it simply asserts that the Board does not "perform adjudicative . . . functions," an assertion that is inconsistent with the terms of the statute.

\* \* \*

1 Here, the justification for insulating the "technical experts" on the Board from fear
2 of losing their jobs due to political influence is particularly strong. Congress
3 deliberately sought to provide that kind of protection. * * * And historically, this
4 regulatory subject matter—financial regulation—has been thought to exhibit a
5 particular need for independence. * * *

6 In sum, Congress and the President could reasonably have thought it prudent to
7 insulate the adjudicative Board members from fear of purely politically based
8 removal. And in a world in which we count on the Federal Government to regulate
9 matters as complex as, say, nuclear-power production, the Court's assertion that
10 we should simply learn to get by "without being" regulated "by experts" is, at best,
11 unrealistic—at worst, dangerously so.

12                                        * * *

13                                         D

14                                        * * *

15 The Court fails to create a bright-line rule because of considerable uncertainty
16 about the scope of its holding—an uncertainty that the Court's opinion both reflects
17 and generates. * * *

18                                        * * *

19 Reading the criteria above as stringently as possible, I still see no way to avoid
20 sweeping hundreds, perhaps thousands of high-level government officials within
21 the scope of the Court's holding, putting their job security and their administrative
22 actions and decisions constitutionally at risk. To make even a conservative
23 estimate, one would have to begin by listing federal departments, offices, bureaus
24 and other agencies whose heads are by statute removable only "for cause." I have
25 found 48 such agencies, which I have listed in Appendix A. Then it would be
26 necessary to identify the senior officials in those agencies (just below the top) who
27 themselves are removable only "for cause." I have identified 573 such high-ranking
28 officials, whom I have listed in Appendix B. They include most of the leadership of
29 the Nuclear Regulatory Commission (including that agency's executive director as
30 well as the directors of its Office of Nuclear Reactor Regulation and Office of
31 Enforcement), virtually all of the leadership of the Social Security Administration,
32 the executive directors of the Federal Energy Regulatory Commission and the
33 Federal Trade Commission, as well as the general counsels of the Chemical Safety
34 Board, the Federal Mine Safety and Health Review Commission, and the National
35 Mediation Board.

36                                        * * *

37 With respect I dissent.

38

1 **Seila Law LLC v. Consumer Financial Protection Bureau**

2 140 S.Ct. 2183 (2020)

3 June 29, 2020

4 CHIEF JUSTICE ROBERTS delivered the opinion of the Court with respect to
5 Parts I, II, and III.

6 In the wake of the 2008 financial crisis, Congress established the Consumer
7 Financial Protection Bureau (CFPB), an independent regulatory agency tasked
8 with ensuring that consumer debt products are safe and transparent. In organizing
9 the CFPB, Congress deviated from the structure of nearly every other independent
10 administrative agency in our history. Instead of placing the agency under the
11 leadership of a board with multiple members, Congress provided that the CFPB
12 would be led by a single Director, who serves for a longer term than the President
13 and cannot be removed by the President except for inefficiency, neglect, or
14 malfeasance. The CFPB Director has no boss, peers, or voters to report to. Yet the
15 Director wields vast rulemaking, enforcement, and adjudicatory authority over a
16 significant portion of the U.S. economy. The question before us is whether this
17 arrangement violates the Constitution's separation of powers.

18 Under our Constitution, the "executive Power"—all of it—is "vested in a President,"
19 who must "take Care that the Laws be faithfully executed." Art. II, § 1, cl. 1; *id.*, § 3.
20 Because no single person could fulfill that responsibility alone, the Framers
21 expected that the President would rely on subordinate officers for assistance. Ten
22 years ago, in *Free Enterprise Fund v. Public Company Accounting Oversight Bd.*
23 (2010), we reiterated that, "as a general matter," the Constitution gives the
24 President "the authority to remove those who assist him in carrying out his duties."
25 "Without such power, the President could not be held fully accountable for
26 discharging his own responsibilities; the buck would stop somewhere else."

27 The President's power to remove—and thus supervise—those who wield executive
28 power on his behalf follows from the text of Article II, was settled by the First
29 Congress, and was confirmed in the landmark decision *Myers v. United States*
30 (1926). Our precedents have recognized only two exceptions to the President's
31 unrestricted removal power. In *Humphrey's Executor v. United States* (1935), we
32 held that Congress could create expert agencies led by a *group* of principal officers
33 removable by the President only for good cause. And in *United States v. Perkins*
34 (1886), and *Morrison v. Olson* (1988), we held that Congress could provide tenure
35 protections to certain *inferior* officers with narrowly defined duties.

36 We are now asked to extend these precedents to a new configuration: an
37 independent agency that wields significant executive power and is run by a single
38 individual who cannot be removed by the President unless certain statutory
39 criteria are met. We decline to take that step. While we need not and do not revisit
40 our prior decisions allowing certain limitations on the President's removal power,
41 there are compelling reasons not to extend those precedents to the novel context

of an independent agency led by a single Director. Such an agency lacks a foundation in historical practice and clashes with constitutional structure by concentrating power in a unilateral actor insulated from Presidential control.

We therefore hold that the structure of the CFPB violates the separation of powers. We go on to hold that the CFPB Director's removal protection is severable from the other statutory provisions bearing on the CFPB's authority. The agency may therefore continue to operate, but its Director, in light of our decision, must be removable by the President at will.

I

A

* * *

In 2010, Congress * * * created the Consumer Financial Protection Bureau (CFPB) as an independent financial regulator within the Federal Reserve System. Dodd-Frank Wall Street Reform and Consumer Protection Act (Dodd-Frank). Congress tasked the CFPB with "implement[ing]" and "enforc[ing]" a large body of financial consumer protection laws to "ensur[e] that all consumers have access to markets for consumer financial products and services and that markets for consumer financial products and services are fair, transparent, and competitive." Congress transferred the administration of 18 existing federal statutes to the CFPB, including the Fair Credit Reporting Act, the Fair Debt Collection Practices Act, and the Truth in Lending Act. * * *

Congress also vested the CFPB with potent enforcement powers. The agency has the authority to conduct investigations, issue subpoenas and civil investigative demands, initiate administrative adjudications, and prosecute civil actions in federal court. * * *

The CFPB's rulemaking and enforcement powers are coupled with extensive adjudicatory authority. The agency may conduct administrative proceedings to "ensure or enforce compliance with" the statutes and regulations it administers.

* * * Rather than create a traditional independent agency headed by a multimember board or commission, Congress elected to place the CFPB under the leadership of a single Director. The CFPB Director is appointed by the President with the advice and consent of the Senate. The Director serves for a term of five years, during which the President may remove the Director from office only for "inefficiency, neglect of duty, or malfeasance in office."

Unlike most other agencies, the CFPB does not rely on the annual appropriations process for funding. Instead, the CFPB receives funding directly from the Federal Reserve, which is itself funded outside the appropriations process through bank assessments. Each year, the CFPB requests an amount that the Director deems "reasonably necessary to carry out" the agency's duties, and the Federal Reserve grants that request so long as it does not exceed 12% of the total operating expenses of the Federal Reserve (inflation adjusted). * * *

* * *

## II

We first consider three threshold arguments raised by the appointed *amicus* for why we may not or should not reach the merits. Each is unavailing.

First, *Amicus* * * * observes that current CFPB Director Kathleen Kraninger, now responsible for enforcing the demand, agrees with the Solicitor General's position in this case that her for-cause removal protection is unconstitutional. In *amicus'* view, these developments reveal that the demand would have been issued—and would continue to be enforced—even in the absence of the CFPB Director's removal protection, making the asserted separation of powers dispute "artificial."

* * * But *amicus'* argument does not cast any doubt on the jurisdiction of the District Court because petitioner is *the defendant* and did not invoke the Court's jurisdiction. See *Bond v. United States* (2011) (When the plaintiff has standing, "Article III does not restrict the opposing party's ability to object to relief being sought at its expense."). * * * Petitioner is compelled to comply with the civil investigative demand and to provide documents it would prefer to withhold, a concrete injury. That injury is traceable to the decision below and would be fully redressed if we were to reverse the judgment of the Court of Appeals and remand with instructions to deny the Government's petition to enforce the demand.

* * *

Second, *amicus* contends that the proper context for assessing the constitutionality of an officer's removal restriction is a contested removal. While that is certainly one way to review a removal restriction, it is not the only way. Our precedents have long permitted private parties aggrieved by an official's exercise of executive power to challenge the official's authority to wield that power while insulated from removal by the President. See *Bowsher* (lawsuit filed by aggrieved third party in the absence of contested removal); *Free Enterprise Fund* (same); *Morrison* (defense to subpoena asserted by third party in the absence of contested removal). Indeed, we have expressly "reject[ed]" the "argument that consideration of the effect of a removal provision is not 'ripe' until that provision is actually used," because when such a provision violates the separation of powers it inflicts a "here-and-now" injury on affected third parties that can be remedied by a court. *Bowsher*. The Court of Appeals therefore correctly entertained petitioner's constitutional defense on the merits.

Lastly, *amicus* contends that we should dismiss the case because the parties agree on the merits of the constitutional question and the case therefore lacks "adverseness." That contention, however, is foreclosed by *United States v. Windsor* (2013). There, we explained that a lower court order that presents real-

1  world consequences for the Government and its adversary suffices to support
2  Article III jurisdiction—even if "the Executive may welcome" an adverse order that
3  "is accompanied by the constitutional ruling it wants." Here, petitioner and the
4  Government disagree about whether petitioner must comply with the civil
5  investigative demand. The lower courts sided with the Government, and the
6  Government has not volunteered to relinquish that victory and withdraw the
7  demand. To the contrary, while the Government agrees that the agency is
8  unconstitutionally structured, it believes it may nevertheless enforce the demand
9  on remand. Accordingly, our "decision will have real meaning" for the parties. *INS
10 v. Chadha* (1983). And, as in *Windsor*, any prudential concerns with deciding an
11 important legal question in this posture can be addressed by "the practice of
12 entertaining arguments made by an *amicus* when the Solicitor General confesses
13 error with respect to a judgment below," which we have done.

14 We therefore turn to the merits of petitioner's constitutional challenge.

15
16                                     III

17 We hold that the CFPB's leadership by a single individual removable only for
18 inefficiency, neglect, or malfeasance violates the separation of powers.

19                                      A

20 Article II provides that "[t]he executive Power shall be vested in a President," who
21 must "take Care that the Laws be faithfully executed." Art. II, § 1, cl. 1; *id.*, § 3. The
22 entire "executive Power" belongs to the President alone. But because it would be
23 "impossib[le]" for "one man" to "perform all the great business of the State," the
24 Constitution assumes that lesser executive officers will "assist the supreme
25 Magistrate in discharging the duties of his trust." Writings of George Washington
26 (1939).

27 These lesser officers must remain accountable to the President, whose authority
28 they wield. As Madison explained, "[I]f any power whatsoever is in its nature
29 Executive, it is the power of appointing, overseeing, and controlling those who
30 execute the laws." That power, in turn, generally includes the ability to remove
31 executive officials, for it is "only the authority that can remove" such officials that
32 they "must fear and, in the performance of [their] functions, obey." *Bowsher*.

33 The President's removal power has long been confirmed by history and precedent.
34 It "was discussed extensively in Congress when the first executive departments
35 were created" in 1789. *Free Enterprise Fund*. * * * The First Congress's recognition
36 of the President's removal power in 1789 "provides contemporaneous and weighty
37 evidence of the Constitution's meaning," *Bowsher*, and has long been the "settled
38 and well understood construction of the Constitution," *Ex parte Hennen* (1839).

39 *Free Enterprise Fund* left in place two exceptions to the President's unrestricted
40 removal power. First, in *Humphrey's Executor*, decided less than a decade after

130

*Myers,* the Court upheld a statute that protected the Commissioners of the FTC from removal except for "inefficiency, neglect of duty, or malfeasance in office." In reaching that conclusion, the Court stressed that Congress's ability to impose such removal restrictions "will depend upon the character of the office."

Because the Court limited its holding "to officers of the kind here under consideration," the contours of the *Humphrey's Executor* exception depend upon the characteristics of the agency before the Court. Rightly or wrongly, the Court viewed the FTC (as it existed in 1935) as exercising "no part of the executive power." Instead, it was "an administrative body" that performed "specified duties as a legislative or as a judicial aid." It acted "as a legislative agency" in "making investigations and reports" to Congress and "as an agency of the judiciary" in making recommendations to courts as a master in chancery. "To the extent that [the FTC] exercise[d] any executive *function*[,] as distinguished from executive *power* in the constitutional sense," it did so only in the discharge of its "quasi-legislative or quasi-judicial powers." *Ibid.* (emphasis added).[2]

The Court identified several organizational features that helped explain its characterization of the FTC as non-executive. Composed of five members—no more than three from the same political party—the Board was designed to be "non-partisan" and to "act with entire impartiality." The FTC's duties were "neither political nor executive," but instead called for "the trained judgment of a body of experts" "informed by experience." And the Commissioners' staggered, seven-year terms enabled the agency to accumulate technical expertise and avoid a "complete change" in leadership "at any one time."

In short, *Humphrey's Executor* permitted Congress to give for-cause removal protections to a multimember body of experts, balanced along partisan lines, that performed legislative and judicial functions and was said not to exercise any executive power.

While recognizing an exception for multimember bodies with "quasi-judicial" or "quasi-legislative" functions, *Humphrey's Executor* reaffirmed the core holding of *Myers* that the President has "unrestrictable power * * * to remove purely executive officers." The Court acknowledged that between purely executive officers on the one hand, and officers that closely resembled the FTC Commissioners on

---

[2] The Court's conclusion that the FTC did not exercise executive power has not withstood the test of time. As we observed in *Morrison* v. *Olson* (1988), "[I]t is hard to dispute that the powers of the FTC at the time of *Humphrey's Executor* would at the present time be considered 'executive,' at least to some degree." See also *Arlington* v. *FCC* (2013) (even though the activities of administrative agencies "take 'legislative' and 'judicial' forms," "they are exercises of—indeed, under our constitutional structure they *must be* exercises of—the 'executive Power' " (quoting Art. II, § 1, cl. 1)).

the other, there existed "a field of doubt" that the Court left "for future consideration."

We have recognized a second exception for *inferior* officers in two cases, *United States v. Perkins* and *Morrison v. Olson*.[3] In *Perkins*, we upheld tenure protections for a naval cadet-engineer. And, in *Morrison*, we upheld a provision granting good-cause tenure protection to an independent counsel appointed to investigate and prosecute particular alleged crimes by high-ranking Government officials. Backing away from the reliance in *Humphrey's Executor* on the concepts of "quasi-legislative" and "quasi-judicial" power, we viewed the ultimate question as whether a removal restriction is of "such a nature that [it] impede[s] the President's ability to perform his constitutional duty." Although the independent counsel was a single person and performed "law enforcement functions that typically have been undertaken by officials within the Executive Branch," we concluded that the removal protections did not unduly interfere with the functioning of the Executive Branch because "the independent counsel [was] an inferior officer under the Appointments Clause, with limited jurisdiction and tenure and lacking policymaking or significant administrative authority." *Ibid.*

These two exceptions—one for multimember expert agencies that do not wield substantial executive power, and one for inferior officers with limited duties and no policymaking or administrative authority— "represent what up to now have been the outermost constitutional limits of permissible congressional restrictions on the President's removal power." *PHH Corp. v. CFPB*, 881 F.3d 75, 165 (D.C. Cir. 2018) ( (KAVANAUGH, J., dissenting).

B

* * *

C

The question * * * is whether to extend those precedents to the "new situation" before us, namely an independent agency led by a single Director and vested with significant executive power. *Free Enterprise Fund v. Public Company Accounting Oversight Bd.*, 561 U.S. 477, 483 (2010). We decline to do so. Such an agency has no basis in history and no place in our constitutional structure.

-----------------

[3] Article II distinguishes between two kinds of officers—principal officers (who must be appointed by the President with the advice and consent of the Senate) and inferior officers (whose appointment Congress may vest in the President, courts, or heads of Departments). § 2, cl. 2. While "[o]ur cases have not set forth an exclusive criterion for distinguishing between principal and inferior officers," we have in the past examined factors such as the nature, scope, and duration of an officer's duties. *Edmond* v. *United States* (1997). More recently, we have focused on whether the officer's work is "directed and supervised" by a principal officer.

1

"Perhaps the most telling indication of [a] severe constitutional problem" with an executive entity "is [a] lack of historical precedent" to support it. *Id.*, at 505. An agency with a structure like that of the CFPB is almost wholly unprecedented.

After years of litigating the agency's constitutionality, the Courts of Appeals, parties, and *amici* have identified "only a handful of isolated" incidents in which Congress has provided good-cause tenure to principal officers who wield power alone rather than as members of a board or commission. "[T]hese few scattered examples"—four to be exact—shed little light. *NLRB v. Noel Canning* (2014).

\* \* \*

2

In addition to being a historical anomaly, the CFPB's single-Director configuration is incompatible with our constitutional structure. Aside from the sole exception of the Presidency, that structure scrupulously avoids concentrating power in the hands of any single individual.

"The Framers recognized that, in the long term, structural protections against abuse of power were critical to preserving liberty." *Bowsher*. Their solution to governmental power and its perils was simple: divide it. To prevent the "gradual concentration" of power in the same hands, they enabled "[a]mbition \* \* \* to counteract ambition" at every turn. The Federalist No. 51 (J. Madison). At the highest level, they "split the atom of sovereignty" itself into one Federal Government and the States. *Gamble v. United States*, (2019). They then divided the "powers of the new Federal Government into three defined categories, Legislative, Executive, and Judicial." *Chadha*.

They did not stop there. Most prominently, the Framers bifurcated the federal legislative power into two Chambers: the House of Representatives and the Senate, each composed of multiple Members and Senators. Art. I, §§ 2, 3.

The Executive Branch is a stark departure from all this division. The Framers viewed the legislative power as a special threat to individual liberty, so they divided that power to ensure that "differences of opinion" and the "jarrings of parties" would "promote deliberation and circumspection" and "check excesses in the majority." See The Federalist No. 70 (A. Hamilton); see also *id.*, No. 51. By contrast, the Framers thought it necessary to secure the authority of the Executive so that he could carry out his unique responsibilities. See No. 70. As Madison put it, while "the weight of the legislative authority requires that it should be \* \* \* divided, the weakness of the executive may require, on the other hand, that it should be fortified." *Id.*, No. 51.

\* \* \*

1  To justify and check *that* authority—unique in our constitutional structure—the
2  Framers made the President the most democratic and politically accountable
3  official in Government. Only the President (along with the Vice President) is
4  elected by the entire Nation. And the President's political accountability is
5  enhanced by the solitary nature of the Executive Branch, which provides "a single
6  object for the jealousy and watchfulness of the people." The President "cannot
7  delegate ultimate responsibility or the active obligation to supervise that goes with
8  it," because Article II "makes a single President responsible for the actions of the
9  Executive Branch." *Free Enterprise Fund*, (quoting *Clinton v. Jones* (1997)
10 (BREYER, J., concurring in judgment)).

11 The resulting constitutional strategy is straightforward: divide power everywhere
12 except for the Presidency, and render the President directly accountable to the
13 people through regular elections. In that scheme, individual executive officials will
14 still wield significant authority, but that authority remains subject to the ongoing
15 supervision and control of the elected President. Through the President's
16 oversight, "the chain of dependence [is] preserved," so that "the lowest officers, the
17 middle grade, and the highest" all "depend, as they ought, on the President, and
18 the President on the community." 1 Annals of Cong. (J. Madison).

19 The CFPB's single-Director structure contravenes this carefully calibrated system
20 by vesting significant governmental power in the hands of a single individual
21 accountable to no one. The Director is neither elected by the people nor
22 meaningfully controlled (through the threat of removal) by someone who is. The
23 Director does not even depend on Congress for annual appropriations. See The
24 Federalist No. 58 (J. Madison) (describing the "power over the purse" as the "most
25 compleat and effectual weapon" in representing the interests of the people). Yet
26 the Director may *unilaterally*, without meaningful supervision, issue final
27 regulations, oversee adjudications, set enforcement priorities, initiate
28 prosecutions, and determine what penalties to impose on private parties. With no
29 colleagues to persuade, and no boss or electorate looking over her shoulder, the
30 Director may dictate and enforce policy for a vital segment of the economy
31 affecting millions of Americans.

32 The CFPB Director's insulation from removal by an accountable President is
33 enough to render the agency's structure unconstitutional. But several other
34 features of the CFPB combine to make the Director's removal protection even more
35 problematic. In addition to lacking the most direct method of presidential
36 control—removal at will—the agency's unique structure also forecloses certain
37 indirect methods of Presidential control.

38 Because the CFPB is headed by a single Director with a five-year term, some
39 Presidents may not have any opportunity to shape its leadership and thereby
40 influence its activities. A President elected in 2020 would likely not appoint a CFPB
41 Director until 2023, and a President elected in 2028 may *never* appoint one. That
42 means an unlucky President might get elected on a consumer-protection platform
43 and enter office only to find herself saddled with a holdover Director from a

competing political party who is dead set *against* that agenda. To make matters worse, the agency's single-Director structure means the President will not have the opportunity to appoint any other leaders—such as a chair or fellow members of a Commission or Board—who can serve as a check on the Director's authority and help bring the agency in line with the President's preferred policies.

The CFPB's receipt of funds outside the appropriations process further aggravates the agency's threat to Presidential control. The President normally has the opportunity to recommend or veto spending bills that affect the operation of administrative agencies. See Art. I, § 7, cl. 2; Art. II, § 3. And, for the past century, the President has annually submitted a proposed budget to Congress for approval. * * * But no similar opportunity exists for the President to influence the CFPB Director. Instead, the Director receives over $500 million per year to fund the agency's chosen priorities. And the Director receives that money from the Federal Reserve, which is itself funded outside of the annual appropriations process. This financial freedom makes it even more likely that the agency will "slip from the Executive's control, and thus from that of the people." *Free Enterprise Fund*, 561 U.S., at 499.

3

\* \* \*

IV

\* \* \*

The judgment of the United States Court of Appeals for the Ninth Circuit is vacated, and the case is remanded for further proceedings consistent with this opinion.

It is so ordered.

JUSTICE THOMAS, with whom JUSTICE GORSUCH joins, concurring in part and dissenting in part. [Omitted.]

JUSTICE KAGAN, with whom JUSTICE GINSBURG, JUSTICE BREYER, and JUSTICE SOTOMAYOR join, concurring in the judgment with respect to severability and dissenting in part.

\* \* \*

The Court today fails to respect its proper role. It recognizes that this Court has approved limits on the President's removal power over heads of agencies much like the CFPB. Agencies possessing similar powers, agencies charged with similar missions, agencies created for similar reasons. The majority's explanation is that the heads of those agencies fall within an "exception"—one for multimember bodies and another for inferior officers—to a "general rule" of unrestricted presidential removal power. And the majority says the CFPB Director does not. That account, though, is wrong in every respect. The majority's general rule does not exist. Its exceptions, likewise, are made up for the occasion—gerrymandered so the CFPB falls outside them. And the distinction doing most of the majority's work—between multimember bodies and single directors—does not respond to the constitutional values at stake. If a removal provision violates the separation of powers, it is because the measure so deprives the President of control over an official as to impede his own constitutional functions. But with or without a for-cause removal provision, the President has at least as much control over an individual as over a commission—and possibly more. That means the constitutional concern is, if anything, ameliorated when the agency has a single head. Unwittingly, the majority shows why courts should stay their hand in these matters. "Compared to Congress and the President, the Judiciary possesses an inferior understanding of the realities of administration" and the way "political power[ ] operates." *Free Enterprise Fund v. Public Company Accounting Oversight Bd.* (2010) (BREYER, J., dissenting).

In second-guessing the political branches, the majority second-guesses as well the wisdom of the Framers and the judgment of history. It writes in rules to the Constitution that the drafters knew well enough not to put there. It repudiates the lessons of American experience, from the 18th century to the present day. And it commits the Nation to a static version of governance, incapable of responding to new conditions and challenges. Congress and the President established the CFPB to address financial practices that had brought on a devastating recession, and could do so again. Today's decision wipes out a feature of that agency its creators thought fundamental to its mission—a measure of independence from political pressure. I respectfully dissent.

I

The text of the Constitution, the history of the country, the precedents of this Court, and the need for sound and adaptable governance—all stand against the majority's opinion. They point not to the majority's "general rule" of "unrestricted removal power" with two grudgingly applied "exceptions." Rather, they bestow discretion on the legislature to structure administrative institutions as the times demand, so long as the President retains the ability to carry out his constitutional duties. And most relevant here, they give Congress wide leeway to limit the President's removal power in the interest of enhancing independence from politics in regulatory bodies like the CFPB.

A

What does the Constitution say about the separation of powers—and particularly about the President's removal authority? (Spoiler alert: about the latter, nothing at all.)

The majority offers the civics class version of separation of powers—call it the Schoolhouse Rock definition of the phrase. See Schoolhouse Rock! Three Ring Government (Mar. 13, 1979), ("Ring one, Executive. Two is Legislative, that's Congress. Ring three, Judiciary"). The Constitution's first three articles, the

1    majority recounts, "split the atom of sovereignty" among Congress, the President,
2    and the courts. And by that mechanism, the Framers provided a "simple" fix "to
3    governmental power and its perils."

4    There is nothing wrong with that as a beginning (except the adjective "simple"). It
5    is of course true that the Framers lodged three different kinds of power in three
6    different entities. And that they did so for a crucial purpose—because, as James
7    Madison wrote, "there can be no liberty where the legislative and executive powers
8    are united in the same person[] or body" or where "the power of judging [is] not
9    separated from the legislative and executive powers." The Federalist No. 47
10    (quoting Baron de Montesquieu).

11    The problem lies in treating the beginning as an ending too—in failing to recognize
12    that the separation of powers is, by design, neither rigid nor complete. Blackstone,
13    whose work influenced the Framers on this subject as on others, observed that
14    "every branch" of government "supports and is supported, regulates and is
15    regulated, by the rest." W. Blackstone, Commentaries on the Laws of England
16    (1765). So as James Madison stated, the creation of distinct branches "did not
17    mean that these departments ought to have no partial agency in, or no controul
18    over the acts of each other." The Federalist No. 47. To the contrary, Madison
19    explained, the drafters of the Constitution—like those of then-existing state
20    constitutions—opted against keeping the branches of government "absolutely
21    separate and distinct." Or as Justice Story reiterated a half-century later: "[W]hen
22    we speak of a separation of the three great departments of government," it is "not
23    meant to affirm, that they must be kept wholly and entirely separate." J. Story,
24    Commentaries on the Constitution of the United States (1833). Instead, the
25    branches have—as they must for the whole arrangement to work—"common link[s]
26    of connexion [and] dependence."

27    One way the Constitution reflects that vision is by giving Congress broad authority
28    to establish and organize the Executive Branch. Article II presumes the existence
29    of "Officer[s]" in "executive Departments." § 2, cl. 1. But it does not, as you might
30    think from reading the majority opinion, give the President authority to decide
31    what kinds of officers—in what departments, with what responsibilities—the
32    Executive Branch requires. See *ante* ("The entire 'executive Power' belongs to the
33    President alone"). Instead, Article I's Necessary and Proper Clause puts those
34    decisions in the legislature's hands. Congress has the power "[t]o make all Laws
35    which shall be necessary and proper for carrying into Execution" not just its own
36    enumerated powers but also "all other Powers vested by this Constitution in the
37    Government of the United States, or in any Department or Officer thereof." § 8, cl.
38    18. Similarly, the Appointments Clause reflects Congress's central role in
39    structuring the Executive Branch. Yes, the President can appoint principal officers,
40    but only as the legislature "shall * * * establish[ ] by Law" (and of course subject to
41    the Senate's advice and consent). Art. II, § 2, cl. 2. And Congress has plenary power
42    to decide not only what inferior officers will exist but also who (the President or a
43    head of department) will appoint them. So as Madison told the first Congress, the
44    legislature gets to "create[ ] the office, define[ ] the powers, [and] limit[ ] its

1  duration." The President, as to the construction of his own branch of government,
2  can only try to work his will through the legislative process.

3  The majority relies for its contrary vision on Article II's Vesting Clause, but the
4  provision can't carry all that weight. Or as Chief Justice Rehnquist wrote of a
5  similar claim in *Morrison v. Olson* (1988), "extrapolat[ing]" an unrestricted
6  removal power from such "general constitutional language"—which says only that
7  "[t]he executive Power shall be vested in a President"—is "more than the text will
8  bear." Dean John Manning has well explained why, even were it not obvious from
9  the Clause's "open-ended language." Separation of Powers as Ordinary
10 Interpretation (2011). * * * For now, note two points about practice before the
11 Constitution's drafting. First, in that era, Parliament often restricted the King's
12 power to remove royal officers—and the President, needless to say, wasn't
13 supposed to be a king. Second, many States at the time allowed limits on
14 gubernatorial removal power even though their constitutions had similar vesting
15 clauses. Historical understandings thus belie the majority's "general rule."

16 Nor can the Take Care Clause come to the majority's rescue. That Clause cannot
17 properly serve as a "placeholder for broad judicial judgments" about presidential
18 control. Goldsmith & Manning, The Protean Take Care Clause (2016). To begin
19 with, the provision—"he shall take Care that the Laws be faithfully executed"—
20 speaks of duty, not power. Art. II, § 3. New scholarship suggests the language came
21 from English and colonial oaths taken by, and placing fiduciary obligations on, all
22 manner and rank of executive officers. * * * And yet more important, the text of the
23 Take Care Clause requires only enough authority to make sure "the laws [are]
24 faithfully executed"—meaning with fidelity to the law itself, not to every
25 presidential policy preference. As this Court has held, a President can ensure
26 "'faithful execution' of the laws"—thereby satisfying his "take care" obligation—
27 with a removal provision like the one here. *Morrison*. A for-cause standard gives
28 him "ample authority to assure that [an official] is competently performing [his]
29 statutory responsibilities in a manner that comports with the [relevant
30 legislation's] provisions."

31 Finally, recall the Constitution's telltale silence: Nowhere does the text say
32 anything about the President's power to remove subordinate officials at will. The
33 majority professes unconcern. After all, it says, "neither is there a 'separation of
34 powers clause' or a 'federalism clause.'" But those concepts are carved into the
35 Constitution's text—the former in its first three articles separating powers, the
36 latter in its enumeration of federal powers and its reservation of all else to the
37 States. And anyway, at-will removal is hardly such a "foundational doctrine[]." You
38 won't find it on a civics class syllabus. That's because removal is a *tool*— one means
39 among many, even if sometimes an important one, for a President to control
40 executive officials. See generally *Free Enterprise Fund* (BREYER, J., dissenting).
41 To find that authority hidden in the Constitution as a "general rule" is to discover
42 what is nowhere there.

43                                    B

1 * * *

2 C

3 What is more, the Court's precedents before today have accepted the role of
4 independent agencies in our governmental system. To be sure, the line of our
5 decisions has not run altogether straight. But we have repeatedly upheld provisions
6 that prevent the President from firing regulatory officials except for such matters
7 as neglect or malfeasance. * * *

8 * * *

9 D

10 The deferential approach this Court has taken gives Congress the flexibility it needs
11 to craft administrative agencies. Diverse problems of government demand diverse
12 solutions. They call for varied measures and mixtures of democratic accountability
13 and technical expertise, energy and efficiency. Sometimes, the arguments push
14 toward tight presidential control of agencies. The President's engagement, some
15 people say, can disrupt bureaucratic stagnation, counter industry capture, and
16 make agencies more responsive to public interests. See, well, Kagan, Presidential
17 Administration, 114 Harv. L. Rev. 2245, 2331–2346 (2001). At other times, the
18 arguments favor greater independence from presidential involvement. Insulation
19 from political pressure helps ensure impartial adjudications. It places technical
20 issues in the hands of those most capable of addressing them. It promotes
21 continuity, and prevents short-term electoral interests from distorting policy.
22 (Consider, for example, how the Federal Reserve's independence stops a President
23 trying to win a second term from manipulating interest rates.) Of course, the right
24 balance between presidential control and independence is often uncertain,
25 contested, and value-laden. No mathematical formula governs institutional
26 design; trade-offs are endemic to the enterprise. But that is precisely why the issue
27 is one for the political branches to debate—and then debate again as times change.
28 And it's why courts should stay (mostly) out of the way. Rather than impose rigid
29 rules like the majority's, they should let Congress and the President figure out what
30 blend of independence and political control will best enable an agency to perform
31 its intended functions.

32 Judicial intrusion into this field usually reveals only how little courts know about
33 governance. Even everything I just said is an over-simplification. It suggests that
34 agencies can easily be arranged on a spectrum, from the most to the least
35 presidentially controlled. But that is not so. A given agency's independence (or lack
36 of it) depends on a wealth of features, relating not just to removal standards, but
37 also to appointments practices, procedural rules, internal organization, oversight
38 regimes, historical traditions, cultural norms, and (inevitably) personal
39 relationships. * * * Of course no court, as *Free Enterprise Fund* noted, can
40 accurately assess the "bureaucratic minutiae" affecting a President's influence over
41 an agency. But that is yet more reason for courts to defer to the branches charged

1  with fashioning administrative structures, and to hesitate before ruling out agency
2  design specs like for-cause removal standards.

3  Our Constitution, as shown earlier, entrusts such decisions to more accountable
4  and knowledgeable actors. The document—with great good sense—sets out almost
5  no rules about the administrative sphere. As Chief Justice Marshall wrote when he
6  upheld the first independent financial agency: "To have prescribed the means by
7  which government should, in all future time, execute its powers, would have been
8  to change, entirely, the character of the instrument." *McCulloch.* That would have
9  been, he continued, "an unwise attempt to provide, by immutable rules, for
10 exigencies which, if foreseen at all, must have been seen dimly." And if the
11 Constitution, for those reasons, does not lay out immutable rules, then neither
12 should judges. * * *

13                                        II

14 No one had a doubt that the [CFPB] should be independent. As explained already,
15 Congress has historically given—with this Court's permission—a measure of
16 independence to financial regulators like the Federal Reserve Board and the FTC.
17 And agencies of that kind had administered most of the legislation whose
18 enforcement the new statute transferred to the CFPB. The law thus included an
19 ordinary for-cause provision—once again, that the President could fire the CFPB's
20 Director only for "inefficiency, neglect of duty, or malfeasance in office." That
21 standard would allow the President to discharge the Director for a failure to
22 "faithfully execute[]" the law, as well as for basic incompetence. U.S. Const., Art.
23 II, § 3. But it would not permit removal for policy differences.

24 The question here, which by now you're well equipped to answer, is whether
25 including that for-cause standard in the statute creating the CFPB violates the
26 Constitution.

27                                        A

28 Applying our longstanding precedent, the answer is clear: It does not. This Court,
29 as the majority acknowledges, has sustained the constitutionality of the FTC and
30 similar independent agencies. The for-cause protections for the heads of those
31 agencies, the Court has found, do not impede the President's ability to perform his
32 own constitutional duties, and so do not breach the separation of powers. There is
33 nothing different here. The CFPB wields the same kind of power as the FTC and
34 similar agencies. And all of their heads receive the same kind of removal
35 protection. No less than those other entities—by now part of the fabric of
36 government—the CFPB is thus a permissible exercise of Congress's power under
37 the Necessary and Proper Clause to structure administration.

38                                     * * *

39 The analysis is as simple as simple can be. The CFPB Director exercises the same
40 powers, and receives the same removal protections, as the heads of other,

constitutionally permissible independent agencies. How could it be that this opinion is a dissent?

B

The majority focuses on one (it says sufficient) reason: The CFPB Director is singular, not plural. And a solo CFPB Director does not fit within either of the majority's supposed exceptions. He is not an inferior officer, so (the majority says) *Morrison* does not apply; and he is not a multimember board, so (the majority says) neither does *Humphrey's*. Further, the majority argues, "[a]n agency with a [unitary] structure like that of the CFPB" is "novel"—or, if not quite that, "almost wholly unprecedented." Finally, the CFPB's organizational form violates the "constitutional structure" because it vests power in a "single individual" who is "insulated from Presidential control."

\* \* \*

\* \* \* [N]ovelty is not the test of constitutionality when it comes to structuring agencies. See *Mistretta v. United States* (1989) ("[M]ere anomaly or innovation" does not violate the separation of powers). Congress regulates in that sphere under the Necessary and Proper Clause, not (as the majority seems to think) a Rinse and Repeat Clause. The Framers understood that new times would often require new measures, and exigencies often demand innovation. See *McCulloch*. In line with that belief, the history of the administrative sphere—its rules, its practices, its institutions—is replete with experiment and change. Indeed, each of the agencies the majority says now fits within its "exceptions" was once new; there is, as the saying goes, "a first time for everything." *National Federation of Independent Business v. Sebelius* (2012). So even if the CFPB differs from its forebears in having a single director, that departure is not itself "telling" of a "constitutional problem." In deciding what *this* moment demanded, Congress had no obligation to make a carbon copy of a design from a bygone era. \* \* \*

But if the demand is for generalization, then the majority's distinction cuts the opposite way: More powerful control mechanisms are needed (if anything) for commissions. Holding everything else equal, those are the agencies more likely to "slip from the Executive's control." Just consider your everyday experience: It's easier to get one person to do what you want than a gaggle. So too, you know exactly whom to blame when an individual—but not when a group—does a job badly. The same is true in bureaucracies. A multimember structure reduces accountability to the President because it's harder for him to oversee, to influence—or to remove, if necessary—a group of five or more commissioners than a single director. Indeed, that is *why* Congress so often resorts to hydra-headed agencies. \* \* \*

Because it has no answer on that score, the majority slides to a different question: Assuming presidential control of any independent agency is vanishingly slim, is a single-head or a multi-head agency more capable of exercising power, and so of endangering liberty? The majority says a single head is the greater threat because he may wield power "*unilaterally*" and "[w]ith no colleagues to persuade." So the

141

CFPB falls victim to what the majority sees as a constitutional anti-power-concentration principle (with an exception for the President).

If you've never heard of a statute being struck down on that ground, you're not alone. It is bad enough to "extrapolat[e]" from the "general constitutional language" of Article II's Vesting Clause an unrestricted removal power constraining Congress's ability to legislate under the Necessary and Proper Clause. It is still worse to extrapolate from the Constitution's general structure (division of powers) and implicit values (liberty) a limit on Congress's express power to create administrative bodies. * * *

And in doing so, the majority again reveals its lack of interest in how agencies work. First, the premise of the majority's argument—that the CFPB head is a mini-dictator, not subject to meaningful presidential control—is wrong. As this Court has seen in the past, independent agencies are not fully independent. A for-cause removal provision, as noted earlier, leaves "ample" control over agency heads in the hands of the President. He can discharge them for failing to perform their duties competently or in accordance with law, and so ensure that the laws are "faithfully executed." U.S. Const., Art. II, § 3. * * * Second, the majority has nothing but intuition to back up its essentially functionalist claim that the CFPB would be less capable of exercising power if it had more than one Director (even supposing that were a suitable issue for a court to address). *Ante*, at 21, 23. Maybe the CFPB would be. Or maybe not. * * * At the least: If the Court is going to invalidate statutes based on empirical assertions like this one, it should offer some empirical support. It should not pretend that its assessment that the CFPB wields more power more dangerously than the SEC comes from someplace in the Constitution. But today the majority fails to accord even that minimal respect to Congress.

### III

Recall again how this dispute got started. In the midst of the Great Recession, Congress and the President came together to create an agency with an important mission. It would protect consumers from the reckless financial practices that had caused the then-ongoing economic collapse. Not only Congress but also the President thought that the new agency, to fulfill its mandate, needed a measure of independence. So the two political branches, acting together, gave the CFPB Director the same job protection that innumerable other agency heads possess. All in all, those branches must have thought, they had done a good day's work. Relying on their experience and knowledge of administration, they had built an agency in the way best suited to carry out its functions. They had protected the public from financial chicanery and crisis. They had governed.

And now consider how the dispute ends—with five unelected judges rejecting the result of that democratic process. The outcome today will not shut down the CFPB: A different majority of this Court, including all those who join this opinion, believes that *if* the agency's removal provision is unconstitutional, it should be severed. But the majority on constitutionality jettisons a measure Congress and the President viewed as integral to the way the agency should operate. The majority does so even though the Constitution grants to Congress, acting with the President's approval, the authority to create and shape administrative bodies. And even though those branches, as compared to courts, have far greater understanding of political control mechanisms and agency design.

Nothing in the Constitution requires that outcome; to the contrary. "While the Constitution diffuses power the better to secure liberty, it also contemplates that practice will integrate the dispersed powers into a workable government." *Youngstown Sheet & Tube Co. v. Sawyer* (1952) (Jackson, J., concurring). The Framers took pains to craft a document that would allow the structures of governance to change, as times and needs change. The Constitution says only a few words about administration. As Chief Justice Marshall wrote: Rather than prescribing "immutable rules," it enables Congress to choose "the means by which government should, in all future time, execute its powers." *McCulloch*. It authorizes Congress to meet new exigencies with new devices. So Article II does not generally prohibit independent agencies. Nor do any supposed structural principles. Nor do any odors wafting from the document. Save for when those agencies impede the President's performance of his own constitutional duties, the matter is left up to Congress.

Our history has stayed true to the Framers' vision. Congress has accepted their invitation to experiment with administrative forms—nowhere more so than in the field of financial regulation. And this Court has mostly allowed it to do so. The result is a broad array of independent agencies, no two exactly alike but all with a measure of insulation from the President's removal power. The Federal Reserve Board; the FTC; the SEC; maybe some you've never heard of. As to each, Congress thought that formal job protection for policymaking would produce regulatory outcomes in greater accord with the long-term public interest. Congress may have been right; or it may have been wrong; or maybe it was some of both. No matter— the branches accountable to the people have decided how the people should be governed.

The CFPB should have joined the ranks. Maybe it will still do so, even under today's opinion: The majority tells Congress that it may "pursu[e] alternative responses" to the identified constitutional defect—"for example, converting the CFPB into a multimember agency." *Ante*, at 36. But there was no need to send Congress back to the drawing board. The Constitution does not distinguish between single-director and multimember independent agencies. It instructs Congress, not this Court, to decide on agency design. Because this Court ignores that sensible— indeed, that obvious—division of tasks, I respectfully dissent.

# C. Agencies and the Judicial Power

1 Under Article III of the Constitution, "the judicial power of the United States shall
2 be vested in one Supreme Court, and in such inferior courts as the Congress may
3 from time to time ordain and establish." What is more, Article II of the Constitution
4 makes clear that federal judges are to be nominated by the President and
5 confirmed by the Senate, and serve until they die, resign, or are impeached.

6 Here's the problem. If the judicial power is the power to decide cases, agencies
7 decide cases all the time. But agencies are not courts within the meaning of Article
8 III, and the agency personnel who decide them are not Article III judges nominated
9 by the President and confirmed by the Senate. Why is it constitutional for
10 Administrative Law Judges in the Social Security Administration to make
11 disability determinations, for instance? And if that is constitutional, are there
12 limits to what kinds of matters agencies can adjudicate? If something like the Tax
13 Court—whose judges don't enjoy Article III protections—isn't really a court within
14 the meaning of Article III, what is it exactly?

15 The cases in this section take up these questions. Watch in particular for how the
16 Supreme Court's answer to the second question shifts between *Crowell* and
17 *Commodity Futures Trading Commission.*

18 *Freytag* is really an Appointments Clause case, but it exposes a deep rift among
19 the Justices about how we should think about agencies that are in the business of
20 deciding cases. The majority concludes that the Tax Court is a "Court of the United
21 States" for Appointment Clause purposes, possessed of the judicial power. Justice
22 Scalia is quite certain that the Tax Court is a Department in the executive branch
23 that disposes over executive power only. Who has the better side of the argument?

24

25 **Crowell v. Benson**

26 285 U.S. 22 (1932)

27 February 23, 1932

28 MR. CHIEF JUSTICE HUGHES delivered the opinion of the Court.

29 This suit was brought in the District Court to enjoin the enforcement of an award
30 made by petitioner Crowell, as Deputy Commissioner of the United States
31 Employees' Compensation Commission, in favor of the petitioner Knudsen and
32 against the respondent Benson. The award was made under the Longshoremen's
33 and Harbor Workers' Compensation Act, and rested upon the finding of the deputy
34 commissioner that Knudsen was injured while in the employ of Benson and
35 performing service upon the navigable waters of the United States. The
36 complainant alleged that the award was contrary to law for the reason that
37 Knudsen was not at the time of his injury an employee of the complainant, and his
38 claim was not "within the jurisdiction" of the Deputy Commissioner. An amended
39 complaint charged that the Act was unconstitutional upon the grounds that it
40 violated the due process clause of the Fifth Amendment, the provision of the

144

Seventh Amendment as to trial by jury, that of the Fourth Amendment as to unreasonable search and seizure, and the provisions of Article III with respect to the judicial power of the United States. The District Judge denied motions to dismiss and granted a hearing *de novo* upon the facts and the law, expressing the opinion that the Act would be invalid if not construed to permit such a hearing. * * *

* * *

* * * The Act has two limitations that are fundamental. It deals exclusively with compensation in respect of disability or death resulting "from an injury occurring upon the navigable waters of the United States" if recovery "through workmen's compensation proceedings may not validly be provided by State law," and it applies only when the relation of master and servant exists. "Injury," within the statute, "means accidental injury or death arising out of and in the course of employment," and the term "employer" means one "any of whose employees are employed in maritime employment, in whole or in part," upon such navigable waters. Employers are made liable for the payment to their employees of prescribed compensation "irrespective of fault as a cause for the injury." * * *

* * *

The contention under the due process clause of the Fifth Amendment relates to the determination of questions of fact. Rulings of the deputy commissioner upon questions of law are without finality. So far as the latter are concerned, full opportunity is afforded for their determination by the Federal courts through proceedings to suspend or to set aside a compensation order, by the requirement that judgment is to be entered on a supplementary order declaring default only in case the order follows the law, and by the provision that the issue of injunction or other process in a proceeding by a beneficiary to compel obedience to a compensation order is dependent upon a determination by the court that the order was lawfully made and served. Moreover, the statute contains no express limitation attempting to preclude the court, in proceedings to set aside an order as not in accordance with law, from making its own examination and determination of facts whenever that is deemed to be necessary to enforce a constitutional right properly asserted. As the statute is to be construed so as to support rather than to defeat it, no such limitation is to be implied.

Apart from cases involving constitutional rights to be appropriately enforced by proceedings in court, there can be no doubt that the Act contemplates that as to questions of fact, arising with respect to injuries to employees within the purview of the Act, the findings of the deputy commissioner, supported by evidence and within the scope of his authority, shall be final. To hold otherwise would be to defeat the obvious purpose of the legislation to furnish a prompt, continuous, expert, and inexpensive method for dealing with a class of questions of fact which are peculiarly suited to examination and determination by an administrative agency specially assigned to that task. * * *

1                                    * * *

2   As to determinations of fact, the distinction is at once apparent between cases of
3   private right and those which arise between the government and persons subject
4   to its authority in connection with the performance of the constitutional functions
5   of the executive or legislative departments. The Court referred to this distinction
6   in *Murray's Lessee v. Hoboken Land & Improvement Co.*, 59 U.S. 272 (1856),
7   pointing out that "there are matters, involving public rights, which may be
8   presented in such form that the judicial power is capable of acting on them, and
9   which are susceptible of judicial determination, but which Congress may or may
10  not bring within the cognizance of the courts of the United States, as it may deem
11  proper." Thus the Congress, in exercising the powers confided to it, may establish
12  "legislative" courts (as distinguished from "constitutional courts in which the
13  judicial power conferred by the Constitution can be deposited") which are to form
14  part of the government of territories or of the District of Columbia, or to serve as
15  special tribunals "to examine and determine various matters, arising between the
16  government and others, which, from their nature, do not require judicial
17  determination and yet are susceptible of it." But "the mode of determining matters
18  of this class is completely within congressional control. Congress may reserve to
19  itself the power to decide, may delegate that power to executive officers, or may
20  commit it to judicial tribunals." *Ex parte Bakelite Corporation*, 279 U.S. 438, 451
21  (1929). Familiar illustrations of administrative agencies created for the
22  determination of such matters are found in connection with the exercise of the
23  congressional power as to interstate and foreign commerce, taxation, immigration,
24  the public lands, public health, the facilities of the post office, pensions, and
25  payments to veterans.

26  The present case does not fall within the categories just described, but is one of
27  private right, that is, of the liability of one individual to another under the law as
28  defined. But, in cases of that sort, there is no requirement that, in order to maintain
29  the essential attributes of the judicial power, all determinations of fact in
30  constitutional courts shall be made by judges. On the common law side of the
31  federal courts, the aid of juries is not only deemed appropriate, but is required by
32  the Constitution itself. In cases of equity and admiralty, it is historic practice to call
33  to the assistance of the courts, without the consent of the parties, masters, and
34  commissioners or assessors, to pass upon certain classes of questions, as, for
35  example, to take and state an account or to find the amount of damages. While the
36  reports of masters and commissioners in such cases are essentially of an advisory
37  nature, it has not been the practice to disturb their findings when they are properly
38  based upon evidence, in the absence of errors of law, and the parties have no right
39  to demand that the court shall redetermine the facts thus found. * * *

40                                   * * *

41  In deciding whether the Congress, in enacting the statute under review, has
42  exceeded the limits of its authority to prescribe procedure in cases of injury upon
43  navigable waters, regard must be had, as in other cases where constitutional limits

1   are invoked, not to mere matters of form, but to the substance of what is required.
2   The statute has a limited application, being confined to the relation of master and
3   servant, and the method of determining the questions of fact, which arise in the
4   routine of making compensation awards to employees under the Act, is necessary
5   to its effective enforcement. The Act itself, where it applies, establishes the
6   measure of the employer's liability, thus leaving open for determination the
7   questions of fact as to the circumstances, nature, extent, and consequences of the
8   injuries sustained by the employee for which compensation is to be made in
9   accordance with the prescribed standards. Findings of fact by the deputy
10  commissioner upon such questions are closely analogous to the findings of the
11  amount of damages that are made according to familiar practice by commissioners
12  or assessors, and the reservation of full authority to the court to deal with matters
13  of law provides for the appropriate exercise of the judicial function in this class of
14  cases. For the purposes stated, we are unable to find any constitutional obstacle to
15  the action of the Congress in availing itself of a method shown by experience to be
16  essential in order to apply its standards to the thousands of cases involved, thus
17  relieving the courts of a most serious burden while preserving their complete
18  authority to insure the proper application of the law.

19  What has been said thus far relates to the determination of claims of employees
20  within the purview of the Act. A different question is presented where the
21  determinations of fact are fundamental or "jurisdictional," in the sense that their
22  existence is a condition precedent to the operation of the statutory scheme. These
23  fundamental requirements are that the injury occurs upon the navigable waters of
24  the United States, and that the relation of master and servant exists. These
25  conditions are indispensable to the application of the statute not only because the
26  Congress has so provided explicitly, but also because the power of the Congress to
27  enact the legislation turns upon the existence of these conditions.

28                                    * * *

29  * * * In the present instance, the Congress has imposed liability without fault only
30  where the relation of master and servant exists in maritime employment, and,
31  while we hold that the Congress could do this, the fact of that relation is the pivot
32  of the statute, and, in the absence of any other justification, underlies the
33  constitutionality of this enactment. If the person injured was not an employee of
34  the person sought to be held, or if the injury did not occur upon the navigable
35  waters of the United States, there is no ground for an assertion that the person
36  against whom the proceeding was directed could constitutionally be subjected, in
37  the absence of fault upon his part, to the liability which the statute creates.

38  In relation to these basic facts, the question is not the ordinary one as to the
39  propriety of provision for administrative determinations. Nor have we simply the
40  question of due process in relation to notice and hearing. It is, rather, a question
41  of the appropriate maintenance of the federal judicial power in requiring the
42  observance of constitutional restrictions. It is the question whether the Congress
43  may substitute for constitutional courts, in which the judicial power of the United

1 States is vested, an administrative agency—in this instance, a single deputy
2 commissioner—for the final determination of the existence of the facts upon which
3 the enforcement of the constitutional rights of the citizen depend. The recognition
4 of the utility and convenience of administrative agencies for the investigation and
5 finding of facts within their proper province, and the support of their authorized
6 action, does not require the conclusion that there is no limitation of their use, and
7 that the Congress could completely oust the courts of all determinations of fact by
8 vesting the authority to make them with finality in its own instrumentalities or in
9 the executive department. That would be to sap the judicial power as it exists under
10 the Federal Constitution, and to establish a government of a bureaucratic character
11 alien to our system, wherever fundamental rights depend, as not infrequently they
12 do depend, upon the facts, and finality as to facts becomes in effect finality in law.

13 * * *

14 * * * [W]here administrative bodies have been appropriately created to meet the
15 exigencies of certain classes of cases and their action is of a judicial character, the
16 question of the conclusiveness of their administrative findings of fact generally
17 arises where the facts are clearly not jurisdictional and the scope of review as to
18 such facts has been determined by the applicable legislation. None of the decisions
19 of this sort touch the question which is presented where the facts involved are
20 jurisdictional, or where the question concerns the proper exercise of the judicial
21 power of the United States in enforcing constitutional limitations. Even where the
22 subject lies within the general authority of the Congress, the propriety of a
23 challenge by judicial proceedings of the determinations of fact deemed to be
24 jurisdictional, as underlying the authority of executive officers, has been
25 recognized. * * *

26 * * *

27 In the present instance, the argument that the Congress has constituted the deputy
28 commissioner a fact-finding tribunal is unavailing, as the contention makes the
29 untenable assumption that the constitutional courts may be deprived in all cases
30 of the determination of facts upon evidence even though a constitutional right may
31 be involved. * * *

32 * * *

33 Assuming that the Federal court may determine for itself the existence of these
34 fundamental or jurisdictional facts, we come to the question: Upon what record is
35 the determination to be made? There is no provision of the statute which seeks to
36 confine the court in such a case to the record before the deputy commissioner or
37 to the evidence which he has taken. The remedy which the statute makes available
38 is not by an appeal or by a writ of certiorari for a review of his determination upon
39 the record before him. The remedy is "through injunction proceedings mandatory
40 or otherwise." The question in the instant case is not whether the deputy
41 commissioner has acted improperly or arbitrarily as shown by the record of his
42 proceedings in the course of administration in cases contemplated by the statute,

but whether he has acted in a case to which the statute is inapplicable. By providing for injunction proceedings, the Congress evidently contemplated a suit as in equity, and, in such a suit, the complainant would have full opportunity to plead and prove either that the injury did not occur upon the navigable waters of the United States or that the relation of master and servant did not exist, and hence that the case lay outside the purview of the statute. As the question is one of the constitutional authority of the deputy commissioner as an administrative agency, the court is under no obligation to give weight to his proceedings pending the determination of that question. If the court finds that the facts existed which gave the deputy commissioner jurisdiction to pass upon the claim for compensation, the injunction will be denied insofar as these fundamental questions are concerned; if, on the contrary, the court is satisfied that the deputy commissioner had no jurisdiction of the proceedings before him, that determination will deprive them of their effectiveness for any purpose. We think that the essential independence of the exercise of the judicial power of the United States in the enforcement of constitutional rights requires that the federal court should determine such an issue upon its own record and the facts elicited before it.

\* \* \*

We are of the opinion that the District Court did not err in permitting a trial *de novo* on the issue of employment. \* \* \*

Decree affirmed.

MR. JUSTICE BRANDEIS, dissenting [Omitted.]


## Commodity Futures Trading Commission v. Schor

478 U.S. 833 (1986)

July 7, 1986

JUSTICE O'CONNOR delivered the opinion of the Court.

The question presented is whether the Commodity Exchange Act (CEA or Act), 7 U.S.C. § 1 et seq., empowers the Commodity Futures Trading Commission (CFTC or Commission) to entertain state law counterclaims in reparation proceedings and, if so, whether that grant of authority violates Article III of the Constitution.

I

The CEA broadly prohibits fraudulent and manipulative conduct in connection with commodity futures transactions. In 1974, Congress "overhaul[ed]" the Act in order to institute a more "comprehensive regulatory structure to oversee the volatile and esoteric futures trading complex." Congress also determined that the broad regulatory powers of the CEA were most appropriately vested in an agency which would be relatively immune from the "political winds that sweep

1    Washington." It therefore created an independent agency, the CFTC, and entrusted
2    to it sweeping authority to implement the CEA.

3    Among the duties assigned to the CFTC was the administration of a reparations
4    procedure through which disgruntled customers of professional commodity
5    brokers could seek redress for the brokers' violations of the Act or CFTC
6    regulations. Thus, § 14 of the CEA, provides that any person injured by such
7    violations may apply to the Commission for an order directing the offender to pay
8    reparations to the complainant and may enforce that order in federal district court.
9    Congress intended this administrative procedure to be an "inexpensive and
10   expeditious" alternative to existing fora available to aggrieved customers, namely,
11   the courts and arbitration.

12   In conformance with the congressional goal of promoting efficient dispute
13   resolution, the CFTC promulgated a regulation in 1976 which allows it to
14   adjudicate counterclaims "aris[ing] out of the transaction or occurrence or series
15   of transactions or occurrences set forth in the complaint." 17 CFR § 12.23(b)(2)
16   (1983). This permissive counterclaim rule leaves the respondent in a reparations
17   proceeding free to seek relief against the reparations complainant in other fora.

18   The instant dispute arose in February, 1980, when respondents Schor and
19   Mortgage Services of America, Inc., invoked the CFTC's reparations jurisdiction by
20   filing complaints against petitioner Conti Commodity Services, Inc. (Conti), a
21   commodity futures broker, and Richard L. Sandor, a Conti employee. Schor had an
22   account with Conti which contained a debit balance because Schor's net futures
23   trading losses and expenses, such as commissions, exceeded the funds deposited
24   in the account. Schor alleged that this debit balance was the result of Conti's
25   numerous violations of the CEA.

26   Before receiving notice that Schor had commenced the reparations proceeding,
27   Conti had filed a diversity action in Federal District Court to recover the debit
28   balance. * * *

29   Although the District Court declined to stay or dismiss the suit, Conti voluntarily
30   dismissed the federal court action and presented its debit balance claim by way of
31   a counterclaim in the CFTC reparations proceeding. Conti denied violating the
32   CEA, and instead insisted that the debit balance resulted from Schor's trading, and
33   was therefore a simple debt owed by Schor.

34   After discovery, briefing, and a hearing, the Administrative Law Judge (ALJ) in
35   Schor's reparations proceeding ruled in Conti's favor on both Schor's claims and
36   Conti's counterclaims. After this ruling, Schor for the first time challenged the
37   CFTC's statutory authority to adjudicate Conti's counterclaim. The ALJ rejected
38   Schor's challenge, stating himself "bound by agency regulations and published
39   agency policies." The Commission declined to review the decision, and allowed it
40   to become final, at which point Schor filed a petition for review with the Court of
41   Appeals for the District of Columbia Circuit. Prior to oral argument, the Court of
42   Appeals, *sua sponte*, raised the question whether CFTC could constitutionally

adjudicate Conti's counterclaims in light of *Northern Pipeline Construction Co. v. Marathon Pipe Line Co.*, 458 U.S. 50 (1982), in which this Court held that "Congress may not vest in a non-Article III court the power to adjudicate, render final judgment, and issue binding orders in a traditional contract action arising under state law, without consent of the litigants, and subject only to ordinary appellate review." *Thomas v. Union Carbide Agricultural Products Co.*, 473 U.S. 568, 584 (1985).

After briefing and argument, the Court of Appeals upheld the CFTC's decision on Schor's claim in most respects, but ordered the dismissal of Conti's counterclaims on the ground that "the CFTC lacks authority (subject matter competence) to adjudicate" common law counterclaims. * * *

* * *

[T]he broad grant of power in § 12a(5) clearly authorizes the promulgation of regulations providing for adjudication of common law counterclaims arising out of the same transaction as a reparations complaint, because such jurisdiction is necessary, if not critical, to accomplish the purposes behind the reparations program.

Reference to the instant controversy illustrates the crippling effect that the Court of Appeals' restrictive reading of the CFTC's counterclaim jurisdiction would have on the efficacy of the reparations remedy. The dispute between Schor and Conti is typical of the disputes adjudicated in reparations proceedings: a customer and a professional commodities broker agree that there is a debit balance in the customer's account, but the customer attributes the deficit to the broker's alleged CEA violations and the broker attributes it to the customer's lack of success in the market. The customer brings a reparations claim; the broker counterclaims for the amount of the debit balance. In the usual case, then, the counterclaim "arises out of precisely the same course of events" as the principal claim, and requires resolution of many of the same disputed factual issues.

Under the Court of Appeals' approach, the entire dispute may not be resolved in the administrative forum. Consequently, the entire dispute will typically end up in court, for when the broker files suit to recover the debit balance, the customer will normally be compelled either by compulsory counterclaim rules or by the expense and inconvenience of litigating the same issues in two fora, to forgo his reparations remedy and to litigate his claim in court. In sum, as Schor himself aptly summarized, to require a bifurcated examination of the single dispute "would be to emasculate, if not destroy, the purposes of the Commodity Exchange Act to provide an efficient and relatively inexpensive forum for the resolution of disputes in futures trading."

As our discussion makes manifest, the CFTC's long-held position that it has the power to take jurisdiction over counterclaims such as Conti's is eminently reasonable, and well within the scope of its delegated authority. * * *

1        \* \* \*

2                            III

3    Article III, § 1, directs that the "judicial Power of the United States shall be vested
4    in one supreme Court and in such inferior Courts as the Congress may from time
5    to time ordain and establish," and provides that these federal courts shall be staffed
6    by judges who hold office during good behavior, and whose compensation shall not
7    be diminished during tenure in office. Schor claims that these provisions prohibit
8    Congress from authorizing the initial adjudication of common law counterclaims
9    by the CFTC, an administrative agency whose adjudicatory officers do not enjoy
10   the tenure and salary protections embodied in Article III.

11   Although our precedents in this area do not admit of easy synthesis, they do
12   establish that the resolution of claims such as Schor's cannot turn on conclusory
13   reference to the language of Article III. *See, e.g., Thomas,* 473 U.S., at 583. Rather,
14   the constitutionality of a given congressional delegation of adjudicative functions
15   to a non-Article III body must be assessed by reference to the purposes underlying
16   the requirements of Article III. *See, e.g., id.* at 473 U.S. 590; *Northern Pipeline,*
17   458 U.S., atU.S. 64. This inquiry, in turn, is guided by the principle that "practical
18   attention to substance, rather than doctrinaire reliance on formal categories,
19   should inform application of Article III." *Thomas, supra,* at 473 U.S. 587. *See also*
20   *Crowell v. Benson,* 285 U.S., at 53 (1932).

21                            A

22   Article III, § 1, serves both to protect "the role of the independent judiciary within
23   the constitutional scheme of tripartite government," *Thomas, supra,* at 473 U.S.
24   583, and to safeguard litigants' "right to have claims decided before judges who are
25   free from potential domination by other branches of government." *United States*
26   *v. Will,* 449 U.S. 200, 218 (1980). \* \* \*

27   Our precedents also demonstrate, however, that Article III does not confer on
28   litigants an absolute right to the plenary consideration of every nature of claim by
29   an Article III court. Moreover, as a personal right, Article III's guarantee of an
30   impartial and independent federal adjudication is subject to waiver, just as are
31   other personal constitutional rights that dictate the procedures by which civil and
32   criminal matters must be tried. \* \* \*

33   In the instant cases, Schor indisputably waived any right he may have possessed to
34   the full trial of Conti's counterclaim before an Article III court. Schor expressly
35   demanded that Conti proceed on its counterclaim in the reparations proceeding,
36   rather than before the District Court, and was content to have the entire dispute
37   settled in the forum he had selected until the ALJ ruled against him on all counts;
38   it was only after the ALJ rendered a decision to which he objected that Schor raised
39   any challenge to the CFTC's consideration of Conti's counterclaim.

40                           \* \* \*

B

[O]ur precedents establish that Article III, § 1, not only preserves to litigants their interest in an impartial and independent federal adjudication of claims within the judicial power of the United States, but also serves as "an inseparable element of the constitutional system of checks and balances." Article III, § 1, safeguards the role of the Judicial Branch in our tripartite system by barring congressional attempts "to transfer jurisdiction [to non-Article III tribunals] for the purpose of emasculating" constitutional courts, *National Insurance Co. v. Tidewater Co.*, 337 U.S. 582, 644 (1949) (VINSON, C.J., dissenting), and thereby preventing "the encroachment or aggrandizement of one branch at the expense of the other." *Buckley v. Valeo*, 424 U.S. 1, 122 (1976) (*per curiam*). To the extent that this structural principle is implicated in a given case, the parties cannot by consent cure the constitutional difficulty, for the same reason that the parties, by consent, cannot confer on federal courts subject matter jurisdiction beyond the limitations imposed by Article III, § 2. When these Article III limitations are at issue, notions of consent and waiver cannot be dispositive, because the limitations serve institutional interests that the parties cannot be expected to protect.

In determining the extent to which a given congressional decision to authorize the adjudication of Article III business in a non-Article III tribunal impermissibly threatens the institutional integrity of the Judicial Branch, the Court has declined to adopt formalistic and unbending rules. Although such rules might lend a greater degree of coherence to this area of the law, they might also unduly constrict Congress' ability to take needed and innovative action pursuant to its Article I powers. Thus, in reviewing Article III challenges, we have weighed a number of factors, none of which has been deemed determinative, with an eye to the practical effect that the congressional action will have on the constitutionally assigned role of the federal judiciary. Among the factors upon which we have focused are the extent to which the "essential attributes of judicial power" are reserved to Article III courts, and, conversely, the extent to which the non-Article III forum exercises the range of jurisdiction and powers normally vested only in Article III courts, the origins and importance of the right to be adjudicated, and the concerns that drove Congress to depart from the requirements of Article III. An examination of the relative allocation of powers between the CFTC and Article III courts in light of the considerations given prominence in our precedents demonstrates that the congressional scheme does not impermissibly intrude on the province of the judiciary. The CFTC's adjudicatory powers depart from the traditional agency model in just one respect: the CFTC's jurisdiction over common law counterclaims. While wholesale importation of concepts of pendent or ancillary jurisdiction into the agency context may create greater constitutional difficulties, we decline to endorse an absolute prohibition on such jurisdiction out of fear of where some hypothetical "slippery slope" may deposit us. * * *

* * *

The CFTC, like the agency in *Crowell*, deals only with a "particularized area of law," whereas the jurisdiction of the bankruptcy courts found unconstitutional in *Northern Pipeline* extended to broadly "all civil proceedings arising under title 11 or arising in or *related* to cases under title 11." 28 U.S.C. § 1471(b) (quoted in *Northern Pipeline*, 458 U.S., at 85) (emphasis added). CFTC orders, like those of the agency in *Crowell*, but unlike those of the bankruptcy courts under the 1978 Act, are enforceable only by order of the district court. CFTC orders are also reviewed under the same "weight of the evidence" standard sustained in *Crowell*, rather than the more deferential standard found lacking in *Northern Pipeline*. The legal rulings of the CFTC, like the legal determinations of the agency in *Crowell*, are subject to *de novo* review. Finally, the CFTC, unlike the bankruptcy courts under the 1978 Act, does not exercise "all ordinary powers of district courts," and thus may not, for instance, preside over jury trials or issue writs of habeas corpus.

Of course, the nature of the claim has significance in our Article III analysis quite apart from the method prescribed for its adjudication. The counterclaim asserted in this litigation is a "private" right for which state law provides the rule of decision. It is therefore a claim of the kind assumed to be at the "core" of matters normally reserved to Article III courts. Yet this conclusion does not end our inquiry; just as this Court has rejected any attempt to make determinative for Article III purposes the distinction between public rights and private rights, there is no reason inherent in separation of powers principles to accord the state law character of a claim talismanic power in Article III inquiries.

We have explained that "the public rights doctrine reflects simply a pragmatic understanding that, when Congress selects a quasi-judicial method of resolving matters that 'could be conclusively determined by the Executive and Legislative Branches,' the danger of encroaching on the judicial powers" is less than when private rights, which are normally within the purview of the judiciary, are relegated as an initial matter to administrative adjudication. *Thomas*, 473 U.S. at 4589 (quoting *Northern Pipeline, supra*, at 458 U.S. 68). * * *

* * *

* * * [O]ur Article III precedents * * * counsel that bright-line rules cannot effectively be employed to yield broad principles applicable in all Article III inquiries. Rather, due regard must be given in each case to the unique aspects of the congressional plan at issue, and its practical consequences in light of the larger concerns that underlie Article III. We conclude that the limited jurisdiction that the CFTC asserts over state law claims as a necessary incident to the adjudication of federal claims willingly submitted by the parties for initial agency adjudication does not contravene separation of powers principles or Article III.

* * *

JUSTICE BRENNAN, with whom JUSTICE MARSHALL joins, dissenting.

* * *

On its face, Article III, § 1, seems to prohibit the vesting of *any* judicial functions in either the Legislative or the Executive Branch. The Court has, however, recognized three narrow exceptions to the otherwise absolute mandate of Article III: territorial courts, courts-martial, and courts that adjudicate certain disputes concerning public rights. Unlike the Court, I would limit the judicial authority of non-Article III federal tribunals to these few, long-established exceptions, and would countenance no further erosion of Article III's mandate.

* * *

## Freytag v. Commissioner

501 U.S. 868 (1991)

June 27, 1991

JUSTICE BLACKMUN delivered the opinion of the Court.

* * * In this litigation, we must decide whether the authority that Congress has granted the Chief Judge of the United States Tax Court to appoint special trial judges transgresses our structure of separated powers. We answer that inquiry in the negative.

### I

By the Tax Reform Act of 1969, Congress "established, under article I of the Constitution of the United States, a court of record to be known as the United States Tax Court." It also empowered the Tax Court to appoint commissioners to assist its judges. By the Tax Reform Act of 1984, the title "commissioner" was changed to "special trial judge." By § 463(a) of that Act, and by § 1556(a) of the Tax Reform Act of 1986, Congress authorized the Chief Judge of the Tax Court to appoint and assign these special trial judges to hear certain specifically described proceedings and "any other proceeding which the chief judge may designate." The Tax Court presently consists of 19 judges appointed to 15-year terms by the President, by and with the advice and consent of the Senate.

### II

This complex litigation began with determinations of federal income tax deficiencies against the several petitioners, who had deducted on their returns approximately $1.5 billion in losses allegedly realized in a tax shelter scheme. When petitioners sought review in the Tax Court in March, 1982, their cases were assigned to Tax Court Judge Richard C. Wilbur. Trial began in 1984. Judge Wilbur became ill in November, 1985, and the Chief Judge of the Tax Court assigned Special Trial Judge Carleton D. Powell to preside over the trial as evidentiary referee, with the proceedings videotaped. When Judge Wilbur's illness forced his retirement and assumption of senior status effective April 1, 1986, the cases were

1    reassigned, with petitioners' specified consent, to Judge Powell for preparation of
2    written findings and an opinion. The judge concluded that petitioners' tax shelter
3    scheme consisted of sham transactions and that petitioners owed additional taxes.
4    The Chief Judge adopted Judge Powell's opinion as that of the Tax Court.

5    Petitioners took an appeal to the Court of Appeals for the Fifth Circuit. It affirmed.
6    Petitioners did not argue to the Court of Appeals, nor do they argue here, that the
7    Tax Court is not a legitimate body. Rather, they contended that the assignment of
8    cases as complex as theirs to a special trial judge was not authorized by § 7443A,
9    and that this violated the Appointments Clause of the Constitution, Art. II, § 2, cl.
10   2. * * *

11   We granted certiorari, 498 U.S. 1066 (1991), to resolve the important questions the
12   litigation raises about the Constitution's structural separation of powers.

13                                  III

14                                  * * *

15   * * * Can the Chief Judge of the Tax Court constitutionally be vested by Congress
16   with the power to appoint? The Appointments Clause names the possible
17   repositories for the appointment power. It is beyond question in this litigation that
18   Congress did not intend to grant to the President the power to appoint special trial
19   judges. We therefore are left with three other possibilities. First, as the
20   Commissioner urges, the Tax Court could be treated as a department with the Chief
21   Judge as its head. Second, as the amicus suggests, the Tax Court could be
22   considered one of "the Courts of Law." Third, we could agree with petitioners that
23   the Tax Court is neither a "Departmen[t]" nor a "Cour[t] of Law." Should we agree
24   with petitioners, it would follow that the appointment power could not be vested
25   in the Chief Judge of the Tax Court.

26                                  * * *

27   We cannot accept the Commissioner's assumption that every part of the Executive
28   Branch is a department, the head of which is eligible to receive the appointment
29   power. The Appointments Clause prevents Congress from distributing power too
30   widely by limiting the actors in whom Congress may vest the power to appoint. The
31   Clause reflects our Framers' conclusion that widely distributed appointment power
32   subverts democratic government. Given the inexorable presence of the
33   administrative state, a holding that every organ in the Executive Branch is a
34   department would multiply indefinitely the number of actors eligible to appoint.
35   The Framers recognized the dangers posed by an excessively diffuse appointment
36   power and rejected efforts to expand that power. So do we. For the Chief Judge of
37   the Tax Court to qualify as a "Head of [a] Department," the Commissioner must
38   demonstrate not only that the Tax Court is a part of the Executive Branch, but also
39   that it is a department.

1   We are not so persuaded. This Court for more than a century has held that the term
2   "Department" refers only to "a part or division of the executive government, as the
3   Department of State, or of the Treasury,'" expressly "creat[ed]" and "giv[en] . . . the
4   name of a department" by Congress. *Germaine*, 99 U.S., at 510-511. Accordingly,
5   the term "Heads of Departments" does not embrace "inferior commissioners and
6   bureau officers." *Germaine*, 99 U.S., at 511.

7   Confining the term "Heads of Departments" in the Appointments Clause to
8   executive divisions like the Cabinet-level departments constrains the distribution
9   of the appointment power just as the Commissioner's interpretation, in contrast,
10  would diffuse it. The Cabinet-level departments are limited in number, and easily
11  identified. Their heads are subject to the exercise of political oversight, and share
12  the President's accountability to the people.

13                                          * * *

14  Even if we were not persuaded that the Commissioner's view threatened to diffuse
15  the appointment power and was contrary to the meaning of "Department" in the
16  Constitution, we still could not accept his treatment of the intent of Congress,
17  which enacted legislation in 1969 with the express purpose of "making the Tax
18  Court an Article I court, rather than an executive agency." S.Rep. No. 91-552, p.
19  303 (1969). Congress deemed it "anomalous to continue to classify" the Tax Court
20  with executive agencies and questioned whether it was "appropriate for one
21  executive agency [the pre-1969 tribunal] to be sitting in judgment on the
22  determinations of another executive agency [the IRS]." *Ibid.*

23  Treating the Tax Court as a "Department" and its chief judge as its "Head" would
24  defy the purpose of the Appointments Clause, the meaning of the Constitution's
25  text, and the clear intent of Congress to transform the Tax Court into an Article I
26  legislative court. The Tax Court is not a "Department."

27  Having so concluded, we now must determine whether it is one of the "Courts of
28  Law," as amicus suggests. Petitioners and the Commissioner both take the position
29  that the Tax Court cannot be a "Court of Law" within the meaning of the
30  Appointments Clause because, they say, that term is limited to Article III courts.

31  The text of the Clause does not limit the "Courts of Law" to those courts established
32  under Article III of the Constitution. The Appointments Clause does not provide
33  that Congress can vest appointment power only in "one supreme Court" and other
34  courts established under Article III, or only in tribunals that exercise broad
35  common law jurisdiction. * * *

36

37  Our cases involving non-Article III tribunals have held that these courts exercise
38  the judicial power of the United States. In both *Canter* and *Williams*, this Court
39  rejected arguments similar to the literalistic one now advanced by petitioners, that
40  only Article III courts could exercise the judicial power because the term "judicial

1  Power" appears only in Article III. In *Williams*, this Court explained that the power
2  exercised by some non-Article III tribunals is judicial power:

3     "The Court of Claims . . . undoubtedly . . . exercises judicial power, but the
4     question still remains—and is the vital question—whether it is the judicial
5     power defined by Art. III of the Constitution."

6     "That judicial power apart from that article may be conferred by Congress
7     upon legislative courts . . . is plainly apparent from the opinion of CHIEF
8     JUSTICE MARSHALL in *American Insurance Co. v. Canter* . . . dealing
9     with the territorial courts. . . . [T]he legislative courts possess and exercise
10    judicial power . . . , although not conferred in virtue of the third article of
11    the Constitution."

12  We cannot hold that an Article I court, such as the Court of Claims in *Williams* or
13  the Territorial Court of Florida in *Canter*, can exercise the judicial power of the
14  United States, and yet cannot be one of the "Courts of Law."

15                                              * * *

16  The Tax Court exercises judicial power to the exclusion of any other function. It is
17  neither advocate nor rulemaker. As an adjudicative body, it construes statutes
18  passed by Congress and regulations promulgated by the Internal Revenue Service.
19  It does not make political decisions.

20  The Tax Court's function and role in the federal judicial scheme closely resemble
21  those of the federal district courts, which indisputably are "Courts of Law."
22  Furthermore, the Tax Court exercises its judicial power in much the same way as
23  the federal district courts exercise theirs. It has authority to punish contempts by
24  fine or imprisonment, 26 U.S.C. § 7456(c); to grant certain injunctive relief, §
25  6213(a); to order the Secretary of the Treasury to refund an overpayment
26  determined by the court, § 6512(b)(2); and to subpoena and examine witnesses,
27  order production of documents, and administer oaths, § 7456(a). All these powers
28  are quintessentially judicial in nature.

29  The Tax Court remains independent of the Executive and Legislative Branches. Its
30  decisions are not subject to review by either the Congress or the President. Nor has
31  Congress made Tax Court decisions subject to review in the federal district courts.
32  Rather, like the judgments of the district courts, the decisions of the Tax Court are
33  appealable only to the regional United States courts of appeals, with ultimate
34  review in this Court. The courts of appeals, moreover, review those decisions "in
35  the same manner and to the same extent as decisions of the district courts in civil
36  actions tried without a jury." § 7482(a). This standard of review contrasts with the
37  standard applied to agency rulemaking by the courts of appeals under § 10(e) of
38  the Administrative Procedure Act.

39  The Tax Court's exclusively judicial role distinguishes it from other non-Article III
40  tribunals that perform multiple functions and provides the limit on the diffusion

1  of appointment power that the Constitution demands. * * * Including Article I
2  courts, such as the Tax Court, that exercise judicial power and perform exclusively
3  judicial functions among the "Courts of Law" does not significantly expand the
4  universe of actors eligible to receive the appointment power.

5                                  * * *

6  JUSTICE SCALIA, with whom JUSTICE O'CONNOR, JUSTICE KENNEDY, and
7  JUSTICE SOUTER join, concurring in part and concurring in the judgment.

8                                  * * *

9  The Appointments Clause provides:

10      "The Congress may by Law vest the Appointment of such inferior Officers,
11          as they think proper, in the President alone, in the Courts of Law, or in the
12          Heads of Departments." Art. II, § 2, cl. 2.

13  I agree with the Court that a special trial judge is an "inferior Office[r]" within the
14  meaning of this Clause, with the result that, absent Presidential appointment, he
15  must be appointed by a court of law or the head of a department. I do not agree,
16  however, with the Court's conclusion that the Tax Court is a "Court of Law" within
17  the meaning of this provision. I would find the appointment valid because the Tax
18  Court is a "Department" and the Chief Judge is its head.

19                                   A

20  A careful reading of the Constitution and attention to the apparent purpose of the
21  Appointments Clause make it clear that the Tax Court cannot be one of those
22  "Courts of Law" referred to there. The Clause does not refer generally to "Bodies
23  exercising judicial Functions," or even to "Courts" generally, or even to "Courts of
24  Law" generally. It refers to "the Courts of Law." Certainly this does not mean *any*
25  "Court of Law" (the Supreme Court of Rhode Island would not do). The definite
26  article "the" obviously narrows the class of eligible "Courts of Law" to those courts
27  of law envisioned by the Constitution. Those are Article III courts, and the Tax
28  Court is not one of them.

29      The Court rejects this conclusion because the Appointments Clause does not (in
30      the style of the Uniform Commercial Code) contain an explicit cross-reference to
31      Article III. Ante at 501 U.S. §§ 888-889. This is no doubt true, but irrelevant. It is
32      equally true that Article I, § 8, cl. 9, which provides that Congress may "constitute
33      Tribunals inferior to the Supreme Court," does not explicitly say "Tribunals under
34      Article III, below." Yet this power "plainly relates to the 'inferior Courts' provided
35      for in Article III, § 1; it has never been relied on for establishment of any other
36      tribunals." * * * The Framers contemplated no other national judicial tribunals.
37                                  * * *

159

We recognized this in *Buckley*, and it was indeed an essential part of our reasoning. Responding to the argument that a select group of Congressmen was a "Department," we said:

> "The phrase 'Heads of Departments,' used as it is in conjunction with the phrase 'Courts of Law,' suggests that the Departments referred to are themselves in the Executive Branch or at least have some connection with that branch. While the Clause expressly authorizes Congress to vest the appointment of certain officers in the 'Courts of Law,' the absence of similar language to include Congress must mean that neither Congress nor its officers were included within the language 'Heads of Departments' in this part of cl. 2.

> "Thus, with respect to four of the six voting members of the Commission, neither the President, the head of any department, *nor the Judiciary* has any voice in their selection." *Buckley v.* Valeo, 424 U.S. 1, 127 (1976) (emphasis added).

The whole point of this passage is that "the Heads of Departments" must reasonably be understood to refer exclusively to the Executive Branch (thereby excluding officers of Congress) because "the Courts of Law" obviously refers exclusively to the Judicial Branch. We were right in *Buckley*, and the Court is wrong today.

\* \* \*

### B

Having concluded, against all odds, that "the Courts of Law" referred to in Article II, § 2, are not the courts of law established by Article III, the Court is confronted with the difficult problem of determining what courts of law they are. It acknowledges that they must be courts which exercise "the judicial power of the United States" and concludes that the Tax Court is such a court—even though it is not an Article III court. This is quite a feat, considering that Article III begins "The judicial Power of the United States"—not *Some* of the judicial Power of the United States," or even *Most* of the judicial Power of the United States"—"shall be vested in one supreme Court, and in such inferior Courts as the Congress may from time to time ordain and establish." Despite this unequivocal text, the Court sets forth the startling proposition that "the judicial power of the United States is not limited to the judicial power defined under Article III." It turns out, however—to our relief, I suppose it must be said—that this is really only a pun. "The judicial power," as the Court uses it, bears no resemblance to the constitutional term of art we are all familiar with, but means only "the power to adjudicate in the manner of courts." So used, as I shall proceed to explain, the phrase covers an infinite variety of individuals exercising executive, rather than judicial, power (in the constitutional sense), and has nothing to do with the separation of powers or with any other characteristic that might cause one to believe that is what was meant by "the Courts

160

1   of Law." As far as I can tell, the only thing to be said for this approach is that it
2   makes the Tax Court a "Court of Law"—which is perhaps the object of the exercise.

3   I agree with the unremarkable proposition that "Congress [has] wide discretion to
4   assign the task of adjudication in cases arising under federal law to legislative
5   tribunals." Congress may also assign that task to subdivisions of traditional
6   executive departments, as it did in 1924 when it created the Tax Court's
7   predecessor, the Tax Board of Appeals—or to take a more venerable example, as it
8   did in 1791 when it created within the Treasury Department the Comptroller of the
9   United States, who "decide[d] on appeal, without further review by the Secretary,
10  all claims concerning the settlement of accounts." Such tribunals, like any other
11  administrative board, exercise the executive power, not the judicial power of the
12  United States. They are, in the words of the great Chief Justice, "incapable of
13  receiving [the judicial power]"—unless their members serve for life during good
14  behavior and receive permanent salary. *American Ins. Co. v. Canter*, 26 U.S. 546
15  (1828) (MARSHALL, C.J.).

16  It is no doubt true that all such bodies "adjudicate," *i.e.*, they determine facts, apply
17  a rule of law to those facts, and thus arrive at a decision. But there is nothing
18  "inherently judicial" about "adjudication." To be a federal officer and to adjudicate
19  are necessary but not sufficient conditions for the exercise of federal judicial
20  power, as we recognized almost a century and a half ago. * * *

21  * * * Today, the Federal Government has a corps of administrative law judges
22  numbering more than 1,000, whose principal statutory function is the conduct of
23  adjudication under the Administrative Procedure Act (APA). They are all *executive*
24  officers. "Adjudication," in other words, is no more an "inherently" judicial
25  function than the promulgation of rules governing primary conduct is an
26  "inherently" legislative one.

27  It is true that Congress *may* commit the sorts of matters administrative law judges
28  and other executive adjudicators now handle to Article III courts—just as some of
29  the matters now in Article III courts could instead be committed to executive
30  adjudicators. "There are matters, involving public rights, which may be presented
31  in such form that the judicial power is capable of acting on them, and which are
32  susceptible of judicial determination, but which Congress may or may not bring
33  within the cognizance of the courts of the United States, as it may deem proper."
34  *Murray's Lessee*, 59 U.S. 284. Congress could, for instance, allow direct review by
35  the Courts of Appeals of denials of Social Security benefits. It could instead
36  establish the Social Security Court—composed of judges serving 5-year terms—
37  within the Social Security Administration. Both tribunals would perform identical
38  functions, but only the former would exercise the judicial power.

39  In short, given the performance of adjudicatory functions by a federal officer, it is
40  the identity of the officer—not something intrinsic about the mode of
41  decisionmaking or type of decision—that tells us whether the judicial power is
42  being exercised. "[O]ur cases demonstrate [that] a particular function, like a

chameleon, will often take on the aspect of the office to which it is assigned." *Bowsher v. Synar*, 478 U.S. 714, 749 (1986) (STEVENS, J., concurring in judgment). * * *

The Tax Court is indistinguishable from my hypothetical Social Security Court. It reviews determinations by Executive Branch officials (the Internal Revenue Service) that this much or that much tax is owed—a classic executive function. For 18 years its predecessor, the Board of Tax Appeals, did the very same thing, and no one suggested that body exercised "the judicial power." We held just the opposite:

> "The Board of Tax Appeals is not a court. It is an executive or administrative board, upon the decision of which the parties are given an opportunity to base a petition for review to the courts after the administrative inquiry of the Board has been had and decided." *Old Colony Trust Co. v. Commissioner*, 279 U.S. 716, 725 (1929) (TAFT, C.J.).

* * *

When the Tax Court was statutorily denominated an "Article I Court" in 1969, its judges did not magically acquire the judicial power. They still lack life tenure; their salaries may still be diminished; they are still removable by the President for "inefficiency, neglect of duty, or malfeasance in office." 26 U.S.C. § 7443(f). (In *Bowsher v. Synar*, 478 U.S. 729, we held that these latter terms are "very broad" and "could sustain removal ... for any number of actual or perceived transgressions.") How anyone with these characteristics can exercise judicial power "independent . . . [of] the Executive Branch" is a complete mystery. It seems to me entirely obvious that the Tax Court, like the Internal Revenue Service, the FCC, and the NLRB, exercises executive power. * * *

* * *

### III

Since the Tax Court is not a court of law, unless the Chief Judge is the head of a department, the appointment of the Special Trial Judge was void. Unlike the Court, I think he is.

I have already explained that the Tax Court, like its predecessors, exercises the executive power of the United States. This does not, of course, suffice to market a "Department" for purposes of the Appointments Clause. If, for instance, the Tax Court were a subdivision of the Department of the Treasury—as the Board of Tax Appeals used to be—it would not qualify. In fact, however, the Tax Court is a freestanding, self-contained entity in the Executive Branch, whose Chief Judge is removable by the President (and, save impeachment, no one else). Nevertheless, the Court holds that the Chief Judge is not the head of a department.

It is not at all clear what the Court's reason for this conclusion is. I had originally thought that the Court was adopting petitioners' theory—wrong, but at least

1    coherent—that "Heads of Departments" means Cabinet officers * * *, but this hint
2    is canceled by a footnote * * *. The Court reserves the right to consider as "Cabinet-
3    like," and hence as "Departments," those agencies which, above all others, are at
4    the farthest remove from Cabinet status, and whose heads are specifically designed
5    *not* to have the quality that the Court earlier thinks important, of being "subject to
6    the exercise of political oversight and shar[ing] the President's accountability to
7    the people,"—namely, independent regulatory agencies such as the Federal Trade
8    Commission and the Securities and Exchange Commission. Indeed, lest any
9    conceivable improbability be excluded, the Court even reserves the right to
10   consider as a "Department" an entity that is not headed by an officer of the United
11   States—the Federal Reserve Bank of St. Louis, whose president is appointed in
12   none of the manners constitutionally permitted for federal officers, but rather by a
13   Board of Directors, two-thirds of whom are elected by regional banks,. It is as
14   impossible to respond to this random argumentation as it is to derive a
15   comprehensible theory of the appointments power from it. I shall address,
16   therefore, what was petitioners' point, what I originally took to be the point of the
17   Court's opinion, and what is the only trace of a flesh-and-blood point that subsists:
18   the proposition that "Department" means "Cabinet-level agency."

19   There is no basis in text or precedent for this position. The term "Cabinet" does not
20   appear in the Constitution, the Founders having rejected proposals to create a
21   Cabinet-like entity. The existence of a Cabinet, its membership, and its
22   prerogatives (except to the extent the Twenty-fifth Amendment speaks to them),
23   are entirely matters of Presidential discretion. Nor does any of our cases hold that
24   "the Heads of Departments" are Cabinet members. * * *

25                                          * * *

26   * * * [T]here is no reason, in text, judicial decision, history, or policy, to limit the
27   phrase "the Heads of Departments" in the Appointments Clause to those officials
28   who are members of the President's Cabinet. I would give the term its ordinary
29   meaning, something which Congress has apparently been doing for decades
30   without complaint. As an American dictionary roughly contemporaneous with
31   adoption of the Appointments Clause provided, and as remains the case, a
32   department is "[a] separate allotment or part of business; a distinct province, in
33   which a class of duties are allotted to a particular person. . . ." 1 N. Webster,
34   American Dictionary 58 (1828). I readily acknowledge that applying this word to
35   an entity such as the Tax Court would have seemed strange to the Founders, as it
36   continues to seem strange to modern ears. But that is only because the Founders
37   did not envision that an independent establishment of such small size and
38   specialized function would be created. They chose the word "Department,"
39   however, not to connote size or function (much less Cabinet status), but separate
40   organization—a connotation that still endures even in colloquial usage today ("that
41   is not my department"). The Constitution is clear, I think, about the chain of
42   appointment and supervision that it envisions: principal officers could be
43   permitted by law to appoint their subordinates. That should subsist, however much
44   the nature of federal business or of federal organizational structure may alter.

I must confess that, in the case of the Tax Court, as with some other independent establishments (notably, the so-called "independent regulatory agencies" such as the FCC and the Federal Trade Commission) permitting appointment of inferior officers by the agency head may not ensure the high degree of insulation from congressional control that was the purpose of the appointments scheme elaborated in the Constitution. That is a consequence of our decision in *Humphrey's Executor v. United States*, 295 U.S. 602 (1935), which approved congressional restriction upon arbitrary dismissal of the heads of such agencies by the President, a scheme avowedly designed to made such agencies less accountable to him, and hence he less responsible for them. Depending upon how broadly one reads the President's power to dismiss "for cause," it may be that he has no control over the appointment of inferior officers in such agencies; and if those agencies are publicly regarded as beyond his control—a "headless Fourth Branch"—he may have less incentive to care about such appointments. It could be argued, then, that much of the *raison d'etre* for permitting appointive power to be lodged in "Heads of Departments" does not exist with respect to the heads of *these* agencies, because they, in fact, will not be shored up by the President, and are thus not resistant to congressional pressures. That is a reasonable position—though I tend to the view that adjusting the remainder of the Constitution to compensate for *Humphrey's Executor* is a fruitless endeavor. But, in any event, it is not a reasonable position that supports the Court's decision today—both because a "Court of Law" artificially defined as the Court defines it is even less resistant to those pressures, and because the distinction between those agencies that are subject to full Presidential control and those that are not is entirely unrelated to the distinction between Cabinet agencies and non-Cabinet agencies, and to all the other distinctions that the Court successively embraces. (The Central Intelligence Agency and the Environmental Protection Agency, for example, though not Cabinet agencies or components of Cabinet agencies, are not "independent" agencies in the sense of independence from Presidential control.)

In sum, whatever may be the distorting effects of later innovations that this Court has approved, considering the Chief Judge of the Tax Court to be the head of a department seems to me the only reasonable construction of Article II, § 2.

\* \* \*

# D. Agencies and Due Process

The Due Process Clause of the Fifth Amendment provides that "[n]o person shall . . . be deprived of life, liberty, or property, without due process of law." The Fifth Amendment applies to the national government; the Due Process of Clause of the Fourteenth Amendment guarantees the same right as against the states. Agencies are depriving people of things all the time: denying their claims for disability benefits or asylum; determining that they owe back taxes to the United States;

preventing them from building on their property because it contains protected wetlands. What kinds of protections does the due process clause offer?

In the following materials, I break this up into, depending on how you count, four or five subsidiary questions:

1.  what triggers due process protections?
    a.  what kinds of **decisions** trigger due process protections?
    b.  what kinds of **interests** are protected by due process?
2.  how do we determine how much process is due?
3.  when must the process be provided?
4.  what kind of decision maker are you entitled to?

## 1. Scope of Application

When are you entitled to due process at all? Agencies have come up with an extraordinary variety of ways to affect people adversely, and they don't always cash out neatly into a deprivation of life, liberty, or property. Which of these implicate our rights to due process at all? In other words, what is the scope of the due process protection, as it applies to agencies?

There are two different aspects to this scope question. The first is, what kinds of decisions trigger due process protections? No one would claim she is entitled to an individual hearing in front of Congress before Congress passes a law that affects her directly—for instance, by changing an income tax rate applicable to her. But surely you are entitled to a hearing of some sort, at some point, if you dispute what the government says you owe in taxes. What's the difference? And how does this apply to agencies? We see the Supreme Court attempt to answer these questions in a pair of very old cases, *Londoner* and *Bimetallic*.

The other question is, what kinds of interests are protected by due process? If the government takes my property, that clearly fits the bill. But what about if the government takes my job, or damages my reputation? The cases on this topic track the evolution of the Supreme Court's thinking on how to handle these questions.

Note that some of these cases involve actions by state agencies. Because states are also subject to a due process guarantee, the analysis for states and the federal government is the same.

### a. <u>Actions that Trigger Due Process Protections</u>

## Londoner v. Denver

210 U.S. 373 (1908)

June 1, 1908

1    MR. JUSTICE MOODY delivered the opinion of the court:

2    The plaintiffs in error began this proceeding in a state court of Colorado to relieve
3    lands owned by them from an assessment of a tax for the cost of paving a street
4    upon which the lands abutted. The relief sought was granted by the trial court, but
5    its action was reversed by the Supreme Court of the State, which ordered judgment
6    for the defendants. The case is here on writ of error. The Supreme Court held that
7    the tax was assessed in conformity with the Constitution and laws of the State, and
8    its decision of that question is conclusive.

9                                    * * *

10   The tax complained of was assessed under the provisions of the charter of the city
11   of Denver, which confers upon the city the power to make local improvements and
12   to assess the cost upon property specially benefited. It does not seem necessary to
13   set forth fully the elaborate provisions of the charter regulating the exercise of this
14   power, except where they call for special examination. The board of public works,
15   upon the petition of a majority of the owners of the frontage to be assessed, may
16   order the paving of a street. The board must, however, first adopt specifications,
17   mark out a district of assessment, cause a map to be made and an estimate of the
18   cost, with the approximate amount to be assessed upon each lot of land. Before
19   action, notice by publication and an opportunity to be heard to any person
20   interested must be given by the board.

21   The board may then order the improvement, but must recommend to the city
22   council a form of ordinance authorizing it, and establishing an assessment district,
23   which is not amendable by the council. The council may then, in its discretion, pass
24   or refuse to pass the ordinance. If the ordinance is passed, the contract for the work
25   is made by the mayor. The charter provides that "the finding of the city council, by
26   ordinance, that any improvements provided for in this article were duly ordered
27   after notice duly given, or that a petition or remonstrance was or was not filed as
28   above provided, or was or was not subscribed by the required number of owners
29   aforesaid, shall be conclusive in every court or other tribunal." The charter then
30   provides for the assessment of the cost in the following sections:

31       "Sec. 29. Upon completion of any local improvement, or, in the case of
32       sewers, upon completion from time to time of any part or parts thereof,
33       affording complete drainage for any part or parts of the district, and
34       acceptance thereof by the board of public works, or whenever the total cost
35       of any such improvement, or of any such part or parts of any sewer, can be
36       definitely ascertained, the board of public works shall prepare a statement
37       therein, showing the whole cost of the improvement, or such parts thereof,
38       including six per cent additional for costs of collection and other
39       incidentals, and interest to the next succeeding date upon which general
40       taxes, or the first instalment thereof, are, by the laws of this state, made
41       payable; and apportioning the same upon each lot or tract of land to be

1      assessed for the same, as hereinabove provided; and shall cause the same
2      to be certified by the president and filed in the office of the city clerk.

3      "Sec. 30. The city clerk shall thereupon, by advertisement for ten days in
4      some newspaper of general circulation, published in the city of Denver,
5      notify the owners of the real estate to be assessed that said improvements
6      have been, or are about to be, completed and accepted, therein specifying
7      the whole cost of the improvements and the share so apportioned to each
8      lot or tract of land; and that any complaints or objections that may be made
9      in writing, by the owners, to the city council and filed with the city clerk
10     within thirty days from the first publication of such notice, will be heard
11     and determined by the city council before the passage of any ordinance
12     assessing the cost of said improvements.

13     "Sec. 31. After the period specified in said notice the city council, sitting as
14     a board of equalization, shall hear and determine all such complaints and
15     objections, and may recommend to the board of public works any
16     modification of the apportionments made by said board; the board may
17     thereupon make such modifications and changes as to them may seem
18     equitable and just, or may confirm the first apportionment, and shall notify
19     the city council of their final decision; and the city council shall thereupon
20     by ordinance assess the cost of said improvements against all the real estate
21     in said district respectively in the proportions above mentioned."

22 It appears from the charter that, in the execution of the power to make local
23 improvements and assess the cost upon the property specially benefited, the main
24 steps to be taken by the city authorities are plainly marked and separated: 1. The
25 board of public works must transmit to the city council a resolution ordering the
26 work to be done and the form of an ordinance authorizing it and creating an
27 assessment district. This it can do only upon certain conditions, one of which is
28 that there shall first be filed a petition asking the improvement, signed by the
29 owners of the majority of the frontage to be assessed. 2. The passage of that
30 ordinance by the city council, which is given authority to determine conclusively
31 whether the action of the board was duly taken. 3. The assessment of the cost upon
32 the landowners after due notice and opportunity for hearing.

33                                  \* \* \*

34 The fifth assignment, though general, vague, and obscure, fairly raises, we think,
35 the question whether the assessment was made without notice and opportunity for
36 hearing to those affected by it, thereby denying to them due process of law. The
37 trial court found as a fact that no opportunity for hearing was afforded, and the
38 supreme court did not disturb this finding. The record discloses what was actually
39 done, and there seems to be no dispute about it. After the improvement was
40 completed, the board of public works, in compliance with § 29 of the charter,
41 certified to the city clerk a statement of the cost, and an apportionment of it to the
42 lots of land to be assessed. Thereupon the city clerk, in compliance with § 30,

1    published a notice, stating, inter alia, that the written complaints or objections of
2    the owners, if filed within thirty days, would be "heard and determined by the city
3    council before the passage of any ordinance assessing the cost." Those interested,
4    therefore, were informed that if they reduced their complaints and objections to
5    writing, and filed them within thirty days, those complaints and objections would
6    be heard, and would be heard before any assessment was made. * * * Resting upon
7    the assurance that they would be heard, the plaintiffs in error filed within the thirty
8    days the following paper:

9    "Denver, Colorado, January 13, 1900.

10    "To the Honorable Board of Public Works and the Honorable Mayor and
11    City Council of the City of Denver:

12    "The undersigned, by Joshua Grozier, their attorney, do hereby most
13    earnestly and strenuously protest and object to the passage of the
14    contemplated or any assessing ordinance against the property in Eighth
15    avenue paving district No. 1, so called, for each of the following reasons, to
16    wit:

17    "1st. That said assessment and all and each of the proceedings leading up
18    to the same were and are illegal, voidable, and void; and the attempted
19    assessment, if made, will be void and uncollectible.

20    "2d. That said assessment and the cost of said pretended improvement
21    should be collected, if at all, as a general tax against the city at large, and
22    not as a special assessment.

23    "3d. That property in said city not assessed is benefited by the said
24    pretended improvement, and certain property assessed is not benefited by
25    said pretended improvement, and other property assessed is not benefited
26    by said pretended improvement to the extent of the assessment; that the
27    individual pieces of property in said district are not benefited to the extent
28    assessed against them and each of them respectively; that the assessment
29    is arbitrary, and property assessed in an equal amount is not benefited
30    equally; that the boundaries of said pretended district were arbitrarily
31    created without regard to the benefits or any other method of assessment
32    known to law; that said assessment is outrageously large.

33    * * *

34    "8th. Because the city had no jurisdiction in the premises. No petition
35    subscribed by the owners of a majority of the frontage in the district to be
36    assessed for said improvements was ever obtained or presented.

37    * * *

"Wherefore, because of the foregoing and numerous other good and sufficient reasons, the undersigned object and protest against the passage of the said proposed assessing ordinance."

This certainly was a complaint against an objection to the proposed assessment. Instead of affording the plaintiffs in error an opportunity to be heard upon its allegations, the city council, without notice to them, met as a board of equalization, not in a stated, but in a specially called, session, and, without any hearing, adopted the following resolution:

"Whereas, complaints have been filed by the various persons and firms as the owners of real estate included within the Eighth Avenue paving district No. 1, of the city of Denver, against the proposed assessments on said property for the cost of said paving, * * * and

"Whereas, no complaint or objection has been filed or made against the apportionment of said assessment made by the board of public works of the city of Denver, but the complaints and objections filed deny wholly the right of the city to assess any district or portion of the assessable property of the city of Denver; therefore, be it

"Resolved, by the city council of the city of Denver, sitting as a board of equalization, that the apportionments of said assessment made by said board of public works be, and the same are hereby, confirmed and approved."

Subsequently, without further notice or hearing, the city council enacted the ordinance of assessment whose validity is to be determined in this case. The facts out of which the question on this assignment arises may be compressed into small compass. The first step in the assessment proceedings was by the certificate of the board of public works of the cost of the improvement and a preliminary apportionment of it. The last step was the enactment of the assessment ordinance. From beginning to end of the proceedings the landowners, although allowed to formulate and file complaints and objections, were not afforded an opportunity to be heard upon them. Upon these facts, was there a denial by the state of the due process of law guaranteed by the Fourteenth Amendment to the Constitution of the United States?

In the assessment, apportionment, and collection of taxes upon property within their jurisdiction, the Constitution of the United States imposes few restrictions upon the states. In the enforcement of such restrictions as the Constitution does impose, this court has regarded substance, and not form. But where the legislature of a State, instead of fixing the tax itself, commits to some subordinate body the duty of determining whether, in what amount, and upon whom it shall be levied, and of making its assessment and apportionment, due process of law requires that, at some stage of the proceedings, before the tax becomes irrevocably fixed, the taxpayer shall have an opportunity to be heard, of which he must have notice, either personal, by publication, or by a law fixing the time and place of the hearing.

169

1  It must be remembered that the law of Colorado denies the landowner the right to
2  object in the courts to the assessment, upon the ground that the objections are
3  cognizable only by the board of equalization.

4  If it is enough that, under such circumstances, an opportunity is given to submit in
5  writing all objections to and complaints of the tax to the board, then there was a
6  hearing afforded in the case at bar. But we think that something more than that,
7  even in proceedings for taxation, is required by due process of law. Many
8  requirements essential in strictly judicial proceedings may be dispensed with in
9  proceedings of this nature. But even here a hearing, in its very essence, demands
10 that he who is entitled to it shall have the right to support his allegations by
11 argument, however brief: and, if need be, by proof, however informal. It is
12 apparent that such a hearing was denied to the plaintiffs in error. The denial was
13 by the city council, which, while acting as a board of equalization, represents the
14 state. The assessment was therefore void, and the plaintiffs in error were entitled
15 to a decree discharging their lands from a lien on account of it. * * *

16 Judgment reversed.

17 MR. CHIEF JUSTICE FULLER, dissenting. [Omitted.]

18 MR. JUSTICE HOLMES, dissenting. [Omitted.]

19

20 **Bi-Metallic Investment Company v. State Board of Equalization**

21 239 U.S. 441 (1915)

22 December 20, 1915

23 MR. JUSTICE HOLMES delivered the opinion of the court:

24 This is a suit to enjoin the State Board of Equalization and the Colorado Tax
25 Commission from putting in force, and the defendant Pitcher as assessor of Denver
26 from obeying, an order of the boards, increasing the valuation of all taxable
27 property in Denver forty per cent. The order was sustained and the suit directed to
28 be dismissed by the supreme court of the state. The plaintiff is the owner of real
29 estate in Denver, and brings the case here on the ground that it was given no
30 opportunity to be heard, and that therefore its property will be taken without due
31 process of law, contrary to the Fourteenth Amendment of the Constitution of the
32 United States. That is the only question with which we have to deal. There are
33 suggestions on the one side that the construction of the state Constitution and laws
34 was an unwarranted surprise, and on the other, that the decision might have been
35 placed, although it was not, on the ground that there was an adequate remedy at
36 law. With these suggestions we have nothing to do. They are matters purely of state
37 law. The answer to the former needs no amplification; that to the latter is that the
38 allowance of equitable relief is a question of state policy, and that as the Supreme
39 Court of the State treated the merits as legitimately before it, we are not to

1 speculate whether it might or might not have thrown out the suit upon the
2 preliminary ground.

3 For the purposes of decision we assume that the constitutional question is
4 presented in the baldest way,—that neither the plaintiff nor the assessor of Denver,
5 who presents a brief on the plaintiff's side, nor any representative of the city and
6 county, was given an opportunity to be heard, other than such as they may have
7 had by reason of the fact that the time of meeting of the boards is fixed by law. On
8 this assumption it is obvious that injustice may be suffered if some property in the
9 county already has been valued at its full worth. But if certain property has been
10 valued at a rate different from that generally prevailing in the county, the owner
11 has had his opportunity to protest and appeal as usual in our system of taxation,
12 so that it must be assumed that the property owners in the county all stand alike.
13 The question, then, is whether all individuals have a constitutional right to be
14 heard before a matter can be decided in which all are equally concerned,—here, for
15 instance, before a superior board decides that the local taxing officers have adopted
16 a system of undervaluation throughout a county, as notoriously often has been the
17 case. The answer of this court in the *State Railroad Tax Cases*, 92 U.S. 575, at least,
18 as to any further notice, was that it was hard to believe that the proposition was
19 seriously made.

20 Where a rule of conduct applies to more than a few people, it is impracticable that
21 everyone should have a direct voice in its adoption. The Constitution does not
22 require all public acts to be done in town meeting or an assembly of the whole.
23 General statutes within the state power are passed that affect the person or
24 property of individuals, sometimes to the point of ruin, without giving them a
25 chance to be heard. Their rights are protected in the only way that they can be in a
26 complex society, by their power, immediate or remote, over those who make the
27 rule. If the result in this case had been reached, as it might have been by the state's
28 doubling the rate of taxation, no one would suggest that the Fourteenth
29 Amendment was violated unless every person affected had been allowed an
30 opportunity to raise his voice against it before the body entrusted by the state
31 constitution with the power. In considering this case in this court we must assume
32 that the proper state machinery has been used, and the question is whether, if the
33 state Constitution had declared that Denver had been undervalued as compared
34 with the rest of the state, and had decreed that for the current year the valuation
35 should be forty per cent higher, the objection now urged could prevail. It appears
36 to us that to put the question is to answer it. There must be a limit to individual
37 argument in such matters if government is to go on. In *Londoner v. Denver*, 210
38 U.S. 373, 385, a local board had to determine 'whether, in what amount, and upon
39 whom' a tax for paving a street should be levied for special benefits. A relatively
40 small number of persons was concerned, who were exceptionally affected, in each
41 case upon individual grounds, and it was held that they had a right to a hearing.
42 But that decision is far from reaching a general determination dealing only with
43 the principle upon which all the assessments in a county had been laid.

44 Judgment affirmed.

1

2     b.  Interests Protected by the Due Process Clause

3  **Joint Anti-Fascist Refugee Committee v. McGrath**

4  341 U.S. 123 (1951)

5  April 30, 1951

6  MR. JUSTICE BURTON announced the judgment of the Court and delivered the
7  following opinion, in which MR. JUSTICE DOUGLAS joins.

8  In each of these cases the same issue is raised by the dismissal of a complaint for
9  its failure to state a claim upon which relief can be granted. That issue is whether,
10 in the face of the facts alleged in the complaint and therefore admitted by the
11 motion to dismiss, the Attorney General of the United States has authority to
12 include the complaining organization in a list of organizations designated by him
13 as Communist and furnished by him to the Loyalty Review Board of the United
14 States Civil Service Commission. He claims to derive authority to do this from the
15 following provisions in Part III, § 3, of Executive Order No. 9835, issued by the
16 President, March 21, 1947:

17  "PART III—RESPONSIBILITIES OF THE CIVIL SERVICE COMMISSION

18  "3. The Loyalty Review Board shall currently be furnished by the
19  Department of Justice the name of each foreign or domestic organization,
20  association, movement, group or combination of persons which the
21  Attorney General, after appropriate investigation and determination,
22  designates as totalitarian, fascist, communist or subversive, or as having
23  adopted a policy of advocating or approving the commission of acts of force
24  or violence to deny others their rights under the Constitution of the United
25  States, or as seeking to alter the form of government of the United States
26  by unconstitutional means.

27  "a. The Loyalty Review Board shall disseminate such information to all
28  departments and agencies."

29 The respective complaints describe the complaining organizations as engaged in
30 charitable or civic activities or in the business of fraternal insurance. Each implies
31 an attitude of cooperation and helpfulness, rather than one of hostility or
32 disloyalty, on the part of the organization toward the United States. Two of the
33 complaints deny expressly that the organization is within any classification
34 specified in Part III, § 3, of the order.

35                               * * *

36 If, upon the allegations in any of these complaints, it had appeared that the acts of
37 the respondents, from which relief was sought, were authorized by the President
38 under his Executive Order No. 9835, the case would have bristled with

172

1    constitutional issues. On that basis, the complaint would have raised questions as
2    to the justiciability and merit of claims based upon the First, Fifth, Ninth, and
3    Tenth Amendments to the Constitution. It is our obligation, however, not to reach
4    those issues unless the allegations before us squarely present them.

5    The Executive Order contains no express or implied attempt to confer power on
6    anyone to act arbitrarily or capriciously—even assuming a constitutional power to
7    do so. The order includes in the purposes of the President's program not only the
8    protection of the United States against disloyal employees, but the "equal
9    protection" of loyal employees against unfounded accusations of disloyalty. * * *
10   Obviously it would be contrary to the purpose of that order to place on a list to be
11   disseminated under the Loyalty Program any designation of an organization that
12   was patently arbitrary and contrary to the uncontroverted material facts. * * *

13                                         * * *

14   For these reasons, we find it necessary to reverse the judgments of the Court of
15   Appeals in the respective cases, and to remand each case to the District Court with
16   instructions to deny the respondents' motion that the complaint be dismissed for
17   failure to state a claim upon which relief can be granted.

18   Reversed and remanded.

19   MR. JUSTICE CLARK took no part in the consideration or decision of any of these
20   cases.

21   MR. JUSTICE BLACK, concurring. [Omitted.]

22   MR. JUSTICE FRANKFURTER, concurring.

23   The more issues of law are inescapably entangled in political controversies,
24   especially those that touch the passions of the day, the more the Court is under
25   duty to dispose of a controversy within the narrowest confines that intellectual
26   integrity permits. And so I sympathize with the endeavor of my brother BURTON
27   to decide these cases on a ground as limited as that which has commended itself to
28   him. Unfortunately, I am unable to read the pleadings as he does. Therefore, I must
29   face up to larger issues. * * *

30                                         * * *

31   * * * Petitioners are organizations which, on the face of the record, are engaged
32   solely in charitable or insurance activities. They have been designated
33   "communist" by the Attorney General of the United States. This designation
34   imposes no legal sanction on these organizations other than that it serves as
35   evidence in ridding the Government of persons reasonably suspected of disloyalty.
36   It would be blindness, however, not to recognize that, in the conditions of our time,
37   such designation drastically restricts the organizations, if it does not proscribe
38   them. Potential members, contributors or beneficiaries of listed organizations may
39   well be influenced by use of the designation, for instance, as ground for rejection

1 of applications for commissions in the armed forces or for permits for meetings in
2 the auditoriums of public housing projects. Yet designation has been made without
3 notice, without disclosure of any reasons justifying it, without opportunity to meet
4 the undisclosed evidence or suspicion on which designation may have been based,
5 and without opportunity to establish affirmatively that the aims and acts of the
6 organization are innocent. It is claimed that thus to maim or decapitate, on the
7 mere say-so of the Attorney General, an organization to all outward-seeming
8 engaged in lawful objectives is so devoid of fundamental fairness as to offend the
9 Due Process Clause of the Fifth Amendment.

10 Fairness of procedure is "due process in the primary sense." *Brinkerhoff-Faris Co.*
11 *v. Hill*, 281 U.S. 673, 681. It is ingrained in our national traditions, and is designed
12 to maintain them. In a variety of situations, the Court has enforced this
13 requirement by checking attempts of executives, legislatures, and lower courts to
14 disregard the deep-rooted demands of fair play enshrined in the Constitution. * * *

15 The requirement of "due process" is not a fair-weather or timid assurance. It must
16 be respected in periods of calm and in times of trouble; it protects aliens as well as
17 citizens. But "due process," unlike some legal rules, is not a technical conception
18 with a fixed content unrelated to time, place and circumstances. Expressing, as it
19 does in its ultimate analysis, respect enforced by law for that feeling of just
20 treatment which has been evolved through centuries of Anglo-American
21 constitutional history and civilization, "due process" cannot be imprisoned within
22 the treacherous limits of any formula. Representing a profound attitude of fairness
23 between man and man, and more particularly between the individual and
24 government, "due process" is compounded of history, reason, the past course of
25 decisions, and stout confidence in the strength of the democratic faith which we
26 profess. Due process is not a mechanical instrument. It is not a yardstick. It is a
27 process. It is a delicate process of adjustment inescapably involving the exercise of
28 judgment by those whom the Constitution entrusted with the unfolding of the
29 process.

30                                          * * *

31 It may fairly be said that, barring only occasional and temporary lapses, this Court
32 has not sought unduly to confine those who have the responsibility of governing by
33 giving the great concept of due process doctrinaire scope. The Court has responded
34 to the infinite variety and perplexity of the tasks of government by recognizing that
35 what is unfair in one situation may be fair in another. Whether the *ex parte*
36 procedure to which the petitioners were subjected duly observed "the rudiments of
37 fair play", *Chicago, M. & St. P. R. Co. v. Polt*, 232 U.S. 165, 168, cannot, therefore,
38 be tested by mere generalities or sentiments abstractly appealing. The precise
39 nature of the interest that has been adversely affected, the manner in which this
40 was done, the reasons for doing it, the available alternatives to the procedure that
41 was followed, the protection implicit in the office of the functionary whose conduct
42 is challenged, the balance of hurt complained of and good accomplished—these are
43 some of the considerations that must enter into the judicial judgment.

1   Applying them to the immediate situation, we note that publicly designating an
2   organization as within the proscribed categories of the Loyalty Order does not
3   directly deprive anyone of liberty or property. Weight must also be given to the fact
4   that such designation is not made by a minor official, but by the highest law officer
5   of the Government. Again, it is fair to emphasize that the individual's interest is
6   here to be weighed against a claim of the greatest of all public interests, that of
7   national security. In striking the balance, the relevant considerations must be
8   fairly, which means coolly, weighed with due regard to the fact that this Court is
9   not exercising a primary judgment, but is sitting in judgment upon those who also
10   have taken the oath to observe the Constitution and who have the responsibility
11   for carrying on government.

12   But the significance we attach to general principles may turn the scale when
13   competing claims appeal for supremacy. Achievements of our civilization as
14   precious as they were hard won were summarized by MR. JUSTICE BRANDEIS
15   when he wrote that, "in the development of our liberty, insistence upon procedural
16   regularity has been a large factor." It is noteworthy that procedural safeguards
17   constitute the major portion of our Bill of Rights. And so no one now doubts that,
18   in the criminal law, a "person's right to reasonable notice of a charge against him,
19   and an opportunity to be heard in his defense—a right to his day in court—are basic
20   in our system of jurisprudence." "The hearing, moreover, must be a real one, not a
21   sham or a pretense." Nor is there doubt that notice and hearing are prerequisite to
22   due process in civil proceedings. Only the narrowest exceptions, justified by
23   history, become part of the habits of our people or, by obvious necessity, are
24   tolerated.

25   It is against this background of guiding considerations that we must view the rather
26   novel aspects of the situation at hand. * * *

27                                          * * *

28   This Court is not alone in recognizing that the right to be heard before being
29   condemned to suffer grievous loss of any kind, even though it may not involve the
30   stigma and hardships of a criminal conviction, is a principle basic to our society.
31   Regard for this principle has guided Congress and the Executive. Congress has
32   often entrusted, as it may, protection of interests which it has created to
33   administrative agencies, rather than to the courts. But rarely has it authorized such
34   agencies to act without those essential safeguards for fair judgment which in the
35   course of centuries have come to be associated with due process. And when
36   Congress has given an administrative agency discretion to determine its own
37   procedure, the agency has rarely chosen to dispose of the rights of individuals
38   without a hearing, however informal.

39                                          * * *

40   The strength and significance of these considerations—considerations which go to
41   the very ethos of the scheme of our society—give a ready answer to the problem
42   before us. That a hearing has been thought indispensable in so many other

situations, leaving the cases of denial exceptional, does not of itself prove that it must be found essential here. But it does place upon the Attorney General the burden of showing weighty reason for departing in this instance from a rule so deeply imbedded in history and in the demands of justice. Nothing in the Loyalty Order requires him to deny organizations opportunity to present their case. * * *

\* \* \*

We are not here dealing with the grant of Government largess. We have not before us the measured action of Congress, with the pause that is properly engendered when the validity of legislation is assailed. The Attorney General is certainly not immune from the historic requirements of fairness merely because he acts, however conscientiously, in the name of security. Nor does he obtain immunity on the ground that designation is not an "adjudication" or a "regulation" in the conventional use of those terms. Due process is not confined in its scope to the particular forms in which rights have heretofore been found to have been curtailed for want of procedural fairness. Due process is perhaps the most majestic concept in our whole constitutional system. While it contains the garnered wisdom of the past in assuring fundamental justice, it is also a living principle not confined to past instances.

Therefore the petitioners did set forth causes of action which the District Court should have entertained.

MR. JUSTICE DOUGLAS, concurring. [Omitted.]

MR. JUSTICE JACKSON, concurring.

\* \* \*

Ordinary dismissals from government service which violate no fixed tenure concern only the Executive branch, and courts will not review such discretionary action. However, these are not discretionary discharges, but discharges pursuant to an order having force of law. Administrative machinery is publicly set up to comb the whole government service to discharge persons or to declare them ineligible for employment upon an incontestable finding, made without hearing, that some organization is subversive. To be deprived not only of present government employment, but of future opportunity for it, certainly is no small injury when government employment so dominates the field of opportunity.

The fact that one may not have a legal right to get or keep a government post does not mean that he can be adjudged ineligible illegally.

\* \* \*

MR. JUSTICE REED, with whom THE CHIEF JUSTICE and MR. JUSTICE MINTON join, dissenting.

\* \* \*

1   The absence of any provision in the Order or rules for notice to suspected
2   organizations, for hearings with privilege to the organizations to confront
3   witnesses, cross-examine, produce evidence, and have representation of counsel
4   or judicial review of the conclusion reached by the Attorney General is urged by
5   the petitioners as a procedure so fundamentally unfair and restrictive of personal
6   freedoms as to violate the Federal Constitution, specifically the Due Process Clause
7   and the First Amendment. No opportunity was allowed by the Attorney General
8   for petitioners to offer proof of the legality of their purposes or to disprove charges
9   of subversive operations. This is the real gravamen of each complaint, the basis
10  upon which the determination of unconstitutionality is sought.

11                                      * * *

12  Does due process require notice and hearing for the Department of Justice
13  investigation under Executive Order No. 9835, Part III, § 3, note 3, preliminary to
14  listing? As a standard for due process, one cannot do better than to accept as a
15  measure that no one may be deprived of liberty or property without such
16  reasonable notice and hearing as fairness requires. This is my understanding of the
17  meaning of the opinions upon due process cited in the concurring opinions. We
18  are not here concerned with the rightfulness of the extent of participation in the
19  investigations that might be claimed by petitioners. They were given no chance to
20  take part. Their claim is that the listing resulted in a deprivation of liberty or
21  property contrary to the procedure required by the Fifth Amendment.

22  The contention can be answered summarily by saying that there is no deprivation
23  of any property or liberty of any listed organization by the Attorney General's
24  designation. It may be assumed that the listing is hurtful to their prestige,
25  reputation and earning power. It may be such an injury as would entitle
26  organizations to damages in a tort action against persons not protected by
27  privilege. This designation, however, does not prohibit any business of the
28  organizations, subject them to any punishment, or deprive them of liberty of
29  speech or other freedom. The cases relied upon in the briefs and opinions of the
30  majority as requiring notice and hearing before valid action can be taken by
31  administrative officers are where complainant will lose some property or
32  enforceable civil or statutory right by the action taken or proposed. "[A] mere
33  abstract declaration" by an administrator regarding the character of an
34  organization, without the effect of forbidding or compelling conduct on the part of
35  complainant, ought not to be subject to judicial interference. *Rochester Telephone*
36  *Corp. v. United States*, 307 U.S. 125, 129. That is, it does not require notice and
37  hearing.

38  These petitioners are not ordered to do anything, and are not punished for
39  anything. Their position may be analogized to that of persons under grand jury
40  investigation. Such persons have no right to notice by and hearing before a grand
41  jury—only a right to defend the charge at trial. * * *

42                                      * * *

1

## Cafeteria & Restaurant Workers Union v. McElroy

367 U.S. 886 (1961)

June 19, 1961

MR. JUSTICE STEWART delivered the opinion of the Court.

In 1956, the petitioner Rachel Brawner was a short-order cook at a cafeteria operated by her employer, M & M Restaurants, Inc., on the premises of the Naval Gun Factory in the City of Washington. She had worked there for more than six years, and, from her employer's point of view, her record was entirely satisfactory.

The Gun Factory was engaged in designing, producing, and inspecting naval ordnance, including the development of weapons systems of a highly classified nature. Located on property owned by the United States, the installation was under the command of Rear Admiral D. M. Tyree, Superintendent. Access to it was restricted, and guards were posted at all points of entry. Identification badges were issued to persons authorized to enter the premises by the Security Officer, a naval officer subordinate to the Superintendent. In 1956, the Security Officer was Lieutenant Commander H. C. Williams. Rachel Brawner had been issued such a badge.

The cafeteria where she worked was operated by M & M under a contract with the Board of Governors of the Gun Factory. Section 5(b) of the contract provided:

> ". . . In no event shall the Concessionaire engage, or continue to engage, for operations under this Agreement, personnel who"

> * * * *

> "(iii) fail to meet the security requirements or other requirements under applicable regulations of the Activity, as determined by the Security Officer of the Activity."

On November 15, 1956, Mrs. Brawner was required to turn in her identification badge because of Lieutenant Commander Williams' determination that she had failed to meet the security requirements of the installation. The Security Officer's determination was subsequently approved by Admiral Tyree, who cited § 5(b)(iii) of the contract as the basis for his action. At the request of the petitioner Union, which represented the employees at the cafeteria, M & M sought to arrange a meeting with officials of the Gun Factory "for the purpose of a hearing regarding the denial of admittance to the Naval Gun Factory of Rachel Brawner." This request was denied by Admiral Tyree on the ground that such a meeting would "serve no useful purpose."

1 Since the day her identification badge was withdrawn, Mrs. Brawner has not been
2 permitted to enter the Gun Factory. M & M offered to employ her in another
3 restaurant which the company operated in the suburban Washington area, but she
4 refused on the ground that the location was inconvenient.

5 The petitioners brought this action in the District Court against the Secretary of
6 Defense, Admiral Tyree, and Lieutenant Commander Williams, in their individual
7 and official capacities, seeking, among other things, to compel the return to Mrs.
8 Brawner of her identification badge, so that she might be permitted to enter the
9 Gun Factory and resume her former employment. The defendants filed a motion
10 for summary judgment, supported by various affidavits and exhibits. The motion
11 was granted, and the complaint dismissed by the District Court. This judgment was
12 affirmed by the Court of Appeals for the District of Columbia, sitting *en banc*. Four
13 judges dissented. We granted certiorari * * *.

14 As the case comes here, two basic questions are presented. Was the commanding
15 officer of the Gun Factory authorized to deny Rachel Brawner access to the
16 installation in the way he did? If he was so authorized, did his action in excluding
17 her operate to deprive her of any right secured to her by the Constitution?

18 [In Part I, the Court concluded that applicable regulations authorized the
19 commanding officer's denial of Brawner's access to the installation.]

20 * * *

21 II

22 The question remains whether Admiral Tyree's action in summarily denying
23 Rachel Brawner access to the site of her former employment violated the
24 requirements of the Due Process Clause of the Fifth Amendment. This question
25 cannot be answered by easy assertion that, because she had no constitutional right
26 to be there in the first place, she was not deprived of liberty or property by the
27 Superintendent's action. "One may not have a constitutional right to go to Bagdad,
28 but the Government may not prohibit one from going there unless by means
29 consonant with due process of law." *Homer v. Richmond*, 292 F.2d 719, 722. It is
30 the petitioners' claim that due process in this case required that Rachel Brawner
31 be advised of the specific grounds for her exclusion and be accorded a hearing at
32 which she might refute them. We are satisfied, however, that, under the
33 circumstances of this case, such a procedure was not constitutionally required.

34 The Fifth Amendment does not require a trial-type hearing in every conceivable
35 case of government impairment of private interest. "For, though 'due process of
36 law' generally implies and includes *actor, reus, judex*, regular allegations,
37 opportunity to answer, and a trial according to some settled course of judicial
38 proceedings, ... yet, this is not universally true." *Murray's Lessee v. Hoboken
39 Land and Improvement Co.*, 59 U.S. 272, 280 (1856). The very nature of due
40 process negates any concept of inflexible procedures universally applicable to
41 every imaginable situation. * * *

1 As these and other cases make clear, consideration of what procedures due process
2 may require under any given set of circumstances must begin with a determination
3 of the precise nature of the government function involved, as well as of the private
4 interest that has been affected by governmental action. Where it has been possible
5 to characterize that private interest (perhaps in oversimplification) as a mere
6 privilege subject to the Executive's plenary power, it has traditionally been held
7 that notice and hearing are not constitutionally required.

8 What, then, was the private interest affected by Admiral Tyree's action in the
9 present case? It most assuredly was not the right to follow a chosen trade or
10 profession. Rachel Brawner remained entirely free to obtain employment as a
11 short-order cook or to get any other job, either with M & M or with any other
12 employer. All that was denied her was the opportunity to work at one isolated and
13 specific military installation.

14 Moreover, the governmental function operating here was not the power to regulate
15 or license, as lawmaker, an entire trade or profession, or to control an entire branch
16 of private business, but, rather, as proprietor, to manage the internal operation of
17 an important federal military establishment. In that proprietary military capacity,
18 the Federal Government, as has been pointed out, has traditionally exercised
19 unfettered control.

20 * * * The Court has consistently recognized that an interest closely analogous to
21 Rachel Brawner's, the interest of a government employee in retaining his job, can
22 be summarily denied. It has become a settled principle that government
23 employment, in the absence of legislation, can be revoked at the will of the
24 appointing officer. * * *

25                                        * * *

26 Nothing that was said or decided in [prior cases] would lead to the conclusion that
27 Rachel Brawner could not be denied access to the Gun Factory without notice and
28 an opportunity to be heard. Those cases demonstrate only that the state and federal
29 governments, even in the exercise of their internal operations, do not
30 constitutionally have the complete freedom of action enjoyed by a private
31 employer. But to acknowledge that there exist constitutional restraints upon state
32 and federal governments in dealing with their employees is not to say that all such
33 employees have a constitutional right to notice and a hearing before they can be
34 removed. We may assume that Rachel Brawner could not constitutionally have
35 been excluded from the Gun Factory if the announced grounds for her exclusion
36 had been patently arbitrary or discriminatory—that she could not have been kept
37 out because she was a Democrat or a Methodist. It does not follow, however, that
38 she was entitled to notice and a hearing when the reason advanced for her
39 exclusion was, as here, entirely rational and in accord with the contract with M &
40 M.

41 Finally, it is to be noted that this is not a case where government action has
42 operated to bestow a badge of disloyalty or infamy, with an attendant foreclosure
180

1  from other employment opportunity. All this record shows is that, in the opinion
2  of the Security Officer of the Gun Factory, concurred in by the Superintendent,
3  Rachel Brawner failed to meet the particular security requirements of that specific
4  military installation. There is nothing to indicate that this determination would in
5  any way impair Rachel Brawner's employment opportunities anywhere else. * * *

6  For these reasons, we conclude that the Due Process Clause of the Fifth
7  Amendment was not violated in this case.

8  MR. JUSTICE BRENNAN, with whom THE CHIEF JUSTICE, MR. JUSTICE
9  BLACK and MR. JUSTICE DOUGLAS join, dissenting.

10                                    * * *

11  I read the Court's opinion to acknowledge that petitioner's status as an employee
12  at the Gun Factory was an interest of sufficient definiteness to be protected by the
13  Federal Constitution from some kinds of governmental injury. Indeed, this
14  acknowledgment seems compelled by our cases. In other words, if petitioner
15  Brawner's badge had been lifted avowedly on grounds of her race, religion, or
16  political opinions, the Court would concede that some constitutionally protected
17  interest—whether "liberty" or "property" it is unnecessary to state—had been
18  injured. But, as the Court says, there has been no such open discrimination here.
19  The expressed ground of exclusion was the obscuring formulation that petitioner
20  failed to meet the "security requirements" of the naval installation where she
21  worked. I assume for present purposes that separation as a "security risk," if the
22  charge is properly established, is not unconstitutional. But the Court goes beyond
23  that. It holds that the mere assertion by government that exclusion is for a valid
24  reason forecloses further inquiry. That is, unless the government official is foolish
25  enough to admit what he is doing—and few will be so foolish after today's
26  decision—he may employ "security requirements" as a blind behind which to
27  dismiss at will for the most discriminatory of causes.

28  Such a result in effect nullifies the substantive right—not to be arbitrarily injured
29  by Government—which the Court purports to recognize. What sort of right is it
30  which enjoys absolutely no procedural protection? I do not mean to imply that
31  petitioner could not have been excluded from the installation without the full
32  procedural panoply of first having been subjected to a trial, with cross-examination
33  and confrontation of accusers, and proof of guilt beyond a reasonable doubt. I need
34  not go so far in this case. For, under today's holding, petitioner is entitled to no
35  process at all. She is not told what she did wrong; she is not given a chance to
36  defend herself. She may be the victim of the basest calumny, perhaps even the
37  caprice of the government officials in whose power her status rested completely. In
38  such a case, I cannot believe that she is not entitled to some procedures. "[T]he
39  right to be heard before being condemned to suffer grievous loss of any kind, even
40  though it may not involve the stigma and hardships of a criminal conviction, is a
41  principle basic to our society." *Joint Anti-Fascist Refugee Committee v. McGrath*,
42  341 U.S. 123, 168 (concurring opinion). In sum, the Court holds that petitioner has

a right not to have her identification badge taken away for an "arbitrary" reason, but no right to be told in detail what the reason is, or to defend her own innocence, in order to show, perhaps, that the true reason for deprivation was one forbidden by the Constitution. That is an internal contradiction to which I cannot subscribe.

One further circumstance makes this particularly a case where procedural requirements of fairness are essential. Petitioner was not simply excluded from the base summarily, without a notice and chance to defend herself. She was excluded as a "security risk"—that designation most odious in our times. The Court consoles itself with the speculation that she may have been merely garrulous, or careless with her identification badge, and indeed she might, although she will never find out. But, in the common understanding of the public with whom petitioner must hereafter live and work, the term "security risk" carries a much more sinister meaning. It is far more likely to be taken as an accusation of communism or disloyalty than imputation of some small personal fault. Perhaps the Government has reasons for lumping such a multitude of sins under a misleading term. But it ought not to affix a "badge of infamy," *Wieman v. Updegraff*, 344 U.S. 183, 191 (1952), to a person without some statement of charges and some opportunity to speak in reply.

It may be, of course, that petitioner was justly excluded from the Gun Factory. But, in my view, it is fundamentally unfair, and therefore violative of the Due Process Clause of the Fifth Amendment, to deprive her of a valuable relationship so summarily.

## Board of Regents of State Colleges v. Roth

408 U.S. 564 (1972)

June 29, 1972

MR. JUSTICE STEWART delivered the opinion of the Court.

In 1968, the respondent, David Roth, was hired for his first teaching job as assistant professor of political science at Wisconsin State University-Oshkosh. He was hired for a fixed term of one academic year. The notice of his faculty appointment specified that his employment would begin on September 1, 1968, and would end on June 30, 1969. The respondent completed that term. But he was informed that he would not be rehired for the next academic year.

The respondent had no tenure rights to continued employment. Under Wisconsin statutory law, a state university teacher can acquire tenure as a "permanent" employee only after four years of year-to-year employment. Having acquired tenure, a teacher is entitled to continued employment "during efficiency and good behavior." A relatively new teacher without tenure, however, is, under Wisconsin law, entitled to nothing beyond his one-year appointment. There are no statutory or administrative standards defining eligibility for re-employment. State law thus clearly leaves the decision whether to rehire a nontenured teacher for another year to the unfettered discretion of university officials.

The procedural protection afforded a Wisconsin State University teacher before he is separated from the University corresponds to his job security. As a matter of statutory law, a tenured teacher cannot be "discharged except for cause upon written charges" and pursuant to certain procedures. A nontenured teacher, similarly, is protected to some extent *during* his one-year term. Rules promulgated by the Board of Regents provide that a nontenured teacher "dismissed" before the end of the year may have some opportunity for review of the "dismissal." But the Rules provide no real protection for a nontenured teacher who simply is not reemployed for the next year. He must be informed by February 1 "concerning retention or non-retention for the ensuing year." But "no reason for non-retention need be given. No review or appeal is provided in such case."

In conformance with these Rules, the President of Wisconsin State University-Oshkosh informed the respondent before February 1, 1969, that he would not be rehired for the 1969-1970 academic year. He gave the respondent no reason for the decision and no opportunity to challenge it at any sort of hearing.

The respondent then brought this action in Federal District Court alleging that the decision not to rehire him for the next year infringed his Fourteenth Amendment rights. He attacked the decision both in substance and procedure. First, he alleged that the true reason for the decision was to punish him for certain statements critical of the University administration, and that it therefore violated his right to freedom of speech. Second, he alleged that the failure of University officials to give him notice of any reason for non-retention and an opportunity for a hearing violated his right, to procedural due process of law.

* * * The only question presented to us at this stage in the case is whether the respondent had a constitutional right to a statement of reasons and a hearing on the University's decision not to rehire him for another year. We hold that he did not.

I

The requirements of procedural due process apply only to the deprivation of interests encompassed by the Fourteenth Amendment's protection of liberty and property. When protected interests are implicated, the right to some kind of prior hearing is paramount. But the range of interests protected by procedural due process is not infinite.

The District Court decided that procedural due process guarantees apply in this case by assessing and balancing the weights of the particular interests involved. It concluded that the respondent's interest in re-employment at Wisconsin State University-Oshkosh outweighed the University's interest in denying him reemployment summarily. Undeniably, the respondent's re-employment prospects were of major concern to him—concern that we surely cannot say was

1 insignificant. And a weighing process has long been a part of any determination of
2 the form of hearing required in particular situations by procedural due process.
3 But, to determine whether due process requirements apply in the first place, we
4 must look not to the "weight," but to the nature, of the interest at stake. We must
5 look to see if the interest is within the Fourteenth Amendment's protection of
6 liberty and property.

7 "Liberty" and "property" are broad and majestic terms. * * * For that reason, the
8 Court has fully and finally rejected the wooden distinction between "rights" and
9 "privileges" that once seemed to govern the applicability of procedural due process
10 rights. The Court has also made clear that the property interests protected by
11 procedural due process extend well beyond actual ownership of real estate,
12 chattels, or money. By the same token, the Court has required due process
13 protection for deprivations of liberty beyond the sort of formal constraints imposed
14 by the criminal process.

15 Yet, while the Court has eschewed rigid or formalistic limitations on the protection
16 of procedural due process, it has at the same time observed certain boundaries. For
17 the words "liberty" and "property" in the Due Process Clause of the Fourteenth
18 Amendment must be given some meaning.

19 II

20 * * *

21 There might be cases in which a State refused to re-employ a person under such
22 circumstances that interests in liberty would be implicated. But this is not such a
23 case.

24 The State, in declining to rehire the respondent, did not make any charge against
25 him that might seriously damage his standing and associations in his community.
26 It did not base the nonrenewal of his contract on a charge, for example, that he had
27 been guilty of dishonesty, or immorality. Had it done so, this would be a different
28 case. For "[w]here a person's good name, reputation, honor, or integrity is at stake
29 because of what the government is doing to him, notice and an opportunity to be
30 heard are essential." *Wisconsin v. Constantineau*, 400 U.S. 433, 437 [(1970)]. In
31 such a case, due process would accord an opportunity to refute the charge before
32 University officials. In the present case, however, there is no suggestion whatever
33 that the respondent's "good name, reputation, honor, or integrity" is at stake.

34 Similarly, there is no suggestion that the State, in declining to re-employ the
35 respondent, imposed on him a stigma or other disability that foreclosed his
36 freedom to take advantage of other employment opportunities. The State, for
37 example, did not invoke any regulations to bar the respondent from all other public
38 employment in state universities. Had it done so, this, again, would be a different
39 case. For "[t]o be deprived not only of present government employment but of
40 future opportunity for it certainly is no small injury.... ." *Joint Anti-Fascist*

1    *Refugee Committee v. McGrath*, 341 U.S. 123, 185 (JACKSON, J., concurring).
2    * * * In the present case, however, this principle does not come into play.

3    To be sure, the respondent has alleged that the nonrenewal of his contract was
4    based on his exercise of his right to freedom of speech. But this allegation is not
5    now before us. The District Court stayed proceedings on this issue, and the
6    respondent has yet to prove that the decision not to rehire him was, in fact, based
7    on his free speech activities.

8    Hence, on the record before us, all that clearly appears is that the respondent was
9    not rehired for one year at one university. It stretches the concept too far to suggest
10    that a person is deprived of "liberty" when he simply is not rehired in one job, but
11    remains as free as before to seek another. *Cafeteria Workers v. McElroy*, 367 U.S.
12    886, 895-896.

13    III

14    The Fourteenth Amendment's procedural protection of property is a safeguard of
15    the security of interests that a person has already acquired in specific benefits.
16    These interests—property interests—may take many forms.

17    Thus, the Court has held that a person receiving welfare benefits under statutory
18    and administrative standards defining eligibility for them has an interest in
19    continued receipt of those benefits that is safeguarded by procedural due process.
20    Similarly, in the area of public employment, the Court has held that a public college
21    professor dismissed from an office held under tenure provisions and college
22    professors and staff members dismissed during the terms of their contracts have
23    interests in continued employment that are safeguarded by due process. Only last
24    year, the Court held that this principle "proscribing summary dismissal from
25    public employment without hearing or inquiry required by due process" also
26    applied to a teacher recently hired without tenure or a formal contract, but
27    nonetheless with a clearly implied promise of continued employment.

28    Certain attributes of "property" interests protected by procedural due process
29    emerge from these decisions. To have a property interest in a benefit, a person
30    clearly must have more than an abstract need or desire for it. He must have more
31    than a unilateral expectation of it. He must, instead, have a legitimate claim of
32    entitlement to it. It is a purpose of the ancient institution of property to protect
33    those claims upon which people rely in their daily lives, reliance that must not be
34    arbitrarily undermined. It is a purpose of the constitutional right to a hearing to
35    provide an opportunity for a person to vindicate those claims.

36    Property interests, of course, are not created by the Constitution. Rather, they are
37    created and their dimensions are defined by existing rules or understandings that
38    stem from an independent source such as state law—rules or understandings that
39    secure certain benefits and that support claims of entitlement to those benefits.
40    Thus, the welfare recipients in *Goldberg v. Kelly,* 397 U.S. 254 (1969), had a claim
41    of entitlement to welfare payments that was grounded in the statute defining

1 eligibility for them. The recipients had not yet shown that they were, in fact, within
2 the statutory terms of eligibility. But we held that they had a right to a hearing at
3 which they might attempt to do so.

4 Just as the welfare recipients' "property" interest in welfare payments was created
5 and defined by statutory terms, so the respondent's "property" interest in
6 employment at Wisconsin State University-Oshkosh was created and defined by
7 the terms of his appointment. Those terms secured his interest in employment up
8 to June 30, 1969. But the important fact in this case is that they specifically
9 provided that the respondent's employment was to terminate on June 30. They did
10 not provide for contract renewal absent "sufficient cause." Indeed, they made no
11 provision for renewal whatsoever.

12 Thus, the terms of the respondent's appointment secured absolutely no interest in
13 re-employment for the next year. They supported absolutely no possible claim of
14 entitlement to re-employment. Nor, significantly, was there any state statute or
15 University rule or policy that secured his interest in re-employment or that created
16 any legitimate claim to it. In these circumstances, the respondent surely had an
17 abstract concern in being rehired, but he did not have a *property* interest sufficient
18 to require the University authorities to give him a hearing when they declined to
19 renew his contract of employment.

20 IV

21 * * *

22 * * * The judgment of the Court of Appeals, accordingly, is reversed, and the case
23 is remanded for further proceedings consistent with this opinion.

24 *It is so ordered.*

25 MR. JUSTICE POWELL took no part in the decision of this case.

26 MR. JUSTICE MARSHALL, dissenting.

27 * * *

28 While I agree with Part I of the Court's opinion, setting forth the proper framework
29 for consideration of the issue presented, and also with those portions of Parts II
30 and III of the Court's opinion that assert that a public employee is entitled to
31 procedural due process whenever a State stigmatizes him by denying employment,
32 or injures his future employment prospects severely, or whenever the State
33 deprives him of a property interest, I would go further than the Court does in
34 defining the terms "liberty" and "property."

35 The prior decisions of this Court, discussed at length in the opinion of the Court,
36 establish a principle that is as obvious as it is compelling—*i.e.*, federal and state
37 governments and governmental agencies are restrained by the Constitution from
38 acting arbitrarily with respect to employment opportunities that they either offer

or control. Hence, it is now firmly established that whether or not a private employer is free to act capriciously or unreasonably with respect to employment practices, at least absent statutory or contractual controls, a government employer is different. The government may only act fairly and reasonably.

\* \* \*

In my view, every citizen who applies for a government job is entitled to it unless the government can establish some reason for denying the employment. This is the "property" right that I believe is protected by the Fourteenth Amendment and that cannot be denied "without due process of law." And it is also liberty—liberty to work—which is the "very essence of the personal freedom and opportunity" secured by the Fourteenth Amendment.

\* \* \*

Employment is one of the greatest, if not the greatest, benefits that governments offer in modern-day life. When something as valuable as the opportunity to work is at stake, the government may not reward some citizens and not others without demonstrating that its actions are fair and equitable. And it is procedural due process that is our fundamental guarantee of fairness, our protection against arbitrary, capricious, and unreasonable government action.

\* \* \*

It may be argued that to provide procedural due process to all public employees or prospective employees would place an intolerable burden on the machinery of government. The short answer to that argument is that it is not burdensome to give reasons when reasons exist. Whenever an application for employment is denied, an employee is discharged, or a decision not to rehire an employee is made, there should be some reason for the decision. It can scarcely be argued that government would be crippled by a requirement that the reason be communicated to the person most directly affected by the government's action.

Where there are numerous applicants for jobs, it is likely that few will choose to demand reasons for not being hired. But, if the demand for reasons is exceptionally great, summary procedures can be devised that would provide fair and adequate information to all persons. As long as the government has a good reason for its actions it need not fear disclosure. It is only where the government acts improperly that procedural due process is truly burdensome. And that is precisely when it is most necessary.

It might also be argued that to require a hearing and a statement of reasons is to require a useless act, because a government bent on denying employment to one or more persons will do so regardless of the procedural hurdles that are placed in its path. Perhaps this is so, but a requirement of procedural regularity at least renders arbitrary action more difficult. Moreover, proper procedures will surely

1 eliminate some of the arbitrariness that results, not from malice, but from innocent
2 error. * * *

3                                                    * * *

4 MR JUSTICE DOUGLAS dissenting. [Omitted.]

5

## 6 Perry v. Sindermann

7 408 U.S. 593 (1972)

8 June 29, 1972

9 MR. JUSTICE STEWART delivered the opinion of the Court.

10 From 1959 to 1969, the respondent, Robert Sindermann, was a teacher in the state
11 college system of the State of Texas. After teaching for two years at the University
12 of Texas and for four years at San Antonio Junior College, he became a professor
13 of Government and Social Science at Odessa Junior College in 1965. He was
14 employed at the college for four successive years, under a series of one-year
15 contracts. He was successful enough to be appointed, for a time, the co-chairman
16 of his department.

17 During the 1968-1969 academic year, however, controversy arose between the
18 respondent and the college administration. The respondent was elected president
19 of the Texas Junior College Teachers Association. In this capacity, he left his
20 teaching duties on several occasions to testify before committees of the Texas
21 Legislature, and he became involved in public disagreements with the policies of
22 the college's Board of Regents. In particular, he aligned himself with a group
23 advocating the elevation of the college to four-year status—a change opposed by
24 the Regents. And, on one occasion, a newspaper advertisement appeared over his
25 name that was highly critical of the Regents.

26 Finally, in May, 1969, the respondent's one-year employment contract terminated
27 and the Board of Regents voted not to offer him a new contract for the next
28 academic year. The Regents issued a press release setting forth allegations of the
29 respondent's insubordination. But they provided him no official statement of the
30 reasons for the nonrenewal of his contract. And they allowed him no opportunity
31 for a hearing to challenge the basis of the nonrenewal.

32 The respondent then brought this action in Federal District Court. He alleged
33 primarily that the Regents' decision not to rehire him was based on his public
34 criticism of the policies of the college administration, and thus infringed his right
35 to freedom of speech. He also alleged that their failure to provide him an
36 opportunity for a hearing violated the Fourteenth Amendment's guarantee of
37 procedural due process. * * *

38                                                    * * *

1                                            I

2    The first question presented is whether the respondent's lack of a contractual or
3    tenure right to re-employment, taken alone, defeats his claim that the nonrenewal
4    of his contract violated the First and Fourteenth Amendments. We hold that it does
5    not.

6    For at least a quarter-century, this Court has made clear that, even though a person
7    has no "right" to a valuable governmental benefit, and even though the government
8    may deny him the benefit for any number of reasons, there are some reasons upon
9    which the government may not rely. It may not deny a benefit to a person on a
10   basis that infringes his constitutionally protected interest, especially his interest in
11   freedom of speech. For if the government could deny a benefit to a person because
12   of his constitutionally protected speech or associations, his exercise of those
13   freedoms would in effect be penalized and inhibited. This would allow the
14   government to "produce a result which [it] could not command directly." *Speiser*
15   *v. Randall*, 357 U.S. 513, 526 (1958). Such interference with constitutional rights
16   is impermissible.

17                                          * * *

18                                          II

19   The respondent's lack of formal contractual or tenure security in continued
20   employment at Odessa Junior College, though irrelevant to his free speech claim,
21   is highly relevant to his procedural due process claim. But it may not be entirely
22   dispositive.

23   We have held today in *Board of Regents v. Roth*, 408 U.S. 564, that the
24   Constitution does not require opportunity for a hearing before the nonrenewal of
25   a nontenured teacher's contract unless he can show that the decision not to rehire
26   him somehow deprived him of an interest in "liberty" or that he had a "property"
27   interest in continued employment, despite the lack of tenure or a formal contract.
28   In *Roth*, the teacher had not made a showing on either point to justify summary
29   judgment in his favor.

30   Similarly, the respondent here has yet to show that he has been deprived of an
31   interest that could invoke procedural due process protection. As in *Roth*, the mere
32   showing that he was not rehired in one particular job, without more, did not
33   amount to a showing of a loss of liberty. Nor did it amount to a showing of a loss of
34   property.

35   But the respondent's allegations—which we must construe most favorably to the
36   respondent at this stage of the litigation—do raise a genuine issue as to his interest
37   in continued employment at Odessa Junior College. He alleged that this interest,
38   though not secured by a formal contractual tenure provision, was secured by a no
39   less binding understanding fostered by the college administration. In particular,
40   the respondent alleged that the college had a *de facto* tenure program, and that he

had tenure under that program. He claimed that he and others legitimately relied upon an unusual provision that had been in the college's official Faculty Guide for many years:

> "*Teacher Tenure*: Odessa College has no tenure system. The Administration of the College wishes the faculty member to feel that he has permanent tenure as long as his teaching services are satisfactory and as long as he displays a cooperative attitude toward his coworkers and his superiors, and as long as he is happy in his work."

Moreover, the respondent claimed legitimate reliance upon guidelines promulgated by the Coordinating Board of the Texas College and University System that provided that a person, like himself. who had been employed as a teacher in the state college and university system for seven years or more has some form of job tenure. Thus, the respondent offered to prove that a teacher with his long period of service at this particular State College had no less a "property" interest in continued employment than a formally tenured teacher at other colleges, and had no less a procedural due process right to a statement of reasons and a hearing before college officials upon their decision not to retain him.

We have made clear in *Roth* that "property" interests subject to procedural due process protection are not limited by a few rigid, technical forms. Rather, "property" denotes a broad range of interests that are secured by "existing rules or understandings." A person's interest in a benefit is a "property" interest for due process purposes if there are such rules or mutually explicit understandings that support his claim of entitlement to the benefit and that he may invoke at a hearing.

A written contract with an explicit tenure provision clearly is evidence of a formal understanding that supports a teacher's claim of entitlement to continued employment unless sufficient "cause" is shown. Yet absence of such an explicit contractual provision may not always foreclose the possibility that a teacher has a "property" interest in reemployment. For example, the law of contracts in most, if not all, jurisdictions long has employed a process by which agreements, though not formalized in writing, may be "implied." Explicit contractual provisions may be supplemented by other agreements implied from "the promisor's words and conduct in the light of the surrounding circumstances." 3 A. Corbin on Contracts § 562. And "[t]he meaning of [the promisor's] words and acts is found by relating them to the usage of the past." *Ibid*.

A teacher, like the respondent, who has held his position for a number of years, might be able to show from the circumstances of this service—and from other relevant facts—that he has a legitimate claim of entitlement to job tenure. Just as this Court has found there to be a "common law of a particular industry or of a particular plant" that may supplement a collective bargaining agreement, *Steelworkers v. Warrior & Gulf Co.*, 363 U.S. 574, 579 (1960), so there may be an unwritten "common law" in a particular university that certain employees shall have the equivalent of tenure. This is particularly likely in a college or university, like Odessa Junior College, that has no explicit tenure system even for senior members of its faculty, but that nonetheless may have created such a system in practice.

In this case, the respondent has alleged the existence of rules and understandings, promulgated and fostered by state officials, that may justify his legitimate claim of entitlement to continued employment absent "sufficient cause." * * * Proof of such a property interest would not, of course, entitle him to reinstatement. But such proof would obligate college officials to grant a hearing at his request, where he could be informed of the grounds for his nonretention and challenge their sufficiency.

Therefore, while we do not wholly agree with the opinion of the Court of Appeals, its judgment remanding this case to the District Court is

Affirmed.

MR. JUSTICE POWELL took no part in the decision of this case.

MR. CHIEF JUSTICE BURGER, concurring. [Omitted.]

MR. JUSTICE MARSHALL, dissenting in part.

* * * I agree with Part I of the Court's opinion holding that respondent has presented a bona fide First Amendment claim that should be considered fully by the District Court. But, for the reasons stated in my dissenting opinion in *Board of Regents v. Roth*, 408 U.S. 587, I would modify the judgment of the Court of Appeals to direct the District Court to enter summary judgment for respondent entitling him to a statement of reasons why his contract was not renewed and a hearing on disputed issues of fact.

MR. JUSTICE BRENNAN, with whom MR. JUSTICE DOUGLAS joins, dissenting in part. [Omitted.]

## Paul v. Davis

424 U.S. 693 (1976)

March 23, 1976

MR. JUSTICE REHNQUIST delivered the opinion of the Court.

We granted certiorari, 421 U.S. 909 (1975), in this case to consider whether respondent's charge that petitioners' defamation of him, standing alone and apart from any other governmental action with respect to him, stated a claim for relief under 42 U.S.C. § 1983 and the Fourteenth Amendment. For the reasons hereinafter stated, we conclude that it does not.

1  Petitioner Paul is the Chief of Police of the Louisville, Ky., Division of Police, while
2  petitioner McDaniel occupies the same position in the Jefferson County, Ky.,
3  Division of Police. In late 1972, they agreed to combine their efforts for the purpose
4  of alerting local area merchants to possible shoplifters who might be operating
5  during the Christmas season. In early December, petitioners distributed to
6  approximately 800 merchants in the Louisville metropolitan area a "flyer," which
7  began as follows:

8  "TO: BUSINESS MEN IN THE METROPOLITAN AREA

9  "The Chiefs of The Jefferson County and City of Louisville Police
10  Departments, in an effort to keep their officers advised on shoplifting
11  activity, have approved the attached alphabetically arranged flyer of
12  subjects known to be active in this criminal field.

13  "This flyer is being distributed to you, the business man, so that you may
14  inform your security personnel to watch for these subjects. These persons
15  have been arrested during 1971 and 1972 or have been active in various
16  criminal fields in high density shopping areas.

17  "Only the photograph and name of the subject is shown on this flyer; if
18  additional information is desired, please forward a request in writing. . . ."

19  The flyer consisted of five pages of "mug shot" photos, arranged alphabetically.
20  Each page was headed:

21  "NOVEMBER 1972

22  CITY OF LOUISVILLE

23  JEFFERSON COUNTY

24  POLICE DEPARTMENTS

25  ACTIVE SHOPLIFTERS"

26  In approximately the center of page 2 there appeared photos and the name of the
27  respondent, Edward Charles Davis III.

28  Respondent appeared on the flyer because, on June 14, 1971, he had been arrested
29  in Louisville on a charge of shoplifting. He had been arraigned on this charge in
30  September, 1971, and, upon his plea of not guilty, the charge had been "filed away
31  with leave [to reinstate]," a disposition which left the charge outstanding. Thus, at
32  the time petitioners caused the flyer to be prepared and circulated, respondent had
33  been charged with shoplifting but his guilt or innocence of that offense had never
34  been resolved. Shortly after circulation of the flyer, the charge against respondent
35  was finally dismissed by a judge of the Louisville Police Court.

1   At the time the flyer was circulated, respondent was employed as a photographer
2   by the Louisville Courier-Journal and Times. The flyer, and respondent's inclusion
3   therein, soon came to the attention of respondent's supervisor, the executive
4   director of photography for the two newspapers. This individual called respondent
5   in to hear his version of the events leading to his appearing in the flyer. Following
6   this discussion, the supervisor informed respondent that, although he would not
7   be fired, he "had best not find himself in a similar situation" in the future.

8                                          * * *

9   * * * The Court of Appeals concluded that respondent had set forth a § 1983 claim
10  "in that he has alleged facts that constitute a denial of due process of law." * * *

11                                           I

12  Respondent's due process claim is grounded upon his assertion that the flyer, and
13  in particular the phrase "Active Shoplifters" appearing at the head of the page upon
14  which his name and photograph appear, impermissibly deprived him of some
15  "liberty" protected by the Fourteenth Amendment. His complaint asserted that the
16  "active shoplifter" designation would inhibit him from entering business
17  establishments for fear of being suspected of shoplifting and possibly
18  apprehended, and would seriously impair his future employment opportunities.
19  Accepting that such consequences may flow from the flyer in question,
20  respondent's complaint would appear to state a classical claim for defamation
21  actionable in the courts of virtually every State. Imputing criminal behavior to an
22  individual is generally considered defamatory per se, and actionable without proof
23  of special damages.

24  Respondent brought his action, however, not in the state courts of Kentucky, but
25  in a United States District Court for that State. He asserted not a claim for
26  defamation under the laws of Kentucky, but a claim that he had been deprived of
27  rights secured to him by the Fourteenth Amendment of the United States
28  Constitution. Concededly, if the same allegations had been made about respondent
29  by a private individual, he would have nothing more than a claim for defamation
30  under state law. But, he contends, since petitioners are, respectively, an official of
31  city and of county government, his action is thereby transmuted into one for
32  deprivation by the State of rights secured under the Fourteenth Amendment.

33                                         * * *

34                                          II

35                                          B

36  * * * The words "liberty" and "property," as used in the Fourteenth Amendment,
37  do not, in terms, single out reputation as a candidate for special protection over
38  and above other interests that may be protected by state law. While we have in a
39  number of our prior cases pointed out the frequently drastic effect of the "stigma"
40  which may result from defamation by the government in a variety of contexts, this

1 line of cases does not establish the proposition that reputation alone, apart from
2 some more tangible interests such as employment, is either "liberty" or "property"
3 by itself sufficient to invoke the procedural protection of the Due Process Clause.
4 As we have said, the Court of Appeals, in reaching a contrary conclusion, relied
5 primarily upon *Wisconsin v. Constantineau*, 400 U.S. 433 (1971). [In
6 *Constantineau*, the Supreme Court held unconstitutional a Wisconsin state law
7 authorizing law enforcement to post, without prior proceedings or subsequent
8 review, notifying identifying individuals as "excessive drinkers," with the
9 consequence that they could purchase liquor.] We think the correct import of that
10 decision, however, must be derived from an examination of the precedents upon
11 which it relied, as well as consideration of the other decisions by this Court, before
12 and after *Constantineau*, which bear upon the relationship between governmental
13 defamation and the guarantees of the Constitution. While not uniform in their
14 treatment of the subject, we think that the weight of our decisions establishes no
15 constitutional doctrine converting every defamation by a public official into a
16 deprivation of liberty within the meaning of the Due Process Clause of the Fifth or
17 Fourteenth Amendment.

18 * * *

19 There is undoubtedly language in *Constantineau*, which is sufficiently ambiguous
20 to justify the reliance upon it by the Court of Appeals:

21 "Yet certainly where the state attaches 'a badge of infamy' to the citizen, due
22 process comes into play. *Wieman v. Updegraff*, 344 U.S. 183, 191. '[T]he
23 right to be heard before being condemned to suffer grievous loss of any
24 kind, even though it may not involve the stigma and hardships of a criminal
25 conviction, is a principle basic to our society.' *Joint Anti-Fascist Committee
26 v. McGrath*, 341 U.S. 123, 168 (FRANKFURTER, J., concurring).

27 "Where a person's good name, reputation, honor, or integrity is at stake
28 *because of what the government is doing to him*, notice and an opportunity
29 to be heard are essential." *Wisconsin v. Constantineau*, 400 U.S. 433, 437
30 (emphasis supplied).

31 The last paragraph of the quotation could be taken to mean that, if a government
32 official defames a person, without more, the procedural requirements of the Due
33 Process Clause of the Fourteenth Amendment are brought into play. If read that
34 way, it would represent a significant broadening of the holdings of *Wieman v.
35 Updegraff*, 344 U.S. 183 (1952), and *Joint Anti-Fascist Refugee Comm. v.
36 McGrath*, 341 U.S. 123 (1951), relied upon by the *Constantineau* Court in its
37 analysis in the immediately preceding paragraph. We should not read this
38 language as significantly broadening those holdings without in any way adverting
39 to the fact if there is any other possible interpretation of *Constantineau*'s language.
40 We believe there is.

We think that the italicized language in the last sentence quoted, "because of what the government is doing to him," referred to the fact that the governmental action taken in that case deprived the individual of a right previously held under state law—the right to purchase or obtain liquor in common with the rest of the citizenry. "Posting," therefore, significantly altered her status as a matter of state law, and it was that alteration of legal status which, combined with the injury resulting from the defamation, justified the invocation of procedural safeguards. The "stigma" resulting from the defamatory character of the posting was doubtless an important factor in evaluating the extent of harm worked by that act, but we do not think that such defamation, standing alone, deprived Constantineau of any "liberty" protected by the procedural guarantees of the Fourteenth Amendment.

\* \* \*

IV

Petitioners therefore were not liable to him under § 1983. The judgment of the Court of Appeals holding otherwise is

Reversed.

MR. JUSTICE STEVENS took no part in the consideration or decision of this case.

MR. JUSTICE BRENNAN, with whom MR. JUSTICE MARSHALL concurs and MR. JUSTICE WHITE concurs in part, dissenting. [Omitted.]

## 2. What Process Is Due

The Supreme Court addressed the key question of how to decide how much process is due in a famous pair of cases from the 1970s, *Goldberg v. Kelly* and *Mathews v. Eldridge*. How does the analysis shift from the first case to the second? Is there anything left of *Goldberg* after *Mathews*?

## Goldberg v. Kelly

397 U.S. 254 (1970)

March 23, 1970

MR. JUSTICE BRENNAN delivered the opinion of the Court.

The question for decision is whether a State that terminates public assistance payments to a particular recipient without affording him the opportunity for an evidentiary hearing prior to termination denies the recipient procedural due process in violation of the Due Process Clause of the Fourteenth Amendment.

1   This action was brought in the District Court for the Southern District of New York
2   by residents of New York City receiving financial aid under the federally assisted
3   program of Aid to Families with Dependent Children (AFDC) or under New York
4   State's general Home Relief program. Their complaint alleged that the New York
5   State and New York City officials administering these programs terminated, or
6   were about to terminate, such aid without prior notice and hearing, thereby
7   denying them due process of law. At the time the suits were filed, there was no
8   requirement of prior notice or hearing of any kind before termination of financial
9   aid. However, the State and city adopted procedures for notice and hearing after
10  the suits were brought, and the plaintiffs, appellees here, then challenged the
11  constitutional adequacy of those procedures.

12                                        * * *

13  Pursuant to subdivision (b) [of section 351.26 of State Department of Social
14  Services regulations], the New York City Department of Social Services
15  promulgated Procedure No. 68-18. A caseworker who has doubts about the
16  recipient's continued eligibility must first discuss them with the recipient. If the
17  caseworker concludes that the recipient is no longer eligible, he recommends
18  termination of aid to a unit supervisor. If the latter concurs, he sends the recipient
19  a letter stating the reasons for proposing to terminate aid and notifying him that,
20  within seven days, he may request that a higher official review the record, and may
21  support the request with a written statement, prepared personally or with the aid
22  of an attorney or other person. If the reviewing official affirms the determination
23  of ineligibility, aid is stopped immediately and the recipient is informed by letter
24  of the reasons for the action. Appellees' challenge to this procedure emphasizes the
25  absence of any provisions for the personal appearance of the recipient before the
26  reviewing official, for oral presentation of evidence, and for confrontation and
27  cross-examination of adverse witnesses. However, the letter does inform the
28  recipient that he may request a post-termination "fair hearing." This is a
29  proceeding before an independent state hearing officer at which the recipient may
30  appear personally, offer oral evidence, confront and cross-examine the witnesses
31  against him, and have a record made of the hearing. If the recipient prevails at the
32  "fair hearing," he is paid all funds erroneously withheld. A recipient whose aid is
33  not restored by a "fair hearing" decision may have judicial review. The recipient is
34  so notified.

35                                          I

36  The constitutional issue to be decided, therefore, is the narrow one whether the
37  Due Process Clause requires that the recipient be afforded an evidentiary hearing
38  *before* the termination of benefits. The District Court held that only a pre-
39  termination evidentiary hearing would satisfy the constitutional command, and
40  rejected the argument of the state and city officials that the combination of the
41  post-termination "fair hearing" with the informal pre-termination review disposed
42  of all due process claims. The court said: "While post-termination review is
43  relevant, there is one overpowering fact which controls here. By hypothesis, a
44  welfare recipient is destitute, without funds or assets. . . . Suffice it to say that to
    196

1    cut off a welfare recipient in the face of . . . 'brutal need' without a prior hearing of
2    some sort is unconscionable unless overwhelming considerations justify it." *Kelly*
3    *v. Wyman*, 294 F.Supp. 893, 899, 900 (1968). The court rejected the argument
4    that the need to protect the public's tax revenues supplied the requisite
5    "overwhelming consideration." "Against the justified desire to protect public funds
6    must be weighed the individual's overpowering need in this unique situation not
7    to be wrongfully deprived of assistance. . . . While the problem of additional
8    expense must be kept in mind, it does not justify denying a hearing meeting the
9    ordinary standards of due process. Under all the circumstances, we hold that due
10   process requires an adequate hearing before termination of welfare benefits, and
11   the fact that there is a later constitutionally fair proceeding does not alter the
12   result." *Id.* at 901. Although state officials were party defendants in the action, only
13   the Commissioner of Social Services of the City of New York appealed. * * *

14   Appellant does not contend that procedural due process is not applicable to the
15   termination of welfare benefits. Such benefits are a matter of statutory entitlement
16   for persons qualified to receive them.[8] Their termination involves state action that
17   adjudicates important rights. The constitutional challenge cannot be answered by
18   an argument that public assistance benefits are "a 'privilege,' and not a 'right.'"
19   *Shapiro v. Thompson*, 394 U.S. 618, 627 n. 6 (1969). Relevant constitutional
20   restraints apply as much to the withdrawal of public assistance benefits as to
21   disqualification for unemployment compensation, *Sherbert v. Verner*, 374 U.S.
22   398 (1963); or to denial of a tax exemption, *Speiser v. Randall*, 357 U.S. 513 (1958);
23   or to discharge from public employment, *Slochower v. Board of Higher Education*,

---

[8] It may be realistic today to regard welfare entitlements as more like "property"
than a "gratuity." Much of the existing wealth in this country takes the form of
rights that do not fall within traditional common law concepts of property. It has
been aptly noted that

"[s]ociety today is built around entitlement. The automobile dealer has his
franchise, the doctor and lawyer their professional licenses, the worker his
union membership, contract, and pension rights, the executive his contract
and stock options; all are devices to aid security and independence. Many
of the most important of these entitlements now flow from government:
subsidies to farmers and businessmen, routes for airlines and channels for
television stations; long-term contracts for defense, space, and education;
social security pensions for individuals. Such sources of security, whether
private or public, are no longer regarded as luxuries or gratuities; to the
recipients, they are essentials, fully deserved, and in no sense a form of
charity. It is only the poor whose entitlements, although recognized by
public policy, have not been effectively enforced."

Reich, *Individual Rights and Social Welfare: The Emerging Legal Issues*, 74 Yale
L.J. 1245, 1255 (1965). See also *Reich, The New Property*, 73 Yale L.J. 733 (1964).

1    350 U.S. 551 (1956). The extent to which procedural due process must be afforded
2    the recipient is influenced by the extent to which he may be "condemned to suffer
3    grievous loss," *Joint Anti-Fascist Refugee Committee v. McGrath*, 341 U.S. 123,
4    168 (1951) (FRANKFURTER, J., concurring), and depends upon whether the
5    recipient's interest in avoiding that loss outweighs the governmental interest in
6    summary adjudication. Accordingly, as we said in *Cafeteria & Restaurant Workers*
7    *Union v. McElroy*, 367 U.S. 886, 895 (1961), "consideration of what procedures
8    due process may require under any given set of circumstances must begin with a
9    determination of the precise nature of the government function involved, as well
10   as of the private interest that has been affected by governmental action."

11   It is true, of course, that some governmental benefits may be administratively
12   terminated without affording the recipient a pre-termination evidentiary hearing.
13   But we agree with the District Court that, when welfare is discontinued, only a pre-
14   termination evidentiary hearing provides the recipient with procedural due
15   process. For qualified recipients, welfare provides the means to obtain essential
16   food, clothing, housing, and medical care. Thus, the crucial factor in this context—
17   a factor not present in the case of the blacklisted government contractor, the
18   discharged government employee, the taxpayer denied a tax exemption, or
19   virtually anyone else whose governmental entitlements are ended—is that
20   termination of aid pending resolution of a controversy over eligibility may deprive
21   an *eligible* recipient of the very means by which to live while he waits. Since he
22   lacks independent resources, his situation becomes immediately desperate. His
23   need to concentrate upon finding the means for daily subsistence, in turn,
24   adversely affects his ability to seek redress from the welfare bureaucracy.

25   Moreover, important governmental interests are promoted by affording recipients
26   a pre-termination evidentiary hearing. From its founding, the Nation's basic
27   commitment has been to foster the dignity and wellbeing of all persons within its
28   borders. We have come to recognize that forces not within the control of the poor
29   contribute to their poverty. This perception, against the background of our
30   traditions, has significantly influenced the development of the contemporary
31   public assistance system. Welfare, by meeting the basic demands of subsistence,
32   can help bring within the reach of the poor the same opportunities that are
33   available to others to participate meaningfully in the life of the community. At the
34   same time, welfare guards against the societal malaise that may flow from a
35   widespread sense of unjustified frustration and insecurity. Public assistance, then,
36   is not mere charity, but a means to "promote the general Welfare, and secure the
37   Blessings of Liberty to ourselves and our Posterity." The same governmental
38   interests that counsel the provision of welfare, counsel as well its uninterrupted
39   provision to those eligible to receive it; pre-termination evidentiary hearings are
40   indispensable to that end.

41   Appellant does not challenge the force of these considerations but argues that they
42   are outweighed by countervailing governmental interests in conserving fiscal and
43   administrative resources. These interests, the argument goes, justify the delay of
44   any evidentiary hearing until after discontinuance of the grants. Summary

adjudication protects the public fisc by stopping payments promptly upon discovery of reason to believe that a recipient is no longer eligible. Since most terminations are accepted without challenge, summary adjudication also conserves both the fisc and administrative time and energy by reducing the number of evidentiary hearings actually held.

We agree with the District Court, however, that these governmental interests are not overriding in the welfare context. The requirement of a prior hearing doubtless involves some greater expense, and the benefits paid to ineligible recipients pending decision at the hearing probably cannot he recouped, since these recipients are likely to be judgment-proof. But the State is not without weapons to minimize these increased costs. Much of the drain on fiscal and administrative resources can be reduced by developing procedures for prompt pre-termination hearings and by skillful use of personnel and facilities. Indeed, the very provision for a post-termination evidentiary hearing in New York's Home Relief program is itself cogent evidence that the State recognizes the primacy of the public interest in correct eligibility determinations, and therefore in the provision of procedural safeguards. Thus, the interest of the eligible recipient in uninterrupted receipt of public assistance, coupled with the State's interest that his payments not be erroneously terminated, clearly outweighs the State's competing concern to prevent any increase in its fiscal and administrative burdens. As the District Court correctly concluded, "[t]he stakes are simply too high for the welfare recipient, and the possibility for honest error or irritable misjudgment too great, to allow termination of aid without giving the recipient a chance, if he so desires, to be fully informed of the case against him so that he may contest its basis and produce evidence in rebuttal."

## II

We also agree with the District Court, however, that the pre-termination hearing need not take the form of a judicial or quasi-judicial trial. We bear in mind that the statutory "fair hearing" will provide the recipient with a full administrative review. Accordingly, the pre-termination hearing has one function only: to produce an initial determination of the validity of the welfare department's grounds for discontinuance of payments in order to protect a recipient against an erroneous termination of his benefits. Thus, a complete record and a comprehensive opinion, which would serve primarily to facilitate judicial review and to guide future decisions, need not be provided at the pre-termination stage. We recognize, too, that both welfare authorities and recipients have an interest in relatively speedy resolution of questions of eligibility, that they are used to dealing with one another informally, and that some welfare departments have very burdensome caseloads. These considerations justify the limitation of the pre-termination hearing to minimum procedural safeguards, adapted to the particular characteristics of welfare recipients, and to the limited nature of the controversies to be resolved. We wish to add that we, no less than the dissenters, recognize the importance of not imposing upon the States or the Federal Government in this developing field of law

1  any procedural requirements beyond those demanded by rudimentary due
2  process.

3  "The fundamental requisite of due process of law is the opportunity to be heard."
4  *Grannis v. Ordean*, 234 U.S. 385, 394 (1914). The hearing must be "at a meaningful
5  time and in a meaningful manner." *Armstrong v. Manzo*, 380 U.S. 545, 552 (1965).
6  In the present context, these principles require that a recipient have timely and
7  adequate notice detailing the reasons for a proposed termination, and an effective
8  opportunity to defend by confronting any adverse witnesses and by presenting his
9  own arguments and evidence orally. These rights are important in cases such as
10 those before us, where recipients have challenged proposed terminations as resting
11 on incorrect or misleading factual premises or on misapplication of rules or
12 policies to the facts of particular cases.

13 We are not prepared to say that the seven-day notice currently provided by New
14 York City is constitutionally insufficient *per se*, although there may be cases where
15 fairness would require that a longer time be given. Nor do we see any constitutional
16 deficiency in the content or form of the notice. New York employs both a letter and
17 a personal conference with a caseworker to inform a recipient of the precise
18 questions raised about his continued eligibility. Evidently the recipient is told the
19 legal and factual bases for the Department's doubts. This combination is probably
20 the most effective method of communicating with recipients.

21 The city's procedures presently do not permit recipients to appear personally, with
22 or without counsel, before the official who finally determines continued eligibility.
23 Thus, a recipient is not permitted to present evidence to that official orally, or to
24 confront or cross-examine adverse witnesses. These omissions are fatal to the
25 constitutional adequacy of the procedures.

26 The opportunity to be heard must be tailored to the capacities and circumstances
27 of those who are to be heard. It is not enough that a welfare recipient may present
28 his position to the decisionmaker in writing or second-hand through his
29 caseworker. Written submissions are an unrealistic option for most recipients, who
30 lack the educational attainment necessary to write effectively and who cannot
31 obtain professional assistance. Moreover, written submissions do not afford the
32 flexibility of oral presentations; they do not permit the recipient to mold his
33 argument to the issues the decisionmaker appears to regard as important.
34 Particularly where credibility and veracity are at issue, as they must be in many
35 termination proceedings, written submissions are a wholly unsatisfactory basis for
36 decision. The second-hand presentation to the decisionmaker by the caseworker
37 has its own deficiencies; since the caseworker usually gathers the facts upon which
38 the charge of ineligibility rests, the presentation of the recipient's side of the
39 controversy cannot safely be left to him. Therefore, a recipient must be allowed to
40 state his position orally. Informal procedures will suffice; in this context, due
41 process does not require a particular order of proof or mode of offering evidence.

42 In almost every setting where important decisions turn on questions of fact, due
43 process requires an opportunity to confront and cross-examine adverse witnesses.

1 * * * Welfare recipients must therefore be given an opportunity to confront and
2 cross-examine the witnesses relied on by the department.

3 "The right to be heard would be, in many cases, of little avail if it did not
4 comprehend the right to be heard by counsel." *Powell v. Alabama*, 287 U.S. 45, 68,
5 69 (1932). We do not say that counsel must be provided at the pre-termination
6 hearing, but only that the recipient must be allowed to retain an attorney if he so
7 desires. Counsel can help delineate the issues, present the factual contentions in
8 an orderly manner, conduct cross-examination, and generally safeguard the
9 interests of the recipient. We do not anticipate that this assistance will unduly
10 prolong or otherwise encumber the hearing. * * *

11 Finally, the decisionmaker's conclusion as to a recipient's eligibility must rest
12 solely on the legal rules and evidence adduced at the hearing. To demonstrate
13 compliance with this elementary requirement, the decisionmaker should state the
14 reasons for his determination and indicate the evidence he relied on, though his
15 statement need not amount to a full opinion, or even formal findings of fact and
16 conclusions of law. And, of course, an impartial decisionmaker is essential. We
17 agree with the District Court that prior involvement in some aspects of a case will
18 not necessarily bar a welfare official from acting as a decisionmaker. He should
19 not, however, have participated in making the determination under review.

20 *Affirmed.*

21 MR. JUSTICE BLACK, dissenting.

22 In the last half century, the United States, along with many, perhaps most, other
23 nations of the world, has moved far toward becoming a welfare state, that is, a
24 nation that, for one reason or another, taxes its most affluent people to help
25 support, feed, clothe, and shelter its less fortunate citizens. The result is that, today,
26 more than nine million men, women, and children in the United States receive
27 some kind of state or federally financed public assistance in the form of allowances
28 or gratuities, generally paid them periodically, usually by the week, month, or
29 quarter. Since these gratuities are paid on the basis of need, the list of recipients is
30 not static, and some people go off the lists and others are added from time to time.
31 These ever-changing lists put a constant administrative burden on government,
32 and it certainly could not have reasonably anticipated that this burden would
33 include the additional procedural expense imposed by the Court today.

34 * * *

35 Representatives of the people of the Thirteen Original Colonies spent long, hot
36 months in the summer of 1787 in Philadelphia, Pennsylvania, creating a
37 government of limited powers. They divided it into three departments—
38 Legislative, Judicial, and Executive. The Judicial Department was to have no part
39 whatever in making any laws. In fact, proposals looking to vesting some power in
40 the Judiciary to take part in the legislative process and veto laws were offered,
41 considered, and rejected by the Constitutional Convention. In my judgment, there
42 is not one word, phrase, or sentence from the beginning to the end of the

1 Constitution from which it can be inferred that judges were granted any such
2 legislative power. True, *Marbury v. Madison* held, and properly, I think, that
3 courts must be the final interpreters of the Constitution, and I recognize that the
4 holding can provide an opportunity to slide imperceptibly into constitutional
5 amendment and law-making. But when federal judges use this judicial power for
6 legislative purposes, I think they wander out of their field of vested powers and
7 transgress into the area constitutionally assigned to the Congress and the people.
8 That is precisely what I believe the Court is doing in this case. Hence, my dissent.

9 The more than a million names on the relief rolls in New York, and the more than
10 nine million names on the rolls of all the 50 States were not put there at random.
11 The names are there because state welfare officials believed that those people were
12 eligible for assistance. Probably, in the officials' haste to make out the lists, many
13 names were put there erroneously in order to alleviate immediate suffering, and
14 undoubtedly some people are drawing relief who are not entitled under the law to
15 do so. Doubtless some draw relief checks from time to time who know they are not
16 eligible, either because they are not actually in need or for some other reason. Many
17 of those who thus draw undeserved gratuities are without sufficient property to
18 enable the government to collect back from them any money they wrongfully
19 receive. But the Court today holds that it would violate the Due Process Clause of
20 the Fourteenth Amendment to stop paying those people weekly or monthly
21 allowances unless the government first affords them a full "evidentiary hearing,"
22 even though welfare officials are persuaded that the recipients are not rightfully
23 entitled to receive a penny under the law. In other words, although some recipients
24 might be on the lists for payment wholly because of deliberate fraud on their part,
25 the Court holds that the government is helpless, and must continue, until after an
26 evidentiary hearing, to pay money that it does not owe, never has owed, and never
27 could owe. I do not believe there is any provision in our Constitution that should
28 thus paralyze the government's efforts to protect itself against making payments
29 to people who are not entitled to them.

30                                           \* \* \*

31 The Court apparently feels that this decision will benefit the poor and needy. In my
32 judgment, the eventual result will be just the opposite. While today's decision
33 requires only an administrative, evidentiary hearing, the inevitable logic of the
34 approach taken will lead to constitutionally imposed, time-consuming delays of a
35 full adversary process of administrative and judicial review. In the next case, the
36 welfare recipients are bound to argue that cutting off benefits before judicial review
37 of the agency's decision is also a denial of due process. Since, by hypothesis,
38 termination of aid at that point may still "deprive an *eligible* recipient of the very
39 means by which to live while he waits," I would be surprised if the weighing process
40 did not compel the conclusion that termination without full judicial review would
41 be unconscionable. After all, at each step, as the majority seems to feel, the issue is
42 only one of weighing the government's pocketbook against the actual survival of
43 the recipient, and surely that balance must always tip in favor of the individual.
44 Similarly today's decision requires only the opportunity to have the benefit of

1  counsel at the administrative hearing, but it is difficult to believe that the same
2  reasoning process would not require the appointment of counsel, for otherwise the
3  right to counsel is a meaningless one, since these people are too poor to hire their
4  own advocates. *Cf. Gideon v. Wainwright*, 372 U.S. 335, 344 (1963). Thus, the end
5  result of today's decision may well be that the government, once it decides to give
6  welfare benefits, cannot reverse that decision until the recipient has had the
7  benefits of full administrative and Judicial review, including, of course, the
8  opportunity to present his case to this Court. Since this process will usually entail
9  a delay of several years, the inevitable result of such a constitutionally imposed
10 burden will be that the government will not put a claimant on the rolls initially
11 until it has made an exhaustive investigation to determine his eligibility. While this
12 Court will perhaps have insured that no needy person will be taken off the rolls
13 without a full "due process" proceeding, it will also have insured that many will
14 never get on the rolls, or at least that they will remain destitute during the lengthy
15 proceedings followed to determine initial eligibility.

16                                         * * *

17

18 ## Mathews v. Eldridge

19 424 U.S. 319 (1976)

20 February 24, 1976

21 MR. JUSTICE POWELL delivered the opinion of the Court.

22 The issue in this case is whether the Due Process Clause of the Fifth Amendment
23 requires that, prior to the termination of Social Security disability benefit
24 payments, the recipient be afforded an opportunity for an evidentiary hearing.

25                                          I

26 Cash benefits are provided to workers during periods in which they are completely
27 disabled under the disability insurance benefits program created by the 1956
28 amendments to Title II of the Social Security Act. Respondent Eldridge was first
29 awarded benefits in June, 1968. In March, 1972, he received a questionnaire from
30 the state agency charged with monitoring his medical condition. Eldridge
31 completed the questionnaire, indicating that his condition had not improved and
32 identifying the medical sources, including physicians, from whom he had received
33 treatment recently. The state agency then obtained reports from his physician and
34 a psychiatric consultant. After considering these reports and other information in
35 his file, the agency informed Eldridge by letter that it had made a tentative
36 determination that his disability had ceased in May, 1972. The letter included a
37 statement of reasons for the proposed termination of benefits, and advised
38 Eldridge that he might request reasonable time in which to obtain and submit
39 additional information pertaining to his condition.

In his written response, Eldridge disputed one characterization of his medical condition and indicated that the agency already had enough evidence to establish his disability. The state agency then made its final determination that he had ceased to be disabled in May, 1972. This determination was accepted by the Social Security Administration (SSA), which notified Eldridge in July that his benefits would terminate after that month. The notification also advised him of his right to seek reconsideration by the state agency of this initial determination within six months.

Instead of requesting reconsideration, Eldridge commenced this action challenging the constitutional validity of the administrative procedures established by the Secretary of Health, Education, and Welfare for assessing whether there exists a continuing disability. He sought an immediate reinstatement of benefits pending a hearing on the issue of his disability. The Secretary moved to dismiss on the grounds that Eldridge's benefits had been terminated in accordance with valid administrative regulations and procedures and that he had failed to exhaust available remedies. In support of his contention that due process requires a pre-termination hearing, Eldridge relied exclusively upon this Court's decision in *Goldberg v. Kelly*, 397 U.S. 254 (1970), which established a right to an "evidentiary hearing" prior to termination of welfare benefits. The Secretary contended that *Goldberg* was not controlling, since eligibility for disability benefits, unlike eligibility for welfare benefits, is not based on financial need, and since issues of credibility and veracity do not play a significant role in the disability entitlement decision, which turns primarily on medical evidence.

The District Court concluded that the administrative procedures pursuant to which the Secretary had terminated Eldridge's benefits abridged his right to procedural due process. The court viewed the interest of the disability recipient in uninterrupted benefits as indistinguishable from that of the welfare recipient in *Goldberg*. It further noted that decisions subsequent to *Goldberg* demonstrated that the due process requirement of pre-termination hearings is not limited to situations involving the deprivation of vital necessities. Reasoning that disability determinations may involve subjective judgments based on conflicting medical and nonmedical evidence, the District Court held that, prior to termination of benefits, Eldridge had to be afforded an evidentiary hearing of the type required for welfare beneficiaries under Title IV of the Social Security Act. Relying entirely upon the District Court's opinion, the Court of Appeals for the Fourth Circuit affirmed the injunction barring termination of Eldridge's benefits prior to an evidentiary hearing. We reverse.

* * *

III

A

Procedural due process imposes constraints on governmental decisions which deprive individuals of "liberty" or "property" interests within the meaning of the Due Process Clause of the Fifth or Fourteenth Amendment. The Secretary does not

1  contend that procedural due process is inapplicable to terminations of Social
2  Security disability benefits. He recognizes, as has been implicit in our prior
3  decisions, that the interest of an individual in continued receipt of these benefits is
4  a statutorily created "property" interest protected by the Fifth Amendment.
5  Rather, the Secretary contends that the existing administrative procedures,
6  detailed below, provide all the process that is constitutionally due before a
7  recipient can be deprived of that interest.

8  This Court consistently has held that some form of hearing is required before an
9  individual is finally deprived of a property interest. The "right to be heard before
10  being condemned to suffer grievous loss of any kind, even though it may not
11  involve the stigma and hardships of a criminal conviction, is a principle basic to
12  our society." *Joint Anti-Fascist Comm. v. McGrath*, 341 U.S. 123, 168 (1951)
13  (FRANKFURTER, J., concurring). The fundamental requirement of due process is
14  the opportunity to be heard "at a meaningful time and in a meaningful manner."
15  *Armstrong v. Manzo*, 380 U.S. 545, 552 (1965). Eldridge agrees that the review
16  procedures available to a claimant before the initial determination of ineligibility
17  becomes final would be adequate if disability benefits were not terminated until
18  after the evidentiary hearing stage of the administrative process. The dispute
19  centers upon what process is due prior to the initial termination of benefits,
20  pending review.

21  In recent years, this Court increasingly has had occasion to consider the extent to
22  which due process requires an evidentiary hearing prior to the deprivation of some
23  type of property interest even if such a hearing is provided thereafter. In only one
24  case, *Goldberg v. Kelly*, 397 U.S., at 266-271, has the Court held that a hearing
25  closely approximating a judicial trial is necessary. In other cases requiring some
26  type of pre-termination hearing as a matter of constitutional right, the Court has
27  spoken sparingly about the requisite procedures. * * *

28  These decisions underscore the truism that "'[d]ue process,' unlike some legal
29  rules, is not a technical conception with a fixed content unrelated to time, place
30  and circumstances." *Cafeteria Workers v. McElroy*, 367 U.S. 886, 895 (1961).
31  "[D]ue process is flexible, and calls for such procedural protections as the
32  particular situation demands." *Morrissey v. Brewer*, 408 U.S. 471, 481 (1972).
33  Accordingly, resolution of the issue whether the administrative procedures
34  provided here are constitutionally sufficient requires analysis of the governmental
35  and private interests that are affected. More precisely, our prior decisions indicate
36  that identification of the specific dictates of due process generally requires
37  consideration of three distinct factors: first, the private interest that will be affected
38  by the official action; second, the risk of an erroneous deprivation of such interest
39  through the procedures used, and the probable value, if any, of additional or
40  substitute procedural safeguards; and, finally, the Government's interest,
41  including the function involved and the fiscal and administrative burdens that the
42  additional or substitute procedural requirement would entail.

1   We turn first to a description of the procedures for the termination of Social
2   Security disability benefits, and thereafter consider the factors bearing upon the
3   constitutional adequacy of these procedures.

4                                     B

5   The disability insurance program is administered jointly by state and federal
6   agencies. State agencies make the initial determination whether a disability exists,
7   when it began, and when it ceased. 42 U.S.C. § 421(a). The standards applied and
8   the procedures followed are prescribed by the Secretary, see § 421(b), who has
9   delegated his responsibilities and powers under the Act to the SSA.

10   In order to establish initial and continued entitlement to disability benefits, a
11   worker must demonstrate that he is unable:

12      "to engage in any substantial gainful activity by reason of any medically
13      determinable physical or mental impairment which can be expected to
14      result in death or which has lasted or can be expected to last for a
15      continuous period of not less than 12 months. . . ." 42 U.S.C. § 423(d)(1)(A).

16   To satisfy this test, the worker bears a continuing burden of showing, by means of
17   "medically acceptable clinical and laboratory diagnostic techniques," § 423(d)(3),
18   that he has a physical or mental impairment of such severity that:

19      "he is not only unable to do his previous work, but cannot, considering his
20      age, education, and work experience, engage in any other kind of
21      substantial gainful work which exists in the national economy, regardless
22      of whether such work exists in the immediate area in which he lives, or
23      whether a specific job vacancy exists for him, or whether he would be hired
24      if he applied for work." § 423(d)(2)(A).

25   The principal reasons for benefits terminations are that the worker is no longer
26   disabled or has returned to work. As Eldridge's benefits were terminated because
27   he was determined to be no longer disabled, we consider only the sufficiency of the
28   procedures involved in such cases.

29   The continuing-eligibility investigation is made by a state agency acting through a
30   "team" consisting of a physician and a nonmedical person trained in disability
31   evaluation. The agency periodically communicates with the disabled worker,
32   usually by mail—in which case he is sent a detailed questionnaire—or by telephone,
33   and requests information concerning his present condition, including current
34   medical restrictions and sources of treatment, and any additional information that
35   he considers relevant to his continued entitlement to benefits.

36   Information regarding the recipient's current condition is also obtained from his
37   sources of medical treatment. If there is a conflict between the information
38   provided by the beneficiary and that obtained from medical sources such as his
39   physician, or between two sources of treatment, the agency may arrange for an
40   examination by an independent consulting physician. Whenever the agency's
41   tentative assessment of the beneficiary's condition differs from his own

assessment, the beneficiary is informed that benefits may be terminated, provided a summary of the evidence upon which the proposed determination to terminate is based, and afforded an opportunity to review the medical reports and other evidence in his case file. He also may respond in writing and submit additional evidence.

The state agency then makes its final determination, which is reviewed by an examiner in the SSA Bureau of Disability Insurance. If, as is usually the case, the SSA accepts the agency determination, it notifies the recipient in writing, informing him of the reasons for the decision, and of his right to seek de novo reconsideration by the state agency. Upon acceptance by the SSA, benefits are terminated effective two months after the month in which medical recovery is found to have occurred.

If the recipient seeks reconsideration by the state agency and the determination is adverse, the SSA reviews the reconsideration determination and notices the recipient of the decision. He then has a right to an evidentiary hearing before an SSA administrative law judge. The hearing is nonadversary, and the SSA is not represented by counsel. As at all prior and subsequent stages of the administrative process, however, the claimant may be represented by counsel or other spokesmen. If this hearing results in an adverse decision, the claimant is entitled to request discretionary review by the SSA Appeals Council, and finally may obtain judicial review.

Should it be determined at any point after termination of benefits, that the claimant's disability extended beyond the date of cessation initially established, the worker is entitled to retroactive payments. If, on the other hand, a beneficiary receives any payments to which he is later determined not to be entitled, the statute authorizes the Secretary to attempt to recoup these funds in specified circumstances.

C

Despite the elaborate character of the administrative procedures provided by the Secretary, the courts below held them to be constitutionally inadequate, concluding that due process requires an evidentiary hearing prior to termination. In light of the private and governmental interests at stake here and the nature of the existing procedures, we think this was error.

Since a recipient whose benefits are terminated is awarded full retroactive relief if he ultimately prevails, his sole interest is in the uninterrupted receipt of this source of income pending final administrative decision on his claim. His potential injury is thus similar in nature to that of the welfare recipient in *Goldberg*. * * * .

Only in *Goldberg* has the Court held that due process requires an evidentiary hearing prior to a temporary deprivation. It was emphasized there that welfare assistance is given to persons on the very margin of subsistence:

"The crucial factor in this context—a factor not present in the case of . . . virtually anyone else whose governmental entitlements are ended—is that

1 termination of aid pending resolution of a controversy over eligibility may
2 deprive an *eligible* recipient of the very means by which to live while he
3 waits." 397 U.S., at 264 (emphasis in original).

4 Eligibility for disability benefits, in contrast, is not based upon financial need.
5 Indeed, it is wholly unrelated to the worker's income or support from many other
6 sources, such as earnings of other family members, workmen's compensation
7 awards, tort claims awards, sayings, private insurance, public or private pensions,
8 veterans' benefits, food stamps, public assistance, or the "many other important
9 programs, both public and private, which contain provisions for disability
10 payments affecting a substantial portion of the workforce. . . ." *Richardson v.*
11 *Belcher*, 404 U.S. 78, 85-87 (DOUGLAS, J., dissenting).

12 As *Goldberg* illustrates, the degree of potential deprivation that may be created by
13 a particular decision is a factor to be considered in assessing the validity of any
14 administrative decisionmaking process. The potential deprivation here is generally
15 likely to be less than in *Goldberg*, although the degree of difference can be
16 overstated. As the District Court emphasized, to remain eligible for benefits, a
17 recipient must be "unable to engage in substantial gainful activity." Thus, in
18 contrast to the discharged federal employee in *Arnett*, there is little possibility that
19 the terminated recipient will be able to find even temporary employment to
20 ameliorate the interim loss.

21 As we recognized last Term in *Fusari v. Steinberg*, 419 U.S. 379, 389 (1975), "the
22 possible length of wrongful deprivation of . . . benefits [also] is an important factor
23 in assessing the impact of official action on the private interests." The Secretary
24 concedes that the delay between a request for a hearing before an administrative
25 law judge and a decision on the claim is currently between 10 and 11 months. Since
26 a terminated recipient must first obtain a reconsideration decision as a
27 prerequisite to invoking his right to an evidentiary hearing, the delay between the
28 actual cutoff of benefits and final decision after a hearing exceeds one year.

29 In view of the torpidity of this administrative review process, and the typically
30 modest resources of the family unit of the physically disabled worker, the hardship
31 imposed upon the erroneously terminated disability recipient may be significant.
32 Still, the disabled worker's need is likely to be less than that of a welfare recipient.
33 In addition to the possibility of access to private resources, other forms of
34 government assistance will become available where the termination of disability
35 benefits places a worker or his family below the subsistence level. In view of these
36 potential sources of temporary income, there is less reason here than in *Goldberg*
37 to depart from the ordinary principle, established by our decisions, that something
38 less than an evidentiary hearing is sufficient prior to adverse administrative action.

39 D

40 An additional factor to be considered here is the fairness and reliability of the
41 existing pre-termination procedures, and the probable value, if any, of additional
42 procedural safeguards. Central to the evaluation of any administrative process is

1   the nature of the relevant inquiry. In order to remain eligible for benefits, the
2   disabled worker must demonstrate by means of "medically acceptable clinical and
3   laboratory diagnostic techniques," 42 U.S.C. § 423(d)(3), that he is unable "to
4   engage in any substantial gainful activity by reason of any *medically determinable*
5   physical or mental impairment. . . ." § 423(d)(1)(A) (emphasis supplied). In short,
6   a medical assessment of the worker's physical or mental condition is required. This
7   is a more sharply focused and easily documented decision than the typical
8   determination of welfare entitlement. In the latter case, a wide variety of
9   information may be deemed relevant, and issues of witness credibility and veracity
10  often are critical to the decisionmaking process. *Goldberg* noted that, in such
11  circumstances "written submissions are a wholly unsatisfactory basis for decision."
12  397 U.S., at 269.

13  By contrast, the decision whether to discontinue disability benefits will turn, in
14  most cases, upon "routine, standard, and unbiased medical reports by physician
15  specialists," *Richardson v. Perales*, 402 U.S. 389, 404, concerning a subject whom
16  they have personally examined. In *Richardson*, the Court recognized the
17  "reliability and probative worth of written medical reports," emphasizing that,
18  while there may be "professional disagreement with the medical conclusions" the
19  "specter of questionable credibility and veracity is not present." *Id.* at 405, 407. To
20  be sure, credibility and veracity may be a factor in the ultimate disability
21  assessment in some cases. But procedural due process rules are shaped by the risk
22  of error inherent in the truthfinding process as applied to the generality of cases,
23  not the rare exceptions. The potential value of an evidentiary hearing, or even oral
24  presentation to the decisionmaker, is substantially less in this context than in
25  *Goldberg*.

26  The decision in *Goldberg* also was based on the Court's conclusion that written
27  submissions were an inadequate substitute for oral presentation because they did
28  not provide an effective means for the recipient to communicate his case to the
29  decisionmaker. Written submissions were viewed as an unrealistic option, for most
30  recipients lacked the "educational attainment necessary to write effectively," and
31  could not afford professional assistance. In addition, such submissions would not
32  provide the "flexibility of oral presentations" or "permit the recipient to mold his
33  argument to the issues the decisionmaker appears to regard as important."
34  *Goldberg v. Kelly*, 397 U.S. 254, 269. In the context of the disability benefits
35  entitlement assessment, the administrative procedures under review here fully
36  answer these objections.

37  The detailed questionnaire which the state agency periodically sends the recipient
38  identifies with particularity the information relevant to the entitlement decision,
39  and the recipient is invited to obtain assistance from the local SSA office in
40  completing the questionnaire. More important, the information critical to the
41  entitlement decision usually is derived from medical sources, such as the treating
42  physician. Such sources are likely to be able to communicate more effectively
43  through written documents than are welfare recipients or the lay witnesses
44  supporting their cause. The conclusions of physicians often are supported by X-

1  rays and the results of clinical or laboratory tests, information typically more
2  amenable to written than to oral presentation.

3  A further safeguard against mistake is the policy of allowing the disability
4  recipient's representative full access to all information relied upon by the state
5  agency. In addition, prior to the cutoff of benefits, the agency informs the recipient
6  of its tentative assessment, the reasons therefor, and provides a summary of the
7  evidence that it considers most relevant. Opportunity is then afforded the recipient
8  to submit additional evidence or arguments, enabling him to challenge directly the
9  accuracy of information in his file, as well as the correctness of the agency's
10 tentative conclusions. These procedures, again as contrasted with those before the
11 Court in *Goldberg*, enable the recipient to "mold" his argument to respond to the
12 precise issues which the decisionmaker regards as crucial.

13 Despite these carefully structured procedures, *amici* point to the significant
14 reversal rate for appealed cases as clear evidence that the current process is
15 inadequate. Depending upon the base selected and the line of analysis followed,
16 the relevant reversal rates urged by the contending parties vary from a high of
17 58.6% for appealed reconsideration decisions to an overall reversal rate of only
18 3.3%.[29] Bare statistics rarely provide a satisfactory measure of the fairness of a
19 decisionmaking process. Their adequacy is especially suspect here, since the
20 administrative review system is operated on an open file basis. A recipient may
21 always submit new evidence, and such submissions may result in additional
22 medical examinations. Such fresh examinations were held in approximately 30%
23 to 40% of the appealed cases in fiscal 1973, either at the reconsideration or
24 evidentiary hearing stage of the administrative process. Staff Report 238. In this
25 context, the value of reversal rate statistics as one means of evaluating the
26 adequacy of the pre-termination process is diminished. Thus, although we view
27 such information as relevant, it is certainly not controlling in this case.

28                                          E

---

[29] By focusing solely on the reversal rate for appealed reconsideration
determinations, *amici* overstate the relevant reversal rate. As we indicated last
Term in *Fusari v. Steinberg,* 419 U.S. 379, 383 n. 6 (1975), in order fully to assess
the reliability and fairness of a system of procedure, one must also consider the
overall rate of error for all denials of benefits. Here, that overall rate is 12.2%.
Moreover, about 75% of these reversals occur at the reconsideration stage of the
administrative process. Since the median period between a request for
reconsideration review and decision is only two months, Brief for AFL-CIO *et
al.* as *Amici Curiae,* App. 4a, the deprivation is significantly less than that
concomitant to the lengthier delay before an evidentiary hearing. Netting out these
reconsideration reversals, the overall reversal rate falls to 3.3%. *See* Supplemental
and Reply Brief for Petitioner 14.

In striking the appropriate due process balance, the final factor to be assessed is the public interest. This includes the administrative burden and other societal costs that would be associated with requiring, as a matter of constitutional right, an evidentiary hearing upon demand in all cases prior to the termination of disability benefits. The most visible burden would be the incremental cost resulting from the increased number of hearings and the expense of providing benefits to ineligible recipients pending decision. No one can predict the extent of the increase, but the fact that full benefits would continue until after such hearings would assure the exhaustion in most cases of this attractive option. Nor would the theoretical right of the Secretary to recover undeserved benefits result, as a practical matter, in any substantial offset to the added outlay of public funds. The parties submit widely varying estimates of the probable additional financial cost. We only need say that experience with the constitutionalizing of government procedures suggests that the ultimate additional cost in terms of money and administrative burden would not be insubstantial.

Financial cost alone is not a controlling weight in determining whether due process requires a particular procedural safeguard prior to some administrative decision. But the Government's interest, and hence that of the public, in conserving scarce fiscal and administrative resources is a factor that must be weighed. At some point, the benefit of an additional safeguard to the individual affected by the administrative action and to society in terms of increased assurance that the action is just may be outweighed by the cost. Significantly, the cost of protecting those whom the preliminary administrative process has identified as likely to be found undeserving may, in the end, come out of the pockets of the deserving, since resources available for any particular program of social welfare are not unlimited.

But more is implicated in cases of this type than ad hoc weighing of fiscal and administrative burdens against the interests of a particular category of claimants. The ultimate balance involves a determination as to when, under our constitutional system, judicial-type procedures must be imposed upon administrative action to assure fairness. We reiterate the wise admonishment of MR. JUSTICE FRANKFURTER that differences in the origin and function of administrative agencies "preclude wholesale transplantation of the rules of procedure, trial, and review which have evolved from the history and experience of courts." *FCC v. Pottsville Broadcasting Co.*, 309 U.S. 134, 143 (1940). The judicial model of an evidentiary hearing is neither a required, nor even the most effective, method of decisionmaking in all circumstances. The essence of due process is the requirement that "a person in jeopardy of serious loss [be given] notice of the case against him and opportunity to meet it." *Joint Anti-Fascist Comm. v. McGrath*, 341 U.S., at 171-172 (FRANKFURTER, J., concurring). All that is necessary is that the procedures be tailored, in light of the decision to be made, to "the capacities and circumstances of those who are to be heard," *Goldberg v. Kelly*, 397 U.S., at 268, 269 (footnote omitted), to [e]nsure that they are given a meaningful opportunity to present their case. In assessing what process is due in this case, substantial weight must be given to the good faith judgments of the individuals charged by Congress with the administration of social welfare programs that the procedures they have provided assure fair consideration of the entitlement claims of individuals. This is especially so where, as here, the prescribed procedures not only provide the claimant with an effective process for asserting his claim prior to any administrative action, but also assure a right to an evidentiary hearing, as well as to subsequent judicial review, before the denial of his claim becomes final.

We conclude that an evidentiary hearing is not required prior to the termination of disability benefits, and that the present administrative procedures fully comport with due process.

The judgment of the Court of Appeals is

Reversed.

MR. JUSTICE STEVENS took no part in the consideration or decision of this case.

MR. JUSTICE BRENNAN, with whom MR. JUSTICE MARSHALL concurs, dissenting.

* * * I agree with the District Court and the Court of Appeals that, prior to termination of benefits, Eldridge must be afforded an evidentiary hearing of the type required for welfare beneficiaries under Title IV of the Social Security Act. I would add that the Court's consideration that a discontinuance of disability benefits may cause the recipient to suffer only a limited deprivation is no argument. It is speculative. Moreover, the very legislative determination to provide disability benefits, without any prerequisite determination of need in fact, presumes a need by the recipient which is not this Court's function to denigrate. Indeed, in the present case, it is indicated that, because disability benefits were terminated, there was a foreclosure upon the Eldridge home and the family's furniture was repossessed, forcing Eldridge, his wife, and their children to sleep in one bed. Finally, it is also no argument that a worker, who has been placed in the untenable position of having been denied disability benefits may still seek other forms of public assistance.

## 3. When Process is Due

Much of due process is about timing: getting a hearing *before* your disability benefits are cut off is very different than getting a hearing after. Indeed, there's not always a bright line between the "what" and "when" questions of due process: *Goldberg v. Kelly* and *Mathews v. Eldridge*, for instance, are really cases about when the hearing must be provided. The time dimension is especially prominent in the cases that follow.

## North American Cold Storage Co. v. Chicago

1     211 U.S. 306 (1908)

2     December 7, 1908

3     The bill [of complaint] was filed against the City of Chicago and the various
4     individual defendants in their official capacities—Commissioner of Health of the
5     City of Chicago, Secretary of the Department of Health, Chief Food Inspector of the
6     Department of Health, and inspectors of that department, and policemen of the
7     city—for the purpose of obtaining an injunction under the circumstances set forth
8     in the bill. It was therein alleged that the complainant was a cold storage company,
9     having a cold storage plant in the City of Chicago, and that it received, for the
10     purpose of keeping in cold storage, food products and goods as bailee for hire; that,
11     on an average, it received $20,000 worth of goods per day, and returned a like
12     amount to its customers, daily, and that it had on an average in storage about two
13     million dollars' worth of goods; that it received some forty-seven barrels of poultry
14     on or about October 2, 1906, from a wholesale dealer, in due course of business, to
15     be kept by it and returned to such dealer on demand; that the poultry was, when
16     received, in good condition and wholesome for human food, and had been so
17     maintained by it in cold storage from that time, and it would remain so, if
18     undisturbed, for three months; that, on the second of October, 1906, the individual
19     defendants appeared at complainant's place of business and demanded of it that it
20     forthwith deliver the forty-seven barrels of poultry for the purpose of being by them
21     destroyed, the defendants alleging that the poultry had become putrid, decayed,
22     poisonous, or infected in such a manner as to render it unsafe or unwholesome for
23     human food. The demand was made under § 1161 of the Revised Municipal Code
24     of the City of Chicago for 1905, which reads as follows:

25       "Every person being the owner, lessee, or occupant of any room, stall,
26       freight house, cold storage house, or other place, other than a private
27       dwelling, where any meat, fish, poultry, game, vegetables, fruit, or other
28       perishable article adapted or designed to be used for human food shall be
29       stored or kept, whether temporarily or otherwise, and every person having
30       charge of, or being interested or engaged, whether as principal or agent, in
31       the care of or in respect to the custody or sale of any such article of food
32       supply, shall put, preserve, and keep such article of food supply in a clean
33       and wholesome condition, and shall not allow the same, nor any part
34       thereof, to become putrid, decayed, poisoned, infected, or in any other
35       manner rendered or made unsafe or unwholesome for human food, and it
36       shall be the duty of the meat and food inspectors and other duly authorized
37       employees of the health department of the city to enter any and all such
38       premises above specified at any time of any day, and to forthwith seize,
39       condemn, and destroy any such putrid, decayed, poisoned, and infected
40       food, which any such inspector may find in and upon said premises."

41     The complainant refused to deliver up the poultry, on the ground that the section
42     above quoted of the Municipal Code of Chicago, insofar as it allows the city or its
43     agents to seize, condemn, or destroy food or other food products, was in conflict

1  with that portion of the Fourteenth Amendment which provides that no state shall
2  deprive any person of life, liberty, or property without due process of law; nor deny
3  to any person within its jurisdiction the equal protection of the laws.

4  After the refusal of the complainant to deliver the poultry, the defendants stated
5  that they would not permit the complainant's business to be further conducted
6  until it complied with the demand of the defendants and delivered up the poultry,
7  nor would they permit any more goods to be received into the warehouse or taken
8  from the same, and that they would arrest and imprison any person who attempted
9  to do so until complainant complied with their demand and delivered up the
10 poultry. Since that time, the complainant's business has been stopped and the
11 complainant has been unable to deliver any goods from its plant or receive the
12 same.

13 The bill averred that the attempt to seize, condemn, and destroy the poultry
14 without a judicial determination of the fact that the same was putrid, decayed,
15 poisonous, or infected was illegal, and it asked that the defendants, and each of
16 them, might be enjoined from taking or removing the poultry from the warehouse
17 or from destroying the same, and that they also be enjoined from preventing
18 complainant delivering its goods and receiving from its customers, in due course
19 of business, the goods committed to its care for storage.

20 In an amendment to the bill, the complainant further stated that the defendants
21 are now threatening to summarily destroy, from time to time, pursuant to the
22 provisions of the above-mentioned section, any and all food products which may
23 be deemed by them, or either of them, as being putrid, decayed, poisonous, or
24 infected in such manner as to be unfit for human food, without any judicial
25 determination of the fact that such food products are in such condition.

26 The defendants demurred to the bill on the ground, among others, that the court
27 had no jurisdiction of the action. The injunction was not issued, but, upon
28 argument of the case upon the demurrer, the bill was dismissed by the circuit court
29 for want of jurisdiction, as already stated.

30 MR. JUSTICE PECKHAM, after making the foregoing statement, delivered the
31 opinion of the Court.

32 In this case, the ordinance in question is to be regarded as in effect a statute of the
33 state, adopted under a power granted it by the state legislature, and hence it is an
34 act of the state within the Fourteenth Amendment.

35                                    * * *

36 We think there was jurisdiction, and that it was error for the court to dismiss the
37 bill on that ground. The court seems to have proceeded upon the theory that, as
38 the complainant's assertion of jurisdiction was based upon an alleged federal
39 question which was not well founded, there was no jurisdiction. In this we think
40 that the court erred. The bill contained a plain averment that the ordinance in

1     question violated the Fourteenth Amendment because it provided for no notice to
2     the complainant or opportunity for a hearing before the seizure and destruction of
3     the food. A constitutional question was thus presented to the court over which it
4     had jurisdiction, and it was bound to decide the same on its merits. * * *

5                                * * *

6     * * * The action of the defendants, which is admitted by the demurrer, in refusing
7     to permit the complainant to carry on its ordinary business until it delivered the
8     poultry, would seem to have been arbitrary and wholly indefensible. Counsel for
9     the complainant, however, for the purpose of obtaining a decision in regard to the
10    constitutional question as to the right to seize and destroy property without a prior
11    hearing, states that he will lay no stress here upon that portion of the bill which
12    alleges the unlawful and forcible taking possession of complainant's business by
13    the defendants. * * *

14                               * * *

15    The general power of the state to legislate upon the subject embraced in the above
16    ordinance of the City of Chicago counsel does not deny. Nor does he deny the right
17    to seize and destroy unwholesome or putrid food, provided that notice and
18    opportunity to be heard be given the owner or custodian of the property before it
19    is destroyed. We are of opinion, however, that provision for a hearing before
20    seizure and condemnation and destruction of food which is unwholesome and
21    unfit for use is not necessary. The right to so seize is based upon the right and duty
22    of the State to protect and guard, as far as possible, the lives and health of its
23    inhabitants, and that it is proper to provide that food which is unfit for human
24    consumption should be summarily seized and destroyed to prevent the danger
25    which would arise from eating it. The right to so seize and destroy is, of course,
26    based upon the fact that the food is not fit to be eaten. Food that is in such a
27    condition, if kept for sale or in danger of being sold, is, in itself, a nuisance, and a
28    nuisance of the most dangerous kind, involving, as it does, the health, if not the
29    lives, of persons who may eat it. A determination on the part of the seizing officers
30    that food is in an unfit condition to be eaten is not a decision which concludes the
31    owner. The *ex parte* finding of the health officers as to the fact is not in any way
32    binding upon those who own or claim the right to sell the food. If a party cannot
33    get his hearing in advance of the seizure and destruction, he has the right to have
34    it afterward, which right may be claimed upon the trial in an action brought for the
35    destruction of his property, and in that action those who destroyed it can only
36    successfully defend if the jury shall find the fact of unwholesomeness, as claimed
37    by them. * * *

38                               * * *

39    Complainant, however, contends that there was no emergency requiring speedy
40    action for the destruction of the poultry in order to protect the public health from
41    danger resulting from consumption of such poultry. It is said that the food was in
42    cold storage, and that it would continue in the same condition it then was for three

months, if properly stored, and that therefore the defendants had ample time in which to give notice to complainant or the owner and have a hearing of the question as to the condition of the poultry; and, as the ordinance provided for no hearing, it was void. But we think this is not required. The power of the legislature to enact laws in relation to the public health being conceded, as it must be, it is to a great extent within legislative discretion as to whether any hearing need be given before the destruction of unwholesome food which is unfit for human consumption. If a hearing were to be always necessary, even under the circumstances of this case, the question at once arises as to what is to be done with the food in the meantime. Is it to remain with the cold storage company, and, if so, under what security that it will not be removed? To be sure that it will not be removed during the time necessary for the hearing, which might frequently be indefinitely prolonged, some guard would probably have to be placed over the subject matter of investigation, which would involve expense, and might not even then prove effectual. What is the emergency which would render a hearing unnecessary? We think when the question is one regarding the destruction of food which is not fit for human use, the emergency must be one which would fairly appeal to the reasonable discretion of the legislature as to the necessity for a prior hearing, and in that case its decision would not be a subject for review by the courts. As the owner of the food or its custodian is amply protected against the party seizing the food, who must, in a subsequent action against him, show as a fact that it was within the statute, we think that due process of law is not denied the owner or custodian by the destruction of the food alleged to be unwholesome and unfit for human food without a preliminary hearing. * * *

* * *

The decree of the court below is modified by striking out the ground for dismissal of the bill as being for want of jurisdiction, and, as modified, is

Affirmed.

MR. JUSTICE BREWER dissenting. [Omitted.]


## Phillips v. Commissioner of Internal Revenue

283 U.S. 589 (1931)

May 25, 1931.

Mr. Justice BRANDEIS delivered the opinion of the Court.

In 1919, the Coombe Garment Company, a Pennsylvania corporation, distributed all of its assets among its stockholders, and then dissolved. Thereafter, the Commissioner of Internal Revenue made deficiency assessments against it for income and profits taxes for the years 1918 and 1919. A small part of these assessments was collected, leaving an unpaid balance of $9,306.36. I. L. Phillips,

1   of New York City, had owned one-fourth of the company's stock and had received
2   $17,139.61 as his distributive dividend. Pursuant to § 280(a)(1) of the Revenue Act
3   of 1926, the Commissioner sent due notice that he proposed to assess against, and
4   collect from, Phillips the entire remaining amount of the deficiencies. No notice of
5   such deficiencies was sent to any of the other transferees, and no suit or
6   proceedings for collection was instituted against them. Upon petition by Phillips'
7   executors for a redetermination, the Board of Tax Appeals held that the estate was
8   liable for the full amount. Its order was affirmed by the United States Circuit Court
9   of Appeals for the Second Circuit. Because of conflict in the decisions of the lower
10  courts a writ of certiorari was granted.

11  Stockholders who have received the assets of a dissolved corporation may
12  confessedly be compelled, in an appropriate proceeding, to discharge unpaid
13  corporate taxes. Before the enactment of § 280(a)(1), such payment by the
14  stockholders could be enforced only by bill in equity or action at law. Section
15  280(a)(1) provides that the liability of the transferee for such taxes may be
16  enforced in the same manner as that of any delinquent taxpayer.

17  The procedure prescribed for collection of the tax from a stockholder is thus the
18  same as that now followed when payment is sought directly from the corporate
19  taxpayer. * * * As applied directly to the taxpayer, its constitutionality is not now
20  assailed. But it is contended that to apply it to stockholder transferees violates
21  several constitutional guaranties; that additional obstacles are encountered if it is
22  applied to transfers made before the enactment of § 280(a)(1); that the specific
23  liability here sought to be enforced is governed by the law of Pennsylvania and
24  barred by its statute of limitations; and that, in no event, can the stockholder be
25  held liable for more than his pro rata share of the unpaid corporate tax.

26  * * * The contention mainly urged is that the summary procedure permitted by the
27  section violates the Constitution because it does not provide for a judicial
28  determination of the transferee's liability at the outset. * * *

29                                    * * *

30  The right of the United States to collect its internal revenue by summary
31  administrative proceedings has long been settled. Where, as here, adequate
32  opportunity is afforded for a later judicial determination of the legal rights,
33  summary proceedings to secure prompt performance of pecuniary obligations to
34  the government have been consistently sustained. Property rights must yield
35  provisionally to governmental need. Thus, while protection of life and liberty from
36  administrative action alleged to be illegal may be obtained promptly by the writ of
37  habeas corpus, the statutory prohibition of any 'suit for the purpose of restraining
38  the assessment or collection of any tax' postpones redress for the alleged invasion
39  of property rights if the exaction is made under color of their offices by revenue
40  officers charged with the general authority to assess and collect the revenue. This
41  prohibition of injunctive relief is applicable in the case of summary proceedings
42  against a transferee. Proceedings more summary in character than that provided

1 in § 280, and involving less directly the obligation of the taxpayer, were sustained
2 in *Murray's Lessee v. Hoboken Land & Improvement Co.*, 59 U.S. 272 (1856). It is
3 urged that the decision in the *Murray* Case was based upon the peculiar
4 relationship of a collector of revenue to his government. The underlying principle
5 in that case was not such relation, but the need of the government promptly to
6 secure its revenues.

7 Where only property rights are involved, mere postponement of the judicial
8 enquiry is not a denial of due process, if the opportunity given for the ultimate
9 judicial determination of the liability is adequate. Delay in the judicial
10 determination of property rights is not uncommon where it is essential that
11 governmental needs be immediately satisfied. For the protection of public health,
12 a state may order the summary destruction of property by administrative
13 authorities without antecedent notice of hearing. *Compare North American Cold*
14 *Storage Co. v. Chicago*, 211 U.S. 306 (1908). Because of the public necessity, the
15 property of citizens may be summarily seized in war-time. And at any time, the
16 United States may acquire property by eminent domain, without paying, or
17 determining the amount of the compensation before the taking.

18 The procedure provided in § 280(a)(1) satisfies the requirements of due process
19 because two alternative methods of eventual judicial review are available to the
20 transferee. He may contest his liability by bringing an action, either against the
21 United States or the collector, to recover the amount paid. This remedy is available
22 where the transferee does not appeal from the determination of the Commissioner,
23 and the latter makes an assessment and enforces payment by distraint; or where
24 the transferee voluntarily pays the tax and is thereafter denied administrative
25 relief. Or the transferee may avail himself of the provisions for immediate
26 redetermination of the liability by the Board of Tax Appeals, since all provisions
27 governing this mode of review are made applicable by § 280. Thus within sixty days
28 after the Commissioner determines that the transferee is liable for an unpaid
29 deficiency, and gives due notice thereof, the latter may file a petition with the Board
30 of Tax Appeals. Formal notice of the tax liability is thus given; the Commissioner
31 is required to answer; and there is a complete hearing *de novo* according to the
32 rules of evidence applicable in courts of equity of the District of Columbia. This
33 remedy may be had before payment, without giving bond (unless the
34 Commissioner in his discretion deems a jeopardy assessment necessary). The
35 transferee has the right to a preliminary examination of books, papers, and other
36 evidence of the taxpayer; and the burden of proof is on the Commissioner to show
37 that the appellant is liable as a transferee of property, though not to show that the
38 taxpayer was liable for the tax. A review by the Circuit Court of Appeals of an
39 adverse determination may be had; and assessment and collection meanwhile may
40 be stayed by giving a bond to secure payment. There may be a further review by
41 this Court on certiorari. These provisions amply protect the transferee against
42 improper administrative action.

43 It is argued that such review by the Board of Tax Appeals and Circuit Court of
44 Appeals is constitutionally inadequate because of the conditions and limitations

1 imposed. Specific objection is made to the provision that collection will not be
2 stayed while the case is pending before the Circuit Court of Appeals, unless a bond
3 is filed; and also to the rule under which the Board's findings of fact are treated by
4 that court as final if there is any evidence to support them. As to the first of these
5 objections, it has already been shown that the right of the United States to exact
6 immediate payment and to relegate the taxpayer to a suit for recovery is
7 paramount. The privilege of delaying payment pending immediate judicial review,
8 by filing a bond, was granted by the sovereign as a matter of grace solely for the
9 convenience of the taxpayer. Nor is the second objection of weight. It has long been
10 settled that determinations of fact for ordinary administrative purposes are not
11 subject to review. Save as there may be an exception for issues presenting claims
12 of constitutional right, such administrative findings on issues of fact are accepted
13 by the court as conclusive if the evidence was legally sufficient to sustain them and
14 there was no irregularity in the proceedings. * * * The alternative judicial review
15 provided is adequate in both cases.

16                 * * *

17 Affirmed.

18

19 **Gilbert v. Homar**

20 520 U.S. 924 (1997)

21 June 9, 1997

22 JUSTICE SCALIA delivered the opinion of the Court.

23 This case presents the question whether a State violates the Due Process Clause of
24 the Fourteenth Amendment by failing to provide notice and a hearing before
25 suspending a tenured public employee without pay.

26                 I

27 Respondent Richard J. Homar was employed as a police officer at East
28 Stroudsburg University (ESU), a branch of Pennsylvania's State System of Higher
29 Education. On August 26, 1992, when respondent was at the home of a family
30 friend, he was arrested by the Pennsylvania State Police in a drug raid. Later that
31 day, the state police filed a criminal complaint charging respondent with
32 possession of marijuana, possession with intent to deliver, and criminal conspiracy
33 to violate the controlled substance law, which is a felony. The state police notified
34 respondent's supervisor, University Police Chief David Marazas, of the arrest and
35 charges. Chief Marazas in turn informed Gerald Levanowitz, ESU's Director of
36 Human Resources, to whom ESU President James Gilbert had delegated authority
37 to discipline ESU employees. Levanowitz suspended respondent without pay
38 effective immediately. Respondent failed to report to work on the day of his arrest,
39 and learned of his suspension the next day, when he called Chief Marazas to

1    inquire whether he had been suspended. That same day, respondent received a
2    letter from Levanowitz confirming that he had been suspended effective August 26
3    pending an investigation into the criminal charges filed against him. The letter
4    explained that any action taken by ESU would not necessarily coincide with the
5    disposition of the criminal charges.

6    Although the criminal charges were dismissed on September 1, respondent's
7    suspension remained in effect while ESU continued with its own investigation. On
8    September 18, Levanowitz and Chief Marazas met with respondent in order to give
9    him an opportunity to tell his side of the story. Respondent was informed at the
10   meeting that the state police had given ESU information that was "very serious in
11   nature," but he was not informed that that included a report of an alleged
12   confession he had made on the day of his arrest; he was consequently unable to
13   respond to damaging statements attributed to him in the police report.

14   In a letter dated September 23, Levanowitz notified respondent that he was being
15   demoted to the position of groundskeeper effective the next day, and that he would
16   receive backpay from the date the suspension took effect at the rate of pay of a
17   groundskeeper. (Respondent eventually received backpay for the period of his
18   suspension at the rate of pay of a university police officer.) The letter maintained
19   that the demotion was being imposed "as a result of admissions made by yourself
20   to the Pennsylvania State Police on August 26, 1992 that you maintained
21   associations with individuals whom you knew were dealing in large quantities of
22   marijuana and that you obtained marijuana from one of those individuals for your
23   own use. Your actions constitute a clear and flagrant violation of Sections 200 and
24   200.2 of the [ESU] Police Department Manual." Upon receipt of this letter, the
25   president of respondent's union requested a meeting with President Gilbert. The
26   requested meeting took place on September 24, at which point respondent had
27   received and read the police report containing the alleged confession. After
28   providing respondent with an opportunity to respond to the charges, Gilbert
29   sustained the demotion.

30   Respondent filed this suit under 42 U.S.C. § 1983 in the United States District
31   Court for the Middle District of Pennsylvania against President Gilbert, Chief
32   Marazas, Levanowitz, and a Vice President of ESU, Curtis English, all in both their
33   individual and official capacities. He contended, *inter alia*, that petitioners' failure
34   to provide him with notice and an opportunity to be heard before suspending him
35   without pay violated due process. The District Court entered summary judgment
36   for petitioners. A divided Court of Appeals reversed the District Court's
37   determination that it was permissible for ESU to suspend respondent without pay
38   without first providing a hearing. We granted certiorari.

39                                    II

40   The protections of the Due Process Clause apply to government deprivation of
41   those perquisites of government employment in which the employee has a
42   constitutionally protected "property" interest. Although we have previously held

1   that public employees who can be discharged only for cause have a constitutionally
2   protected property interest in their tenure and cannot be fired without due process,
3   *see Board of Regents of State Colleges v. Roth*, 408 U.S. 564, 578 (1972); *Perry v.*
4   *Sindermann*, 408 U.S. 593, 602-603 (1972), we have not had occasion to decide
5   whether the protections of the Due Process Clause extend to discipline of tenured
6   public employees short of termination. Petitioners, however, do not contest this
7   preliminary point, and so without deciding it we will, like the District Court,
8   "[a]ssum[e] that the suspension infringed a protected property interest," and turn
9   at once to petitioners' contention that respondent received all the process he was
10  due.

11                                           A

12  In *Cleveland Bd. of Ed. v. Loudermill*, 470 U.S. 532 (1985), we concluded that a
13  public employee dismissible only for cause was entitled to a very limited hearing
14  prior to his termination, to be followed by a more comprehensive post-termination
15  hearing. Stressing that the pretermination hearing "should be an initial check
16  against mistaken decisions—essentially, a determination of whether there are
17  reasonable grounds to believe that the charges against the employee are true and
18  support the proposed action," *id.*, at 545-546, we held that pretermination process
19  need only include oral or written notice of the charges, an explanation of the
20  employer's evidence, and an opportunity for the employee to tell his side of the
21  story. In the course of our assessment of the governmental interest in immediate
22  termination of a tenured employee, we observed that "in those situations where
23  the employer perceives a significant hazard in keeping the employee on the job, it
24  can avoid the problem by suspending *with pay.*" *Id.*, at 544-545 (emphasis added).

25  Relying on this dictum, which it read as "strongly suggest[ing] that suspension
26  without pay must be preceded by notice and an opportunity to be heard *in all*
27  *instances*," and determining on its own that such a rule would be "eminently
28  sensible," the Court of Appeals adopted a categorical prohibition: "[A]
29  governmental employer may not suspend an employee without pay unless that
30  suspension is preceded by some kind of presuspension hearing, providing the
31  employee with notice and an opportunity to be heard." Respondent (as well as most
32  of his *amici*) makes no attempt to defend this absolute rule, which spans all types
33  of government employment and all types of unpaid suspensions. This is eminently
34  wise, since under our precedents such an absolute rule is indefensible.

35  It is by now well established that "'due process,' unlike some legal rules, is not a
36  technical conception with a fixed content unrelated to time, place and
37  circumstances." *Cafeteria & Restaurant Workers v. McElroy*, 367 U.S. 886, 895
38  (1961). "[D]ue process is flexible and calls for such procedural protections as the
39  particular situation demands." *Morrissey v. Brewer*, 408 U.S. 471, 481 (1972). This
40  Court has recognized, on many occasions, that where a State must act quickly, or
41  where it would be impractical to provide predeprivation process, postdeprivation
42  process satisfies the requirements of the Due Process Clause. * * * [I]n *FDIC v.*
43  *Mallen*, 486 U.S. 230 (1988), where we unanimously approved the Federal Deposit

1 Insurance Corporation's (FDIC's) suspension, without prior hearing, of an indicted
2 private bank employee, we said: "An important government interest, accompanied
3 by a substantial assurance that the deprivation is not baseless or unwarranted, may
4 in limited cases demanding prompt action justify postponing the opportunity to be
5 heard until after the initial deprivation." *Id.*, at 240.

6 The dictum in *Loudermill* relied upon by the Court of Appeals is of course not
7 inconsistent with these precedents. To say that when the government employer
8 perceives a hazard in leaving the employee on the job it "can avoid the problem by
9 suspending with pay" is not to say that that is the only way of avoiding the problem.
10 Whatever implication the phrase "with pay" might have conveyed is far outweighed
11 by the clarity of our precedents which emphasize the flexibility of due process as
12 contrasted with the sweeping and categorical rule adopted by the Court of Appeals.

13 B

14 To determine what process is constitutionally due, we have generally balanced
15 three distinct factors:

16 "First, the private interest that will be affected by the official action; second,
17 the risk of an erroneous deprivation of such interest through the
18 procedures used, and the probable value, if any, of additional or substitute
19 procedural safeguards; and finally, the Government's interest."

20 *Mathews v. Eldridge*, 424 U.S. 319, 335 (1976).

21 Respondent contends that he has a significant private interest in the uninterrupted
22 receipt of his paycheck. But while our opinions have recognized the severity of
23 depriving someone of the means of his livelihood, they have also emphasized that
24 in determining what process is due, account must be taken of "the *length*" and
25 "*finality* of the deprivation." Unlike the employee in *Loudermill*, who faced
26 *termination*, respondent faced only a *temporary suspension* without pay. So long
27 as the suspended employee receives a sufficiently prompt postsuspension hearing,
28 the lost income is relatively insubstantial (compared with termination), and fringe
29 benefits such as health and life insurance are often not affected at all.

30 On the other side of the balance, the State has a significant interest in immediately
31 suspending, when felony charges are filed against them, employees who occupy
32 positions of great public trust and high public visibility, such as police officers.
33 Respondent contends that this interest in maintaining public confidence could
34 have been accommodated by suspending him *with* pay until he had a hearing. We
35 think, however, that the government does not have to give an employee charged
36 with a felony a paid leave at taxpayer expense. If his services to the government are
37 no longer useful once the felony charge has been filed, the Constitution does not
38 require the government to bear the added expense of hiring a replacement while
39 still paying him. * * *

1     The last factor in the *Mathews* balancing, and the factor most important to
2     resolution of this case, is the risk of erroneous deprivation and the likely value of
3     any additional procedures. * * * We noted in *Loudermill* that the purpose of a pre-
4     *termination* hearing is to determine "whether there are reasonable grounds to
5     believe that the charges against the employee are true and support the proposed
6     action." 470 U.S., at 545-546. By parity of reasoning, the purpose of any pre-
7     *suspension* hearing would be to assure that there are reasonable grounds to
8     support the suspension without pay. But here that has already been assured by the
9     arrest and the filing of charges.

10     In *Mallen*, we concluded that an "*ex parte* finding of probable cause" such as a
11     grand jury indictment provides adequate assurance that the suspension is not
12     unjustified. The same is true when an employee is arrested and then formally
13     charged with a felony. First, as with an indictment, the arrest and formal charges
14     imposed upon respondent "by an independent body demonstrat[e] that the
15     suspension is not arbitrary." *Id.*, at 244. Second, like an indictment, the imposition
16     of felony charges "itself is an objective fact that will in most cases raise serious
17     public concern." *Id.*, at 244-245. It is true, as respondent argues, that there is more
18     reason to believe an employee has committed a felony when he is indicted rather
19     than merely arrested and formally charged; but for present purposes arrest and
20     charge give reason enough. They serve to assure that the state employer's decision
21     to suspend the employee is not "baseless or unwarranted," in that an independent
22     third party has determined that there is probable cause to believe the employee
23     committed a serious crime.

24     Respondent further contends that since (as we have agreed to assume) Levanowitz
25     had discretion *not* to suspend despite the arrest and filing of charges, he had to be
26     given an opportunity to persuade Levanowitz of his innocence before the decision
27     was made. We disagree. * * * Unlike in the case of a termination, where we have
28     recognized that "the only meaningful opportunity to invoke the discretion of the
29     decisionmaker is likely to be before the termination takes effect," *Loudermill*,
30     *supra*, at 543, in the case of a suspension there will be ample opportunity to invoke
31     discretion later—and a short delay actually benefits the employee by allowing state
32     officials to obtain more accurate information about the arrest and charges.
33     Respondent "has an interest in seeing that a decision concerning his or her
34     continued suspension is not made with excessive haste." *Mallen*, 486 U.S., at 243.
35     If the State is forced to act too quickly, the decisionmaker "may give greater weight
36     to the public interest and leave the suspension in place." *Ibid.*

37     C

38     Much of respondent's argument is dedicated to the proposition that he had a due
39     process right to a presuspension hearing because the suspension was open-ended
40     and he "theoretically may not have had the opportunity to be heard for weeks,
41     months, or even years after his initial suspension without pay." But, as respondent
42     himself asserts in his attempt to downplay the governmental interest, "[b]ecause
43     the employee is entitled, in any event, to a prompt post-suspension opportunity to

be heard, the period of the suspension should be short and the amount of pay during the suspension minimal." *Id.*, at 24-25.

Whether respondent was provided an adequately prompt post-suspension hearing in the present case is a separate question. Although the charges against respondent were dropped on September 1 (petitioners apparently learned of this on September 2), he did not receive any sort of hearing until September 18. Once the charges were dropped, the risk of erroneous deprivation increased substantially, and, as petitioners conceded at oral argument, there was likely value in holding a prompt hearing. Compare *Mallen*, 486 U.S., at 243 (holding that 90 days before the agency hears and decides the propriety of a suspension does not exceed the permissible limits where coupled with factors that minimize the risk of an erroneous deprivation). Because neither the Court of Appeals nor the District Court addressed whether, under the particular facts of this case, petitioners violated due process by failing to provide a sufficiently prompt postsuspension hearing, we will not consider this issue in the first instance, but remand for consideration by the Court of Appeals.

The judgment of the Court of Appeals is reversed, and the case is remanded for further proceedings consistent with this opinion.

It is so ordered.


## General Electric Company v. Jackson

610 F.3d 110 (D.C. Cir. 2010)

June 29, 2010

Before: ROGERS, TATEL, and GRIFFITH, Circuit Judges.

TATEL, Circuit Judge: In this case, appellant challenges the constitutionality of a statutory scheme that authorizes the Environmental Protection Agency to issue orders, known as unilateral administrative orders (UAOs), directing companies and others to clean up hazardous waste for which they are responsible. Appellant argues that the statute, as well as the way in which EPA administers it, violates the Due Process Clause because EPA issues UAOs without a hearing before a neutral decisionmaker. We disagree. To the extent the UAO regime implicates constitutionally protected property interests by imposing compliance costs and threatening fines and punitive damages, it satisfies due process because UAO recipients may obtain a pre-deprivation hearing by refusing to comply and forcing EPA to sue in federal court. Appellant insists that the UAO scheme and EPA's implementation of it nonetheless violate due process because the mere issuance of a UAO can inflict immediate, serious, and irreparable damage by depressing the recipient's stock price, harming its brand value, and increasing its cost of financing. But such "consequential" injuries—injuries resulting not from EPA's issuance of the UAO, but from market reactions to it—are insufficient to merit Due Process

224

1 Clause protection. We therefore affirm the district court's grant of summary
2 judgment to EPA.

3                                    I.

4 Congress enacted the Comprehensive Environmental Response, Compensation,
5 and Liability Act (CERCLA) "in response to the serious environmental and health
6 risks posed by industrial pollution." *United States v. Bestfoods*, 524 U.S. 51, 55
7 (1998). CERCLA seeks to promote prompt cleanup of hazardous waste sites and to
8 ensure that responsible parties foot the bill. * * *

9                                  * * *

10 When EPA determines that an environmental cleanup is necessary at a
11 contaminated site, CERCLA gives the agency four options: (1) it may negotiate a
12 settlement with potentially responsible parties (PRPs); (2) it may conduct the
13 cleanup with "Superfund" money and then seek reimbursement from PRPs by
14 filing suit; (3) it may file an abatement action in federal district court to compel
15 PRPs to conduct the cleanup,; or (4) it may issue a UAO instructing PRPs to clean
16 the site. This last option, authorized by CERCLA section 106, is the focus of this
17 case.

18 * * * For remedial actions, the longer-term option, CERCLA requires EPA to
19 "provide for the participation of interested persons, including [PRPs], in the
20 development of the administrative record." 42 U.S.C. § 9613(k)(2)(B). Specifically,
21 EPA must provide "[n]otice to potentially affected persons and the public," "[a]
22 reasonable opportunity to comment and provide information regarding the
23 [remedial] plan," "[a]n opportunity for a public meeting in the affected area," "[a]
24 response to each of the significant comments, criticisms, and new data submitted
25 in written or oral presentations," and "[a] statement of the basis and purpose of
26 the selected action." *Id.*; see also § 9617(a)(b) (requiring public notice of all
27 remedial actions).

28 Once EPA issues a UAO, the recipient PRP has two choices. It may comply and,
29 after completing the cleanup, seek reimbursement from EPA. If EPA refuses
30 reimbursement, the PRP may sue the agency in federal district court to recover its
31 costs on the grounds that (1) it was not liable for the cleanup; or (2) it was liable
32 but EPA's selected response action (or some portion thereof) was "arbitrary and
33 capricious or . . . otherwise not in accordance with law." Alternatively, the PRP
34 may refuse to comply with the UAO, in which case EPA may either bring an action
35 in federal district court to enforce the UAO against the noncomplying PRP, or clean
36 the site itself and then sue the PRP to recover its costs. In either proceeding, if the
37 court concludes that the PRP "willfully" failed to comply with an order "without
38 sufficient cause," it "may" (but need not) impose fines, which are currently set at
39 $37,500 per day, and accumulate until EPA brings a recovery or enforcement
40 action—a period of up to six years. If EPA itself undertakes the cleanup and the
41 district court finds that the PRP "fail[ed] without sufficient cause" to comply with

1    the UAO, the court "may" impose punitive damages of up to "three times [ ] the
2    amount of any costs" the agency incurs. 42 U.S.C. § 9607(c)(3).

3    Central to this case, these two options—comply and seek reimbursement, or refuse
4    to comply and wait for EPA to bring an enforcement or cost recovery action—are
5    exclusive. CERCLA section 113(h) bars PRPs from obtaining immediate judicial
6    review of a UAO. That section provides that "No Federal court shall have
7    jurisdiction . . . to review any order issued under section [106]" until the PRP
8    completes the work and seeks reimbursement, or until EPA brings an enforcement
9    action or seeks to recover fines and damages for noncompliance.

10    Over the years, appellant General Electric (GE) has received at least 68 UAOs. In
11    addition, GE "is currently participating in response actions at 79 active CERCLA
12    sites" where UAOs may issue * * * .

13    In 2000, GE filed suit in the United States District Court for the District of
14    Columbia challenging CERCLA's UAO regime. In its amended complaint, GE
15    alleged that the statute violates the Fifth Amendment to the United States
16    Constitution because it "deprive[s] persons of their fundamental right to liberty
17    and property without . . . constitutionally adequate procedural safeguards."
18    According to GE, "[t]he unilateral orders regime . . . imposes a classic and
19    unconstitutional Hobson's choice": because refusing to comply "risk[s] severe
20    punishment [i.e., fines and treble damages]," UAO recipients' only real option is to
21    "comply . . . before having any opportunity to be heard on the legality and
22    rationality of the underlying order." GE also alleged that it "has been and is
23    aggrieved by CERCLA's fundamental constitutional deficiencies" because it has
24    repeatedly received UAOs and is likely to receive them in the future. GE sought "[a]
25    declaratory judgment that the provisions of CERCLA relating to unilateral
26    administrative orders . . . are unconstitutional."

27                                            * * *

28                                            II

29                                          * * *

30    The Fifth Amendment to the United States Constitution provides that "No person
31    shall . . . be deprived of life, liberty, or property, without due process of law." "The
32    first inquiry in every due process challenge is whether the plaintiff has been
33    deprived of a protected interest in 'liberty' or 'property.' Only after finding the
34    deprivation of a protected interest do we look to see if the [government's]
35    procedures comport with due process." *American Manufacturers Mut. Ins. Co. v.*
36    *Sullivan*, 526 U.S. 40, 59 (1999). At this second step, we apply the now-familiar
37    *Mathews v. Eldridge* balancing test, considering (1) the significance of the private
38    party's protected interest, (2) the government's interest, and (3) the risk of
39    erroneous deprivation and "the probable value, if any, of additional or substitute
40    procedural safeguards."

1    GE asserts that UAOs deprive PRPs of two types of protected property: (1) the
2    money PRPs must spend to comply with a UAO or the daily fines and treble
3    damages they face should they refuse to comply; and (2) the PRPs' stock price,
4    brand value, and cost of financing, all of which, GE contends, are adversely affected
5    by the issuance of a UAO. We address each of these alleged deprivations in turn.

6    *Costs of Compliance, Fines, and Damages*

7    The parties agree that the costs of compliance and the monetary fines and damages
8    associated with noncompliance qualify as protected property interests. They
9    disagree, however, as to whether judicial review is available before any deprivation
10   occurs. EPA contends that CERCLA gives PRPs the right to pre-deprivation judicial
11   review: by refusing to comply with a UAO, a PRP can force EPA to file suit in federal
12   court, where the PRP can challenge the order's validity before spending a single
13   dollar on compliance costs, damages, or fines. GE responds that noncompliance—
14   and thus pre-deprivation judicial review—is but a theoretical option. According to
15   GE, daily fines and treble damages "are so severe that they . . . intimidate [ ] PRPs
16   from exercising the purported option of electing not to comply with a UAO so as to
17   test an order's validity" via judicial review. * * *

18   GE's argument hinges on the Supreme Court's decision in *Ex parte Young*, 209
19   U.S. 123 (1908), and its progeny. Under those cases, a statutory scheme violates
20   due process if "the penalties for disobedience are by fines so enormous . . . as to
21   intimidate the [affected party] from resorting to the courts to test the validity of
22   the legislation [because] the result is the same as if the law in terms prohibited the
23   [party] from seeking judicial [review]" at all. *Id.* at 147. The Supreme Court has
24   made clear, however, that statutes imposing fines—even "enormous" fines—on
25   noncomplying parties may satisfy due process if such fines are subject to a "good
26   faith" or "reasonable ground[s]" defense. Courts have also held that "there is no
27   constitutional violation if the imposition of penalties is subject to judicial
28   discretion."

29   CERCLA guarantees these safeguards. Indeed, the statute offers noncomplying
30   PRPs several levels of protection: a PRP faces daily fines and treble damages only
31   if a federal court finds (1) that the UAO was proper; (2) that the PRP "willfully"
32   failed to comply "without sufficient cause"; and (3) that, in the court's discretion,
33   fines and treble damages are appropriate. As to the first of these findings—the
34   propriety of the UAO—the district court reviews EPA's determination de novo:
35   although the PRP must prove that it is not liable by a preponderance of the
36   evidence, EPA's liability determination warrants no judicial deference. As to the
37   second, CERCLA's "willfulness" and "sufficient cause" requirements are quite
38   similar to the good faith and reasonable grounds defenses the Supreme Court has
39   found sufficient to satisfy due process, and GE does not argue otherwise. * * *
40   Given these safeguards, we have no basis for concluding that "[t]he necessary effect
41   and result of [CERCLA] must be to preclude a resort to the courts . . . for the
42   purpose of testing [a UAO's] validity." *Young*, 209 U.S., at 146. Contrary to GE's
43   claim, then, PRPs face no Hobson's choice.

1       * * *

2       *Stock Price, Brand Value, and Cost of Financing*

3   GE contends that, in addition to potential cleanup costs, fines, and damages,
4   issuance of a UAO "immediately tag[s]" a PRP "with a massive contingent liability,"
5   which in turn depresses its stock price, harms its brand value, and increases its
6   cost of financing. According to GE, these adverse impacts are "irreparable and
7   cannot be remedied through a later, delayed challenge to [a] UAO." Perhaps so,
8   but we must first address an antecedent question: does the Due Process Clause
9   protect PRPs' interest in the market's assessment of their stock, brand, and credit
10  worthiness?

11  As the Supreme Court has repeatedly stated, "the range of interests protected by
12  procedural due process is not infinite." *Bd. of Regents of State Colls. v. Roth*, 408
13  U.S. 564, 570 (1972). Moreover, "[p]roperty interests . . . are not created by the
14  Constitution. Rather they are created and their dimensions are defined by existing
15  rules or understandings that stem from an independent source such as state law—
16  rules or understandings that secure certain benefits and that support claims of
17  entitlement to those benefits." *Id.* at 577; see also *Paul v. Davis*, 424 U.S. 693, 710
18  (1976). For due process purposes, then, it is not enough that one has "an abstract
19  need or desire" for the asserted property; to merit due process protection, "[h]e
20  must . . . have a legitimate claim for entitlement to it." *Roth*, 408 U.S., at 577.

21  GE points to no "independent source such as state law," for its purported property
22  interests. * * *

23      * * *

24  Stripped of its reliance on [cases distinguished by the Court], GE's case boils down
25  to this: by declaring that a PRP is responsible for cleaning up a hazardous waste
26  site, a UAO harms the PRP's reputation, and the market, in turn, devalues its stock,
27  brand, and credit rating. Viewed this way, GE's argument is foreclosed by *Paul v.*
28  *Davis*, 424 U.S. 693. There the Supreme Court held that a sheriff's inclusion of
29  Davis's name and photograph on a flyer captioned "Active Shoplifters" implicated
30  no due process interest. * * * In so holding, the Court distinguished *Wisconsin v.*
31  *Constantineau*, 400 U.S. 433 (1971), which ruled that a law allowing for
32  "posting"—forbidding the sale of alcoholic beverages to persons determined to
33  have become hazards based on their "excessive drinking"—violated due process.
34  As the Court explained in *Davis*, the law at issue in *Constantineau* went beyond
35  mere stigma, depriving the plaintiff "of a right previously held under state law . . .
36  to purchase or obtain liquor in common with the rest of the citizenry." *Davis*, 424
37  U.S., at 708. "[I]t was that alteration of legal status which, combined with the
38  injury resulting from the defamation, justified the invocation of procedural
39  safeguards" in *Constantineau. Id.* at 708-09. *Davis*'s rule is thus clear: stigma
40  alone is insufficient to invoke due process protections.

41      * * *

1   Our conclusion is unaffected by the fact that GE alleges "property" harm while
2   Davis addresses a "liberty" claim. Like other circuits, we have applied the stigma-
3   plus framework to property claims, requiring plaintiffs to show that alleged
4   reputational harm completely destroys the value of their property. * * *

5                                     * * *

6   Finally, * * * GE insists that the issuance of a UAO triggers due process protections
7   because it follows a factfinding, adjudicatory proceeding. * * *

8   GE argues that [two 1960s Supreme Court decisions,] *Hannah* and *Jenkins*, taken
9   together, establish that "where government action moves from investigatory to
10  adjudicatory, the government must provide pre-deprivation hearings." . * * * [I]n
11  the forty years since the Court decided *Jenkins*, it has never cited the case for the
12  broader proposition advocated by GE, i.e., that the Due Process Clause is
13  implicated whenever the government uses an adjudicatory process to find facts
14  with respect to a particular individual or corporation. * * *

15                                     III

16                                    * * *

17  * * * GE also contends that even if CERCLA is not facially coercive, EPA
18  administers the statute in a way that "intimidate[s] PRPs from exercising the
19  purported option of electing not to comply with a UAO so as to test an order's
20  validity, giving rise to an independent due process violation under *Ex parte*
21  *Young*." To the extent GE makes this argument, it urges us to infer coercion from
22  the fact that the vast majority of PRPs elect to comply with UAOs. * * *

23  Rejecting this argument, the district court began by explaining, properly in our
24  view, that the pattern and practice claim added little to GE's facial *Ex parte Young*
25  challenge: regardless of EPA's policies—for example, GE alleges that the agency
26  coerces PRPs into compliance by threatening to seek multiple penalties for
27  violations at a single UAO site—"a judge ultimately decides what, if any, penalty to
28  impose." As noted above, moreover, CERCLA's sufficient cause and willfulness
29  defenses protect PRPs from unwarranted fines and damages. As to GE's argument
30  that the high incidence of UAO compliance evidences coercion, the district court
31  found that "GE's own expert . . . demonstrate[d] that instances of noncompliance
32  are sufficiently numerous to suggest that PRPs are not, in fact, forced to comply."
33  *GE IV*, 595 F.Supp.2d at 28-29 (GE's expert found that "of the 1,638 PRPs who
34  have been issued UAOs most recently, there were 75 instances of noncompliance—
35  a rate of 4.6 percent."). And for our part, we observe that in light of the extensive
36  procedures CERCLA requires EPA to follow before issuing a UAO, including notice
37  and comment, recipients may be complying in large numbers not because they feel
38  coerced, but because they believe that UAOs are generally accurate and would
39  withstand judicial review. * * *

40                                     IV

We fully understand, as GE argues, that the financial consequences of UAOs can be substantial. We also understand that other administrative enforcement schemes that address matters of public health and safety may provide greater process than does CERCLA. Such concerns, however, do not implicate the constitutionality of CERCLA or of the policies and practices by which EPA implements it. * * * Because our judicial task is limited to determining whether CERCLA's UAO provisions violate the Fifth Amendment either on their face or as administered by EPA, we affirm the decisions of the district court.

*So ordered.*


## 4. Right to an Unbiased Decisionmaker

Does the due process clause entitle us to an unbiased decisionmaker? All of the procedural protections in the world have little value if the decisionmaker's mind is made up before the case begins. But how would judges possibly detect decisionmakers' unstated biases?

Many administrative agencies combine investigatory, prosecutorial, and adjudicatory functions. Does an agency tip its hand as to the merits of a matter by bringing charges? The Supreme Court addresses the question in *FTC v. Cement Institute* with respect to the Federal Trade Commission, and later in *Withrow v. Larkin* in the context of a state regulatory agency. Is the Court's response convincing?

The *Cement Institute* litigation arose before the Administrative Procedure Act was enacted, and *Withrow* involves a constitutional challenge to a state regulatory regime. Note that the Administrative Procedure Act imposes additional requirements on decisionmakers, and that the rules are different for rulemaking and adjudication.




### FTC v. Cement Institute

333 U.S. 683 (1948)

April 26, 1948

MR. JUSTICE BLACK delivered the opinion of the Court.

We granted certiorari to review the decree of the Circuit Court of Appeals which, with one judge dissenting, vacated and set aside a cease and desist order issued by the Federal Trade Commission against the respondents. Those respondents are: The Cement Institute, an unincorporated trade association composed of 74

1    corporations which manufacture, sell and distribute cement; the 74 corporate
2    members of the Institute; and 21 individuals who are associated with the Institute.
3    It took three years for a trial examiner to hear the evidence, which consists of about
4    49,000 pages of oral testimony and 50,000 pages of exhibits. Even the findings
5    and conclusions of the Commission cover 176 pages. The briefs, with
6    accompanying appendixes submitted by the parties, contain more than 4,000
7    pages. The legal questions raised by the Commission and by the different
8    respondents are many and varied. Some contentions are urged by all respondents,
9    and can be jointly considered. Others require separate treatment. In order to keep
10   our opinion within reasonable limits, we must restrict our record references to the
11   minimum consistent with an adequate consideration of the legal questions we
12   discuss.

13   The proceedings were begun by a Commission complaint of two counts. The first
14   charged that certain alleged conduct set out at length constituted an unfair method
15   of competition in violation of § 5 of the Federal Trade Commission Act. 38 Stat.
16   719, 15 U.S.C. § 45. The core of the charge was that the respondents had restrained
17   and hindered competition in the sale and distribution of cement by means of a
18   combination among themselves made effective through mutual understanding or
19   agreement to employ a multiple basing point system of pricing. It was alleged that
20   this system resulted in the quotation of identical terms of sale and identical prices
21   for cement by the respondents at any given point in the United States. This system
22   had worked so successfully, it was further charged, that, for many years prior to
23   the filing of the complaint, all cement buyers throughout the nation, with rare
24   exceptions, had been unable to purchase cement for delivery in any given locality
25   from any one of the respondents at a lower price or on more favorable terms than
26   from any of the other respondents.

27   The second count of the complaint, resting chiefly on the same allegations of fact
28   set out in Count I, charged that the multiple basing point system of sales resulted
29   in systematic price discriminations between the customers of each respondent.
30   These discriminations were made, it was alleged, with the purpose of destroying
31   competition in price between the various respondents in violation of § 2 of the
32   Clayton Act, 38 Stat. 730, as amended by the Robinson-Patman Act, 49 Stat. 1526.
33   That section, with certain conditions which need not here be set out, makes it

34       "unlawful for any person engaged in commerce, . . . either directly or
35       indirectly, to discriminate in price between different purchasers of
36       commodities of like grade and quality. . . ."

37   15 U.S.C. § 13.

38   Resting upon its findings, the Commission ordered that respondents cease and
39   desist from "carrying out any planned common course of action, understanding,

1   agreement, combination, or conspiracy" to do a number of things, 37 F.T.C. 97,
2   258-262, all of which things, the Commission argues, had to be restrained in order
3   effectively to restore individual freedom of action among the separate units in the
4   cement industry. Certain contentions with reference to the order will later require
5   a more detailed discussion of its terms. For the present, it is sufficient to say that,
6   if the order stands, its terms are broad enough to bar respondents from acting in
7   concert to sell cement on a basing point delivered price plan which so eliminates
8   competition that respondents' prices are always identical at any given point in the
9   United States.

10                                      * * *

11  *Alleged Bias of the Commission.* — One year after the taking of testimony had been
12  concluded, and while these proceedings were still pending before the Commission,
13  the respondent Marquette asked the Commission to disqualify itself from passing
14  upon the issues involved. Marquette charged that the Commission had previously
15  prejudged the issues, was "prejudiced and biased against the Portland cement
16  industry generally," and that the industry and Marquette in particular could not
17  receive a fair hearing from the Commission. After hearing oral argument, the
18  Commission refused to disqualify itself. This contention, repeated here, was also
19  urged and rejected in the Circuit Court of Appeals one year before that court
20  reviewed the merits of the Commission's order.

21  Marquette introduced numerous exhibits intended to support its charges. In the
22  main, these exhibits were copies of the Commission's reports made to Congress or
23  to the President, as required by § 6 of the Trade Commission Act. 15 U.S.C. § 46.
24  These reports, as well as the testimony given by members of the Commission
25  before congressional committees, make it clear that, long before the filing of this
26  complaint, the members of the Commission at that time, or at least some of them,
27  were of the opinion that the operation of the multiple basing point system, as they
28  had studied it, was the equivalent of a price-fixing restraint of trade in violation of
29  the Sherman Act. We therefore decide this contention, as did the Circuit Court of
30  Appeals, on the assumption that such an opinion had been formed by the entire
31  membership of the Commission as a result of its prior official investigations. But
32  we also agree with that court's holding that this belief did not disqualify the
33  Commission. In the first place, the fact that the Commission had entertained such
34  views as the result of its prior *ex parte* investigations did not necessarily mean that
35  the minds of its members were irrevocably closed on the subject of the
36  respondents' basing point practices. Here, in contrast to the Commission's
37  investigations, members of the cement industry were legally authorized
38  participants in the hearings. They produced evidence -- volumes of it. They were
39  free to point out to the Commission by testimony, by cross-examination of
40  witnesses, and by arguments, conditions of the trade practices under attack which

they thought kept these practices within the range of legally permissible business activities.

Moreover, Marquette's position, if sustained, would to a large extent defeat the congressional purposes which prompted passage of the Trade Commission Act. Had the entire membership of the Commission disqualified in the proceedings against these respondents, this complaint could not have been acted upon by the Commission or by any other government agency. Congress has provided for no such contingency. It has not directed that the Commission disqualify itself under any circumstances, has not provided for substitute commissioners should any of its members disqualify, and has not authorized any other government agency to hold hearings, make findings, and issue cease and desist orders in proceedings against unfair trade practices. Yet, if Marquette is right, the Commission, by making studies and filing reports in obedience to congressional command, completely immunized the practices investigated, even though they are "unfair," from any cease and desist order by the Commission or any other governmental agency. There is no warrant in the Act for reaching a conclusion which would thus frustrate its purposes. If the Commission's opinions expressed in congressionally required reports would bar its members from acting in unfair trade proceedings, it would appear that opinions expressed in the first basing point unfair trade proceeding would similarly disqualify them from ever passing on another. *See Morgan v. United States,* 313 U.S. 409, 313 U.S. 421. Thus, experience acquired from their work as commissioners would be a handicap, instead of an advantage. Such was not the intendment of Congress. For Congress acted on a committee report stating:

> "It is manifestly desirable that the terms of the commissioners shall be long enough to give them an opportunity to acquire the expertness in dealing with these special questions concerning industry that comes from experience."

Report of Committee on Interstate Commerce, No. 597, June 13, 1914, 63d Cong., 2d Sess. 10-11.

Marquette also seems to argue that it was a denial of due process for the Commission to act in these proceedings after having expressed the view that industry-wide use of the basing point system was illegal. A number of cases are cited as giving support to this contention. *Tumey v. Ohio,* 273 U.S. 510, is among them. But it provides no support for the contention. In that case, Tumey had been convicted of a criminal offense, fined, and committed to jail by a judge who had a direct, personal, substantial pecuniary interest in reaching his conclusion to convict. A criminal conviction by such a tribunal was held to violate procedural due process. But the Court there pointed out that most matters relating to judicial disqualification did not rise to a constitutional level. *Id.* at 273 U.S. 523.

1    Neither the *Tumey* decision nor any other decision of this Court would require us
2    to hold that it would be a violation of procedural due process for a judge to sit in a
3    case after he had expressed an opinion as to whether certain types of conduct were
4    prohibited by law. In fact, judges frequently try the same case more than once, and
5    decide identical issues each time, although these issues involved questions both of
6    law and fact. Certainly the Federal Trade Commission cannot possibly be under
7    stronger constitutional compulsions in this respect than a court.

8    The Commission properly refused to disqualify itself. We thus need not review the
9    additional holding of the Circuit Court of Appeals that Marquette's objection on
10    the ground of the alleged bias of the Commission was filed too late in the
11    proceedings before that agency to warrant consideration.

12    <center>* * *</center>

13    Many other arguments have been presented by respondents. All have been
14    examined, but we find them without merit. The Commission's order should not
15    have been set aside by the Circuit Court of Appeals. Its judgment is reversed, and
16    the cause is remanded to that court with directions to enforce the order.

17    *It is so ordered.*

18    MR. JUSTICE DOUGLAS and MR. JUSTICE JACKSON took no part in the
19    consideration or decision of these cases.

20    MR. JUSTICE BURTON, dissenting.

21    [Omitted]

22

23    **Withrow v. Larkin**

24    421 U.S. 35 (1975)

25    April 16, 1975

26    MR. JUSTICE WHITE delivered the opinion of the Court.

27    The statutes of the State of Wisconsin forbid the practice of medicine without a
28    license from an Examining Board composed of practicing physicians. The statutes
29    also define and forbid various acts of professional misconduct, proscribe fee
30    splitting, and make illegal the practice of medicine under any name other than the
31    name under which a license has issued if the public would be misled, such practice
32    would constitute unfair competition with another physician, or other detriment to
33    the profession would result. To enforce these provisions, the Examining Board is
34    empowered under Wis. Stat. Ann. §§ 448.17 and 448.18 (1974) to warn and

1 reprimand, temporarily to suspend the license, and "to institute criminal action or
2 action to revoke license when it finds probable cause therefor under criminal or
3 revocation statute . . . ." When an investigative proceeding before the Examining
4 Board was commenced against him, appellee brought this suit against appellants,
5 the individual members of the Board, seeking an injunction against the
6 enforcement of the statutes. The District Court issued a preliminary injunction, the
7 appellants appealed, and we noted probable jurisdiction.

8 I

9 Appellee, a resident of Michigan and licensed to practice medicine there, obtained
10 a Wisconsin license in August 1971 under a reciprocity agreement between
11 Michigan and Wisconsin governing medical licensing. His practice in Wisconsin
12 consisted of performing abortions at an office in Milwaukee. On June 20, 1973, the
13 Board sent to appellee a notice that it would hold an investigative hearing on July
14 12, 1973 to determine whether he had engaged in certain proscribed acts. The
15 hearing would be closed to the public, although appellee and his attorney could
16 attend. They would not, however, be permitted to cross-examine witnesses. Based
17 upon the evidence presented at the hearing, the Board would decide "whether to
18 warn or reprimand if it finds such practice and whether to institute criminal action
19 or action to revoke license if probable cause therefor exists under criminal or
20 revocation statutes."

21 On July 6, 1973, appellee filed his complaint in this action under 42 U.S.C. § 1983
22 seeking preliminary and permanent injunctive relief and a temporary restraining
23 order preventing the Board from investigating him and from conducting the
24 investigative hearing. The District Court denied the motion for a temporary
25 restraining order.

26 On July 12, 1973, appellants moved to dismiss the complaint. * * *

27 The Board proceeded with its investigative hearing on July 12 and 13, 1973;
28 numerous witnesses testified and appellee's counsel was present throughout the
29 proceedings. Appellee's counsel was subsequently informed that appellee could, if
30 he wished, appear before the Board to explain any of the evidence which had been
31 presented.

32 On September 18, 1973, the Board sent to appellee a notice that a "contested
33 hearing" would be held on October 4, 1973, to determine whether appellee had
34 engaged in certain prohibited acts and that based upon the evidence adduced at
35 the hearing the Board would determine whether his license would be suspended
36 temporarily under Wis. Stat. Ann. § 448.18 (7). Appellee moved for a restraining
37 order against the contested hearing. The District Court granted the motion on

October 1, 1973. Because the Board had moved from purely investigative proceedings to a hearing aimed at deciding whether suspension of appellee's license was appropriate, the District Court concluded that a substantial federal question had arisen, namely, whether the authority given to appellants both "to investigate physicians and present charges [and] to rule on those charges and impose punishment, at least to the extent of reprimanding or temporarily suspending" violated appellee's due process rights. Appellee's motion to request the convening of a three-judge court was also granted, and appellants' motion to dismiss was denied.

The Board complied and did not go forward with the contested hearing. Instead, it noticed and held a final investigative session on October 4, 1973, at which appellee's attorney, but not appellee, appeared. The Board thereupon issued "Findings of Fact," "Conclusions of Law," and a "Decision" in which the Board found that appellee had engaged in specified conduct proscribed by the statute. The operative portion of its "Decision" was the following:

> "Within the meaning of sec. 448.17, Stats., it is hereby determined that there is probable cause to believe that licensee has violated the criminal provisions of ch. 448, Stats., and that there is probable cause for an action to revoke the license of the licensee for engaging in unprofessional conduct.

> "Therefore, it is the decision of this Board that the secretary verify this document and file it as a verified complaint with the District Attorney of Milwaukee County in accordance with sec. 448.18 (2), Stats., for the purpose of initiating an action to revoke the license of Duane R. Larkin, M.D., to practice medicine and surgery in the State of Wisconsin and initiating appropriate actions for violation of the criminal laws relating to the practice of medicine."

On November 19, 1973, the three-judge District Court found (with an opinion following on December 21, 1973) that § 448.18 (7) was unconstitutional as a violation of due process guarantees and enjoined the Board from enforcing it. Its holding was:

> "[F]or the board temporarily to suspend Dr. Larkin's license at its own contested hearing on charges evolving from its own investigation would constitute a denial to him of his rights to procedural due process. Insofar as § 448.18 (7) authorizes a procedure wherein a physician stands to lose his liberty or property, absent the intervention of an independent, neutral and detached decision maker, we concluded that it was unconstitutional and unenforceable." 368 F. Supp. 796, 797 (ED Wis. 1973).

* * *

1                                II

2                              * * *

3                              III

The District Court framed the constitutional issue, which it addressed as being whether "for the board temporarily to suspend Dr. Larkin's license at its own contested hearing on charges evolving from its own investigation would constitute a denial to him of his rights to procedural due process." The question was initially answered affirmatively, and in its amended judgment the court asserted that there was a high probability that appellee would prevail on the question. Its opinion stated that the "state medical examining board [did] not qualify as [an independent] decisionmaker [and could not] properly rule with regard to the merits of the same charges it investigated and, as in this case, presented to the district attorney." We disagree. On the present record, it is quite unlikely that appellee would ultimately prevail on the merits of the due process issue presented to the District Court, and it was an abuse of discretion to issue the preliminary injunction.

Concededly, a "fair trial in a fair tribunal is a basic requirement of due process." *In re Murchison*, 349 U.S. 133, 136 (1955). This applies to administrative agencies which adjudicate as well as to courts. Not only is a biased decisionmaker constitutionally unacceptable but "our system of law has always endeavored to prevent even the probability of unfairness." *In re Murchison*, supra, at 136. In pursuit of this end, various situations have been identified in which experience teaches that the probability of actual bias on the part of the judge or decisionmaker is too high to be constitutionally tolerable. Among these cases are those in which the adjudicator has a pecuniary interest in the outcome and in which he has been the target of personal abuse or criticism from the party before him.

The contention that the combination of investigative and adjudicative functions necessarily creates an unconstitutional risk of bias in administrative adjudication has a much more difficult burden of persuasion to carry. It must overcome a presumption of honesty and integrity in those serving as adjudicators; and it must convince that, under a realistic appraisal of psychological tendencies and human weakness, conferring investigative and adjudicative powers on the same individuals poses such a risk of actual bias or prejudgment that the practice must be forbidden if the guarantee of due process is to be adequately implemented.

Very similar claims have been squarely rejected in prior decisions of this Court. In *FTC v. Cement Institute*, 333 U.S. 683 (1948), the Federal Trade Commission had instituted proceedings concerning the respondents' multiple basing-point delivered-price system. It was demanded that the Commission members disqualify themselves because long before the Commission had filed its complaint it had investigated the parties and reported to Congress and to the President, and its members had testified before congressional committees concerning the legality of such a pricing system. At least some of the members had disclosed their opinion that the system was illegal. The issue of bias was brought here and confronted "on the assumption that such an opinion had been formed by the entire membership of the Commission as a result of its prior official investigations." *Id.*, at 700.

The Court rejected the claim, saying:

> "[T]he fact that the Commission had entertained such views as the result of its prior *ex parte* investigations did not necessarily mean that the minds of its members were irrevocably closed on the subject of the respondents' basing point practices. Here, in contrast to the Commission's investigations, members of the cement industry were legally authorized participants in the hearings. They produced evidence—volumes of it. They were free to point out to the Commission by testimony, by cross-examination of witnesses, and by arguments, conditions of the trade practices under attack which they thought kept these practices within the range of legally permissible business activities." *Id.*, at 701.

In specific response to a due process argument, the Court asserted:

> "No decision of this Court would require us to hold that it would be a violation of procedural due process for a judge to sit in a case after he had expressed an opinion as to whether certain types of conduct were prohibited by law. In fact, judges frequently try the same case more than once and decide identical issues each time, although these issues involve questions both of law and fact. Certainly, the Federal Trade Commission cannot possibly be under stronger constitutional compulsions in this respect than a court." *Id.*, at 702-703.

This Court has also ruled that a hearing examiner who has recommended findings of fact after rejecting certain evidence as not being probative was not disqualified to preside at further hearings that were required when reviewing courts held that the evidence had been erroneously excluded. The Court of Appeals had decided that the examiner should not again sit because it would be unfair to require the parties to try "issues of fact to those who may have prejudged them . . . ." But this Court unanimously reversed, saying:

> "Certainly it is not the rule of judicial administration that, statutory requirements apart . . . . a judge is disqualified from sitting in a retrial because he was reversed on earlier rulings. We find no warrant for

238

imposing upon administrative agencies a stiffer rule, whereby examiners would be disentitled to sit because they ruled strongly against a party in the first hearing." NLRB *v. Donnelly Garment Co.*, 330 U.S. 219, 236, 237 (1947).

More recently we have sustained against due process objection a system in which a Social Security examiner has responsibility for developing the facts and making a decision as to disability claims, and observed that the challenge to this combination of functions "assumes too much and would bring down too many procedures designed, and working well, for a governmental structure of great and growing complexity." *Richardson v. Perales*, 402 U.S. 389, 410 (1971).

That is not to say that there is nothing to the argument that those who have investigated should not then adjudicate. The issue is substantial, it is not new, and legislators and others concerned with the operations of administrative agencies have given much attention to whether and to what extent distinctive administrative functions should be performed by the same persons. No single answer has been reached. Indeed, the growth, variety, and complexity of the administrative processes have made any one solution highly unlikely. Within the Federal Government itself, Congress has addressed the issue in several different ways, providing for varying degrees of separation from complete separation of functions to virtually none at all. For the generality of agencies, Congress has been content with § 5 of the Administrative Procedure Act, which provides that no employee engaged in investigating or prosecuting may also participate or advise in the adjudicating function, but which also expressly exempts from this prohibition "the agency or a member or members of the body comprising the agency."

It is not surprising, therefore, to find that "[t]he case law, both federal and state, generally rejects the idea that the combination [of] judging [and] investigating functions is a denial of due process . . . ." 2 K. Davis, Administrative Law Treatise § 13.02, p. 175 (1958). Similarly, our cases, although they reflect the substance of the problem, offer no support for the bald proposition applied in this case by the District Court that agency members who participate in an investigation are disqualified from adjudicating. The incredible variety of administrative mechanisms in this country will not yield to any single organizing principle.

\* \* \*

\* \* \* When the Board instituted its investigative procedures, it stated only that it would investigate whether proscribed conduct had occurred. Later in noticing the adversary hearing, it asserted only that it would determine if violations had been committed which would warrant suspension of appellee's license. Without doubt, the Board then anticipated that the proceeding would eventuate in an adjudication

1   of the issue; but there was no more evidence of bias or the risk of bias or
2   prejudgment than inhered in the very fact that the Board had investigated and
3   would now adjudicate. Of course, we should be alert to the possibilities of bias that
4   may lurk in the way particular procedures actually work in practice. The processes
5   utilized by the Board, however, do not in themselves contain an unacceptable risk
6   of bias. The investigative proceeding had been closed to the public, but appellee
7   and his counsel were permitted to be present throughout; counsel actually
8   attended the hearings and knew the facts presented to the Board. No specific
9   foundation has been presented for suspecting that the Board had been prejudiced
10  by its investigation or would be disabled from hearing and deciding on the basis of
11  the evidence to be presented at the contested hearing. The mere exposure to
12  evidence presented in nonadversary investigative procedures is insufficient in
13  itself to impugn the fairness of the Board members at a later adversary hearing.
14  Without a showing to the contrary, state administrators "are assumed to be men of
15  conscience and intellectual discipline, capable of judging a particular controversy
16  fairly on the basis of its own circumstances." *United States v. Morgan*, 313 U.S.
17  409, 421 (1941).

18                                    * * *

19                                     IV

20  Nor do we think the situation substantially different because the Board, when it
21  was prevented from going forward with the contested hearing, proceeded to make
22  and issue formal findings of fact and conclusions of law asserting that there was
23  probable cause to believe that appellee had engaged in various acts prohibited by
24  the Wisconsin statutes. These findings and conclusions were verified and filed with
25  the district attorney for the purpose of initiating revocation and criminal
26  proceedings. Although the District Court did not emphasize this aspect of the case
27  before it, appellee stresses it in attempting to show prejudice and prejudgment. We
28  are not persuaded.

29  Judges repeatedly issue arrest warrants on the basis that there is probable cause
30  to believe that a crime has been committed and that the person named in the
31  warrant has committed it. Judges also preside at preliminary hearings where they
32  must decide whether the evidence is sufficient to hold a defendant for trial. Neither
33  of these pretrial involvements has been thought to raise any constitutional barrier
34  against the judge's presiding over the criminal trial and, if the trial is without a
35  jury, against making the necessary determination of guilt or innocence. Nor has it
36  been thought that a judge is disqualified from presiding over injunction
37  proceedings because he has initially assessed the facts in issuing or denying a
38  temporary restraining order or a preliminary injunction. It is also very typical for
39  the members of administrative agencies to receive the results of investigations, to

240

approve the filing of charges or formal complaints instituting enforcement proceedings, and then to participate in the ensuing hearings. This mode of procedure does not violate the Administrative Procedure Act, and it does not violate due process of law. We should also remember that it is not contrary to due process to allow judges and administrators who have had their initial decisions reversed on appeal to confront and decide the same questions a second time around. See *Cement Institute*, 333 U.S., at 702-703; *Donnelly Garment Co.*, 330 U.S., at 236-237.

Here, the Board stayed within the accepted bounds of due process. Having investigated, it issued findings and conclusions asserting the commission of certain acts and ultimately concluding that there was probable cause to believe that appellee had violated the statutes.

The risk of bias or prejudgment in this sequence of functions has not been considered to be intolerably high or to raise a sufficiently great possibility that the adjudicators would be so psychologically wedded to their complaints that they would consciously or unconsciously avoid the appearance of having erred or changed position. Indeed, just as there is no logical inconsistency between a finding of probable cause and an acquittal in a criminal proceeding, there is no incompatibility between the agency filing a complaint based on probable cause and a subsequent decision, when all the evidence is in, that there has been no violation of the statute. Here, if the Board now proceeded after an adversary hearing to determine that appellee's license to practice should not be temporarily suspended, it would not implicitly be admitting error in its prior finding of probable cause. Its position most probably would merely reflect the benefit of a more complete view of the evidence afforded by an adversary hearing.

The initial charge or determination of probable cause and the ultimate adjudication have different bases and purposes. The fact that the same agency makes them in tandem and that they relate to the same issues does not result in a procedural due process violation. Clearly, if the initial view of the facts based on the evidence derived from nonadversarial processes as a practical or legal matter foreclosed fair and effective consideration at a subsequent adversary hearing leading to ultimate decision, a substantial due process question would be raised. But in our view, that is not this case.

* * * The judgment of the District Court is reversed and the case is remanded to that court for further proceedings consistent with this opinion.

*So ordered.*

# CHAPTER 2: FORMS OF AGENCY ACTION

This part of the book examines the two key forms agency activity—rulemaking and adjudication—and the body of law that govern them.

The first section takes a look at how these are defined in the Administrative Procedure Act (APA)—the framework statute that lays out many of the core concepts and processes of administrative law—and how they relate to one another. The subsequent two sections explore the requirements that the APA and courts have imposed on agencies when they engage in rulemaking and adjudication, respectively.

## A. Meet the Administrative Procedure Act

Passed in 1946,[1] the Administrative Procedure Act (APA) is a bit like the Constitution for administrative law in several respects. One, it is very old (though not as old as the Constitution). Two, it is (relatively) short. Three, it has not been amended much. And four, like the Constitution, it lays out a framework for how government operates. Specifically, the APA lays out the rules for how agencies enact regulations and decide cases that come before them.

Because, like the Constitution, the APA is old, short, and infrequently amended, it largely falls to the courts to give content to it. While we will pay attention to what the statute says, this part of the course focuses more on what some have called administrative common law: in essence, the body of caselaw that builds on the APA.

Almost everything in the APA revolves around two sets of binaries: a distinction between rulemaking and adjudication, and a distinction between formal (or on-the-record, or trial-type) and informal (or not-on-the-record, or non-trial-type) proceedings. In principle, then, there are four kinds of agency action:

| formal rulemaking | formal adjudication |
|---|---|
| informal rulemaking | informal adjudication |

---

[1] Pub.L. 79–404, 60 Stat. 237. The APA is codified in Title 5 of the U.S. Code at § 551ff.

These distinctions give rise to some important questions: how do we know when agencies must act through rulemaking, and when through adjudication? How do we know when agencies need to use formal, instead of informal, proceedings?

One more quick thing to note about the APA before we begin. If you want to look like you know your way around administrative law, don't refer to the statute as the Administrative Procedures Act: it's the Administrative Procedure Act. The singular form is a subtle reminder of the ambition of the statute: to come up with a unified approach to the governance of a diverse set of agencies.

The APA is codified in Title 5 of the U.S. Code, starting at section 551. (If you *really* want to look like you know your way around administrative law, you can refer to the statute not only by the codified sections, but also by the parallel sections in the original statute—although you might just look like you are showing off.)[2]

## 1. Rulemaking Versus Adjudication

When agencies have been granted authority by Congress to engage in both rulemaking and adjudication, do they have *carte blanche* to decide which one to

---

[2] In case you are curious, here are some of the most important provisions in the U.S. Code and their parallel sections in the statute:

| Codified section | Title | Parallel in statute |
|---|---|---|
| § 551 | Definitions | § 2 |
| § 552 | Public information; agency rules, opinion, orders, records, and proceedings (Freedom of Information Act) | § 3 (as amended) |
| § 553 | Rule making | § 4 |
| § 554 | Adjudications | § 5 |
| § 555 | Ancillary matters | § 6 |
| § 556 | Hearings; presiding employees; powers and duties; burden of proof; evidence; record as basis of decision | § 7 |
| § 557 | Initial decisions; conclusiveness; review by agency; submissions by parties; contents of decision; record | § 8 |
| § 701 | Application; definitions | § 10 |
| § 702 | Right of review | § 10(a) |
| § 703 | Form and venue of proceeding | § 10(b) |
| § 704 | Actions reviewable | § 10(c) |
| § 705 | Relief pending review | § 10(d) |
| § 706 | Scope of review | § 10(e) |

use in a given situation? In particular, may agencies make policy through adjudication? (Another question to consider is why agencies might want to.)

The Supreme Court first addressed these questions in the *Chenery* cases, which preceded the APA. The Court returned to them in the 1970s, in *Wyman-Gordon* and *Bell Aerospace*. (The *Excelsior Underwear* decision by the National Labor Relations Board is related to the *Wyman-Gordon* case.) In *Wyman-Gordon*, the Supreme Court split three ways on whether the NLRB behaved properly. Who has the best argument?

In *National Petroleum Refiners*, the D.C. Circuit finds that the Federal Trade Commission does have the authority to issue substantive rules pursuant to Section 6(g) of the Trade Commission Act. Do you find the court's analysis persuasive?

In November 2019, the EPA issued a proposed rule that would allow the use in rulemaking of only those scientific studies where researchers had disclosed their raw data, including confidential medical records. In promulgating the rule, the EPA relied solely on the so-called "Federal Housekeeping Statute," 5 U.S.C. section 301, which authorizes an agency to make internal rules to regulate "the conduct of its employees, the distribution and performance of its business, and the custody, use, and preservation of its records, papers, and property." Does the EPA have the authority to promulgate this rule? If not, why is the outcome here different from in *National Petroleum Refiners*?

## Excelsior Underwear Inc.

156 N.L.R.B. 1236 (1966)

February 4, 1966

NATIONAL LABOR RELATIONS BOARD (N.L.R.B.)

DECISIONS AND CERTIFICATIONS OF RESULTS OF ELECTIONS

In the *Excelsior* case, pursuant to a stipulation for certification upon consent election, an election by secret ballot was conducted by the Regional Director for Region 11 on December 6, 1963, among the employees in the unit described below. After the election, the parties were furnished with a tally of ballots which showed that of approximately 247 eligible voters, 246 cast ballots, of which 35 were for, and 206 against, the Petitioner, and 5 challenged. The challenges were insufficient in number to affect the results of the election. The Petitioner filed timely objections to conduct affecting the results.

The objections, as summarized by the Regional Director, related to the following:

> (1) The Employer's conduct on November 29 in mailing to all employees an 8-page letter allegedly containing material misstatements as to Union dues and initiation fees, as well as provisions of the National Labor

244

1 Relations Act, threats of plant closings, strikes and violence, and a
2 predetermined position of refusing to bargain in the event the Union were
3 to be selected as bargaining representative.

4 (2) The Employer's conduct in refusing to supply the Union with a list of
5 employees and their addresses for the purpose of allowing the Union to
6 answer the letter referred to in Objection No. 1.

7 (3) The Employer's conduct on or about December 4, in posting a notice at
8 its plants materially misrepresenting Union officials' salaries.

9                                    * * *

10 After investigation, the Regional Director, on January 10, 1964, issued and served
11 upon the parties his report and recommendation on objections, in which he
12 recommended that the objections be overruled and that a certification of election
13 results be issued. Petitioner filed timely exceptions to the Regional Director's
14 report.

15                                    * * *

16 [The Board described a second case, also raising an employer's refusal to provide
17 employee name and addresses to a union.]

18 On April 2, 1965, the National Labor Relations Board, having determined that the
19 Employers' denial of the Petitioners' request for the names and addresses of
20 employees eligible to vote in the elections in these two cases presented a question
21 of substantial importance in the administration of the National Labor Relations
22 Act, as amended, ordered that the two cases be consolidated, and that oral
23 argument be heard before the Board on May 20, 1965. The parties were given
24 permission to file further briefs and directed to focus their attention, in briefs and
25 argument, on the following questions:

26 I. Can a fair and free election be held when the union involved lacks the
27 names and addresses of employees eligible to vote in that election, and the
28 employer refuses to accede to the union's request therefor?

29 II. If such information should be made available, should the requirement
30 be limited to situations in which the employer has utilized his knowledge
31 of these names and addresses to mail anti-union letters or literature to
32 employees' homes?

33 III. If some requirement that the employer make addresses available is to
34 be imposed, how should this be implemented? For example, should such
35 names and addresses be furnished to a mailing service with instructions to
36 mail, at the union's expense, such materials as the union may furnish? Or,
37 should the union be entitled to have the names and addresses?

38                                    * * *

1    Upon the entire record in each of these cases, the Board finds:

2                                          * * *

3    6. Objection No. 2 in each of these cases poses the question whether an
4    employer's refusal to provide a union with the names and addresses of
5    employees eligible to vote in a representation election should be grounds
6    on which to set that election aside. The Board has not in the past set
7    elections aside on this ground. For, while the Board has required that an
8    employer, shortly before an election, make available for inspection by the
9    parties and the Regional Director a list of employees claimed by him to be
10   eligible to vote in that election, there has been no requirement that this list
11   contain addresses in addition to names. The rules governing representation
12   elections are not, however, "fixed and immutable. They have been changed
13   and refined, generally in the direction of higher standards."

14   We are persuaded * * * that higher standards of disclosure than we have heretofore
15   imposed are necessary, and that prompt disclosure of the information here sought
16   by the Petitioners should be required in all representation elections. Accordingly,
17   we now establish a requirement that will be applied in all election cases. That is,
18   within 7 days after the Regional Director has approved a consent-election
19   agreement entered into by the parties * * *, or after the Regional Director or the
20   Board has directed an election * * * the employer must file with the Regional
21   Director an election eligibility list, containing the names and addresses of all the
22   eligible voters. The Regional Director, in turn, shall make this information
23   available to all parties in the case. Failure to comply with this requirement shall be
24   grounds for setting aside the election whenever proper objections are filed.[5]

25   The considerations that impel us to adopt the foregoing rule are these: "The control
26   of the election proceeding, and the determination of the steps necessary to conduct
27   that election fairly [are] matters which Congress entrusted to the Board alone." In
28   discharging that trust, we regard it as the Board's function to conduct elections in
29   which employees have the opportunity to cast their ballots for or against
30   representation under circumstances that are free not only from interference,
31   restraint, or coercion violative of the Act, but also from other elements that prevent
32   or impede a free and reasoned choice. Among the factors that undoubtedly tend to
33   impede such a choice is a lack of information with respect to one of the choices
34   available. In other words, an employee who has had an effective opportunity to
35   hear the arguments concerning representation is in a better position to make a

---

[5] * * * [T]he rule we have here announced is to be applied prospectively only. It will
not apply in the instant cases but only in those elections that are directed, or
consented to, subsequent to 30 days from the date of this Decision We impose this
brief period of delay to insure that all parties to forthcoming representation
elections are fully aware of their rights and obligations as here stated.

more fully informed and reasonable choice. Accordingly, we think that it is appropriate for us to remove the impediment to communication to which our new rule is directed.

As a practical matter, an employer, through his possession of employee names and home addresses as well as his ability to communicate with employees on plant premises, is assured of the continuing opportunity to inform the entire electorate of his views with respect to union representation. On the other hand, without a list of employee names and addresses, a labor organization, whose organizers normally have no right of access to plant premises, has no method by which it can be certain of reaching all the employees with its arguments in favor of representation, and, as a result, employees are often completely unaware of that point of view. This is not, of course, to deny the existence of various means by which a party *might* be able to communicate with a substantial portion of the electorate even without possessing their names and addresses. It is rather to say what seems to us obvious—that the access of all employees to such communications can be insured only if all parties have the names and addresses of all the voters. In other words, by providing all parties with employes' names and addresses, we maximize the likelihood that all the voters will be exposed to the arguments for, as well as against, union representation.

Nor are employee names and addresses readily available from sources other than the employer. * * *

* * *

The arguments against imposing a requirement of disclosure are of little force especially when weighed against the benefits resulting therefrom. Initially, we are able to perceive no substantial infringement of employer interests that would flow from such a requirement. A list of employee names and addresses is not like a customer list, and an employer would appear to have no significant interest in keeping the names and addresses of his employees secret (other than a desire to prevent the union from communicating with his employees—an interest we see no reason to protect). Such legitimate interest in secrecy as an employer may have is, in any event, plainly outweighed by the substantial public interest in favor of disclosure where, as here, disclosure is a key factor in insuring a fair and free electorate.

The main arguments that have been presented to us by the Employers and the *amici curiae* supporting the Employers relate not to any infringement of *employer* rights flowing from a disclosure requirement but rather to an asserted infringement of *employee* rights. Thus, it is argued that if employees wished an organizing union to have their names and addresses they would present the union with that information. By compelling the employer to provide the union with information that the employees have chosen not to divulge, the Board, it is asserted, compels employer interference with the Section 7 rights of employees to refrain from union activities. We regard this argument as without merit. * * *

Similarly, we reject the argument that to provide the union with employee names and addresses subjects employees to the dangers of harassment and coercion in their homes. We cannot assume that a union, seeking to obtain employees' votes in a secret ballot election, will engage in conduct of this nature; if it does, we shall provide an appropriate remedy." We do not, in any event, regard the mere possibility that a union will abuse the opportunity to communicate with employees in their homes as sufficient basis for denying this opportunity altogether.

* * *


## National Labor Relations Board v. Wyman-Gordon Co.

394 U.S. 759 (1969)

April 23, 1969

MR. JUSTICE FORTAS announced the judgment of the Court and delivered an opinion in which THE CHIEF JUSTICE, MR. JUSTICE STEWART, and MR. JUSTICE WHITE join.

On the petition of the International Brotherhood of Boilermakers and pursuant to its powers under 9 of the National Labor Relations Act, 29 U.S.C. § 159, the National Labor Relations Board ordered an election among the production and maintenance employees of the respondent company. At the election, the employees were to select one of two labor unions as their exclusive bargaining representative, or to choose not to be represented by a union at all. In connection with the election, the Board ordered the respondent to furnish a list of the names and addresses of its employees who could vote in the election, so that the unions could use the list for election purposes. The respondent refused to comply with the order, and the election was held without the list. Both unions were defeated in the election.

The Board upheld the unions' objections to the election because the respondent had not furnished the list, and the Board ordered a new election. The respondent again refused to obey a Board order to supply a list of employees, and the Board issued a subpoena ordering the respondent to provide the list or else produce its personnel and payroll records showing the employees' names and addresses. The Board filed an action in the United States District Court for the District of Massachusetts seeking to have its subpoena enforced or to have a mandatory injunction issued to compel the respondent to comply with its order.

The District Court held the Board's order valid and directed the respondent to comply. The United States Court of Appeals for the First Circuit reversed. The Court of Appeals thought that the order in this case was invalid because it was based on a rule laid down in an earlier decision by the Board, *Excelsior Underwear Inc.*, 156 N. L. R. B. 1236 (1966), and the *Excelsior* rule had not been promulgated in accordance with the requirements that the Administrative Procedure Act

248

1  prescribes for rule making, 5 U.S.C. 553. We granted certiorari to resolve a conflict
2  among the circuits concerning the validity and effect of the *Excelsior* rule. 393 U.S.
3  932 (1968).

4  I

5  \* \* \*

6  Section 6 of the National Labor Relations Act empowers the Board "to make . . . ,
7  in the manner prescribed by the Administrative Procedure Act, such rules and
8  regulations as may be necessary to carry out the provisions of this Act." 29 U.S.C.
9  § 156. The Administrative Procedure Act contains specific provisions governing
10 agency rule making, which it defines as "an agency statement of general or
11 particular applicability and future effect," 5 U.S.C. § 551(4). The Act requires,
12 among other things, publication in the Federal Register of notice of proposed rule
13 making and of hearing; opportunity to be heard; a statement in the rule of its basis
14 and purposes; and publication in the Federal Register of the rule as adopted. The
15 Board asks us to hold that it has discretion to promulgate new rules in adjudicatory
16 proceedings, without complying with the requirements of the Administrative
17 Procedure Act.

18 The rule-making provisions of that Act, which the Board would avoid, were
19 designed to assure fairness and mature consideration of rules of general
20 application. They may not be avoided by the process of making rules in the course
21 of adjudicatory proceedings. There is no warrant in law for the Board to replace
22 the statutory scheme with a rule-making procedure of its own invention. Apart
23 from the fact that the device fashioned by the Board does not comply with statutory
24 command, it obviously falls short of the substance of the requirements of the
25 Administrative Procedure Act. The "rule" created in *Excelsior* was not published
26 in the Federal Register, which is the statutory and accepted means of giving notice
27 of a rule as adopted; only selected organizations were given notice of the "hearing,"
28 whereas notice in the Federal Register would have been general in character; under
29 the Administrative Procedure Act, the terms or substance of the rule would have
30 to be stated in the notice of hearing, and all interested parties would have an
31 opportunity to participate in the rule making.

32 The Solicitor General does not deny that the Board ignored the rule-making
33 provisions of the Administrative Procedure Act. But he appears to argue that
34 *Excelsior*'s command is a valid substantive regulation, binding upon this
35 respondent as such, because the Board promulgated it in the *Excelsior* proceeding,
36 in which the requirements for valid adjudication had been met. This argument
37 misses the point. There is no question that, in an adjudicatory hearing, the Board
38 could validly decide the issue whether the employer must furnish a list of
39 employees to the union. But that is not what the Board did in *Excelsior*. The Board
40 did not even apply the rule it made to the parties in the adjudicatory proceeding,
41 the only entities that could properly be subject to the order in that case. Instead,
42 the Board purported to make a rule: *i.e.*, to exercise its quasi-legislative power.

1  Adjudicated cases may and do, of course, serve as vehicles for the formulation of
2  agency policies, which are applied and announced therein. They generally provide
3  a guide to action that the agency may be expected to take in future cases. Subject
4  to the qualified role of *stare decisis* in the administrative process, they may serve
5  as precedents. But this is far from saying, as the Solicitor General suggests, that
6  commands, decisions, or policies announced in adjudication are "rules" in the
7  sense that they must, without more, be obeyed by the affected public.

8  In the present case, however, the respondent itself was specifically directed by the
9  Board to submit a list of the names and addresses of its employees for use by the
10  unions in connection with the election. This direction, which was part of the order
11  directing that an election be held, is unquestionably valid. Even though the
12  direction to furnish the list was followed by citation to "*Excelsior Underwear Inc.*,
13  156 NLRB No. 111," it is an order in the present case that the respondent was
14  required to obey. Absent this direction by the Board, the respondent was under no
15  compulsion to furnish the list because no statute and no validly adopted rule
16  required it to do so.

17  Because the Board in an adjudicatory proceeding directed the respondent itself to
18  furnish the list, the decision of the Court of Appeals for the First Circuit must be
19  reversed.

20                                    II

21  The respondent also argues that it need not obey the Board's order because the
22  requirement of disclosure of employees' names and addresses is substantively
23  invalid. This argument lacks merit. The objections that the respondent raises to
24  the requirement of disclosure were clearly and correctly answered by the Board in
25  its *Excelsior* decision. * * *

26                                  * * *

27  We have held in a number of cases that Congress granted the Board a wide
28  discretion to ensure the fair and free choice of bargaining representatives. The
29  disclosure requirement furthers this objective by encouraging an informed
30  employee electorate and by allowing unions the right of access to employees that
31  management already possesses. It is for the Board and not for this Court to weigh
32  against this interest the asserted interest of employees in avoiding the problems
33  that union solicitation may present.

34                                   III

35                                  * * *

36  * * * The District Court held * * * that "in the context of § 11 of the Act, 'evidence'
37  means not only proof at a hearing but also books and records and other papers
38  which will be of assistance to the Board in conducting a particular investigation."
39  The courts of appeals that have passed on the question have construed the term

1 "evidence" in a similar manner. We agree that the list here in issue is within the
2 scope of § 11 so that the Board's subpoena power may be validly exercised.

3 The judgment of the Court of Appeals is reversed, and the case is remanded to the
4 District Court with directions to reinstate its judgment.

5 *It is so ordered.*

6 MR. JUSTICE BLACK, with whom MR. JUSTICE BRENNAN and MR. JUSTICE
7 MARSHALL join, concurring in the result.

8 I agree with Parts II and III of the prevailing opinion of MR. JUSTICE FORTAS,
9 holding that the *Excelsior* requirement that an employer supply the union with the
10 names and addresses of its employees prior to an election is valid on its merits and
11 can be enforced by a subpoena. But I cannot subscribe to the criticism in that
12 opinion of the procedure followed by the Board in adopting that requirement in
13 the *Excelsior* case, 156 N.L.R.B. 1236 (1966). Nor can I accept the novel theory by
14 which the opinion manages to uphold enforcement of the *Excelsior* practice in
15 spite of what it considers to be statutory violations present in the procedure by
16 which the requirement was adopted. Although the opinion is apparently intended
17 to rebuke the Board and encourage it to follow the plurality's conception of proper
18 administrative practice, the result instead is to free the Board from all judicial
19 control whatsoever regarding compliance with procedures specifically required by
20 applicable federal statutes such as the National Labor Relations Act, 29 U.S.C. §
21 151 *et seq.*, and the Administrative Procedure Act, 5 U.S.C. § 551 *et seq.* Apparently,
22 under the prevailing opinion, courts must enforce any requirement announced in
23 a purported "adjudication" even if it clearly was not adopted as an incident to the
24 decision of a case before the agency, and must enforce "rules" adopted in a
25 purported "rule making" even if the agency materially violated the specific
26 requirements that Congress has directed for such proceedings in the
27 Administrative Procedure Act. I for one would not give judicial sanction to any
28 such illegal agency action.

29 In the present case, however, I am convinced that the *Excelsior* practice was
30 adopted by the Board as a legitimate incident to the adjudication of a specific case
31 before it, and for that reason I would hold that the Board properly followed the
32 procedures applicable to "adjudication" rather than "rule making." Since my
33 reasons for joining in reversal of the Court of Appeals differ so substantially from
34 those set forth in the prevailing opinion, I will spell them out at some length.

35 Most administrative agencies, like the Labor Board here, are granted two functions
36 by the legislation creating them: (1) the power under certain conditions to make
37 rules having the effect of laws, that is, generally speaking, quasi-legislative power;
38 and (2) the power to hear and adjudicate particular controversies, that is quasi-
39 judicial power. The line between these two functions is not always a clear one and
40 in fact the two functions merge at many points. For example, in exercising its
41 quasi-judicial function an agency must frequently decide controversies on the basis
42 of new doctrines, not theretofore applied to a specific problem, though drawn to

1  be sure from broader principles reflecting the purposes of the statutes involved and
2  from the rules invoked in dealing with related problems. If the agency decision
3  reached under the adjudicatory power becomes a precedent, it guides future
4  conduct in much the same way as though it were a new rule promulgated under
5  the rule-making power, and both an adjudicatory order and a formal "rule" are
6  alike subject to judicial review. Congress gave the Labor Board both of these
7  separate but almost inseparably related powers. No language in the National Labor
8  Relations Act requires that the grant or the exercise of one power was intended to
9  exclude the Board's use of the other.

10  Nor does any language in the Administrative Procedure Act require such a
11  conclusion. The Act does specify the procedure by which the rule-making power is
12  to be exercised, requiring publication of notice for the benefit of interested parties
13  and provision of an opportunity for them to be heard, and, after establishment of
14  a rule as provided in the Act, it is then to be published in the Federal Register.
15  Congress had a laudable purpose in prescribing these requirements, and it was
16  evidently contemplated that administrative agencies like the Labor Board would
17  follow them when setting out to announce a new rule of law to govern parties in
18  the future. In this same statute, however, Congress also conferred on the affected
19  administrative agencies the power to proceed by adjudication, and Congress
20  specified a distinct procedure by which this adjudicatory power is to be exercised.
21  The Act defines "adjudication" as "agency process for the formulation of an order,"
22  and "order" is defined as "the whole or a part of a final disposition, whether
23  affirmative, negative, injunctive, or declaratory in form, of an agency in a matter
24  other than rule making but including licensing." 5 U.S.C. § 551 (7), (6). Thus,
25  although it is true that the adjudicatory approach frees an administrative agency
26  from the procedural requirements specified for rule making, the Act permits this
27  to be done whenever the action involved can satisfy the definition of "adjudication"
28  and then imposes separate procedural requirements that must be met in
29  adjudication. Under these circumstances, so long as the matter involved can be
30  dealt with in a way satisfying the definition of either "rule making" or
31  "adjudication" under the Administrative Procedure Act, that Act, along with the
32  Labor Relations Act, should be read as conferring upon the Board the authority to
33  decide, within its informed discretion, whether to proceed by rule making or
34  adjudication. Our decision in *SEC v. Chenery Corp.*, 332 U.S. 194 (1947), though
35  it did not involve the Labor Board or the Administrative Procedure Act, is
36  nonetheless equally applicable here. As we explained in that case, "the choice made
37  between proceeding by general rule or by individual, ad hoc litigation is one that
38  lies primarily in the informed discretion of the administrative agency."

39  In the present case there is no dispute that all the procedural safeguards required
40  for "adjudication" were fully satisfied in connection with the Board's Excelsior
41  decision, and it seems plain to me that that decision did constitute "adjudication"
42  within the meaning of the Administrative Procedure Act, even though the
43  requirement was to be prospectively applied. *See Great Northern R. Co. v.*
44  *Sunburst Co.*, 287 U.S. 358 (1932). The Board did not abstractly decide out of the

1   blue to announce a brand new rule of law to govern labor activities in the future,
2   but rather established the procedure as a direct consequence of the proper exercise
3   of its adjudicatory powers. * * * A controversy arose between the Excelsior
4   Company and its employees as to the bargaining agent the employees desired to
5   act for them. The Board's power to provide the procedures for the election was
6   invoked, an election was held, and the losing unions sought to have that election
7   set aside. Undoubtedly the Board proceeding for determination of whether to
8   confirm or set aside that election was "agency process for the formulation of an
9   order" and thus was "adjudication" within the meaning of the Administrative
10   Procedure Act.

11   The prevailing opinion seems to hold that the *Excelsior* requirement cannot be
12   considered the result of adjudication because the Board did not apply it to the
13   parties in the *Excelsior* case itself, but rather announced that it would be applied
14   only to elections called 30 days after the date of the *Excelsior* decision. But the
15   *Excelsior* order was nonetheless an inseparable part of the adjudicatory process.
16   The principal issue before the Board in the *Excelsior* case was whether the election
17   should be set aside on the ground, urged by the unions, that the employer had
18   refused to make the employee lists available to them. The Board decided that the
19   election involved there should not be set aside and thus rejected the contention of
20   the unions. In doing so, the Board chose to explain the reasons for its rejection of
21   their claim, and it is this explanation, the Board's written opinion, which is the
22   source of the *Excelsior* requirement. The Board's opinion should not be regarded
23   as any less an appropriate part of the adjudicatory process merely because the
24   reason it gave for rejecting the unions' position was not that the Board disagreed
25   with them as to the merits of the disclosure procedure but rather, that while fully
26   agreeing that disclosure should be required, the Board did not feel that it should
27   upset the Excelsior Company's justified reliance on previous refusals to compel
28   disclosure by setting aside this particular election.

29   Apart from the fact that the decisions whether to accept a "new" requirement urged
30   by one party and, if so, whether to apply it retroactively to the other party are
31   inherent parts of the adjudicatory process, I think the opposing theory accepted by
32   the Court of Appeals and by the prevailing opinion today is a highly impractical
33   one. In effect, it would require an agency like the Labor Board to proceed by
34   adjudication only when it could decide, *prior* to adjudicating a particular case, that
35   any new practice to be adopted would be applied retroactively. Obviously, this
36   decision cannot properly be made until all the issues relevant to adoption of the
37   practice are fully considered in connection with the final decision of that case. If
38   the Board were to decide, after careful evaluation of all the arguments presented
39   to it in the adjudicatory proceeding, that it might be fairer to apply the practice
40   only prospectively, it would be faced with the unpleasant choice of either starting
41   all over again to evaluate the merits of the question, this time in a "rule-making"
42   proceeding, or overriding the considerations of fairness and applying its order
43   retroactively anyway, in order to preserve the validity of the new practice and avoid

duplication of effort. I see no good reason to impose any such inflexible requirement on the administrative agencies.

For all of the foregoing reasons I would hold that the Board acted well within its discretion in choosing to proceed as it did, and I would reverse the judgment of the Court of Appeals on this basis.

MR. JUSTICE DOUGLAS, dissenting.

* * *

I am willing to assume that, if the Board decided to treat each case on its special facts and perform its adjudicatory function in the conventional way, we should have no difficulty in affirming its action. The difficulty is that it chose a different course in the *Excelsior* case and, having done so, it should be bound to follow the procedures prescribed in the Act as my Brother HARLAN has outlined them. When we hold otherwise, we let the Board "have its cake and eat it too."

* * *

The "substantive" rules described by § 553 (d) may possibly cover "adjudications," even though they represent performance of the "judicial" function. But it is no answer to say that the order under review was "adjudicatory." For as my Brother HARLAN says, an agency is not adjudicating when it is making a rule to fit future cases. A rule like the one in *Excelsior* is designed to fit all cases at all times. It is not particularized to special facts. It is a statement of far-reaching policy covering all future representation elections.

It should therefore have been put down for the public hearing prescribed by the Act.

The rule-making procedure performs important functions. It gives notice to an entire segment of society of those controls or regimentation that is forthcoming. It gives an opportunity for persons affected to be heard. Recently the proposed Rules of the Federal Highway Administration governing the location and design of freeways were put down for a hearing; and the Governor of every State appeared or sent an emissary. The result was a revision of the Rules before they were promulgated.

That is not an uncommon experience. Agencies discover that they are not always repositories of ultimate wisdom; they learn from the suggestions of outsiders and often benefit from that advice. This is a healthy process that helps make a society viable. The multiplication of agencies and their growing power make them more and more remote from the people affected by what they do and make more likely the arbitrary exercise of their powers. Public airing of problems through rule making makes the bureaucracy more responsive to public needs and is an important brake on the growth of absolutism in the regime that now governs all of us.

1            * * *

Rule making is no cure-all; but it does force important issues into full public display and in that sense makes for more responsible administrative action.

I would hold the agencies governed by the rule-making procedure strictly to its requirements and not allow them to play fast and loose as the National Labor Relations Board apparently likes to do.

           * * *

MR. JUSTICE HARLAN, dissenting.

The language of the Administrative Procedure Act does not support the Government's claim that an agency is "adjudicating" when it announces a rule which it refuses to apply in the dispute before it. The Act makes it clear that an agency "adjudicates" only when its procedures result in the "formulation of an *order*." 5 U.S.C. § 551 (7). (Emphasis supplied.) An "order" is defined to include "the whole or a *part* of a final disposition . . . of an agency *in a matter other than rule making* . . . ." 5 U.S.C. § 551 (6). (Emphasis supplied.) This definition makes it apparent that an agency is not adjudicating when it is making a rule, which the Act defines as "an agency statement of general or particular applicability and *future effect* . . . ." 5 U.S.C. § 551 (4). (Emphasis supplied.) Since the Labor Board's Excelsior rule was to be effective only 30 days after its promulgation, it clearly falls within the rule-making requirements of the Act. [1]

Nor can I agree that the natural interpretation of the statute should be rejected because it requires the agency to choose between giving its rules immediate effect or initiating a separate rule-making proceeding. An agency chooses to apply a rule prospectively only because it represents such a departure from pre-existing understandings that it would be unfair to impose the rule upon the parties in pending matters. But it is precisely in these situations, in which established patterns of conduct are revolutionized, that rule-making procedures perform the vital functions that my Brother DOUGLAS describes so well in a dissenting opinion with which I basically agree.

Given the fact that the Labor Board has promulgated a rule in violation of the governing statute, I believe that there is no alternative but to affirm the judgment of the Court of Appeals in this case. If, as the plurality opinion suggests, the NLRB may properly enforce an invalid rule in subsequent adjudications, the rule-making provisions of the Administrative Procedure Act are completely trivialized. Under today's prevailing approach, the agency may evade the commands of the Act whenever it desires and yet coerce the regulated industry into compliance. It is no answer to say that "respondent was under no compulsion to furnish the list because no statute and no validly adopted rule required it to do so," when the Labor Board was threatening to issue a subpoena which the courts would enforce. In what other way would the administrative agency compel obedience to its invalid rule?

255

One cannot always have the best of both worlds. Either the rule-making provisions are to be enforced or they are not. Before the Board may be permitted to adopt a rule that so significantly alters pre-existing labor-management understandings, it must be required to conduct a satisfactory rule-making proceeding, so that it will have the benefit of wide-ranging argument before it enacts its proposed solution to an important problem.

\* \* \*

I would affirm the judgment of the Court of Appeals.


## NLRB v. Bell Aerospace Co.

416 U.S. 267 (1974)

April 23, 1974

MR. JUSTICE POWELL delivered the opinion of the Court.

This case presents two questions: first, whether the National Labor Relations Board properly determined that all "managerial employees," except those whose participation in a labor organization would create a conflict of interest with their job responsibilities, are covered by the National Labor Relations Act; and second, whether the Board must proceed by rulemaking, rather than by adjudication, in determining whether certain buyers are "managerial employees." We answer both questions in the negative.

\* \* \*

II

\* \* \*

In sum, the Board's early decisions, the purpose and legislative history of the Taft-Hartley Act of 1947, the Board's subsequent and consistent construction of the Act for more than two decades, and the decisions of the courts of appeals all point unmistakably to the conclusion that "managerial employees" are not covered by the Act. We agree with the Court of Appeals below that the Board "is not now free" to read a new and more restrictive meaning into the Act.

In view of our conclusion, the case must be remanded to permit the Board to apply the proper legal standard in determining the status of these buyers. *SEC v. Chenery Corp.*, 318 U.S. 80, 85 (1943). We express no opinion as to whether these buyers fall within the category of "managerial employees."

III

The Court of Appeals also held that, although the Board was not precluded from determining that buyers or some types of buyers were not "managerial employees," it could do so only by invoking its rulemaking procedures under § 6 of the Act, 29 U.S.C. § 156.[21] We disagree.

At the outset, the precise nature of the present issue must be noted. The question is not whether the Board should have resorted to rulemaking, or, in fact, improperly promulgated a "rule," when, in the context of the prior representation proceeding, it held that the Act covers all "managerial employees" except those meeting the new "conflict of interest in labor relations" touchstone. Our conclusion that the Board applied the wrong legal standard makes consideration of that issue unnecessary. Rather, the present question is whether, on remand, the Board must invoke its rulemaking procedures if it determines, in light of our opinion, that these buyers are not "managerial employees" under the Act. The Court of Appeals thought that rulemaking was required because any Board finding that the company's buyers are not "managerial" would be contrary to its prior decisions, and would presumably be in the nature of a general rule designed "to fit all cases at all times."

\* \* \*

The views expressed in *Chenery II* and *Wyman-Gordon* make plain that the Board is not precluded from announcing new principles in an adjudicative proceeding, and that the choice between rulemaking and adjudication lies in the first instance within the Board's discretion. Although there may be situations where the Board's reliance on adjudication would amount to an abuse of discretion or a violation of the Act, nothing in the present case would justify such a conclusion. Indeed, there is ample indication that adjudication is especially appropriate in the instant context. As the Court of Appeals noted, "[t]here must be tens of thousands of manufacturing, wholesale and retail units which employ buyers, and hundreds of

---

[21] Section 6 provides:

"The Board shall have authority from time to time to make, amend, and rescind, in the manner prescribed by the Administrative Procedure Act, such rules and regulations as may be necessary to carry out the provisions of this subchapter." 29 U.S.C. § 156.

\* \* \*

Sections 9(c)(1) and (2) of the National Labor Relations Act (NLRA) empower the Board to investigate petitions involving questions of unit representation, to conduct hearings on such petitions, to direct representation elections, and to certify the results thereof. 29 U.S.C. §§ 159(c)(1) and (2).

\* \* \*

\* \* \* Board determinations on such representation questions would appear to constitute "orders" within the meaning of the APA. See 5 U.S.C. §§ 551(6), (7).
The NLRA does not specify in what instances the Board must resort to rulemaking.

\* \* \*

thousands of the latter." Moreover, duties of buyers vary widely depending on the company or industry. It is doubtful whether any generalized standard could be framed which would have more than marginal utility. The Board thus has reason to proceed with caution, developing its standards in a case-by-case manner with attention to the specific character of the buyers' authority and duties in each company. The Board's judgment that adjudication best serves this purpose is entitled to great weight.

The possible reliance of industry on the Board's past decisions with respect to buyers does not require a different result. It has not been shown that the adverse consequences ensuing from such reliance are so substantial that the Board should be precluded from reconsidering the issue in an adjudicative proceeding. Furthermore, this is not a case in which some new liability is sought to be imposed on individuals for past actions which were taken in good faith reliance on Board pronouncements. Nor are fines or damages involved here. In any event, concern about such consequences is largely speculative, for the Board has not yet finally determined whether these buyers are "managerial."

It is true, of course, that rulemaking would provide the Board with a forum for soliciting the informed views of those affected in industry and labor before embarking on a new course. But surely the Board has discretion to decide that the adjudicative procedures in this case may also produce the relevant information necessary to mature and fair consideration of the issues. Those most immediately affected, the buyers and the company in the particular case, are accorded a full opportunity to be heard before the Board makes its determination.

The judgment of the Court of Appeals is therefore affirmed in part and reversed in part, and the cause remanded to that court with directions to remand to the Board for further proceedings in conformity with this opinion.

*It is so ordered.*


MR. JUSTICE WHITE, with whom MR. JUSTICE BRENNAN, MR. JUSTICE STEWART, and MR. JUSTICE MARSHALL join, dissenting in part.


I concur in Part III of the Court's opinion insofar as it holds that the Board was not required to resort to rulemaking in deciding this case, but I dissent from its holding in Part II that managerial employees as a class are not "employees" within the meaning of the National Labor Relations Act.

\* \* \*

1  **National Petroleum Refiners Association v. Federal Trade**
2  **Commission**

3  482 F.2d 672 (D.C. Cir. 1973)

4  June 27, 1973

5  Before BAZELON, Chief Judge, and WRIGHT and ROBINSON, Circuit Judges.

6  J. SKELLY WRIGHT, Circuit Judge.

7  This case presents an important question concerning the powers and procedures
8  of the Federal Trade Commission. We are asked to determine whether the
9  Commission, under its governing statute, the Trade Commission Act, 15 U.S.C. §
10  41 *et seq.* (1970), and specifically 15 U.S.C. § 46(g), is empowered to promulgate
11  substantive rules of business conduct or, as it terms them, "Trade Regulation
12  Rules." The effect of these rules would be to give greater specificity and clarity to
13  the broad standard of illegality—"unfair methods of competition in commerce, and
14  unfair or deceptive acts or practices in commerce"—which the agency is
15  empowered to prevent. 15 U.S.C. § 45(a). Once promulgated, the rules would be
16  used by the agency in adjudicatory proceedings aimed at producing cease and
17  desist orders against violations of the statutory standard. The central question in
18  such adjudicatory proceedings would be whether the particular defendant's
19  conduct violated the rule in question.

20  The case is here on appeal from a District Court ruling that the Commission lacks
21  authority under its governing statute to issue rules of this sort. *National Petroleum*
22  *Refiners Assn v. FTC*, 340 F. Supp. 1343 (D.D.C. 1972). Specifically at issue in the
23  District Court was the Commission's rule declaring that failure to post octane
24  rating numbers on gasoline pumps at service stations was an unfair method of
25  competition and an unfair or deceptive act or practice. The plaintiffs in the District
26  Court, appellees here, are two trade associations and 34 gasoline refining
27  companies. Plaintiffs attacked the rule on several grounds, but the District Court
28  disposed of the case solely on the question of the Commission's statutory authority
29  to issue such rules. That is the only question presented for our consideration on
30  appeal. We reverse and remand to the District Court for further consideration of
31  appellees' challenge to the validity of the procedure before the Commission which
32  resulted in the rule.

33  I

34  * * *

35  As always, we must begin with the words of the statute creating the Commission
36  and delineating its powers. Section 5 directs the Commission to "prevent persons,
37  partnerships, or corporations from using unfair methods of competition in
38  commerce and unfair or deceptive acts or practices in commerce." Section 5(b) of
39  the Trade Commission Act specifies that the Commission is to accomplish this goal
40  by means of issuance of a complaint, a hearing, findings as to the facts, and

259

1  issuance of a cease and desist order. The Commission's assertion that it is
2  empowered by Section 6(g) to issue substantive rules defining the statutory
3  standard of illegality in advance of specific adjudications does not in any formal
4  sense circumvent this method of enforcement. For after the rules are issued, their
5  mode of enforcement remains what it has always been under Section 5: the
6  sequence of complaint, hearing, findings, and issuance of a cease and desist order.
7  What rule-making does do, functionally, is to narrow the inquiry conducted in
8  proceedings under Section 5(b). It is the legality of this practice which we must
9  judge.

10  Appellees argue that since Section 5 mentions only adjudication as the means of
11  enforcing the statutory standard, any supplemental means of putting flesh on that
12  standard, such as rulemaking, is contrary to the overt legislative design. But
13  Section 5(b) does not use limiting language suggesting that adjudication alone is
14  the only proper means of elaborating the statutory standard. It merely makes clear
15  that a Commission decision, after complaint and hearing, followed by a cease and
16  desist order, is the way to force an offender to halt his illegal activities.[6] Nor are we
17  persuaded by appellees' argument that, despite the absence of limiting language in
18  Section 5 regarding the role of adjudication in defining the meaning of the
19  statutory standard, we should apply the maxim of statutory construction *expressio*

---

[6] Section 5(b) provides:

"Whenever the Commission shall have reason to believe that any such person, partnership, or corporation has been or is using any unfair method of competition or unfair or deceptive act or practice in commerce, and if it shall appear to the Commission that a proceeding by it in respect thereof would be to the interest of the public, it shall issue * * * a complaint stating its charges in that respect and containing a notice of a hearing upon a day and at a place therein fixed * * * . The person, partnership, or corporation so complained of shall have the right to appear at the place and time so fixed and show cause why an order should not be entered by the Commission requiring such person, partnership, or corporation to cease and desist from the violation of the law so charged in said complaint. * * *

If upon such hearing the Commission shall be of the opinion that the method of competition or the act or practice in question is prohibited by sections 41 to 46 and 47 to 58 of this title, it shall make a report in writing in which it shall state its findings as to the facts and shall issue and cause to be served on such person, partnership, or corporation an order requiring such person, partnership, or corporation to cease and desist from using such method of competition or such act or practice. * * * "

1   *unius est exclusio alterius* and conclude that adjudication is the *only* means of
2   defining the statutory standard. * * * Here we have particularly good reason on the
3   face of the statute to reject such arguments. For the Trade Commission Act
4   includes a provision which specifically provides for rule-making by the
5   Commission to implement its adjudicatory functions under Section 5 of the Act.
6   Section 6(g) of the Act, 15 U.S.C. § 46(g), states that the Commission may " [f]rom
7   time to time . . . classify corporations and . . . make rules and regulations for the
8   purpose of carrying out the provisions of sections 41 to 46 and 47 to 58 of this title."

9   According to appellees, however, this rule-making power is limited to specifying
10  the details of the Commission's non-adjudicatory, investigative and informative
11  functions spelled out in the other provisions of Section 6 and should not be read to
12  encompass substantive rulemaking in implementation of Section 5 adjudications.
13  We disagree for the simple reason that Section 6(g) clearly states that the
14  Commission "may" make rules and regulations for the purpose of carrying out the
15  provisions of Section 5 and it has been so applied. For example, the Commission
16  has issued rules specifying in greater detail than the statute the mode of
17  Commission procedure under Section 5 in matters involving service of process,
18  requirements as to the filing of answers, and other litigation details necessarily
19  involved in the Commission's work of prosecuting its complaints under Section 5.
20  Such rulemaking by the Commission has been upheld.

21                                    * * *

22  Of course, it is at least arguable that these cases go no farther than to justify
23  utilizing Section 6(g) to promulgate procedural, as opposed to substantive, rules
24  for administration of the Section 5 adjudication and enforcement powers. But we
25  see no reason to import such a restriction on the "rules and regulations" permitted
26  by Section 6(g). On the contrary, as we shall see, judicial precedents concerning
27  rule-making by other agencies and the background and purpose of the Federal
28  Trade Commission Act lead us liberally to construe the term "rules and
29  regulations." The substantive rule here unquestionably implements the statutory
30  plan. Section 5 adjudications—trial type proceedings—will still be necessary to
31  obtain cease and desist orders against offenders, but Section 5 enforcement
32  through adjudication will be expedited, simplified, and thus "carried out" by use of
33  this substantive rule. And the overt language of both Section 5 and Section 6, read
34  together, supports its use in Section 5 proceedings.

35                                     II

36  Our belief that "rules and regulations" in Section 6(g) should be construed to
37  permit the Commission to promulgate binding substantive rules as well as rules of
38  procedure is reinforced by the construction courts have given similar provisions in
39  the authorizing statutes of other administrative agencies. There is, of course, no
40  doubt that the approved practices of agencies with similar statutory provisions is a
41  relevant factor in arriving at a sound interpretation of the Federal Trade
42  Commission's power here. * * *

1                                    * * *

2   * * * [T]here is little question that the availability of substantive rule-making gives
3   any agency an invaluable resource-saving flexibility in carrying out its task of
4   regulating parties subject to its statutory mandate. More than merely expediting
5   the agency's job, use of substantive rule-making is increasingly felt to yield
6   significant benefits to those the agency regulates. Increasingly, courts are
7   recognizing that use of rule-making to make innovations in agency policy may
8   actually be fairer to regulated parties than total reliance on case-by-case
9   adjudication.

10                                   * * *

11  * * * As *Wyman-Gordon* and *Bell Aerospace* explicitly noted, utilizing rule-making
12  procedures opens up the process of agency policy innovation to a broad range of
13  criticism, advice and data that is ordinarily less likely to be forthcoming in
14  adjudication. Moreover, the availability of notice before promulgation and wide
15  public participation in rule-making avoids the problem of singling out a single
16  defendant among a group of competitors for initial imposition of a new and
17  inevitably costly legal obligation.

18                                   * * *

19                                    IV

20  Although we believe there are thus persuasive considerations for accepting the
21  FTC's view that the plain meaning of the statute supports substantive rule-making,
22  the question is not necessarily closed. For appellees' contention—that the phrase
23  "rules and regulations for the purpose of carrying out" Section 5 refers only to rules
24  of procedure and practice for carrying out the Commission's adjudicatory
25  responsibility—is not implausible. The opinion of the District Court argues
26  forcefully that, in spite of the clear and unlimited language of Section 6(g) granting
27  rule-making authority to the Commission, the Congress that enacted Section 5 and
28  Section 6(g) gave clear indications of its intent to reject substantive rule-making,
29  that the FTC's own behavior in the years since that time supports a narrow
30  interpretation of its mandate to promulgate "rules and regulations," and that
31  where Congress desired to give the FTC substantive rule-making authority in
32  discrete areas it did so in subsequent years in unambiguous terms. Our own
33  conclusion, based on an independent review of this history, is different. We believe
34  that, while the legislative history of Section 5 and Section 6(g) is ambiguous, it
35  certainly does not compel the conclusion that the Commission was not meant to
36  exercise the power to make substantive rules with binding effect in Section 5(a)
37  adjudications. We also believe that the plain language of Section 6(g), read in light
38  of the broad, clearly agreed-upon concerns that motivated passage of the Trade
39  Commission Act, confirms the framers' intent to allow exercise of the power
40  claimed here. * * *

41                                   * * *

1  Moreover, while we believe the historical evidence is indecisive of the question
2  before us, we are convinced that the broad, undisputed policies which clearly
3  motivated the framers of the Federal Trade Commission Act of 1914 would indeed
4  be furthered by our view as to the proper scope of the Commission's rule-making
5  authority. * * *

6  In determining the legislative intent, our duty is to favor an interpretation which
7  would render the statutory design effective in terms of the policies behind its
8  enactment and to avoid an interpretation which would make such policies more
9  difficult of fulfillment, particularly where, as here, that interpretation is consistent
10 with the plain language of the statute. * * *

11                                          * * *

12 The problems of delay and inefficiency that proponents of both a strong and a weak
13 commission aimed to eliminate or minimize have plagued the Trade Commission
14 down to the present. While the Commission has broad common law-like authority
15 to delineate the scope of the statute's prohibitions, like the federal courts it was
16 designed to supplement, it has remained hobbled in its task by the delay inherent
17 in repetitious, lengthy litigation of cases involving complex factual questions under
18 a broad legal standard. Close students of the agency agree that the historic case-
19 by-case purely adjudicatory method of elaborating the Section 5 standard and
20 applying it to discrete business practices has not only produced considerable
21 uncertainty, but also has helped to spawn litigation the length of which has
22 frequently been noted ruefully by commentators on the Commission's
23 performance. We believe that, to the extent substantive rule-making to implement
24 Section 5 proceedings is likely to deal with these problems given the statutory
25 authority provided in Section 6(g), the Commission's position should be upheld as
26 a reasonable means of attacking ills the Commission was created to cure.

27                                          * * *

28 Moreover, when delay in agency proceedings is minimized by using rules, those
29 violating the statutory standard lose an opportunity to turn litigation into a
30 profitable and lengthy game of postponing the effect of the rule on their current
31 practice. As a result, substantive rules will protect the companies which willingly
32 comply with the law against what amounts to the unfair competition of those who
33 would profit from delayed enforcement as to them. This, too, will minimize useless
34 litigation and is likely to assist the Commission in more effectively allocating its
35 resources. In addition, whatever form rules take, whether bright-line standards or
36 presumptions that are rebuttable, they are likely to decrease the current
37 uncertainty many businesses are said to feel over the current scope and
38 applicability of Section 5. But the important point here is not that rule-making is
39 assuredly going to solve the Commission's problems. It is rather than recognition
40 and use of rule-making by the Commission is convincingly linked to the goals of
41 agency expedition, efficiency, and certainty of regulatory standards that loomed in
42 the background of the 1914 passage of the Federal Trade Commission Act.

1                                          * * *

2                                            V

3                                          * * *

4     * * * The rule here does not bypass the Commission's statute-based cease-and-
5     desist proceedings. It merely supplements them. Moreover, in light of the concern
6     evident in the legislative history that the Commission give attention to the special
7     circumstances of individual businesses in proceeding against them, the
8     Commission should administer any rules it might promulgate in much the same
9     way that courts have ordinarily required other agencies to administer rules that
10    operate to modify a regulated party's rights to a full hearing. That is, some
11    opportunity must be given for a defendant in a Section 5 proceeding to
12    demonstrate that the special circumstances of his case warrant waiving the rule's
13    applicability, as where the rationale of the rule does not appear to apply to his own
14    situation or a compelling case of hardship can be made out. * * *

15    * * * Furthermore, under the Administrative Procedure Act the public, including
16    all parties in the industry who might be affected, are given a significant opportunity
17    prior to promulgation of a rule to ventilate the policy and empirical issues at stake
18    through written submissions, at a minimum, or more, as here, where the agency
19    permitted oral argument in a non-adjudicatory setting. Finally, any rules
20    promulgated by the agency are subject to judicial review testing their legality and
21    ensuring that they are within the scope of the broad statutory prohibition they
22    purport to define.

23                                         * * *

24                                           VI

25    Our conclusion as to the scope of Section 6(g) is not disturbed by the fact that the
26    agency itself did not assert the power to promulgate substantive rules until 1962
27    and indeed indicated intermittently before that time that it lacked such power. * * *
28    Here, the question is simply one of statutory interpretation concerning the
29    procedures and setting in which the Commission may elaborate its statutory
30    standard. Since this sort of question calls largely for the exercise of historical
31    analysis and logical and analogical reasoning, it is the everyday staple of judges as
32    well as agencies. Thus we feel confident in making our own judgment as to the
33    proper construction of Section 6(g). * * *

34    * * * So far as we can tell, the earlier assertions of lack of rule-making power were
35    based on an unduly crabbed and cautious analysis of the legislative background,
36    an analysis that we have conducted independently and that has brought us to an
37    opposite but, in our judgment, correct conclusion.

38    A more troubling obstacle to the Commission's position here is the argument that
39    Congress was made fully aware of the formerly restrictive view of the Commission's
40    power and passed a series of laws granting limited substantive rule-making

      264

authority to the Commission in discrete areas allegedly on the premise that the 1914 debate withheld such authority. * * *

* * *

* * * The view that the Commission lacked substantive rule-making power has been clearly brought to the attention of Congress and, rather than simply failing to act on the question, Congress, in expanding the agency's powers in several discrete areas of marketing regulation, affirmatively enacted limited grants of substantive rule-making authority in the Wool Products Act of 1939, the Fur Products Labeling Act of 1951, the Flammable Fabrics Act of 1953 as amended in 1967, the Textile Fiber Products Identification Act of 1958, and the Fair Packaging and Labeling Act of 1967. Thus it is argued that Congress would not have granted the agency such powers unless it had felt that otherwise the agency lacked rule-making authority.

Conceding the greater force of this argument than one premised on congressional inaction, we believe it must not be accepted blindly. In such circumstances, it is equally possible that Congress granted the power out of uncertainty, understandable caution, and a desire to avoid litigation. While this argument, like any theory requiring us to draw inferences from congressional action or inaction, may be speculative, we believe it cannot be ignored here. * * * Where there is solid reason, as there plainly is here, to believe that Congress, in fact, has not wholeheartedly accepted the agency's viewpoint and instead enacted legislation out of caution and to eliminate the kind of disputes that invariably attend statutory ambiguity, we believe that relying on the de facto ratification argument is unwise. In such circumstances, we must perform our customary task of coming to an independent judgment as to the statute's meaning, confident that if Congress believes that its creature, the Commission, thus exercises too much power, it will repeal the grant.[40]

## VII

In sum, we must respectfully register our disagreement with the District Court's painstaking opinion. Its result would render the Commission ineffective to do the job assigned it by Congress. * * * We hold that under the terms of its governing statute, and under Section 6(g), in particular, the Federal Trade Commission is authorized to promulgate rules defining the meaning of the statutory standards of the illegality the Commission is empowered to prevent. Thus we must reverse the District Court's judgment and remand this case for further proceedings.

It is so ordered.

---

[40] We are aware, of course, that in both the just concluded 92nd Congress and the current 93rd Congress legislation granting the FTC limited substantive rule-making power in the area of "unfair and deceptive practices" has been under consideration. * * *

**Heckler v. Campbell**

461 U.S. 458 (1983)

May 16, 1983

JUSTICE POWELL delivered the opinion of the Court.

The issue is whether the Secretary of Health and Human Services may rely on published medical-vocational guidelines to determine a claimant's right to Social Security disability benefits.

I

The Social Security Act defines "disability" in terms of the effect a physical or mental impairment has on a person's ability to function in the workplace. It provides disability benefits only to persons who are unable "to engage in any substantial gainful activity by reason of any medically determinable physical or mental impairment." 42 U.S.C. § 423(d)(1)(A). And it specifies that a person must "not only [be] unable to do his previous work but [must be unable], considering his age, education, and work experience, [to] engage in any other kind of substantial gainful work which exists in the national economy, regardless of whether such work exists in the immediate area in which he lives, or whether a specific job vacancy exists for him, or whether he would be hired if he applied for work."

In 1978, the Secretary of Health and Human Services promulgated regulations implementing this definition. *See* 43 Fed.Reg. 55349 (1978). The regulations recognize that certain impairments are so severe that they prevent a person from pursuing any gainful work. A claimant who establishes that he suffers from one of these impairments will be considered disabled without further inquiry. If a claimant suffers from a less severe impairment, the Secretary must determine whether the claimant retains the ability to perform either his former work or some less demanding employment. If a claimant can pursue his former occupation, he is not entitled to disability benefits. If he cannot, the Secretary must determine whether the claimant retains the capacity to pursue less demanding work.

The regulations divide this last inquiry into two stages. First, the Secretary must assess each claimant's present job qualifications. The regulations direct the Secretary to consider the factors Congress has identified as relevant: physical ability, age, education, and work experience. Second, she must consider whether jobs exist in the national economy that a person having the claimant's qualifications could perform.

Prior to 1978, the Secretary relied on vocational experts to establish the existence of suitable jobs in the national economy. After a claimant's limitations and abilities had been determined at a hearing, a vocational expert ordinarily would testify

266

1   whether work existed that the claimant could perform. Although this testimony
2   often was based on standardized guides, vocational experts frequently were
3   criticized for their inconsistent treatment of similarly situated claimants. To
4   improve both the uniformity and efficiency of this determination, the Secretary
5   promulgated medical-vocational guidelines as part of the 1978 regulations.

6   These guidelines relieve the Secretary of the need to rely on vocational experts by
7   establishing through rulemaking the types and numbers of jobs that exist in the
8   national economy. They consist of a matrix of the four factors identified by
9   Congress—physical ability, age, education, and work experience—and set forth
10  rules that identify whether jobs requiring specific combinations of these factors
11  exist in significant numbers in the national economy. Where a claimant's
12  qualifications correspond to the job requirements identified by a rule, the
13  guidelines direct a conclusion as to whether work exists that the claimant could
14  perform.[5] If such work exists, the claimant is not considered disabled.

15                                    II

16  In 1979, Calmen Campbell applied for disability benefits because a back condition
17  and hypertension prevented her from continuing her work as a hotel maid. After
18  her application was denied, she requested a hearing *de novo* before an
19  Administrative Law Judge. He determined that her back problem was not severe
20  enough to find her disabled without further inquiry, and accordingly considered
21  whether she retained the ability to perform either her past work or some less
22  strenuous job. He concluded that, even though Campbell's back condition
23  prevented her from returning to her work as a maid, she retained the physical
24  capacity to do light work. In accordance with the regulations, he found that
25  Campbell was 52 years old, that her previous employment consisted of unskilled
26  jobs, and that she had a limited education. He noted that Campbell, who had been
27  born in Panama, experienced difficulty in speaking and writing English. She was
28  able, however, to understand and read English fairly well. Relying on the medical-
29  vocational guidelines, the Administrative Law Judge found that a significant

---

[5] The regulations recognize that the rules only describe "major functional and vocational patterns." 20 CFR pt. 404, subpt. P, app. 2, § 200.00(a) (1982). If an individual's capabilities are not described accurately by a rule, the regulations make clear that the individual's particular limitations must be considered. *See* app. 2, §§ 200.00(a), (d). Additionally, the regulations declare that the administrative law judge will not apply the age categories "mechanically in a borderline situation," 20 CFR § 404.1563(a) (1982), and recognize that some claimants may possess limitations that are not factored into the guidelines, *see* app. 2, § 200.00(e). Thus, the regulations provide that the rules will be applied only when they describe a claimant's abilities and limitations accurately.

1 number of jobs existed that a person of Campbell's qualifications could perform.
2 Accordingly, he concluded that she was not disabled.

3 This determination was upheld by both the Social Security Appeals Council and
4 the District Court for the Eastern District of New York. The Court of Appeals for
5 the Second Circuit reversed. * * *

6 The court found that the medical-vocational guidelines did not provide the specific
7 evidence that it previously had required. It explained that, in the absence of such a
8 showing, "the claimant is deprived of any real chance to present evidence showing
9 that she cannot in fact perform the types of jobs that are administratively noticed
10 by the guidelines." The court concluded that, because the Secretary had failed to
11 introduce evidence that specific alternative jobs existed, the determination that
12 Campbell was not disabled was not supported by substantial evidence.

13 We granted certiorari to resolve a conflict among the Courts of Appeals. We now
14 reverse.

15 III

16 * * *

17 The Social Security Act directs the Secretary to "adopt reasonable and proper rules
18 and regulations to regulate and provide for the nature and extent of the proofs and
19 evidence and the method of taking and furnishing the same" in disability cases. 42
20 U.S.C. § 405(a). As we previously have recognized, Congress has "conferred on the
21 Secretary exceptionally broad authority to prescribe standards for applying certain
22 sections of the [Social Security] Act." *Schweiker v. Gray Panthers*, 453 U.S. 34, 43
23 (1981). Where, as here, the statute expressly entrusts the Secretary with the
24 responsibility for implementing a provision by regulation, our review is limited to
25 determining whether the regulations promulgated exceeded the Secretary's
26 statutory authority and whether they are arbitrary and capricious.

27 We do not think that the Secretary's reliance on medical-vocational guidelines is
28 inconsistent with the Social Security Act. It is true that the statutory scheme
29 contemplates that disability hearings will be individualized determinations based
30 on evidence adduced at a hearing. But this does not bar the Secretary from relying
31 on rulemaking to resolve certain classes of issues. The Court has recognized that,
32 even where an agency's enabling statute expressly requires it to hold a hearing, the
33 agency may rely on its rulemaking authority to determine issues that do not require
34 case-by-case consideration. *See FPC v. Texaco Inc.*, 377 U.S. 33, 41-44 (1964);
35 *United States v. Storer Broadcasting Co.*, 351 U.S. 192, 205 (1956). A contrary
36 holding would require the agency continually to relitigate issues that may be
37 established fairly and efficiently in a single rulemaking proceeding. *See FPC v.*
38 *Texaco Inc.*, at 377 U.S. 44.

39 The Secretary's decision to rely on medical-vocational guidelines is consistent with
40 *Texaco* and *Storer*. As noted above, in determining whether a claimant can

perform less strenuous work, the Secretary must make two determinations. She must assess each claimant's individual abilities and then determine whether jobs exist that a person having the claimant's qualifications could perform. The first inquiry involves a determination of historic facts, and the regulations properly require the Secretary to make these findings on the basis of evidence adduced at a hearing. We note that the regulations afford claimants ample opportunity both to present evidence relating to their own abilities and to offer evidence that the guidelines do not apply to them.[12] The second inquiry requires the Secretary to determine an issue that is not unique to each claimant—the types and numbers of jobs that exist in the national economy. This type of general factual issue may be resolved as fairly through rulemaking as by introducing the testimony of vocational experts at each disability hearing. *See American Airlines, Inc. v. CAB*, 319, 359 F.2d 624, 633 (D.C. Cir. 1966) (*en banc*).

As the Secretary has argued, the use of published guidelines brings with it a uniformity that previously had been perceived as lacking. To require the Secretary to relitigate the existence of jobs in the national economy at each hearing would hinder needlessly an already overburdened agency. We conclude that the Secretary's use of medical-vocational guidelines does not conflict with the statute, nor can we say on the record before us that they are arbitrary and capricious.

* * *

IV

The Court of Appeals' decision would require the Secretary to introduce evidence of specific available jobs that respondent could perform. It would limit severely her ability to rely on the medical-vocational guidelines. We think the Secretary reasonably could choose to rely on these guidelines in appropriate cases, rather than on the testimony of a vocational expert in each case. Accordingly, the judgment of the Court of Appeals is

*Reversed.*

JUSTICE BRENNAN, concurring. [Omitted.]

JUSTICE MARSHALL, concurring in part and dissenting in part. [Omitted.]

---

[12] Both *FPC v. Texaco Inc.*, 377 U.S. 33, 40 (1964), and *United States v. Storer Broadcasting Co.*, 351 U.S. 192, 205 (1956), were careful to note that the statutory scheme at issue allowed an individual applicant to show that the rule promulgated should not be applied to him. The regulations here provide a claimant with equal or greater protection since they state that an administrative law judge will not apply the rules contained in the guidelines when they fail to describe a claimant's particular limitations.

MEET THE ADMINISTRATIVE PROCEDURE ACT

## 2. On-the-Record Versus Informal Actions

Because the procedures of on-the-record actions are more burdensome, agencies generally would prefer to proceed informally where they may. When do they have to engage in on-the-record proceedings? These cases, *Florida East Coast Railway* and *Dominion Point*, address that question in the context of rulemaking. *Dominion Point* makes reference to an earlier case, *Seacoast*, which had left agencies less latitude in choosing between formal and informal adjudication. One thing that had changed between *Seacoast* and *Dominion Point* was the Supreme Court's *Chevron* case, which we will discuss—at length!—later in the course. This is a first taste of *Chevron*, and the impact it has had on how courts review agency choices.

### United States v. Florida East Coast Railway Co.

410 U.S. 224 (1973)

January 22, 1973

MR. JUSTICE REHNQUIST delivered the opinion of the Court.

Appellees, two railroad companies, brought this action in the District Court for the Middle District of Florida to set aside the incentive per diem rates established by appellant Interstate Commerce Commission in a rulemaking proceeding. They challenged the order of the Commission on both substantive and procedural grounds. The District Court sustained appellees' position that the Commission had failed to comply with the applicable provisions of the Administrative Procedure Act, and therefore set aside the order without dealing with the railroads' other contentions. The District Court held that the language of § 1(14)(a) of the Interstate Commerce Act required the Commission in a proceeding such as this to act in accordance with the Administrative Procedure Act, 5 U.S.C. § 556(d), and that the Commission's determination to receive submissions from the appellees only in written form was a violation of that section because the appellees were "prejudiced" by that determination within the meaning of that section.

* * *

I.

BACKGROUND OF CHRONIC FREIGHT CAR SHORTAGES

This case arises from the factual background of a chronic freight-car shortage on the Nation's railroads, which we described in *United States v. Allegheny-Ludlum Steel Corp.* Judge Simpson, writing for the District Court in this case, noted that "[f]or a number of years portions of the nation have been plagued with seasonal

1  shortages of freight cars in which to ship goods." Judge Friendly, writing for a
2  three-judge District Court in the Eastern District of New York in the related case
3  of *Long Island R. Co. v. United States*, 318 F.Supp. 490, 491 (EDNY 1970),
4  described the Commission's order as "the latest chapter in a long history of freight
5  car shortages in certain regions and seasons and of attempts to ease them."
6  Congressional concern for the problem was manifested in the enactment in 1966
7  of an amendment to § 1(14)(a) of the Interstate Commerce Act, enlarging the
8  Commission's authority to prescribe per diem charges for the use by one railroad
9  of freight cars owned by another. * * *

10  The Commission, in 1966, commenced an investigation, "to determine whether
11  information presently available warranted the establishment of an incentive
12  element increase, on an interim basis, to apply pending further study and
13  investigation." Statements of position were received from the Commission staff
14  and a number of railroads. Hearings were conducted at which witnesses were
15  examined. In October, 1967, the Commission rendered a decision discontinuing
16  the earlier proceeding, but announcing a program of further investigation into the
17  general subject.

18  In December, 1967, the Commission initiated the rulemaking procedure giving rise
19  to the order that appellees here challenge. It directed Class I and Class II line-haul
20  railroads to compile and report detailed information with respect to freight car
21  demand and supply at numerous sample stations for selected days of the week
22  during 12 four-week periods, beginning January 29, 1968.

23  Some of the affected railroads voiced questions about the proposed study or
24  requested modification in the study procedures outlined by the Commission in its
25  notice of proposed rulemaking. In response to petitions setting forth these carriers'
26  views, the Commission staff held an informal conference in April, 1968, at which
27  the objections and proposed modifications were discussed. Twenty railroads,
28  including appellee Seaboard, were represented at this conference, at which the
29  Commission's staff sought to answer questions about reporting methods to
30  accommodate individual circumstances of particular railroads. The conference
31  adjourned on a note that undoubtedly left the impression that hearings would be
32  held at some future date. A detailed report of the conference was sent to all parties
33  to the proceeding before the Commission.

34  The results of the information thus collected were analyzed and presented to
35  Congress by the Commission during a hearing before the Subcommittee on Surface
36  Transportation of the Senate Committee on Commerce in May, 1969. Members of
37  the Subcommittee expressed dissatisfaction with the Commission's slow pace in
38  exercising the authority that had been conferred upon it by the 1966 Amendments
39  to the Interstate Commerce Act. Judge Simpson, in his opinion for the District
40  Court, said:

41  "Members of the Senate Subcommittee on Surface Transportation
42  expressed considerable dissatisfaction with the Commission's apparent

inability to take effective steps toward eliminating the national shortage of freight cars. Comments were general that the Commission was conducting too many hearings and taking too little action. Senators pressed for more action and less talk, but Commission counsel expressed doubt respecting the Commission's statutory power to act without additional hearings." 322 F.Supp. at 727.

Judge Friendly, describing the same event in *Long Island R. Co. v. United States* said:

"To say that the presentation was not received with enthusiasm would be a considerable understatement. Senators voiced displeasure at the Commission's long delay at taking action under the 1966 amendment, engaged in some merriment over what was regarded as an unintelligible discussion of methodology . . . and expressed doubt about the need for a hearing. . . . But the Commission's general counsel insisted that a hearing was needed . . . and the Chairman of the Commission agreed. . . ." 318 F.Supp. at 494.

The Commission, now apparently imbued with a new sense of mission, issued in December, 1969, an interim report announcing its tentative decision to adopt incentive per diem charges on standard boxcars based on the information compiled by the railroads. The substantive decision reached by the Commission was that so-called "incentive" per diem charges should be paid by any railroad using on its lines a standard boxcar owned by another railroad. Before the enactment of the 1966 amendment to the Interstate Commerce Act, it was generally thought that the Commission's authority to fix per diem payments for freight car use was limited to setting an amount that reflected fair return on investment for the owning railroad, without any regard being had for the desirability of prompt return to the owning line or for the encouragement of additional purchases of freight cars by the railroads as a method of investing capital. The Commission concluded, however, that, in view of the 1966 amendment, it could impose additional "incentive" per diem charges to spur prompt return of existing cars and to make acquisition of new cars financially attractive to the railroads. It did so by means of a proposed schedule that established such charges on an across-the-board basis for all common carriers by railroads subject to the Interstate Commerce Act. Embodied in the report was a proposed rule adopting the Commission's tentative conclusions and a notice to the railroads to file statements of position within 60 days, couched in the following language:

"That verified statements of facts, briefs, and statements of position respecting the tentative conclusions reached in the said interim report, the rules and regulations proposed in the appendix to this order, and any other pertinent matter, are hereby invited to be submitted pursuant to the filing schedule set forth below by an interested person whether or not such person is already a party to this proceeding.

272

1     * * * *

2     "That any party requesting oral hearing shall set forth with specificity the
3     need therefor and the evidence to be adduced." 337 I.C.C. 183, 213.

4     Both appellee railroads filed statements objecting to the Commission's proposal
5     and requesting an oral hearing, as did numerous other railroads. In April, 1970,
6     the Commission, without having held further "hearings," issued a supplemental
7     report making some modifications in the tentative conclusions earlier reached, but
8     overruling *in toto* the requests of appellees.

9     The District Court held that, in so doing, the Commission violated § 556(d) of the
10    Administrative Procedure Act, and it was on this basis that it set aside the order of
11    the Commission.

12    II.

13    APPLICABILITY OF ADMINISTRATIVE PROCEDURE ACT

14    In *United States v. Allegheny-Ludlum Steel Corp.*, 406 U.S. 742 (1972), we held
15    that the language of § 1(14)(a) of the Interstate Commerce Act authorizing the
16    Commission to act "after hearing" was not the equivalent of a requirement that a
17    rule be made "on the record after opportunity for an agency hearing" as the latter
18    term is used in § 53(c) of the Administrative Procedure Act. Since the 1966
19    amendment to § 1(14)(a), under which the Commission was here proceeding, does
20    not, by its terms, add to the hearing requirement contained in the earlier language,
21    the same result should obtain here unless that amendment contains language that
22    is tantamount to such a requirement. Appellees contend that such language is
23    found in the provisions of that Act requiring that:

24        "The Commission shall give consideration to the national level of
25        ownership of such type of freight car and to other factors affecting the
26        adequacy of the national freight car supply, and shall, on the basis of such
27        consideration, determine whether compensation should be computed. . . ."

28    While this language is undoubtedly a mandate to the Commission to consider the
29    factors there set forth in reaching any conclusion as to imposition of per diem
30    incentive charges, it adds to the hearing requirements of the section neither
31    expressly nor by implication. We know of no reason to think that an administrative
32    agency, in reaching a decision, cannot accord consideration to factors such as those
33    set forth in the 1966 amendment by means other than a trial-type hearing or the
34    presentation of oral argument by the affected parties. Congress by that amendment
35    specified necessary components of the ultimate decision, but it did not specify the
36    method by which the Commission should acquire information about those
37    components.

38    Both of the district courts that reviewed this order of the Commission concluded
39    that its proceedings were governed by the stricter requirement of §§ 556 and 557
40    of the Administrative Procedure Act, rather than by the provisions of § 553 alone.

The conclusion of the District Court for the Middle District of Florida, which we here review, was based on the assumption that the language in § 1(14)(a) of the Interstate Commerce Act requiring rulemaking under that section to be done "after hearing" was the equivalent of a statutory requirement that the rule "be made on the record after opportunity for an agency hearing." Such an assumption is inconsistent with our decision in *Allegheny-Ludlum.*

The District Court for the Eastern District of New York reached the same conclusion by a somewhat different line of reasoning. That court felt that, because § 1(14)(a) of the Interstate Commerce Act had required a "hearing," and because that section was originally enacted in 1917, Congress was probably thinking in terms of a "hearing" such as that described in the opinion of this Court in the roughly contemporaneous case of *ICC v. Louisville & Nashville R. Co.,* 227 U.S. 88, 93 (1913). The ingredients of the "hearing" were there said to be that "[a]ll parties must be fully apprised of the evidence submitted or to be considered, and must be given opportunity to cross-examine witnesses, to inspect documents and to offer evidence in explanation or rebuttal." Combining this view of congressional understanding of the term "hearing" with comments by the Chairman of the Commission at the time of the adoption of the 1966 legislation regarding the necessity for "hearings," that court concluded that Congress had, in effect, required that these proceedings be "on the record after opportunity for an agency hearing" within the meaning of § 553(c) of the Administrative Procedure Act.

Insofar as this conclusion is grounded on the belief that the language "after hearing" of § 1(14)(a), without more, would trigger the applicability of §§ 556 and 557, it, too, is contrary to our decision in *Allegheny-Ludlum.* The District Court observed that it was "rather hard to believe that the last sentence of § 553(c) was directed only to the few legislative sports where the words 'on the record' or their equivalent had found their way into the statute book." This is, however, the language which Congress used, and since there are statutes on the books that do use these very words the regulations provision of the Food and Drug Act, adherence to that language cannot be said to render the provision nugatory or ineffectual. We recognized in *Allegheny-Ludlum* that the actual words "on the record" and "after . . . hearing" used in § 553 were not words of art, and that other statutory language having the same meaning could trigger the provisions of §§ 556 and 557 in rulemaking proceedings. But we adhere to our conclusion, expressed in that case, that the phrase "after hearing" in § 1(14)(a) of the Interstate Commerce Act does not have such an effect.

### III.

### "HEARING" REQUIREMENT OF § 1(14)(a) OF THE INTERSTATE COMMERCE ACT

Inextricably intertwined with the hearing requirement of the Administrative Procedure Act in this case is the meaning to be given to the language "after hearing" in § 1(14)(a) of the Interstate Commerce Act. Appellees, both here and in the court

1  below, contend that the Commission procedure here fell short of that mandated by
2  the "hearing" requirement of § 1(14)(a), even though it may have satisfied § 553 of
3  the Administrative Procedure Act. The Administrative Procedure Act states that
4  none of its provisions "limit or repeal additional requirements imposed by statute
5  or otherwise recognized by law." 5 U.S.C. § 559. Thus, even though the Commission
6  was not required to comply with §§ 556 and 557 of that Act, it was required to
7  accord the "hearing" specified in § 1(14)(a) of the Interstate Commerce Act. Though
8  the District Court did not pass on this contention, it is so closely related to the claim
9  based on the Administrative Procedure Act that we proceed to decide it now.

10  If we were to agree with the reasoning of the District Court for the Eastern District
11  of New York with respect to the type of hearing required by the Interstate
12  Commerce Act, the Commission's action might well violate those requirements,
13  even though it was consistent with the requirements of the Administrative
14  Procedure Act.

15  The term "hearing" in its legal context undoubtedly has a host of meanings. Its
16  meaning undoubtedly will vary, depending on whether it is used in the context of
17  a rulemaking-type proceeding or in the context of a proceeding devoted to the
18  adjudication of particular disputed facts. It is by no means apparent what the
19  drafters of the Esch Car Service Act of 1917, which became the first part of § 1(14)(a)
20  of the Interstate Commerce Act, meant by the term. Such an intent would surely
21  be an ephemeral one if, indeed, Congress in 1917 had in mind anything more
22  specific than the language it actually used, for none of the parties refer to any
23  legislative history that would shed light on the intended meaning of the words
24  "after hearing." What is apparent, though, is that the term was used in granting
25  authority to the Commission to make rules and regulations of a prospective nature.

26                                    * * *

27  Under these circumstances, confronted with a grant of substantive authority made
28  after the Administrative Procedure Act was enacted, we think that reference to that
29  Act, in which Congress devoted itself exclusively to questions such as the nature
30  and scope of hearings, is a satisfactory basis for determining what is meant by the
31  term "hearing" used in another statute. Turning to that Act, we are convinced that
32  the term "hearing," as used therein, does not necessarily embrace either the right
33  to present evidence orally and to cross-examine opposing witnesses, or the right to
34  present oral argument to the agency's decisionmaker.

35  Section 553 excepts from its requirements rulemaking devoted to "interpretative
36  rules, general statements of policy, or rules of agency organization, procedure, or
37  practice," and rulemaking "when the agency for good cause finds . . . that notice
38  and public procedure thereon are impracticable, unnecessary, or contrary to the
39  public interest." This exception does not apply, however, "when notice or hearing
40  is required by statute"; in those cases, even though interpretative rulemaking be
41  involved, the requirements of § 553 apply. But since these requirements
42  themselves do not mandate any oral presentation, it cannot be doubted that a

statute that requires a "hearing" prior to rulemaking may in some circumstances be satisfied by procedures that meet only the standards of § 553. * * *

Similarly, even where the statute requires that the rulemaking procedure take place "on the record after opportunity for an agency hearing," thus triggering the applicability of § 656, subsection (d) provides that the agency may proceed by the submission of all or part of the evidence in written form if a party will not be "prejudiced thereby." Again, the Act makes it plain that a specific statutory mandate that the proceedings take place on the record after hearing may be satisfied in some circumstances by evidentiary submission in written form only.

We think this treatment of the term "hearing" in the Administrative Procedure Act affords a sufficient basis for concluding that the requirement of a "hearing" contained in § 1(14)(a), in a situation where the Commission was acting under the 1966 statutory rulemaking authority that Congress had conferred upon it, did not by its own force require the Commission either to hear oral testimony, to permit cross-examination of Commission witnesses, or to hear oral argument. * * *

Appellee railroads cite a number of our previous decisions dealing in some manner with the right to a hearing in an administrative proceeding. Although appellees have asserted no claim of constitutional deprivation in this proceeding, some of the cases they rely upon expressly speak in constitutional terms, while others are less than clear as to whether they depend upon the Due Process Clause of the Fifth and Fourteenth Amendments to the Constitution, or upon generalized principles of administrative law formulated prior to the adoption of the Administrative Procedure Act.

* * *

Here, the incentive payments proposed by the Commission * * * were applicable across the board to all of the common carriers by railroad subject to the Interstate Commerce Act. No effort was made to single out any particular railroad for special consideration based on its own peculiar circumstances. Indeed, one of the objections of appellee Florida East Coast was that it and other terminating carriers should have been treated differently from the generality of the railroads. But the fact that the order may, in its effects, have been thought more disadvantageous by some railroads than by others does not change its generalized nature. Though the Commission obviously relied on factual inferences as a basis for its order, the source of these factual inferences was apparent to anyone who read the order of December, 1969. The factual inferences were used in the formulation of a basically legislative-type judgment, for prospective application only, rather than in adjudicating a particular set of disputed facts.

The Commission's procedure satisfied both the provisions of § 1(14)(a) of the Interstate Commerce Act and of the Administrative Procedure Act, and were not inconsistent with prior decisions of this Court. We, therefore, reverse the judgment of the District Court, and remand the case so that it may consider those contentions of the parties that are not disposed of by this opinion.

1 *It is so ordered.*

2 MR. JUSTICE POWELL took no part in the consideration or decision of this case.

3 MR. JUSTICE DOUGLAS, with whom MR. JUSTICE STEWART concurs,
4 dissenting.

5 The present decision makes a sharp break with traditional concepts of procedural
6 due process. The Commission order under attack is tantamount to a rate order.
7 Charges are fixed that nonowning railroads must pay owning railroads for boxcars
8 of the latter that are on the tracks of the former. * * * This is the imposition on
9 carriers by administrative fiat of a new financial liability. I do not believe it is within
10 our traditional concepts of due process to allow an administrative agency to saddle
11 anyone with a new rate, charge, or fee without a full hearing that includes the right
12 to present oral testimony, cross-examine witnesses, and present oral argument.
13 That is required by the Administrative Procedure Act, 5 U.S.C. § 556(d); § 556(a)
14 states that § 556 applies to hearings required by § 553. Section 553(c) provides that
15 § 556 applies "[w]hen rules are required by statute to be made on the record after
16 opportunity for an agency hearing." A hearing under § 1(14)(a) of the Interstate
17 Commerce Act fixing rates, charges, or fees is certainly adjudicatory, not legislative
18 in the customary sense.

19 * * *

20 The more exacting hearing provisions of the Administrative Procedure Act, 5
21 U.S.C. §§ 556-557, are only applicable, of course, if the "rules are required by
22 statute to be made on the record after opportunity for an agency hearing." *Id.* §
23 553(c).

24 * * *

25 The rules in question here established "incentive" per diem charges to spur the
26 prompt return of existing cars and to make the acquisition of new cars financially
27 attractive to the railroads. Unlike those we considered in *Allegheny-Ludlum*, these
28 rules involve the creation of a new financial liability. Although quasi-legislative,
29 they are also adjudicatory in the sense that they determine the measure of the
30 financial responsibility of one road for its use of the rolling stock of another road.
31 * * *

32 * * *

33 Accordingly, I would hold that appellees were not afforded the hearing guaranteed
34 by § 1(14)(a) of the Interstate Commerce Act and 5 U.S.C. §§ 553, 556, and 557, and
35 would affirm the decision of the District Court.

36

37 **Dominion Energy Brayton Point, LLC v. Johnson**

38 443 F.3d 12 (1st Cir. 2006)

1    March 30, 2006

2    Before SELYA, LIPEZ and HOWARD, Circuit Judges.

3    SELYA, Circuit Judge.

4    USGen New England, Inc., now Dominion Energy Brayton Point, LLC (Dominion),
5    filed suit against the U.S. Environmental Protection Agency, its administrator, and
6    its regional office (collectively, the EPA), alleging that the EPA failed to perform a
7    non-discretionary duty when it refused to grant Dominion's request for a formal
8    evidentiary hearing after issuing a proposed final National Pollution Discharge
9    Elimination System (NPDES) permit. The district court dismissed the case for
10   want of subject matter jurisdiction. On appeal, the central question presented
11   concerns the effect of this court's decision in *Seacoast Anti-Pollution League v.*
12   *Costle*, 572 F.2d 872 (1st Cir. 1978), in light of the Supreme Court's subsequent
13   decision in *Chevron U.S.A. Inc. v. Natural Resources Defense Council, Inc.*, 467
14   U.S. 837 (1984). Concluding, as we do, that *Seacoast* does not control, we affirm
15   the judgment below.

## I. Background

17   Dominion owns an electrical generating facility in Somerset, Massachusetts (the
18   station). The station opened in the 1960s and, like most power plants of its era,
19   utilizes an "open-cycle" cooling system. Specifically, the station withdraws water
20   from the Lees and Taunton Rivers, circulates that water through the plant's
21   generating equipment as a coolant, and then discharges the water (which, by then,
22   has attained an elevated temperature) into Mount Hope Bay.

23   The withdrawals and discharges of water are regulated by the Clean Water Act
24   (CWA), 33 U.S.C. §§ 1251-1387. For the last three decades, these actions have been
25   authorized by a series of NPDES permits issued by the EPA pursuant to section
26   402(a) of the CWA. The standards incorporated into those permits are determined
27   under the thermal variance procedures laid out in section 316(a).

28   In 1998, the station applied for renewal of its NPDES permit and thermal variance
29   authorization. The EPA issued a proposed final permit on October 6, 2003, in
30   which it rejected the requested thermal variance. On November 4, Dominion
31   sought review before the Environmental Appeals Board (the Board) and asked for
32   an evidentiary hearing. The Board accepted the petition for review but declined to
33   convene an evidentiary hearing.

34                                    * * *

## II. The Legal Landscape

36   Before the EPA either issues an NPDES permit or authorizes a thermal variance, it
37   must offer an "opportunity for public hearing." No definition of "public hearing" is
38   contained within the four corners of the CWA.

1    The Administrative Procedure Act (APA), 5 U.S.C. § 551 *et seq.*, is also part of the
2    relevant legal landscape. Most pertinent here are those sections that combine to
3    describe the procedures for formal administrative adjudications. These procedures
4    apply "in every case of adjudication required by statute to be determined on the
5    record after opportunity for an agency hearing." *Id.* § 554(a). The APA does not
6    directly address whether these procedures apply when a statute simply calls for an
7    "opportunity for public hearing" without any specific indication that the hearing
8    should be "on the record."

9    In *Seacoast*, this court interpreted "public hearing" (as used in sections 402(a) and
10   316(a) of the CWA) to mean "evidentiary hearing"—in other words, a hearing that
11   comports with the APA's requirements for a formal adjudication. Examining the
12   legislative history of the APA, we adopted a presumption that "unless a statute
13   otherwise specifies, an adjudicatory hearing subject to judicial review must be [an
14   evidentiary hearing] on the record." Applying that presumption to the CWA, we
15   concluded that "the statute certainly does not indicate that the determination need
16   *not* be on the record." 572 F.2d, at 878 (emphasis in original).

17   So viewed, *Seacoast* established a rebuttable presumption that, in the context of
18   an adjudication, an organic statute that calls for a "public hearing" should be read
19   to require an evidentiary hearing in compliance with the formal adjudication
20   provisions of the APA. Two other circuit courts reached the same conclusion, albeit
21   through different reasoning. Acquiescing in this construction, the EPA
22   promulgated regulations that memorialized the use of formal evidentiary hearings
23   in the NPDES permit process.

24   In 1984, a sea change occurred in administrative law and, specifically, in the
25   interpretation of organic statutes such as the CWA. The Supreme Court held that
26   "[w]hen a court reviews an agency's construction of the statute which it
27   administers," the reviewing court first must ask "whether Congress has directly
28   spoken to the precise question at issue." *Chevron*, 467 U.S., at 842. If Congress's
29   intent is clear, that intent governs—both the court and the agency must give it full
30   effect. If, however, Congress has not directly addressed the question and the
31   agency has stepped into the vacuum by promulgating an interpretive regulation, a
32   reviewing court may "not simply impose its own construction on the statute," but,
33   rather, ought to ask "whether the agency's answer is based on a permissible
34   construction of the statute." *Id.* at 843.

35   This paradigm, sometimes called the *Chevron* two-step, increases the sphere of
36   influence of agency action. If congressional intent is unclear and an agency's
37   interpretation of a statute that it administers is reasonable, an inquiring court must
38   defer to that interpretation. That is so even if the agency's interpretation is not the
39   one that the court considers to be the best available interpretation.

40   Armed with the *Chevron* decision and a presidential directive to streamline
41   regulatory programs, the EPA advanced a proposal to eliminate formal evidentiary

hearings from the NPDES permitting process. In due course, the EPA adopted that proposal as a final rule.

This revision depended heavily on a *Chevron* analysis. The agency began by "finding no evidence that Congress intended to require formal evidentiary hearings or that the text [of section 402(a)] precludes informal adjudication of permit review petitions." Then, it weighed the risks and benefits of employing informal hearing procedures for NPDES permit review, "determining that these procedures would not violate the Due Process Clause." Finally, it "concluded that informal hearing procedures satisfy the hearing requirement of section 402(a)."

It was under this new regulatory scheme that the EPA considered Dominion's request to renew its NPDES permit and to authorize a thermal variance. Thus, it was under this scheme that the EPA denied Dominion's request for an evidentiary hearing.

\* \* \*

## III. Analysis

\* \* \*

One thing is crystal clear: on their face, the current EPA regulations do not establish a non-discretionary duty to provide the evidentiary hearing that Dominion seeks. Prior to the date of Dominion's request, the EPA vitiated the preexisting rule introducing evidentiary hearings into the NPDES permitting process. Dominion concedes this fact, but nonetheless relies on *Seacoast* as the source of a non-discretionary duty to convene an evidentiary hearing.

This reliance is misplaced. Even if *Seacoast* established a non-discretionary duty for section 505(a)(2) purposes when it was decided—a matter upon which we need not opine—Dominion's position ignores two important post-*Seacoast* changes in the legal landscape: the Supreme Court's decision in *Chevron* and the agency's subsequent promulgation of the current "no evidentiary hearing" rule.

\* \* \*

For present purposes, the critical precedent is *National Cable & Telecommunications Ass'n v. Brand X Internet Services*, 545 U.S. 967 (2005). There, the Court examined the relationship between the stare decisis effect of an appellate court's statutory interpretation and the *Chevron* deference due to an administrative agency's subsequent, but contrary, interpretation. Echoing *Chevron*, the Court reiterated that "[f]illing [statutory] gaps . . . involves difficult policy choices that agencies are better equipped to make than courts." Then, concluding that *Chevron*'s application should not turn on the order in which judicial and agency interpretations issue, the Justices held squarely that "[a] court's prior judicial construction of a statute trumps an agency construction otherwise entitled to *Chevron* deference only if the prior court decision holds that its construction follows from the unambiguous terms of the statute and thus leaves

1  no room for agency discretion." This approach "hold[s] judicial interpretations
2  contained in precedents to the same demanding *Chevron* . . . standard that applies
3  if the court is reviewing the agency's construction on a blank slate."

4  *Brand X* demands that we reexamine pre-*Chevron* precedents through a *Chevron*
5  lens. The *Chevron* two-step applies. At the first step, a court "must look primarily
6  to the plain meaning of the statute, drawing its essence from the particular
7  statutory language at issue, as well as the language and design of the statute as a
8  whole." *Strickland v. Comm'r, Me. Dep't of Human Servs.*, 48 F.3d 12, 16 (1st Cir.
9  1995) (citation and internal quotation marks omitted). At this step, the court may
10 "examine the legislative history, albeit skeptically, in search of an unmistakable
11 expression of congressional intent." *Id.* at 17. If the precedent at issue finds clarity
12 at step one—that is, if the holding of the case rests on a perception of clear and
13 unambiguous congressional intent—that precedent will govern. *See Brand X*, 545
14 U.S., at 982. If, however, the precedent operates at *Chevron* step two—that is, if
15 the case holds, in effect, that congressional intent is less than pellucid and proceeds
16 to choose a "*best* reading" rather than "the *only permissible* reading," *id.* at 984
17 (emphasis in original)—its stare decisis effect will, through *Chevron* deference,
18 yield to a contrary but plausible agency interpretation.

19 Once this mode of analysis is understood and applied, Dominion's argument
20 collapses. *Seacoast* simply does not hold that Congress clearly intended the term
21 "public hearing" in sections 402(a) and 316(a) of the CWA to mean "evidentiary
22 hearing." To the contrary, the *Seacoast* court based its interpretation of the CWA
23 on a presumption derived from the legislative history of the APA—a presumption
24 that would hold sway only in the absence of a showing of a contrary congressional
25 intent. In other words, the court resorted to the presumption only because it could
26 find no sign of a plainly discernible congressional intent. A statutory interpretation
27 constructed on such a negative finding is antithetic to a conclusion that Congress's
28 intent was clear and unambiguous.

29 The short of it is that the *Seacoast* court, faced with an opaque statute, settled upon
30 what it sensibly thought was the best construction of the CWA's "public hearing"
31 language. Such a holding is appropriate at step two of the *Chevron* pavane, not at
32 step one. Consequently, under *Brand X*, *Seacoast* must yield to a reasonable
33 agency interpretation of the CWA's "public hearing" requirement.

34 The only piece left to this puzzle is to confirm that the EPA's new regulations are,
35 in fact, entitled to *Chevron* deference. This inquiry is a straightforward one. As our
36 earlier discussion suggests (and as the *Seacoast* court correctly deduced), Congress
37 has not spoken directly to the precise question at issue here. Accordingly, we must
38 defer to the EPA's interpretation of the CWA as long as that interpretation is
39 reasonable. *See Chevron*, 467 U.S., at 843-44.

40 In this instance, the administrative interpretation took into account the relevant
41 universe of factors. *See* 65 Fed. Reg. at 30,898-30,900 (considering "(1) [t]he
42 private interests at stake, (2) the risk of erroneous decision-making, and (3) the

nature of the government interest," and concluding that its new regulation was a reasonable interpretation of the CWA). The agency's conclusion that evidentiary hearings are unnecessary and that Congress, in using the phrase "opportunity for public hearing," did not mean to mandate evidentiary hearings seems reasonable— and Dominion, to its credit, has conceded the point.

\* \* \*

\* \* \* For the reasons elucidated above, we conclude that the district court did not err in dismissing Dominion's action.

## B. Rulemaking

### 1. Notice-and-Comment Rulemaking Under the APA

Especially after *United States v. Florida East Coast Railway Co.,* formal rulemaking is a rarity. The conventional wisdom is that trial-type procedures are ill-suited to deciding policy questions involving a multiplicity of stakeholders and interests. For a colorful description of some formal rulemaking trainwrecks, see Robert Hamilton, *Procedures for the Adoption of Rules of General Applicability: The Need for Procedural Innovation in Administrative Rulemaking,* 60 Cal. L. Rev. 1276 (1972).[3] Today, for the most part, when we are talking about rulemaking, we are talking about informal rulemaking.

Informal rulemaking is often called notice-and-comment rulemaking for a reason: the basic process, as laid down in 5 U.S.C. § 553, is that the agency gives notice of its intention to adopt a rule, receives public comment, and then officially promulgates the rule. You can find the full text of § 553 in the Appendix. Clocking in at 372 words, it does not provide a lot of detail. As we shall see, courts have elaborated on the skeletal process defined in the APA considerably over the years.

The rulemaking process outlined by § 553 has essentially three components:

- **Notice** (§553(b): "[g]eneral notice of proposed rule making shall be published in the Federal Register.")
- **Participation** (§553(c): "the agency shall give interested persons an opportunity to participate in the rule making through submission of written data, views, or arguments with or without opportunity for oral presentation.")
- **Justification** (§553(c): "After consideration of the relevant matter presented, the agency shall incorporate in the rules adopted a concise general statement of their basis and purpose.")

---

[3] Not everyone agrees with the conventional wisdom. *See* Aaron L. Nielson, *In Defense of Formal Rulemaking,* 75 Ohio State L.J. 237 (2014).

1  What do these requirements mean in practice? The cases in this section address
2  that question.

3

4  **Chocolate Manufacturers Association v. Block**

5  755 F.2d 1098 (4th Cir. 1985)

6  February 27, 1985

7  Before RUSSELL and SPROUSE, Circuit Judges, and HARGROVE, United States
8  District Judge for the District of Maryland, sitting by designation.

9  SPROUSE, Circuit Judge:

10  Chocolate Manufacturers Association (CMA) appeals from the decision of the
11  district court denying it relief from a rule promulgated by the Food and Nutrition
12  Services of the United States Department of Agriculture (USDA or Department).
13  CMA protests that part of the rule that prohibits the use of chocolate flavored milk
14  in the federally funded Special Supplemental Food Program for Women, Infants
15  and Children (WIC Program). Holding that the Department's proposed
16  rulemaking did not provide adequate notice that the elimination of flavored milk
17  would be considered in the rulemaking procedure, we reverse.

18                                    I

19                                  * * *

20  The WIC Program was established by Congress in 1972 to assist pregnant,
21  postpartum, and breastfeeding women, infants and young children from families
22  with inadequate income whose physical and mental health is in danger because of
23  inadequate nutrition or health care. Under the program, the Department designs
24  food packages reflecting the different nutritional needs of women, infants, and
25  children and provides cash grants to state or local agencies, which distribute cash
26  or vouchers to qualifying individuals in accordance with Departmental regulations
27  as to the type and quantity of food.

28  In 1975 Congress revised and extended the WIC Program through fiscal year 1978
29  and, for the first time, defined the "supplemental foods" which the program was
30  established to provide. The term

31      "shall mean those foods containing nutrients known to be lacking in the
32      diets of populations at nutritional risk and, in particular, those foods and
33      food products containing high-quality protein, iron, calcium, vitamin A,
34      and vitamin C. . . . The contents of the food package shall be made available
35      in such a manner as to provide flexibility, taking into account medical and
36      nutritional objectives and cultural eating patterns."

1  Pub. L. No. 94-105, Sec. 17(g) (3), 89 Stat. 511, 520 (1975) (codified at 42 U.S.C. §
2  1786(g) (3) (1976)) (replaced by 42 U.S.C. § 1786(b) (14) (1982)).

3  Pursuant to this statutory definition, the Department promulgated new
4  regulations specifying the contents of WIC Program food packages. These
5  regulations specified that flavored milk was an acceptable substitute for fluid
6  whole milk in the food packages for women and children, but not infants. This
7  regulation formalized the Department's practice of permitting the substitution of
8  flavored milk, a practice observed in the WIC Program since its inception in 1973
9  as well as in several of the other food programs administered by the Department.

10  In 1978 Congress, in extending the WIC Program through fiscal year 1982,
11  redefined the term "supplemental foods" to mean:

12       those foods containing nutrients determined by nutritional research to be
13       lacking in the diets of pregnant, breastfeeding, and postpartum women,
14       infants, and children, as prescribed by the Secretary. State agencies may,
15       with the approval of the Secretary, substitute different foods providing the
16       nutritional equivalent of foods prescribed by the Secretary, to allow for
17       different cultural eating patterns.

18  Pub. L. No. 95-627, Sec. 17(b) (14), 92 Stat. 3603, 3613 (1978) (codified at 42 U.S.C.
19  § 1786(b) (14) (1982)).

20                                          * * *

21  Congress stated further:

22       "The Secretary shall prescribe by regulation supplemental foods to be made
23       available in the program under this section. To the degree possible, the
24       Secretary shall assure that the fat, sugar, and salt content of the prescribed
25       foods is appropriate."

26  *Id.*at Sec. 17(f) (12), 92 Stat. at 3616 (codified at 42 U.S.C. § 1786(f) (12) (1982)).
27  To comply with this statutory redefinition, the Department * * *, in November
28  1979, published for comment the proposed rule at issue in this case. 44 Fed.Reg.
29  69254 (1979). Along with the proposed rule, the Department published a preamble
30  discussing the general purpose of the rule and acknowledging the congressional
31  directive that the Department design food packages containing the requisite
32  nutritional value and appropriate levels of fat, sugar, and salt. Discussing the issue
33  of sugar at length, it noted, for example, that continued inclusion of high sugar
34  cereals may be "contrary to nutrition education principles and may lead to
35  unsound eating practices." It also noted that high sugar foods are more expensive
36  than foods with lower sugar content, and that allowing them would be
37  "inconsistent with the goal of teaching participants economical food buying
38  patterns."

39  The rule proposed a maximum sugar content specifically for authorized cereals.
40  The preamble also contained a discussion of the sugar content in juice, but the

284

1   Department did not propose to reduce the allowable amount of sugar in juice
2   because of technical problems involved in any reduction. Neither the rule nor the
3   preamble discussed sugar in relation to flavoring in milk. Under the proposed rule,
4   the food packages for women and children without special dietary needs included
5   milk that could be "flavored or unflavored."

6   The notice allowed sixty days for comment and specifically invited comment on the
7   entire scope of the proposed rules: "The public is invited to submit written
8   comments in favor of or in objection to the proposed regulations or to make
9   recommendations for alternatives not considered in the proposed regulations."
10  Over 1,000 comments were received from state and local agencies, congressional
11  offices, interest groups, and WIC Program participants and others. Seventy-eight
12  commenters, mostly local WIC administrators, recommended that the agency
13  delete flavored milk from the list of approved supplemental foods.

14  In promulgating the final rule, the Department, responding to these public
15  comments, deleted flavored milk from the list, explaining:

16      "In the previous regulations, women and children were allowed to receive
17      flavored or unflavored milk. No change in this provision was proposed by
18      the Department. However, 78 commenters requested the deletion of
19      flavored milk from the food packages since flavored milk has a higher sugar
20      content than unflavored milk. They indicated that providing flavored milk
21      contradicts nutrition education and the Department's proposal to limit
22      sugar in the food packages. Furthermore, flavored milk is more expensive
23      than unflavored milk. The Department agrees with these concerns. There
24      are significant differences in the sugar content of fluid whole milk and low
25      fat chocolate milk. Fluid whole milk supplies 12.0 grams of carbohydrate
26      per cup compared to 27.3 grams of carbohydrate per cup provided by low
27      fat chocolate milk. If we assume that the major portion of carbohydrate in
28      milk is in the form of simple sugar, fluid whole milk contains 4.9% sugar
29      contrasted with 10.9% sugar in low fat chocolate milk. Therefore, to
30      reinforce nutrition education, for consistency with the Department's
31      philosophy about sugar in the food packages, and to maintain food package
32      costs at economic levels, the Department is deleting flavored milk from the
33      food packages for women and children. Although the deletion of flavored
34      milk was not proposed, the comments and the Department's policy on
35      sugar validate this change."

36  45 Fed.Reg. 74854, 74865-66 (1980).

37                                        * * *

38  On this appeal, CMA contends that the Department did not provide notice that the
39  disallowance of flavored milk would be considered * * * .

40                                        II

1                           \* \* \*

2 Section 4 of the Administrative Procedure Act (APA) requires that the notice in the
3 Federal Register of a proposed rulemaking contain "either the terms or substance
4 of the proposed rule or a description of the subjects and issues involved." 5 U.S.C.
5 § 553(b) (3) (1982). The purpose of the notice-and-comment procedure is both "to
6 allow the agency to benefit from the experience and input of the parties who file
7 comments . . . and to see to it that the agency maintains a flexible and open-minded
8 attitude towards its own rules." *National Tour Brokers Ass'n v. United States*, 591
9 F.2d 896, 902 (D.C. Cir. 1978). The notice-and-comment procedure encourages
10 public participation in the administrative process and educates the agency, thereby
11 helping to ensure informed agency decisionmaking.

12                           \* \* \*

13 There is no question that an agency may promulgate a final rule that differs in some
14 particulars from its proposal. Otherwise the agency "can learn from the comments
15 on its proposals only at the peril of starting a new procedural round of
16 commentary." *International Harvester Co. v. Ruckelshaus*, 478 F.2d 615, 632 n.
17 51 (D.C. Cir. 1973). An agency, however, does not have carte blanche to establish a
18 rule contrary to its original proposal simply because it receives suggestions to alter
19 it during the comment period. An interested party must have been alerted by the
20 notice to the possibility of the changes eventually adopted from the comments.
21 \* \* \*

22                           \* \* \*

23 The test devised by the First Circuit for determining adequacy of notice of a change
24 in a proposed rule occurring after comments appears to us to be sound: notice is
25 adequate if the changes in the original plan "are in character with the original
26 scheme," and the final rule is a "logical outgrowth" of the notice and comments
27 already given. Other circuits also have adopted some form of the "logical
28 outgrowth" test. Stated differently, if the final rule materially alters the issues
29 involved in the rulemaking or, as stated in *Rowell v. Andrus*, 631 F.2d 699, 702 n.
30 2 (10th Cir. 1980), if the final rule "substantially departs from the terms or
31 substance of the proposed rule," the notice is inadequate.

32 There can be no doubt that the final rule in the instant case was the "outgrowth" of
33 the original rule proposed by the agency, but the question of whether the change
34 in it was in character with the original scheme and whether it was a *"logical*
35 outgrowth" is not easy to answer. \* \* \*

36 It is apparent that for many years the Department of Agriculture has permitted the
37 use of chocolate in some form in the food distribution programs that it administers.
38 The only time the Department has proposed to remove chocolate in any form from
39 its programs was in April 1978 when it sought to characterize chocolate as a candy
40 and remove it from the School Lunch Program. That proposal was withdrawn after
41 CMA commented, supporting chocolate as a part of the diet. Chocolate flavored

1   milk has been a permissible part of the WIC Program diet since its inception and
2   there have been no proposals for its removal until the present controversy.

3   The Department sponsored commendable information-gathering proceedings
4   prior to publishing its proposed rule. Together with its own research, the
5   information gathered in the pre-publication information solicitations formed the
6   basis for the proposed rule. Most of the same information was presented to
7   Congress prior to enactment of the 1978 statute that precipitated the 1979
8   rulemaking here in controversy. The National Advisory Council on Maternal,
9   Infant, and Fetal Nutrition provided information and advice. Regional council
10  meetings were open to the public and held in diverse areas of the country.
11  Department of Agriculture personnel attended a number of regional, state, and
12  local meetings and gathered opinions concerning possible changes in the food
13  packages. The agency also gathered a food package advisory panel of experts
14  seeking their recommendations. Food packages were designed based on the
15  information and advice gleaned from these sources. In all of these activities setting
16  out and discussing food packages, including the proposed rule and its preamble,
17  the Department never suggested that flavored milk be removed from the WIC
18  Program.

19  The published preamble to the proposed rule consisted of twelve pages in the
20  Federal Register discussing in detail factors that would be considered in making
21  the final rule. Two pages were devoted to a general discussion of nutrients,
22  including protein, iron, calcium, vitamin A, vitamin C, folic acid, zinc, and fiber,
23  and the dangers of overconsumption of sugar, fat, and salt. The preamble discussed
24  some foods containing these ingredients and foods posing specific problems. It did
25  not discuss flavored milk.

26  In the next eight pages of the preamble, the nutrition content of food packages was
27  discussed—under the general headings of "cereal" and "juice" for infants; and
28  "eggs," "milk," "cheese," "peanut butter and mature dried beans and peas," "juice,"
29  "additional foods," "cereals," "iron," "sugar," "whole grain cereals," "highly
30  fortified cereals," and "artificial flavors and colors" for women and children. The
31  only reference to milk concerned the correct quantity to be provided to children,
32  *i.e.*, 24 quarts per month instead of 28 quarts. Although there was considerable
33  discussion of the sugar content of juice and cereal, there was none concerning
34  flavored milk. Likewise, there was considerable discussion of artificial flavor and
35  color in cereal but none concerning flavored milk. The only reference to flavored
36  milk was in the two-page discussion of the individual food packages, which noted
37  that the proposed rule would permit the milk to be flavored or unflavored. The
38  proposed rule which followed the preamble expressly noted that flavored or
39  unflavored milk was permitted in the individual food packages for women and
40  children without special dietary needs.

41  At the time the proposed rulemaking was published, neither CMA nor the public
42  in general could have had any indication from the history of either the WIC
43  Program or any other food distribution programs that flavored milk was not part

of the acceptable diet for women and children without special dietary needs. The discussion in the preamble to the proposed rule was very detailed and identified specific foods which the agency was examining for excess sugar. This specificity, together with total silence concerning any suggestion of eliminating flavored milk, strongly indicated that flavored milk was not at issue. The proposed rule positively and unqualifiedly approved the continued use of flavored milk. Under the specific circumstances of this case, it cannot be said that the ultimate changes in the proposed rule were in character with the original scheme or a logical outgrowth of the notice. We can well accept that, in general, an approval of a practice in a proposed rule may properly alert interested parties that the practice may be disapproved in the final rule in the event of adverse comments. The total effect of the history of the use of flavored milk, the preamble discussion, and the proposed rule, however, could have led interested persons only to conclude that a change in flavored milk would not be considered. Although ultimately their comments may well have been futile, CMA and other interested persons at least should have had the opportunity to make them. We believe that there was insufficient notice that the deletion of flavored milk from the WIC Program would be considered if adverse comments were received, and, therefore, that affected parties did not receive a fair opportunity to contribute to the administrative rulemaking process. That process was ill-served by the misleading or inadequate notice concerning the permissibility of chocolate flavored milk in the WIC Program and "does not serve the policy underlying the notice requirement."

The judgment of the district court is therefore reversed, and the case is remanded to the administrative agency with instructions to reopen the comment period and thereby afford interested parties a fair opportunity to comment on the proposed changes in the rule.

REVERSED AND REMANDED WITH INSTRUCTIONS.

## Portland Cement Association v. Ruckelshaus

486 F.2d 375 (D.C. Cir. 1973)

June 29, 1973

LEVENTHAL, Circuit Judge:

Portland Cement Association seeks review of the action of the Administrator of the Environmental Protection Agency (EPA) in promulgating stationary source standards for new or modified portland cement plants, pursuant to the provisions of Section 111 of the Clean Air Act. * * *

### I. STATEMENT OF THE CASE

Section 111 of the Clean Air Act directs the Administrator to promulgate "standards of performance" governing emissions of air pollutants by new stationary sources

1   constructed or modified after the effective date of pertinent regulations. The focus
2   of dispute in this case concerns EPA compliance with the statutory language of
3   Section 111(a) which defines "standard of performance" as follows:

4       "(1) The term 'standard of performance' means a standard for emissions of
5       air pollutants which reflects the degree of emission limitation achievable
6       through the application of the best system of emission reduction which
7       (taking into account the cost of achieving such reduction) the
8       Administrator determines has been adequately demonstrated."

9   After designating portland cement plants as a stationary source of air pollution
10  which may "contribute significantly to air pollution which causes or contributes to
11  the endangerment of public health or welfare", under Section 111(b)(1)(A) of the
12  Act, the Administrator published a proposed regulation establishing standards of
13  performance for portland cement plants. The proposed regulation was
14  accompanied by a document entitled "Background Information For Proposed
15  New-Source Performance Standards," which set forth the justification. Interested
16  parties were afforded an opportunity to participate in the rule making by
17  submitting comments, and more than 200 interested parties did so. The
18  "standards of performance" were adopted by a regulation, issued December 16,
19  1971, which requires, inter alia, that particulate matter emitted from portland
20  cement plants shall not be:

21      "(1) In excess of 0.30 lb. per ton of feed to the kiln (0.15 Kg. per metric ton),
22      maximum 2-hour average.

23      "(2) Greater than 10% opacity, except that where the presence of
24      uncombined water is the only reason for failure to meet the requirements
25      for this subparagraph, such failure shall not be a violation of this section."

26  The standards were justified by the EPA as follows:

27      "The standards of performance are based on stationary source testing
28      conducted by the Environmental Protection Agency and/or contractors
29      and on data derived from various other sources, including the available
30      technical literature. In the comments of the proposed standards, many
31      questions were raised as to costs and demonstrated capability of control
32      systems to meet the standards. These comments have been evaluated and
33      investigated, and it is the Administrator's judgment that emission control
34      systems capable of meeting the standards have been adequately
35      demonstrated and that the standards promulgated herein are achievable at
36      reasonable costs."

37                                      * * *

38                      IV. ACHIEVABILITY OF EMISSION STANDARD

39                                      * * *

C. Right to Comment on EPA Methodology

We find a critical defect in the decision-making process in arriving at the standard under review in the initial inability of petitioners to obtain—in timely fashion—the test results and procedures used on existing plants which formed a partial basis for the emission control level adopted, and in the subsequent seeming refusal of the agency to respond to what seem to be legitimate problems with the methodology of these tests.

1. *Unavailability of Test Methodology*

The regulations under review were first proposed on August 3, 1971 and then adopted on December 16, 1971. Both the proposed and adopted rule cited certain portland cement testing as forming a basis for the standards. In the statements accompanying the proposed rule, the Administrator stated:

> "The standards of performance set forth herein are based on stationary source testing conducted by the Environmental Protection Agency and/or contractors . . . ."

On December 16, this test reliance was reiterated:

> "The standards of performance are based on stationary source testing conducted by the Environmental Protection Agency and/or contractors . . . ."

As indicated in the earlier statement of the case, the proposed standard was accompanied by a Background Document which disclosed some information about the tests, but did not identify the location or methodology used in the one successful test conducted on a dry-process kiln. Further indication was given to petitioners that the Administrator was relying on the tests referred to in the Background Document, when the statement of reasons accompanying the adopted standard were expanded in mid-March of 1972, in the supplemental statement filed while this case was pending on appeal to our court. The Administrator there stated:

> "The proposed standard was based principally on particulate levels achieved at a kiln controlled by a fabric filter."

For the first time, however, another set of tests was referred to, as follows:

> "After proposal [of the regulation], but prior to promulgation a second kiln controlled by a fabric filter was tested and found to have particulate emissions in excess of the proposed standard. However, based on the revised particulate test method, the second installation showed particulate emissions to be less than 0.3 pound per ton of kiln feed."

These two testing programs were referred to in the March 1972 supplemental statement, but the details, aside from a summary of test results, were not made available to petitioners until mid-April 1972. At that time, it was revealed that the first set of tests was conducted April 29-30, 1971, by a contractor for EPA, at the Dragon Cement Plant, a dry process plant in Northampton, Pennsylvania, and that the second set was performed at the Oregon Portland Cement plant, at Lake Oswego, Oregon, a wet process plant, on October 7 and 8, 1971. The full disclosure of the methodology followed in these tests raised certain problems, in the view of petitioners, on which they had not yet had the opportunity to comment. Their original comments in the period between the proposal and promulgation of the regulation could only respond to the brief summary of the results of the tests that had been disclosed at that time.

After intervenor Northwestern States Portland Cement Company received the detailed test information in mid-April 1972, it submitted the test data, for analysis of reliability and accuracy, to Ralph H. Striker, an engineer experienced in the design of emission control systems for portland cement plants. He concluded that the first series of tests run at the Dragon Cement Company were "grossly erroneous" due to inaccurate sampling techniques to measure particulate matter. Northwestern States then moved this Court to remand the record to EPA so that the agency might consider the additional comments on the tests. This motion was granted on October 31, 1972. This action by the Court was based on "the flexibility and capacity of reexamination that is rooted in the administrative process". We considered this opportunity to make further comments necessary to sound execution of our judicial review function.

We are aware that EPA was required to issue its standards within 90 days of the issuance of the proposed regulation, and that this time might not have sufficed to make an adequate compilation of the data from the initial tests, or to fully describe the methodology employed. This was more likely as to the second tests, which were begun during the pendency of the proposed regulation. In contrast, more than three months intervened between the conduct of the first tests and the issuance of the proposed regulation. Even as to the second tests however, as we indicated in *International Harvester*, which involved the issue of the availability of the Technical Appendix upon which the auto emission suspension decision was based, the fact that the agency chose to perform additional tests and release the results indicates that it did not believe possible agency consideration was frozen. It is not consonant with the purpose of a rule-making proceeding to promulgate rules on the basis of inadequate data, or on data that, critical degree, is known only to the agency.

\* \* \*

We have identified a number of matters that require consideration and clarification on remand. While we remain diffident in approaching problems of this technical complexity, if it is to be more than a meaningless exercise, requires enough steeping in technical matters to determine whether the agency "has exercised a reasoned discretion." We cannot substitute our judgment for that of the agency, but it is our duty to consider whether "the decision was based on a

1 consideration of the relevant factors and whether there has been a clear error of
2 judgment." *Citizens To Preserve Overton Park v. Volpe*, 401 U.S. 402, 416 (1971).
3 Ultimately, we believe, that the cause of a clean environment is best served by
4 reasoned decision-making. The record is remanded for further proceedings not
5 inconsistent with this opinion.

6 So ordered.

7

## 8 United States v. Nova Scotia Food Products Corp.

9 568 F.2d 240 (2d Cir. 1977)

10 December 15, 1977

11 Before WATERMAN and GURFEIN, Circuit Judges, and BLUMENFELD, District
12 Judge.

13 GURFEIN, Circuit Judge:

14 This appeal involving a regulation of the Food and Drug Administration is not here
15 upon a direct review of agency action. It is an appeal from a judgment of the
16 District Court for the Eastern District of New York enjoining the appellants, after
17 a hearing, from processing hot smoked whitefish except in accordance with time-
18 temperature-salinity (T-T-S) regulations contained in 21 C.F.R. Part 122 (1977).

19 The injunction was sought and granted on the ground that smoked whitefish which
20 has been processed in violation of the T-T-S regulation is "adulterated." Food, Drug
21 and Cosmetics Act ("the Act") §§ 302(a) and 301(k), 21 U.S.C. §§ 332(a), 331(k).

22 Appellant Nova Scotia receives frozen or iced whitefish in interstate commerce
23 which it processes by brining, smoking and cooking. The fish are then sold as
24 smoked whitefish.

25 The regulations cited above require that hot-process smoked fish be heated by a
26 controlled heat process that provides a monitoring system positioned in as many
27 strategic locations in the oven as necessary to assure a continuous temperature
28 through each fish of not less than 180° F. for a minimum of 30 minutes for fish
29 which have been brined to contain 3.5% water phase salt or at 150° F. for a
30 minimum of 30 minutes if the salinity was at 5% water phase. Since *each* fish must
31 meet these requirements, it is necessary to heat an entire batch of fish to even
32 higher temperatures so that the lowest temperature for *any* fish will meet the
33 minimum requirements.

34 Government inspection of appellants' plant established without question that the
35 minimum T-T-S requirements were not being met. There is no substantial claim
36 that the plant was processing whitefish under "insanitary conditions" in any other
37 material respect. Appellants, on their part, do not defend on the ground that they
38 were in compliance, but rather that the requirements could not be met if a

1 marketable whitefish was to be produced. * * * We reject the contention that the
2 regulation is beyond the authority delegated by the statute, but we find serious
3 inadequacies in the procedure followed in the promulgation of the regulation and
4 hold it to be invalid as applied to the appellants herein.

5 The hazard which the FDA sought to minimize was the outgrowth and toxin
6 formation of Clostridium botulinum Type E spores of the bacteria which
7 sometimes inhabit fish. There had been an occurrence of several cases of botulism
8 traced to consumption of fish from inland waters in 1960 and 1963 which
9 stimulated considerable bacteriological research. These bacteria can be present in
10 the soil and water of various regions. They can invade fish in their natural habitat
11 and can be further disseminated in the course of evisceration and preparation of
12 the fish for cooking. A failure to destroy such spores through an adequate brining,
13 thermal, and refrigeration process was found to be dangerous to public health.

14 The Commissioner of Food and Drugs ("Commissioner"), employing informal
15 "notice-and-comment" procedures under 21 U.S.C. § 371(a), issued a proposal for
16 the control of C. botulinum bacteria Type E in fish. * * *

17 Similar guidelines for smoking fish had been suggested by the FDA several years
18 earlier, and were generally made known to people in the industry. At that stage,
19 however, they were merely guidelines without substantive effect as law.
20 Responding to the Commissioner's invitation in the notice of proposed
21 rulemaking, members of the industry, including appellants and the intervenor-
22 appellant, submitted comments on the proposed regulation.

23 The Commissioner thereafter issued the final regulations in which he adopted
24 certain suggestions made in the comments, including a suggestion by the National
25 Fisheries Institute, Inc. ("the Institute"), the intervenor herein. The original
26 proposal provided that the fish would have to be cooked to a temperature of 180°
27 F. for at least 30 minutes, if the fish have been brined to contain 3.5% Water phase
28 salt, with no alternative. In the final regulation, an alternative suggested by the
29 intervenor "that the parameter of 150° F. for 30 minutes and 5% Salt in the water
30 phase be established as an alternate procedure to that stated in the proposed
31 regulation for an interim period until specific parameters can be established" was
32 accepted, but as a permanent part of the regulation rather than for an interim
33 period.

34 The intervenor suggested that "specific parameters" be established. This referred
35 to particular processing parameters for different species of fish on a "species by
36 species" basis. Such "species by species" determination was proposed not only by
37 the intervenor but also by the Bureau of Commercial Fisheries of the Department
38 of the Interior. That Bureau objected to the general application of the T-T-S
39 requirement proposed by the FDA on the ground that application of the regulation
40 to all species of fish being smoked was not commercially feasible, and that the
41 regulation should therefore specify time-temperature-salinity requirements, as
42 developed by research and study, on a species-by-species basis. The Bureau

suggested that "wholesomeness considerations could be more practically and adequately realized by reducing processing temperature and using suitable concentrations of nitrite and salt." The Commissioner took cognizance of the suggestion, but decided, nevertheless, to impose the T-T-S requirement on *all* species of fish (except chub, which were regulated by 21 C.F.R. 172.177 (1977) (dealing with food additives)).

He did acknowledge, however, in his "basis and purpose" statement required by the Administrative Procedure Act ("APA") that "adequate times, temperatures and salt concentrations have not been demonstrated for each individual species of fish presently smoked". 35 F.R. 17,401 (Nov. 13, 1970). The Commissioner concluded, nevertheless, that "the processing requirements of the proposed regulations are the safest now known to prevent the outgrowth and toxin formation of C. botulinum Type E". He determined that "the conditions of current good manufacturing practice for this industry should be established without further delay." *Id.*

The Commissioner did not answer the suggestion by the Bureau of Fisheries that nitrite and salt as additives could safely lower the high temperature otherwise required, a solution which the FDA had accepted in the case of chub. Nor did the Commissioner respond to the claim of Nova Scotia through its trade association, the Association of Smoked Fish Processors, Inc., Technical Center that "(t)he proposed process requirements suggested by the FDA for hot processed smoked fish are neither commercially feasible nor based on sound scientific evidence obtained with the variety of smoked fish products to be included under this regulation."

Nova Scotia, in its own comment, wrote to the Commissioner that "the heating of certain types of fish to high temperatures will completely destroy the product". It suggested, as an alternative, that "specific processing procedures could be established for each species after adequate work and experimention [sic] has been done but not before." We have noted above that the response given by the Commissioner was in general terms. He did not specifically aver that the T-T-S requirements as applied to whitefish were, in fact, commercially feasible.

When, after several inspections and warnings, Nova Scotia failed to comply with the regulation, an action by the United States Attorney for injunctive relief was filed on April 7, 1976, six years later, and resulted in the judgment here on appeal. The District Court denied a stay pending appeal, and no application for a stay was made to this court.

\* \* \*

### 1. The History of Botulism in Whitefish

The history of botulism occurrence in whitefish, as established in the trial record, which we must assume was available to the FDA in 1970, is as follows. Between 1899 and 1964 there were only eight cases of botulism reported as attributable to

1  hot-smoked whitefish. In all eight instances, vacuum-packed whitefish was
2  involved. All of the eight cases occurred in 1960 and 1963. The industry has
3  abandoned vacuum-packing, and there has not been a single case of botulism
4  associated with commercially prepared whitefish since 1963, though 2,750,000
5  pounds of whitefish are processed annually. Thus, in the seven-year period from
6  1964 through 1970, 17.25 million pounds of whitefish have been commercially
7  processed in the United States without a single reported case of botulism. The
8  evidence also disclosed that defendant Nova Scotia has been in business some 56
9  years, and that there has never been a case of botulism illness from the whitefish
10 processed by it.

11                          2. The Scientific Data

12 Interested parties were not informed of the scientific data, or at least of a selection
13 of such data deemed important by the agency, so that comments could be
14 addressed to the data. Appellants argue that unless the scientific data relied upon
15 by the agency are spread upon the public records, criticism of the methodology
16 used or the meaning to be inferred from the data is rendered impossible.

17 We agree with appellants in this case, for although we recognize that an agency
18 may resort to its own expertise outside the record in an informal rulemaking
19 procedure, we do not believe that when the pertinent research material is readily
20 available and the agency has no special expertise on the precise parameters
21 involved, there is any reason to conceal the scientific data relied upon from the
22 interested parties. As Judge Leventhal said in *Portland Cement Ass'n v.*
23 *Ruckelhaus*, 486 F.2d 375, 393 (1973): "It is not consonant with the purpose of a
24 rulemaking proceeding to promulgate rules on the basis of inadequate data, or on
25 data that [in] critical degree, *is known only to the agency*." (Emphasis added.) This
26 is not a case where the agency methodology was based on material supplied by the
27 interested parties themselves. Here all the scientific research was collected by the
28 agency, and none of it was disclosed to interested parties as the material upon
29 which the proposed rule would be fashioned. * * *

30                             * * *

31 If the failure to notify interested persons of the scientific research upon which the
32 agency was relying actually prevented the presentation of relevant comment, the
33 agency may be held not to have considered all "the relevant factors." We can think
34 of no sound reasons for secrecy or reluctance to expose to public view (with an
35 exception for trade secrets or national security) the ingredients of the deliberative
36 process. Indeed, the FDA's own regulations now specifically require that every
37 notice of proposed rulemaking contain "references to all data and information on
38 which the Commissioner relies for the proposal (copies or a full list of which shall
39 be a part of the administrative file on the matter . . .) ." 21 C.F.R. § 10.40(b) (1)
40 (1977). * * *

41 We think that the scientific data should have been disclosed to focus on the proper
42 interpretation of "insanitary conditions." When the basis for a proposed rule is a

295

1  scientific decision, the scientific material which is believed to support the rule
2  should be exposed to the view of interested parties for their comment. One cannot
3  ask for comment on a scientific paper without allowing the participants to read the
4  paper. Scientific research is sometimes rejected for diverse inadequacies of
5  methodology; and statistical results are sometimes rebutted because of a lack of
6  adequate gathering technique or of supportable extrapolation. Such is the stuff of
7  scientific debate. To suppress meaningful comment by failure to disclose the basic
8  data relied upon is akin to rejecting comment altogether. For unless there is
9  common ground, the comments are unlikely to be of a quality that might impress
10 a careful agency. The inadequacy of comment in turn leads in the direction of
11 arbitrary decision-making. We do not speak of findings of fact, for such are not
12 technically required in the informal rulemaking procedures. We speak rather of
13 what the agency should make known so as to elicit comments that probe the
14 fundamentals. Informal rulemaking does not lend itself to a rigid pattern.
15 Especially, in the circumstance of our broad reading of statutory authority in
16 support of the agency, we conclude that the failure to disclose to interested persons
17 the scientific data upon which the FDA relied was procedurally erroneous.
18 Moreover, the burden was upon the agency to articulate rationally why the rule
19 should apply to a large and diverse class, with the same T-T-S parameters made
20 applicable to *all* species.

21                                        C

22 Appellants additionally attack the "concise general statement" required by APA, 5
23 U.S.C. § 553, as inadequate. We think that, in the circumstances, it was less than
24 adequate. It is not in keeping with the rational process to leave vital questions,
25 raised by comments which are of cogent materiality, completely unanswered. The
26 agencies certainly have a good deal of discretion in expressing the basis of a rule,
27 but the agencies do not have quite the prerogative of obscurantism reserved to
28 legislatures. "Congress did not purport to transfer its legislative power to the
29 unbounded discretion of the regulatory body." *F.C.C. v. RCA Communications,
30 Inc.*, 346 U.S. 86, 90, (1953) (FRANKFURTER, J.). As was said in *Environmental
31 Defense Fund, Inc. v. EPA*, 465 F.2d 528, 540-51 (1972): "We cannot discharge our
32 role adequately unless we hold EPA to a high standard of articulation."

33 The test of adequacy of the "concise general statement" was expressed by Judge
34 McGowan in the following terms:

35     "We do not expect the agency to discuss every item of fact or opinion
36     included in the submissions made to it in informal rulemaking. We do
37     expect that, if the judicial review which Congress has thought it important
38     to provide is to be meaningful, the 'concise general statement of . . . basis
39     and purpose' mandated by Section 4 will enable us to see what major issues
40     of policy were ventilated by the informal proceedings and why the agency
41     reacted to them as it did." *Automotive Parts & Accessories Ass'n v. Boyd*,
42     407 F.2d 330, 338 (1968).

1 * * *

2 The Secretary was squarely faced with the question whether it was necessary to
3 formulate a rule with specific parameters that applied to all species of fish, and
4 particularly whether lower temperatures with the addition of nitrite and salt would
5 not be sufficient. Though this alternative was suggested by an agency of the federal
6 government, its suggestion, though acknowledged, was never answered.

7 Moreover, the comment that to apply the proposed T-T-S requirements to
8 whitefish would destroy the commercial product was neither discussed nor
9 answered. We think that to sanction silence in the face of such vital questions
10 would be to make the statutory requirement of a "concise general statement" less
11 than an adequate safeguard against arbitrary decision-making.

12 We cannot improve on the statement of the District of Columbia Circuit in
13 *Industrial Union Dep't, AFL-CIO v. Hodgson*, 499 F.2d 467, 475 (1974).

14 "What we are entitled to at all events is a careful identification by the
15 Secretary, when his proposed standards are challenged, of the reasons why
16 he chooses to follow one course rather than another. Where that choice
17 purports to be based on the existence of certain determinable facts, the
18 Secretary must, in form as well as in substance, find those facts from
19 evidence in the record. By the same token, when the Secretary is obliged to
20 make policy judgments where no factual certainties exist or where facts
21 alone do not provide the answer, he should so state and go on to identify
22 the considerations he found to be persuasive."

23 One may recognize that even commercial infeasibility cannot stand in the way of
24 an overwhelming public interest. Yet the administrative process should disclose,
25 at least, whether the proposed regulation is considered to be commercially feasible,
26 or whether other considerations prevail even if commercial infeasibility is
27 acknowledged. This kind of forthright disclosure and basic statement was lacking
28 in the formulation of the T-T-S standard made applicable to whitefish. It is easy
29 enough for an administrator to ban everything. In the regulation of food
30 processing, the worldwide need for food also must be taken into account in
31 formulating measures taken for the protection of health. In the light of the history
32 of smoked whitefish to which we have referred, we find no articulate balancing here
33 sufficient to make the procedure followed less than arbitrary.

34 * * *

35 When the District Court held the regulation to be valid, it properly exercised its
36 discretion to grant the injunction. In view of our conclusion to the contrary, we
37 must reverse the grant of the injunction and direct that the complaint be

38 *dismissed.*

39

# 2. "Hybrid" Rulemaking?

As we have seen, appeals courts in the 1970s began imposing obligations on agencies that were not explicitly rooted in the text of the APA, on the grounds that they were necessary for the public to have a meaningful opportunity to participate in rulemaking. So in *Portland Cement*, the D.C. Circuit held that agencies must disclose to the public the scientific evidence they rely on, and in *Nova Scotia Food Products*, the Second Circuit required that agencies respond, in the statement of basis and purpose accompanying a final rule, to comments of "cogent materiality."

How much latitude do courts have to impose extrastatutory obligations such as these on agencies? In particular, when courts conclude that informal rulemaking would benefit from some of the procedural features associated with on-the-record proceedings, such as hearings with opportunities for cross examination, can they require a sort of "hybrid" rulemaking that is somewhere between informal and formal? The Supreme Court addressed this issue in *Vermont Yankee*, one of the landmark administrative law decisions of the twentieth century.

## Vermont Yankee Nuclear Power Corp. v. NRDC

435 U.S. 519 (1978)

April 3, 1978

MR. JUSTICE REHNQUIST delivered the opinion of the Court.

In 1946, Congress enacted the Administrative Procedure Act, which, as we have noted elsewhere, was not only "a new, basic and comprehensive regulation of procedures in many agencies," *Won Yang Sung v. McGrath*, 339 U.S. 33 (1950), but was also a legislative enactment which settled "long-continued and hard-fought contentions, and enacts a formula upon which opposing social and political forces have come to rest." *Id.*, at 40. Section 4 of the Act, 5 U.S.C. § 553 (1976 ed.), dealing with rulemaking, requires in subsection (b) that "notice of proposed rule making shall be published in the Federal Register . . . ," describes the contents of that notice, and goes on to require in subsection (c) that, after the notice, the agency "shall give interested persons an opportunity to participate in the rule making through submission of written data, views, or arguments with or without opportunity for oral presentation. After consideration of the relevant matter presented, the agency shall incorporate in the rules adopted a concise general statement of their basis and purpose." Interpreting this provision of the Act in *United States v. Allegheny-Ludlum Steel Corp.*, 406 U.S. 742 (1972), and *United States v. Florida East Coast R. Co.*, 410 U.S. 224 (1973), we held that, generally speaking, this section of the Act established the maximum procedural requirements which Congress was willing to have the courts impose upon agencies in conducting rulemaking procedures. Agencies are free to grant additional procedural rights in the exercise of their discretion, but reviewing courts are

1 generally not free to impose them if the agencies have not chosen to grant them.
2 This is not to say necessarily that there are no circumstances which would ever
3 justify a court in overturning agency action because of a failure to employ
4 procedures beyond those required by the statute. But such circumstances, if they
5 exist, are extremely rare.

6 Even apart from the Administrative Procedure Act, this Court has, for more than
7 four decades, emphasized that the formulation of procedures was basically to be
8 left within the discretion of the agencies to which Congress had confided the
9 responsibility for substantive judgments. * * *

10 It is in the light of this background of statutory and decisional law that we granted
11 certiorari to review two judgments of the Court of Appeals for the District of
12 Columbia Circuit because of our concern that they had seriously misread or
13 misapplied this statutory and decisional law cautioning reviewing courts against
14 engrafting their own notions of proper procedures upon agencies entrusted with
15 substantive functions by Congress. We conclude that the Court of Appeals has done
16 just that in these cases, and we therefore remand them to it for further proceedings.
17 We also find it necessary to examine the Court of Appeals' decision with respect to
18 agency action taken after full adjudicatory hearings. We again conclude that the
19 court improperly intruded into the agency's decisionmaking process, making it
20 necessary for us to reverse and remand with respect to this part of the case also.

21                                         I

22                                         A

23 Under the Atomic Energy Act of 1954, the Atomic Energy Commission[2] was given
24 broad regulatory authority over the development of nuclear energy. Under the
25 terms of the Act, a utility seeking to construct and operate a nuclear power plant
26 must obtain a separate permit or license at both the construction and the operation
27 stage of the project. In order to obtain the construction permit, the utility must file
28 a preliminary safety analysis report, an environmental report, and certain
29 information regarding the antitrust implications of the proposed project. This
30 application then undergoes exhaustive review by the Commission's staff and by the
31 Advisory Committee on Reactor Safeguards (ACRS), a group of distinguished
32 experts in the field of atomic energy. Both groups submit to the Commission their
33 own evaluations, which then become part of the record of the utility's application.
34 The Commission staff also undertakes the review required by the National
35 Environmental Policy Act of 1969 (NEPA), and prepares a draft
36 environmental impact statement which, after being circulated for comment, is
37 revised and becomes a final environmental impact statement. Thereupon a three-

---

[2] The licensing and regulatory functions of the Atomic Energy Commission (AEC) were transferred to the Nuclear Regulatory Commission (NRC) by the Energy Reorganization Act of 1974, 42 U.S.C. § 5801 et seq. (1970 ed., Supp. V). Hereinafter, both the AEC and NRC will be referred to as the Commission.

1      member Atomic Safety and Licensing Board conducts a public adjudicatory
2      hearing, and reaches a decision[4] which can be appealed to the Atomic Safety and
3      Licensing Appeal Board, and currently, in the Commission's discretion, to the
4      Commission itself. The final agency decision may be appealed to the courts of
5      appeals. The same sort of process occurs when the utility applies for a license to
6      operate the plant, except that a hearing need only be held in contested cases, and
7      may be limited to the matters in controversy.

8      These cases arise from two separate decisions of the Court of Appeals for the
9      District of Columbia Circuit. In the first, the court remanded a decision of the
10     Commission to grant a license to petitioner Vermont Yankee Nuclear Power Corp.
11     to operate a nuclear power plant. In the second, the court remanded a decision of
12     that same agency to grant a permit to petitioner Consumers Power Co. to construct
13     two pressurized water nuclear reactors to generate electricity and steam.

14                                       B

15     In December, 1967, after the mandatory adjudicatory hearing and necessary
16     review, the Commission granted petitioner Vermont Yankee a permit to build a
17     nuclear power plant in Vernon, Vt. Thereafter, Vermont Yankee applied for an
18     operating license. Respondent Natural Resources Defense Council (NRDC)
19     objected to the granting of a license, however, and therefore a hearing on the
20     application commenced on August 10, 1971. Excluded from consideration at the
21     hearings, over NRDC's objection, was the issue of the environmental effects of
22     operations to reprocess fuel or dispose of wastes resulting from the reprocessing
23     operations. This ruling was affirmed by the Appeal Board in June 1972.

24     In November 1972, however, the Commission, making specific reference to the
25     Appeal Board's decision with respect to the Vermont Yankee license, instituted
26     rulemaking proceedings "that would specifically deal with the question of
27     consideration of environmental effects associated with the uranium fuel cycle in
28     the individual cost-benefit analyses for light water cooled nuclear power reactors."
29     The notice of proposed rulemaking offered two alternatives, both predicated on a
30     report prepared by the Commission's staff entitled Environmental Survey of the
31     Nuclear Fuel Cycle. The first would have required no quantitative evaluation of the
32     environmental hazards of fuel reprocessing or disposal. because the
33     Environmental Survey had found them to be slight. The second would have
34     specified numerical values for the environmental impact of this part of the fuel
35     cycle, which values would then be incorporated into a table, along with the other
36     relevant factors, to determine the overall cost-benefit balance for each operating
37     license.

---

[4] The Licensing Board issues a permit if it concludes that there is a reasonable
assurance that the proposed plant can be constructed and operated without undue
risk, and that the environmental cost-benefit balance favors the issuance of a
permit.

1   Much of the controversy in this case revolves around the procedures used in the
2   rulemaking hearing which commenced in February, 1973. In a supplemental notice
3   of hearing, the Commission indicated that, while discovery or cross-examination
4   would not be utilized, the Environmental Survey would be available to the public
5   before the hearing, along with the extensive background documents cited therein.
6   All participants would be given a reasonable opportunity to present their position,
7   and could be represented by counsel if they so desired. Written and, time
8   permitting, oral statements would be received and incorporated into the record.
9   All persons giving oral statements would be subject to questioning by the
10  Commission. At the conclusion of the hearing, a transcript would be made
11  available to the public, and the record would remain open for 30 days to allow the
12  filing of supplemental written statements. More than 40 individuals and
13  organizations representing a wide variety of interests submitted written
14  comments. On January 17, 1973, the Licensing Board held a planning session to
15  schedule the appearance of witnesses and to discuss methods for compiling a
16  record. The hearing was held on February 1 and 2, with participation by a number
17  of groups, including the Commission's staff, the United States Environmental
18  Protection Agency, a manufacturer of reactor equipment, a trade association from
19  the nuclear industry, a group of electric utility companies, and a group called
20  Consolidated National Intervenors, which represented 79 groups and individuals,
21  including respondent NRDC.

22  After the hearing, the Commission's staff filed a supplemental document for the
23  purpose of clarifying and revising the Environmental Survey. Then the Licensing
24  Board forwarded its report to the Commission without rendering any decision. The
25  Licensing Board identified as the principal procedural question the propriety of
26  declining to use full formal adjudicatory procedures. The major substantive issue
27  was the technical adequacy of the Environmental Survey.

28  In April, 1974, the Commission issued a rule which adopted the second of the two
29  proposed alternatives described above. The Commission also approved the
30  procedures used at the hearing, and indicated that the record, including the
31  Environmental Survey, provided an "adequate data base for the regulation
32  adopted." Finally, the Commission ruled that, to the extent the rule differed from
33  the Appeal Board decisions in *Vermont Yankee*, "those decisions have no further
34  precedential significance," but that, since "the environmental effects of the
35  uranium fuel cycle have been shown to be relatively insignificant, ... it is
36  unnecessary to apply the amendment to applicant's environmental reports
37  submitted prior to its effective date or to Final Environmental Statements for
38  which Draft Environmental Statements have been circulated for comment prior to
39  the effective date."

40  Respondents appealed from both the Commission's adoption of the rule and its
41  decision to grant Vermont Yankee's license to the Court of Appeals for the District
42  of Columbia Circuit.

43                                        * * *

1

## D

2    With respect to the challenge of Vermont Yankee's license, the court first ruled
3    that, in the absence of effective rulemaking proceedings, the Commission must
4    deal with the environmental impact of fuel reprocessing and disposal in individual
5    licensing proceedings. The court then examined the rulemaking proceedings and,
6    despite the fact that it appeared that the agency employed all the procedures
7    required by 5 U.S.C. § 553 (1976 ed.) and more, the court determined the
8    proceedings to be inadequate, and overturned the rule. Accordingly, the
9    Commission's determination with respect to Vermont Yankee's license was also
10   remanded for further proceedings.

11                                    * * *

12                                     II

13                                    * * *

14                                     B

15   We next turn to the invalidation of the fuel cycle rule. But before determining
16   whether the Court of Appeals reached a permissible result, we must determine
17   exactly what result it did reach, and, in this case, that is no mean feat. Vermont
18   Yankee argues that the court invalidated the rule because of the inadequacy of the
19   procedures employed in the proceedings. Respondents, on the other hand, labeling
20   petitioner's view of the decision a "straw man," argue to this Court that the court
21   merely held that the record was inadequate to enable the reviewing court to
22   determine whether the agency had fulfilled its statutory obligation. But we
23   unfortunately have not found the parties' characterization of the opinion to be
24   entirely reliable; it appears here, as in *Orloff v. Willoughby*, 345 U.S. 83, 87 (1953),
25   that, "in this Court, the parties changed positions as nimbly as if dancing a
26   quadrille."[15]

---

[15] Vermont Yankee's interpretation has been consistent throughout the litigation.
That cannot be said of the other parties, however. The Government, Janus-like,
initially took both positions. While the petition for certiorari was pending, a brief
was filed on behalf of the United States and the Commission, with the former
indicating that it believed the court had unanimously held the record to be
inadequate, while the latter took Vermont Yankee's view of the matter. See Brief
for Federal Respondents 5-9 (filed Jan. 10, 1977). When announcing its intention
to undertake licensing of reactors pending the promulgation of an "interim" fuel
cycle rule, however, the Commission said:

> "[T]he court found that the rule was inadequately supported by the record
> insofar as it treated two particular aspects of the fuel cycle—the impacts

1     After a thorough examination of the opinion itself, we conclude that, while the
2     matter is not entirely free from doubt, the majority of the Court of Appeals struck
3     down the rule because of the perceived inadequacies of the procedures employed
4     in the rulemaking proceedings. The court first determined the intervenors' primary
5     argument to be "that the decision to preclude 'discovery or cross-examination'
6     denied them a meaningful opportunity to participate in the proceedings as

---

> from reprocessing of spent fuel and the impacts from radioactive waste
> management."

41 Fed.Reg. 45850 (1976).

And even more recently, in opening another rulemaking proceeding to replace the
rule overturned by the Court of Appeals, the Commission stated:

> "The original procedures proved adequate for the development and
> illumination of a wide range of fuel cycle impact issues. . . . "

> ". . . The court here indicated that the procedures previously employed
> could suffice, and indeed did for other issues."

> "Accordingly, notice is hereby given that the rules for the conduct of the
> reopened hearing and the authorities and responsibilities of the Hearing
> Board will be the same as originally applied in this matter (38 Fed.Reg. 49,
> January 3, 1973) except that specific provision is hereby made for the
> Hearing Board to entertain suggestions from participants as to questions
> which the Board should ask of witnesses for other participants." 42
> Fed.Reg. 26988-26989 (1977).

Respondent NRDC likewise happily switches sides depending on the forum. As
indicated above, it argues here that the Court of Appeals held only that the record
was inadequate. Almost immediately after the Court of Appeals rendered its
decision, however, NRDC filed a petition for rulemaking with the Commission
which listed over 13 pages of procedural suggestions it thought "necessary to
comply with the Court's order and with the mandate of [NEPA]." These proposals
include cross-examination, discovery, and subpoena power. NRDC likewise
challenged the interim fuel cycle rule, and suggested to the Court of Appeals that
it hold the case pending our decision in this case because the interim rules were
"defective due to the inadequacy of the procedures used in developing the rule. . .
." NRDC has likewise challenged the procedures being used in the final rulemaking
proceeding as being "no more than a re-run of hearing procedures which were
found inadequate [by the Court of Appeals]."

1  guaranteed by due process." The court then went on to frame the issue for decision
2  thus:

> 3  "Thus, we are called upon to decide whether the procedures provided by
> 4  the agency were sufficient to ventilate the issues."

5  The court conceded that, absent extraordinary circumstances, it is improper for a
6  reviewing court to prescribe the procedural format an agency must follow, but it
7  likewise clearly thought it entirely appropriate to "scrutinize the record as a whole
8  to insure that genuine opportunities to participate in a meaningful way were
9  provided. . . ." The court also refrained from actually ordering the agency to follow
10 any specific procedures, but there is little doubt in our minds that the ineluctable
11 mandate of the court's decision is that the procedures afforded during the hearings
12 were inadequate. This conclusion is particularly buttressed by the fact that after
13 the court examined the record, particularly the testimony of Dr. Pittman, and
14 declared it insufficient, the court proceeded to discuss at some length the necessity
15 for further procedural devices or a more "sensitive" application of those devices
16 employed during the proceedings. The exploration of the record and the statement
17 regarding its insufficiency might initially lead one to conclude that the court was
18 only examining the sufficiency of the evidence, but the remaining portions of the
19 opinion dispel any doubt that this was certainly not the sole, or even the principal,
20 basis of the decision. Accordingly, we feel compelled to address the opinion on its
21 own terms, and we conclude that it was wrong.

22 In prior opinions, we have intimated that, even in a rulemaking proceeding, when
23 an agency is making a "quasi-judicial'" determination by which a very small
24 number of persons are "'exceptionally affected, in each case upon individual
25 grounds,'" in some circumstances, additional procedures may be required in order
26 to afford the aggrieved individuals due process. *United States v. Florida East*
27 *Coast R. Co.*, 410 U.S. 424, 242-245 (1973), quoting from *Bi-Metallic Investment*
28 *Co. v. State Board of Equalization*, 239 U.S. 441, 446 (1915). It might also be true,
29 although we do not think the issue is presented in this case, and accordingly do not
30 decide it, that a totally unjustified departure from well settled agency procedures
31 of long standing might require judicial correction.

32 But this much is absolutely clear. Absent constitutional constraints or extremely
33 compelling circumstances, the "administrative agencies 'should be free to fashion
34 their own rules of procedure, and to pursue method of inquiry capable of
35 permitting them to discharge their multitudinous duties.'" *FCC v. Schreiber*, 381
36 U.S., at 290, quoting from *FCC v. Pottsville Broadcasting Co.*, 309 U.S., at 143.
37 Indeed, our cases could hardly be more explicit in this regard. * * *

38                                    * * *

39 Respondent NRDC argues that § 4 of the Administrative Procedure Act merely
40 establishes lower procedural bounds, and that a court may routinely require more
41 than the minimum when an agency's proposed rule addresses complex or technical
42 factual issues or "Issues of Great Public Import." We have, however, previously

1  shown that our decisions reject this view. We also think the legislative history, even
2  the part which it cites, does not bear out its contention. * * *

3  　　　　　　　　　　　　　　　　　* * *

4  And the Attorney General's Manual on the Administrative Procedure Act 31, 35
5  (1947), a contemporaneous interpretation previously given some deference by this
6  Court because of the role played by the Department of Justice in drafting the
7  legislation, further confirms that view. In short, all of this leaves little doubt that
8  Congress intended that the discretion of the agencies, and not that of the courts,
9  be exercised in determining when extra procedural devices should be employed.

10  There are compelling reasons for construing § 4 in this manner. In the first place,
11  if courts continually review agency proceedings to determine whether the agency
12  employed procedures which were, in the court's opinion, perfectly tailored to reach
13  what the court perceives to be the "best" or "correct" result, judicial review would
14  be totally unpredictable. And the agencies, operating under this vague injunction
15  to employ the "best" procedures and facing the threat of reversal if they did not,
16  would undoubtedly adopt full adjudicatory procedures in every instance. Not only
17  would this totally disrupt the statutory scheme, through which Congress enacted
18  "a formula upon which opposing social and political forces have come to rest,"
19  *Wong Yang Sung v. McGrath*, 339 U.S., at 40, but all the inherent advantages of
20  informal rulemaking would be totally lost.

21  Secondly, it is obvious that the court in these cases reviewed the agency's choice of
22  procedures on the basis of the record actually produced at the hearing, and not on
23  the basis of the information available to the agency when it made the decision to
24  structure the proceedings in a certain way. This sort of Monday morning
25  quarterbacking not only encourages, but almost compels, the agency to conduct all
26  rulemaking proceedings with the full panoply of procedural devices normally
27  associated only with adjudicatory hearings.

28  Finally, and perhaps most importantly, this sort of review fundamentally
29  misconceives the nature of the standard for judicial review of an agency rule. The
30  court below uncritically assumed that additional procedures will automatically
31  result in a more adequate record because it will give interested parties more of an
32  opportunity to participate in and contribute to the proceedings. But informal
33  rulemaking need not be based solely on the transcript of a hearing held before an
34  agency. Indeed, the agency need not even hold a formal hearing. Thus, the
35  adequacy of the "record" in this type of proceeding is not correlated directly to the
36  type of procedural devices employed, but rather turns on whether the agency has
37  followed the statutory mandate of the Administrative Procedure Act or other
38  relevant statutes. If the agency is compelled to support the rule which it ultimately
39  adopts with the type of record produced only after a full adjudicatory hearing, it
40  simply will have no choice but to conduct a full adjudicatory hearing prior to
41  promulgating every rule. In sum, this sort of unwarranted judicial examination of

perceived procedural shortcomings of a rulemaking proceeding can do nothing but seriously interfere with that process prescribed by Congress.

Respondent NRDC also argues that the fact that the Commission's inquiry was undertaken in the context of NEPA somehow permits a court to require procedures beyond those specified in § 4 of the APA when investigating factual issues through rulemaking. The Court of Appeals was apparently also of this view, indicating that agencies may be required to "develop new procedures to accomplish the innovative task of implementing NEPA through rulemaking." But we search in vain for something in NEPA which would mandate such a result. * * * In fact, just two Terms ago, we emphasized that the only procedural requirements imposed by NEPA are those stated in the plain language of the Act. *Kleppe v. Sierra Club*, 427 U.S. 390, 405-406 (1976). Thus, it is clear NEPA cannot serve as the basis for a substantial revision of the carefully constructed procedural specifications of the APA.

In short, nothing in the APA, NEPA, the circumstances of this case, the nature of the issues being considered, past agency practice, or the statutory mandate under which the Commission operates permitted the court to review and overturn the rulemaking proceeding on the basis of the procedural devices employed (or not employed) by the Commission so long as the Commission employed at least the statutory *minima*, a matter about which there is no doubt in this case.

There remains, of course, the question of whether the challenged rule finds sufficient justification in the administrative proceedings that it should be upheld by the reviewing court. Judge Tamm, concurring in the result reached by the majority of the Court of Appeals, thought that it did not. There are also intimations in the majority opinion which suggest that the judges who joined it likewise may have thought the administrative proceedings an insufficient basis upon which to predicate the rule in question. We accordingly remand so that the Court of Appeals may review the rule as the Administrative Procedure Act provides. We have made it abundantly clear before that, when there is a contemporaneous explanation of the agency decision, the validity of that action must "stand or fall on the propriety of that finding, judged, of course, by the appropriate standard of review. If that finding is not sustainable on the administrative record made, then the Comptroller's decision must be vacated and the matter remanded to him for further consideration." *Camp v. Pitts*, 411 U.S. 138, 143 (1973). The court should engage in this kind of review and not stray beyond the judicial province to explore the procedural format or to impose upon the agency its own notion of which procedures are "best" or most likely to further some vague, undefined public good.

* * *

*Reversed and remanded.*

## 3. Exceptions to Rulemaking Requirements

1  Section 553 provides a number of exceptions to the rulemaking requirements. The
2  provision as a whole exempts military and foreign affairs functions plus agency
3  management, personnel, and property. The notice and comment requirements do
4  not apply to "interpretative rules, general statements of policy, or rules of agency
5  organization, procedure, or practice," or when the agency "for good cause" finds
6  the requirements are "impracticable, unnecessary, or contrary to the public
7  interest."

8  What do these exceptions mean? This section addresses that issue, focusing on a
9  few key categories.

10

11      a.  Procedural Rules

12  **Air Transport Association of America v. Department of**
13  **Transportation**

14  900 F.2d 369 (D.C. Cir. 1990)

15  April 13, 1990.

16  Before MIKVA, HARRY T. EDWARDS and SILBERMAN, Circuit Judges.

17  HARRY T. EDWARDS, Circuit Judge:

18  The issue in this case is whether respondent governmental agencies (collectively
19  "Federal Aviation Administration" or "FAA") were obliged to engage in notice and
20  comment procedures before promulgating a body of regulations governing the
21  adjudication of administrative civil penalty actions. The FAA issued the Penalty
22  Rules pursuant to a temporary enabling statute intended to augment the agency's
23  authority to enforce compliance with aviation safety standards. Petitioner Air
24  Transport Association of America ("Air Transport") contends that the FAA's failure
25  to comply with the notice and comment requirements of the Administrative
26  Procedure Act ("APA") renders the Penalty Rules invalid. The FAA maintains that
27  it was justified in dispensing with notice and comment under the "rules of agency
28  organization, procedure, or practice" and "good cause" exceptions to section 553.

29  We grant the petition for review. It is well established that the exemption under
30  section 553(b)(A), for "rules of agency organization, procedure, or practice," does
31  not apply to agency action that "substantially alter[s] the rights or interests of
32  regulated" parties. *American Hosp. Ass'n v. Bowen*, 834 F.2d 1037, 1041
33  (D.C.Cir.1987). The Penalty Rules fall outside the scope of the exception because
34  they substantially affect civil penalty defendants' "right to avail [themselves] of an
35  administrative adjudication." *National Motor Freight Traffic Ass'n v. United*
36  *States*, 268 F.Supp. 90, 96 (D.D.C.1967) (three-judge panel), aff'd mem., 393 U.S.
37  18 (1968). Moreover, because we find that the time constraints of the enabling
38  statute did not impose an insurmountable obstacle to complying with the
39  applicable notice and comment requirements of the APA, we also reject the FAA's

1  reliance on the "good cause" exception under section 553(b)(B). Consequently, we
2  hold that the Penalty Rules are invalid and that the FAA may not initiate new
3  prosecutions until it has complied with the procedural requirements of the APA.

4  I.

5  BACKGROUND

6  In December of 1987, Congress enacted a series of amendments to the Federal
7  Aviation Act relating to civil penalties. Among other things, these amendments
8  raised to $10,000 the maximum penalty for a single violation of aviation safety
9  standards and established a "demonstration program" authorizing the FAA to
10  prosecute and adjudicate administrative penalty actions involving less than
11  $50,000. Under the terms of the demonstration program, the FAA was granted the
12  authority to assess administrative penalties for a two-year period beginning on
13  December 30, 1987 and was to report to Congress on the effectiveness of the
14  program within eighteen months.

15  Congress' goal in enacting this legislation was to strengthen the enforcement
16  powers of the Federal Aviation Administration. Before the 1987 amendments, the
17  FAA could propose a maximum civil penalty of only $1,000 per violation and had
18  no enforcement authority of its own. When an alleged violator disputed a penalty,
19  the FAA was obliged to refer the case to the United States Attorney's office for
20  prosecution in federal district court; relatively few such cases were prosecuted,
21  however, because of competing work obligations facing U.S. Attorneys. * * * At the
22  same time, however, Congress remained attentive to the adjudicative rights of civil
23  penalty defendants. Congress provided that the FAA could assess a civil penalty
24  "only after notice and opportunity for a hearing on the record in accordance with
25  section 554 of [the APA]." 49 U.S.C. app. Sec. 1475(d)(1). As the conference report
26  accompanying section 1475 explained, the express incorporation of the APA's
27  procedural protections was designed to achieve two purposes:

28      First, the requirement is intended to advise the FAA of the appropriate level
29      of procedural formality and attention to the rights of those assessed civil
30      penalties under this demonstration program. Secondly, this requirement is
31      intended to provide reasonable assurance to the potential subjects of such
32      civil penalties that their due process rights are not compromised.

33  H.R. CONF.REP. No. 484, 100th Cong., 1st Sess. 81 (1987).

34  Approximately nine months after enactment of section 1475, the FAA promulgated
35  the Penalty Rules. See 53 Fed.Reg. 34,646 (1988) (codified at 14 C.F.R. pt. 13).
36  Effective immediately upon their issuance, the Penalty Rules established a
37  schedule of civil penalties, including fines of up to $10,000 for violations of the
38  safety standards of the Federal Aviation Act and related regulations. The Penalty
39  Rules also established a comprehensive adjudicatory scheme providing for formal
40  notice, settlement procedures, discovery, an adversary hearing before an ALJ and
41  an administrative appeal. In explaining why it dispensed with prepromulgation
    308

1   notice and comment, the FAA emphasized the procedural character of the Penalty
2   Rules and the time constraints of section 1475. The FAA did respond to post
3   promulgation comments but declined to make any amendments to the Rules.

4   * * *

5   In its petition for review, Air Transport * * * attacks the procedural adequacy of the
6   Rules, arguing that the FAA was obliged by section 553 of the APA to permit notice
7   and comment before the Rules became effective. * * *

8   II. ANALYSIS

9   * * *

10   B. The Merits

11   Section 553 of the APA obliges an agency to provide notice and an opportunity to
12   comment before promulgating a final rule. No question exists that the Penalty
13   Rules fall within the scope of the APA's rulemaking provisions. Nonetheless, the
14   FAA maintains that the Penalty Rules were exempt from the notice and comment
15   requirements for two, independent reasons: first, because they are "rules of agency
16   organization, procedure, or practice," id. Sec. 553(b)(A); and second, because the
17   time constraints of section 1475 gave the FAA "good cause" to find that
18   prepromulgation notice and comment would be "impracticable, unnecessary, or
19   contrary to the public interest," id. Sec. 553(b)(B). The FAA also argues that its
20   entertainment of post promulgation comments cured any violation of section 553.

21   Section 553's notice and comment requirements are essential to the scheme of
22   administrative governance established by the APA. These procedures reflect
23   Congress' "judgment that . . . informed administrative decisionmaking require[s]
24   that agency decisions be made only after affording interested persons" an
25   opportunity to communicate their views to the agency. *Chrysler Corp. v.*
26   *Brown*, 441 U.S. 281 (1979). Equally important, by mandating "openness,
27   explanation, and participatory democracy" in the rulemaking process, these
28   procedures assure the legitimacy of administrative norms. *Weyerhaeuser Co. v.*
29   *Costle*, 590 F.2d 1011, 1027 (D.C.Cir.1978). For these reasons, we have consistently
30   afforded a narrow cast to the exceptions to section 553, permitting an agency to
31   forgo notice and comment only when the subject matter or the circumstances of
32   the rulemaking divest the public of any legitimate stake in influencing the outcome.
33   In the instant case, because the Penalty Rules substantially affected civil penalty
34   defendants' right to avail themselves of an administrative adjudication, we cannot
35   accept the FAA's contention that the Rules could be promulgated without notice
36   and comment.

37   1. "Rules of Agency Organization, Procedure, or Practice"

38   The FAA argues that the Penalty Rules are exempt as "rules of agency organization,
39   procedure, or practice" because they establish "procedures" for adjudicating civil
40   penalty actions. According to the FAA, it would have been obliged to permit public

309

1 participation in the rulemaking process only if the Penalty Rules affected aviators'
2 "substantive" obligations under the Federal Aviation Act. We find this analysis
3 unpersuasive.

4 Our cases construing section 553(b)(A) have long emphasized that a rule does not
5 fall within the scope of the exception merely because it is capable of bearing the
6 label "procedural." *See, e.g., Reeder v. FCC*, 865 F.2d 1298 (D.C.Cir.1989) (per
7 curiam ). * * *

8 Rather than focus on whether a particular rule is "procedural" or "substantive,"
9 these decisions employ a functional analysis. Section 553(b)(A) has been described
10 as essentially a "housekeeping" measure, *Chrysler Corp. v. Brown*, 441 U.S. at 310,
11 "[t]he distinctive purpose of . . . [which] is to ensure 'that agencies retain latitude
12 in organizing their *internal* operations,'" *American Hosp. Ass'n v. Bowen*, 834
13 F.2d 1037, 1047 (D.C.Cir.1987). Where nominally "procedural" rules "encode[ ] a
14 substantive value judgment" or "substantially alter the rights or interests of
15 regulated" parties, however, the rules must be preceded by notice and comment.
16 *Id.* at 1047, 1041.

17 The Penalty Rules fall outside the scope of section 553(b)(A) because they
18 substantially affect a civil penalty defendant's right to an administrative
19 adjudication. Under both the due process clause and the APA, a party has a right
20 to notice and a hearing before being forced to pay a monetary penalty. Congress
21 expressly directed the FAA to incorporate these rights into its civil penalty
22 program. In implementing this mandate, the FAA made discretionary—indeed, in
23 many cases, highly contentious—choices concerning what process civil penalty
24 defendants are due. Each one of these choices "encode[d] a substantive value
25 judgment," *American Hosp. Ass'n*, 834 F.2d at 1047, on the appropriate balance
26 between a defendant's rights to adjudicatory procedures and the agency's interest
27 in efficient prosecution. The FAA was no less obliged to engage in notice and
28 comment before taking action affecting these adjudicatory rights than it would
29 have been had it taken action affecting aviators' "substantive" obligations under
30 the Federal Aviation Act.

31 * * *

32 The dissent also contends that we have "obliterated" the distinction between
33 substance and procedure. But, as the case law clearly illustrates, there is no such
34 "distinction" to obliterate for purposes of section 553(b)(A). The dissent refuses to
35 come to terms with the precedent characterizing this exception to notice and
36 comment rulemaking as a mere "housekeeping" measure, *Brown*, 441 U.S. at 310,
37 99 S.Ct. at 1721, applicable to rules "'organizing [agencies'] *internal* operations.'"
38 *American Hosp. Ass'n*, 834 F.2d at 1047 (quoting *Batterton v. Marshall*, 648 F.2d
39 694, 707 (D.C.Cir.1980) (emphasis added). The dissent's infusion of a rigid
40 "procedure"—"substance" distinction is not only inconsistent with our precedent,
41 but is also inconsistent with the statutory text. Section 553(b)(A) does not exempt
42 "rules of procedure" per se, but rather "rules of agency organization, procedure, or

1  practice." * * * In using the terms "rules of agency organization, procedure, or
2  practice," Congress intended to distinguish not between rules affecting different
3  classes of rights —"substantive" and "procedural"—but rather to distinguish
4  between rules affecting different subject matters —"the rights or interests of
5  regulated" parties, *American Hosp. Ass'n*, 834 F.2d at 1041, and agencies'
6  "'internal operations,'" *id.* at 1047 (quoting *Batterton*, 648 F.2d at 707). Because
7  the Penalty Rules substantially affect civil penalty defendants' "right to avail
8  [themselves] of an administrative adjudication," members of the aviation
9  community had a legitimate interest in participating in the rulemaking process.
10 *National Motor Freight*, 268 F.Supp. at 96.

## 2. "Good Cause"

12 We also disagree that the two-year duration of section 1475's demonstration
13 program furnished the FAA with "good cause" to dispense with notice and
14 comment procedures. Like the other exceptions, the good cause exception is to "be
15 narrowly construed and only reluctantly countenanced." *New Jersey v. EPA*, 626
16 F.2d 1038, 1045 (D.C.Cir.1980). In particular, we have explained that statutory
17 time limits do not ordinarily excuse compliance with the APA's procedural
18 requirements. In *New Jersey v. EPA*, we reviewed a set of regulations issued
19 pursuant to a six-month time limit. Adopting the reasoning of two of our sister
20 circuits, we held that the statutory deadline did not constitute good cause to forgo
21 notice and comment absent "'any express indication'" by Congress to this effect.
22 *Id.* at 1043.

23                                        * * *

## 3. Postpromulgation Comment

25 Finally, we reject the FAA's contention that its response to comments after
26 promulgation of the Penalty Rules cured any noncompliance with section 553.
27 Section 553 provides "that notice and an opportunity for comment are to precede
28 rule-making." *New Jersey v. EPA*, 626 F.2d at 1050. We strictly enforce this
29 requirement because we recognize that an agency is not likely to be receptive to
30 suggested changes once the agency "put[s] its credibility on the line in the form of
31 'final' rules. People naturally tend to be more close-minded and defensive once
32 they have made a 'final' determination." *National Tour Brokers Ass'n v. United*
33 *States*, 591 F.2d 896, 902 (D.C.Cir.1978). Although we have suggested that there
34 might be circumstances in which "defects in an original notice [could] be cured by
35 an adequate later notice" and opportunity to comment, we have emphasized that
36 we could reach such a conclusion only upon a compelling showing that "the
37 agency's mind remain[ed] open enough at the later stage." *McLouth Steel Prods.*
38 *Corp. v. Thomas*, 838 F.2d 1317, 1323 (D.C.Cir.1988).

39 The FAA has not come close to overcoming the presumption of closed-mindedness
40 in this case. It made no changes in the Penalty Rules in response to public
41 comments. Nor did the language of FAA's published replies suggest that the agency
42 had afforded the comments particularly searching consideration.

1  Under the circumstances, then, we cannot discount the possibility that, had the
2  FAA entertained comments before the Penalty Rules became final, it "might have
3  decided [on] a different accommodation" of the agency's enforcement needs and
4  civil penalty defendants' procedural rights. *Brown*, 441 U.S. at 316, 99 S.Ct. at 1725.
5  Indeed, if the FAA had entertained prepromulgation comments and taken those
6  comments seriously, it might very well have averted the public outcry underlying
7  the agency's pending notice of proposed rulemaking.

8  * * *

9  SILBERMAN, Circuit Judge, dissenting:

10  * * * I disagree with the majority's answer to the question because I think the rules
11  fall, by ample measure, within the "procedural" exemption of section 553(b)(A),
12  which exempts from notice and comment "rules of agency organization, procedure,
13  or practice." To be sure, the rules in this case could as well be described as rules of
14  "practice" (covering the practice of the parties and attorneys before the FAA) and
15  also in some respects rules of "agency organization" (dealing with the
16  interrelationship between the administrative law judges and the Administrator). I
17  use the term "procedure" here to cover all three concepts.

18  Lines between substance and procedure in various areas of the law are difficult to
19  draw and therefore often perplex scholars and judges. But Congress, when it
20  passed the Administrative Procedure Act, made that difference critical, and we are
21  therefore obliged to implement a viable distinction between "procedural" rules and
22  those that are substantive. The majority opinion, in effect, abandons the effort * * *
23  . Accordingly, it will be impossible for any agency general counsel, in the future,
24  safely to advise agency heads that a given set of proposed rules are procedural and
25  do not have to be published for comment. Therefore, I dissent.

26  If we assume a spectrum of rules running from the most substantive to the most
27  procedural, I would describe the former as those that regulate "primary conduct"
28  in the way that term is used in *Toilet Goods Ass'n, Inc. v. Gardner*, 387 U.S. 158,
29  164 (1967), and the latter are those furthest away from primary conduct. In other
30  words, if a given regulation purports to direct, control, or condition the behavior
31  of those institutions or individuals subject to regulation by the authorizing statute
32  it is not procedural, it is substantive. At the other end of the spectrum are those
33  rules, such as the ones before us in this case, which deal with enforcement or
34  adjudication of claims of violations of the substantive norm but which do not
35  purport to affect the substantive norm. These kinds of rules are, in my view, clearly
36  procedural.

37  Rules are no less procedural because they are thought to be important or affect
38  outcomes. Congress did not state, when it passed the APA, that all but insignificant
39  rules must be put out for notice and comment. And to say, as does the majority,
40  that the rules are covered by section 553's notice and comment requirement
41  because they "substantially affect a civil defendant's *right to an administrative*
42  *adjudication*," Maj. Op. at 378 (emphasis in original), is, I respectfully submit,

312

1 circular reasoning. It assumes the conclusion by describing petitioner's interest in
2 the agency's adjudicatory procedures as if it were a substantive right. It also
3 implicitly suggests that petitioner is correct on the merits in claiming the agency's
4 adjudicatory procedures are illegal. In determining whether particular rules must
5 be put out for comment, surely the APA does not contemplate that a reviewing
6 court would be influenced by whether or not it thought procedural rules were
7 illegal. If, as argued by petitioner, the rules violate its rather ill-defined notion of
8 administrative due process (petitioner's primary claim on the merits seems to be
9 that the rules offend the views of the American Bar Association) or even
10 constitutional due process, that is an entirely separate matter which can be raised
11 in a concrete setting.

12                                             * * *

13 It might be thought that there is something vaguely underhanded about an agency
14 publishing important rules without an opportunity for those affected to comment.
15 And lawyers and judges tend to prefer, on the margin, added procedure. But as
16 *Cabais* makes clear, *Cabais v. Egger*, 690 F.2d 234 (D.C.Cir.1982), we have been
17 admonished somewhat dramatically by *Vermont Yankee* to not add more
18 procedure to the APA than Congress required. I am afraid the majority opinion by
19 obliterating the distinction between substance and procedure in section 553 does
20 just that.

21                                             * * *

22

23          b.  Interpretative Rules

24 **American Mining Congress v. Mine Safety and Health**
25 **Administration**

26 995 F.2d 1106 (D.C. Cir. 1993)

27 June 15, 1993

28 Before WILLIAMS, SENTELLE and RANDOLPH, Circuit Judges.

29 STEPHEN F. WILLIAMS, Circuit Judge:

30 This case presents a single issue: whether Program Policy Letters of the Mine
31 Safety and Health Administration, stating the agency's position that certain x-ray
32 readings qualify as "diagnose[s]" of lung disease within the meaning of agency
33 reporting regulations, are interpretive rules under the Administrative Procedure
34 Act. We hold that they are.

35 The Federal Mine Safety and Health Act, 30 U.S.C. § 801 *et seq.*, extensively
36 regulates health and safety conditions in the nation's mines and empowers the
37 Secretary of Labor to enforce the statute and relevant regulations. In addition, the
38 Act requires "every operator of a . . . mine . . . [to] establish and maintain such

1    records, make such reports, and provide such information, as the Secretary . . . may
2    reasonably require from time to time to enable him to perform his functions." *Id.*
3    at § 813(h). The Act makes a general grant of authority to the Secretary to issue
4    "such regulations as . . . [he] deems appropriate to carry out" any of its provisions.
5    *Id.* at § 957.

6    Pursuant to its statutory authority, the Mine Safety and Health Administration
7    (acting on behalf of the Secretary of Labor) maintains regulations known as "Part
8    50" regulations, which cover the "Notification, Investigation, Reports and Records
9    of Accidents, Injuries, Illnesses, Employment, and Coal Production in Mines." *See*
10    30 CFR Part 50. These were adopted via notice-and-comment rulemaking. Subpart
11    C deals with the "Reporting of Accidents, Injuries, and Illnesses" and requires mine
12    operators to report to the MSHA within ten days "each accident, occupational
13    injury, or occupational illness" that occurs at a mine. *See* 30 CFR § 50.20(a). Of
14    central importance here, the regulation also says that whenever any of certain
15    occupational illnesses are "*diagnosed*," the operator must similarly report the
16    diagnosis within ten days. *Id.* (emphasis added). Among the occupational illnesses
17    covered are " [s]ilicosis, asbestosis, coal worker's pneumoconiosis, and other
18    pneumoconioses." *Id.* at § 50.20-6(b)(7)(ii). An operator's failure to report may
19    lead to citation and penalty.

20    As the statute and formal regulations contain ambiguities, the MSHA from time to
21    time issues Program Policy Letters ("PPLs") intended to coordinate and convey
22    agency policies, guidelines, and interpretations to agency employees and
23    interested members of the public. One subject on which it has done so—apparently
24    in response to inquiries from mine operators about whether certain x-ray results
25    needed to be reported as "diagnos[es]"—has been the meaning of the term
26    diagnosis for purposes of Part 50.

27    The first of the PPLs at issue here, PPL No. 91-III-2 (effective September 6, 1991),
28    stated that any chest x-ray of a miner who had a history of exposure to
29    pneumonoconiosis-causing dust that rated 1/0 or higher on the International
30    Labor Office (ILO) classification system would be considered a "diagnosis that the
31    x-rayed miner has silicosis or one of the other pneumonoconioses" for the purposes
32    of the Part 50 reporting requirements. (The ILO classification system uses a 12-
33    step scale to measure the concentration of opacities (i.e., areas of darkness or
34    shading) on chest x-rays. A 1/0 rating is the fourth most severe of the ratings.) The
35    1991 PPL also set up a procedure whereby, if a mine operator had a chest x-ray
36    initially evaluated by a relatively unskilled reader, the operator could seek a
37    reading by a more skilled one; if the latter rated the x-ray below 1/0, the MSHA
38    would delete the "diagnosis" from its files. We explain the multiple-reader rules
39    further in the context of the third PPL, where they took their final form (so far).

40    The second letter, PPL No. P92-III-2 (effective May 6, 1992), superseded the 1991
41    PPL but largely repeated its view about a Part 50 diagnosis. * * *

1 The final PPL under dispute, PPL No. P92-III-2 (effective August 1, 1992), replaced
2 the May 1992 PPL and again restated the MSHA's basic view that a chest x-ray
3 rating above 1/0 on the ILO scale constituted a "diagnosis" of silicosis or some
4 other pneumoconiosis. The August 1992 PPL also modified the MSHA's position
5 on additional readings. Specifically, when the first reader is not a "B" reader (i.e.,
6 one certified by the National Institute of Occupational Safety and Health to
7 perform ILO ratings), and the operator seeks a reading from a "B" reader, the
8 MSHA will stay enforcement for failure to report the first reading. If the "B" reader
9 concurs with the initial determination that the x-ray should be scored a 1/0 or
10 higher, the mine operator must report the "diagnosis". If the "B" reader scores the
11 x-ray below 1/0, the MSHA will continue to stay enforcement if the operator gets a
12 third reading, again from a "B" reader; the MSHA then will accept the majority
13 opinion of the three readers.

14 The MSHA did not follow the notice and comment requirements of 5 U.S.C. § 553
15 [the Administrative Procedure Act] in issuing any of the three PPLs. In defending
16 its omission of notice and comment, the agency relies solely on the interpretive
17 rule exemption of § 553(b)(3)(A).

18 We note parenthetically that the agency also neglected to publish any of the PPLs
19 in the Federal Register, but distributed them to all mine operators and
20 independent contractors with MSHA identification numbers, as well as to
21 interested operator associations and trade unions. Compare 5 U.S.C. §
22 552(a)(1)(D) (requiring publication in the Federal Register of all "interpretations
23 of general applicability") with *id.* at § 552(a)(2)(B) (requiring agencies to make
24 available for public inspection and copying "those statements of policy and
25 interpretations which have been adopted by the agency and are not published in
26 the Federal Register"). Petitioners here make no issue of the failure to publish in
27 the Federal Register.

28 The distinction between those agency pronouncements subject to APA notice-and-
29 comment requirements and those that are exempt has been aptly described as
30 "enshrouded in considerable smog," Given the confusion, it makes some sense to
31 go back to the origins of the distinction in the legislative history of the
32 Administrative Procedure Act. Here the key document is the *Attorney General's*
33 *Manual on the Administrative Procedure Act* (1947), which offers "the following
34 working definitions":

35     "*Substantive rules*—rules, other than organizational or procedural under
36     section 3(a)(1) and (2), issued by an agency pursuant to statutory authority
37     and which implement the statute, as, for example, the proxy rules issued by
38     the Securities and Exchange Commission pursuant to section 14 of the
39     Securities Exchange Act of 1934. Such rules have the force and effect of law.

40     "*Interpretative rules*—rules or statements issued by an agency to advise the
41     public of the agency's construction of the statutes and rules which it
42     administers. . . .

> *"General statements of policy*—statements issued by an agency to advise the public prospectively of the manner in which the agency proposes to exercise a discretionary power."

*Id.* at 30 n. 3. *See also* Michael Asimow, *Public Participation in the Adoption of Interpretive Rules and Policy Statements*, 75 Mich. L. Rev. 520, 542 & n. 95 (1977) (reading legislative history of Administrative Procedure Act as "suggest[ing] an intent to adopt the legal effect test" as marking the line between substantive and interpretive rules).

See, e.g., *National Latino Media Coalition v. FCC,* 816 F.2d 785, 787–88 (D.C.Cir.1987). We have said that a rule has such force only if Congress has delegated legislative power to the agency and if the agency intended to exercise that power in promulgating the rule. See, e.g., *American Postal Workers Union v. U.S. Postal Service,* 707 F.2d 548, 558 (D.C.Cir.1983).

On its face, the "intent to exercise" language may seem to lead only to more smog, but in fact there are a substantial number of instances where such "intent" can be found with some confidence. The first and clearest case is where, in the absence of a legislative rule by the agency, the legislative basis for agency enforcement would be inadequate. The example used by the Attorney General's Manual fits exactly— the SEC's proxy authority under § 14 of the Securities Exchange Act of 1934, for example, forbids certain persons, "to give, or to refrain from giving a proxy" "in contravention of such rules and regulations as the Commission may prescribe." 15 U.S.C. § 78n(b). The statute itself forbids nothing except acts or omissions to be spelled out by the Commission in "rules or regulations". The present case is similar, as to Part 50 itself, in that § 813(h) merely requires an operator to maintain "such records . . . as the Secretary . . . may reasonably require from time to time." 30 U.S.C. § 813(h). Although the Secretary might conceivably create some "require[ments]" ad hoc, clearly some agency creation of a duty is a necessary predicate to any enforcement against an operator for failure to keep records. Analogous cases may exist in which an agency may offer a government benefit only after it formalizes the prerequisites.

Second, an agency seems likely to have intended a rule to be legislative if it has the rule published in the Code of Federal Regulations; 44 U.S.C. § 1510 limits publication in that code to rules "having general applicability and legal effect."

Third, "'[i]f a second rule repudiates or is irreconcilable with [a prior legislative rule], the second rule must be an amendment of the first; and, of course, an amendment to a legislative rule must itself be legislative.'" *National Family Planning & Reproductive Health Ass'n v. Sullivan,* 979 F.2d 227, 235 (D.C. Cir. 1992) (quoting Michael Asimow, *Nonlegislative Rulemaking and Regulatory Reform*, 1985 Duke L.J. 381, 396).

\* \* \*

1    This focus on whether the agency *needs* to exercise legislative power (to provide a
2    basis for enforcement actions or agency decisions conferring benefits) helps
3    explain some distinctions that may, out of context, appear rather metaphysical. For
4    example, in *Fertilizer Institute* we drew a distinction between instances where an
5    agency merely "declare[s] its understanding of what a statute requires"
6    (interpretive), and ones where an agency "go[es] beyond the text of a statute"
7    (legislative). 935 F.2d 1303, 1308 (1991). The difficulty with the distinction is that
8    almost every rule may seem to do both. But if the dividing line is the necessity for
9    agency legislative action, then a rule supplying that action will be legislative no
10    matter how grounded in the agency's "understanding of what the statute requires",
11    and an interpretation that spells out the scope of an agency's or regulated entity's
12    pre-existing duty (such as EPA's interpretation of "release" in *Fertilizer Institute*),
13    will be interpretive, even if, as in that case itself, it widens that duty even beyond
14    the scope allowed to the agency under *Chevron U.S.A., Inc. v. NRDC*, 467 U.S. 837
15    (1984).

16    Similarly, we have distinguished between cases where a rule is "based on specific
17    statutory provisions" (interpretive), and where one is instead "based on an
18    agency's power to exercise its judgment as to how best to implement a general
19    statutory mandate" (legislative). *United Technologies Corp. v. EPA*, 821 F.2d 714,
20    719, 720 (D.C. Cir. 1987). A statute or legislative rule that actually establishes a
21    duty or a right is likely to be relatively specific (and the agency's refinement will be
22    interpretive), whereas an agency's authority to create rights and duties will
23    typically be relatively broad (and the agency's actual establishment of rights and
24    duties will be legislative). But the legislative or interpretive status of the agency
25    rules turns not in some general sense on the narrowness or breadth of the statutory
26    (or regulatory) term in question, but on the prior existence or non-existence of
27    legal duties and rights.

28    Of course an agency may for reasons of its own choose explicitly to invoke its
29    general legislating authority—perhaps, for example, out of concern that its
30    proposed action might be invalid as an interpretation of some existing mandate
31    * * * . In that event, even if a court believed that the agency had been unduly
32    cautious about the legislative background, it would presumably treat the rule as an
33    attempted exercise of legislative power.

34    In an occasional case we have appeared to stress whether the disputed rule is one
35    with "binding effect"—"binding" in the sense that the rule does not "'genuinely
36    leave[ ] the agency . . . free to exercise discretion.'" *State of Alaska v. DOT*, 868
37    F.2d at 445 (quoting *Community Nutrition Institute v. Young*, 818 F.2d 943, 945,
38    946 (D.C. Cir. 1987)). That inquiry arose in a quite different context, that of
39    distinguishing policy statements, rather than interpretive rules, from legislative
40    norms. The classic application is *Pacific Gas & Electric Co. v. FPC*, 506 F.2d 33, 38
41    (D.C. Cir. 1974); *see also American Bus Ass'n v. United States*, 627 F.2d 525, 529
42    (D.C. Cir. 1980) (following *PG & E*, again in policy statement context). Indeed, the
43    agency's theory in *Community Nutrition* was that its pronouncement had been a
44    policy statement.

1    But while a good rule of thumb is that a norm is less likely to be a general policy
2    statement when it purports (or, even better, has proven) to restrict agency
3    discretion, restricting discretion tells one little about whether a rule is interpretive.
4    See *Attorney General's Manual*, supra, at 30 n. 3 (discussing exercise of discretion
5    only in definition of policy statements). Nor is there much explanatory power in
6    any distinction that looks to the use of mandatory as opposed to permissive
7    language. While an agency's decision to use "will" instead of "may" may be of use
8    when drawing a line between policy statements and legislative rules, the endeavor
9    miscarries in the interpretive/legislative rule context. Interpretation is a
10   chameleon that takes its color from its context; therefore, an interpretation will use
11   imperative language—or at least have imperative meaning—if the interpreted term
12   is part of a command; it will use permissive language—or at least have a permissive
13   meaning—if the interpreted term is in a permissive provision.

14   A non-legislative rule's capacity to have a binding effect is limited in practice by
15   the fact that agency personnel at every level act under the shadow of judicial
16   review. If they believe that courts may fault them for brushing aside the arguments
17   of persons who contest the rule or statement, they are obviously far more likely to
18   entertain those arguments. And, as failure to provide notice-and-comment
19   rulemaking will usually mean that affected parties have had no prior formal
20   opportunity to present their contentions, judicial review for want of reasoned
21   decisionmaking is likely, in effect, to take place in review of specific agency actions
22   implementing the rule. Similarly, where the agency must defend its view as an
23   application of *Chevron* "prong two" (i.e., where Congress has not "clearly" decided
24   for or against the agency interpretation), so that only reasonableness is at issue,
25   agency disregard of significant policy arguments will clearly count against it. As
26   Donald Elliott has said, agency attentiveness to parties' arguments must come
27   sooner or later. * * * Because the threat of judicial review provides a spur to the
28   agency to pay attention to facts and arguments submitted in derogation of any rule
29   not supported by notice and comment, even as late as the enforcement stage, any
30   agency statement not subjected to notice-and-comment rulemaking will be more
31   vulnerable to attack not only in court but also within the agency itself.

32   Not only does an agency have an incentive to entertain objections to an interpretive
33   rule, but the ability to promulgate such rules, without notice and comment, does
34   not appear more hazardous to affected parties than the likely alternative. Where a
35   statute or legislative rule has created a legal basis for enforcement, an agency can
36   simply let its interpretation evolve ad hoc in the process of enforcement or other
37   applications (e.g., grants). The protection that Congress sought to secure by
38   requiring notice and comment for legislative rules is not advanced by reading the
39   exemption for "interpretive rule" so narrowly as to drive agencies into pure *ad*
40   *hocery*—an *ad hocery*, moreover, that affords less notice, or less convenient notice,
41   to affected parties.

42   Accordingly, insofar as our cases can be reconciled at all, we think it almost
43   exclusively on the basis of whether the purported interpretive rule has "legal
44   effect," which in turn is best ascertained by asking (1) whether in the absence of

1  the rule there would not be an adequate legislative basis for enforcement action or
2  other agency action to confer benefits or ensure the performance of duties, (2)
3  whether the agency has published the rule in the Code of Federal Regulations, (3)
4  whether the agency has explicitly invoked its general legislative authority, or (4)
5  whether the rule effectively amends a prior legislative rule. If the answer to any of
6  these questions is affirmative, we have a legislative, not an interpretive rule.

7  Here we conclude that the August 1992 PPL is an interpretive rule. The Part 50
8  regulations themselves require the reporting of diagnoses of the specified diseases,
9  so there is no legislative gap that required the PPL as a predicate to enforcement
10  action. Nor did the agency purport to act legislatively, either by including the letter
11  in the Code of Federal Regulations, or by invoking its general legislative authority
12  under 30 U.S.C. § 811(a). The remaining possibility therefore is that the August
13  1992 PPL is a de facto amendment of prior legislative rules, namely the Part 50
14  regulations.

15  A rule does not, in this inquiry, become an amendment merely because it supplies
16  crisper and more detailed lines than the authority being interpreted. If that were
17  so, no rule could pass as an interpretation of a legislative rule unless it were
18  confined to parroting the rule or replacing the original vagueness with another.

19  Although petitioners cite some definitions of "diagnosis" suggesting that with
20  pneumoconiosis and silicosis, a diagnosis requires more than a chest x-ray—
21  specifically, additional diagnostic tools as tissue examination or at least an
22  occupational history—MSHA points to some administrative rules that make x-rays
23  at the level specified here the basis for a finding of pneumoconiosis. A finding of a
24  disease is surely equivalent, in normal terminology, to a diagnosis, and thus the
25  PPLs certainly offer no interpretation that repudiates or is irreconcilable with an
26  existing legislative rule.

27                                    * * *

28  Accordingly, the petitions for review are

29  *Dismissed.*

30

31  ## Hoctor v. United States Department of Agriculture

32  82 F.3d 165 (7th Cir. 1996)

33  April 25, 1996

34  Before POSNER, Chief Judge, and DIANE P. WOOD and EVANS, Circuit Judges.

35  POSNER, Chief Judge.

36  A rule promulgated by an agency that is subject to the Administrative Procedure
37  Act is invalid unless the agency first issues a public notice of proposed rulemaking,

1    describing the substance of the proposed rule, and gives the public an opportunity
2    to submit written comments; and if after receiving the comments it decides to
3    promulgate the rule it must set forth the basis and purpose of the rule in a public
4    statement. These procedural requirements do not apply, however, to
5    "interpretative rules, general statements of policy, or rules of agency organization,
6    procedure, or practice." 5 U.S.C. § 553(b)(A). Distinguishing between a
7    "legislative" rule, to which the notice and comment provisions of the Act apply, and
8    an interpretive rule, to which these provisions do not apply, is often very difficult—
9    and often very important to regulated firms, the public, and the agency. Notice and
10    comment rulemaking is time-consuming, facilitates the marshaling of opposition
11    to a proposed rule, and may result in the creation of a very long record that may in
12    turn provide a basis for a judicial challenge to the rule if the agency decides to
13    promulgate it. There are no formalities attendant upon the promulgation of an
14    interpretive rule, but this is tolerable because such a rule is "only" an
15    interpretation. Every governmental agency that enforces a less than crystalline
16    statute must interpret the statute, and it does the public a favor if it announces the
17    interpretation in advance of enforcement, whether the announcement takes the
18    form of a rule or of a policy statement, which the Administrative Procedure Act
19    assimilates to an interpretive rule. It would be no favor to the public to discourage
20    the announcement of agencies' interpretations by burdening the interpretive
21    process with cumbersome formalities.

22    The question presented by this appeal from an order of the Department of
23    Agriculture is whether a rule for the secure containment of animals, a rule
24    promulgated by the Department under the Animal Welfare Act, 7 U.S.C. §§ 2131 *et*
25    *seq.*, without compliance with the notice and comment requirements of the
26    Administrative Procedure Act, is nevertheless valid because it is merely an
27    interpretive rule. Enacted in 1966, the Animal Welfare Act, as its title implies, is
28    primarily designed to assure the humane treatment of animals. The Act requires
29    the licensing of dealers (with obvious exceptions, for example retail pet stores) and
30    exhibitors, and authorizes the Department to impose sanctions on licensees who
31    violate either the statute itself or the rules promulgated by the Department under
32    the authority of 7 U.S.C. § 2151, which authorizes the Secretary of Agriculture "to
33    promulgate such rules, regulations, and orders as he may deem necessary in order
34    to effectuate the purposes of [the Act]." The Act provides guidance to the exercise
35    of this rulemaking authority by requiring the Department to formulate standards
36    "to govern the humane handling, care, treatment, and transportation of animals
37    by dealers," and these standards must include minimum requirements "for
38    handling, housing, feeding, watering, sanitation," etc. 7 U.S.C. § 2143(a).

39    The Department has employed the notice and comment procedure to promulgate
40    a regulation, the validity of which is not questioned, that is entitled "structural
41    strength" and that provides that "the facility [housing the animals] must be
42    constructed of such material and of such strength as appropriate for the animals
43    involved. The indoor and outdoor housing facilities shall be structurally sound and

1   shall be maintained in good repair to protect the animals from injury and to
2   contain the animals." 9 C.F.R. § 3.125(a).

3   Enter the petitioner, Patrick Hoctor, who in 1982 began dealing in exotic animals
4   on his farm outside of Terre Haute. In a 25-acre compound he raised a variety of
5   animals including "Big Cats"—a typical inventory included three lions, two tigers,
6   seven ligers (a liger is a cross between a male lion and a female tiger, and is thus to
7   be distinguished from a tigon), six cougars, and two snow leopards. The animals
8   were in pens ("primary enclosures" in the jargon of the administration of the
9   Animal Welfare Act). The area in which the pens were located was surrounded by
10   a fence ("containment fence"). In addition, Hoctor erected a fence around the
11   entire compound ("perimeter fence"). At the suggestion of a veterinarian employed
12   by the Agriculture Department who was assigned to inspect the facility when
13   Hoctor started his animal dealership in 1982, Hoctor made the perimeter fence six
14   feet high.

15   The following year the Department issued an internal memorandum addressed to
16   its force of inspectors in which it said that all "dangerous animals," defined as
17   including, among members of the cat family, lions, tigers, and leopards, must be
18   inside a perimeter fence at least eight feet high. This provision is the so-called
19   interpretive rule, interpreting the housing regulation quoted above. An agency has,
20   of course, the power, indeed the inescapable duty, to interpret its own legislative
21   rules, such as the housing standard, just as it has the power and duty to interpret
22   a statute that it enforces.

23   On several occasions beginning in 1990, Hoctor was cited by a Department of
24   Agriculture inspector for violating 9 C.F.R. § 3.125(a), the housing standard, by
25   failing to have an eight-foot perimeter fence. Eventually the Department
26   sanctioned Hoctor for this and other alleged violations, and he has sought judicial
27   review limited, however, to the perimeter fence. He is a small dealer and it would
28   cost him many thousands of dollars to replace his six-foot-high fence with an eight-
29   foot-high fence. Indeed, we were told at argument that pending the resolution of
30   his dispute over the fence he has discontinued dealing in Big Cats. The parties
31   agree that unless the rule requiring a perimeter fence at least eight feet high is a
32   valid interpretive rule, the sanction for violating it was improper.

33   We may assume, though we need not decide, that the Department of Agriculture
34   has the statutory authority to require dealers in dangerous animals to enclose their
35   compounds with eight-foot-high fences. The fence is a backup fail-safe device,
36   since the animals are kept in pens, cages, or other enclosures within the compound,
37   in an area that is itself fenced, rather than being free to roam throughout the
38   compound. Since animals sometimes break out or are carelessly let out of their
39   pens, a fail-safe device seems highly appropriate, to say the least. Two lions once
40   got out of their pen on Hoctor's property, and he had to shoot them. Yet, when he
41   did so, they were still within the containment fence. The Department's regulations
42   do not require a containment fence, and it is unclear to us why, if that fence was
43   adequate—and we are given no reason to suppose it was not—Hoctor should have

had to put up an additional fence, let alone one eight-feet high. But we lay any doubts on this score to one side. And we may also assume that the containment of dangerous animals is a proper concern of the Department in the enforcement of the Animal Welfare Act, even though the purpose of the Act is to protect animals from people rather than people from animals. Even Big Cats are not safe outside their compounds, and with a lawyer's ingenuity the Department's able counsel reminded us at argument that if one of those Cats mauled or threatened a human being, the Cat might get into serious trouble and thus it is necessary to protect human beings from Big Cats *in order to protect the Cats from human beings*, which is the important thing under the Act. In fact Hoctor had shot the two lions because they were dangerously close to one of his employees. Since tort liability for injury caused by a wild animal is strict, the common law, at least, is solicitous for the protection of the citizens of Terre Haute against escapees from Hoctor's menagerie even if the Animal Welfare Act is not. The internal memorandum also justifies the eight-foot requirement as a means of protecting the animals from animal predators, though one might have supposed the Big Cats able to protect themselves against the native Indiana fauna.

Another issue that we need not resolve besides the issue of the statutory authority for the challenged rule is whether the Department might have cited Hoctor for having a perimeter fence that was *in fact*, considering the number and type of his animals, the topography of the compound, the design and structure of the protective enclosures and the containment fence, the proximity of highways or inhabited areas, and the design of the perimeter fence itself, too low to be safe, as distinct from merely being lower than eight feet. No regulation is targeted on the problem of containment other than 9 C.F.R. § 3.125, which seems to be concerned with the strength of enclosures rather than their height. But maybe there is some implicit statutory duty of containment that Hoctor might have been thought to have violated even if there were no rule requiring an eight-foot-high perimeter fence.

The only ground on which the Department defends sanctioning Hoctor for not having a high enough fence is that requiring an eight-foot-high perimeter fence for dangerous animals is an interpretation of the Department's own structural-strength regulation, and "provided an agency's interpretation of its own regulations does not violate the Constitution or a federal statute, it must be given 'controlling weight unless it is plainly erroneous or inconsistent with the regulation.'" *Stinson v. United States*, 508 U.S. 36, 44-46 (1993).[*] The "provided" clause does not announce a demanding standard of judicial review, although the absence of any reference in the housing regulation to fences or height must give us pause. The regulation appears only to require that pens and other animal housing be sturdy enough in design and construction, and sufficiently well maintained, to

---

[*] [note: this statement of the law is no longer completely accurate; see *Kisor v. Wilkie*, No. 18-15, 588 U.S. ___ (2019). – ed.]

1   prevent the animals from breaking *through* the enclosure—not that any enclosure,
2   whether a pen or a perimeter fence, be high enough to prevent the animals from
3   escaping by jumping *over* the enclosure. The Department's counsel made the
4   wonderful lawyer's argument that the eight-foot rule is consistent with the
5   regulation because a fence lower than eight feet has zero structural strength
6   between its height (here six feet) and the eight-foot required minimum. The two
7   feet by which Hoctor's fence fell short could not have contained a groundhog, let
8   alone a liger, since it was empty space.

9   Our doubts about the scope of the regulation that the eight-foot rule is said to be
10  "interpreting" might seem irrelevant, since even if a rule requiring an eight-foot
11  perimeter fence could not be based on the regulation, it could be based on the
12  statute itself, which in requiring the Department to establish minimum standards
13  for the housing of animals presumably authorizes it to promulgate standards for
14  secure containment. But if the eight-foot rule were deemed one of those minimum
15  standards that the Department is required by statute to create, it could not possibly
16  be thought an *interpretive* rule. For what would it be interpreting? When Congress
17  authorizes an agency to create standards, it is delegating legislative authority,
18  rather than itself setting forth a standard which the agency might then
19  particularize through interpretation. Put differently, when a statute does not
20  impose a duty on the persons subject to it but instead authorizes (or requires—it
21  makes no difference) an agency to impose a duty, the formulation of that duty
22  becomes a legislative task entrusted to the agency. Provided that a rule
23  promulgated pursuant to such a delegation is intended to bind, and not merely to
24  be a tentative statement of the agency's view, which would make it just a policy
25  statement, and not a rule at all, the rule would be the clearest possible example of
26  a legislative rule, as to which the notice and comment procedure not followed here
27  is mandatory, as distinct from an interpretive rule; for there would be nothing to
28  interpret. *American Mining Congress v. Mine Safety & Health Administration*,
29  995 F.2d 1106, 1109 (D.C.Cir.1993). That is why the Department must argue that
30  its eight-foot rule is an interpretation of the structural-strength regulation—itself
31  a standard, and therefore interpretable —in order to avoid reversal.

32  Even if, despite the doubts that we expressed earlier, the eight-foot rule is
33  consistent with, even in some sense authorized by, the structural-strength
34  regulation, it would not necessarily follow that it is an interpretive rule. It is that
35  only if it can be derived from the regulation by a process reasonably described as
36  interpretation. Supposing that the regulation imposes a general duty of secure
37  containment, the question is, then, Can a requirement that the duty be
38  implemented by erecting an eight-foot-high perimeter fence be thought an
39  interpretation of that general duty?

40  "Interpretation" in the narrow sense is the ascertainment of meaning. It is obvious
41  that eight feet is not part of the meaning of secure containment. But
42  "interpretation" is often used in a much broader sense. A process of
43  "interpretation" has transformed the Constitution into a body of law undreamt of
44  by the framers. To skeptics the *Miranda* rule is as remote from the text of the Fifth

1 Amendment as the eight-foot rule is from the text of 9 C.F.R. § 3.125(a). But our
2 task in this case is not to plumb the mysteries of legal theory; it is merely to give
3 effect to a distinction that the Administrative Procedure Act makes, and we can do
4 this by referring to the purpose of the distinction. The purpose is to separate the
5 cases in which notice and comment rulemaking is required from the cases in which
6 it is not required. As we noted at the outset, unless a statute or regulation is of
7 crystalline transparency, the agency enforcing it cannot avoid interpreting it, and
8 the agency would be stymied in its enforcement duties if every time it brought a
9 case on a new theory it had to pause for a bout, possibly lasting several years, of
10 notice and comment rulemaking. * * *

11 At the other extreme from what might be called normal or routine interpretation
12 is the making of reasonable but arbitrary (not in the "arbitrary or capricious"
13 sense) rules that are consistent with the statute or regulation under which the rules
14 are promulgated but not derived from it, because they represent an arbitrary
15 choice among methods of implementation. A rule that turns on a number is likely
16 to be arbitrary in this sense. There is no way to reason to an eight-foot perimeter-
17 fence rule as opposed to a seven-and-a-half foot fence or a nine-foot fence or a ten-
18 foot fence. None of these candidates for a rule is uniquely appropriate to, and in
19 that sense derivable from, the duty of secure containment. This point becomes
20 even clearer if we note that the eight-foot rule actually has another component—
21 the fence must be at least three feet from any animal's pen. Why three feet? Why
22 not four? Or two?

23 The reason courts refuse to create statutes of limitations is precisely the difficulty
24 of reasoning to a number by the methods of reasoning used by courts. One cannot
25 extract from the concept of a tort that a tort suit should be barred unless brought
26 within one, or two, or three, or five years. The choice is arbitrary and courts are
27 uncomfortable with making arbitrary choices. They see this as a legislative
28 function. Legislators have the democratic legitimacy to make choices among value
29 judgments, choices based on hunch or guesswork or even the toss of a coin, and
30 other arbitrary choices. When agencies base rules on arbitrary choices they are
31 legislating, and so these rules are legislative or substantive and require notice and
32 comment rulemaking, a procedure that is analogous to the procedure employed by
33 legislatures in making statutes. The notice of proposed rulemaking corresponds to
34 the bill and the reception of written comments to the hearing on the bill.

35 The common sense of requiring notice and comment rulemaking for legislative
36 rules is well illustrated by the facts of this case. There is no process of cloistered,
37 appellate-court type reasoning by which the Department of Agriculture could have
38 excogitated the eight-foot rule from the structural-strength regulation. The rule is
39 arbitrary in the sense that it could well be different without significant impairment
40 of any regulatory purpose. But this does not make the rule a matter of indifference
41 to the people subject to it. There are thousands of animal dealers, and some
42 unknown fraction of these face the prospect of having to tear down their existing
43 fences and build new, higher ones at great cost. The concerns of these dealers are
44 legitimate and since, as we are stressing, the rule could well be otherwise, the

324

1    agency was obliged to listen to them before settling on a final rule and to provide
2    some justification for that rule, though not so tight or logical a justification as a
3    court would be expected to offer for a new judge-made rule. Notice and comment
4    is the procedure by which the persons affected by legislative rules are enabled to
5    communicate their concerns in a comprehensive and systematic fashion to the
6    legislating agency. The Department's lawyer speculated that if the notice and
7    comment route had been followed in this case the Department would have received
8    thousands of comments. The greater the public interest in a rule, the greater reason
9    to allow the public to participate in its formation.

10    We are not saying that an interpretive rule can never have a numerical component.
11    There is merely an empirical relation between interpretation and generality on the
12    one hand, and legislation and specificity on the other. Especially in scientific and
13    other technical areas, where quantitative criteria are common, a rule that
14    translates a general norm into a number may be justifiable as interpretation. The
15    mine safety agency in the *American Mining* case could refer to established medical
16    criteria, expressed in terms of numerical evaluations of x-rays, for diagnosing
17    black-lung disease. Even in a nontechnical area the use of a number as a rule of
18    thumb to guide the application of a general norm will often be legitimately
19    interpretive. Had the Department of Agriculture said in the internal memorandum
20    that it could not imagine a case in which a perimeter fence for dangerous animals
21    that was lower than eight feet would provide secure containment, and would
22    therefore presume, subject to rebuttal, that a lower fence was insecure, it would
23    have been on stronger ground. For it would have been tying the rule to the
24    animating standard, that of secure containment, rather than making it stand free
25    of the standard, self-contained, unbending, arbitrary. To switch metaphors, the
26    "flatter" a rule is, the harder it is to conceive of it as merely spelling out what is in
27    some sense latent in a statute or regulation, and the eight-foot rule in its present
28    form is as flat as they come. At argument the Department's lawyer tried to loosen
29    up the rule, implying that the Department might have bent it if Hoctor proposed
30    to dig a moat or to electrify his six-foot fence. But an agency's lawyer is not
31    authorized to amend its rules in order to make them more palatable to the
32    reviewing court.

33    The Department's position might seem further undermined by the fact that it has
34    used the notice and comment procedure to promulgate rules prescribing perimeter
35    fences for dogs and monkeys. Why it proceeded differently for dangerous animals
36    is unexplained. But we attach no weight to the Department's inconsistency, not
37    only because it would be unwise to penalize the Department for having at least
38    partially complied with the requirements of the Administrative Procedure Act, but
39    also because there is nothing in the Act to forbid an agency to use the notice and
40    comment procedure in cases in which it is not *required* to do so. * * * The order
41    under review, based as it was on a rule that is invalid because not promulgated in
42    accordance with the required procedure, is therefore

43    Vacated.

1

## Syncor International Corp. v. Shalala

127 F.3d 90 (D.C. Cir. 1997)

October 28, 1997

Before SILBERMAN, ROGERS and TATEL, Circuit Judges.

Opinion for the Court filed by Circuit Judge SILBERMAN.

Appellants Syncor International Corporation, American College of Nuclear Physicians, Society of Nuclear Medicine, and American Pharmaceutical Association (collectively, Syncor) appeal the district court's decision that FDA's 1995 "Notice," entitled "Regulation of Positron Emission Tomography Radiopharmaceutical Drug Products; Guidance; Public Workshop," was a "non-substantive" rule not subject to notice and comment rulemaking. We reverse.

                                    I

Positron emission tomography (PET) is a diagnostic imaging method that uses a subset of radioactive pharmaceuticals, called PET drugs, to determine biochemistry, physiology, anatomy, and pathology within various body organs and tissues by measuring the concentration of radioactivity in a targeted area of the body. The active component of PET drugs is a positron-emitting isotope. This component has a short half-life, so the drug remains effective for only brief periods of time. As a consequence, PET drugs are not manufactured by pharmaceutical companies; instead, they are prepared by physicians and pharmacists operating accelerators in facilities known as nuclear pharmacies, which most often are part of major teaching hospitals or their adjacent universities, and always are located very near to the place where the PET drug will be administered to patients. These nuclear pharmacists compound the isotope with a chemical solution called a substrate. The substrate is used to carry the isotope to the targeted organ or tissue, and the precise solution used depends on the targeted area. For example, a nuclear pharmacist might combine an isotope with a glucose substrate if the brain was being targeted, since the brain is an area of high glucose uptake. In part for this reason, PET drugs are compounded pursuant to a prescription.

On February 25, 1995, FDA announced that PET radiopharmaceuticals "should be regulated" under the drug provisions of the Federal Food, Drug, and Cosmetic Act. In this publication, labeled a "Notice," and referred to alternatively in its text as "guidance" and a "policy statement," FDA indicated that it would require PET "radiopharmaceutical manufacturers" to comply with the adulteration provision * * * ); the misbranding provision * * * ; the new drug provision * * * ; and the registration and listing provisions of the Act * * * .

FDA indicated that its 1995 publication was to supersede its prior 1984 publication—directed at all nuclear pharmacies, not just those compounding PET

326

1 radiopharmaceuticals—entitled "Nuclear Pharmacy Guideline; Criteria for
2 Determining When to Register as a Drug Establishment." The 1984 Guideline had
3 unequivocally stated that nuclear pharmacists who operated an accelerator to
4 produce radioactive drugs to be dispensed under a prescription—which precisely
5 describes the process by which nuclear pharmacies compound PET
6 radiopharmaceuticals—were not required to register under § 510 of the Act. The
7 Guideline also indicated that if a nuclear pharmacist was not required to register,
8 that other of the Act's requirements, including the new drug provision and
9 compliance with current good manufacturing practices, would not apply.

10 Syncor filed suit in the district court challenging FDA's 1995 publication. Syncor
11 brought three claims * * * [including that] FDA violated the Administrative
12 Procedure Act's requirement that an agency engaged in rulemaking give notice of
13 its proposed rulemaking to the public, and "give interested persons an opportunity
14 to participate in the rule making through submission of written data, views, or
15 arguments." The district judge granted summary judgment in FDA's favor on all
16 three claims. We consider the APA claim first since if notice and comment are
17 required we think it prudent to defer deciding the other two issues which
18 presumably would be explored in a future rulemaking.

19                                        II

20 The APA exempts from notice and comment interpretative rules or general
21 statements of policy. Before the district court the FDA characterized its 1995
22 publication as merely "guidance" (a general statement of policy). The district judge
23 disagreed, concluding that it was a rule, but an interpretative one. Here, FDA
24 concedes that the publication is a "rule," and adopts the district court's conclusion.
25 Syncor still contends that the publication is a substantive regulation.

26 We have long recognized that it is quite difficult to distinguish between substantive
27 and interpretative rules. *See American Mining Congress v. Mine Safety & Health*
28 *Admin.*, 995 F.2d 1106, 1108, 1109 (D.C. Cir. 1993). Further confusing the matter
29 is the tendency of courts and litigants to lump interpretative rules and policy
30 statements together in contrast to substantive rules, a tendency to which we have
31 ourselves succumbed on occasion. *See Community Nutrition Inst. v. Young*, 818
32 F.2d 943, 946 (D.C. Cir. 1987). That causes added confusion because interpretative
33 rules and policy statements are quite different agency instruments. An agency
34 policy statement does not seek to impose or elaborate or interpret a legal norm. It
35 merely represents an agency position with respect to how it will treat—typically
36 enforce—the governing legal norm. By issuing a policy statement, an agency simply
37 lets the public know its current enforcement or adjudicatory approach. The agency
38 retains the discretion and the authority to change its position—even abruptly—in
39 any specific case because a change in its policy does not affect the legal norm. We
40 thus have said that policy statements are binding on neither the public, nor the
41 agency. The primary distinction between a substantive rule—really any rule—and
42 a general statement of policy, then, turns on whether an agency intends to bind

1    itself to a particular legal position. *See United States Tel. Ass'n v. FCC*, 28 F.3d
2    1232, 1234 (D.C. Cir. 1994).

3    An interpretative rule, on the other hand, typically reflects an agency's
4    construction of a statute that has been entrusted to the agency to administer. The
5    legal norm is one that Congress has devised; the agency does not purport to modify
6    that norm, in other words, to engage in lawmaking. To be sure, since an agency's
7    interpretation of an ambiguous statute is entitled to judicial deference under
8    *Chevron*, it might be thought that the interpretative rule—particularly if it changes
9    a prior statutory interpretation as an agency may do without notice and comment—
10   is, in reality, a change in the legal norm. Still, in such a situation the agency does
11   not claim to be exercising authority to itself make positive law. Instead, it is
12   construing the product of congressional lawmaking "based on specific statutory
13   provisions." That is why we have said that "[t]he distinction between an
14   interpretative rule and substantive rule . . . likely turns on how tightly the agency's
15   interpretation is drawn linguistically from the actual language of the statute."
16   *Paralyzed Veterans of Am. v. D.C. Arena L.P.*, 117 F.3d 579, 588 (D.C. Cir. 1997).

17                             \* \* \*

18   A substantive rule has characteristics of both the policy statement and the
19   interpretative rule; it is certainly in part an exercise of policy, and it is a rule. But
20   the crucial distinction between it and the other two techniques is that a substantive
21   rule *modifies* or *adds* to a legal norm based on the agency's *own authority*. That
22   authority flows from a congressional delegation to promulgate substantive rules,
23   to engage in supplementary lawmaking. And, it is because the agency is engaged in
24   lawmaking that the APA requires it to comply with notice and comment.

25   It is apparent to us, in light of the foregoing discussion, that FDA's 1995 publication
26   is not an interpretative rule. It does not purport to construe any language in a
27   relevant statute or regulation; it does not interpret anything. Instead, FDA's rule
28   uses wording consistent only with the invocation of its general rulemaking
29   authority to extend its regulatory reach. *See American Mining Congress*, 995 F.2d
30   at 1112. The publication is entitled "*Regulation* of Positron Emission Tomography
31   Radiopharmaceutical Drug Products." In the text, FDA explained that "as [PET]
32   technology has advanced, questions have been raised about the most appropriate
33   approach to *regulation* of PET radiopharmaceuticals." And then FDA stated,
34   "[h]aving considered the available information, including that presented to the
35   agency at the hearing and in written materials, FDA has *concluded* that
36   radiopharmaceuticals should be regulated under the drug provisions of the Federal
37   Food, Drug, and Cosmetic Act."

38   FDA made a careful, considered decision not to exercise the full extent of its
39   regulatory authority—whatever that may be—over nuclear pharmacies in 1984. In
40   its "Nuclear Pharmacy Guideline; Criteria for Determining When to Register as a
41   Drug Establishment," it said that "the criteria for registration as a drug
42   establishment for nuclear pharmacies should be the same as those for traditional

1 pharmacies" under the pharmacy exemption of § 510(g)(1) of the Act. And,
2 therefore, "in a situation where the nuclear pharmacy is operating within
3 applicable local laws regulating the practice of pharmacy and only prepares and
4 dispenses a radioactive drug upon receipt of a 'valid prescription,' the pharmacy
5 exemption clearly applies." Persons who simply operated an accelerator in the
6 course of compounding radioactive drugs to be dispensed under a prescription
7 specifically were found not to be required to register.

8 Syncor tells us, and FDA does not dispute, that PET manufacturers today operate
9 within applicable local laws governing pharmacy, and only prepare and dispense
10 PET radiopharmaceuticals under a prescription, as they did in 1984. FDA does
11 claim that PET technology has advanced and that PET has many more applications
12 today than it did in 1984. And, after "[h]aving considered the available
13 information," FDA has concluded, by way of its challenged rule, that PET
14 manufacturers *should* be regulated." Their activities—which clearly fell within the
15 scope of the regular course of the practice of the profession of pharmacy in 1984—
16 are thought no longer to fall within that scope. This is not a change in
17 interpretation or in enforcement policy, but rather, is fundamentally new
18 regulation. The reasons FDA has advanced for its rule—advancement in PET
19 technology, the expansion of procedures in which PET is used, and the unique
20 nature of PET radiopharmaceuticals—are exactly the sorts of changes in fact and
21 circumstance which notice and comment rulemaking is meant to inform.

22 The FDA nevertheless focuses on *American Mining Congress*, in which,
23 recognizing that an agency often has an option to proceed through *adjudication*,
24 we warned against construing the interpretative rule exception to the APA's notice
25 and comment provisions "so narrowly as to drive agencies into pure [adjudicatory]
26 ad hocery—an ad hocery, moreover, that affords less notice, or less convenient
27 notice, to affected parties." *American Mining Congress*, 995 F.2d at 1112.
28 Accordingly, we identified four factors, any one of which, if present, would identify
29 a supposed interpretative rule as really legislative. The first of those factors, on
30 which FDA concentrates, is whether in the absence of the rule there would not have
31 been "an adequate legislative basis for enforcement action or other agency action
32 to confer benefits or ensure the performance of duties," which is another way of
33 asking whether the disputed rule really adds content to the governing legal norms.

34 The government contends that the rule in question qualifies as an interpretative
35 rule, under that factor, because in the absence of its issuance the government could
36 have proceeded to enforce regulatory requirements against manufacturers of PET
37 drugs. In the past, pursuant to FDA's 1984 Guideline, those requirements were
38 merely "deferred." The government does not clearly explain what it means by
39 "deferred," but seems to suggest that it exercised enforcement discretion in not
40 asserting regulatory authority over appellants until 1995, and therefore simply is
41 reversing that discretionary decision. The obvious difficulty with the government's
42 argument is that it is supportive of a claim that the rule was really a policy
43 statement—a claim which the government abandoned on appeal. As we have said,
44 enforcement discretion is relevant in determining whether an agency intended to

1  bind itself, and therefore, in determining whether a pronouncement is a legislative
2  rule or a general statement of policy, but "tells one little about whether a rule is
3  interpretive." *American Mining Congress*, 995 F.2d at 1111.

4  In any event, we think the government misreads *American Mining Congress*. We
5  never suggested in that case that a rule that does not purport to interpret *any*
6  language in a statute or regulation could be thought an interpretative rule. We do
7  not have to decide, therefore, whether FDA could have succeeded in an
8  enforcement proceeding against a nuclear pharmacy that was operating pursuant
9  to the 1984 Guideline, under the secure impression that their activities were totally
10 unregulated (although we find it hard to imagine the government facing a
11 hospitable reception in any federal district court). We think it a kindness also to
12 say that we doubt that the government would have done any better in this case to
13 have relied on the policy statement exception on appeal. The 1995 publication is as
14 far removed from the typical policy statement as it is from an interpretative rule; it
15 drew a boundary to the agency's regulatory reach.

16 Accordingly, we reverse and remand to the district court with instructions to enter
17 summary judgment in Syncor's favor, and to vacate FDA's rule as not in accordance
18 with law. * * *

19

20      c.  <u>Statements of Policy</u>

21 **Pacific Gas and Electric Company v. Federal Power Commission**

22 506 F.2d 33 (D.C. Cir. 1974)

23 June 26, 1974

24 Before BAZELON, Chief Judge, and MacKINNON, Circuit Judge, and A.
25 SHERMAN CHRISTENSEN,* United States Senior District Judge for the District
26 of Utah.

27 MacKINNON, Circuit Judge:

28 Petitioners assert that we have jurisdiction under section 19(b) of the Natural Gas
29 Act to review Order No. 467, which the Federal Power Commission issued on
30 January 8, 1973. Order No. 467 is a 'Statement of Policy' on 'priorities-of-deliveries
31 by jurisdictional pipelines during periods of curtailment' which the Commission
32 indicated it proposes to implement in all matters arising under the Act. The
33 petitioning customers of pipeline companies, whose deliveries are subject to
34 curtailment during natural gas shortages, contend that Order No. 467 is
35 procedurally defective for failure to comply with the Administrative Procedure Act
36 * * * .

37 We hold that as a general statement of policy, Order No. 467 is exempt from the
38 rulemaking requirements of the Administrative Procedure Act. * * *

330

1 I. Background

2 This country appears to be experiencing a natural gas shortage which necessitates
3 the curtailment of supplies to certain customers during peak demand periods. The
4 problem confronting many pipeline companies is whether to curtail on the basis of
5 existing contractual commitments or on the basis of the most efficient end use of
6 the gas. In some instances the pipeline companies are concerned that withholding
7 gas due under existing contracts may subject them to civil liability.

8 Recognizing these uncertainties and mindful of the desirability of providing
9 uniform curtailment regulation, the FPC in 1971 issued a Statement of General
10 Policy in the form of Order No. 431 directing jurisdictional pipeline companies
11 which expected periods of shortages to file tariff sheets containing a curtailment
12 plan. Order No. 431 hinted that curtailment priorities should be based on the end
13 use of the gas and stated that curtailment plans approved by the Commission "will
14 control in all respects notwithstanding inconsistent provisions in [prior] sales
15 contracts . . . ." In response to Order No. 431, numerous pipeline companies which
16 had not already done so submitted a variety of curtailment plans for the
17 Commission's approval. As could be expected, the curtailment plans reflected a
18 wide range of views as to the proper priorities for delivery. Some plans were based
19 on end use; others, on contract entitlements. The industry was forced to speculate
20 as to which priorities would later be found to be just and reasonable by the
21 Commission, and the absence of any stated Commission policy hindered effective
22 long range planning by pipelines, distributors and consumers.

23 Sensing a need for guidance and uniformity in the curtailment area, on January 8,
24 1973 the Commission promulgated Order No. 467, the order presently under
25 review * * * . Entitled "Statement of Policy," Order No. 467 was issued without
26 prior notice or opportunity for comment. The statement sets forth the
27 Commission's view of a proper priority schedule and expresses the Commission's
28 policy that the national interest would be best served by assigning curtailment
29 priorities on the basis of end use rather than on the basis of prior contractual
30 commitments. Order No. 467 further states the Commission's intent to follow this
31 priority schedule unless a particular pipeline company demonstrates that a
32 different curtailment plan is more in the public interest. * * *

33 * * *

34 Petitioners seek review of Order No. 467 in this court under section 19(b) of the
35 Natural Gas Act and advance the following * * * argument * * * : that Order No.
36 467 is in effect a substantive rule which the Commission should have promulgated
37 after a rulemaking proceeding under the Administrative Procedure Act (APA) * * *
38 .

39 II. Statements of Policy

40 * * *

1   The APA never defines "general statements of policy" but it does define "rule" to

2   "[mean] the whole or a part of an agency statement of general or particular
3   applicability and future effect designed to implement, interpret, or
4   prescribe law or policy or describing the organization, procedure, or
5   practice requirements of an agency . . . ."

6   5 U.S.C. § 551(4). This broad definition obviously could be read literally to
7   encompass virtually any utterance by an agency, including statements of general
8   policy. But the statutory provision of an exception to the rulemaking requirements
9   for "general statements of policy" indicates that Congress did not intend the
10  definition of "rule" to be construed so broadly. Congress recognized that certain
11  administrative pronouncements did not require public participation in their
12  formulation. These types of pronouncements are listed in section 553(b)(A) and
13  include "general statements of policy."

14  Professor Davis has described the distinction between substantive rules and
15  general statements of policy as a "fuzzy product." Unfortunately the issues in this
16  case compel us to attempt to define the fuzzy perimeters of a general statement of
17  policy.

18  An administrative agency has available two methods for formulating policy that
19  will have the force of law. An agency may establish binding policy through
20  rulemaking procedures by which it promulgates substantive rules, or through
21  adjudications which constitute binding precedents. A general statement of policy
22  is the outcome of neither a rulemaking nor an adjudication; it is neither a rule nor
23  a precedent but is merely an announcement to the public of the policy which the
24  agency hopes to implement in future rulemakings or adjudications. A general
25  statement of policy, like a press release, presages an upcoming rulemaking or
26  announces the course which the agency intends to follow in future adjudications.

27  As an informational device, the general statement of policy serves several
28  beneficial functions. By providing a formal method by which an agency can express
29  its views, the general statement of policy encourages public dissemination of the
30  agency's policies prior to their actual application in particular situations. Thus the
31  agency's initial views do not remain secret but are disclosed well in advance of their
32  actual application. Additionally, the publication of a general statement of policy
33  facilitates long range planning within the regulated industry and promotes
34  uniformity in areas of national concern.

35  The critical distinction between a substantive rule and a general statement of policy
36  is the different practical effect that these two types of pronouncements have in
37  subsequent administrative proceedings. A properly adopted substantive rule
38  establishes a standard of conduct which has the force of law. In subsequent
39  administrative proceedings involving a substantive rule, the issues are whether the
40  adjudicated facts conform to the rule and whether the rule should be waived or
41  applied in that particular instance. The underlying policy embodied in the rule is
42  not generally subject to challenge before the agency.

1 A general statement of policy, on the other hand, does not establish a "binding
2 norm." It is not finally determinative of the issues or rights to which it is addressed.
3 The agency cannot apply or rely upon a general statement of policy as law because
4 a general statement of policy only announces what the agency seeks to establish as
5 policy. A policy statement announces the agency's tentative intentions for the
6 future. When the agency applies the policy in a particular situation, it must be
7 prepared to support the policy just as if the policy statement had never been issued.
8 An agency cannot escape its responsibility to present evidence and reasoning
9 supporting its substantive rules by announcing binding precedent in the form of a
10 general statement of policy.

11 Often the agency's own characterization of a particular order provides some
12 indication of the nature of the announcement. The agency's express purpose may
13 be to establish a binding rule of law not subject to challenge in particular cases. On
14 the other hand the agency may intend merely to publish a policy guideline that is
15 subject to complete attack before it is finally applied in future cases. When the
16 agency states that in subsequent proceedings it will thoroughly consider not only
17 the policy's applicability to the facts of a given case but also the underlying validity
18 of the policy itself, then the agency intends to treat the order as a general statement
19 of policy.

20 * * *

21 The tentative effect of a general statement of policy has ramifications in
22 subsequent judicial review proceedings as well as in administrative proceedings.
23 Because a general statement of policy is adopted without public participation, the
24 scope of review may be broader than the scope of review for a substantive rule. The
25 rulemaking process prescribed by the APA insures a thorough exploration of the
26 relevant issues. The public is notified of the proposed rule and interested parties
27 submit arguments supporting their positions. The rulemaking process culminates
28 in the agency applying its experience and expertise to the issues. A court reviewing
29 a rule that was adopted pursuant to this extensive rulemaking process will defer to
30 the agency's judgment if the rule satisfies the minimal criterion of reasonableness.

31 But when an agency promulgates a general statement of policy, the agency does
32 not have the benefit of public exploration of the issues. Judicial review may be the
33 first stage at which the policy is subjected to full criticism by interested parties.
34 Consequently a policy judgment expressed as a general statement of policy is
35 entitled to less deference than a decision expressed as a rule or an adjudicative
36 order. Although the agency's expertise and experience cannot be ignored, the
37 reviewing court has some leeway to assess the underlying wisdom of the policy and
38 need not affirm a general statement of policy that merely satisfies the test of
39 reasonableness.

40 Applying these general principles to the problem at hand, we conclude that Order
41 No. 467 is a general statement of policy. Order No. 467 is entitled and consistently
42 referred to by the Commission as a general statement of policy. Recognizing the

1  "need for Commission guidance in curtailment planning," the Commission
2  announced in Order No. 467 the curtailment policy which it "proposes to
3  implement," the "plan preferred by the Commission" which "will serve as a guide
4  in other proceedings." Thus, the stated purpose of Order No. 467 was not to
5  provide an inflexible, binding rule but to give advance notice of the general policy
6  with respect to curtailment priorities that the Commission prefers.

7  Order No. 467 does not establish a curtailment plan for any particular pipeline.
8  The effect of the order is to inform the public of the types of plans which will receive
9  initial and tentative FPC approval, but there is no assurance that any such plan will
10 be finally approved. As the Commission stated:

11     "When applied in specific cases, opportunity will be afforded interested
12     parties to challenge or support this policy through factual or legal
13     presentation as may be appropriate in the circumstances presented."

14 49 F.P.C. at 85.

15     "[Order No. 467 is] not finally determinative of the rights and duties of a
16     given pipeline, its customers or ultimate consumers; it expressly envisions
17     further proceedings."

18 49 F.P.C. at 585.

19                              * * *

20 The FPC of course was under no compulsion to issue Order No. 467. The
21 Commission issued the policy statement because the curtailment plans being
22 submitted reflected sharp differences in philosophy which necessitated
23 Commission guidance in the curtailment area. In the absence of such a policy
24 statement, the Commission could have proceeded on an ad hoc basis and
25 tentatively approved curtailment plans filed under section 4 of the Act which the
26 Commission found to be just and reasonable. In following such a course the only
27 difference from the present situation would be that the Commission would be
28 acting under a secret policy rather than under the publicized guidelines of Order
29 No. 467. The argument that an agency must follow rulemaking procedures when it
30 elects to formulate policy by a substantive rule has no application in this case.
31 Order No. 467 does not establish a substantive rule. Although the Commission is
32 free to initiate a rulemaking proceeding to establish a binding substantive rule, the
33 Commission apparently intends to establish its curtailment policies by proceeding
34 through individual adjudications. Order No. 467 merely announces the general
35 policy which the Commission hopes to establish in subsequent proceedings.

36                              * * *

37 We conclude that Order No. 467 is a general statement of policy and that it was
38 therefore unnecessary for the Commission to conduct rulemaking proceedings
39 under the Administrative Procedure Act.

1            * * *

2    The petitions for review are therefore dismissed.

3    Judgment accordingly.

4

5    **Community Nutrition Institute v. Young**

6    818 F.2d 943 (D.C. Cir 1987)

7    May 15, 1987.

8    Before MIKVA, EDWARDS and STARR, Circuit Judges.

9    PER CURIAM:

10   This case makes its second appearance before this court. It presents a challenge by
11   a consortium of organizations and private citizens (collectively referred to as CNI)
12   to the Food and Drug Administration's regulation of certain unavoidable
13   contaminants in food, most particularly, aflatoxins in corn. Pursuant to its
14   statutory mandate to limit the amount of "poisonous or deleterious substances" in
15   food FDA establishes "action levels" informing food producers of the allowable
16   levels of unavoidable contaminants such as aflatoxins. Producers who sell products
17   that are contaminated above the action level, which for aflatoxins in corn is
18   currently set at 20 parts per billion, are subject to enforcement proceedings
19   initiated by FDA.

20   CNI filed suit in federal district court, launching a three-pronged attack on FDA's
21   action level for aflatoxins in corn: (1) in issuing the action level, FDA failed to
22   comply with the rulemaking requirements of the Food, Drug and Cosmetic Act
23   (FDC Act), (2) the action level violated the Administrative Procedure Act because
24   it constitutes a legislative rule issued without the requisite notice-and-comment
25   procedures, and (3) FDA's decision to permit adulterated corn to be blended with
26   unadulterated corn to bring the total contamination within the action level violated
27   the FDC Act. The District Court granted summary judgment in favor of FDA on
28   each issue.

29           * * *

30           I

31   Under the APA, agency rules may be issued only after the familiar notice-and-
32   comment procedures enumerated in the statute are completed. See 5 U.S.C. § 553.
33   It is undisputed that the action level at issue here was promulgated *sans* those
34   procedures. FDA, however, argues that notice-and-comment requirements do not
35   apply by virtue of subsection (b)(3)(A) of section 553, which carves out an
36   exception for "interpretative rules [and] general statements of policy." According
37   to the FDA, action levels represent nothing more than nonbinding statements of

1 agency enforcement policy. CNI, on the other hand, argues that the action levels
2 restrict enforcement discretion to such a degree as to constitute legislative rules.

3 The distinction between legislative rules and interpretative rules or policy
4 statements has been described at various times as "tenuous," "fuzzy," "blurred,"
5 and, perhaps most picturesquely, "enshrouded in considerable smog." As
6 Professor Davis puts it, "the problem is baffling." 2 K. Davis, *Administrative Law*
7 *Treatise* 32 (2d ed. 1979). By virtue of Congress' silence with respect to this matter,
8 it has fallen to the courts to discern the line through the painstaking exercise of,
9 hopefully, sound judgment.

10 Despite the difficulty of the terrain, prior cases do provide some useful guideposts.
11 In this circuit, we are particularly guided by *American Bus Ass'n v. United States*,
12 627 F.2d 625 (D.C. Cir. 1980). There, in speaking for the court, JUDGE McGOWAN
13 identified "two criteria" that courts have used in their efforts to fathom the
14 interpretative/legislative distinction:

15     First, courts have said that, unless a pronouncement acts prospectively, it
16     is a binding norm. Thus . . . a statement of policy may not have a present
17     effect: "a 'general statement of policy' is one that does not impose any rights
18     and obligations" . . . .

19     The second criterion is whether a purported policy statement genuinely
20     leaves the agency and its decisionmakers free to exercise discretion.

21 627 F.2d at 529 (quoting *Texaco v. FPC*, 412 F.2d 740, 744 (3d Cir.1969)).

22 In conducting our analysis of these two criteria, we consider and give some, albeit
23 "not overwhelming," deference to an agency's characterization of its statement. As
24 befits a principled exercise in interpretation, courts are to give far greater weight
25 to the language actually used by the agency; we have, for example, found decisive
26 the choice between the words "will" and "may." Compare *American Bus*, 627 F.2d
27 at 532 (use of "will" indicates statement is in fact a binding norm) with *Guardian*
28 *Federal*, 589 F.2d at 666 (use of "may" indicates statement is a "general statement
29 of policy").

30 Applying these principles to the case at hand, we are persuaded that the FDA action
31 levels are legislative rules and thus subject to the notice-and-comment
32 requirements of section 553. While FDA now characterizes the action levels as
33 policy statements, a variety of factors, when considered in light of the criteria set
34 out in *American Bus*, indicate otherwise.

35 *First*. The language employed by FDA in creating and describing action levels
36 suggests that those levels both have a present effect and are binding. Specifically,
37 the agency's regulations on action levels explain an action level in the following
38 way:

39     [A]n action level for an added poisonous or deleterious substance . . . may
40     be established to define the level of contamination at which food *will be*

336

1 *deemed to be adulterated.* An action level *may prohibit any detectable*
2 *amount of substance in food.*

3 21 C.F.R. § 109.4 (1986) (emphasis added). This language, speaking as it does of
4 an action level "defin[ing]" the acceptable level and "prohibit[ing]" substances,
5 clearly reflects an interpretation of action levels as presently binding norms. This
6 type of mandatory, definitive language is a powerful, even potentially dispositive,
7 factor suggesting that action levels are substantive rules. * * *

8 *Second.* This view of action levels—as having a present, binding effect—is
9 confirmed by the fact that FDA considers it necessary for food producers to secure
10 *exceptions* to the action levels. A specific regulatory provision allows FDA to
11 "exempt from regulatory action and permit the marketing of any food that is
12 unlawfully contaminated with a poisonous or deleterious substance" if certain
13 conditions exist. *Id.* § 109.8(a). This language implies that in the absence of an
14 exemption, food with aflatoxin contamination over the action level is "unlawful."
15 This putatively unlawful status can derive only from the action level, which, again,
16 indicates that the action level is a presently binding norm. If, as the agency would
17 have it, action levels did indeed "not bind courts, food producers or FDA," it would
18 scarcely be necessary to require that "exceptions" be obtained.

19 *Third.* On several occasions, in authorizing blending of adulterated with
20 unadulterated corn, the FDA has made statements indicating that action levels
21 establish a binding form. For example, in a telegram to the Commissioner of the
22 South Carolina Department of Agriculture, in which it indicated its approval of a
23 blending plan, the FDA stated that "[a]ny shipments made independent of this
24 plan *would*, if found to exceed the 20 ppb level, *be considered adulterated and*
25 *subject to* condemnation." . But we need not resort to informal communications,
26 where precision of draftsmanship may understandably be wanting. For, in a formal
27 notice published in the Federal Register of a decision to permit blending and
28 interstate shipment, FDA wrote:

29 "Any food that contains aflatoxin in excess of 20 ppb . . . *is considered by*
30 *FDA to be adulterated* under section 402(a)(1) of the Federal Food, Drug,
31 and Cosmetic Act, and *therefore may not be shipped in interstate*
32 *commerce.*"

33 46 Fed.Reg. 7447 (1981) (emphasis added). Both statements, one informal and the
34 other elaborately formal, indicate that, when judged under the *American Bus*
35 criteria, action levels constitute substantive rules. The agency's own words strongly
36 suggest that action levels are not musings about what the FDA might do in the
37 future but rather that they set a precise level of aflatoxin contamination that FDA
38 has presently deemed permissible. Action levels inform food producers what this
39 level is; indeed, that is their very purpose.

40 We are not unmindful that in a suit to enjoin shipment of allegedly contaminated
41 corn, it appears that FDA would be obliged to prove that the corn is "adulterated,"
42 within the meaning of the FDC Act, rather than merely prove non-compliance with

337

1   the action level. The action level thus does not bind food producers in the sense
2   that producers are automatically subject to enforcement proceedings for violating
3   the action level. This factor, accordingly, points in favor of the agency's
4   characterization. But the fact that action levels do not completely bind food
5   producers as would a more classic legislative rule (where the only issue before the
6   court would be if the agency rule were in fact violated) is not determinative of the
7   issue. For here, we are convinced that FDA has bound itself. As FDA conceded at
8   oral argument, it would be daunting indeed to try to convince a court that the
9   agency could appropriately prosecute a producer for shipping corn with less than
10   20 ppb aflatoxin. And this type of cabining of an agency's prosecutorial discretion
11   can in fact rise to the level of a substantive, legislative rule. That is exactly what has
12   happened here.

13                                  \* \* \*

14                                  III

15   In conclusion, we find FDA's action levels to be invalid in that they were issued
16   without the requisite notice-and-comment procedures, but we reject CNI's
17   challenge to FDA's disinclination to initiate enforcement action against certain
18   blended corn. Accordingly, the case is remanded to the District Court for further
19   proceedings not inconsistent with this opinion.

20   *It is so ordered.*

21   STARR, Circuit Judge, concurring in part and dissenting in part:

22   I fully concur in section II of the panel opinion, holding that FDA's decision to
23   permit blending fell within the agency's enforcement discretion. I am also
24   persuaded that the majority's careful treatment of the substantive rules-policy
25   statements distinction is not unfaithful to the teachings of this circuit's more recent
26   precedents. Nonetheless, I am constrained to conclude that the correct rule was
27   that laid down by our court thirteen years ago in *Pacific Gas & Electric Co. v. FPC*,
28   where we held:

29       "The critical distinction between a substantive rule and a general statement
30       of policy is the different practical effect that these two types of
31       pronouncements have in subsequent administrative proceedings. . . . A
32       properly adopted substantive rule establishes a standard of conduct which
33       has the force of law."

34   506 F.2d 33, 38 (D.C. Cir. 1974). The *Pacific Gas*-enunciated factor—whether the
35   pronouncement has the force of law in subsequent proceedings—should be
36   deemed determinative of the issue. Because there is no doubt that the agency
37   pronouncements at issue here have no such effect, I respectfully dissent from
38   section I of the panel opinion.

39                                    I

1　The abiding characteristic of a legislative rule is that it is law. It defines a standard
2　of conduct that regulated individuals or entities ignore at their peril, in the face of
3　possible enforcement action. Significantly, the only issue in any such proceeding is
4　whether the rule applies to the facts at hand. "The underlying policy embodied in
5　the rule is not generally subject to challenge before the agency." *Id.*, at 38.

6　Before such rules are sanctioned one would think that they should be carefully
7　crafted, with the "underlying polic[ies] embodied in the rule" recognized, openly
8　discussed, and deliberately weighed. To return to basic civics for a moment,
9　statutes passed by Congress have been refined in this manner by the very nature of
10　the legislative process. Bills are considered by committees, hearings are held,
11　debate is conducted, compromises are reached, and votes are taken. And all this is
12　carried on in a bicameral legislative body with the final result presented to the
13　President for his approval or rejection. A statute therefore possesses important
14　attributes justifying placement of the coercive power of the state behind a
15　particular policy framed in accordance with the process ordained at the Founding.

16　In the modern administrative state, many "laws" emanate not from Congress but
17　from administrative agencies, inasmuch as Congress has seen fit to vest broad
18　rulemaking power in the executive branch, including independent agencies. This
19　rulemaking power is obviously cabined by whatever requirements may exist in the
20　particular statute delegating rulemaking authority, a subject which we treated in
21　our initial decision in this case. But Congress has also provided in the APA for
22　certain procedural protections before that which achieves the lofty status of "law"
23　is promulgated by an agency acting in its Congressionally authorized lawmaking
24　capacity. Chief among these protections are the notice-and-comment
25　requirements laid down in the familiar provision of 5 U.S.C. § 553. In a sense,
26　notice-and-comment procedures serve as a Congressionally mandated proxy for
27　the procedures which Congress itself employs in fashioning its "rules," as it were,
28　thereby insuring that agency "rules" are also carefully crafted (with democratic
29　values served by public participation) and developed only after assessment of
30　relevant considerations. It is thus, in theory, important for APA procedures to be
31　followed before an agency pronouncement is deemed a binding legislative rule not
32　merely because the APA says so, but because in saying so the APA is protecting a
33　free people from the danger of coercive state power undergirding pronouncements
34　that lack the essential attributes of deliberativeness present in statutes. Because of
35　the value inhering in such procedures, it is well-established that "only reluctantly
36　should courts recognize exceptions therefrom."

37　Nonetheless, in crafting the APA, Congress directed that courts should recognize
38　certain exceptions to the statute's notice-and-comment requirements. Specifically,
39　Congress recognized that not all agency pronouncements, even those of
40　considerable moment, rise to the dignity of law. Thus, the APA excepts, as the panel
41　opinion recounts, interpretative rules and general statements of policy from the
42　general notice-and-comment requirements. While it is no doubt true, and indeed
43　is frequently recognized, that such agency pronouncements may have a direct
44　effect on the regulated community, and may even be judicially reviewable, these

1 pronouncements still lack the dignity of "law." Before that status can be achieved,
2 the agency must run its policies through the notice-and-comment gantlet. Perhaps
3 in part because the agency here has avoided testing its pronouncements in this
4 way, it must in any future proceeding defend and justify its chosen standard in the
5 face of a challenge to that standard.

6                                       II

7 The majority is quite correct when it chronicles the difficulty courts have found in
8 attempting to fathom the distinction between legislative or substantive rules on
9 one hand, and interpretative rules or policy statements on the other. Inasmuch as
10 our decisional law over the last decade avowedly reflects considerable uncertainty
11 in discerning the line between agency pronouncements that are "law" and those
12 that are "policy," it seems advisable to return to the pristine teaching of *Pacific
13 Gas*. In that case, this court articulated a rule which is clearly preferable to the
14 present muddy state of the law. The wisdom of the *Pacific Gas* principle is in no
15 small measure found in the fact that the case reflects the "core principles" which I
16 sought briefly to adumbrate in the preceding section of this opinion. As I read the
17 case, *Pacific Gas* deems as "critical" the effect of the agency pronouncement in
18 future proceedings. This is as it should be, for as I discussed above, it is this
19 element that is the essence of "law." Not only is the *Pacific Gas* approach therefore
20 the most principled manner in which to draw the legislative-interpretative line (in
21 view of the fact that the determination is whether a pronouncement is "law" or
22 not), but it has the not insignificant practical benefit in an unclear world of
23 providing great clarity where previously there has been "considerable smog."

24 We should reembrace our *Pacific Gas* test as the determinative factor in analyzing
25 whether a particular pronouncement is legislative or interpretative in nature. If the
26 pronouncement has the force of law in future proceedings, it is a legislative rule.
27 Unless that critical feature is present, however, the agency statement should be
28 considered to be a lower form of pronouncement, a "non-law" as it were, or in APA
29 terms an "interpretative rule" or "general statement of policy." The correct
30 measure of a pronouncement's force in subsequent proceedings is a practical one:
31 must the agency merely show that the pronouncement has been violated or must
32 the agency, if its hand is called, show that the pronouncement itself is justified in
33 light of the underlying statute and the facts.

34 Application of this test can readily be illustrated by the case at hand. Action levels
35 offer guidance to the regulated community with respect to what products FDA
36 deems adulterated within the meaning of the FDC Act. But in an enforcement
37 proceeding in which FDA seeks either to impose sanctions for shipment of an
38 adulterated product or to enjoin shipment of an adulterated product, the agency
39 must prove the product is "adulterated." That is, FDA cannot merely show that the
40 product at issue fails to comply with the action level. Rather, FDA must offer
41 scientific or other probative evidence to support its contention that the product is
42 adulterated. Thus, the action level does not have the force of law in the subsequent
43 proceeding. Indeed, it has no "force" at all.

1                                \* \* \*

2

## 3 United States Telephone Association v. Federal Communications
## 4 Commission

5   28 F.3d 1232 (D.C. Cir. 1994)

6   July 12, 1994

7   Before: WALD, SILBERMAN, and HENDERSON, Circuit Judges.

8   SILBERMAN, Circuit Judge:

9   The Commission issued, without notice and comment, a schedule of base penalties
10  and adjustments to determine the appropriate fines for violations of the
11  Communications Act. We conclude that the penalty schedule is not a policy
12  statement and, therefore, should have been put out for comment under the
13  Administrative Procedure Act.

14                                I

15  Section 503(b) of the Communications Act authorizes the FCC to impose
16  "monetary forfeitures" (fines) on licensees for violations of the Act or of regulations
17  promulgated thereunder \* \* \* . The statute provides a maximum fine schedule in
18  accordance with classification of licensee: $25,000 for broadcasters and cable
19  television operators, $100,000 for common carriers (such as telephone
20  companies), and $10,000 for other service providers. For each day of a continuing
21  violation, the Commission may assess up to $250,000 for broadcasters,
22  $1,000,000 for common carriers, and $75,000 for others.

23  The FCC decided in 1991 to abandon its traditional case-by-case approach to
24  implementing section 503(b) and issued an order to "adopt more specific
25  standards for assessing forfeitures." *Standards for Assessing Forfeitures*, 6
26  F.C.C.R. 4695 (1991), *revised*, 8 F.C.C.R. 6215 (1993). The forfeiture standards, set
27  forth in a schedule appended to its order, contemplate a base forfeiture amount for
28  each type of violation, which amount is calculated as a percentage (varying on the
29  violation) of the statutory maxima for the different services. Thus, the base
30  forfeiture amount for false distress communications is 80% of the statutory
31  maxima: *i.e.*, $20,000 per violation for broadcasters, $80,000 for common
32  carriers, and $8,000 for others. The FCC asserted that setting the base amounts as
33  a percentage of the maximum fines permitted by Congress for each category of
34  licensee best furthered the goals of the statute. The fines schedule also provides for
35  adjustments to the base amount depending on various aggravating or mitigating
36  factors. The base amount, for instance, is increased 20-50% for "substantial
37  economic gain" and reduced 30-60% for "good faith or voluntary disclosure."

1 Petitioner, a trade group of telephone companies that unsuccessfully sought
2 reconsideration before the agency, * * * claims that the Commission violated the
3 Administrative Procedure Act by issuing the standards without notice and an
4 opportunity to comment. * * *

5 II

6 * * *

7 The Commission claims that the standards are only general statements of policy
8 exempt from the notice and comment obligation that the APA imposes on the
9 adoption of substantive rules. The distinction between the two types of agency
10 pronouncements has not proved an easy one to draw, but we have said repeatedly
11 that it turns on an agency's intention to bind itself to a particular legal policy
12 position. The Commission, mindful of this precedent, labeled the standards as a
13 policy statement and reiterated 12 times that it retained discretion to depart from
14 the standards in specific applications.

15 The difficulty we see in the Commission's position is that the appendix affixed to
16 the short "policy statement" sets forth a detailed schedule of penalties applicable
17 to specific infractions as well as the appropriate adjustments for particular
18 situations. It is rather hard to imagine an agency wishing to publish such an
19 exhaustive framework for sanctions if it did not intend to use that framework to
20 cabin its discretion. Indeed, no agency to our knowledge has ever claimed that such
21 a schedule of fines was a policy statement. It simply does not fit the paradigm of a
22 policy statement, namely, an indication of an agency's current position on a
23 particular regulatory issue.

24 Although sometimes we face the difficulty of reviewing a statement before it has
25 been applied and therefore are unsure whether the agency intends to be bound,
26 that is not so in this case. The schedule of fines has been employed in over 300
27 cases and only in 8 does the Commission even claim that it departed from the
28 schedule. In three cases, the Commission maintains that it did not apply the
29 guidelines at all to certain violations of a new tariff-filing requirement. That,
30 however, is a mischaracterization. * * * The most that could be said about these
31 cases is that the Commission exercised enforcement discretion *not to prosecute*—
32 but adhered to the standards when it calculated the penalties that would have
33 applied had it prosecuted.

34 In *Cargo Vessel Kodiak Enterprise*, 7 F.C.C.R. 1847 (1992), the Commission
35 ordered a forfeiture of $50,000 where strict application of the standards would
36 have amounted to $155,000. The reason given, however, was that " [w]hen an
37 inspection certificate expires while a vessel is at sea, our policy is not to assess a
38 forfeiture for the period between the expiration of the certificate and the vessel's
39 arrival in port." 7 F.C.C.R. at 1848. The deviation thus resulted not from relaxation
40 of the standards but again from a non-prosecution policy independent of the
41 standards—that under certain conditions no fines at all, however they are
42 calculated, will attach. In three other cases, the Commission applied the base

342

1 amounts under the forfeiture standards but did not insist on upward adjustments.
2 That the Commission deviated from a minor portion of the standards, while
3 probative, does not vitiate its adherence to the schedule of base amounts.

4 The Commission is left to rely on a single opinion, *James Scott Martin*, 7 F.C.C.R.
5 3524 (1992), in which it noted that under the standards, the base forfeiture amount
6 would have been $8000. "Under the circumstances of this case," however, the
7 Commission imposed a fine of $1000. The decision admittedly is ambiguous as to
8 whether the Commission applied downward adjustment criteria under the
9 standards (which, petitioner contends, could yield a $1000 bottom line) or
10 exercised independent discretion in reaching that amount. But even if we resolved
11 the ambiguity in the Commission's favor, that would mean that the Commission
12 exercised discretion in only one out of over 300 cases, which is little support for
13 the Commission's assertion that it intended not to be bound by the forfeiture
14 standards.

15 If there were any doubt as to the nature of the standards—and we do not think
16 there is—the Commission's own Common Carrier Bureau in *David L.*
17 *Hollingsworth*, 7 F.C.C.R. 6640 (Com. Car. Bur. 1992) supported petitioner's
18 argument by refusing to consider a claim that the fine set forth in the schedule was
19 inequitable as applied to a particular respondent. The Bureau responded to this
20 challenge to the substance of the policy statement by asserting that the argument
21 "should have been raised in a petition by [respondent] for reconsideration of the
22 Policy Statement." *Id*. That certainly indicates that the Bureau thought the "Policy
23 Statement" was a rule in masquerade. For " [w]hen the agency applies the policy
24 in a particular situation, it must be prepared to support the policy just as if the
25 policy statement had never been issued." *Pacific Gas & Elec. Co. v. Federal Power*
26 *Comm'n*, 506 F.2d 33, 38 (D.C. Cir. 1974). Otherwise, a party would not be able to
27 challenge the policy either when issued as a statement or when applied in an
28 individual case. Indeed, the Commission rejected petitioner USTA's petition for
29 reconsideration of the standards:

30     "In light of the fact that the *Policy Statement* simply provides some general
31     guidance that may be used in particular cases, we believe such concerns are
32     more appropriately addressed in the context of specific cases. Accordingly,
33     we will not address such implementation matters here." 7 F.C.C.R. at 5340.

34 It seems that the Commissioner has sought to accomplish the agency hat trick—
35 avoid defense of its policy at any stage. To be sure, the Commission disavows the
36 Bureau's opinion, suggesting that if review to the full Commission had been
37 sought, *Hollingsworth* would have been decided somewhat differently. But the
38 Bureau's decision is certainly a powerful indication that the Commission's own
39 staff thought the schedule of fines was intended to bind, no matter what "policy
40 statement" clothing it wore.

41 The Commission appears to wish to avoid grappling with the issue which we noted
42 at the outset is quite vexing—whether the disparate treatment of different classes

of licensees in the forfeiture schedule is reasonable and authorized under the statute. Neither in a direct challenge to the policy nor in an individual enforcement proceeding, according to the Commission, would common carriers be entitled to claim that their treatment visa-vis broadcasters or other licensees is arbitrary. Not in the former because the policy statement is supposedly not binding, and not in the latter because the conceptual framework for the schedule of fines—at least the comparison between the base levels for different classes of licensees—is somehow not germane in an individual case. That simply will not do. The FCC cannot determine that common carriers as a class will pay heavier fines than other licensees and not explain their reasons for that position or subject that explanation to judicial review. The Commission will, thus, have to put its proposed position out for comment and be prepared to justify whatever rule it fashions to the public and, if necessary, to the judiciary.

Accordingly, we grant the petition for review and set aside the forfeiture standards.

*So ordered.*

### d.  Good Cause

5 U.S.C. § 553(b)(3)(B) broadly provides that notice and comment are not required "when the agency for good cause finds . . . [notice and comment] are impracticable, unnecessary, or contrary to the public interest." What counts as a good cause?

## Mack Trucks, Inc. v. EPA

682 F.3d 87 (D.C. Cir. 2012)

June 12, 2012

Before: SENTELLE, Chief Judge, BROWN and GRIFFITH, Circuit Judges.

BROWN, Circuit Judge: In January 2012, EPA promulgated an interim final rule (IFR) to permit manufacturers of heavy-duty diesel engines to pay nonconformance penalties (NCPs) in exchange for the right to sell noncompliant engines. EPA took this action without providing formal notice or an opportunity for comment, invoking the "good cause" exception provided in the Administrative Procedure Act (APA). Because we find that none of the statutory criteria for "good cause" are satisfied, we vacate the IFR.

I

In 2001, pursuant to Section 202 of the Clean Air Act ("the Act"), EPA enacted a rule requiring a 95 percent reduction in the emissions of nitrogen oxide from heavy-duty diesel engines. 66 Fed. Reg. 5,002 (Jan. 18, 2001). By delaying the effective date until 2010, EPA gave industry nine years to innovate the necessary new technologies. *Id.* at 5,010. (EPA and manufacturers refer to the rule as the "2010 NOx standard." 77 Fed. Reg. 4,678, 4,681 (Jan. 31, 2012).) During those nine years, most manufacturers of heavy-duty diesel engines, including Petitioners, invested hundreds of millions of dollars to develop a technology called "selective catalytic reduction." This technology converts nitrogen oxide into nitrogen and water by using a special aftertreatment system and a diesel-based chemical agent. With selective catalytic reduction, manufacturers have managed to meet the 2010 NOx standard.

One manufacturer, Navistar, took a different approach. For its domestic sales, Navistar opted for a form of "exhaust gas recirculation," but this technology proved less successful; Navistar's engines do not meet the 2010 NOx standard. All else being equal, Navistar would therefore be unable to sell these engines in the United States—unless, of course, it adopted a different, compliant technology. But for the last few years, Navistar has been able to lawfully forestall that result and continue selling its noncompliant engines by using banked emission credits. Simply put, it bet on finding a way to make exhaust gas recirculation a feasible and compliant technology before its finite supply of credits ran out.

Navistar's day of reckoning is fast approaching: its supply of credits is dwindling and its engines remain noncompliant. In October 2011, Navistar informed EPA that it would run out of credits sometime in 2012. EPA, estimating that Navistar "might have as little as three to four months" of available credits before it "would be forced to stop introducing its engines into commerce," leapt into action. Without formal notice and comment, EPA hurriedly promulgated the IFR on January 31, 2012, pursuant to its authority under 42 U.S.C. § 7525(g), to make NCPs available to Navistar.

To issue NCPs under its regulations, EPA must first find that a new emissions standard is "more stringent" or "more difficult to achieve" than a prior standard, that "substantial work will be required to meet the standard for which the NCP is offered," and that "there is likely to be a technological laggard." 40 C.F.R. § 86.1103-87. EPA found these criteria were met. The 2010 NOx standard permits a significantly smaller amount of emissions than the prior standard, so the first criterion is easily satisfied. As for the second, EPA simply said that, because compliant engines (like Petitioners') use new technologies to be compliant, "[i]t is therefore logical to conclude . . . that substantial work was required to meet the emission standard." 77 Fed. Reg. at 4,681. Finally, EPA determined that there was likely to be a technological laggard because "an engine manufacturer [Navistar] . . . has not yet met the requirements for technological reasons" and because "it is a reasonable possibility that this manufacturer may not be able to comply for technological reasons." *Id.*

Having determined that NCPs are appropriate, EPA proceeded to set the amount of the penalty and establish the "upper limit" of emissions permitted even by a penalty-paying manufacturer. The IFR provides that manufacturers may sell heavy-duty diesel engines in model years 2012 and 2013 as long as they pay a

1 penalty of $1,919 per engine and as long as the engines emit fewer than 0.50 grams
2 of nitrogen oxide per horsepower-hour. *Id.* at 4,682–83. This "upper limit" thus
3 permits emissions of up to two-and-a-half times the 0.20 grams permitted under
4 the 2010 NOx standard with which Navistar is meant to comply and with which
5 Petitioners do comply. *See id.* at 4,681.

6 EPA explained its decision to forego notice and comment procedures by invoking
7 the "good cause" exception of the APA, *id.* at 4,680, which provides that an agency
8 may dispense with formal notice and comment procedures if the agency "for good
9 cause finds . . . that notice and public procedure thereon are impracticable,
10 unnecessary, or contrary to the public interest," 5 U.S.C. § 553(b)(B). EPA cited
11 four factors to show the existence of good cause: (1) notice and comment would
12 mean "the possibility of an engine manufacturer [Navistar] . . . being unable to
13 certify a complete product line of engines for model year 2012 and/or 2013," (2)
14 EPA was only "amending limited provisions in existing NCP regulations," (3) the
15 IFR's "duration is limited," and (4) "there is no risk to the public interest in
16 allowing manufacturers to certify using NCPs before the point at which EPA could
17 make them available through a full notice-and- comment rulemaking." 77 Fed.
18 Reg. at 4,680.

19 Petitioners each requested administrative stays of the IFR, protesting that EPA
20 lacked good cause within the meaning of the APA. Petitioners also objected to the
21 substance of the NCP, arguing that EPA misapplied its own regulatory criteria for
22 determining when such a penalty is warranted, and that EPA arbitrarily and
23 capriciously set the amount of the penalty and the "upper limit" level of permissible
24 emissions. EPA denied those requests. Petitioners promptly filed an emergency
25 motion with this Court to expedite review, which we granted.

26 * * *

27 III

28 Petitioners argue first that Section 206 of the Act requires notice and comment;
29 alternatively, they claim EPA lacked good cause in any event. The APA provides
30 that, "[e]xcept when notice or hearing is required by statute," an agency is relieved
31 of its obligation to provide notice and an opportunity to comment "when the
32 agency for good cause finds (and incorporates the finding and a brief statement of
33 reasons therefor in the rules issued) that notice and public procedure thereon are
34 impracticable, unnecessary, or contrary to the public interest." 5 U.S.C. §
35 553(b)(B).

36 A

37 [The court concludes notice or hearing is not expressly required by the statute.]

38 * * *

39 B

1  Because the Act does not contain any notice-and- comment requirement
2  applicable to the IFR, EPA may invoke the APA's good cause exception. We must
3  therefore determine whether notice and comment were "impracticable,
4  unnecessary, or contrary to the public interest." 5 U.S.C. § 553(b)(B). On that
5  question, it would appear we owe EPA's findings no particular deference. *See Jifry
6  v. FAA*, 370 F.3d 1174, 1178–79 (D.C. Cir. 2004) (finding good cause without
7  resorting to deference); *Util. Solid Waste Activities Grp. v. EPA*, 236 F.3d 749, 754
8  (D.C. Cir. 2001) (finding no good cause without invoking deference). But we need
9  not decide the standard of review since, even if we were to review EPA's assertion
10  of "good cause" simply to determine if it is arbitrary or capricious, 5 U.S.C. §
11  706(2)(A), we would still find it lacking.

12  We have repeatedly made clear that the good cause exception "is to be narrowly
13  construed and only reluctantly countenanced." *Util. Solid Waste Activities Grp.*,
14  236 F.3d at 754; *Tenn. Gas Pipeline Co. v. FERC*, 969 F.2d 1141, 1144 (D.C. Cir.
15  1992); *New Jersey v. EPA*, 626 F.2d 1038, 1045 (D.C. Cir. 1980); *see also Jifry*,
16  370 F.3d at 1179 ("The exception excuses notice and comment in emergency
17  situations, or where delay could result in serious harm."); *Am. Fed. of Gov't Emps.
18  v. Block*, 655 F.2d 1153, 1156 (D.C. Cir. 1981) ("As the legislative history of the APA
19  makes clear, moreover, the exceptions at issue here are not 'escape clauses' that
20  may be arbitrarily utilized at the agency's whim. Rather, use of these exceptions by
21  administrative agencies should be limited to emergency situations . . . .").

22  First, an agency may invoke the impracticability of notice and comment. 5 U.S.C.
23  § 553(b)(B). Our inquiry into impracticability "is inevitably fact- or context-
24  dependent," *Mid-Tex Electric Coop. v. FERC*, 822 F.2d 1123, 1132 (D.C. Cir. 1987).
25  For the sake of comparison, we have suggested agency action could be sustained
26  on this basis if, for example, air travel security agencies would be unable to address
27  threats posing "a possible imminent hazard to aircraft, persons, and property
28  within the United States," *Jifry*, 370 F.3d at 1179, or if "a safety investigation shows
29  that a new safety rule must be put in place immediately," *Util. Solid Waste
30  Activities Grp.*, 236 F.3d at 755 (ultimately finding that not to be the case and
31  rejecting the agency's argument), or if a rule was of "life- saving importance" to
32  mine workers in the event of a mine explosion, *Council of the S. Mountains, Inc. v.
33  Donovan*, 653 F.2d 573, 581 (D.C. Cir. 1981) (describing that circumstance as "a
34  special, possibly unique, case").

35  By contrast, the context of this case reveals that the only purpose of the IFR is, as
36  Petitioners put it, "to rescue a lone manufacturer from the folly of its own choices."
37  Pet. Br. at 29; *see* 77 Fed. Reg. at 4,680 (expressing EPA's concern that providing
38  notice and comment would mean "the possibility of an engine manufacturer
39  [Navistar] . . . being unable to certify a complete product line of engines for model
40  year 2012 and/or 2013"). The IFR does not stave off any imminent threat to the
41  environment or safety or national security. It does not remedy any real emergency
42  at all, save the "emergency" facing Navistar's bottom line. Indeed, all EPA points
43  to is "the serious harm to Navistar and its employees" and "the ripple effect on its

1    customers and suppliers," Resp't Br. at 28, but the same could be said for any
2    manufacturer facing a standard with which its product does not comply.

3    EPA claims the harm to Navistar and the resulting up- and down-stream impacts
4    should still be enough under our precedents. The only case on which it relies,
5    however, is one in which an entire industry and its customers were imperiled. *See*
6    *Am. Fed. of Gov't Emps.*, 655 F.2d at 1157. Navistar's plight is not even remotely
7    close to such a weighty, systemic interest, especially since it is a consequence
8    brought about by Navistar's own choice to continue to pursue a technology which,
9    so far, is noncompliant. At bottom, EPA's approach would give agencies "good
10    cause" under the APA every time a manufacturer in a regulated field felt a new
11    regulation imposed some degree of economic hardship, even if the company could
12    have avoided that hardship had it made different business choices. This is both
13    nonsensical and in direct tension with our longstanding position that the exception
14    should be "narrowly construed and only reluctantly countenanced." *Util. Solid*
15    *Waste Activities Grp.*, 236 F.3d at 754.

16    Second, an agency may claim notice and comment were "unnecessary." 5 U.S.C. §
17    553(b)(B). This prong of the good cause inquiry is "confined to those situations in
18    which the administrative rule is a routine determination, insignificant in nature
19    and impact, and inconsequential to the industry and to the public." *Util. Solid*
20    *Waste Activities Grp.*, 236 F.3d at 755. This case does not present such a situation.
21    Just as in *Utility Solid Waste*, the IFR is a rule "about which these members of the
22    public [the petitioners] were greatly interested," so notice and comment were not
23    "unnecessary." *Id.* EPA argues that since the IFR is just an interim rule, good cause
24    is satisfied because "the interim status of the challenged rule is a significant factor"
25    in determining whether notice and comment are unnecessary. Resp't Br. at 35; 77
26    Fed. Reg. at 4,680 (finding good cause because the IFR's "duration is limited").
27    But we held, in the very case on which EPA relies, that "the limited nature of the
28    rule cannot in itself justify a failure to follow notice and comment procedures."
29    *Mid-Tex Electric Coop.*, 822 F.2d at 1132. And for good reason: if a rule's interim
30    nature were enough to satisfy the element of good cause, then "agencies could issue
31    interim rules of limited effect for any plausible reason, irrespective of the degree of
32    urgency" and "the good cause exception would soon swallow the notice and
33    comment rule." *Tenn. Gas Pipeline*, 969 F.2d at 1145. EPA's remaining argument
34    that notice and comment were "unnecessary" is that the IFR was essentially
35    ministerial: EPA simply input numbers into an NCP-setting formula without
36    substantially amending the NCP regime. Resp't Br. at 36; 77 Fed. Reg. at 4,680.
37    But even if it were true that EPA arrived at the level of the penalty and the upper
38    limit in this way (and Petitioners strenuously argue that EPA actually *amended* the
39    NCP regime in order to arrive at the upper limit level in the IFR5), that argument
40    does not account for how EPA determined NCPs were warranted in this case in the
41    first place—another finding to which Petitioners object. EPA's decision to
42    implement an NCP, perhaps even more than the level of the penalty itself, is far
43    from inconsequential or routine, and EPA does not even attempt to defend it as
44    such.

Finally, an agency may invoke the good cause exception if providing notice and comment would be contrary to the public interest. 5 U.S.C. § 553(b)(B). In the IFR, EPA says it has good cause since "there is no risk to the public interest in allowing manufacturers to [use] NCPs before the point at which EPA could make them available through a full notice- and-comment rulemaking," 77 Fed. Reg. at 4,680, but this misstates the statutory criterion. The question is not whether *dispensing* with notice and comment would be contrary to the public interest, but whether *providing* notice and comment would be contrary to the public interest. By improperly framing the question in this way, the IFR inverts the presumption, apparently suggesting that notice and comment is usually unnecessary. We cannot permit this subtle malformation of the APA. The public interest prong of the good cause exception is met only in the rare circumstance when ordinary procedures— generally presumed to serve the public interest—would in fact harm that interest. It is appropriately invoked when the timing and disclosure requirements of the usual procedures would defeat the purpose of the proposal—if, for example, "announcement of a proposed rule would enable the sort of financial manipulation the rule sought to prevent." *Util. Solid Waste Activities Grp.*, 236 F.3d at 755. In such a circumstance, notice and comment could be dispensed with "in order to prevent the amended rule from being evaded." *Id.* * * *

IV

Because EPA lacked good cause to dispense with required notice and comment procedures, we conclude the IFR must be vacated without reaching Petitioners' alternative arguments. We are aware EPA is currently in the process of promulgating a final rule—with the benefit of notice and comment—on this precise issue. However, we strongly reject EPA's claim that the challenged errors are harmless simply because of the pendency of a properly-noticed final rule. Were that true, agencies would have no use for the APA when promulgating any interim rules. So long as the agency eventually opened a final rule for comment, every error in every interim rule—no matter how egregious—could be excused as a harmless error. * * *

* * * For now, therefore, we simply hold that EPA lacked good cause for not providing formal notice-and-comment rulemaking, and accordingly vacate the IFR and remand for further proceedings.

*So ordered.*

## C. Adjudication

Agencies adjudicate millions of matters every year. The basic idea, as already discussed, is that adjudications are similar to judicial proceedings. This picture may roughly capture what happens in many on-the-record proceedings—think a claim for disability benefits before an ALJ working for the Social Security

1 Administration, or a removal proceeding before an Immigration Judge—but there
2 are aspects to adjudication quite different from what happens in courts. Courts do
3 not initiate litigation, but many agencies act as both prosecutor and judge.
4 (Provisions of the APA seek to guarantee that agencies decide fairly
5 notwithstanding this combination of functions, see 5 U.S.C.§§ 556-557, and
6 *Withrow v. Larkin, supra*, absolves this arrangement of constitutional suspicion.)
7 The "agencies as courts" picture also fails to capture the extraordinary number of
8 *informal* adjudications every year.

9 On-the-record adjudications are regulated in substantial detail by 5 U.S.C. § 554,
10 § 556, and § 557. This section addresses some questions raised or left open by these
11 provisions, including: who has the right to participate in an adjudication? What
12 guarantees the independence of adjudicators? And, what procedural requirements
13 apply to informal adjudications?

14 *Association of Administrative Law Judges, Inc. v. Heckler* concludes that ALJs
15 have a qualified right to decisional independence. In keeping with the idea that
16 ALJs should enjoy a substantial measure of independence, they may only be
17 removed for cause, and only by the Merit System Protections Board, an
18 independent "quasi-judicial" agency.* The Supreme Court ruled in *Lucia* that ALJs
19 working for the Securities and Exchange Commission are officers of the United
20 States, and in *Free Enterprise Fund* that officers cannot be insulated against
21 removal by more than one layer of for-cause protection. All this is to say, a broader
22 reckoning on the professional structure of the ALJ cadre may be coming.

23

24 **Envirocare, Inc., v. Nuclear Regulatory Commission**

25 194 F.3d 72 (D.C. Cir. 1999)

26 October 22, 1999

27 Before EDWARDS, Chief Judge, SENTELLE and RANDOLPH, Circuit Judges.

28 RANDOLPH, Circuit Judge:

29 Federal agencies may, and sometimes do, permit persons to intervene in
30 administrative proceedings even though these persons would not have standing to
31 challenge the agency's final action in federal court. Agencies, of course, are not

---

* Members of the Merit Systems Protection Board can only be removed for cause.
5 U.S.C. § 1202(d). It is particularly difficult to remove them at present, because
the Board has had *no members* since February 2019.

constrained by Article III of the Constitution; nor are they governed by judicially-created standing doctrines restricting access to the federal courts. The criteria for establishing "administrative standing" therefore may permissibly be less demanding than the criteria for "judicial standing." *See, e.g., Alexander Sprunt & Son, Inc. v. United States*, 281 U.S. 249, 255 (1930).

Is the converse true? May an agency refuse to grant a hearing to persons who would satisfy the criteria for judicial standing and refuse to allow them to intervene in administrative proceedings? This is the ultimate question posed in these consolidated petitions for judicial review of two orders of the Nuclear Regulatory Commission refusing to grant Envirocare of Utah, Inc.'s requests for a hearing and for intervention in licensing proceedings.

## I

Envirocare was the first commercial facility in the nation the Commission licensed to dispose of certain radioactive by-product material from offsite sources. The Commission had licensed other companies to dispose of such radioactive waste, but only if the waste was produced onsite. In the late 1990s, the Commission granted the applications of two such companies for amended licenses to allow them to dispose of radioactive waste received from other sites. International Uranium (USA) Corporation's facility in Utah became licensed to receive and dispose of approximately 25,000 dry tons of waste still remaining from the Manhattan Project and currently stored in New York State. Quivira Mining Company's facility in New Mexico, some 500 miles from Envirocare's operation, also became licensed to dispose of specified amounts of such material from offsite sources.

In both licensing proceedings before the Atomic Safety and Licensing Board, Envirocare requested a hearing and sought leave to intervene to oppose the amendment. Envirocare's basic complaint was "that the license amendment permits [the company] to become a general commercial facility like Envirocare, but that the NRC did not require [the company] to meet the same regulatory standards the agency imposed upon Envirocare when Envirocare sought *its* license to become a commercial disposal facility for" radioactive waste. The Licensing Board rejected Envirocare's requests for a hearing and for leave to intervene in both cases, and in separate opinions several months apart, the Commission affirmed.

With respect to the proceedings to amend Quivira's license, the Commission ruled that Envirocare did not come within the following "standing" provision in the Atomic Energy Act: when the Commission institutes a proceeding for the granting or amending of a license, "the Commission shall grant a hearing upon the request

1    of any person whose interest may be affected by the proceeding, and shall admit

2    any such person as a party to such proceeding." 42 U.S.C. § 2239(a)(1)(A). In

3    determining whether Envirocare possessed the requisite "interest" under this

4    provision, the Commission looked to "current judicial concepts of standing."

5    Envirocare alleged economic injury, claiming that the less stringent application of

6    regulations to Quivira placed Envirocare at a competitive disadvantage. This

7    allegation was sufficient, the Commission held, to meet the injury-in-fact

8    requirements of constitutional standing. On the question of prudential standing,

9    however, the Commission determined that "Envirocare's purely competitive

10    interests, unrelated to any radiological harm to itself, do not bring it within the

11    zone of interests of the AEA for the purpose of policing the license requirements of

12    a competitor."

13    With respect to International Uranium's license, the Commission agreed with the

14    Licensing Board that the case was "on all fours" with [a prior N.R.C case,] *Quivira*.

15    As in that case, Envirocare's injury from International Uranium's competition was

16    not within the Atomic Energy Act's zone of interests. In addition, the Commission

17    made explicit its view that judicial standing doctrines were not controlling in the

18    administrative context and that its duty was to interpret the "interests" Congress

19    intended to recognize in § 2239(a)(1)(A) * * *.

20                                   II

21    Envirocare spends all of its time arguing that in light of decisions of the Supreme

22    Court and of this court, its status as a competitor satisfies the "zone of interests"

23    test for standing, as the test was formulated in *Association of Data Processing*

24    *Service Organizations v. Camp*, 397 U.S. 150, (1970), and as it was refined in

25    *National Credit Union Administration v. First National Bank & Trust Co.*, 522

26    U.S. 479 (1998). We shall assume that Envirocare is correct. It does not follow that

27    the Commission erred in refusing the company's motions for a hearing and for

28    leave to intervene, at least in regard to International Uranium's license

29    amendment. The Commission rightly pointed out, in *International Uranium* and

30    in *Quivira*, that it is not an Article III court and thus is not bound to follow the law

31    of standing derived from the "case or controversy" requirement. Judicially-devised

32    prudential standing requirements, of which the "zone of interests" test is one, are

33    also inapplicable to an administrative agency acting within the jurisdiction

34    Congress assigned to it. * * *

35    Whether the Commission erred in excluding Envirocare from participating in

36    International Uranium's licensing proceeding therefore turns not on judicial

37    decisions dealing with standing to sue, but on familiar principles of administrative

38    law regarding an agency's interpretation of the statutes it alone administers. The

39    governing provision—42 U.S.C. § 2239(a)(1)(A)—requires the Commission to hold

1  a hearing "on the request of any person whose interest may be affected by the
2  proceeding" and to allow such a person to intervene. The term "interest" is not
3  defined in the Act and it is scarcely self-defining. It could mean merely an academic
4  or organizational interest in a problem or subject, as in *Sierra Club v. Morton*, 405
5  U.S. 727, 738-40 (1972). Or an interest in avoiding economic harm or in gaining
6  an economic benefit from agency action directed at others. *See Association of Data
7  Processing Serv. Orgs.*, 397 U.S., at 154. Or an "interest" in "aesthetic,
8  conservational and recreational values." *Id.* Or all of these. But whatever the
9  judicial mind thinks of today as an "interest" affected by a proceeding is not
10  necessarily what Congress meant when it enacted this provision in 1954. At the
11  time, judicial notions of standing were considerably more restrictive than they are
12  now. * * *

13  Because we cannot be confident of what kinds of interests the 1954 Congress meant
14  to recognize in § 2239(a)(1)(A)—because, in other words, the statute is
15  ambiguous—the Commission's interpretation of this provision must be sustained
16  if it is reasonable. *See Chevron*, 467 U.S., at 843. We think it is. For one thing,
17  excluding competitors who allege only economic injury from the class of persons
18  entitled to intervene in licensing proceedings is consistent with the Atomic Energy
19  Act. The Act meant to increase private competition in the industry, not limit it.
20  Before its passage in 1954, the federal government completely controlled nuclear
21  energy. Through the Act, Congress sought to foster a private nuclear industry for
22  peaceful purposes. In order to ensure that private industry would not undermine
23  nuclear safety, the Act created an agency—what is today the Nuclear Regulatory
24  Commission—to regulate the private sector. One of the Commission's statutory
25  duties is authorizing the transfer and receipt of radioactive by-product material.
26  *See* 42 U.S.C. § 2111. The statute describes the Commission's responsibility in this
27  area as follows: "The Commission shall insure that the management of any by-
28  product material . . . is carried out in such a manner as the Commission deems
29  appropriate to protect the public health and safety and the environment from
30  radiological and nonradiological hazards associated with the processing and with
31  the possession and transfer of such material . . . ." 42 U.S.C. § 2114(a)(1).

32  Nothing in this provision, or in the rest of the Act, indicates that the license
33  requirement was intended to protect market participants from new entrants.
34  Envirocare points to the Act's policy statement which mentions "strengthening free
35  competition in private enterprise." This statement refers to the Act's goal of
36  creating a private nuclear energy industry. Allowing new competitors to enter the
37  market strengthens competition. Permitting current license holders to initiate
38  hearings for the purpose of imposing burdens on potential competitors does the
39  opposite.

1    In rendering its interpretation of § 2239(a)(1)(A), the Commission also properly
2    took account of regulatory burdens on the agency. It wrote: "Competitors, though,
3    whose only 'interest' is lost business opportunities, could readily burden our
4    adjudicatory process with open-ended allegations designed not to advance public
5    health and safety but as a dilatory tactic to interfere with and impose costs upon a
6    competitor. Such an abuse of our hearing process would significantly divert limited
7    agency resources, which ought to be squarely—genuinely—focused upon health
8    and safety concerns." * * *

9    For these reasons, the view the Commission expressed in its *International*
10    *Uranium* opinion—that competitors asserting economic injury do not demonstrate
11    the type of interest necessary under § 2239(a)(1)(A)—is a permissible construction
12    of the statute. And it appears to be a construction the Commission has adhered to
13    for some time. *See Virginia Elec. & Power Co.,* 4 N.R.C. 98, 105-06 (1976). The
14    Commission stated that it has long been its practice to deny requests for a hearing
15    under § 2239(a)(1)(A) when the petitioner alleged only economic injury.
16    Envirocare has cited nothing to the contrary. In any event, even if the
17    Commission's refusal to follow the developing law of judicial standing had been a
18    departure from its usual practice, it gave adequate reasons for changing course.

19                                             * * *

20    *The petitions for judicial review are denied.*

21

22    **Association of Administrative Law Judges, Inc. v. Heckler**

23    594 F. Supp. 1132 (D.D.C. 1984)

24    September 10, 1984

25    MEMORANDUM OPINION AND ORDER

26    GREEN, District Judge.

27    Plaintiff, the Association of Administrative Law Judges, is a not-for-profit
28    corporation whose members are administrative law judges (ALJs) employed by the
29    Department of Health and Human Services (HHS) and assigned to the Office of
30    Hearings and Appeals (OHA) of the Social Security Administration (SSA).
31    Plaintiff's members adjudicate claims for disability benefits under Titles II and XVI
32    of the Social Security Act. Plaintiff brought this lawsuit to challenge the "Bellmon
33    Review Program", which defendants instituted to implement Section 304(q) of the
34    Social Security Disability Amendments of 1980, the "Bellmon Amendment".
35    Plaintiff alleges that this program violates the rights of its members to decisional

1 independence under the Administrative Procedure Act (APA), 5 U.S.C. § 551 *et seq.*
2 (1982).

3 State agencies administer the Social Security Disability Insurance Program
4 pursuant to agreements with the SSA. Based upon medical information received
5 from various sources and applying SSA guidelines, the state disability
6 determination service issues the decision of SSA. A claimant who is denied benefits
7 may file for reconsideration at the state level and if dissatisfied may then seek relief
8 on the federal level. The ALJ hearing is a *de novo* proceeding. The ALJ is the first
9 agency personnel in the review process to interview the claimant in person. The
10 claimant may submit additional evidence, produce expert witnesses, and be
11 represented by counsel. If his or her claim is denied by the ALJ, the claimant may
12 appeal to the Appeals Council, which is the last step in the administrative process.

13 The Appeals Council has the authority to review all decisions of ALJs, at its own
14 discretion ("own motion"), or at the request of a claimant. In either case, the
15 Appeals Council is authorized to exercise jurisdiction only when: (1) there appears
16 to be an abuse of discretion by the ALJ; (2) there is an error of law; (3) the action,
17 findings or conclusions of the ALJ are not supported by substantial evidence; or
18 (4) there is a broad policy or procedural issue that may affect the general public
19 interest. 20 C.F.R. § 404.970(a), 416.1470(a) (1984). Based upon its review, the
20 Appeals Council may modify, affirm, reverse or remand the ALJ's decision. When
21 the Appeals Council reverses or remands an ALJ's decision, it issues an opinion
22 stating the grounds for reversal or remand and identifying dispositive abuses of
23 discretion, errors of law, problems with conclusions of law and findings of fact,
24 insufficiencies of evidence, and policy or procedural issues of concern to SSA. If a
25 case is remanded, the ALJ must take any action ordered by the Appeals Council,
26 but may also take any additional action that is not inconsistent with the remand
27 order.

28 The Bellmon Amendment directed the Secretary of HHS to resume review of
29 decisions of ALJs on her own motion. Congress expressed concern at that time
30 about the high rate at which ALJs were reversing determinations made at the state
31 level and the variance in these rates among ALJs.

32 A study performed pursuant to the Bellmon Amendment and described in a report
33 to Congress in January 1982, indicated that the Appeals Council more often would
34 have changed decisions by ALJs allowing benefits made by ALJs with above
35 average allowance rates than allowance decisions made by ALJs with average or
36 below-average allowance rates. The Bellmon Review Program, a series of measures
37 designed to improve decisional quality and accuracy, began in October, 1981.
38 Associate Commissioner of SSA, Louis B. Hays, announced that four categories of
39 cases would be selected for possible "own motion" review:

| | |
|---|---|
| (1) National random sample | 21% |
| (2) Allowance decisions of new ALJs | |
| (3) Decisions referred by SSA's | 16% |

| Office of Disability Operations | |
|---|---|
| (4) Individual ALJs | 63% |

Initially, individual ALJs with allowance rates of 70% or higher were to have 100% of their allowance decisions reviewed for accuracy and hearing offices with allowance rates of 74% or higher would also be reviewed. 106 ALJs, or approximately 13% of all ALJs in SSA, were placed on Bellmon Review because of their high allowance rates. The selection of entire hearing offices for review was soon discontinued. The other three categories of review were not yet operative.

An overview of the program was communicated to the ALJ corps in a Memorandum dated September 24, 1982 from Mr. Hays. ("Hays Memorandum"). That Memorandum explained that Bellmon Review was being instituted because of Congressional concern about high allowance rates and because only ALJ decisions denying benefits were generally subject to further review. Allowance rates were used as the basis for selecting the initial review group, in part, because studies had shown that decisions in this group would be the most likely to contain errors which would otherwise go uncorrected.

Based upon own-motion rates (the frequency with which the Appeals Council takes action to correct an ALJs decision, as calculated by the Office of Appraisal) the individual ALJs were divided into four groups: 100% review; 75% review; 50% review; and 25% review. In determining whether an ALJ should be removed from review, the Appeals Council considered only decisional accuracy, defined as a 5% own motion rate for three consecutive months. An ALJ with a 5% own motion rate could be said to be 95% accurate. Shortly after implementation, the criteria for removing targeted ALJs from review were amended. The 5% own motion rate was abandoned in favor of an own motion rate approximating that of the national random sample.

\* \* \*

[The court describes other aspects of the Hays Memorandum that were never implemented: a system for providing additional feedback and counseling for ALJs based on performance, and the possibility that "other steps" could be taken with respect to underperforming ALJs.] The Bellmon Review Program has evolved substantially since the Hays Memorandum was issued. Significantly, in April 1982, before this lawsuit was filed, defendants stopped using allowance rates to target ALJs for Bellmon Review once own motion data became available. The ALJs whose allowance decisions were reviewed were selected for individual review solely on the basis of their own motion rates under the national random sample.

\* \* \*

Most recently, OHA, under a new Associate Commissioner, has eliminated entirely the individual ALJ portion of Bellmon Review. Notice of Filing June 22, 1984,

1   Memorandum to all ALJs, June 21, 1984. This Memorandum indicates that the
2   number of cases reviewed under the national random sample will be increased.
3   Apparently, the results of Bellmon Review demonstrated that the difference
4   between the own motion rates of the selected ALJ and national random sample
5   portions of the review had progressively narrowed, which suggested that overall,
6   decisional quality and consistency had improved. * * *

7   Plaintiff charged that the targeting of individual ALJs under Bellmon Review,
8   based upon allowance rates and then own motion rates, was in essence an attempt
9   to influence ALJs to reduce their allowance rates and thereby compromise their
10  decisional independence.

11                                          * * *

12  It was plaintiff's view that Mr. Hays had a financial incentive to pressure ALJs to
13  reduce their allowance rates. As a member of the Senior Executive Service, he had
14  a performance plan which stated as one of its goals or objectives, the reduction of
15  allowance rates. Mr. Hays' performance was rated higher in FY 1981, a year in
16  which such a reduction took place, than in FY 1982, when it did not. Mr. Hays
17  stressed that his performance plan goal, to improve the quality of adjudication in
18  OHA, was derived in response to Congressional criticism. Studies had shown a
19  correlation between high allowance rates and high error rates. Thus, Mr. Hays
20  expected that improved quality of adjudication would lead to some reduction in
21  allowance rates, particularly since allowance decisions had not been subject to
22  review by the Appeals Council for several years. Mr. Hays denied that the reduction
23  of allowance rates was an independent goal in the performance plan.

24                                          * * *

25  Evidence apart from the budgetary projections cumulatively, and strongly,
26  suggested that OHA had an ulterior goal to reduce ALJ allowance rates. When Mr.
27  Hays first became Associate Commissioner, he issued a memorandum to the ALJs,
28  in which he noted a perception that ALJ allowance rates were "untenable".
29  Sometime later, he sent a memorandum to SSA, in which he described as "good
30  news" a decline in allowance rates. Mr. Hays received a memorandum from SSA's
31  Office of Management Coordination, which requested a decrease in the variance
32  among allowance rates and a decrease in allowance rates overall.

33  Much of the testimony in this case involved the Fort Smith, Arkansas Hearing
34  Office. On December 10, 1980, prior to the institution of the Bellmon Review
35  Program, Deputy Chief ALJ J. Robert Brown visited the Fort Smith Hearing Office
36  to discuss with ALJs Jerry Thomasson, Francis Mayhue, and David Hubbard the
37  possible reasons why the allowance rate of the Fort Smith Hearing Office was
38  significantly higher than the allowance rate of the Little Rock, Arkansas Hearing
39  Office, which received cases from the same state agency. The allowance rate at Fort
40  Smith was approximately 90%. * * *

## ADJUDICATION

1  The Fort Smith ALJs were subsequently advised by Chief ALJ Phillip Brown, that
2  effective August 17, 1981, the Appeals Council would begin reviewing all of their
3  decisions. The Fort Smith Review was a separate program entirely from Bellmon
4  Review. During the course of its review OHA discovered significant deficiencies in
5  the quality and accuracy of the Fort Smith Hearing Office decisions. OHA decided
6  to provide training to ALJs Thomasson and Mayhue on the application of the
7  Social Security disability regulations and the sequential evaluation process of
8  adjudicating cases. Judge Hubbard was not included in the training because he
9  appeared generally to understand the regulatory scheme.

10                                    * * *

11  Defendants' position throughout this litigation, expressed by Mr. Hays
12  emphatically at trial, has been that there is no agency policy to reduce allowance
13  rates. The agency's policy is to reduce inconsistency in the application of law and
14  regulations both within the ALJ corps and in the different levels of the adjudicatory
15  process, and to reduce the number of decisions that do not correctly apply
16  substantive agency policy. In keeping with this policy, OHA recognized that high
17  allowance rates may indicate undue inconsistency of adjudicatory standards
18  within SSA and that a reduction of that inconsistency may result in or be reflected
19  by some reduction in allowance rates, among other things. Defendants maintained
20  that ALJs were not ranked by allowance rates.

21                                    * * *

22  The APA contains a number of provisions designed to safeguard the decisional
23  independence of ALJs. Although employees of the selecting agency, ALJs are
24  entitled to pay prescribed by the Office of Personnel Management independently
25  of agency recommendations or ratings. They are exempted from the performance
26  appraisals to which other Civil Service employees are subject. 5 U.S.C. § 4301(2)(D)
27  (1982). ALJs do not receive monetary awards or periodic step increases based upon
28  performance. Cases must be assigned whenever possible, in rotation, an ALJ may
29  not be assigned duties inconsistent with his or her responsibilities as an ALJ, and
30  an ALJ may not communicate *ex parte* with anyone inside or outside the agency
31  about the facts of a particular case. 5 U.S.C. §§ 3105, 557(d) (1) (1982).

32                                    * * *

33  While the position of an ALJ is not "constitutionally protected," *Ramspeck v.*
34  *Federal Trial Examiners Conference*, 345 U.S., at 133, in many respects, it is
35  "functionally comparable" to that of a federal judge. *Butz v. Economou*, 438 U.S.,
36  at 513. * * *

37  On matters of law and policy, however, ALJs are entirely subject to the agency.
38  Although an ALJ may dispute the validity of agency policy, the agency may impose
39  its policy through the administrative appeals process. In reviewing an ALJ's
40  decision the agency retains "all the powers which it would have in making the

358

1 initial decision." 5 U.S.C. § 557(b) (1982). * * * In sum, the ALJ's right to decisional
2 independence is qualified.

3 The sole issue in this case is whether that qualified right has been violated by the
4 now discontinued individual ALJ portion of the Bellmon Review Program, which
5 targeted individual ALJs initially on the basis of their allowance rates and then on
6 the basis of their own motion rates. Although the evidence at trial did not suggest
7 that defendants intend to resume the practice of targeting high allowance ALJs for
8 Bellmon Review, and although targeted review based upon own motion rates and
9 grant-review rates of individual ALJs is no longer in effect, defendants have
10 advised the ALJ corps of the possibility that Bellmon Review could be resumed.
11 For this reason, there remains a live controversy between the parties.

12 At the same time, perhaps in response to this litigation, defendants have modified
13 the Bellmon Review Program significantly for the better. The worthiness of
14 defendants' stated goal of improving the quality and accuracy of decisions
15 notwithstanding, targeting high allowance ALJs for review, counseling and
16 possible disciplinary action was of dubious legality for at least two reasons. First,
17 that practice was not consistent with the language of the Bellmon Amendment nor
18 its sparse legislative history. Neither directed SSA to focus on allowance decisions
19 or target for review only ALJs with high allowance rates. In his introductory
20 remarks, Senator Bellmon did state that SSA was to review the allowance decisions
21 of those ALJs with high allowance rates but those remarks were not incorporated
22 into the law. Second, high allowance ALJs were initially targeted for review without
23 regard to their actual own motion rates in an overbroad sweep.

24 The practice of targeting ALJs on the basis of own motion rates, once that data
25 became available, did reflect defendants' stated goal of improving the quality and
26 accuracy of ALJ decisions. However, the evidence as a whole, persuasively
27 demonstrated that defendants retained an unjustifiable preoccupation with
28 allowance rates, to the extent that ALJs could reasonably feel pressure to issue
29 fewer allowance decisions in the name of accuracy. While there was no evidence
30 that an ALJ consciously succumbed to such pressure, in close cases, and, in
31 particular, where the determination of disability may have been based largely on
32 subjective factors, as a matter of common sense, that pressure may have intruded
33 upon the factfinding process and may have influenced some outcomes. * * *

34                                          * * *

35 In sum, the Court concludes, that defendants' unremitting focus on allowance rates
36 in the individual ALJ portion of the Bellmon Review Program created an untenable
37 atmosphere of tension and unfairness which violated the spirit of the APA, if no
38 specific provision thereof. Defendants' insensitivity to that degree of decisional
39 independence the APA affords to administrative law judges and the injudicious use
40 of phrases such as "targeting", "goals" and "behavior modification" could have
41 tended to corrupt the ability of administrative law judges to exercise that
42 independence in the vital cases that they decide. However, defendants appear to

1 have shifted their focus, obviating the need for any injunctive relief or restructuring
2 of the agency at this time. While it is incumbent upon the agency to reexamine the
3 role and function of the Appeals Council and its relationship to the ALJs in light of
4 this litigation, it would be unsuitable for the Court to order any affirmative relief
5 under the present circumstances. Plaintiff has achieved considerable success in its
6 valid attempt to reveal and change agency practices.

7 It is, therefore, by the Court, this 10th day of September, 1984

8 ORDERED that judgment be entered in favor of defendants and that this cause
9 stands dismissed.

10

## 11 Pension Benefit Guaranty Corporation v. LTV Corporation

12 496 U.S. 633 (1990)

13 June 18, 1990

14 Justice BLACKMUN delivered the opinion of the Court.

15 In this case, we must determine whether the decision of the Pension Benefit
16 Guaranty Corporation (PBGC) to restore certain pension plans under § 4047 of the
17 Employee Retirement Income Security Act of 1974 (ERISA), was, as the Court of
18 Appeals concluded, arbitrary and capricious or contrary to law within the meaning
19 of § 706 of the Administrative Procedure Act (APA), 5 U.S.C. § 706.

20                                        I

21 Petitioner PBGC is a wholly owned United States Government corporation,
22 modeled after the Federal Deposit Insurance Corporation. The Board of Directors
23 of the PBGC consists of the Secretaries of the Treasury, Labor, and Commerce. The
24 PBGC administers and enforces Title IV of ERISA. Title IV includes a mandatory
25 Government insurance program that protects the pension benefits of over 30
26 million private-sector American workers who participate in plans covered by the
27 Title. In enacting Title IV, Congress sought to ensure that employees and their
28 beneficiaries would not be completely "deprived of anticipated retirement benefits
29 by the termination of pension plans before sufficient funds have been accumulated
30 in the plans." *Pension Benefit Guaranty Corp. v. R.A. Gray & Co.*, 467 U.S. 717,
31 720 (1984).

32 When a plan covered under Title IV terminates with insufficient assets to satisfy
33 its pension obligations to the employees, the PBGC becomes trustee of the plan,
34 taking over the plan's assets and liabilities. The PBGC then uses the plan's assets
35 to cover what it can of the benefit obligations. The PBGC then must add its own
36 funds to ensure payment of most of the remaining "nonforfeitable" benefits, *i.e.*,
37 those benefits to which participants have earned entitlement under the plan terms
38 as of the date of termination. ERISA does place limits on the benefits PBGC may

guarantee upon plan termination, however, even if an employee is entitled to greater benefits under the terms of the plan. * * *

The cost of the PBGC insurance is borne primarily by employers that maintain ongoing pension plans. Sections 4006 and 4007 of ERISA require these employers to pay annual premiums. The insurance program is also financed by statutory liability imposed on employers who terminate under-funded pension plans. Upon termination, the employer becomes liable to the PBGC for the benefits that the PBGC will pay out. Because the PBGC historically has recovered only a small portion of that liability, Congress repeatedly has been forced to increase the annual premiums. Even with these increases, the PBGC in its most recent Annual Report noted liabilities of $4 billion and assets of only $2.4 billion, leaving a deficit of over $1.5 billion.

As noted above, plan termination is the insurable event under Title IV. Plans may be terminated "voluntarily" by an employer or "involuntarily" by the PBGC. An employer may terminate a plan voluntarily in one of two ways. It may proceed with a "standard termination" only if it has sufficient assets to pay all benefit commitments. A standard termination thus does not implicate PBGC insurance responsibilities. If an employer wishes to terminate a plan whose assets are insufficient to pay all benefits, the employer must demonstrate that it is in financial "distress" as defined in 29 U.S.C. § 1341(c). Neither a standard nor a distress termination by the employer, however, is permitted if termination would violate the terms of an existing collective bargaining agreement.

The PBGC, though, may terminate a plan "involuntarily," notwithstanding the existence of a collective bargaining agreement. Section 4042 of ERISA provides that the PBGC may terminate a plan whenever it determines that:

"(1) the plan has not met the minimum funding standard required under section 412 of title 26, or has been notified by the Secretary of the Treasury that a notice of deficiency under section 6212 of title 26 has been mailed with respect to the tax imposed under section 4971(a) of title 26,

"(2) the plan will be unable to pay benefits when due,

"(3) the reportable event described in section 1343(b)(7) of this title has occurred, or

"(4) the possible long-run loss of the [PBGC] with respect to the plan may reasonably be expected to increase unreasonably if the plan is not terminated." 29 U.S.C. § 1342(a) (1982 ed. Supp. IV).

Termination can be undone by PBGC. Section 4047 of ERISA, 29 U.S.C. § 1347, provides:

"In the case of a plan which has been terminated under section 1341 or 1342 of this title the [PBGC] is authorized in any such case in which [it]

1     determines such action to be appropriate and consistent with its duties
2     under this subchapter, to take such action as may be necessary to restore
3     the plan to its pretermination status, including, but not limited to, the
4     transfer to the employer or a plan administrator of control of part or all of
5     the remaining assets and liabilities of the plan."

6     When a plan is restored, full benefits are reinstated and the employer, rather than
7     the PBGC, again is responsible for the plan's unfunded liabilities.

8                                         II

9     This case arose after respondent The LTV Corporation (LTV Corp.) and many of
10    its subsidiaries, including LTV Steel Company Inc. (LTV Steel) (collectively LTV),
11    in July, 1986, filed petitions for reorganization under Chapter 11 of the Bankruptcy
12    Code. At that time, LTV Steel was the sponsor of three defined benefit pension
13    plans (the Plans) covered by Title IV of ERISA. Two of the Plans were the products
14    of collective bargaining negotiations with the United Steelworkers of America. The
15    third was for nonunion salaried employees. Chronically underfunded, the Plans,
16    by late 1986, had unfunded liabilities for promised benefits of almost $2.3 billion.
17    Approximately $2.1 billion of this amount was covered by PBGC insurance.

18    It is undisputed that one of LTV Corp.'s principal goals in filing the Chapter 11
19    petitions was the restructuring of LTV Steel's pension obligations, a goal which
20    could be accomplished if the Plans were terminated and responsibility for the
21    unfunded liabilities was placed on the PBGC. LTV Steel then could negotiate with
22    its employees for new pension arrangements. LTV, however, could not voluntarily
23    terminate the Plans because two of them had been negotiated in collective
24    bargaining. LTV therefore sought to have the PBGC terminate the Plans.

25    To that end, LTV advised the PBGC in 1986 that it could not continue to provide
26    complete funding for the Plans. PBGC estimated that, without continued funding,
27    the Plans' $2.1 billion underfunding could increase by as much as $65 million by
28    December, 1987, and by another $63 million by December, 1988, unless the Plans
29    were terminated. Moreover, extensive plant shutdowns were anticipated. These
30    shut-downs, if they occurred before the Plans were terminated, would have
31    required the payment of significant "shutdown benefits." The PBGC estimated that
32    such benefits could increase the Plans' liabilities by as much as $300 million to
33    $700 million, of which up to $500 million was covered by PBGC insurance.
34    Confronted with this information, the PBGC, invoking § 4042(a)(4) of ERISA,
35    determined that the Plans should be terminated in order to protect the insurance
36    program from the unreasonable risk of large losses, and commenced termination
37    proceedings in the District Court. With LTV's consent, the Plans were terminated
38    effective January 13, 1987.

39                                        \* \* \*

40    In early August, 1987, the PBGC determined that the financial factors on which it
41    had relied in terminating the Plans had changed significantly. Of particular

362

significance to the PBGC was its belief that the steel industry, including LTV Steel, was experiencing a dramatic turnaround. As a result, the PBGC concluded it no longer faced the imminent risk, central to its original termination decision, of large unfunded liabilities stemming from plant shutdowns. * * *

The Director issued a Notice Of Restoration on September 22, 1987, indicating the PBGC's intent to restore the terminated Plans. The PBGC Notice explained that the restoration decision was based on (1) LTV's establishment of "a retirement program that results in an abuse of the pension plan termination insurance system established by Title IV of ERISA," and (2) LTV's "improved financial circumstances." Restoration meant that the Plans were ongoing, and that LTV again would be responsible for administering and funding them.

LTV refused to comply with the restoration decision. This prompted the PBGC to initiate an enforcement action in the District Court. The court vacated the PBGC's restoration decision, finding, among other things, that the PBGC had exceeded its authority under § 4047.

The Court of Appeals for the Second Circuit affirmed, holding that the PBGC's restoration decision was "arbitrary and capricious" or contrary to law under § 706(2)(A) of the APA in various ways. * * * Finally, the court concluded that the agency's restoration decision was arbitrary and capricious because the PBGC's decisionmaking process of informal adjudication lacked adequate procedural safeguards.

* * *

III

* * *

C

Finally, we consider the Court of Appeals' ruling that the agency procedures were inadequate in this particular case. Relying upon a passage in *Bowman Transportation, Inc. v. Arkansas-Best Freight System, Inc.*, 419 U.S. 281, 288, n. 4 (1974), the court held that the PBGC's decision was arbitrary and capricious because the "PBGC neither apprised LTV of the material on which it was to base its decision, gave LTV an adequate opportunity to offer contrary evidence, proceeded in accordance with ascertainable standards . . . , nor provided [LTV] a statement showing its reasoning in applying those standards." The court suggested that, on remand, the agency was required to do each of these things.

The PBGC argues that this holding conflicts with *Vermont Yankee Nuclear Power Corp. v. Natural Resources Defense Council, Inc.*, 435 U.S. 519 (1978), where, the PBGC contends, this Court made clear that, when the Due Process Clause is not implicated and an agency's governing statute contains no specific procedural mandates, the Administrative Procedure Act establishes the maximum procedural requirements a reviewing court may impose on agencies. Although *Vermont*

1    *Yankee* concerned additional procedures imposed by the Court of Appeals for the
2    District of Columbia Circuit on the Atomic Energy Commission when the agency
3    was engaging in informal rulemaking, the PBGC argues that the informal
4    adjudication process by which the restoration decision was made should be
5    governed by the same principles.

6    Respondents counter by arguing that courts, under some circumstances, do
7    require agencies to undertake additional procedures. As support for this
8    proposition, they rely on *Citizens to Preserve Overton Park, Inc. v. Volpe*, 401 U.S.
9    402 (1971). In *Overton Park*, the Court concluded that the Secretary of
10    Transportation's "*post hoc* rationalizations" regarding a decision to authorize the
11    construction of a highway did not provide "an [a]dequate basis for [judicial]
12    review" for purposes of § 706 of the APA. *Id.* at. 419. Accordingly, the Court
13    directed the District Court on remand to consider evidence that shed light on the
14    Secretary's reasoning at the time he made the decision. Of particular relevance for
15    present purposes, the Court in *Overton Park* intimated that one recourse for the
16    District Court might be a remand to the agency for a fuller explanation of the
17    agency's reasoning at the time of the agency action. Subsequent cases have made
18    clear that remanding to the agency in fact is the preferred course. *See Florida
19    Power & Light Co. v. Lorion*, 470 U.S. 729, 744 (1985) ("[I]f the reviewing court
20    simply cannot evaluate the challenged agency action on the basis of the record
21    before it, the proper course, except in rare circumstances, is to remand to the
22    agency for additional investigation or explanation"). Respondents contend that the
23    instant case is controlled by *Overton Park* rather than *Vermont Yankee*, and that
24    the Court of Appeals' ruling was thus correct.

25    We believe that respondents' argument is wide of the mark. We begin by noting
26    that, although one initially might feel that there is some tension between *Vermont
27    Yankee* and *Overton Park*, the two cases are not necessarily inconsistent. *Vermont
28    Yankee* stands for the general proposition that courts are not free to impose upon
29    agencies specific procedural requirements that have no basis in the APA. At most,
30    *Overton Park* suggests that § 706(2)(A) of the APA, which directs a court to ensure
31    that an agency action is not arbitrary and capricious or otherwise contrary to law,
32    imposes a general "procedural" requirement of sorts by mandating that an agency
33    take whatever steps it needs to provide an explanation that will enable the court to
34    evaluate the agency's rationale at the time of decision.

35    Here, unlike in *Overton Park*, the Court of Appeals did not suggest that the
36    administrative record was inadequate to enable the court to fulfill its duties under
37    § 706. Rather, to support its ruling, the court focused on "fundamental fairness" to
38    LTV. With the possible exception of the absence of "ascertainable standards"—by
39    which we are not exactly sure what the Court of Appeals meant—the procedural
40    inadequacies cited by the court all relate to LTV's role in the PBGC's
41    decisionmaking process. But the court did not point to any provision in ERISA or
42    the APA which gives LTV the procedural rights the court identified. Thus, the
43    court's holding runs afoul of *Vermont Yankee*, and finds no support in *Overton
44    Park.*

364

Nor is *Arkansas-Best*, the case on which the Court of Appeals relied, to the contrary. The statement relied upon (which was dictum) said: "A party is entitled, of course, to know the issues on which decision will turn and to be apprised of the factual material on which the agency relies for decision so that he may rebut it." 419 U.S., at 288, n. 4. That statement was entirely correct in the context of *Arkansas-Best*, which involved a formal adjudication by the Interstate Commerce Commission pursuant to the trial-type procedures set forth in §§ 5, 7 and 8 of the APA, 5 U.S.C. §§ 554, 556-557, which include requirements that parties be given notice of "the matters of fact and law asserted," § 554(b)(3), an opportunity for "the submission and consideration of facts [and] arguments," § 554(c)(1), and an opportunity to submit "proposed findings and conclusions" or "exceptions," § 557(c)(1), (2). The determination in this case, however, was lawfully made by informal adjudication, the minimal requirements for which are set forth in § 555 of the APA, and do not include such elements. A failure to provide them where the Due Process Clause itself does not require them (which has not been asserted here) is therefore not unlawful.

IV

* * * [W]e find the procedures employed by the PBGC to be consistent with the APA. Accordingly, the judgment of the Court of Appeals is reversed and the case is remanded for further proceedings consistent with this opinion.

*It is so ordered.*

JUSTICE WHITE, with whom JUSTICE O'CONNOR joins, concurring in part and dissenting in part. [Omitted.]

JUSTICE STEVENS, dissenting. [Omitted.]

# D. Fairness in Administrative Proceedings

The APA imposes heightened fairness requirements for on-the-record proceedings (prototypically adjudications). The D.C. Circuit in *Home Box Office* applied a presumption against "*ex parte*" contacts[*] to notice-and-comment rulemakings as well, only to retreat from that position in *Sierra Club*. Does the D.C. Circuit's first approach or its second make more sense? If you believe the court overreached in *Home Box Office* by going beyond the requirements of the APA, what do you think

---

[*] In *Sierra Club v. Costle*, the D.C. Circuit declines to label all contacts that between an agency and interested parties about a rulemaking outside the official rulemaking channels "*ex parte*." What's the Court's reasoning?

of that's court's decision in *Volpe* to overturn the agency action at issue—an informal adjudication—on the basis of improper outside influence?

### 1. *"Ex parte"* Contacts

## Home Box Office, Inc. v. Federal Communications Commission

567 F.2d 9 (D.C. Cir. 1977)

March 25, 1977

Before WRIGHT and MacKINNON, Circuit Judges, and WEIGEL, District judge.

PER CURIAM:

In these 15 cases, consolidated for purposes of argument and decision, petitioners challenge various facets of four orders of the Federal Communications Commission which, taken together, regulate and limit the program fare "cablecasters" and "subscription broadcast television stations" may offer to the public for a fee set on a per-program or per-channel basis. * * *

At the heart of these cases are the Commission's "pay cable" rules * * * . The effect of these rules is to restrict sharply the ability of cablecasters to present feature film and sports programs if a separate program or channel charge is made for this material. In addition, the rules prohibit cablecasters from devoting more than 90 percent of their cablecast hours to movie and sports programs and further bar cablecasters from showing commercial advertising on cable channels on which programs are presented for a direct charge to the viewer. Virtually identical restrictions apply to subscription broadcast television. * * *

\* \* \*

### IV. *EX PARTE* CONTACTS

During the pendency of this proceeding Mr. Henry Geller, a participant before the Commission and an *amicus* here, filed with the Commission a "Petition for Revision of Procedures or for Issuance of Notice of Inquiry or Proposed Rule Making." In this petition amicus Geller sought to call the Commission's attention to what were alleged to be violations in these proceedings of the *ex parte* communications doctrine set out by this court in *Sangamon Valley Television Corp. v. United States*, 269 F.2d 221 (1959). The Commission took no action in response to the petition, and *amicus* now presses us to set aside the orders under review here because of procedural infirmity in their promulgation.

It is apparently uncontested that a number of participants before the Commission sought out individual commissioners or Commission employees for the purpose of discussing *ex parte* and in confidence the merits of the rules under review here. In fact, the Commission itself solicited such communications in its notices of proposed rulemaking and, without discussing the nature, substance, or importance of what was said, argues before us that we should simply ignore these communications because *amicus'* petition was untimely, because *amicus* is estopped from complaining about a course of conduct in which he also participated, or, alternatively, because *Sangamon* does not apply. In an attempt to clarify the facts this court *sua sponte* ordered the Commission to provide "a list of all of the *ex parte* presentations, together with the details of each, made to it, or to any of its members or representatives, during the rulemaking proceedings." In response to this order the Commission filed a document over 60 pages long which revealed, albeit imprecisely, widespread *ex parte* communications involving virtually every party before this court, including *amicus* Geller.

Unfortunately, the document filed with this court does not allow an assessment of what was said to the Commission by the various persons who engaged in *ex parte* contacts. To give a flavor of the effect of these contacts, however, we think it useful to quote at length from the brief of *amicus* Geller:

> [*Ex parte*] presentations have in fact been made at crucial stages of the proceeding. Thus, in early 1974, then-Chairman Burch sought to complete action in this proceeding. Because the Commission was "leaning" in its deliberations towards relaxing the existing rules "with 'wildcard' rights for 'blockbuster' movies," American Broadcasting Company's representatives contacted "key members of Congress," who in turn successfully pressured the Commission not to take such action. Further, in the final crucial decisional period, the tentative course to be taken by the Commission would leak after each non-public meeting, and industry representatives would rush to make *ex parte* presentations to the Commissioners and staff. On March 10, 1975, the trade journals state that "word of last week's changes . . . got out during the week, and both broadcast and cable lobbyists rushed to the Commission, unhappy with some facets" that broadcast representatives ". . . were calling on commissioners on Friday . . ." to oppose the changes. The following week, the trade press again reported that "various [industry] groups lobbied the Commission, pressing for changes in the tentative decision" that National Association of Broadcasters ". . . staff members met with [FCC] Broadcast Bureau staffers to present data backing up [an] asserted need for [a more restrictive] standard."

It is important to note that many contacts occurred in the crucial period between the close of oral argument on October 25, 1974 and the adoption of the *First Report and Order* on March 20, 1975, when the rulemaking record should have been closed while the Commission was deciding what rules to promulgate. The information submitted to this court by the Commission indicates that during this period broadcast interests met some 18 times with Commission personnel, cable interests some nine times, motion picture and sports interests five times each, and "public interest" intervenors not at all.

1   Although it is impossible to draw any firm conclusions about the effect of *ex parte*
2   presentations upon the ultimate shape of the pay cable rules, the evidence is
3   certainly consistent with often-voiced claims of undue industry influence over
4   Commission proceedings, and we are particularly concerned that the final shaping
5   of the rules we are reviewing here may have been by compromise among the
6   contending industry forces, rather than by exercise of the independent discretion
7   in the public interest the Communications Act vests in individual commissioners.
8   Our concern is heightened by the submission of the Commission's Broadcast
9   Bureau to this court which states that in December 1974 broadcast representatives
10  "described the kind of pay cable regulation that, in their view, broadcasters 'could
11  live with.'" If actual positions were not revealed in public comments, as this
12  statement would suggest, and, further, if the Commission relied on these
13  apparently more candid private discussions in framing the final pay cable rules,
14  then the elaborate public discussion in these dockets has been reduced to a sham.

15  Even the possibility that there is here one administrative record for the public and
16  this court and another for the Commission and those "in the know" is intolerable.
17  Whatever the law may have been in the past, there can now be no doubt that
18  implicit in the decision to treat the promulgation of rules as a "final" event in an
19  ongoing process of administration is an assumption that an act of reasoned
20  judgment has occurred, an assumption which further contemplates the existence
21  of a body of material—documents, comments, transcripts, and statements in
22  various forms declaring agency expertise or policy—with reference to which such
23  judgment was exercised. Against this material, "the full administrative record that
24  was before [an agency official] at the time he made his decision," *Citizens to*
25  *Preserve Overton Park, Inc. v. Volpe, supra*, 401 U.S., at 420, it is the obligation
26  of this court to test the actions of the Commission for arbitrariness or inconsistency
27  with delegated authority. Yet here agency secrecy stands between us and
28  fulfillment of our obligation. As a practical matter, *Overton Park*'s mandate means
29  that the public record must reflect what representations were made to an agency
30  so that relevant information supporting or refuting those representations may be
31  brought to the attention of the reviewing courts by persons participating in agency
32  proceedings. This course is obviously foreclosed if communications are made to
33  the agency in secret and the agency itself does not disclose the information
34  presented. Moreover, where, as here, an agency justifies its actions by reference
35  only to information in the public file while failing to disclose the substance of other
36  relevant information that has been presented to it, a reviewing court cannot
37  presume that the agency has acted properly, *Citizens to Preserve Overton Park,*
38  *Inc. v. Volpe, supra*, 401 U.S., at 415, but must treat the agency's justifications as a
39  fictional account of the actual decisionmaking process and must perforce find its
40  actions arbitrary.

41  The failure of the public record in this proceeding to disclose all the information
42  made available to the Commission is not the only inadequacy we find here. Even if
43  the Commission had disclosed to this court the substance of what was said to it *ex*
44  *parte*, it would still be difficult to judge the truth of what the Commission asserted

1    it knew about the television industry because we would not have the benefit of an
2    adversarial discussion among the parties. The importance of such discussion to the
3    proper functioning of the agency decisionmaking and judicial review processes is
4    evident in our cases. We have insisted, for example, that information in agency files
5    or consultants' reports which the agency has identified as relevant to the
6    proceeding be disclosed to the parties for adversarial comment. Similarly, we have
7    required agencies to set out their thinking in notices of proposed rulemaking. This
8    requirement not only allows adversarial critique of the agency but is perhaps one
9    of the few ways that the public may be apprised of what the agency thinks it knows
10    in its capacity as a repository of expert opinion. From a functional standpoint, we
11    see no difference between assertions of fact and expert opinion tendered by the
12    public, as here, and that generated internally in an agency: each may be biased,
13    inaccurate, or incomplete—failings which adversary comment may illuminate.
14    Indeed, the potential for bias in private presentations in rulemakings which resolve
15    "conflicting private claims to a valuable privilege," *Sangamon Valley Television*
16    *Corp. v. United States, supra,* 269 F.2d at 224, seems to us greater than in cases
17    where we have reversed agencies for failure to disclose internal studies. * * *

18    Equally important is the inconsistency of secrecy with fundamental notions of
19    fairness implicit in due process and with the ideal of reasoned decisionmaking on
20    the merits which undergirds all of our administrative law. This inconsistency was
21    recognized in *Sangamon,* and we would have thought that the principles
22    announced there so clearly governed the instant proceeding that there could be no
23    question of the impropriety of *ex parte* contacts here. Certainly any ambiguity in
24    how *Sangamon* should be interpreted has been removed by recent congressional
25    and presidential actions. In the Government in the Sunshine Act, for example,
26    Congress has declared it to be "the policy of the United States that the public is
27    entitled to the fullest practicable information regarding the decisionmaking
28    processes of the Federal Government," and has taken steps to guard against *ex*
29    *parte* contacts in formal agency proceedings. Perhaps more closely on point is
30    Executive Order 11920, 12 Weekly Comp. of Presidential Documents 1040 (1976),
31    which prohibits *ex parte* contacts with members of the White House staff by those
32    seeking to influence allocation of international air routes during the time route
33    certifications are before the President for his approval. The President's actions
34    under Section 801 of the Federal Aviation Act are clearly not adjudication, nor even
35    quasi-judicial. Instead, the closest analogue is precisely that of *Sangamon*:
36    informal official action allocating valuable privileges among competing private
37    parties. Thus this is a time when all branches of government have taken steps
38    "designed to better assure fairness and to avoid suspicions of impropriety," White
39    House Fact Sheet on Executive Order 11920 (June 10, 1976), and consequently we
40    have no hesitation in concluding with *Sangamon* that due process requires us to
41    set aside the Commission's rules here.

42    From what has been said above, it should be clear that information gathered *ex*
43    *parte* from the public which becomes relevant to a rulemaking will have to be
44    disclosed at some time. On the other hand, we recognize that informal contacts

between agencies and the public are the "bread and butter" of the process of administration and are completely appropriate so long as they do not frustrate judicial review or raise serious questions of fairness. Reconciliation of these considerations in a manner which will reduce procedural uncertainty leads us to conclude that communications which are received prior to issuance of a formal notice of rulemaking do not, in general, have to be put in a public file. Of course, if the information contained in such a communication forms the basis for agency action, then, under well established principles, that information must be disclosed to the public in some form. Once a notice of proposed rulemaking has been issued, however, any agency official or employee who is or may reasonably be expected to be involved in the decisional process of the rulemaking proceeding, should "refus(e) to discuss matters relating to the disposition of a (rulemaking proceeding) with any interested private party, or an attorney or agent for any such party, prior to the (agency's) decision . . . ," Executive Order 11920, § 4, supra, at 1041. If *ex parte* contacts nonetheless occur, we think that any written document or a summary of any oral communication must be placed in the public file established for each rulemaking docket immediately after the communication is received so that interested parties may comment thereon.

\* \* \* Therefore, we today remand the record to the Commission for supplementation with instructions "to hold, with the aid of a specially appointed hearing examiner, an evidential hearing to determine the nature and source of all *ex parte* pleas and other approaches that were made to "the Commission or its employees after the issuance of the first notice of proposed rulemaking in these dockets." All parties to the former proceeding and to the present review may on request participate fully in the evidential hearing," and may further participate in any proceedings before the Commission which it may hold for the purpose of evaluating the report of the hearing examiner. \* \* \*

* * *

*So ordered.*

DISTRICT JUDGE WEIGEL, concurring. [Omitted.]

JUDGE MacKINNON, concurring. [Omitted.]


## Sierra Club v. Costle

 657 F.2d 298 (D.C. Cir. 1981)

April 29, 1981

Before ROBB, WALD and GINSBURG, Circuit Judges.

WALD, Circuit Judge:

1   This case concerns the extent to which new coal-fired steam generators that
2   produce electricity must control their emissions of sulfur dioxide and particulate
3   matter into the air. In June of 1979 EPA revised the regulations called "new source
4   performance standards" ("NSPS" or "standards") governing emission control by
5   coal burning power plants. On this appeal we consider challenges to the revised
6   NSPS brought by environmental groups which contend that the standards are too
7   lax and by electric utilities which contend that the standards are too rigorous.
8   Together these petitioners present an array of statutory, substantive, and
9   procedural grounds for overturning the challenged standards. For the reasons
10  stated below, we hold that EPA did not exceed its statutory authority under the
11  Clean Air Act in promulgating the NSPS, and we decline to set aside the standards.

12                              I. INTRODUCTION

13                          A. The Challenged Standards

14  The Clean Air Act provides for direct federal regulation of emissions from new
15  stationary sources of air pollution by authorizing EPA to set performance
16  standards for significant sources of air pollution which may be reasonably
17  anticipated to endanger public health or welfare. In June 1979 EPA promulgated
18  the NSPS involved in this case. The new standards increase pollution controls for
19  new coal-fired electric power plants by tightening restrictions on emissions of
20  sulfur dioxide and particulate matter. Sulfur dioxide emissions are limited to a
21  maximum of 1.2 lbs./MBtu (or 520 ng/j) and a 90 percent reduction of potential
22  uncontrolled sulfur dioxide emissions is required except when emissions to the
23  atmosphere are less than 0.60 lbs./MBtu (or 260 ng/j). When sulfur dioxide
24  emissions are less than 0.60 lbs./MBtu potential emissions must be reduced by no
25  less than 70 percent. In addition, emissions of particulate matter are limited to
26  0.03 lbs./MBtu (or 13 ng/j).

27                                  * * *

28              V. THE 1.2 LBS./MBTU EMISSION CEILING

29  EPA proposed and ultimately adopted a 1.2 lbs./MBtu ceiling for total sulfur
30  dioxide emissions which is applicable regardless of the percentage of sulfur dioxide
31  reduction attained. The 1.2 lbs./MBtu standard is identical to the emission ceiling
32  required by the former standard. The achievability of the standard is undisputed.

33  EDF [Environmental Defense Foundation] challenges this part of the final NSPS
34  on procedural grounds, contending that although there may be evidence
35  supporting the 1.2 lbs./MBtu standard, EPA should have and would have adopted
36  a stricter standard if it had not engaged in post-comment period irregularities and
37  succumbed to political pressures. * * *

38                                  * * *

39                        B. EDF'S PROCEDURAL ATTACK

EDF alleges that as a result of an "*ex parte* blitz" by coal industry advocates conducted after the close of the comment period, EPA backed away from adopting the .55 lbs./MBtu limit, and instead adopted the higher 1.2 lbs./MBtu restriction. * * *

In order for this court to assess these claims, we must identify the particular actions and incidents which gave rise to EDF's complaints. Aside from a passing reference to a telephone call from an EPA official to the Chief Executive Officer of NCAEDF's procedural objections stem from either (1) comments filed after the close of the official comment period, or (2) meetings between EPA officials and various government and private parties interested in the outcome of the final rule, all of which took place after the close of the comment period.

### 1. LATE COMMENTS

The comment period for the NSPS began on September 19, 1978, and closed on January 15, 1979. After January 15, EPA received almost 300 written submissions on the proposed rule from a broad range of interests. EPA accepted these comments and entered them all on its administrative docket. EPA did not, however, officially reopen the comment period, nor did it notify the public through the Federal Register or by other means that it had received and was entering the "late" comments. According to EDF, most of the approximately 300 late comments were received after the "leak" of the new .55 lbs./MBtu proposal. EDF claims that of the 138 late comments from non-government sources, at least 30 were from "representatives of the coal or utility industries," and of the 53 comments from members of Congress, 22 were either forwarded by the Congressmen from industry interests, or else were prepared and submitted by Congressmen as advocates of those interests.

### 2. MEETINGS

EDF objects to nine different meetings. A chronological list and synopsis of the challenged meetings follows:

> 1. *March 14, 1979*—This was a one and a half hour briefing at the White House for high-level officials from the Department of Energy (DOE), the Council of Economic Advisers (CEA), the White House staff, the Department of Interior, the Council on Environmental Quality (CEQ), the Office of Management and Budget (OMB), and the National Park Service. The meeting was reported in a May 9, 1979 memorandum from EPA to Senator Muskie's staff, responding to the Senator's request for a monthly report of contacts between EPA staff and other federal officials concerning the NSPS. A summary of the meeting and the materials distributed were docketed on May 30, 1979. EDF also obtained, after promulgation of the final rule, a copy of the memorandum to Senator Muskie in response to its Freedom of Information Act ("FOIA") request.

2. *April 5, 1979*— * * * The meeting was attended by representatives of EPA, DOE, NCA, EDF, Congressman Paul Simon's office, ICF, Inc. (who performed the microanalysis), and Hunton & Williams (who represented the Electric Utilities). The participants were notified in advance of the agenda for the meeting. Materials relating to EPA's and NCA's presentations during the meeting were distributed and copies were later put into the docket along with detailed minutes of the meeting. Follow-up calls and letters between NCA and EPA came on April 20, 23, and 29, commenting or elaborating upon the April 5 data. All of these follow-up contacts were recorded in the docket.

3. *April 23, 1979*—This was a 30-45 minute meeting held at then Senate Majority Leader Robert Byrd's request, in his office, attended by EPA Administrator Douglas Costle, Chief Presidential Assistant Stuart Eizenstat, and NCA officials. A summary of this meeting was put in the docket on May 1, 1979, and copies of the summary were sent to EDF and to other parties. In its denial of the petition for reconsideration, EPA was adamant that no new information was transmitted to EPA at this meeting.

4. *April 27, 1979*—This was a briefing on dry scrubbing technology conducted by EPA for representatives of the Office of Science and Technology Policy, the Council on Wage and Price Stability, DOE, the President's domestic policy staff, OMB, and various offices within EPA. A description of this briefing and copies of the material distributed were docketed on May 1, 1979.

5. *April 30, 1979*—At 10:00 a. m., a one hour White House briefing was held for the President, the White House staff, and high ranking members of the Executive Branch "concerning the issues and options presented by the rulemaking." This meeting was noted on an EPA official's personal calendar which EDF obtained after promulgation in response to its FOIA request, but was never noted in the rulemaking docket.

6. *April 30, 1979*—At 2:30 p. m., a technical briefing on dry scrubbing technology at the White House was conducted by EPA for the White House staff. A short memorandum describing this briefing was docketed on May 30, 1979.

7. *May 1, 1979*—Another White House briefing was held on the subject of FGD technology. A description of the meeting and materials distributed were docketed on May 30, 1979.

8. *May 1, 1979*—EPA conducted a one hour briefing of staff members of the Senate Committee on Environmental and Public Works concerning EPA's analysis of the effect of alternative emission ceilings on coal reserves. The briefing was "substantially the same as the briefing given to Senator Byrd on May 2, 1980." No persons other than Committee staff members and EPA officials attended the briefing. This meeting, like the one at 10:00 a. m. on

April 30, was never entered on the rulemaking docket but was listed on an EPA official's calendar obtained by EDF in response to its FOIA request. This EPA official has since stated that it was an oversight not to have a memorandum of this briefing prepared for the docket.

9. *May 2, 1979*—This was a brief meeting between Senator Byrd, EPA, DOE and NCA officials held ostensibly for Senator Byrd to hear EPA's comments on the NCA data. A 49 word, not very informative, memorandum describing the meeting was entered on the docket on June 1, 1979.

On June 16, 1980, responding to motions filed by EDF, this court ordered EPA to file affidavits providing additional information regarding five of these nine meetings (March 14, April 23, April 27, April 30, and May 2, 1979). After EPA complied with the order, EDF argued that the other meetings held on April 30 and May 1 were still undocumented, whereupon EPA voluntarily filed an affidavit describing them.

EDF believes that the communications just outlined, when taken as a whole, were so extensive and had such a serious impact on the NSPS rulemaking, that they violated EDF's rights to due process in the proceeding, and that these *"ex parte"* contacts were procedural errors of such magnitude that this court must reverse. EDF does not specify which particular features in each of the above-enumerated communications violated due process or constituted errors under the statute; indeed, EDF nowhere lists the communications in a form designed to clarify why any particular communication was unlawful. Instead, EDF labels all post-comment communications with EPA from whatever source and in whatever form as *"ex parte,"* and claims that "this court has repeatedly stated that *ex parte* contacts of substance violate due process."

At the outset, we decline to begin our task of reviewing EPA's procedures by labeling all post-comment communications with the agency as *"ex parte."* Such an approach essentially begs the question whether these particular communications in an informal rulemaking proceeding were unlawful. Instead of beginning with a conclusion that these communications were *"ex parte,"* we must evaluate the various communications in terms of their timing, source, mode, content, and the extent of their disclosure on the docket, in order to discover whether any of them violated the procedural requirements of the Clean Air Act, or of due process.

\* \* \*

E. Validity of EPA's Procedures During the Post-Comment Period

The post-comment period communications about which EDF complains vary widely in their content and mode; some are written documents or letters, others are oral conversations and briefings, while still others are meetings where alleged political arm-twisting took place. For analytical purposes we have grouped the communications into categories and shall discuss each of them separately. As a general matter, however, we note at the outset that nothing in the statute prohibits

374

EPA from admitting all post-comment communications into the record; nothing expressly requires it, either. Most likely the drafters envisioned promulgation of a rule soon after the close of the public comment period, and did not envision a months-long hiatus where continued outside communications with the agency would continue unabated. We must therefore attempt to glean the law for this case by inference from the procedural framework provided in the statute.

### 1. Written Comments Submitted During Post-Comment Period

Although no express authority to admit post-comment documents exists, the [Clean Air Act] statute does provide that:

> "All documents which become available after the proposed rule has been published and which the Administrator determines are of central relevance to the rulemaking shall be placed in the docket as soon as possible after their availability."[482]

This provision, in contrast to others in the same subparagraph, is not limited to the comment period. Apparently it allows EPA not only to put documents into the record after the comment period is over, but also to define which documents are "of central relevance" so as to require that they be placed in the docket. The principal purpose of the drafters was to define in advance, for the benefit of reviewing courts, the record upon which EPA would rely in defending the rule it finally adopted; it was not their purpose to guarantee that every piece of paper or phone call related to the rule which was received by EPA during the post-comment period be included in the docket. EPA thus has authority to place post-comment documents into the docket, but it need not do so in all instances.

Such a reading of the statute accords well with the realities of Washington administrative policymaking, where rumors, leaks, and overreactions by concerned groups abound, particularly as the time for promulgation draws near. In a proceeding such as this, one of vital concern to so many interests industry, environmental groups, as well as Congress and the Administration it would be unrealistic to think there would not naturally be attempts on all sides to stay in contact with EPA right up to the moment the final rule is promulgated. The drafters of the 1977 Amendments were practical people, well versed in such activity, and we decline now to infer from their silence that they intended to prohibit the lodging of documents with the agency at any time prior to promulgation. Common sense, after all, must play a part in our interpretation of these statutory procedures.

EPA of course could have extended, or reopened, the comment period after January 15 in order formally to accommodate the flood of new documents; it has done so in other cases. But under the circumstances of this case, we do not find

---

[482] 42 U.S.C. § 7607(d)(4)(B)(i).

\* \* \*

that it was necessary for EPA to reopen the formal comment period. In the first place, the comment period lasted over four months, and although the length of the comment period was not specified in the 1977 Amendments, the statute did put a premium on speedy decisionmaking by setting a one year deadline from the Amendments' enactment to the rules' promulgation. EPA failed to meet that deadline, and subsequently entered into a consent decree where it promised to adopt the final rules by March 19, 1979, over seven months late. EPA also failed to meet that deadline, and it was once more extended until June 1, 1979 upon agreement of the parties pursuant to court order. Reopening the formal comment period in the late spring of 1979 would have confronted the agency with a possible violation of the court order, and would further have frustrated the Congressional intent that these rules be promulgated expeditiously.

If, however, documents of central importance upon which EPA intended to rely had been entered on the docket too late for any meaningful public comment prior to promulgation, then both the structure and spirit of section 307 would have been violated. The Congressional drafters, after all, intended to provide "thorough and careful procedural safeguards . . . [to] insure an effective opportunity for public participation in the rulemaking process." Indeed the Administrator is obligated by the statute to convene a proceeding to reconsider the rule where an objection of central importance to it is proffered, and the basis of the objection arose after the comment period had closed. Thus we do not hold that there are no circumstances in which reopening the comment period would ever be required.

The case before us, however, does not present an instance where documents vital to EPA's support for its rule were submitted so late as to preclude any effective public comment. The vast majority of the written comments * * * were submitted in ample time to afford an opportunity for response. Regarding those documents submitted closer to the promulgation date, our review does not reveal that they played any significant role in the agency's support for the rule. The decisive point, however, is that EDF itself has failed to show us any particular document or documents to which it lacked an opportunity to respond, and which also were vital to EPA's support for the rule.

EDF makes only one particularized allegation concerning its inability to respond adequately to documents submitted during the post-comment period. It argues that at the April 5 meeting called by EPA, representatives of NCA produced new data purporting to show a significant impact upon available coal reserves of more restrictive emissions ceilings. EDF alleges that additional documents supporting a higher ceiling were thereafter forwarded by NCA to EPA following the April 5 meeting. We find, however, that EDF was not denied an adequate opportunity to respond to this material. EDF was provided with advance notice of the April 5 meeting's time, place, and agenda. At the meeting EDF proceeded to question the assumptions used in the coal industry's studies. After the meeting, on April 19, 1979, it sent a detailed memorandum to EPA asserting that NCA's new claims were "false" and "unsupported by the sheaves of new data the Coal Association has hastened to submit. . . ." Of course EDF would have preferred "additional time" to be able to furnish a "more complete evaluation" of the studies, but we do not find that EDF's preference for more time constitutes substantial evidence of an inability to respond. * * *

We therefore conclude that it was not improper in this case for EPA to docket and consider the post-comment documents submitted to it. Nor was it improper for EPA to decline to reopen the formal comment period and delay promulgation, since there was no proof that evidence crucial to the rule's validity was entered too late for any effective public comment.

### 2. Meetings Held With Individuals Outside EPA

The statute does not explicitly treat the issue of post-comment period meetings with individuals outside EPA. Oral face-to-face discussions are not prohibited anywhere, anytime, in the Act. The absence of such prohibition may have arisen from the nature of the informal rulemaking procedures Congress had in mind. Where agency action resembles judicial action, where it involves formal rulemaking, adjudication, or quasi-adjudication among "conflicting private claims to a valuable privilege," the insulation of the decisionmaker from *ex parte* contacts is justified by basic notions of due process to the parties involved. But where agency action involves informal rulemaking of a policymaking sort, the concept of *ex parte* contacts is of more questionable utility.

Under our system of government, the very legitimacy of general policymaking performed by unelected administrators depends in no small part upon the openness, accessibility, and amenability of these officials to the needs and ideas of the public from whom their ultimate authority derives, and upon whom their commands must fall. As judges we are insulated from these pressures because of the nature of the judicial process in which we participate; but we must refrain from the easy temptation to look askance at all face-to-face lobbying efforts, regardless of the forum in which they occur, merely because we see them as inappropriate in the judicial context. Furthermore, the importance to effective regulation of continuing contact with a regulated industry, other affected groups, and the public cannot be underestimated. Informal contacts may enable the agency to win needed support for its program, reduce future enforcement requirements by helping those regulated to anticipate and shape their plans for the future, and spur the provision of information which the agency needs. The possibility of course exists that in permitting *ex parte* communications with rulemakers we create the danger of "one administrative record for the public and this court and another for the Commission." Under the Clean Air Act procedures, however, "[t]he promulgated rule may not be based (in part or whole) on any information or data which has not been placed in the docket. . . ." Thus EPA must justify its rulemaking solely on the basis of the record it compiles and makes public.

Regardless of this court's views on the need to restrict all post-comment contacts in the informal rulemaking context, however, it is clear to us that Congress has decided not to do so in the statute which controls this case. As we have previously noted:

> "Where Congress wanted to prohibit *ex parte* contacts it clearly did so. Thus APA § 5(c) forbids *ex parte* contacts when an 'adjudication' is underway, but even that prohibition does not apply to 'the agency or a member or members of the body comprising the agency.' 5 U.S.C. § 554(d)(C) (1970). . . . If Congress wanted to forbid or limit *ex parte* contact in every case of informal rulemaking, it certainly had a perfect opportunity of doing so when it enacted the Government in the Sunshine Act, Pub.L. No. 94-409 (Sept. 13, 1976). . . . That it did not extend the *ex parte* contact provisions of the amended section 557 to section 553 even though such an extension was urged upon it during the hearing is a sound indication that Congress still does not favor a per se prohibition or even a 'logging' requirement in all such proceedings.

*Action for Children's Television v. FCC*, 564 F.2d 458, 474-75 n. 28 (D.C. Cir. 1977)

Lacking a statutory basis for its position, EDF would have us extend our decision in *Home Box Office, Inc. v. FCC* to cover all meetings with individuals outside EPA during the post-comment period. Later decisions of this court, however, have declined to apply *Home Box Office* to informal rulemaking of the general policymaking sort involved here, and there is no precedent for applying it to the procedures found in the Clean Air Act Amendments of 1977.

It still can be argued, however, that if oral communications are to be freely permitted after the close of the comment period, then at least some adequate summary of them must be made in order to preserve the integrity of the rulemaking docket, which under the statute must be the sole repository of material upon which EPA intends to rely. The statute does not require the docketing of all post-comment period conversations and meetings, but we believe that a fair inference can be drawn that in some instances such docketing may be needed in order to give practical effect to section 307(d)(4)(B)(i), which provides that all documents "of central relevance to the rulemaking" shall be placed in the docket as soon as possible after their availability. This is so because unless oral communications of central relevance to the rulemaking are also docketed in some fashion or other, information central to the justification of the rule could be obtained without ever appearing on the docket, simply by communicating it by voice rather than by pen, thereby frustrating the command of section 307 that the final rule not be "based (in part or whole) on any information or data which has not been placed in the docket . . . ."

EDF is understandably wary of a rule which permits the agency to decide for itself when oral communications are of such central relevance that a docket entry for them is required. Yet the statute itself vests EPA with discretion to decide whether "documents" are of central relevance and therefore must be placed in the docket; surely EPA can be given no less discretion in docketing oral communications,

1  concerning which the statute has no explicit requirements whatsoever.
2  Furthermore, this court has already recognized that the relative significance of
3  various communications to the outcome of the rule is a factor in determining
4  whether their disclosure is required. A judicially imposed blanket requirement that
5  all post-comment period oral communications be docketed would, on the other
6  hand, contravene our limited powers of review, would stifle desirable
7  experimentation in the area by Congress and the agencies, and is unnecessary for
8  achieving the goal of an established, procedure-defined docket to enable reviewing
9  courts to fully evaluate the stated justification given by the agency for its final rule.

10  Turning to the particular oral communications in this case, we find that only two
11  of the nine contested meetings were undocketed by EPA. The agency has
12  maintained that, as to the May 1 meeting where Senate staff people were briefed
13  on EPA's analysis concerning the impact of alternative emissions ceilings upon
14  coal reserves, its failure to place a summary of the briefing in the docket was an
15  oversight. We find no evidence that this oversight was anything but an honest
16  inadvertence; furthermore, a briefing of this sort by EPA which simply provides
17  background information about an upcoming rule is not the type of oral
18  communication which would require a docket entry under the statute.

19  The other undocketed meeting occurred at the White House and involved the
20  President and his White House staff. Because this meeting involves considerations
21  unique to intra-executive meetings, it is discussed in the section immediately *infra*.

22              (a) Intra-Executive Branch Meetings

23  We have already held that a blanket prohibition against meetings during the post-
24  comment period with individuals outside EPA is unwarranted, and this perforce
25  applies to meetings with White House officials. We have not yet addressed,
26  however, the issue whether such oral communications with White House staff, or
27  the President himself, must be docketed on the rulemaking record, and we now
28  turn to that issue. The facts, as noted earlier, present us with a single undocketed
29  meeting held on April 30, 1979, at 10:00 a. m., attended by the President, White
30  House staff, other high ranking members of the Executive Branch, as well as EPA
31  officials, and which concerned the issues and options presented by the rulemaking.

32  * * * [I]t is hard to believe Congress was unaware that intra-executive meetings and
33  oral comments would occur throughout the rulemaking process. We assume,
34  therefore, that unless expressly forbidden by Congress, such intra-executive
35  contacts may take place, both during and after the public comment period; the only
36  real issue is whether they must be noted and summarized in the docket.

37  The court recognizes the basic need of the President and his White House staff to
38  monitor the consistency of executive agency regulations with Administration
39  policy. He and his White House advisers surely must be briefed fully and frequently
40  about rules in the making, and their contributions to policymaking considered. The
41  executive power under our Constitution, after all, is not shared it rests exclusively
42  with the President. The idea of a "plural executive," or a President with a council

379

1   of state, was considered and rejected by the Constitutional Convention. Instead the
2   Founders chose to risk the potential for tyranny inherent in placing power in one
3   person, in order to gain the advantages of accountability fixed on a single source.
4   To ensure the President's control and supervision over the Executive Branch, the
5   Constitution—and its judicial gloss—vests him with the powers of appointment and
6   removal, the power to demand written opinions from executive officers, and the
7   right to invoke executive privilege to protect consultative privacy. In the particular
8   case of EPA, Presidential authority is clear since it has never been considered an
9   "independent agency," but always part of the Executive Branch.

10  The authority of the President to control and supervise executive policymaking is
11  derived from the Constitution; the desirability of such control is demonstrable
12  from the practical realities of administrative rulemaking. Regulations such as those
13  involved here demand a careful weighing of cost, environmental, and energy
14  considerations. They also have broad implications for national economic policy.
15  Our form of government simply could not function effectively or rationally if key
16  executive policymakers were isolated from each other and from the Chief
17  Executive. Single mission agencies do not always have the answers to complex
18  regulatory problems. An overworked administrator exposed on a 24-hour basis to
19  a dedicated but zealous staff needs to know the arguments and ideas of
20  policymakers in other agencies as well as in the White House.

21  We recognize, however, that there may be instances where the docketing of
22  conversations between the President or his staff and other Executive Branch
23  officers or rulemakers may be necessary to ensure due process. This may be true,
24  for example, where such conversations directly concern the outcome of
25  adjudications or quasi-adjudicatory proceedings; there is no inherent executive
26  power to control the rights of individuals in such settings. Docketing may also be
27  necessary in some circumstances where a statute like this one specifically requires
28  that essential "information or data" upon which a rule is based be docketed. But in
29  the absence of any further Congressional requirements, we hold that it was not
30  unlawful in this case for EPA not to docket a face-to-face policy session involving
31  the President and EPA officials during the post-comment period, since EPA makes
32  no effort to base the rule on any "information or data" arising from that meeting.
33  Where the President himself is directly involved in oral communications with
34  Executive Branch officials, Article II considerations—combined with the strictures
35  of *Vermont Yankee*—require that courts tread with extraordinary caution in
36  mandating disclosure beyond that already required by statute.

37  The purposes of full-record review which underlie the need for disclosing *ex parte*
38  conversations in some settings do not require that courts know the details of every
39  White House contact, including a Presidential one, in this informal rulemaking
40  setting. After all, any rule issued here with or without White House assistance must
41  have the requisite *factual support* in the rulemaking record, and under this
42  particular statute the Administrator may not base the rule in whole or in part on
43  any "information or data" which is not in the record, no matter what the source.
44  The courts will monitor all this, but they need not be omniscient to perform their

1   role effectively. Of course, it is always possible that undisclosed Presidential
2   prodding may direct an outcome that is factually based on the record, but different
3   from the outcome that would have obtained in the absence of Presidential
4   involvement. In such a case, it would be true that the political process did affect
5   the outcome in a way the courts could not police. But we do not believe that
6   Congress intended that the courts convert informal rulemaking into a rarified
7   technocratic process, unaffected by political considerations or the presence of
8   Presidential power. In sum, we find that the existence of intra-Executive Branch
9   meetings during the post-comment period, and the failure to docket one such
10  meeting involving the President, violated neither the procedures mandated by the
11  Clean Air Act nor due process.

12          (b) Meetings Involving Alleged Congressional Pressure

13  Finally, EDF challenges the rulemaking on the basis of alleged Congressional
14  pressure, citing principally two meetings with Senator Byrd. EDF asserts that
15  under the controlling case law the political interference demonstrated in this case
16  represents a separate and independent ground for invalidating this rulemaking.
17  But among the cases EDF cites in support of its position, only *D. C. Federation of*
18  *Civil Associations v. Volpe* seems relevant to the facts here.

19  In *D. C. Federation the Secretary of Transportation*, pursuant to applicable
20  federal statutes, made certain safety and environmental findings in designating a
21  proposed bridge as part of the interstate highway system. Civic associations sought
22  to have these determinations set aside for their failure to meet certain statutory
23  standards, and because of possible tainting by reason of improper Congressional
24  influence. * * *

25  *D. C. Federation* * * * requires that two conditions be met before an administrative
26  rulemaking may be overturned simply on the grounds of Congressional pressure.
27  First, the content of the pressure upon the Secretary is designed to force him to
28  decide upon factors not made relevant by Congress in the applicable statute. * * *
29  Second, the Secretary's determination must be affected by those extraneous
30  considerations.

31  In the case before us, there is no persuasive evidence that either criterion is
32  satisfied. Senator Byrd requested a meeting in order to express "strongly" his
33  already well-known views that the $SO_2$ standards' impact on coal reserves was a
34  matter of concern to him. EPA initiated a second responsive meeting to report its
35  reaction to the reserve data submitted by the NCA. In neither meeting is there any
36  allegation that EPA made any commitments to Senator Byrd. The meetings did
37  underscore Senator Byrd's deep concerns for EPA, but there is no evidence he
38  attempted actively to use "extraneous" pressures to further his position. Americans
39  rightly expect their elected representatives to voice their grievances and
40  preferences concerning the administration of our laws. We believe it entirely
41  proper for Congressional representatives vigorously to represent the interests of
42  their constituents before administrative agencies engaged in informal, general

1   policy rulemaking, so long as individual Congressmen do not frustrate the intent
2   of Congress as a whole as expressed in statute, nor undermine applicable rules of
3   procedure. Where Congressmen keep their comments focused on the substance of
4   the proposed rule and we have no substantial evidence to cause us to believe
5   Senator Byrd did not do so here administrative agencies are expected to balance
6   Congressional pressure with the pressures emanating from all other sources. To
7   hold otherwise would deprive the agencies of legitimate sources of information and
8   call into question the validity of nearly every controversial rulemaking.

9   In sum, we conclude that EPA's adoption of the 1.2 lbs./MBtu emissions ceiling
10   was free from procedural error. The post-comment period contacts here violated
11   neither the statute nor the integrity of the proceeding. We also hold that it was not
12   improper for the agency to docket and consider documents submitted to it during
13   the post-comment period, since no document vital to EPA's support for the rule
14   was submitted so late as to preclude any effective public comment. Hence we find
15   no reason under section 307 to overturn the 1.2 lbs./MBtu standard. The field of
16   course is open for Congress or the agency to formulate further procedural rules in
17   this area.

18   CONCLUSION

19   Since the issues in this proceeding were joined in 1973 when the Navajo Indians
20   first complained about sulfur dioxide fumes over their Southwest homes, we have
21   had several lawsuits, almost four years of substantive and procedural maneuvering
22   before the EPA, and now this extended court challenge. In the interim, Congress
23   has amended the Clean Air Act once and may be ready to do so again. The standard
24   we uphold has already been in effect for almost two years, and could be revised
25   within another two years.

26   We reach our decision after interminable record searching (and considerable soul
27   searching). We have read the record with as hard a look as mortal judges can
28   probably give its thousands of pages. We have adopted a simple and straight-
29   forward standard of review, probed the agency's rationale, studied its references
30   (and those of appellants), endeavored to understand them where they were
31   intelligible (parts were simply impenetrable), and on close questions given the
32   agency the benefit of the doubt out of deference for the terrible complexity of its
33   job. We are not engineers, computer modelers, economists or statisticians,
34   although many of the documents in this record require such expertise and more.

35   Cases like this highlight the critical responsibilities Congress has entrusted to the
36   courts in proceedings of such length, complexity and disorder. Conflicting interests
37   play fiercely for enormous stakes, advocates are prolific and agile, obfuscation runs
38   high, common sense correspondingly low, the public interest is often obscured.

39   We cannot redo the agency's job; Congress has told us, at least in proceedings
40   under this Act, that it will not brook reversal for small procedural errors; *Vermont*
41   *Yankee* reinforces the admonition. So in the end we can only make our best effort
42   to understand, to see if the result makes sense, and to assure that nothing unlawful

1 or irrational has taken place. In this case, we have taken a long while to come to a
2 short conclusion: the rule is reasonable.

3 Affirmed.

4

5 ## D.C. Federation of Civic Associations v. Volpe

6 459 F.2d 1231 (D.C. Cir. 1971)

7 October 11, 1971

8 Before BAZELON, Chief Judge, FAHY, Senior Circuit Judge, and MacKINNON,
9 Circuit Judge.

10 BAZELON, Chief Judge:

11 This appeal injects us back into the midst of a long and sometimes acrimonious
12 imbroglio over the proposed construction of a bridge across the Potomac River
13 from Virginia into the District of Columbia. In an earlier appeal we held that the
14 so-called Three Sisters Bridge could not be built except in compliance with the
15 hearing, environmental protection, safety, and other provisions of federal law
16 applicable to the construction of federally-assisted highway projects. That
17 question, accordingly, is no longer open. We must now decide whether the
18 Department of Transportation did, in fact and in law, heed the applicable federal
19 statutes when it decided that the bridge should be built. * * *

20 * * * Briefly stated, the controversy concerns a projected bridge between the
21 Georgetown waterfront in the District of Columbia and Spout Run in Virginia. The
22 bridge, which would be part of the Interstate Highway System and would be built
23 largely with federal funds, would traverse the Three Sisters Islands, would "affect
24 the Georgetown Historic District," and would use some parkland. The precise
25 amount of harm to parkland and historic sites has not yet been determined,
26 however, since the planning of the bridge—including the approaches and access
27 roads—is not yet finalized. A source of continuous controversy since its conception,
28 the proposed bridge was deleted from the Interstate Highway System in January,
29 1969, when the National Capital Planning Commission, the official planning body
30 for the District, adopted "a comprehensive transportation plan which did not
31 include the Three Sisters Bridge." The bridge was redesignated part of the
32 Interstate System six months later after Representative Natcher, Chairman of the
33 Subcommittee on the District of Columbia of the House Appropriations
34 Committee, indicated unmistakably that money for construction of the District's
35 subway system would be withheld if the bridge plan were not revived. To satisfy
36 the Chairman, it was necessary, first, for the District of Columbia City Council to

1   reverse its earlier position,[9] and vote to approve the project. On August 9, 1969,
2   the District government so voted, with the swing members loudly protesting that
3   they would not have changed their votes but for the pressures exerted by
4   Representative Natcher. The second prerequisite of redesignation was a decision
5   by Transportation Secretary Volpe that the project should go ahead as part of the
6   Interstate System. He announced that decision on August 12, 1969, and the project
7   sprang full-blown back to life on the following day.

8                         I

9   Given our earlier decision, the Secretary's approval of the bridge must be
10  predicated on compliance with a number of statutory provisions. Plaintiffs
11  challenged with two lines of argument the District Court's finding of compliance.
12  First, they maintain that the Secretary's determinations under the statute were
13  tainted by his consideration of extraneous factors unrelated to the merits of the
14  questions presented. They allege—and argue, moreover, that the District Court
15  specifically found—that pressures exerted by Representative Natcher contributed
16  to the decision to approve the bridge. Second, they argue that quite apart from the
17  allegations of pressure, the record and applicable legal principles do not support a
18  finding of compliance. The two strands of argument are plainly related, in
19  plaintiffs' view, since the alleged shortcomings under each statutory provision
20  illustrate and lend substance to the argument that the rational, impartial
21  evaluation of the project envisioned by the statute was impermissibly distorted by
22  extraneous pressures. We consider first plaintiffs' argument that the
23  determinations could not stand even if there were no issue of extraneous pressure.

24                       * * *

25                        II

26  As Part I of this opinion makes clear, the Secretary's determinations failed to
27  comply with a significant number of title 23 provisions applicable to the Three
28  Sisters Bridge. Taken as a whole, the defects in the Secretary's determinations—in
29  particular, his effort to make the determinations before plans for the bridge were
30  complete—lend color to plaintiffs' contention that the repeated and public threats
31  by a few Congressional voices did have an impact on the Secretary's decisions. * * *

32                       * * *

33  The author of this opinion is convinced that the impact of this pressure is sufficient,
34  standing alone, to invalidate the Secretary's action. Even if the Secretary had taken
35  every formal step required by every applicable statutory provision, reversal would

---

[19] On Jan. 17, 1969, the District's City Council had voted to approve the NCPC
transportation plan which rejected the Three Sisters Bridge as unnecessary and
undesirable.

be required, in my opinion, because extraneous pressure intruded into the calculus of considerations on which the Secretary's decision was based. * * *

\* \* \*

The District Court was surely correct in concluding that the Secretary's action was not judicial or quasi-judicial, and for that reason we agree that much of the doctrine cited by plaintiffs is inapposite. If he had been acting in such a capacity, plaintiffs could have forcefully argued that the decision was invalid because of the decisionmaker's bias, or because he had received *ex parte* communications. Well-established principles could have been invoked to support these arguments, and plaintiffs might have prevailed even without showing that the pressure had actually influenced the Secretary's decision. With regard to judicial decisionmaking, whether by court or agency, the appearance of bias or pressure may be no less objectionable than the reality. But since the Secretary's action was not judicial, that rationale has no application here.

If, on the other hand, the Secretary's action had been purely legislative, we might have agreed with the District Court that his decision could stand in spite of a finding that he had considered extraneous pressures. Beginning with *Fletcher v. Peck*, the Supreme Court has maintained that a statute cannot be invalidated merely because the legislature's action was motivated by impermissible considerations (except, perhaps, in special circumstances not applicable here). Indeed, that very principle requires us to reject plaintiffs' argument that the approval of the bridge by the District of Columbia City Council was in some sense invalid. We do not sit in judgment of the motives of the District's legislative body, nor do we have authority to review its decisions. The City Council's action constituted, in our view, the approval of the project required by statute.

Thus, the underlying problem cannot be illuminated by a simplistic effort to force the Secretary's action into a purely judicial or purely legislative mold. His decision was not "judicial" in that he was not required to base it solely on a formal record established at a public hearing. At the same time, it was not purely "legislative" since Congress had already established the boundaries within which his discretion could operate. But even though his action fell between these two conceptual extremes, it is still governed by principles that we had thought elementary and beyond dispute. If, in the course of reaching his decision, Secretary Volpe took into account "considerations that Congress could not have intended to make relevant,"[82] his action proceeded from an erroneous premise and his decision cannot stand. The error would be more flagrant, of course, if the Secretary had based his decision solely on the pressures generated by Representative Natcher. But it should be clear that his action would not be immunized merely because he also considered some relevant factors.

---

[82] United States ex rel. Kaloudis v. Shaughnessy, 180 F.2d 489, 491 (2d Cir. 1950).

1  It is plainly not our function to establish the parameters of relevance. Congress has
2  carried out that task in its delegation of authority to the Secretary of
3  Transportation. Nor are we charged with the power to decide where or when
4  bridges should be built. That responsibility has been entrusted by Congress to,
5  among others, the Secretary, who has the expertise and information to make a
6  decision pursuant to the statutory standards. So long as the Secretary applies his
7  expertise to considerations Congress intended to make relevant, he acts within his
8  discretion and our role as a reviewing court is constrained. We do not hold, in other
9  words that the bridge can never be built. Nor do we know or mean to suggest that
10 the information now available to the Secretary is necessarily insufficient to justify
11 construction of the bridge. We hold only that the Secretary must reach his decision
12 strictly on the merits and in the manner prescribed by statute, without reference
13 to irrelevant or extraneous considerations.

14                                          * * *

15 To avoid any misconceptions about the nature of our holding, we emphasize that
16 we have not found—nor, for that matter, have we sought—any suggestion of
17 impropriety or illegality in the actions of Representative Natcher and others who
18 strongly advocate the bridge. They are surely entitled to their own views on the
19 need for the Three Sisters Bridge, and we indicate no opinion on their authority to
20 exert pressure on Secretary Volpe. Nor do we mean to suggest that Secretary Volpe
21 acted in bad faith or in deliberate disregard of his statutory responsibilities. He was
22 placed, through the action of others, in an extremely treacherous position. Our
23 holding is designed, if not to extricate him from that position, at least to enhance
24 his ability to obey the statutory command notwithstanding the difficult position in
25 which he was placed.

26                                          III

27 We conclude that the case should be remanded to the District Court with directions
28 that it return the case to the Secretary for him to perform his statutory function in
29 accordance with this opinion. It seems clear that even though formal
30 administrative findings are not required by statute, the Secretary could best serve
31 the interests of the parties as well as the reviewing court by establishing a full-scale
32 administrative record which might dispel any doubts about the true basis of his
33 action. Accordingly, the District Court is directed to enjoin construction of the
34 bridge until the defendants have complied with the applicable statutory provisions
35 as set forth in our opinion.

36 Reversed and remanded.

37 FAHY, Senior Circuit Judge, with whom BAZELTON, Chief Judge, joins,
38 concurring. [Omitted.]

39

40    ## 2. Impartiality and Agency Decisionmaking

1 The APA states that the functions of decisionmakers in on-the-record proceedings
2 "shall be conducted in an impartial manner." 5 U.S.C. § 556(b)(3). However, the
3 APA has nothing to say about the impartiality of decisionmakers in informal
4 proceedings (which include notice-and-comment rulemaking). Does this mean it
5 is permissible for administrators to approach rulemakings with their minds made
6 up before they begin? Compare how Judge Tamm of the D.C. Circuit handles
7 claims that Federal Trade Commissioners should recuse themselves in *Cinderella*
8 *Career and Finishing Schools, Inc.* and *Association of National Advertisers.*

9

## 10 Cinderella Career and Finishing Schools, Inc. v. Federal Trade
## 11 Commission

12 425 F.2d 583 (D.C. Cir. 1970)

13 March 20, 1970

14 Before TAMM, MacKINNON and ROBB, Circuit Judges.

15 TAMM, Circuit Judge:

16 This is a petition to review orders of the Federal Trade Commission which required
17 petitioners Cinderella Career College and Finishing Schools, Inc. (hereinafter
18 Cinderella), Stephen Corporation (the corporate entity which operates Cinderella),
19 and Vincent Melzac (the sole owner of the stock of Cinderella and Stephen
20 Corporation), to cease and desist from engaging in certain practices which were
21 allegedly unfair and deceptive.

22 After the Commission filed its complaint under section 5 of the Federal Trade
23 Commission Act, 15 U.S.C. § 45 (1964), which charged Cinderella with making
24 representations and advertising in a manner which was false, misleading and
25 deceptive, a hearing examiner held a lengthy series of hearings which consumed a
26 total of sixteen days; these proceedings are reported in 1,810 pages of transcript.
27 After the Commission had called twenty-nine witnesses and the petitioners
28 twenty-three, and after the FTC had introduced 157 exhibits and petitioners 90
29 (Petitioners' Brief at 7), the hearing examiner ruled in a ninety-three page initial
30 decision that the charges in the complaint should be dismissed.

31 Complaint counsel appealed the hearing examiner's initial decision to the full
32 Commission * * *. For the reasons which follow we remand to the Commission for
33 further proceedings.

34 We are faced with two principal issues on this appeal: whether the action of the
35 Commission in reversing the hearing examiner comports with standards of due
36 process, and whether then Chairman Paul Rand Dixon should have recused
37 himself from participation in the review of the initial decision due to public
38 statements he had previously made which allegedly indicated pre-judgment of the
39 case on his part.

1 ## I. Procedural Irregularity and Due Process

2     * * * [T]he hearing on the complaint against petitioners was exhaustive. The
3 important question raised by petitioners here is whether the full Commission, in
4 reviewing an initial decision, may consider the advertisements de novo,
5 disregarding entirely the evidence adduced at a lengthy hearing, and arrive at
6 independent findings of fact and conclusions of law, or whether the Commission is
7 bound by its own rules and regulations, as well as concepts of due process, to
8 review the conclusions of the hearing examiner in light of the evidence.

9     In their final decision the Commissioners first criticized the hearing examiner for
10 his handling of some of the testimony, stating that " [f]rom the initial decision it
11 appears that the examiner ignored some of this testimony and some of it was given
12 little or no weight because the examiner either questioned the credibility of the
13 witness or considered their testimony hearsay." The Commissioners themselves
14 then proceeded to ignore all testimony completely: " [I]n view of our decision to
15 independently analyze—and without assistance from consumer or other
16 witnesses—the challenged advertisements and their impact ... *it becomes*
17 *unnecessary to review the testimony of these expert and consumer witnesses.*"
18 (emphasis added.) Later in the opinion they again noted that "for the reasons
19 stated above *the Commission will rely on its own reading and study of the*
20 *advertisements to determine whether the questioned representation has the*
21 *capacity to deceive.*" (emphasis added.) The hearing examiner in a Federal Trade
22 Commission proceeding has both the right and duty to make determinations
23 concerning the credibility of witnesses and the exclusion of hearsay evidence; while
24 the Commissioners may review those determinations on appeal, in light of the
25 record, they may not choose to ignore completely the testimony adduced at the
26 hearing. A further example of the Commissioners' determination to make a de
27 novo review of the advertisements rather than considering the record as developed
28 during the hearing is the statement that:

29      "A review of the examiner's initial decision has persuaded the members of
30      the Commission to *examine* firsthand and *independently* the challenged
31      representations contained in respondents' advertisements rather than
32      relying on the analysis thereof contained in the initial decision." (emphasis
33      added)

34     Not only do we find this conduct on the part of the Commissioners a violation of
35 their own rules and hence of due process, but we also seriously question their
36 ability to make the determination called for without the aid of the testimony in the
37 record. It should be noted that the advertisements here in question are directed at
38 a specific, narrow part of the public—teenage girls who are recent high school
39 graduates and who do not intend to pursue their formal education in college. While
40 it may be true that some advertisements are so glaringly misleading that anyone
41 can recognize that fact, we think it could only benefit the ultimate determination if
42 the Commissioners had before them the testimony both of experts on youth and of
43 teenage girls themselves, in addition to their own reading of the statements alleged

388

1    to be misleading. While they might initially decide that a given statement had the
2    capacity to mislead, perhaps testimony of experts and consumers would reveal that
3    the group at which the statements were directed was in fact more knowledgeable
4    and sophisticated than the Commissioners had originally anticipated. In any event,
5    we think it can only help, and certainly it will not hurt, to have the testimony before
6    the reviewing Commissioners as well as their own reading of the advertisements.

7    As authority for the proposition that they could properly ignore the record and
8    make a de novo determination of the capacity of the statement to mislead, the
9    Commissioners state only that "[t]he Commission's authority to predicate a finding
10   of deception on its own examination and study is too well settled to require further
11   comment." * * *

12                                                   * * *

13   * * * We are unable to find any authority for their proposition—that a sixteen-day
14   hearing may be completely ignored if the Commissioners are dissatisfied with the
15   result reached by their hearing examiner. In fact, language in an opinion which the
16   Commission cites cuts decidedly the other way:

17        This finding [that advertising tended to deceive] was amply supported by
18        *evidence adduced in the proceedings before the Commission* .... The
19        applicable section of the Act provides ... that upon a review of this kind "
20        [t]he findings of the Commission as to the facts, *if supported by evidence*,
21        shall be conclusive."

22   *Stauffer Laboratories, Inc. v. FTC*, 343 F.2d 75, 79 (9th Cir. 1965) (emphasis
23   added).

24                                                  * * *

25   The procedures for decision on appeal have been established for the Federal Trade
26   Commission as follows:

27        "Upon appeal from or review of an initial decision, the Commission *will*
28        *consider* such parts of the record as are cited or as may be necessary to
29        resolve the issues presented and, *in addition*, will, to the extent necessary
30        or desirable, exercise all the power which it could have exercised *if* it had
31        made the initial decision."

32   16 C.F.R. § 3.54(a) (1969) (emphasis added). Surely this language makes it clear
33   that the five Commissioners, in reviewing an initial decision, are not to speak as
34   *verbum regis*, but must consider the evidence adduced at the hearing. The
35   regulation makes it clear that the Commissioners will consider the record, and that
36   they may *additionally* exercise the powers they could have exercised had they
37   made the initial decision. * * *

38   The regulations establish the procedure the Commission is to follow:

"In rendering its decision [on appeal or review], the Commission will adopt, modify, or set aside the findings, conclusions, and rule or order contained in the initial decision, and will include in the decision a statement of the reasons or basis for its action."

16 C.F.R. § 3.54(b) (1969). This gives the reviewing Commissioners great latitude to disagree with their hearing examiner; it does not, however, give them the option of completely ignoring the testimony of many witnesses and the findings of the examiner on premises which are legally evanescent. If they choose to modify or set aside his conclusions they must state that they are doing so and they must give reasons for so doing. To hold otherwise is to ignore the objectives of adversary proceedings before the Commission. Only if such rules are carefully adhered to can a reviewing court properly analyze the action taken by the Commission; only then can the wheat of meaningful agency action be separated from the chaff of arbitrary and capricious conduct. The Commissioners may not turn away in haughty administrative aloofness from the entire body of law governing their procedures.

## II. Disqualification of Chairman Dixon

An additional ground which requires remand of these proceedings—and which would have required reversal even in the absence of the above-described procedural irregularities—is participation in the proceedings by the then Chairman of the Federal Trade Commission, Paul Rand Dixon.

* * * [W]hile the appeal from the examiner's decision was pending before him, Chairman Dixon made a speech before the Government Relations Workshop of the National Newspaper Association in which he stated:

"What kind of vigor can a reputable newspaper exhibit? The quick answer, of course, pertains to its editorial policy, its willingness to present the news without bias. However, that is only half the coin. How about ethics on the business side of running a paper? What standards are maintained on advertising acceptance? What would be the attitude toward accepting good money for advertising by a merchant who conducts a 'going out of business' sale every five months? *What about carrying ads that offer college educations in five weeks*, fortunes by raising mushrooms in the basement, getting rid of pimples with a magic lotion, or becoming an airline's hostess by attending a charm school? Or, to raise the target a bit, how many newspapers would hesitate to accept an ad promising an unqualified guarantee for a product when the guarantee is subject to many limitations? Without belaboring the point, I'm sure you're aware that advertising acceptance standards could stand more tightening by many newspapers. *Granted that newspapers are not in the advertising policing business, their advertising managers are savvy enough to smell deception when the odor is strong enough.* And it is in the public interest, as well as their own, that their sensory organs become more discriminating. The Federal Trade

1     Commission, even where it has jurisdiction, could not protect the public as
2     quickly.

3     It requires no superior olfactory powers to recognize that the danger of unfairness
4     through prejudgment is not diminished by a cloak of self-righteousness. We have
5     no concern for or interest in the public statements of government officers, but we
6     are charged with the responsibility of making certain that the image of the
7     administrative process is not transformed from a Rubens to a Modigliani.

8     We indicated in our earlier opinion in this case that "there is in fact and law
9     authority in the Commission, acting in the public interest, to alert the public to
10     *suspected* violations of the law by *factual press releases* whenever the Commission
11     shall have reason to believe that a respondent is engaged in activities made
12     unlawful by the Act . . .." *FTC v. Cinderella Career & Finishing Schools, Inc.*, 404
13     F.2d 1308, 1314 (1968) (emphasis added). This does not give individual
14     Commissioners license to prejudge cases or to make speeches which give the
15     appearance that the case has been prejudged. * * * There is a marked difference
16     between the issuance of a press release which states that the Commission has filed
17     a complaint because it has "reason to believe" that there have been violations, and
18     statements by a Commissioner after an appeal has been filed which give the
19     appearance that he has already prejudged the case and that the ultimate
20     determination of the merits will move in predestined grooves. While these two
21     situations—Commission press releases and a Commissioner's pre-decision public
22     statements—are similar in appearance, they are obviously of a different order of
23     merit.

24     As we noted in our earlier opinion, Congress has specifically vested the
25     administrative agencies both with the "power to act in an accusatory capacity" and
26     with the "responsibility of ultimately determining the merits of the charges so
27     presented."

28     Chairman Dixon, sensitive to theory but insensitive to reality, made the following
29     statement in declining to recuse himself from this case after petitioners requested
30     that he withdraw:

31         "As . . . I have stated . . . this principle 'is not a rigid command of the law,
32         compelling disqualification for trifling causes, but a consideration
33         addressed to the discretion and sound judgment of the administrator,
34         himself in determining whether, irrespective of the law's requirements, he
35         should disqualify himself.'"

36     To this tenet of self-appraisal we apply Lord Macaulay's evaluation more than 100
37     years ago of our American government: "It has one drawback—it is all sail and no
38     anchor." We find it hard to believe that former Chairman Dixon is so indifferent to
39     the dictates of the Courts of Appeals that he has chosen once again to put his
40     personal determination of what the law requires ahead of what the courts have
41     time and again told him the law requires. If this is a question of "discretion and
42     judgment," Commissioner Dixon has exercised questionable discretion and very

poor judgment indeed, in directing his shafts and squibs at a case awaiting his official action. We can use his own words in telling Commissioner Dixon that he has acted "irrespective of the law's requirements"; we will spell out for him once again, avoiding tired cliche and weary generalization, in no uncertain terms, exactly what those requirements are, in the fervent hope that this will be the last time we have to travel this wearisome road.

The test for disqualification has been succinctly stated as being whether "a disinterested observer may conclude that [the agency] has in some measure adjudged the facts as well as the law of a particular case in advance of hearing it." *Gilligan, Will & Co. v. SEC*, 267 F.2d 461, 469 (2d Cir.).

\* \* \*

It is appalling to witness such insensitivity to the requirements of due process; it is even more remarkable to find ourselves once again confronted with a situation in which Mr. Dixon, pouncing on the most convenient victim, has determined either to distort the holdings in the cited cases beyond all reasonable interpretation or to ignore them altogether. We are constrained to this harshness of language because of Mr. Dixon's flagrant disregard of prior decisions.

The rationale for remanding the case despite the fact that former Chairman Dixon's vote was not necessary for a majority is well established:

> "Litigants are entitled to an impartial tribunal whether it consists of one man or twenty and there is no way which we know of whereby the influence of one upon the others can be quantitatively measured."

*Berkshire Employees Ass'n of Berkshire Knitting Mills v. NLRB*, 121 F.2d 235, 239 (3d Cir. 1941). \* \* \*

### III. Conclusion

For the reasons set forth above we vacate the order of the Commission and remand with instructions that the Commissioners consider the record and evidence in reviewing the initial decision, without the participation of Commissioner Dixon.

*Vacated and remanded.*


## Association of National Advertisers, Inc. v. Federal Trade Commission

627 F.2d 1151 (D.C. Cir. 1980)

December 27, 1979

Before TAMM, LEVENTHAL, and MacKINNON, Circuit Judges.

TAMM, Circuit Judge:

1  Plaintiffs, appellees here, brought an action in the United States District Court for
2  the District of Columbia to prohibit Michael Pertschuk, Chairman of the Federal
3  Trade Commission (Commission), from participating in a pending rulemaking
4  proceeding concerning children's advertising. The district court, citing this court's
5  decision in *Cinderella Career & Finishing Schools, Inc. v. FTC*, 425 F.2d 583 (D.C.
6  Cir. 1970), found that Chairman Pertschuk had prejudged issues involved in the
7  rulemaking and ordered him disqualified. We hold that the *Cinderella* standard is
8  not applicable to the Commission's rulemaking proceeding. An agency member
9  may be disqualified from such a proceeding only when there is a clear and
10 convincing showing that he has an unalterably closed mind on matters critical to
11 the disposition of the rulemaking. Because we find that the appellees have failed to
12 demonstrate the requisite prejudgment, the order of the district court is reversed.

13                                          I

14 On April 27, 1978, the Commission issued a Notice of Proposed Rulemaking that
15 suggested restrictions regarding television advertising directed toward children.
16 The decision to commence rulemaking under section 18 of the Federal Trade
17 Commission (FTC) Act was accompanied by a statement setting forth "with
18 particularity the reason for the proposed rule." The Commission explained that it
19 had decided to propose a rule limiting children's advertising after consideration of
20 a staff report that discussed

21     "facts which suggest that the televised advertising of any product directed
22     to young children who are too young to understand the selling purpose of,
23     or otherwise comprehend or evaluate, commercials may be unfair and
24     deceptive within the meaning of Section 5 of the Federal Trade Commission
25     Act, requiring appropriate remedy. The Report also discloses facts which
26     suggest that the current televised advertising of sugared products directed
27     to older children may be unfair and deceptive, again requiring appropriate
28     remedy."

29 43 Fed.Reg. 17,967, 17,969 (1978) (footnotes omitted). The Commission invited
30 interested persons to comment upon any issue raised by the staff proposal.

31 On May 8, 1978, the Association of National Advertisers, Inc. (ANA), the American
32 Association of Advertising Agencies (AAAA), the American Advertising Federation
33 (AAF), and the Toy Manufacturers of America, Inc. (TMA) petitioned Chairman
34 Pertschuk to recuse himself from participation in the children's advertising
35 inquiry. The petition charged that Pertschuk had made public statements
36 concerning regulation of children's advertising that demonstrated prejudgment of
37 specific factual issues sufficient to preclude his ability to serve as an impartial
38 arbiter. The charges were based on a speech Pertschuk delivered to the Action for
39 Children's Television (ACT) Research Conference in November 1977, on several
40 newspaper and magazine articles quoting Chairman Pertschuk's views on
41 children's television, on the transcript of a televised interview, and on a press
42 release issued by the Commission during the summer of 1977.

1   On July 13, 1978, Chairman Pertschuk declined to recuse himself from the
2   proceeding. Pertschuk stated his belief that the disqualification standard
3   appropriate for administrative adjudications did not apply to administrative
4   rulemaking, and that, even if adjudicative criteria were relevant, his remarks did
5   not warrant disqualification because they did not concern the petitioners in
6   particular; rather, they addressed the "issue of advertising to children and the
7   *policy* questions raised by it," (emphasis in original). Five days later, the
8   Commission, without Pertschuk participating, also determined that Pertschuk
9   need not be disqualified.

10               \* \* \*

11               III

12   The Commission attacks the substance of the district court's decision on two
13   grounds. First, it insists that the standard for disqualification of an administrative
14   decisionmaker in rulemaking differs from the standard in adjudication. The
15   Commission's view rests on the different purposes of rulemaking and adjudication
16   and on the long-standing rule that due process requirements are not the same in
17   the two contexts. Second, the Commission asserts that under any disqualification
18   standard, Chairman Pertschuk cannot be found to have prejudged issues in
19   contravention of due process.

20   The appellees respond with two contentions. First, they support the district court's
21   conclusion that *Cinderella Career & Finishing Schools, Inc. v. FTC*, 425 F.2d 583
22   (D.C. Cir. 1970), applies to Commission rulemaking under section 18 of the FTC
23   Act. Although *Cinderella* involved an adjudication, the appellees claim that the
24   existence of procedures in section 18 rulemaking proceedings that are not required
25   in informal notice-and-comment rulemaking under section 553 of the
26   Administrative Procedure Act, 5 U.S.C. § 553 (1976), mandates application of the
27   standard set out in that case. Second, they argue that Chairman Pertschuk's
28   statements indicate prejudgment sufficient to bar him from further participation
29   in the children's advertising proceeding.

30   We are, therefore, called upon to resolve two questions: (1) What is the appropriate
31   standard by which to decide prejudgment in the context of a section 18 proceeding?
32   (2) Has Chairman Pertschuk made statements that demonstrate prejudgment
33   under that standard?

34               A

35   Before we examine either the structure of section 18 or the content of Pertschuk's
36   statements, we review our decision in *Cinderella Career & Finishing Schools, Inc.*
37   *v. FTC*. In *Cinderella*, we held that the standard for disqualifying an administrator
38   in an adjudicatory proceeding because of prejudgment is whether "'a disinterested
39   observer may conclude that [the decisionmaker] has in some measure adjudged
40   the facts as well as the law of a particular case in advance of hearing it.'" This
41   standard guarantees that the adjudicative hearing of a person facing

1 administrative prosecution for past behavior is before a decisionmaker who has
2 not prejudged facts concerning the events under review.

3 * * *

4 B

5 The district court in the case now before us held that "the standard of conduct
6 delineated in *Cinderella*" governs agency decisionmakers participating in a section
7 18 proceeding. Section 18 authorizes the Commission to promulgate rules designed
8 to "define with specificity acts or practices which are unfair or deceptive." Basically,
9 it allows the Commission to enforce the broad command of section 5 of the FTC
10 Act, which declares "unfair or deceptive acts or practices in or affecting commerce
11 ... unlawful." The district court ruled that a section 18 proceeding,
12 notwithstanding the appellation rulemaking, "is neither wholly legislative nor
13 wholly adjudicative." According to the district court, the "adjudicative aspects" of
14 the proceeding render *Cinderella* applicable.

15 The appellees urge us to uphold the district court's analysis of section 18. They
16 emphasize two allegedly "adjudicatory aspects" of a section 18 proceeding: (1)
17 interested persons are entitled to limited cross-examination of those who testify to
18 disputed issues of material fact, and (2) a reviewing court must set aside any rule
19 not supported by substantial evidence in the rulemaking record taken as a whole.

20 The district court's characterization of section 18 rulemaking as a "hybrid" or
21 quasi-adjudicative proceeding ignores the clear scheme of the APA. Administrative
22 action pursuant to the APA is either adjudication or rulemaking. The two processes
23 differ fundamentally in purpose and focus:

24 "The object of the rule making proceeding is the implementation or
25 prescription of law or policy for the future, rather than the evaluation of a
26 respondent's past conduct. Typically, the issues relate not to the evidentiary
27 facts, as to which the veracity and demeanor of witnesses would often be
28 important, but rather to the policy-making conclusions to be drawn from
29 the facts. . . . Conversely, adjudication is concerned with the determination
30 of past and present rights and liabilities. Normally, there is involved a
31 decision as to whether past conduct was unlawful, so that the proceeding is
32 characterized by an accusatory flavor and may result in disciplinary action."

33 Attorney General's Manual on the Administrative Procedure Act 14 (1947).

34 Adjudication and rulemaking may be conducted pursuant to either informal or
35 formal procedures. Informal rulemaking requires the administrative agency to
36 provide "interested persons an opportunity to participate in the rule making
37 through submission of written data, views, or arguments." 5 U.S.C. § 553(c). Under
38 section 706(2) (A), reviewing courts are required to uphold informal rulemaking
39 decisions unless those decisions are "arbitrary, capricious, an abuse of discretion,
40 or otherwise not in accordance with law." 5 U.S.C. § 706(2) (A) (1976).

1  Formal rulemaking is invoked when "rules are required by statute to be made on
2  the record after opportunity for an agency hearing." 5 U.S.C. § 553(c). Under
3  sections 556 and 557 of the APA, formal rulemaking must include a trial-type
4  hearing at which a "party is entitled to present his case or defense or oral or
5  documentary evidence, to submit rebuttal evidence, and to conduct such cross-
6  examination as may be required for a full and true disclosure of the facts." Section
7  706(2)(E) governs judicial review of formal rulemaking and requires a court to set
8  aside a rule that is "unsupported by substantial evidence."

9  Formal adjudication is governed by section 554 of the APA and arises in "every case
10 of adjudication required by statute to be determined on the record after
11 opportunity for an agency hearing." Section 554 incorporates the procedural
12 requirements of sections 556 and 557 and affords parties to a formal adjudication
13 the right to present evidence and to conduct cross-examination. Judicial review of
14 formal adjudication, like that of formal rulemaking, is governed by the substantial
15 evidence standard.

16 The foregoing descriptions merely outline the basic parameters of administrative
17 action. Congress has, in the Magnuson-Moss Warranty Federal Trade Commission
18 Improvement (Magnuson-Moss) Act § 202(a), 15 U.S.C. § 57a (1976), and
19 elsewhere, enacted specific statutory rulemaking provisions that require more
20 procedures than those of section 553 but less than the full procedures required
21 under sections 556 and 557. The presence of procedures not mandated by section
22 553, however, does not, as the appellees urge, convert rulemaking into quasi-
23 adjudication. The appellees err by focusing on the details of administrative process
24 rather than the nature of administrative action.

25 * * * [T]he Commission's children's advertising inquiry is designed to determine
26 whether certain acts or practices will, in the future, be considered to contravene
27 the FTC Act. The proceeding is not adjudication or quasi-adjudication. It is a clear
28 exercise of the Commission's rulemaking authority.

29                                      * * *

30                                       IV

31                                        A

32 Had Congress amended section 5 of the FTC Act to declare certain types of
33 children's advertising unfair or deceptive, we would barely pause to consider a due
34 process challenge. No court to our knowledge has imposed procedural
35 requirements upon a legislature before it may act. Indeed, any suggestion that
36 congressmen may not prejudge factual and policy issues is fanciful. A legislator
37 must have the ability to exchange views with constituents and to suggest public
38 policy that is dependent upon factual assumptions. Individual interests impinged
39 upon by the legislative process are protected, as Justice Holmes wrote, "in the only
40 way that they can be in a complex society, by [the individual's] power, immediate

or remote, over those who make the rule." *Bi-Metallic Investment Co. v. State Board of Equalization*, 239 U.S. 441, 445 (1915).

Congress chose, however, to delegate its power to proscribe unfair or deceptive acts or practices to the Commission because "there were too many unfair practices for it to define." S.Rep.No. 597, 63d Cong., 2d Sess. 13 (1914). In determining the due process standards applicable in a section 18 proceeding, we are guided by its nature as rulemaking. When a proceeding is classified as rulemaking, due process ordinarily does not demand procedures more rigorous than those provided by Congress. * * *

* * *

B

We never intended the *Cinderella* rule to apply to a rulemaking procedure such as the one under review. The *Cinderella* rule disqualifies a decisionmaker if "'a disinterested observer may conclude that (he) has in some measure adjudged the facts as well as the law of a particular case in advance of hearing it.'" 425 F.2d at 591 (quoting *Gilligan, Will & Co. v. SEC*, 267 F.2d at 469). As we already have noted, legislative facts adduced in rulemaking partake of agency expertise, prediction, and risk assessment. In *Cinderella*, the court was able to cleave fact from law in deciding whether Chairman Dixon had prejudged particular factual issues. In the rulemaking context, however, the factual component of the policy decision is not easily assessed in terms of an empirically verifiable condition. Rulemaking involves the kind of issues "where a month of experience will be worth a year of hearings." Application of *Cinderella*'s strict law-fact dichotomy would necessarily limit the ability of administrators to discuss policy questions.

The legitimate functions of a policymaker, unlike an adjudicator, demand interchange and discussion about important issues. We must not impose judicial roles upon administrators when they perform functions very different from those of judges. * * *

The *Cinderella* view of a neutral and detached adjudicator is simply an inapposite role model for an administrator who must translate broad statutory commands into concrete social policies. If an agency official is to be effective he must engage in debate and discussion about the policy matters before him. As this court has recognized before, "informal contacts between agencies and the public are the 'bread and butter' of the process of administration." *Home Box Office, Inc. v. FCC*, 567 F.2d 9, 57 (D.C. Cir.).

* * *

Accordingly, a Commissioner should be disqualified only when there has been a clear and convincing showing that the agency member has an unalterably closed mind on matters critical to the disposition of the proceeding. The "clear and convincing" test is necessary to rebut the presumption of administrative regularity.

1  The "unalterably closed mind" test is necessary to permit rulemakers to carry out
2  their proper policy-based functions while disqualifying those unable to consider
3  meaningfully a section 18 hearing.

4                                          V

5  We view the statements offered as grounds for disqualification as a whole to
6  discern whether they evidence a clear and convincing showing that Chairman
7  Pertschuk has an unalterably closed mind on matters critical to the children's
8  television proceeding. * * *

9                                        * * *

10  Chairman Pertschuk's remarks, considered as a whole, represent discussion, and
11  perhaps advocacy, of the legal theory that might support exercise of the
12  Commission's jurisdiction over children's advertising. The mere discussion of
13  policy or advocacy on a legal question, however, is not sufficient to disqualify an
14  administrator. To present legal and policy arguments, Pertschuk not unnaturally
15  employed the factual assumptions that underlie the rationale for Commission
16  action. The simple fact that the Chairman explored issues based on legal and
17  factual assumptions, however, did not necessarily bind him to them forever.
18  Rather, he remained free, both in theory and in reality, to change his mind upon
19  consideration of the presentations made by those who would be affected.

20  In outlining his legal theory of "unfairness," Pertschuk suggested that children
21  might be harmed by overconsumption of sugared products and that they might not
22  be able to comprehend the purpose of advertising. Insofar as these conclusions are
23  ones of fact, they are certainly of legislative facts. Neither conclusion bears on the
24  particular activities of any specific advertiser or food manufacturer or makes
25  reference to the health or comprehension of any particular child. These
26  conclusions are broad and general, far removed from the narrow, detailed facts
27  that were at the heart of the *Cinderella* case.

28                                        * * *

29  We also note that Chairman Pertschuk made the challenged comments before the
30  Commission adopted its notice of proposed rulemaking. This court has never
31  suggested that the interchange between rulemaker and the public should be
32  limited prior to the initiation of agency action. The period before the Commission
33  first decides to take action on a perceived problem is, in fact, the best time for a
34  rulemaker to engage in dialogue with concerned citizens. Discussion would be
35  futile, of course, if the administrator could not test his own views on different
36  audiences. Moreover, as we stated earlier, an expression of opinion prior to the
37  issuance of a proposed rulemaking does not, without more, show that an agency
38  member cannot maintain an open mind during the hearing stage of the proceeding.

39  Indeed, section 18 in effect requires the Commission to formulate tentative
40  judgments on suggested rules. Before the Commission initiates rulemaking

proceedings, it must "publish a notice of proposed rulemaking stating with particularity the reason for the proposed rule prior to the comment stage of the proceeding." 15 U.S.C. § 57a(b). * * * Congress intended for the Commission to develop proposals that subsequently would be published and discussed openly. To perform this task intelligently necessarily involves making tentative conclusions of fact, even if they later are open to public challenge.

In sum, we hold that the materials adduced by the appellees are insufficient to rebut the strong presumption of administrative regularity. The materials, as a whole, merely demonstrate that Pertschuk discussed a legal theory by which the Commission could adopt a rule, if circumstances warranted. The statements do not demonstrate that Chairman Pertschuk is unwilling or unable to consider rationally argument that a final rule is unnecessary because children are either unharmed by sugared products or are able to understand advertising. The appellees have failed to make a clear and convincing showing that Chairman Pertschuk has an unalterably closed mind on matters critical to the children's television proceeding.

## VI

The appellees have a right to a fair and open proceeding; that right includes access to an impartial decisionmaker. Impartial, however, does not mean uninformed, unthinking, or inarticulate. The requirements of due process clearly recognize the necessity for rulemakers to formulate policy in a manner similar to legislative action. The standard enunciated [sic] today will protect the purposes of a section 18 proceeding, and, in so doing, will guarantee the appellees a fair hearing.

We would eviscerate the proper evolution of policymaking were we to disqualify every administrator who has opinions on the correct course of his agency's future action. Administrators, and even judges, may hold policy views on questions of law prior to participating in a proceeding. The factual basis for a rulemaking is so closely intertwined with policy judgments that we would obliterate rulemaking were we to equate a statement on an issue of legislative fact with unconstitutional prejudgment. The importance and legitimacy of rulemaking procedures are too well established to deny administrators such a fundamental tool.

Finally, we eschew formulation of a disqualification standard that impinges upon the political process. An administrator's presence within an agency reflects the political judgment of the President and Senate. As Judge Prettyman of this court aptly noted, a "Commission's view of what is best in the public interest may change from time to time. Commissions themselves change, underlying philosophies differ, and experience often dictates changes." *Pinellas Broadcasting Co. v. FCC*, 230 F.2d 204, 206 (D.C. Cir.). We are concerned that implementation of the *Cinderella* standard in the rulemaking context would plunge courts into the midst of political battles concerning the proper formulation of administrative policy. We serve as guarantors of statutory and constitutional rights, but not as arbiters of the political process. Accordingly, we will not order the disqualification of a rulemaker

1  absent the most compelling proof that he is unable to carry out his duties in a
2  constitutionally permissible manner.

3  Reversed.

4

5  LEVENTHAL, Circuit Judge, concurring. [Omitted.]

6

# CHAPTER 3: JUDICIAL REVIEW

The APA provides a number of bases on which agencies actions may be challenged in court. Although we have not discussed the various grounds for review until this point in the course, judicial review has been with us all semester: as you have no doubt noticed, your diet of readings to this point has consisted mostly of cases.

So what do courts do when they review agencies? The APA provides at least the beginnings of an answer, in §706, "Scope of Review." If you're looking to challenge an agency action, §706 is your menu: here are the different grounds on which you could sue, together with the types of relief available. For instance, you could seek to compel agency action on the ground that it is unreasonably delayed (§706(1), although, as we will see, you're not likely to win on this one). Alternatively, you could try to get the agency action set aside on the ground that it's in violation of the Constitution (§706(2)(B)) or that the agency didn't follow the required procedures (§706(2)(D)).

Note also that some of the grounds for review effectively build in their own standards of review. For instance, agency actions generally can be set aside if "arbitrary, capricious, an abuse of discretion, or otherwise not in accordance with law" (§706(2)(A)), but on-the-record proceedings in particular will be set aside if "unsupported by substantial evidence" (§706(2)(F)).

This part of the course explores how courts review different kinds of agency determinations in practice. Simplifying some, we can divide agency determinations into three categories: agencies make determinations of fact, of law, and of policy. Simplifying some more, each has its own body of judicial review doctrine. Substantial evidence review is the most important for agency fact determinations, and arbitrary and capricious review is for agency policy judgments. The body of doctrine that governs agency determinations of law is vast, but at its center is the endlessly debated *Chevron* doctrine.

Before we get into the specifics of these forms of review, we start with an introductory unit containing some landmark cases that establish fundamental principles governing judicial review of agencies.


## A. Foundations of Judicial Review

The cases in this section highlight some of the key characteristics of judicial review in administrative law.

In some ways, administrative law requires courts to play roles outside of their comfort zone. Reviewing the work of agencies is different in important respects from the appellate review courts conduct of other courts' rulings. The cases in this section are all classics, and they showcase the Supreme Court figuring out how to play this unfamiliar role in which administrative law has cast it.

The *Morgan* saga is an epic, in which we see the Court facing up to realities of its role vis-à-vis administrative decision making. In the first case, Chief Justice Hughes articulated a sensible sounding claim: "he who decides must hear." What would that mean in practice for the Department of Agriculture program described in the cases? Before long, the Supreme Court ended up articulating a very differently proposition: that "it was not the function of the court to probe the mental processes of the Secretary in reaching his conclusions" so long as he followed the required procedures. How did the Court end up in that very different place?

In *Chenery I*, the Supreme Court seems to be saying that it respects the SEC's authority so much that it must vacate the agency's order. What's the logic to the Court's ruling? Is this the administrative law equivalent of destroying a town in order to save it (as a U.S. army officer infamously described an operation in the Vietnam conflict)?

Although written almost a quarter century after the enactment of the APA, *Citizens to Preserve Overton Park* is one of the first Supreme Court decisions to engage extensively with the different provisions of the statute relating to judicial review. The decision is a treasure trove on APA judicial review, but at one point is misstates what the statute says. Can you spot the error?

In *New York v. Department of Commerce*, the Supreme Court affirmed a lower court's ruling that struck a citizenship question from the 2020 census form on the grounds that the reasons the Secretary of Commerce gave for adding the question were "pretextual." How is this consistent with *Morgan IV*? Under what circumstances is it permissible for a court to reject the reasons offered by an agency on the grounds that they aren't the agency's *real* reasons for acting? Under what circumstances is it permissible for a court to take discovery into an agency's decision-making process, as opposed to relying on the administrative record? This case also offers a preview of "arbitrary and capricious" review, which is covered at length later.

## Morgan v. United States (*Morgan I*)

298 U.S. 468 (1936)

May 25, 1936

MR. CHIEF JUSTICE HUGHES delivered the opinion of the Court.

These are fifty suits, consolidated for the purpose of trial, to restrain the enforcement of an order of the Secretary of Agriculture fixing the maximum rates

1   to be charged by market agencies for buying and selling livestock at the Kansas City
2   Stock Yards.

3   The proceeding was instituted by an order of the Secretary of Agriculture in April,
4   1930, directing an inquiry into the reasonableness of existing rates. Testimony was
5   taken, and an order prescribing rates followed in May, 1932. An application for
6   rehearing, in view of changed economic conditions, was granted in July, 1932.
7   After the taking of voluminous testimony, which was concluded in November,
8   1932, the order in question was made on June 14, 1933. Rehearing was refused on
9   July 6, 1933.

10  Plaintiffs then brought these suits attacking the order, so far as it prescribed
11  maximum charges for selling livestock, as illegal and arbitrary and as depriving
12  plaintiffs of their property without due process of law in violation of the Fifth
13  Amendment of the Constitution. The District Court of three judges entered decrees
14  sustaining the order and dismissing the bills of complaint. Motions for rehearing
15  were denied and, by stipulation, the separate decrees were set aside and a joint and
16  final decree was entered to the same effect. Plaintiffs bring this direct appeal.

17  On the merits, plaintiffs assert that the ultimate basis for the reduction in
18  commission rates is the Secretary's opinion that there are too many market
19  agencies, too many salesmen, and too much competition in the business; that the
20  Secretary has departed entirely from the evidence as to the actual cost of employing
21  salesmen in selling cattle at these yards, and has made an allowance for salaries
22  which is based on pure speculation and is wholly inadequate to meet the cost of the
23  service; that he has substituted in place of his accountants' figures as to actual
24  expenditures, with respect to the item entitled "Business Getting and Maintaining
25  Expense," a hypothetical allowance greatly less than actual cost, and that the
26  Secretary has thus made findings without evidence, and an order, essentially
27  arbitrary, which prescribes unreasonable rates. * * *

28  Before reaching these questions, we meet at the threshold of the controversy
29  plaintiffs' additional contention that they have not been accorded the hearing
30  which the statute requires. They rightly assert that the granting of that hearing is
31  a prerequisite to the making of a valid order. The statute provides (42 Stat. 159,
32  166, § 310; 7 U.S.C. § 211):

33      "Sec. 310. Whenever after full hearing upon a complaint made as provided
34      in § 309, or after full hearing under an order for investigation and hearing
35      made by the Secretary on his own initiative, either in extension of any
36      pending complaint or without any complaint whatever, the Secretary is of
37      the opinion that any rate, charge, regulation, or practice of a stockyard
38      owner or market agency, for or in connection with the furnishing of
39      stockyard services, is or will be unjust, unreasonable, or discriminatory, the
40      Secretary—

41      "(a) May determine and prescribe what will be the just and reasonable rate
42      or charge, or rates or charges, to be thereafter observed in such case, or the

maximum or minimum, or maximum and minimum, to be charged, and what regulation or practice is or will be just, reasonable, and nondiscriminatory to be thereafter followed; . . ."

The allegations as to the failure to give a proper hearing are set forth in paragraph IV of the bill of complaint * * * . The allegations in substance are: * * * That the Secretary, without warrant of law, delegated to Acting Secretaries the determination of issues with respect to the reasonableness of the rates involved. That, when the oral arguments were presented after the original hearing, and after the rehearing, the Secretary was neither sick, absent, nor otherwise disabled, but was at his office in the Department of Agriculture, and the appointment of any other person as Acting Secretary was illegal. That the Secretary, at the time he signed the order in question, had not personally heard or read any of the evidence presented at any hearing in connection with the proceeding, and had not heard or considered oral arguments relating thereto or briefs submitted on behalf of the plaintiffs, but that the sole information of the Secretary with respect to the proceeding was derived from consultation with employees in the Department of Agriculture out of the presence of the plaintiffs or any of their representatives.

On motion of the government, the District Court struck out all the allegations in paragraph IV of the bill of complaint, and the plaintiffs were thus denied opportunity to require an answer to these allegations or to prove the facts alleged.

* * *

First. * * * All questions touching the regularity and validity of the proceeding before the Secretary are open to review. When the Secretary acts within the authority conferred by the statute, his findings of fact are conclusive. But, in determining whether, in conducting an administrative proceeding of this sort, the Secretary has complied with the statutory prerequisites, the recitals of his procedure cannot be regarded as conclusive. Otherwise, the statutory conditions could be set at naught by mere assertion. If, upon the facts alleged, the "full hearing" required by the statute was not given, plaintiffs were entitled to prove the facts and have the Secretary's order set aside. Nor is it necessary to go beyond the terms of the statute in order to consider the constitutional requirement of due process as to notice and hearing. For the statute itself demands a full hearing, and the order is void if such a hearing was denied.

Second. The outstanding allegation, which the District Court struck out, is that the Secretary made the rate order without having heard or read any of the evidence, and without having heard the oral arguments or having read or considered the briefs which the plaintiffs submitted. That the only information which the Secretary had as to the proceeding was what he derived from consultation with employees of the Department.

The other allegations of the stricken paragraph do not go to the root of the matter. Thus, it cannot be said that the failure to hear the respondents separately was an abuse of discretion. Again, while it would have been good practice to have the

404

examiner prepare a report and submit it to the Secretary and the parties, and to permit exceptions and arguments addressed to the points thus presented—a practice found to be of great value in proceedings before the Interstate Commerce Commission—we cannot say that that particular type of procedure was essential to the validity of the hearing. The statute does not require it, and what the statute does require relates to substance, and not form.

Nor should the fundamental question be confused with one of mere delegation of authority. The government urges that the Acting Secretary who heard the oral argument was in fact the Assistant Secretary of Agriculture, whose duties are prescribed by the Act of February 9, 1889 (5 U.S.C. § 517), providing for his appointment and authorizing him to perform such duties in the conduct of the business of the Department of Agriculture as may be assigned to him by the Secretary. If the Secretary had assigned to the Assistant Secretary the duty of holding the hearing, and the Assistant Secretary accordingly had received the evidence taken by the examiner, had heard argument thereon, and had then found the essential facts and made the order upon his findings, we should have had simply the question of delegation. But, while the Assistant Secretary heard argument, he did not make the decision. The Secretary who, according to the allegation, had neither heard nor read evidence or argument, undertook to make the findings and fix the rates. The Assistant Secretary, who had heard, assumed no responsibility for the findings or order, and the Secretary, who had not heard, did assume that responsibility.

* * *

Third. What is the essential quality of the proceeding under review, and what is the nature of the hearing which the statute prescribes?

The proceeding is not one of ordinary administration, conformable to the standards governing duties of a purely executive character. It is a proceeding looking to legislative action in the fixing of rates of market agencies. And, while the order is legislative and gives to the proceeding its distinctive character (*Louisville & Nashville R. Co. v. Garrett*, 231 U.S. 298, 307), it is a proceeding which, by virtue of the authority conferred, has special attributes. The Secretary, as the agent of Congress in making the rates, must make them in accordance with the standards and under the limitations which Congress has prescribed. Congress has required the Secretary to determine, as a condition of his action, that the existing rates are or will be "unjust, unreasonable, or discriminatory." If and when he so finds, he may "determine and prescribe" what shall be the just and reasonable rate, or the maximum or minimum rate, thereafter to be charged. That duty is widely different from ordinary executive action. It is a duty which carries with it fundamental procedural requirements. There must be a full hearing. There must be evidence adequate to support pertinent and necessary findings of fact. Nothing can be treated as evidence which is not introduced as such. Facts and circumstances which ought to be considered must not be excluded. Facts and circumstances must not be considered which should not legally influence the conclusion. Findings

1    based on the evidence must embrace the basic facts which are needed to sustain
2    the order.

3    A proceeding of this sort requiring the taking and weighing of evidence,
4    determinations of fact based upon the consideration of the evidence, and the
5    making of an order supported by such findings, has a quality resembling that of a
6    judicial proceeding. Hence, it is frequently described as a proceeding of a *quasi-
7    judicial* character. The requirement of a "full hearing" has obvious reference to the
8    tradition of judicial proceedings in which evidence is received and weighed by the
9    trier of the facts. The "hearing" is designed to afford the safeguard that the one who
10   decides shall be bound in good conscience to consider the evidence, to be guided
11   by that alone, and to reach his conclusion uninfluenced by extraneous
12   considerations which, in other fields, might have play in determining purely
13   executive action. The "hearing" is the hearing of evidence and argument. If the one
14   who determines the facts which underlie the order has not considered evidence or
15   argument, it is manifest that the hearing has not been given.

16   There is thus no basis for the contention that the authority conferred by § 310 of
17   the Packers and Stockyards Act is given to the Department of Agriculture, as a
18   department in the administrative sense, so that one official may examine evidence,
19   and another official who has not considered the evidence may make the findings
20   and order. In such a view, it would be possible, for example, for one official to hear
21   the evidence and argument and arrive at certain conclusions of fact and another
22   official who had not heard or considered either evidence or argument to overrule
23   those conclusions and, for reasons of policy, to announce entirely different ones. It
24   is no answer to say that the question for the court is whether the evidence supports
25   the findings and the findings support the order. For the weight ascribed by the law
26   to the findings—their conclusiveness when made within the sphere of the authority
27   conferred—rests upon the assumption that the officer who makes the findings has
28   addressed himself to the evidence, and, upon that evidence, has conscientiously
29   reached the conclusions which he deems it to justify. That duty cannot be
30   performed by one who has not considered evidence or argument. It is not an
31   impersonal obligation. It is a duty akin to that of a judge. The one who decides
32   must hear.

33   This necessary rule does not preclude practicable administrative procedure in
34   obtaining the aid of assistants in the department. Assistants may prosecute
35   inquiries. Evidence may be taken by an examiner. Evidence thus taken may be
36   sifted and analyzed by competent subordinates. Argument may be oral or written.
37   The requirements are not technical. But there must be a hearing in a substantial
38   sense. And to give the substance of a hearing, which is for the purpose of making
39   determinations upon evidence, the officer who makes the determinations must
40   consider and appraise the evidence which justifies them. That duty undoubtedly
41   may be an onerous one, but the performance of it in a substantial manner is
42   inseparable from the exercise of the important authority conferred.

43                                    * * *

Our conclusion is that the District Court erred in striking out the allegations of Paragraph IV of the bill of complaint with respect to the Secretary's action. The defendants should be required to answer these allegations, and the question whether plaintiffs had a proper hearing should be determined.

The decree is reversed, and the cause is remanded for further proceedings in conformity with this opinion.

*Reversed.*

## Morgan v. United States (*Morgan II*)

304 U.S. 1 (1938)

April 25, 1938

MR. CHIEF JUSTICE HUGHES delivered the opinion of the Court.

This case presents the question of the validity of an order of the Secretary of Agriculture fixing maximum rates to be charged by market agencies at the Kansas City Stockyards. * * *

The case comes here for the second time. On the former appeal, we met at the threshold of the controversy the contention that the plaintiffs had not been accorded the hearing which the statute made a prerequisite to a valid order. The District Court had struck from plaintiffs' bills the allegations that the Secretary had made the order without having heard or read the evidence and without having heard or considered the arguments submitted, and that his sole information with respect to the proceeding was derived from consultation with employees in the Department of Agriculture. We held that it was error to strike these allegations, that the defendant should be required to answer them, and that the question whether plaintiffs had a proper hearing should be determined.

After the remand, the bills were amended and interrogatories were directed to the Secretary which he answered. The court received the evidence which had been introduced at its previous hearing, together with additional testimony bearing upon the nature of the hearing accorded by the Secretary. This evidence embraced the testimony of the Secretary and of several of his assistants. The District Court rendered an opinion, with findings of fact and conclusions of law, holding that the hearing before the Secretary was adequate and, on the merits, that his order was lawful.

On this appeal, plaintiffs again contend (1) that the Secretary's order was made without the hearing required by the statute, and (2) that the order was arbitrary, and unsupported by substantial evidence.

The first question goes to the very foundation of the action of administrative agencies entrusted by the Congress with broad control over activities which in their

1   detail cannot be dealt with directly by the Legislature. The vast expansion of this
2   field of administrative regulation in response to the pressure of social needs is
3   made possible under our system by adherence to the basic principles that the
4   Legislature shall appropriately determine the standards of administrative action
5   and that, in administrative proceedings of a quasi-judicial character, the liberty
6   and property of the citizen shall be protected by the rudimentary requirements of
7   fair play. These demand "a fair and open hearing," essential alike to the legal
8   validity of the administrative regulation and to the maintenance of public
9   confidence in the value and soundness of this important governmental process.
10   * * *

11   In the record now before us, the controlling facts stand out clearly. The original
12   administrative proceeding was begun on April 7, 1930, when the Secretary of
13   Agriculture issued an order of inquiry and notice of hearing with respect to the
14   reasonableness of the charges of appellants for stockyards services at Kansas City.
15   The taking of evidence before an examiner of the Department was begun on
16   December 3, 1930, and continued until February 10, 1931. The Government and
17   appellants were represented by counsel, and voluminous testimony and exhibits
18   were introduced. In March, 1931, oral argument was had before the Acting
19   Secretary of Agriculture and appellants submitted a brief. On May 18, 1932, the
20   Secretary issued his findings and an order prescribing maximum rates. In view of
21   changed economic conditions, the Secretary vacated that order and granted a
22   rehearing. That was begun on October 6, 1932, and the taking of evidence was
23   concluded on November 16, 1932. The evidence received at the first hearing was
24   resubmitted, and this was supplemented by additional testimony and exhibits. On
25   March 24, 1933, oral argument was had before Rexford G. Tugwell as Acting
26   Secretary.

27   It appears that there were about 10,000 pages of transcript of oral evidence and
28   over 1,000 pages of statistical exhibits. The oral argument was general and sketchy.
29   Appellants submitted the brief which they had presented after the first
30   administrative hearing and a supplemental brief dealing with the evidence
31   introduced upon the rehearing. No brief was at any time supplied by the
32   Government. Apart from what was said on its behalf in the oral argument, the
33   Government formulated no issues and furnished appellants no statement or
34   summary of its contentions and no proposed findings. Appellants' request that the
35   examiner prepare a tentative report, to be submitted as a basis for exceptions and
36   argument, was refused.

37   Findings were prepared in the Bureau of Animal Industry, Department of
38   Agriculture, whose representatives had conducted the proceedings for the
39   Government, and were submitted to the Secretary, who signed them, with a few
40   changes in the rates, when his order was made on June 14, 1933. These findings,
41   180 in number, were elaborate. They dealt with the practices and facilities at the
42   Kansas City livestock market, the character of appellants' business and services,
43   their rates and the volume of their transactions, their gross revenues, their
44   methods in getting and maintaining business, their joint activities, the economic

1    changes since the year 1929, the principles which governed the determination of
2    reasonable commission rates, the classification of cost items, the reasonable unit
3    costs plus a reasonable amount of profits to be covered into reasonable
4    commission rates, the reasonable amounts to be included for salesmanship,
5    yarding salaries and expenses, office salaries and expenses, business getting and
6    maintaining expenses, administrative and general expenses, insurance, interest on
7    capital, and profits, together with summary and the establishment of the rate
8    structure. Upon the basis of the reasonable costs as thus determined, the Secretary
9    found that appellants' schedules of rates were unreasonable and unjustly
10    discriminatory, and fixed the maximum schedules of the just and reasonable rates
11    thereafter to be charged.

12    No opportunity was afforded to appellants for the examination of the findings thus
13    prepared in the Bureau of Animal Industry until they were served with the order.
14    Appellants sought a rehearing by the Secretary, but their application was denied
15    on July 6, 1933, and these suits followed.

16    The part taken by the Secretary himself in the departmental proceedings is shown
17    by his full and candid testimony. The evidence had been received before he took
18    office. He did not hear the oral argument. The bulky record was placed upon his
19    desk and he dipped into it from time to time to get its drift. He decided that
20    probably the essence of the evidence was contained in appellants' briefs. These,
21    together with the transcript of the oral argument, he took home with him and read.
22    He had several conferences with the Solicitor of the Department and with the
23    officials in the Bureau of Animal Industry, and discussed the proposed findings.
24    He testified that he considered the evidence before signing the order. The
25    substance of his action is stated in his answer to the question whether the order
26    represented his independent conclusion, as follows:

27       "My answer to the question would be that that very definitely was my
28       independent conclusion as based on the findings of the men in the Bureau
29       of Animal Industry. I would say, I will try to put it as accurately as possible,
30       that it represented my own independent reactions to the findings of the
31       men in the Bureau of Animal Industry."

32    Save for certain rate alterations, he "accepted the findings."

33    In the light of this testimony, there is no occasion to discuss the extent to which
34    the Secretary examined the evidence, and we agree with the Government's
35    contention that it was not the function of the court to probe the mental processes
36    of the Secretary in reaching his conclusions if he gave the hearing which the law
37    required. The Secretary read the summary presented by appellants' briefs, and he
38    conferred with his subordinates, who had sifted and analyzed the evidence. We
39    assume that the Secretary sufficiently understood its purport. But a "full hearing"
40    —a fair and open hearing—requires more than that. The right to a hearing
41    embraces not only the right to present evidence, but also a reasonable opportunity
42    to know the claims of the opposing party and to meet them. The right to submit

1 argument implies that opportunity; otherwise, the right may be but a barren one.
2 Those who are brought into contest with the Government in a quasi-judicial
3 proceeding aimed at the control of their activities are entitled to be fairly advised
4 of what the Government proposes, and to be heard upon its proposals before it
5 issues its final command.

6 No such reasonable opportunity was accorded appellants. The administrative
7 proceeding was initiated by a notice of inquiry into the reasonableness of
8 appellants' rates. No specific complaint was formulated * * * . [I]n the absence of
9 any report by the examiner or any findings proposed by the Government, and thus
10 without any concrete statement of the Government's claims, the parties
11 approached the oral argument.

12 Nor did the oral argument reveal these claims in any appropriate manner. The
13 discussion by counsel for the Government was "very general," as he said, in order
14 not to take up "too much time." It dealt with generalities both as to principles and
15 procedure. Counsel for appellants then discussed the evidence from his
16 standpoint. The Government's counsel closed briefly, with a few additional and
17 general observations. The oral argument was of the sort which might serve as a
18 preface to a discussion of definite points in a brief, but the Government did not
19 submit a brief. And the appellants had no further information of the Government's
20 concrete claims until they were served with the Secretary's order.

21 Congress, in requiring a "full hearing," had regard to judicial standards—not in any
22 technical sense but with respect to those fundamental requirements of fairness
23 which are of the essence of due process in a proceeding of a judicial nature. If, in
24 an equity cause, a special master or the trial judge permitted the plaintiff's attorney
25 to formulate the findings upon the evidence, conferred *ex parte* with the plaintiff's
26 attorney regarding them, and then adopted his proposals without affording an
27 opportunity to his opponent to know their contents and present objections, there
28 would be no hesitation in setting aside the report or decree as having been made
29 without a fair hearing. The requirements of fairness are not exhausted in the taking
30 or consideration of evidence, but extend to the concluding parts of the procedure
31 as well as to the beginning and intermediate steps.

32 The answer that the proceeding before the Secretary was not of an adversary
33 character, as it was not upon complaint, but was initiated as a general inquiry, is
34 futile. * * * In all substantial respects, the Government, acting through the Bureau
35 of Animal Industry of the Department, was prosecuting the proceeding against the
36 owners of the market agencies. The proceeding had all the essential elements of
37 contested litigation, with the Government and its counsel on the one side and the
38 appellants and their counsel on the other. It is idle to say that this was not a
39 proceeding in reality against the appellants when the very existence of their
40 agencies was put in jeopardy. Upon the rates for their services the owners
41 depended for their livelihood, and the proceeding attacked them at a vital spot.
42 * * *

410

1                                    * * *

2   As the hearing was fatally defective, the order of the Secretary was invalid. In this
3   view, we express no opinion upon the merits. The decree of the District Court is

4   *Reversed.*

5   MR. JUSTICE CARDOZO and MR. JUSTICE REED too no part in the
6   consideration of this case.

7   MR. JUSTICE BLACK, dissenting. [Omitted.]

8

9   **United States v. Morgan (*Morgan IV*)**

10  313 U.S. 409 (1941)

11  May 26, 1941

12  MR. JUSTICE FRANKFURTER delivered the opinion of the Court.

13  * * * The case is now here for the fourth time.

14  The validity of the Secretary's order has undergone the closest scrutiny in elaborate
15  briefs and extended oral arguments. Nothing has been overlooked. However, in the
16  final stage of this long drawn out litigation, critical examination reveals only a few
17  issues demanding attention.

18                                   * * *

19  An[] attack upon the Secretary's order is the conventional objection that the
20  findings were not rooted in proof. To reexamine here with particularity the
21  extensive findings made by the Secretary, and to test them by a record of 1340
22  printed pages and thousands of pages of additional exhibits would, in itself, go a
23  long way to convert a contest before the Secretary into one before the courts. We
24  have canvassed too fully in the past the duties respectively allotted to the Secretary
25  of Agriculture and the courts in the enforcement of the Packers and Stockyards Act
26  to justify extended discussion of the governing principles. We are in the legislative
27  realm of fixing rates. This is a task of striking a balance and reaching a judgment
28  on factors beset with doubts and difficulties, uncertainty and speculation. On
29  ultimate analysis, the real question is whether the Secretary or a court should make
30  an appraisal of elements having delusive certainty. Congress has put the
31  responsibility on the Secretary, and the Constitution does not deny the assignment.

32  The objection that the proof does not support the findings is really a repetition in
33  disguise of the unfounded claim that the Secretary misconceived his duty and made
34  his order in 1939 as though he were acting in 1933. The bedrock of these variously
35  phrased attacks upon the order is the contention that the Secretary was indifferent
36  to events occurring after 1933. The short answer is that he was not. * * *

1                         \* \* \*

2 And so we conclude that the order of the Secretary furnishes "the appropriate basis
3 for action in the district court in making distribution of the fund in its custody."
4 *United States v. Morgan*, 307 U.S. 183, 198. But, finally, a matter not touching the
5 validity of the order requires consideration. Over the Government's objection, the
6 district court authorized the market agencies to take the deposition of the
7 Secretary. The Secretary thereupon appeared in person at the trial. He was
8 questioned at length regarding the process by which he reached the conclusions of
9 his order, including the manner and extent of his study of the record and his
10 consultation with subordinates. His testimony shows that he dealt with the
11 enormous record in a manner not unlike the practice of judges in similar
12 situations, and that he held various conferences with the examiner who heard the
13 evidence. Much was made of his disregard of a memorandum from one of his
14 officials who, on reading the proposed order, urged considerations favorable to the
15 market agencies. But the short of the business is that the Secretary should never
16 have been subjected to this examination. The proceeding before the Secretary "has
17 a quality resembling that of a judicial proceeding." *Morgan v. United States*, 298
18 U.S. 468, 480. Such an examination of a judge would be destructive of judicial
19 responsibility. We have explicitly held in this very litigation that "it was not the
20 function of the court to probe the mental processes of the Secretary." *Morgan v.*
21 *United States*, 304 U.S. 1, 18. Just as a judge cannot be subjected to such a scrutiny,
22 so the integrity of the administrative process must be equally respected. It will bear
23 repeating that, although the administrative process has had a different
24 development and pursues somewhat different ways from those of courts, they are
25 to be deemed collaborative instrumentalities of justice, and the appropriate
26 independence of each should be respected by the other.

27 *Reversed.*

28 MR. JUSTICE REED did not participate in the consideration or decision of this
29 case.

30 MR. JUSTICE ROBERTS, dissenting. [Omitted.]

31

32 **SEC v. Chenery Corp. (*Chenery I*)**

33 318 U.S. 80 (1943)

34 February 1, 1943

35 MR. JUSTICE FRANKFURTER delivered the opinion of the Court.

36 The respondents, who were officers, directors, and controlling stockholders of the
37 Federal Water Service Corporation (hereafter called Federal), a holding company
38 registered under the Public Utility Holding Company Act of 1935 brought this
39 proceeding under § 24(a) of the Act to review an order made by the Securities and

Exchange Commission on September 24, 1941, approving a plan of reorganization for the company. Under the Commission's order, preferred stock acquired by the respondents during the period in which successive reorganization plans proposed by the management of the company were before the Commission was not permitted to participate in the reorganization on an equal footing with all other preferred stock. The Court of Appeals for the District of Columbia, with one judge dissenting, set the Commission's order aside, and, because the question presented looms large in the administration of the Act, we brought the case here.

The relevant facts are as follows. In 1937, Federal was a typical public utility holding company. Incorporated in Delaware, its assets consisted of securities of subsidiary water, gas, electric, and other companies in thirteen states and one foreign country. The respondents controlled Federal through their control of its parent, Utility Operators Company, which owned all of the outstanding shares of Federal's Class B common stock, representing the controlling voting power in the company. On November 8, 1937, when Federal registered as a holding company under the Public Utility Holding Company Act of 1935, its management filed a plan for reorganization under §§ 7 and 11 of the Act, the relevant portions of which are copied in the margin. This plan, as well as two other plans later submitted by Federal, provided for participation by Class B stockholders in the equity of the proposed reorganized company. This feature of the plans was unacceptable to the Commission, and all were ultimately withdrawn. On March 30, 1940, a fourth plan was filed by Federal. This plan, proposing a merger of Federal, Utility Operators Company, and Federal Water and Gas Corporation, a wholly owned inactive subsidiary of Federal, contained no provision for participation by the Class B stock. Instead, that class of stock was to be surrendered for cancellation, and the preferred and Class A common stock of Federal were to be converted into common stock of the new corporation. As the Commission pointed out in its analysis of the proposed plan, "except for the 5.3% of new common allocated to the present holders of Class A stock, substantially all of the equity of the reorganized company will be given to the present preferred stockholders."

During the period from November 8, 1937, to June 30, 1940, while the successive reorganization plans were before the Commission, the respondents purchased a total of 12,407 shares of Federal's preferred stock. (The total number of outstanding shares of Federal's preferred stock was 159,269.) These purchases were made on the over-the-counter market through brokers at prices lower than the book value of the common stock of the new corporation into which the preferred stock would have been converted under the proposed plan. If this feature of the plan had been approved by the Commission, the respondents, through their holdings of Federal's preferred stock, would have acquired more than 10 percent of the common stock of the new corporation. The respondents frankly admitted that their purpose in buying the preferred stock was to protect their interests in the company.

In ascertaining whether the terms of issuance of the new common stock were "fair and equitable" or "detrimental to the interest of investors" within § 7 of the Act,

413

1  the Commission found that it could not approve the proposed plan so long as the
2  preferred stock acquired by the respondents would be permitted to share on a
3  parity with other preferred stock. The Commission did not find fraud or lack of
4  disclosure, but it concluded that the respondents, as Federal's managers, were
5  fiduciaries, and hence under a "duty of fair dealing" not to trade in the securities
6  of the corporation while plans for its reorganization were before the Commission.
7  It recommended that a formula be devised under which the respondents' preferred
8  stock would participate only to the extent of the purchase prices paid plus
9  accumulated dividends since the dates of such purchases. Accordingly, the plan
10  was thereafter amended to provide that the preferred stock acquired by the
11  respondents, unlike the preferred stock held by others, would not be converted into
12  stock of the reorganized company, but could only be surrendered at cost plus 4
13  percent interest. The Commission, over the respondents' objections, approved the
14  plan as thus amended, and it is this order which is now under review.

15                                     * * *

16  The Commission did not find that the respondents, as managers of Federal, acted
17  covertly or traded on inside knowledge, or that their position as reorganization
18  managers enabled them to purchase the preferred stock at prices lower than they
19  would otherwise have had to pay, or that their acquisition of the stock in any way
20  prejudiced the interests of the corporation or its stockholders. To be sure, the new
21  stock into which the respondents' preferred stock would be converted under the
22  plan of reorganization would have a book value—which may or may not represent
23  market value—considerably greater than the prices paid for the preferred stock.
24  But that would equally be true of purchases of preferred stock made by other
25  investors. * * * The Commission did not suggest that, as a result of their purchases
26  of preferred stock, the respondents would be unjustly enriched. On the contrary,
27  the question before the Commission was whether the respondents, simply because
28  they were reorganization managers, should be denied the benefits to be received
29  by the 6,000 other preferred stockholders. Some technical rule of law must have
30  moved the Commission to single out the respondents and deny their preferred
31  stock the right to participate equally in the reorganization. To ascertain the precise
32  basis of its determination, we must look to the Commission's opinion.

33  The Commission stated that, "in the process of formulation of a 'voluntary'
34  reorganization plan, the management of a corporation occupies a fiduciary
35  position toward all of the security holders to be affected, and that it is subjected to
36  the same standards as other fiduciaries with respect to dealing with the property
37  which is the subject matter of the trust." Applying by analogy the restrictions
38  imposed on trustees in trafficking in property held by them in trust for others, the
39  Commission ruled that, even though the management does not hold the stock of
40  the corporation in trust for the stockholders, nevertheless the "duty of fair dealing"
41  which the management owes to the stockholders is violated if those in control of
42  the corporation purchase its stock, even at a fair price, openly and without fraud.
43  The Commission concluded that "honesty, full disclosure, and purchase at a fair
44  price do not take the case outside the rule."

414

In reaching this result, the Commission stated that it was merely applying "the broad equitable principles enunciated in the cases heretofore cited," * * * . Its opinion plainly shows that the Commission purported to be acting only as it assumed a court of equity would have acted in a similar case. Since the decision of the Commission was explicitly based upon the applicability of principles of equity announced by courts, its validity must likewise be judged on that basis. The grounds upon which an administrative order must be judged are those upon which the record discloses that its action was based.

In confining our review to a judgment upon the validity of the grounds upon which the Commission itself based its action, we do not disturb the settled rule that, in reviewing the decision of a lower court, it must be affirmed if the result is correct "although the lower court relied upon a wrong ground or gave a wrong reason." *Helvering v. Gowran*, 302 U.S. 238, 245 (1937). The reason for this rule is obvious. It would be wasteful to send a case back to a lower court to reinstate a decision which it had already made, but which the appellate court concluded should properly be based on another ground within the power of the appellate court to formulate. But it is also familiar appellate procedure that, where the correctness of the lower court's decision depends upon a determination of fact which only a jury could make, but which has not been made, the appellate court cannot take the place of the jury. Like considerations govern review of administrative orders. If an order is valid only as a determination of policy or judgment which the agency alone is authorized to make and which it has not made, a judicial judgment cannot be made to do service for an administrative judgment. For purposes of affirming, no less than reversing, its orders, an appellate court cannot intrude upon the domain which Congress has exclusively entrusted to an administrative agency.

If, therefore, the rule applied by the Commission is to be judged solely on the basis of its adherence to principles of equity derived from judicial decisions, its order plainly cannot stand. As the Commission concedes here, the courts do not impose upon officers and directors of a corporation any fiduciary duty to its stockholders which precludes them, merely because they are officers and directors, from buying and selling the corporation's stock. The cases upon which the Commission relied do not establish principles of law and equity which, in themselves, are sufficient to sustain its order. The only question in *Pepper v. Litton*, 308 U.S. 295, was whether claims obtained by the controlling stockholders of a bankrupt corporation were to be treated equally with the claims of other creditors where the evidence revealed "a scheme to defraud creditors reminiscent of some of the evils with which 13 Eliz, c. 5 was designed to cope," 308 U.S., at 296. Another case relied upon, *Woods v. City Bank Co.*, 312 U.S. 262, held only that a bankruptcy court, in the exercise of its plenary power to review fees and expenses in connection with a reorganization proceeding under Chapter X of the Chandler Act, 52 Stat. 840, could deny compensation to protective committees representing conflicting interests. *Michoud v. Girod*, 4 How. 503, and *Magruder v. Drury*, 235 U.S. 106, dealt with the specific obligations of express trustees, and not with those of persons in control of a corporate enterprise toward its stockholders.

1   Determination of what is "fair and equitable" calls for the application of ethical
2   standards to particular sets of facts. But these standards are not static. In evolving
3   standards of fairness and equity, the Commission is not bound by settled judicial
4   precedents. Congress certainly did not mean to preclude the formulation by the
5   Commission of standards expressing a more sensitive regard for what is right and
6   what is wrong than those prevalent at the time the Public Utility Holding Company
7   Act of 1935 became law. But the Commission did not, in this case, proffer new
8   standards reflecting the experience gained by it in effectuating the legislative
9   policy. On the contrary, it explicitly disavowed any purpose of going beyond those
10   which the courts had theretofore recognized. Since the Commission professed to
11   decide the case before it according to settled judicial doctrines, its action must be
12   judged by the standards which the Commission itself invoked. And, judged by
13   those standards, *i.e.*, those which would be enforced by a court of equity, we must
14   conclude that the Commission was in error in deeming its action controlled by
15   established judicial principles.

16   But the Commission urges here that the order should nevertheless be sustained
17   because "the effect of trading by management is not measured by the fairness
18   of individual transactions between buyer and seller, but by its relation to the
19   timing and dynamics of the reorganization which the management itself
20   initiates and so largely controls." * * *

21                                               * * *

22   * * * [T]he Commission could take appropriate action for the correction of
23   reorganization abuses found to be "detrimental to the public interest or the interest
24   of investors or consumers." It was entitled to take into account those more subtle
25   factors in the marketing of utility company securities that gave rise to the very
26   grave evils which the Public Utility Holding Act of 1935 was designed to correct.

27   But the difficulty remains that the considerations urged here in support of the
28   Commission's order were not those upon which its action was based. The
29   Commission did not rely upon "its special administrative competence"; it
30   formulated no judgment upon the requirements of the "public interest or the
31   interest of investors or consumers" in the situation before it. Through its
32   preoccupation with the special problems of utility reorganizations, the
33   Commission accumulates an experience and insight denied to others. Had the
34   Commission, acting upon its experience and peculiar competence, promulgated a
35   general rule of which its order here was a particular application, the problem for
36   our consideration would be very different. Whether and to what extent directors
37   or officers should be prohibited from buying or selling stock of the corporation
38   during its reorganization presents problems of policy for the judgment of Congress
39   or of the body to which it has delegated power to deal with the matter. Abuse of
40   corporate position, influence, and access to information may raise questions so
41   subtle that the law can deal with them effectively only by prohibitions not
42   concerned with the fairness of a particular transaction. But before transactions
43   otherwise legal can be outlawed or denied their usual business consequences, they

1   must fall under the ban of some standards of conduct prescribed by an agency of
2   government authorized to prescribe such standards—either the courts or Congress
3   or an agency to which Congress has delegated its authority. Congress itself did not
4   proscribe the respondents' purchases of preferred stock in Federal. Established
5   judicial doctrines do not condemn these transactions. Nor has the Commission,
6   acting under the rulemaking powers delegated to it by § 11(e), promulgated new
7   general standards of conduct. It purported merely to be applying an existing judge-
8   made rule of equity. The Commission's determination can stand, therefore, only if
9   it found that the specific transactions under scrutiny showed misuse by the
10  respondents of their position as reorganization managers, in that, as such
11  managers, they took advantage of the corporation or the other stockholders or the
12  investing public. The record is utterly barren of any such showing. Indeed, such a
13  claim against the respondents was explicitly disavowed by the Commission.

14                                  * * *

15  Judged, therefore, as a determination based upon judge-made rules of equity, the
16  Commission's order cannot be upheld. Its action must be measured by what the
17  Commission did, not by what it might have done. It is not for us to determine
18  independently what is "detrimental to the public interest or the interest of
19  investors or consumers" or "fair and equitable" within the meaning of §§ 7 and 11
20  of the Public Utility Holding Company Act of 1935. The Commission's action
21  cannot be upheld merely because findings might have been made and
22  considerations disclosed which would justify its order as an appropriate safeguard
23  for the interests protected by the Act. There must be such a responsible finding.
24  There is no such finding here.

25  Congress has seen fit to subject to judicial review such orders of the Securities and
26  Exchange Commission as the one before us. That the scope of such review is
27  narrowly circumscribed is beside the point. For the courts cannot exercise their
28  duty of review unless they are advised of the considerations underlying the action
29  under review. If the action rests upon an administrative determination—an
30  exercise of judgment in an area which Congress has entrusted to the agency—of
31  course it must not be set aside, because the reviewing court might have made a
32  different determination were it empowered to do so. But if the action is based upon
33  a determination of law as to which the reviewing authority of the courts does come
34  into play, an order may not stand if the agency has misconceived the law. In either
35  event, the orderly functioning of the process of review requires that the grounds
36  upon which the administrative agency acted by clearly disclosed and adequately
37  sustained. "The administrative process will best be vindicated by clarity in its
38  exercise." *Phelps Dodge Corp. v. Labor Board*, 313 U.S. 177, 197. What was said in
39  that case is equally applicable here:

40      "We do not intend to enter the province the belongs to the Board, nor do
41      we do so. All we ask of the Board is to give clear indication that it has
42      exercised the discretion with which Congress has empowered it. This is to
43      affirm most emphatically the authority of the Board."

1   *Ibid.* In finding that the Commission's order cannot be sustained, we are not
2   imposing any trammels on its powers. We are not enforcing formal requirements.
3   We are not suggesting that the Commission must justify its exercise of
4   administrative discretion in any particular manner or with artistic refinement. We
5   are not sticking in the bark of words. We merely hold that an administrative order
6   cannot be upheld unless the grounds upon which the agency acted in exercising its
7   powers were those upon which its action can be sustained.

8   The cause should therefore be remanded to the Court to Appeals with directions to
9   remand to the Commission for such further proceedings, not inconsistent with this
10  opinion, as may be appropriate.

11  *So ordered.*

12  MR. JUSTICE BLACK, with whom MR. JUSTICE REED and MR. JUSTICE
13  MURPHY concur, dissenting. [Omitted.]

14

15  **SEC v. Chenery Corp. (*Chenery II*)**

16  332 U.S. 194 (1947)

17  June 23, 1947

18  MR. JUSTICE MURPHY delivered the opinion of the Court.

19  This case is here for the second time. In *SEC v. Chenery Corp.*, 318 U.S. 80 (1943),
20  we held that an order of the Securities and Exchange Commission could not be
21  sustained on the grounds upon which that agency acted. We therefore directed that
22  the case be remanded to the Commission for such further proceedings as might be
23  appropriate. On remand, the Commission reexamined the problem, recast its
24  rationale, and reached the same result. The issue now is whether the Commission's
25  action is proper in light of the principles established in our prior decision.

26                                              * * *

27  The latest order of the Commission definitely avoids the fatal error of relying on
28  judicial precedents which do not sustain it. This time, after a thorough
29  reexamination of the problem in light of the purposes and standards of the Holding
30  Company Act, the Commission has concluded that the proposed transaction is
31  inconsistent with the standards of §§ 7 and 11 of the Act. It has drawn heavily upon
32  its accumulated experience in dealing with utility reorganizations. And it has
33  expressed its reasons with a clarity and thoroughness that admit of no doubt as to
34  the underlying basis of its order.

35  The argument is pressed upon us, however, that the Commission was foreclosed
36  from taking such a step following our prior decision. It is said that, in the absence
37  of findings of conscious wrongdoing on the part of Federal's management, the
38  Commission could not determine by an order in this particular case that it was
39  inconsistent with the statutory standards to permit Federal's management to
    418

1 realize a profit through the reorganization purchases. All that it could do was to
2 enter an order allowing an amendment to the plan so that the proposed transaction
3 could be consummated. Under this view, the Commission would be free only to
4 promulgate a general rule outlawing such profits in future utility reorganizations;
5 but such a rule would have to be prospective in nature, and have no retroactive
6 effect upon the instant situation.

7 We reject this contention, for it grows out of a misapprehension of our prior
8 decision and of the Commission's statutory duties. We held no more and no less
9 than that the Commission's first order was unsupportable for the reasons supplied
10 by that agency. But when the case left this Court, the problem whether Federal's
11 management should be treated equally with other preferred stockholders still
12 lacked a final and complete answer. It was clear that the Commission could not
13 give a negative answer by resort to prior judicial declarations. And it was also clear
14 that the Commission was not bound by settled judicial precedents in a situation of
15 this nature. Still unsettled, however, was the answer the Commission might give
16 were it to bring to bear on the facts the proper administrative and statutory
17 considerations, a function which belongs exclusively to the Commission in the first
18 instance. The administrative process had taken an erroneous, rather than a final,
19 turn. Hence, we carefully refrained from expressing any views as to the propriety
20 of an order rooted in the proper and relevant considerations.

21 When the case was directed to be remanded to the Commission for such further
22 proceedings as might be appropriate, it was with the thought that the Commission
23 would give full effect to its duties in harmony with the views we had expressed.
24 This obviously meant something more than the entry of a perfunctory order giving
25 parity treatment to the management holdings of preferred stock. The fact that the
26 Commission had committed a legal error in its first disposition of the case certainly
27 gave Federal's management no vested right to receive the benefits of such an order.
28 After the remand was made, therefore, the Commission was bound to deal with the
29 problem afresh, performing the function delegated to it by Congress. It was again
30 charged with the duty of measuring the proposed treatment of the management's
31 preferred stock holdings by relevant and proper standards. Only in that way could
32 the legislative policies embodied in the Act be effectuated.

33 The absence of a general rule or regulation governing management trading during
34 reorganization did not affect the Commission's duties in relation to the particular
35 proposal before it. The Commission was asked to grant or deny effectiveness to a
36 proposed amendment to Federal's reorganization plan whereby the management
37 would be accorded parity treatment on its holdings. It could do that only in the
38 form of an order, entered after a due consideration of the particular facts in light
39 of the relevant and proper standards. That was true regardless of whether those
40 standards previously had been spelled out in a general rule or regulation. Indeed,
41 if the Commission rightly felt that the proposed amendment was inconsistent with
42 those standards, an order giving effect to the amendment merely because there was
43 no general rule or regulation covering the matter would be unjustified.

1   It is true that our prior decision explicitly recognized the possibility that the
2   Commission might have promulgated a general rule dealing with this problem
3   under its statutory rulemaking powers, in which case the issue for our
4   consideration would have been entirely different from that which did confront us.
5   But we did not mean to imply thereby that the failure of the Commission to
6   anticipate this problem and to promulgate a general rule withdrew all power from
7   that agency to perform its statutory duty in this case. To hold that the Commission
8   had no alternative in this proceeding but to approve the proposed transaction,
9   while formulating any general rules it might desire for use in future cases of this
10  nature, would be to stultify the administrative process. That we refuse to do.

11  Since the Commission, unlike a court, does have the ability to make new law
12  prospectively through the exercise of its rulemaking powers, it has less reason to
13  rely upon *ad hoc* adjudication to formulate new standards of conduct within the
14  framework of the Holding Company Act. The function of filling in the interstices of
15  the Act should be performed, as much as possible, through this *quasi*-legislative
16  promulgation of rules to be applied in the future. But any rigid requirement to that
17  effect would make the administrative process inflexible and incapable of dealing
18  with many of the specialized problems which arise. *See* Report of the Attorney
19  General's Committee on Administrative Procedure in Government Agencies,
20  S.Doc. No. 8, 77th Cong., 1st Sess., p. 29. Not every principle essential to the
21  effective administration of a statute can or should be cast immediately into the
22  mold of a general rule. Some principles must await their own development, while
23  others must be adjusted to meet particular unforeseeable situations. In performing
24  its important functions in these respects, therefore, an administrative agency must
25  be equipped to act either by general rule or by individual order. To insist upon one
26  form of action to the exclusion of the other is to exalt form over necessity.

27  In other words, problems may arise in a case which the administrative agency
28  could not reasonably foresee, problems which must be solved despite the absence
29  of a relevant general rule. Or the agency may not have had sufficient experience
30  with a particular problem to warrant rigidifying its tentative judgment into a hard
31  and fast rule. Or the problem may be so specialized and varying in nature as to be
32  impossible of capture within the boundaries of a general rule. In those situations,
33  the agency must retain power to deal with the problems on a case-to-case basis if
34  the administrative process is to be effective. There is thus a very definite place for
35  the case-by-case evolution of statutory standards. And the choice made between
36  proceeding by general rule or by individual, *ad hoc* litigation is one that lies
37  primarily in the informed discretion of the administrative agency. *See Columbia
38  Broadcasting System v. United States,* 316 U.S. 407, 421 (1942).

39  Hence, we refuse to say that the Commission, which had not previously been
40  confronted with the problem of management trading during reorganization, was
41  forbidden from utilizing this particular proceeding for announcing and applying a
42  new standard of conduct. That such action might have a retroactive effect was not
43  necessarily fatal to its validity. Every case of first impression has a retroactive
44  effect, whether the new principle is announced by a court or by an administrative

1    agency. But such retroactivity must be balanced against the mischief of producing
2    a result which is contrary to a statutory design or to legal and equitable principles.
3    If that mischief is greater than the ill effect of the retroactive application of a new
4    standard, it is not the type of retroactivity which is condemned by law.

5                                    * * *

6    The problem in this case thus resolves itself into a determination of whether the
7    Commission's action in denying effectiveness to the proposed amendment to the
8    Federal reorganization plan can be justified on the basis upon which it clearly rests.
9    As we have noted, the Commission avoided placing its sole reliance on inapplicable
10   judicial precedents. Rather, it has derived its conclusions from the particular facts
11   in the case, its general experience in reorganization matters, and its informed view
12   of statutory requirements. It is those matters which are the guide for our review.

13   The Commission concluded that it could not find that the reorganization plan, if
14   amended as proposed, would be "fair and equitable to the persons affected
15   [thereby]" within the meaning of § 11(e) of the Act, under which the reorganization
16   was taking place. Its view was that the amended plan would involve the issuance
17   of securities on terms "detrimental to the public interest or the interest of
18   investors" contrary to §§ 7(d)(6) and 7(e), and would result in an "unfair or
19   inequitable distribution of voting power" among the Federal security holders
20   within the meaning of § 7(e). It was led to this result

21   "not by proof that the interveners [Federal's management] committed acts of
22   conscious wrongdoing, but by the character of the conflicting interests created by
23   the interveners' program of stock purchases carried out while plans for
24   reorganization were under consideration."

25                                   * * *

26   Federal's management had thus placed itself in a position where it was "peculiarly
27   susceptible to temptation to conduct the reorganization for personal gain, rather
28   than the public good," and where its desire to make advantageous purchases of
29   stock could have an important influence, even though subconsciously, upon many
30   of the decisions to be made in the course of the reorganization. Accordingly, the
31   Commission felt that all of its general considerations of the problem were
32   applicable to this case.

33   The scope of our review of an administrative order wherein a new principle is
34   announced and applied is no different from that which pertains to ordinary
35   administrative action. The wisdom of the principle adopted is none of our concern.
36   *See Board of Trade v. United States*, 314 U.S. 534, 548 (1942). Our duty is at an
37   end when it becomes evident that the Commission's action is based upon
38   substantial evidence and is consistent with the authority granted by Congress. *See*
39   *National Broadcasting Co. v. United States*, 319 U.S. 190, 224 (1943).

40   We are unable to say in this case that the Commission erred in reaching the result
41   it did. The facts being undisputed, we are free to disturb the Commission's

conclusion only if it lacks any rational and statutory foundation. In that connection, the Commission has made a thorough examination of the problem, utilizing statutory standards and its own accumulated experience with reorganization matters. In essence, it has made what we indicated in our prior opinion would be an informed, expert judgment on the problem. It has taken into account

> "those more subtle factors in the marketing of utility company securities that gave rise to the very grave evils which the Public Utility Holding Company Act of 1935 was designed to correct,"

and has relied upon the fact that

> "[a]buse of corporate position, influence, and access to information may raise questions so subtle that the law can deal with them effectively only by prohibitions not concerned with the fairness of a particular transaction."

318 U.S. at 92.

Such factors may properly be considered by the Commission in determining whether to approve a plan of reorganization of a utility holding company, or an amendment to such a plan. The "fair and equitable" rule of § 11(e) and the standard of what is "detrimental to the public interest or the interest of investors or consumers" under § 7(d)(6) and § 7(e) were inserted by the framers of the Act in order that the Commission might have broad powers to protect the various interests at stake. 318 U.S. at 90-91. The application of those criteria, whether in the form of a particular order or a general regulation, necessarily requires the use of informal discretion by the Commission. The very breath of the statutory language precludes a reversal of the Commission's judgment save where it has plainly abused its discretion in these matters. *See United States v. Lowden,* 308 U.S. 225 (1939); *ICC v. Railway Labor Executives Ass'n,* 315 U.S. 373 (1942). Such an abuse is not present in this case.

\* \* \*

The Commission's conclusion here rests squarely in that area where administrative judgments are entitled to the greatest amount of weight by appellate courts. It is the product of administrative experience, appreciation of the complexities of the problem, realization of the statutory policies, and responsible treatment of the uncontested facts. It is the type of judgment which administrative agencies are best equipped to make and which justifies the use of the administrative process. *See Republic Aviation Corporation v. Labor Board,* 324 U.S. 793, 800 (1945). Whether we agree or disagree with the result reached, it is an allowable judgment which we cannot disturb.

*Reversed.*

MR. JUSTICE BURTON concurs in the result.

422

1 THE CHIEF JUSTICE and MR. JUSTICE DOUGLAS took no part in the
2 consideration or decision of this case.

3 MR. JUSTICE JACKSON, dissenting.

4 The Court by this present decision sustains the identical administrative order
5 which only recently it held invalid. *Securities and Exchange Commission v.*
6 *Chenery Corp.,* 318 U.S. 80. As the Court correctly notes, the Commission has only
7 "recast its rationale and reached the same result." (Par. 1.) There being no change
8 in the order, no additional evidence in the record, and no amendment of relevant
9 legislation, it is clear that there has been a shift in attitude between that of the
10 controlling membership of the Court when the case was first here and that of those
11 who have the power of decision on this second review.

12 I feel constrained to disagree with the reasoning offered to rationalize this shift. It
13 makes judicial review of administrative orders a hopeless formality for the litigant,
14 even where granted to him by Congress. It reduces the judicial process in such
15 cases to a mere feint. While the opinion does not have the adherence of a majority
16 of the full Court, if its pronouncements should become governing principles, they
17 would, in practice, put most administrative orders over and above the law.

18                              \* \* \*

19 MR. JUSTICE FRANKFURTER joins in this opinion.

20

21 ## Citizens to Preserve Overton Park v. Volpe

22 401 U.S. 402 (1971)

23 March 2, 1971

24 Opinion of the Court by MR. JUSTICE MARSHALL, announced by MR. JUSTICE
25 STEWART.

26 The growing public concern about the quality of our natural environment has
27 prompted Congress in recent years to enact legislation designed to curb the
28 accelerating destruction of our country's natural beauty. We are concerned in this
29 case with § 4(f) of the Department of Transportation Act of 1966, as amended, and
30 § 18(a) of the Federal-Aid Highway Act of 1968, 82 Stat. 823, 23 U.S.C. § 138 (1964
31 ed., Supp. V) (hereafter § 138). These statutes prohibit the Secretary of
32 Transportation from authorizing the use of federal funds to finance the
33 construction of highways through public parks if a "feasible and prudent"
34 alternative route exists. If no such route is available, the statutes allow him to
35 approve construction through parks only if there has been "all possible planning
36 to minimize harm" to the park.

37 Petitioners, private citizens as well as local and national conservation
38 organizations, contend that the Secretary has violated these statutes by authorizing
39 the expenditure of federal funds for the construction of a six-lane interstate

1 highway through a public park in Memphis, Tennessee. Their claim was rejected
2 by the District Court, which granted the Secretary's motion for summary judgment,
3 and the Court of Appeals for the Sixth Circuit affirmed. After oral argument, this
4 Court granted a stay that halted construction and, treating the application for the
5 stay as a petition for certiorari, granted review. We now reverse the judgment
6 below and remand for further proceedings in the District Court.

7 Overton Park is a 342-acre city park located near the center of Memphis. The park
8 contains a zoo, a nine-hole municipal golf course, an outdoor theater, nature trails,
9 a bridle path, an art academy, picnic areas, and 170 acres of forest. The proposed
10 highway, which is to be a six-lane, high-speed, expressway, will sever the zoo from
11 the rest of the park. Although the roadway will be depressed below ground level
12 except where it crosses a small creek, 26 acres of the park will be destroyed. The
13 highway is to be a segment of Interstate Highway I-40, part of the National System
14 of Interstate and Defense Highways. I-40 will provide Memphis with a major east-
15 west expressway which will allow easier access to downtown Memphis from the
16 residential areas on the eastern edge of the city.

17 Although the route through the park was approved by the Bureau of Public Roads
18 in 1956 and by the Federal Highway Administrator in 1966, the enactment of § 4(f)
19 of the Department of Transportation Act prevented distribution of federal funds
20 for the section of the highway designated to go through Overton Park until the
21 Secretary of Transportation determined whether the requirements of § 4(f) had
22 been met. Federal funding for the rest of the project was, however, available; and
23 the state acquired a right-of-way on both sides of the park. In April, 1968, the
24 Secretary announced that he concurred in the judgment of local officials that I-40
25 should be built through the park. And in September, 1969, the State acquired the
26 right-of-way inside Overton Park from the city. Final approval for the project—the
27 route as well as the design—was not announced until November, 1969, after
28 Congress had reiterated in § 138 of the Federal-Aid Highway Act that highway
29 construction through public parks was to be restricted. Neither announcement
30 approving the route and design of I-40 was accompanied by a statement of the
31 Secretary's factual findings. He did not indicate why he believed there were no
32 feasible and prudent alternative routes, or why design changes could not be made
33 to reduce the harm to the park.

34 Petitioners contend that the Secretary's action is invalid without such formal
35 findings, and that the Secretary did not make an independent determination, but
36 merely relied on the judgment of the Memphis City Council. They also contend that
37 it would be "feasible and prudent" to route I-40 around Overton Park either to the
38 north or to the south. And they argue that, if these alternative routes are not
39 "feasible and prudent," the present plan does not include "all possible" methods
40 for reducing harm to the park. Petitioners claim that I-40 could be built under the
41 park by using either of two possible tunneling methods, and they claim that, at a
42 minimum, by using advanced drainage techniques, the expressway could be
43 depressed below ground level along the entire route through the park, including
44 the section that crosses the small creek.

424

Respondents argue that it was unnecessary for the Secretary to make formal findings, and that he did, in fact, exercise his own independent judgment, which was supported by the facts. In the District Court, respondents introduced affidavits, prepared specifically for this litigation, which indicated that the Secretary had made the decision and that the decision was supportable. These affidavits were contradicted by affidavits introduced by petitioners, who also sought to take the deposition of a former Federal Highway Administrator who had participated in the decision to route I-40 through Overton Park.

The District Court and the Court of Appeals found that formal findings by the Secretary were not necessary, and refused to order the deposition of the former Federal Highway Administrator because those courts believed that probing of the mental processes of an administrative decisionmaker was prohibited. And, believing that the Secretary's authority was wide, and reviewing courts' authority narrow, in the approval of highway routes, the lower courts held that the affidavits contained no basis for a determination that the Secretary had exceeded his authority.

We agree that formal findings were not required. But we do not believe that, in this case, judicial review based solely on litigation affidavits was adequate.

A threshold question—whether petitioners are entitled to any judicial review—is easily answered. Section 701 of the Administrative Procedure Act, 5 U.S.C. § 701 (1964 ed., Supp. V), provides that the action of "each authority of the Government of the United States," which includes the Department of Transportation, is subject to judicial review except where there is a statutory prohibition on review or where "agency action is committed to agency discretion by law." In this case, there is no indication that Congress sought to prohibit judicial review, and there is most certainly no "showing of clear and convincing evidence' of a . . . legislative intent" to restrict access to judicial review. *Abbott Laboratories v. Gardner*, 387 U.S. 136, 387 U.S. 141 (1967).

Similarly, the Secretary's decision here does not fall within the exception for action "committed to agency discretion." This is a very narrow exception. The legislative history of the Administrative Procedure Act indicates that it is applicable in those rare instances where "statutes are drawn in such broad terms that, in a given case, there is no law to apply." S.Rep. No. 752, 79th Cong., 1st Sess., 26 (1945).

Section 4(f) of the Department of Transportation Act and § 138 of the Federal-Aid Highway Act are clear and specific directives. Both the Department of Transportation Act and the Federal-Aid Highway Act provide that the Secretary "shall not approve any program or project" that requires the use of any public park land "unless (1) there is no feasible and prudent alternative to the use of such land, and (2) such program includes all possible planning to minimize harm to such park. . . ." 23 U.S.C. § 138; 49 U.S.C. § 1653(f). This language is a plain and explicit bar to the use of federal funds for construction of highways through parks—only the most unusual situations are exempted.

1  Despite the clarity of the statutory language, respondents argue that the Secretary
2  has wide discretion. They recognize that the requirement that there be no "feasible"
3  alternative route admits of little administrative discretion. For this exemption to
4  apply, the Secretary must find that, as a matter of sound engineering, it would not
5  be feasible to build the highway along any other route. Respondents argue,
6  however, that the requirement that there be no other "prudent" route requires the
7  Secretary to engage in a wide-ranging balancing of competing interests. They
8  contend that the Secretary should weigh the detriment resulting from the
9  destruction of park land against the cost of other routes, safety considerations, and
10 other factors, and determine on the basis of the importance that he attaches to
11 these other factors whether, on balance, alternative feasible routes would be
12 "prudent."

13 But no such wide-ranging endeavor was intended. It is obvious that, in most cases,
14 considerations of cost, directness of route, and community disruption will indicate
15 that park land should be used for highway construction whenever possible.
16 Although it may be necessary to transfer funds from one jurisdiction to another,
17 there will always be a smaller outlay required from the public purse when park land
18 is used, since the public already owns the land, and there will be no need to pay for
19 right-of-way. And since people do not live or work in parks, if a highway is built on
20 park land, no one will have to leave his home or give up his business. Such factors
21 are common to substantially all highway construction. Thus, if Congress intended
22 these factors to be on an equal footing with preservation of park land, there would
23 have been no need for the statutes.

24 Congress clearly did not intend that cost and disruption of the community were to
25 be ignored by the Secretary. But the very existence of the statutes indicates that
26 protection of park land was to be given paramount importance. The few green
27 havens that are public parks were not to be lost unless there were truly unusual
28 factors present in a particular case or the cost or community disruption resulting
29 from alternative routes reached extraordinary magnitudes. If the statutes are to
30 have any meaning, the Secretary cannot approve the destruction of park land
31 unless he finds that alternative routes present unique problems.

32 Plainly, there is "law to apply," and thus the exemption for action "committed to
33 agency discretion" is inapplicable. But the existence of judicial review is only the
34 start: the standard for review must also be determined. For that, we must look to §
35 706 of the Administrative Procedure Act, which provides that a "reviewing court
36 shall . . . hold unlawful and set aside agency action, findings, and conclusions
37 found" not to meet six separate standards. In all cases, agency action must be set
38 aside if the action was "arbitrary, capricious, an abuse of discretion, or otherwise
39 not in accordance with law" or if the action failed to meet statutory, procedural, or
40 constitutional requirements. In certain narrow, specifically limited situations, the
41 agency action is to be set aside if the action was not supported by "substantial
42 evidence." And in other equally narrow circumstances, the reviewing court is to
43 engage in a de novo review of the action and set it aside if it was "unwarranted by
44 the facts." 5 U.S.C. §§ 706(2)(E), (F).

426

1     Petitioners argue that the Secretary's approval of the construction of I-40 through
2     Overton Park is subject to one or the other of these latter two standards of limited
3     applicability. First, they contend that the "substantial evidence" standard of §
4     706(2)(E) must be applied. In the alternative, they claim that § 706(2)(F) applies,
5     and that there must be a *de novo* review to determine if the Secretary's action was
6     "unwarranted by the facts." Neither of these standards is, however, applicable.

7     Review under the substantial evidence test is authorized only when the agency
8     action is taken pursuant to a rulemaking provision of the Administrative Procedure
9     Act itself or when the agency action is based on a public adjudicatory hearing. The
10    Secretary's decision to allow the expenditure of federal funds to build I-40 through
11    Overton Park was plainly not an exercise of a rulemaking function. And the only
12    hearing that is required by either the Administrative Procedure Act or the statutes
13    regulating the distribution of federal funds for highway construction is a public
14    hearing conducted by local officials for the purpose of informing the community
15    about the proposed project and eliciting community views on the design and route.
16    The hearing is nonadjudicatory, quasi-legislative in nature. It is not designed to
17    produce a record that is to be the basis of agency action—the basic requirement for
18    substantial evidence review.

19    Petitioners' alternative argument also fails. *De novo review* of whether the
20    Secretary's decision was "unwarranted by the facts" is authorized by § 706(2)(F) in
21    only two circumstances. First, such *de novo* review is authorized when the action
22    is adjudicatory in nature and the agency factfinding procedures are inadequate.
23    And there may be independent judicial factfinding when issues that were not
24    before the agency are raised in a proceeding to enforce nonadjudicatory agency
25    action. Neither situation exists here.

26    Even though there is no *de novo* review in this case and the Secretary's approval of
27    the route of I-40 does not have ultimately to meet the substantial evidence test, the
28    generally applicable standards of § 706 require the reviewing court to engage in a
29    substantial inquiry. Certainly, the Secretary's decision is entitled to a presumption
30    of regularity. But that presumption is not to shield his action from a thorough,
31    probing, in-depth review.

32    The court is first required to decide whether the Secretary acted within the scope
33    of his authority. This determination naturally begins with a delineation of the
34    scope of the Secretary's authority and discretion. As has been shown, Congress has
35    specified only a small range of choices that the Secretary can make. Also involved
36    in this initial inquiry is a determination of whether, on the facts, the Secretary's
37    decision can reasonably be said to be within that range. The reviewing court must
38    consider whether the Secretary properly construed his authority to approve the use
39    of park land as limited to situations where there are no feasible alternative routes
40    or where feasible alternative routes involve uniquely difficult problems. And the
41    reviewing court must be able to find that the Secretary could have reasonably
42    believed that, in this case, there are no feasible alternatives, or that alternatives do
43    involve unique problems.

1  Scrutiny of the facts does not end, however, with the determination that the
2  Secretary has acted within the scope of his statutory authority. Section 706(2)(A)
3  requires a finding that the actual choice made was not "arbitrary, capricious, an
4  abuse of discretion, or otherwise not in accordance with law." To make this finding,
5  the court must consider whether the decision was based on a consideration of the
6  relevant factors and whether there has been a clear error of judgment. Although
7  this inquiry into the facts is to be searching and careful, the ultimate standard of
8  review is a narrow one. The court is not empowered to substitute its judgment for
9  that of the agency.

10  The final inquiry is whether the Secretary's action followed the necessary
11  procedural requirements. Here, the only procedural error alleged is the failure of
12  the Secretary to make formal findings and state his reason for allowing the highway
13  to be built through the park.

14  Undoubtedly, review of the Secretary's action is hampered by his failure to make
15  such findings, but the absence of formal findings does not necessarily require that
16  the case be remanded to the Secretary. Neither the Department of Transportation
17  Act nor the Federal-Aid Highway Act requires such formal findings. Moreover, the
18  Administrative Procedure Act requirements that there be formal findings in
19  certain rulemaking and adjudicatory proceedings do not apply to the Secretary's
20  action here. And, although formal findings may be required in some cases in the
21  absence of statutory directives when the nature of the agency action is ambiguous,
22  those situations are rare. Plainly, there is no ambiguity here; the Secretary has
23  approved the construction of I-40 through Overton Park, and has approved a
24  specific design for the project.

25                                        * * *

26  * * * [T]here is an administrative record that allows the full, prompt review of the
27  Secretary's action that is sought without additional delay which would result from
28  having a remand to the Secretary.

29  That administrative record is not, however, before us. The lower courts based their
30  review on the litigation affidavits that were presented. These affidavits were merely
31  "*post hoc*" rationalizations, which have traditionally been found to be an
32  inadequate basis for review. And they clearly do not constitute the "whole record"
33  compiled by the agency: the basis for review required by § 706 of the
34  Administrative Procedure Act.

35  Thus, it is necessary to remand this case to the District Court for plenary review of
36  the Secretary's decision. That review is to be based on the full administrative record
37  that was before the Secretary at the time he made his decision. But since the bare
38  record may not disclose the factors that were considered or the Secretary's
39  construction of the evidence, it may be necessary for the District Court to require
40  some explanation in order to determine if the Secretary acted within the scope of
41  his authority and if the Secretary's action was justifiable under the applicable
42  standard.

The court may require the administrative officials who participated in the decision to give testimony explaining their action. Of course, such inquiry into the mental processes of administrative decisionmakers is usually to be avoided. *United States v. Morgan*, 313 U.S. 409. 422 (1941). And where there are administrative findings that were made at the same time as the decision, as was the case in *Morgan*, there must be a strong showing of bad faith or improper behavior before such inquiry may be made. But here there are no such formal findings, and it may be that the only way there can be effective judicial review is by examining the decisionmakers themselves.

The District Court is not, however, required to make such an inquiry. It may be that the Secretary can prepare formal findings * * * that will provide an adequate explanation for his action. Such an explanation will, to some extent, be a "*post hoc* rationalization," and thus must be viewed critically. If the District Court decides that additional explanation is necessary, that court should consider which method will prove the most expeditious so that full review may be had as soon as possible.

*Reversed and remanded.*

MR. JUSTICE DOUGLAS took no part in the consideration or decision of this case.

MR. JUSTICE BLACK, with whom MR. JUSTICE BRENNAN joins, concurring.

I agree with the Court that the judgment of the Court of Appeals is wrong, and that its action should be reversed. I do not agree that the whole matter should be remanded to the District Court. I think the case should be sent back to the Secretary of Transportation. * * * The Act of Congress, in connection with other federal highway aid legislation, it seems to me, calls for hearings—hearings that a court can review, hearings that demonstrate more than mere arbitrary defiance by the Secretary. Whether the findings growing out of such hearings are labeled "formal" or "informal" appears to me to be no more than an exercise in semantics. Whatever the hearing requirements might be, the Department of Transportation failed to meet them in this case. * * * I dissent from the Court's failure to send the case back to the Secretary, whose duty has not yet been performed.

MR JUSTICE BLACKMUN, concurring. [Omitted.]

## Department of Commerce v. New York

139 S.Ct. 2551 (2019)

June 27, 2019

CHIEF JUSTICE ROBERTS delivered the opinion of the Court.

1  The Secretary of Commerce decided to reinstate a question about citizenship on
2  the 2020 census questionnaire. A group of plaintiffs challenged that decision on
3  constitutional and statutory grounds. We now decide whether the Secretary
4  violated the Enumeration Clause of the Constitution, the Census Act, or otherwise
5  abused his discretion.

6  I

7  A

8  In order to apportion Members of the House of Representatives among the States,
9  the Constitution requires an "Enumeration" of the population every 10 years, to be
10  made "in such Manner" as Congress "shall by Law direct." Art. I, § 2, cl. 3; Amdt.
11  14, § 2. In the Census Act, Congress delegated to the Secretary of Commerce the
12  task of conducting the decennial census "in such form and content as he may
13  determine." 13 U.S.C. § 141(a). The Secretary is aided in that task by the Census
14  Bureau, a statistical agency housed within the Department of Commerce.

15  The population count derived from the census is used not only to apportion
16  representatives but also to allocate federal funds to the States and to draw electoral
17  districts. The census additionally serves as a means of collecting demographic
18  information, which "is used for such varied purposes as computing federal grant-
19  in-aid benefits, drafting of legislation, urban and regional planning, business
20  planning, and academic and social studies." *Baldrige v. Shapiro*, 455 U.S. 345,
21  353-354, n. 9 (1982). Over the years, the census has asked questions about (for
22  example) race, sex, age, health, education, occupation, housing, and military
23  service. It has also asked about radio ownership, age at first marriage, and native
24  tongue. The Census Act obliges everyone to answer census questions truthfully and
25  requires the Secretary to keep individual answers confidential, including from
26  other Government agencies.

27  There have been 23 decennial censuses from the first census in 1790 to the most
28  recent in 2010. Every census between 1820 and 2000 (with the exception of 1840)
29  asked at least some of the population about their citizenship or place of birth.
30  Between 1820 and 1950, the question was asked of all households. Between 1960
31  and 2000, it was asked of about one-fourth to one-sixth of the population. That
32  change was part of a larger effort to simplify the census by asking most people a
33  few basic demographic questions (such as sex, age, race, and marital status) on a
34  short-form questionnaire, while asking a sample of the population more detailed
35  demographic questions on a long-form questionnaire. In explaining the decision
36  to move the citizenship question to the long-form questionnaire, the Census
37  Bureau opined that "general census information on citizenship had become of less
38  importance compared with other possible questions to be included in the census,

430

1   particularly in view of the recent statutory requirement for annual alien
2   registration which could provide the Immigration and Naturalization Service, the
3   principal user of such data, with the information it needed." Dept. of Commerce,
4   Bureau of Census, *1960 Censuses of Population and Housing* 194 (1966).

5   In 2010, the year of the latest census, the format changed again. All households
6   received the same questionnaire, which asked about sex, age, race, Hispanic origin,
7   and living arrangements. The more detailed demographic questions previously
8   asked on the long-form questionnaire, including the question about citizenship,
9   were instead asked in the American Community Survey (or ACS), which is sent
10  each year to a rotating sample of about 2.6% of households.

11  The Census Bureau and former Bureau officials have resisted occasional proposals
12  to resume asking a citizenship question of everyone, on the ground that doing so
13  would discourage noncitizens from responding to the census and lead to a less
14  accurate count of the total population. *See, e.g., Federation of Am. Immigration
15  Reform v. Klutznick,* 486 F. Supp. 564, 568 (DC 1980) ("[A]ccording to the
16  Bureau[,] any effort to ascertain citizenship will inevitably jeopardize the overall
17  accuracy of the population count").

18                                            B

19  In March 2018, Secretary of Commerce Wilbur Ross announced in a memo that he
20  had decided to reinstate a question about citizenship on the 2020 decennial census
21  questionnaire. The Secretary stated that he was acting at the request of the
22  Department of Justice (DOJ), which sought improved data about citizen voting-
23  age population for purposes of enforcing the Voting Rights Act (or VRA)—
24  specifically the Act's ban on diluting the influence of minority voters by depriving
25  them of single-member districts in which they can elect their preferred candidates.
26  DOJ explained that federal courts determine whether a minority group could
27  constitute a majority in a particular district by looking to the citizen voting-age
28  population of the group. According to DOJ, the existing citizenship data from the
29  American Community Survey was not ideal: It was not reported at the level of the
30  census block, the basic component of legislative districting plans; it had substantial
31  margins of error; and it did not align in time with the census-based population
32  counts used to draw legislative districts. DOJ therefore formally requested
33  reinstatement of the citizenship question on the census questionnaire.

34  The Secretary's memo explained that the Census Bureau initially analyzed, and the
35  Secretary considered, three possible courses of action. * * *

36  The Secretary "carefully considered" the possibility that reinstating a citizenship
37  question would depress the response rate. But after evaluating the Bureau's

1 "limited empirical evidence" on the question— evidence drawn from estimated
2 non-response rates to previous American Community Surveys and census
3 questionnaires—the Secretary concluded that it was not possible to "determine
4 definitively" whether inquiring about citizenship in the census would materially
5 affect response rates. He also noted the long history of the citizenship question on
6 the census, as well as the facts that the United Nations recommends collecting
7 census-based citizenship information, and other major democracies such as
8 Australia, Canada, France, Indonesia, Ireland, Germany, Mexico, Spain, and the
9 United Kingdom inquire about citizenship in their censuses. Altogether, the
10 Secretary determined that "the need for accurate citizenship data and the limited
11 burden that the reinstatement of the citizenship question would impose outweigh
12 fears about a potentially lower response rate."

13                                              C

14 Shortly after the Secretary announced his decision, two groups of plaintiffs filed
15 suit in Federal District Court in New York, challenging the decision on several
16 grounds. The first group of plaintiffs included 18 States, the District of Columbia,
17 various counties and cities, and the United States Conference of Mayors. They
18 alleged that the Secretary's decision violated the Enumeration Clause of the
19 Constitution and the requirements of the Administrative Procedure Act. The
20 second group of plaintiffs consisted of several non-governmental organizations
21 that work with immigrant and minority communities. They added an equal
22 protection claim. The District Court consolidated the two cases. Both groups of
23 plaintiffs are respondents here. * * *The District Court dismissed the Enumeration
24 Clause claim but allowed the other claims to proceed.

25 In June 2018, the Government submitted to the District Court the Commerce
26 Department's "administrative record": the materials that Secretary Ross
27 considered in making his decision. That record included DOJ's December 2017
28 letter requesting reinstatement of the citizenship question, as well as several
29 memos from the Census Bureau analyzing the predicted effects of reinstating the
30 question. Shortly thereafter, at DOJ's urging, the Government supplemented the
31 record with a new memo from the Secretary, "intended to provide further
32 background and context regarding" his March 2018 memo. The supplemental
33 memo stated that the Secretary had begun considering whether to add the
34 citizenship question in early 2017, and had inquired whether DOJ "would support,
35 and if so would request, inclusion of a citizenship question as consistent with and
36 useful for enforcement of the Voting Rights Act." According to the Secretary, DOJ
37 "formally" requested reinstatement of the citizenship question after that inquiry.

38 Respondents argued that the supplemental memo indicated that the Government
39 had submitted an incomplete record of the materials considered by the Secretary.

1   They asked the District Court to compel the Government to complete the
2   administrative record. The court granted that request, and the parties jointly
3   stipulated to the inclusion of more than 12,000 pages of additional materials in the
4   administrative record. Among those materials were emails and other records
5   confirming that the Secretary and his staff began exploring the possibility of
6   reinstating a citizenship question shortly after he was confirmed in early 2017,
7   attempted to elicit requests for citizenship data from other agencies, and
8   eventually persuaded DOJ to request reinstatement of the question for VRA
9   enforcement purposes.

10   In addition, respondents asked the court to authorize discovery outside the
11   administrative record. They claimed that such an unusual step was warranted
12   because they had made a strong preliminary showing that the Secretary had acted
13   in bad faith. *See Citizens to Preserve Overton Park, Inc. v. Volpe*, 401 U.S. 402,
14   420 (1971). The court also granted that request, authorizing expert discovery and
15   depositions of certain DOJ and Commerce Department officials.

16   In August and September 2018, the District Court issued orders compelling
17   depositions of Secretary Ross and of the Acting Assistant Attorney General for
18   DOJ's Civil Rights Division. We granted the Government's request to stay the
19   Secretary's deposition pending further review, but we declined to stay the Acting
20   AAG's deposition or the other extra-record discovery that the District Court had
21   authorized.

22   The District Court held a bench trial and issued findings of fact and conclusions of
23   law on respondents' statutory and equal protection claims. * * *[T]he District
24   Court ruled that the Secretary's action was arbitrary and capricious, based on a
25   pretextual rationale, and violated certain provisions of the Census Act. On the
26   equal protection claim, however, the District Court concluded that respondents
27   had not met their burden of showing that the Secretary was motivated by
28   discriminatory animus. The court granted judgment to respondents on their
29   statutory claims, vacated the Secretary's decision, and enjoined him from
30   reinstating the citizenship question until he cured the legal errors the court had
31   identified.

32   The Government appealed to the Second Circuit, but also filed a petition for writ
33   of certiorari before judgment, asking this Court to review the District Court's
34   decision directly because the case involved an issue of imperative public
35   importance, and the census questionnaire needed to be finalized for printing by
36   the end of June 2019. We granted the petition. At the Government's request, we
37   later ordered the parties to address whether the Enumeration Clause provided an
38   alternative basis to affirm.

1                                    * * *

2                                     IV

3    The District Court set aside the Secretary's decision to reinstate a citizenship
4    question on the grounds that the Secretary acted arbitrarily and violated certain
5    provisions of the Census Act. The Government contests those rulings, but also
6    argues that the Secretary's decision was not judicially reviewable under the
7    Administrative Procedure Act in the first place. We begin with that contention.

8                                      A

9    The Administrative Procedure Act embodies a "basic presumption of judicial
10   review," *Abbott Laboratories v. Gardner*, 387 U.S. 136, 140 (1967), and instructs
11   reviewing courts to set aside agency action that is "arbitrary, capricious, an abuse
12   of discretion, or otherwise not in accordance with law," 5 U.S.C. §706(2)(A).
13   Review is not available, however, "to the extent that" a relevant statute precludes
14   it, §701(a)(1), or the agency action is "committed to agency discretion by law,"
15   §701(a)(2). The Government argues that the Census Act commits to the Secretary's
16   unreviewable discretion decisions about what questions to include on the
17   decennial census questionnaire.

18   We disagree. To be sure, the Act confers broad authority on the Secretary. Section
19   141(a) instructs him to take "a decennial census of population" in "such form and
20   content as he may determine, including the use of sampling procedures and special
21   surveys." 13 U.S.C. §141. The Act defines "census of population" to mean "a census
22   of population, housing, and matters relating to population and housing," §141(g),
23   and it authorizes the Secretary, in "connection with any such census," to "obtain
24   such other census information as necessary," §141(a). It also states that the
25   "Secretary shall prepare questionnaires, and shall determine the inquiries, and the
26   number, form, and subdivisions thereof, for the statistics, surveys, and censuses
27   provided for in this title." §5. And it authorizes him to acquire materials, such as
28   administrative records, from other federal, state, and local agencies in aid of
29   conducting the census. §6. Those provisions leave much to the Secretary's
30   discretion.

31   But they do not leave his discretion unbounded. In order to give effect to the
32   command that courts set aside agency action that is an abuse of discretion, and to
33   honor the presumption of judicial review, we have read the §701(a)(2) exception
34   for action committed to agency discretion "quite narrowly, restricting it to 'those
35   rare circumstances where the relevant statute is drawn so that a court would have
36   no meaningful standard against which to judge the agency's exercise of
37   discretion.'" *Weyerhaeuser Co. v. United States Fish & Wildlife Serv.*, 113 S. Ct.

434

1    2024 (2018). And we have generally limited the exception to "certain categories of
2    administrative decisions that courts traditionally have regarded as 'committed to
3    agency discretion,'" *id.*, at 191, such as a decision not to institute enforcement
4    proceedings, *Heckler v. Chaney*, 470 U.S. 821, 831, 832 (1985), or a decision by an
5    intelligence agency to terminate an employee in the interest of national security,
6    *Webster v. Doe*, 486 U.S. 592, 600, 601 (1988).

7    The taking of the census is not one of those areas traditionally committed to agency
8    discretion. We and other courts have entertained both constitutional and statutory
9    challenges to census-related decisionmaking.

10    Nor is the statute here drawn so that it furnishes no meaningful standard by which
11    to judge the Secretary's action. In contrast to the National Security Act in *Webster*,
12    which gave the Director of Central Intelligence discretion to terminate employees
13    whenever he "deem[ed]" it "advisable," 486 U.S., at 594, the Census Act constrains
14    the Secretary's authority to determine the form and content of the census in a
15    number of ways. Section 195, for example, governs the extent to which he can use
16    statistical sampling. Section 6(c), which will be considered in more detail below,
17    circumscribes his power in certain circumstances to collect information through
18    direct inquiries when administrative records are available. More generally, by
19    mandating a population count that will be used to apportion representatives, see
20    §141(b), 2 U.S.C. §2a, the Act imposes "a duty to conduct a census that is accurate
21    and that fairly accounts for the crucial representational rights that depend on the
22    census and the apportionment." *Franklin*, 505 U.S., at 819-820 (STEVENS, J.,
23    concurring in part and concurring in judgment).

24    The Secretary's decision to reinstate a citizenship question is amenable to review
25    for compliance with those and other provisions of the Census Act, according to the
26    general requirements of reasoned agency decisionmaking. Because this is not a
27    case in which there is "no law to apply," *Overton Park*, 401 U.S., at 410, the
28    Secretary's decision is subject to judicial review.

29                                                          B

30    At the heart of this suit is respondents' claim that the Secretary abused his
31    discretion in deciding to reinstate a citizenship question. We review the Secretary's
32    exercise of discretion under the deferential "arbitrary and capricious" standard.
33    Our scope of review is "narrow": we determine only whether the Secretary
34    examined "the relevant data" and articulated "a satisfactory explanation" for his
35    decision, "including a rational connection between the facts found and the choice
36    made." *Motor Vehicle Mfrs. Ass'n v. State Farm Mut. Automobile Ins. Co.*, 463
37    U.S. 29, 43 (1983). We may not substitute our judgment for that of the Secretary,

1     but instead must confine ourselves to ensuring that he remained "within the
2     bounds of reasoned decisionmaking,"

3     The District Court set aside the Secretary's decision for two independent reasons:
4     His course of action was not supported by the evidence before him, and his stated
5     rationale was pretextual. We focus on the first point here and take up the question
6     of pretext later.

7     The Secretary examined the Bureau's analysis of various ways to collect improved
8     citizenship data and explained why he thought the best course was to both reinstate
9     a citizenship question and use citizenship data from administrative records to fill
10    in the gaps. He considered but rejected the Bureau's recommendation to use
11    administrative records alone. As he explained, records are lacking for about 10%
12    of the population, so the Bureau would still need to estimate citizenship for
13    millions of voting-age people. Asking a citizenship question of everyone, the
14    Secretary reasoned, would eliminate the need to estimate citizenship for many of
15    those people. And supplementing census responses with administrative record
16    data would help complete the picture and allow the Bureau to better estimate
17    citizenship for the smaller set of cases where it was still necessary to do so.

18    The evidence before the Secretary supported that decision. As the Bureau
19    acknowledged, each approach—using administrative records alone, or asking
20    about citizenship and using records to fill in the gaps—entailed tradeoffs between
21    accuracy and completeness. Without a citizenship question, the Bureau would
22    need to estimate the citizenship of about 35 million people; with a citizenship
23    question, it would need to estimate the citizenship of only 13.8 million. Under
24    either approach, there would be some errors in both the administrative records
25    and the Bureau's estimates. With a citizenship question, there would also be some
26    erroneous self-responses (about 500,000) and some conflicts between responses
27    and administrative record data (about 9.5 million).

28    The Bureau explained that the "relative quality" of the citizenship data generated
29    by each approach would depend on the "relative importance of the errors" in each,
30    but it was not able to "quantify the relative magnitude of the errors across the
31    alternatives." The Bureau nonetheless recommended using administrative records
32    alone because it had "high confidence" that it could develop an accurate model for
33    estimating the citizenship of the 35 million people for whom administrative
34    records were not available, and it thought the resulting citizenship data] would be
35    of superior quality. But when the time came for the Secretary to make a decision,
36    the model did not yet exist, and even if it had, there was no way to gauge its relative
37    accuracy. As the Bureau put it, "we will most likely never possess a fully adequate
38    truth deck to benchmark" the model—which appears to be bureaucratese for
39    "maybe, maybe not." Secretary opted instead for the approach that would yield a

1 more complete set of data at an acceptable rate of accuracy, and would require
2 estimating the citizenship of fewer people.

3 The District Court overruled that choice, agreeing with the Bureau's assessment
4 that its recommended approach would yield higher quality citizenship data on the
5 whole. But the choice between reasonable policy alternatives in the face of
6 uncertainty was the Secretary's to make. He considered the relevant factors,
7 weighed risks and benefits, and articulated a satisfactory explanation for his
8 decision. In overriding that reasonable exercise of discretion, the court improperly
9 substituted its judgment for that of the agency.

10 The Secretary then weighed the benefit of collecting more complete and accurate
11 citizenship data against the risk that inquiring about citizenship would depress
12 census response rates, particularly among noncitizen households. In the
13 Secretary's view, that risk was difficult to assess. The Bureau predicted a 5.1%
14 decline in response rates among noncitizen households if the citizenship question
15 were reinstated. It relied for that prediction primarily on studies showing that,
16 while noncitizens had responded at lower rates than citizens to the 2000 short-
17 form and 2010 censuses, which did not ask about citizenship, they responded at
18 even lower rates than citizens to the 2000 long-form census and the 2010
19 American Community Survey, which did ask about citizenship. The Bureau
20 thought it was reasonable to infer that the citizenship question accounted for the
21 differential decline in noncitizen responses. But, the Secretary explained, the
22 Bureau was unable to rule out other causes. For one thing, the evidence before the
23 Secretary suggested that noncitizen households tend to be more distrustful of, and
24 less likely to respond to, any government effort to collect information. For another,
25 both the 2000 long-form census and 2010 ACS asked over 45 questions on a range
26 of topics, including employment, income, and housing characteristics. Noncitizen
27 households might disproportionately fail to respond to a lengthy and intrusive
28 Government questionnaire for a number of reasons besides reluctance to answer a
29 citizenship question—reasons relating to education level, socioeconomic status,
30 and less exposure to Government outreach efforts.

31 The Secretary justifiably found the Bureau's analysis inconclusive. Weighing that
32 uncertainty against the value of obtaining more complete and accurate citizenship
33 data, he determined that reinstating a citizenship question was worth the risk of a
34 potentially lower response rate. That decision was reasonable and reasonably
35 explained, particularly in light of the long history of the citizenship question on the
36 census.

37 JUSTICE BREYER would conclude otherwise, but only by subordinating the
38 Secretary's policymaking discretion to the Bureau's technocratic expertise.
39 JUSTICE BREYER's analysis treats the Bureau's (pessimistic) prediction about

437

1     response rates and (optimistic) assumptions about its data modeling abilities as
2     touchstones of substantive reasonableness rather than simply evidence for the
3     Secretary to consider. He suggests that the Secretary should have deferred to the
4     Bureau or at least offered some special justification for drawing his own inferences
5     and adopting his own assumptions. But the Census Act authorizes the Secretary,
6     not the Bureau, to make policy choices within the range of reasonable options. And
7     the evidence before the Secretary hardly led ineluctably to just one reasonable
8     course of action. It called for value-laden decisionmaking and the weighing of
9     incommensurables under conditions of uncertainty. The Secretary was required to
10     consider the evidence and give reasons for his chosen course of action. He did so.
11     It is not for us to ask whether his decision was "the best one possible" or even
12     whether it was "better than the alternatives." *FERC v. Elec. Power Supply Ass'n,*
13     136 S. Ct. 760 (2016) (slip op., at 30). By second-guessing the Secretary's weighing
14     of risks and benefits and penalizing him for departing from the Bureau's inferences
15     and assumptions, JUSTICE BREYER—like the District Court—substitutes his
16     judgment for that of the agency.

17                                       \* \* \*

18                                       V

19     We now consider the District Court's determination that the Secretary's decision
20     must be set aside because it rested on a pretextual basis, which the Government
21     conceded below would warrant a remand to the agency.

22     We start with settled propositions. First, in order to permit meaningful judicial
23     review, an agency must "disclose the basis" of its action. *Burlington Truck Lines,*
24     *Inc. v. United States,* 371 U.S. 156, 167-169, (1962) (internal quotation marks
25     omitted); *see also SEC v. Chenery Corp.,* 318 U.S. 80, 94 (1943) ("[T]he orderly
26     functioning of the process of review requires that the grounds upon which the
27     administrative agency acted be clearly disclosed and adequately sustained.").

28     Second, in reviewing agency action, a court is ordinarily limited to evaluating the
29     agency's contemporaneous explanation in light of the existing administrative
30     record. *Vermont Yankee Nuclear Power Corp. v. Natural Resources Defense*
31     *Council, Inc.,* 435 U.S. 519, 549 (1978); *Camp v. Pitts,* 411 U.S. 138, 142-143 (1973)
32     (per curiam). That principle reflects the recognition that further judicial inquiry
33     into "executive motivation" represents "a substantial intrusion" into the workings
34     of another branch of Government and should normally be avoided.

35     Third, a court may not reject an agency's stated reasons for acting simply because
36     the agency might also have had other unstated reasons. *See Jagers v. Federal Crop*
37     *Ins. Corp.,* 758 F. 3d 1179, 1185-1186 (CA10 2014) (rejecting argument that "the

agency's subjective desire to reach a particular result must necessarily invalidate the result, regardless of the objective evidence supporting the agency's conclusion"). Relatedly, a court may not set aside an agency's policymaking decision solely because it might have been influenced by political considerations or prompted by an Administration's priorities. Agency policymaking is not a "rarified technocratic process, unaffected by political considerations or the presence of Presidential power." *Sierra Club v. Costle*, 657 F. 2d 298, 408 (CADC 1981). Such decisions are routinely informed by unstated considerations of politics, the legislative process, public relations, interest group relations, foreign relations, and national security concerns (among others).

Finally, we have recognized a narrow exception to the general rule against inquiring into "the mental processes of administrative decisionmakers." *Overton Park*, 401 U.S., at 420. On a "strong showing of bad faith or improper behavior," such an inquiry may be warranted and may justify extra-record discovery. *Ibid.*

The District Court invoked that exception in ordering extra-record discovery here. Although that order was premature, we think it was ultimately justified in light of the expanded administrative record. * * *

We agree with the Government that the District Court should not have ordered extra-record discovery when it did. At that time, the most that was warranted was the order to complete the administrative record. But the new material that the parties stipulated should have been part of the administrative record—which showed, among other things, that the VRA played an insignificant role in the decisionmaking process—largely justified such extra-record discovery as occurred (which did not include the deposition of the Secretary himself). We accordingly review the District Court's ruling on pretext in light of all the evidence in the record before the court, including the extra-record discovery.

That evidence showed that the Secretary was determined to reinstate a citizenship question from the time he entered office; instructed his staff to make it happen; waited while Commerce officials explored whether another agency would request census-based citizenship data; subsequently contacted the Attorney General himself to ask if DOJ would make the request; and adopted the Voting Rights Act rationale late in the process. In the District Court's view, this evidence established that the Secretary had made up his mind to reinstate a citizenship question "well before" receiving DOJ's request, and did so for reasons unknown but unrelated to the VRA.

The Government, on the other hand, contends that there was nothing objectionable or even surprising in this. And we agree—to a point. It is hardly improper for an agency head to come into office with policy preferences and ideas,

1   discuss them with affected parties, sound out other agencies for support, and work
2   with staff attorneys to substantiate the legal basis for a preferred policy. The record
3   here reflects the sometimes-involved nature of Executive Branch decisionmaking,
4   but no particular step in the process stands out as inappropriate or defective.

5   And yet, viewing the evidence as a whole, we share the District Court's conviction
6   that the decision to reinstate a citizenship question cannot be adequately explained
7   in terms of DOJ's request for improved citizenship data to better enforce the VRA.
8   Several points, considered together, reveal a significant mismatch between the
9   decision the Secretary made and the rationale he provided.

10   The record shows that the Secretary began taking steps to reinstate a citizenship
11   question about a week into his tenure, but it contains no hint that he was
12   considering VRA enforcement in connection with that project. * * *

13   * * * [I]t was not until the Secretary contacted the Attorney General directly that
14   DOJ's Civil Rights Division expressed interest in acquiring census-based
15   citizenship data to better enforce the VRA. And even then, the record suggests that
16   DOJ's interest was directed more to helping the Commerce Department than to
17   securing the data. The December 2017 letter from DOJ drew heavily on
18   contributions from Commerce staff and advisors. Their influence may explain why
19   the letter went beyond a simple entreaty for better citizenship data—what one
20   might expect of a typical request from another agency—to a specific request that
21   Commerce collect the data by means of reinstating a citizenship question on the
22   census. Finally, after sending the letter, DOJ declined the Census Bureau's offer to
23   discuss alternative ways to meet DOJ's stated need for improved citizenship data,
24   further suggesting a lack of interest on DOJ's part.

25   Altogether, the evidence tells a story that does not match the explanation the
26   Secretary gave for his decision. In the Secretary's telling, Commerce was simply
27   acting on a routine data request from another agency. Yet the materials before us
28   indicate that Commerce went to great lengths to elicit the request from DOJ (or
29   any other willing agency). And unlike a typical case in which an agency may have
30   both stated and unstated reasons for a decision, here the VRA enforcement
31   rationale—the sole stated reason—seems to have been contrived.

32   We are presented, in other words, with an explanation for agency action that is
33   incongruent with what the record reveals about the agency's priorities and
34   decisionmaking process. It is rare to review a record as extensive as the one before
35   us when evaluating informal agency action—and it should be. But having done so
36   for the sufficient reasons we have explained, we cannot ignore the disconnect
37   between the decision made and the explanation given. Our review is deferential,
38   but we are "not required to exhibit a naiveté from which ordinary citizens are free."

*United States v. Stanchich*, 550 F. 2d 1294, 1300 (CA2 1977) (Friendly, J.). The reasoned explanation requirement of administrative law, after all, is meant to ensure that agencies offer genuine justifications for important decisions, reasons that can be scrutinized by courts and the interested public. Accepting contrived reasons would defeat the purpose of the enterprise. If judicial review is to be more than an empty ritual, it must demand something better than the explanation offered for the action taken in this case.

In these unusual circumstances, the District Court was warranted in remanding to the agency, and we affirm that disposition. We do not hold that the agency decision here was substantively invalid. But agencies must pursue their goals reasonably. Reasoned decisionmaking under the Administrative Procedure Act calls for an explanation for agency action. What was provided here was more of a distraction.

The judgment of the United States District Court for the Southern District of New York is affirmed in part and reversed in part, and the case is remanded for further proceedings consistent with this opinion.

*It is so ordered.*

JUSTICE THOMAS, with whom JUSTICE GORSUCH and JUSTICE KAVANAUGH join, concurring in part and dissenting in part.

In March 2018, the Secretary of Commerce exercised his broad discretion over the administration of the decennial census to resume a nearly unbroken practice of asking a question relating to citizenship. Our only role in this case is to decide whether the Secretary complied with the law and gave a reasoned explanation for his decision. The Court correctly answers these questions in the affirmative. That ought to end our inquiry.

The Court, however, goes further. For the first time ever, the Court invalidates an agency action solely because it questions the sincerity of the agency's otherwise adequate rationale. Echoing the din of suspicion and distrust that seems to typify modern discourse, the Court declares the Secretary's memorandum "pretextual" because, "viewing the evidence as a whole," his explanation that including a citizenship question on the census would help enforce the Voting Rights Act (VRA) "seems to have been contrived." The Court does not hold that the Secretary merely had additional, unstated reasons for reinstating the citizenship question. Rather, it holds that the Secretary's stated rationale did not factor at all into his decision.

1   The Court's holding reflects an unprecedented departure from our deferential
2   review of discretionary agency decisions. And, if taken seriously as a rule of
3   decision, this holding would transform administrative law. It is not difficult for
4   political opponents of executive actions to generate controversy with accusations
5   of pretext, deceit, and illicit motives. Significant policy decisions are regularly
6   criticized as products of partisan influence, interest-group pressure, corruption,
7   and animus. Crediting these accusations on evidence as thin as the evidence here
8   could lead judicial review of administrative proceedings to devolve into an endless
9   morass of discovery and policy disputes not contemplated by the Administrative
10  Procedure Act (APA).

11  Unable to identify any legal problem with the Secretary's reasoning, the Court
12  imputes one by concluding that he must not be telling the truth. The Court
13  therefore upholds the decision of the District Court—which, in turn, was
14  transparently based on the application of an administration-specific standard.

15  The law requires a more impartial approach. Even assuming we are authorized to
16  engage in the review undertaken by the Court—which is far from clear—we have
17  often stated that courts reviewing agency action owe the Executive a "presumption
18  of regularity." *Citizens to Preserve Overton Park, Inc. v. Volpe*, 401 U.S. 402, 415
19  (1971). The Court pays only lipservice to this principle. But, the evidence falls far
20  short of supporting its decision. The Court, I fear, will come to regret inventing the
21  principles it uses to achieve today's result. I respectfully dissent from Part V of the
22  opinion of the Court.

23                                    * * *

24  JUSTICE BREYER, with whom JUSTICE GINSBURG, JUSTICE SOTOMAYOR,
25  and JUSTICE KAGAN join, concurring in part and dissenting in part.

26  I join Parts I, II, IV-A, and V of the Court's opinion (except as otherwise indicated
27  in this opinion). I dissent, however, from the conclusion the Court reaches in Part
28  IV-B. To be more specific, I agree with the Court that the Secretary of Commerce
29  provided a pretextual reason for placing a question about citizenship on the short-
30  form census questionnaire and that a remand to the agency is appropriate on that
31  ground. But I write separately because I also believe that the Secretary's decision
32  to add the citizenship question was arbitrary and capricious and therefore violated
33  the Administrative Procedure Act (APA).

34  There is no serious dispute that adding a citizenship question would diminish the
35  accuracy of the enumeration of the population—the sole constitutional function of
36  the census and a task of great practical importance. The record demonstrates that
37  the question would likely cause a disproportionate number of noncitizens and

442

1   Hispanics to go uncounted in the upcoming census. That, in turn, would create a
2   risk that some States would wrongfully lose a congressional representative and
3   funding for a host of federal programs. And, the Secretary was told, the adverse
4   consequences would fall most heavily on minority communities. The Secretary
5   decided to ask the question anyway, citing a need for more accurate citizenship
6   data. But the evidence indicated that asking the question would produce
7   citizenship data that is less accurate, not more. And the reason the Secretary gave
8   for needing better citizenship data in the first place—to help enforce the Voting
9   Rights Act of 1965—was not convincing.

10  In short, the Secretary's decision to add a citizenship question created a severe risk
11  of harmful consequences, yet he did not adequately consider whether the question
12  was necessary or whether it was an appropriate means of achieving his stated goal.
13  The Secretary thus failed to "articulate a satisfactory explanation" for his decision,
14  "failed to consider . . . important aspect[s] of the problem," and "offered an
15  explanation for [his] decision that runs counter to the evidence," all in violation of
16  the APA. *Motor Vehicle Mfrs. Ass'n, Inc. v. State Farm Mut. Auto. Ins. Co.*, 463
17  U.S. 29, 43 (1983). These failures, in my view, risked undermining public
18  confidence in the integrity of our democratic system itself. I would therefore hold
19  that the Secretary's decision—whether pretextual or not—was arbitrary,
20  capricious, and an abuse of discretion.

21                                    * * *

22  JUSTICE ALITO, concurring in part and dissenting in part.

23  It is a sign of our time that the inclusion of a question about citizenship on the
24  census has become a subject of bitter public controversy and has led to today's
25  regrettable decision. While the decision to place such a question on the 2020
26  census questionnaire is attacked as racist, there is a broad international consensus
27  that inquiring about citizenship on a census is not just appropriate but advisable.
28  No one disputes that it is important to know how many inhabitants of this country
29  are citizens. And the most direct way to gather this information is to ask for it in a
30  census. The United Nations recommends that a census inquire about citizenship,
31  and many countries do so.

32                                    * * *

33  Now, for the first time, this Court has seen fit to claim a role with respect to the
34  inclusion of a citizenship question on the census, and in doing so, the Court has set
35  a dangerous precedent, both with regard to the census itself and with regard to
36  judicial review of all other executive agency actions. For the reasons ably stated by
37  JUSTICE THOMAS, today's decision is either an aberration or a license for

widespread judicial inquiry into the motivations of Executive Branch officials. If this case is taken as a model, then any one of the approximately 1,000 district court judges in this country, upon receiving information that a controversial agency decision might have been motivated by some unstated consideration, may order the questioning of Cabinet officers and other high-ranking Executive Branch officials, and the judge may then pass judgment on whether the decision was pretextual. What Bismarck is reputed to have said about laws and sausages comes to mind. And that goes for decisionmaking by all three branches.

To put the point bluntly, the Federal Judiciary has no authority to stick its nose into the question whether it is good policy to include a citizenship question on the census or whether the reasons given by Secretary Ross for that decision were his only reasons or his real reasons. Of course, we may determine whether the decision is constitutional. But under the considerations that typically guide this Court in the exercise of its power of judicial review of agency action, we have no authority to decide whether the Secretary's decision was rendered in compliance with the Administrative Procedure Act (APA).

* * *

I join Parts I, II, III, IV-B, and IV-C of the opinion of the Court. I do not join the remainder, and insofar as the Court holds that the Secretary's decision is reviewable under the APA, I respectfully dissent.

# B. Arbitrary and Capricious Review

Under the APA, different kinds of agency actions receive different forms of review by courts. The most encompassing scope-of-review provision in the APA is found in 5 U.S.C. § 706(2)(A), which empowers courts to "hold unlawful and set aside agency action, findings, and conclusions found to be . . . arbitrary, capricious, an abuse of discretion, or otherwise not in accordance with law." Administrative lawyers call this "arbitrary and capricious review" for short, or "arbitrariness review" for shorter.

Just how much scrutiny does arbitrary and capricious review entail? Are courts reviewing for arbitrariness supposed to set aside only those agency actions that lack any rational basis? That seems to have been the original idea; see, e.g., *Pac. States Box & Basket Co. v. White*, 296 U.S. 176, 185 (1935). But in the late 1960s and early 1970s, appeals courts—the D.C. Circuit Court of Appeals in particular—began to give arbitrary and capricious review more teeth. In a 1970 opinion, Judge Harold Leventhal wrote that agencies have a duty to engage in reasoned decision making, and a court is obliged to reverse when it "becomes aware . . . that the

444

1 agency has not really taken a 'hard look' at the salient problems" before it. The
2 stepped-up version of arbitrariness review this entails became known as "hard
3 look" review.

4 In a case like *Brinegar*, is the reviewing court appropriately holding the agency to
5 account, or is it overstepping the role envisioned for it in the administrative
6 process? The Supreme Court famously boarded the hard look review train in *State*
7 *Farm*. Judging by *Fox TV*, is it still on it?

8 Chances are, you have never seen any of the pre-airbag safety features. If you
9 search for "automatic seatbelt" in YouTube, you will find videos showing them in
10 action. Some passenger cars manufactured as late as 1997 contained detachable
11 safety belts instead of airbags. As some of the videos reflect, these American safety
12 innovations baffled and amused the international visitors to the United States who
13 encountered them in their rental cars.

14

15 **Motor Vehicle Manufacturers Association of the United States,**
16 **Inc. v. State Farm Mutual Automobile Insurance Co.**

17 463 U.S. 29 (1983)

18 June 24, 1983

19 JUSTICE WHITE delivered the opinion of the Court.

20 The development of the automobile gave Americans unprecedented freedom to
21 travel, but exacted a high price for enhanced mobility. Since 1929, motor vehicles
22 have been the leading cause of accidental deaths and injuries in the United States.
23 In 1982, 46,300 Americans died in motor vehicle accidents, and hundreds of
24 thousands more were maimed and injured. While a consensus exists that the
25 current loss of life on our highways is unacceptably high, improving safety does not
26 admit to easy solution. In 1966, Congress decided that at least part of the answer
27 lies in improving the design and safety features of the vehicle itself. But much of
28 the technology for building safer cars was undeveloped or untested. Before changes
29 in automobile design could be mandated, the effectiveness of these changes had to
30 be studied, their costs examined, and public acceptance considered. This task
31 called for considerable expertise, and Congress responded by enacting the National
32 Traffic and Motor Vehicle Safety Act of 1966. The Act, created for the purpose of
33 "reduc[ing] traffic accidents and deaths and injuries to persons resulting from
34 traffic accidents," 15 U.S.C. §1381, directs the Secretary of Transportation or his
35 delegate to issue motor vehicle safety standards that "shall be practicable, shall
36 meet the need for motor vehicle safety, and shall be stated in objective terms." 15
37 U.S.C. §1392(a). In issuing these standards, the Secretary is directed to consider
38 "relevant available motor vehicle safety data," whether the proposed standard "is
39 reasonable, practicable and appropriate" for the particular type of motor vehicle,

and the "extent to which such standards will contribute to carrying out the purposes" of the Act. 15 U.S.C. §§ 1392(f)(1), (3), (4).

The Act also authorizes judicial review under the provisions of the Administrative Procedure Act (APA), of all "orders establishing, amending, or revoking a Federal motor vehicle safety standard," 15 U.S.C. § 1392(b). Under this authority, we review today whether NHTSA acted arbitrarily and capriciously in revoking the requirement in Motor Vehicle Safety Standard 208 that new motor vehicles produced after September, 1982, be equipped with passive restraints to protect the safety of the occupants of the vehicle in the event of a collision. Briefly summarized, we hold that the agency failed to present an adequate basis and explanation for rescinding the passive restraint requirement, and that the agency must either consider the matter further or adhere to or amend Standard 208 along lines which its analysis supports.

I

The regulation whose rescission is at issue bears a complex and convoluted history. Over the course of approximately 60 rulemaking notices, the requirement has been imposed, amended, rescinded, reimposed, and now rescinded again.

As originally issued by the Department of Transportation in 1967, Standard 208 simply required the installation of seatbelts in all automobiles. It soon became apparent that the level of seatbelt use was too low to reduce traffic injuries to an acceptable level. The Department therefore began consideration of "passive occupant restraint systems"—devices that do not depend for their effectiveness upon any action taken by the occupant except that necessary to operate the vehicle. Two types of automatic crash protection emerged: automatic seatbelts and airbags. The automatic seatbelt is a traditional safety belt, which, when fastened to the interior of the door, remains attached without impeding entry or exit from the vehicle and deploys automatically without any action on the part of the passenger. The airbag is an inflatable device concealed in the dashboard and steering column. It automatically inflates when a sensor indicates that deceleration forces from an accident have exceeded a preset minimum, then rapidly deflates to dissipate those forces. The lifesaving potential of these devices was immediately recognized, and in 1977, after substantial on-the-road experience with both devices, it was estimated by NHTSA that passive restraints could prevent approximately 12,000 deaths and over 100,000 serious injuries annually.

In 1969, the Department formally proposed a standard requiring the installation of passive restraints, thereby commencing a lengthy series of proceedings. In 1970, the agency revised Standard 208 to include passive protection requirements, and in 1972, the agency amended the Standard to require full passive protection for all front seat occupants of vehicles manufactured after August 15, 1975. In the interim, vehicles built between August, 1973, and August, 1975, were to carry either passive restraints or lap and shoulder belts coupled with an "ignition interlock" that would prevent starting the vehicle if the belts were not connected. On review, the agency's decision to require passive restraints was found to be supported by "substantial evidence," and upheld.

In preparing for the upcoming model year, most car makers chose the "ignition interlock" option, a decision which was highly unpopular and led Congress to amend the Act to prohibit a motor vehicle safety standard from requiring or permitting compliance by means of an ignition interlock or a continuous buzzer designed to indicate that safety belts were not in use. * * *

The effective date for mandatory passive restraint systems was extended for a year until August 31, 1976. But in June, 1976, Secretary of Transportation William T. Coleman, Jr., initiated a new rulemaking on the issue. After hearing testimony and reviewing written comments, Coleman extended the optional alternatives indefinitely and suspended the passive restraint requirement. Although he found passive restraints technologically and economically feasible, the Secretary based his decision on the expectation that there would be widespread public resistance to the new systems. He instead proposed a demonstration project involving up to 500,000 cars installed with passive restraints, in order to smooth the way for public acceptance of mandatory passive restraints at a later date.

Coleman's successor as Secretary of Transportation disagreed. Within months of assuming office, Secretary Brock Adams decided that the demonstration project was unnecessary. He issued a new mandatory passive restraint regulation, known as Modified Standard 208. The Modified Standard mandated the phasing in of passive restraints beginning with large cars in model year 1982 and extending to all cars by model year 1984. The two principal systems that would satisfy the Standard were airbags and passive belts; the choice of which system to install was left to the manufacturers. In *Pacific Legal Foundation v. Department of Transportation*, 593 F.2d 1338 (1979), the Court of Appeals upheld Modified Standard 208 as a rational, nonarbitrary regulation consistent with the agency's mandate under the Act. The Standard also survived scrutiny by Congress, which did not exercise its authority under the legislative veto provision of the 1974 Amendments.

Over the next several years, the automobile industry geared up to comply with Modified Standard 208. As late as July, 1980, NHTSA reported:

> "On-the-road experience in thousands of vehicles equipped with air bags and automatic safety belts has confirmed agency estimates of the life-saving and injury-preventing benefits of such systems. When all cars are equipped with automatic crash protection systems, each year an estimated 9,000 more lives will be saved, and tens of thousands of serious injuries will be prevented."

In February, 1981, however, Secretary of Transportation Andrew Lewis reopened the rulemaking due to changed economic circumstances and, in particular, the difficulties of the automobile industry. Two months later, the agency ordered a one-year delay in the application of the Standard to large cars, extending the deadline to September 1982, and at the same time, proposed the possible rescission of the entire Standard. After receiving written comments and holding public hearings, NHTSA issued a final rule (Notice 25) that rescinded the passive restraint requirement contained in Modified Standard 208.

## II

In a statement explaining the rescission, NHTSA maintained that it was no longer able to find, as it had in 1977, that the automatic restraint requirement would produce significant safety benefits. This judgment reflected not a change of opinion on the effectiveness of the technology, but a change in plans by the automobile industry. In 1977, the agency had assumed that airbags would be installed in 60% of all new cars and automatic seatbelts in 40%. By 1981, it became apparent that automobile manufacturers planned to install the automatic seatbelts in approximately 99% of the new cars. For this reason, the lifesaving potential of airbags would not be realized. Moreover, it now appeared that the overwhelming majority of passive belts planned to be installed by manufacturers could be detached easily and left that way permanently. Passive belts, once detached, then required "the same type of affirmative action that is the stumbling block to obtaining high usage levels of manual belts." For this reason, the agency concluded that there was no longer a basis for reliably predicting that the Standard would lead to any significant increased usage of restraints at all.

In view of the possibly minimal safety benefits, the automatic restraint requirement no longer was reasonable or practicable in the agency's view. The requirement would require approximately $1 billion to implement, and the agency did not believe it would be reasonable to impose such substantial costs on manufacturers and consumers without more adequate assurance that sufficient safety benefits would accrue. In addition, NHTSA concluded that automatic restraints might have an adverse effect on the public's attitude toward safety. Given the high expense and limited benefits of detachable belts, NHTSA feared that many consumers would regard the Standard as an instance of ineffective regulation, adversely affecting the public's view of safety regulation and, in particular, "poisoning ... popular sentiment toward efforts to improve occupant restraint systems in the future."

\* \* \*

## III

Unlike the Court of Appeals, we do not find the appropriate scope of judicial review to be the "most troublesome question" in these cases. Both the Act and the 1974 Amendments concerning occupant crash protection standards indicate that motor vehicle safety standards are to be promulgated under the informal rulemaking procedures of the Administrative Procedure Act. 5 U.S.C. § 553. The agency's action in promulgating such standards therefore may be set aside if found to be "arbitrary, capricious, an abuse of discretion, or otherwise not in accordance with law." 5 U.S.C. § 706(2)(A). We believe that the rescission or modification of an occupant protection standard is subject to the same test. Section 103(b) of the Act, 15 U.S.C. § 1392(b), states that the procedural and judicial review provisions of the Administrative Procedure Act "shall apply to all orders establishing, amending, or revoking a Federal motor vehicle safety standard," and suggests no difference in the scope of judicial review depending upon the nature of the agency's action.

Petitioner Motor Vehicle Manufacturers Association (MVMA) disagrees, contending that the rescission of an agency rule should be judged by the same standard a court would use to judge an agency's refusal to promulgate a rule in the first place—a standard petitioner believes considerably narrower than the traditional arbitrary and capricious test. We reject this view. The Act expressly equates orders "revoking" and "establishing" safety standards; neither that Act nor the APA suggests that revocations are to be treated as refusals to promulgate standards. Petitioner's view would render meaningless Congress' authorization for judicial review of orders revoking safety rules. Moreover, the revocation of an extant regulation is substantially different than a failure to act. Revocation constitutes a reversal of the agency's former views as to the proper course. A "settled course of behavior embodies the agency's informed judgment that, by pursuing that course, it will carry out the policies committed to it by Congress. There is, then, at least a presumption that those policies will be carried out best if the settled rule is adhered to." *Atchison, T. & S. F. R. Co. v. Wichita Bd. of Trade*, 412 U.S. 800, 808 (1973). Accordingly, an agency changing its course by rescinding a rule is obligated to supply a reasoned analysis for the change beyond that which may be required when an agency does not act in the first instance.

In so holding, we fully recognize that "[r]egulatory agencies do not establish rules of conduct to last forever," *American Trucking Assns., Inc. v. Atchison, T. & S. F. R. Co.*, 387 U.S. 397, 416 (1967), and that an agency must be given ample latitude to "adapt their rules and policies to the demands of changing circumstances." *Permian Basin Area Rate Cases*, 390 U.S. 747, 784 (1968). But the forces of change do not always or necessarily point in the direction of deregulation. In the abstract, there is no more reason to presume that changing circumstances require the rescission of prior action, instead of a revision in or even the extension of current regulation. If Congress established a presumption from which judicial review should start, that presumption—contrary to petitioners' views—is not *against* safety regulation, but against changes in current policy that are not justified by the rulemaking record. While the removal of a regulation may not entail the monetary expenditures and other costs of enacting a new standard, and, accordingly, it may be easier for an agency to justify a deregulatory action, the direction in which an agency chooses to move does not alter the standard of judicial review established by law.

The Department of Transportation accepts the applicability of the "arbitrary and capricious" standard. It argues that, under this standard, a reviewing court may not set aside an agency rule that is rational, based on consideration of the relevant factors, and within the scope of the authority delegated to the agency by the statute.

449

1 We do not disagree with this formulation. The scope of review under the "arbitrary
2 and capricious" standard is narrow, and a court is not to substitute its judgment
3 for that of the agency. Nevertheless, the agency must examine the relevant data
4 and articulate a satisfactory explanation for its action, including a "rational
5 connection between the facts found and the choice made." *Burlington Truck Lines,*
6 *Inc. v. United States,* 371 U.S. 156, 168 (1962). In reviewing that explanation, we
7 must "consider whether the decision was based on a consideration of the relevant
8 factors and whether there has been a clear error of judgment." *Bowman*
9 *Transportation, Inc. v. Arkansas-Best Freight System, Inc., supra,* 419 U.S., at
10 285; *Citizens to Preserve Overton Park v. Volpe, supra,* 401 U.S., at 416. Normally,
11 an agency rule would be arbitrary and capricious if the agency has relied on factors
12 which Congress has not intended it to consider, entirely failed to consider an
13 important aspect of the problem, offered an explanation for its decision that runs
14 counter to the evidence before the agency, or is so implausible that it could not be
15 ascribed to a difference in view or the product of agency expertise. The reviewing
16 court should not attempt itself to make up for such deficiencies; we may not supply
17 a reasoned basis for the agency's action that the agency itself has not given. *SEC v.*
18 *Chenery Corp.,* 332 U.S. 194, 196 (1947). * * *

19                                         * * *

20                                          V

21 The ultimate question before us is whether NHTSA's rescission of the passive
22 restraint requirement of Standard 208 was arbitrary and capricious. We conclude,
23 as did the Court of Appeals, that it was. We also conclude, but for somewhat
24 different reasons, that further consideration of the issue by the agency is therefore
25 required. We deal separately with the rescission as it applies to airbags and as it
26 applies to seatbelts.

27                                          A

28 The first and most obvious reason for finding the rescission arbitrary and
29 capricious is that NHTSA apparently gave no consideration whatever to modifying
30 the Standard to require that airbag technology be utilized. Standard 208 sought to
31 achieve automatic crash protection by requiring automobile manufacturers to
32 install either of two passive restraint devices: airbags or automatic seatbelts. There
33 was no suggestion in the long rulemaking process that led to Standard 208 that, if
34 only one of these options were feasible, no passive restraint standard should be
35 promulgated. Indeed, the agency's original proposed Standard contemplated the
36 installation of inflatable restraints in all cars. Automatic belts were added as a
37 means of complying with the Standard because they were believed to be as effective
38 as airbags in achieving the goal of occupant crash protection. At that time, the
39 passive belt approved by the agency could not be detached. Only later, at a
40 manufacturer's behest, did the agency approve of the detachability feature—and
41 only after assurances that the feature would not compromise the safety benefits of
42 the restraint. Although it was then foreseen that 60% of the new cars would contain

1 airbags and 40% would have automatic seatbelts, the ratio between the two was
2 not significant as long as the passive belt would also assure greater passenger
3 safety.

4 The agency has now determined that the detachable automatic belts will not attain
5 anticipated safety benefits, because so many individuals will detach the
6 mechanism. Even if this conclusion were acceptable in its entirety, standing alone,
7 it would not justify any more than an amendment of Standard 208 to disallow
8 compliance by means of the one technology which will not provide effective
9 passenger protection. It does not cast doubt on the need for a passive restraint
10 standard or upon the efficacy of airbag technology. * * *

11 Given the effectiveness ascribed to airbag technology by the agency, the mandate
12 of the Act to achieve traffic safety would suggest that the logical response to the
13 faults of detachable seatbelts would be to require the installation of airbags. At the
14 very least, this alternative way of achieving the objectives of the Act should have
15 been addressed and adequate reasons given for its abandonment. But the agency
16 not only did not require compliance through airbags, it also did not even consider
17 the possibility in its 1981 rulemaking. Not one sentence of its rulemaking statement
18 discusses the airbags-only option. * * * We have frequently reiterated that an
19 agency must cogently explain why it has exercised its discretion in a given manner,
20 and we reaffirm this principle again today.

21                                       * * *

22 Although the agency did not address the mandatory airbag option and the Court of
23 Appeals noted that "airbags seem to have none of the problems that NHTSA
24 identified in passive seatbelts," petitioners recite a number of difficulties that they
25 believe would be posed by a mandatory airbag standard. These range from
26 questions concerning the installation of airbags in small cars to that of adverse
27 public reaction. But these are not the agency's reasons for rejecting a mandatory
28 airbag standard. Not having discussed the possibility, the agency submitted no
29 reasons at all. The short—and sufficient—answer to petitioners' submission is that
30 the courts may not accept appellate counsel's *post hoc* rationalizations for agency
31 action. *Burlington Truck Lines, Inc. v. United States*, 371 U.S., at. 168. It is well
32 established that an agency's action must be upheld, if at all, on the basis articulated
33 by the agency itself. *Ibid.*; *SEC v. Chenery Corp.*, 332 U.S., at 196.

34                                       * * *

35                                        B

36 Although the issue is closer, we also find that the agency was too quick to dismiss
37 the safety benefits of automatic seatbelts. NHTSA's critical finding was that, in
38 light of the industry's plans to install readily detachable passive belts, it could not
39 reliably predict "even a 5 percentage point increase as the minimum level of
40 expected usage increase." 46 Fed.Reg. 53423 (1981). The Court of Appeals rejected
41 this finding because there is "not one iota" of evidence that Modified Standard 208

1  will fail to increase nationwide seatbelt use by at least 13 percentage points, the
2  level of increased usage necessary for the Standard to justify its cost. Given the lack
3  of probative evidence, the court held that "only a well justified refusal to seek more
4  evidence could render rescission nonarbitrary."

5  Petitioners object to this conclusion. In their view, "substantial uncertainty" that a
6  regulation will accomplish its intended purpose is sufficient reason, without more,
7  to rescind a regulation. We agree with petitioners that, just as an agency reasonably
8  may decline to issue a safety standard if it is uncertain about its efficacy, an agency
9  may also revoke a standard on the basis of serious uncertainties if supported by the
10  record and reasonably explained. * * *

11  In these cases, the agency's explanation for rescission of the passive restraint
12  requirement is *not* sufficient to enable us to conclude that the rescission was the
13  product of reasoned decisionmaking. To reach this conclusion, we do not upset the
14  agency's view of the facts, but we do appreciate the limitations of this record in
15  supporting the agency's decision. * * * The empirical evidence on the record,
16  consisting of surveys of drivers of automobiles equipped with passive belts, reveals
17  more than a doubling of the usage rate experienced with manual belts. Much of the
18  agency's rulemaking statement—and much of the controversy in these cases—
19  centers on the conclusions that should be drawn from these studies. The agency
20  maintained that the doubling of seatbelt usage in these studies could not be
21  extrapolated to an across-the-board mandatory standard because the passive
22  seatbelts were guarded by ignition interlocks and purchasers of the tested cars are
23  somewhat atypical. Respondents insist these studies demonstrate that Modified
24  Standard 208 will substantially increase seatbelt usage. We believe that it is within
25  the agency's discretion to pass upon the generalizability of these field studies. This
26  is precisely the type of issue which rests within the expertise of NHTSA, and upon
27  which a reviewing court must be most hesitant to intrude.

28  But accepting the agency's view of the field tests on passive restraints indicates
29  only that there is no reliable real-world experience that usage rates will
30  substantially increase. To be sure, NHTSA opines that "it cannot reliably predict
31  even a 5 percentage point increase as the minimum level of expected increased
32  usage." Notice 25, 46 Fed.Reg. 53423 (1981). But this and other statements that
33  passive belts will not yield substantial increases in seatbelt usage apparently take
34  no account of the critical difference between detachable automatic belts and
35  current manual belts. A detached passive belt does require an affirmative act to
36  reconnect it, but—unlike a manual seatbelt—the passive belt, once reattached, will
37  continue to function automatically unless again disconnected. Thus, inertia—a
38  factor which the agency's own studies have found significant in explaining the
39  current low usage rates for seatbelts—works in *favor* of, not *against*, use of the
40  protective device. Since 20% to 50% of motorists currently wear seatbelts on some
41  occasions, there would seem to be grounds to believe that seatbelt use by
42  occasional users will be substantially increased by the detachable passive belts.
43  Whether this is in fact the case is a matter for the agency to decide, but it must
44  bring its expertise to bear on the question.

1                                   * * *

2    The agency also failed to articulate a basis for not requiring nondetachable belts
3    under Standard 208. It is argued that the concern of the agency with the easy
4    detachability of the currently favored design would be readily solved by a
5    continuous passive belt, which allows the occupant to "spool out" the belt and
6    create the necessary slack for easy extrication from the vehicle. The agency did not
7    separately consider the continuous belt option, but treated it together with the
8    ignition interlock device in a category it titled "Option of Adopting Use-Compelling
9    Features." The agency was concerned that use-compelling devices would
10   "complicate the extrication of [an] occupant from his or her car." "[T]o require that
11   passive belts contain use-compelling features," the agency observed, "could be
12   counterproductive [, given] . . . widespread, latent and irrational fear in many
13   members of the public that they could be trapped by the seat belt after a crash." In
14   addition, based on the experience with the ignition interlock, the agency feared
15   that use-compelling features might trigger adverse public reaction.

16   By failing to analyze the continuous seatbelts option in its own right, the agency
17   has failed to offer the rational connection between facts and judgment required to
18   pass muster under the arbitrary and capricious standard. We agree with the Court
19   of Appeals that NHTSA did not suggest that the emergency release mechanisms
20   used in nondetachable belts are any less effective for emergency egress than the
21   buckle release system used in detachable belts. In 1978, when General Motors
22   obtained the agency's approval to install a continuous passive belt, it assured the
23   agency that nondetachable belts with spool releases were as safe as detachable
24   belts with buckle releases. NHTSA was satisfied that this belt design assured easy
25   extricability * * * While the agency is entitled to change its view on the acceptability
26   of continuous passive belts, it is obligated to explain its reasons for doing so.

27   The agency also failed to offer any explanation why a continuous passive belt would
28   engender the same adverse public reaction as the ignition interlock, and, as the
29   Court of Appeals concluded, "every indication in the record points the other way."
30   We see no basis for equating the two devices: the continuous belt, unlike the
31   ignition interlock, does not interfere with the operation of the vehicle. More
32   importantly, it is the agency's responsibility, not this Court's, to explain its
33   decision.

34                                    VI

35   "An agency's view of what is in the public interest may change, either with or
36   without a change in circumstances. But an agency changing its course must supply
37   a reasoned analysis. . . ." *Greater Boston Television Corp. v. FCC*, 444 F.2d 841,
38   852 (1970) (footnote omitted). We do not accept all of the reasoning of the Court
39   of Appeals, but we do conclude that the agency has failed to supply the requisite
40   "reasoned analysis" in this case. Accordingly, we vacate the judgment of the Court
41   of Appeals and remand the cases to that court with directions to remand the matter
42   to the NHTSA for further consideration consistent with this opinion.

*So ordered.*

JUSTICE REHNQUIST, with whom THE CHIEF JUSTICE, JUSTICE POWELL, and JUSTICE O'CONNOR join, concurring in part and dissenting in part.

I join Parts I, II, III, IV, and V-A of the Court's opinion. In particular, I agree that, since the airbag and continuous spool automatic seatbelt were explicitly approved in the Standard the agency was rescinding, the agency should explain why it declined to leave those requirements intact. In this case, the agency gave no explanation at all. Of course, if the agency can provide a rational explanation, it may adhere to its decision to rescind the entire Standard.

I do not believe, however, that NHTSA's view of detachable automatic seatbelts was arbitrary and capricious. The agency adequately explained its decision to rescind the Standard insofar as it was satisfied by detachable belts.

\* \* \*

\* \* \* It seems to me that the agency's explanation, while by no means a model, is adequate. The agency acknowledged that there would probably be some increase in belt usage, but concluded that the increase would be small, and not worth the cost of mandatory detachable automatic belts. The agency's obligation is to articulate a "rational connection between the facts found and the choice made." I believe it has met this standard.

\* \* \*

The agency's changed view of the standard seems to be related to the election of a new President of a different political party. It is readily apparent that the responsible members of one administration may consider public resistance and uncertainties to be more important than do their counterparts in a previous administration. A change in administration brought about by the people casting their votes is a perfectly reasonable basis for an executive agency's reappraisal of the costs and benefits of its programs and regulations. As long as the agency remains within the bounds established by Congress, it is entitled to assess administrative records and evaluate priorities in light of the philosophy of the administration.\* Of course, a new administration may not refuse to enforce laws of which it does not approve, or to ignore statutory standards in carrying out its regulatory functions. But in this case, as the Court correctly concludes Congress has not required the agency to require passive restraints.

# Federal Communications Commission v. Fox Television Stations, Inc.

556 U.S. 502 (2009)

454

1    April 28, 2009

2    JUSTICE SCALIA delivered the opinion of the Court, except as to Part III-E.

3    Federal law prohibits the broadcasting of "any . . . indecent . . . language," 18 U.S.C.
4    §1464, which includes expletives referring to sexual or excretory activity or organs,
5    *see FCC v. Pacifica Foundation*, 438 U.S. 726 (1978). This case concerns the
6    adequacy of the Federal Communications Commission's explanation of its decision
7    that this sometimes forbids the broadcasting of indecent expletives even when the
8    offensive words are not repeated.

9    I.

10    Statutory and Regulatory Background

11    * * *

12    The Communications Act of 1934, 48 Stat. 1064, 47 U.S.C. §151 et seq., established
13    a system of limited-term broadcast licenses subject to various "conditions"
14    designed "to maintain the control of the United States over all the channels of radio
15    transmission," §301. Twenty-seven years ago we said that "[a] licensed broadcaster
16    is granted the free and exclusive use of a limited and valuable part of the public
17    domain; when he accepts that franchise it is burdened by enforceable public
18    obligations." *CBS, Inc. v. FCC*, 453 U.S. 367, 395 (1981) (internal quotation marks
19    omitted).

20    One of the burdens that licensees shoulder is the indecency ban—the statutory
21    proscription against "utter[ing] any obscene, indecent, or profane language by
22    means of radio communication," 18 U.S.C. §1464—which Congress has instructed
23    the Commission to enforce between the hours of 6 a.m. and 10 p.m. * * * The
24    Commission first invoked the statutory ban on indecent broadcasts in 1975,
25    declaring a daytime broadcast of George Carlin's "Filthy Words" monologue
26    actionably indecent. *Pacifica Foundation*, 56 F. C. C. 2d 94. * * *

27    * * *

28    In the ensuing years, the Commission took a cautious, but gradually expanding,
29    approach to enforcing the statutory prohibition against indecent broadcasts. * * *

30    Although the Commission had expanded its enforcement beyond the "repetitive
31    use of specific words or phrases," it preserved a distinction between literal and
32    nonliteral (or "expletive") uses of evocative language. *In re Pacifica Foundation,
33    Inc.*, 2 FCC Rcd., at 2699, ¶13. The Commission explained that each literal
34    "description or depiction of sexual or excretory functions must be examined in
35    context to determine whether it is patently offensive," but that "deliberate and
36    repetitive use . . . is a requisite to a finding of indecency" when a complaint focuses
37    solely on the use of nonliteral expletives. *Ibid.*

38    * * *

1    In 2004, the Commission took one step further by declaring for the first time that
2    a nonliteral (expletive) use of the F- and S-Words could be actionably indecent,
3    even when the word is used only once. The first order to this effect dealt with an
4    NBC broadcast of the Golden Globe Awards, in which the performer Bono
5    commented, "This is really, really, f * * * ing brilliant." *In re Complaints Against*
6    *Various Broadcast Licensees Regarding Their Airing of the "Golden Globe*
7    *Awards" Program*, 19 FCC Rcd. 4975, 4976, n. 4 (2004) (Golden Globes Order).
8    Although the Commission had received numerous complaints directed at the
9    broadcast, its enforcement bureau had concluded that the material was not
10    indecent because "Bono did not describe, in context, sexual or excretory organs or
11    activities and . . . the utterance was fleeting and isolated." The full Commission
12    reviewed and reversed the staff ruling.

13    The Commission first declared that Bono's use of the F-Word fell within its
14    indecency definition, even though the word was used as an intensifier rather than
15    a literal descriptor. "[G]iven the core meaning of the 'F-Word,'" it said, "any use of
16    that word . . . inherently has a sexual connotation." The Commission determined,
17    moreover, that the broadcast was "patently offensive" because the F-Word "is one
18    of the most vulgar, graphic and explicit descriptions of sexual activity in the
19    English language," because "[i]ts use invariably invokes a coarse sexual image,"
20    and because Bono's use of the word was entirely "shocking and gratuitous."

21    The Commission observed that categorically exempting such language from
22    enforcement actions would "likely lead to more widespread use." Commission
23    action was necessary to "safeguard the well-being of the nation's children from the
24    most objectionable, most offensive language." The order noted that technological
25    advances have made it far easier to delete ("bleep out") a "single and gratuitous use
26    of a vulgar expletive," without adulterating the content of a broadcast.

27    The order acknowledged that "prior Commission and staff action have indicated
28    that isolated or fleeting broadcasts of the 'F-Word' . . . are not indecent or would
29    not be acted upon." It explicitly ruled that "any such interpretation is no longer
30    good law." * * *

31    ## II. The Present Case

32    This case concerns utterances in two live broadcasts aired by Fox Television
33    Stations, Inc., and its affiliates prior to the Commission's *Golden Globes Order.*
34    The first occurred during the 2002 Billboard Music Awards, when the singer Cher
35    exclaimed, "I've also had critics for the last 40 years saying that I was on my way
36    out every year. Right. So f * * * 'em." The second involved a segment of the 2003
37    Billboard Music Awards, during the presentation of an award by Nicole Richie and
38    Paris Hilton, principals in a Fox television series called "The Simple Life." Ms.
39    Hilton began their interchange by reminding Ms. Richie to "watch the bad
40    language," but Ms. Richie proceeded to ask the audience, "Why do they even call it
41    'The Simple Life?' Have you ever tried to get cow s * * * out of a Prada purse? It's
42    not so f * * * ing simple." Following each of these broadcasts, the Commission

received numerous complaints from parents whose children were exposed to the language.

On March 15, 2006, the Commission released Notices of Apparent Liability for a number of broadcasts that the Commission deemed actionably indecent, including the two described above. * * * . The Commission's order on remand upheld the indecency findings for the broadcasts described above.

* * *

The order asserted that both broadcasts under review would have been actionably indecent under the staff rulings and Commission dicta in effect prior to the *Golden Globes Order*—the 2003 broadcast because it involved a literal description of excrement, rather than a mere expletive, because it used more than one offensive word, and because it was planned, and the 2002 broadcast because Cher used the F-Word not as a mere intensifier, but as a description of the sexual act to express hostility to her critics. The order stated, however, that the pre-*Golden Globes* regime of immunity for isolated indecent expletives rested only upon staff rulings and Commission dicta, and that the Commission itself had never held "that the isolated use of an expletive . . . was not indecent or could not be indecent," 21 FCC Rcd., at 13307. In any event, the order made clear, the *Golden Globes Order* eliminated any doubt that fleeting expletives could be actionably indecent, and the Commission disavowed the bureau-level decisions and its own dicta that had said otherwise. Under the new policy, a lack of repetition "weigh[s] against a finding of indecency," *id.*, at 13325, but is not a safe harbor.

* * *

III. Analysis

A. Governing Principles

The Administrative Procedure Act, which sets forth the full extent of judicial authority to review executive agency action for procedural correctness permits (insofar as relevant here) the setting aside of agency action that is "arbitrary" or "capricious," 5 U.S.C. §706(2)(A). Under what we have called this "narrow" standard of review, we insist that an agency "examine the relevant data and articulate a satisfactory explanation for its action." *Motor Vehicle Mfrs. Assn. of United States, Inc. v. State Farm Mut. Automobile Ins. Co.*, 463 U.S. 29, 43 (1983). We have made clear, however, that "a court is not to substitute its judgment for that of the agency," *ibid.*, and should "uphold a decision of less than ideal clarity if the agency's path may reasonably be discerned," *Bowman Transp., Inc. v. Arkansas-Best Freight System, Inc.*, 419 U.S. 281, 286 (1974).

In overturning the Commission's judgment, the Court of Appeals here relied in part on Circuit precedent requiring a more substantial explanation for agency action that changes prior policy. The Second Circuit has interpreted the Administrative Procedure Act and our opinion in *State Farm* as requiring agencies to make clear "'why the original reasons for adopting the [displaced] rule or policy are no longer dispositive'" as well as "'why the new rule effectuates the statute as well as or better than the old rule.'" 489 F. 3d, at 456-457 (quoting *New York Council, Assn. of Civilian Technicians v. FLRA*, 757 F. 2d 502, 508 (CA2 1985); emphasis deleted). The Court of Appeals for the District of Columbia Circuit has similarly indicated that a court's standard of review is "heightened somewhat" when an agency reverses course. *NAACP v. FCC*, 682 F. 2d 993, 998 (1982).

We find no basis in the Administrative Procedure Act or in our opinions for a requirement that all agency change be subjected to more searching review. The Act mentions no such heightened standard. And our opinion in *State Farm* neither held nor implied that every agency action representing a policy change must be justified by reasons more substantial than those required to adopt a policy in the first instance. That case, which involved the rescission of a prior regulation, said only that such action requires "a reasoned analysis for the change beyond that which may be required when an agency *does not act* in the first instance." 463 U.S., at 42 (emphasis added). Treating failures to act and rescissions of prior action differently for purposes of the standard of review makes good sense, and has basis in the text of the statute, which likewise treats the two separately. It instructs a reviewing court to "compel agency action unlawfully withheld or unreasonably delayed," 5 U.S.C. §706(1), and to "hold unlawful and set aside agency action, findings, and conclusions found to be [among other things] ... arbitrary [or] capricious," §706(2)(A). The statute makes no distinction, however, between initial agency action and subsequent agency action undoing or revising that action.

To be sure, the requirement that an agency provide reasoned explanation for its action would ordinarily demand that it display awareness that it is changing position. An agency may not, for example, depart from a prior policy *sub silentio* or simply disregard rules that are still on the books. And of course the agency must show that there are good reasons for the new policy. But it need not demonstrate to a court's satisfaction that the reasons for the new policy are *better* than the reasons for the old one; it suffices that the new policy is permissible under the statute, that there are good reasons for it, and that the agency *believes* it to be better, which the conscious change of course adequately indicates. This means that the agency need not always provide a more detailed justification than what would suffice for a new policy created on a blank slate. Sometimes it must—when, for example, its new policy rests upon factual findings that contradict those which underlay its prior policy; or when its prior policy has engendered serious reliance interests that must be taken into account. It would be arbitrary or capricious to ignore such matters. In such cases it is not that further justification is demanded by the mere fact of policy change; but that a reasoned explanation is needed for disregarding facts and circumstances that underlay or were engendered by the prior policy.

In this appeal from the Second Circuit's setting aside of Commission action for failure to comply with a procedural requirement of the Administrative Procedure Act, the broadcasters' arguments have repeatedly referred to the First Amendment.

1   If they mean to invite us to apply a more stringent arbitrary-and-capricious review
2   to agency actions that implicate constitutional liberties, we reject the invitation.
3   The so-called canon of constitutional avoidance is an interpretive tool, counseling
4   that ambiguous statutory language be construed to avoid serious constitutional
5   doubts. We know of no precedent for applying it to limit the scope of authorized
6   executive action. In the same section authorizing courts to set aside "arbitrary [or]
7   capricious" agency action, the Administrative Procedure Act separately provides
8   for setting aside agency action that is "unlawful," 5 U.S.C. §706(2)(A), which of
9   course includes unconstitutional action. We think that is the only context in which
10  constitutionality bears upon judicial review of authorized agency action. If the
11  Commission's action here was not arbitrary or capricious in the ordinary sense, it
12  satisfies the Administrative Procedure Act's "arbitrary [or] capricious" standard;
13  its lawfulness under the Constitution is a separate question to be addressed in a
14  constitutional challenge.

15                          B.  Application to This Case

16  Judged under the above described standards, the Commission's new enforcement
17  policy and its order finding the broadcasts actionably indecent were neither
18  arbitrary nor capricious. First, the Commission forthrightly acknowledged that its
19  recent actions have broken new ground, taking account of inconsistent "prior
20  Commission and staff action" and explicitly disavowing them as "no longer good
21  law." *Golden Globes Order*, 19 FCC Rcd., at 4980. To be sure, the (superfluous)
22  explanation in its *Remand Order* of why the Cher broadcast would even have
23  violated its earlier policy may not be entirely convincing. But that unnecessary
24  detour is irrelevant. There is no doubt that the Commission knew it was making a
25  change. That is why it declined to assess penalties; and it relied on the *Golden
26  Globes Order* as removing any lingering doubt.

27  Moreover, the agency's reasons for expanding the scope of its enforcement activity
28  were entirely rational. It was certainly reasonable to determine that it made no
29  sense to distinguish between literal and nonliteral uses of offensive words,
30  requiring repetitive use to render only the latter indecent. As the Commission said
31  with regard to expletive use of the F-Word, "the word's power to insult and offend
32  derives from its sexual meaning." And the Commission's decision to look at the
33  patent offensiveness of even isolated uses of sexual and excretory words fits with
34  the context-based approach we sanctioned in *Pacifica*, 438 U.S., at 750. Even
35  isolated utterances can be made in "pander[ing,] . . . vulgar and shocking"
36  manners, *Remand Order*, 21 FCC Rcd., at 13305, and can constitute harmful " 'first
37  blow[s]' " to children, *id.*, at 13309. It is surely rational (if not inescapable) to
38  believe that a safe harbor for single words would "likely lead to more widespread
39  use of the offensive language."

40  When confronting other requests for *per se* rules governing its enforcement of the
41  indecency prohibition, the Commission has declined to create safe harbors for
42  particular types of broadcasts. The Commission could rationally decide it needed
43  to step away from its old regime where nonrepetitive use of an expletive was *per se*

1  nonactionable because that was "at odds with the Commission's overall
2  enforcement policy."

3  The fact that technological advances have made it easier for broadcasters to bleep
4  out offending words further supports the Commission's stepped-up enforcement
5  policy. And the agency's decision not to impose any forfeiture or other sanction
6  precludes any argument that it is arbitrarily punishing parties without notice of the
7  potential consequences of their action.

8  * * *

9  E. The Dissents' Arguments

10  JUSTICE BREYER purports to "begin with applicable law," but in fact begins by
11  stacking the deck. He claims that the FCC's status as an "independent" agency
12  sheltered from political oversight requires courts to be "all the more" vigilant in
13  ensuring "that major policy decisions be based upon articulable reasons." Not so.
14  The independent agencies are sheltered not from politics but from the President,
15  and it has often been observed that their freedom from presidential oversight (and
16  protection) has simply been replaced by increased subservience to congressional
17  direction. Indeed, the precise policy change at issue here was spurred by significant
18  political pressure from Congress.

19  * * *

20  Regardless, it is assuredly not "applicable law" that rulemaking by independent
21  regulatory agencies is subject to heightened scrutiny. The Administrative
22  Procedure Act, which provides judicial review, makes no distinction between
23  independent and other agencies, neither in its definition of agency, 5 U.S.C.
24  §701(b)(1), nor in the standards for reviewing agency action, §706. Nor does any
25  case of ours express or reflect the "heightened scrutiny" JUSTICE BREYER and
26  JUSTICE STEVENS would impose. Indeed, it is hard to imagine any closer scrutiny
27  than that we have given to the Environmental Protection Agency, which is not an
28  independent agency. *See Massachusetts v. EPA*, 549 U.S. 497, 533-535 (2007);
29  *Whitman v. American Trucking Assns., Inc.*, 531 U.S. 457, 481-486 (2001). There
30  is no reason to magnify the separation-of-powers dilemma posed by the Headless
31  Fourth Branch, *see Freytag v. Commissioner*, 501 U.S. 868, 921 (1991) (SCALIA,
32  J., concurring in part and concurring in judgment), by letting Article III judges—
33  like jackals stealing the lion's kill—expropriate some of the power that Congress
34  has wrested from the unitary Executive.

35  JUSTICE BREYER and JUSTICE STEVENS rely upon two supposed omissions in
36  the FCC's analysis that they believe preclude a finding that the agency did not act
37  arbitrarily. Neither of these omissions could undermine the coherence of the
38  rationale the agency gave, but the dissenters' evaluation of each is flawed in its own
39  right.

1  First, both claim that the Commission failed adequately to explain its
2  consideration of the constitutional issues inherent in its regulation. We are
3  unaware that we have ever before reversed an executive agency, not for violating
4  our cases, but for failure to discuss them adequately. But leave that aside.
5  According to JUSTICE BREYER, the agency said "next to nothing about the
6  relation between the change it made in its prior 'fleeting expletive' policy and the
7  First-Amendment-related need to avoid 'censorship,' " The *Remand Order* does,
8  however, devote four full pages of small-type, single-spaced text (over 1,300 words
9  not counting the footnotes) to explaining why the Commission believes that its
10 indecency-enforcement regime (which includes its change in policy) is consistent
11 with the First Amendment—and therefore not censorship as the term is
12 understood. * * *

13 Second, JUSTICE BREYER looks over the vast field of particular factual scenarios
14 unaddressed by the FCC's 35-page *Remand Order* and finds one that is fatal: the
15 plight of the small local broadcaster who cannot afford the new technology that
16 enables the screening of live broadcasts for indecent utterances. The Commission
17 has failed to address the fate of this unfortunate, who will, he believes, be subject
18 to sanction.

19 We doubt, to begin with, that small-town broadcasters run a heightened risk of
20 liability for indecent utterances. In programming that they originate, their down-
21 home local guests probably employ vulgarity less than big-city folks; and small-
22 town stations generally cannot afford or cannot attract foul-mouthed glitteratae
23 from Hollywood. Their main exposure with regard to self-originated programming
24 is live coverage of news and public affairs. But the Remand Order went out of its
25 way to note that the case at hand did not involve "breaking news coverage," and
26 that "it may be inequitable to hold a licensee responsible for airing offensive speech
27 during live coverage of a public event," 21 FCC Rcd., at 13311, ¶33. * * *

28 But never mind the detail of whether small broadcasters are uniquely subject to a
29 great risk of punishment for fleeting expletives. The fundamental fallacy of
30 JUSTICE BREYER's small-broadcaster gloomy scenario is its demonstrably false
31 assumption that the Remand Order makes no provision for the avoidance of
32 unfairness—that the single-utterance prohibition will be invoked uniformly, in all
33 situations. The Remand Order made very clear that this is not the case. It said that
34 in determining "what, if any, remedy is appropriate" the Commission would
35 consider the facts of each individual case, such as the "possibility of human error
36 in using delay equipment," *id.*, at 13313. * * *

37 There was, in sum, no need for the Commission to compose a special treatise on
38 local broadcasters. And JUSTICE BREYER can safely defer his concern for those
39 yeomen of the airwaves until we have before us a case that involves one.

40                                        * * *

461

1 The judgment of the United States Court of Appeals for the Second Circuit is
2 reversed, and the case is remanded for further proceedings consistent with this
3 opinion.

4 *It is so ordered.*

5

6 JUSTICE BREYER, with whom JUSTICE STEVENS, JUSTICE SOUTER, and
7 JUSTICE GINSBURG join, dissenting.

8 In my view, the Federal Communications Commission failed adequately to explain
9 *why* it *changed* its indecency policy from a policy permitting a single "fleeting use"
10 of an expletive, to a policy that made no such exception. Its explanation fails to
11 discuss two critical factors, at least one of which directly underlay its original policy
12 decision. Its explanation instead discussed several factors well known to it the first
13 time around, which by themselves provide no significant justification for a *change*
14 of policy. Consequently, the FCC decision is "arbitrary, capricious, an abuse of
15 discretion." And I would affirm the Second Circuit's similar determination.

16 I

17 I begin with applicable law. That law grants those in charge of independent
18 administrative agencies broad authority to determine relevant policy. But it does
19 not permit them to make policy choices for purely political reasons nor to rest them
20 primarily upon unexplained policy preferences. Federal Communications
21 Commissioners have fixed terms of office; they are not directly responsible to the
22 voters; and they enjoy an independence expressly designed to insulate them, to a
23 degree, from " 'the exercise of political oversight.'" *Freytag v. Commissioner*, 501
24 U.S. 868, 916 (1991) (SCALIA, J., concurring in part and concurring in judgment).
25 That insulation helps to secure important governmental objectives, such as the
26 constitutionally related objective of maintaining broadcast regulation that does not
27 bend too readily before the political winds. But that agency's comparative freedom
28 from ballot-box control makes it all the more important that courts review its
29 decisionmaking to assure compliance with applicable provisions of the law—
30 including law requiring that major policy decisions be based upon articulable
31 reasons.

32 The statutory provision applicable here is the Administrative Procedure Act's
33 (APA) prohibition of agency action that is "arbitrary, capricious, [or] an abuse of
34 discretion," 5 U.S.C. §706(2)(A). This legal requirement helps assure agency
35 decisionmaking based upon more than the personal preferences of the
36 decisionmakers. Courts have applied the provision sparingly, granting agencies
37 broad policymaking leeway. But they have also made clear that agency discretion
38 is not "'unbounded.'" *Burlington Truck Lines, Inc. v. United States*, 371 U.S. 156,
39 167, 168 (1962). * * *

1 The law has also recognized that it is not so much a particular set of substantive
2 commands but rather it is a *process*, a process of learning through reasoned
3 argument, that is the antithesis of the "arbitrary." This means agencies must follow
4 a "logical and rational" decisionmaking "process." *Allentown Mack Sales &*
5 *Service, Inc. v. NLRB*, 522 U.S. 359, 374 (1998). An agency's policy decisions must
6 reflect the reasoned exercise of expert judgment. And, as this Court has specified,
7 in determining whether an agency's policy choice was "arbitrary," a reviewing court
8 "must consider whether the decision was based on a consideration of the relevant
9 factors and whether there has been a clear error of judgment." *Overton* Park, 401
10 U.S. 402, 416 (1971).

11 Moreover, an agency must act consistently. The agency must follow its own rules.
12 And when an agency seeks to change those rules, it must focus on the fact of change
13 and explain the basis for that change.

14 To explain a change requires more than setting forth reasons why the new policy
15 is a good one. It also requires the agency to answer the question, "Why did you
16 change?" And a rational answer to this question typically requires a more complete
17 explanation than would prove satisfactory were change itself not at issue. An
18 (imaginary) administrator explaining why he chose a policy that requires driving
19 on the right-side, rather than the left-side, of the road might say, "Well, one side
20 seemed as good as the other, so I flipped a coin." But even assuming the rationality
21 of that explanation for an *initial choice*, that explanation is not at all rational if
22 offered to explain why the administrator changed driving practice, from right-side
23 to left-side, 25 years later.

24         * * *

25 Contrary to the majority's characterization of this dissent, it would not (and *State*
26 *Farm* does not) require a "*heightened standard*" of review. Rather, the law
27 requires application of the same standard of review to different circumstances,
28 namely circumstances characterized by the fact that *change* is at issue. It requires
29 the agency to focus upon the fact of change where change is relevant, just as it must
30 focus upon any other relevant circumstance. It requires the agency here to focus
31 upon the reasons that led the agency to adopt the initial policy, and to explain why
32 it now comes to a new judgment.

33 I recognize that *sometimes* the ultimate explanation for a change may have to be,
34 "We now weigh the relevant considerations differently." But at other times, an
35 agency can and should say more. Where, for example, the agency rested its
36 previous policy on particular factual findings, or where an agency rested its prior
37 policy on its view of the governing law, or where an agency rested its previous
38 policy on, say, a special need to coordinate with another agency, one would
39 normally expect the agency to focus upon those earlier views of fact, of law, or of
40 policy and explain why they are no longer controlling. Regardless, to say that the
41 agency here must answer the question "why change" is not to require the agency to
42 provide a justification that is "*better* than the reasons for the old [policy]." It is only

to recognize the obvious fact that *change* is sometimes (not always) a relevant background feature that sometimes (not always) requires focus (upon prior justifications) and explanation lest the adoption of the new policy (in that circumstance) be "arbitrary, capricious, an abuse of discretion." * * *

* * *

V

* * *

With respect, I dissent.

JUSTICE THOMAS, concurring. [Omitted.]

JUSTICE KENNEDY, concurring in part and concurring in the judgment. [Omitted.]

JUSTICE STEVENS, dissenting. [Omitted.]

JUSTICE GINSBURG, dissenting. [Omitted.]


## DHS v. Regents of the University of California

140 S. Ct. 1891 (2020)

June 18, 2020

CHIEF JUSTICE ROBERTS delivered the opinion of the Court, except as to Part IV.

In the summer of 2012, the Department of Homeland Security (DHS) announced an immigration program known as Deferred Action for Childhood Arrivals, or DACA. That program allows certain unauthorized aliens who entered the United States as children to apply for a two-year forbearance of removal. Those granted such relief are also eligible for work authorization and various federal benefits. Some 700,000 aliens have availed themselves of this opportunity.

Five years later, the Attorney General advised DHS to rescind DACA, based on his conclusion that it was unlawful. The Department's Acting Secretary issued a memorandum terminating the program on that basis. The termination was challenged by affected individuals and third parties who alleged, among other things, that the Acting Secretary had violated the Administrative Procedure Act (APA) by failing to adequately address important factors bearing on her decision. For the reasons that follow, we conclude that the Acting Secretary did violate the APA, and that the rescission must be vacated.

I

1        A

2    In June 2012, the Secretary of Homeland Security issued a memorandum
3    announcing an immigration relief program for "certain young people who were
4    brought to this country as children." Known as DACA, the program applies to
5    childhood arrivals who were under age 31 in 2012; have continuously resided here
6    since 2007; are current students, have completed high school, or are honorably
7    discharged veterans; have not been convicted of any serious crimes; and do not
8    threaten national security or public safety. DHS concluded that individuals who
9    meet these criteria warrant favorable treatment under the immigration laws
10   because they "lacked the intent to violate the law," are "productive" contributors to
11   our society, and "know only this country as home."

12   "[T]o prevent [these] low priority individuals from being removed from the United
13   States," the DACA Memorandum instructs Immigration and Customs
14   Enforcement to "exercise prosecutorial discretion[] on an individual basis . . . by
15   deferring action for a period of two years, subject to renewal." In addition, it directs
16   U.S. Citizenship and Immigration Services (USCIS) to "accept applications to
17   determine whether these individuals qualify for work authorization during this
18   period of deferred action," as permitted under regulations long predating DACA's
19   creation, see 8 CFR §274a.12(c)(14) (2012) (permitting work authorization for
20   deferred action recipients who establish "economic necessity"); 46 Fed. Reg.
21   25080-25081 (1981) (similar). Pursuant to other regulations, deferred action
22   recipients are considered "lawfully present" for purposes of, and therefore eligible
23   to receive, Social Security and Medicare benefits. See 8 CFR §1.3(a)(4)(vi); 42 CFR
24   §417.422(h) (2012).

25   In November 2014, two years after DACA was promulgated, DHS issued a
26   memorandum announcing that it would expand DACA eligibility by removing the
27   age cap, shifting the date-of-entry requirement from 2007 to 2010, and extending
28   the deferred action and work authorization period to three years. In the same
29   memorandum, DHS created a new, related program known as Deferred Action for
30   Parents of Americans and Lawful Permanent Residents, or DAPA. That program
31   would have authorized deferred action for up to 4.3 million parents whose children
32   were U.S. citizens or lawful permanent residents. These parents were to enjoy the
33   same forbearance, work eligibility, and other benefits as DACA recipients.

34   Before the DAPA Memorandum was implemented, 26 States, led by Texas, filed
35   suit in the Southern District of Texas. The States contended that DAPA and the
36   DACA expansion violated the APA's notice and comment requirement, the
37   Immigration and Nationality Act (INA), and the Executive's duty under the Take
38   Care Clause of the Constitution. The District Court found that the States were likely
39   to succeed on the merits of at least one of their claims and entered a nationwide
40   preliminary injunction barring implementation of both DAPA and the DACA
41   expansion.

1  A divided panel of the Court of Appeals for the Fifth Circuit affirmed the
2  preliminary injunction. In opposing the injunction, the Government argued that
3  the DAPA Memorandum reflected an unreviewable exercise of the Government's
4  enforcement discretion. The Fifth Circuit majority disagreed. It reasoned that the
5  deferred action described in the DAPA Memorandum was "much more than
6  nonenforcement: It would affirmatively confer 'lawful presence' and associated
7  benefits on a class of unlawfully present aliens." From this, the majority concluded
8  that the creation of the DAPA program was not an unreviewable action "committed
9  to agency discretion by law."

10  The majority then upheld the injunction on two grounds. It first concluded the
11  States were likely to succeed on their procedural claim that the DAPA
12  Memorandum was a substantive rule that was required to undergo notice and
13  comment. It then held that the APA required DAPA to be set aside because the
14  program was "manifestly contrary" to the INA, which "expressly and carefully
15  provides legal designations allowing defined classes" to "receive the benefits"
16  associated with "lawful presence" and to qualify for work authorization, Judge
17  King dissented.

18  This Court affirmed the Fifth Circuit's judgment by an equally divided vote, which
19  meant that no opinion was issued. *United States v. Texas*, 579 U.S. ____ (2016)
20  (*per curiam*). For the next year, litigation over DAPA and the DACA expansion
21  continued in the Southern District of Texas, while implementation of those policies
22  remained enjoined.

23  Then, in June 2017, following a change in Presidential administrations, DHS
24  rescinded the DAPA Memorandum. In explaining that decision, DHS cited the
25  preliminary injunction and ongoing litigation in Texas, the fact that DAPA had
26  never taken effect, and the new administration's immigration enforcement
27  priorities.

28  Three months later, in September 2017, Attorney General Jefferson B. Sessions III
29  sent a letter to Acting Secretary of Homeland Security Elaine C. Duke, "advis[ing]"
30  that DHS "should rescind" DACA as well. Citing the Fifth Circuit's opinion and this
31  Court's equally divided affirmance, the Attorney General concluded that DACA
32  shared the "same legal . . . defects that the courts recognized as to DAPA" and was
33  "likely" to meet a similar fate. "In light of the costs and burdens" that a rescission
34  would "impose[] on DHS," the Attorney General urged DHS to "consider an orderly
35  and efficient wind-down process."

36  The next day, Duke acted on the Attorney General's advice. In her decision
37  memorandum, Duke summarized the history of the DACA and DAPA programs,
38  the Fifth Circuit opinion and ensuing affirmance, and the contents of the Attorney
39  General's letter. "Taking into consideration the Supreme Court's and the Fifth
40  Circuit's rulings" and the "letter from the Attorney General," she concluded that
41  the "DACA program should be terminated." Duke then detailed how the program
42  would be wound down: No new applications would be accepted, but DHS would

1  entertain applications for two-year renewals from DACA recipients whose benefits
2  were set to expire within six months. For all other DACA recipients, previously
3  issued grants of deferred action and work authorization would not be revoked but
4  would expire on their own terms, with no prospect for renewal.

5  <center>B</center>

6  Within days of Acting Secretary Duke's rescission announcement, multiple groups
7  of plaintiffs ranging from individual DACA recipients and States to the Regents of
8  the University of California and the National Association for the Advancement of
9  Colored People challenged her decision in the U.S. District Courts for the Northern
10  District of California (*Regents*, No. 18-587), the Eastern District of New York
11  (*Batalla Vidal*, No. 18-589), and the District of Columbia (*NAACP*, No. 18-588).
12  The relevant claims are that the rescission was arbitrary and capricious in violation
13  of the APA and that it infringed the equal protection guarantee of the Fifth
14  Amendment's Due Process Clause.

15  Plaintiffs also raised notice and comment claims, which uniformly failed below,
16  and assorted due process challenges, some of which survived motions to dismiss.
17  Those claims are not before us.

18  All three District Courts ruled for the plaintiffs, albeit at different stages of the
19  proceedings. In doing so, each court rejected the Government's threshold
20  arguments that the claims were unreviewable under the APA and that the INA
21  deprived the court of jurisdiction.

22  In a related challenge not at issue here, the District Court for the District of
23  Maryland granted partial summary judgment in favor of the Government. After
24  the Government filed petitions for certiorari in the instant cases, the Fourth Circuit
25  reversed that decision and vacated Acting Secretary Duke's rescission as arbitrary
26  and capricious. The Fourth Circuit has since stayed its mandate.

27  In *Regents* and *Batalla Vidal*, the District Courts held that the equal protection
28  claims were adequately alleged. Those courts also entered coextensive nationwide
29  preliminary injunctions, based on the conclusion that the plaintiffs were likely to
30  succeed on the merits of their claims that the rescission was arbitrary and
31  capricious. These injunctions did not require DHS to accept new applications, but
32  did order the agency to allow DACA recipients to "renew their enrollments."

33  In *NAACP*, the D.C. District Court took a different course. In April 2018, it deferred
34  ruling on the equal protection challenge but granted partial summary judgment to
35  the plaintiffs on their APA claim, holding that Acting Secretary Duke's "conclusory
36  statements were insufficient to explain the change in [the agency's] view of DACA's
37  lawfulness." The District Court stayed its order for 90 days to permit DHS to
38  "reissue a memorandum rescinding DACA, this time providing a fuller explanation
39  for the determination that the program lacks statutory and constitutional
40  authority."

1    Two months later, Duke's successor, Secretary Kirstjen M. Nielsen, responded via
2    memorandum. She explained that, "[h]aving considered the Duke memorandum,"
3    she "decline[d] to disturb" the rescission. Secretary Nielsen went on to articulate
4    her "understanding" of Duke's memorandum, identifying three reasons why, in
5    Nielsen's estimation, "the decision to rescind the DACA policy was, and remains,
6    sound." First, she reiterated that, "as the Attorney General concluded, the DACA
7    policy was contrary to law." Second, she added that, regardless, the agency had
8    "serious doubts about [DACA's] legality" and, for law enforcement reasons, wanted
9    to avoid "legally questionable" policies. Third, she identified multiple policy
10    reasons for rescinding DACA, including (1) the belief that any class-based
11    immigration relief should come from Congress, not through executive non-
12    enforcement; (2) DHS's preference for exercising prosecutorial discretion on "a
13    truly individualized, case-by-case basis"; and (3) the importance of "project[ing] a
14    message" that immigration laws would be enforced against all classes and
15    categories of aliens. *Id.*, In her final paragraph, Secretary Nielsen acknowledged
16    the "asserted reliance interests" in DACA's continuation but concluded that they
17    did not "outweigh the questionable legality of the DACA policy and the other
18    reasons" for the rescission discussed in her memorandum.

19    The Government asked the D. C. District Court to revise its prior order in light of
20    the reasons provided by Secretary Nielsen, but the court declined. In the court's
21    view, the new memorandum, which "fail[ed] to elaborate meaningfully" on the
22    agency's illegality rationale, still did not provide an adequate explanation for the
23    September 2017 rescission.

24    The Government appealed the various District Court decisions to the Second,
25    Ninth, and D. C. Circuits, respectively. In November 2018, while those appeals
26    were pending, the Government simultaneously filed three petitions for certiorari
27    before judgment. After the Ninth Circuit affirmed the nationwide injunction
28    in *Regents*, but before rulings from the other two Circuits, we granted the petitions
29    and consolidated the cases for argument. The issues raised here are (1) whether the
30    APA claims are reviewable, (2) if so, whether the rescission was arbitrary and
31    capricious in violation of the APA, and (3) whether the plaintiffs have stated an
32    equal protection claim.

33                                              II

34    The dispute before the Court is not whether DHS may rescind DACA. All parties
35    agree that it may. The dispute is instead primarily about the procedure the agency
36    followed in doing so.

37    The APA "sets forth the procedures by which federal agencies are accountable to
38    the public and their actions subject to review by the courts." *Franklin* v.
39    *Massachusetts*, 505 U.S. 788, 796 (1992). It requires agencies to engage in
40    "reasoned decisionmaking," *Michigan* v. *EPA*, 576 U.S. 743, 750 (2015) (internal
41    quotation marks omitted), and directs that agency actions be "set aside" if they are
42    "arbitrary" or "capricious," 5 U.S. C. §706(2)(A). Under this "narrow standard of

1 review, . . . a court is not to substitute its judgment for that of the agency," *FCC v.*
2 *Fox Television Stations, Inc.*, 556 U.S. 502, 513 (2009) (internal quotation marks
3 omitted), but instead to assess only whether the decision was "based on a
4 consideration of the relevant factors and whether there has been a clear error of
5 judgment," *Citizens to Preserve Overton Park, Inc. v. Volpe*, 401 U.S. 402, 416
6 (1971).

7 But before determining whether the rescission was arbitrary and capricious, we
8 must first address the Government's contentions that DHS's decision is
9 unreviewable under the APA and outside this Court's jurisdiction.

10 A

11 The APA establishes a "basic presumption of judicial review [for] one 'suffering
12 legal wrong because of agency action.'" *Abbott Laboratories* v. *Gardner*, 387 U.S.
13 136, 140 (1967) (quoting §702). That presumption can be rebutted by a showing
14 that the relevant statute "preclude[s]" review, §701(a)(1), or that the "agency action
15 is committed to agency discretion by law," §701(a)(2). The latter exception is at
16 issue here.

17 To "honor the presumption of review, we have read the exception in §701(a)(2)
18 quite narrowly," *Weyerhaeuser Co. v. United States Fish and Wildlife Serv.*, 586
19 U.S. ___, ___ (2018) (slip op., at 12), confining it to those rare "administrative
20 decision[s] traditionally left to agency discretion," *Lincoln* v. *Vigil*, 508 U.S. 182,
21 191 (1993). This limited category of unreviewable actions includes an agency's
22 decision not to institute enforcement proceedings, *Heckler v. Chaney*, 470 U.S.
23 821, 831-832 (1985), and it is on that exception that the Government primarily
24 relies.

25 In *Chaney*, several death-row inmates petitioned the Food and Drug
26 Administration (FDA) to take enforcement action against two States to prevent
27 their use of certain drugs for lethal injection. The Court held that the FDA's denial
28 of that petition was presumptively unreviewable in light of the well-established
29 "tradition" that "an agency's decision not to prosecute or enforce" is "generally
30 committed to an agency's absolute discretion." *Id.*, at 831. We identified a
31 constellation of reasons that underpin this tradition. To start, a non-enforcement
32 decision "often involves a complicated balancing of a number of factors which are
33 peculiarly within [the agency's] expertise," such as "whether the particular
34 enforcement action requested best fits the agency's overall policies." *Ibid*. The
35 decision also mirrors, "to some extent," a prosecutor's decision not to indict, which
36 has "long been regarded as the special province of the Executive Branch." *Id.*, at
37 832. And, as a practical matter, "when an agency refuses to act" there is no action
38 to "provide[] a focus for judicial review." *Ibid*.

39 The Government contends that a general non-enforcement policy is equivalent to
40 the individual non-enforcement decision at issue in *Chaney*. In each case, the
41 Government argues, the agency must balance factors peculiarly within its
42 expertise, and does so in a manner akin to a criminal prosecutor. Building on that

premise, the Government argues that the rescission of a non-enforcement policy is no different—for purposes of reviewability—from the adoption of that policy. While the rescission may lead to increased enforcement, it does not, by itself, constitute a particular enforcement action. Applying this logic to the facts here, the Government submits that DACA is a non-enforcement policy and that its rescission is therefore unreviewable.

But we need not test this chain of reasoning because DACA is not simply a non-enforcement policy. For starters, the DACA Memorandum did not merely "refus[e] to institute proceedings" against a particular entity or even a particular class. *Ibid.* Instead, it directed USCIS to "establish a clear and efficient process" for identifying individuals who met the enumerated criteria. Based on this directive, USCIS solicited applications from eligible aliens, instituted a standardized review process, and sent formal notices indicating whether the alien would receive the two-year forbearance. These proceedings are effectively "adjudicat[ions]." And the result of these adjudications—DHS's decision to "grant deferred action," Brief for Petitioners 45—is an "affirmative act of approval," the very opposite of a "refus[al] to act," *Chaney*, 470 U.S., at 831-832. In short, the DACA Memorandum does not announce a passive non-enforcement policy; it created a program for conferring affirmative immigration relief. The creation of that program—and its rescission—is an "action [that] provides a focus for judicial review." *Id.*, at 832.

The benefits attendant to deferred action provide further confirmation that DACA is more than simply a non-enforcement policy. As described above, by virtue of receiving deferred action, the 700,000 DACA recipients may request work authorization and are eligible for Social Security and Medicare. See *supra*, at 3. Unlike an agency's refusal to take requested enforcement action, access to these types of benefits is an interest "courts often are called upon to protect." *Chaney*, 470 U.S., at 832. See also *Barnhart v. Thomas*, 540 U.S. 20 (2003) (reviewing eligibility determination for Social Security benefits).

Because the DACA program is more than a non-enforcement policy, its rescission is subject to review under the APA.

B

The Government also invokes two jurisdictional provisions of the INA as independent bars to review. Neither applies.

Section 1252(b)(9) bars review of claims arising from "action[s]" or "proceeding[s] brought to remove an alien." 66 Stat. 209, as amended, 8 U.S. C. §1252(b)(9). That targeted language is not aimed at this sort of case. As we have said before, §1252(b)(9) "does not present a jurisdictional bar" where those bringing suit "are not asking for review of an order of removal," "the decision . . . to seek removal," or "the process by which . . . removability will be determined." *Jennings v. Rodriguez*, 583 U.S. ___, ___-___ (2018) (plurality opinion) (slip op., at 10-11); *id.*, at ___ (BREYER, J., dissenting) (slip op., at 31). And it is certainly not a bar where, as here, the parties are not challenging any removal proceedings.

Section 1252(g) is similarly narrow. That provision limits review of cases "arising from" decisions "to commence proceedings, adjudicate cases, or execute removal orders." §1252(g). We have previously rejected as "implausible" the Government's suggestion that §1252(g) covers "all claims arising from deportation proceedings" or imposes "a general jurisdictional limitation." *Reno v. American-Arab Anti Discrimination Comm.*, 525 U.S. 471, 482 (1999). The rescission, which revokes a deferred action program with associated benefits, is not a decision to "commence proceedings," much less to "adjudicate" a case or "execute" a removal order.

With these preliminary arguments out of the way, we proceed to the merits.

### III

### A

Deciding whether agency action was adequately explained requires, first, knowing where to look for the agency's explanation. The natural starting point here is the explanation provided by Acting Secretary Duke when she announced the rescission in September 2017. But the Government urges us to go on and consider the June 2018 memorandum submitted by Secretary Nielsen as well. That memo was prepared after the D. C. District Court vacated the Duke rescission and gave DHS an opportunity to "reissue a memorandum rescinding DACA, this time providing a fuller explanation for the determination that the program lacks statutory and constitutional authority." According to the Government, the Nielsen Memorandum is properly before us because it was invited by the District Court and reflects the views of the Secretary of Homeland Security—the official responsible for immigration policy. Respondents disagree, arguing that the Nielsen Memorandum, issued nine months after the rescission, impermissibly asserts prudential and policy reasons not relied upon by Duke.

It is a "foundational principle of administrative law" that judicial review of agency action is limited to "the grounds that the agency invoked when it took the action." *Michigan*, 576 U.S. at 758. If those grounds are inadequate, a court may remand for the agency to do one of two things: First, the agency can offer "a fuller explanation of the agency's reasoning *at the time of the agency action*." *Pension Benefit Guaranty Corporation v. LTV Corp.*, 496 U.S. 633, 654 (1990) (emphasis added). This route has important limitations. When an agency's initial explanation "indicate[s] the determinative reason for the final action taken," the agency may elaborate later on that reason (or reasons) but may not provide new ones. *Camp v. Pitts*, 411 U.S. 138, 143 (1973) (*per curiam*). Alternatively, the agency can "deal with the problem afresh" by taking *new* agency action. *SEC v. Chenery Corp.*, 332 U.S. 194, 201 (1947) (*Chenery II*). An agency taking this route is not limited to its prior reasons but must comply with the procedural requirements for new agency action.

The District Court's remand thus presented DHS with a choice: rest on the Duke Memorandum while elaborating on its prior reasoning, or issue a new rescission bolstered by new reasons absent from the Duke Memorandum. Secretary Nielsen took the first path. Rather than making a new decision, she "decline[d] to disturb the Duke memorandum's rescission" and instead "provide[d] further explanation" for that action. Indeed, the Government's subsequent request for reconsideration described the Nielsen Memorandum as "additional explanation for [Duke's] decision" and asked the District Court to "leave in place [Duke's] September 5, 2017 decision to rescind the DACA policy." Motion to Revise Order in No. 17-cv-1907 etc. (D DC), pp. 2, 19. Contrary to the position of the Government before this Court, and of JUSTICE KAVANAUGH in dissent, (opinion concurring in judgment in part and dissenting in part), the Nielsen Memorandum was by its own terms not a new rule implementing a new policy.

Because Secretary Nielsen chose to elaborate on the reasons for the initial rescission rather than take new administrative action, she was limited to the agency's original reasons, and her explanation "must be viewed critically" to ensure that the rescission is not upheld on the basis of impermissible "*post hoc* rationalization." *Overton Park*, 401 U.S., at 420. But despite purporting to explain the Duke Memorandum, Secretary Nielsen's reasoning bears little relationship to that of her predecessor. Acting Secretary Duke rested the rescission on the conclusion that DACA is unlawful. Period. By contrast, Secretary Nielsen's new memorandum offered three "separate and independently sufficient reasons" for the rescission, only the first of which is the conclusion that DACA is illegal.

Her second reason is that DACA is, at minimum, legally *questionable* and should be terminated to maintain public confidence in the rule of law and avoid burdensome litigation. No such justification can be found in the Duke Memorandum. Legal uncertainty is, of course, related to illegality. But the two justifications are meaningfully distinct, especially in this context. While an agency might, for one reason or another, choose to do nothing in the face of uncertainty, illegality presumably requires remedial action of some sort.

The policy reasons that Secretary Nielsen cites as a third basis for the rescission are also nowhere to be found in the Duke Memorandum. That document makes no mention of a preference for legislative fixes, the superiority of case-by-case decisionmaking, the importance of sending a message of robust enforcement, or any other policy consideration. Nor are these points included in the legal analysis from the Fifth Circuit and the Attorney General. They can be viewed only as impermissible *post hoc* rationalizations and thus are not properly before us.

The Government, echoed by JUSTICE KAVANAUGH, protests that requiring a new decision before considering Nielsen's new justifications would be "an idle and useless formality." *NLRB v. Wyman-Gordon Co.*, 394 U.S. 759, 766, n. 6 (1969) (plurality opinion). Procedural requirements can often seem such. But here the rule serves important values of administrative law. Requiring a new decision before considering new reasons promotes "agency accountability," *Bowen v. American Hospital Assn.*, 476 U.S. 610, 643 (1986), by ensuring that parties and the public can respond fully and in a timely manner to an agency's exercise of authority. Considering only contemporaneous explanations for agency action also

1  instills confidence that the reasons given are not simply "convenient litigating
2  position[s]." *Christopher v. SmithKline Beecham Corp.*, 567 U.S. 142, 155 (2012)
3  (internal quotation marks omitted). Permitting agencies to invoke belated
4  justifications, on the other hand, can upset "the orderly functioning of the process
5  of review," *SEC v. Chenery Corp.*, 318 U.S. 80, 94 (1943), forcing both litigants and
6  courts to chase a moving target. Each of these values would be markedly
7  undermined were we to allow DHS to rely on reasons offered nine months after
8  Duke announced the rescission and after three different courts had identified flaws
9  in the original explanation.

10  * * *

11  Justice Holmes famously wrote that "[m]en must turn square corners when they
12  deal with the Government." *Rock Island, A. & L. R. Co. v. United States*, 254 U.S.
13  141, 143 (1920). But it is also true, particularly when so much is at stake, that "the
14  Government should turn square corners in dealing with the people." *St. Regis
15  Paper Co. v. United States*, 368 U.S. 208, 229 (1961) (BLACK, J., dissenting). The
16  basic rule here is clear: An agency must defend its actions based on the reasons it
17  gave when it acted. This is not the case for cutting corners to allow DHS to rely
18  upon reasons absent from its original decision.

19  B

20  We turn, finally, to whether DHS's decision to rescind DACA was arbitrary and
21  capricious. As noted earlier, Acting Secretary Duke's justification for the rescission
22  was succinct: "Taking into consideration" the Fifth Circuit's conclusion that DAPA
23  was unlawful because it conferred benefits in violation of the INA, and the Attorney
24  General's conclusion that DACA was unlawful for the same reason, she
25  concluded—without elaboration—that the "DACA program should be terminated."

26  * * *

27  Respondents maintain that this explanation is deficient for three reasons. Their
28  first and second arguments work in tandem, claiming that the Duke Memorandum
29  does not adequately explain the conclusion that DACA is unlawful, and that this
30  conclusion is, in any event, wrong. While those arguments carried the day in the
31  lower courts, in our view they overlook an important constraint on Acting
32  Secretary Duke's decisionmaking authority—she was *bound* by the Attorney
33  General's legal determination.

34  The same statutory provision that establishes the Secretary of Homeland Security's
35  authority to administer and enforce immigration laws limits that authority,
36  specifying that, with respect to "all questions of law," the determinations of the
37  Attorney General "shall be controlling." 8 U. S. C. §1103(a)(1). Respondents are
38  aware of this constraint. Indeed they emphasized the point in the reviewability
39  sections of their briefs. But in their merits arguments, respondents never
40  addressed whether or how this unique statutory provision might affect our review.
41  They did not discuss whether Duke was required to explain a legal conclusion that

1  was not hers to make. Nor did they discuss whether the current suits challenging
2  Duke's rescission decision, which everyone agrees was within her legal authority
3  under the INA, are proper vehicles for attacking the Attorney General's legal
4  conclusion.

5  Because of these gaps in respondents' briefing, we do not evaluate the claims
6  challenging the explanation and correctness of the illegality conclusion. Instead we
7  focus our attention on respondents' third argument—that Acting Secretary Duke
8  "failed to consider . . . important aspect[s] of the problem" before her. *Motor*
9  *Vehicle Mfrs. Assn. of United States, Inc. v. State Farm Mut. Automobile*
10 *Ins. Co.*, 463 U.S. 29, 43 (1983).

11 Whether DACA is illegal is, of course, a legal determination, and therefore a
12 question for the Attorney General. But deciding how best to address a finding of
13 illegality moving forward can involve important policy choices, especially when the
14 finding concerns a program with the breadth of DACA. Those policy choices are for
15 DHS.

16 Acting Secretary Duke plainly exercised such discretionary authority in winding
17 down the program. Among other things, she specified that those DACA recipients
18 whose benefits were set to expire within six months were eligible for two-year
19 renewals.

20 But Duke did not appear to appreciate the full scope of her discretion, which picked
21 up where the Attorney General's legal reasoning left off. The Attorney General
22 concluded that "the DACA policy has the same legal . . . defects that the courts
23 recognized as to DAPA." So, to understand those defects, we look to the Fifth
24 Circuit, the highest court to offer a reasoned opinion on the legality of DAPA. That
25 court described the "core" issue before it as the "Secretary's decision" to grant
26 "eligibility for benefits"—including work authorization, Social Security, and
27 Medicare—to unauthorized aliens on "a class-wide basis." *Texas*, 809 F. 3d, at 170;
28 see *id.*, at 148, 184. * * *

29 But there is more to DAPA (and DACA) than such benefits. The defining feature of
30 deferred action is the decision to defer removal (and to notify the affected alien of
31 that decision). See App. to Pet. for Cert. 99a. And the Fifth Circuit was careful to
32 distinguish that forbearance component from eligibility for benefits. * * *
33 Borrowing from this Court's prior description of deferred action, the Fifth Circuit
34 observed that "the states do not challenge the Secretary's decision to 'decline to
35 institute proceedings, terminate proceedings, or decline to execute a final order of
36 deportation.'" *Id.*, at 168 (quoting *Reno*, 525 U.S., at 484). And the Fifth Circuit
37 underscored that nothing in its decision or the preliminary injunction "requires
38 the Secretary to remove any alien or to alter" the Secretary's class-based
39 "enforcement priorities." *Texas*, 809 F. 3d, at 166, 169. In other words, the
40 Secretary's forbearance authority was unimpaired.

41 Acting Secretary Duke recognized that the Fifth Circuit's holding addressed the
42 benefits associated with DAPA. In her memorandum she explained that the Fifth

Circuit concluded that DAPA "conflicted with the discretion authorized by Congress" because the INA "'flatly does not permit the reclassification of millions of illegal aliens as lawfully present and thereby make them newly eligible for a host of federal and state benefits, including work authorization.'". Duke did not characterize the opinion as one about forbearance.

In short, the Attorney General neither addressed the forbearance policy at the heart of DACA nor compelled DHS to abandon that policy. Thus, removing benefits eligibility while continuing forbearance remained squarely within the discretion of Acting Secretary Duke, who was responsible for "[e]stablishing national immigration enforcement policies and priorities." 116 Stat. 2178, 6 U.S.C. §202(5). But Duke's memo offers no reason for terminating forbearance. She instead treated the Attorney General's conclusion regarding the illegality of benefits as sufficient to rescind both benefits and forbearance, without explanation.

That reasoning repeated the error we identified in one of our leading modern administrative law cases, *Motor Vehicle Manufacturers Association of the United States, Inc. v. State Farm Mutual Automobile Insurance Co.* There, the National Highway Traffic Safety Administration (NHTSA) promulgated a requirement that motor vehicles produced after 1982 be equipped with one of two passive restraints: airbags or automatic seatbelts. 463 U.S., at 37-38, 46. Four years later, before the requirement went into effect, NHTSA concluded that automatic seatbelts, the restraint of choice for most manufacturers, would not provide effective protection. Based on that premise, NHTSA rescinded the passive restraint requirement in full. *Id.*, at 38.

We concluded that the total rescission was arbitrary and capricious. As we explained, NHTSA's justification supported only "disallow[ing] compliance by means of" automatic seatbelts. *Id.*, at 47. It did "not cast doubt" on the "efficacy of airbag technology" or upon "the need for a passive restraint standard." *Ibid.* Given NHTSA's prior judgment that "airbags are an effective and cost-beneficial lifesaving technology," we held that "the mandatory passive restraint rule [could] not be abandoned without any consideration whatsoever of an airbags-only requirement." *Id.*, at 51.

While the factual setting is different here, the error is the same. Even if it is illegal for DHS to extend work authorization and other benefits to DACA recipients, that conclusion supported only "disallow[ing]" benefits. *Id.*, at 47. It did "not cast doubt" on the legality of forbearance or upon DHS's original reasons for extending forbearance to childhood arrivals. *Ibid.* Thus, given DHS's earlier judgment that forbearance is "especially justified" for "productive young people" who were brought here as children and "know only this country as home," the DACA Memorandum could not be rescinded in full "without any consideration whatsoever" of a forbearance-only policy, *State Farm*, 463 U.S., at 51.

The three-page memorandum that established DACA is devoted entirely to forbearance, save for one sentence directing USCIS to "determine whether [DACA

1   recipients] qualify for work authorization." The benefits associated with DACA
2   flow from a separate regulation. See 8 CFR §1.3(a)(4)(vi); see also 42 CFR
3   §417.422(h) (cross-referencing 8 CFR §1.3). Thus, DHS could have addressed the
4   Attorney General's determination that such benefits were impermissible under the
5   INA by amending 8 CFR §1.3 to exclude DACA recipients from those benefits
6   without rescinding the DACA Memorandum and the forbearance policy it
7   established. But Duke's rescission memo shows no cognizance of this possibility.

8   The Government acknowledges that "[d]eferred action coupled with the associated
9   benefits are the two legs upon which the DACA policy stands." It insists, however,
10   that "DHS was not required to consider whether DACA's illegality could be
11   addressed by separating" the two. According to the Government, "It was not
12   arbitrary and capricious for DHS to view deferred action and its collateral benefits
13   as importantly linked." Perhaps. But that response misses the point. The fact that
14   there may be a valid reason not to separate deferred action from benefits does not
15   establish that DHS considered that option or that such consideration was
16   unnecessary.

17                                   \* \* \*

18   That omission alone renders Acting Secretary Duke's decision arbitrary and
19   capricious. But it is not the only defect. Duke also failed to address whether there
20   was "legitimate reliance" on the DACA Memorandum. *Smiley* v. *Citibank (South*
21   *Dakota), N. A.*, 517 U.S. 735, 742 (1996). When an agency changes course, as DHS
22   did here, it must "be cognizant that longstanding policies may have 'engendered
23   serious reliance interests that must be taken into account.'" *Encino Motorcars,*
24   *LLC v. Navarro*, 579 U.S. \_\_\_, \_\_\_ (2016) (slip op., at 9) (quoting *Fox*
25   *Television*, 556 U.S., at 515). "It would be arbitrary and capricious to ignore such
26   matters." *Id.*, at 515. Yet that is what the Duke Memorandum did.

27   For its part, the Government does not contend that Duke considered potential
28   reliance interests; it counters that she did not need to. In the Government's view,
29   shared by the lead dissent, DACA recipients have no "legally cognizable reliance
30   interests" because the DACA Memorandum stated that the program "conferred no
31   substantive rights" and provided benefits only in two-year increments. Reply Brief
32   16-17; App. to Pet. for Cert. 125a. See also *post*, at 23-24 (opinion of THOMAS, J).
33   But neither the Government nor the lead dissent cites any legal authority
34   establishing that such features automatically preclude reliance interests, and we
35   are not aware of any. These disclaimers are surely pertinent in considering the
36   strength of any reliance interests, but that consideration must be undertaken by
37   the agency in the first instance, subject to normal APA review. There was no such
38   consideration in the Duke Memorandum.

39                                   \* \* \*

40   DHS has considerable flexibility in carrying out its responsibility. The wind-down
41   here is a good example of the kind of options available. Acting Secretary Duke
42   authorized DHS to process two-year renewals for those DACA recipients whose

benefits were set to expire within six months. But Duke's consideration was solely for the purpose of assisting the agency in dealing with "administrative complexities." She should have considered whether she had similar flexibility in addressing any reliance interests of DACA recipients. * * *

* * *

The lead dissent sees all the foregoing differently. In its view, DACA is illegal, so any actions under DACA are themselves illegal. Such actions, it argues, must cease immediately and the APA should not be construed to impede that result.

The dissent is correct that DACA was rescinded because of the Attorney General's illegality determination. But nothing about that determination foreclosed or even addressed the options of retaining forbearance or accommodating particular reliance interests. Acting Secretary Duke should have considered those matters but did not. That failure was arbitrary and capricious in violation of the APA.

IV

* * *

We do not decide whether DACA or its rescission are sound policies. "The wisdom" of those decisions "is none of our concern." *Chenery II*, 332 U.S., at 207. We address only whether the agency complied with the procedural requirement that it provide a reasoned explanation for its action. Here the agency failed to consider the conspicuous issues of whether to retain forbearance and what if anything to do about the hardship to DACA recipients. That dual failure raises doubts about whether the agency appreciated the scope of its discretion or exercised that discretion in a reasonable manner. The appropriate recourse is therefore to remand to DHS so that it may consider the problem anew.

* * *

*It is so ordered.*

JUSTICE SOTOMAYOR, concurring in part, concurring in the judgment in part, and dissenting in part. [omitted]

JUSTICE THOMAS, with whom JUSTICE ALITO and JUSTICE GORSUCH join, concurring in the judgment in part and dissenting in part.

Between 2001 and 2011, Congress considered over two dozen bills that would have granted lawful status to millions of aliens who were illegally brought to this country as children. Each of those legislative efforts failed. In the wake of this impasse, the Department of Homeland Security (DHS) under President Barack Obama took matters into its own hands. Without any purported delegation of authority from Congress and without undertaking a rulemaking, DHS unilaterally created a program known as Deferred Action for Childhood Arrivals (DACA). The three-page DACA memorandum made it possible for approximately 1.7 million illegal aliens to qualify for temporary lawful presence and certain federal and state benefits. When President Donald Trump took office in 2017, his Acting Secretary of Homeland Security, acting through yet another memorandum, rescinded the DACA memorandum. To state it plainly, the Trump administration rescinded DACA the same way that the Obama administration created it: unilaterally, and through a mere memorandum.

Today the majority makes the mystifying determination that this rescission of DACA was unlawful. In reaching that conclusion, the majority acts as though it is engaging in the routine application of standard principles of administrative law. On the contrary, this is anything but a standard administrative law case.

DHS created DACA during the Obama administration without any statutory authorization and without going through the requisite rulemaking process. As a result, the program was unlawful from its inception. The majority does not even attempt to explain why a court has the authority to scrutinize an agency's policy reasons for rescinding an unlawful program under the arbitrary and capricious microscope. The decision to countermand an unlawful agency action is clearly reasonable. So long as the agency's determination of illegality is sound, our review should be at an end.

Today's decision must be recognized for what it is: an effort to avoid a politically controversial but legally correct decision. The Court could have made clear that the solution respondents seek must come from the Legislative Branch. Instead, the majority has decided to prolong DHS' initial overreach by providing a stopgap measure of its own. In doing so, it has given the green light for future political battles to be fought in this Court rather than where they rightfully belong—the political branches. Such timidity forsakes the Court's duty to apply the law according to neutral principles, and the ripple effects of the majority's error will be felt throughout our system of self-government.

Perhaps even more unfortunately, the majority's holding creates perverse incentives, particularly for outgoing administrations. Under the auspices of today's decision, administrations can bind their successors by unlawfully adopting significant legal changes through Executive Branch agency memoranda. Even if the agency lacked authority to effectuate the changes, the changes cannot be undone by the same agency in a successor administration unless the successor provides sufficient policy justifications to the satisfaction of this Court. In other words, the majority erroneously holds that the agency is not only permitted, but required, to continue administering unlawful programs that it inherited from a previous administration. I respectfully dissent in part.

I concur in the judgment insofar as the majority rejects respondents' equal protection claim.

* * *

JUSTICE KAVANAUGH, concurring in the judgment in part and dissenting in part. [Omitted.]


# C. Substantial Evidence Review

5 U.S.C. §706(2)(E) provides that reviewing courts should set aside agency actions "unsupported by substantial evidence in a case subject to sections 556 and 557 of this title or otherwise reviewed on the record of an agency hearing provided by statute." The restriction to matters subject to 556 and 557 means that substantial evidence review only applies to on-the-record proceedings (unless Congress stipulates by statute that it applies in other circumstances, as Congress sometimes does: see, *e.g.*, 29 U.S.C. § 655(f)).

What does substantial evidence review mean as a practical matter? Is it tougher to survive than arbitrary and capricious review, or easier, or equally stringent, or different in some other way?

In applying the substantial evidence standard, as in many other administrative law contexts, courts must figure out where they stand in relation to other decision makers who have considered the same matter. In the classic *Universal Camera* case, for instance, the Supreme Court is reviewing an appeals court reviewing the National Labor Relations Board's review of its own hearing examiner's findings. The NLRB order and the appeals court's opinion are included below.

*Universal Camera* demands that the Supreme Court wrestle with important questions. These include: in determining whether an agency's action is supported by substantial evidence, should the court look only to the agency in the record that supports the agency's conclusion, as a literal reading of the statute might suggest, or should it consider evidence that points the other way as well? And: when different agency actors have participated in the agency's decision making—for instance, when an ALJ has rendered a decision that agency higher-ups have then reversed—what weight, if any, is it proper for a reviewing court to give to the earlier decisions?


## In The Matter Of Universal Camera Corporation

79 N.L.R.B. 379 (1948)

August 31, 1948

DECISION AND ORDER

On February 18, 1947, Trial Examiner Sidney L. Feiler issued his Intermediate Report in the above-entitled proceeding, finding that the Respondent had not engaged in the unfair labor practices alleged in the complaint and recommending

1  that the complaint be dismissed. * * * Thereafter, the complainant and counsel for
2  the Board filed exceptions and supporting briefs. * * *

3                                                        * * *

4   The Trial Examiner found that the evidence failed to sustain the allegation of the
5   complaint that Chairman was discharged in violation of Section 8 (4) of the Act.
6   We disagree. In our opinion, a preponderance of the evidence shows that
7   Chairman's discharge was due to the Respondent's resentment against Chairman
8   because he had testified for the Union at a representation hearing on November
9   30, 1943. We believe that the Trial Examiner, in finding otherwise, failed to
10  appreciate the strength of the *prima facie* case against the Respondent established
11  by the evidence, and erroneously credited certain implausible testimony adduced
12  by the Respondent in explanation of the circumstances leading up to Chairman's
13  discharge.

14  As fully detailed in the Intermediate Report, the record shows conclusively that
15  Chairman incurred the hostility of the Respondent, and especially of Chief
16  Engineer Kende, who ultimately discharged him, by testifying favorably to the
17  Union's position, and unfavorably to the Respondent's at the Board hearing in a
18  representation case on November 30, 1943. Politzer, Chairman's immediate
19  superior, warned Chairman in advance not to testify for the Union; and a few hours
20  after Chairman's appearance as a witness, Kende angrily upbraided him for
21  testifying. On the following day, Kende, in conference with Politzer and Personnel
22  Manager Weintraub, launched an investigation of Chairman's record for the
23  purpose of finding an excuse to discharge him. Both Kende's own testimony and
24  Politzer's contemporaneous statements to Chairman and Goldson show beyond
25  any reasonable doubt that this search for a pretext was motivated by Kende's
26  indignation over Chairman's testimony. The net result of this conference on
27  December 1 was that neither of the causes for discharging Chairman then
28  suggested by Kende proved feasible. Politzer assured Kende that Chairman was
29  efficient and a few days later also reported, after making inquiry as he was
30  instructed to do, that Chairman was not a Communist. Nothing, therefore, was
31  done about Chairman at that time.

32  In the face of this clear evidence of the Respondent's animus against Chairman and
33  its desire and intention to discharge him because of his testimony at the Board
34  hearing if a pretext could be found, it was incumbent upon the Respondent to go
35  forward to show convincingly that when Chairman was actually discharged—by
36  Kende himself—8 weeks later, ostensibly because of an episode that was then stale,
37  the real reason was something other than Chairman's appearance as a witness.
38  Contrary to the Trial Examiner, we find the Respondent's explanation of the
39  discharge implausible.

40  Kende ordered Chairman's discharge on January 24, 1944, ostensibly because of a
41  complaint lodged against Chairman by Personnel Manager Weintraub, to the effect
42  that Chairman had been guilty of "gross insubordination" in an encounter with

1    Weintraub in the plant on the night of December 30, more than 3 weeks before.
2    Politzer, who was Chairman's immediate superior, and was himself responsible
3    directly to Kende, opposed Weintraub's demand for the discharge. Kende
4    nevertheless ruled peremptorily in Weintraub's favor, without questioning
5    Chairman himself or otherwise independently investigating the December 30
6    incident. That episode itself was a heated argument between Weintraub and
7    Chairman, precipitated by Weintraub's order that Chairman send home an
8    employee whom Chairman had stationed on stand-by duty. The record shows that
9    Weintraub's authority to give Chairman such an order was at least questionable.
10    Moreover, whether or not Weintraub had this authority, the dispute ended with
11    the two men shaking hands and agreeing to "forget" their differences. It was, at
12    most, only a squabble between two supervisors, one of whom, Chairman,
13    reasonably questioned the other's authority in the circumstances; it was not an
14    instance of "gross insubordination" on Chairman's part.

15    During the next 3½ weeks, the Respondent neither reprimanded Chairman for his
16    supposed impertinence to Weintraub, nor took any disciplinary action against him.
17    Indeed, Politzer, when Chairman reported the affair to him on December 31,
18    assured Chairman that it was Weintraub, rather than Chairman, who had been
19    "out of order." The only testimony offered by the Respondent in explanation of the
20    long delay between Chairman's alleged misconduct and his punishment, is that of
21    Weintraub and Politzer to the effect that Politzer assured Weintraub, within a day
22    or two after December 30, that Chairman intended to resign in about 10 days. The
23    Respondent asserts that Weintraub thereupon lodged no complaint against
24    Chairman until January 24 because he had in the meantime been expecting
25    Chairman to leave, and only noticed, on or about January 24, that Chairman was
26    still at work. The Trial Examiner believed this testimony, although he flatly
27    discredited Politzer's statement, contradicted by Chairman, that Chairman had in
28    fact agreed to resign, and although he also found both Weintraub and Politzer to
29    be unreliable witnesses in many respects. We cannot accept the Trial Examiner's
30    finding that Politzer, in effect, invented the story that Chairman intended to resign
31    in order to appease Weintraub and gain time for Chairman, for this finding is
32    irreconcilable with the other related facts, and all the other evidence bearing on
33    Politzer's behavior and attitudes at that time. We find, then, that the record
34    contains no credible explanation of Weintraub's failure to call for disciplinary
35    action against Chairman, on account of their quarrel on December 30, until about
36    a month after the event. We think that on this record, Weintraub's revival of the
37    December 30 episode as a basis for demanding Chairman's discharge, and Kende's
38    summary ruling on that demand, despite Politzer's opposition, are reasonably
39    explained only by the other facts to which we previously adverted: The
40    Respondent's extreme animus against Chairman because of his testimony at the
41    Board hearing despite its prior warning, and its promptly conceived plan—which
42    was initially frustrated, but not shown to have been abandoned—to find a pretext
43    for discharging him. * * * We find, on the entire record, that Chairman was
44    discharged for testifying at the Board hearing, in violation of Section 8 (4) of the
45    Act. * * *

1                                             * * *

2   As it has been found that the Respondent discriminated against Chairman for
3   having given testimony under the Act and thereby violated Section 8 (4) of the Act,
4   we shall direct that the Respondent offer him immediate and full reinstatement to
5   his former or a substantially equivalent position without prejudice to his seniority
6   or other rights or privileges. We shall also order that the Respondent make
7   Chairman whole for any loss of pay he may have suffered by reason of his
8   discriminatory discharge by payment to him of a sum equal to the amount he
9   would normally have earned as wages during the periods * * * .

10  * * * In order to effectuate the policies of the Act, we shall order the Respondent to
11  cease and desist from discharging, or otherwise discriminating against any
12  employee because he has filed charges or given testimony under the Act, or in any
13  other manner interfering with the rights of employees to file and prosecute charges
14  and to give testimony under the Act.

15                                            * * *

16  MEMBER REYNOLDS, dissenting. [Omitted.]

17

18  **National Labor Relations Board v. Universal Camera**
19  **Corporation**

20  179 F.2d 749 (2d Cir. 1950)

21  January 10, 1950

22  Before L. HAND, Chief Judge, and SWAN and FRANK, Circuit Judges.

23  L. HAND, Chief Judge.

24                                            * * *

25  This case arises upon a petition to enforce an order of the Labor Board, whose only
26  direction that we need consider was to reinstate with back pay a "supervisory
27  employee," named [Imre] Chairman, whom the respondent discharged on January
28  24, 1944, avowedly for insubordination. * * *

29                                            * * *

30  * * * [T]he examiner was not satisfied that the Board had proved that Chairman's
31  testimony at the representation proceeding had been an actuating cause of his
32  discharge; but, not only did the majority of the Board reverse his ruling as to that,
33  but they also overruled his finding that Politzer had told Weintraub on January
34  first that Chairman was going to resign. They then found that Kende and
35  Weintraub had agreed to bring about Chairman's discharge, at some undefined
36  time after December first, because of Chairman's testimony; and that Weintraub's

1    complaint on January 24 was a cover for affecting that purpose. Whether these
2    findings were justified is the first, and indeed the only important, question of fact;
3    and as a preliminary point arises the extent of our review.

4    This has been the subject of so much uncertainty that we shall not try to clarify it;
5    but we must decide what change, if any, the amendment of 1947 has made. Section
6    10(e) now reads that the findings "shall be conclusive" "if supported by substantial
7    evidence on the record considered as a whole"; and the original was merely that
8    they should be conclusive, "if supported by evidence." * * * It is true that there were
9    efforts, especially in the House, to give to courts of appeal a wider review than
10   before; but the Senate opposed these, and, so far as concerns the adjective,
11   "substantial," it added nothing to the interpretation which the Supreme Court had
12   already put upon the earlier language. The most probable intent in adding the
13   phrase, "on the record considered as a whole," was to overrule what Congress
14   apparently supposed—perhaps rightly—had been the understanding of some
15   courts: *i.e.* that, if any passage could be found in the testimony to support a finding,
16   the review was to stop, no matter how much other parts of the testimony
17   contradicted, or outweighed, it. That the words throughout section ten were chosen
18   with deliberation and care is evident from the changes in § 10(c), apparently
19   intended to confine the Board to the record before it, and in § 10(b), restricting it
20   in the admission of evidence to Rule 43(a) of the Federal Rules of Civil Procedure.
21   It appears to us that, had it been intended to set up a new measure of review by the
22   courts, the matter would not have been left so at large. We cannot agree that our
23   review has been "broadened"; we hold that no more was done than to make definite
24   what was already implied.

25   Just what that review was is another and much more difficult matter—particularly,
26   when it comes to deciding how to treat a reversal by the Board of a finding of one
27   of its own examiners. Obviously no printed record preserves all the evidence, on
28   which any judicial officer bases his findings; and it is principally on that account
29   that upon an appeal from the judgment of a district court, a court of appeals will
30   hesitate to reverse. Its position must be: "No matter what you saw of the witnesses
31   and what else you heard than these written words, we are satisfied from them alone
32   that you were clearly wrong. Nothing which could have happened that is not
33   recorded, could have justified your conclusion in the face of what is before us."
34   That gives such findings great immunity, which the Rules extend even to the
35   findings of masters, when reviewed by a district judge. The standing of an
36   examiner's findings under the Labor Relations Act is not plain; but it appears to us
37   at least clear that they were not intended to be as unassailable as a master's. * * *
38   We hold that, although the Board would be wrong in totally disregarding his
39   findings, it is practically impossible for a court, upon review of those findings
40   which the Board itself substitutes, to consider the Board's reversal as a factor in
41   the court's own decision. This we say, because we cannot find any middle ground
42   between doing that and treating such a reversal as error, whenever it would be
43   such, if done by a judge to a master in equity.

1 The foregoing discussion is relevant in the case at bar for the following reason. One
2 ground why the evidence failed to convince the examiner of any agreement
3 between Kende and Weintraub to discharge Chairman, was that he thought it quite
4 as likely that the quarrel between Weintraub and Chairman at the end of December
5 still rankled in Weintraub's mind, and induced him to insist upon Chairman's
6 discharge on January 24, 1944. It became important in this view to explain why
7 Weintraub waited for over three weeks; and this the examiner did explain because
8 he believed that Politzer had told Weintraub that Chairman was going to resign.
9 When the majority of the Board refused to accept this finding, they concluded that,
10 since this left Weintraub's delay unexplained, his motive was to be related back to
11 the quarrel of Kende and Chairman on November 30. We should feel obliged in
12 our turn to reverse the reversal of this finding, if we were dealing with the finding
13 of a judge who had reversed the finding of a master, because the reasons given do
14 not seem to us enough to overbear the evidence which the record did not preserve
15 and which may have convinced the examiner. * * *

16                                     * * *

17 Nevertheless, in spite of all this we shall direct the Board's order to be enforced. If
18 by special verdict a jury had made either the express finding of the majority that
19 there was an agreement between Kende and Weintraub, or the alternate finding, if
20 there be one, that Kende without Weintraub's concurrence used Weintraub's
21 complaint as an excuse, we should not reverse the verdict; and we understand our
22 function in cases of this kind to be the same. Such a verdict would be within the
23 bounds of rational entertainment. When all is said, Kende had been greatly
24 outraged at Chairman's testimony; he then did propose to get him out of the
25 factory; he still thought at the hearings that he was unfit to remain; and he had told
26 Weintraub to keep watch on him. We cannot say that, with all these circumstances
27 before him, no reasonable person could have concluded that Chairman's testimony
28 was one of the causes of his discharge, little as it would have convinced us, were we
29 free to pass upon the evidence in the first instance.

30                                     * * *

31 An enforcement order will issue.

32 SWAN, Circuit Judge (dissenting).

33 In *National Labor Relations Board v. A. Sartorius & Co.*, 140 F.2d 203, 205 (2d
34 Cir. 1944), we said that "if an administrative agency ignores all the evidence given
35 by one side in a controversy and with studied design gives credence to the
36 testimony of the other side, the findings would be arbitrary and not in accord with
37 the legal requirement." I think that is what the majority of the board has done in
38 the case at bar. I would reverse its finding of motive and deny enforcement of the
39 order.

40

1    **Universal Camera Corp. v. National Labor Relations Board**

2    340 U.S. 474 (1951)

3    February 26, 1951

4    MR. JUSTICE FRANKFURTER delivered the opinion of the Court.

5    The essential issue raised by this case * * * is the effect of the Administrative
6    Procedure Act and the legislation colloquially known as the Taft-Hartley Act on the
7    duty of Courts of Appeals when called upon to review orders of the National Labor
8    Relations Board.

9    The Court of Appeals for the Second Circuit granted enforcement of an order
10   directing, in the main, that petitioner reinstate with back pay an employee found
11   to have been discharged because he gave testimony under the Wagner Act, and
12   cease and desist from discriminating against any employee who files charges or
13   gives testimony under that Act. * * *

14                                          I

15   Want of certainty in judicial review of Labor Board decisions partly reflects the
16   intractability of any formula to furnish definiteness of content for all the
17   impalpable factors involved in judicial review. But, in part, doubts as to the nature
18   of the reviewing power and uncertainties in its application derive from history,
19   and, to that extent, an elucidation of this history may clear them away.

20   The Wagner Act provided: "The findings of the Board as to the facts, if supported
21   by evidence, shall be conclusive." 29 U.S.C. § 160(e). This Court read "evidence" to
22   mean "substantial evidence," *Washington, V. & M. Coach Co. v. Labor Board*, 301
23   U.S. 142 (1937), and we said that "[s]ubstantial evidence is more than a mere
24   scintilla. It means such relevant evidence as a reasonable mind might accept as
25   adequate to support a conclusion." *Consolidated Edison Co. v. Labor Board*, 305
26   U.S. 197, 229 (1938). Accordingly, it "must do more than create a suspicion of the
27   existence of the fact to be established. . . . [I]t must be enough to justify, if the trial
28   were to a jury, a refusal to direct a verdict when the conclusion sought to be drawn
29   from it is one of fact for the jury." *Labor Board v. Columbian Enameling &
30   Stamping Co.*, 306 U.S. 292, 300 (1939).

31   The very smoothness of the "substantial evidence" formula as the standard for
32   reviewing the evidentiary validity of the Board's findings established its currency.
33   But the inevitably variant applications of the standard to conflicting evidence soon
34   brought contrariety of views, and, in due course, bred criticism. Even though the
35   whole record may have been canvassed in order to determine whether the
36   evidentiary foundation of a determination by the Board was "substantial," the
37   phrasing of this Court's process of review readily lent itself to the notion that it was
38   enough that the evidence supporting the Board's result was "substantial" when
39   considered by itself. It is fair to say that, by imperceptible steps, regard for the fact-
40   finding function of the Board led to the assumption that the requirements of the

485

Wagner Act were met when the reviewing court could find in the record evidence which, when viewed in isolation, substantiated the Board's findings. * * *

Criticism of so contracted a reviewing power reinforced dissatisfaction felt in various quarters with the Board's administration of the Wagner Act in the years preceding the war. The scheme of the Act was attacked as an inherently unfair fusion of the functions of prosecutor and judge. Accusations of partisan bias were not wanting. * * *

The strength of these pressures was reflected in the passage in 1940 of the Walter-Logan Bill. It was vetoed by President Roosevelt * * * .

* * *

Similar dissatisfaction with too restricted application of the "substantial evidence" test is reflected in the legislative history of the Taft-Hartley Act. The bill as reported to the House provided that the "findings of the Board as to the facts shall be conclusive unless it is made to appear to the satisfaction of the court either (1) that the findings of fact are against the manifest weight of the evidence, or (2) that the findings of fact are not supported by substantial evidence." The bill left the House with this provision. Early committee prints in the Senate provided for review by "weight of the evidence" or "clearly erroneous" standards. But, as the Senate Committee Report relates, "it was finally decided to conform the statute to the corresponding section of the Administrative Procedure Act, where the substantial evidence test prevails. In order to clarify any ambiguity in that statute, however, the committee inserted the words 'questions of fact, if supported by substantial evidence on the record considered as a *whole*. . . .'"

This phraseology was adopted by the Senate. * * * The Senate version became the law.

It is fair to say that, in all this, Congress expressed a mood. And it expressed its mood not merely by oratory, but by legislation. As legislation, that mood must be respected, even though it can only serve as a standard for judgment, and not as a body of rigid rules assuring sameness of applications. Enforcement of such broad standards implies subtlety of mind and solidity of judgment. But it is not for us to question that Congress may assume such qualities in the federal judiciary.

From the legislative story we have summarized, two concrete conclusions do emerge. One is the identity of aim of the Administrative Procedure Act and the Taft-Hartley Act regarding the proof with which the Labor Board must support a decision. The other is that, now, Congress has left no room for doubt as to the kind of scrutiny which a court of appeals must give the record before the Board to satisfy itself that the Board's order rests on adequate proof.

* * *

Whether or not it was ever permissible for courts to determine the substantiality of evidence supporting a Labor Board decision merely on the basis of evidence

1    which, in and of itself, justified it, without taking into account contradictory
2    evidence or evidence from which conflicting inferences could be drawn, the new
3    legislation definitively precludes such a theory of review and bars its practice. The
4    substantiality of evidence must take into account whatever in the record fairly
5    detracts from its weight. This is clearly the significance of the requirement in both
6    statutes that courts consider the whole record. * * *

7    To be sure, the requirement for canvassing "the whole record" in order to ascertain
8    substantiality does not furnish a calculus of value by which a reviewing court can
9    assess the evidence. Nor was it intended to negative the function of the Labor
10    Board as one of those agencies presumably equipped or informed by experience to
11    deal with a specialized field of knowledge, whose findings within that field carry
12    the authority of an expertness which courts do not possess, and therefore must
13    respect. Nor does it mean that, even as to matters not requiring expertise, a court
14    may displace the Board's choice between two fairly conflicting views even though
15    the court would justifiably have made a different choice had the matter been before
16    it *de novo*. Congress has merely made it clear that a reviewing court is not barred
17    from setting aside a Board decision when it cannot conscientiously find that the
18    evidence supporting that decision is substantial when viewed in the light that the
19    record in its entirety furnishes, including the body of evidence opposed to the
20    Board's view.

21                                               * * *

22    Whatever changes were made by the Administrative Procedure and Taft-Hartley
23    Acts are clearly within this area where precise definition is impossible. Retention
24    of the familiar "substantial evidence" terminology indicates that no drastic reversal
25    of attitude was intended.

26    But a standard leaving an unavoidable margin for individual judgment does not
27    leave the judicial judgment at large, even though the phrasing of the standard does
28    not wholly fence it in. The legislative history of these Acts demonstrates a purpose
29    to impose on courts a responsibility which has not always been recognized. * * *

30    We conclude, therefore, that the Administrative Procedure Act and the Taft-
31    Hartley Act direct that courts must now assume more responsibility for the
32    reasonableness and fairness of Labor Board decisions than some courts have
33    shown in the past. Reviewing courts must be influenced by a feeling that they are
34    not to abdicate the conventional judicial function. Congress has imposed on them
35    responsibility for assuring that the Board keeps within reasonable grounds. That
36    responsibility is not less real because it is limited to enforcing the requirement that
37    evidence appear substantial when viewed, on the record as a whole, by courts
38    invested with the authority and enjoying the prestige of the Courts of Appeals. The
39    Board's findings are entitled to respect, but they must nonetheless be set aside
40    when the record before a Court of Appeals clearly precludes the Board's decision
41    from being justified by a fair estimate of the worth of the testimony of witnesses or
42    its informed judgment on matters within its special competence or both.

1                                          * * *

2                                           II

3                                          * * *

4    The decision of the Court of Appeals is assailed on two grounds. It is said (1) that
5    the court erred in holding that it was barred from taking into account the report of
6    the examiner on questions of fact insofar as that report was rejected by the Board,
7    and (2) that the Board's order was not supported by substantial evidence on the
8    record, considered as a whole, even apart from the validity of the court's refusal to
9    consider the rejected portions of the examiner's report.

10   The latter contention is easily met. * * * [I]t is clear from the court's opinion in this
11   case that it, in fact, did consider the "record as a whole," and did not deem itself
12   merely the judicial echo of the Board's conclusion. The testimony of the company's
13   witnesses was inconsistent, and there was clear evidence that the complaining
14   employee had been discharged by an officer who was at one time influenced against
15   him because of his appearance at the Board hearing. On such a record, we could
16   not say that it would be error to grant enforcement.

17   The first contention, however, raises serious questions, to which we now turn.

18                                          III

19   The Court of Appeals deemed itself bound by the Board's rejection of the
20   examiner's findings because the court considered these findings not "as
21   unassailable as a master's." They are not. Section 10(c) of the Labor Management
22   Relations Act provides that "If upon the preponderance of the testimony taken, the
23   Board shall be of the opinion that any person named in the complaint has engaged
24   in or is engaging in any such unfair labor practice, then the Board shall state its
25   findings of fact. . . ." 61 Stat. 147, 29 U.S.C. (Supp. III) § 160(c). The responsibility
26   for decision thus placed on the Board is wholly inconsistent with the notion that it
27   has power to reverse an examiner's findings only when they are "clearly
28   erroneous." Such a limitation would make so drastic a departure from prior
29   administrative practice that explicitness would be required.

30   The Court of Appeals concluded from this premise "that, although the Board would
31   be wrong in totally disregarding his findings, it is practically impossible for a court,
32   upon review of those findings which the Board itself substitutes, to consider the
33   Board's reversal as a factor in the court's own decision. This we say because we
34   cannot find any middle ground between doing that and treating such a reversal as
35   error, whenever it would be such, if done by a judge to a master in equity." Much
36   as we respect the logical acumen of the Chief Judge of the Court of Appeals, we do
37   not find ourselves pinioned between the horns of his dilemma.

38   We are aware that to give the examiner's findings less finality than a master's, and
39   yet entitle them to consideration in striking the account, is to introduce another
40   and an unruly factor into the judgmatical process of review. But we ought not to

1   fashion an exclusionary rule merely to reduce the number of imponderables to be
2   considered by reviewing courts.

3   The Taft-Hartley Act provides that "The findings of the Board with respect to
4   questions of fact if supported by substantial evidence on the record considered as
5   a whole shall be conclusive." 61 Stat. 148, 29 U.S.C. (Supp. III) § 160(e). Surely an
6   examiner's report is as much a part of the record as the complaint or the testimony.
7   According to the Administrative Procedure Act, "All decisions (including initial,
8   recommended, or tentative decisions) shall become a part of the record. . . ." 5
9   U.S.C. § 1007(b). We found that this Act's provision for judicial review has the
10  same meaning as that in the Taft-Hartley Act. The similarity of the two statutes in
11  language and purpose also requires that the definition of "record" found in the
12  Administrative Procedure Act be construed to be applicable as well to the term
13  "record" as used in the Taft-Hartley Act.

14  It is therefore difficult to escape the conclusion that the plain language of the
15  statutes directs a reviewing court to determine the substantiality of evidence on the
16  record including the examiner's report. * * *

17                                      * * *

18  * * * Nothing in the statutes suggests that the Labor Board should not be
19  influenced by the examiner's opportunity to observe the witnesses he hears and
20  sees and the Board does not. Nothing suggests that reviewing courts should not
21  give to the examiner's report such probative force as it intrinsically commands. To
22  the contrary, § 11 of the Administrative Procedure Act contains detailed provisions
23  designed to maintain high standards of independence and competence in
24  examiners. Section 10(c) of the Labor Management Relations Act requires that
25  examiners "shall issue . . . a proposed report, together with a recommended order."
26  Both statutes thus evince a purpose to increase the importance of the role of
27  examiners in the administrative process. High standards of public administration
28  counsel that we attribute to the Labor Board's examiners both due regard for the
29  responsibility which Congress imposes on them and the competence to discharge
30  it.

31                                      * * *

32  We do not require that the examiner's findings be given more weight than, in
33  reason and in the light of judicial experience, they deserve. The "substantial
34  evidence" standard is not modified in any way when the Board and its examiner
35  disagree. We intend only to recognize that evidence supporting a conclusion may
36  be less substantial when an impartial, experienced examiner who has observed the
37  witnesses and lived with the case has drawn conclusions different from the Board's
38  than when he has reached the same conclusion. The findings of the examiner are
39  to be considered along with the consistency and inherent probability of testimony.
40  The significance of his report, of course, depends largely on the importance of
41  credibility in the particular case. To give it this significance does not seem to us

materially more difficult than to heed the other factors which in sum determine whether evidence is "substantial."

\* \* \*

We therefore remand the cause to the Court of Appeals. On reconsideration of the record, it should accord the findings of the trial examiner the relevance that they reasonably command in answering the comprehensive question whether the evidence supporting the Board's order is substantial. But the court need not limit its reexamination of the case to the effect of that report on its decision. We leave it free to grant or deny enforcement as it thinks the principles expressed in this opinion dictate.

*Judgment vacated that cause remanded.*

MR. JUSTICE BLACK and MR. JUSTICE DOUGLAS concur with parts I and II of this opinion, but, as to part III, agree with the opinion of the court below, 179 F.2d 749, 753.

## National Labor Relations Board v. Universal Camera Corporation

190 F.2d 429 (1951)

July 13, 1951.

Before SWAN, Chief Judge, and FRANK and L. HAND, Circuit Judges.

L. HAND, Circuit Judge.

By a divided vote we decided this appeal last year upon the same record that is now before us, holding that the Board's order should be "enforced." The Supreme Court vacated our order and remanded the cause to us for reconsideration in two particulars. \* \* \* [T]he Court \* \* \* held that the [Taft-Hartley] amendment \* \* \* was intended to prescribe an attitude in courts of appeal less compliant towards the Board's findings than had been proper before; not only were they to look to the record as a whole, but they were to be less ready to yield their personal judgment on the facts; at least less ready than many at times had been. Presumably that does not extend to those issues on which the Board's specialized experience equips it with major premises inaccessible to judges, but as to matters of common knowledge we are to use a somewhat stiffer standard. Just where the Board's specialized experience ends it may no doubt be hard to say; but we are to find the boundary and beyond it to deem ourselves as competent as the Board to pass upon issues of fact. We hold that all the issues at bar are beyond the boundary and for that reason we cannot accept the Board's argument that we are not in as good a position as itself to decide what witnesses were more likely to be telling the truth in this labor dispute.

1 * * * Perhaps as good a way as any to state the change effected by the amendment
2 is to say that we are not to be reluctant to insist that an examiner's findings on
3 veracity must not be overruled without a very substantial preponderance in the
4 testimony as recorded.

5 In the case at bar the examiner came to the conclusion that Chairman's discharge
6 on January 24, 1944, was not because of his testimony two months before. He
7 believed that Politzer had told Weintraub, a day or two after Weintraub's quarrel
8 with Chairman at the end of December, that Chairman had said he was going to
9 resign; and, although he did not believe that Chairman had in fact said so, he found
10 that Politzer either thought he had, or told Weintraub that he had in the hope of
11 smoothing over their quarrel. We see nothing improbable in this story, nor can we
12 find any contradiction of it in Chairman's testimony that on January 11th Politzer
13 asked him if he were going to resign. * * *

14 * * * It is of course true that no one can be sure what may have actuated Kende at
15 least in part; nothing is more difficult than to disentangle the motives of another's
16 conduct—motives frequently unknown even to the actor himself. But for that very
17 reason those parts of the evidence which are lost in print become especially
18 pregnant, and the Board which had no access to them should have hesitated to
19 assume that the examiner was not right to act upon them. A story may indeed be
20 so unreasonable on its face that no plausibility in its telling will make it tenable,
21 but that is seldom true and certainly was not true here. In appeals from the Board
22 we have over and over again refused to upset findings which in cold type seemed
23 to us extremely doubtful just because we were aware that we could not know what
24 may have been the proper deciding factors. However limited should be the regard
25 which the Board must give to the findings of its examiner, we cannot escape the
26 conclusion that the record in the case at bar was such that the following finding of
27 the examiner should have turned the scale; "the undersigned is not persuaded that
28 Kende based his decision upon any animus against Chairman for testifying rather
29 than on an evaluation of Weintraub's request based upon the merits." * * * [U]pon
30 a reexamination of the record as a whole, and upon giving weight to the examiner's
31 findings—now in compliance with the Court's directions as we understand them—
32 we think that our first disposition of the appeal was wrong, and we hold that the
33 Board should have dismissed the complaint.

34 Order reversed; complaint to be dismissed.

35 FRANK, Circuit Judge, concurring.

36 Recognizing, as only a singularly stupid man would not, Judge HAND's superior
37 wisdom, intelligence and learning, I seldom disagree with him, and then with
38 serious misgivings. In this instance, I have overcome my misgivings because I
39 think that his modesty has moved him to interpret too sweepingly the Supreme
40 Court's criticism of our earlier opinion written by him. I read the Supreme Court's
41 opinion as saying that we had obeyed the new statute with but one exception: We
42 had wholly disregarded the examiner's finding which the Board rejected.

\* \* \*

Concerning our error in disregarding the examiner's findings, Judge HAND, as I understand him, interprets as follows the Supreme Court's ruling: The Board may never reject an examiner's finding if it rests on his evaluation of the credibility of oral testimony unless (1) that rejection results from the Board's rational use of the Board's specialized knowledge or (2) the examiner has been absurdly naive in believing a witness. This, I think, is somewhat more restrictive of the Board's powers than the Supreme Court suggested, for it said: "The responsibility for decision thus placed on the Board is wholly inconsistent with the notion that it has power to reverse an examiner's findings only when they are 'clearly erroneous.'"

I would also, by way of caution, add this qualification (to which, judging from his opinions elsewhere, I gather Judge HAND will not demur): An examiner's finding binds the Board only to the extent that it is a "testimonial inference," or "primary inference," i.e., an inference that a fact to which a witness orally testified is an actual fact because that witness so testified and because observation of the witness induces a belief in that testimony. The Board, however, is not bound by the examiner's "secondary inferences," or "derivative inferences," i.e., facts to which no witness orally testified but which the examiner inferred from facts orally testified by witnesses whom the examiner believed. The Board may reach its own "secondary inferences," and we must abide by them unless they are irrational; in that way, the Board differs from a trial judge (in a juryless case) who hears and sees the witnesses, for, although we are usually bound by his "testimonial inferences," we need not accept his "secondary inferences" even if rational, but, where other rational "secondary inferences" are possible, we may substitute our own. Since that is true, it is also true that we must not interfere when the Board adopts either (1) its examiner's "testimonial inferences" and they are not absurd, or (2) his rational "secondary inferences."

Except as noted above, I concur.

## D. Review of Agency Interpretations of Law

### 1. The Law B.C. (Before *Chevron*)

These days, conversations about how courts review agency interpretations of law all begin with the 1984 Supreme Court decision *NRDC v. Chevron*. Courts do not apply *Chevron* review to all agency constructions of law, but it is the starting point for the modern analysis—and, increasingly, the target of criticism. But while some have referred to the "*Chevron* Revolution," the opinion's author, Justice Stevens, did not regard the case as sweeping away all of the law that came before it. This unit explores how courts reviewed agencies' constructions of law prior to *Chevron*. A key question is just how much *Chevron* changed things as a practical matter.

1 While reading the *Gray v. Powell* decision, try not to get lost in the weeds of the
2 legal disputes, and focus instead on figuring out where the Court defers to the
3 agency, and where it does not. Can you account for the difference?

4

5 **Gray v. Powell**

6 314 U.S. 402 (1941)

7 December 1, 1941

8 MR. JUSTICE REED delivered the opinion of the Court.

9 Respondents, receivers of the Seaboard Air Line Railway Company, seek from the
10 Bituminous Coal Division of the Department of the Interior an exemption of
11 certain coal from the Bituminous Coal Code on the ground that they were both the
12 producer and consumer of the coal. If Seaboard is held to be a producer-consumer,
13 it is entitled to an exemption by virtue of § 4-II(l) and § 4-A. These sections,
14 together with others pertinent to the discussion, are set out in a note below.[1]

15 * * *

16 Seaboard, a coal-burning railroad, is a large consumer of bituminous coal. The
17 arrangements here in question are with three mines, but, as there are no significant
18 difference in the plans by which the coal is extracted, we shall describe the
19 contracts relating to one only, the William-Ann Mine, owned by the United
20 Thacker Coal Company and the Cole and Crane Real Estate Trust.

21 This was the earliest arrangement. * * * The first step was a lease of coal lands by
22 the Seaboard from the landowners which granted to Seaboard the right to mine
23 coal for fourteen months, with the privilege of yearly renewals, which originally
24 were not to run beyond June 30, 1939. Successive extensions have continued its
25 effect since that time. * * *

26 The second step in this arrangement was for the landowner lessors of the lease just
27 described to lease simultaneously to a contractor selected by Seaboard the mining
28 equipment on the demised premises, consisting of buildings, tipples, machinery
29 and other appurtenances necessary or convenient for extracting the coal. This
30 equipment was sufficient for reasonably economical mining. It was further

---

[1] Bituminous Coal Act of 1937, 50 Stat. 72, 15 U.S.C. § 828 *et seq.* (1940).

"SEC. 3. (a) There is hereby imposed upon the sale or other disposal of
bituminous coal produced within the United States when sold or otherwise
disposed of by the producer thereof an excise tax of 1 cent per ton of two
thousand pounds."

* * *

provided in the coal lease that the term and the renewal privileges of the equipment lease should be coextensive with those of the coal lease.

The final step was an operating contract between the contractor, Daniel H. Pritchard, referred to in the land lease as the lessee of the facilities for mining, and Seaboard for the extraction of the coal by the contractor or supplier and the delivery of it to Seaboard for consumption. This contract also was made simultaneously with the coal lease. It contained a provision requiring the contractor to obtain a lease of the mining equipment in accordance with that segment of the entire plan referred to in the preceding paragraph. For a flat per ton cost on a sliding scale dependent upon volume, the supplier agreed to mine the coal. * * *

The landowner, the contractor, and Seaboard, by this series of coordinated and synchronized contracts, caused the entire output of the mine to be delivered to Seaboard for its consumption at a fixed price, subject to variations for factors beyond the supplier contractor's control. The alternative cost-plus plan was not employed. Under the contractor's agreement, the contractor assumed all risks of operation, as heretofore explained, and all obligations of Seaboard to the landowner except the royalty payments. This made a fixed cost to Seaboard for coal of supplier's contract price plus the royalty per ton as rent. * * *

* * *

From the several arrangements, the Seaboard obtained about half of its annual requirements, estimated for 1936 at one million tons. There is no question as to the interstate character of the commerce involved. The coal is mined in Virginia and West Virginia, and consumed in a number of other South Atlantic states.

The Bituminous Coal Act of 1937 followed the invalidation of the Bituminous Coal Conservation Act of 1935 by *Carter v. Carter Coal Co.*, 298 U.S. 238 (1936), and the abandonment of the N.R.A. Code of Fair Competition after the decision in *Schechter Corp. v. United States,* 295 U.S. 495 (1935). These legislative enactments sought a solution of the economic difficulties of the soft coal industry which were bringing bankruptcy to operators and an even worse condition— unemployment—to the miners. Each time legislation was attempted, the conclusion was reached that price stabilization offered the best remedy. The industry found the same answer. This Court has determined that the present 1937 act is within the constitutional powers of Congress.

This purpose of stabilization of conditions through a fixed price scheme met a difficult problem in the captive coal mines. The 1935 act taxed the value of such coal at the mine. It defined captive coal as including "all coal produced at a mine for consumption by the producer or by a subsidiary or affiliate thereof." 49 Stat. 1008. As the coal consumed by a producer apparently was deemed by Congress, when considering the present act, not to offer the same disturbing effect to prices as non-code, open market coal, a method of exemption was provided. Congress, however, did not define exempt coal as it had captive coal in the 1935 act. While a

494

1  definition was inserted in the Senate, it was eliminated in the conference report.
2  As a result, the determination of exempt coal was left to the administrative body.

3  *Determination of Producer.* We are thus brought squarely to decide whether the
4  Director's finding that Seaboard is not the producer of this coal is to be sustained.
5  By § 4-A, note 1, the determination of this issue rests with the Director, subject to
6  the review, as obtained herein, by a Circuit Court of Appeals, provided by § 6(b).
7  * * * In a matter left specifically by Congress to the determination of an
8  administrative body, as the question of exemption was here by §§4-II(l) and 4-A,
9  the function of review placed upon the courts by § 6(b) is fully performed when
10  they determine that there has been a fair hearing, with notice and an opportunity
11  to present the circumstances and arguments to the decisive body, and an
12  application of the statute in a just and reasoned manner.

13  Such a determination as is here involved belongs to the usual administrative
14  routine. Congress, which could have legislated specifically as to the individual
15  exemptions from the code, found it more efficient to delegate that function to those
16  whose experience in a particular field gave promise of a better informed, more
17  equitable, adjustment of the conflicting interests of price stabilization, upon the
18  one hand, and producer consumption, upon the other. By thus committing the
19  execution of its policies to the specialized personnel of the Bituminous Coal
20  Division, the Congress followed a familiar practice. Of course, there is no difference
21  between the skill of employees in a division of a department and those in a board,
22  commission, or administration.

23  Where, as here, a determination has been left to an administrative body, this
24  delegation will be respected, and the administrative conclusion left untouched.
25  Certainly, a finding on Congressional reference that an admittedly constitutional
26  act is applicable to a particular situation does not require such further scrutiny.
27  Although we have here no dispute as to the evidentiary facts, that does not permit
28  a court to substitute its judgment for that of the Director. It is not the province of
29  a court to absorb the administrative functions to such an extent that the executive
30  or legislative agencies become mere factfinding bodies deprived of the advantages
31  of prompt and definite action.

32  Congress could not "define the whole gamut of remedies to effectuate these policies
33  in an infinite variety of specific situations." *Phelps Dodge Corp. v. Labor Board,*
34  313 U.S. 177, 194 (1941). Just as, in the *Adkins* case, the determination of the sweep
35  of the term "bituminous coal" was for this same administrative agency, so here
36  there must be left to it, subject to the basic prerequisites of lawful adjudication, the
37  determination of "producer." The separation of production and consumption is
38  complete when a buyer obtains supplies from a seller totally free from buyer
39  connection. Their identity is undoubted when the consumer extracts coal from its
40  own land with its own employees. Between the two extremes are the innumerable
41  variations that bring the arrangements closer to one pole or the other of the range
42  between exemption and inclusion. To determine upon which side of the median
43  line the particular instance falls calls for the expert experienced judgment of those

1  familiar with the industry. Unless we can say that a set of circumstances deemed
2  by the Commission to bring them within the concept "producer" is so unrelated to
3  the tasks entrusted by Congress to the Commission as in effect to deny a sensible
4  exercise of judgment, it is the Court's duty to leave the Commission's judgment
5  undisturbed.

6  * * *

7  *Code Coverage.* Seaboard contends that the coal here involved is not affected by
8  the code § 4-II because there is no sale or other transfer of the title to the coal by
9  the producer. As to this point, in Seaboard's view, since it, as lessee of the mineral
10  rights, is the owner of the coal when it is extracted and until it is consumed, and
11  therefore no title ever passes, it is immaterial whether or not it or its suppliers of
12  the coal are determined to be the producer. Support for the conclusion that there
13  must be a transfer of title to bring the coal under the Code, § 4-II, is found by
14  Seaboard in the preoccupation of Congress in sales, which attitude it feels is shown
15  by the continuous reference in the provisions of the Act to sales or other transfers
16  of title. Further support is drawn for the position by reference to Section 3(a),
17  where "disposal" is declared to include consumption by a producer or any transfer
18  of title other than by sale. Reliance is placed also on Section 3(b), which, by a tax
19  of 19 1/2 percent of the selling price, impels adherence to the code when coal
20  "which would be subject to the application of the conditions and provisions of the
21  code provided for in section 4, or of the provisions of section 4-A," is sold or
22  otherwise disposed of by the producer.

23  Had we held that Seaboard was the producer, the pertinency of this argument
24  would disappear, because Seaboard would be both producer and consumer, and
25  therefore this coal would be entitled to exemption under §§ 4-II(l) and 4-A. As we
26  determine otherwise, however, it is essential to examine the soundness of the
27  position asserted by Seaboard, to-wit, that coal produced by the instrumentalities
28  is not subject to the provisions of § 4-II for the reason that it is not sold not
29  otherwise disposed of by the producers. We conclude that coal extracted under the
30  circumstances of this case is within the scope of the code provisions of § 4-II.

31  Examination of the code discloses that minimum prices for code coal are fixed by
32  joint action of the district boards and the Director. § 4-I(a), II(a). Thereafter, no
33  code coal may be sold at prices less than the fixed minimum except at the risk of
34  severe penalties. Code coal is that produced by code members—*i.e.,* coal producers
35  who accept membership in the code. § 5(a). All producers of bituminous coal
36  within the statutory districts are eligible for membership, and therefore all coal
37  produced by any of these producers is potentially code coal. The code regulates the
38  coal, and not the producer. In order to force the eligible coal within the code, an
39  excise tax of 19 1/2% of the sale price is placed upon all bituminous coal "sold or
40  otherwise disposed of by the producer thereof which would be subject to the
41  application of the conditions and provisions of the code," with a blanket exemption
42  from this tax of sales or other disposal by code members.

1   The core of the Act is the requirement that coal be put under the code or pay the 19
2   1/2 percent exercise. We said in *Sunshine Coal Co. v. Adkins,* 310 U.S. 381, 392,
3   that the sanction tax applied to non-code members. Since they were not members,
4   it was there contended that their coal would not be subject to the code, but it was
5   explained in the *Adkins* case that the code was intended to apply to sales "in or
6   directly affecting interstate commerce in bituminous coal," § 4, 3rd paragraph, and
7   that non-code coal "would be" subject to the code when it was interstate coal or
8   coal affecting interstate commerce, and therefore subject to the regulatory power
9   of Congress. So here, the purpose of Congress which was to stabilize the industry
10  through price regulation, would be hampered by an interpretation that required a
11  transfer of title, in the technical sense, to bring a producer's coal, consumed by
12  another party, within the ambit of the coal code. We find no necessity to so
13  interpret the act. This conclusion seems to us in accord with the plain language of
14  § 3(a) and (b) providing for a tax on "other disposal" as well as sale. The definition
15  of disposal as including "consumption or use . . . by a producer, and any transfer
16  of title by the producer other than by sale" cannot be said to put a meaning on
17  disposal limited to the inclusion. It is true that § 4-II(e) speaks of a violation of the
18  price provisions by "sale or delivery or offer for sale of coal at a price below" the
19  minimum, without reference to "other disposition," the phrase generally used; but
20  the failure to include those words at that point does not, we think, justify an
21  interpretation that coal covered by the code may be disposed of otherwise than by
22  a transfer of title without penalty. We think the language of § 5(b) relating to
23  findings on orders punishing for violation of the code shows this to be true. It
24  reads, so far as pertinent, as follows:

25      ". . . the Commission shall specifically find . . . the quantity of coal sold or
26      otherwise disposed of in violation of the code . . . ; the sales price at the
27      mine or the market value at the mine if disposed of otherwise than by sale
28      at the mine, or if sold otherwise than through an arms' length transaction,
29      of the coal sold or otherwise disposed of by such code member in violation
30      of the code or regulations thereunder."

31  This conclusion is fortified by an examination of the tax section of the 1935 act,
32  from which the present § 3 is obviously derived. In the first, or 1935, act, captive
33  coal was taxed along with other coal. The tax was laid upon the "sale or other
34  disposal of all bituminous coal produced within the United States." It was "15 per
35  centum on the sale price at the mine, or in the case of captive coal the fair market
36  value of such coal at the mine." 49 Stat. 993, § 3. Evidently the draftsman thought
37  of the sale of free coal and of the "other disposal" of captive coal.

38  Finally, respondent contends that, if the act is construed to apply to the contractual
39  arrangements just considered, it is beyond the power of Congress under the
40  Commerce and Due Process Clauses of the Constitution. This is said to be so
41  because there is no power in Congress to regulate the price paid for the service of
42  mining coal or the consideration for mining rights, and to do so would violate the
43  Fifth Amendment. We are, in this review by certiorari, determining only the

497

question of whether the Seaboard is a producer under the act. Congressional power over that problem is beyond dispute.

*Reversed.*

MR. JUSTICE JACKSON took no part in the consideration or decision of the case.

MR. JUSTICE ROBERTS, dissenting.

I think the judgment should be affirmed. There are limits to which administrative officers and courts may appropriately go in reconstructing a statute so as to accomplish aims which the legislature might have had, but which the statute itself, and its legislative history, do not disclose. The present decision, it seems to me, passes that limitation.

\* \* \*

THE CHIEF JUSTICE and MR. JUSTICE BYRNES join in this opinion.


## National Labor Relations Board v. Hearst Publications, Inc.

322 U.S. 111 (1944)

April 24, 1944

MR. JUSTICE RUTLEDGE delivered the opinion of the Court.

These cases arise from the refusal of respondents, publishers of four Los Angeles daily newspapers, to bargain collectively with a union representing newsboys who distribute their papers on the streets of that city. Respondents' contention that they were not required to bargain because the newsboys are not their "employees" within the meaning of that term in the National Labor Relations Act, 29 U.S.C. § 152, presents the important question which we granted certiorari to resolve.

The proceedings before the National Labor Relations Board were begun with the filing of four petitions for investigation and certification by Los Angeles Newsboys Local Industrial Union No. 75. Hearings were held in a consolidated proceeding, after which the Board made findings of fact and concluded that the regular full-time newsboys selling each paper were employees within the Act and that questions affecting commerce concerning the representation of employees had arisen. It designated appropriate units and ordered elections. At these, the union was selected as their representative by majorities of the eligible newsboys. After the union was appropriately certified, the respondents refused to bargain with it. Thereupon, proceedings under § 10, 49 Stat. 453-455, 29 U.S.C. § 160, were instituted, a hearing was held, and respondents were found to have violated §§ 8(1) and (5) of the Act, 29 U.S.C. § 158(1), (5). They were ordered to cease and desist from such violations and to bargain collectively with the union upon request.

* * *

The newsboys work under varying terms and conditions. They may be "bootjackers," selling to the general public at places other than established corners, or they may sell at fixed "spots." They may sell only casually or part-time, or full-time; and they may be employed regularly and continuously or only temporarily. The units which the Board determined to be appropriate are composed of those who sell full-time at established spots. Those vendors, misnamed boys, are generally mature men, dependent upon the proceeds of their sales for their sustenance, and frequently supporters of families. Working thus as news vendors on a regular basis often for a number of years, they form a stable group with relatively little turnover, in contrast to schoolboys and others who sell as bootjackers, temporary and casual distributors.

Over-all circulation and distribution of the papers are under the general supervision of circulation managers. But, for purposes of street distribution, each paper has divided metropolitan Los Angeles into geographic districts. Each district is under the direct and close supervision of a district manager. His function in the mechanics of distribution is to supply the newsboys in his district with papers which he obtains from the publisher and to turn over to the publisher the receipts which he collects from their sales, either directly or with the assistance of "checkmen" or "main spot" boys. The latter, stationed at the important corners or "spots" in the district, are newsboys who, among other things, receive delivery of the papers, redistribute them to other newsboys stationed at less important corners, and collect receipts from their sales. For that service, which occupies a minor portion of their working day, the checkmen receive a small salary from the publisher. The bulk of their day, however, they spend in hawking papers at their "spots" like other full-time newsboys. A large part of the appropriate units selected by the Board for the News and the Herald are checkmen who, in that capacity, clearly are employees of those papers.

The newsboys' compensation consists in the difference between the prices at which they sell the papers and the prices they pay for them. The former are fixed by the publishers, and the latter are fixed either by the publishers or, in the case of the News, by the district manager. In practice, the newsboys receive their papers on credit. They pay for those sold either sometime during or after the close of their selling day, returning for credit all unsold papers. Lost or otherwise unreturned papers, however, must be paid for as though sold. Not only is the "profit" per paper thus effectively fixed by the publisher, but substantial control of the newsboys' total "take home" can be effected through the ability to designate their sales areas and the power to determine the number of papers allocated to each. While, as a practical matter, this power is not exercised fully, the newsboys' "right" to decide how many papers they will take is also not absolute. In practice, the Board found, they cannot determine the size of their established order without the cooperation of the district manager. And often the number of papers they must take is determined unilaterally by the district managers.

In addition to effectively fixing the compensation, respondents in a variety of ways prescribe, if not the minutiae of daily activities, at least the broad terms and conditions of work. This is accomplished largely through the supervisory efforts of the district managers, who serve as the nexus between the publishers and the newsboys. The district managers assign "spots" or corners to which the newsboys are expected to confine their selling activities. Transfers from one "spot" to another may be ordered by the district manager for reasons of discipline or efficiency or other cause. Transportation to the spots from the newspaper building is offered by each of respondents. Hours of work on the spots are determined not simply by the impersonal pressures of the market, but to a real extent by explicit instructions from the district managers. Adherence to the prescribed hours is observed closely by the district managers or other supervisory agents of the publishers. Sanctions, varying in severity from reprimand to dismissal, are visited on the tardy and the delinquent. By similar supervisory controls, minimum standards of diligence and good conduct while at work are sought to be enforced. However wide may be the latitude for individual initiative beyond those standards, district managers' instructions in what the publishers apparently regard as helpful sales technique are expected to be followed. Such varied items as the manner of displaying the paper, of emphasizing current features and headlines, and of placing advertising placards, or the advantages of soliciting customers at specific stores or in the traffic lanes are among the subjects of this instruction. Moreover, newsboys are furnished with sales equipment, such as racks, boxes and change aprons, and advertising placards by the publishers. In this pattern of employment, the Board found that the newsboys are an integral part of the publishers' distribution system and circulation organization. And the record discloses that the newsboys and checkmen feel they are employees of the papers, and respondents' supervisory employees, if not respondents themselves, regard them as such.

In addition to questioning the sufficiency of the evidence to sustain these findings, respondents point to a number of other attributes characterizing their relationship with the newsboys, and urge that, on the entire record, the latter cannot be considered their employees. They base this conclusion on the argument that, by common-law standards, the extent of their control and direction of the newsboys' working activities creates no more than an "independent contractor" relationship, and that common-law standards determine the "employee" relationship under the Act. They further urge that the Board's selection of a collective bargaining unit is neither appropriate nor supported by substantial evidence.

I

The principal question is whether the newsboys are "employees." Because Congress did not explicitly define the term, respondents say its meaning must be determined by reference to common-law standards. In their view, "common-law standards" are those the courts have applied in distinguishing between "employees" and "independent contractors" when working out various problems unrelated to the Wagner Act's purposes and provisions.

The argument assumes that there is some simple, uniform and easily applicable test which the courts have used, in dealing with such problems, to determine whether persons doing work for others fall in one class or the other. Unfortunately this is not true. Only by a long and tortuous history was the simple formulation worked out which has been stated most frequently as "the test" for deciding whether one who hires another is responsible in tort for his wrongdoing. But this formula has been by no means exclusively controlling in the solution of other problems. And its simplicity has been illusory because it is more largely simplicity of formulation than of application. Few problems in the law have given greater variety of application and conflict in results than the cases arising in the borderland between what is clearly an employer-employee relationship and what is clearly one of independent entrepreneurial dealing. This is true within the limited field of determining vicarious liability in tort. It becomes more so when the field is expanded to include all of the possible applications of the distinction.

It is hardly necessary to stress particular instances of these variations or to emphasize that they have arisen principally, first, in the struggle of the courts to work out common law liabilities where the legislature has given no guides for judgment, more recently also under statutes which have posed the same problem for solution in the light of the enactment's particular terms and purposes. It is enough to point out that, with reference to an identical problem, results may be contrary over a very considerable region of doubt in applying the distinction, depending upon the state or jurisdiction where the determination is made; and that, within a single jurisdiction, a person who, for instance, is held to be an "independent contractor" for the purpose of imposing vicarious liability in tort may be an "employee" for the purposes of particular legislation, such as unemployment compensation. In short, the assumed simplicity and uniformity, resulting from application of "common-law standards," does not exist.

* * *

Both the terms and the purposes of the statute, as well as the legislative history, show that Congress had in mind no such patchwork plan for securing freedom of employees' organization and of collective bargaining. The Wagner Act is federal legislation, administered by a national agency, intended to solve a national problem on a national scale. It is an Act, therefore, in reference to which it is not only proper, but necessary for us to assume, "in the absence of a plain indication to the contrary, that Congress . . . is not making the application of the federal act dependent on state law." *Jerome v. United States*, 318 U.S. 101, 104 (1943). Nothing in the statute's background, history, terms or purposes indicates its scope is to be limited by such varying local conceptions, either statutory or judicial, or that it is to be administered in accordance with whatever different standards the respective states may see fit to adopt for the disposition of unrelated, local problems. Consequently, so far as the meaning of "employee" in this statute is concerned, "the federal law must prevail no matter what name is given to the interest or right by state law." *Morgan v. Commissioner*, 309 U.S. 78, 81 (1940).

REVIEW OF AGENCY INTERPRETATIONS OF LAW

## II

* * *

To eliminate the causes of labor disputes and industrial strife, Congress thought it necessary to create a balance of forces in certain types of economic relationships. These do not embrace simply employment associations in which controversies could be limited to disputes over proper "physical conduct in the performance of the service." On the contrary, Congress recognized those economic relationships cannot be fitted neatly into the containers designated "employee" and "employer" which an earlier law had shaped for different purposes. Its Reports on the bill disclose clearly the understanding that "employers and employees not in proximate relationship may be drawn into common controversies by economic forces," and that the very disputes sought to be avoided might involve "employees [who] are at times brought into an economic relationship with employers who are not their employers." In this light, the broad language of the Act's definitions, which in terms reject conventional limitations on such conceptions as "employee," "employer," and "labor dispute," leaves no doubt that its applicability is to be determined broadly, in doubtful situations, by underlying economic facts, rather than technically and exclusively by previously established legal classifications.

Hence "technical concepts pertinent to an employer's legal responsibility to third persons for the acts of his servants" have been rejected in various applications of this Act both here and in other federal courts. There is no good reason for invoking them to restrict the scope of the term "employee" sought to be done in this case. That term, like other provisions, must be understood with reference to the purpose of the Act and the facts involved in the economic relationship. "Where all the conditions of the relation require protection, protection ought to be given."

It is not necessary in this case to make a completely definitive limitation around the term "employee." That task has been assigned primarily to the agency created by Congress to administer the Act. Determination of "where all the conditions of the relation require protection" involves inquiries for the Board charged with this duty. Everyday experience in the administration of the statute gives it familiarity with the circumstances and backgrounds of employment relationships in various industries, with the abilities and needs of the workers for self-organization and collective action, and with the adaptability of collective bargaining for the peaceful settlement of their disputes with their employers. The experience thus acquired must be brought frequently to bear on the question who is an employee under the Act. Resolving that question, like determining whether unfair labor practices have been committed, "belongs to the usual administrative routine" of the Board. *Gray v. Powell*, 314 U.S. 402, 411.

In making that body's determinations as to the facts in these matters conclusive, if supported by evidence, Congress entrusted to it primarily the decision whether the evidence establishes the material facts. Hence, in reviewing the Board's ultimate conclusions, it is not the court's function to substitute its own inferences of fact for

502

the Board's when the latter have support in the record. Undoubtedly questions of statutory interpretation, especially when arising in the first instance in judicial proceedings, are for the courts to resolve, giving appropriate weight to the judgment of those whose special duty is to administer the questioned statute. But where the question is one of specific application of a broad statutory term in a proceeding in which the agency administering the statute must determine it initially, the reviewing court's function is limited. Like the commissioner's determination under the Longshoremen's & Harbor Workers' Act, that a man is not a "member of a crew" (*South Chicago Coal & Dock Co. v. Bassett*, 309 U.S. 251) or that he was injured "in the course of his employment" (*Parker v. Motor Boat Sales, Inc.*, 314 U.S. 244) and the Federal Communications Commission's determination that one company is under the "control" of another (*Rochester Telephone Corp. v. United States*, 307 U.S. 125), the Board's determination that specified persons are "employees" under this Act is to be accepted if it has "warrant in the record" and a reasonable basis in law.

In this case the Board found that the designated newsboys work continuously and regularly, rely upon their earnings for the support of themselves and their families, and have their total wages influenced in large measure by the publishers who dictate their buying and selling prices, fix their markets, and control their supply of papers. Their hours of work and their efforts on the job are supervised and to some extent prescribed by the publishers or their agents. Much of their sales equipment and advertising materials is furnished by the publishers with the intention that it be used for the publisher's benefit. Stating that "the primary consideration in the determination of the applicability of the statutory definition is whether effectuation of the declared policy and purposes of the Act comprehends securing to the individual the rights guaranteed and protection afforded by the Act," the Board concluded that the newsboys are employees. The record sustains the Board's findings, and there is ample basis in the law for its conclusion.

\* \* \*

*Reversed.*

MR. JUSTICE REED concurs in the result. \* \* \*

MR. JUSTICE ROBERTS, dissenting.

I think the judgment of the Circuit Court of Appeals should be affirmed. The opinion of that court \* \* \* seems to me adequately to state the controlling facts and correctly to deal with the question of law presented for decision. I should not add anything were it not for certain arguments presented here and apparently accepted by the court.

I think it plain that newsboys are not "employees" of the respondents within the meaning and intent of the National Labor Relations Act. When Congress, in § 2(3), said: "The term 'employee' shall include any employee, . . ." it stated as clearly as language could do it that the provisions of the Act were to extend to those who, as

1 a result of decades of tradition which had become part of the common
2 understanding of our people, bear the named relationship. Clearly also, Congress
3 did not delegate to the National Labor Relations Board the function of defining the
4 relationship of employment so as to promote what the Board understood to be the
5 underlying purpose of the statute. The question who is an employee, so as to make
6 the statute applicable to him, is a question of the meaning of the Act, and therefore
7 is a judicial, and not an administrative, question.

8 * * *

9

## 10 Skidmore v. Swift & Co.

11 323 U.S. 134 (1944)

12 December 4, 1944

13 MR. JUSTICE JACKSON delivered the opinion of the Court.

14 Seven employees of the Swift and Company packing plant at Fort Worth, Texas,
15 brought an action under the Fair Labor Standards Act to recover overtime,
16 liquidated damages, and attorneys' fees totaling approximately $77,000. The
17 District Court rendered judgment denying this claim wholly, and the Circuit Court
18 of Appeals for the Fifth Circuit affirmed.

19 It is not denied that the daytime employment of these persons was working time
20 within the Act. Two were engaged in general fire-hall duties and maintenance of
21 firefighting equipment of the Swift plant. The others operated elevators or acted as
22 relief men in fire duties. They worked from 7:00 a.m. to 3:30 p.m., with a half-hour
23 lunch period, five days a week. They were paid weekly salaries.

24 Under their oral agreement of employment, however, petitioners undertook to stay
25 in the fire hall on the Company premises, or within hailing distance, three and a
26 half to four nights a week. This involved no task except to answer alarms, either
27 because of fire or because the sprinkler was set off for some other reason. No fires
28 occurred during the period in issue, the alarms were rare, and the time required
29 for their answer rarely exceeded an hour. For each alarm answered, the employees
30 were paid, in addition to their fixed compensation, an agreed amount, fifty cents
31 at first, and later sixty-four cents. The Company provided a brick fire hall equipped
32 with steam heat and air-conditioned rooms. It provided sleeping quarters, a pool
33 table, a domino table, and a radio. The men used their time in sleep or amusement
34 as they saw fit, except that they were required to stay in or close by the fire hall and
35 be ready to respond to alarms. It is stipulated that "they agreed to remain in the
36 fire hall and stay in it or within hailing distance, subject to call, in event of fire or
37 other casualty, but were not required to perform any specific tasks during these
38 periods of time, except in answering alarms." The trial court found the evidentiary
39 facts as stipulated; it made no findings of fact, as such, as to whether, under the
40 arrangement of the parties and the circumstances of this case, which, in some
504

1    respects, differ from those of the *Armour* case (323 U.S. 126), the fire-hall duty or
2    any part thereof constituted working time. It said, however, as a "conclusion of
3    law" that "the time plaintiffs spent in the fire hall subject to call to answer fire
4    alarms does not constitute hours worked for which overtime compensation is due
5    them under the Fair Labor Standards Act, as interpreted by the Administrator and
6    the Courts," and in its opinion observed, "of course, we know pursuing such
7    pleasurable occupations or performing such personal chores does not constitute
8    work." The Circuit Court of Appeals affirmed.

9    For reasons set forth in the *Armour* case, decided herewith, we hold that no
10    principle of law found either in the statute or in Court decisions precludes waiting
11    time from also being working time. We have not attempted to, and we cannot, lay
12    down a legal formula to resolve cases so varied in their facts as are the many
13    situations in which employment involves waiting time. Whether, in a concrete
14    case, such time falls within or without the Act is a question of fact to be resolved by
15    appropriate findings of the trial court. This involves scrutiny and construction of
16    the agreements between the particular parties, appraisal of their practical
17    construction of the working agreement by conduct, consideration of the nature of
18    the service, and its relation to the waiting time, and all of the surrounding
19    circumstances. Facts may show that the employee was engaged to wait, or they may
20    show that he waited to be engaged. His compensation may cover both waiting and
21    task, or only performance of the task itself. Living quarters may in some situations
22    be furnished as a facility of the task and in another as a part of its compensation.
23    The law does not impose an arrangement upon the parties. It imposes upon the
24    courts the task of finding what the arrangement was.

25    We do not minimize the difficulty of such an inquiry where the arrangements of
26    the parties have not contemplated the problem posed by the statute. But it does
27    not differ in nature or in the standards to guide judgment from that which
28    frequently confronts courts where they must find retrospectively the effect of
29    contracts as to matters which the parties failed to anticipate or explicitly to provide
30    for.

31    Congress did not utilize the services of an administrative agency to find facts and
32    to determine in the first instance whether particular cases fall within or without
33    the Act. Instead, it put this responsibility on the courts. *Kirschbaum v. Walling*,
34    316 U.S. 517, 523 (1942). But it did create the office of Administrator, impose upon
35    him a variety of duties, endow him with powers to inform himself of conditions in
36    industries and employments subject to the Act, and put on him the duties of
37    bringing injunction actions to restrain violations. Pursuit of his duties has
38    accumulated a considerable experience in the problems of ascertaining working
39    time in employments involving periods of inactivity and a knowledge of the
40    customs prevailing in reference to their solution. From these he is obliged to reach
41    conclusions as to conduct without the law, so that he should seek injunctions to
42    stop it, and that within the law, so that he has no call to interfere. He has set forth
43    his views of the application of the Act under different circumstances in an
44    interpretative bulletin and in informal rulings. They provide a practical guide to

employers and employees as to how the office representing the public interest in its enforcement will seek to apply it.

The Administrator thinks the problems presented by inactive duty require a flexible solution, rather than the all-in or all-out rules respectively urged by the parties in this case, and his Bulletin endeavors to suggest standards and examples to guide in particular situations. In some occupations, it says, periods of inactivity are not properly counted as working time even though the employee is subject to call. Examples are an operator of a small telephone exchange where the switchboard is in her home and she ordinarily gets several hours of uninterrupted sleep each night; or a pumper of a stripper well or watchman of a lumber camp during the off season, who may be on duty twenty-four hours a day but ordinarily "has a normal night's sleep, has ample time in which to eat his meals, and has a certain amount of time for relaxation and entirely private pursuits." Exclusion of all such hours the Administrator thinks may be justified. In general, the answer depends "upon the degree to which the employee is free to engage in personal activities during periods of idleness when he is subject to call and the number of consecutive hours that the employee is subject to call without being required to perform active work." "Hours worked are not limited to the time spent in active labor, but include time given by the employee to the employer. . . ."

The facts of this case do not fall within any of the specific examples given, but the conclusion of the Administrator, as expressed in the brief amicus curiae, is that the general tests which he has suggested point to the exclusion of sleeping and eating time of these employees from the work-week and the inclusion of all other on-call time: although the employees were required to remain on the premises during the entire time, the evidence shows that they were very rarely interrupted in their normal sleeping and eating time, and these are pursuits of a purely private nature which would presumably occupy the employees' time whether they were on duty or not, and which apparently could be pursued adequately and comfortably in the required circumstances; the rest of the time is different, because there is nothing in the record to suggest that, even though pleasurably spent, it was spent in the ways the men would have chosen had they been free to do so.

There is no statutory provision as to what, if any, deference courts should pay to the Administrator's conclusions. And while we have given them notice, we have had no occasion to try to prescribe their influence. The rulings of this Administrator are not reached as a result of hearing adversary proceedings in which he finds facts from evidence and reaches conclusions of law from findings of fact. They are not, of course, conclusive, even in the cases with which they directly deal, much less in those to which they apply only by analogy. They do not constitute an interpretation of the Act or a standard for judging factual situations which binds a district court's processes, as an authoritative pronouncement of a higher court might do. But the Administrator's policies are made in pursuance of official duty, based upon more specialized experience and broader investigations and information than is likely to come to a judge in a particular case. They do determine the policy which will guide applications for enforcement by injunction on behalf of the Government. Good administration of the Act and good judicial administration alike require that the standards of public enforcement and those for determining private rights shall be at variance only where justified by very good reasons. The fact that the Administrator's policies and standards are not reached by trial in adversary form does not mean that they are not entitled to respect. This Court has long given considerable, and in some cases decisive, weight to Treasury Decisions and to interpretative regulations of the Treasury and of other bodies that were not of adversary origin.

We consider that the rulings, interpretations, and opinions of the Administrator under this Act, while not controlling upon the courts by reason of their authority, do constitute a body of experience and informed judgment to which courts and litigants may properly resort for guidance. The weight of such a judgment in a particular case will depend upon the thoroughness evident in its consideration, the validity of its reasoning, its consistency with earlier and later pronouncements, and all those factors which give it power to persuade, if lacking power to control.

The courts in the *Armour* case weighed the evidence in the particular case in the light of the Administrator's rulings and reached a result consistent therewith. The evidence in this case, in some respects, such as the understanding as to separate compensation for answering alarms, is different. Each case must stand on its own facts. But, in this case, although the District Court referred to the Administrator's Bulletin, its evaluation and inquiry were apparently restricted by its notion that waiting time may not be work, an understanding of the law which we hold to be erroneous. Accordingly, the judgment is reversed and the cause remanded for further proceedings consistent herewith.

*Reversed.*

## 2. Chevron and Its Domain

As already noted, *Chevron* is central to modern doctrine governing judicial review of agencies' statutory interpretations. An initial question to consider is: what makes *Chevron* such a big deal?

*Mead* addresses the question of when courts should apply *Chevron*. What is *Mead*'s central holding? How much guidance does *Mead* actually give courts?

## Chevron U.S.A., Inc. v. Natural Resources Defense Council, Inc.

467 U.S. 837 (1984)

June 25, 1984

JUSTICE STEVENS delivered the opinion of the Court.

1    In the Clean Air Act Amendments of 1977, Congress enacted certain requirements
2    applicable to States that had not achieved the national air quality standards
3    established by the Environmental Protection Agency (EPA) pursuant to earlier
4    legislation. The amended Clean Air Act required these "nonattainment" States to
5    establish a permit program regulating "new or modified major stationary sources"
6    of air pollution. Generally, a permit may not be issued for a new or modified major
7    stationary source unless several stringent conditions are met. The EPA regulation
8    promulgated to implement this permit requirement allows a State to adopt a
9    plantwide definition of the term "stationary source." Under this definition, an
10   existing plant that contains several pollution-emitting devices may install or
11   modify one piece of equipment without meeting the permit conditions if the
12   alteration will not increase the total emissions from the plant. The question
13   presented by these cases is whether EPA's decision to allow States to treat all of the
14   pollution-emitting devices within the same industrial grouping as though they
15   were encased within a single "bubble" is based on a reasonable construction of the
16   statutory term "stationary source."

17                                        I

18   The EPA regulations containing the plantwide definition of the term stationary
19   source were promulgated on October 14, 1981. Respondents filed a timely petition
20   for review in the United States Court of Appeals for the District of Columbia Circuit
21   pursuant to 42 U.S.C. § 7607(b)(1). The Court of Appeals set aside the regulations.

22   The court observed that the relevant part of the amended Clean Air Act "does not
23   explicitly define what Congress envisioned as a 'stationary source,' to which the
24   permit program . . . should apply," and further stated that the precise issue was not
25   "squarely addressed in the legislative history." In light of its conclusion that the
26   legislative history bearing on the question was "at best contradictory," it reasoned
27   that "the purposes of the nonattainment program should guide our decision here."
28   Based on two of its precedents concerning the applicability of the bubble concept
29   to certain Clean Air Act programs, the court stated that the bubble concept was
30   "mandatory" in programs designed merely to maintain existing air quality, but
31   held that it was "inappropriate" in programs enacted to improve air quality. Since
32   the purpose of the permit program—its "*raison d'etre*," in the court's view—was to
33   improve air quality, the court held that the bubble concept was inapplicable in
34   these cases under its prior precedents. It therefore set aside the regulations
35   embodying the bubble concept as contrary to law. We granted certiorari to review
36   that judgment, and we now reverse.

37                                       * * *

38                                        II

39   When a court reviews an agency's construction of the statute which it administers,
40   it is confronted with two questions. First, always, is the question whether Congress
41   has directly spoken to the precise question at issue. If the intent of Congress is
42   clear, that is the end of the matter; for the court, as well as the agency, must give

1     effect to the unambiguously expressed intent of Congress.[21] If, however, the court
2     determines Congress has not directly addressed the precise question at issue, the
3     court does not simply impose its own construction on the statute, as would be
4     necessary in the absence of an administrative interpretation. Rather, if the statute
5     is silent or ambiguous with respect to the specific issue, the question for the court
6     is whether the agency's answer is based on a permissible construction of the
7     statute.

8     "The power of an administrative agency to administer a congressionally created . . .
9     program necessarily requires the formulation of policy and the making of rules to
10    fill any gap left, implicitly or explicitly, by Congress." *Morton v. Ruiz*, 415 U.S. 199,
11    231 (1974). If Congress has explicitly left a gap for the agency to fill, there is an
12    express delegation of authority to the agency to elucidate a specific provision of the
13    statute by regulation. Such legislative regulations are given controlling weight
14    unless they are arbitrary, capricious, or manifestly contrary to the statute.
15    Sometimes the legislative delegation to an agency on a particular question is
16    implicit, rather than explicit. In such a case, a court may not substitute its own
17    construction of a statutory provision for a reasonable interpretation made by the
18    administrator of an agency.

19    We have long recognized that considerable weight should be accorded to an
20    executive department's construction of a statutory scheme it is entrusted to
21    administer, and the principle of deference to administrative interpretations

22        "has been consistently followed by this Court whenever decision as to the
23        meaning or reach of a statute has involved reconciling conflicting policies,
24        and a full understanding of the force of the statutory policy in the given
25        situation has depended upon more than ordinary knowledge respecting the
26        matters subjected to agency regulations."

27        ". . . If this choice represents a reasonable accommodation of conflicting
28        policies that were committed to the agency's care by the statute, we should
29        not disturb it unless it appears from the statute or its legislative history that
30        the accommodation is not one that Congress would have sanctioned."
31        *United States v. Shimer*, 367 U.S. 374, 382, 383 (1961).

32    In light of these well-settled principles, it is clear that the Court of Appeals
33    misconceived the nature of its role in reviewing the regulations at issue. Once it
34    determined, after its own examination of the legislation, that Congress did not
35    actually have an intent regarding the applicability of the bubble concept to the

---

[21] The judiciary is the final authority on issues of statutory construction, and must reject administrative constructions which are contrary to clear congressional intent. If a court, employing traditional tools of statutory construction, ascertains that Congress had an intention on the precise question at issue, that intention is the law, and must be given effect.

permit program, the question before it was not whether, in its view, the concept is "inappropriate" in the general context of a program designed to improve air quality, but whether the Administrator's view that it is appropriate in the context of this particular program is a reasonable one. Based on the examination of the legislation and its history which follows, we agree with the Court of Appeals that Congress did not have a specific intention on the applicability of the bubble concept in these cases, and conclude that the EPA's use of that concept here is a reasonable policy choice for the agency to make.

\* \* \*

## IV

The Clean Air Act Amendments of 1977 are a lengthy, detailed, technical, complex, and comprehensive response to a major social issue. A small portion of the statute expressly deals with nonattainment areas. The focal point of this controversy is one phrase in that portion of the Amendments.

\* \* \*

Most significantly for our purposes, the statute provided that each plan shall:

> "(6) require permits for the construction and operation of new or modified major stationary sources in accordance with section 173. . . ." *Federal Maritime Com. v. Seatrain Lines, Inc.*, 411 U.S. 726, 747 (1973).

Before issuing a permit, § 173 requires (1) the state agency to determine that there will be sufficient emissions reductions in the region to offset the emissions from the new source and also to allow for reasonable further progress toward attainment, or that the increased emissions will not exceed an allowance for growth established pursuant to § 172(b)(5); (2) the applicant to certify that his other sources in the State are in compliance with the SIP, (3) the agency to determine that the applicable SIP is otherwise being implemented, and (4) the proposed source to comply with the lowest achievable emission rate (LAER).

The 1977 Amendments contain no specific reference to the "bubble concept." Nor do they contain a specific definition of the term "stationary source," though they did not disturb the definition of "stationary source" contained in § 111(a)(3), applicable by the terms of the Act to the NSPS program. Section 302(j), however, defines the term "major stationary source" as follows:

> "(j) Except as otherwise expressly provided, the terms 'major stationary source' and 'major emitting facility' mean any stationary facility or source of air pollutants which directly emits, or has the potential to emit, one hundred tons per year or more of any air pollutant (including any major emitting facility or source of fugitive emissions of any such pollutant, as determined by rule by the Administrator)."

510

V

The legislative history of the portion of the 1977 Amendments dealing with nonattainment areas does not contain any specific comment on the "bubble concept" or the question whether a plantwide definition of a stationary source is permissible under the permit program. It does, however, plainly disclose that in the permit program Congress sought to accommodate the conflict between the economic interest in permitting capital improvements to continue and the environmental interest in improving air quality. Indeed, the House Committee Report identified the economic interest as one of the "two main purposes" of this section of the bill. * * *

* * *

VII

In this Court, respondents expressly reject the basic rationale of the Court of Appeals' decision. That court viewed the statutory definition of the term "source" as sufficiently flexible to cover either a plantwide definition, a narrower definition covering each unit within a plant, or a dual definition that could apply to both the entire "bubble" and its components. It interpreted the policies of the statute, however, to mandate the plantwide definition in programs designed to maintain clean air and to forbid it in programs designed to improve air quality. Respondents place a fundamentally different construction on the statute. They contend that the text of the Act requires the EPA to use a dual definition—if either a component of a plant, or the plant as a whole, emits over 100 tons of pollutant, it is a major stationary source. They thus contend that the EPA rules adopted in 1980, insofar as they apply to the maintenance of the quality of clean air, as well as the 1981 rules which apply to nonattainment areas, violate the statute.

### Statutory Language

The definition of the term "stationary source" in § 111(a)(3) refers to "any building, structure, facility, or installation" which emits air pollution. This definition is applicable only to the NSPS program by the express terms of the statute; the text of the statute does not make this definition applicable to the permit program. Petitioners therefore maintain that there is no statutory language even relevant to ascertaining the meaning of stationary source in the permit program aside from § 302(j), which defines the term "major stationary source." We disagree with petitioners on this point.

The definition in § 302(j) tells us what the word "major" means—a source must emit at least 100 tons of pollution to qualify—but it sheds virtually no light on the meaning of the term "stationary source." It does equate a source with a facility—a "major emitting facility" and a "major stationary source" are synonymous under § 302(j). The ordinary meaning of the term "facility" is some collection of integrated elements which has been designed and constructed to achieve some purpose. Moreover, it is certainly no affront to common English usage to take a reference to

1    a major facility or a major source to connote an entire plant, as opposed to its
2    constituent parts. Basically, however, the language of § 302(j) simply does not
3    compel any given interpretation of the term "source."

4    Respondents recognize that, and hence point to § 111(a)(3). Although the definition
5    in that section is not literally applicable to the permit program, it sheds as much
6    light on the meaning of the word "source" as anything in the statute. * * * As
7    respondents point out, use of the words "building, structure, facility, or
8    installation," as the definition of source, could be read to impose the permit
9    conditions on an individual building that is a part of a plant. A "word may have a
10    character of its own not to be submerged by its association." *Russell Motor Car Co.*
11    *v. United States*, 261 U.S. 514, 519 (1923). On the other hand, the meaning of a
12    word must be ascertained in the context of achieving particular objectives, and the
13    words associated with it may indicate that the true meaning of the series is to
14    convey a common idea. The language may reasonably be interpreted to impose the
15    requirement on any discrete, but integrated, operation which pollutes. This gives
16    meaning to all of the terms—a single building, not part of a larger operation, would
17    be covered if it emits more than 100 tons of pollution, as would any facility,
18    structure, or installation. Indeed, the language itself implies a "bubble concept" of
19    sorts: each enumerated item would seem to be treated as if it were encased in a
20    bubble. While respondents insist that each of these terms must be given a discrete
21    meaning, they also argue that § 111(a)(3) defines "source" as that term is used in §
22    302(j). The latter section, however, equates a source with a facility, whereas the
23    former defines "source" as a facility, among other items.

24    We are not persuaded that parsing of general terms in the text of the statute will
25    reveal an actual intent of Congress. We know full well that this language is not
26    dispositive; the terms are overlapping, and the language is not precisely directed
27    to the question of the applicability of a given term in the context of a larger
28    operation. To the extent any congressional "intent" can be discerned from this
29    language, it would appear that the listing of overlapping, illustrative terms was
30    intended to enlarge, rather than to confine, the scope of the agency's power to
31    regulate particular sources in order to effectuate the policies of the Act.

32    *Legislative History*

33    In addition, respondents argue that the legislative history and policies of the Act
34    foreclose the plantwide definition, and that the EPA's interpretation is not entitled
35    to deference, because it represents a sharp break with prior interpretations of the
36    Act.

37    Based on our examination of the legislative history, we agree with the Court of
38    Appeals that it is unilluminating. The general remarks pointed to by respondents
39    "were obviously not made with this narrow issue in mind, and they cannot be said
40    to demonstrate a Congressional desire. . . ." *Jewell Ridge Coal Corp. v. Mine*
41    *Workers*, 325 U.S. 161, 168, 169 (1945). * * *

42    * * *

1   Our review of the EPA's varying interpretations of the word "source"—both before
2   and after the 1977 Amendments—convinces us that the agency primarily
3   responsible for administering this important legislation has consistently
4   interpreted it flexibly—not in a sterile textual vacuum, but in the context of
5   implementing policy decisions in a technical and complex arena. The fact that the
6   agency has from time to time changed its interpretation of the term "source" does
7   not, as respondents argue, lead us to conclude that no deference should be
8   accorded the agency's interpretation of the statute. An initial agency interpretation
9   is not instantly carved in stone. On the contrary, the agency, to engage in informed
10  rulemaking, must consider varying interpretations and the wisdom of its policy on
11  a continuing basis. Moreover, the fact that the agency has adopted different
12  definitions in different contexts adds force to the argument that the definition itself
13  is flexible, particularly since Congress has never indicated any disapproval of a
14  flexible reading of the statute.

15  Significantly, it was not the agency in 1980, but rather the Court of Appeals that
16  read the statute inflexibly to command a plantwide definition for programs
17  designed to maintain clean air and to forbid such a definition for programs
18  designed to improve air quality. The distinction the court drew may well be a
19  sensible one, but our labored review of the problem has surely disclosed that it is
20  not a distinction that Congress ever articulated itself, or one that the EPA found in
21  the statute before the courts began to review the legislative work product. We
22  conclude that it was the Court of Appeals, rather than Congress or any of the
23  decisionmakers who are authorized by Congress to administer this legislation, that
24  was primarily responsible for the 1980 position taken by the agency.

25                                  *Policy*

26  The arguments over policy that are advanced in the parties' briefs create the
27  impression that respondents are now waging in a judicial forum a specific policy
28  battle which they ultimately lost in the agency and in the 32 jurisdictions opting
29  for the "bubble concept," but one which was never waged in the Congress. Such
30  policy arguments are more properly addressed to legislators or administrators, not
31  to judges.

32  In these cases, the Administrator's interpretation represents a reasonable
33  accommodation of manifestly competing interests, and is entitled to deference: the
34  regulatory scheme is technical and complex, the agency considered the matter in a
35  detailed and reasoned fashion, and the decision involves reconciling conflicting
36  policies. Congress intended to accommodate both interests, but did not do so itself
37  on the level of specificity presented by these cases. Perhaps that body consciously
38  desired the Administrator to strike the balance at this level, thinking that those
39  with great expertise and charged with responsibility for administering the
40  provision would be in a better position to do so; perhaps it simply did not consider
41  the question at this level; and perhaps Congress was unable to forge a coalition on
42  either side of the question, and those on each side decided to take their chances

with the scheme devised by the agency. For judicial purposes, it matters not which of these things occurred.

Judges are not experts in the field, and are not part of either political branch of the Government. Courts must, in some cases, reconcile competing political interests, but not on the basis of the judges' personal policy preferences. In contrast, an agency to which Congress has delegated policymaking responsibilities may, within the limits of that delegation, properly rely upon the incumbent administration's views of wise policy to inform its judgments. While agencies are not directly accountable to the people, the Chief Executive is, and it is entirely appropriate for this political branch of the Government to make such policy choices—resolving the competing interests which Congress itself either inadvertently did not resolve, or intentionally left to be resolved by the agency charged with the administration of the statute in light of everyday realities.

When a challenge to an agency construction of a statutory provision, fairly conceptualized, really centers on the wisdom of the agency's policy, rather than whether it is a reasonable choice within a gap left open by Congress, the challenge must fail. In such a case, federal judges—who have no constituency—have a duty to respect legitimate policy choices made by those who do. The responsibilities for assessing the wisdom of such policy choices and resolving the struggle between competing views of the public interest are not judicial ones: "Our Constitution vests such responsibilities in the political branches." *TVA v. Hill*, 437 U.S. 153, 195 (1978).

We hold that the EPA's definition of the term "source" is a permissible construction of the statute which seeks to accommodate progress in reducing air pollution with economic growth. "The Regulations which the Administrator has adopted provide what the agency could allowably view as . . . [an] effective reconciliation of these twofold ends. . . ." *United States v. Shimer*, 367 U.S. 374, 383 (1961).

The judgment of the Court of Appeals is reversed.

*It is so ordered.*

JUSTICE MARSHALL and JUSTICE REHNQUIST took no part in the consideration or decision of these cases.

JUSTICE O'CONNOR took no part in the decision of these cases.

## United States v. Mead Corp.

533 U.S. 218 (2001)

June 18, 2001

JUSTICE SOUTER delivered the opinion of the Court.

1 The question is whether a tariff classification ruling by the United States Customs
2 Service deserves judicial deference. The Federal Circuit rejected Customs'
3 invocation of *Chevron U.S.A. Inc. v. Natural Resources Defense Council, Inc.*, 467
4 U.S. 837 (1984), in support of such a ruling, to which it gave no deference. We agree
5 that a tariff classification has no claim to judicial deference under *Chevron*, there
6 being no indication that Congress intended such a ruling to carry the force of law,
7 but we hold that under *Skidmore v. Swift & Co.*, 323 U.S. 134 (1944), the ruling is
8 eligible to claim respect according to its persuasiveness.

9 ## I

10 ## A

11 Imports are taxed under the Harmonized Tariff Schedule of the United States
12 (HTSUS), 19 U.S.C. § 1202. Title 19 U.S.C. § 1500(b) provides that Customs "shall,
13 under rules and regulations prescribed by the Secretary [of the Treasury,] . . . fix
14 the final classification and rate of duty applicable to . . . merchandise" under the
15 HTSDS. Section 1502(a) provides that

16 "[t]he Secretary of the Treasury shall establish and promulgate such rules
17 and regulations not inconsistent with the law (including regulations
18 establishing procedures for the issuance of binding rulings prior to the
19 entry of the merchandise concerned), and may disseminate such
20 information as may be necessary to secure a just, impartial, and uniform
21 appraisement of imported merchandise and the classification and
22 assessment of duties thereon at the various ports of entry."[1]

23 The Secretary provides for tariff rulings before the entry of goods by regulations
24 authorizing "ruling letters" setting tariff classifications for particular imports. 19
25 CFR § 177.8 (2000). A ruling letter

26 "represents the official position of the Customs Service with respect to the
27 particular transaction or issue described therein and is binding on all
28 Customs Service personnel in accordance with the provisions of this section
29 until modified or revoked. In the absence of a change of practice or other
30 modification or revocation which affects the principle of the ruling set forth
31 in the ruling letter, that principle may be cited as authority in the
32 disposition of transactions involving the same circumstances." § 177.9(a).

33 After the transaction that gives it birth, a ruling letter is to "be applied only with
34 respect to transactions involving articles identical to the sample submitted with
35 the ruling request or to articles whose description is identical to the description set

---

[1] The statutory term "ruling" is defined by regulation as "a written statement . . .
that interprets and applies the provisions of the Customs and related laws to a
specific set of facts." 19 CFR § 177.1(d)(1) (2000).

forth in the ruling letter." § 177.9(b)(2). As a general matter, such a letter is "subject to modification or revocation without notice to any person, except the person to whom the letter was addressed," § 177.9(c), and the regulations consequently provide that "no other person should rely on the ruling letter or assume that the principles of that ruling will be applied in connection with any transaction other than the one described in the letter," *ibid.* Since ruling letters respond to transactions of the moment, they are not subject to notice and comment before being issued, may be published but need only be made "available for public inspection," 19 U.S.C. § 1625(a), and, at the time this action arose, could be modified without notice and comment under most circumstances, 19 CFR § 177.10(c) (2000). A broader notice-and-comment requirement for modification of prior rulings was added by statute in 1993, and took effect after this case arose.

Any of the 46 port-of-entry Customs offices may issue ruling letters, and so may the Customs Headquarters Office, in providing "advice or guidance as to the interpretation or proper application of the Customs and related laws with respect to a specific Customs transaction [which] may be requested by Customs Service field offices . . . at any time, whether the transaction is prospective, current, or completed," 19 CFR § 177.11(a) (2000). Most ruling letters contain little or no reasoning, but simply describe goods and state the appropriate category and tariff. A few letters, like the Headquarters ruling at issue here, set out a rationale in some detail.

B

Respondent, the Mead Corporation, imports "day planners," three-ring binders with pages having room for notes of daily schedules and phone numbers and addresses, together with a calendar and suchlike. The tariff schedule on point falls under the HTSUS heading for "[r]egisters, account books, notebooks, order books, receipt books, letter pads, memorandum pads, diaries and similar articles," HTSUS subheading 4820.10, which comprises two subcategories. Items in the first, "[d]iaries, notebooks and address books, bound; memorandum pads, letter pads and similar articles," were subject to a tariff of 4.0% at the time in controversy. Objects in the second, covering "[o]ther" items, were free of duty.

Between 1989 and 1993, Customs repeatedly treated day planners under the "other" HTSUS subheading. In January 1993, however, Customs changed its position, and issued a Headquarters ruling letter classifying Mead's day planners as "Diaries . . . , bound" subject to tariff under subheading 4820.10.20. That letter was short on explanation, but after Mead's protest, Customs Headquarters issued a new letter, carefully reasoned but never published, reaching the same conclusion. This letter considered two definitions of "diary" from the Oxford English Dictionary, the first covering a daily journal of the past day's events, the second a book including "'printed dates for daily memoranda and jottings; also . . . calendars . . . .'" Customs concluded that "diary" was not confined to the first, in part because the broader definition reflects commercial usage and hence the "commercial identity of these items in the marketplace." As for the definition of "bound,"

1  Customs concluded that HTSUS was not referring to "bookbinding," but to a less
2  exact sort of fastening described in the Harmonized Commodity Description and
3  Coding System Explanatory Notes to Heading 4820, which spoke of binding by
4  "'reinforcements or fittings of metal, plastics, etc.'"

5  Customs rejected Mead's further protest of the second Headquarters ruling letter,
6  and Mead filed suit in the Court of International Trade (CIT). The CIT granted the
7  Government's motion for summary judgment, adopting Customs' reasoning
8  without saying anything about deference.

9  Mead then went to the United States Court of Appeals for the Federal Circuit.
10  While the case was pending there this Court decided *United States v. Haggar*
11  *Apparel Co.*, 526 U.S. 380 (1999), holding that Customs regulations receive the
12  deference described in *Chevron*. The appeals court requested briefing on the
13  impact of *Haggar*, and the Government argued that classification rulings, like
14  Customs regulations, deserve *Chevron* deference.

15  The Federal Circuit, however, reversed the CIT and held that Customs
16  classification rulings should not get *Chevron* deference, owing to differences from
17  the regulations at issue in *Haggar*. Rulings are not preceded by notice and
18  comment as under the Administrative Procedure Act (APA), 5 U.S.C. § 553, they
19  "do not carry the force of law and are not, like regulations, intended to clarify the
20  rights and obligations of importers beyond the specific case under review." The
21  appeals court thought classification rulings had a weaker *Chevron* claim even than
22  Internal Revenue Service interpretive rulings, to which that court gives no
23  deference; unlike rulings by the IRS, Customs rulings issue from many locations
24  and need not be published.

25  The Court of Appeals accordingly gave no deference at all to the ruling classifying
26  the Mead day planners and rejected the agency's reasoning as to both "diary" and
27  "bound." * * *

28  We granted certiorari in order to consider the limits of *Chevron* deference owed to
29  administrative practice in applying a statute. We hold that administrative
30  implementation of a particular statutory provision qualifies for *Chevron* deference
31  when it appears that Congress delegated authority to the agency generally to make
32  rules carrying the force of law, and that the agency interpretation claiming
33  deference was promulgated in the exercise of that authority. Delegation of such
34  authority may be shown in a variety of ways, as by an agency's power to engage in
35  adjudication or notice-and-comment rulemaking, or by some other indication of a
36  comparable congressional intent. The Customs ruling at issue here fails to qualify,
37  although the possibility that it deserves some deference under *Skidmore* leads us
38  to vacate and remand.

39                                    II

40                                    A

1  When Congress has "explicitly left a gap for an agency to fill, there is an express
2  delegation of authority to the agency to elucidate a specific provision of the statute
3  by regulation," *Chevron*, 467 U.S., at 843844, and any ensuing regulation is
4  binding in the courts unless procedurally defective, arbitrary or capricious in
5  substance, or manifestly contrary to the statute. But whether or not they enjoy any
6  express delegation of authority on a particular question, agencies charged with
7  applying a statute necessarily make all sorts of interpretive choices, and while not
8  all of those choices bind judges to follow them, they certainly may influence courts
9  facing questions the agencies have already answered. "The well-reasoned views of
10 the agencies implementing a statute 'constitute a body of experience and informed
11 judgment to which courts and litigants may properly resort for guidance,'"
12 *Bragdon v. Abbott*, 524 U.S. 624, 642 (1998) (quoting *Skidmore*, 323 U.S., at 139-
13 140), and "[w]e have long recognized that considerable weight should be accorded
14 to an executive department's construction of a statutory scheme it is entrusted to
15 administer . . . . " *Chevron, supra*, at 844 (footnote omitted). The fair measure of
16 deference to an agency administering its own statute has been understood to vary
17 with circumstances, and courts have looked to the degree of the agency's care, its
18 consistency, formality, and relative expertness, and to the persuasiveness of the
19 agency's position. The approach has produced a spectrum of judicial responses,
20 from great respect at one end to near indifference at the other. JUSTICE JACKSON
21 summed things up in *Skidmore v. Swift & Co.*:

22    "The weight [accorded to an administrative] judgment in a particular case
23    will depend upon the thoroughness evident in its consideration, the validity
24    of its reasoning, its consistency with earlier and later pronouncements, and
25    all those factors which give it power to persuade, if lacking power to
26    control." 323 U.S., at 140.

27 Since 1984, we have identified a category of interpretive choices distinguished by
28 an additional reason for judicial deference. This Court in *Chevron* recognized that
29 Congress not only engages in express delegation of specific interpretive authority,
30 but that "[s]ometimes the legislative delegation to an agency on a particular
31 question is implicit." 467 U.S., at 844. Congress, that is, may not have expressly
32 delegated authority or responsibility to implement a particular provision or fill a
33 particular gap. Yet it can still be apparent from the agency's generally conferred
34 authority and other statutory circumstances that Congress would expect the
35 agency to be able to speak with the force of law when it addresses ambiguity in the
36 statute or fills a space in the enacted law, even one about which "Congress did not
37 actually have an intent" as to a particular result. *Id.*, at 845. When circumstances
38 implying such an expectation exist, a reviewing court has no business rejecting an
39 agency's exercise of its generally conferred authority to resolve a particular
40 statutory ambiguity simply because the agency's chosen resolution seems unwise,
41 but is obliged to accept the agency's position if Congress has not previously spoken
42 to the point at issue and the agency's interpretation is reasonable.

We have recognized a very good indicator of delegation meriting *Chevron* treatment in express congressional authorizations to engage in the process of rulemaking or adjudication that produces regulations or rulings for which deference is claimed. It is fair to assume generally that Congress contemplates administrative action with the effect of law when it provides for a relatively formal administrative procedure tending to foster the fairness and deliberation that should underlie a pronouncement of such force. Thus, the overwhelming number of our cases applying *Chevron* deference have reviewed the fruits of notice-and-comment rulemaking or formal adjudication. That said, and as significant as notice-and-comment is in pointing to *Chevron* authority, the want of that procedure here does not decide the case, for we have sometimes found reasons for *Chevron* deference even when no such administrative formality was required and none was afforded. The fact that the tariff classification here was not a product of such formal process does not alone, therefore, bar the application of *Chevron*.

There are, nonetheless, ample reasons to deny *Chevron* deference here. The authorization for classification rulings, and Customs' practice in making them, present a case far removed not only from notice-and-comment process, but from any other circumstances reasonably suggesting that Congress ever thought of classification rulings as deserving the deference claimed for them here.

B

No matter which angle we choose for viewing the Customs ruling letter in this case, it fails to qualify under *Chevron*. On the face of the statute, to begin with, the terms of the congressional delegation give no indication that Congress meant to delegate authority to Customs to issue classification rulings with the force of law. We are not, of course, here making any global statement about Customs' authority, for it is true that the general rulemaking power conferred on Customs authorizes some regulation with the force of law, or "legal norms," as we put it in *Haggar*, 526 U.S., at 391. It is true as well that Congress had classification rulings in mind when it explicitly authorized, in a parenthetical, the issuance of "regulations establishing procedures for the issuance of binding rulings prior to the entry of the merchandise concerned," 19 U.S.C. § 1502(a). The reference to binding classifications does not, however, bespeak the legislative type of activity that would naturally bind more than the parties to the ruling, once the goods classified are admitted into this country. And though the statute's direction to disseminate "information" necessary to "secure" uniformity, seems to assume that a ruling may be precedent in later transactions, precedential value alone does not add up to *Chevron* entitlement; interpretive rules may sometimes function as precedents, and they enjoy no Chevron status as a class. In any event, any precedential claim of a classification ruling is counterbalanced by the provision for independent review of Customs classifications by the CIT, *see* 28 U.S.C. §§ 2638-2640; the scheme for CIT review includes a provision that treats classification rulings on par with the Secretary's rulings on "valuation, rate of duty, marking, restricted merchandise, entry requirements, drawbacks, vessel repairs, or similar matters," § 1581(h); *see* §

2639(b). It is hard to imagine a congressional understanding more at odds with the *Chevron* regime.

It is difficult, in fact, to see in the agency practice itself any indication that Customs ever set out with a lawmaking pretense in mind when it undertook to make classifications like these. Customs does not generally engage in notice-and-comment practice when issuing them, and their treatment by the agency makes it clear that a letter's binding character as a ruling stops short of third parties; Customs has regarded a classification as conclusive only as between itself and the importer to whom it was issued, and even then only until Customs has given advance notice of intended change. Other importers are in fact warned against assuming any right of detrimental reliance.

Indeed, to claim that classifications have legal force is to ignore the reality that 46 different Customs offices issue 10,000 to 15,000 of them each year. Any suggestion that rulings intended to have the force of law are being churned out at a rate of 10,000 a year at an agency's 46 scattered offices is simply self-refuting. Although the circumstances are less startling here, with a Headquarters letter in issue, none of the relevant statutes recognizes this category of rulings as separate or different from others; there is thus no indication that a more potent delegation might have been understood as going to Headquarters even when Headquarters provides developed reasoning, as it did in this instance.

Nor do the amendments to the statute made effective after this case arose disturb our conclusion. The new law requires Customs to provide notice-and-comment procedures only when modifying or revoking a prior classification ruling or modifying the treatment accorded to substantially identical transactions; and under its regulations, Customs sees itself obliged to provide notice-and-comment procedures only when "changing a practice" so as to produce a tariff increase, or in the imposition of a restriction or prohibition, or when Customs Headquarters determines that "the matter is of sufficient importance to involve the interests of domestic industry," 19 CFR §§ 177.10(c)(1), (2) (2000). The statutory changes reveal no new congressional objective of treating classification decisions generally as rulemaking with force of law, nor do they suggest any intent to create a *Chevron* patchwork of classification rulings, some with force of law, some without.

In sum, classification rulings are best treated like "interpretations contained in policy statements, agency manuals, and enforcement guidelines." *Christensen*, 529 U.S., at 587. They are beyond the *Chevron* pale.

C

To agree with the Court of Appeals that Customs ruling letters do not fall within *Chevron* is not, however, to place them outside the pale of any deference whatever. *Chevron* did nothing to eliminate *Skidmore*'s holding that an agency's interpretation may merit some deference whatever its form, given the "specialized experience and broader investigations and information" available to the agency,

323 U.S., at 139, and given the value of uniformity in its administrative and judicial understandings of what a national law requires, *id.*, at 140.

There is room at least to raise a *Skidmore* claim here, where the regulatory scheme is highly detailed, and Customs can bring the benefit of specialized experience to bear on the subtle questions in this case: whether the daily planner with room for brief daily entries falls under "diaries," when diaries are grouped with "notebooks and address books, bound; memorandum pads, letter pads and similar articles," and whether a planner with a ring binding should qualify as "bound," when a binding may be typified by a book, but also may have "reinforcements or fittings of metal, plastics, etc.." A classification ruling in this situation may therefore at least seek a respect proportional to its "power to persuade," *Skidmore, supra*, at 140. Such a ruling may surely claim the merit of its writer's thoroughness, logic, and expertness, its fit with prior interpretations, and any other sources of weight.

## D

Underlying the position we take here, like the position expressed by JUSTICE SCALIA in dissent, is a choice about the best way to deal with an inescapable feature of the body of congressional legislation authorizing administrative action. That feature is the great variety of ways in which the laws invest the Government's administrative arms with discretion, and with procedures for exercising it, in giving meaning to Acts of Congress. Implementation of a statute may occur in formal adjudication or the choice to defend against judicial challenge; it may occur in a central board or office or in dozens of enforcement agencies dotted across the country; its institutional lawmaking may be confined to the resolution of minute detail or extend to legislative rulemaking on matters intentionally left by Congress to be worked out at the agency level.

Although we all accept the position that the Judiciary should defer to at least some of this multifarious administrative action, we have to decide how to take account of the great range of its variety. If the primary objective is to simplify the judicial process of giving or withholding deference, then the diversity of statutes authorizing discretionary administrative action must be declared irrelevant or minimized. If, on the other hand, it is simply implausible that Congress intended such a broad range of statutory authority to produce only two varieties of administrative action, demanding either *Chevron* deference or none at all, then the breadth of the spectrum of possible agency action must be taken into account. JUSTICE SCALIA'S first priority over the years has been to limit and simplify. The Court's choice has been to tailor deference to variety. This acceptance of the range of statutory variation has led the Court to recognize more than one variety of judicial deference, just as the Court has recognized a variety of indicators that Congress would expect *Chevron* deference.

Our respective choices are repeated today. JUSTICE SCALIA would pose the question of deference as an either-or choice. * * *

* * *

We think, in sum, that JUSTICE SCALIA'S efforts to simplify ultimately run afoul of Congress's indications that different statutes present different reasons for considering respect for the exercise of administrative authority or deference to it. Without being at odds with congressional intent much of the time, we believe that judicial responses to administrative action must continue to differentiate between *Chevron* and *Skidmore*, and that continued recognition of *Skidmore* is necessary for just the reasons Justice Jackson gave when that case was decided.

Since the *Skidmore* assessment called for here ought to be made in the first instance by the Court of Appeals for the Federal Circuit or the CIT, we go no further than to vacate the judgment and remand the case for further proceedings consistent with this opinion.

*It is so ordered.*

JUSTICE SCALIA, dissenting.

Today's opinion makes an avulsive change in judicial review of federal administrative action. Whereas previously a reasonable agency application of an ambiguous statutory provision had to be sustained so long as it represented the agency's authoritative interpretation, henceforth such an application can be set aside unless "it appears that Congress delegated authority to the agency generally to make rules carrying the force of law," as by giving an agency "power to engage in adjudication or notice-and-comment rulemaking, or . . . some other [procedure] indicati[ng] comparable congressional intent," and "the agency interpretation claiming deference was promulgated in the exercise of that authority." What was previously a general presumption of authority in agencies to resolve ambiguity in the statutes they have been authorized to enforce has been changed to a presumption of no such authority, which must be overcome by affirmative legislative intent to the contrary. And whereas previously, when agency authority to resolve ambiguity did not exist the court was free to give the statute what it considered the best interpretation, henceforth the court must supposedly give the agency view some indeterminate amount of so-called *Skidmore* deference. We will be sorting out the consequences of the *Mead* doctrine, which has today replaced the *Chevron* doctrine, for years to come. I would adhere to our established jurisprudence, defer to the reasonable interpretation the Customs Service has given to the statute it is charged with enforcing, and reverse the judgment of the Court of Appeals.

I

Only five years ago, the Court described the *Chevron* doctrine as follows: "We accord deference to agencies under *Chevron* . . . because of a presumption that Congress, when it left ambiguity in a statute meant for implementation by an agency, understood that the ambiguity would be resolved, first and foremost, by the agency, and desired the agency (rather than the courts) to possess whatever degree of discretion the ambiguity allows," *Smiley v. Citibank* (South Dakota), N. A., 517 U.S. 735, 740-741 (1996). Today the Court collapses this doctrine,

522

announcing instead a presumption that agency discretion does not exist unless the statute, expressly or impliedly, says so. While the Court disclaims any hard-and-fast rule for determining the existence of discretion-conferring intent, it asserts that "a very good indicator [is] express congressional authorizations to engage in the process of rulemaking or adjudication that produces regulations or rulings for which deference is claimed." Only when agencies act through "adjudication[,] notice-and-comment rulemaking, or ... some other [procedure] indicati[ng] comparable congressional intent [whatever that means]" is *Chevron* deference applicable—because these "relatively formal administrative procedures [designed] to foster ... fairness and deliberation" bespeak (according to the Court) congressional willingness to have the agency, rather than the courts, resolve statutory ambiguities. Once it is determined that *Chevron* deference is not in order, the uncertainty is not at an end—and indeed is just beginning. Litigants cannot then assume that the statutory question is one for the courts to determine, according to traditional interpretive principles and by their own judicial lights. No, the Court now resurrects, in full force, the pre-*Chevron* doctrine of *Skidmore* deference, whereby "[t]he fair measure of deference to an agency administering its own statute ... var[ies] with circumstances," including "the degree of the agency's care, its consistency, formality, and relative expertness, and ... the persuasiveness of the agency's position." The Court has largely replaced *Chevron*, in other words, with that test most beloved by a court unwilling to be held to rules (and most feared by litigants who want to know what to expect): th' ol' "totality of the circumstances" test.

The Court's new doctrine is neither sound in principle nor sustainable in practice.

## A

As to principle: The doctrine of *Chevron*—that all authoritative agency interpretations of statutes they are charged with administering deserve deference—was rooted in a legal presumption of congressional intent, important to the division of powers between the Second and Third Branches. When, *Chevron* said, Congress leaves an ambiguity in a statute that is to be administered by an executive agency, it is presumed that Congress meant to give the agency discretion, within the limits of reasonable interpretation, as to how the ambiguity is to be resolved. By committing enforcement of the statute to an agency rather than the courts, Congress committed its initial and primary interpretation to that branch as well.

\* \* \*

Statutory ambiguities, in other words, were left to reasonable resolution by the Executive.

The basis in principle for today's new doctrine can be described as follows: The background rule is that ambiguity in legislative instructions to agencies is to be resolved not by the agencies but by the judges. Specific congressional intent to depart from this rule must be found—and while there is no single touchstone for such intent it can generally be found when Congress has authorized the agency to act through (what the Court says is) relatively formal procedures such as informal rulemaking and formal (and informal?) adjudication, and when the agency in fact employs such procedures. The Court's background rule is contradicted by the origins of judicial review of administrative action. But in addition, the Court's principal criterion of congressional intent to supplant its background rule seems to me quite implausible. There is no necessary connection between the formality of procedure and the power of the entity administering the procedure to resolve authoritatively questions of law. The most formal of the procedures the Court refers to—formal adjudication—is modeled after the process used in trial courts, which of course are not generally accorded deference on questions of law. The purpose of such a procedure is to produce a closed record for determination and review of the facts—which implies nothing about the power of the agency subjected to the procedure to resolve authoritatively questions of law.

As for informal rulemaking: While formal adjudication procedures are *prescribed* (either by statute or by the Constitution), informal rulemaking is more typically *authorized* but not required. Agencies with such authority are free to give guidance through rulemaking, but they may proceed to administer their statute case-by-case, "making law" as they implement their program (not necessarily through formal adjudication). Is it likely—or indeed even plausible—that Congress meant, when such an agency chooses rulemaking, to accord the administrators of that agency, and their successors, the flexibility of interpreting the ambiguous statute now one way, and later another; but, when such an agency chooses case-by-case administration, to eliminate all future agency discretion by having that same ambiguity resolved authoritatively (and forever) by the courts? Surely that makes no sense. It is also the case that certain significant categories of rules—those involving grant and benefit programs, for example, are exempt from the requirements of informal rulemaking. Under the Court's novel theory, when an agency takes advantage of that exemption its rules will be deprived of *Chevron* deference, *i.e.*, authoritative effect. Was this either the plausible intent of the APA rulemaking exemption, or the plausible intent of the Congress that established the grant or benefit program?

Some decisions that are neither informal rulemaking nor formal adjudication are required to be made personally by a Cabinet Secretary, without any prescribed procedures. * * * Is it conceivable that decisions specifically committed to these high-level officers are meant to be accorded no deference, while decisions by an administrative law judge left in place without further discretionary agency review are authoritative? This seems to me quite absurd, and not at all in accord with any plausible actual intent of Congress.

B

As for the practical effects of the new rule:

(1)

The principal effect will be protracted confusion. As noted above, the one test for *Chevron* deference that the Court enunciates is wonderfully imprecise: whether "Congress delegated authority to the agency generally to make rules carrying the force of law, ... as by ... adjudication[,] notice-and-comment rulemaking, or ... some other [procedure] indicati[ng] comparable congressional intent." But even this description does not do justice to the utter flabbiness of the Court's criterion, since, in order to maintain the fiction that the new test is really just the old one, applied consistently throughout our case law, the Court must make a virtually open-ended exception to its already imprecise guidance: In the present case, it tells us, the absence of notice-and-comment rulemaking (and "[who knows?] [of] some other [procedure] indicati[ng] comparable congressional intent") is not enough to decide the question of *Chevron* deference, "for we have sometimes found reasons for *Chevron* deference even when no such administrative formality was required and none was afforded." The opinion then goes on to consider a grab bag of other factors—including the factor that used to be the sole criterion for *Chevron* deference: whether the interpretation represented the *authoritative* position of the agency. It is hard to know what the lower courts are to make of today's guidance.

(2)

Another practical effect of today's opinion will be an artificially induced increase in informal rulemaking. Buy stock in the GPO. Since informal rulemaking and formal adjudication are the only more-or-less safe harbors from the storm that the Court has unleashed; and since formal adjudication is not an option but must be mandated by statute or constitutional command; informal rulemaking-which the Court was once careful to make voluntary unless required by statute—will now become a virtual necessity. As I have described, the Court's safe harbor requires not merely that the agency have been given rulemaking authority, but also that the agency have *employed* rulemaking as the means of resolving the statutory ambiguity. (It is hard to understand why that should be so. Surely the mere *conferral* of rulemaking authority demonstrates—if one accepts the Court's logic— a congressional intent to allow the agency to resolve ambiguities. And given that intent, what difference does it make that the agency chooses instead to use another perfectly permissible means for that purpose?) Moreover, the majority's approach will have a perverse effect on the rules that do emerge, given the principle (which the Court leaves untouched today) that judges must defer to reasonable agency interpretations of their own regulations. Agencies will now have high incentive to rush out barebones, ambiguous rules construing statutory ambiguities, which they can then in turn further clarify through informal rulings entitled to judicial respect.

(3)

Worst of all, the majority's approach will lead to the ossification of large portions of our statutory law. Where *Chevron* applies, statutory ambiguities remain ambiguities subject to the agency's ongoing clarification. They create a space, so to speak, for the exercise of continuing agency discretion. As *Chevron* itself held, the Environmental Protection Agency can interpret "stationary source" to mean a single smokestack, can later replace that interpretation with the "bubble concept" embracing an entire plant, and if that proves undesirable can return again to the original interpretation. 467 U.S., at 853-859, 865-866. For the indeterminately large number of statutes taken out of *Chevron* by today's decision, however, ambiguity (and hence flexibility) will cease with the first judicial resolution. *Skidmore* deference gives the agency's current position some vague and uncertain amount of respect, but it does not, like *Chevron*, leave the matter within the control of the Executive Branch for the future. Once the court has spoken, it becomes *unlawful* for the agency to take a contradictory position; the statute now says what the court has prescribed. It will be bad enough when this ossification occurs as a result of judicial determination (under today's new principles) that there is no affirmative indication of congressional intent to "delegate"; but it will be positively bizarre when it occurs simply because of an agency's failure to act by rulemaking (rather than informal adjudication) before the issue is presented to the courts.

\* \* \*

(4)

And finally, the majority's approach compounds the confusion it creates by breathing new life into the anachronism of *Skidmore*, which sets forth a sliding scale of deference owed an agency's interpretation of a statute that is dependent "upon the thoroughness evident in [the agency's] consideration, the validity of its reasoning, its consistency with earlier and later pronouncements, and all those factors which give it power to persuade, if lacking power to control"; in this way, the appropriate measure of deference will be accorded the "body of experience and informed judgment" that such interpretations often embody, 323 U.S., at 140. JUSTICE JACKSON's eloquence notwithstanding, the rule of *Skidmore* deference is an empty truism and a trifling statement of the obvious: A judge should take into account the well-considered views of expert observers.

It was possible to live with the indeterminacy of *Skidmore* deference in earlier times. But in an era when federal statutory law administered by federal agencies is pervasive, and when the ambiguities (intended or unintended) that those statutes contain are innumerable, totality-of-the-circumstances *Skidmore* deference is a recipe for uncertainty, unpredictability, and endless litigation. To condemn a vast body of agency action to that regime (all except rulemaking, formal (and informal?) adjudication, and whatever else might now and then be included within today's intentionally vague formulation of affirmative congressional intent to "delegate") is irresponsible.

\* \* \*

III

To decide the present case, I would adhere to the original formulation of *Chevron*. "'The power of an administrative agency to administer a congressionally created . . . program necessarily requires the formulation of policy and the making of rules

526

1  to fill any gap left, implicitly or explicitly, by Congress,'" 467 U.S., at 843. We
2  accordingly presume—and our precedents have made clear to Congress that we
3  presume —that, absent some clear textual indication to the contrary, "Congress,
4  when it left ambiguity in a statute meant for implementation by an agency,
5  understood that the ambiguity would be resolved, first and foremost, by the
6  agency, and desired the agency (rather than the courts) to possess whatever degree
7  of discretion the ambiguity allows," *Smiley*, 517 U.S., at 740-741. *Chevron* sets
8  forth an across-the-board presumption, which operates as a background rule of
9  law against which Congress legislates: Ambiguity means Congress intended agency
10 discretion. Any resolution of the ambiguity by the administering agency that is
11 authoritative—that represents the official position of the agency—must be accepted
12 by the courts if it is reasonable.

13 Nothing in the statute at issue here displays an intent to modify the background
14 presumption on which *Chevron* deference is based. * * *

15 There is no doubt that the Customs Service's interpretation represents the
16 authoritative view of the agency. Although the actual ruling letter was signed by
17 only the Director of the Commercial Rulings Branch of Customs Headquarters'
18 Office of Regulations and Rulings, the Solicitor General of the United States has
19 filed a brief, cosigned by the General Counsel of the Department of the Treasury,
20 that represents the position set forth in the ruling letter to be the official position
21 of the Customs Service.[6]

---

[6] * * * The "authoritativeness" of an agency interpretation does not turn upon
whether it has been enunciated by someone who is actually employed by the
agency. It must represent the judgment of central agency management, approved
at the highest levels. I would find that condition to have been satisfied when, a
ruling having been attacked in court, the general counsel of the agency has
determined that it should be defended. If one thinks that that does not impart
sufficient authoritativeness, then surely the line has been crossed when, as here,
the General Counsel of the agency and the Solicitor General of the United States
have assured this Court that the position represents the agency's authoritative
view. (Contrary to the Court's suggestion, there would be nothing bizarre about the
fact that this latter approach would entitle the ruling to deference here, though it
would not have been entitled to deference in the lower courts. Afirmation of the
official agency position before this court—if that is thought necessary—is no
different from the agency's issuing a new rule after the Court of Appeals
determination. It establishes a new legal basis for the decision, which this Court
must take into account (or remand for that purpose), even though the Court of
Appeals could not.
The *authoritativeness* of the agency ruling may not be a bright-line standard—but
it is infinitely brighter than the line the Court asks us to draw today, * * * And, most
important of all, it is a line that focuses attention on the right question: not whether
Congress "affirmatively intended" to delegate interpretive authority (if it entrusted

527

There is also no doubt that the Customs Service's interpretation is a reasonable one, whether or not judges would consider it the best. I will not belabor this point, since the Court evidently agrees: An interpretation that was unreasonable would not merit the remand that the Court decrees for consideration of *Skidmore* deference.

IV

Finally, and least importantly, even were I to accept the Court's revised version of *Chevron* as a correct statement of the law, I would still accord deference to the tariff classification ruling at issue in this case. For the case is indistinguishable, in that regard, from *NationsBank of N.C., N.A. v. Variable Annuity Life Ins. Co.*, 513 U.S. 251 (1995), which the Court acknowledges as an instance in which *Chevron* deference is warranted notwithstanding the absence of formal adjudication, notice-and-comment rulemaking, or comparable "administrative formality." Here, as in *NationsBank*, there is a tradition of great deference to the opinions of the agency head * * * . And here, as in *NationsBank*, the agency interpretation in question is officially that of the agency head. Consequently, even on the Court's own terms, the Customs ruling at issue in this case should be given *Chevron* deference.

For the reasons stated, I respectfully dissent from the Court's judgment. * * * I dissent even more vigorously from the reasoning that produces the Court's judgment, and that makes today's decision one of the most significant opinions ever rendered by the Court dealing with the judicial review of administrative action. Its consequences will be enormous, and almost uniformly bad.

## 3.  Chevron Step One

Under the first step of the *Chevron* analysis, courts ask whether Congress has "directly spoken to the precise question at issue." If Congress has, then that's the end of the matter: what Congress says is the law. If, on the other hand, Congress has not directly spoken to the legal question presented in the case—"if the statute is silent or ambiguous with respect to the specific issue"—then the Court will move on to Step Two of the *Chevron* analysis, asking whether the agency's answer to the statutory interpretation question is permissible (*i.e.*, reasonable).

Sounds straightforward, right? The cases that follow indicate that, in fact, *Chevron* Step One can be difficult and controversial.

---

administration of the statute to an agency, it did, because that is how our system works); but whether it is truly the agency's considered view, or just the opinions of some underlings, that are at issue.

1

## 2 Dole v. United Steelworkers

3 494 U.S. 26 (1990)

4 February 21, 1990

5 Justice BRENNAN delivered the opinion of the Court.

6 Among the regulatory tools available to government agencies charged with
7 protecting public health and safety are rules which require regulated entities to
8 disclose information directly to employees, consumers, or others. Disclosure rules
9 protect by providing access to information about what dangers exist and how these
10 dangers can be avoided. Today we decide whether the Office of Management and
11 Budget (OMB) has the authority under the Paperwork Reduction Act of 1980 (Act),
12 44 U.S.C. § 3501 *et seq.*, to review such regulations.

13                                             I

14 In 1983, pursuant to the Occupational Safety and Health Act of 1970 (OSH Act),
15 84 Stat. 1590, 29 U.S.C. § 651 et seq. which authorizes the Department of Labor
16 (DOL) to set health and safety standards for workplaces, DOL promulgated a
17 Hazard Communications Standard. 29 CFR § 1910.1200 (1984). The Standard
18 imposed various requirements on manufacturers aimed at ensuring that their
19 employees were informed of the potential hazards posed by chemicals found at
20 their workplace. Specifically, the Standard required chemical manufacturers to
21 label containers of hazardous chemicals with appropriate warnings. "Downstream"
22 manufacturers—commercial purchasers who used the chemicals in their
23 manufacturing plants—were obliged to keep the original labels intact or else
24 transfer the information onto any substitute containers. The Standard also
25 required chemical manufacturers to provide "material safety data sheets" to
26 downstream manufacturers. The data sheets were to list the physical
27 characteristics and hazards of each chemical, the symptoms caused by
28 overexposure, and any preexisting medical conditions aggravated by exposure. In
29 addition, the data sheets were to recommend safety precautions and first aid and
30 emergency procedures in case of overexposure, and provide a source for additional
31 information. Both chemical manufacturers and downstream manufacturers were
32 required to make the data sheets available to their employees and to provide
33 training on the dangers of the particular hazardous chemicals found at each
34 workplace.

35 Respondent United Steelworkers of America, among others, challenged the
36 Standard in the Court of Appeals for the Third Circuit. That court held that the

1   Occupational Safety and Health Administration (OSHA) had not adequately
2   explained why the regulation was limited to the manufacturing sector * * * .

3                                    * * *

4   DOL complied by issuing a revised Hazard Communications Standard that applied
5   to worksites in all sectors of the economy. At the same time, DOL submitted the
6   Standard to OMB for review of any paperwork requirements. After holding a public
7   hearing, OMB approved all but three of its provisions. * * *

8   OMB disapproved these provisions based on its determination that the
9   requirements were not necessary to protect employees. * * * DOL disagreed with
10  OMB's assessment, but it published notice that the three provisions were
11  withdrawn. DOL added its reasons for believing that the provisions were
12  necessary, proposed that they be retained, and invited public comment.

13  The union and its co-petitioners responded by filing a motion for further relief with
14  the Third Circuit. That court ordered DOL to reinstate the OMB-disapproved
15  provisions. The court reasoned that the provisions represented good faith
16  compliance by DOL with the court's prior orders, that OMB lacked authority under
17  the Paperwork Reduction Act to disapprove the provisions and that, therefore,
18  DOL had no legitimate basis for withdrawing them.

19  Petitioners sought review in this Court. We granted certiorari to answer the
20  important question whether the Paperwork Reduction Act authorizes OMB to
21  review and countermand agency regulations mandating disclosure by regulated
22  entities directly to third parties. We hold that the Paperwork Reduction Act does
23  not give OMB that authority, and therefore affirm.

24                                    II

25  The Paperwork Reduction Act was enacted in response to one of the less auspicious
26  aspects of the enormous growth of our federal bureaucracy: its seemingly
27  insatiable appetite for data. Outcries from small businesses, individuals, and state
28  and local governments that they were being buried under demands for paperwork
29  led Congress to institute controls. Congress designated OMB the overseer of other
30  agencies with respect to paperwork, and set forth a comprehensive scheme
31  designed to reduce the paperwork burden. The Act charges OMB with developing
32  uniform policies for efficient information processing, storage and transmittal
33  systems, both within and among agencies. * * *

34  The Act prohibits any federal agency from adopting regulations which impose
35  paperwork requirements on the public unless the information is not available to
36  the agency from another source within the Federal Government, and the agency
37  must formulate a plan for tabulating the information in a useful manner. Agencies

are also required to minimize the burden on the public to the extent practicable. In addition, the Act institutes a second layer of review by OMB for new paperwork requirements. After an agency has satisfied itself that an instrument for collecting information—termed an "information collection request"—is needed, the agency must submit the request to OMB for approval. If OMB disapproves the request, the agency may not collect the information.

Typical information collection requests include tax forms, Medicare forms, financial loan applications, job applications, questionnaires, compliance reports and tax or business records. These information requests share at least one characteristic: The information requested is provided to a federal agency, either directly or indirectly. Agencies impose the requirements on private parties in order to generate information to be used by the agency in pursuing some other purpose. For instance, agencies use these information requests in gathering background on a particular subject to develop the expertise with which to devise or fine-tune appropriate regulations, amassing diffuse data for processing into useful statistical form, and monitoring business records and compliance reports for signs or proof of nonfeasance to determine when to initiate enforcement measures.

By contrast, disclosure rules do not result in information being made available for agency personnel to use. The promulgation of a disclosure rule is a final agency action that represents a substantive regulatory choice. An agency charged with protecting employees from hazardous chemicals has a variety of regulatory weapons from which to choose: it can ban the chemical altogether; it can mandate specified safety measures, such as gloves or goggles; or it can require labels or other warnings alerting users to dangers and recommended precautions. An agency chooses to impose a warning requirement because it believes that such a requirement is the least intrusive measure that will sufficiently protect the public, not because the measure is a means of acquiring information useful in performing some other agency function.

No provision of the Act expressly declares whether Congress intended the Paperwork Reduction Act to apply to disclosure rules as well as information-gathering rules. The Act applies to "information collection requests" by a federal agency which are defined as

> "a written report form, application form, schedule, questionnaire, reporting or recordkeeping requirement, collection of information requirement, or other similar method calling for the collection of information." 44 U.S.C. § 3502(11)

"Collection of information," in turn, is defined as

> "the obtaining or soliciting of facts or opinions by an agency through the use of written report forms, application forms, schedules, questionnaires,

1    reporting or recordkeeping requirements, or other similar methods calling
2    for either—

3    "(A) answers to identical questions posed to, or identical reporting or
4    recordkeeping requirements imposed on, ten or more persons, other than
5    agencies, instrumentalities, or employees of the United States; or

6    "(B) answers to questions posed to agencies, instrumentalities, or
7    employees of the United States which are to be used for general statistical
8    purposes." 44 U.S.C. § 3502(4).

9    Petitioners urge us to read the words "obtaining or soliciting of facts by an agency
10   through . . . reporting or recordkeeping requirements" as encompassing disclosure
11   rules. They contend that an agency is "soliciting facts" when it requires someone
12   to communicate specified data to a third party and that the Hazard
13   Communications Standard's rules are "reporting and recordkeeping
14   requirements" within the meaning of the Act because the employer is required to
15   report hazard information to employees. Petitioner submits that the provisions
16   requiring labeling and employee training are "reporting requirements" and that
17   the provision requiring accessible data sheets containing health and safety
18   information is a "recordkeeping requirement." We believe, however, that the
19   language, structure, and purpose of the Paperwork Reduction Act reveal that
20   petitioners' position is untenable because Congress did not intend the Act to
21   encompass these or any other third-party disclosure rules.

22   "On a pure question of statutory construction, our first job is to try to determine
23   congressional intent, using traditional tools of statutory construction." *NLRB v.*
24   *Food & Commercial Workers*, 484 U.S. 112, 123 (1987). Our "starting point is the
25   language of the statute," *Schreiber v. Burlington Northern, Inc.*, 472 U.S. 1, 5
26   (1985), but "'in expounding a statute, we are not guided by a single sentence or
27   member of a sentence, but look to the provisions of the whole law, and to its object
28   and policy.'" *Massachusetts v. Morash*, 490 U.S. 107, 115 (1989), quoting *Pilot Life*
29   *Ins. Co. v. Dedeaux*, 481 U.S. 41, 51 (1987).

30   Petitioners' interpretation of "obtaining or soliciting facts by an agency through . . .
31   reporting or recordkeeping requirements" is not the most natural reading of this
32   language. The common-sense view of "obtaining or soliciting facts *by an agency*"
33   is that the phrase refers to an agency's efforts to gather facts for its own use, and
34   that Congress used the word "solicit" in addition to the word "obtain" in order to
35   cover information requests that rely on the voluntary cooperation of information
36   suppliers as well as rules which make compliance mandatory. Similarly, data
37   sheets consisting of advisory material on health and safety do not fall within the
38   normal meaning of "records," and a government-imposed reporting requirement

customarily requires reports to be made to the government, not training and labels to be given to someone else altogether.

That a more limited reading of the phrase "reporting and recordkeeping requirement" was intended derives some further support from the words surrounding it. The traditional canon of construction, *noscitur a sociis*, dictates that "words grouped in a list should be given related meaning.'" *Massachusetts v. Morash, supra,* 490 U.S., at 114-115, quoting *Schreiber, supra,* 472 U.S., at 8. The other examples listed in the definitions of "information collection request" and "collection of information" are forms for communicating information to the party requesting that information. If "reporting and recordkeeping requirement" is understood to be analogous to the examples surrounding it, the phrase would comprise only rules requiring information to be sent or made available to a federal agency, not disclosure rules.

The same conclusion is produced by a consideration of the object and structure of the Act as a whole. Particularly useful is the provision detailing Congress' purposes in enacting the statute. The Act declares that its purposes are:

"(1) to minimize the Federal paperwork burden for individuals, small businesses, State and local governments, and other persons;

"(2) to minimize the cost *to the Federal Government* of collecting, maintaining, using, and disseminating information;

"(3) to maximize the usefulness of information collected, maintained, and disseminated *by the Federal Government*;

"(4) to coordinate, integrate and, to the extent practicable and appropriate, make uniform Federal information policies and practices;

"(5) to ensure that automatic data processing, telecommunications, and other information technologies are acquired and used by the Federal Government in a manner which improves service delivery and program management, increases productivity, improves the quality of decisionmaking, reduces waste and fraud, and wherever practicable and appropriate, reduces the information processing burden for the Federal Government and *for persons who provide information to and for the Federal Government*; and

"(6) to ensure that the collection, maintenance, use and dissemination of information by the *Federal Government* is consistent with applicable laws relating to confidentiality, including . . . the Privacy Act." 44 U.S.C. § 3501 (1982 ed, and Supp. V) (emphasis added).

1 Disclosure rules present none of the problems Congress sought to solve through
2 the Paperwork Reduction Act, and none of Congress' enumerated purposes would
3 be served by subjecting disclosure rules to the provisions of the Act. The statute
4 makes clear that the first purpose—avoiding a burden on private parties and state
5 and local governments—refers to avoiding "the time, effort, or financial resources
6 expended by persons to provide information to a *Federal agency.*" 44 U.S.C. §
7 3502(3) (1982 ed.) (defining "burden") (emphasis added). Because Congress
8 expressed concern only for the burden imposed by requirements to provide
9 information to a federal agency, and not for any burden imposed by requirements
10 to provide information to a third party, OMB review of disclosure rules would not
11 further this congressional aim.

12 Congress' second purpose—minimizing the Federal Government's cost of handling
13 information—also would not be advanced by review of disclosure rules, because
14 such rules do not impose any information processing costs on the Federal
15 Government. Because the Federal Government is not the consumer of information
16 "requested" by a disclosure rule nor an intermediary in its dissemination, OMB
17 review of disclosure rules would not serve Congress' third, fourth, fifth, or sixth
18 purposes. Thus, nothing in Congress' itemized and exhaustive textual description
19 of its reasons for enacting this particular Act indicates any legislative purpose to
20 have OMB screen proposed disclosure rules. We find this to be strong evidence
21 that Congress did not intend the Act to authorize OMB review of such regulations.

22 This conclusion is buttressed by the language and import of other provisions of the
23 Act. * * *

24                                             * * *

25 * * * [The Paperwork Reduction Act's] meaning is clear: the public is protected
26 under the Paperwork Reduction Act from paperwork regulations not issued in
27 compliance with the Act, only when those regulations dictate that a person
28 maintain information *for an agency* or provide information to an agency. By its
29 very terms, the statute's enforcement mechanism does not apply to rules which
30 require disclosure to a third party rather than to a federal agency. Thus either
31 Congress intended the Paperwork Reduction Act to cover information-gathering
32 rules only, or Congress intended the Act to cover disclosure rules, but intended to
33 exempt them from this agency compliance mechanism. Because the latter is
34 counterintuitive and contrary to clear legislative history, § 3512 is further evidence
35 that Congress did not intend the Act to cover disclosure rules.

36                                             III

37 For the foregoing reasons, we find that the terms "collection of information" and
38 "information collection request," when considered in light of the language and
39 structure of the Act as a whole, refer solely to the collection of information by, or

for the use of, a federal agency; they cannot reasonably be interpreted to cover rules mandating disclosure of information to a third party. In addition, we find unpersuasive petitioners' claims that there is a "clearly expressed legislative intention [to the] contrary."

Petitioners rely on statements from various stages of the Act's legislative history as evidence that Congress intended "collection of information" to include disclosure rules. However, the statements show merely that the Act was intended to reach not only statistical compilations but also information collected for law enforcement purposes and information filed with an agency for possible dissemination to the public (*i.e.*, when the agency is an intermediary in the process of data dissemination). This sheds no light on the issue before this Court: Whether the Act reaches rules mandating disclosure by one party directly to a third party. Moreover, other statements in the committee reports reinforce respondents' position.

Because we find that the statute, as a whole, clearly expresses Congress' intention, we decline to defer to OMB's interpretation. *See Board of Governors of the Federal Reserve System v. Dimension Financial Corp.*, 474 U.S. 361, 368 (1986) ("The traditional deference courts pay to agency interpretation is not to be applied to alter the clearly expressed intent of Congress"); *Chevron U.S.A. Inc. v. Natural Resources Defense Council, Inc.*, 467 U.S. 837, 842-843 (1984) ("If the intent of Congress is clear, that is the end of the matter"). We affirm the judgment of the Third Circuit insofar as it held that the Paperwork Reduction Act does not give OMB the authority to review agency rules mandating disclosure by regulated entities to third parties.

*It is so ordered.*

Justice WHITE, with whom THE CHIEF JUSTICE joins, dissenting.

The Court's opinion today requires more than ten pages, including a review of numerous statutory provisions and legislative history, to conclude that the Paperwork Reduction Act of 1980 (PRA or Act) is clear and unambiguous on the question of whether it applies to agency directives to private parties to collect specified information and disseminate or make it available to third parties. On the basis of that questionable conclusion, the Court refuses to give *any* deference to the Office of Management and Budget's (OMB's) longstanding and consistently applied interpretation that such requirements fall within the Act's scope. Because in my view the Act is not clear in that regard and deference is due OMB under *Chevron U.S.A. Inc. v. Natural Resources Defense Council, Inc.*, 467 U.S. 837 (1984), I respectfully dissent.

\* \* \*

1  As the Court acknowledges, there is no question in this case that OMB is the agency
2  charged with administering the PRA. Unless Congress has directly spoken to the
3  issue of whether an agency request that private parties disclose to or maintain for
4  third parties information such as material safety data sheets (MSDS's) is an
5  "information collection request" or a "recordkeeping requirement" within the Act's
6  scope, OMB's interpretation of the Act is entitled to deference, provided of course
7  that it is based on a permissible construction of the statute.

8  The Court concedes that the Act does not expressly address "whether Congress
9  intended the Paperwork Reduction Act to apply to disclosure rules as well as
10 information-gathering rules." Curiously, the Court then almost immediately
11 asserts that interpreting the Act to provide coverage for disclosure requests is
12 untenable. The plain language of the Act, however, suggests the contrary. Indeed,
13 the Court appears to acknowledge that Petitioners' interpretation of the Act,
14 although not the one the Court prefers, is nonetheless reasonable: "Petitioner's
15 interpretation . . . is not the *most* natural reading of this language." (emphasis
16 added). The Court goes on to arrive at what it believes is the *most* reasonable of
17 plausible interpretations; it cannot rationally conclude that its interpretation is the
18 *only* one that Congress could possibly have intended. The Court neglects to even
19 mention that the only other Court of Appeals besides the Third Circuit in this case
20 to address a similar question rejected the interpretation that the Court now adopts.
21 In addition, there is evidence that for years OMB has been reviewing proposals
22 similar to the standard at issue in this case routinely and without objection from
23 other agencies. As I see it, by independently construing the statute rather than
24 asking if the agency's interpretation is a permissible one and deferring to it if that
25 is the case, the Court's approach is clearly contrary to *Chevron*.

26                                         * * *

27

## Pauley v. BethEnergy Mines, Inc.

29   501 U.S. 680 (1991)

30  June 24, 1991

31  JUSTICE BLACKMUN delivered the opinion of the Court.

32  The black lung benefits program, created by Congress, was to be administered first
33  by the Social Security Administration (SSA) under the auspices of the then-existent
34  Department of Health, Education, and Welfare (HEW), and later by the
35  Department of Labor (DOL). Congress authorized these Departments, during their
36  respective tenures, to adopt interim regulations governing the adjudication of
37  claims for black lung benefits, but constrained the Secretary of Labor by providing

that the DOL regulations "shall not be more restrictive than" HEW's. This litigation calls upon us to determine whether the Secretary of Labor has complied with that constraint.

I

A

The black lung benefits program was enacted originally as Title IV of the Federal Coal Mine Health and Safety Act of 1969 (FCMHSA) to provide benefits for miners totally disabled due at least in part to pneumoconiosis arising out of coal mine employment, and to the dependents and survivors of such miners.

Through FCMHSA, Congress established a bifurcated system of compensating miners disabled by pneumoconiosis. Part B thereof created a temporary program administered by the Social Security Administration under the auspices of the Secretary of Health, Education, and Welfare. This program was intended for the processing of claims filed on or before December 31, 1972. Benefits awarded under part B were paid by the Federal Government. For claims filed after 1972, part C originally authorized a permanent program, administered by the Secretary of Labor, to be coordinated with federally approved state workmen's compensation programs. Benefits awarded under part C were to be paid by the claimants' coal mining employers.

Under FCMHSA, the Secretary of HEW was authorized to promulgate permanent regulations regarding the determination and adjudication of part B claims. 30 U.S.C. § 921(b). The Secretary's discretion was limited, however, by three statutory presumptions defining eligibility under the part B program. § 921(c). For a claimant suffering from pneumoconiosis who could establish 10 years of coal mine employment, there "shall be a rebuttable presumption that his pneumoconiosis arose out of such employment." § 921(c)(1). Similarly, for a miner with at least 10 years of coal mine employment who "died from a respirable disease there shall be a rebuttable presumption that his death was due to pneumoconiosis." § 921(c)(2). Finally, there was an irrebuttable presumption that a miner presenting medical evidence demonstrating complicated pneumoconiosis was totally disabled as a result of that condition. § 921(c)(3). Consistent with these presumptions, HEW promulgated permanent regulations prescribing the methods and standards for establishing entitlement to black lung benefits under part B. See 20 CFR §§ 410.401 to 410.476 (1990).

B

Dissatisfied with the increasing backlog of unadjudicated claims and the relatively high rate of claim denials resulting from the application of the HEW permanent regulations, Congress in 1972 amended FCMSHA and redesignated Title IV of that

537

Act as the Black Lung Benefits Act of 1972. 86 Stat. 150. In addition to extending the coverage of part B to those claims filed by living miners prior to July 1, 1973, and those filed by survivors before January 1, 1974, the 1972 amendments liberalized in several ways the criteria and procedures applicable to part B claims. * * *

In response to these amendments, the Secretary of HEW adopted interim regulations "designed to 'permit prompt and vigorous processing of the large backlog of claims' that had developed during the early phases of administering part B." These interim regulations established adjudicatory rules for processing part B claims that permit the invocation of a presumption of eligibility upon demonstration by the claimant of specified factors, and a subsequent opportunity for the SSA [Social Security Administration], in administering the program, to rebut the presumption.

* * *

Once a claimant invokes the presumption of eligibility under § 410.490(b), the HEW interim regulations permit rebuttal by the SSA upon a showing that the miner is doing his usual coal mine work or comparable and gainful work, or is capable of doing such work.

The statutory changes adopted by the 1972 amendments and the application of HEW's interim regulations resulted in a surge of claims approvals under part B. Because the HEW interim regulations expired with the part B program, however, the Secretary of Labor was constrained to adjudicate all part C claims, *i.e.*, those filed after June 30, 1973, by living miners, and after December 31, 1973, by survivors, under the more stringent permanent HEW regulations. Neither the Congress nor the Secretary of Labor was content with the application to part C claims of the unwieldy and restrictive permanent regulations. Not only did the application of the permanent regulations cause the DOL to process claims slowly, but the DOL's claims approval rate was significantly below that of the SSA. Accordingly, Congress turned its attention once again to the black lung benefits program.

C

The Black Lung Benefits Reform Act of 1977 (BLBRA), 92 Stat. 95, approved and effective Mar. 1, 1978, further liberalized the criteria for eligibility for black lung benefits in several ways. * * *

In addition to liberalizing the statutory prerequisites to benefit entitlement, the BLBRA authorized the DOL to adopt its own interim regulations for processing part C claims filed before March 31, 1980. In so doing, Congress required that the "[c]riteria applied by the Secretary of Labor . . . shall not be more restrictive than the criteria applicable to a claim filed on June 30, 1973." § 902(f)(2).

The Secretary of Labor, pursuant to this authorization, adopted interim regulations governing the adjudication of part C claims. These regulations differ significantly from the HEW interim regulations. See 20 CFR § 727.203 (1990). The DOL regulations include two presumption provisions similar to the two presumption provisions in the HEW interim regulations. Compare §§ 727.203(a)(1) and (2) with §§ 410.490(b)(1)(i) and (ii). To invoke the presumption of eligibility under these two provisions, however, a claimant need not prove that the "impairment . . . arose out of coal mine employment," as was required under the HEW interim regulations.

In addition, the DOL interim regulations add three methods of invoking the presumption of eligibility not included in the HEW interim regulations. * * * Finally, the DOL interim regulations provide four methods for rebutting the presumptions established under § 727.203. Two of the rebuttal provisions mimic those in the HEW regulations, permitting rebuttal upon a showing that the miner is performing or is able to perform his coal mining or comparable work. See §§ 727.203(b)(1) and (2). The other two rebuttal provisions are at issue in these cases. Under these provisions, a presumption of total disability due to pneumoconiosis can be rebutted if "[t]he evidence establishes that the total disability or death of the miner did not arise in whole or in part out of coal mine employment," or if "[t]he evidence establishes that the miner does not, or did not, have pneumoconiosis." See §§ 727.203(b)(3) and (4).

## II

The three cases before us present the question whether the DOL's interim regulations are "more restrictive than" the HEW's interim regulations by virtue of the third and fourth rebuttal provisions, and therefore are inconsistent with the agency's statutory authority. * * *

* * *

## III

We turn to the statutory text that provides that "[c]riteria applied by the Secretary of Labor . . . shall not be more restrictive than the criteria applicable" under the interim HEW regulations. 30 U.S.C. § 902(f)(2). Specifically, we must determine whether the third and fourth rebuttal provisions in the DOL regulations render the DOL regulations more restrictive than were the HEW regulations. These provisions permit rebuttal of the presumption of eligibility upon a showing that the miner's disability did not arise in whole or in part out of coal mine employment or that the miner does not have pneumoconiosis.

A

In the BLBRA, Congress specifically constrained the Secretary of Labor's discretion through the directive that the criteria applied to part C claims could "not be more restrictive than" that applied to part B claims. 30 U.S.C. § 902(f)(2). The claimants and the dissent urge that this restriction is unambiguous, and that no deference is due the Secretary's determination that her interim regulations are not more restrictive than the HEW's. * * *

Judicial deference to an agency's interpretation of ambiguous provisions of the statutes it is authorized to implement reflects a sensitivity to the proper roles of the political and judicial branches. *See Chevron U.S.A. Inc. v. Natural Resources Defense Council, Inc.*, 467 U.S. 837, 866 (1984). When Congress, through express delegation or the introduction of an interpretive gap in the statutory structure, has delegated policymaking authority to an administrative agency, the extent of judicial review of the agency's policy determinations is limited.

It is precisely this recognition that informs our determination that deference to the Secretary is appropriate here. The Black Lung Benefits Act has produced a complex and highly technical regulatory program. The identification and classification of medical eligibility criteria necessarily require significant expertise, and entail the exercise of judgment grounded in policy concerns. In those circumstances, courts appropriately defer to the agency entrusted by Congress to make such policy determinations.

* * *

B

Having determined that the Secretary's position is entitled to deference, we must decide whether this position is reasonable. *See Chevron*, 467 U.S., at 845. The claimants and the dissent argue that this issue can be resolved simply by comparing the two interim regulations. This argument is straightforward; it reasons that the mere existence of regulatory provisions permitting rebuttal of statutory elements not rebuttable under the HEW interim regulations renders the DOL interim regulations more restrictive than HEW's and, as a consequence renders the Secretary's interpretation unreasonable. Specifically, the claimants and the dissent assert that the HEW interim regulations plainly contain no provision, either in the invocation subsection or in the rebuttal subsection, that directs factual inquiry into the issue of disability causation or the existence of pneumoconiosis. Accordingly, under the claimants' reading of the regulations, there is no manner in which the DOL interim regulations can be seen to be "not . . . more restrictive than" the HEW regulations.

The regulatory scheme, however, is not so straightforward as the claimants would make it out to be. We have noted before the Byzantine character of these regulations. In our view, the Secretary presents the more reasoned interpretation of this complex regulatory structure, an interpretation that has the additional benefit of providing coherence among the statute and the two interim regulations.

The premise underlying the Secretary's interpretation of the HEW interim regulations is that the regulations were adopted to ensure that miners who were disabled due to pneumoconiosis arising out of coal mine employment would receive benefits from the black lung program. Under the Secretary's view, it disserves congressional intent to interpret HEW's interim regulations to allow recovery by miners who do not have pneumoconiosis or whose total disability did not arise, at least in part, from their coal mine employment. We agree.

\* \* \*

The claimants respond that the Secretary has not adopted the most natural reading of subsection (b)(2). Specifically, the claimants argue that miners who have 10 years of coal mine experience and satisfy the requirements of subsection (b)(1) automatically obtain the presumption of causation that § 410.416 or § 410.456 confers, and thereby satisfy the causation requirement inherent in the Act. In addition, the claimants point out that the reference in the HEW rebuttal provisions to § 410.412(a)(1) may best be read as a reference only to the definition of the term "comparable and gainful work," not to the disability causation provision of § 410.412(a). While it is possible that the claimants' parsing of these impenetrable regulations would be consistent with accepted canons of construction, it is axiomatic that the Secretary's interpretation need not be the best or most natural one by grammatical or other standards. *EEOC v. Commercial Office Products Co.*, 486 U.S. 107, 115 (1988). Rather, the Secretary's view need be only reasonable to warrant deference. *Ibid.*; *Mullins*, 484 U.S., at 159.

\* \* \*

IV

We conclude that the Secretary of Labor has not acted unreasonably, or inconsistently with [§ 402(f)(2) of the Federal Mine Safety and Health Act of 1977 as amended by the Black Lung Benefits Act] in promulgating interim regulations that permit the presumption of entitlement to black lung benefits to be rebutted with evidence demonstrating that the miner does not, or did not, have pneumoconiosis, or that the miner's disability does not, or did not, arise out of coal mine employment. Accordingly, we affirm the judgment of the Third Circuit in No. 89-1714. The judgments of the Fourth Circuit in No. 90-113 and No. 90-114 are reversed, and those cases are remanded for further proceedings consistent with this opinion. No costs are allowed in any of these cases.

1   *It is so ordered.*

2   JUSTICE KENNEDY took no part in the consideration or decision of this litigation.

3   JUSTICE SCALIA, dissenting.

4   I respectfully dissent. The disputed regulatory language is complex, but it is not
5   ambiguous, and I do not think *Chevron* deference requires us to accept the strained
6   and implausible construction advanced by the Department of Labor (DOL). In my
7   judgment, at least one of the claimants before us is entitled to benefits under the
8   statute.

9                                    I

10                                   A

11  As an initial matter, the Court misconstrues our *Chevron* jurisprudence. *Chevron*
12  requires that we defer to an agency's interpretation of its organic statute once we
13  determine that that statute is ambiguous. No one contends that the relevant
14  *statutory* language ("shall not be more restrictive than") is ambiguous. The only
15  serious question surrounds the regulations of the then-extant Department of
16  Health, Education, and Welfare (HEW) to which the statute refers. I agree that
17  those regulations are complex, perhaps even "Byzantine," but that alone is
18  insufficient to invoke *Chevron* deference. Deference is appropriate where the
19  relevant language, carefully considered, can yield more than one reasonable
20  interpretation, not where discerning the only possible interpretation requires a
21  taxing inquiry. *Chevron* is a recognition that the ambiguities in statutes are to be
22  resolved by the agencies charged with implementing them, not a declaration that,
23  when statutory construction becomes difficult, we will throw up our hands and let
24  regulatory agencies do it for us. In my view, the HEW regulations referred to by
25  the present statute are susceptible of only one meaning, although they are so
26  intricate that that meaning is not immediately accessible.

27                                  * * *

28                                   B

29                                  * * *

30  The relationship between the two regulations is apparent because they use a
31  similar structure and, in large part, similar language. Both allow claimants to
32  invoke a presumption of disability due to pneumoconiosis upon the presentation
33  of certain medical evidence (the HEW regulations provide for two types of medical
34  evidence while the DOL regulations provide for four). Both specify certain ways in
35  which that presumption may be rebutted. The HEW regulations, however, specify
36  only two methods of rebuttal (both relating to the extent of the disability), while

the DOL regulations authorize four methods (the two expressed in the HEW regulations plus two more: (1) that pneumoconiosis did not cause the disability, and (2) that the miner does not have pneumoconiosis).

Obviously, if the DOL regulations provide more opportunities for rebuttal, they are less favorable to claimants. I think it quite apparent that they do. The present case is illustrative. Claimant Pauley invoked the presumption by submitting X-ray evidence of pneumoconiosis * * * BethEnergy, the employer, rebutted the presumption by arguing * * * that, although Pauley had pneumoconiosis, it did not cause his disability. Had the case proceeded under the HEW regulations, Pauley's presentation would have been the same * * * . For BethEnergy, however, things would have been different. * * * The only rebuttal expressly contemplated by the HEW regulations is that the claimant is not in fact disabled—but Pauley concededly was. It appears, therefore, that BethEnergy could not have challenged the causal link between the pneumoconiosis and the disability under the HEW regulations, and thus would have had no defense.

In my view, this argument is self-evidently correct, and is obscured only by the technical complexity of the regulatory provisions. But the statutory structure, as opposed to the actual language, is simple. Under the HEW regulations, we assume "x," but "x" may be rebutted by a showing of "a" or "b." Under the DOL regulations, we likewise assume "x," but "x" may be rebutted by a showing of "a" or "b" or "c" or "d." It defies common sense to argue that, given this structure, the two regulations are in fact identical, and that Pauley, whose claim could be defeated by a showing of "c" but not by a showing of "a" or "b," was no worse off under the latter regime. Yet that is precisely the argument the Court accepts.

* * *

## General Dynamics Land Systems, Inc. v. Cline

540 U.S. 581 (2004)

February 24, 2004

JUSTICE SOUTER delivered the opinion of the Court.

The Age Discrimination in Employment Act of 1967 (ADEA or Act) forbids discriminatory preference for the young over the old. The question in this case is whether it also prohibits favoring the old over the young. We hold it does not.

I

In 1997, a collective-bargaining agreement between petitioner General Dynamics and the United Auto Workers eliminated the company's obligation to provide

1  health benefits to subsequently retired employees, except as to then-current
2  workers at least 50 years old. Respondents (collectively, Cline) were then at least
3  40 and thus protected by the Act, but under 50 and so without promise of the
4  benefits. All of them objected to the new terms, although some had retired before
5  the change in order to get the prior advantage, some retired afterwards with no
6  benefit, and some worked on, knowing the new contract would give them no health
7  coverage when they were through.

8  Before the Equal Employment Opportunity Commission (EEOC or Commission)
9  they claimed that the agreement violated the ADEA, because it "discriminate[d
10 against them] . . . with respect to . . . compensation, terms, conditions, or privileges
11 of employment, because of [their] age," § 623(a)(1). The EEOC agreed, and invited
12 General Dynamics and the union to settle informally with Cline.

13 When they failed, Cline brought this action against General Dynamics, combining
14 claims under the ADEA and state law. The District Court called the federal claim
15 one of "reverse age discrimination," upon which, it observed, no court had ever
16 granted relief under the ADEA. It dismissed in reliance on the Seventh Circuit's
17 opinion in *Hamilton v. Caterpillar Inc.*, 966 F. 2d 1226 (1992), that "the ADEA
18 'does not protect . . . the younger against the older,'" *id.*, at 1227 (quoting *Karlen v.*
19 *City Colleges of Chicago*, 837 F. 2d 314, 318 (CA7)).

20 A divided panel of the Sixth Circuit reversed, with the majority reasoning that the
21 prohibition of § 623(a)(1), covering discrimination against "any individual . . .
22 because of such individual's age," is so clear on its face that if Congress had meant
23 to limit its coverage to protect only the older worker against the younger, it would
24 have said so. * * *

25                                          * * *

26 We granted certiorari to resolve the conflict among the Circuits, and now reverse.

27                                          II

28 The common ground in this case is the generalization that the ADEA's prohibition
29 covers "discriminat[ion] . . . because of [an] individual's age," 29 U. S. C. §
30 623(a)(1), that helps the younger by hurting the older. In the abstract, the phrase
31 is open to an argument for a broader construction, since reference to "age" carries
32 no express modifier and the word could be read to look two ways. This more
33 expansive possible understanding does not, however, square with the natural
34 reading of the whole provision prohibiting discrimination, and in fact Congress's
35 interpretive clues speak almost unanimously to an understanding of
36 discrimination as directed against workers who are older than the ones getting
37 treated better.

Congress chose not to include age within discrimination forbidden by Title VII of the Civil Rights Act of 1964, being aware that there were legitimate reasons as well as invidious ones for making employment decisions on age. Instead it called for a study of the issue by the Secretary of Labor, who concluded that age discrimination was a serious problem, but one different in kind from discrimination on account of race. The Secretary spoke of disadvantage to older individuals from arbitrary and stereotypical employment distinctions (including then-common policies of age ceilings on hiring), but he examined the problem in light of rational considerations of increased pension cost and, in some cases, legitimate concerns about an older person's ability to do the job. When the Secretary ultimately took the position that arbitrary discrimination against older workers was widespread and persistent enough to call for a federal legislative remedy, he placed his recommendation against the background of common experience that the potential cost of employing someone rises with age, so that the older an employee is, the greater the inducement to prefer a younger substitute. The report contains no suggestion that reactions to age level off at some point, and it was devoid of any indication that the Secretary had noticed unfair advantages accruing to older employees at the expense of their juniors.

Congress then asked for a specific proposal, which the Secretary provided in January 1967. Extensive House and Senate hearings ensued.

The testimony at both hearings dwelled on unjustified assumptions about the effect of age on ability to work. The hearings specifically addressed higher pension and benefit costs as heavier drags on hiring workers the older they got. The record thus reflects the common facts that an individual's chances to find and keep a job get worse over time; as between any two people, the younger is in the stronger position, the older more apt to be tagged with demeaning stereotype. Not surprisingly, from the voluminous records of the hearings, we have found (and Cline has cited) nothing suggesting that any workers were registering complaints about discrimination in favor of their seniors.

Nor is there any such suggestion in the introductory provisions of the ADEA, 81 Stat. 602, which begins with statements of purpose and findings that mirror the Wirtz Report and the committee transcripts. The findings stress the impediments suffered by "older workers . . . in their efforts to retain . . . and especially to regain employment," *id.*, § 2(a)(1); "the [burdens] of arbitrary age limits regardless of potential for job performance," *id.*, § 2(a)(2); the costs of "otherwise desirable practices [that] may work to the disadvantage of older persons," *ibid.*; and "the incidence of unemployment, especially long-term unemployment[, which] is, relative to the younger ages, high among older workers," *id.*, § 2(a)(3). The statutory objects were "to promote employment of older persons based on their ability rather than age; to prohibit arbitrary age discrimination in employment;

[and] to help employers and workers find ways of meeting problems arising from the impact of age on employment." *Id.*, § 2(b).

In sum, except on one point, all the findings and statements of objectives are either cast in terms of the effects of age as intensifying over time, or are couched in terms that refer to "older" workers, explicitly or implicitly relative to "younger" ones. The single subject on which the statute speaks less specifically is that of "arbitrary limits" or "arbitrary age discrimination." But these are unmistakable references to the Wirtz Report's finding that "[a]lmost three out of every five employers covered by [a] 1965 survey have in effect age limitations (most frequently between 45 and 55) on new hires which they apply without consideration of an applicant's other qualifications." The ADEA's ban on "arbitrary limits" thus applies to age caps that exclude older applicants, necessarily to the advantage of younger ones.

Such is the setting of the ADEA's core substantive provision, § 4 (as amended, 29 U.S.C. § 623), prohibiting employers and certain others from "discriminat[ion] . . . because of [an] individual's age," whenever (as originally enacted) the individual is "at least forty years of age but less than sixty-five years of age," § 12, 81 Stat. 607. The prefatory provisions and their legislative history make a case that we think is beyond reasonable doubt, that the ADEA was concerned to protect a relatively old worker from discrimination that works to the advantage of the relatively young.

Nor is it remarkable that the record is devoid of any evidence that younger workers were suffering at the expense of their elders, let alone that a social problem required a federal statute to place a younger worker in parity with an older one. Common experience is to the contrary, and the testimony, reports, and congressional findings simply confirm that Congress used the phrase "discriminat[ion] . . . because of [an] individual's age" the same way that ordinary people in common usage might speak of age discrimination any day of the week. One commonplace conception of American society in recent decades is its character as a "youth culture," and in a world where younger is better, talk about discrimination because of age is naturally understood to refer to discrimination against the older.

This same, idiomatic sense of the statutory phrase is confirmed by the statute's restriction of the protected class to those 40 and above. If Congress had been worrying about protecting the younger against the older, it would not likely have ignored everyone under 40. The youthful deficiencies of inexperience and unsteadiness invite stereotypical and discriminatory thinking about those a lot younger than 40, and prejudice suffered by a 40-year-old is not typically owing to youth, as 40-year-olds sadly tend to find out. The enemy of 40 is 30, not 50. Even so, the 40-year threshold was adopted over the objection that some discrimination against older people begins at an even younger age; female flight attendants were not fired at 32 because they were too young. Thus, the 40-year threshold makes sense as identifying a class requiring protection against preference for their juniors, not as defining a class that might be threatened by favoritism toward seniors.

The federal reports are as replete with cases taking this position as they are nearly devoid of decisions like the one reviewed here. * * *

The Courts of Appeals and the District Courts have read the law the same way, and prior to this case have enjoyed virtually unanimous accord in understanding the ADEA to forbid only discrimination preferring young to old. So the Seventh Circuit held in *Hamilton*, and the First Circuit said in *Schuler*, and so the District Courts have ruled in cases too numerous for citation here in the text. The very strength of this consensus is enough to rule out any serious claim of ambiguity, and congressional silence after years of judicial interpretation supports adherence to the traditional view.

III

Cline and *amicus* EEOC proffer three rejoinders in favor of their competing view that the prohibition works both ways. First, they say (as does JUSTICE THOMAS) that the statute's meaning is plain when the word "age" receives its natural and ordinary meaning and the statute is read as a whole giving "age" the same meaning throughout. And even if the text does not plainly mean what they say it means, they argue that the soundness of their version is shown by a colloquy on the floor of the Senate involving Senator Yarborough, a sponsor of the bill that became the ADEA. Finally, they fall back to the position (fortified by JUSTICE SCALIA's dissent) that we should defer to the EEOC's reading of the statute. On each point, however, we think the argument falls short of unsettling our view of the natural meaning of the phrase speaking of discrimination, read in light of the statute's manifest purpose.

A

The first response to our reading is the dictionary argument that "age" means the length of a person's life, with the phrase "because of such individual's age" stating a simple test of causation: "discriminat[ion] . . . because of [an] individual's age" is treatment that would not have occurred if the individual's span of years had been longer or shorter. The case for this reading calls attention to the other instances of "age" in the ADEA that are not limited to old age, such as 29 U.S.C. § 623(f), which gives an employer a defense to charges of age discrimination when "age is a bona fide occupational qualification." Cline and the EEOC argue that if "age" meant old age, § 623(f) would then provide a defense (old age is a bona fide qualification) only for an employer's action that on our reading would never clash with the statute (because preferring the older is not forbidden).

The argument rests on two mistakes. First, it assumes that the word "age" has the same meaning wherever the ADEA uses it. But this is not so, and Cline simply misemploys the "presumption that identical words used in different parts of the same act are intended to have the same meaning." *Atlantic Cleaners & Dyers, Inc. v. United States*, 286 U.S. 427, 433 (1932). Cline forgets that "the presumption is not rigid and readily yields whenever there is such variation in the connection in which the words are used as reasonably to warrant the conclusion that they were employed in different parts of the act with different intent." *Ibid.* The presumption of uniform usage thus relents when a word used has several commonly understood meanings among which a speaker can alternate in the course of an ordinary conversation, without being confused or getting confusing.

"Age" is that kind of word. As JUSTICE THOMAS agrees, the word "age" standing alone can be readily understood either as pointing to any number of years lived, or as common shorthand for the longer span and concurrent aches that make youth look good. Which alternative was probably intended is a matter of context; we understand the different choices of meaning that lie behind a sentence like "Age can be shown by a driver's license," and the statement, "Age has left him a shut-in." So it is easy to understand that Congress chose different meanings at different places in the ADEA, as the different settings readily show. Hence the second flaw in Cline's argument for uniform usage: it ignores the cardinal rule that "[s]tatutory language must be read in context [since] a phrase 'gathers meaning from the words around it.'" *Jones v. United States*, 527 U.S. 373, 389 (1999) (quoting Jarecki v. G. D. Searle & Co., 367 U.S. 303, 307 (1961)). The point here is that we are not asking an abstract question about the meaning of "age"; we are seeking the meaning of the whole phrase "discriminate . . . because of such individual's age," where it occurs in the ADEA, 29 U.S.C. § 623(a)(1). As we have said, social history emphatically reveals an understanding of age discrimination as aimed against the old, and the statutory reference to age discrimination in this idiomatic sense is confirmed by legislative history. For the very reason that reference to context shows that "age" means "old age" when teamed with "discrimination," the provision of an affirmative defense when age is a bona fide occupational qualification readily shows that "age" as a qualification means comparative youth. As context tells us that "age" means one thing in § 623(a)(1) and another in § 623(f), so it also tells us that the presumption of uniformity cannot sensibly operate here.

* * *

## B

The second objection has more substance than the first, but still not enough. The record of congressional action reports a colloquy on the Senate floor between two of the legislators most active in pushing for the ADEA, Senators Javits and

Yarborough. Senator Javits began the exchange by raising a concern mentioned by Senator Dominick, that "the bill might not forbid discrimination between two persons each of whom would be between the ages of 40 and 65." 113 Cong. Rec. 31255 (1967). Senator Javits then gave his own view that, "if two individuals ages 52 and 42 apply for the same job, and the employer selected the man aged 42 solely . . . because he is younger than the man 52, then he will have violated the act," and asked Senator Yarborough for his opinion. *Ibid.* Senator Yarborough answered that "[t]he law prohibits age being a factor in the decision to hire, as to one age over the other, whichever way [the] decision went." *Ibid.*

Although in the past we have given weight to Senator Yarborough's views on the construction of the ADEA because he was a sponsor, his side of this exchange is not enough to unsettle our reading of the statute. . . . What matters is that the Senator's remark, "whichever way [the] decision went," is the only item in all the 1967 hearings, reports, and debates going against the grain of the common understanding of age discrimination. Even from a sponsor, a single outlying statement cannot stand against a tide of context and history, not to mention 30 years of judicial interpretation producing no apparent legislative qualms.

## C

The third objection relies on a reading consistent with the Yarborough comment, adopted by the agency now charged with enforcing the statute, as set out at 29 CFR § 1625.2(a) (2003). When the EEOC adopted § 1625.2(a) in 1981, shortly after assuming administrative responsibility for the ADEA, it gave no reasons for the view expressed, beyond noting that the provision was carried forward from an earlier Department of Labor regulation; that earlier regulation itself gave no reasons.

The parties contest the degree of weight owed to the EEOC's reading, with General Dynamics urging us that *Skidmore v. Swift & Co.*, 323 U.S. 134 (1944), sets the limit, while Cline and the EEOC say that § 1625.2(a) deserves greater deference under *Chevron U.S.A. Inc. v. Natural Resources Defense Council, Inc.*, 467 U.S. 837 (1984). Although we have devoted a fair amount of attention lately to the varying degrees of deference deserved by agency pronouncements of different sorts, *see United States v. Mead Corp.*, 533 U.S. 218 (2001); *Christensen v. Harris County*, 529 U.S. 576 (2000), the recent cases are not on point here. In *Edelman v. Lynchburg College*, 535 U.S. 106, 114 (2002), we found no need to choose between *Skidmore* and *Chevron*, or even to defer, because the EEOC was clearly right; today, we neither defer nor settle on any degree of deference because the Commission is clearly wrong.

Even for an agency able to claim all the authority possible under *Chevron*, deference to its statutory interpretation is called for only when the devices of

1 judicial construction have been tried and found to yield no clear sense of
2 congressional intent. Here, regular interpretive method leaves no serious question,
3 not even about purely textual ambiguity in the ADEA. The word "age" takes on a
4 definite meaning from being in the phrase "discriminat[ion] ... because of such
5 individual's age," occurring as that phrase does in a statute structured and
6 manifestly intended to protect the older from arbitrary favor for the younger.

7 IV

8 We see the text, structure, purpose, and history of the ADEA, along with its
9 relationship to other federal statutes, as showing that the statute does not mean to
10 stop an employer from favoring an older employee over a younger one. The
11 judgment of the Court of Appeals is

12 *Reversed.*

13 JUSTICE SCALIA, dissenting.

14 The Age Discrimination in Employment Act of 1967 (ADEA), 29 U.S.C. §§ 621–
15 634, makes it unlawful for an employer to "discriminate against any individual
16 with respect to his compensation, terms, conditions, or privileges of employment,
17 because of such individual's age." § 623(a)(1). The question in this case is whether,
18 in the absence of an affirmative defense, the ADEA prohibits an employer from
19 favoring older over younger workers when both are protected by the Act, *i.e.*, are
20 40 years of age or older.

21 The Equal Employment Opportunity Commission (EEOC) has answered this
22 question in the affirmative. In 1981, the agency adopted a regulation which states,
23 in pertinent part:

24 "It is unlawful in situations where this Act applies, for an employer to
25 discriminate in hiring or in any other way by giving preference because of
26 age between individuals 40 and over. Thus, if two people apply for the same
27 position, and one is 42 and the other 52, the employer may not lawfully
28 turn down either one on the basis of age, but must make such decision on
29 the basis of some other factor." 29 C.F.R. § 1625.2(a) (2003).

30 This regulation represents the interpretation of the agency tasked by Congress with
31 enforcing the ADEA. See 29 U.S.C. § 628.

32 The Court brushes aside the EEOC's interpretation as "clearly wrong." I cannot
33 agree with the contention upon which that rejection rests: that "regular
34 interpretive method leaves no serious question, not even about purely textual
35 ambiguity in the ADEA." It is evident, for the reasons given in Part II of Justice
36 Thomas's dissenting opinion, that the Court's interpretive method is anything but

"regular." And for the reasons given in Part I of that opinion, the EEOC's interpretation is neither foreclosed by the statute nor unreasonable.

Because § 623(a) "does not unambiguously require a different interpretation, and . . . the [EEOC's] regulation is an entirely reasonable interpretation of the text," *Barnhart v. Thomas*, 540 U.S. 20, 290-30 (2003), I would defer to the agency's authoritative conclusion. See *United States v. Mead Corp.*, 533 U.S. 218, 257 (2001) (Scalia, J., dissenting). I respectfully dissent.

Justice THOMAS, with whom Justice KENNEDY joins, dissenting.

This should have been an easy case. The plain language of 29 U.S.C. § 623(a)(1) mandates a particular outcome: that the respondents are able to sue for discrimination against them in favor of older workers. The agency charged with enforcing the statute has adopted a regulation and issued an opinion as an adjudicator, both of which adopt this natural interpretation of the provision. And the only portion of legislative history relevant to the question before us is consistent with this outcome. Despite the fact that these traditional tools of statutory interpretation lead inexorably to the conclusion that respondents can state a claim for discrimination against the relatively young, the Court, apparently disappointed by this result, today adopts a different interpretation. In doing so, the Court, of necessity, creates a new tool of statutory interpretation, and then proceeds to give this newly created "social history" analysis dispositive weight. Because I cannot agree with the Court's new approach to interpreting antidiscrimination statutes, I respectfully dissent.

\* \* \*

## 4. Chevron Step Two

Courts very rarely overturn agencies at Chevron Step Two. That is, they very rarely conclude that the statute in question is capable of more than one reading, but the agency's is unreasonable. Indeed, an empirical study finds that, when agencies make it to *Chevron* Step Two, they win 94% of the time.

The *Utility Air Regulatory Group* case is one of the rare ones in which the agency loses at *Chevron* Step Two. Justice Scalia concludes that the Clean Air Act permits an interpretation of pollutant that includes greenhouse gases (*i.e.*, agency passes Step One), but that it was unreasonable for the EPA to adopt such an interpretation (*i.e.*, agency fails Step Two). Is there some tension between these two conclusions? Do they reflect a broader tension between the two steps of *Chevron* analysis?

## Utility Air Regulatory Group v. EPA

1    573 U.S. 302

2    June 23, 2014

3    JUSTICE SCALIA announced the judgment of the Court and delivered the opinion
4    of the Court with respect to Parts I and II.

5    Acting pursuant to the Clean Air Act, 69 Stat. 322, as amended, 42 U.S.C. §§ 7401-
6    7671q, the Environmental Protection Agency recently set standards for emissions
7    of "greenhouse gases" (substances it believes contribute to "global climate
8    change") from new motor vehicles. We must decide whether it was permissible for
9    EPA to determine that its motor-vehicle greenhouse-gas regulations automatically
10   triggered permitting requirements under the Act for stationary sources that emit
11   greenhouse gases.

12                            I. Background

13                 A. Stationary-Source Permitting

14   The Clean Air Act regulates pollution-generating emissions from both stationary
15   sources, such as factories and powerplants, and moving sources, such as cars,
16   trucks, and aircraft. This litigation concerns permitting obligations imposed on
17   stationary sources under Titles I and V of the Act.

18   Title I charges EPA with formulating national ambient air-quality standards
19   (NAAQS) for air pollutants. §§ 7408-7409. To date, EPA has issued NAAQS for six
20   pollutants: sulfur dioxide, particulate matter, nitrogen dioxide, carbon monoxide,
21   ozone, and lead. States have primary responsibility for implementing the NAAQS
22   by developing "State implementation plans." 42 U.S.C. § 7410. A State must
23   designate every area within its borders as "attainment," "nonattainment," or
24   "unclassifiable" with respect to each NAAQS, § 7407(d), and the State's
25   implementation plan must include permitting programs for stationary sources that
26   vary according to the classification of the area where the source is or is proposed
27   to be located. § 7410(a)(2)(C), (I).

28   Stationary sources in areas designated attainment or unclassifiable are subject to
29   the Act's provisions relating to "Prevention of Significant Deterioration" (PSD). §§
30   7470-7492. EPA interprets the PSD provisions to apply to sources located in areas
31   that are designated attainment or unclassifiable for any NAAQS pollutant,
32   regardless of whether the source emits that specific pollutant. Since the inception
33   of the PSD program, every area of the country has been designated attainment or
34   unclassifiable for at least one NAAQS pollutant; thus, on EPA's view, all stationary
35   sources are potentially subject to PSD review.

36   It is unlawful to construct or modify a "major emitting facility" in "any area to
37   which [the PSD program] applies" without first obtaining a permit. §§ 7475(a)(1),

7479(2)(C). To qualify for a permit, the facility must not cause or contribute to the violation of any applicable air-quality standard, § 7475(a)(3), and it must comply with emissions limitations that reflect the "best available control technology" (or BACT) for "each pollutant subject to regulation under" the Act. § 7475(a)(4). The Act defines a "major emitting facility" as any stationary source with the potential to emit 250 tons per year of "any air pollutant" (or 100 tons per year for certain types of sources). § 7479(1). It defines "modification" as a physical or operational change that causes the facility to emit more of "any air pollutant." § 7411(a)(4).

In addition to the PSD permitting requirements for construction and modification, Title V of the Act makes it unlawful to operate any "major source," wherever located, without a comprehensive operating permit. § 7661a(a). Unlike the PSD program, Title V generally does not impose any substantive pollution-control requirements. Instead, it is designed to facilitate compliance and enforcement by consolidating into a single document all of a facility's obligations under the Act. The permit must include all "emissions limitations and standards" that apply to the source, as well as associated inspection, monitoring, and reporting requirements. § 7661c(a)-(c). Title V defines a "major source" by reference to the Act-wide definition of "major stationary source," which in turn means any stationary source with the potential to emit 100 tons per year of "any air pollutant." §§ 7661(2)(B), 7602(j).

## B. EPA's Greenhouse-Gas Regulations

In 2007, the Court held that Title II of the Act "authorize[d] EPA to regulate greenhouse gas emissions from new motor vehicles" if the Agency "form[ed] a 'judgment' that such emissions contribute to climate change." *Massachusetts v. EPA*, 549 U.S. 497, 528 (quoting § 7521(a)(1)). In response to that decision, EPA embarked on a course of regulation resulting in "the single largest expansion in the scope of the [Act] in its history." Clean Air Act Handbook, at xxi.

\* \* \*

In 2009, EPA announced its determination regarding the danger posed by motor-vehicle greenhouse-gas emissions. EPA found that greenhouse-gas emissions from new motor vehicles contribute to elevated atmospheric concentrations of greenhouse gases, which endanger public health and welfare by fostering global "climate change." 74 Fed. Reg. 66523, 66537 (hereinafter Endangerment Finding). It denominated a "single air pollutant" the "combined mix" of six greenhouse gases that it identified as "the root cause of human-induced climate change": carbon dioxide, methane, nitrous oxide, hydrofluorocarbons, perfluorocarbons, and sulfur hexafluoride. *Id.*, at 66526, 66537. A source's greenhouse-gas emissions would be measured in "carbon dioxide equivalent units" ($CO_2e$), which would be calculated based on each gas's "global warming potential." *Id.*, at 66499, n. 4.

Next, EPA issued its "final decision" regarding the prospect that motor-vehicle greenhouse-gas standards would trigger stationary-source permitting requirements. 75 Fed. Reg. 17004 (2010) (hereinafter Triggering Rule). EPA announced that beginning on the effective date of its greenhouse-gas standards for motor vehicles, stationary sources would be subject to the PSD program and Title V on the basis of their potential to emit greenhouse gases. As expected, EPA in short order promulgated greenhouse-gas emission standards for passenger cars, light-duty trucks, and medium-duty passenger vehicles to take effect on January 2, 2011. 75 Fed. Reg. 25324 (hereinafter Tailpipe Rule).

EPA then announced steps it was taking to "tailor" the PSD program and Title V to greenhouse gases. 75 Fed. Reg. 31514 (hereinafter Tailoring Rule). Those steps were necessary, it said, because the PSD program and Title V were designed to regulate "a relatively small number of large industrial sources," and requiring permits for all sources with greenhouse-gas emissions above the statutory thresholds would radically expand those programs, making them both unadministrable and "unrecognizable to the Congress that designed" them. *Id.*, at 31555, 31562. EPA nonetheless rejected calls to exclude greenhouse gases entirely from those programs, asserting that the Act is not "ambiguous with respect to the need to cover [greenhouse-gas] sources under either the PSD or title V program." *Id.*, at 31548, n. 31. Instead, EPA adopted a "phase-in approach" that it said would "appl[y] PSD and title V at threshold levels that are as close to the statutory levels as possible, and do so as quickly as possible, at least to a certain point." *Id.*, at 31523.

\* \* \*

## C. Decision Below

Numerous parties, including several States, filed petitions for review in the D. C. Circuit under 42 U.S.C. § 7607(b), challenging EPA's greenhouse-gas-related actions. The Court of Appeals dismissed some of the petitions for lack of jurisdiction and denied the remainder. *Coalition for Responsible Regulation, Inc. v. EPA*, 684 F. 3d 102 (2012) (per curiam). First, it upheld the Endangerment Finding and Tailpipe Rule. *Id.*, at 119, 126. Next, it held that EPA's interpretation of the PSD permitting requirement as applying to "any regulated air pollutant," including greenhouse gases, was "compelled by the statute." *Id.*, at 133-134. The court also found it "crystal clear that PSD permittees must install BACT for greenhouse gases." *Id.*, at 137. Because it deemed petitioners' arguments about the PSD program insufficiently applicable to Title V, it held they had "forfeited any challenges to EPA's greenhouse gas-inclusive interpretation of Title V." *Id.*, at 136. Finally, it held that petitioners were without Article III standing to challenge EPA's efforts to limit the reach of the PSD program and Title V through the Triggering and Tailoring Rules. *Id.*, at 146. The court denied rehearing en banc, with Judges Brown and Kavanaugh each dissenting. No. 09-1322 etc. (Dec. 20, 2012).

We granted six petitions for certiorari but agreed to decide only one question: "'Whether EPA permissibly determined that its regulation of greenhouse gas emissions from new motor vehicles triggered permitting requirements under the Clean Air Act for stationary sources that emit greenhouse gases.'" 571 U.S. 951 (2013).

## II. Analysis

This litigation presents two distinct challenges to EPA's stance on greenhouse-gas permitting for stationary sources. First, we must decide whether EPA permissibly determined that a source may be subject to the PSD and Title V permitting requirements on the sole basis of the source's potential to emit greenhouse gases. Second, we must decide whether EPA permissibly determined that a source already subject to the PSD program because of its emission of conventional pollutants (an "anyway" source) may be required to limit its greenhouse-gas emissions by employing the "best available control technology" for greenhouse gases. The Solicitor General joins issue on both points but evidently regards the second as more important; he informs us that "anyway" sources account for roughly 83% of American stationary-source greenhouse-gas emissions, compared to just 3% for the additional, non-"anyway" sources EPA sought to regulate at Steps 2 and 3 of the Tailoring Rule. Tr. of Oral Arg. 52.

We review EPA's interpretations of the Clean Air Act using the standard set forth in *Chevron U.S. A. Inc. v. Natural Resources Defense Council, Inc.*, 467 U.S. 837, 842-843 (1984). Under *Chevron*, we presume that when an agency-administered statute is ambiguous with respect to what it prescribes, Congress has empowered the agency to resolve the ambiguity. The question for a reviewing court is whether in doing so the agency has acted reasonably and thus has "stayed within the bounds of its statutory authority." *Arlington v. FCC*, 569 U.S. 290, 297 (2013) (emphasis deleted).

## A. The PSD and Title V Triggers

We first decide whether EPA permissibly interpreted the statute to provide that a source may be required to obtain a PSD or Title V permit on the sole basis of its potential greenhouse-gas emissions.

1

EPA thought its conclusion that a source's greenhouse-gas emissions may necessitate a PSD or Title V permit followed from the Act's unambiguous language. The Court of Appeals agreed and held that the statute "compelled" EPA's

1  interpretation. 684 F. 3d, at 134. We disagree. The statute compelled EPA's
2  greenhouse-gas-inclusive interpretation with respect to neither the PSD program
3  nor Title V.

4  The Court of Appeals reasoned by way of a flawed syllogism: Under
5  *Massachusetts*, the general, Act-wide definition of "air pollutant" includes
6  greenhouse gases; the Act requires permits for major emitters of "any air
7  pollutant"; therefore, the Act requires permits for major emitters of greenhouse
8  gases. The conclusion follows from the premises only if the air pollutants referred
9  to in the permit-requiring provisions (the minor premise) are the same air
10 pollutants encompassed by the Act-wide definition as interpreted in
11 *Massachusetts* (the major premise). Yet no one—least of all EPA—endorses that
12 proposition, and it is obviously untenable.

13 The Act-wide definition says that an air pollutant is "any air pollution agent or
14 combination of such agents, including any physical, chemical, biological, [or]
15 radioactive . . . substance or matter which is emitted into or otherwise enters the
16 ambient air." § 7602(g). In *Massachusetts*, the Court held that the Act-wide
17 definition includes greenhouse gases because it is all-encompassing; it "embraces
18 all airborne compounds of whatever stripe." 549 U.S., at 529. But where the term
19 "air pollutant" appears in the Act's operative provisions, EPA has routinely given
20 it a narrower, context-appropriate meaning.

21 That is certainly true of the provisions that require PSD and Title V permitting for
22 major emitters of "any air pollutant." Since 1978, EPA's regulations have
23 interpreted "air pollutant" in the PSD permitting trigger as limited to regulated air
24 pollutants, 43 Fed. Reg. 26403, codified, as amended, 40 CFR § 52.21(b)(1)-(2),
25 (50)—a class much narrower than *Massachusetts*' "all airborne compounds of
26 whatever stripe," 549 U.S., at 529. And since 1993 EPA has informally taken the
27 same position with regard to the Title V permitting trigger, a position the Agency
28 ultimately incorporated into some of the regulations at issue here. Those
29 interpretations were appropriate: It is plain as day that the Act does not envision
30 an elaborate, burdensome permitting process for major emitters of steam, oxygen,
31 or other harmless airborne substances. It takes some cheek for EPA to insist that
32 it cannot possibly give "air pollutant" a reasonable, context-appropriate meaning
33 in the PSD and Title V contexts when it has been doing precisely that for decades.

34                          * * *

35 *Massachusetts* did not invalidate all these longstanding constructions. * * *

36 *Massachusetts* does not strip EPA of authority to exclude greenhouse gases from
37 the class of regulable air pollutants under other parts of the Act where their
38 inclusion would be inconsistent with the statutory scheme. The Act-wide definition
39 to which the Court gave a "sweeping" and "capacious" interpretation, *id.*, at 528,
   556

532, is not a command to regulate, but a description of the universe of substances EPA may consider regulating under the Act's operative provisions.

* * *

In sum, there is no insuperable textual barrier to EPA's interpreting "any air pollutant" in the permitting triggers of PSD and Title V to encompass only pollutants emitted in quantities that enable them to be sensibly regulated at the statutory thresholds, and to exclude those atypical pollutants that, like greenhouse gases, are emitted in such vast quantities that their inclusion would radically transform those programs and render them unworkable as written.

2

Having determined that EPA was mistaken in thinking the Act compelled a greenhouse-gas-inclusive interpretation of the PSD and Title V triggers, we next consider the Agency's alternative position that its interpretation was justified as an exercise of its "discretion" to adopt "a reasonable construction of the statute." Tailoring Rule 31517. We conclude that EPA's interpretation is not permissible.

Even under *Chevron*'s deferential framework, agencies must operate "within the bounds of reasonable interpretation." *Arlington*, 569 U.S., at 296. And reasonable statutory interpretation must account for both "the specific context in which . . . language is used" and "the broader context of the statute as a whole." *Robinson v. Shell Oil Co.*, 519 U.S. 337, 341 (1997). A statutory "provision that may seem ambiguous in isolation is often clarified by the remainder of the statutory scheme . . . because only one of the permissible meanings produces a substantive effect that is compatible with the rest of the law." *United Sav. Assn. of Tex. v. Timbers of Inwood Forest Associates, Ltd.*, 484 U.S. 365, 371 (1988). Thus, an agency interpretation that is "inconsisten[t] with the design and structure of the statute as a whole," *University of Tex. Southwestern Medical Center v. Nassar*, 570 U.S. 338, 353 (2013), does not merit deference.

EPA itself has repeatedly acknowledged that applying the PSD and Title V permitting requirements to greenhouse gases would be inconsistent with—in fact, would overthrow—the Act's structure and design. In the Tailoring Rule, EPA described the calamitous consequences of interpreting the Act in that way. Under the PSD program, annual permit applications would jump from about 800 to nearly 82,000; annual administrative costs would swell from $12 million to over $1.5 billion; and decade-long delays in issuing permits would become common, causing construction projects to grind to a halt nationwide. Tailoring Rule 31557. The picture under Title V was equally bleak: The number of sources required to have permits would jump from fewer than 15,000 to about 6.1 million; annual administrative costs would balloon from $62 million to $21 billion; and collectively the newly covered sources would face permitting costs of $147 billion. *Id.*, at 31562-

31563. Moreover, "the great majority of additional sources brought into the PSD and title V programs would be small sources that Congress did not expect would need to undergo permitting." *Id.*, at 31533. EPA stated that these results would be so "contrary to congressional intent," and would so "severely undermine what Congress sought to accomplish," that they necessitated as much as a 1,000-fold increase in the permitting thresholds set forth in the statute. *Id.*, at 31554, 31562.

Like EPA, we think it beyond reasonable debate that requiring permits for sources based solely on their emission of greenhouse gases at the 100- and 250-tons-per-year levels set forth in the statute would be "incompatible" with "the substance of Congress' regulatory scheme." *Brown & Williamson*, 529 U.S., at 156. A brief review of the relevant statutory provisions leaves no doubt that the PSD program and Title V are designed to apply to, and cannot rationally be extended beyond, a relative handful of large sources capable of shouldering heavy substantive and procedural burdens.

\* \* \*

The fact that EPA's greenhouse-gas-inclusive interpretation of the PSD and Title V triggers would place plainly excessive demands on limited governmental resources is alone a good reason for rejecting it; but that is not the only reason. EPA's interpretation is also unreasonable because it would bring about an enormous and transformative expansion in EPA's regulatory authority without clear congressional authorization. When an agency claims to discover in a long-extant statute an unheralded power to regulate "a significant portion of the American economy," *Brown & Williamson*, 529 U.S., at 159, we typically greet its announcement with a measure of skepticism. We expect Congress to speak clearly if it wishes to assign to an agency decisions of vast "economic and political significance." *Id.*, at 160; see also *MCI Telecommunications Corp. v. American Telephone & Telegraph Co.*, 512 U.S. 218, 231 (1994); *Industrial Union Dept., AFL-CIO v. American Petroleum Institute*, 448 U.S. 607, 645-646 (1980) (plurality opinion). \* \* \* Since, as we hold above, the statute does not compel EPA's interpretation, it would be patently unreasonable—not to say outrageous—for EPA to insist on seizing expansive power that it admits the statute is not designed to grant.

\* \* \*

### B. BACT for "Anyway" Sources

For the reasons we have given, EPA overstepped its statutory authority when it decided that a source could become subject to PSD or Title V permitting by reason of its greenhouse-gas emissions. But what about "anyway" sources, those that would need permits based on their emissions of more conventional pollutants (such as particulate matter)? We now consider whether EPA reasonably

558

interpreted the Act to require those sources to comply with "best available control technology" emission standards for greenhouse gases.

1

* * *

2

The question before us is whether EPA's decision to require BACT for greenhouse gases emitted by sources otherwise subject to PSD review is, as a general matter, a permissible interpretation of the statute under Chevron. We conclude that it is.

The text of the BACT provision is far less open-ended than the text of the PSD and Title V permitting triggers. It states that BACT is required "for each pollutant subject to regulation under this chapter" (i.e., the entire Act), § 7475(a)(4), a phrase that—as the D. C. Circuit wrote 35 years ago—"would not seem readily susceptible [of] misinterpretation." *Alabama Power Co. v. Costle*, 636 F. 2d 323, 404 (1979). Whereas the dubious breadth of "any air pollutant" in the permitting triggers suggests a role for agency judgment in identifying the subset of pollutants covered by the particular regulatory program at issue, the more specific phrasing of the BACT provision suggests that the necessary judgment has already been made by Congress. The wider statutory context likewise does not suggest that the BACT provision can bear a narrowing construction: There is no indication that the Act elsewhere uses, or that EPA has interpreted, "each pollutant subject to regulation under this chapter" to mean anything other than what it says.

Even if the text were not clear, applying BACT to greenhouse gases is not so disastrously unworkable, and need not result in such a dramatic expansion of agency authority, as to convince us that EPA's interpretation is unreasonable. We are not talking about extending EPA jurisdiction over millions of previously unregulated entities, but about moderately increasing the demands EPA (or a state permitting authority) can make of entities already subject to its regulation. And it is not yet clear that EPA's demands will be of a significantly different character from those traditionally associated with PSD review. In short, the record before us does not establish that the BACT provision as written is incapable of being sensibly applied to greenhouse gases.

* * *

To sum up: We hold that EPA exceeded its statutory authority when it interpreted the Clean Air Act to require PSD and Title V permitting for stationary sources based on their greenhouse-gas emissions. Specifically, the Agency may not treat greenhouse gases as a pollutant for purposes of defining a "major emitting facility" (or a "modification" thereof) in the PSD context or a "major source" in the Title V context. To the extent its regulations purport to do so, they are invalid. EPA may, however, continue to treat greenhouse gases as a "pollutant subject to regulation under this chapter" for purposes of requiring BACT for "anyway" sources. The judgment of the Court of Appeals is affirmed in part and reversed in part.

It is so ordered.

Justice Breyer, with whom Justice Ginsburg, Justice Sotomayor, and Justice Kagan join, concurring in part and dissenting in part.

\* \* \*

I agree with the Court's holding that stationary sources that are subject to the PSD program because they emit other (non-greenhouse-gas) pollutants in quantities above the statutory threshold—those facilities that the Court refers to as "anyway" sources—must meet the "best available control technology" requirement of § 7475(a)(4) with respect to greenhouse gas emissions. I therefore join Part II-B-2 of the Court's opinion. But as for the Court's holding that the EPA cannot interpret the language at issue here to cover facilities that emit more than 100,000 tpy of greenhouse gases by virtue of those emissions, I respectfully dissent.

Justice Alito, with whom Justice Thomas joins, concurring in part and dissenting in part.

In *Massachusetts v. EPA*, 549 U.S. 497 (2007), this Court considered whether greenhouse gases fall within the Clean Air Act's general definition of an air "pollutant." *Id.*, at 528-529. The Environmental Protection Agency cautioned us that "key provisions of the [Act] cannot cogently be applied to [greenhouse gas] emissions," Brief for Federal Respondent in *Massachusetts v. EPA*, p. 22, but the Court brushed the warning aside and had "little trouble" concluding that the Act's "sweeping definition" of a pollutant encompasses greenhouse gases. 549 U.S., at 528-529. I believed *Massachusetts v. EPA* was wrongly decided at the time, and these cases further expose the flaws with that decision.

\* \* \*


## 5. Chevron's Limits

How big is "*Chevron*'s Domain"? The Supreme Court addressed an important aspect of this question in *Mead*, back in 2001, holding that *Chevron* did not apply every time an agency interpreted a statute it administered, but only where agencies offered interpretations with the force of law pursuant to a congressional delegation of power.

1 The cases in this unit also raise questions about *Chevron*'s domain. Some statutes
2 administered by agencies also come up in litigation not involving the agencies. Can
3 an agency adopt any "reasonable" interpretation of an ambiguous statute even
4 when there is a contrary judicial interpretation already on the books? Does
5 *Chevron* also apply to "jurisdictional" issues: when the agency is determining
6 whether or not it has authority under a statute? If so, aren't courts really giving
7 away the store to agencies? If so, how confident are we that we can distinguish
8 "jurisdictional" issues from "non-jurisdictional" ones?

9

## National Cable & Telecommunications Assn. v. Brand X Internet Services

12 545 U.S. 967 (2005)

13 June 27, 2005

14 JUSTICE THOMAS delivered the opinion of the Court.

15 Title II of the Communications Act of 1934, 48 Stat. 1064, as amended, 47 U.S.C. §
16 151 *et seq.*, subjects all providers of "telecommunications servic[e]" to mandatory
17 common-carrier regulation, § 153(44). In the order under review, the Federal
18 Communications Commission concluded that cable companies that sell broadband
19 Internet service do not provide "telecommunications servic[e]" as the
20 Communications Act defines that term, and hence are exempt from mandatory
21 common-carrier regulation under Title II. We must decide whether that conclusion
22 is a lawful construction of the Communications Act under *Chevron U.S.A. Inc. v.*
23 *Natural Resources Defense Council, Inc.*, 467 U.S. 837 (1984), and the
24 Administrative Procedure Act. We hold that it is.

25 I

26 The traditional means by which consumers in the United States access the network
27 of interconnected computers that make up the Internet is through "dial-up"
28 connections provided over local telephone facilities. Using these connections,
29 consumers access the Internet by making calls with computer modems through the
30 telephone wires owned by local phone companies. Internet service providers
31 (ISPs), in turn, link those calls to the Internet network, not only by providing a
32 physical connection, but also by offering consumers the ability to translate raw
33 Internet data into information they may both view on their personal computers
34 and transmit to other computers connected to the Internet. Technological
35 limitations of local telephone wires, however, retard the speed at which data from
36 the Internet may be transmitted through end users' dial-up connections. Dial-up
37 connections are therefore known as "narrowband," or slower speed, connections.

"Broadband" Internet service, by contrast, transmits data at much higher speeds. There are two principal kinds of broadband Internet service: cable modem service and Digital Subscriber Line (DSL) service. Cable modem service transmits data between the Internet and users' computers via the network of television cable lines owned by cable companies. DSL service provides high-speed access using the local telephone wires owned by local telephone companies. Cable companies and telephone companies can either provide Internet access directly to consumers, thus acting as ISPs themselves, or can lease their transmission facilities to independent ISPs that then use the facilities to provide consumers with Internet access. Other ways of transmitting high-speed Internet data into homes, including terrestrial- and satellite-based wireless networks, are also emerging.

## II

At issue in these cases is the proper regulatory classification under the Communications Act of broadband cable Internet service. The Act, as amended by the Telecommunications Act of 1996, 110 Stat. 56, defines two categories of regulated entities relevant to these cases: telecommunications carriers and information-service providers. The Act regulates telecommunications carriers, but not information-service providers, as common carriers. Telecommunications carriers, for example, must charge just and reasonable, nondiscriminatory rates to their customers, 47 U.S.C. §§201–209, design their systems so that other carriers can interconnect with their communications networks, § 251(a)(1), and contribute to the federal "universal service" fund, § 254(d). These provisions are mandatory, but the Commission must forbear from applying them if it determines that the public interest requires it. §§ 160(a), (b). Information-service providers, by contrast, are not subject to mandatory common-carrier regulation under Title II, though the Commission has jurisdiction to impose additional regulatory obligations under its Title I ancillary jurisdiction to regulate interstate and foreign communications.

\* \* \*

In September 2000, the Commission initiated a rulemaking proceeding to, among other things, apply these classifications to cable companies that offer broadband Internet service directly to consumers. In March 2002, that rulemaking culminated in the *Declaratory Ruling* under review in these cases. In the *Declaratory Ruling*, the Commission concluded that broadband Internet service provided by cable companies is an "information service" but not a "telecommunications service" under the Act, and therefore not subject to mandatory Title II common-carrier regulation. \* \* \*

\* \* \*

* * * Though the Commission declined to apply mandatory Title II common-carrier regulation to cable companies, it invited comment on whether under its Title I jurisdiction it should require cable companies to offer other ISPs access to their facilities on common-carrier terms. Numerous parties petitioned for judicial review, challenging the Commission's conclusion that cable modem service was not telecommunications service. By judicial lottery, the Court of Appeals for the Ninth Circuit was selected as the venue for the challenge.

The Court of Appeals granted the petitions in part, vacated the *Declaratory Ruling* in part, and remanded to the Commission for further proceedings. In particular, the Court of Appeals vacated the ruling to the extent it concluded that cable modem service was not "telecommunications service" under the Communications Act. It held that the Commission could not permissibly construe the Communications Act to exempt cable companies providing Internet service from Title II regulation. Rather than analyzing the permissibility of that construction under the deferential framework of *Chevron*, however, the Court of Appeals grounded its holding in the *stare decisis* effect of *AT&T Corp. v. Portland*, 216 F. 3d 871 (CA9 2000). *Portland* held that cable modem service was a "telecommunications service," though the court in that case was not reviewing an administrative proceeding and the Commission was not a party to the case. Nevertheless, *Portland*'s holding, the Court of Appeals reasoned, overrode the contrary interpretation reached by the Commission in the *Declaratory Ruling*.

We granted certiorari to settle the important questions of federal law that these cases present.

### III

We first consider whether we should apply *Chevron*'s framework to the Commission's interpretation of the term "telecommunications service." We conclude that we should. We also conclude that the Court of Appeals should have done the same, instead of following the contrary construction it adopted in *Portland*.

### A

In *Chevron*, this Court held that ambiguities in statutes within an agency's jurisdiction to administer are delegations of authority to the agency to fill the statutory gap in reasonable fashion. Filling these gaps, the Court explained, involves difficult policy choices that agencies are better equipped to make than courts. If a statute is ambiguous, and if the implementing agency's construction is reasonable, *Chevron* requires a federal court to accept the agency's construction of the statute, even if the agency's reading differs from what the court believes is the best statutory interpretation.

The *Chevron* framework governs our review of the Commission's construction. Congress has delegated to the Commission the authority to "execute and enforce" the Communications Act, and to "prescribe such rules and regulations as may be necessary in the public interest to carry out the provisions" of the Act. These provisions give the Commission the authority to promulgate binding legal rules; the Commission issued the order under review in the exercise of that authority; and no one questions that the order is within the Commission's jurisdiction. Hence, as we have in the past, we apply the *Chevron* framework to the Commission's interpretation of the Communications Act. * * *

\* \* \*

B

The Court of Appeals declined to apply *Chevron* because it thought the Commission's interpretation of the Communications Act foreclosed by the conflicting construction of the Act it had adopted in *Portland*. It based that holding on the assumption that *Portland*'s construction overrode the Commission's, regardless of whether *Portland* had held the statute to be unambiguous. That reasoning was incorrect.

A court's prior judicial construction of a statute trumps an agency construction otherwise entitled to *Chevron* deference only if the prior court decision holds that its construction follows from the unambiguous terms of the statute and thus leaves no room for agency discretion. This principle follows from *Chevron* itself. * * * [A]llowing a judicial precedent to foreclose an agency from interpreting an ambiguous statute, as the Court of Appeals assumed it could, would allow a court's interpretation to override an agency's. *Chevron*'s premise is that it is for agencies, not courts, to fill statutory gaps. The better rule is to hold judicial interpretations contained in precedents to the same demanding *Chevron* step one standard that applies if the court is reviewing the agency's construction on a blank slate: Only a judicial precedent holding that the statute unambiguously forecloses the agency's interpretation, and therefore contains no gap for the agency to fill, displaces a conflicting agency construction.

A contrary rule would produce anomalous results. It would mean that whether an agency's interpretation of an ambiguous statute is entitled to *Chevron* deference would turn on the order in which the interpretations issue: If the court's construction came first, its construction would prevail, whereas if the agency's came first, the agency's construction would command *Chevron* deference. Yet whether Congress has delegated to an agency the authority to interpret a statute does not depend on the order in which the judicial and administrative constructions occur. * * *

1    The dissent answers that allowing an agency to override what a court believes to
2    be the best interpretation of a statute makes "judicial decisions subject to reversal
3    by Executive officers." It does not. Since *Chevron* teaches that a court's opinion as
4    to the best reading of an ambiguous statute an agency is charged with
5    administering is not authoritative, the agency's decision to construe that statute
6    differently from a court does not say that the court's holding was legally wrong.
7    Instead, the agency may, consistent with the court's holding, choose a different
8    construction, since the agency remains the authoritative interpreter (within the
9    limits of reason) of such statutes. In all other respects, the court's prior ruling
10   remains binding law (for example, as to agency interpretations to which *Chevron*
11   is inapplicable). The precedent has not been "reversed" by the agency, any more
12   than a federal court's interpretation of a State's law can be said to have been
13   "reversed" by a state court that adopts a conflicting (yet authoritative)
14   interpretation of state law.

15                                            * * *

16   Against this background, the Court of Appeals erred in refusing to apply *Chevron*
17   to the Commission's interpretation of the definition of "telecommunications
18   service." Its prior decision in *Portland* held only that the *best* reading of §153(46)
19   was that cable modem service was a "telecommunications service," not that it was
20   the *only permissible* reading of the statute. Nothing in *Portland* held that the
21   Communications Act unambiguously required treating cable Internet providers as
22   telecommunications carriers. Instead, the court noted that it was "not presented
23   with a case involving potential deference to an administrative agency's statutory
24   construction pursuant to the *Chevron* doctrine," and the court invoked no other
25   rule of construction requiring it to conclude that the statute was unambiguous to
26   reach its judgment. Before a judicial construction of a statute, whether contained
27   in a precedent or not, may trump an agency's, the court must hold that the statute
28   unambiguously requires the court's construction. *Portland* did not do so.

29                                            * * *

30                                            IV

31   We next address whether the Commission's construction of the definition of
32   "telecommunications service" is a permissible reading of the Communications Act
33   under the *Chevron* framework. *Chevron* established a familiar two-step procedure
34   for evaluating whether an agency's interpretation of a statute is lawful. At the first
35   step, we ask whether the statute's plain terms "directly addres[s] the precise
36   question at issue." If the statute is ambiguous on the point, we defer at step two to
37   the agency's interpretation so long as the construction is "a reasonable policy
38   choice for the agency to make." The Commission's interpretation is permissible at
39   both steps.

1                                          A

2    * * * The issue before the Commission was whether cable companies providing
3    cable modem service are providing a "telecommunications service" in addition to
4    an "information service."

5    The Commission first concluded that cable modem service is an "information
6    service," a conclusion unchallenged here. The Act defines "information service" as
7    "the offering of a capability for generating, acquiring, storing, transforming,
8    processing, retrieving, utilizing, or making available information via
9    telecommunications . . . ." §153(20). Cable modem service is an information
10   service, the Commission reasoned, because it provides consumers with a
11   comprehensive capability for manipulating information using the Internet via
12   high-speed telecommunications. * * *

13   At the same time, the Commission concluded that cable modem service was not
14   "telecommunications service." "Telecommunications service" is "the offering of
15   telecommunications for a fee directly to the public." 47 U.S.C. §153(46).
16   "Telecommunications," in turn, is defined as "the transmission, between or among
17   points specified by the user, of information of the user's choosing, without change
18   in the form or content of the information as sent and received." §153(43). The
19   Commission conceded that, like all information-service providers, cable
20   companies use "telecommunications" to provide consumers with Internet service;
21   cable companies provide such service via the high-speed wire that transmits
22   signals to and from an end user's computer. For the Commission, however, the
23   question whether cable broadband Internet providers "offer" telecommunications
24   involved more than whether telecommunications was one necessary component of
25   cable modem service. Instead, whether that service also includes a
26   telecommunications "offering" "tur[ned] on the nature of the functions the *end*
27   *user* is offered," for the statutory definition of "telecommunications service" does
28   not "res[t] on the particular types of facilities used."

29   Seen from the consumer's point of view, the Commission concluded, cable modem
30   service is not a telecommunications offering because the consumer uses the high-
31   speed wire always in connection with the information-processing capabilities
32   provided by Internet access, and because the transmission is a necessary
33   component of Internet access: "As provided to the end user the
34   telecommunications is part and parcel of cable modem service and is integral to its
35   other capabilities." * * *

36                                          B

37   This construction passes *Chevron*'s first step. Respondents argue that it does not,
38   on the ground that cable companies providing Internet service necessarily "offe[r]"
39   the underlying telecommunications used to transmit that service. The word

"offering" as used in §153(46), however, does not unambiguously require that result. Instead, "offering" can reasonably be read to mean a "stand-alone" offering of telecommunications, *i.e.*, an offered service that, from the user's perspective, transmits messages unadulterated by computer processing. That conclusion follows not only from the ordinary meaning of the word "offering," but also from the regulatory history of the Communications Act.

\* \* \*

\* \* \*

## C

We also conclude that the Commission's construction was "a reasonable policy choice for the [Commission] to make" at *Chevron*'s second step.

Respondents argue that the Commission's construction is unreasonable because it allows any communications provider to "evade" common-carrier regulation by the expedient of bundling information service with telecommunications. \* \* \*

We need not decide whether a construction that resulted in these consequences would be unreasonable because we do not believe that these results follow from the construction the Commission adopted. As we understand the *Declaratory Ruling*, the Commission did not say that any telecommunications service that is priced or bundled with an information service is automatically unregulated under Title II. \* \* \*

\* \* \*

\* \* \* The judgment of the Court of Appeals is reversed, and the cases are remanded for further proceedings consistent with this opinion.

It is so ordered.

JUSTICE STEVENS, concurring. [Omitted.]

JUSTICE BREYER, concurring. [Omitted.]

JUSTICE SCALIA, with whom JUSTICE SOUTER and JUSTICE GINSBURG join as to Part I, dissenting.

\* \* \*

## II

In Part III-B of its opinion, the Court continues the administrative-law improvisation project it began four years ago in *United States v. Mead Corp.*, 533 U.S. 218 (2001). To the extent it set forth a comprehensible rule, *Mead* drastically

1   limited the categories of agency action that would qualify for deference under
2   *Chevron U.S.A. Inc. v. Natural Resources Defense Council, Inc.,* 467 U.S. 837
3   (1984). For example, the position taken by an agency before the Supreme Court,
4   with full approval of the agency head, would not qualify. Rather, some unspecified
5   degree of formal process was required—or was at least the only safe harbor. See
6   *Mead, supra,* at 245-246 (SCALIA, J., dissenting).

7   This meant that many more issues appropriate for agency determination would
8   reach the courts without benefit of an agency position entitled to *Chevron*
9   deference, requiring the courts to rule on these issues *de novo.* As I pointed out in
10  dissent, this in turn meant (under the law as it was understood until today) that
11  many statutory ambiguities that might be resolved in varying fashions by
12  successive agency administrations, would be resolved finally, conclusively, and
13  forever, by federal judges—producing an "ossification of large portions of our
14  statutory law," 533 U.S., at 247. The Court today moves to solve this problem of its
15  own creation by inventing yet another breathtaking novelty: judicial decisions
16  subject to reversal by Executive officers.

17  Imagine the following sequence of events: FCC action is challenged as ultra vires
18  under the governing statute; the litigation reaches all the way to the Supreme Court
19  of the United States. The Solicitor General sets forth the FCC's official position
20  (approved by the Commission) regarding interpretation of the statute. Applying
21  *Mead,* however, the Court denies the agency position *Chevron* deference, finds that
22  the *best* interpretation of the statute contradicts the agency's position, and holds
23  the challenged agency action unlawful. The agency promptly conducts a
24  rulemaking, and adopts a rule that comports with its earlier position—in effect
25  disagreeing with the Supreme Court concerning the best interpretation of the
26  statute. According to today's opinion, the agency is thereupon free to take the
27  action that the Supreme Court found unlawful.

28  This is not only bizarre. It is probably unconstitutional. Article III courts do not sit
29  to render decisions that can be reversed or ignored by Executive officers. Even
30  when the agency itself is party to the case in which the Court construes a statute,
31  the agency will be able to disregard that construction and seek *Chevron* deference
32  for its contrary construction the next time around.

33                                        * * *

34  I would adhere to what has been the rule in the past: When a court interprets a
35  statute without *Chevron* deference to agency views, its interpretation is the law. I
36  might add that it is a great mystery why any of this is relevant here. *Whatever* the
37  *stare decisis* effect of *AT&T Corp. v. Portland,* 216 F. 3d 871 (CA9 2000), in the
38  Ninth Circuit, it surely does not govern this Court's decision. And—despite the
39  Court's peculiar, self-abnegating suggestion to the contrary, the Ninth Circuit

would already be obliged to abandon *Portland*'s holding in the face of *this Court's* decision that the Commission's construction of "telecommunications service" is entitled to deference and is reasonable. It is a sadness that the Court should go so far out of its way to make bad law.

I respectfully dissent.

## United States v. Home Concrete & Supply, LLC

566 U.S. 478

April 25, 2012

JUSTICE BREYER delivered the opinion of the Court, except as to Part IV–C.

Ordinarily, the Government must assess a deficiency against a taxpayer within "3 years after the return was filed." 26 U.S.C. § 6501(a) (2000 ed.). The 3-year period is extended to 6 years, however, when a taxpayer "*omits from gross income an amount properly includible therein* which is in excess of 25 percent of the amount of gross income stated in the return." § 6501(e)(1)(A) (emphasis added). The question before us is whether this latter provision applies (and extends the ordinary 3-year limitations period) when the taxpayer overstates his basis in property that he has sold, thereby understating the gain that he received from its sale. Following *Colony, Inc. v. Commissioner*, 357 U.S. 28 (1958), we hold that the provision does not apply to an overstatement of basis. Hence the 6-year period does not apply.

I

For present purposes the relevant underlying circumstances are not in dispute. We consequently assume that (1) the respondent taxpayers filed their relevant tax returns in April 2000; (2) the returns overstated the basis of certain property that the taxpayers had sold; (3) as a result the returns understated the gross income that the taxpayers received from the sale of the property; and (4) the understatement exceeded the statute's 25% threshold. We also take as undisputed that the Commissioner asserted the relevant deficiency within the extended 6-year limitations period, but outside the default 3-year period. Thus, unless the 6-year statute of limitations applies, the Government's efforts to assert a tax deficiency came too late. Our conclusion—that the extended limitations period does not apply—follows directly from this Court's earlier decision in *Colony*.

II

1    In *Colony* this Court interpreted a provision of the Internal Revenue Code of 1939,
2    the operative language of which is identical to the language now before us. The
3    Commissioner there had determined

4        "that the taxpayer had understated the gross profits on the sales of certain
5        lots of land for residential purposes as a result of having overstated the
6        'basis' of such lots by erroneously including in their cost certain
7        unallowable items of development expense."

8    The Commissioner's assessment came after the ordinary 3-year limitations period
9    had run. And, it was consequently timely only if the taxpayer, in the words of the
10   1939 Code, had "omit[ted] from gross income an amount properly includible
11   therein which is in excess of 25 per centum of the amount of gross income stated
12   in the return . . . ." 26 U.S.C. § 275(c) (1940 ed.). The Code provision applicable to
13   this case, adopted in 1954, contains materially indistinguishable language.

14   In *Colony* this Court held that taxpayer misstatements, overstating the basis in
15   property, do not fall within the scope of the statute. But the Court recognized the
16   Commissioner's contrary argument for inclusion. Then as now, the Code itself
17   defined "gross income" in this context as the difference between gross revenue
18   (often the amount the taxpayer received upon selling the property) and basis (often
19   the amount the taxpayer paid for the property). And, the Commissioner pointed
20   out, an overstatement of basis can diminish the "amount" of the gain just as leaving
21   the item entirely off the return might do. Either way, the error wrongly understates
22   the taxpayer's income.

23   But, the Court added, the Commissioner's argument did not fully account for the
24   provision's language, in particular the word "omit." The key phrase says "omits . . .
25   an amount." The word "omits" (unlike, say, "reduces" or "understates") means
26   "'[t]o leave out or unmentioned; not to insert, include, or name.'" Thus, taken
27   literally, "omit" limits the statute's scope to situations in which specific receipts or
28   accruals of income are left out of the computation of gross income; to inflate the
29   basis, however, is not to "omit" a specific item, not even of profit.

30   While finding this latter interpretation of the language the "more plausibl[e]," the
31   Court also noted that the language was not "unambiguous." *Colony*, 357 U.S., at
32   33. It then examined various congressional Reports discussing the relevant
33   statutory language. It found in those Reports

34       "persuasive indications that Congress merely had in mind failures to report
35       particular income receipts and accruals, and did not intend the [extended]
36       limitation to apply whenever gross income was understated . . . ." *Id.*, at 35.

37   This "history," the Court said, "shows . . . that the Congress intended an exception
38   to the usual three-year statute of limitations only in the restricted type of situation

1 already described," a situation that did not include overstatements of basis. *Id.*, at
2 36.

3 * * *

4 Finally, the Court noted that Congress had recently enacted the Internal Revenue
5 Code of 1954. And the Court observed that "the conclusion we reach is in harmony
6 with the unambiguous language of § 6501(e)(1)(A)," i.e., the provision relevant in
7 this present case.

8 III

9 In our view, *Colony* determines the outcome in this case. The provision before us
10 is a 1954 reenactment of the 1939 provision that *Colony* interpreted. The operative
11 language is identical. It would be difficult, perhaps impossible, to give the same
12 language here a different interpretation without effectively overruling *Colony*, a
13 course of action that basic principles of stare decisis wisely counsel us not to take.

14 The Government, in an effort to convince us to interpret the operative language
15 before us differently, points to differences in other nearby parts of the 1954 Code.
16 It suggests that these differences counsel in favor of a different interpretation than
17 the one adopted in *Colony*. * * *

18 * * *

19 In our view, these points are too fragile to bear the significant argumentative
20 weight the Government seeks to place upon them. * * *

21 * * *

22 IV

23 A

24 Finally, the Government points to Treasury Regulation § 301.6501(e)–1, which was
25 promulgated in final form in December 2010. See 26 CFR § 301.6501(e)–1 (2011).
26 The regulation, as relevant here, departs from *Colony* and interprets the operative
27 language of the statute in the Government's favor. The regulation says that "an
28 understated amount of gross income resulting from an overstatement of
29 unrecovered cost or other basis constitutes an omission from gross income."
30 §301.6501(e)–1(a)(1)(iii). In the Government's view this new regulation in effect
31 overturns *Colony*'s interpretation of this statute.

32 The Government points out that the Treasury Regulation constitutes "an agency's
33 construction of a statute which it administers." *Chevron, U.S.A. Inc. v. Natural*
34 *Resources Defense Council, Inc.*, 467 U.S. 837, 842 (1984). The Court has written
35 that a "court's prior judicial construction of a statute trumps an agency

construction otherwise entitled to *Chevron* deference only if the prior court decision holds that its construction follows from the *unambiguous* terms of the statute . . . ." *National Cable & Telecommunications Assn. v. Brand X Internet Services*, 545 U.S. 967, 982 (2005) (emphasis added). And, as the Government notes, in *Colony* itself the Court wrote that "it cannot be said that the language is unambiguous." Hence, the Government concludes, *Colony* cannot govern the outcome in this case. The question, rather, is whether the agency's construction is a "permissible construction of the statute." *Chevron, supra*, at 843. And, since the Government argues that the regulation embodies a reasonable, hence permissible, construction of the statute, the Government believes it must win.

## B

We do not accept this argument. In our view, *Colony* has already interpreted the statute, and there is no longer any different construction that is consistent with *Colony* and available for adoption by the agency.

## C

The fatal flaw in the Government's contrary argument is that it overlooks the reason why *Brand X* held that a "prior judicial construction," unless reflecting an "unambiguous" statute, does not trump a different agency construction of that statute. 545 U.S., at 982. The Court reveals that reason when it points out that "it is for agencies, not courts, to fill statutory gaps." *Ibid*. The fact that a statute is unambiguous means that there is "no gap for the agency to fill" and thus "no room for agency discretion." *Id.*, at 982–983.

In so stating, the Court sought to encapsulate what earlier opinions, including *Chevron*, made clear. Those opinions identify the underlying interpretive problem as that of deciding whether, or when, a particular statute in effect delegates to an agency the power to fill a gap, thereby implicitly taking from a court the power to void a reasonable gap-filling interpretation. Thus, in *Chevron* the Court said that, when

> "Congress has explicitly left a gap for the agency to fill, there is an express delegation of authority to the agency to elucidate a specific provision of the statute by regulation. . . . Sometimes the legislative delegation to an agency on a particular question is implicit rather than explicit. [But in either instance], a court may not substitute its own construction of a statutory provision for a reasonable interpretation made by the administrator of an agency."

*Chevron* and later cases find in unambiguous language a clear sign that Congress did *not* delegate gap-filling authority to an agency; and they find in ambiguous language at least a presumptive indication that Congress did delegate that gap-

1 filling authority. Thus, in *Chevron* the Court wrote that a statute's silence or
2 ambiguity as to a particular issue means that Congress has not "directly addressed
3 the precise question at issue" (thus likely delegating gap-filling power to the
4 agency). 467 U.S., at 843. * * *

5 *Chevron* added that "[i]f a court, employing traditional tools of statutory
6 construction, ascertains that Congress had an intention on the precise question at
7 issue, that intention is the law and must be given effect."

8 As the Government points out, the Court in *Colony* stated that the statutory
9 language at issue is not "unambiguous." But the Court decided that case nearly 30
10 years before it decided *Chevron*. There is no reason to believe that the linguistic
11 ambiguity noted by *Colony* reflects a post-*Chevron* conclusion that Congress had
12 delegated gap-filling power to the agency. At the same time, there is every reason
13 to believe that the Court thought that Congress had "directly spoken to the question
14 at hand," and thus left "[no] gap for the agency to fill."

15 For one thing, the Court said that the taxpayer had the better side of the textual
16 argument. *Colony*. For another, its examination of legislative history led it to
17 believe that Congress had decided the question definitively, leaving no room for
18 the agency to reach a contrary result. It found in that history "persuasive
19 indications" that Congress intended overstatements of basis to fall outside the
20 statute's scope, and it said that it was satisfied that Congress "intended an
21 exception . . . only in the restricted type of situation" it had already described. *Id.*,
22 at 35–36. Further, it thought that the Commissioner's interpretation (the
23 interpretation once again advanced here) would "create a patent incongruity in the
24 tax law." *Id.*, at 36–37. And it reached this conclusion despite the fact that, in the
25 years leading up to *Colony*, the Commissioner had consistently advocated the
26 opposite in the circuit courts. Thus, the Court was aware it was rejecting the expert
27 opinion of the Commissioner of Internal Revenue. And finally, after completing its
28 analysis, *Colony* found its interpretation of the 1939 Code "in harmony with the
29 [now] unambiguous language" of the 1954 Code, which at a minimum suggests that
30 the Court saw nothing in the 1954 Code as inconsistent with its conclusion.

31 * * * The question is whether the Court in *Colony* concluded that the statute left
32 such a gap. And, in our view, the opinion (written by JUSTICE HARLAN for the
33 Court) makes clear that it did not.

34 * * * We agree with the taxpayer that overstatements of basis, and the resulting
35 understatement of gross income, do not trigger the extended limitations period of
36 § 6501(e)(1)(A). The Court of Appeals reached the same conclusion. And its
37 judgment is affirmed.

38 It is so ordered.

1 JUSTICE SCALIA, concurring in part and concurring in the judgment.

2 It would be reasonable, I think, to deny all precedential effect to *Colony, Inc. v.*
3 *Commissioner*, to overrule its holding as obviously contrary to our later law that
4 agency resolutions of ambiguities are to be accorded deference. Because of
5 justifiable taxpayer reliance I would not take that course—and neither does the
6 Court's opinion, which says that "*Colony* determines the outcome in this case."
7 That should be the end of the matter.

8 The plurality, however, goes on to address the Government's argument that
9 Treasury Regulation § 301.6501(e)–1 effectively overturned *Colony*. In my view,
10 that cannot be: "Once a court has decided upon its de novo construction of the
11 statute, there no longer is a different construction that is consistent with the court's
12 holding and available for adoption by the agency." *National Cable &*
13 *Telecommunications Assn. v. Brand X Internet Services*, 545 U.S. 967, n. 12
14 (2005) (SCALIA, J., dissenting). That view, of course, did not carry the day in
15 *Brand X*, and the Government quite reasonably relies on the *Brand X* majority's
16 innovative pronouncement that a "court's prior judicial construction of a statute
17 trumps an agency construction otherwise entitled to *Chevron* deference only if the
18 prior court decision holds that its construction follows from the unambiguous
19 terms of the statute."

20 In cases decided pre-*Brand X*, the Court had no inkling that it must utter the magic
21 words "ambiguous" or "unambiguous" in order to (poof!) expand or abridge
22 executive power, and (poof!) enable or disable administrative contradiction of the
23 Supreme Court. Indeed, the Court was unaware of even the utility (much less the
24 necessity) of making the ambiguous/nonambiguous determination in cases
25 decided pre-*Chevron*, before that opinion made the so-called "Step 1"
26 determination of ambiguity *vel non* a customary (though hardly mandatory) part
27 of judicial-review analysis. For many of those earlier cases, therefore, it will be
28 incredibly difficult to determine whether the decision purported to be giving
29 meaning to an ambiguous, or rather an unambiguous, statute.

30 Thus, one would have thought that the *Brand X* majority would breathe a sigh of
31 relief in the present case, involving a pre-*Chevron* opinion that (*mirabile dictu*)
32 makes it inescapably clear that the Court thought the statute ambiguous: "It cannot
33 be said that the language is unambiguous." *Colony, supra*, at 33 (emphasis added).
34 As today's plurality opinion explains, *Colony* "said that the taxpayer had the better
35 side of the textual argument,"—not what *Brand X* requires to foreclose
36 administrative revision of our decisions: "the only permissible reading of the
37 statute." Thus, having decided to stand by *Colony* and to stand by *Brand X* as well,
38 the plurality should have found—in order to reach the decision it did—that the
39 Treasury Department's current interpretation was unreasonable.

Instead of doing what *Brand X* would require, however, the plurality manages to sustain the justifiable reliance of taxpayers by revising *yet again* the meaning of *Chevron*—and revising it yet again in a direction that will create confusion and uncertainty. Of course there is no doubt that, with regard to the Internal Revenue Code, the Treasury Department satisfies the *Mead* requirement of some indication "that Congress delegated authority to the agency generally to make rules carrying the force of law." We have given *Chevron* deference to a Treasury Regulation before. But in order to evade *Brand X* and yet reaffirm *Colony*, the plurality would add yet another lop-sided story to the ugly and improbable structure that our law of administrative review has become: To trigger the *Brand X* power of an authorized "gap-filling" agency to give content to an ambiguous text, a pre-*Chevron* determination that language is ambiguous does not alone suffice; the pre-*Chevron* Court must in addition have found that Congress wanted the particular ambiguity in question to be resolved by the agency. And here, today's plurality opinion finds, "[t]here is no reason to believe that the linguistic ambiguity noted by *Colony* reflects a post-*Chevron* conclusion that Congress had delegated gap-filling power to the agency." The notion, seemingly, is that post-*Chevron* a finding of ambiguity is accompanied by a finding of agency authority to resolve the ambiguity, but pre-*Chevron* that was not so. The premise is false. Post-*Chevron* cases do not "conclude" that Congress wanted the particular ambiguity resolved by the agency; that is simply the legal effect of ambiguity—a legal effect that should obtain whenever the language is in fact (as *Colony* found) ambiguous.

\* \* \*

Rather than making our judicial-review jurisprudence curiouser and curiouser, the Court should abandon the opinion that produces these contortions, *Brand X*. I join the judgment announced by the Court because it is indisputable that *Colony* resolved the construction of the statutory language at issue here, and that construction must therefore control. And I join the Court's opinion except for Part IV–C.

JUSTICE KENNEDY, with whom JUSTICE GINSBURG, JUSTICE SOTOMAYOR, and JUSTICE KAGAN join, dissenting. [Omitted.]

### City of Arlington v. Federal Communications Commission

569 U.S. 290 (2013)

May 20, 2013

JUSTICE SCALIA delivered the opinion of the Court.

1   We consider whether an agency's interpretation of a statutory ambiguity that
2   concerns the scope of its regulatory authority (that is, its jurisdiction) is entitled to
3   deference under *Chevron U.S.A. Inc. v. Natural Resources Defense Council, Inc.*,
4   467 U.S. 837 (1984).

5                                          I

6   Wireless telecommunications networks require towers and antennas; proposed
7   sites for those towers and antennas must be approved by local zoning authorities.
8   In the Telecommunications Act of 1996, Congress "impose[d] specific limitations
9   on the traditional authority of state and local governments to regulate the location,
10  construction, and modification of such facilities," *Rancho Palos Verdes v. Abrams*,
11  544 U.S. 113, 115 (2005), and incorporated those limitations into the
12  Communications Act of 1934, see 110 Stat. 56, 151. Section 201(b) of that Act
13  empowers the Federal Communications Commission to "prescribe such rules and
14  regulations as may be necessary in the public interest to carry out [its] provisions."
15  Ch. 296, 52 Stat. 588, codified at 47 U.S.C. § 201(b). Of course, that rulemaking
16  authority extends to the subsequently added portions of the Act.

17  The Act imposes five substantive limitations, which are codified in 47 U.S.C. §
18  332(c)(7)(B); only one of them, § 332(c)(7)(B)(ii), is at issue here. That provision
19  requires state or local governments to act on wireless siting applications "within a
20  reasonable period of time after the request is duly filed." Two other features of §
21  332(c)(7) are relevant. First, subparagraph (A), known as the "saving clause,"
22  provides that nothing in the Act, *except* those limitations provided in
23  §332(c)(7)(B), "shall limit or affect the authority of a State or local government"
24  over siting decisions. Second, § 332(c)(7)(B)(v) authorizes a person who believes a
25  state or local government's wireless-siting decision to be inconsistent with any of
26  the limitations in § 332(c)(7)(B) to "commence an action in any court of competent
27  jurisdiction."

28  In theory, § 332(c)(7)(B)(ii) requires state and local zoning authorities to take
29  prompt action on siting applications for wireless facilities. But in practice, wireless
30  providers often faced long delays. * * * In November 2009, the Commission,
31  relying on its broad statutory authority to implement the provisions of the
32  Communications Act, issued a declaratory ruling responding to CTIA's petition. *In*
33  *re Petition for Declaratory Ruling*, 24 FCC Rcd. 13994, 14001. The Commission
34  found that the "record evidence demonstrates that unreasonable delays in the
35  personal wireless service facility siting process have obstructed the provision of
36  wireless services" and that such delays "impede the promotion of advanced
37  services and competition that Congress deemed critical in the Telecommunications
38  Act of 1996." *Id.*, at 14006, 14008. A "reasonable period of time" under §
39  332(c)(7)(B)(ii), the Commission determined, is presumptively (but rebuttably) 90
40  days to process a collocation application (that is, an application to place a new

1  antenna on an existing tower) and 150 days to process all other applications. *Id.,*
2  at 14005.

3  Some state and local governments opposed adoption of the *Declaratory Ruling* on
4  the ground that the Commission lacked "authority to interpret ambiguous
5  provisions of Section 332(c)(7)." *Id.,* at 14000. Specifically, they argued that the
6  saving clause, § 332(c)(7)(A), and the judicial review provision, § 337(c)(7)(B)(v),
7  together display a congressional intent to withhold from the Commission authority
8  to interpret the limitations in § 332(c)(7)(B). Asserting that ground of objection,
9  the cities of Arlington and San Antonio, Texas, petitioned for review of the
10  *Declaratory Ruling* in the Court of Appeals for the Fifth Circuit.

11  Relying on Circuit precedent, the Court of Appeals held that the *Chevron*
12  framework applied to the threshold question whether the FCC possessed statutory
13  authority to adopt the 90- and 150-day timeframes. Applying *Chevron*, the Court
14  of Appeals found "§332(c)(7)(A)'s effect on the FCC's authority to administer §
15  332(c)(7)(B)'s limitations ambiguous," and held that "the FCC's interpretation of
16  its statutory authority" was a permissible construction of the statute. On the
17  merits, the court upheld the presumptive 90- and 150-day deadlines as a
18  "permissible construction of § 332(c)(7)(B)(ii) and (v) . . . entitled to *Chevron*
19  deference."

20  We granted certiorari limited to the first question presented: "Whether . . . a court
21  should apply *Chevron* to . . . an agency's determination of its own jurisdiction."

22                                     II

23                                     A

24  As this case turns on the scope of the doctrine enshrined in *Chevron*, we begin with
25  a description of that case's now-canonical formulation. "When a court reviews an
26  agency's construction of the statute which it administers, it is confronted with two
27  questions." 467 U.S., at 842. First, applying the ordinary tools of statutory
28  construction, the court must determine "whether Congress has directly spoken to
29  the precise question at issue. If the intent of Congress is clear, that is the end of the
30  matter; for the court, as well as the agency, must give effect to the unambiguously
31  expressed intent of Congress." *Id.,* at 842-843. But "if the statute is silent or
32  ambiguous with respect to the specific issue, the question for the court is whether
33  the agency's answer is based on a permissible construction of the statute." *Id.,* at
34  843.

35  *Chevron* is rooted in a background presumption of congressional intent: namely,
36  "that Congress, when it left ambiguity in a statute" administered by an agency,
37  "understood that the ambiguity would be resolved, first and foremost, by the
38  agency, and desired the agency (rather than the courts) to possess whatever degree

577

of discretion the ambiguity allows." *Smiley v. Citibank (South Dakota), N. A.*, 517 U.S. 735, 740-741 (1996). *Chevron* thus provides a stable background rule against which Congress can legislate: Statutory ambiguities will be resolved, within the bounds of reasonable interpretation, not by the courts but by the administering agency. Congress knows to speak in plain terms when it wishes to circumscribe, and in capacious terms when it wishes to enlarge, agency discretion.

B

The question here is whether a court must defer under *Chevron* to an agency's interpretation of a statutory ambiguity that concerns the scope of the agency's statutory authority (that is, its jurisdiction). The argument against deference rests on the premise that there exist two distinct classes of agency interpretations: Some interpretations—the big, important ones, presumably—define the agency's "jurisdiction." Others—humdrum, run-of-the-mill stuff—are simply applications of jurisdiction the agency plainly has. That premise is false, because the distinction between "jurisdictional" and "nonjurisdictional" interpretations is a mirage. No matter how it is framed, the question a court faces when confronted with an agency's interpretation of a statute it administers is always, simply, *whether the agency has stayed within the bounds of its statutory authority.*

The misconception that there are, for *Chevron* purposes, separate "jurisdictional" questions on which no deference is due derives, perhaps, from a reflexive extension to agencies of the very real division between the jurisdictional and nonjurisdictional that is applicable to courts. In the judicial context, there *is* a meaningful line: Whether the court decided *correctly* is a question that has different consequences from the question whether it had the power to decide *at all.* Congress has the power (within limits) to tell the courts what classes of cases they may decide, but not to prescribe or superintend how they decide those cases. A court's power to decide a case is independent of whether its decision is correct, which is why even an erroneous judgment is entitled to res judicata effect. Put differently, a jurisdictionally proper but substantively incorrect judicial decision is not ultra vires.

That is not so for agencies charged with administering congressional statutes. Both their power to act and how they are to act is authoritatively prescribed by Congress, so that when they act improperly, no less than when they act beyond their jurisdiction, what they do is ultra vires. Because the question—whether framed as an incorrect application of agency authority or an assertion of authority not conferred—is always whether the agency has gone beyond what Congress has permitted it to do, there is no principled basis for carving out some arbitrary subset of such claims as "jurisdictional."

An example will illustrate just how illusory the proposed line between "jurisdictional" and "nonjurisdictional" agency interpretations is. Imagine the following validly-enacted statute:

"COMMON CARRIER ACT

"SECTION 1. The Agency shall have jurisdiction to prohibit any common carrier from imposing an unreasonable condition upon access to its facilities."

There is no question that this provision—including the terms "common carrier" and "unreasonable condition"—defines the Agency's jurisdiction. Surely, the argument goes, a court must determine *de novo* the scope of that jurisdiction.

Consider, however, this alternative formulation of the statute:

"COMMON CARRIER ACT

"SECTION 1. No common carrier shall impose an unreasonable condition upon access to its facilities.

"SECTION 2. The Agency may prescribe rules and regulations necessary in the public interest to effectuate Section 1 of this Act."

Now imagine that the Agency, invoking its Section 2 authority, promulgates this Rule: "(1) The term 'common carrier' in Section 1 includes Internet Service Providers. (2) The term 'unreasonable condition' in Section 1 includes unreasonably high prices. (3) A monthly fee greater than $25 is an unreasonable condition on access to Internet service." By this Rule, the Agency has claimed for itself jurisdiction that is doubly questionable: Does its authority extend to Internet Service Providers? And does it extend to setting prices? Yet Section 2 makes clear that Congress, in petitioners' words, "conferred interpretive power on the agency" with respect to Section 1. Brief for Petitioners in No. 1545, p. 14. Even under petitioners' theory, then, a court should defer to the Agency's interpretation of the terms "common carrier" and "unreasonable condition"—that is to say, its assertion that its "jurisdiction" extends to regulating Internet Service Providers and setting prices.

In the first case, by contrast, petitioners' theory would accord the agency no deference. The trouble with this is that in both cases, the underlying question is *exactly the same*: Does the statute give the agency authority to regulate Internet Service Providers and cap prices, or not? The reality, laid bare, is that there is *no difference*, insofar as the validity of agency action is concerned, between an agency's exceeding the scope of its authority (its "jurisdiction") and its exceeding authorized application of authority that it unquestionably has. "To exceed authorized application is to exceed authority. Virtually any administrative action

1 can be characterized as either the one or the other, depending on how generally
2 one wishes to describe the 'authority.'" *Mississippi Power & Light Co. v.*
3 *Mississippi ex rel. Moore*, 487 U.S. 354, 381 (1988) (SCALIA, J., concurring in
4 judgment); see also Monaghan, Marbury and the Administrative State, 83 Colum.
5 L. Rev. 1, 29 (1983) ("Administrative application of law is administrative
6 formulation of law whenever it involves elaboration of the statutory norm.").

7 * * *

8 In sum, judges should not waste their time in the mental acrobatics needed to
9 decide whether an agency's interpretation of a statutory provision is
10 "jurisdictional" or "nonjurisdictional." Once those labels are sheared away, it
11 becomes clear that the question in every case is, simply, whether the statutory text
12 forecloses the agency's assertion of authority, or not. * * *

13 C

14 Fortunately, then, we have consistently held "that *Chevron* applies to cases in
15 which an agency adopts a construction of a jurisdictional provision of a statute it
16 administers." 1 R. Pierce, Administrative Law Treatise § 3.5, p. 187 (2010). One of
17 our opinions explicitly says that no "exception exists to the normal [deferential]
18 standard of review" for "'jurisdictional or legal question[s] concerning the
19 coverage'" of an Act. *NLRB v. City Disposal Systems, Inc.*, 465 U.S. 822, 830, n. 7
20 (1984). * * *

21 * * *

22 The false dichotomy between "jurisdictional" and "nonjurisdictional" agency
23 interpretations may be no more than a bogeyman, but it is dangerous all the same.
24 Like the Hound of the Baskervilles, it is conjured by those with greater quarry in
25 sight: Make no mistake—the ultimate target here is *Chevron* itself. Savvy
26 challengers of agency action would play the "jurisdictional" card in every case.
27 Some judges would be deceived by the specious, but scary-sounding,
28 "jurisdictional-nonjurisdictional" line; others tempted by the prospect of making
29 public policy by prescribing the meaning of ambiguous statutory commands. The
30 effect would be to transfer any number of interpretive decisions—archetypal
31 *Chevron* questions, about how best to construe an ambiguous term in light of
32 competing policy interests—from the agencies that administer the statutes to
33 federal courts. We have cautioned that "judges ought to refrain from substituting
34 their own interstitial lawmaking" for that of an agency. *Ford Motor Credit Co. v.*
35 *Milhollin*, 444 U.S. 555, 568 (1980). That is precisely what *Chevron* prevents.

36 III

37 A

One group of respondents contends that *Chevron* deference is inappropriate here because the FCC has "assert[ed] jurisdiction over matters of traditional state and local concern." But this case has nothing to do with federalism. Section 332(c)(7)(B)(ii) explicitly supplants state authority by *requiring* zoning authorities to render a decision "within a reasonable period of time," and the meaning of that phrase is indisputably a question of federal law. We rejected a similar faux-federalism argument in the *Iowa Utilities Board* case, in terms that apply equally here: "This is, at bottom, a debate not about whether the States will be allowed to do their own thing, but about whether it will be the FCC or the federal courts that draw the lines to which they must hew." 525 U.S., at 379, n. 6. * * *

B

A few words in response to the dissent. The question on which we granted certiorari was whether "a court should apply *Chevron* to review an agency's determination of its own jurisdiction." Perhaps sensing the incoherence of the "jurisdictional-nonjurisdictional" line, the dissent does not even attempt to defend it, but proposes a much broader scope for *de novo* judicial review: Jurisdictional or not, and even where a rule is at issue and the statute contains a broad grant of rulemaking authority, the dissent would have a court search provision-by-provision to determine "whether [that] delegation covers the 'specific provision' and 'particular question' before the court."

The dissent is correct that *United States v. Mead Corp.*, 533 U.S. 218 (2001), requires that, for *Chevron* deference to apply, the agency must have received congressional authority to determine the particular matter at issue in the particular manner adopted. No one disputes that. But *Mead* denied *Chevron* deference to action, by an agency with rulemaking authority, that was not rulemaking. What the dissent needs, and fails to produce, is a single case in which a general conferral of rulemaking or adjudicative authority has been held insufficient to support *Chevron* deference for an exercise of that authority within the agency's substantive field. There is no such case, and what the dissent proposes is a massive revision of our *Chevron* jurisprudence.

* * *

The judgment of the Court of Appeals is affirmed.

*It is so ordered.*

JUSTICE BREYER, concurring in part and concurring in the judgment. [Omitted.]

CHIEF JUSTICE ROBERTS, with whom JUSTICE KENNEDY and JUSTICE ALITO join, dissenting.

My disagreement with the Court is fundamental. It is also easily expressed: A court should not defer to an agency until the court decides, on its own, that the agency is entitled to deference. Courts defer to an agency's interpretation of law when and because Congress has conferred on the agency interpretive authority over the question at issue. An agency cannot exercise interpretive authority until it has it; the question whether an agency enjoys that authority must be decided by a court, without deference to the agency.

I

One of the principal authors of the Constitution famously wrote that the "accumulation of all powers, legislative, executive, and judiciary, in the same hands, . . . may justly be pronounced the very definition of tyranny." The Federalist No. 47 (J. Madison). Although modern administrative agencies fit most comfortably within the Executive Branch, as a practical matter they exercise legislative power, by promulgating regulations with the force of law; executive power, by policing compliance with those regulations; and judicial power, by adjudicating enforcement actions and imposing sanctions on those found to have violated their rules. The accumulation of these powers in the same hands is not an occasional or isolated exception to the constitutional plan; it is a central feature of modern American government.

\* \* \*

As for judicial oversight, agencies enjoy broad power to construe statutory provisions over which they have been given interpretive authority. In *Chevron U.S.A. Inc. v. Natural Resources Defense Council, Inc.*, we established a test for reviewing "an agency's construction of the statute which it administers." 467 U.S. 837, 842 (1984). If Congress has "directly spoken to the precise question at issue," we said, "that is the end of the matter." *Ibid.* A contrary agency interpretation must give way. But if Congress has not expressed a specific intent, a court is bound to defer to any "permissible construction of the statute," even if that is not "the reading the court would have reached if the question initially had arisen in a judicial proceeding." *Id.*, at 843, and n. 11.

When it applies, *Chevron* is a powerful weapon in an agency's regulatory arsenal. Congressional delegations to agencies are often ambiguous—expressing "a mood rather than a message." Friendly, The Federal Administrative Agencies: The Need for Better Definition of Standards, 75 Harv. L. Rev. 1263, 1311 (1962). By design or default, Congress often fails to speak to "the precise question" before an agency. In the absence of such an answer, an agency's interpretation has the full force and effect of law, unless it "exceeds the bounds of the permissible." *Barnhart v. Walton*, 535 U.S. 212, 218 (2002).

\* \* \*

The Court states that the question "is whether a court must defer under *Chevron* to an agency's interpretation of a statutory ambiguity that concerns the scope of the agency's statutory authority (that is, its jurisdiction)." That is fine—until the parenthetical. The parties, *amici*, and court below too often use the term "jurisdiction" imprecisely, which leads the Court to misunderstand the argument it must confront. * * * The argument is that a court should not defer to an agency on whether Congress has granted the agency interpretive authority over the statutory ambiguity at issue.

You can call that "jurisdiction" if you'd like, as petitioners do in the question presented. But given that the term is ambiguous, more is required to understand its use in that question than simply "having read it." It is important to keep in mind that the term, in the present context, has the more precise meaning noted above, encompassing congressionally delegated authority to issue interpretations with the force and effect of law. See 668 F. 3d 229, 248 (CA5 2012) ("The issue in the instant case is whether the FCC possessed statutory authority to administer § 332(c)(7)(B)(ii) and (v) by adopting the 90- and 150-day time frames"). And that has nothing do with whether the statutory provisions at issue are "big" or "small."

## II

"It is emphatically the province and duty of the judicial department to say what the law is." The rise of the modern administrative state has not changed that duty. Indeed, the Administrative Procedure Act, governing judicial review of most agency action, instructs reviewing courts to decide "all relevant questions of law." 5 U.S.C. § 706.

We do not ignore that command when we afford an agency's statutory interpretation *Chevron* deference; we respect it. We give binding deference to permissible agency interpretations of statutory ambiguities *because* Congress has delegated to the agency the authority to interpret those ambiguities "with the force of law."

But before a court may grant such deference, it must on its own decide whether Congress—the branch vested with lawmaking authority under the Constitution—has in fact delegated to the agency lawmaking power over the ambiguity at issue. * * *

## III

* * *

## B

We have never faltered in our understanding of this straightforward principle, that whether a particular agency interpretation warrants *Chevron* deference turns on

1   the court's determination whether Congress has delegated to the agency the
2   authority to interpret the statutory ambiguity at issue. * * *

3                                      * * *

4   In other words, we do not defer to an agency's interpretation of an ambiguous
5   provision unless Congress wants us to, and whether Congress wants us to is a
6   question that courts, not agencies, must decide. Simply put, that question is
7   "beyond the *Chevron* pale." *Mead, supra,* at 234.

8                                       IV

9   Despite these precedents, the FCC argues that a court need only locate an agency
10  and a grant of general rulemaking authority over a statute. *Chevron* deference then
11  applies, it contends, to the agency's interpretation of any ambiguity in the Act,
12  including ambiguity in a provision said to carve out specific provisions from the
13  agency's general rulemaking authority. If Congress intends to exempt part of the
14  statute from the agency's interpretive authority, the FCC says, Congress "can
15  ordinarily be expected to state that intent explicitly."

16  If a congressional delegation of interpretive authority is to support *Chevron*
17  deference, however, that delegation must extend to the specific statutory
18  ambiguity at issue. The appropriate question is whether the delegation covers the
19  "specific provision" and "particular question" before the court. *Chevron,* 467 U.S.,
20  at 844. A congressional grant of authority over some portion of a statute does not
21  necessarily mean that Congress granted the agency interpretive authority over all
22  its provisions.

23                                     * * *

24  I respectfully dissent.

25

26  ## 6. Major Questions Doctrine

27  In *Food and Drug Administration v. Brown & Williamson Tobacco Corp.,* 529
28  U.S. 120 (2000), the Supreme Court rejected the FDA's effort to regulate the sale
29  of cigarettes. The agency based its regulation on its conclusion that nicotine
30  constituted a "drug," and cigarettes, "drug delivery devices," within the meaning of
31  the Food, Drug, and Cosmetic Act. The Court declined to give *Chevron* deference
32  to this interpretation because it did not believe that Congress in fact intended this
33  statutory language to grant the FDA jurisdiction over something economically and
34  politically significant as the regulation of cigarettes.

1     Initially. it appeared that this "extraordinary cases" or "major questions" approach
2     to statutory interpretation might be a one-off, but several times in recent years the
3     Court has declined to defer on similar grounds. For the first time in 2022, the Court
4     embraced the "major question doctrine" by name, in the course of invalidating the
5     EPA's Clean Power Plan, in *West Virginia v. EPA*. The concurrence from Justice
6     Gorsuch, not excerpted here, gives a non-delegation doctrine twist to the major
7     questions doctrine: the Court should construe narrowly delegations that otherwise
8     could be constitutionally overbroad. (Recall, from *Gundy*, that Justice Gorsuch
9     favors significantly tightening up the non-delegation doctrine.)

10    Note that *Chevron* is not mentioned once in the majority opinion, although the
11    core question in the case is the meaning of the statutory term "best system of
12    emission reduction." (The dissent discusses *Chevron* briefly, in a passage not
13    included in the excerpt below.) How, if it all, is the "major questions doctrine" to
14    be integrated with *Chevron*? How major does a question need to be before a court
15    skips *Chevron*?

16    **West Virginia v. EPA**

17    142 U.S. 2587

18    June 30, 2022

19    CHIEF JUSTICE ROBERTS delivered the opinion of the Court.

20    The Clean Air Act authorizes the Environmental Protection Agency to regulate
21    power plants by setting a "standard of performance" for their emission of certain
22    pollutants into the air. 84 Stat. 1683, 42 U.S.C. §7411(a)(1). That standard may be
23    different for new and existing plants, but in each case it must reflect the "best
24    system of emission reduction" that the Agency has determined to be "adequately
25    demonstrated" for the particular category. §§7411(a)(1), (b)(1), (d). For existing
26    plants, the States then implement that requirement by issuing rules restricting
27    emissions from sources within their borders.

28    Since passage of the Act 50 years ago, EPA has exercised this authority by setting
29    performance standards based on measures that would reduce pollution by causing
30    plants to operate more cleanly. In 2015, however, EPA issued a new rule concluding
31    that the "best system of emission reduction" for existing coal-fired power plants
32    included a requirement that such facilities reduce their own production of
33    electricity, or subsidize increased generation by natural gas, wind, or solar sources.

34    The question before us is whether this broader conception of EPA's authority is
35    within the power granted to it by the Clean Air Act.

36    I

37    A

The Clean Air Act establishes three main regulatory programs to control air pollution from stationary sources such as power plants. One program is the New Source Performance Standards program of Section 111, at issue here. The other two are the National Ambient Air Quality Standards (NAAQS) program * * * and the Hazardous Air Pollutants (HAP) program, set out in Section 112, §7412. To understand the place and function of Section 111 in the statutory scheme, some background on the other two programs is in order.

The NAAQS program addresses air pollutants that "may reasonably be anticipated to endanger public health or welfare," and "the presence of which in the ambient air results from numerous or diverse mobile or stationary sources." §7408(a)(1). After identifying such pollutants, EPA establishes a NAAQS for each. The NAAQS represents "the maximum airborne concentration of [the] pollutant that the public health can tolerate." *Whitman v. American Trucking Assns., Inc.*, 531 U.S. 457; see §7409(b). EPA, though, does not choose which sources must reduce their pollution and by how much to meet the ambient pollution target. Instead, Section 110 of the Act leaves that task in the first instance to the States, requiring each "to submit to [EPA] a plan designed to implement and maintain such standards within its boundaries." *Train v. Natural Resources Defense Council, Inc.*, 421 U.S. 60, 65 (1975); §7410.

The second major program governing stationary sources is the HAP program. The HAP program primarily targets pollutants, other than those already covered by a NAAQS, that present "a threat of adverse human health effects," including substances known or anticipated to be "carcinogenic, mutagenic, teratogenic, neurotoxic," or otherwise "acutely or chronically toxic." §7412(b)(2).

EPA's regulatory role with respect to these toxic pollutants is different in kind from its role in administering the NAAQS program. There, EPA is generally limited to determining the maximum safe amount of covered pollutants in the air. As to each hazardous pollutant, by contrast, the Agency must promulgate emissions standards for both new and existing major sources. §7412(d)(1). Those standards must "require the maximum degree of reduction in emissions . . . that the [EPA] Administrator, taking into consideration the cost of achieving such emission reduction, and any non-air quality health and environmental impacts and energy requirements, determines is achievable . . . through application of measures, processes, methods, systems or techniques" of emission reduction. §7412(d)(2). In other words, EPA must directly require all covered sources to reduce their emissions to a certain level. And it chooses that level by determining the "maximum degree of reduction" it considers "achievable" in practice by using the best existing technologies and methods. §7412(d)(3).

Thus, in the parlance of environmental law, Section 112 directs the Agency to impose "*technology-based* standard[s] for hazardous emissions," *Alaska Dept. of Environmental Conservation v. EPA*, 540 U.S. 461, 485, n. 12 (2004) (emphasis added). This sort of "'technology-based' approach focuses upon the control technologies that are available to industrial entities and requires the agency to . . .

ensur[e] that regulated firms adopt the appropriate cleanup technology." T. McGarity, Media-Quality, Technology, and CostBenefit Balancing Strategies for Health and Environmental Regulation, 46 Law & Contemp. Prob. 159, 160 (Summer 1983) (McGarity). * * *

The third air pollution control scheme is the New Source Performance Standards program of Section 111. §7411. That section directs EPA to list "categories of stationary sources" that it determines "cause[], or contribute[] significantly to, air pollution which may reasonably be anticipated to endanger public health or welfare." §7411(b)(1)(A). Under Section 111(b), the Agency must then promulgate for each category "Federal standards of performance for new sources," §7411(b)(1)(B). A "standard of performance" is one that "reflects the degree of emission limitation achievable through the application of the best system of emission reduction which (taking into account the cost of achieving such reduction and any non-air quality health and environmental impact and energy requirements) the [EPA] Administrator determines has been adequately demonstrated." §7411(a)(1).

Thus, the statute directs EPA to (1) "determine[]," taking into account various factors, the "best system of emission reduction which . . . has been adequately demonstrated," (2) ascertain the "degree of emission limitation achievable through the application" of that system, and (3) impose an emissions limit on new stationary sources that "reflects" that amount. *Ibid.*; see also 80 Fed. Reg. 64538 (2015). Generally speaking, a source may achieve that emissions cap any way it chooses; the key is that its pollution be no more than the amount "achievable through the application of the best system of emission reduction . . . adequately demonstrated," or the BSER. §7411(a)(1); see §7411(b)(5). * * *

Although the thrust of Section 111 focuses on emissions limits for new and modified sources—as its title indicates—the statute also authorizes regulation of certain pollutants from existing sources. Under Section 111(d), once EPA "has set new source standards addressing emissions of a particular pollutant under . . . section 111(b)," 80 Fed. Reg. 64711, it must then address emissions of that same pollutant by existing sources—but only if they are not already regulated under the NAAQS or HAP programs. §7411(d)(1). * * * Section 111(d) thus "operates as a gap-filler," empowering EPA to regulate harmful emissions not already controlled under the Agency's other authorities. *American Lung Assn. v. EPA*, 985 F. 3d 914, 932 (CADC 2021).

Although the States set the actual rules governing existing power plants, EPA itself still retains the primary regulatory role in Section 111(d). The Agency, not the States, decides the amount of pollution reduction that must ultimately be achieved. It does so by again determining, as when setting the new source rules, "the best system of emission reduction . . . that has been adequately demonstrated for [existing covered] facilities." 40 CFR §60.22(b)(5) (2021). The States then submit plans containing the emissions restrictions that they intend to adopt and enforce in order not to exceed the permissible level of pollution established by EPA.

Reflecting the ancillary nature of Section 111(d), EPA has used it only a handful of times since the enactment of the statute in 1970. See 80 Fed. Reg. 64703, and n. 275 (past regulations pertained to "four pollutants from five source categories").

\* \* \*

B

Things changed in October 2015, when EPA promulgated two rules addressing carbon dioxide pollution from power plants—one for new plants under Section 111(b), the other for existing plants under Section 111(d). Both were premised on the Agency's earlier finding that carbon dioxide is an "air pollutant" that "may reasonably be anticipated to endanger public health or welfare" by causing climate change. 80 Fed. Reg. 64530. Carbon dioxide is not subject to a NAAQS and has not been listed as a toxic pollutant.

The first rule announced by EPA established federal carbon emissions limits for new power plants of two varieties: fossil-fuel-fired electric steam generating units (mostly coal fired) and natural-gas-fired stationary combustion turbines. *Id.*, at 64512. Following the statutory process set out above, the Agency determined the BSER for the two categories of sources. \* \* \* The second rule was triggered by the first: Because EPA was now regulating carbon dioxide from new coal and gas plants, Section 111(d) required EPA to also address carbon emissions from existing coal and gas plants. See §7411(d)(1). It did so through what it called the Clean Power Plan rule.

In that rule, EPA established "final emission guidelines for states to follow in developing plans" to regulate existing power plants within their borders. *Id.*, at 64662. To arrive at the guideline limits, EPA did the same thing it does when imposing federal regulations on new sources: It identified the BSER.

The BSER that the Agency selected for existing coal-fired power plants, however, was quite different from the BSER it had chosen for new sources. The BSER for existing plants included three types of measures, which the Agency called "building blocks." *Id.*, at 64667. The first building block was "heat rate improvements" at coal-fired plants—essentially practices such plants could undertake to burn coal more efficiently. *Id.*, at 64727. But such improvements, EPA stated, would "lead to only small emission reductions," because coal-fired power plants were already operating near optimum efficiency. *Ibid.* On the Agency's view, "much larger emission reductions [were] needed from [coal-fired plants] to address climate change." *Ibid.*

So the Agency included two additional building blocks in its BSER, both of which involve what it called "generation shifting from higher-emitting to lower-emitting" producers of electricity. *Id.*, at 64728. Building block two was a shift in electricity production from existing coal-fired power plants to natural-gas-fired plants. *Ibid.* Because natural gas plants produce "typically less than half as much" carbon dioxide per unit of electricity created as coal-fired plants, the Agency explained, "this generation shift [would] reduce[ ] $CO_2$ emissions." *Ibid.* Building block three

588

worked the same way, except that the shift was from both coal- and gas-fired plants to "new lowor zero-carbon generating capacity," mainly wind and solar. *Id.*, at 64729, 64748. "Most of the $CO_2$ controls" in the rule came from the application of building blocks two and three. *Id.*, at 64728.

The Agency identified three ways in which a regulated plant operator could implement a shift in generation to cleaner sources. *Id.*, at 64731. First, an operator could simply reduce the regulated plant's own production of electricity. Second, it could build a new natural gas plant, wind farm, or solar installation, or invest in someone else's existing facility and then increase generation there. *Ibid.* Finally, operators could purchase emission allowances or credits as part of a cap-and-trade regime. *Id.*, at 64731– 64732. Under such a scheme, sources that achieve a reduction in their emissions can sell a credit representing the value of that reduction to others, who are able to count it toward their own applicable emissions caps.

EPA explained that taking any of these steps would implement a sector-wide shift in electricity production from coal to natural gas and renewables. *Id.*, at 64731. Given the integrated nature of the power grid, "adding electricity to the grid from one generator will result in the instantaneous reduction in generation from other generators," and "reductions in generation from one generator lead to the instantaneous increase in generation" by others. *Id.*, at 64769. So coal plants, whether by reducing their own production, subsidizing an increase in production by cleaner sources, or both, would cause a shift toward wind, solar, and natural gas.

Having decided that the "best system of emission reduction . . . adequately demonstrated" was one that would reduce carbon pollution mostly by moving production to cleaner sources, EPA then set about determining "the degree of emission limitation achievable through the application" of that system. 42 U.S.C. §7411(a)(1). * * * The Agency settled on what it regarded as a "reasonable" amount of shift * * *. *Id.*, at 64797–64811. Based on these changes, EPA projected that by 2030, it would be feasible to have coal provide 27% of national electricity generation, down from 38% in 2014.

From these significant projected reductions in generation, EPA developed a series of complex equations to "determine the emission performance rates" that States would be required to implement. 80 Fed. Reg. 64815. The calculations resulted in numerical emissions ceilings so strict that no existing coal plant would have been able to achieve them without engaging in one of the three means of shifting generation described above. Indeed, the emissions limit the Clean Power Plan established for existing power plants was actually stricter than the cap imposed by the simultaneously published standards for new plants.

The point, after all, was to compel the transfer of power generating capacity from existing sources to wind and solar. The White House stated that the Clean Power Plan would "drive a[n] . . . aggressive transformation in the domestic energy industry." White House Fact Sheet, App. in American Lung Assn. v. EPA, No. 19–

589

1140 etc. (CADC), p. 2076. EPA's own modeling concluded that the rule would entail billions of dollars in compliance costs (to be paid in the form of higher energy prices), require the retirement of dozens of coal-fired plants, and eliminate tens of thousands of jobs across various sectors. The Energy Information Administration reached similar conclusions, projecting that the rule would cause retail electricity prices to remain persistently 10% higher in many States, and would reduce GDP by at least a trillion 2009 dollars by 2040.

\* \* \*

## II

\* \* \*

## III

### A

In devising emissions limits for power plants, EPA first "determines" the "best system of emission reduction" that—taking into account cost, health, and other factors—it finds "has been adequately demonstrated." 42 U.S.C. §7411(a)(1). \* \* \* The issue here is whether restructuring the Nation's overall mix of electricity generation, to transition from 38% coal to 27% coal by 2030, can be the "best system of emission reduction" within the meaning of Section 111.

"It is a fundamental canon of statutory construction that the words of a statute must be read in their context and with a view to their place in the overall statutory scheme." *Davis v. Michigan Dept. of Treasury*, 489 U.S. 803, 809 (1989). Where the statute at issue is one that confers authority upon an administrative agency, that inquiry must be "shaped, at least in some measure, by the nature of the question presented"—whether Congress in fact meant to confer the power the agency has asserted. *FDA v. Brown & Williamson Tobacco Corp.*, 529 U.S. 120, 159 (2000). In the ordinary case, that context has no great effect on the appropriate analysis. Nonetheless, our precedent teaches that there are "extraordinary cases" that call for a different approach—cases in which the "history and the breadth of the authority that [the agency] has asserted," and the "economic and political significance" of that assertion, provide a "reason to hesitate before concluding that Congress" meant to confer such authority. *Id.*, at 159–160.

Such cases have arisen from all corners of the administrative state. In *Brown & Williamson*, for instance, the Food and Drug Administration claimed that its authority over "drugs" and "devices" included the power to regulate, and even ban, tobacco products. *Id.*, at 126–127. We rejected that "expansive construction of the statute," concluding that "Congress could not have intended to delegate" such a sweeping and consequential authority "in so cryptic a fashion." *Id.*, at 160. In *Alabama Assn. of Realtors v. Department of Health and Human Servs.*, 594 U.S., (2021) (per curiam) (slip op., at 3), we concluded that the Centers for Disease Control and Prevention could not, under its authority to adopt measures "necessary to prevent the . . . spread of" disease, institute a nationwide eviction moratorium in response to the COVID–19 pandemic. We found the statute's language a "wafer-thin reed" on which to rest such a measure, given "the sheer scope of the CDC's claimed authority," its "unprecedented" nature, and the fact that Congress had failed to extend the moratorium after previously having done so. *Id.,* at ____. Our decision in *Utility Air* addressed another question regarding EPA's authority—namely, whether EPA could construe the term "air pollutant," in a specific provision of the Clean Air Act, to cover greenhouse gases. 573 U.S., at 310. Despite its textual plausibility, we noted that the Agency's interpretation would have given it permitting authority over millions of small sources, such as hotels and office buildings, that had never before been subject to such requirements. *Id.,* at 310, 324. We declined to uphold EPA's claim of "unheralded" regulatory power over "a significant portion of the American economy." *Id.,* at 324. In *Gonzales v. Oregon,* 546 U.S. 243 (2006), we confronted the Attorney General's assertion that he could rescind the license of any physician who prescribed a controlled substance for assisted suicide, even in a State where such action was legal. The Attorney General argued that this came within his statutory power to revoke licenses where he found them "inconsistent with the public interest," 21 U.S.C. §823(f ). We considered the "idea that Congress gave [him] such broad and unusual authority through an implicit delegation . . . not sustainable." 546 U.S., at 267. Similar considerations informed our recent decision invalidating the Occupational Safety and Health Administration's mandate that "84 million Americans . . . either obtain a COVID–19 vaccine or undergo weekly medical testing at their own expense." *National Federation of Independent Business v. Occupational Safety and Health Administration,* 595 U.S.____, ____ (2022) (per curiam) (slip op., at 5). We found it "telling that OSHA, in its half century of existence," had never relied on its authority to regulate occupational hazards to impose such a remarkable measure. *Id.,* at ____ (slip op., at 8).

All of these regulatory assertions had a colorable textual basis. And yet, in each case, given the various circumstances, "common sense as to the manner in which Congress [would have been] likely to delegate" such power to the agency at issue, *Brown & Williamson,* 529 U.S., at 133, made it very unlikely that Congress had actually done so. Extraordinary grants of regulatory authority are rarely accomplished through "modest words," "vague terms," or "subtle device[s]." *Whitman,* 531 U.S., at 468. Nor does Congress typically use oblique or elliptical language to empower an agency to make a "radical or fundamental change" to a statutory scheme. *MCI Telecommunications Corp. v. American Telephone & Telegraph Co.,* 512 U.S. 218, 229 (1994). Agencies have only those powers given to them by Congress, and "enabling legislation" is generally not an "open book to which the agency [may] add pages and change the plot line." E. Gellhorn & P. Verkuil, Controlling Chevron-Based Delegations, 20 Cardozo L. Rev. 989, 1011 (1999). We presume that "Congress intends to make major policy decisions itself, not leave those decisions to agencies." *United States Telecom Assn. v. FCC,* 855 F. 3d 381, 419 (CADC 2017) (Kavanaugh, J., dissenting from denial of rehearing en banc).

1 Thus, in certain extraordinary cases, both separation of powers principles and a
2 practical understanding of legislative intent make us "reluctant to read into
3 ambiguous statutory text" the delegation claimed to be lurking there. *Utility Air*,
4 573 U.S., at 324. To convince us otherwise, something more than a merely plausible
5 textual basis for the agency action is necessary. The agency instead must point to
6 "clear congressional authorization" for the power it claims. *Ibid.*

7 * * *

8 B

9 Under our precedents, this is a major questions case. In arguing that Section 111(d)
10 empowers it to substantially restructure the American energy market, EPA
11 "claim[ed] to discover in a long-extant statute an unheralded power" representing
12 a "transformative expansion in [its] regulatory authority." *Utility Air*, 573 U.S., at
13 324. It located that newfound power in the vague language of an "ancillary
14 provision[]" of the Act, *Whitman*, 531 U.S., at 468, one that was designed to
15 function as a gap filler and had rarely been used in the preceding decades. And the
16 Agency's discovery allowed it to adopt a regulatory program that Congress had
17 conspicuously and repeatedly declined to enact itself. *Brown & Williamson*, 529
18 U.S., at 159–160; *Gonzales*, 546 U.S., at 267–268; *Alabama Assn.*, 594 U.S., at
19 ___, ___ (slip op., at 2, 8). Given these circumstances, there is every reason to
20 "hesitate before concluding that Congress" meant to confer on EPA the authority it
21 claims under Section 111(d). *Brown & Williamson*, 529 U.S., at 159–160.

22 Prior to 2015, EPA had always set emissions limits under Section 111 based on the
23 application of measures that would reduce pollution by causing the regulated
24 source to operate more cleanly. And as Justice Frankfurter has noted, "just as
25 established practice may shed light on the extent of power conveyed by general
26 statutory language, so the want of assertion of power by those who presumably
27 would be alert to exercise it, is equally significant in determining whether such
28 power was actually conferred." *FTC v. Bunte Brothers, Inc.*, 312 U.S. 349, 352
29 (1941).

30 * * *

31 This consistent understanding of "system[s] of emission reduction" tracked the
32 seemingly universal view, as stated by EPA in its inaugural Section 111(d)
33 rulemaking, that "Congress intended a technology-based approach" to regulation
34 in that Section. 40 Fed. Reg. 53343 (1975). A technology-based standard, recall, is
35 one that focuses on improving the emissions performance of individual sources.
36 EPA "commonly referred to" the "level of control" required as a "best demonstrated
37 technology (BDT)" standard, 73 Fed. Reg. 34073, and consistently applied it as
38 such.

39 Indeed, EPA nodded to this history in the Clean Power Plan itself, describing the
40 sort of "systems of emission reduction" it had always before selected—"efficiency
41 improvements, fuel-switching," and "add-on controls"—as "more traditional air

1   pollution control measures." 80 Fed. Reg. 64784. * * *

2   But, the Agency explained, in order to "control[] CO$_2$ from affected [plants] at levels
3   . . . necessary to mitigate the dangers presented by climate change," it could not
4   base the emissions limit on "measures that improve efficiency at the power plants."
5   *Id.*, at 64728. * * * Rather than focus on improving the performance of individual
6   sources, it would "improve the *overall power system* by lowering the carbon
7   intensity of power generation." *Ibid.* (emphasis added). And it would do that by
8   forcing a shift throughout the power grid from one type of energy source to another.
9   In the words of the then-EPA Administrator, the rule was "not about pollution
10  control" so much as it was "an investment opportunity" for States, especially
11  "investments in renewables and clean energy." Oversight Hearing on EPA's
12  Proposed Carbon Pollution Standards for Existing Power Plants before the Senate
13  Committee on Environment and Public Works, 113th Cong., 2d Sess., p. 33 (2014).

14  This view of EPA's authority was not only unprecedented; it also effected a
15  "fundamental revision of the statute, changing it from [one sort of] scheme of . . .
16  regulation" into an entirely different kind. *MCI*, 512 U.S., at 231. * * * [O]n this view
17  of EPA's authority, it could go further, perhaps forcing coal plants to "shift" away
18  virtually all of their generation—*i.e.*, to cease making power altogether.

19                                    * * *

20  There is little reason to think Congress assigned such decisions to the Agency. * * *
21  "When [an] agency has no comparative expertise" in making certain policy
22  judgments, we have said, "Congress presumably would not" task it with doing so.
23  *Kisor v. Wilkie*, 588 U.S. ___, ___ (2019) (slip op., at 17); see also *Gonzales*, 546
24  U.S., at 266–267.

25  We also find it "highly unlikely that Congress would leave" to "agency discretion"
26  the decision of how much coal-based generation there should be over the coming
27  decades. *MCI*, 512 U.S., at 231; see also *Brown & Williamson*, 529 U.S., at 160 ("We
28  are confident that Congress could not have intended to delegate a decision of such
29  economic and political significance to an agency in so cryptic a fashion."). The basic
30  and consequential tradeoffs involved in such a choice are ones that Congress would
31  likely have intended for itself. Congress certainly has not conferred a like authority
32  upon EPA anywhere else in the Clean Air Act. The last place one would expect to
33  find it is in the previously little-used backwater of Section 111(d).

34                                    * * *

35  Finally, we cannot ignore that the regulatory writ EPA newly uncovered
36  conveniently enabled it to enact a program that, long after the dangers posed by
37  greenhouse gas emissions "had become well known, Congress considered and
38  rejected" multiple times. *Brown & Williamson*, 529 U.S., at 144. At bottom, the
39  Clean Power Plan essentially adopted a cap-and-trade scheme, or set of state cap-
40  and-trade schemes, for carbon. Congress, however, has consistently rejected
41  proposals to amend the Clean Air Act to create such a program. * * *

1

## C

2 Given these circumstances, our precedent counsels skepticism toward EPA's claim
3 that Section 111 empowers it to devise carbon emissions caps based on a generation
4 shifting approach. To overcome that skepticism, the Government must—under the
5 major questions doctrine—point to "clear congressional authorization" to regulate
6 in that manner. *Utility Air*, 573 U.S., at 324.

7 All the Government can offer, however, is the Agency's authority to establish
8 emissions caps at a level reflecting "the application of the best system of emission
9 reduction . . . adequately demonstrated." 42 U.S.C. §7411(a)(1). As a matter of
10 "definitional possibilities," *FCC v. AT&T Inc.*, 562 U.S. 397, 407 (2011), generation
11 shifting can be described as a "system"—"an aggregation or assemblage of objects
12 united by some form of regular interaction," Brief for Federal Respondents 31—
13 capable of reducing emissions. But of course almost anything could constitute such
14 a "system"; shorn of all context, the word is an empty vessel. Such a vague statutory
15 grant is not close to the sort of clear authorization required by our precedents.

16 * * *

17 Capping carbon dioxide emissions at a level that will force a nationwide transition
18 away from the use of coal to generate electricity may be a sensible "solution to the
19 crisis of the day." *New York v. United States*, 505 U.S. 144, 187 (1992). But it is not
20 plausible that Congress gave EPA the authority to adopt on its own such a
21 regulatory scheme in Section 111(d). A decision of such magnitude and
22 consequence rests with Congress itself, or an agency acting pursuant to a clear
23 delegation from that representative body. The judgment of the Court of Appeals for
24 the District of Columbia Circuit is reversed, and the cases are remanded for further
25 proceedings consistent with this opinion.

26 It is so ordered.

27 JUSTICE GORSUCH, with whom JUSTICE ALITO joins, concurring. [omitted]

28 [The concurrence presents the major questions doctrine as a clear statement rule
29 for the Article I vesting clause: the Court will give a narrow construction to
30 statutory delegations of power so broad as to be constitutionally questionable,
31 unless the statute makes it unmistakably clear that Congress does wish to delegate
32 that matter to an agency.]

33

34 JUSTICE KAGAN, with whom JUSTICE BREYER and JUSTICE SOTOMAYOR
35 join, dissenting.

36 Today, the Court strips the Environmental Protection Agency (EPA) of the power
37 Congress gave it to respond to "the most pressing environmental challenge of our
38 time." *Massachusetts v. EPA*, 549 U.S. 497, 505 (2007).

* * *

Congress charged EPA with addressing those potentially catastrophic harms, including through regulation of fossil-fuel-fired power plants. Section 111 of the Clean Air Act directs EPA to regulate stationary sources of any substance that "causes, or contributes significantly to, air pollution" and that "may reasonably be anticipated to endanger public health or welfare." 42 U.S.C. §7411(b)(1)(A). Carbon dioxide and other greenhouse gases fit that description. EPA thus serves as the Nation's "primary regulator of greenhouse gas emissions." *American Elec. Power*, 564 U.S., at 428. And among the most significant of the entities it regulates are fossil-fuel-fired (mainly coal- and natural-gas-fired) power plants. * * *

To carry out its Section 111 responsibility, EPA issued the Clean Power Plan in 2015. The premise of the Plan— which no one really disputes—was that operational improvements at the individual-plant level would either "lead to only small emission reductions" or would cost far more than a readily available regulatory alternative. 80 Fed. Reg. 64727–64728 (2015). That alternative—which fossil-fuel-fired plants were "already using to reduce their [carbon dioxide] emissions" in "a cost effective manner"—is called generation shifting. *Id.*, at 64728, 64769. * * *

* * *

The limits the majority now puts on EPA's authority fly in the face of the statute Congress wrote. The majority says it is simply "not plausible" that Congress enabled EPA to regulate power plants' emissions through generation shifting. *Ante*, at 31. But that is just what Congress did when it broadly authorized EPA in Section 111 to select the "best system of emission reduction" for power plants.

§7411(a)(1). The "best system" full stop—no ifs, ands, or buts of any kind relevant here. The parties do not dispute that generation shifting is indeed the "best system"—the most effective and efficient way to reduce power plants' carbon dioxide emissions. And no other provision in the Clean Air Act suggests that Congress meant to foreclose EPA from selecting that system; to the contrary, the Plan's regulatory approach fits hand-in-glove with the rest of the statute. The majority's decision rests on one claim alone: that generation shifting is just too new and too big a deal for Congress to have authorized it in Section 111's general terms. But that is wrong. A key reason Congress makes broad delegations like Section 111 is so an agency can respond, appropriately and commensurately, to new and big problems. Congress knows what it doesn't and can't know when it drafts a statute; and Congress therefore gives an expert agency the power to address issues—even significant ones—as and when they arise. That is what Congress did in enacting Section 111. The majority today overrides that legislative choice. In so doing, it deprives EPA of the power needed—and the power granted—to curb the emission of greenhouse gases.

I

* * *

1            II

2            \* \* \*

3            A

4            \* \* \*

5 The majority today \* \* \* announces the arrival of the "major questions doctrine,"
6 which replaces normal text-in-context statutory interpretation with some tougher-
7 to-satisfy set of rules. *Ante*, at 16–31. Apparently, there is now a two-step inquiry.
8 First, a court must decide, by looking at some panoply of factors, whether agency
9 action presents an "extraordinary case[]." *Ante*, at 17; see *ante*, at 20–28. If it does,
10 the agency "must point to clear congressional authorization for the power it
11 claims," someplace over and above the normal statutory basis we require. *Ante*, at
12 19 (internal quotation marks omitted); see *ante*, at 28–31. The result is statutory
13 interpretation of an unusual kind. It is not until page 28 of a 31-page opinion that
14 the majority begins to seriously discuss the meaning of Section 111. And even then,
15 it does not address straight-up what should be the question: Does the text of that
16 provision, when read in context and with a commonsense awareness of how
17 Congress delegates, authorize the agency action here?

18 The majority claims it is just following precedent, but that is not so. The Court has
19 never even used the term "major questions doctrine" before. And in the relevant
20 cases, the Court has done statutory construction of a familiar sort. It has looked to
21 the text of a delegation. It has addressed how an agency's view of that text works—
22 or fails to do so— in the context of a broader statutory scheme. And it has asked, in
23 a common-sensical (or call it purposive) vein, about what Congress would have
24 made of the agency's view—otherwise said, whether Congress would naturally have
25 delegated authority over some important question to the agency, given its expertise
26 and experience. In short, in assessing the scope of a delegation, the Court has
27 considered—without multiple steps, triggers, or special presumptions—the fit
28 between the power claimed, the agency claiming it, and the broader statutory
29 design.

30            \* \* \*

31            B

32 \* \* \* Of course, [the majority] views Section 111 (if for unexplained reasons) as less
33 clear than I do. But nowhere does the majority provide evidence from within the
34 statute itself that the Clean Power Plan conflicts with or undermines Congress's
35 design. That fact alone makes this case different from all the cases described above.
36 As to the other critical matter in those cases—is the agency operating outside its
37 sphere of expertise?—the majority at least tries to say something. It claims EPA has
38 no "comparative expertise" in "balancing the many vital considerations of national
39 policy" implicated in regulating electricity sources. *Ante*, at 25–26. But that is
40 wrong.

Start with what this Court has said before on the subject, reflecting Congress's view of the matter. About a decade ago, we recognized that Congress had "delegated to EPA" in Section 111 "the decision whether and how to regulate carbon-dioxide emissions from powerplants." *American Elec. Power*, 564 U.S., at 426. * * * So the balancing—including of the Nation's "energy requirements"—that the majority says EPA has no "comparative expertise" in? §7411(a)(1); *ante*, at 25. We explained 11 short years ago, citing Congress, that it was smack in the middle of EPA's wheelhouse.

And we were right. * * * This is not the Attorney General regulating medical care, or even the CDC regulating landlord-tenant relations. It is EPA (that's the Environmental Protection Agency, in case the majority forgot) acting to address the greatest environmental challenge of our time. * * *

\* \* \*

### III

Some years ago, I remarked that "[w]e're all textualists now." Harvard Law School, The Antonin Scalia Lecture Series: A Dialogue with Justice Elena Kagan on the Reading of Statutes (Nov. 25, 2015). It seems I was wrong. The current Court is textualist only when being so suits it. When that method would frustrate broader goals, special canons like the "major questions doctrine" magically appear as get-out-of-text-free cards. Today, one of those broader goals makes itself clear: Prevent agencies from doing important work, even though that is what Congress directed. That anti-administrative-state stance shows up in the majority opinion, and it suffuses the concurrence. The kind of agency delegations at issue here go all the way back to this Nation's founding. * * *

\* \* \*

Over time, the administrative delegations Congress has made have helped to build a modern Nation. Congress wanted fewer workers killed in industrial accidents. It wanted to prevent plane crashes, and reduce the deadliness of car wrecks. It wanted to ensure that consumer products didn't catch fire. It wanted to stop the routine adulteration of food and improve the safety and efficacy of medications. And it wanted cleaner air and water. If an American could go back in time, she might be astonished by how much progress has occurred in all those areas. It didn't happen through legislation alone. It happened because Congress gave broad-ranging powers to administrative agencies, and those agencies then filled in—rule by rule by rule—Congress's policy outlines.

This Court has historically known enough not to get in the way. * * *

\* \* \*

In short, when it comes to delegations, there are good reasons for Congress (within extremely broad limits) to get to call the shots. Congress knows about how government works in ways courts don't. More specifically, Congress knows what mix of legislative and administrative action conduces to good policy. Courts should be modest.

Today, the Court is not. * * * The Court, rather than Congress, will decide how much regulation is too much.

The subject matter of the regulation here makes the Court's intervention all the more troubling. Whatever else this Court may know about, it does not have a clue about how to address climate change. And let's say the obvious: The stakes here are high. Yet the Court today prevents congressionally authorized agency action to curb power plants' carbon dioxide emissions. The Court appoints itself—instead of Congress or the expert agency—the decisionmaker on climate policy. I cannot think of many things more frightening. Respectfully, I dissent.

## 7. Agencies Interpreting Their Own Regulations

*Chevron* and related cases address the question of how courts should evaluate agencies' interpretations of *statutes that they administer*. The *Auer* Doctrine (also known as the *Seminole Rock* Doctrine, for the 1944 case that first announced it) concerns the question of how courts should evaluate agencies' interpretations of *their own regulations.* Can you think of reasons why courts would approach these two questions differently? If so, do those reasons counsel in favor of greater deference to agency interpretations of statutes, or regulations?

*Kisor* is the latest in a series of Supreme Court decisions that limit the use of *Auer* deference. What is left of *Auer* after *Kisor*?

### Auer v. Robbins

519 U.S. 452 (1997)

February 19, 1997

JUSTICE SCALIA delivered the opinion of the Court.

The Fair Labor Standards Act of 1938 (FLSA), 52 Stat. 1060, as amended, 29 U.S.C. §§ 201 *et seq.,* exempts "bona fide executive, administrative, or professional" employees from overtime pay requirements. This case presents the question whether the Secretary of Labor's "salary-basis" test for determining an employee's exempt status reflects a permissible reading of the statute as it applies to public sector employees. We also consider whether the Secretary has reasonably interpreted the salary-basis test to deny an employee salaried status (and thus

1    grant him overtime pay) when his compensation may "as a practical matter" be
2    adjusted in ways inconsistent with the test.

3                                    I

4    Petitioners are sergeants and a lieutenant employed by the St. Louis Police
5    Department. They brought suit in 1988 against respondents, members of the St.
6    Louis Board of Police Commissioners, seeking payment of overtime pay that they
7    claimed was owed under § 7(a)(1) of the FLSA, 29 U.S.C. § 207(a)(1). Respondents
8    argued that petitioners were not entitled to such pay because they came within the
9    exemption provided by § 213(a)(1) for "bona fide executive, administrative, or
10   professional" employees.

11   Under regulations promulgated by the Secretary, one requirement for exempt
12   status under § 213(a)(1) is that the employee earn a specified minimum amount on
13   a "salary basis." 29 CFR §§ 541.1(f), 541.2(e), 541.3(e) (1996). According to the
14   regulations, "[a]n employee will be considered to be paid 'on a salary basis' . . . if
15   under his employment agreement he regularly receives each pay period on a
16   weekly, or less frequent basis, a predetermined amount constituting all or part of
17   his compensation, which amount is not subject to reduction because of variations
18   in the quality or quantity of the work performed." § 541.118(a). Petitioners
19   contended that the salary-basis test was not met in their case because, under the
20   terms of the St. Louis Metropolitan Police Department Manual, their
21   compensation could be reduced for a variety of disciplinary infractions related to
22   the "quality or quantity" of work performed. Petitioners also claimed that they did
23   not meet the other requirement for exempt status under § 213(a)(1): that their
24   duties be of an executive, administrative, or professional nature.

25   The District Court found that petitioners were paid on a salary basis and that most,
26   though not all, also satisfied the duties criterion. The Court of Appeals affirmed in
27   part and reversed in part, holding that both the salary-basis test and the duties test
28   were satisfied as to all petitioners. We granted certiorari.

29                                   II

30   The FLSA grants the Secretary broad authority to "defin[e] and delimi[t]" the scope
31   of the exemption for executive, administrative, and professional employees. §
32   213(a)(1). Under the Secretary's chosen approach, exempt status requires that the
33   employee be paid on a salary basis, which in turn requires that his compensation
34   not be subject to reduction because of variations in the "quality or quantity of the
35   work performed," 29 CFR § 541.118(a) (1996). Because the regulation goes on to
36   carve out an exception from this rule for "[p]enalties imposed . . . for infractions of
37   safety rules of major significance," § 541.118(a)(5), it is clear that the rule embraces
38   reductions in pay for disciplinary violations. The Secretary is of the view that
39   employees whose pay is adjusted for disciplinary reasons do not deserve exempt

1  status because as a general matter true "executive, administrative, or professional"
2  employees are not "disciplined" by piecemeal deductions from their pay, but are
3  terminated, demoted, or given restricted assignments.

4  A

5  * * * The salary-basis test has existed largely in its present form since 1954, see 19
6  Fed. Reg. 4405 (1954), and is expressly applicable to public-sector employees, see
7  29 CFR §§ 553.2(b), 553.32(c) (1996).

8  Respondents concede that the FLSA may validly be applied to the public sector,
9  and they also do not raise any general challenge to the Secretary's reliance on the
10  salary-basis test. They contend, however, that the "no disciplinary deductions"
11  element of the salary-basis test is invalid for public-sector employees because as
12  applied to them it reflects an unreasonable interpretation of the statutory
13  exemption. That is so, they say, because the ability to adjust public-sector
14  employees' pay—even executive, administrative or professional employees' pay—
15  as a means of enforcing compliance with work rules is a necessary component of
16  effective government. In the public-sector context, they contend, fewer disciplinary
17  alternatives to deductions in pay are available.

18  Because Congress has not "directly spoken to the precise question at issue," we
19  must sustain the Secretary's approach so long as it is "based on a permissible
20  construction of the statute." *Chevron U.S.A. Inc. v. Natural Resources Defense*
21  *Council, Inc.,* 467 U.S. 837, 842-843 (1984). While respondents' objections would
22  perhaps support a different application of the salary-basis test for public
23  employees, we cannot conclude that they compel it. The Secretary's view that
24  public employers are not *so* differently situated with regard to disciplining their
25  employees as to require wholesale revision of his time-tested rule simply cannot be
26  said to be unreasonable. * * *

27  Respondents appeal to the "quasi military" nature of law enforcement agencies
28  such as the St. Louis Police Department. The ability to use the full range of
29  disciplinary tools against even relatively senior law enforcement personnel is
30  essential, they say, to maintaining control and discipline in organizations in which
31  human lives are on the line daily. It is far from clear, however, that only a pay
32  deduction, and not some other form of discipline-for example, placing the
33  offending officer on restricted duties-will have the necessary effect. Because the
34  FLSA entrusts matters of judgment such as this to the Secretary, not the federal
35  courts, we cannot say that the disciplinary-deduction rule is invalid as applied to
36  law enforcement personnel.

37  * * *

38  III

A primary issue in the litigation unleashed by application of the salary-basis test to public-sector employees has been whether, under that test, an employee's pay is "subject to" disciplinary or other deductions whenever there exists a theoretical possibility of such deductions, or rather only when there is something more to suggest that the employee is actually vulnerable to having his pay reduced. Petitioners in effect argue for something close to the former view; they contend that because the police manual nominally subjects all department employees to a range of disciplinary sanctions that includes disciplinary deductions in pay, and because a single sergeant was actually subjected to a disciplinary deduction, they are "subject to" such deductions and hence nonexempt under the FLSA.

The Court of Appeals rejected petitioners' approach, saying that "[t]he mere possibility of an improper deduction in pay does not defeat an employee's salaried status" if no practice of making deductions exists. 65 F. 3d, at 710-711. In the Court of Appeals' view, a "one-time incident" in which a disciplinary deduction is taken under "unique circumstances" does not defeat the salaried status of employees. * * *

The Secretary of Labor, in an *amicus* brief filed at the request of the Court, interprets the salary-basis test to deny exempt status when employees are covered by a policy that permits disciplinary or other deductions in pay "as a practical matter." That standard is met, the Secretary says, if there is either an actual practice of making such deductions or an employment policy that creates a "significant likelihood" of such deductions. The Secretary's approach rejects a wooden requirement of actual deductions, but in their absence it requires a clear and particularized policy-one which "effectively communicates" that deductions will be made in specified circumstances. This avoids the imposition of massive and unanticipated overtime liability (including the possibility of substantial liquidated damages) in situations in which a vague or broadly worded policy is nominally applicable to a whole range of personnel but is not "significantly likely" to be invoked against salaried employees.

Because the salary-basis test is a creature of the Secretary's own regulations, his interpretation of it is, under our jurisprudence, controlling unless "'plainly erroneous or inconsistent with the regulation.'" *Robertson v. Methow Valley Citizens Council,* 490 U.S. 332, 359 (1989) (quoting *Bowles v. Seminole Rock & Sand Co.,* 325 U.S. 410, 414 (1945)). That deferential standard is easily met here. The critical phrase "subject to" comfortably bears the meaning the Secretary assigns. See American Heritage Dictionary 1788 (3d ed. 1992) (def. 2: defining "subject to" to mean "prone; disposed"; giving as an example "a child who is subject to colds"); Webster's New International Dictionary 2509 (2d ed. 1950) (def. 3: defining "subject to" to mean "[e]xposed; liable; prone; disposed"; giving as an example "a country subject to extreme heat").

1    * * *

2    Petitioners complain that the Secretary's interpretation comes to us in the form of
3    a legal brief; but that does not, in the circumstances of this case, make it unworthy
4    of deference. The Secretary's position is in no sense a *"post hoc* rationalization"
5    advanced by an agency seeking to defend past agency action against attack, *Bowen*
6    *v. Georgetown Univ. Hospital,* 488 U.S. 204, 212 (1988). There is simply no
7    reason to suspect that the interpretation does not reflect the agency's fair and
8    considered judgment on the matter in question. Petitioners also suggest that the
9    Secretary's approach contravenes the rule that FLSA exemptions are to be
10   "narrowly construed against . . . employers" and are to be withheld except as to
11   persons "plainly and unmistakably within their terms and spirit." *Arnold v. Ben*
12   *Kanowsky, Inc.,* 361 U.S. 388, 392 (1960). But that is a rule governing judicial
13   interpretation of statutes and regulations, not a limitation on the Secretary's power
14   to resolve ambiguities in his own regulations. A rule requiring the Secretary to
15   construe his own regulations narrowly would make little sense, since he is free to
16   write the regulations as broadly as he wishes, subject only to the limits imposed by
17   the statute.

18   * * *

19   * * * The judgment of the Court of Appeals is affirmed.

20   *It is so ordered.*

21

22   **Kisor v. Wilkie**

23   139 S. Ct. 2400 (2019)

24   June 26, 2019

25   JUSTICE KAGAN announced the judgment of the Court and delivered the opinion
26   of the Court with respect to Parts I, II–B, III–B, and IV, and an opinion with
27   respect to Parts II–A and III–A, in which JUSTICE GINSBURG, JUSTICE
28   BREYER, and JUSTICE SOTOMAYOR join.

29   This Court has often deferred to agencies' reasonable readings of genuinely
30   ambiguous regulations. We call that practice *Auer* deference, or sometimes
31   *Seminole Rock* deference, after two cases in which we employed it. See *Auer v.*
32   *Robbins,* 519 U.S. 452 (1997); *Bowles v. Seminole Rock & Sand Co.,* 325 U.S. 410
33   (1945). The only question presented here is whether we should overrule those
34   decisions, discarding the deference they give to agencies. We answer that question
35   no. *Auer* deference retains an important role in construing agency regulations. But
36   even as we uphold it, we reinforce its limits. *Auer* deference is sometimes

appropriate and sometimes not. Whether to apply it depends on a range of considerations that we have noted now and again, but compile and further develop today. The deference doctrine we describe is potent in its place, but cabined in its scope. On remand, the Court of Appeals should decide whether it applies to the agency interpretation at issue.

I

\* \* \*

Kisor is a Vietnam War veteran seeking disability benefits from the Department of Veterans Affairs (VA). He first applied in 1982, alleging that he had developed post-traumatic stress disorder (PTSD) as a result of his participation in a military action called Operation Harvest Moon. The report of the agency's evaluating psychiatrist noted Kisor's involvement in that battle, but found that he "d[id] not suffer from PTSD." The VA thus denied Kisor benefits. There matters stood until 2006, when Kisor moved to reopen his claim. Based on a new psychiatric report, the VA this time agreed that Kisor suffered from PTSD. But it granted him benefits only from the date of his motion to reopen, rather than (as he requested) from the date of his first application.

The Board of Veterans' Appeals—a part of the VA, represented in Kisor's case by a single administrative judge—affirmed that timing decision, based on its interpretation of an agency rule. Under the VA's regulation, the agency could grant Kisor retroactive benefits if it found there were "relevant official service department records" that it had not considered in its initial denial. See 38 CFR §3.156(c)(1) (2013). The Board acknowledged that Kisor had come up with two new service records, both confirming his participation in Operation Harvest Moon. But according to the Board, those records were not "relevant" because they did not go to the reason for the denial—that Kisor did not have PTSD. The Court of Appeals for Veterans Claims, an independent Article I court that initially reviews the Board's decisions, affirmed for the same reason.

The Court of Appeals for the Federal Circuit also affirmed, but it did so based on deference to the Board's interpretation of the VA rule. Kisor had argued to the Federal Circuit that to count as "relevant," a service record need not (as the Board thought) "counter[ ] the basis of the prior denial"; instead, it could relate to some other criterion for obtaining disability benefits. The Federal Circuit found the regulation "ambiguous" as between the two readings. The rule, said the court, does not specifically address "whether 'relevant' records are those casting doubt on the agency's prior [rationale or] those relating to the veteran's claim more broadly." So how to choose between the two views? The court continued: "Both parties insist that the plain regulatory language supports their case, and neither party's position strikes us as unreasonable." Because that was so, the court believed *Auer* deference appropriate: The agency's construction of its own regulation would govern unless "plainly erroneous or inconsistent with the VA's regulatory framework." Applying that standard, the court upheld the Board's reading—and so approved the denial of retroactive benefits.

We then granted certiorari to decide whether to overrule *Auer* and (its predecessor) *Seminole Rock*.

## II

Before addressing that question directly, we spend some time describing what *Auer* deference is, and is not, for. * * *

## A

Begin with a familiar problem in administrative law: For various reasons, regulations may be genuinely ambiguous. They may not directly or clearly address every issue; when applied to some fact patterns, they may prove susceptible to more than one reasonable reading. Sometimes, this sort of ambiguity arises from careless drafting—the use of a dangling modifier, an awkward word, an opaque construction. But often, ambiguity reflects the well-known limits of expression or knowledge. The subject matter of a rule "may be so specialized and varying in nature as to be impossible"—or at any rate, impracticable—to capture in its every detail. *SEC v. Chenery Corp.*, 332 U.S. 194, 203 (1947). Or a "problem[ ] may arise" that the agency, when drafting the rule, "could not [have] reasonably foresee[n]." *Id.*, at 202. Whichever the case, the result is to create real uncertainties about a regulation's meaning.

Consider these examples:

> In a rule issued to implement the Americans with Disabilities Act (ADA), the Department of Justice requires theaters and stadiums to provide people with disabilities "lines of sight comparable to those for members of the general public." 28 CFR pt. 36, App. A, p. 563 (1996). Must the Washington Wizards construct wheelchair seating to offer lines of sight over spectators when they rise to their feet? Or is it enough that the facility offers comparable views so long as everyone remains seated? See *Paralyzed Veterans of Am. v. D. C. Arena L. P.*, 117 F.3d 579, 581–582 (CADC 1997).

> The Transportation Security Administration (TSA) requires that liquids, gels, and aerosols in carry-on baggage be packed in containers smaller than 3.4 ounces and carried in a clear plastic bag. Does a traveler have to pack his jar of truffle pâté in that way? See *Laba v. Copeland*, 2016 WL 5958241, *1 (WDNC, Oct. 13, 2016).

The Mine Safety and Health Administration issues a rule requiring employers to report occupational diseases within two weeks after they are "diagnosed." 30 CFR §50.20(a) (1993). Do chest X-ray results that "scor[e]" above some level of opacity count as a "diagnosis"? What level, exactly? See *American Min. Congress* v. *Mine Safety and Health Admin.*, 995 F.2d 1106, 1107–1108 (CADC 1993).

An FDA regulation gives pharmaceutical companies exclusive rights to drug products if they contain "no active moiety that has been approved by FDA in any other" new drug application. 21 CFR §314.108(a) (2010). Has a company created a new "active moiety" by joining a previously approved moiety to lysine through a non-ester covalent bond? See *Actavis Elizabeth LLC v. FDA*, 625 F.3d 760, 762–763 (CADC 2010).

Or take the facts of *Auer* itself. An agency must decide whether police captains are eligible for overtime under the Fair Labor Standards Act. According to the agency's regulations, employees cannot receive overtime if they are paid on a "salary basis." 29 CFR §541.118(a) (1996). And in deciding whether an employee is salaried, one question is whether his pay is "subject to reduction" based on performance. A police department's manual informs its officers that their pay might be docked if they commit a disciplinary infraction. Does that fact alone make them "subject to" pay deductions? Or must the department have a practice of docking officer pay, so that the possibility of that happening is more than theoretical? 519 U.S., at 459–462.

In each case, interpreting the regulation involves a choice between (or among) more than one reasonable reading. To apply the rule to some unanticipated or unresolved situation, the court must make a judgment call. How should it do so?

In answering that question, we have often thought that a court should defer to the agency's construction of its own regulation. For the last 20 or so years, we have referred to that doctrine as *Auer* deference, and applied it often. * * * Deference to administrative agencies traces back to the late nineteenth century, and perhaps beyond.

We have explained *Auer* deference (as we now call it) as rooted in a presumption about congressional intent—a presumption that Congress would generally want the agency to play the primary role in resolving regulatory ambiguities. Congress, we have pointed out, routinely delegates to agencies the power to implement statutes by issuing rules. In doing so, Congress knows (how could it not?) that regulations will sometimes contain ambiguities. But Congress almost never explicitly assigns responsibility to deal with that problem, either to agencies or to courts. Hence the need to presume, one way or the other, what Congress would want. And as between those two choices, agencies have gotten the nod. We have adopted the presumption—though it is always rebuttable—that "the power authoritatively to interpret its own regulations is a component of the agency's delegated lawmaking powers." *Martin v. Occupational Safety and Health Review Comm'n*, 499 U.S., 144, 151 (1991). Or otherwise said, we have thought that when granting rulemaking power to agencies, Congress usually intends to give them, too, considerable latitude to interpret the ambiguous rules they issue.

In part, that is because the agency that promulgated a rule is in the "better position [to] reconstruct" its original meaning. *Id.,* at 152. Consider that if you don't know what some text (say, a memo or an e-mail) means, you would probably want to ask the person who wrote it. And for the same reasons, we have thought, Congress would too (though the person is here a collective actor). * * * Want to know what a rule means? Ask its author.

In still greater measure, the presumption that Congress intended *Auer* deference stems from the awareness that resolving genuine regulatory ambiguities often "entail[s] the exercise of judgment grounded in policy concerns." *Thomas Jefferson Univ. v. Shalala*, 512 U.S. 504, 512 (1994) (internal quotation marks omitted). Return to our TSA example. In most of their applications, terms like "liquids" and "gels" are clear enough. (Traveler checklist: Pretzels OK; water not.) But resolving the uncertain issues—the truffle pâtés or olive tapenades of the world—requires getting in the weeds of the rule's policy: Why does TSA ban liquids and gels in the first instance? What makes them dangerous? Can a potential hijacker use pâté jars in the same way as soda cans? * * * Or finally, take the more technical "moiety" example. Or maybe, don't. If you are a judge, you probably have no idea of what the FDA's rule means, or whether its policy is implicated when a previously approved moiety is connected to lysine through a non-ester covalent bond.

And Congress, we have thought, knows just that: It is attuned to the comparative advantages of agencies over courts in making such policy judgments. Agencies (unlike courts) have "unique expertise," often of a scientific or technical nature, relevant to applying a regulation "to complex or changing circumstances." *Martin*, 499 U.S., at 151; see *Thomas Jefferson*, 512 U.S., at 512. Agencies (unlike courts) can conduct factual investigations, can consult with affected parties, can consider how their experts have handled similar issues over the long course of administering a regulatory program. See *Long Island Care at Home, Ltd. v. Coke*, 551 U.S. 158, 167–168 (2007). And agencies (again unlike courts) have political accountability, because they are subject to the supervision of the President, who in turn answers to the public. See *Free Enterprise Fund v. Public Company Accounting Oversight Bd.*, 561 U.S. 477, 499 (2010); *Pauley v. BethEnergy Mines, Inc.*, 501 U.S. 680, 696 (1991) (discussing as a matter of democratic accountability

1   the "proper roles of the political and judicial branches" in filling regulatory gaps).
2   It is because of those features that Congress, when first enacting a statute, assigns
3   rulemaking power to an agency and thus authorizes it to fill out the statutory
4   scheme. And so too, when new issues demanding new policy calls come up within
5   that scheme, Congress presumably wants the same agency, rather than any court,
6   to take the laboring oar.

7   Finally, the presumption we use reflects the well-known benefits of uniformity in
8   interpreting genuinely ambiguous rules. * * *

9                                       B

10   But all that said, *Auer* deference is not the answer to every question of interpreting
11   an agency's rules. Far from it. As we explain in this section, the possibility of
12   deference can arise only if a regulation is genuinely ambiguous. And when we use
13   that term, we mean it—genuinely ambiguous, even after a court has resorted to all
14   the standard tools of interpretation. Still more, not all reasonable agency
15   constructions of those truly ambiguous rules are entitled to deference. As just
16   explained, we presume that Congress intended for courts to defer to agencies when
17   they interpret their own ambiguous rules. But when the reasons for that
18   presumption do not apply, or countervailing reasons outweigh them, courts should
19   not give deference to an agency's reading, except to the extent it has the "power to
20   persuade." *Christopher*, 567 U.S., at 159 (quoting *Skidmore v. Swift & Co.*, 323
21   U.S. 134, 140 (1944)). * * *

22   We take the opportunity to restate, and somewhat expand on, those principles here
23   to clear up some mixed messages we have sent. At times, this Court has applied
24   *Auer* deference without significant analysis of the underlying regulation. See, *e.g.*,
25   *United States v. Larionoff*, 431 U.S. 864, 872 (1977) (stating that the Court "need
26   not tarry" over the regulation's language given *Seminole Rock*). At other times, the
27   Court has given *Auer* deference without careful attention to the nature and context
28   of the interpretation. See, *e.g.*, *Thorpe v. Housing Authority of Durham*, 393 U.S.
29   268, 276, and nn. 22–23 (1969) (deferring to an agency's view as expressed in
30   letters to third parties). And in a vacuum, our most classic formulation of the test—
31   whether an agency's construction is "plainly erroneous or inconsistent with the
32   regulation," *Seminole Rock*, 325 U.S., at 414—may suggest a caricature of the
33   doctrine, in which deference is "reflexive." *Pereira v. Sessions*, 138 S. Ct. 2105
34   (2018) (KENNEDY, J., concurring). So we cannot deny that Kisor has a bit of grist
35   for his claim that *Auer* "bestows on agencies expansive, unreviewable" authority.
36   But in fact *Auer* does no such thing: It gives agencies their due, while also
37   allowing—indeed, obligating—courts to perform their reviewing and restraining
38   functions. So before we turn to Kisor's specific grievances, we think it worth
39   reinforcing some of the limits inherent in the *Auer* doctrine.

1    First and foremost, a court should not afford *Auer* deference unless the regulation
2    is genuinely ambiguous. See *Christensen v. Harris County*, 529 U.S. 576, 588
3    (2000); *Seminole Rock*, 325 U.S., at 414 (deferring only "if the meaning of the
4    words used is in doubt"). * * *

5    And before concluding that a rule is genuinely ambiguous, a court must exhaust all
6    the "traditional tools" of construction. *Chevron U.S.A. Inc. v. Natural Resources*
7    *Defense Council, Inc.*, 467 U.S. 837, 843, n. 9 (1984) (adopting the same approach
8    for ambiguous statutes). For again, only when that legal toolkit is empty and the
9    interpretive question still has no single right answer can a judge conclude that it is
10    "more [one] of policy than of law." *Pauley*, 501 U.S., at 696. That means a court
11    cannot wave the ambiguity flag just because it found the regulation impenetrable
12    on first read. Agency regulations can sometimes make the eyes glaze over. But hard
13    interpretive conundrums, even relating to complex rules, can often be solved. * * *

14    If genuine ambiguity remains, moreover, the agency's reading must still be
15    "reasonable." *Thomas Jefferson*, 512 U.S., at 515. * * * Some courts have thought
16    (perhaps because of *Seminole Rock*'s "plainly erroneous" formulation) that at this
17    stage of the analysis, agency constructions of rules receive greater deference than
18    agency constructions of statutes. But that is not so. Under *Auer*, as under *Chevron*,
19    the agency's reading must fall "within the bounds of reasonable interpretation."
20    *Arlington v. FCC*, 569 U.S. 290, 296 (2013). And let there be no mistake: That is a
21    requirement an agency can fail.

22    Still, we are not done—for not every reasonable agency reading of a genuinely
23    ambiguous rule should receive *Auer* deference. We have recognized in applying
24    *Auer* that a court must make an independent inquiry into whether the character
25    and context of the agency interpretation entitles it to controlling weight. As
26    explained above, we give *Auer* deference because we presume, for a set of reasons
27    relating to the comparative attributes of courts and agencies, that Congress would
28    have wanted us to. But the administrative realm is vast and varied, and we have
29    understood that such a presumption cannot always hold. The inquiry on this
30    dimension does not reduce to any exhaustive test. But we have laid out some
31    especially important markers for identifying when *Auer* deference is and is not
32    appropriate.

33    To begin with, the regulatory interpretation must be one actually made by the
34    agency. In other words, it must be the agency's "authoritative" or "official position,"
35    rather than any more ad hoc statement not reflecting the agency's views. *Mead*,
36    533 U.S., at 257–259, and n. 6 (SCALIA, J., dissenting). That constraint follows
37    from the logic of *Auer* deference—because Congress has delegated rulemaking
38    power, and all that typically goes with it, to the agency alone. Of course, the
39    requirement of "authoritative" action must recognize a reality of bureaucratic life:
40    Not everything the agency does comes from, or is even in the name of, the Secretary

or his chief advisers. So, for example, we have deferred to "official staff memoranda" that were "published in the Federal Register," even though never approved by the agency head. *Ford Motor Credit*, 444 U.S., at 566, n. 9, 567, n. 10 (declining to "draw a radical distinction between" agency heads and staff for *Auer* deference). But there are limits. The interpretation must at the least emanate from those actors, using those vehicles, understood to make authoritative policy in the relevant context. See, *e.g., Paralyzed Veterans*, 117 F. 3d, at 587 (refusing to consider a "speech of a mid-level official" as an "authoritative departmental position"); *N. Y. State Dept. of Social Servs. v. Bowen*, 835 F.2d 360, 365–366 (CADC 1987) (rejecting the idea that an "informal memorandum" recounting a telephone conversation between employees could count as an "authoritative pronouncement"); *Exelon Generation Co. v. Local 15, Int'l Brotherhood of Elec. Workers, AFL–CIO*, 676 F.3d 566, 576–578 (CA7 2012) (declining deference when the agency had itself "disclaimed the use of regulatory guides as authoritative"). If the interpretation does not do so, a court may not defer.

Next, the agency's interpretation must in some way implicate its substantive expertise. Administrative knowledge and experience largely "account [for] the presumption that Congress delegates interpretive lawmaking power to the agency." *Martin*, 499 U.S., at 153. So the basis for deference ebbs when "[t]he subject matter of the [dispute is] distan[t] from the agency's ordinary" duties or "fall[s] within the scope of another agency's authority." *Arlington*, 569 U.S., at 309 (opinion of BREYER, J.). * * *

Finally, an agency's reading of a rule must reflect "fair and considered judgment" to receive *Auer* deference. *Christopher*, 567 U.S., at 155 (quoting *Auer*, 519 U.S., at 462). That means, we have stated, that a court should decline to defer to a merely "convenient litigating position" or "*post hoc* rationalizatio[n] advanced" to "defend past agency action against attack." *Christopher*, 567 U.S., at 155 (quoting *Bowen v. Georgetown Univ. Hospital*, 488 U.S. 204, 213 (1988) and *Auer*, 519 U.S., at 462). And a court may not defer to a new interpretation, whether or not introduced in litigation, that creates "unfair surprise" to regulated parties. *Long Island Care*, 551 U.S., at 170. * * * The upshot of all this goes something as follows. When it applies, *Auer* deference gives an agency significant leeway to say what its own rules mean. In so doing, the doctrine enables the agency to fill out the regulatory scheme Congress has placed under its supervision. But that phrase "when it applies" is important—because it often doesn't. As described above, this Court has cabined *Auer*'s scope in varied and critical ways—and in exactly that measure, has maintained a strong judicial role in interpreting rules. What emerges is a deference doctrine not quite so tame as some might hope, but not nearly so menacing as they might fear.

III

1   That brings us to the lone question presented here—whether we should abandon
2   the longstanding doctrine just described. In contending that we should, Kisor
3   raises statutory, policy, and constitutional claims (in that order). * * *

4                                        A

5   Kisor first attacks *Auer* as inconsistent with the judicial review provision of the
6   Administrative Procedure Act (APA). See 5 U.S.C. §706. As Kisor notes, Congress
7   enacted the APA in 1946—the year after *Seminole Rock*—to serve as "the
8   fundamental charter of the administrative state." Brief for Petitioner 26 (internal
9   quotation marks omitted). Section 706 of the Act, governing judicial review of
10  agency action, states (among other things) that reviewing courts shall "determine
11  the meaning or applicability of the terms of an agency action" (including a
12  regulation). According to Kisor, *Auer* violates that edict by thwarting "meaningful
13  judicial review" of agency rules. * * *

14  To begin with, that argument ignores the many ways, discussed above, that courts
15  exercise independent review over the meaning of agency rules. * * *

16  And even when a court defers to a regulatory reading, it acts consistently with
17  Section 706. That provision does not specify the standard of review a court should
18  use in "determin[ing] the meaning" of an ambiguous rule. 5 U.S.C. §706. * * *
19  [C]ourts do not violate Section 706 by applying *Auer*. To the contrary, they fulfill
20  their duty to "determine the meaning" of a rule precisely by deferring to the
21  agency's reasonable reading. See Sunstein & Vermeule, The Unbearable Rightness
22  of *Auer*, 84 U. Chi. L. Rev. 297, 306 (2017) (If Congress intends "that the meaning
23  of a regulation turns on the agency's interpretation of its meaning," then courts
24  comply with Section 706's command to "'determine the meaning' [of the
25  regulation] by deferring to that view"); cf. *Arlington*, 569 U.S., at 317 (Roberts, C.
26  J., dissenting) (similarly addressing why *Chevron* deference comports with Section
27  706). Section 706 and *Auer* thus go hand in hand.

28                                      * * *

29  Kisor next claims that *Auer* circumvents the APA's rulemaking requirements.
30  Section 553, as Kisor notes, mandates that an agency use notice-and-comment
31  procedures before issuing legislative rules. See 5 U.S.C. §§553(b), (c). But the
32  section allows agencies to issue "interpret[ive]" rules without notice and comment.
33  See §553(b)(A). A key feature of those rules is that (unlike legislative rules) they
34  are not supposed to "have the force and effect of law"—or, otherwise said, to bind
35  private parties. *Perez v. Mortgage Bankers Assn.*, 575 U.S. 92 (2015) (internal
36  quotation marks omitted). Instead, interpretive rules are meant only to "advise the
37  public" of how the agency understands, and is likely to apply, its binding statutes
38  and legislative rules. *Ibid.* But consider, Kisor argues, what happens when a court
39  gives *Auer* deference to an interpretive rule. The result, he asserts, is to make a rule
    610

CHAPTER 3: JUDICIAL REVIEW

that has never gone through notice and comment binding on the public. Or put another way, the interpretive rule ends up having the "force and effect of law" without ever paying the procedural cost. But this Court rejected the identical argument just a few years ago, and for good reason. In *Mortgage Bankers*, we held that interpretive rules, even when given *Auer* deference, do *not* have the force of law. An interpretive rule itself never forms "the basis for an enforcement action"— because, as just noted, such a rule does not impose any "legally binding requirements" on private parties. *National Min. Assn. v. McCarthy*, 758 F.3d 243, 251 (CADC 2014). An enforcement action must instead rely on a legislative rule, which (to be valid) must go through notice and comment. * * * In short, courts retain the final authority to approve—or not—the agency's reading of a notice-and-comment rule. See *Mortgage Bankers*, 575 U.S., at ___, n. 4 (slip op., at 10, n. 4) ("[I]t is the court that ultimately decides whether a given regulation means what the agency says"). No binding of anyone occurs merely by the agency's say-so.

And indeed, a court deciding whether to give *Auer* deference must heed the same procedural values as Section 553 reflects. Remember that a court may defer to only an agency's authoritative and considered judgments. No *ad hoc* statements or *post hoc* rationalizations need apply. And recall too that deference turns on whether an agency's interpretation creates unfair surprise or upsets reliance interests. So an agency has a strong incentive to circulate its interpretations early and widely. In such ways, the doctrine of *Auer* deference reinforces, rather than undermines, the ideas of fairness and informed decisionmaking at the core of the APA.

To supplement his two APA arguments, Kisor turns to policy, leaning on a familiar claim about the incentives *Auer* creates. According to Kisor, *Auer* encourages agencies to issue vague and open-ended regulations, confident that they can later impose whatever interpretation of those rules they prefer. * * *

But the claim has notable weaknesses, empirical and theoretical alike. First, it does not survive an encounter with experience. No real evidence—indeed, scarcely an anecdote—backs up the assertion. As two noted scholars (one of whom reviewed thousands of rules during four years of government service) have written: "[W]e are unaware of, and no one has pointed to, any regulation in American history that, because of *Auer*, was designed vaguely." Sunstein & Vermeule, 84 U. Chi. L. Rev., at 308. * * *

Finally, Kisor goes big, asserting (though fleetingly) that *Auer* deference violates "separation-of-powers principles." In his view, those principles prohibit "vest[ing] in a single branch the law-making and law-interpreting functions." If that objection is to agencies' usurping the interpretive role of courts, this opinion has already met it head-on. Properly understood and applied, *Auer* does no such thing. In all the ways we have described, courts retain a firm grip on the interpretive function. If Kisor's objection is instead to the supposed commingling of functions

611

(that is, the legislative and judicial) within an agency, this Court has answered it often before. See, *e.g., Withrow v. Larkin,* 421 U.S. 35, 54 (1975) (permitting such a combination of functions); *FTC v. Cement Institute,* 333 U.S. 683, 702 (1948) (same). That sort of mixing is endemic in agencies, and has been "since the beginning of the Republic." *Arlington,* 569 U.S., at 304–305, n. 4. It does not violate the separation of powers, we have explained, because even when agency "activities take 'legislative' and 'judicial' forms," they continue to be "exercises of[ ] the 'executive Power'"—or otherwise said, ways of executing a statutory plan. *Ibid.* (quoting U.S. Const., Art. II, § 1, cl. 1). So Kisor's last argument to dispatch *Auer* deference fails as roundly as the rest.

B

If all that were not enough, *stare decisis* cuts strongly against Kisor's position. "Overruling precedent is never a small matter." *Kimble v. Marvel Entertainment, LLC,* 576 U.S. 446, 455 (2015). * * *

And that is even more than usually so in the circumstances here. First, Kisor asks us to overrule not a single case, but a "long line of precedents"—each one reaffirming the rest and going back 75 years or more. *Bay Mills,* 572 U.S., at 798. This Court alone has applied *Auer* or *Seminole Rock* in dozens of cases, and lower courts have done so thousands of times. Deference to reasonable agency interpretations of ambiguous rules pervades the whole corpus of administrative law. Second, because that is so, abandoning *Auer* deference would cast doubt on many settled constructions of rules. * * *

And third, even if we are wrong about *Auer,* "Congress remains free to alter what we have done." *Patterson v. McLean Credit Union,* 491 U.S. 164, 172–173 (1989) (stating that when that is so, "[c]onsiderations of *stare decisis* have special force"). In a constitutional case, only we can correct our error. But that is not so here. Our deference decisions are "balls tossed into Congress's court, for acceptance or not as that branch elects." *Kimble,* 576 U.S., at 456. * * *

* * *

IV

With that, we can finally return to Kisor's own case. You may remember that his retroactive benefits depend on the meaning of the term "relevant" records in a VA regulation. The Board of Veterans' Appeals, through a single judge's opinion, understood records to be relevant only if they relate to the basis of the VA's initial denial of benefits. By contrast, Kisor argued that records are relevant if they go to any benefits criterion, even one that was uncontested. The Federal Circuit upheld the Board's interpretation based on *Auer* deference.

1 Applying the principles outlined in this opinion, we hold that a redo is necessary
2 for two reasons. First, the Federal Circuit jumped the gun in declaring the
3 regulation ambiguous. We have insisted that a court bring all its interpretive tools
4 to bear before finding that to be so. It is not enough to casually remark, as the court
5 did here, that "[b]oth parties insist that the plain regulatory language supports
6 their case, and neither party's position strikes us as unreasonable." 869 F. 3d, at
7 1368. Rather, the court must make a conscientious effort to determine, based on
8 indicia like text, structure, history, and purpose, whether the regulation really has
9 more than one reasonable meaning. The Solicitor General argued in this Court that
10 the Board's reading is the only reasonable one. Perhaps Kisor will make the
11 converse claim below. Before even considering deference, the court must seriously
12 think through those positions.

13 And second, the Federal Circuit assumed too fast that *Auer* deference should apply
14 in the event of genuine ambiguity. As we have explained, that is not always true. A
15 court must assess whether the interpretation is of the sort that Congress would
16 want to receive deference. The Solicitor General suggested at oral argument that
17 the answer in this case might be no. He explained that all 100 or so members of the
18 VA Board act individually (rather than in panels) and that their roughly 80,000
19 annual decisions have no "precedential value." He thus questioned whether a
20 Board member's ruling "reflects the considered judgment of the agency as a
21 whole." Cf. *Mead*, 533 U.S., at 233 (declining to give *Chevron* deference to rulings
22 "being churned out at a rate of 10,000 a year at an agency's 46 scattered offices").
23 We do not know what position the Government will take on that issue below. But
24 the questions the Solicitor General raised are exactly the kind the court must
25 consider in deciding whether to award *Auer* deference to the Board's
26 interpretation.

27 We accordingly vacate the judgment below and remand the case for further
28 proceedings.

29 *It is so ordered.*

30 CHIEF JUSTICE ROBERTS, concurring in part.

31 I join Parts I, II–B, III–B, and IV of the Court's opinion. We took this case to
32 consider whether to overrule *Auer v. Robbins*, 519 U.S. 452 (1997), and *Bowles v.*
33 *Seminole Rock & Sand Co.*, 325 U.S. 410 (1945). For the reasons the Court
34 discusses in Part III–B, I agree that overruling those precedents is not warranted.
35 I also agree with the Court's treatment in Part II–B of the bounds of *Auer*
36 deference.

37 I write separately to suggest that the distance between the majority and JUSTICE
38 GORSUCH is not as great as it may initially appear. The majority catalogs the
39 prerequisites for, and limitations on, *Auer* deference: The underlying regulation

1  must be genuinely ambiguous; the agency's interpretation must be reasonable and
2  must reflect its authoritative, expertise-based, and fair and considered judgment;
3  and the agency must take account of reliance interests and avoid unfair surprise.
4  JUSTICE GORSUCH, meanwhile, lists the reasons that a court might be persuaded
5  to adopt an agency's interpretation of its own regulation: The agency thoroughly
6  considered the problem, offered a valid rationale, brought its expertise to bear, and
7  interpreted the regulation in a manner consistent with earlier and later
8  pronouncements. Accounting for variations in verbal formulation, those lists have
9  much in common.

10  That is not to say that *Auer* deference is just the same as the power of persuasion
11  discussed in *Skidmore v. Swift & Co.*, 323 U.S. 134 (1944); there is a difference
12  between holding that a court ought to be persuaded by an agency's interpretation
13  and holding that it should defer to that interpretation under certain conditions.
14  But it is to say that the cases in which *Auer* deference is warranted largely overlap
15  with the cases in which it would be unreasonable for a court not to be persuaded
16  by an agency's interpretation of its own regulation.

17  * * *

18  JUSTICE GORSUCH, with whom JUSTICE THOMAS joins, with whom JUSTICE
19  KAVANAUGH joins as to Parts I, II, III, IV, and V, and with whom JUSTICE
20  ALITO joins as to Parts I, II, and III, concurring in the judgment.

21  It should have been easy for the Court to say goodbye to *Auer v. Robbins*. In
22  disputes involving the relationship between the government and the people, *Auer*
23  requires judges to accept an executive agency's interpretation of its own
24  regulations even when that interpretation doesn't represent the best and fairest
25  reading. This rule creates a "systematic judicial bias in favor of the federal
26  government, the most powerful of parties, and against everyone else."[2] Nor is
27  *Auer*'s biased rule the product of some congressional mandate we are powerless to
28  correct: This Court invented it, almost by accident and without any meaningful
29  effort to reconcile it with the Administrative Procedure Act or the Constitution. A
30  legion of academics, lower court judges, and Members of this Court—even *Auer*'s
31  author—has called on us to abandon *Auer*. Yet today a bare majority flinches, and
32  *Auer* lives on.

33  Still, today's decision is more a stay of execution than a pardon. The Court cannot
34  muster even five votes to say that *Auer* is lawful or wise. Instead, a majority retains
35  *Auer* only because of *stare decisis*. And yet, far from standing by that precedent,
36  the majority proceeds to impose so many new and nebulous qualifications and

---

[2] Larkin & Slattery, The World After Seminole Rock and Auer, 42 Harv. J. L. & Pub. Pol'y 625, 641 (2019) (internal quotation marks omitted).

1    limitations on *Auer* that THE CHIEF JUSTICE claims to see little practical
2    difference between keeping it on life support in this way and overruling it entirely.
3    So the doctrine emerges maimed and enfeebled—in truth, zombified.

4    Respectfully, we owe our colleagues on the lower courts more candid and useful
5    guidance than this. And judges owe the people who come before them nothing less
6    than a fair contest, where every party has an equal chance to persuade the court of
7    its interpretation of the law's demands. One can hope that THE CHIEF JUSTICE
8    is right, and that whether we formally overrule *Auer* or merely neuter it, the results
9    in most cases will prove the same. But means, not just ends, matter, and retaining
10   even this debilitated version of *Auer* threatens to force litigants and lower courts
11   to jump through needless and perplexing new hoops and in the process deny the
12   people the independent judicial decisions they deserve. All to what end? So that we
13   may *pretend* to abide *stare decisis*?

14   Consider this case. Mr. Kisor is a Marine who lost out on benefits for post-
15   traumatic stress disorder when the court of appeals deferred to a regulatory
16   interpretation advanced by the Department of Veterans Affairs. The court of
17   appeals was guilty of nothing more than faithfully following *Auer*. But the majority
18   today invokes *stare decisis*, of all things, to vacate that judgment and tell the court
19   of appeals to try again using its newly retooled, multi-factored, and far less
20   determinate version of *Auer*. Respectfully, I would stop this business of making up
21   excuses for judges to abdicate their job of interpreting the law, and simply allow
22   the court of appeals to afford Mr. Kisor its best independent judgment of the law's
23   meaning.

24   The Court's failure to be done with *Auer*, and its decision to adorn *Auer* with so
25   many new and ambiguous limitations, all but guarantees we will have to pass this
26   way again. When that day comes, I hope this Court will find the nerve it lacks today
27   and inter *Auer* at last. Until then, I hope that our judicial colleagues on other courts
28   will take courage from today's ruling and realize that it has transformed *Auer* into
29   a paper tiger.

## I. How We Got Here

31   Where did *Auer* come from? Not from the Constitution, some ancient common law
32   tradition, or even a modern statute. Instead, it began as an unexplained aside in a
33   decision about emergency price controls at the height of the Second World War.
34   Even then, the dictum sat on the shelf, little noticed, for years. Only in the last few
35   decades of the 20th century did lawyers and courts really begin to dust it off and
36   shape it into the reflexive rule of deference to regulatory agencies we know today.
37   And they did so without ever pausing to consider whether a rule like that could be
38   legally justified or even made sense. *Auer* is really little more than an accident.

39                  A

Before the mid-20th century, few federal agencies engaged in extensive rulemaking, and those that did rarely sought deference for their regulatory interpretations.[3] But when the question arose, this Court did not hesitate to say that judges reviewing administrative action should decide all questions of law, including questions concerning the meaning of regulations. As JUSTICE BRANDEIS put it, "[t]he inexorable safeguard which the due process clause assures is . . . that there will be opportunity for a court to determine whether the applicable rules of law . . . were observed."[4] Unsurprisingly, the government's early, longstanding, and consistent interpretation of a statute, regulation, or other legal instrument could count as powerful *evidence*.[5] But courts respected executive interpretations only because and to the extent "they embodied understandings made roughly contemporaneously with . . . enactment and stably maintained and practiced since that time," not "because they were executive as such.[6]

\* \* \*

## B

In truth, the seeds of the *Auer* doctrine were first planted only in 1945, in *Bowles v. Seminole Rock & Sand Co.* \* \* \*

Yet even then it was far from clear how much weight the Court really placed on the agency's interpretation. \* \* \*

\* \* \*

---

[3] See Knudsen & Wildermuth, Unearthing the Lost History of *Seminole Rock*, 65 Emory L.J. 47, 55, 65, 68 (2015) (Lost History).

[4] *St. Joseph Stock Yards Co.* v. *United States*, 298 U.S. 38, 73 (1936) (concurring opinion). See also *FTC* v. *Gratz,*253 U.S. 421, 427 (1920); *ICC* v. *Union Pacific R. Co.*, 222 U.S. 541, 547 (1912); *Belden* v. *Chase*, 150 U.S. 674, 698 (1893); *Decatur* v. *Paulding*, 14 Pet. 497, 515 (1840); accord, Woolhandler, Judicial Deference to Administrative Action—A Revisionist History, 43 Admin. L. Rev. 197, 206–207 (1991).

[5] Bamzai, The Origins of Judicial Deference to Executive Interpretation, 126 Yale L. J. 908, 930–947 (2017) (Origins).

[6] *Id.*, at 943, 962; cf. *NLRB* v. *Noel Canning*, 573 U.S. 513, 572–573 (2014) (SCALIA, J., concurring in judgment) (an "open, widespread, and unchallenged" governmental practice can "guide [courts'] interpretation" of an ambiguous text, but it cannot "alter" the meaning of that text); *Edward's Lessee* v. *Darby*, 12 Wheat. 206, 210 (1827) ("In the construction of a doubtful and ambiguous law, the cotemporaneous construction of those who were called upon to act under the law, and were appointed to carry its provisions into effect, is entitled to very great respect").

1

C

2    \* \* \* From the 1960s on, this Court and lower courts began to cite the *Seminole*
3    *Rock* dictum with increasing frequency and in a wider variety of circumstances,
4    but still without much explanation. \* \* \*

5    *Auer* represents the apotheosis of this line of cases. \* \* \*

6                                        \* \* \*

7

II. The Administrative Procedure Act

8    When this Court speaks about the rules governing judicial review of federal agency
9    action, we are not (or shouldn't be) writing on a blank slate or exercising some
10    common-law-making power. We are supposed to be applying the Administrative
11    Procedure Act. \* \* \*

12

A

13    The first problem lies in § 706. That provision instructs reviewing courts to "decide
14    all relevant questions of law" and "set aside agency action . . . found to be . . . not
15    in accordance with law." Determining the meaning of a statute or regulation, of
16    course, presents a classic legal question. But in case these directives were not clear
17    enough, the APA further directs courts to "determine the meaning" of any relevant
18    "agency action," including any rule issued by the agency. The APA thus requires a
19    reviewing court to resolve for itself any dispute over the proper interpretation of
20    an agency regulation. A court that, in deference to an agency, adopts something
21    other than the best reading of a regulation isn't "decid[ing]" the relevant
22    "questio[n] of law" or "determin[ing] the meaning" of the regulation. Instead, it's
23    allowing the agency to dictate the answer to that question. In doing so, the court is
24    abdicating the duty Congress assigned to it in the APA.

25                                       \* \* \*

26

B

27    The problems don't end there. *Auer* is also incompatible with the APA's
28    instructions in § 553. That provision requires agencies to follow notice-and-
29    comment procedures when issuing or amending legally binding regulations (what
30    the APA calls "substantive rules"), but not when offering mere interpretations of
31    those regulations. An agency wishing to adopt or amend a binding regulation thus
32    must publish a proposal in the Federal Register, give interested members of the
33    public an opportunity to submit written comments on the proposal, and consider
34    those comments before issuing the final regulation. Under the APA, that regulation
35    then carries the force of law unless and until it is amended or repealed. By contrast,

an agency can announce an interpretation of an existing substantive regulation without advance warning and in pretty much whatever form it chooses.

*Auer* effectively nullifies the distinction Congress drew here. Under *Auer*, courts must treat as "controlling" not only an agency's duly promulgated rules but also its mere interpretations—even ones that appear only in a legal brief, press release, or guidance document issued without affording the public advance notice or a chance to comment. * * *

* * *

* * * JUSTICE KAGAN tries an alternative argument from nearly the opposite direction. She replies that affording *Auer* deference to an agency's interpretation of its own rules never offends the APA because the agency's interpretation lacks "the force of law" associated with substantive rules. Agency interpretations lack this force, we are told, because a court always retains the power to decide at least whether the interpretation is entitled to deference. But this argument rests on an implausibly narrow understanding of what it means for an agency action to bear the force of law. Under JUSTICE KAGAN's logic, even a binding substantive rule would lack the force of law because a court retains the power to decide whether the rule is arbitrary and capricious and thus invalid under the APA. But no one believes that. While an agency interpretation, just like a substantive rule, "must meet certain conditions before it gets deference," "once it does so [*Auer* makes it] every bit as binding as a substantive rule."[61] To suggest that *Auer* does not make an agency's interpretive guidance "binding o[n] anyone," is linguistic hocus-pocus.

* * *

### III. The Constitution

Not only is *Auer* incompatible with the APA; it also sits uneasily with the Constitution. Article III, § 1 provides that the "judicial Power of the United States" is vested exclusively in this Court and the lower federal courts. * * * And never, this Court has warned, should the "judicial power . . . be shared with [the] Executive Branch."[72] Yet that seems to be exactly what *Auer* requires.

* * *

### IV. Policy Arguments

Lacking support elsewhere, JUSTICE KAGAN is forced to resort to policy arguments to defend *Auer*. * * *

---

[61] *Perez*, 575 U.S., at ____ (Scalia, J., concurring in judgment) (slip op., at 3).
[72] *Miller* v. *Johnson*, 515 U.S. 900, 922 (1995).

Take the first and boldest offering. JUSTICE KAGAN suggests that determining the meaning of a regulation is largely a matter of figuring out what the "person who wrote it . . . intended." In this way, we're told, a legally binding regulation isn't all that different from "a memo or an e-mail"—if you "[w]ant to know what [it] means," you'd better "[a]sk its author." But the federal government's substantive rules are not like memos or e-mails; they are binding edicts that carry the force of law for all citizens. And if the rule of law means anything, it means that we are governed by the public meaning of the words found in statutes and regulations, not by their authors' private intentions. This is a vital part of what it means to have "a government of laws, and not of men."[95] When judges interpret a regulation, what we are trying to get at, as Justice Holmes explained long ago, is not the "particular intent" of those who wrote it, but "what [its] words would mean [to] a normal speaker of English . . . in the circumstances in which they were used."[96] If the best reading of the regulation turns out to be something other than what the agency claims to have intended, the agency is free to rewrite the regulation; but its secret intentions are not the law.

\* \* \*

Proceeding farther down this doubtful path, JUSTICE KAGAN asserts that resolving ambiguities in a regulation "sounds more in policy than in law" and is thus a task more suited to executive officials than judges. But this claim, too, contradicts a basic premise of our legal order: that we are governed not by the shifting whims of politicians and bureaucrats, but by written laws whose meaning is fixed and ascertainable—if not by all members of the public, then at least by lawyers who can advise them and judges who must apply the law to individual cases guided by the neutral principles found in our traditional tools of interpretation. The text of the regulation is treated *as* the law, and the agency's policy judgment has the force of law *only* insofar as it is embodied in the regulatory text. \* \* \*

\* \* \*

JUSTICE KAVANAUGH, with whom JUSTICE ALITO joins, concurring in the judgment.

---

[95] *Marbury*, 5 U.S., at 163.

[96] Holmes, The Theory of Legal Interpretation, 12 Harv. L. Rev. 417, 417–418 (1899); see *INS* v. *Cardoza-Fonseca*, 480 U.S. 421, 452–453 (1987) (Scalia, J., concurring in judgment) ("Judges interpret laws rather than reconstruct legislators' intentions"); H. Hart & A. Sacks, The Legal Process 1375 (1994) ("Unenacted intentions or wishes cannot be given effect as law").

I agree with JUSTICE GORSUCH's conclusion that the *Auer* deference doctrine should be formally retired. I write separately to emphasize two points.

*First*, I agree with The Chief Justice that "the distance between the majority and Justice Gorsuch is not as great as it may initially appear." The majority's approach in Part II–B of its opinion closely resembles the argument advanced by the Solicitor General to "clarif[y] and narro[w]" *Auer*. Importantly, the majority borrows from footnote 9 of this Court's opinion in *Chevron* to say that a reviewing court must "exhaust all the 'traditional tools' of construction" before concluding that an agency rule is ambiguous and deferring to an agency's reasonable interpretation. *Ante,* (quoting *Chevron U.S.A. Inc. v. Natural Resources Defense Council, Inc.*, 467 U.S. 837, 843, n. 9 (1984)). If a reviewing court employs all of the traditional tools of construction, the court will almost always reach a conclusion about the best interpretation of the regulation at issue. After doing so, the court then will have no need to adopt or defer to an agency's contrary interpretation. In other words, the footnote 9 principle, taken seriously, means that courts will have no reason or basis to put a thumb on the scale in favor of an agency when courts interpret agency regulations.

Formally rejecting *Auer* would have been a more direct approach, but rigorously applying footnote 9 should lead in most cases to the same general destination. Umpires in games at Wrigley Field do not defer to the Cubs manager's in-game interpretation of Wrigley's ground rules. So too here.

To be sure, some cases involve regulations that employ broad and open-ended terms like "reasonable," "appropriate," "feasible," or "practicable." Those kinds of terms afford agencies broad policy discretion, and courts allow an agency to reasonably exercise its discretion to choose among the options allowed by the text of the rule. But that is more *State Farm* than *Auer*. See *Motor Vehicle Mfrs. Assn. of United States, Inc. v. State Farm Mut. Automobile Ins. Co.*, 463 U.S. 29 (1983).

In short, after today's decision, a judge should engage in appropriately rigorous scrutiny of an agency's interpretation of a regulation, and can simultaneously be appropriately deferential to an agency's reasonable policy choices within the discretion allowed by a regulation.

*Second*, I also agree with The Chief Justice that "[i]ssues surrounding judicial deference to agency interpretations of their own regulations are distinct from those raised in connection with judicial deference to agency interpretations of statutes enacted by Congress." Like THE CHIEF JUSTICE, "I do not regard the Court's decision" not to formally overrule *Auer* "to touch upon the latter question."

1 # CHAPTER 4: AVAILABILITY OF JUDICIAL REVIEW

2

3 The unit on Judicial Review explains how courts review agency actions. But *when*
4 do courts review agency actions? That is the subject of this unit.

5 Final agency actions are presumptively reviewable under the APA—but this does
6 not mean that anyone with a gripe against an agency can litigate it in court. As the
7 readings in this unit reveal, there are a number of exceptions to the presumption
8 of reviewability, either in the text of the APA itself, or created by courts.

9 There are a number of different reviewability doctrines: covered in the pages that
10 follow: preclusion, commitment to agency discretion, finality, ripeness, standing
11 (in two flavors!), primary jurisdiction, and exhaustion. Not surprising for such a
12 crowded area, there can be some overlap between the different doctrines.

13

14 ## A. Preclusion of Judicial Review

15 The APA provides that judicial review is available except, among other things, "to
16 the extent that . . . statutes preclude judicial review."

17 Sometimes, a statute will just straightforwardly say, judicial review is not available.
18 Those are the easy cases. The ones you will encounter in this set of readings are the
19 harder ones.

20 The cases covered in this section all involve statutes that preclude review: the
21 questions in these cases are just whether the statutes cover the claims at issue here.
22 The Supreme Court has also found judicial review to be *impliedly* precluded
23 before, see *Block v. Community Nutrition Institute*, 467 U.S. 340 (1984).

24

25 ### Johnson v. Robison

26 415 U.S. 361 (1974)

27 March 4, 1974

28 MR. JUSTICE BRENNAN delivered the opinion of the Court.

29 A draftee accorded Class I-O conscientious objector status and completing
30 performance of required alternative civilian service does not qualify under 38
31 U.S.C. § 1652(a)(1) as a "veteran who . . . served on active duty" as "full-time duty
32 in the Armed Forces"), and is therefore not an "eligible veteran" entitled under 38
33 U.S.C. § 1661(a) to veterans' educational benefits provided by the Veterans'

621

1 Readjustment Benefits Act of 1966. Appellants, the Veterans' Administration and
2 the Administrator of Veterans' Affairs, for that reason, denied the application for
3 educational assistance of appellee Robison, a conscientious objector who filed his
4 application after he satisfactorily completed two years of alternative civilian service
5 at the Peter Bent Brigham Hospital, Boston. Robison thereafter commenced this
6 class action in the United States District Court for the District of Massachusetts,
7 seeking a declaratory judgment that 38 U.S.C. §§ 101 (21), 1652(a)(1), and 1661(a),
8 read together, violated the First Amendment's guarantee of religious freedom and
9 the Fifth Amendment's guarantee of equal protection of the laws. Appellants
10 moved to dismiss the action on the ground, among others, that the District Court
11 lacked jurisdiction because of 38 U.S.C. § 211(a), which prohibits judicial review of
12 decisions of the Administrator. The District Court denied the motion, and, on the
13 merits, rejected appellee's First Amendment claim, but sustained the equal
14 protection claim and entered a judgment declaring

15 "that 38 U.S.C. §§ 1652(a)(1) and 1661(a), defining 'eligible veteran' and
16 providing for entitlement to educational assistance are unconstitutional
17 and that 38 U.S.C. 101(21), defining 'active duty' is unconstitutional with
18 respect to chapter 34 of Title 38, United States Code, 38 U.S.C. § 1651-1697,
19 conferring Veterans' Educational Assistance, for the reason that said
20 sections deny plaintiff and members of his class due process of law in
21 violation of the Fifth Amendment to the Constitution of the United
22 States. . . ."

23 352 F. Supp. 848, 862 (1973). * * *

24 We hold, in agreement with the District Court, that § 211(a) is inapplicable to this
25 action, and therefore that appellants' motion to dismiss for lack of jurisdiction of
26 the subject matter was properly denied. On the merits, we agree that appellee's
27 First Amendment claim is without merit, but disagree that §§ 1652(a)(1), 1661(a),
28 and 101(21) violate the Fifth Amendment, and therefore reverse the judgment of
29 the District Court.

30 I

31 We consider first appellants' contention that § 211(a) bars federal courts from
32 deciding the constitutionality of veterans' benefits legislation. Such a construction
33 would, of course, raise serious questions concerning the constitutionality of §
34 211(a) and, in such case, "it is a cardinal principle that this Court will first ascertain
35 whether a construction of the statute is fairly possible by which the [constitutional]
36 question[s] may be avoided."

37 Plainly, no explicit provision of § 211(a) bars judicial consideration of appellee's
38 constitutional claims. That section provides that "the *decisions* of the
39 Administrator on any question of law or fact *under* any law administered by the

Veterans' Administration providing benefits for veterans . . . shall be final and conclusive and no . . . court of the United States shall have power or jurisdiction to review any such decision. . ." (Emphasis added.) The prohibitions would appear to be aimed at review only of those decisions of law or fact that arise in the *administration* by the Veterans' Administration of a *statute* providing benefits for veterans. A decision of law or fact "under" a statute is made by the Administrator in the interpretation or application of a particular provision of the statute to a particular set of facts. Appellee's constitutional challenge is not to any such decision of the *Administrator,* but rather to a decision of *Congress* to create a statutory class entitled to benefits that does not include I-O conscientious objectors who performed alternative civilian service. Thus, as the District Court stated: "The questions of law presented in these proceedings arise under the Constitution, not under the statute whose validity is challenged."

This construction is also supported by the administrative practice of the Veterans' Administration." When faced with a problem of statutory construction, this Court shows great deference to the interpretation given the statute by the officers or agency charged with its administration." The Board of Veterans' Appeals expressly disclaimed authority to decide constitutional questions in *Appeal of Sly,* C-27 593 725 (May 10, 1972). There, the Board, denying a claim for educational assistance by a I-O conscientious objector, held that "[t]his decision does not reach the issue of the constitutionality of the pertinent laws, as this matter is not within the jurisdiction of this Board." *Sly* thus accepts and follows the principle that "adjudication of the constitutionality of congressional enactments has generally been thought beyond the jurisdiction of administrative agencies.

Nor does the legislative history accompanying the 1970 amendment of § 211(a) demonstrate a congressional intention to bar judicial review even of constitutional questions. No-review clauses similar to § 211(a) have been a part of veterans' benefits legislation since 1933. While the legislative history accompanying these precursor no-review clauses is almost nonexistent, the Administrator, in a letter written in 1952 in connection with a revision of the clause under consideration by the Subcommittee of the House Committee on Veterans' Affairs, comprehensively explained the policies necessitating the no review clause and identified two primary purposes: (1) to insure that veterans' benefits claims will not burden the courts and the Veterans' Administration with expensive and time-consuming litigation, and (2) to insure that the technical and complex determinations and applications of Veterans' Administration policy connected with veterans' benefits decision will be adequately and uniformly made.

The legislative history of the 1970 amendment indicates nothing more than a congressional intent to preserve these two primary purposes. Before amendment, the no-review clause made final "the decisions of the Administrator on any question of law or fact *concerning a claim for benefits or payments* under [certain] law[s] administered by the Veterans' Administration" (emphasis added), 38 U.S.C. § 211(a) (1964 ed.), 71 Stat. 92. In a series of decisions [between 1958 and 1967], the Court of Appeals for the District of Columbia Circuit interpreted the term "claim" as a limitation upon the reach of § 211(a) and, as a consequence, held that judicial review of actions by the Administrator subsequent to an original grant of benefits was not barred.

Congress perceived this judicial interpretation as a threat to the dual purposes of the no-review clause. First, the interpretation would lead to an inevitable increase in litigation, with consequent burdens upon the courts and the Veterans' Administration. In its House Report, the Committee on Veterans' Affairs stated that, "[s]ince the decision in the *Tracy* case—and as the result of that decision and the *Wellman* and *Thompson* decisions—suits in constantly increasing numbers have been filed in the U.S. District Court for the District of Columbia by plaintiffs seeking a resumption of terminated benefits." H.R.Rep. No. 91-1166, p. 10 (1970). This same concern over the rising number of court cases was expressed by the Administrator in a letter to the Committee:

> "The *Wellman, Thompson,* and *Tracy* decisions have not been followed in any of the other 10 Federal judicial circuits throughout the country. Nevertheless, soon after the *Tracy* decision, suits in the nature of mandamus or for declaratory judgment commenced to be filed in the U.S. District Court for the District of Columbia in constantly increasing numbers by plaintiffs seeking resumption of terminated benefits. As of March 8, 1970, 353 suits of this type had been filed in the District of Columbia circuit." "The scope of the *Tracy* decision and the decisions upon which it is based is so broad that it could well afford a basis for judicial review of millions of decisions terminating or reducing many types of benefits provided under laws administered by the Veterans' Administration. Such review might even extend to the decisions of predecessor agencies made many years ago."

*Id.* at 21, 24.

Second, Congress was concerned that the judicial interpretation of § 211(a) would involve the courts in day-to-day determination and interpretation of Veterans' Administration policy. The House Report states that the cases already filed in the courts in response to *Wellman, Thompson,* and *Tracy*

> "involve a large variety of matters—a 1930's termination of a widow's pension payments under a statute then extant, because of her open and notorious adulterous cohabitation; invalid marriage to a veteran; severance of a veteran's service connection for disability compensation; reduction of

1 such compensation because of lessened disability ... [and] suits ...
2 brought by [Filipino] widows of World War II servicemen seeking
3 restoration of death compensation or pension benefits terminated after the
4 Administrator raised a presumption of their remarriage on the basis of
5 evidence gathered through field examination. Notwithstanding the 1962
6 endorsement by the Congress of the Veterans' Administrations [*sic*]
7 administrative presumption of remarriage rule, most of [the suits brought
8 by Filipino widows] have resulted in judgments adverse to the
9 Government."

10 *Id.* at 10.

11 The Administrator voiced similar concerns, stating that "it seems obvious that suits
12 similar to the several hundred already filed can—and undoubtedly will—subject
13 nearly every aspect of our benefit determinations to judicial review, including
14 rating decisions, related Veterans' Administration regulations, Administrator's
15 decisions, and various adjudication procedures." Letter to the Committee on
16 Veterans' Affairs 23-24.

17 Thus, the 1970 amendment was enacted to overrule the interpretation of the Court
18 of Appeals for the District of Columbia Circuit, and thereby restore vitality to the
19 two primary purposes to be served by the no-review clause. Nothing whatsoever in
20 the legislative history of the 1970 amendment, or predecessor no-review clauses,
21 suggests any congressional intent to preclude judicial cognizance of constitutional
22 challenges to veterans' benefits legislation. Such challenges obviously do not
23 contravene the purposes of the no-review clause, for they cannot be expected to
24 burden the courts by their volume, nor do they involve technical considerations of
25 Veterans' Administration policy. We therefore conclude, in agreement with the
26 District Court, that a construction of § 211(a) that does not extend the prohibitions
27 of that section to actions challenging the constitutionality of laws providing
28 benefits for veterans is not only "fairly possible," but is the most reasonable
29 construction, for neither the text nor the scant legislative history of § 211(a)
30 provides the "clear and convincing" evidence of congressional intent required by
31 this Court before a statute will be construed to restrict access to judicial review. *See*
32 *Abbott Laboratories v. Gardner*, 387 U.S. 136, 141 (1967).

33 * * *

34 *Reversed.*

35 MR. JUSTICE DOUGLAS, dissenting. [Omitted.]

36

37 **Bowen v. Michigan Academy of Family Physicians**

1    476 U.S. 667 (1986)

2    June 9, 1986

3    JUSTICE STEVENS delivered the opinion of the Court.

4    The question presented in this case is whether Congress, in either § 1395ff or §
5    1395ii of Title 42 of the United States Code, barred judicial review of regulations
6    promulgated under Part B of the Medicare program.

7    Respondents, who include an association of family physicians and several
8    individual doctors, filed suit to challenge the validity of 42 CFR § 405.504(b)
9    (1985), which authorizes the payment of benefits in different amounts for similar
10   physicians' services. The District Court held that the regulation contravened
11   several provisions of the statute governing the Medicare program:

12       "There is no basis to justify the segregation of allopathic family physicians
13       from all other types of physicians. Such segregation is not rationally related
14       to any legitimate purpose of the Medicare statute. To lump MDs who are
15       family physicians, but who have chosen not to become board certified
16       family physicians for whatever motive, with chiropractors, dentists, and
17       podiatrists for the purpose of determining Medicare reimbursement defies
18       all reason."

19   Because it ruled in favor of respondents on statutory grounds, the District Court
20   did not reach their constitutional claims. The Court of Appeals agreed with the
21   District Court that the Secretary's regulation was "obvious[ly] inconsisten[t] with
22   the plain language of the Medicare statute," and held that "this regulation is
23   irrational and is invalid." Like the District Court, it too declined to reach
24   respondents' constitutional claims.

25   The Secretary of Health and Human Services has not sought review of the decision
26   on the merits invalidating the regulation. Instead, he renews the contention,
27   rejected by both the District Court and the Court of Appeals, that Congress has
28   forbidden judicial review of all questions affecting the amount of benefits payable
29   under Part B of the Medicare program. Because the question is important and has
30   divided the Courts of Appeals, we granted the petition for a writ of certiorari. We
31   now affirm.

32                                          I

33   We begin with the strong presumption that Congress intends judicial review of
34   administrative action. From the beginning, "our cases [have established] that
35   judicial review of a final agency action by an aggrieved person will not be cut off
36   unless there is persuasive reason to believe that such was the purpose of Congress."
37   *Abbott Laboratories v. Gardner,* 387 U.S. 136, 140 (1967). In *Marbury v.*

     626

1  *Madison,* 5 U.S. 163 (1803), a case itself involving review of executive action,
2  CHIEF JUSTICE MARSHALL insisted that "[t]he very essence of civil liberty
3  certainly consists in the right of every individual to claim the protection of the
4  laws." Later, in the lesser known but nonetheless important case of *United States*
5  *v. Nourse,* 34 U.S. 8, 28-29 (1835), the Chief Justice noted the traditional
6  observance of this right and laid the foundation for the modern presumption of
7  judicial review:

8  "It would excite some surprise if, in a government of laws and of principle,
9  furnished with a department whose appropriate duty it is to decide
10  questions of right, not only between individuals, but between the
11  government and individuals; a ministerial officer might, at his discretion,
12  issue this powerful process . . . leaving to the debtor no remedy, no appeal
13  to the laws of his country, if he should believe the claim to be unjust. But
14  this anomaly does not exist; this imputation cannot be cast on the
15  legislature of the United States."

16  Committees of both Houses of Congress have endorsed this view. * * *

17  * * *

18  Subject to constitutional constraints, Congress can, of course, make exceptions to
19  the historic practice whereby courts review agency action. The presumption of
20  judicial review is, after all, a presumption, and "like all presumptions used in
21  interpreting statutes, may be overcome by," *inter alia,* "specific language or
22  specific legislative history that is a reliable indicator of congressional intent," or a
23  specific congressional intent to preclude judicial review that is "'fairly discernible'
24  in the detail of the legislative scheme."

25  In this case, the Government asserts that two statutory provisions remove the
26  Secretary's regulation from review under the grant of general federal question
27  jurisdiction found in 28 U.S.C. § 1331. First, the Government contends that 42
28  U.S.C. § 1395ff(b), which authorizes "Appeal by individuals," impliedly forecloses
29  administrative or judicial review of any action taken under Part B of the Medicare
30  program by failing to authorize such review while simultaneously authorizing
31  administrative and judicial review of "any determination . . . as to . . . the amount
32  of benefits under part A." Second, the Government asserts that 42 U.S.C. § 1395ii,
33  which makes applicable 42 U.S.C. § 405(h), of the Social Security Act to the
34  Medicare program, expressly precludes all administrative or judicial review not
35  otherwise provided in that statute. We find neither argument persuasive.

36  II

37  Section 1395ff on its face is an explicit authorization of judicial review, not a bar.
38  As a general matter, "'[t]he mere fact that some acts are made reviewable should

627

1     not suffice to support an implication of exclusion as to others. The right to review
2     is too important to be excluded on such slender and indeterminate evidence of
3     legislative intent.'" *Abbott Laboratories v. Gardner,* 387 U.S., at 141 (quoting L.
4     Jaffe, Judicial Control of Administrative Action 357 (1965)).

5     In the Medicare program, however, the situation is somewhat more complex.
6     Under Part B of that program, which is at issue here, the Secretary contracts with
7     private health insurance carriers to provide benefits for which individuals
8     voluntarily remit premiums. This optional coverage, which is federally subsidized,
9     supplements the mandatory institutional health benefits (such as coverage for
10    hospital expenses) provided by Part A. Subject to an amount-in-controversy
11    requirement, individuals aggrieved by delayed or insufficient payment with respect
12    to benefits payable under Part B are afforded an "opportunity for a fair hearing by
13    the *carrier,*" 42 U.S.C. § 1395u(b)(3)(C) (emphasis added); in comparison, and
14    subject to a like amount-in-controversy requirement, a similarly aggrieved
15    individual under Part A is entitled "to a hearing thereon by the *Secretary . . .* and
16    to judicial review," § 1395ff(b). "In the context of the statute's precisely drawn
17    provisions," we held in *United States v. Erika, Inc.,* 456 U.S. 201, 208 (1982), that
18    the failure "to authorize further review for determinations of the amount of Part B
19    awards . . . provides persuasive evidence that Congress deliberately intended to
20    foreclose further review of such claims." * * *

21    Respondents' federal court challenge to the validity of the Secretary's regulation is
22    not foreclosed by § 1395ff as we construed that provision in *Erika.* The reticulated
23    statutory scheme, which carefully details the forum and limits of review of "any
24    determination . . . of . . . the amount of benefits under part A," and of the "amount
25    of . . . payment" of benefits under Part B, simply does not speak to challenges
26    mounted against the *method* by which such amounts are to be determined, rather
27    than the *determinations* themselves. As the Secretary has made clear, "the legality,
28    constitutional or otherwise, of any provision of the Act or regulations relevant to
29    the Medicare Program" is not considered in a "fair hearing" held by a carrier to
30    resolve a grievance related to a determination of the amount of a Part B award. As
31    a result, an attack on the validity of a regulation is not the kind of administrative
32    action that we described in *Erika* as an "amount determination" which decides "the
33    amount of the Medicare payment to be made on a particular claim" and with
34    respect to which the Act impliedly denies judicial review.

35    That Congress did not preclude review of the method by which Part B awards are
36    computed is borne out by the very legislative history we found persuasive in *Erika.*
37    * * *

38    Careful analysis of the governing statutory provisions and their legislative history
39    thus reveals that Congress intended to bar judicial review only of determinations
40    of the amount of benefits to be awarded under Part B. Congress delegated this task

1  to carriers who would finally determine such matters in conformity with the
2  regulations and instructions of the Secretary. We conclude, therefore, that those
3  matters which Congress did *not* leave to be determined in a "fair hearing"
4  conducted by the carrier—including challenges to the validity of the Secretary's
5  instructions and regulations—are not impliedly insulated from judicial review by
6  42 U.S.C. § 1395ff.

7  III

8  In light of Congress' express provision for carrier review of millions of what it
9  characterized as "trivial" claims, it is implausible to think it intended that there be
10  *no* forum to adjudicate statutory and constitutional challenges to regulations
11  promulgated by the Secretary. The Government nevertheless maintains that this is
12  precisely what Congress intended to accomplish in 42 U.S.C. § 1395ii. That section
13  states that 42 U.S.C. § 405(h), along with a string citation of 10 other provisions of
14  Title II of the Social Security Act, "shall also apply with respect to this subchapter
15  to the same extent as they are applicable with respect to subchapter II of this
16  chapter." Section 405(h), in turn, reads in full as follows:

17  "(h) Finality of Secretary's decision"

18  "The findings and decision of the Secretary after a hearing shall be binding
19  upon all individuals who were parties to such hearing. No findings of fact
20  or decision of the Secretary shall be reviewed by any person, tribunal, or
21  governmental agency except as herein provided. No action against the
22  United States, the Secretary, or any officer or employee thereof shall be
23  brought under section 1331 or 1346 of title 28 to recover on any claim
24  arising under this subchapter."

25  The Government contends that the third sentence of § 405(h) by its terms prevents
26  any resort to the grant of general federal question jurisdiction contained in 28
27  U.S.C. § 1331.It finds support for this construction in *Weinberger v. Salfi,* 422 U.S.
28  749, 756-762 (1975), and *Heckler v. Ringer,* 466 U.S. 602, 614-616, 620-626
29  (1984). Respondents counter that the dispositions in these two cases are consistent
30  with the view that Congress' purpose was to make clear that whatever specific
31  procedures it provided for judicial review of final action by the Secretary were
32  exclusive, and could not be circumvented by resort to the general jurisdiction of
33  the federal courts.

34  Whichever may be the better reading of *Salfi* and *Ringer,* we need not pass on the
35  meaning of § 405(h) in the abstract to resolve this case. Section 405(h) does not
36  apply on its own terms to Part B of the Medicare program, but is instead
37  incorporated *mutatis mutandis* by § 1395ii. The legislative history of both the
38  statute establishing the Medicare program and the 1972 amendments thereto
39  provides specific evidence of Congress' intent to foreclose review only of "amount

1   determinations"—*i.e.*, those "quite minor matters," remitted finally and
2   exclusively to adjudication by private insurance carriers in a "fair hearing." By the
3   same token, matters which Congress did *not* delegate to private carriers, such as
4   challenges to the validity of the Secretary's instructions and regulations, are
5   cognizable in courts of law. In the face of this persuasive evidence of legislative
6   intent, we will not indulge the Government's assumption that Congress
7   contemplated review by carriers of "trivial" monetary claims, but intended no
8   review at all of substantial statutory and constitutional challenges to the
9   Secretary's administration of Part B of the Medicare program. This is an extreme
10   position, and one we would be most reluctant to adopt without "a showing of clear
11   and convincing evidence,'" to overcome the "strong presumption that Congress did
12   not mean to prohibit all judicial review" of executive action, *Dunlop v. Bachowski,*
13   421 U.S., at. 567. We ordinarily presume that Congress intends the executive to
14   obey its statutory commands and, accordingly, that it expects the courts to grant
15   relief when an executive agency violates such a command. That presumption has
16   not been surmounted here.

17   The judgment of the Court of Appeals is

18   *Affirmed.*

19   JUSTICE REHNQUIST took no part in the consideration or decision of this case.

20

## 21   McNary v. Haitian Refugee Center, Inc.

22   498 U.S. 479 (1991)

23   February 20, 1991

24   Justice STEVENS delivered the opinion of the Court.

25   The Immigration Reform and Control Act of 1986 (Reform Act) constituted a
26   major statutory response to the vast tide of illegal immigration that had produced
27   a "shadow population" of literally millions of undocumented aliens in the United
28   States. On the one hand, Congress sought to stem the tide by making the plight of
29   the undocumented alien even more onerous in the future than it had been in the
30   past; thus, the Reform Act imposed criminal sanctions on employers who hired
31   undocumented workers and made a number of federally funded welfare benefits
32   unavailable to these aliens. On the other hand, in recognition that a large segment
33   of the shadow population played a useful and constructive role in the American
34   economy, but continued to reside in perpetual fear, the Reform Act established two
35   broad amnesty programs to allow existing undocumented aliens to emerge from
36   the shadows.

1   The first amnesty program permitted any alien who had resided in the United
2   States continuously and unlawfully since January 1, 1982, to qualify for an
3   adjustment of his or her status to that of a lawful permanent resident. The second
4   program required the Attorney General to adjust the status of any alien
5   farmworker who could establish that he or she had resided in the United States
6   and performed at least 90 days of qualifying agricultural work during the 12-month
7   period prior to May 1, 1986, provided that the alien could also establish his or her
8   admissibility in the United States as an immigrant. The Reform Act required the
9   Attorney General first to adjust the status of these aliens to "Special Agricultural
10  Workers" (SAW) lawfully admitted for temporary residence, and then eventually
11  to aliens lawfully admitted for permanent residence.

12  This case relates only to the SAW amnesty program. Although additional issues
13  were resolved by the District Court and the Court of Appeals, the only question
14  presented to us is whether § 210(e) of the Immigration and Nationality Act (INA),
15  which was added by § 302(a) of the Reform Act and sets forth the administrative
16  and judicial review provisions of the SAW program, precludes a federal district
17  court from exercising general federal question jurisdiction over an action alleging
18  a pattern or practice of procedural due process violations by the Immigration and
19  Naturalization Service (INS) in its administration of the SAW program. We hold
20  that, given the absence of clear congressional language mandating preclusion of
21  federal jurisdiction and the nature of respondents' requested relief, the District
22  Court had jurisdiction to hear respondents' constitutional and statutory challenges
23  to INS procedures. Were we to hold otherwise and instead require respondents to
24  avail themselves of the limited judicial review procedures set forth in § 210(e) of
25  the INA, meaningful judicial review of their statutory and constitutional claims
26  would be foreclosed.

27                                    I

28                                   * * *

29  The Reform Act provided that SAW status applications could be filed with a
30  specially created Legalization Office (LO), or with a QDE [Qualified Designated
31  Entity], which would forward applications to the appropriate LO, during an 18-
32  month period commencing on June 1, 1987. Regulations adopted by the INS to
33  administer the program provided for a personal interview of each applicant at an
34  LO. In the application, the alien had to prove by a preponderance of the evidence
35  that he or she worked the requisite 90 days of qualifying seasonal agricultural
36  services. To meet the burden of proof, the applicant was required to present
37  evidence of eligibility independent of his or her own testimony. The applicant could
38  meet this burden through production of his or her employer's payroll records, or
39  through submission of affidavits "by agricultural producers, foremen, farm labor

1   contractors, union officials, fellow employees, or other persons with specific
2   knowledge of the applicant's employment."

3   At the conclusion of the interview and of the review of the application materials,
4   the LO could deny the application or make a recommendation to a regional
5   processing facility that the application be either granted or denied. A denial,
6   whether at the regional or local level, could be appealed to the legalization appeals
7   unit, which was authorized to make the final administrative decision in each
8   individual case.

9   The Reform Act expressly prohibited judicial review of such a final administrative
10   determination of SAW status except as authorized by § 210(e)(3)(A) of the
11   amended INA. That subsection permitted "judicial review of such a denial only in
12   the judicial review of an order of exclusion or deportation." In view of the fact that
13   the courts of appeals constitute the only fora for judicial review of deportation
14   orders, the statute plainly foreclosed any review in the district courts of individual
15   denials of SAW status applications. Moreover, absent initiation of a deportation
16   proceeding against an unsuccessful applicant, judicial review of such individual
17   determinations was completely foreclosed.

18                          II

19   This action was filed in the District Court for the Southern District of Florida by
20   the Haitian Refugee Center, the Migration and Refugee Services of the Roman
21   Catholic Diocese of Palm Beach, and 17 unsuccessful individual SAW applicants.
22   The plaintiffs sought relief on behalf of a class of alien farmworkers who either had
23   been or would be injured by unlawful practices and policies adopted by the INS in
24   its administration of the SAW program. The complaint alleged that the interview
25   process was conducted in an arbitrary fashion that deprived applicants of the due
26   process guaranteed by the Fifth Amendment to the Constitution. Among other
27   charges, the plaintiffs alleged that INS procedures did not allow SAW applicants to
28   be apprised of or to be given opportunity to challenge adverse evidence on which
29   denials were predicated, that applicants were denied the opportunity to present
30   witnesses on their own behalf, that non-English speaking Haitian applicants were
31   unable to communicate effectively with LOs because competent interpreters were
32   not provided, and that no verbatim recording of the interview was made, thus
33   inhibiting even any meaningful administrative review of application denials by LOs
34   or regional processing facilities.

35                         * * *

36                         III

37   We preface our analysis of petitioners' position with an identification of matters
38   that are not in issue. First, it is undisputed that SAW status is an important benefit

1  for a previously undocumented alien. This status not only protects the alien from
2  deportation; it also creates job opportunities that are not available to an alien
3  whose application is denied. Indeed, the denial of SAW status places the alien in
4  an even worse position than he or she was in before the Reform Act was passed,
5  because lawful employment opportunities are no longer available to such persons.
6  Thus, the successful applicant for SAW status acquires a measure of freedom to
7  work and to live openly without fear of deportation or arrest that is markedly
8  different from that of the unsuccessful applicant. Even disregarding the risk of
9  deportation, the impact of a denial on the opportunity to obtain gainful
10  employment is plainly sufficient to mandate constitutionally fair procedures in the
11  application process. At no time in this litigation have petitioners asserted a right
12  to employ arbitrary procedures or questioned their obligation to afford SAW status
13  applicants due process of law.

14  Nor, at this stage of the litigation, is there any dispute that the INS routinely and
15  persistently violated the Constitution and statutes in processing SAW applications.
16  Petitioners do not deny that those violations caused injury in fact to the two
17  organizational plaintiffs as well as to the individual members of the plaintiff class.
18  Although it does not do so explicitly, petitioners' argument assumes that the
19  District Court would have federal question jurisdiction over the entire case if
20  Congress had not, through the Reform Act, added § 210(e) to the INA. The narrow
21  issue, therefore, is whether §210(e), which bars judicial review of individual
22  determinations except in deportation proceedings, also forecloses this general
23  challenge to the INS's unconstitutional practices.

24                                          IV

25  Petitioners' entire jurisdictional argument rests on their view that respondents'
26  constitutional challenge is an action seeking "judicial review of a determination
27  respecting an application for adjustment of status," and that district court
28  jurisdiction over the action is therefore barred by the plain language of § 210(e)(1)
29  of the amended INA. The critical words in §210(e)(1), however, describe the
30  provision as referring only to review "of *a determination* respecting an
31  *application*" for SAW status. Significantly, the reference to "a determination"
32  describes a single act, rather than a group of decisions or a practice or procedure
33  employed in making decisions. Moreover, the only judicial review permitted is in
34  the context of a deportation proceeding, it refers to "judicial review of *such a*
35  *denial*"—again referring to a single act, and again making clear that the earlier
36  reference to "a determination respecting an application" describes the denial of an
37  individual application. We therefore agree with the District Court's and the Court
38  of Appeals' reading of this language as describing the process of direct review of
39  individual denials of SAW status, rather than as referring to general collateral

1    challenges to unconstitutional practices and policies used by the agency in
2    processing applications.

3    This reading of the Reform Act's review provision is supported by the language in
4    § 210(e)(3)(B) of the INA, which provides that judicial review "shall be based solely
5    upon the administrative record established at the time of the review by the
6    appellate authority and the findings of fact and determinations contained in such
7    record shall be conclusive unless the applicant can establish abuse of discretion or
8    that the findings are directly contrary to clear and convincing facts contained in
9    the record considered as a whole." This provision incorporates an assumption that
10   the limited review provisions of § 210(e) apply only to claims that have been
11   subjected to administrative consideration and that have resulted in the creation of
12   an adequate administrative record. However, the record created during the SAW
13   administrative review process consists solely of a completed application form, a
14   report of medical examination, any documents or affidavits that evidence an
15   applicant's agricultural employment and residence, and notes, if any, from an LO
16   interview—all relating to a single SAW applicant. Because the administrative
17   appeals process does not address the kind of procedural and constitutional claims
18   respondents bring in this action, limiting judicial review of these claims to the
19   procedures set forth in § 210(e) is not contemplated by the language of that
20   provision.

21   Moreover, the "abuse of discretion" standard of judicial review under §
22   210(e)(3)(B) would make no sense if we were to read the Reform Act as requiring
23   constitutional and statutory challenges to INS procedures to be subject to its
24   specialized review provision. Although the abuse-of-discretion standard is
25   appropriate for judicial review of an administrative adjudication of the facts of an
26   individual application for SAW status, such a standard does not apply to
27   constitutional or statutory claims, which are reviewed *de novo* by the courts. The
28   language of § 210(e)(3)(B) thus lends substantial credence to the conclusion that
29   the Reform Act's review provision does not apply to challenges to INS's practices
30   and procedures in administering the SAW program.

31   Finally, we note that, had Congress intended the limited review provisions of §
32   210(e) of the INA to encompass challenges to INS procedures and practices, it
33   could easily have used broader statutory language. Congress could, for example,
34   have modeled § 210(e) on the more expansive language in the general grant of
35   district court jurisdiction under Title II of the INA by channeling into the Reform
36   Act's special review procedures "all causes . . . arising under any of the provisions"
37   of the legalization program. It moreover could have modeled § 210(e) on 38 U.S.C.
38   § 211(a), which governs review of veterans' benefits claims, by referring to review
39   "on all questions of law and fact" under the SAW legalization program.

1  Given Congress' choice of statutory language, we conclude that challenges to the
2  procedures used by INS do not fall within the scope of § 210(e). Rather, we hold
3  that § 210(e) applies only to review of denials of individual SAW applications.
4  Because respondents' action does not seek review on the merits of a denial of a
5  particular application, the District Court's general federal question jurisdiction
6  under 28 U.S.C. § 1331 to hear this action remains unimpaired by § 210(e).

7                                         V

8                                       * * *

9   * * * [I]f not allowed to pursue their claims in the District Court, respondents
10  would not as a practical matter be able to obtain meaningful judicial review of their
11  application denials or of their objections to INS procedures, notwithstanding the
12  review provisions of § 210(e) of the amended INA. It is presumable that Congress
13  legislates with knowledge of our basic rules of statutory construction, and, given
14  our well settled presumption favoring interpretations of statutes that allow judicial
15  review of administrative action, see *Bowen v. Michigan Academy of Family*
16  *Physicians,* 476 U.S. 667, 670 (1986), coupled with the limited review provisions
17  of § 210(e), it is most unlikely that Congress intended to foreclose all forms of
18  meaningful judicial review.

19  Several aspects of this statutory scheme would preclude review of respondents'
20  application denials if we were to hold that the District Court lacked jurisdiction to
21  hear this challenge. Initially, administrative or judicial review of an agency
22  decision is almost always confined to the record made in the proceeding at the
23  initial decision making level, and one of the central attacks on INS procedures in
24  this litigation is based on the claim that such procedures do not allow applicants to
25  assemble adequate records. * * *

26  Additionally, because there is no provision for direct judicial review of the denial
27  of SAW status unless the alien is later apprehended, and deportation proceedings
28  are initiated, most aliens denied SAW status can ensure themselves review in
29  courts of appeals only if they voluntarily surrender themselves for deportation.
30  Quite obviously, that price is tantamount to a complete denial of judicial review for
31  most undocumented aliens.

32  Finally, even in the context of a deportation proceeding, it is unlikely that a court
33  of appeals would be in a position to provide meaningful review of the type of claims
34  raised in this litigation. To establish the unfairness of the INS practices,
35  respondents in this case adduced a substantial amount of evidence, most of which
36  would have been irrelevant in the processing of a particular individual application.
37  Not only would a court of appeals reviewing an individual SAW determination
38  therefore most likely not have an adequate record as to the pattern of INS' allegedly
39  unconstitutional practices, but it also would lack the factfinding and record-

developing capabilities of a federal district court. As the American Bar Association, as *amicus,* points out, statutes that provide for only a single level of judicial review in the courts of appeals "are traditionally viewed as warranted only in circumstances where district court factfinding would unnecessarily duplicate an adequate administrative record—circumstances that are not present in 'pattern and practice' cases where district court factfinding is essential [given the inadequate administrative record]." It therefore seems plain to us, as it did to the District Court and the Court of Appeals, that restricting judicial review to the courts of appeals as a component of the review of an individual deportation order is the practical equivalent of a total denial of judicial review of generic constitutional and statutory claims.

\* \* \*

The judgment of the Court of Appeals is affirmed.

*It is so ordered.*

JUSTICE WHITE joins only Parts I, II, III, and IV of this opinion.

CHIEF JUSTICE REHNQUIST, with whom JUSTICE SCALIA joins, dissenting.

Congress has carefully limited the judicial review available under the Immigration Control and Reform Act of 1986 (Reform Act) in language which "he who runs may read." The Court, with considerable and obvious effort, finds a way to avoid this limitation, because to apply the statute as written could bar judicial review of respondents' constitutional claims. The statute as written is, in my view, constitutional, and there is therefore no need to rewrite it.

I

The relevant provisions of the Reform Act dealing with administrative and judicial review are found in 8 U.S.C. § 1160(e):

"(1) Administrative and judicial review

"There shall be no administrative or judicial review of a determination respecting an application for adjustment of status under this section except in accordance with this subsection.

"(2) Administrative review

" (A) Single level of administrative appellate review

"The Attorney General shall establish an appellate authority to provide for a single level of administrative appellate review of such a determination"

. . .

636

1    "(3) Judicial review"

2    "(A) Limitation to review of exclusion or deportation"

3    "There shall be judicial review of such a denial only in the judicial review of
4         an order of exclusion or deportation under section 1105a of this title. "

5    The first of the quoted sentences states, as clearly as any language can, that judicial
6    review of a "determination respecting an application for adjustment of status
7    under this section" may not be had except in accordance with the provisions of the
8    subsection. The plain language of subsection (3)(A) provides that judicial review
9    of a denial may be had only in connection with review of an order of exclusion or
10   deportation. The Court chooses to read this language as dealing only with "direct
11   review of individual denials of SAW status, rather than as referring to general
12   collateral challenges to unconstitutional practices and policies used by the agency
13   in processing applications."

14    But the accepted view of judicial review of administrative action generally—even
15   when there is no express preclusion provision as there is in the present statute—is
16   that only "final actions" are reviewable in court. The Administrative Procedure Act
17   provides:

18        "[F]inal agency action for which there is no other adequate remedy in a
19        court [is] subject to judicial review. A preliminary, procedural, or
20        intermediate agency action or ruling not directly reviewable is subject to
21        review on the review of the final agency action."

22   The Court's reasoning is thus a classic non sequitur. It reasons that, because
23   Congress limited judicial review only of what were in effect final administrative
24   decisions, it must not have intended to preclude separate challenges to procedures
25   used by the agency before it issued any final decision. But the type of judicial review
26   of agency action which the Court finds that Congress failed to preclude is a type
27   not generally available, even without preclusion. In the light of this settled rule, the
28   natural reading of "determination respecting an application" in § 1160(e)
29   encompasses both final decisions and procedures used to reach those decisions.
30   Each of respondents' claims attacks the process used by Immigration and
31   Naturalization Service (INS) to make a determination respecting an application.

32   We have on several occasions rejected the argument advanced by respondents that
33   individual plaintiffs can bypass restrictions on judicial review by purporting to
34   attack general policies, rather than individual results. * * *

35   It is well settled that, when Congress has established a particular review
36   mechanism, courts are not free to fashion alternatives to the specified scheme. In
37   creating the Reform Act and the SAW program, Congress balanced the goals of the

unprecedented amnesty programs with the need "to insure reasonably prompt determinations" in light of the incentives and opportunity for ineligible applicants to delay the disposition of their cases and derail the program. The Court's ponderously reasoned gloss on the statute's plain language sanctions an unwarranted intrusion into a carefully drafted congressional program, a program which placed great emphasis on a minimal amount of paperwork and procedure in an effort to speed the process of adjusting the status of those aliens who demonstrated their entitlement to adjustment. "If the balance is to be struck anew, the decision must come from Congress, and not from this Court." *Heckler v. Ringer,* 466 U.S. 602, 627.

II

The Court bases its conclusion that district courts have jurisdiction to entertain respondents' pattern and practice allegations in part out of respect for the "strong presumption" that Congress intends judicial review of administrative action. This presumption, however, comes into play only where there is a genuine ambiguity as to whether Congress intended to preclude judicial review of administrative action. In this case, two things are evident: first, in drafting the Reform Act, Congress did not preclude all judicial review of administrative action; as detailed earlier, Congress provided for judicial review of INS action in the courts of appeals in deportation proceedings, and in the district courts in orders of exclusion. Second, by enacting such a scheme, Congress intended to foreclose all other avenues of relief. Therefore, since the statute is not ambiguous, the presumption has no force here.

The Court states that this presumption of judicial review is particularly applicable in cases raising constitutional challenges to agency action. I believe that Congress intended to preclude judicial review of such claims in this instance, and that, in this context, it is permissible for it to do so.

In the Reform Act, Congress enacted a one-time amnesty program to process claims of illegal aliens, allowing them to obtain status as lawful residents. Congress intended aliens to come forward during the limited, 12-month eligibility period because "[t]his is the first call and the last call, a one-shot deal." 132 Cong. Rec. 33217 (1986) (remarks of Sen. Simpson). If an alien failed to file a legalization application within the 12-month period, the opportunity was lost forever. To further expedite this unique and unprecedented amnesty program and to minimize the burden on the federal courts, Congress provided for limited judicial review.

Given the structure of the Act and the status of these alien respondents, it is extremely doubtful that the operation of the administrative process in their cases would give rise to any colorable constitutional claims. "'An alien who seeks political rights as a member of this Nation can rightfully obtain them only upon terms and

638

conditions specified by Congress. Courts are without authority to sanction changes or modifications; their duty is rigidly to enforce the legislative will in respect of a matter so vital to the public welfare.'" *INS v. Pangilinan*, 486 U.S. 875, 884 (1988) (quoting *United States v. Ginsberg,* 243 U.S. 472, 474 (1917)).

Respondents are undoubtedly entitled to the benefit of those procedures which Congress has accorded them in the Reform Act. But there is no reason to believe that administrative appeals as provided in the Act—which simply have not been resorted to by these respondents before suing in the District Court—would not have assured them compliance with statutory procedures. The Court never mentions what colorable constitutional claims these aliens, illegally present in the United States, could have had that demand judicial review. The most that can be said for respondents' case in this regard is that it is conceivable, though not likely, that the administrative processing of their claims could be handled in such a way as to deny them some constitutional right, and that the remedy of requesting deportation in order to obtain judicial review is a burdensome one. We have never held, however, that Congress may not, by explicit language, preclude judicial review of constitutional claims, and here, where that body was obviously interested in expeditiously processing an avalanche of claims from noncitizens upon whom it was conferring a substantial benefit, I think it may do so.

## B. Commitment to Agency Discretion By Law

The APA makes two references to "discretion." 5 U.S.C. § 701(a)(2) creates a carve-out from judicial review "to the extent that . . . agency action is committed to agency discretion by law," while U.S.C. § 706(2)(A) empowers courts to set aside agency actions found to be "an abuse of discretion." On their face, the two provisions create something of a puzzle: agencies cannot be challenged for actions committed to their discretion, but their actions can be set aside if agencies abuse their discretion. When does a grant of discretion to an agency render its actions unreviewable? The Supreme Court wrestles with this question in the cases that follow.

## Heckler v. Chaney

470 U.S. 821 (1985)

March 20, 1985

JUSTICE REHNQUIST delivered the opinion of the Court.

1   This case presents the question of the extent to which a decision of an
2   administrative agency to exercise its "discretion" not to undertake certain
3   enforcement actions is subject to judicial review under the Administrative
4   Procedure Act (APA). Respondents are several prison inmates convicted of capital
5   offenses and sentenced to death by lethal injection of drugs. They petitioned the
6   Food and Drug Administration (FDA), alleging that, under the circumstances, the
7   use of these drugs for capital punishment violated the Federal Food, Drug, and
8   Cosmetic Act, (FDCA), and requesting that the FDA take various enforcement
9   actions to prevent these violations. The FDA refused their request. We review here
10  a decision of the Court of Appeals for the District of Columbia Circuit, which held
11  the FDA's refusal to take enforcement actions both reviewable and an abuse of
12  discretion, and remanded the case with directions that the agency be required "to
13  fulfill its statutory function."

14                                          I

15  Respondents have been sentenced to death by lethal injection of drugs under the
16  laws of the States of Oklahoma and Texas. Those States, and several others, have
17  recently adopted this method for carrying out the capital sentence. Respondents
18  first petitioned the FDA, claiming that the drugs used by the States for this
19  purpose, although approved by the FDA for the medical purposes stated on their
20  labels, were not approved for use in human executions. They alleged that the drugs
21  had not been tested for the purpose for which they were to be used, and that, given
22  that the drugs would likely be administered by untrained personnel, it was also
23  likely that the drugs would not induce the quick and painless death intended. They
24  urged that use of these drugs for human execution was the "unapproved use of an
25  approved drug," and constituted a violation of the Act's prohibitions against
26  "misbranding." They also suggested that the FDCA's requirements for approval of
27  "new drugs" applied, since these drugs were now being used for a new purpose.
28  Accordingly, respondents claimed that the FDA was required to approve the drugs
29  as "safe and effective" for human execution before they could be distributed in
30  interstate commerce. They therefore requested the FDA to take various
31  investigatory and enforcement actions to prevent these perceived violations; they
32  requested the FDA to affix warnings to the labels of all the drugs stating that they
33  were unapproved and unsafe for human execution, to send statements to the drug
34  manufacturers and prison administrators stating that the drugs should not be so
35  used, and to adopt procedures for seizing the drugs from state prisons and to
36  recommend the prosecution of all those in the chain of distribution who knowingly
37  distribute or purchase the drugs with intent to use them for human execution.

38  The FDA Commissioner responded, refusing to take the requested actions. The
39  Commissioner first detailed his disagreement with respondents' understanding of
40  the scope of FDA jurisdiction over the unapproved use of approved drugs for

1 human execution, concluding that FDA jurisdiction in the area was generally
2 unclear, but in any event should not be exercised to interfere with this particular
3 aspect of state criminal justice systems. He went on to state:

4 "Were FDA clearly to have jurisdiction in the area, moreover, we believe we
5 would be authorized to decline to exercise it under our inherent discretion
6 to decline to pursue certain enforcement matters. The unapproved use of
7 approved drugs is an area in which the case law is far from uniform.
8 Generally, enforcement proceedings in this area are initiated only when
9 there is a serious danger to the public health or a blatant scheme to defraud.
10 We cannot conclude that those dangers are present under State lethal
11 injection laws, which are duly authorized statutory enactments in
12 furtherance of proper State functions. . . ."

13 Respondents then filed the instant suit in the United States District Court for the
14 District of Columbia, claiming the same violations of the FDCA and asking that the
15 FDA be required to take the same enforcement actions requested in the prior
16 petition. * * * The District Court granted summary judgment for petitioner. It
17 began with the proposition that "decisions of executive departments and agencies
18 to *refrain* from instituting investigative and enforcement proceedings are
19 essentially unreviewable by the courts."

20 * * * A divided panel of the Court of Appeals for the District of Columbia Circuit
21 reversed. * * *

22 *  *  *

23 * * * We granted certiorari to review the implausible result that the FDA is required
24 to exercise its enforcement power to ensure that States only use drugs that are "safe
25 and effective" for human execution. We reverse.

26 II

27 *  *  *

28 * * * Petitioner urges that the decision of the FDA to refuse enforcement is an
29 action "committed to agency discretion by law" under § 701(a)(2).

30 This Court has not had occasion to interpret this second exception in § 701(a) in
31 any great detail. On its face, the section does not obviously lend itself to any
32 particular construction; indeed, one might wonder what difference exists between
33 § (a)(1) and § (a)(2). The former section seems easy in application; it requires
34 construction of the substantive statute involved to determine whether Congress
35 intended to preclude judicial review of certain decisions. * * * But one could read
36 the language "committed to agency discretion *by law*" in § (a)(2) to require a
37 similar inquiry. In addition, commentators have pointed out that construction of §

1   (a)(2) is further complicated by the tension between a literal reading of § (a)(2),
2   which exempts from judicial review those decisions committed to agency
3   "discretion," and the primary scope of review prescribed by § 706(2)(A)—whether
4   the agency's action was "arbitrary, capricious, or an *abuse of discretion.*" * * *

5   This Court first discussed § (a)(2) in *Citizens to Preserve Overton Park v. Volpe*,
6   401 U.S. 402 (1971). That case * * * clearly separates the exception provided by §
7   (a)(1) from the § (a)(2) exception. The former applies when Congress has expressed
8   an intent to preclude judicial review. The latter applies in different circumstances;
9   even where Congress has not affirmatively precluded review, review is not to be
10   had if the statute is drawn so that a court would have no meaningful standard
11   against which to judge the agency's exercise of discretion. In such a case, the statute
12   ("law") can be taken to have "committed" the decision making to the agency's
13   judgment absolutely. This construction avoids conflict with the "abuse of
14   discretion" standard of review in § 706—if no judicially manageable standards are
15   available for judging how and when an agency should exercise its discretion, then
16   it is impossible to evaluate agency action for "abuse of discretion." * * *

17                               * * *

18   *Overton Park* did not involve an agency's refusal to take requested enforcement
19   action. It involved an affirmative act of approval under a statute that set clear
20   guidelines for determining when such approval should be given. Refusals to take
21   enforcement steps generally involve precisely the opposite situation, and, in that
22   situation, we think the presumption is that judicial review is not available. This
23   Court has recognized on several occasions over many years that an agency's
24   decision not to prosecute or enforce, whether through civil or criminal process, is
25   a decision generally committed to an agency's absolute discretion. This recognition
26   of the existence of discretion is attributable in no small part to the general
27   unsuitability for judicial review of agency decisions to refuse enforcement.

28   The reasons for this general unsuitability are many. First, an agency decision not
29   to enforce often involves a complicated balancing of a number of factors which are
30   peculiarly within its expertise. Thus, the agency must not only assess whether a
31   violation has occurred, but whether agency resources are best spent on this
32   violation or another, whether the agency is likely to succeed if it acts, whether the
33   particular enforcement action requested best fits the agency's overall policies, and,
34   indeed, whether the agency has enough resources to undertake the action at all. An
35   agency generally cannot act against each technical violation of the statute it is
36   charged with enforcing. The agency is far better equipped than the courts to deal
37   with the many variables involved in the proper ordering of its priorities. Similar
38   concerns animate the principles of administrative law that courts generally will
39   defer to an agency's construction of the statute it is charged with implementing,
40   and to the procedures it adopts for implementing that statute.

In addition to these administrative concerns, we note that, when an agency refuses to act, it generally does not exercise its *coercive* power over an individual's liberty or property rights, and thus does not infringe upon areas that courts often are called upon to protect. Similarly, when an agency *does* act to enforce, that action itself provides a focus for judicial review, inasmuch as the agency must have exercised its power in some manner. The action at least can be reviewed to determine whether the agency exceeded its statutory powers. Finally, we recognize that an agency's refusal to institute proceedings shares to some extent the characteristics of the decision of a prosecutor in the Executive Branch not to indict—a decision which has long been regarded as the special province of the Executive Branch, inasmuch as it is the Executive who is charged by the Constitution to "take Care that the Laws be faithfully executed."

We of course only list the above concerns to facilitate understanding of our conclusion that an agency's decision not to take enforcement action should be presumed immune from judicial review under § 701(a)(2). For good reasons, such a decision has traditionally been "committed to agency discretion," and we believe that the Congress enacting the APA did not intend to alter that tradition. In so stating, we emphasize that the decision is only presumptively unreviewable; the presumption may be rebutted where the substantive statute has provided guidelines for the agency to follow in exercising its enforcement powers. * * *

*Dunlop v. Bachowski*, 421 U.S. 560 (1975), relied upon heavily by respondents and the majority in the Court of Appeals, presents an example of statutory language which supplied sufficient standards to rebut the presumption of unreviewability. *Dunlop* involved a suit by a union employee, under the Labor-Management Reporting and Disclosure Act, 29 U.S.C. § 481 *et seq.* (LMRDA), asking the Secretary of Labor to investigate and file suit to set aside a union election. Section 482 provided that, upon filing of a complaint by a union member, "[t]he Secretary shall investigate such complaint and, if he finds probable cause to believe that a violation . . . has occurred . . . he shall . . . bring a civil action. . . ." After investigating the plaintiff's claims, the Secretary of Labor declined to file suit, and the plaintiff sought judicial review under the APA. This Court held that review was available. * * * [W]e were content to rely on the Court of Appeals' opinion to hold the * * * "principle of absolute prosecutorial discretion" inapplicable, because the language of the LMRDA indicated that the Secretary was required to file suit if certain "clearly defined" factors were present. The decision therefore was not "'*beyond the judicial capacity to supervise.*'"

*Dunlop* is thus consistent with a general presumption of unreviewability of decisions not to enforce. The statute being administered quite clearly withdrew discretion from the agency and provided guidelines for exercise of its enforcement power. Our decision that review was available was not based on "pragmatic considerations," such as those cited by the Court of Appeals that amount to an assessment of whether the interests at stake are important enough to justify intervention in the agencies' decision-making. The danger that agencies may not carry out their delegated powers with sufficient vigor does not necessarily lead to the conclusion that courts are the most appropriate body to police this aspect of their performance. That decision is in the first instance for Congress, and we therefore turn to the FDCA to determine whether in this case Congress has provided us with "law to apply." If it has indicated an intent to circumscribe agency enforcement discretion, and has provided meaningful standards for defining the limits of that discretion, there is "law to apply" under § 701(a)(2), and courts may require that the agency follow that law; if it has not, then an agency refusal to institute proceedings is a decision "committed to agency discretion by law" within the meaning of that section.

III

To enforce the various substantive prohibitions contained in the FDCA, the Act provides for injunctions, criminal sanctions, and seizure of any offending food, drug, or cosmetic article. The Act's general provision for enforcement, § 372, provides only that "[t]he Secretary is *authorized* to conduct examinations and investigations . . ." Unlike the statute at issue in *Dunlop,* § 332 gives no indication of when an injunction should be sought, and § 334, providing for seizures, is framed in the permissive—the offending food, drug, or cosmetic "shall be liable to be proceeded against." The section on criminal sanctions states baldly that any person who violates the Act's substantive prohibitions "shall be imprisoned . . . or fined." Respondents argue that this statement mandates criminal prosecution of every violator of the Act, but they adduce no indication in case law or legislative history that such was Congress' intention in using this language, which is commonly found in the criminal provisions of Title 18 of the United States Code. We are unwilling to attribute such a sweeping meaning to this language, particularly since the Act charges the Secretary only with recommending prosecution; any criminal prosecutions must be instituted by the Attorney General. The Act's enforcement provisions thus commit complete discretion to the Secretary to decide how and when they should be exercised.

Respondents nevertheless present three separate authorities that they claim provide the courts with sufficient indicia of an intent to circumscribe enforcement discretion. Two of these may be dealt with summarily. First, we reject respondents' argument that the Act's substantive prohibitions of "misbranding" and the introduction of "new drugs" absent agency approval, supply us with "law to apply." These provisions are simply irrelevant to the agency's discretion to refuse to initiate proceedings.

1 We also find singularly unhelpful the agency "policy statement" on which the Court
2 of Appeals placed great reliance. * * * Although the statement indicates that the
3 agency considered itself "obligated" to take certain investigative actions, that
4 language did not arise in the course of discussing the agency's discretion to exercise
5 its enforcement power, but rather in the context of describing agency policy with
6 respect to unapproved uses of approved drugs by physicians. In addition, if read to
7 circumscribe agency enforcement discretion, the statement conflicts with the
8 agency rule on judicial review, 21 CFR § 10.45(d)(2) (1984), which states that "[t]he
9 Commissioner shall object to judicial review . . . if (i) [t]he matter is committed by
10 law to the discretion of the Commissioner, *e.g.*, a decision to recommend or not to
11 recommend civil or criminal enforcement action. . . ." * * *

12 Respondents' third argument based upon § 306 of the FDCA, merits only slightly
13 more consideration. That section provides:

14    "Nothing in this chapter shall be construed as requiring the Secretary to
15    report for prosecution, or for the institution of libel or injunction
16    proceedings, minor violations of this chapter whenever he believes that the
17    public interest will be adequately served by a suitable written notice or
18    ruling."

19 21 U.S.C. § 336.

20 Respondents seek to draw from this section the negative implication that the
21 Secretary is *required* to report for prosecution all "major" violations of the Act,
22 however those might be defined, and that it therefore supplies the needed
23 indication of an intent to limit agency enforcement discretion. We think that this
24 section simply does not give rise to the negative implication which respondents
25 seek to draw from it. The section is not addressed to agency proceedings designed
26 to discover the existence of violations, but applies only to a situation where a
27 violation has already been established to the satisfaction of the agency. We do not
28 believe the section speaks to the criteria which shall be used by the agency for
29 investigating possible violations of the Act.

30                                        IV

31 We therefore conclude that the presumption that agency decisions not to institute
32 proceedings are unreviewable under 5 U.S.C. § 701(a)(2) is not overcome by the
33 enforcement provisions of the FDCA. The FDA's decision not to take the
34 enforcement actions requested by respondents is therefore not subject to judicial
35 review under the APA. The general exception to reviewability provided by §
36 701(a)(2) for action "committed to agency discretion" remains a narrow one, *see*
37 *Citizens to Preserve Overton Park v. Volpe*, 401 U.S. 402 (1971), but within that
38 exception are included agency refusals to institute investigative or enforcement
39 proceedings, unless Congress has indicated otherwise. In so holding, we essentially

1   leave to Congress, and not to the courts, the decision as to whether an agency's
2   refusal to institute proceedings should be judicially reviewable. No colorable claim
3   is made in this case that the agency's refusal to institute proceedings violated any
4   constitutional rights of respondents, and we do not address the issue that would
5   be raised in such a case. The fact that the drugs involved in this case are ultimately
6   to be used in imposing the death penalty must not lead this Court or other courts
7   to import profound differences of opinion over the meaning of the Eighth
8   Amendment to the United States Constitution into the domain of administrative
9   law.

10   The judgment of the Court of Appeals is

11   *Reversed.*

12   JUSTICE BRENNAN, concurring.

13   Today the Court holds that individual decisions of the Food and Drug
14   Administration not to take enforcement action in response to citizen requests are
15   presumptively not reviewable under the Administrative Procedure Act, 5 U.S.C. §§
16   701-706. I concur in this decision. This general presumption is based on the view
17   that, in the normal course of events, Congress intends to allow broad discretion for
18   its administrative agencies to make particular enforcement decisions, and there
19   often may not exist readily discernible "law to apply" for courts to conduct judicial
20   review of nonenforcement decisions.

21   I also agree that, despite this general presumption, "Congress did not set agencies
22   free to disregard legislative direction in the statutory scheme that the agency
23   administers." Thus, the Court properly does not decide today that nonenforcement
24   decisions are unreviewable in cases where (1) an agency flatly claims that it has no
25   statutory jurisdiction to reach certain conduct; (2) an agency engages in a pattern
26   of nonenforcement of clear statutory language; (3) an agency has refused to
27   enforce a regulation lawfully promulgated and still in effect, or (4) a
28   nonenforcement decision violates constitutional rights. It is possible to imagine
29   other nonenforcement decisions made for entirely illegitimate reasons, for
30   example, nonenforcement in return for a bribe, judicial review of which would not
31   be foreclosed by the nonreviewability presumption. It may be presumed that
32   Congress does not intend administrative agencies, agents of Congress' own
33   creation, to ignore clear jurisdictional, regulatory, statutory, or constitutional
34   commands, and in some circumstances, including those listed above, the statutes
35   or regulations at issue may well provide "law to apply" under 5 U.S.C. § 701(a)(2).
36   Individual, isolated nonenforcement decisions, however, must be made by
37   hundreds of agencies each day. It is entirely permissible to presume that Congress
38   has not intended courts to review such mundane matters, absent either some

1   indication of congressional intent to the contrary or proof of circumstances such
2   as those set out above.

3   On this understanding of the scope of today's decision, I join the Court's opinion.

4   JUSTICE MARSHALL, concurring in the judgment.

5   Easy cases at times produce bad law, for in the rush to reach a clearly ordained
6   result, courts may offer up principles, doctrines, and statements that calmer
7   reflection, and a fuller understanding of their implications in concrete settings,
8   would eschew. In my view, the "presumption of unreviewability" announced today
9   is a product of that lack of discipline that easy cases make all too easy. The majority,
10  eager to reverse what it goes out of its way to label as an "implausible result," not
11  only does reverse, as I agree it should, but along the way creates out of whole cloth
12  the notion that agency decisions not to take "enforcement action" are unreviewable
13  unless Congress has rather specifically indicated otherwise. Because this
14  "presumption of unreviewability" is fundamentally at odds with rule-of-law
15  principles firmly embedded in our jurisprudence, because it seeks to truncate an
16  emerging line of judicial authority subjecting enforcement discretion to rational
17  and principled constraint, and because, in the end, the presumption may well be
18  indecipherable, one can only hope that it will come to be understood as a relic of a
19  particular factual setting in which the full implications of such a presumption were
20  neither confronted nor understood.

21  I write separately to argue for a different basis of decision: that refusals to enforce,
22  like other agency actions, are reviewable in the absence of a "clear and convincing"
23  congressional intent to the contrary, but that such refusals warrant deference
24  when, as in this case, there is nothing to suggest that an agency with enforcement
25  discretion has abused that discretion.

26                              * * *

27  * * * [A]rguments about prosecutorial discretion do not necessarily translate into
28  the context of agency refusals to act. * * * Criminal prosecutorial decisions
29  vindicate only intangible interests, common to society as a whole, in the
30  enforcement of the criminal law. The conduct at issue has already occurred; all that
31  remains is society's general interest in assuring that the guilty are punished. In
32  contrast, requests for administrative enforcement typically seek to prevent
33  concrete and future injuries that Congress has made cognizable—injuries that
34  result, for example, from misbranded drugs, such as alleged in this case, or unsafe
35  nuclear powerplants, or to obtain palpable benefits that Congress has intended to
36  bestow—such as labor union elections free of corruption. Entitlements to receive
37  these benefits or to be free of these injuries often run to specific classes of
38  individuals whom Congress has singled out as statutory beneficiaries. The interests
39  at stake in review of administrative enforcement decisions are thus more focused,

647

1  and in many circumstances more pressing, than those at stake in criminal
2  prosecutorial decisions. A request that a nuclear plant be operated safely or that
3  protection be provided against unsafe drugs is quite different from a request that
4  an individual be put in jail or his property confiscated as punishment for past
5  violations of the criminal law. Unlike traditional exercises of prosecutorial
6  discretion, "the decision to enforce—or not to enforce—may itself result in
7  significant burdens on a . . . statutory beneficiary." *Marshall v. Jerrico, Inc.*, 446
8  U.S. 238 249 (1980).

9  * * *

10  **Webster v. Doe**

11  486 U.S. 592 (1988)

12  June 15, 1988

13  CHIEF JUSTICE REHNQUIST delivered the opinion of the Court.

14  Section 102(c) of the National Security Act of 1947, 61 Stat. 498, *as amended,*
15  provides that:

> 16  "[T]he Director of Central Intelligence may, in his discretion, terminate the
> 17  employment of any officer or employee of the Agency whenever he shall
> 18  deem such termination necessary or advisable in the interests of the United
> 19  States. . ."

20  In this case we decide whether, and to what extent, the termination decisions of
21  the Director under § 102(c) are judicially reviewable.

22  I

23  Respondent John Doe was first employed by the Central Intelligence Agency (CIA
24  or Agency) in 1973 as a clerk typist. He received periodic fitness reports that
25  consistently rated him as an excellent or outstanding employee. By 1977,
26  respondent had been promoted to a position as a covert electronics technician.

27  In January, 1982, respondent voluntarily informed a CIA security officer that he
28  was a homosexual. Almost immediately, the Agency placed respondent on paid
29  administrative leave pending an investigation of his sexual orientation and
30  conduct. On February 12 and again on February 17, respondent was extensively
31  questioned by a polygraph officer concerning his homosexuality and possible
32  security violations. Respondent denied having sexual relations with any foreign
33  nationals and maintained that he had not disclosed classified information to any
34  of his sexual partners. After these interviews, the officer told respondent that the
35  polygraph tests indicated that he had truthfully answered all questions. The

648

1  polygraph officer then prepared a five-page summary of his interviews with
2  respondent, to which respondent was allowed to attach a two-page addendum.

3  On April 14, 1982, a CIA security agent informed respondent that the Agency's
4  Office of Security had determined that respondent's homosexuality posed a threat
5  to security but declined to explain the nature of the danger. Respondent was then
6  asked to resign. When he refused to do so, the Office of Security recommended to
7  the CIA Director (petitioner's predecessor) that respondent be dismissed. After
8  reviewing respondent's records and the evaluations of his subordinates, the
9  Director "deemed it necessary and advisable in the interests of the United States
10 to terminate [respondent's] employment with this Agency pursuant to section
11 102(c) of the National Security Act. . ." Respondent was also advised that, while the
12 CIA would give him a positive recommendation in any future job search, if he
13 applied for a job requiring a security clearance, the Agency would inform the
14 prospective employer that it had concluded that respondent's homosexuality
15 presented a security threat.

16 Respondent then filed an action against petitioner in the United States District
17 Court for the District of Columbia. Respondent's amended complaint asserted a
18 variety of statutory and constitutional claims against the Director. Respondent
19 alleged that the Director's decision to terminate his employment violated the
20 Administrative Procedure Act (APA), because it was arbitrary and capricious,
21 represented an abuse of discretion, and was reached without observing the
22 procedures required by law and CIA regulations. He also complained that the
23 Director's termination of his employment deprived him of constitutionally
24 protected rights to property, liberty, and privacy in violation of the First, Fourth,
25 Fifth, and Ninth Amendments. Finally, he asserted that his dismissal transgressed
26 the procedural due process and equal protection of the laws guaranteed by the Fifth
27 Amendment. Respondent requested a declaratory judgment that the Director had
28 violated the APA and the Constitution, and asked the District Court for an
29 injunction ordering petitioner to reinstate him to the position he held with the CIA
30 prior to his dismissal. As an alternative remedy, he suggested that he be returned
31 to paid administrative leave and that petitioner be ordered to reevaluate
32 respondent's employment termination and provide a statement of the reasons for
33 any adverse final determination. Respondent sought no monetary damages in his
34 amended complaint.

35 Petitioner moved to dismiss respondent's amended complaint on the ground that
36 § 102(c) of the National Security Act (NSA) precludes judicial review of the
37 Director's termination decisions under the provisions of the APA set forth in 5
38 U.S.C. §§ 701, 702, and 706. * * *

39 The District Court denied petitioner's motion to dismiss, and granted respondent's
40 motion for partial summary judgment. The court determined that the APA

649

provided judicial review of petitioner's termination decisions made under § 102(c) of the NSA, and found that respondent had been unlawfully discharged because the CIA had not followed the procedures described in its own regulations. The District Court declined, however, to address respondent's constitutional claims. Respondent was ordered reinstated to administrative leave status, and the Agency was instructed to reconsider his case using procedures that would supply him with the reasons supporting any termination decision and provide him with an opportunity to respond.

A divided panel of the Court of Appeals for the District of Columbia Circuit vacated the District Court's judgment and remanded the case for further proceedings. * * *

* * * We granted certiorari to decide the question whether the Director's decision to discharge a CIA employee under § 102(c) of the NSA is judicially reviewable under the APA.

II

The APA's comprehensive provisions, set forth in 5 U.S.C. §§ 701-706, allow any person "adversely affected or aggrieved" by agency action to obtain judicial review thereof, so long as the decision challenged represents a "final agency action for which there is no other adequate remedy in a court." Typically, a litigant will contest an action (or failure to act) by an agency on the ground that the agency has neglected to follow the statutory directives of Congress. Section 701(a), however, limits application of the entire APA to situations in which judicial review is not precluded by statute, and the agency action is not committed to agency discretion by law.

* * *

Both *Overton Park* and *Heckler* emphasized that § 701 (a)(2) requires careful examination of the statute on which the claim of agency illegality is based * * * . In the present case, respondent's claims against the CIA arise from the Director's asserted violation of § 102(c) of the NSA. As an initial matter, it should be noted that § 102(c) allows termination of an Agency employee whenever the Director "shall *deem* such termination necessary or advisable in the interests of the United States" (emphasis added), not simply when the dismissal *is* necessary or advisable to those interests. This standard fairly exudes deference to the Director, and appears to us to foreclose the application of any meaningful judicial standard of review. Short of permitting cross-examination of the Director concerning his views of the Nation's security and whether the discharged employee was inimical to those interests, we see no basis on which a reviewing court could properly assess an Agency termination decision. The language of § 102(c) thus strongly suggests that its implementation was "committed to agency discretion by law."

1   So too does the overall structure of the NSA. Passed shortly after the close of the
2   Second World War, the NSA created the CIA and gave its Director the
3   responsibility "for protecting intelligence sources and methods from unauthorized
4   disclosure." *See* 50 U.S.C. § 403(d)(3). Section 102(c) is an integral part of that
5   statute, because the Agency's efficacy, and the Nation's security, depend in large
6   measure on the reliability and trustworthiness of the Agency's employees. As we
7   recognized in *Snepp v. United States,* 444 U.S. 507, 510 (1980), employment with
8   the CIA entails a high degree of trust that is perhaps unmatched in Government
9   service.

10  This overriding need for ensuring integrity in the Agency led us to uphold the
11  Director's use of § 102(d)(3) of the NSA to withhold the identities of protected
12  intelligence sources in *CIA v. Sims,* 471 U.S. 159 (1985). In denying respondent's
13  Freedom of Information Act requests in *Sims* to produce certain CIA records, we
14  stated that

15      "[t]he plain meaning of the statutory language, as well as the legislative
16      history of the National Security Act, . . . indicates that Congress vested in
17      the Director of Central Intelligence very broad authority to protect all
18      sources of intelligence information from disclosure."

19  *Id.* at 471 U.S. 168,169. Section 102(c), that portion of the NSA under consideration
20  in the present case, is part and parcel of the entire Act, and likewise exhibits the
21  Act's extraordinary deference to the Director in his decision to terminate individual
22  employees.

23  We thus find that the language and structure of § 102(c) indicate that Congress
24  meant to commit individual employee discharges to the Director's discretion, and
25  that § 701(a)(2) accordingly precludes judicial review of these decisions under the
26  APA. We reverse the Court of Appeals to the extent that it found such terminations
27  reviewable by the courts.

28                                  III

29  In addition to his claim that the Director failed to abide by the statutory dictates of
30  § 102(c), respondent also alleged a number of constitutional violations in his
31  amended complaint. Respondent charged that petitioner's termination of his
32  employment deprived him of property and liberty interests under the Due Process
33  Clause of the Fifth Amendment, denied him equal protection of the laws, and
34  unjustifiably burdened his right to privacy. Respondent asserts that he is entitled,
35  under the APA, to judicial consideration of these claimed violations.

36                                  * * *

1   Petitioner maintains that, no matter what the nature of respondent's constitutional
2   claim, judicial review is precluded by the language and intent of § 102(c). In
3   petitioner's view, all Agency employment termination decisions, even those based
4   on policies normally repugnant to the Constitution, are given over to the absolute
5   discretion of the Director, and are hence unreviewable under the APA. We do not
6   think § 102(c) may be read to exclude review of constitutional claims. We
7   emphasized in *Johnson v. Robison,* 415 U.S. 361 (1974), that, where Congress
8   intends to preclude judicial review of constitutional claims, its intent to do so must
9   be clear. In *Weinberger v. Salfi,* 422 U.S. 749 (1975), we reaffirmed that view. We
10  require this heightened showing in part to avoid the "serious constitutional
11  question" that would arise if a federal statute were construed to deny any judicial
12  forum for a colorable constitutional claim. *See Bowen v. Michigan Academy of*
13  *Family Physicians,* 476 U.S. 667, 681, n. 12 (1986).

14  Our review of § 102(c) convinces us that it cannot bear the preclusive weight
15  petitioner would have it support. As detailed above, the section does commit
16  employment termination decisions to the Director's discretion, and precludes
17  challenges to these decisions based upon the statutory language of § 102(c). A
18  discharged employee thus cannot complain that his termination was not
19  "necessary or advisable in the interests of the United States," since that assessment
20  is the Director's alone. Subsections (a)(1) and (a)(2) of § 701, however, remove
21  from judicial review only those determinations specifically identified by Congress
22  or "committed to agency discretion by law." Nothing in § 102(c) persuades us that
23  Congress meant to preclude consideration of colorable constitutional claims
24  arising out of the actions of the Director pursuant to that section; we believe that a
25  constitutional claim based on an individual discharge may be reviewed by the
26  District Court. We agree with the Court of Appeals that there must be further
27  proceedings in the District Court on this issue.

28                                    * * *

29  The judgment of the Court of Appeals is affirmed in part, reversed in part, and the
30  case is remanded for further proceedings consistent with this opinion.

31  *It is so ordered.*

32  JUSTICE KENNEDY took no part in the consideration or decision of this case.

33  JUSTICE O'CONNOR, concurring in part and dissenting in part.

34  I agree that the Administrative Procedure Act (APA) does not authorize judicial
35  review of the employment decisions referred to in § 102(c) of the National Security
36  Act of 1947. * * * I do not understand the Court to say that the exception in §
37  701(a)(2) is necessarily or fully defined by reference to statutes "drawn in such
38  broad terms that in a given case there is no law to apply."

1  I disagree, however, with the Court's conclusion that a constitutional claim
2  challenging the validity of an employment decision covered by § 102(c) may
3  nonetheless be brought in a federal district court. Whatever may be the exact scope
4  of Congress' power to close the lower federal courts to constitutional claims in
5  other contexts, I have no doubt about its authority to do so here.

6  * * *

7  JUSTICE SCALIA, dissenting.

8  I agree with the Court's apparent holding in Part II of its opinion, that the
9  Director's decision to terminate a CIA employee is "committed to agency discretion
10 by law" within the meaning of 5 U.S.C. § 701(a)(2). But because I do not see how a
11 decision can, either practically or legally, be both unreviewable and yet reviewable
12 for constitutional defect, I regard Part III of the opinion as essentially undoing Part
13 II. I therefore respectfully dissent from the judgment of the Court.

14  I

15 Before proceeding to address Part III of the Court's opinion, which I think to be in
16 error, I must discuss one significant element of the analysis in Part II. Though I
17 subscribe to most of that analysis, I disagree with the Court's description of what
18 is required to come within subsection (a)(2) of § 701(a), which provides that
19 judicial review is unavailable "to the extent that . . . agency action is committed to
20 agency discretion by law." The Court's discussion suggests that the Court of
21 Appeals below was correct in holding that this provision is triggered only when
22 there is "no law to apply." Our precedents amply show that "commit[ment] to
23 agency discretion by law" includes, but is not limited to, situations in which there
24 is "no law to apply."

25  * * *

26 The "no law to apply" test can account for the nonreviewability of certain issues,
27 but falls far short of explaining the full scope of the areas from which the courts are
28 excluded. For the fact is that there is no governmental decision that is not subject
29 to a fair number of legal constraints precise enough to be susceptible of judicial
30 application—beginning with the fundamental constraint that the decision must be
31 taken in order to further a public purpose, rather than a purely private interest; yet
32 there are many governmental decisions that are not at all subject to judicial review.
33 A United States Attorney's decision to prosecute, for example, will not be reviewed
34 on the claim that it was prompted by personal animosity. Thus, "no law to apply"
35 provides much less than the full answer to whether § 701(a)(2) applies.

36 The key to understanding the "committed to agency discretion *by law*" provision
37 of § 701(a)(2) lies in contrasting it with the "*statutes* preclude judicial review"

1    provision of § 701(a)(1). Why "statutes" for preclusion, but the much more general
2    term "law" for commission to agency discretion? The answer is, as we implied
3    in *Chaney,* that the latter was intended to refer to "the common law' of judicial
4    review of agency action," 470 U.S., at 832—a body of jurisprudence that had
5    marked out, with more or less precision, certain issues and certain areas that were
6    beyond the range of judicial review. That jurisprudence included principles
7    ranging from the "political question" doctrine, to sovereign immunity (including
8    doctrines determining when a suit against an officer would be deemed to be a suit
9    against the sovereign), to official immunity, to prudential limitations upon the
10    courts' equitable powers, to what can be described no more precisely than a
11    traditional respect for the functions of the other branches reflected in the
12    statement in *Marbury v. Madison,* 5 U.S. 137, 170-171 (1803), that "[w]here the
13    head of a department acts in a case, in which executive discretion is to be exercised;
14    in which he is the mere organ of executive will; it is again repeated, that any
15    application to a court to control, in any respect, his conduct, would be rejected
16    without hesitation."

17    Only if all that "common law" were embraced within § 701 (a)(2) could it have been
18    true that, as was generally understood, "[t]he intended result of [§ 701(a)] is to
19    restate the existing law as to the area of reviewable agency action." Attorney
20    General's Manual on the Administrative Procedure Act 94 (1947). Because that is
21    the meaning of the provision, we have continued to take into account for purposes
22    of determining reviewability, post-APA as before, not only the text and structure
23    of the statute under which the agency acts, but such factors as whether the decision
24    involves "a sensitive and inherently discretionary judgment call," *Department of*
25    *Navy v. Egan,* 484 U.S. 518, 527 (1988), whether it is the sort of decision that has
26    traditionally been nonreviewable, *ICC v. Locomotive Engineers,* 482 U.S. 270,
27    282(1987); *Chaney,* 470 U.S., at 832, and whether review would have "disruptive
28    practical consequences," *see Southern R. Co. v. Seaboard Allied Milling Corp.,* 442
29    U.S. 444, 457 (1979). This explains the seeming contradiction between §
30    701(a)(2)'s disallowance of review to the extent that action is "committed to agency
31    discretion," and § 706's injunction that a court shall set aside agency action that
32    constitutes "an abuse of discretion." Since, in the former provision, "committed to
33    agency discretion by law" means "of the sort that is traditionally unreviewable," it
34    operates to keep certain categories of agency action out of the courts; but when
35    agency action is appropriately in the courts, abuse of discretion is of course
36    grounds for reversal.

37    All this law, shaped over the course of centuries and still developing in its
38    application to new contexts, cannot possibly be contained within the phrase "no
39    law to apply." It is not surprising, then, that although the Court recites the test, it
40    does not really apply it. Like other opinions relying upon it, this one essentially
41    announces the test, declares victory, and moves on. It is not really true "that a court

1  would have no meaningful standard against which to judge the agency's exercise
2  of discretion,'" The standard set forth in § 102(c) of the National Security Act of
3  1947, 50 U.S.C. § 403(c), "necessary or advisable in the interests of the United
4  States," at least excludes dismissal out of personal vindictiveness, or because the
5  Director wants to give the job to his cousin.

6  * * *

7  II

8  Before taking the reader through the terrain of the Court's holding that respondent
9  may assert constitutional claims in this suit, I would like to try to clear some of the
10  underbrush, consisting primarily of the Court's ominous warning that "[a] 'serious
11  constitutional question' . . . would arise if a federal statute were construed to deny
12  any judicial forum for a colorable constitutional claim."

13  The first response to the Court's grave doubt about the constitutionality of denying
14  all judicial review to a "colorable constitutional claim" is that the denial of all
15  judicial review is not at issue here, but merely the denial of review in United States
16  district courts. As to that, the law is, and has long been, clear. * * * [I]f there is any
17  truth to the proposition that judicial cognizance of constitutional claims cannot be
18  eliminated, it is, at most, that they cannot be eliminated from state courts, and
19  from this Court's appellate jurisdiction over cases from state courts (or eases from
20  federal courts, should there be any) involving such claims. * * *

21  * * * I turn, then, to the substance of the Court's warning that judicial review of all
22  "colorable constitutional claims" arising out of the respondent's dismissal may well
23  be constitutionally required. What could possibly be the basis for this fear? Surely
24  not some general principle that *all* constitutional violations must be remediable in
25  the courts. The very text of the Constitution refutes that principle, since it provides
26  that "[e]ach House shall be the Judge of the Elections, Returns and Qualifications
27  of its own Members," Art. I, § 5, and that "for any Speech or Debate in either House,
28  [the Senators and Representatives] shall not be questioned in any other Place," Art.
29  I, § 6. Claims concerning constitutional violations committed in these contexts—
30  for example, the rather grave constitutional claim that an election has been
31  stolen—cannot be addressed to the courts. *See, e.g., Morgan v. United States*, 801
32  F.2d 445 (1986). Even apart from the strict text of the Constitution, we have found
33  some constitutional claims to be beyond judicial review because they involve"
34  political questions." *See, e.g., Coleman v. Miller*, 307 U.S. 433, 443-446
35  (1939); *Ohio ex rel. Bryant v. Akron Metropolitan Park District*, 281 U.S. 74, 79-
36  80 (1930). The doctrine of sovereign immunity—not repealed by the Constitution,
37  but to the contrary at least partly reaffirmed as to the States by the Eleventh
38  Amendment—is a monument to the principle that some constitutional claims can
39  go unheard. No one would suggest that, if Congress had not passed the Tucker Act,

28 U.S.C. § 1491(a)(1), the courts would be able to order disbursements from the Treasury to pay for property taken under lawful authority (and subsequently destroyed) without just compensation. *See Schillinger v. United States*, 155 U.S. 163, 166-169 (1894). * * * In sum, it is simply untenable that there must be a judicial remedy for every constitutional violation. Members of Congress and the supervising officers of the Executive Branch take the same oath to uphold the Constitution that we do, and sometimes they are left to perform that oath unreviewed, as we always are.

Perhaps, then, the Court means to appeal to a more limited principle that, although there may be areas where judicial review of a constitutional claim will be denied, the scope of those areas is fixed by the Constitution and judicial tradition, and cannot be affected by *Congress* through the enactment of a statute such as § 102(c). That would be a rather counterintuitive principle, especially since Congress has in reality been the principal determiner of the scope of review, for constitutional claims as well as all other claims, through its waiver of the preexisting doctrine of sovereign immunity. On the merits of the point, however: It seems to me clear that courts would not entertain, for example, an action for backpay by a dismissed Secretary of State claiming that the reason he lost his Government job was that the President did not like his religious views—surely a colorable violation of the First Amendment. I am confident we would hold that the President's choice of his Secretary of State is a "political question." But what about a similar suit by the Deputy Secretary of State? Or one of the Under Secretaries? Or an Assistant Secretary? Or the head of the European Desk? Is there really a constitutional line that falls at some immutable point between one and another of these offices at which the principle of unreviewability cuts in, and which cannot be altered by congressional prescription? I think not. I think Congress can prescribe, at least within broad limits, that, for certain jobs, the dismissal decision will be unreviewable—that is, will be "committed to agency discretion by law."

Once it is acknowledged, as I think it must be, (1) that not all constitutional claims require a judicial remedy, and (2) that the identification of those that do not can, even if only within narrow limits, be determined by Congress, then it is clear that the "serious constitutional question" feared by the Court is an illusion. Indeed, it seems to me that, if one is in a mood to worry about serious constitutional questions, the one to worry about is not whether Congress can, by enacting § 102(c), give the President, through his Director of Central Intelligence, unreviewable discretion in firing the agents that he employs to gather military and foreign affairs intelligence, but rather whether Congress could constitutionally permit the courts to review all such decisions if it wanted to. * * * We have * * * recognized that the

1  "authority to classify and control access to information bearing on national
2  security and to determine whether an individual is sufficiently trustworthy
3  to occupy a position in the Executive Branch that will give that person
4  access to such information flows primarily from this constitutional
5  investment of power in the President, *and exists quite apart from any*
6  *explicit congressional grant.*"

7  *Department of Navy v. Egan,* 484 U.S., at 527 (emphasis added).

8  I think it entirely beyond doubt that, if Congress intended, by the APA in 5 U.S.C.
9  § 701(a)(2), to exclude judicial review of the President's decision (through the
10 Director of Central Intelligence) to dismiss an officer of the Central Intelligence
11 Agency, that disposition would be constitutionally permissible.

12                                    III

13 I turn, then, to whether that executive action is, within the meaning of § 701(a)(2),
14 "committed to agency discretion by law." My discussion of this point can be brief,
15 because the answer is compellingly obvious. Section 102(c) of the National Security
16 Act of 1947, 61 Stat. 498, states:

17  "*Notwithstanding . . . the provisions of any other law,* the Director of
18  Central Intelligence, *may, in his discretion,* terminate the employment of
19  any officer or employee of the Agency *whenever he shall deem* such
20  termination necessary or advisable in the interests of the United
21  States. . . ."

22 50 U.S.C. § 403(c) (emphasis added).

23 Further, as the Court declares, § 102(c) is an "integral part" of the National Security
24 Act, which throughout exhibits "extraordinary deference to the Director." Given
25 this statutory text, and given (as discussed above) that the area to which the text
26 pertains is one of predominant executive authority and of traditional judicial
27 abstention, it is difficult to conceive of a statutory scheme that more clearly reflects
28 that "commit[ment] to agency discretion by law" to which § 701(a)(2) refers.

29 It is baffling to observe that the Court seems to agree with the foregoing
30 assessment, holding that "the language and structure of § 102(c) indicate that
31 Congress meant to commit individual employee discharges to the Director's
32 discretion." Nevertheless, without explanation, the Court reaches the conclusion
33 that "a constitutional claim based on an individual discharge may be reviewed by
34 the District Court." It seems to me the Court is attempting the impossible feat of
35 having its cake and eating it too. The opinion states that "[a] discharged employee
36 . . . cannot complain that his termination was not 'necessary or advisable in the
37 interests of the United States,' *since that assessment is the Director's alone.*"

1  (emphasis added). But two sentences later, it says that "[n]othing in § 102(c)
2  persuades us that Congress meant to preclude consideration of colorable
3  constitutional claims arising out of the actions of the Director pursuant to that
4  section."

5  Which are we to believe? If the former, the case should be at an end. If the § 102(c)
6  assessment is really "the Director's alone," the only conceivable basis for review of
7  respondent's dismissal (which is what this case is about) would be that the
8  dismissal was not *really* the result of a § 102(c) assessment by the Director. But
9  respondent has never contended that, nor could he. * * *

10  Even if the basis for the Director's assessment was the respondent's homosexuality,
11  and even if the connection between that and the interests of the United States is an
12  irrational, and hence an unconstitutional one, if that assessment is really "the
13  Director's alone," there is nothing more to litigate about. * * *

14  Since the Court's disposition contradicts its fair assurances, I must assume that the
15  § 102(c) judgment is no longer "the Director's alone," but rather only "the
16  Director's alone except to the extent it is colorably claimed that his judgment is
17  unconstitutional." I turn, then, to the question of where this exception comes from.
18  As discussed at length earlier, the Constitution assuredly does not require it. Nor
19  does the text of the statute. * * *

20  Perhaps, then, a constitutional right is by its nature so much more important to
21  the claimant than a statutory right that a statute which plainly excludes the latter
22  should not be read to exclude the former unless it says so. That principle has never
23  been announced—and with good reason, because its premise is not true. An
24  individual's contention that the government has reneged upon a $100,000 debt
25  owing under a contract is much more important to him—both financially and, I
26  suspect, in the sense of injustice that he feels—than the same individual's claim
27  that a particular federal licensing provision requiring a $100 license denies him
28  equal protection of the laws, or that a particular state tax violates the Commerce
29  Clause. A citizen would much rather have his statutory entitlement correctly
30  acknowledged after a constitutionally inadequate hearing than have it incorrectly
31  denied after a proceeding that fulfills all the requirements of the Due Process
32  Clause. The *only* respect in which a constitutional claim is necessarily more
33  significant than any other kind of claim is that, regardless of how trivial its real-life
34  importance may be in the case at hand, it can be asserted against the action of the
35  legislature itself, whereas a nonconstitutional claim (no matter how significant)
36  cannot. That is an important distinction, and one relevant to the constitutional
37  analysis that I conducted above. But it has no relevance to the question whether,
38  as between executive violations of statute and executive violations of the
39  Constitution—both of which are equally unlawful, and neither of which can be

1 said, *a priori,* to be more harmful or more unfair to the plaintiff—one or the other
2 category should be favored by a presumption against exclusion of judicial review.

3 * * *

4 The harm done by today's decision is that, contrary to what Congress knows is
5 preferable, it brings a significant decisionmaking process of our intelligence
6 services into a forum where it does not belong. Neither the Constitution, nor our
7 laws, nor common sense gives an individual a right to come into court to litigate
8 the reasons for his dismissal as an intelligence agent. It is of course not just
9 *valid* constitutional claims that today's decision makes the basis for judicial review
10 of the Director's action, but all *colorable* constitutional claims, whether
11 meritorious or not. And in determining whether what is colorable is in fact
12 meritorious, a court will necessarily have to review the entire decision. * * *
13 Presumably the court would be expected to evaluate whether the agent really did
14 fail in this or that secret mission. The documents needed will make interesting
15 reading for district judges (and perhaps others) throughout the country. Of course,
16 the Agency can seek to protect itself, ultimately, by an authorized assertion of
17 executive privilege, *United States v. Nixon,* 418 U.S. 683 (1974), but that is a power
18 to be invoked only *in extremis,* and any scheme of judicial review of which it is a
19 central feature is extreme. I would, in any event, not like to be the agent who has
20 to explain to the intelligence services of other nations, with which we sometimes
21 cooperate, that they need have no worry that the secret information they give us
22 will be subjected to the notoriously broad discovery powers of our courts, because,
23 although we have to litigate the dismissal of our spies, we have available a
24 protection of somewhat uncertain scope known as executive privilege, which the
25 President can invoke if he is willing to take the political damage that it often entails.

26 Today's result, however, will have ramifications far beyond creation of the world's
27 only secret intelligence agency that must litigate the dismissal of its agents. If
28 constitutional claims can be raised in this highly sensitive context, it is hard to
29 imagine where they cannot. The assumption that there are any executive decisions
30 that cannot be hauled into the courts may no longer be valid. Also obsolete may be
31 the assumption that we are capable of preserving a sensible common law of judicial
32 review.

33 I respectfully dissent.

34

35 **Lincoln v. Vigil**

36 508 U.S. 182 (1993)

37 May 24, 1993

1    JUSTICE SOUTER delivered the opinion of the Court.

2    For several years in the late 1970's and early 1980's, the Indian Health Service
3    provided diagnostic and treatment services, referred to collectively as the Indian
4    Children's Program (Program), to handicapped Indian children in the Southwest.
5    In 1985, the Service decided to reallocate the Program's resources to a nationwide
6    effort to assist such children. We hold that the Service's decision to discontinue the
7    Program was "committed to agency discretion by law" and therefore not subject to
8    judicial review under the Administrative Procedure Act, and that the Service's
9    exercise of that discretion was not subject to the notice-and-comment rulemaking
10   requirements imposed by §553.

11                             I

12   The Indian Health Service, an agency within the Public Health Service of the
13   Department of Health and Human Services, provides health care for some 1.5
14   million American Indian and Alaska Native people. The Service receives yearly
15   lump-sum appropriations from Congress and expends the funds under authority
16   of the Snyder Act, 42 Stat. 208, as amended, 25 U.S.C. § 13, and the Indian Health
17   Care Improvement Act, 90 Stat. 1400, as amended, 25 U.S.C. § 1601 *et seq.* So far
18   as it concerns us here, the Snyder Act authorizes the Service to "expend such
19   moneys as Congress may from time to time appropriate, for the benefit, care, and
20   assistance of the Indians," for the "relief of distress and conservation of health." 25
21   U.S.C. § 13.1 The Improvement Act authorizes expenditures for, *inter alia,* Indian
22   mental-health care, and specifically for "therapeutic and residential treatment
23   centers." § 1621(a)(4)(D).

24   The Service employs roughly 12,000 people and operates more than 500 health-
25   care facilities in the continental United States and Alaska. This case concerns a
26   collection of related services, commonly known as the Indian Children's Program,
27   that the Service provided from 1978 to 1985. In the words of the Court of Appeals,
28   a "clou[d] [of] bureaucratic haze" obscures the history of the Program, *Vigil v.*
29   *Rhoades,* 953 F.2d 1225, 1226 (CA10 1992), which seems to have grown out of a
30   plan "to establish therapeutic and residential treatment centers for disturbed
31   Indian children." H. R. Rep. No. 94-1026, pt. 1, p. 80 (1976) (prepared in
32   conjunction with enactment of the Improvement Act). These centers were to be
33   established under a "major cooperative care agreement" between the Service and
34   the Bureau of Indian Affairs and would have provided such children "with
35   intensive care in a residential setting." *Id.,* at 80-81.

36   Congress never expressly appropriated funds for these centers. In 1978, however,
37   the Service allocated approximately $292,000 from its fiscal year 1978
38   appropriation to its office in Albuquerque, New Mexico, for the planning and
39   development of a pilot project for handicapped Indian children, which became

known as the Indian Children's Program. The pilot project apparently convinced the Service that a building was needed, and, in 1979, the Service requested $3.5 million from Congress to construct a diagnostic and treatment center for handicapped Indian children. The appropriation for fiscal year 1980 did not expressly provide the requested funds, however, and legislative reports indicated only that Congress had increased the Service's funding by $300,000 for nationwide expansion and development of the Program in coordination with the Bureau.

Plans for a national program to be managed jointly by the Service and the Bureau were never fulfilled, however, and the Program continued simply as an offering of the Service's Albuquerque office, from which the Program's staff of 11 to 16 employees would make monthly visits to Indian communities in New Mexico and southern Colorado and on the Navajo and Hopi Reservations. The Program's staff provided "diagnostic, evaluation, treatment planning and followup services" for Indian children with emotional, educational, physical, or mental handicaps. "For parents, community groups, school personnel and health care personnel," the staff provided "training in child development, prevention of handicapping conditions, and care of the handicapped child." Hearings on Department of the Interior and Related Agencies Appropriations for 1984 before a Subcommittee of the House Committee on Appropriations, 98th Cong., 1st Sess., pt. 3, p. 374 (1983) (Service submission) (hereinafter House Hearings (Fiscal Year 1984)). Congress never authorized or appropriated moneys expressly for the Program, and the Service continued to pay for its regional activities out of annual lump-sum appropriations from 1980 to 1985, during which period the Service repeatedly apprised Congress of the Program's continuing operation.

Nevertheless, the Service had not abandoned the proposal for a nationwide treatment program, and in June 1985 it notified those who referred patients to the Program that it was "re-evaluating [the Program's] purpose . . . as a national mental health program for Indian children and adolescents." In August 1985, the Service determined that Program staff hitherto assigned to provide direct clinical services should be reassigned as consultants to other nationwide Service programs, and discontinued the direct clinical services to Indian children in the Southwest. The Service announced its decision in a memorandum, dated August 21, 1985, addressed to Service offices and Program referral sources * * *. * * *

\* \* \*

Respondents, handicapped Indian children eligible to receive services through the Program, subsequently brought this action for declaratory and injunctive relief against petitioners, the Director of the Service and others (collectively, the Service), in the United States District Court for the District of New Mexico. Respondents alleged, *inter alia,* that the Service's decision to discontinue direct

1  clinical services violated the federal trust responsibility to Indians, the Snyder Act,
2  the Improvement Act, the Administrative Procedure Act, various agency
3  regulations, and the Fifth Amendment's Due Process Clause.

4  The District Court granted summary judgment for respondents. The District Court
5  held that the Service's decision to discontinue the Program was subject to judicial
6  review, rejecting the argument that the Service's decision was "committed to
7  agency discretion by law" under the Administrative Procedure Act (APA).The court
8  declined on ripeness grounds, however, to address the merits of the Service's
9  action. It held that the Service's decision to discontinue the Program amounted to
10 the making of a "legislative rule" subject to the APA's notice-and-comment
11 requirements, and that the termination was also subject to the APA's publication
12 requirements for the adoption of "statements of general policy." Because the
13 Service had not met these procedural requirements, the court concluded that the
14 termination was procedurally invalid and that judicial review would be
15 "premature." The court ordered the Service to reinstate the Program, and the
16 Solicitor General has represented that a reinstated Program is now in place.

17 The Court of Appeals affirmed. Like the District Court, it rejected the Service's
18 argument that the decision to discontinue the Program was committed to agency
19 discretion under the APA. Although the court concededly could identify no statute
20 or regulation even mentioning the Program, it believed that the repeated
21 references to it in the legislative history of the annual appropriations Acts, "in
22 combination with the special relationship between the Indian people and the
23 federal government," provided a basis for judicial review. The Court of Appeals also
24 affirmed the District Court's ruling that the Service was subject to the APA's notice-
25 and-comment procedures in terminating the Program. The Court of Appeals did
26 not consider whether the APA's publication requirements applied to the Service's
27 decision to terminate the Program or whether the District Court's order to reinstate
28 the Program was a proper form of relief, an issue the Service had failed to raise. We
29 granted certiorari to address the narrow questions presented by the Court of
30 Appeals' decision.

31                                    II

32 First is the question whether it was error for the Court of Appeals to hold the
33 substance of the Service's decision to terminate the Program reviewable under the
34 APA. The APA provides that "[a] person suffering legal wrong because of agency
35 action, or adversely affected or aggrieved by agency action within the meaning of a
36 relevant statute, is entitled to judicial review thereof," 5 U.S.C. § 702, and we have
37 read the APA as embodying a "basic presumption of judicial review," *Abbott*
38 *Laboratories v. Gardner,* 387 U.S. 136, 140 (1967). This is "just" a presumption,
39 however, and under § 701(a)(2) agency action is not subject to judicial review "to
40 the extent that" such action "is committed to agency discretion by law." * * *

1    Over the years, we have read § 701(a)(2) to preclude judicial review of certain
2    categories of administrative decisions that courts traditionally have regarded as
3    "committed to agency discretion." See *Franklin v. Massachusetts, 505* U.S. 788,
4    817 (1992) (STEVENS, J., concurring in part and concurring in
5    judgment); *Webster, supra,* at 609 (SCALIA, J., dissenting). In *Heckler* itself, we
6    held an agency's decision not to institute enforcement proceedings to be
7    presumptively unreviewable under § 701(a)(2). 470 U.S., at 831. An agency's
8    "decision not to enforce often involves a complicated balancing of a number of
9    factors which are peculiarly within its expertise," *ibid.,* and for this and other good
10   reasons, we concluded, "such a decision has traditionally been 'committed to
11   agency discretion,'" *id.,* at 832. Similarly, in *ICC v. Locomotive Engineers,* 482
12   U.S. 270, 282 (1987), we held that § 701(a)(2) precludes judicial review of another
13   type of administrative decision traditionally left to agency discretion, an agency's
14   refusal to grant reconsideration of an action because of material error. In so
15   holding, we emphasized "the impossibility of devising an adequate standard of
16   review for such agency action." *Ibid.* Finally, in *Webster, supra,* at 599-601, we
17   held that § 701(a)(2) precludes judicial review of a decision by the Director of
18   Central Intelligence to terminate an employee in the interests of national security,
19   an area of executive action "in which courts have long been hesitant to intrude."
20   *Franklin, supra,* at 819 (STEVENS, J., concurring in part and concurring in
21   judgment).

22   The allocation of funds from a lump-sum appropriation is another administrative
23   decision traditionally regarded as committed to agency discretion. After all, the
24   very point of a lump-sum appropriation is to give an agency the capacity to adapt
25   to changing circumstances and meet its statutory responsibilities in what it sees as
26   the most effective or desirable way. For this reason, a fundamental principle of
27   appropriations law is that where "Congress merely appropriates lump-sum
28   amounts without statutorily restricting what can be done with those funds, a clear
29   inference arises that it does not intend to impose legally binding restrictions, and
30   indicia in committee reports and other legislative history as to how the funds
31   should or are expected to be spent do not establish any legal requirements on" the
32   agency. *LTV Aerospace Corp.,* 55 Compo Gen. 307, 319 (1975). Put another way, a
33   lump-sum appropriation reflects a congressional recognition that an agency must
34   be allowed "flexibility to shift . . . funds within a particular . . . appropriation
35   account so that" the agency "can make necessary adjustments for 'unforeseen
36   developments'" and "'changing requirements.'" *LTV Aerospace Corp., supra,* at
37   318.

38   Like the decision against instituting enforcement proceedings, then, an agency's
39   allocation of funds from a lump-sum appropriation requires "a complicated
40   balancing of a number of factors which are peculiarly within its expertise": whether
41   its "resources are best spent" on one program or another; whether it "is likely to

1 succeed" in fulfilling its statutory mandate; whether a particular program "best fits
2 the agency's overall policies"; and, "indeed, whether the agency has enough
3 resources" to fund a program "at all." *Heckler,* 470 U.S., at 831. As in *Heckler,* so
4 here, the "agency is far better equipped than the courts to deal with the many
5 variables involved in the proper ordering of its priorities." *Id.,* at 831-832. Of
6 course, an agency is not free simply to disregard statutory responsibilities:
7 Congress may always circumscribe agency discretion to allocate resources by
8 putting restrictions in the operative statutes (though not, as we have seen, just in
9 the legislative history). And, of course, we hardly need to note that an agency's
10 decision to ignore congressional expectations may expose it to grave political
11 consequences. But as long as the agency allocates funds from a lump-sum
12 appropriation to meet permissible statutory objectives, § 701(a)(2) gives the courts
13 no leave to intrude. "[T]o [that] extent," the decision to allocate funds "is
14 committed to agency discretion by law." § 701(a)(2).

15 The Service's decision to discontinue the Program is accordingly unreviewable
16 under § 701(a)(2). As the Court of Appeals recognized, the appropriations Acts for
17 the relevant period do not so much as mention the Program, and both the Snyder
18 Act and the Improvement Act likewise speak about Indian health only in general
19 terms. It is true that the Service repeatedly apprised Congress of the Program's
20 continued operation, but, as we have explained, these representations do not
21 translate through the medium of legislative history into legally binding obligations.
22 The reallocation of agency resources to assist handicapped Indian children
23 nationwide clearly falls within the Service's statutory mandate to provide health
24 care to Indian people, and respondents, indeed, do not seriously contend
25 otherwise. The decision to terminate the Program was committed to the Service's
26 discretion.

27 The Court of Appeals saw a separate limitation on the Service's discretion in the
28 special trust relationship existing between Indian people and the Federal
29 Government. * * * Whatever the contours of that relationship, though, it could not
30 limit the Service's discretion to reorder its priorities from serving a subgroup of
31 beneficiaries to serving the broader class of all Indians nationwide.

32 One final note: although respondents claimed in the District Court that the
33 Service's termination of the Program violated their rights under the Fifth
34 Amendment's Due Process Clause, that court expressly declined to address
35 respondents' constitutional arguments, as did the Court of Appeals. Thus, while
36 the APA contemplates, in the absence of a clear expression of contrary
37 congressional intent, that judicial review will be available for colorable
38 constitutional claims, see *Webster,* 486 U.S., at 603-604, the record at this stage
39 does not allow mature consideration of constitutional issues, which we leave for
40 the Court of Appeals on remand.

1       * * *

2                                    IV

3   The judgment of the Court of Appeals is reversed, and the case is remanded for
4   further proceedings consistent with this opinion.

5   *It is so ordered.*

6

## C. Final Agency Action

8

9    Under 5 U.S.C. § 702, judicial review is available for "[a]gency action made
10   reviewable by statute and final agency action for which there is no other adequate
11   remedy in a court." "Agency action" is defined in 5 U.S.C. § 551 to include "the
12   whole or a part of an agency rule, order, license, sanction, relief, or the equivalent
13   or denial thereof, or failure to act."

14   The cases in this section address two main questions: under what circumstances is
15   "failure to act" reviewable? And what does it mean for agency action to be "final"?

16

### Dalton v. Specter

18   511 U.S. 462

19   May 23, 1994

20   CHIEF JUSTICE REHNQUIST delivered the opinion of the Court.

21   Respondents sought to enjoin the Secretary of Defense (Secretary) from carrying
22   out a decision by the President to close the Philadelphia Naval Shipyard. This
23   decision was made pursuant to the Defense Base Closure and Realignment Act of
24   1990. The Court of Appeals held that judicial review of the decision was available
25   to ensure that various participants in the selection process had complied with
26   procedural mandates specified by Congress. We hold that such review is not
27   available.

28   The decision to close the shipyard was the end result of an elaborate selection
29   process prescribed by the 1990 Act. Designed "to provide a fair process that will
30   result in the timely closure and realignment of military installations inside the
31   United States," § 2901(b), the Act provides for three successive rounds of base
32   closings—in 1991, 1993, and 1995, § 2903(c)(1). For each round, the Secretary must

1 prepare closure and realignment recommendations, based on selection criteria he
2 establishes after notice and an opportunity for public comment.

3 The Secretary submits his recommendations to Congress and to the Defense Base
4 Closure and Realignment Commission (Commission), an independent body whose
5 eight members are appointed by the President, with the advice and consent of the
6 Senate. The Commission must then hold public hearings and prepare a report,
7 containing both an assessment of the Secretary's recommendations and the
8 Commission's own recommendations for base closures and realignments. Within
9 roughly three months of receiving the Secretary's recommendations, the
10 Commission has to submit its report to the President.

11 Within two weeks of receiving the Commission's report, the President must decide
12 whether to approve or disapprove, in their entirety, the Commission's
13 recommendations. If the President disapproves, the Commission has roughly one
14 month to prepare a new report and submit it to the President. If the President again
15 disapproves, no bases may be closed that year under the Act. If the President
16 approves the initial or revised recommendations, the President must submit the
17 recommendations, along with his certification of approval, to Congress. Congress
18 may, within 45 days of receiving the President's certification (or by the date
19 Congress adjourns for the session, whichever is earlier), enact a joint resolution of
20 disapproval. If such a resolution is passed, the Secretary may not carry out any
21 closures pursuant to the Act; if such a resolution is not passed, the Secretary must
22 close all military installations recommended for closure by the Commission.

23 In April 1991, the Secretary recommended the closure or realignment of a number
24 of military installations, including the Philadelphia Naval Shipyard. After holding
25 public hearings in Washington, D. C., and Philadelphia, the Commission
26 recommended closure or realignment of 82 bases. The Commission did not concur
27 in all of the Secretary's recommendations, but it agreed that the Philadelphia Naval
28 Shipyard should be closed. In July 1991, President Bush approved the
29 Commission's recommendations, and the House of Representatives rejected a
30 proposed joint resolution of disapproval by a vote of 364 to 60.

31 Two days before the President submitted his certification of approval to Congress,
32 respondents filed this action under the Administrative Procedure Act (APA) and
33 the 1990 Act. Their complaint contained three counts, two of which remain at
34 issue. Count I alleged that the Secretaries of Navy and Defense violated substantive
35 and procedural requirements of the 1990 Act in recommending closure of the
36 Philadelphia Naval Shipyard. Count II made similar allegations regarding the
37 Commission's recommendations to the President, asserting specifically that, inter
38 alia, the Commission used improper criteria, failed to place certain information in
39 the record until after the close of public hearings, and held closed meetings with
40 the Navy.

1  The United States District Court for the Eastern District of Pennsylvania dismissed
2  the complaint in its entirety, on the alternative grounds that the 1990 Act itself
3  precluded judicial review and that the political question doctrine foreclosed
4  judicial intervention. A divided panel of the United States Court of Appeals for the
5  Third Circuit affirmed in part and reversed in part. The Court of Appeals first
6  acknowledged that the actions challenged by respondents were not typical of the
7  "agency actions" reviewed under the APA, because the 1990 Act contemplates joint
8  decisionmaking among the Secretary, Commission, President, and Congress. The
9  Court of Appeals then reasoned that because respondents sought to enjoin the
10 implementation of the President's decision, respondents (who had not named the
11 President as a defendant) were asking the Court of Appeals "to review a
12 presidential decision." The Court of Appeals decided that there could be judicial
13 review of the President's decision because the "actions of the President have never
14 been considered immune from judicial review solely because they were taken by
15 the President." It held that certain procedural claims, such as respondents' claim
16 that the Secretary failed to transmit to the Commission all of the information he
17 used in making his recommendations, and their claim that the Commission did not
18 hold public hearings as required by the Act, were thus reviewable. The dissenting
19 judge took the view that the 1990 Act precluded judicial review of all statutory
20 claims, procedural and substantive.

21 Shortly after the Court of Appeals issued its opinion, we decided *Franklin v.*
22 *Massachusetts*, 505 U.S. 788 (1992), in which we addressed the existence of "final
23 agency action" in a suit seeking APA review of the decennial reapportionment of
24 the House of Representatives. The Census Act requires the Secretary of Commerce
25 to submit a census report to the President, who then certifies to Congress the
26 number of Representatives to which each State is entitled pursuant to a statutory
27 formula. We concluded both that the Secretary's report was not "final agency
28 action" reviewable under the APA, and that the APA does not apply to the
29 President. After we rendered our decision in *Franklin*, petitioners sought our
30 review in this case. Because of the similarities between *Franklin* and this case, we
31 granted the petition for certiorari, vacated the judgment of the Court of Appeals,
32 and remanded for further consideration in light of *Franklin*.

33 On remand, the same divided panel of the Court of Appeals adhered to its earlier
34 decision, and held that *Franklin* did not affect the reviewability of respondents'
35 procedural claims. Although apparently recognizing that APA review was
36 unavailable, the Court of Appeals felt that adjudging the President's actions for
37 compliance with the 1990 Act was a "form of constitutional review," and that
38 *Franklin* sanctioned such review. Petitioners again sought our review, and we
39 granted certiorari. We now reverse.

40                                      I

## FINAL AGENCY ACTION

We begin our analysis on common ground with the Court of Appeals. In *Specter II*, that court acknowledged, at least tacitly, that respondents' claims are not reviewable under the APA. A straightforward application of *Franklin* to this case demonstrates why this is so. *Franklin* involved a suit against the President, the Secretary of Commerce, and various public officials, challenging the manner in which seats in the House of Representatives had been apportioned among the States. The plaintiffs challenged the method used by the Secretary of Commerce in preparing her census report, particularly the manner in which she counted federal employees working overseas. The plaintiffs raised claims under both the APA and the Constitution. In reviewing the former, we first sought to determine whether the Secretary's action, in submitting a census report to the President, was "final" for purposes of APA review. (The APA provides for judicial review only of "*final* agency action." 5 U.S.C. § 704 (emphasis added).) Because the President reviewed (and could revise) the Secretary's report, made the apportionment calculations, and submitted the final apportionment report to Congress, we held that the Secretary's report was "not final and therefore not subject to review." 505 U.S., at 798.

We next held that the President's actions were not reviewable under the APA, because the President is not an "agency" within the meaning of the APA. *Id.*, at 801. We thus concluded that the reapportionment determination was not reviewable under the standards of the APA. *Ibid.* In reaching our conclusion, we noted that the "President's actions may still be reviewed for constitutionality." *Ibid.* (citing *Youngstown Sheet & Tube Co. v. Sawyer*, 343 U.S. 579 (1952), and *Panama Refining Co. v. Ryan*, 293 U.S. 388 (1935)).

In this case, respondents brought suit under the APA, alleging that the Secretary and the Commission did not follow the procedural mandates of the 1990 Act. But here, as in *Franklin*, the prerequisite to review under the APA—"final agency action"—is lacking. The reports submitted by the Secretary and the Commission, like the report of the Secretary of Commerce in *Franklin*, "carr[y] no direct consequences" for base closings. 505 U.S., at 798. The action that "will directly affect" the military bases, *id.*, at 797, is taken by the President, when he submits his certification of approval to Congress. Accordingly, the Secretary's and Commission's reports serve "more like a tentative recommendation than a final and binding determination." *Id.*, at 798. The reports are, "like the ruling of a subordinate official, not final and therefore not subject to review." *Ibid.* (internal quotation marks and citation omitted). The actions of the President, in turn, are not reviewable under the APA because, as we concluded in *Franklin*, the President is not an "agency." See *id.*, at 800-801.

Respondents contend that the 1990 Act differs significantly from the Census Act at issue in *Franklin*, and that our decision in *Franklin* therefore does not control the question whether the Commission's actions here are final. Respondents appear to

1 argue that the President, under the 1990 Act, has little authority regarding the
2 closure of bases. Consequently, respondents continue, the Commission's report
3 must be regarded as final. This argument ignores the *ratio decidendi* of *Franklin*.

4 First, respondents underestimate the President's authority under the Act, and the
5 importance of his role in the base closure process. Without the President's
6 approval, no bases are closed under the Act; the Act, in turn, does not by its terms
7 circumscribe the President's discretion to approve or disapprove the Commission's
8 report. Second, and more fundamentally, respondents' argument ignores "[t]he
9 core question" for determining finality: "whether the agency has completed its
10 decision-making process, and whether the result of that process is one that will
11 directly affect the parties." *Franklin*, 505 U.S. at 799. That the President cannot
12 pick and choose among bases, and must accept or reject the entire package offered
13 by the Commission, is immaterial. What is crucial is the fact that "[t]he President,
14 not the [Commission], takes the final action that affects" the military installations.
15 Accordingly, we hold that the decisions made pursuant to the 1990 Act are not
16 reviewable under the APA.

17 Although respondents apparently sought review exclusively under the APA, the
18 Court of Appeals nevertheless sought to determine whether non-APA review,
19 based on either common law or constitutional principles, was available. It focused,
20 moreover, on whether the President's actions under the 1990 Act were reviewable,
21 even though respondents did not name the President as a defendant. The Court of
22 Appeals reasoned that because respondents sought to enjoin the implementation
23 of the President's decision, the legality of that decision would determine whether
24 an injunction should issue. In this rather curious fashion, the case was transmuted
25 into one concerning the reviewability of Presidential decisions.

26 II

27 Seizing upon our statement in *Franklin* that Presidential decisions are reviewable
28 for constitutionality, the Court of Appeals asserted that "there is a constitutional
29 aspect to the exercise of judicial review in this case—an aspect grounded in the
30 separation of powers doctrine." It reasoned, relying primarily on *Youngstown*
31 *Sheet & Tube Co. v. Sawyer*, 343 U.S. 579 (1952), that whenever the President acts
32 in excess of his statutory authority, he also violates the constitutional separation-
33 of-powers doctrine. Thus, judicial review must be available to determine whether
34 the President has statutory authority "for whatever action" he takes. In terms of
35 this case, the Court of Appeals concluded that the President's statutory authority
36 to close and realign bases would be lacking if the Secretary and Commission
37 violated the procedural requirements of the Act in formulating their
38 recommendations.

1 Accepting for purposes of decision here the propriety of examining the President's
2 actions, we nonetheless believe that the Court of Appeals' analysis is flawed. Our
3 cases do not support the proposition that every action by the President, or by
4 another executive official, in excess of his statutory authority is *ipso facto* in
5 violation of the Constitution. * * *

6 * * *

7 * * * [C]laims simply alleging that the President has exceeded his statutory
8 authority are not "constitutional" claims, subject to judicial review. * * *

9 So the claim raised here is a statutory one: The President is said to have violated
10 the terms of the 1990 Act by accepting procedurally flawed recommendations. The
11 exception identified in *Franklin* for review of constitutional claims thus does not
12 apply in this case. We may assume for the sake of argument that some claims that
13 the President has violated a statutory mandate are judicially reviewable outside the
14 framework of the APA. But longstanding authority holds that such review is not
15 available when the statute in question commits the decision to the discretion of the
16 President.

17 As we stated in *Dakota Central Telephone Co. v. South Dakota ex rel. Payne*, 250
18 U.S. 163, 184 (1919), where a claim

19 "concerns not a want of [Presidential] power, but a mere excess or abuse of
20 discretion in exerting a power given, it is clear that it involves
21 considerations which are beyond the reach of judicial power. This must be
22 since, as this court has often pointed out, the judicial may not invade the
23 legislative or executive departments so as to correct alleged mistakes or
24 wrongs arising from asserted abuse of discretion."

25 In a case analogous to the present one, *Chicago & Southern Air Lines, Inc. v.*
26 *Waterman S. S. Corp.*, 333 U.S. 103 (1948), an airline denied a certificate from the
27 Civil Aeronautics Board to establish an international air route sought judicial
28 review of the denial. Although the Civil Aeronautics Act generally allowed for
29 judicial review of the Board's decisions, and did not explicitly exclude judicial
30 review of decisions involving international routes of domestic airlines, we
31 nonetheless held that review was unavailable.

32 In reasoning pertinent to this case, we first held that the Board's certification was
33 not reviewable because it was not final until approved by the President. We then
34 concluded that the President's decision to approve or disapprove the orders was
35 not reviewable, because "the final orders embody Presidential discretion as to
36 political matters beyond the competence of the courts to adjudicate." See *id.,* at
37 114. We fully recognized that the consequence of our decision was to foreclose
38 judicial review * * * .

* * *

## III

In sum, we hold that the actions of the Secretary and the Commission cannot be reviewed under the APA because they are not "final agency actions." The actions of the President cannot be reviewed under the APA because the President is not an "agency" under that Act. The claim that the President exceeded his authority under the 1990 Act is not a constitutional claim, but a statutory one. Where a statute, such as the 1990 Act, commits decisionmaking to the discretion of the President, judicial review of the President's decision is not available.

Respondents tell us that failure to allow judicial review here would virtually repudiate *Marbury v. Madison*, 5 U.S. 137 (1803), and nearly two centuries of constitutional adjudication. But our conclusion that judicial review is not available for respondents' claim follows from our interpretation of an Act of Congress, by which we and all federal courts are bound. The judicial power of the United States conferred by Article III of the Constitution is upheld just as surely by withholding judicial relief where Congress has permissibly foreclosed it, as it is by granting such relief where authorized by the Constitution or by statute.

The judgment of the Court of Appeals is

*Reversed.*

JUSTICE BLACKMUN, concurring in part and concurring in the judgment. [Omitted.]

JUSTICE SOUTER, with whom JUSTICE BLACKMUN, JUSTICE STEVENS, and JUSTICE GINSBURG join, concurring in Part II and concurring in the judgment. [Omitted.]


# Norton v. Southern Utah Wilderness Alliance

542 U.S. 55 (2004)

June 14, 2004

JUSTICE SCALIA delivered the opinion of the Court.

In this case, we must decide whether the authority of a federal court under the Administrative Procedure Act (APA) to "compel agency action unlawfully withheld or unreasonably delayed," extends to the review of the United States Bureau of Land Management's stewardship of public lands under certain statutory provisions and its own planning documents.

1                                        I

2 Almost half the State of Utah, about 23 million acres, is federal land administered
3 by the Bureau of Land Management (BLM), an agency within the Department of
4 Interior. For nearly 30 years, BLM's management of public lands has been
5 governed by the Federal Land Policy and Management Act of 1976 (FLPMA), which
6 "established a policy in favor of retaining public lands for multiple use
7 management." *Lujan v. National Wildlife Federation,* 497 U.S. 871, 877 (1990).
8 "Multiple use management" is a deceptively simple term that describes the
9 enormously complicated task of striking a balance among the many competing
10 uses to which land can be put, "including, but not limited to, recreation, range,
11 timber, minerals, watershed, wildlife and fish, and [uses serving] natural scenic,
12 scientific and historical values." 43 U.S.C. § 1702(c). A second management goal,
13 "sustained yield," requires BLM to control depleting uses over time, so as to ensure
14 a high level of valuable uses in the future. § 1702(h). To these ends, FLPMA
15 establishes a dual regime of inventory and planning. Sections 1711 and 1712,
16 respectively, provide for a comprehensive, ongoing inventory of federal lands, and
17 for a land use planning process that "project[s]" "present and future use," §
18 1701(a)(2), given the lands' inventoried characteristics.

19 Of course not all uses are compatible. Congress made the judgment that some
20 lands should be set aside as wilderness at the expense of commercial and
21 recreational uses. A pre-FLPMA enactment, the Wilderness Act of 1964, 78 Stat.
22 890, provides that designated wilderness areas, subject to certain exceptions,
23 "shall [have] no commercial enterprise and no permanent road," no motorized
24 vehicles, and no manmade structures. 16 U.S.C. § 1133(c). The designation of a
25 wilderness area can be made only by Act of Congress, see 43 U.S.C. § 1782(b).

26 Pursuant to § 1782, the Secretary of the Interior has identified so-called
27 "wilderness study areas" (WSAs), roadless lands of 5,000 acres or more that
28 possess "wilderness characteristics," as determined in the Secretary's land
29 inventory. § 1782(a); see 16 U.S.C. § 1131(c). As the name suggests, WSAs (as well
30 as certain wild lands identified prior to the passage of FLPMA) have been subjected
31 to further examination and public comment in order to evaluate their suitability
32 for designation as wilderness. In 1991, out of 3.3 million acres in Utah that had
33 been identified for study, 2 million were recommended as suitable for wilderness
34 designation. 1 U.S. Dept. of Interior, BLM, Utah Statewide Wilderness Study
35 Report 3 (Oct. 1991). This recommendation was forwarded to Congress, which has
36 not yet acted upon it. Until Congress acts one way or the other, FLPMA provides
37 that "the Secretary shall continue to manage such lands . . . in a manner so as not
38 to impair the suitability of such areas for preservation as wilderness." 43 U.S.C. §
39 1782(c). This nonimpairment mandate applies to all WSAs identified under § 1782,
40 including lands considered unsuitable by the Secretary.

1   Aside from identification of WSAs, the main tool that BLM employs to balance
2   wilderness protection against other uses is a land use plan—what BLM regulations
3   call a "resource management plan." 43 CFR § 1601.0–5(k) (2003). Land use plans,
4   adopted after notice and comment, are "designed to guide and control future
5   management actions," § 1601.0–2. See 43 U.S. C. § 1712; 43 CFR § 1610.2 (2003).
6   Generally, a land use plan describes, for a particular area, allowable uses, goals for
7   future condition of the land, and specific next steps. § 1601.0–5(k). Under FLPMA,
8   "[t]he Secretary shall manage the public lands under principles of multiple use and
9   sustained yield, in accordance with the land use plans . . . when they are available."
10  43 U.S.C. §1732(a).

11  Protection of wilderness has come into increasing conflict with another element
12  of multiple use, recreational use of so-called off-road vehicles (ORVs), which
13  include vehicles primarily designed for off-road use, such as lightweight, four-
14  wheel "all-terrain vehicles," and vehicles capable of such use, such as sport utility
15  vehicles. See 43 CFR §8340.0–5(a) (2003). * * * The use of ORVs on federal land
16  has negative environmental consequences, including soil disruption and
17  compaction, harassment of animals, and annoyance of wilderness lovers. Thus,
18  BLM faces a classic land use dilemma of sharply inconsistent uses, in a context of
19  scarce resources and congressional silence with respect to wilderness designation.

20  In 1999, respondents Southern Utah Wilderness Alliance and other organizations
21  (collectively SUWA) filed this action in the United States District Court for Utah
22  against petitioners BLM, its Director, and the Secretary. In its second amended
23  complaint, SUWA sought declaratory and injunctive relief for BLM's failure to act
24  to protect public lands in Utah from damage caused by ORV use. SUWA made
25  three claims that are relevant here: (1) that BLM had violated its nonimpairment
26  obligation under § 1782(a) by allowing degradation in certain WSAs; (2) that BLM
27  had failed to implement provisions in its land use plans relating to ORV use; (3)
28  that BLM had failed to take a "hard look" at whether, pursuant to the National
29  Environmental Policy Act of 1969 (NEPA), 83 Stat. 852, 42 U.S.C. § 4321 *et seq.*, it
30  should undertake supplemental environmental analyses for areas in which ORV
31  use had increased. SUWA contended that it could sue to remedy these three
32  failures to act pursuant to the APA's provision of a cause of action to "compel
33  agency action unlawfully withheld or unreasonably delayed." 5 U.S.C. § 706(1).

34  The District Court entered a dismissal with respect to the three claims. A divided
35  panel of the Tenth Circuit reversed. The majority acknowledged that under
36  §706(1), "federal courts may order agencies to act only where the agency fails to
37  carry out a mandatory, nondiscretionary duty." It concluded, however, that BLM's
38  nonimpairment obligation was just such a duty, and therefore BLM could be
39  compelled to comply. Under similar reasoning, it reversed the dismissal with

1 respect to the land use plan claim; and likewise reversed dismissal of the NEPA
2 claim. We granted certiorari.

3 II

4 All three claims at issue here involve assertions that BLM failed to take action with
5 respect to ORV use that it was required to take. Failures to act are sometimes
6 remediable under the APA, but not always. We begin by considering what limits
7 the APA places upon judicial review of agency inaction.

8 The APA authorizes suit by "[a] person suffering legal wrong because of agency
9 action, or adversely affected or aggrieved by agency action within the meaning of a
10 relevant statute." 5 U.S.C. §702. Where no other statute provides a private right of
11 action, the "agency action" complained of must be *final* agency action." § 704
12 (emphasis added). "Agency action" is defined in § 551(13) to include "the whole or
13 a part of an agency rule, order, license, sanction, relief, or the equivalent or denial
14 thereof, *or failure to act.*" (Emphasis added.) The APA provides relief for a failure
15 to act in § 706(1): "The reviewing court shall . . . compel agency action unlawfully
16 withheld or unreasonably delayed."

17 Sections 702, 704, and 706(1) all insist upon an "agency action," either as the
18 action complained of (in §§ 702 and 704) or as the action to be compelled (in §
19 706(1)). The definition of that term begins with a list of five categories of decisions
20 made or outcomes implemented by an agency—"agency rule, order, license,
21 sanction [or] relief." § 551(13). All of those categories involve circumscribed,
22 discrete agency actions, as their definitions make clear: "an agency statement of
23 . . . future effect designed to implement, interpret, or prescribe law or policy"
24 (rule); "a final disposition . . . in a matter other than rule making" (order); a
25 "permit . . . or other form of permission" (license); a "prohibition . . . or taking [of]
26 other compulsory or restrictive action" (sanction); or a "grant of money, assistance,
27 license, authority," etc., or "recognition of a claim, right, immunity," etc., or "taking
28 of other action on the application or petition of, and beneficial to, a person" (relief).
29 §§ 551(4), (6), (8), (10), (11).

30 The terms following those five categories of agency action are not defined in the
31 APA: "or the equivalent or denial thereof, or failure to act." § 551(13). But an
32 "equivalent . . . thereof" must also be discrete (or it would not be equivalent), and
33 a "denial thereof" must be the denial of a discrete listed action (and perhaps denial
34 of a discrete equivalent).

35 The final term in the definition, "failure to act," is in our view properly understood
36 as a failure to take an *agency action*—that is, a failure to take one of the agency
37 actions (including their equivalents) earlier defined in § 551(13). Moreover, even
38 without this equation of "act" with "agency action" the interpretive canon of
39 *ejusdem generis* would attribute to the last item ("failure to act") the same
674

1  characteristic of discreteness shared by all the preceding items. A "failure to act" is
2  not the same thing as a "denial." The latter is the agency's act of saying no to a
3  request; the former is simply the omission of an action without formally rejecting
4  a request—for example, the failure to promulgate a rule or take some decision by a
5  statutory deadline. The important point is that a "failure to act" is properly
6  understood to be limited, as are the other items in § 551(13), to a *discrete* action.

7  A second point central to the analysis of the present case is that the only agency
8  action that can be compelled under the APA is action legally *required*. This
9  limitation appears in § 706(1)'s authorization for courts to "compel agency
10 action *unlawfully* withheld." In this regard the APA carried forward the traditional
11 practice prior to its passage, when judicial review was achieved through use of the
12 so-called prerogative writs—principally writs of mandamus under the All Writs
13 Act, now codified at 28 U.S.C. § 1651(a). The mandamus remedy was normally
14 limited to enforcement of "a specific, unequivocal command," *ICC v. New York, N.*
15 *H. & H. R. Co.*, 287 U.S. 178, 204 (1932), the ordering of a "'precise, definite act . . .
16 about which [an official] had no discretion whatever,'" *United States ex rel. Dunlap*
17 *v. Black*, 128 U.S. 40, 46 (1888) (quoting *Kendall* v. *United States ex rel. Stokes*, 12
18 Pet. 524, 613 (1838)). As described in the Attorney General's Manual on the APA,
19 a document whose reasoning we have often found persuasive, § 706(1) empowers
20 a court only to compel an agency "to perform a ministerial or non-discretionary
21 act," or "to take action upon a matter, without directing *how* it shall act." Attorney
22 General's Manual on the Administrative Procedure Act 108 (1947) (emphasis
23 added).

24 Thus, a claim under § 706(1) can proceed only where a plaintiff asserts that an
25 agency failed to take a *discrete* agency action that it is *required to take*. These
26 limitations rule out several kinds of challenges. The limitation to discrete agency
27 action precludes the kind of broad programmatic attack we rejected in *Lujan v.*
28 *National Wildlife Federation*, 497 U.S. 871 (1990). There we considered a
29 challenge to BLM's land withdrawal review program, couched as unlawful agency
30 "action" that the plaintiffs wished to have "set aside" under §706(2). *Id.*, at 879.
31 We concluded that the program was not an "agency action":

32    "[R]espondent cannot seek *wholesale* improvement of this program by
33    court decree, rather than in the offices of the Department or the halls of
34    Congress, where programmatic improvements are normally made. Under
35    the terms of the APA, respondent must direct its attack against some
36    particular 'agency action' that causes it harm."

37 *Id.*, at 891 (emphasis in original).

38                                        * * *

1  The limitation to *required* agency action rules out judicial direction of even
2  discrete agency action that is not demanded by law (which includes, of course,
3  agency regulations that have the force of law). Thus, when an agency is compelled
4  by law to act within a certain time period, but the manner of its action is left to the
5  agency's discretion, a court can compel the agency to act, but has no power to
6  specify what the action must be. * * *

7                                    III

8                                    A

9  With these principles in mind, we turn to SUWA's first claim, that by permitting
10 ORV use in certain WSAs, BLM violated its mandate to "continue to manage
11 [WSAs] ... in a manner so as not to impair the suitability of such areas for
12 preservation as wilderness," 43 U.S.C. § 1782(c). SUWA relies not only upon §
13 1782(c) but also upon a provision of BLM's Interim Management Policy for Lands
14 Under Wilderness Review, which interprets the nonimpairment mandate to
15 require BLM to manage WSAs so as to prevent them from being "degraded so far,
16 compared with the area's values for other purposes, as to significantly constrain
17 the Congress's prerogative to either designate [it] as wilderness or release it for
18 other uses."

19 Section 1782(c) is mandatory as to the object to be achieved, but it leaves BLM a
20 great deal of discretion in deciding how to achieve it. It assuredly does not
21 mandate, with the clarity necessary to support judicial action under §706(1), the
22 total exclusion of ORV use.

23 SUWA argues that § 1782 *does* contain a categorical imperative, namely the
24 command to comply with the nonimpairment mandate. It contends that a federal
25 court could simply enter a general order compelling compliance with that
26 mandate, without suggesting any particular manner of compliance. * * *

27 The principal purpose of the APA limitations we have discussed—and of the
28 traditional limitations upon mandamus from which they were derived—is to
29 protect agencies from undue judicial interference with their lawful discretion, and
30 to avoid judicial entanglement in abstract policy disagreements which courts lack
31 both expertise and information to resolve. If courts were empowered to enter
32 general orders compelling compliance with broad statutory mandates, they would
33 necessarily be empowered, as well, to determine whether compliance was
34 achieved—which would mean that it would ultimately become the task of the
35 supervising court, rather than the agency, to work out compliance with the broad
36 statutory mandate, injecting the judge into day-to-day agency management. To
37 take just a few examples from federal resources management, a plaintiff might
38 allege that the Secretary had failed to "manage wild free-roaming horses and
39 burros in a manner that is designed to achieve and maintain a thriving natural

676

1   ecological balance," or to "manage the [New Orleans Jazz National] [H]istorical
2   [P]ark in such a manner as will preserve and perpetuate knowledge and
3   understanding of the history of jazz," or to "manage the [Steens Mountain]
4   Cooperative Management and Protection Area for the benefit of present and future
5   generations." 16 U.S.C. §§ 1333(a), 410bbb–2(a)(1), 460nnn–12(b). The prospect
6   of pervasive oversight by federal courts over the manner and pace of agency
7   compliance with such congressional directives is not contemplated by the APA.

8                                         B

9   SUWA's second claim is that BLM failed to comply with certain provisions in its
10  land use plans, thus contravening the requirement that "[t]he Secretary shall
11  manage the public lands . . . in accordance with the land use plans . . . when they
12  are available." 43 U.S.C. § 1732(a); see also 43 CFR § 1610.5–3(a) (2003) ("All
13  future resource management authorizations and actions . . . and subsequent more
14  detailed or specific planning, shall conform to the approved plan"). The relevant
15  count in SUWA's second amended complaint alleged that BLM had violated a
16  variety of commitments in its land use plans, but over the course of the litigation
17  these have been reduced to two, one relating to the 1991 resource management
18  plan for the San Rafael area, and the other to various aspects of the 1990 ORV
19  implementation plan for the Henry Mountains area.

20  The actions contemplated by the first of these alleged commitments (completion
21  of a route designation plan in the San Rafael area), and by one aspect of the second
22  (creation of "use supervision files" for designated areas in the Henry Mountains
23  area) have already been completed, and these claims are therefore moot. There
24  remains the claim, with respect to the Henry Mountains plan, that "in light of
25  damage from ORVs in the Factory Butte area," a sub-area of Henry Mountains
26  open to ORV use, "the [plan] obligated BLM to conduct an intensive ORV
27  monitoring program." This claim is based upon the plan's statement that the
28  Factory Butte area "will be monitored and closed if warranted." SUWA does not
29  contest BLM's assertion in the court below that informal monitoring has taken
30  place for some years, but it demands continuing implementation of a monitoring
31  *program.* * * * . SUWA acknowledges that a monitoring program has recently been
32  *commenced.* In light, however, of the continuing action that existence of a
33  "program" contemplates, and in light of BLM's contention that the program cannot
34  be compelled under § 706(1), this claim cannot be considered moot.

35  The statutory directive that BLM manage "in accordance with" land use plans, and
36  the regulatory requirement that authorizations and actions "conform to" those
37  plans, prevent BLM from taking actions inconsistent with the provisions of a land
38  use plan. Unless and until the plan is amended, such actions can be set aside as
39  contrary to law pursuant to 5 U.S.C. § 706(2). The claim presently under
40  discussion, however, would have us go further, and conclude that a statement in a

1    plan that BLM "will" take this, that, or the other action, is a binding commitment
2    that can be compelled under § 706(1). In our view it is not—at least absent clear
3    indication of binding commitment in the terms of the plan.

4    FLPMA describes land use plans as tools by which "present and future use is
5    *projected.*" 43 U.S.C. § 1701(a)(2) (emphasis added). The implementing
6    regulations make clear that land use plans are a preliminary step in the overall
7    process of managing public lands—"designed to guide and control future
8    management actions and the development of subsequent, more detailed and
9    limited scope plans for resources and uses." 43 CFR § 1601.0–2 (2003). The statute
10    and regulations confirm that a land use plan is not ordinarily the medium for
11    affirmative decisions that implement the agency's "project[ions]." Title 43 U.S.C. §
12    1712(e) provides that "[t]he Secretary may issue management decisions to
13    implement land use plans"—the decisions, that is, are distinct from the plan itself.
14    Picking up the same theme, the regulation defining a land use plan declares that a
15    plan "is not a final implementation decision on actions which require further
16    specific plans, process steps, or decisions under specific provisions of law and
17    regulations." 43 CFR § 1601.0–5(k) (2003). * * *

18                                        * * *

19    Quite unlike a specific statutory command requiring an agency to promulgate
20    regulations by a certain date, a land use plan is generally a statement of priorities;
21    it guides and constrains actions, but does not (at least in the usual case) prescribe
22    them. It would be unreasonable to think that either Congress or the agency
23    intended otherwise, since land use plans nationwide would commit the agency to
24    actions far in the future, for which funds have not yet been appropriated. Some
25    plans make explicit that implementation of their programmatic content is subject
26    to budgetary constraints. While the Henry Mountains plan does not contain such
27    a specification, we think it must reasonably be implied. A statement by BLM about
28    what it plans to do, at some point, provided it has the funds and there are not more
29    pressing priorities, cannot be plucked out of context and made a basis for suit
30    under § 706(1).

31    Of course, an action called for in a plan may be compelled when the plan merely
32    reiterates duties the agency is already obligated to perform, or perhaps when
33    language in the plan itself creates a commitment binding on the agency. But
34    allowing general enforcement of plan terms would lead to pervasive interference
35    with BLM's own ordering of priorities. * * *

36    We therefore hold that the Henry Mountains plan's statements to the effect that
37    BLM will conduct "use supervision and monitoring" in designated areas—like
38    other "will do" projections of agency action set forth in land use plans—are not a
39    legally binding commitment enforceable under § 706(1). That being so, we find it

678

1  unnecessary to consider whether the action envisioned by the statements is
2  sufficiently discrete to be amenable to compulsion under the APA.

3  * * *

4  The judgment of the Court of Appeals is reversed, and the case is remanded for
5  further proceedings consistent with this opinion.

6  It is so ordered.

7

## 8  United States Army Corps of Engineers v. Hawkes Co., Inc.

9  578 U.S. ___ (2016)

10  May 31, 2016

11  CHIEF JUSTICE ROBERTS delivered the opinion of the Court.

12  The Clean Water Act regulates the discharge of pollutants into "the waters of the
13  United States." Because it can be difficult to determine whether a particular parcel
14  of property contains such waters, the U.S. Army Corps of Engineers will issue to
15  property owners an "approved jurisdictional determination" stating the agency's
16  definitive view on that matter. The question presented is whether that
17  determination is final agency action judicially reviewable under the Administrative
18  Procedure Act.

19  I

20  A

21  The Clean Water Act prohibits "the discharge of any pollutant" without a permit
22  into "navigable waters," which it defines, in turn, as "the waters of the United
23  States." During the time period relevant to this case, the U.S. Army Corps of
24  Engineers defined the waters of the United States to include land areas
25  occasionally or regularly saturated with water—such as "mudflats, sandflats,
26  wetlands, sloughs, prairie potholes, wet meadows, [and] playa lakes"—the "use,
27  degradation or destruction of which could affect interstate or foreign commerce."
28  33 CFR §328.3(a)(3) (2012). The Corps has applied that definition to assert
29  jurisdiction over "270-to-300 million acres of swampy lands in the United States—
30  including half of Alaska and an area the size of California in the lower 48
31  States." *Rapanos v. United States*, 547 U.S. 715, 722 (2006) (plurality opinion).

32  It is often difficult to determine whether a particular piece of property contains
33  waters of the United States, but there are important consequences if it does. The
34  Clean Water Act imposes substantial criminal and civil penalties for discharging

1 any pollutant into waters covered by the Act without a permit from the Corps. The
2 costs of obtaining such a permit are significant. For a specialized "individual"
3 permit of the sort at issue in this case, for example, one study found that the
4 average applicant "spends 788 days and $271,596 in completing the process,"
5 without "counting costs of mitigation or design changes."*Rapanos*, 547 U.S., at
6 721. Even more readily available "general" permits took applicants, on average, 313
7 days and $28,915 to complete. *Ibid.* See generally 33 CFR §323.2(h) (limiting
8 "general" permits to activities that "cause only minimal individual and cumulative
9 environmental impacts").

10 The Corps specifies whether particular property contains "waters of the United
11 States" by issuing "jurisdictional determinations" (JDs) on a case-by-case basis.
12 §331.2. JDs come in two varieties: "preliminary" and "approved." *Ibid.* While
13 preliminary JDs merely advise a property owner "that there *may* be waters of the
14 United States on a parcel," approved JDs definitively "stat[e] the presence or
15 absence" of such waters. *Ibid.* (emphasis added). Unlike preliminary JDs,
16 approved JDs can be administratively appealed and are defined by regulation to
17 "constitute a Corps final agency action." §§320.1(a)(6), 331.2. They are binding for
18 five years on both the Corps and the Environmental Protection Agency, which
19 share authority to enforce the Clean Water Act. See 33 U.S.C. §§ 1319, 1344(s); 33
20 CFR pt. 331, App. C; EPA, Memorandum of Agreement: Exemptions Under Section
21 404(F) of the Clean Water Act § VI–A (1989) (Memorandum of Agreement).

22 B

23 Respondents are three companies engaged in mining peat in Marshall County,
24 Minnesota. Peat is an organic material that forms in waterlogged grounds, such as
25 wetlands and bogs. It is widely used for soil improvement and burned as fuel. It
26 can also be used to provide structural support and moisture for smooth, stable
27 greens that leave golfers with no one to blame but themselves for errant putts. At
28 the same time, peat mining can have significant environmental and ecological
29 impacts, and therefore is regulated by both federal and state environmental
30 protection agencies.

31 Respondents own a 530-acre tract near their existing mining operations. The tract
32 includes wetlands, which respondents believe contain sufficient high quality peat,
33 suitable for use in golf greens, to extend their mining operations for 10 to 15 years.

34 In December 2010, respondents applied to the Corps for a Section 404 permit for
35 the property. A Section 404 permit authorizes "the discharge of dredged or fill
36 material into the navigable waters at specified disposal sites." 33 U.S.C. § 1344(a).
37 Over the course of several communications with respondents, Corps officials
38 signaled that the permitting process would be very expensive and take years to
39 complete. The Corps also advised respondents that, if they wished to pursue their

1 application, they would have to submit numerous assessments of various features
2 of the property, which respondents estimate would cost more than $100,000.

3 In February 2012, in connection with the permitting process, the Corps issued an
4 approved JD stating that the property contained "water of the United States"
5 because its wetlands had a "significant nexus" to the Red River of the North,
6 located some 120 miles away. Respondents appealed the JD to the Corps'
7 Mississippi Valley Division Commander, who remanded for further factfinding. On
8 remand, the Corps reaffirmed its original conclusion and issued a revised JD to
9 that effect.

10 Respondents then sought judicial review of the revised JD under the
11 Administrative Procedure Act (APA). The District Court dismissed for want of
12 subject matter jurisdiction, holding that the revised JD was not "final agency action
13 for which there is no other adequate remedy in a court," as required by the APA
14 prior to judicial review. The Court of Appeals for the Eighth Circuit reversed, and
15 we granted certiorari.

16 II

17 The Corps contends that the revised JD is not "final agency action" and that, even
18 if it were, there are adequate alternatives for challenging it in court. We disagree
19 at both turns.

20 A

21 In *Bennett v. Spear*, 520 U.S. 154 (1997), we distilled from our precedents two
22 conditions that generally must be satisfied for agency action to be "final" under the
23 APA. "First, the action must mark the consummation of the agency's
24 decisionmaking process—it must not be of a merely tentative or interlocutory
25 nature. And second, the action must be one by which rights or obligations have
26 been determined, or from which legal consequences will flow." *Id.,* at 177–178
27 (internal quotation marks and citation omitted).

28 The Corps does not dispute that an approved JD satisfies the first *Bennett*
29 condition. Unlike preliminary JDs—which are "advisory in nature" and simply
30 indicate that "there may be waters of the United States" on a parcel of property, 33
31 CFR §331.2—an approved JD clearly "mark[s] the consummation" of the Corps'
32 decisionmaking process on that question, *Bennett,* 520 U.S., at 178 (internal
33 quotation marks omitted). It is issued after extensive factfinding by the Corps
34 regarding the physical and hydrological characteristics of the property and is
35 typically not revisited if the permitting process moves forward. Indeed, the Corps
36 itself describes approved JDs as "final agency action," see 33 CFR §320.1(a)(6),
37 and specifies that an approved JD "will remain valid for a period of five years,"

1   Corps, Regulatory Guidance Letter No. 05–02, §1(a), p. 1 (June 14, 2005) (2005
2   Guidance Letter).

3   The Corps may revise an approved JD within the five-year period based on "new
4   information." 2005 Guidance Letter §1(a), at 1. That possibility, however, is a
5   common characteristic of agency action, and does not make an otherwise definitive
6   decision nonfinal. By issuing respondents an approved JD, the Corps for all
7   practical purposes "has ruled definitively" that respondents' property contains
8   jurisdictional waters.

9   The definitive nature of approved JDs also gives rise to "direct and appreciable
10  legal consequences," thereby satisfying the second prong of *Bennett*. 520 U.S., at
11  178. Consider the effect of an approved JD stating that a party's property does *not*
12  contain jurisdictional waters—a "negative" JD, in Corps parlance. As noted, such a
13  JD will generally bind the Corps for five years. Under a longstanding memorandum
14  of agreement between the Corps and EPA, it will also be "binding on the
15  Government and represent the Government's position in any subsequent Federal
16  action or litigation concerning that final determination." Memorandum of
17  Agreement §§IV–C–2, VI–A. A negative JD thus binds the two agencies authorized
18  to bring civil enforcement proceedings under the Clean Water Act, see 33 U.S.C.
19  §1319, creating a five-year safe harbor from such proceedings for a property owner.
20  Additionally, although the property owner may still face a citizen suit under the
21  Act, such a suit—unlike actions brought by the Government—cannot impose civil
22  liability for wholly past violations. See §§1319(d), 1365(a); *Gwaltney of Smithfield,*
23  *Ltd.* v. *Chesapeake Bay Foundation, Inc.*, 484 U.S. 49-59 (1987). In other words,
24  a negative JD both narrows the field of potential plaintiffs and limits the potential
25  liability a landowner faces for discharging pollutants without a permit. Each of
26  those effects is a "legal consequence[ ]" satisfying the second *Bennett* prong. 520
27  U.S., at 178. It follows that affirmative JDs have legal consequences as well: They
28  represent the denial of the safe harbor that negative JDs afford. See 5 U.S.C.
29  §551(13) (defining "agency action" to include an agency "rule, order, license,
30  sanction, relief, or the equivalent," or the "denial thereof"). Because "legal
31  consequences ... flow" from approved JDs, they constitute final agency action.
32  *Bennett*, 520 U.S., at 178 (internal quotation marks omitted).

33  This conclusion tracks the "pragmatic" approach we have long taken to
34  finality. *Abbott Laboratories v. Gardner*, 387 U.S. 136, 149 (1967). For example,
35  in *Frozen Food Express v. United States*, 351 U.S. 40 (1956), we considered the
36  finality of an order specifying which commodities the Interstate Commerce
37  Commission believed were exempt by statute from regulation, and which it
38  believed were not. Although the order "had no authority except to give notice of
39  how the Commission interpreted" the relevant statute, and "would have effect only
40  if and when a particular action was brought against a particular carrier," *Abbott*,

1    387 U.S., at 150, we held that the order was nonetheless immediately reviewable,
2    *Frozen Food*, 351 U.S., at 44, 45. The order, we explained, "warns every carrier,
3    who does not have authority from the Commission to transport those commodities,
4    that it does so at the risk of incurring criminal penalties." *Id.*, at 44. So too here,
5    while no administrative or criminal proceeding can be brought for failure to
6    conform to the approved JD itself, that final agency determination not only
7    deprives respondents of a five-year safe harbor from liability under the Act, but
8    warns that if they discharge pollutants onto their property without obtaining a
9    permit from the Corps, they do so at the risk of significant criminal and civil
10   penalties.

11                                                    B

12   Even if final, an agency action is reviewable under the APA only if there are no
13   adequate alternatives to APA review in court. 5 U.S.C. §704. The Corps contends
14   that respondents have two such alternatives: either discharge fill material without
15   a permit, risking an EPA enforcement action during which they can argue that no
16   permit was required, or apply for a permit and seek judicial review if dissatisfied
17   with the results.

18   Neither alternative is adequate. As we have long held, parties need not await
19   enforcement proceedings before challenging final agency action where such
20   proceedings carry the risk of "serious criminal and civil penalties." *Abbott*, 387
21   U.S., at 153. If respondents discharged fill material without a permit, in the
22   mistaken belief that their property did not contain jurisdictional waters, they
23   would expose themselves to civil penalties of up to $37,500 for each day they
24   violated the Act, to say nothing of potential criminal liability. Respondents need
25   not assume such risks while waiting for EPA to "drop the hammer" in order to have
26   their day in court. *Sackett*, 566 U.S. 120, 127 (2012).

27   Nor is it an adequate alternative to APA review for a landowner to apply for a
28   permit and then seek judicial review in the event of an unfavorable decision. As
29   Corps officials indicated in their discussions with respondents, the permitting
30   process can be arduous, expensive, and long. See *Rapanos*, 547 U.S., at 721
31   (plurality opinion). On top of the standard permit application that respondents
32   were required to submit, see 33 CFR §325.1(d) (detailing contents of permit
33   application), the Corps demanded that they undertake, among other things, a
34   "hydrogeologic assessment of the rich fen system including the mineral/nutrient
35   composition and pH of the groundwater; groundwater flow spatially and vertically;
36   discharge and recharge areas"; a "functional/resource assessment of the site
37   including a vegetation survey and identification of native fen plan communities
38   across the site"; an "inventory of similar wetlands in the general area (watershed),
39   including some analysis of their quality"; and an "inventory of rich fen plant
40   communities that are within sites of High and Outstanding Biodiversity

1 Significance in the area." Respondents estimate that undertaking these analyses
2 alone would cost more than $100,000. And whatever pertinence all this might
3 have to the issuance of a permit, none of it will alter the finality of the approved
4 JD, or affect its suitability for judicial review. The permitting process adds nothing
5 to the JD.

6 The Corps nevertheless argues that Congress made the "evident[ ]" decision in the
7 Clean Water Act that a coverage determination would be made "as part of the
8 permitting process, and that the property owner would obtain any necessary
9 judicial review of that determination at the conclusion of that process." But as the
10 Corps acknowledges, the Clean Water Act makes no reference to standalone
11 jurisdictional determinations, so there is little basis for inferring anything from it
12 concerning the reviewability of such distinct final agency action. * * *

13                                    * * *

14 The judgment of the Court of Appeals for the Eighth Circuit is affirmed.

15 *It is so ordered.*

16 JUSTICE GINSBURG, concurring in part and concurring in the judgment.

17 I join the Court's opinion, save for its reliance upon the Memorandum of
18 Agreement between the Army Corps of Engineers and the Environmental
19 Protection Agency. The Court received scant briefing about this memorandum,
20 and the United States does not share the Court's reading of it. But the JD at issue
21 is "definitive," not "informal" or "tentative," and has "an immediate and practical
22 impact." Accordingly, I agree with the Court that the JD is final.

23 JUSTICE KAGAN, concurring.

24 I join the Court's opinion in full. I write separately to note that for me, unlike for
25 Justice Ginsburg, the memorandum of agreement between the Army Corps of
26 Engineers and the Environmental Protection Agency is central to the disposition
27 of this case. For an agency action to be final, "the action must be one by which
28 rights or obligations have been determined, or from which legal consequences will
29 flow." As the Court states, the memorandum of agreement establishes that
30 jurisdictional determinations (JDs) are "binding on the Government and represent
31 the Government's position in any subsequent Federal action or litigation
32 concerning that final determination." A negative JD thus prevents the Corps and
33 EPA—the two agencies with authority to enforce the Clean Water Act—from
34 bringing a civil action against a property owner for the JD's entire 5-year lifetime.
35 The creation of that safe harbor, which binds the agencies in any subsequent
36 litigation, is a "direct and appreciable legal consequence[ ]" satisfying the second
37 prong of *Bennett*.

1   JUSTICE KENNEDY, with whom JUSTICE THOMAS and JUSTICE ALITO join,
2   concurring. [Omitted.]

3

4   **Air Brake Systems, Inc. v. Mineta**

5   357 F.3d 632 (2004) (6th Cir.)

6   February 11, 2004

7   Before KEITH, MARTIN, and SUTTON, Circuit Judges.

8   SUTTON, J.

9   This case arises from a longstanding dispute between the National Highway Traffic
10  Safety Administration (NHTSA) and Air Brake Systems, Inc. (Air Brake). Air Brake
11  manufactures a "non-electronic" antilock brake system for trucks and trailers,
12  which purports to comply with Federal Motor Vehicle Safety Standard 121, a
13  NHTSA regulation concerning antilock brakes. When an Air Brake customer asked
14  NHTSA whether a vehicle with Air Brake's brake system—the only non-electronic
15  antilock brake system on the market—would comply with Standard 121, NHTSA's
16  Acting Chief Counsel issued two opinion letters stating that the brake system would
17  not satisfy the standard. NHTSA posted the letters on its website (with negative
18  consequences for Air Brake's business), but it did not begin the statutory process
19  for determining whether vehicles carrying such brakes were noncompliant or the
20  statutory process for ordering a recall of vehicles with these brakes.

21  Soon after NHTSA posted the first of these letters on its website, Air Brake filed
22  this action challenging the Chief Counsel's conclusion as well as the Chief Counsel's
23  authority to issue the letter. The district court granted summary judgment in favor
24  of NHTSA, reasoning that interpretive letters issued by NHTSA's Acting Chief
25  Counsel do not constitute "final agency action" subject to judicial review under the
26  Administrative Procedure Act. We agree that the tentative conclusions reached in
27  the letters, which are based in part on Air Brake's representations about its antilock
28  brake system and which NHTSA acknowledges are neither binding on the industry
29  nor entitled to any administrative deference, do not constitute final agency action
30  regarding the meaning of Standard 121 or Air Brake's compliance with that
31  standard. At the same time, however, the letters do reflect final agency action with
32  respect to the distinct question whether the Chief Counsel has authority to issue
33  them, because the practice does not lend itself to further review at the agency level
34  and has legal consequences. Yet because the practice of permitting NHTSA's Chief
35  Counsel to issue advisory opinions in response to inquiries from the public does
36  not exceed the Chief Counsel's authority (and indeed has much to recommend it),
37  we affirm the district court's judgment in favor of the Government.

**FINAL AGENCY ACTION**

1                                                                  I

2 When Congress enacted the National Traffic and Motor Vehicle Safety Act of 1966,
3 80 Stat. 718, 49 U.S.C. § 30101 *et seq.*, it directed the Secretary of Transportation
4 to prescribe motor vehicle safety standards. The Secretary in turn delegated this
5 task to NHTSA. The first Federal Motor Vehicle Safety Standard was promulgated
6 in 1967 and NHTSA has promulgated numerous other standards since then,
7 including Standard 121 (codified at 49 C.F.R. § 571.121), which covers the
8 requirements for air brake systems used in heavy vehicles.

9 In 1995, NHTSA amended Standard 121 to require that trucks, buses and trailers
10 equipped with air brakes have an "antilock brake system." See Standard No. 121,
11 Air Brake Systems, 60 Fed.Reg. 13,216 (Mar. 10, 1995). The standard defines
12 "antilock brake system" as

13     "a portion of a service brake system that automatically controls the degree
14     of rotational wheel slip during braking by:

15     "(1) Sensing the rate of angular rotation of the wheels;

16     "(2) Transmitting signals regarding the rate of wheel angular rotation to
17     one or more controlling devices which interpret those signals and generate
18     responsive controlling output signals; and

19     "(3) Transmitting those controlling signals to one or more modulators
20     which adjust brake actuating forces in response to those signals."

21 49 C.F.R. § 571.121, S4. In accordance with this standard, antilock brakes also
22 must have an electrical circuit capable of signaling a malfunction in the brakes
23 through an external warning light. NHTSA enacted the 1995 amendment amid
24 concerns that only electronic braking systems would satisfy this provision.

25 One company concerned about the impact of the amended standard was Air Brake
26 Systems, which manufactures braking systems installed on trucks and trailers.
27 After devoting ten years to developing a pneumatic antilock brake system for
28 trucks and trailers, Air Brake patented its new brake system—the "MSQR-5000"—
29 in 1992. The MSQR-5000 is a non-electronic brake or, in the words of Air Brake,
30 is a "non-computerized antilock braking system which is a combination differential
31 pressure regulator/quick release valve that is installed at each braking axle into the
32 service air lines centered between the brake chambers." Air Brake initially sold its
33 non-electronic antilock brakes on the retrofit after-market for used trucks and
34 trailers (which is not subject to Standard 121), but not on the original-equipment
35 market for new trucks and trailers (which is subject to Standard 121).

36                                                       \* \* \*

1    In January 2001, Air Brake tried to sell the MSQR-5000 to MAC Trailer
2    Manufacturing, a manufacturer of vehicles subject to Standard 121. Because Air
3    Brake's product was the only non-electronic antilock brake system on the market,
4    MAC Trailer asked NHTSA (orally) whether the device met the requirements of
5    Standard 121. NHTSA responded (also orally) that it did not.

6    A month later, [Air Brake President] William Washington and consultants hired
7    by Air Brake met with NHTSA to explain the operation and features of the MSQR-
8    5000, in an apparent attempt to persuade NHTSA that the braking system
9    complied with the agency's safety standards. During the meeting, NHTSA
10   requested that certain tests be performed on the product and that Air Brake submit
11   the test data to the agency. Air Brake scheduled another meeting with NHTSA for
12   this purpose on June 12, 2001.

13   On June 4, 2001, eight days before the scheduled meeting, NHTSA's Acting Chief
14   Counsel, John Womack, sent a letter to MAC Trailer in response to its earlier oral
15   inquiry and a subsequent written inquiry as to whether the MSQR-5000 satisfied
16   Standard 121. In the letter, the Chief Counsel noted that NHTSA does not pre-
17   approve equipment, and that the applicable statutes make the vehicle
18   manufacturer, not the parts manufacturer, responsible for ensuring compliance
19   with NHTSA's safety standards. Nonetheless, based on NHTSA's review of Air
20   Brake's promotional materials and the "principles involved in [the braking
21   system's] operation," he noted that "the installation of the MSQR-5000 alone
22   would not allow a vehicle to meet [Standard] 121's [antilock brake system]
23   requirement." The Chief Counsel expressed specific concern that (1) "the MSQR-
24   5000 does not seem to have any means of automatically controlling wheel slip
25   during braking by sensing, analyzing, and modulating the rate of angular rotation
26   of the wheel," and (2) "the MSQR-5000 also appears to lack any provision for
27   illuminating a warning light providing notification of an [antilock brake system]
28   malfunction." NHTSA posted the letter on its website.

29   Air Brake met with NHTSA as planned on June 12th. At the meeting NHTSA
30   recommended that Air Brake perform certain tests on the brakes. Air Brake
31   conducted the tests and forwarded the results to NHTSA. At the same time, it asked
32   NHTSA to post a letter from Air Brake's counsel on its website so that Air Brake's
33   views about MSQR-5000 and specifically about the brake system's compliance
34   with Standard 121 could be seen by visitors to NHTSA's website alongside the
35   contrary opinion of NHTSA's Chief Counsel. NHTSA never posted the letter.

36   On August 29, 2001, Air Brake sued Secretary of Transportation Norman Mineta
37   and NHTSA (collectively, NHTSA), challenging the agency's determination that
38   the MSQR-5000 did not comply with Standard 121 and seeking to enjoin NHTSA
39   from continuing to publish the offending letter on its website. The United States
40   District Court for the Eastern District of Michigan denied Air Brake a temporary

1 restraining order, but took Air Brake's motion for a preliminary injunction under
2 consideration and ordered the parties to take the steps necessary for NHTSA to
3 complete its review of Air Brake's product. As a culmination of these steps and as
4 requested by the district court, NHTSA's Acting Chief Counsel issued a letter on
5 December 10, 2001 to Air Brake containing his interpretation and application of
6 Standard 121 to Air Brake's pneumatic brake system. The letter superseded the
7 June 4th letter and essentially reaffirmed the Chief Counsel's conclusion that the
8 MSQR-5000 braking system would not by itself bring a vehicle into compliance
9 with Standard 121.

10 NHTSA then moved for summary judgment, which the district court granted on
11 the ground that neither the June 4th letter nor the December 10th letter issued by
12 the Chief Counsel constituted "final agency action." Because "the letters contain
13 the opinion of NHTSA's acting chief counsel—a subordinate official—that the
14 plaintiff's product 'alone' will not permit a vehicle to comply with [Standard] 121,"
15 the court reasoned that they "represent[ ] the position the Secretary is likely to take
16 if and when proceedings are initiated," not the final action by the Secretary. "More
17 importantly," the court continued, "the Letters do not determine 'rights or
18 obligations' or cause 'legal consequences' to 'flow' [because] [t]he Letters are
19 advisory in nature and have no legal effect." The district court also held that
20 "there is ample authority permitting NHTSA's response to MAC Trailer's inquiry
21 and issuance of the letters was not beyond the authority of the agency." Air Brake
22 appealed the judgment, which we now review de novo.

23                                          II

24                                        * * *

25 Before reaching the merits of either challenge, we must consider whether the
26 federal courts have jurisdiction over them under the right to review created by §
27 10 of the Administrative Procedure Act (APA), 80 Stat. 392, as amended, 5 U.S.C.
28 § 701 *et seq.* In accordance with that provision, federal courts may review two
29 types of agency actions: "[1] Agency action made reviewable by statute and [2] final
30 agency action for which there is no other adequate remedy in a court." 5 U.S.C. §
31 704. In contrast, "[a] preliminary, procedural, or intermediate agency action or
32 ruling [is] not directly reviewable" and may be examined by a federal court only
33 through "review of the final agency action" itself. *Id.* Because no specific statute
34 creates a right to review the agency actions in this case, as the parties agree, the
35 jurisdictional question here is one of statutory interpretation: Do the letters
36 constitute "final" agency action for which no other adequate judicial remedy exists?
37 * * *

38 "As a general matter," the Supreme Court has instructed, "two conditions must be
39 satisfied for agency action to be 'final': First, the action must mark the

688

1  consummation of the agency's decisionmaking process . . . [and] must not be of a
2  tentative or interlocutory nature. And second, the action must be one by which
3  rights or obligations have been determined, or from which legal consequences will
4  flow." *Bennett v. Spear*, 520 U.S. 154, (1997).

5                                   III

6  Air Brake claims that we have jurisdiction to review three distinct actions by the
7  agency: (1) the Chief Counsel's statements (in each letter) that Air Brake's product
8  fails to satisfy the general requirements of Standard 121; (2) the Chief Counsel's
9  legal interpretation (in each letter) of Standard 121's warning-light requirement;
10  and (3) the authority of the Chief Counsel to issue the letters in the first place. As
11  each of these issues presents a distinct finality question, we examine them
12  separately.

13                                   A

14  The essential content of each letter, explaining why Air Brake's product generally
15  does not comply with Standard 121, is not final agency action under § 10 of the
16  APA. First and foremost, "[a]n agency action is not final if it is . . . 'tentative'" in
17  nature. *Franklin v. Massachusetts*, 505 U.S. 788, 797 (1992). And agency letters
18  based on hypothetical facts or facts submitted to the agency, as opposed to fact-
19  findings made by the agency, are classically non-final for this reason. See *Nat'l Res.*
20  *Def. Council v. FAA*, 292 F.3d 875, 882 (D.C.Cir.2002) (holding that an opinion
21  letter issued by the FAA "based on a hypothetical factual situation" presented to
22  the agency by the parties was "not appropriate for review"); *Ass'n of Am. Med.*
23  *Colls. v. United States*, 217 F.3d 770, 780-81 (9th Cir.2000) (holding that a letter
24  from the general counsel of the Department of Health and Human Services was
25  not final where facts remained to be developed).

26  Both letters suffer from this defect. By their terms, they state tentative conclusions
27  based on limited information presented to the agency. For example, the June 4th
28  letter states that it "represents our opinion based on the facts presented in [MAC
29  Trailer's] letter, the attachments provided with [MAC Trailer's] letter and agency
30  review of other data obtained from [Air Brake]." Later, the letter stresses that
31  "NHTSA's view" about the MSQR-5000 is "based on a review of the promotional
32  materials describing the device and the principles involved in its operation." The
33  December 10th letter, too, relies on "materials received or obtained since June 4,
34  as well as those that we had previously obtained," and disclaims any intent to
35  adjudicate factual issues. In this respect, the second letter also expresses an
36  opinion based on "[t]he test data and information provided by [Air Brake]," not
37  based upon any factfinding by the agency.

## FINAL AGENCY ACTION

1   By itself, the conditional nature of the Chief Counsel's advice—conditioned on the
2   untested factual submissions of the parties—suggests that it is non-final and non-
3   reviewable. But the regulatory context in which the issue arises makes that
4   conclusion all the more appropriate. In the world of vehicle safety requirements,
5   fact-specific conclusions about whether a product complies with NHTSA's
6   regulations generally come at the end of a recall proceeding, not before the process
7   for initiating a recall has begun. As the applicable statutes explain, the Secretary
8   generally must follow a carefully-delineated process for reaching a conclusion of
9   non-compliance that has the force of law. * * *

10  Besides being conditional and tentative and besides arising outside of the
11  customary setting for determining safety compliance, the main body of each letter
12  contains a related flaw: "An agency action is not final if it is only 'the ruling of a
13  subordinate official.'" *Franklin*, 505 U.S., at 797. While NHTSA's Chief Counsel
14  has considerable authority over purely legal interpretations of pertinent statutes
15  and regulations, the Secretary has not delegated authority to the Chief Counsel to
16  make final fact-bound determinations of compliance with NHTSA's safety
17  standards. Compare 49 C.F.R. § 501.8(d)(5) (the authority to "[i]ssue
18  authoritative interpretations of the statutes administered by NHTSA and the
19  regulations issued by the agency" is "delegated" to the Chief Counsel), with *id.* §
20  501.7(a)(2) (the authority to "[m]ake final decisions concerning alleged safety-
21  related defects and noncompliance with Federal motor vehicle safety standards" is
22  "reserved to the Administrator"). For this reason as well, the letters do not
23  constitute final agency action with respect to their advice about whether Air
24  Brake's product complies with Standard 121.

25                                          B.

26  A different analysis, but a similar conclusion, applies to the legal interpretation in
27  each letter of Standard 121's warning-light requirement. While the letters in the
28  main address fact-specific issues based upon the materials presented to the agency
29  by the parties requesting the opinion, they also appear to contain a statement of
30  general applicability designed to interpret the law—namely, that Standard 121
31  requires all antilock brake systems, even non-electronic ones, to include a warning
32  light.

33  One cannot lightly dismiss this legal interpretation of Standard 121 as either
34  tentative or as the view of a subordinate agency official. There is nothing
35  provisional about this interpretation of the standard: Either it requires a warning
36  light or it does not. And there is nothing hypothetical or intricately fact dependent
37  about the inquiry: Either Air Brake's product has these features or it does not.
38  Neither are these the views of a subordinate official, at least when it comes to this
39  purely-legal interpretation. The Secretary of Transportation has delegated to
40  NHTSA's Chief Counsel responsibility to "[i]ssue authoritative interpretations of

690

the statutes administered by NHTSA and the regulations [i.e., Safety Standards] issued by the agency." 49 C.F.R. § 501.8(d)(5). So unlike his general take on compliance, the Chief Counsel's views about purely legal questions—does, for example, Standard 121 require a warning light?—may constitute the final word within the agency. Bolstering the point, NHTSA's website states that the Chief Counsel's legal interpretation letters "represent the definitive view of the agency on the question addressed and may be relied upon." In view of the Secretary's delegation of authority to the Chief Counsel over legal issues and in view of NHTSA's public use of that authority through its website, an interpretive letter like this one (or at least partially like this one) may indeed represent the "consummation" of the agency's process as to purely legal questions.

To say that a legal interpretation is final because it is not subject to further review within the agency, however, is not to say that it is "final" in the sense that § 10 of the APA requires it to be. If the interpretation nonetheless (1) does not "determine rights or obligations" or (2) does not have "legal consequences," it remains non-final for purposes of review under the APA. Neither measure of finality is availing to Air Brake here. An agency's determination of "rights or obligations" generally stems from an agency action that is directly binding on the party seeking review, such as an administrative adjudication (like a recall proceeding) or legislative rulemaking, both of which did not happen here.

The harder question is whether the letters, while not directly binding on Air Brake, occasion sufficient "legal consequences" to make them reviewable. One reliable indicator that an agency interpretation still has the requisite legal consequence, we have held, is whether the agency may claim *Chevron* deference for it.

\* \* \*

Air Brake, however, cannot rely upon this principle because the Chief Counsel's legal interpretations have no claim to deference of any sort. For one reason, they are too informal. Congress does not generally expect agencies to make law through general counsel opinion letters. \* \* \*

\* \* \*

### D.

Although the letters do not constitute final agency action with respect to the opinions expressed in them, they do represent final agency action in another respect—namely, as to whether the Chief Counsel has authority to issue advisory opinions in the first instance. In contrast to the contents of the letters, all of the finality factors point to the conclusion that the agency's view regarding the Chief Counsel's authority to issue them is "final" agency action under the APA.

1 First, there is nothing tentative or fact dependent about the authority to issue the
2 letters. The Secretary has delegated this power to the Chief Counsel in concrete and
3 unconditional terms, and the issue is purely a legal one. See 49 C.F.R. §
4 501.8(d)(5) ("The Chief Counsel is delegated authority to . . . [i]ssue authoritative
5 interpretations of the statutes administered by NHTSA and the regulations issued
6 by the agency."). Second, as the head of the Department of Transportation, the
7 Secretary is anything but a subordinate official for these purposes. Third, this
8 decision would receive deference from the federal courts as an interpretation of the
9 agency's regulations under *Seminole Rock*, and (in contrast to the letters) the
10 agency has not disclaimed deference regarding this position. * * *

11 <center>* * *</center>

12 <center>V.</center>

13 For the foregoing reasons, we affirm the judgment of the district court.

14

## D. Ripeness

16 Ripeness is a judge-made doctrine that goes to the timing of judicial review. In the
17 so-called *Toilet Goods Trilogy*, two of whose number you will encounter in this
18 section's reading, the Supreme Court laid out the metes and bounds of ripeness
19 doctrine. If you can understand why did the Court concluded review was available
20 in *Abbott Labs* but not *Toilet Goods*, you are well on your way to understanding
21 ripeness doctrine.

22

### Abbott Laboratories v. Gardner

24 387 U.S. 136 (1967)

25 May 22, 1967

26 MR. JUSTICE HARLAN delivered the opinion of the Court.

27 In 1962, Congress amended the Federal Food, Drug, and Cosmetic Act (52 Stat.
28 1040, as amended by the Drug Amendments of 1962, 76 Stat. 780, 21 U.S.C. § 301
29 *et seq.*), to require manufacturers of prescription drugs to print the "established
30 name" of the drug "prominently and in type at least half as large as that used
31 thereon for any proprietary name or designation for such drug," on labels and
32 other printed material, § 502(e)(1)(B), 21 U.S.C. § 352(e)(1)(B). The "established
33 name" is one designated by the Secretary of Health, Education, and Welfare
34 pursuant to § 502(e)(2) of the Act, 21 U.S.C. § 352(e)(2); the "proprietary name" is
35 usually a trade name under which a particular drug is marketed. The underlying
692

1     purpose of the 1962 amendment was to bring to the attention of doctors and
2     patients the fact that many of the drugs sold under familiar trade names are
3     actually identical to drugs sold under their "established" or less familiar trade
4     names at significantly lower prices. The Commissioner of Food and Drugs,
5     exercising authority delegated to him by the Secretary, published proposed
6     regulations designed to implement the statute, 28 Fed.Reg. 1448. After inviting
7     and considering comments submitted by interested parties, the Commissioner
8     promulgated the following regulation for the "efficient enforcement" of the Act, §
9     701(a), 21 U.S.C. § 371(a):

10     "If the label or labeling of a prescription drug bears a proprietary name or
11     designation for the drug or any ingredient thereof, the established name, if
12     such there be, corresponding to such proprietary name or designation shall
13     accompany each appearance of such proprietary name or designation."

14     21 CFR § 1.104(g)(1). A similar rule was made applicable to advertisements for
15     prescription drugs, 21 CFR § 1.105(b)(1).

16     The present action was brought by a group of 37 individual drug manufacturers
17     and by the Pharmaceutical Manufacturers Association, of which all the petitioner
18     companies are members, and which includes manufacturers of more than 90% of
19     the Nation's supply of prescription drugs. They challenged the regulations on the
20     ground that the Commissioner exceeded his authority under the statute by
21     promulgating an order requiring labels, advertisements, and other printed matter
22     relating to prescription drugs to designate the established name of the particular
23     drug involved every time its trade name is used anywhere in such material.

24     The District Court, on cross-motions for summary judgment, granted the
25     declaratory and injunctive relief sought, finding that the statute did not sweep so
26     broadly as to permit the Commissioner's "every time" interpretation. The Court of
27     Appeals for the Third Circuit reversed without reaching the merits of the case. It
28     held first that, under the statutory scheme provided by the Federal Food, Drug,
29     and Cosmetic Act, pre-enforcement review of these regulations was unauthorized,
30     and therefore beyond the jurisdiction of the District Court. Second, the Court of
31     Appeals held that no "actual case or controversy" existed, and, for that reason, that
32     no relief under the Administrative Procedure Act, or under the Declaratory
33     Judgment Act was, in any event, available. Because of the general importance of
34     the question, and the apparent conflict with the decision of the Court of Appeals
35     for the Second Circuit in *Toilet Goods Assn. v. Gardner*, 360 F.2d 677 (2d Cir.
36     1966) which we also review today, we granted certiorari.

37     I

38     The first question we consider is whether Congress, by the Federal Food, Drug, and
39     Cosmetic Act, intended to forbid pre-enforcement review of this sort of regulation

1 promulgated by the Commissioner. The question is phrased in terms of
2 "prohibition", rather than "authorization," because a survey of our cases shows that
3 judicial review of a final agency action by an aggrieved person will not be cut off
4 unless there is persuasive reason to believe that such was the purpose of
5 Congress. Early cases in which this type of judicial review was entertained, *e.g.,*
6 *Shields v. Utah Idaho Central R. Co.,* 305 U.S. 177 (1938); *Stark v. Wickard,* 321
7 U.S. 288 (1944), have been reinforced by the enactment of the Administrative
8 Procedure Act, which embodies the basic presumption of judicial review to one
9 "suffering legal wrong because of agency action, or adversely affected or aggrieved
10 by agency action within the meaning of a relevant statute," 5 U.S.C. § 702, so long
11 as no statute precludes such relief or the action is not one committed by law to
12 agency discretion, 5 U.S.C. § 701(a). The Administrative Procedure Act provides
13 specifically not only for review of "[a]gency action made reviewable by statute," but
14 also for review of "final agency action for which there is no other adequate remedy
15 in a court," 5 U.S.C. § 704. The legislative material elucidating that seminal act
16 manifests a congressional intention that it cover a broad spectrum of
17 administrative actions, and this Court has echoed that theme by noting that the
18 Administrative Procedure Act's "generous review provisions" must be given a
19 "hospitable" interpretation. *Shaughnessy v. Pedreiro,* 349 U.S. 48, 51 (1955).
20 Again in *Rusk v. Cort,* 369 U.S. 367, 379-380 (1962), the Court held that only upon
21 a showing of "clear and convincing evidence" of a contrary legislative intent should
22 the courts restrict access to judicial review.

23 Given this standard, we are wholly unpersuaded that the statutory scheme in the
24 food and drug area excludes this type of action. The Government relies on no
25 explicit statutory authority for its argument that pre-enforcement review is
26 unavailable, but insists instead that, because the statute includes a specific
27 procedure for such review of certain enumerated kinds of regulations, not
28 encompassing those of the kind involved here, other types were necessarily meant
29 to be excluded from any pre-enforcement review. The issue, however, is not so
30 readily resolved; we must go further and inquire whether, in the context of the
31 entire legislative scheme the existence of that circumscribed remedy evinces a
32 congressional purpose to bar agency action not within its purview from judicial
33 review. As a leading authority in this field has noted,

34 "The mere fact that some acts are made reviewable should not suffice to
35 support an implication of exclusion as to others. The right to review is too
36 important to be excluded on such slender and indeterminate evidence of
37 legislative intent."

38 Jaffe, Judicial Control of Administrative Action, 357 (1965). In this case, the
39 Government has not demonstrated such a purpose; indeed, a study of the
40 legislative history shows rather conclusively that the specific review provisions

694

1    were designed to give an additional remedy and not to cut down more traditional
2    channels of review. At the time the Food, Drug, and Cosmetic Act was under
3    consideration, in the late 1930's, the Administrative Procedure Act had not yet
4    been enacted, the Declaratory Judgment Act was in its infancy, and the scope of
5    judicial review of administrative decisions under the equity power was unclear. It
6    was these factors that led to the form the statute ultimately took. There is no
7    evidence at all that members of Congress meant to preclude traditional avenues of
8    judicial relief. Indeed, throughout the consideration of the various bills submitted
9    to deal with this issue, it was recognized that "There is always an appropriate
10   remedy in equity in cases where an administrative officer has exceeded his
11   authority and there is no adequate remedy of law, . . . [and that] protection is given
12   by the so-called Declaratory Judgments Act. . . ." H.R.Rep. No. 2755, 74th Cong.,
13   2d Sess., 8. It was specifically brought to the attention of Congress that such
14   methods had, in fact, been used in the food and drug area, and the Department of
15   Justice, in opposing the enactment of the special review procedures of § 701,
16   submitted a memorandum which was read on the floor of the House, stating: "As
17   a matter of fact, the entire subsection is really unnecessary, because even without
18   any express provision in the bill for court review, any citizen aggrieved by any order
19   of the Secretary, who contends that the order is invalid, may test the legality of the
20   order by bringing an injunction suit against the Secretary, or the head of the
21   Bureau, under the general equity powers of the court." 83 Cong.Rec. 7892 (1938).

22   The main issue in contention was whether these methods of review were
23   satisfactory. *Compare* the majority and minority reports on the review provisions,
24   H.R.Rep. No. 2139, 75th Cong., 3d Sess. (1938), both of which acknowledged that
25   traditional judicial remedies were available, but disagreed as to the need for
26   additional procedures. The provisions now embodied in a modified form in § 701(f)
27   were supported by those who feared the life-and-death power given by the Act to
28   the executive officials, a fear voiced by many members of Congress. The supporters
29   of the special review section sought to include it in the Act primarily as a method
30   of reviewing agency *factual* determinations. * * *

31   A second reason for the special procedure was to provide broader venue to litigants
32   challenging such technical agency determinations. At that time, a suit against the
33   Secretary was proper only in the District of Columbia, an advantage that the
34   Government sought to preserve. The House bill, however, originally authorized
35   review in any district court, but, in the face of a Senate bill allowing review only in
36   the District of Columbia, the Conference Committee reached the compromise
37   preserved in the present statute authorizing review of such agency actions by the
38   courts of appeals.

39   Against this background, we think it quite apparent that the special review
40   procedures provided in § 701(f), applying to regulations embodying technical

1  factual determinations, were simply intended to assure adequate judicial review of
2  such agency decisions, and that their enactment does not manifest a congressional
3  purpose to eliminate judicial review of other kinds of agency action.

4  This conclusion is strongly buttressed by the fact that the Act itself, in § 701(f)(6),
5  states, "The remedies provided for in this subsection shall be in addition to and not
6  in substitution for any other remedies provided by law." * * *

7  * * *

8  We conclude that nothing in the Food, Drug, and Cosmetic Act itself precludes this
9  action.

10  II

11  A further inquiry must, however, be made. The injunctive and declaratory
12  judgment remedies are discretionary, and courts traditionally have been reluctant
13  to apply them to administrative determinations unless these arise in the context of
14  a controversy "ripe" for judicial resolution. Without undertaking to survey the
15  intricacies of the ripeness doctrine it is fair to say that its basic rationale is to
16  prevent the courts, through avoidance of premature adjudication, from entangling
17  themselves in abstract disagreements over administrative policies, and also to
18  protect the agencies from judicial interference until an administrative decision has
19  been formalized and its effects felt in a concrete way by the challenging parties.
20  The problem is best seen in a two-fold aspect, requiring us to evaluate both the
21  fitness of the issues for judicial decision and the hardship to the parties of
22  withholding court consideration.

23  As to the former factor, we believe the issues presented are appropriate for judicial
24  resolution at this time. First, all parties agree that the issue tendered is a purely
25  legal one: whether the statute was properly construed by the Commissioner to
26  require the established name of the drug to be used *every time* the proprietary
27  name is employed. Both sides moved for summary judgment in the District Court,
28  and no claim is made here that further administrative proceedings are
29  contemplated. * * *

30  Second, the regulations in issue we find to be "final agency action" within the
31  meaning of § 10 of the Administrative Procedure Act, 5 U.S.C. § 704, as construed
32  in judicial decisions. An "agency action" includes any "rule," defined by the Act as
33  "an agency statement of general or particular applicability and future effect
34  designed to implement, interpret, or prescribe law or policy," §§ 2(c), 2(g), 5 U.S.C.
35  §§ 551(4), 551(13). The cases dealing with judicial review of administrative actions
36  have interpreted the "finality" element in a pragmatic way. Thus, in *Columbia*
37  *Broadcasting System v. United States*, 316 U.S. 407 (1942), a suit under the
38  Urgent Deficiencies Act, 38 Stat. 219, this Court held reviewable a regulation of the

Federal Communications Commission setting forth certain proscribed contractual arrangements between chain broadcasters and local stations. The FCC did not have direct authority to regulate these contracts, and its rule asserted only that it would not license stations which maintained such contracts with the networks. Although no license had, in fact, been denied or revoked, and the FCC regulation could properly be characterized as a statement only of its intentions, the Court held that

> "Such regulations have the force of law before their sanctions are invoked as well as after. When, as here, they are promulgated by order of the Commission and the expected conformity to them causes injury cognizable by a court of equity, they are appropriately the subject of attack. . . ."

316 U.S., at 418-419.

Two more recent cases have taken a similarly flexible view of finality. In *Frozen Food Express v. United States,* 351 U.S. 40 (1956), at issue was an Interstate Commerce Commission order specifying commodities that were deemed to fall within the statutory class of "agricultural commodities." Vehicles carrying such commodities were exempt from ICC supervision. An action was brought by a carrier that claimed to be transporting exempt commodities, but which the ICC order had not included in its terms. Although the dissenting opinion noted that this ICC order had no authority except to give notice of how the Commission interpreted the Act, and would have effect only if and when a particular action was brought against a particular carrier, and argued that "judicial intervention [should] be withheld until administrative action has reached its complete development," 351 U.S., at 45, the Court held the order reviewable.

Again, in *United States v. Storer Broadcasting Co.,* 351 U.S. 192, the Court held to be a final agency action within the meaning of the Administrative Procedure Act an FCC regulation announcing a Commission policy that it would not issue a television license to an applicant already owning five such licenses, even though no specific application was before the Commission. The Court stated: "The process of rulemaking was complete. It was final agency action . . . by which Storer claimed to be *aggrieved.*'" 351 U.S., at 351 U.S. 198.

We find decision in the present case following *a fortiori* from these precedents. The regulation challenged here, promulgated in a formal manner after announcement in the Federal Register and consideration of comments by interested parties is quite clearly definitive. There is no hint that this regulation is informal, or only the ruling of a subordinate official, or tentative. It was made effective upon publication, and the Assistant General Counsel for Food and Drugs stated in the District Court that compliance was expected.

The Government argues, however, that the present case can be distinguished from cases like *Frozen Food Express* on the ground that, in those instances, the agency

697

1  involved could implement its policy directly, while here, the Attorney General must
2  authorize criminal and seizure actions for violations of the statute. In the context
3  of this case, we do not find this argument persuasive. These regulations are not
4  meant to advise the Attorney General, but purport to be directly authorized by the
5  statute. Thus, if within the Commissioner's authority, they have the status of law
6  and violations of them carry heavy criminal and civil sanctions. Also, there is no
7  representation that the Attorney General and the Commissioner disagree in this
8  area; the Justice Department is defending this very suit. It would be adherence to
9  a mere technicality to give any credence to this contention. Moreover, the agency
10 does have direct authority to enforce this regulation in the context of passing upon
11 applications for clearance of new drugs, § 505, 21 U.S.C. § 355, or certification of
12 certain antibiotics, § 507, 21 U.S.C. § 357.

13 This is also a case in which the impact of the regulations upon the petitioners is
14 sufficiently direct and immediate as to render the issue appropriate for judicial
15 review at this stage. These regulations purport to give an authoritative
16 interpretation of a statutory provision that has a direct effect on the day-to-day
17 business of all prescription drug companies; its promulgation puts petitioners in a
18 dilemma that it was the very purpose of the Declaratory Judgment Act to
19 ameliorate. As the District Court found on the basis of uncontested allegations,

20    "Either they must comply with the every time requirement and incur the
21    costs of changing over their promotional material and labeling or they must
22    follow their present course and risk prosecution."

23 228 F.Supp. 855, 861. The regulations are clear-cut, and were made effective
24 immediately upon publication; as noted earlier the agency's counsel represented
25 to the District Court that immediate compliance with their terms was expected. If
26 petitioners wish to comply they must change all their labels, advertisements, and
27 promotional materials; they must destroy stocks of printed matter, and they must
28 invest heavily in new printing type and new supplies. The alternative to
29 compliance—continued use of material which they believe in good faith meets the
30 statutory requirements, but which clearly does not meet the regulation of the
31 Commissioner—may be even more costly. That course would risk serious criminal
32 and civil penalties for the unlawful distribution of "misbranded" drugs.

33 It is relevant at this juncture to recognize that petitioners deal in a sensitive
34 industry, in which public confidence in their drug products is especially important.
35 To require them to challenge these regulations only as a defense to an action
36 brought by the Government might harm them severely and unnecessarily. Where
37 the legal issue presented is fit for judicial resolution, and where a regulation
38 requires an immediate and significant change in the plaintiffs' conduct of their
39 affairs with serious penalties attached to noncompliance, access to the courts
40 under the Administrative Procedure Act and the Declaratory Judgment Act must

698

1  be permitted, absent a statutory bar or some other unusual circumstance, neither
2  of which appears here.

3  The Government does not dispute the very real dilemma in which petitioners are
4  placed by the regulation, but contends that "mere financial expense" is not a
5  justification for pre-enforcement judicial review. It is, of course, true that cases in
6  this Court dealing with the standing of particular parties to bring an action have
7  held that a possible financial loss is not, by itself, a sufficient interest to sustain a
8  judicial challenge to governmental action. But there is no question in the present
9  case that petitioners have sufficient standing as plaintiffs: the regulation is directed
10  at them in particular; it requires them to make significant changes in their
11  everyday business practices; if they fail to observe the Commissioner's rule, they
12  are quite clearly exposed to the imposition of strong sanctions. * * *

13  The Government further contends that the threat of criminal sanctions for
14  noncompliance with a judicially untested regulation is unrealistic; the Solicitor
15  General has represented that, if court enforcement becomes necessary, "the
16  Department of Justice will proceed only civilly for an injunction . . . or by
17  condemnation." We cannot accept this argument as a sufficient answer to
18  petitioners' petition. This action at its inception was properly brought and this
19  subsequent representation of the Department of Justice should not suffice to
20  defeat it.

21  Finally, the Government urges that to permit resort to the courts in this type of
22  case may delay or impede effective enforcement of the Act. We fully recognize the
23  important public interest served by assuring prompt and unimpeded
24  administration of the Pure Food, Drug, and Cosmetic Act, but we do not find the
25  Government's argument convincing. First, in this particular case, a pre-
26  enforcement challenge by nearly all prescription drug manufacturers is calculated
27  to speed enforcement. If the Government prevails, a large part of the industry is
28  bound by the decree; if the Government loses, it can more quickly revise its
29  regulation.

30  The Government contends, however, that, if the Court allows this consolidated
31  suit, then nothing will prevent a multiplicity of suits in various jurisdictions
32  challenging other regulations. The short answer to this contention is that the courts
33  are well equipped to deal with such eventualities. The venue transfer provision, 28
34  U.S.C. § 1404(a), may be invoked by the Government to consolidate separate
35  actions. Or actions in all but one jurisdiction might be stayed pending the
36  conclusion of one proceeding. A court may even, in its discretion, dismiss a
37  declaratory judgment or injunctive suit if the same issue is pending in litigation
38  elsewhere. In at least one suit for a declaratory judgment, relief was denied with
39  the suggestion that the plaintiff intervene in a pending action elsewhere.

1  *Automotive Equip., Inc. v. Trico Prods. Corp.*, 11 F. Supp. 292; *see Allstate Ins. Co.*
2  *v. Thompson*, 121 F. Supp. 696.

3  Further, the declaratory judgment and injunctive remedies are equitable in nature,
4  and other equitable defenses may be interposed. If a multiplicity of suits are
5  undertaken in order to harass the Government or to delay enforcement, relief can
6  be denied on this ground alone. * * *

7  In addition to all these safeguards against what the Government fears, it is
8  important to note that the institution of this type of action does not, by itself, stay
9  the effectiveness of the challenged regulation. There is nothing in the record to
10  indicate that petitioners have sought to stay enforcement of the "every time"
11  regulation pending judicial review. If the agency believes that a suit of this type will
12  significantly impede enforcement or will harm the public interest, it need not
13  postpone enforcement of the regulation, and may oppose any motion for a judicial
14  stay on the part of those challenging the regulation. *Ibid.* It is scarcely to be
15  doubted that a court would refuse to postpone the effective date of an agency action
16  if the Government could show, as it made no effort to do here, that delay would be
17  detrimental to the public health or safety.

18  Lastly, although the Government presses us to reach the merits of the challenge to
19  the regulation in the event we find the District Court properly entertained this
20  action, we believe the better practice is to remand the case to the Court of Appeals
21  for the Third Circuit to review the District Court's decision that the regulation was
22  beyond the power of the Commissioner.

23  *Reversed and remanded.*

24  MR. JUSTICE BRENNAN took no part in the consideration or decision of this case.

25  MR. JUSTICE FORTAS, with whom THE CHIEF JUSTICE and MR. JUSTICE
26  CLARK join, concurring in No. 336, and dissenting in Nos. 39 and 438.

27  I am in agreement with the Court in No. 336, *Toilet Goods Assn. v. Gardner*, 387
28  U.S. 158, that we should affirm the decision of the Court of Appeals for the Second
29  Circuit holding that the authority of the Secretary of Health, Education, and
30  Welfare to promulgate the regulation there involved may not be challenged by
31  injunctive or declaratory judgment action. * * *

32  I am, however, compelled to dissent from the decisions of the Court in No. 39,
33  *Abbott Laboratories v. Gardner*, 387 U.S. 136, and No. 438, *Gardner v. Toilet*
34  *Goods Assn.*, 387 U.S. 167. * * *

35  The issues considered by the Court are not constitutional questions. The Court
36  does not rest upon any asserted right to challenge the regulations at this time
37  because the agency lacks authority to promulgate the regulations as to the subject

1  matters involved, or because its procedures have been arbitrary or unreasonable.
2  Its decision is based solely upon the claim of right to challenge these particular
3  regulations at this time on the ground that they are erroneous exercises of the
4  agency's power. It is solely on this point that the Court in these two cases authorizes
5  threshold or pre-enforcement challenge by action for injunction and declaratory
6  relief to suspend the operation of the regulations in their entirety and without
7  reference to particular factual situations.

8  With all respect, I submit that established principles of jurisprudence, solidly
9  rooted in the constitutional structure of our Government, require that the courts
10  should not intervene in the administrative process at this stage, under these facts
11  and in this gross, shotgun fashion. With all respect, I submit that the governing
12  principles of law do not permit a different result in these cases than in No. 336. In
13  none of these cases is judicial interference warranted at this stage, in this fashion,
14  and to test—on a gross, free-wheeling basis—whether the content of these
15  regulations is within the statutory intendment. The contrary is dictated by a proper
16  regard for the purpose of the regulatory statute and the requirements of effective
17  administration; and by regard for the salutary rule that courts should pass upon
18  concrete, specific questions in a particularized setting rather than upon a general
19  controversy divorced from particular facts.

20  The Court, by today's decisions in Nos. 39 and 438, has opened Pandora's box.
21  Federal injunctions will now threaten programs of vast importance to the public
22  welfare. The Court's holding here strikes at programs for the public health. The
23  dangerous precedent goes even further. It is cold comfort-it is little more than
24  delusion-to read in the Court's opinion that "It is scarcely to be doubted that a court
25  would refuse to postpone the effective date of an agency action if the Government
26  could show . . . that delay would be detrimental to the public health or safety."
27  Experience dictates, on the contrary, that it can hardly be hoped that some federal
28  judge somewhere will not be moved as the Court is here, by the cries of anguish
29  and distress of those regulated, to grant a disruptive injunction.

30  The difference between the majority and me in these cases is not with respect to
31  the existence of jurisdiction to enjoin, but to the definition of occasions on which
32  such jurisdiction may be invoked. I do not doubt that there is residual judicial
33  power in some extreme and limited situations to enjoin administrative actions
34  even in the absence of specific statutory provision where the agency has acted
35  unconstitutionally or without jurisdiction—as distinguished from an allegedly
36  erroneous action. But the Court's opinions in No. 39 and No. 438 appear to proceed
37  on the principle that, even where no constitutional issues or questions of
38  administrative jurisdiction or of arbitrary procedure are involved, exercise of
39  judicial power to enjoin allegedly erroneous regulatory action is permissible unless
40  Congress has explicitly prohibited it, provided only that the controversy is "ripe"

1 for judicial determination. This is a rule that is novel in its breadth and destructive
2 in its implications as illustrated by the present application. As will appear, I believe
3 that this approach improperly and unwisely gives individual federal district judges
4 a roving commission to halt the regulatory process, and to do so on the basis of
5 abstractions and generalities instead of concrete fact situations, and that it
6 impermissibly broadens the license of the courts to intervene in administrative
7 action by means of a threshold suit for injunction rather than by the method
8 provided by statute.

9 * * *

10 I

11 Since enactment of the Federal Food, Drug, and Cosmetic Act in 1938, the
12 mechanism for judicial review of agency actions under its provisions has been well
13 understood. Except for specific types of agency regulations and actions to which I
14 shall refer, judicial review has been confined to enforcement actions instituted by
15 the Attorney General on recommendation of the agency. As the recurrent debate
16 over this technique demonstrates, this restricted avenue for challenge has been
17 deemed necessary because of the direct and urgent relationship of the field of
18 regulation to the public health. It is this avenue that applies with respect to the
19 regulations at issue in the present cases.

20 * * *

21 Where a remedy is provided by statute, I submit that it is and has been
22 fundamental to our law, to judicial administration, to the principle of separation
23 of powers in our Constitution, that the courts will withhold equitable or
24 discretionary remedies unless they conclude that the statutory remedy is
25 inadequate. * * *

26 The limited applicability of the Administrative Procedure Act in these cases is
27 entirely clear. That Act requires that unless precluded by Congress final agency
28 action of the sorts involved here must be reviewable at some stage, and it
29 recognizes that such review must be "adequate." It merely presents the question in
30 these cases. It does not supply an answer. Certainly, it would be revolutionary
31 doctrine that the Administrative Procedure Act authorizes threshold suits for
32 injunction even where another and adequate review provision is available. * * *

33 * * *

34 II

35 I come then to the questions whether the review otherwise available under the
36 statute is "adequate," whether the controversies are "ripe" or appropriate for
37 review in terms of the evaluation of the competing private and public interests. I

1  discuss these together because the questions of adequacy and ripeness or
2  appropriateness for review are interrelated. I again note that no constitutional
3  issues are raised, and, indeed, no issues as to the authority of the agency to issue
4  regulations of the general sort involved. The only issue is whether that authority
5  was properly exercised.

6  There is, of course, no abstract or mechanical method for determining the
7  adequacy of review provisions. Where personal status or liberties are involved, the
8  courts may well insist upon a considerable ease of challenging administrative
9  orders or regulations. But in situations where a regulatory scheme designed to
10 protect the public is involved, this Court has held that postponement of the
11 opportunity to obtain judicial relief in the interest of avoiding disruption of the
12 regulatory plan is entirely justifiable. * * *

13                                    * * *

14 The regulation in No. 39 relates to a 1962 amendment to the Act requiring
15 manufacturers of prescription drugs to print on the labels or other printed
16 material, the "established name" of the drug "prominently and in type at least half
17 as large as that used thereon for any proprietary name or designation for such
18 drug." § 502(e)(1), 76 Stat. 790, 21 U.S.C. § 352(e)(1). Obviously, this requires some
19 elucidation, either case-by-case or by general regulation or pronouncement,
20 because the statute does not say that this must be done "every time," or only once
21 on each label or in each pamphlet, or once per panel, etc., or that it must be done
22 differently on labels than on circulars, or doctors' literature than on directions to
23 the patients, etc. This is exactly the traditional purpose and function of an
24 administrative agency. The Commissioner, acting by delegation from the
25 Secretary, took steps to provide for the specification. He invited and considered
26 comments and then issued a regulation requiring that the 'established name'
27 appear every time the proprietary name is used. A manufacturer—or other person
28 who violates this regulation—has mislabeled his product. The product may be
29 seized; or injunction may be sought; or the mislabeler may be criminally
30 prosecuted. In any of these actions he may challenge the regulation and obtain a
31 judicial determination.

32 The Court, however, moved by petitioners' claims as to the expense and
33 inconvenience of compliance and the risks of deferring challenge by
34 noncompliance, decrees that the manufacturers may have their suit for injunction
35 at this time and reverses the Third Circuit. The Court says that this confronts the
36 manufacturer with a "real dilemma." But the fact of the matter is that the dilemma
37 is no more than citizens face in connection with countless statutes and with the
38 rules of the SEC, FTC, FCC, ICC, and other regulatory agencies. This has not
39 heretofore been regarded as a basis for injunctive relief unless Congress has so
40 provided. The overriding fact here is—or should be—that the public interest in

1  avoiding the delay in implementing Congress' program far outweighs the private
2  interest; and that the private interest which has so impressed the Court is no more
3  than that which exists in respect of most regulatory statutes or agency rules.

4                                    * * *

5

6  **Toilet Goods Assn., Inc. v. Gardner**

7  387 U.S. 158 (1967)

8  May 22, 1967

9  MR. JUSTICE HARLAN delivered the opinion of the Court.

10  Petitioners in this case are the Toilet Goods Association, an organization of
11  cosmetics manufacturers accounting for some 90% of annual American sales in
12  this field, and 39 individual cosmetics manufacturers and distributors. They
13  brought this action in the United States District Court for the Southern District of
14  New York seeking declaratory and injunctive relief against the Secretary of Health,
15  Education, and Welfare and the Commissioner of Food and Drugs, on the ground
16  that certain regulations promulgated by the Commissioner exceeded his statutory
17  authority under the Color Additive Amendments to the Federal Food, Drug, and
18  Cosmetic Act.

19  The District Court held that the Act did not prohibit this type of pre-enforcement
20  suit, that a case and controversy existed, that the issues presented were justiciable,
21  and that no reasons had been presented by the Government to warrant declining
22  jurisdiction on discretionary grounds. Recognizing that the subsequent decision of
23  the Court of Appeals for the Third Circuit in *Abbott Laboratories v.*
24  *Celebrezze*, 352 F.2d 286, appeared to conflict with its holding, the District Court
25  reaffirmed its earlier rulings, but certified the question of jurisdiction to the Court
26  of Appeals for the Second Circuit under 28 U.S.C. § 1292(b). The Court of Appeals
27  affirmed the judgment of the District Court that jurisdiction to hear the suit existed
28  as to three of the challenged regulations, but sustained the Government's
29  contention that judicial review was improper as to a fourth.

30  Each side below sought review here from the portions of the Court of Appeals'
31  decision adverse to it, the Government as petitioner in *Gardner v. Toilet Goods*
32  *Assn.*, and the Toilet Goods Association and other plaintiffs in the present case. We
33  granted certiorari in both instances, as we did in *Abbott Laboratories v.*
34  *Gardner*, because of the apparent conflict between the Second and Third Circuits.
35  The two *Toilet Goods* cases were set and argued together with *Abbott*
36  *Laboratories.*

704

1   In our decisions reversing the judgment in *Abbott Laboratories,* and affirming the
2   judgment in *Gardner v. Toilet Goods Assn,* we hold that nothing in the Food, Drug,
3   and Cosmetic Act bars a pre-enforcement suit under the Administrative Procedure
4   Act and the Declaratory Judgment Act. We nevertheless agree with the Court of
5   Appeals that judicial review of this particular regulation in this particular context
6   is inappropriate at this stage because, applying the standards set forth in *Abbott*
7   *Laboratories v. Gardner,* the controversy is not presently ripe for adjudication.

8   The regulation in issue here was promulgated under the Color Additive
9   Amendments of 1960, a statute that revised and somewhat broadened the
10   authority of the Commissioner to control the ingredients added to foods, drugs,
11   and cosmetics that impart color to them. The Commissioner of Food and Drugs,
12   exercising power delegated by the Secretary, under statutory authority "to
13   promulgate regulations for the efficient enforcement" of the Act, § 701(a), 21 U.S.C.
14   § 371(a), issued the following regulation after due public notice, 26 Fed.Reg. 679,
15   and consideration of comments submitted by interested parties:

16      "(a) When it appears to the Commissioner that a person has:

17      ". . ."

18      "(4) Refused to permit duly authorized employees of the Food and Drug
19      Administration free access to all manufacturing facilities, processes, and
20      formulae involved in the manufacture of color additives and intermediates
21      from which such color additives are derived;"

22      "he may immediately suspend certification service to such person and may
23      continue such suspension until adequate corrective action has been taken."

24   28 Fed.Reg. 6445-6446; 21 CFR § 8.28.

25   The petitioners maintain that this regulation is an impermissible exercise of
26   authority, that the FDA has long sought congressional authorization for free access
27   to facilities, processes, and formulae, but that Congress has always denied the
28   agency this power except for prescription drugs. Framed in this way, we agree with
29   petitioners that a "legal" issue is raised, but nevertheless we are not persuaded that
30   the present suit is properly maintainable.

31   In determining whether a challenge to an administrative regulation is ripe for
32   review, a two-fold inquiry must be made: *first,* to determine whether the issues
33   tendered are appropriate for judicial resolution, and *second,* to assess the hardship
34   to the parties if judicial relief is denied at that stage.

35     As to the first of these factors, we agree with the Court of Appeals that the legal
36     issue, as presently framed, is not appropriate for judicial resolution. This is not
37       because the regulation is not the agency's considered and formalized

1  determination, for we are in agreement with petitioners that, under this Court's
2  decisions in *Frozen Food Express v. United States,* 351 U.S. 40, and *United*
3  *States v. Storer Broadcasting Co.,* 351 U.S. 192, there can be no question that
4  this regulation—promulgated in a formal manner after notice and evaluation of
5  submitted comments—is a "final agency action" under § 10 of the Administrative
6  Procedure Act, 5 U.S.C. § 704. * * *

7  These points which support the appropriateness of judicial resolution are,
8  however, outweighed by other considerations. The regulation serves notice only
9  that the Commissioner *may,* under certain circumstances, order inspection of
10 certain facilities and data, and that further certification of additives *may* be refused
11 to those who decline to permit a duly authorized inspection until they have
12 complied in that regard. At this juncture, we have no idea whether or when such
13 an inspection will be ordered and what reasons the Commissioner will give to
14 justify his order. The statutory authority asserted for the regulation is the power to
15 promulgate regulations "for the efficient enforcement" of the Act, § 701(a).
16 Whether the regulation is justified thus depends not only, as petitioners appear to
17 suggest, on whether Congress refused to include a specific section of the Act
18 authorizing such inspections, although this factor is, to be sure, a highly relevant
19 one, but also on whether the statutory scheme as a whole justified promulgation of
20 the regulation. This will depend not merely on an inquiry into statutory purpose,
21 but concurrently on an understanding of what types of enforcement problems are
22 encountered by the FDA, the need for various sorts of supervision in order to
23 effectuate the goals of the Act, and the safeguards devised to protect legitimate
24 trade secrets. We believe that judicial appraisal of these factors is likely to stand on
25 a much surer footing in the context of a specific application of this regulation than
26 could be the case in the framework of the generalized challenge made here.

27 We are also led to this result by considerations of the effect on the petitioners of
28 the regulation, for the test of ripeness, as we have noted, depends not only on how
29 adequately a court can deal with the legal issue presented, but also on the degree
30 and nature of the regulation's present effect on those seeking relief. The regulation
31 challenged here is not analogous to those that were involved in *Columbia*
32 *Broadcasting System, supra,* and *Storer, supra,* and those other color additive
33 regulations with which we deal in *Gardner v. Toilet Goods Assn.,* 387 U.S.167,
34 where the impact of the administrative action could be said to be felt immediately
35 by those subject to it in conducting their day-to-day affairs. *See also Federal*
36 *Communications Comm'n v. American Broadcasting Co.,* 347 U.S. 284.

37 This is not a situation in which primary conduct is affected—when contracts must
38 be negotiated, ingredients tested or substituted, or special records compiled. This
39 regulation merely states that the Commissioner may authorize inspectors to
40 examine certain processes or formulae; no advance action is required of cosmetics

1   manufacturers, who, since the enactment of the 1938 Act, have been under a
2   statutory duty to permit reasonable inspection of a "factory, warehouse,
3   establishment, or vehicle and all pertinent equipment, finished and unfinished
4   materials; containers, and labeling therein." Moreover, no irremediable adverse
5   consequences flow from requiring a later challenge to this regulation by a
6   manufacturer who refuses to allow this type of inspection. Unlike the other
7   regulations challenged in this action, in which seizure of goods, heavy fines,
8   adverse publicity for distributing "adulterated" goods, and possible criminal
9   liability might penalize failure to comply, *see Gardner v. Toilet Goods Assn.*, 387
10   U.S. 167, a refusal to admit an inspector here would, at most, lead only to a
11   suspension of certification services to the particular party, a determination that
12   can then be promptly challenged through an administrative procedure, which in
13   turn is reviewable by a court. Such review will provide an adequate forum for
14   testing the regulation in a concrete situation.

15   It is true that the administrative hearing will deal with the "factual basis" of the
16   suspension, from which petitioners infer that the Commissioner will not entertain
17   and consider a challenge to his statutory authority to promulgate the regulation.
18   Whether or not this assumption is correct, given the fact that only minimal, if any,
19   adverse consequences will face petitioners if they challenge the regulation in this
20   manner, we think it wiser to require them to exhaust this administrative process
21   through which the factual basis of the inspection order will certainly be aired and
22   where more light may be thrown on the Commissioner's statutory and practical
23   justifications for the regulation. Judicial review will then be available, and a court
24   at that juncture will be in a better position to deal with the question of statutory
25   authority. For these reasons the judgment of the Court of Appeals is

26   *Affirmed.*

27   MR. JUSTICE DOUGLAS dissents for the reasons stated by Judge Tyler of the
28   District Court.

29   MR. JUSTICE BRENNAN took no part in the consideration or decision of this case.

30   [For concurring opinion of MR. JUSTICE FORTAS., *see* 387 U.S., at 174.]

31

## 32   E. Standing

33   There are both constitutional and non-constitutional dimensions to standing
34   doctrine, but the commonality is this: both ask whether the parties appearing in
35   court are the right parties to litigate a particular claim.

1 The core idea of constitutional standing is that Article III empowers federal courts
2 to adjudicate cases,[4] and a matter is not really a "case" unless there are two adverse
3 parties that have a stake in the outcome.

4 The idea of non-constitutional (or prudential) standing is that courts are unwilling
5 to hear cases brought by certain parties, even those with a real stake in the matter,
6 if they are nonetheless not the appropriate parties to litigate a challenge to the
7 agency action at issue. Prior to passage of the APA, courts were left to figure out
8 for themselves what kinds of litigants it was "prudent" to admit to court, but the
9 APA provides at least some guidance within the statute as to who can bring suit.

10 "Standing" sounds like an old doctrine, particularly when it goes by its Latin name
11 (*ius standi*), but the Supreme Court has really only developed it since the New Deal.
12 It also has some overlap with other justiciability doctrine, including preclusion and
13 ripeness. Some complain that standing doctrine is hard to follow, and others claim
14 there is a simple principle at work: Justices manipulate the doctrine to kill off cases
15 they disfavor on the merits. Do the cases in this section bear out the critique?

16

## 17   1.  Non-Constitutional Standing Doctrine

18 The judicial review provisions of the APA define who may challenge agency action;
19 *Association of Data Processing Service Organizations* and subsequent cases are
20 building on that statutory language. *Alexander Sprunt & Son* is a pre-APA case.
21 How much, if any, of the *Sprunt* approach survives into the APA era?

22

### 23   Alexander Sprunt & Son, Inc. v. United States

24 281 U.S. 249 (1930)

25 April 14, 1930

26 MR. JUSTICE BRANDEIS delivered the opinion of the Court.

27 The Interstate Commerce Commission entered, on April 4, 1927, an order directed
28 to the railroads operating in Oklahoma, Arkansas, Texas, and Louisiana, which
29 required them to remove, in a manner prescribed, undue prejudice and preference
30 caused by their rates on cotton shipped from interior points to Houston and other
31 ports on the Gulf of Mexico. Two suits, under the Act of June 18, 1910, c. 309, 36
32 Stat. 539, as amended by Urgent Deficiencies Act of October 22, 1913, c. 32, 38

---

[4] Well, "cases" and "controversies," but the standing requirements apply the same
to all of the heads of federal jurisdiction.

1    Stat. 208, 220, were promptly brought in the federal court for Southern Texas, to
2    enjoin the enforcement of the order and to set it aside. The first suit was brought
3    by Alexander Sprunt & Son, Inc., and others interested in cotton compresses and
4    warehouses located at wharves on the waterfront. The second by the Texas & New
5    Orleans Railroad Company and other rail carriers. The two cases were, with the
6    consent of the parties, ordered consolidated as a single cause with a single record.
7    The consolidated case was heard by three judges. An interlocutory injunction
8    issued. Upon final hearing, the district court sustained the validity of the order;
9    dissolved the injunction, and entered a decree dismissing the bills.

10   None of the carriers appealed from the decree. Acquiescing in the decision of the
11   district court and in the order of the Commission, the railroads promptly
12   established the prescribed rate adjustment, and it is now in force. This appeal was
13   taken by Alexander Sprunt & Son, Inc., and those shippers and associations of
14   shippers which had joined below as co-plaintiffs in the bill filed by it. No stay of
15   the decree pending the appeal was granted or sought. And no railroad was made a
16   party to the proceedings on the appeal. At the argument, this court raised the
17   preliminary question whether there is any substantive ground for appeal by the
18   shippers alone. In order to answer that question, a fuller statement is necessary of
19   the matter in controversy before the commission and of the terms of the order
20   entered by it.

21   From interior points in Texas, Louisiana, Oklahoma, and Arkansas to the several
22   ports on the Gulf of Mexico, there were on all the railroads two schedules of rates
23   on cotton—the domestic or city-delivery rates, and the export, or ship-side rates.
24   The latter were, prior to the entry of the order complained of, 3 or 3.5 cents per
25   100 pounds higher than the former. All rates permit concentration and
26   compression in transit, and include free switching to and from the warehouses and
27   compresses. Complaint was made that, in applying these rates, the railroads
28   unjustly discriminated against other shippers and in favor of Alexander Sprunt &
29   Son, Inc., and other owners of warehouses and compresses at the wharves, by
30   applying the domestic rates on shipments to their plants of cotton intended for
31   export or for transshipment by vessel coastwise. It was sought to justify this
32   practice on the ground that the conditions which had led to charging the higher
33   rate for export cotton were absent in the case of these waterfront plants.

34   The difference of about 3.5 cents per 100 pounds between the domestic and the
35   export rates is approximately equal to the cost of transporting the cotton, by dray
36   or by switching, from uptown concentrating and high density compressing plants
37   in the ports to shipside. This difference served to equalize rates as between the
38   uptown plants and the interior plants. In 1921, and later, warehouses and high
39   density compressing plants were located at the waterfront, almost within reach of
40   the ship's tackle. From these plants, there was no need of local transportation, by

1  dray or switching, to shipside. The lower domestic rates were accordingly applied
2  on cotton shipped to them, even though intended for export.

3  This practice gave to the water-front plants an obvious advantage over those
4  located uptown in the ports and over those located in the interior. Widespread
5  complaint of undue prejudice and preference led the Commission to institute,
6  upon its own motion, a general investigation concerning the lawfulness of the
7  practices of the carriers in connection with the application of the city-delivery and
8  shipside rates, with a view to determining, among other things, "whether any
9  change should be made in existing tariff regulations or rates in order to avoid or
10 remove such undue preference, if any, that results or may result in favor of said
11 waterfront shippers or localities." Practically all the railroads operating in the four
12 southwestern states were made respondents to that proceeding.

13 After extended hearings, the Commission found that the existing adjustment of
14 rates to ports was unduly prejudicial to the warehouses and compresses uptown
15 and in the interior; that it was unduly preferential of those at the waterfront, and
16 that the rates should be readjusted so that one rate would apply for all deliveries
17 within the usual switching limits of the respective ports, except that the export
18 rates should be made higher than the domestic rates by an amount equal to the
19 wharfage. The Commission did not, at first, specify the particular rate adjustment
20 to be established to accomplish the result directed. Without inquiring into the
21 reasonableness of the rates, it stated that the equality of treatment might be
22 effected by any readjustment which would preserve, but not increase, the carriers'
23 revenues. But, upon reopening the proceeding pursuant to petitions therefor, the
24 Commission prescribed specifically what the rate adjustment should be. It found
25 that, "for the purposes of this case, a fair and reasonable basis for equalizing the
26 city-delivery and shipside rates will be to increase the city-delivery rates 1 cent per
27 100 pounds and reduce the shipside rates exclusive of wharf or pier terminal
28 charges equivalent to 2 cents per 100 pounds, to the basis of the increased city-
29 delivery rates."

30 *First.* The appellants contend that there is no basis for the Commission's finding
31 of undue prejudice and preference. We are of opinion that appellants have no
32 standing, in their own right, to make this attack. Insofar as the order directs
33 elimination of the rate differential previously existing, it worsened the economic
34 position of the appellants. It deprived them of an advantage over other competitors
35 of almost 3.5 cents per hundred pounds. The enjoyment of this advantage gave
36 them a distinct interest in the proceeding before the Commission under § 3 of the
37 Interstate Commerce Act. For their competitive advantage was threatened. Having
38 this interest, they were entitled to intervene in that administrative proceeding.
39 And, if they did so, they became entitled under § 212 of the Judicial Code to
40 intervene, as of right, in any suit "wherein is involved the validity" of the order

1   entered by the Commission. But that interest alone did not give them the right to
2   maintain an independent suit to vacate and set aside the order. Such a suit can be
3   brought by a shipper only where a right of his own is alleged to have been violated
4   by the order. And his independent right to relief is no greater where, by
5   intervention or otherwise, he has become a party to the proceeding before the
6   Commission or to a suit brought by a carrier. In the case at bar, the appellants have
7   no independent right which is violated by the order to cease and desist. They are
8   entitled as shippers only to reasonable service at reasonable rates and without
9   unjust discrimination. If such service and rates are accorded them, they cannot
10  complain of the rate or practice enjoyed by their competitors or of the retraction of
11  a competitive advantage to which they are not otherwise entitled. The advantage
12  which the appellants enjoyed under the former tariff was merely an incident of,
13  and hence was dependent upon, the right, if any, of the carriers to maintain that
14  tariff in force and their continuing desire to do so.

15  Why the carriers filed the new rate structure now in force is no concern of the
16  appellants. If the carriers had done so wholly of their own motion, obviously these
17  shippers would have had no ground of complaint, before any tribunal, unless the
18  new rates were unreasonable or unjust. If they were believed by the appellants to
19  be so, a complaint before the Commission would be the appropriate remedy.

20  The appellants' position is legally no different from what it would have been if the
21  carriers had filed the rates freely, pursuant to an informal suggestion of the
22  Commission or one of its members; or if the filing had been made by carriers
23  voluntarily after complaint filed before the Commission, which had never reached
24  a hearing, because the rate structure complained of was thus superseded. The
25  carriers who were respondents before the Commission filed the new rates,
26  presumably because they now desire them. Nothing to the contrary is shown. So
27  far as the carriers are concerned, it is as if the new rates had been filed wholly of
28  their own accord, and as if there had never been a controversy before the
29  Commission. Since the appellants' economic advantage as shippers was an
30  incident of the supposed right exercised by the carriers, the appellants cannot
31  complain after the carriers are satisfied or prefer not to press their right, if any.

32  Appellants' present position resembles in all essentials one which was put forward
33  in *Edward Hines Trustees v. United States*, 263 U.S. 143, and *United States v.*
34  *Merchants' & Manufacturers' Traffic Association*, 242 U.S. 178. There, as here,
35  the plaintiffs were deprived by the order of the Commission of a competitive
36  advantage. But the plaintiffs there, as here, were not subjected to or threatened
37  with any legal wrong. And, since the carriers acquiesced in the order of the
38  Commission, the plaintiffs could not maintain an independent action to annul the
39  orders. Appellants' present position is unlike that of the plaintiffs in the cases relied

upon. In each of those cases, an independent legal right of the plaintiff was affected by the order which it was sought to set aside.

Moreover, by the action of the carriers, the issue of undue prejudice and unjust preference, which had been passed upon by the Commission, has become moot. Most of the carriers never sought to annul the order. Those that joined in the suit to set it aside have since voluntarily severed themselves from the shippers who object to it. The fact that some carriers at one time protested is of no significance, among other reasons, because their protest may have been directed not against that part of the order which commanded an equalization of rates, but against the particular figure at which equalization was ordered. There is nothing to show that any carrier is now in sympathy with the appellants' attack on the order. A judgment in appellants' favor would be futile. It would not restore the appellants to the advantage previously enjoyed. If the Commission's order is set aside, the carriers would still be free to continue to equalize the rates, and, for aught that appears, would continue to do so.

*Second.* Appellants complain of the order also on the ground that it authorized an increase in the local or domestic delivery rates without a hearing and findings as to the reasonableness of the level of either the old or the new rates. It is urged that § 15 of the Act does not authorize the Commission to fix the rates necessary to remove undue prejudice without such hearing and findings. But plainly appellants cannot, in their own right, be heard to complain in this suit of this part of the order. The Commission's first order left the carriers free to choose the method for the removal of the preference. If the carriers had, of their own accord, adopted the plan later prescribed by the Commission, appellants could, obviously, not be heard to complain of the reasonableness of the rate adopted, except in a proceeding before the Commission instituted under §§ 13 and 15 of the Act. For reasons which it is unnecessary to detail, the carriers were unable to agree upon a plan. They petitioned the Commission for help. In reopening the proceedings, the Commission notified the parties that one of the issues to be decided was "what rates shall be established to comply with [its] findings and order." The carriers have accepted the rate fixed by the Commission. In prescribing the rate, the Commission in no way prejudiced any preexisting rights or remedies of the appellants. Any question as to the reasonableness of the level of the rate was expressly left open by the Commission. It did not prescribe any rate as the minimum. If appellants are aggrieved by the level of the new rates, they still have their remedy before the Commission under §§ 13 and 15 of the Act.

\* \* \*

*Reversed, with direction to dismiss.*

THE CHIEF JUSTICE did not take part in this case.

1

## Association of Data Processing Service Organizations, Inc. v. Camp

397 U.S. 150 (1970)

March 3, 1970

MR. JUSTICE DOUGLAS delivered the opinion of the Court.

Petitioners sell data processing services to businesses generally. In this suit, they seek to challenge a ruling by respondent Comptroller of the Currency that, as an incident to their banking services, national banks, including respondent American National Bank & Trust Company, may make data processing services available to other banks and to bank customers. The District Court dismissed the complaint for lack of standing of petitioners to bring the suit. The Court of Appeals affirmed. The case is here on a petition for writ of certiorari, which we granted.

Generalizations about standing to sue are largely worthless as such. One generalization is, however, necessary, and that is that the question of standing in the federal courts is to be considered in the framework of Article III, which restricts judicial power to "cases" and "controversies." As we recently stated in *Flast v. Cohen*, 392 U.S. 83, 101 (1968), "[I]n terms of Article III limitations on federal court jurisdiction, the question of standing is related only to whether the dispute sought to be adjudicated will be presented in an adversary context and in a form historically viewed as capable of judicial resolution." *Flast* was a *taxpayer's* suit. The present is a *competitor's* suit. And while the two have the same Article III starting point, they do not necessarily track one another.

The first question is whether the plaintiff alleges that the challenged action has caused him injury in fact, economic or otherwise. There can be no doubt but that petitioners have satisfied this test. The petitioners not only allege that competition by national banks in the business of providing data processing services might entail some future loss of profits for the petitioners, they also allege that respondent American National Bank & Trust Company was performing or preparing to perform such services for two customers for whom petitioner Data Systems, Inc., had previously agreed or negotiated to perform such services. The petitioners' suit was brought not only against the American National Bank & Trust Company, but also against the Comptroller of the Currency. The Comptroller was alleged to have caused petitioners injury in fact by his 1966 ruling, which stated:

> "Incidental to its banking services, a national bank may make available its data processing equipment or perform data processing services on such equipment for other banks and bank customers."

1   Comptroller's Manual for National Banks (October 15, 1966).

2   The Court of Appeals viewed the matter differently, stating:

3   "[A] plaintiff may challenge alleged illegal competition when as
4   complainant it pursues (1) a legal interest by reason of public charter or
5   contract, . . . (2) a legal interest by reason of statutory protection, . . . or (3)
6   a 'public interest' in which Congress has recognized the need for review of
7   administrative action and plaintiff is significantly involved to have standing
8   to represent the public. . . ."

9   406 F.2d at 842-843.[1]

10  Those tests were based on prior decisions of this Court, such as *Tennessee Power*
11  *Co. v. TVA*, 306 U.S. 118 (1939), where private power companies sought to enjoin
12  TVA from operating, claiming that the statutory plan under which it was created
13  was unconstitutional. The Court denied the competitors' standing, holding that
14  they did not have that status "unless the right invaded is a legal right,—one of
15  property, one arising out of contract, one protected against tortious invasion, or
16  one founded on a statute which confers a privilege." *Id.* at 137-138.

17  The "legal interest" test goes to the merits. The question of standing is different. It
18  concerns, apart from the "case" or "controversy" test, the question whether the
19  interest sought to be protected by the complainant is arguably within the zone of
20  interests to be protected or regulated by the statute or constitutional guarantee in
21  question. Thus, the Administrative Procedure Act grants standing to a person
22  "aggrieved by agency action within the meaning of a relevant statute." 5 U.S.C. §
23  702 (1964 ed., Supp. IV). That interest, at times, may reflect "aesthetic,
24  conservational, and recreational," as well as economic, values. *Scenic Hudson*
25  *Preservation Conf. v. FPC,* 354 F.2d 608, 616 (2d Cir. 1965); *Office of*
26  *Communication of United Church of Christ v. FCC,* 359 F.2d 994, 1000-1006 (2d
27  Cir. 1966). A person or a family may have a spiritual stake in First Amendment
28  values sufficient to give standing to raise issues concerning the Establishment
29  Clause and the Free Exercise Clause. *Abington School District v. Schempp,* 374
30  U.S. 203 (1963). We mention these noneconomic values to emphasize that
31  standing may stem from them as well as from the economic injury on which
32  petitioners rely here. Certainly he who is "likely to be financially" injured, *FCC v.*

---

[1] The first two tests applied by the Court of Appeals required a showing of a "legal
interest." But the existence or nonexistence of a "legal interest" is a matter quite
distinct from the problem of standing. *Barlow v. Collins,* 397 U.S. 159. The third
test mentioned by the Court of Appeals, which rests on an explicit provision in a
regulatory statute conferring standing, and is commonly referred to in terms of
allowing suits by "private attorneys general," is inapplicable to the present case.

1    *Sanders Bros. Radio Station,* 309 U.S. 470, 477 (1940), may be a reliable private
2    attorney general to litigate the issues of the public interest in the present case.

3    Apart from Article III jurisdictional questions, problems of standing. as resolved
4    by this Court for its own governance, have involved a "rule of self-restraint."
5    *Barrows v. Jackson,* 346 U.S. 249, 255 (1953). Congress can, of course, resolve the
6    question one way or another, save as the requirements of Article III dictate
7    otherwise. *Muskrat v. United States,* 219 U.S. 346 (1911).

8    Where statutes are concerned, the trend is toward enlargement of the class of
9    people who may protest administrative action. The whole drive for enlarging the
10   category of aggrieved "persons" is symptomatic of that trend. In a closely
11   analogous case, we held that an existing entrepreneur had standing to challenge
12   the legality of the entrance of a newcomer into the business, because the
13   established business was allegedly protected by a valid city ordinance that
14   protected it from unlawful competition. *Chicago v. Atchison, T. & S.F. R. Co.,* 357
15   U.S. 77, 83-84 (1958). In that tradition was *Hardin v. Kentucky Utilities Co.,* 390
16   U.S. 1 (1968), which involved a section of the TVA Act designed primarily to
17   protect, through area limitations, private utilities against TVA competition. We
18   held that no explicit statutory provision was necessary to confer standing, since the
19   private utility bringing suit was within the class of persons that the statutory
20   provision was designed to protect.

21   It is argued that the *Chicago* case and the *Hardin* case are relevant here because
22   of § 4 of the Bank Service Corporation Act of 1962, 76 Stat. 1132, 12 U.S.C. § 1864,
23   which provides:

24       "No bank service corporation may engage in any activity other than the
25       performance of bank services for banks."

26   The Court of Appeals for the First Circuit held in *Arnold Tours, Inc. v. Camp,* 408
27   F.2d 1147, 1153 (1st Cir. 1969), that, by reason of § 4, a data processing company
28   has standing to contest the legality of a national bank performing data processing
29   services for other banks and bank customers:

30       "Section 4 had a broader purpose than regulating only the service
31       corporations. It was also a response to the fears expressed by a few senators
32       that, without such a prohibition, the bill would have enabled 'banks to
33       engage in a nonbanking activity,' S.Rep. No. 2105, [87th Cong., 2d Sess., 7-
34       12] (Supplemental views of Senators Proxmire, Douglas, and Newberger),
35       and thus constitute 'a serious exception to the accepted public policy which
36       strictly limits banks to banking.' (Supplemental views of Senators Muskie
37       and Clark). We think Congress has provided the sufficient statutory aid to
38       standing even though the competition may not be the precise kind
39       Congress legislated against."

1   We do not put the issue in those words, for they implicate the merits. We do think,
2   however, that § 4 arguably brings a competitor within the zone of interests
3   protected by it.

4   That leaves the remaining question, whether judicial review of the Comptroller's
5   action has been precluded. We do not think it has been. There is great contrariety
6   among administrative agencies created by Congress as respects "the extent to
7   which, and the procedures by which, different measures of control afford judicial
8   review of administrative action." *Stark v. Wickard,* 321 U.S. 288, 312 (1944)
9   (FRANKFURTER, J., dissenting). The answer, of course, depends on the particular
10  enactment under which review is sought. It turns on "the existence of courts and
11  the intent of Congress as deduced from the statutes and precedents." *Id.* at 308.

12  The Administrative Procedure Act provides that the provisions of the Act
13  authorizing judicial review apply "except to the extent that—(1) statutes preclude
14  judicial review; or (2) agency action is committed to agency discretion by law." 5
15  U.S.C. § 701(a) (1964 ed., Supp. IV).

16  In *Shaughnessy v. Pedreiro,* 349 U.S. 48, 51 (1955), we referred to "the generous
17  review provisions" of that Act, and, in that case, as well as in others, (*see Rusk v.*
18  *Cort,* 369 U.S. 367, 379-380 (1962)) we have construed that Act not grudgingly,
19  but as serving a broadly remedial purpose.

20  We read § 701(a) as sympathetic to the issue presented in this case. As stated in the
21  House Report:

22      "The statutes of Congress are not merely advisory when they relate to
23      administrative agencies, any more than in other cases. To preclude judicial
24      review under this bill, a statute, if not specific in withholding such review,
25      must, upon its face, give clear and convincing evidence of an intent to
26      withhold it. The mere failure to provide specially by statute for judicial
27      review is certainly no evidence of intent to withhold review."

28  H.R.Rep. No.1980, 79th Cong., 2d Sess., 41.

29  There is no presumption against judicial review and in favor of administrative
30  absolutism (*see Abbott Laboratories v. Gardner,* 387 U.S. 136, 140 (1967)), unless
31  that purpose is fairly discernible in the statutory scheme. *Cf. Switchmen's Union*
32  *v. National Mediation Board,* 320 U.S. 297 (1943).

33  We find no evidence that Congress, in either the Bank Service Corporation Act or
34  the National Bank Act, sought to preclude judicial review of administrative rulings
35  by the Comptroller as to the legitimate scope of activities available to national
36  banks under those statutes. Both Acts are clearly "relevant" statutes within the
37  meaning of § 702. The Acts do not, in terms, protect a specified group. But their

1   general policy is apparent, and those whose interests are directly affected by a
2   broad or narrow interpretation of the Acts are easily identifiable. It is clear that
3   petitioners, as competitors of national banks which are engaging in data processing
4   services, are within that class of "aggrieved" persons who, under § 702, are entitled
5   to judicial review of "agency action."

6   Whether anything in the Bank Service Corporation Act or the National Bank Act
7   gives petitioners a "legal interest" that protects them against violations of those
8   Acts, and whether the actions of respondents did in fact, violate either of those
9   Acts, are questions which go to the merits, and remain to be decided below.

10  We hold that petitioners have standing to sue, and that the case should be
11  remanded for a hearing on the merits.

12  *Reversed and remanded.*

13

14  **Air Courier Conf. v. Postal Workers**

15  498 U.S. 517 (1991)

16  February 26, 1991

17  CHIEF JUSTICE REHNQUIST delivered the opinion of the Court.

18  This case requires us to decide whether postal employees are within the "zone of
19  interests" of the Private Express Statutes, so that they may challenge the action of
20  the United States Postal Service in suspending the operation of the PES with
21  respect to a practice of private courier services called "international remailing." We
22  hold that they are not.

23  Since its establishment, the United States Postal Service has exercised a monopoly
24  over the carriage of letters in and from the United States. The postal monopoly is
25  codified in a group of statutes known as the Private Express Statutes (PES), 18
26  U.S.C. §§ 1693-1699 and 39 U.S.C. §§ 601-606. The monopoly was created by
27  Congress as a revenue protection measure for the Postal Service to enable it to
28  fulfill its mission. It prevents private competitors from offering service on low-cost
29  routes at prices below those of the Postal Service, while leaving the Service with
30  high-cost routes and insufficient means to fulfill its mandate of providing uniform
31  rates and service to patrons in all areas, including those that are remote or less
32  populated.

33  A provision of the PES allows the Postal Service to "suspend [the PES restrictions]
34  upon any mail route where the public interest requires the suspension." 39 U.S.C.
35  § 601(b). In 1979, the Postal Service suspended the PES restrictions for "extremely
36  urgent letters," thereby allowing overnight delivery of letters by private courier

1    services. 39 CFR § 320.6 (1990); 44 Fed.Reg. 61178 (1979). Private courier services,
2    including members of petitioner-intervenor Air Courier Conference of America,
3    relied on that suspension to engage in a practice called "international remailing."
4    This entails bypassing the Postal Service and using private courier systems to
5    deposit with foreign postal systems letters destined for foreign addresses.
6    Believing this international remailing was a misuse of the urgent-letter suspension,
7    the Postal Service issued a proposed modification and clarification of its regulation
8    in order to make clear that the suspension for extremely urgent letters did not
9    cover this practice. The comments received in response to the proposed rule were
10   overwhelmingly negative, and focused on the perceived benefits of international
11   remailing: Lower cost, faster delivery, greater reliability, and enhanced ability of
12   United States companies to remain competitive in the international market.
13   Because of the vigorous opposition to the proposed rule, the Postal Service agreed
14   to reconsider its position, and instituted a rulemaking "to remove the cloud" over
15   the validity of the international remailing services. 51 Fed.Reg. 9852, 9853 (1986).
16   After receiving additional comments and holding a public meeting on the subject,
17   on June 17, 1986, the Postal Service issued a proposal to suspend operation of the
18   PES for international remailing. Additional comments were received, and after
19   consideration of the record it had compiled, the Postal Service issued a final rule
20   suspending the operation of the PES with respect to international remailing.

21   Respondents, the American Postal Workers Union, AFL-CIO and the National
22   Association of Letter Carriers, AFL-CIO (Unions), sued in the United States
23   District Court for the District of Columbia, challenging the international remailing
24   regulation pursuant to the judicial review provisions of the Administrative
25   Procedure Act. They claimed that the rulemaking record was inadequate to support
26   a finding that the suspension of the PES for international remailing was in the
27   public interest. Petitioner Air Courier Conference of America (ACCA) intervened.

28   On December 20, 1988, the District Court granted summary judgment in favor of
29   the Postal Service and ACCA. The Unions appealed to the Court of Appeals for the
30   District of Columbia Circuit, and that court vacated the grant of summary
31   judgment. It held that the Unions satisfied the zone-of-interests requirement for
32   APA review and that the Postal Service's regulation was arbitrary and capricious
33   because it relied on too narrow an interpretation of "the public interest." In
34   determining that the Unions' interest in employment opportunities was protected
35   by the PES, the Court of Appeals noted that the PES were reenacted as part of the
36   Postal Reorganization Act (PRA), Pub.L. 91-375, 84 Stat. 719, *codified at* 39 U.S.C.
37   § 101 *et seq*. The Court of Appeals found that a "key impetus" and "principal
38   purpose" of the PRA was "to implement various labor reforms that would improve
39   pay, working conditions and labor-management relations for postal employees."
40   891 F.2d, at 309-310. Reasoning that "[t]he Unions' asserted interest is embraced
41   directly by the labor reform provisions of the PRA," 891 F.2d, at 310, and that "[t]he

1  PES constitute the linchpin in a statutory scheme concerned with maintaining an
2  effective, financially viable Postal Service," *ibid.*, the court concluded that "[t]he
3  interplay between the PES and the entire PRA persuades us that there is an
4  'arguable' or 'plausible' relationship between the purposes of the PES and the
5  interests of the Union[s]." 891 F.2d, at 309-310. The Court of Appeals also held
6  that "the revenue protective purposes of the PES, standing alone, plausibly relate
7  to the Unions' interest in preventing the reduction of employment opportunities,"
8  since "postal workers benefit from the PES's function in ensuring a sufficient
9  revenue base" for the Postal Service's activities. *Ibid.*

10  Addressing the merits of the Unions' challenge to the suspension order, the Court
11  of Appeals held that it was arbitrary and capricious, because the Postal Service had
12  applied § 601(b)'s public interest test too narrowly by considering only the benefits
13  of the international remail rule to the small segment of the Postal Service's
14  consumer base that engages in international commerce. We granted certiorari, and
15  we now reverse.

16  The United States Postal Service, nominally a respondent, argues along with ACCA
17  that the Unions do not have standing to challenge the Postal Service's suspension
18  of the PES for international remailing. * * *

19                                      * * *

20  To establish standing to sue under § 702 of the APA, respondents must establish
21  that they have suffered a legal wrong because of the challenged agency action, or
22  are adversely affected or "aggrieved by agency action within the meaning of a
23  relevant statute." Once they have shown that they are adversely affected, *i.e.*, have
24  suffered an "injury in fact," *see Allen v. Wright,* 468 U.S. 737, 751 (1984), the
25  Unions must show that they are within the zone of interests sought to be protected
26  through the PES. *Lujan v. National Wildlife Federation,* 497 U.S.
27  871 (1990); *Clarke v. Securities Industry Assn.,* 479 U.S. 388 (1987); *Association*
28  *of Data Processing Service Organizations, Inc. v. Camp,* 397 U.S. 150 (1970).
29  Specifically, "the plaintiff must establish that the injury he complains of (*his*
30  aggrievement, or the adverse effect *upon him*) falls within the 'zone of interests'
31  sought to be protected by the statutory provision whose violation forms the legal
32  basis of his complaint." *Lujan, supra,* at 883 (citing *Clarke, supra,* 479 U.S., at
33  396-397).

34  The District Court found that the Unions had satisfied the injury-in-fact test
35  because increased competition through international remailing services might
36  have an adverse effect on employment opportunities of postal workers. This
37  finding of injury in fact was not appealed. The question before us, then, is whether
38  the adverse effects on the employment opportunities of postal workers resulting
39  from the suspension is within the zone of interests encompassed by the PES—the

1 statutes which the Unions assert the Postal Service has violated in promulgating
2 the international remailing rule.

3 The Court of Appeals found that the Unions had standing because "the revenue-
4 protective purposes of the PES, standing alone, plausibly relate to the Unions'
5 interest in preventing the reduction of employment opportunities." 891 F.2d, at
6 310. This view is mistaken, for it conflates the zone-of-interests test with injury in
7 fact. In *Lujan*, this Court gave the following example illustrating how injury in fact
8 does not necessarily mean one is within the zone of interests to be protected by a
9 given statute:

> "The failure of an agency to comply with a statutory provision requiring 'on
> the record' hearings would assuredly have an adverse effect upon the
> company that has the contract to record and transcribe the agency's
> proceedings; but since the provision was obviously enacted to protect the
> interests of the parties to the proceedings, and not those of the reporters,
> that company would not be 'adversely affected within the meaning' of the
> statute."

17 497 U.S., at 883.

18 We must inquire then, as to Congress' intent in enacting the PES in order to
19 determine whether postal workers were meant to be within the zone of interests
20 protected by those statutes. The particular language of the statutes provides no
21 support for respondents' assertion that Congress intended to protect jobs with the
22 Postal Service. In fact, the provisions of 18 U.S.C. § 1696(c), allowing private
23 conveyance of letters if done on a one-time basis or without compensation, and 39
24 U.S.C. § 601(a), allowing letters to be carried out of the mails if certain procedures
25 are followed, indicate that the congressional concern was not with opportunities
26 for postal workers, but with the receipt of necessary revenues for the Postal Service.

27 Nor does the history of this legislation—such as it is—indicate that the PES were
28 intended for the benefit of postal workers. * * *

29                                        * * *

30 The PES enable the Postal Service to fulfill its responsibility to provide service to
31 all communities at a uniform rate by preventing private courier services from
32 competing selectively with the Postal Service on its most profitable routes. If
33 competitors could serve the lower cost segment of the market, leaving the Postal
34 Service to handle the high-cost services, the Service would lose lucrative portions
35 of its business, thereby increasing its average unit cost and requiring higher prices
36 to all users. The postal monopoly, therefore, exists to ensure that postal services
37 will be provided to the citizenry at large, and not to secure employment for postal
38 workers.

1  The Unions' claim on the merits is that the Postal Service has failed to comply with
2  the mandate of 39 U.S.C. § 601(b) that the PES be suspended only if the public
3  interest requires. The foregoing discussion has demonstrated that the PES were
4  not designed to protect postal employment or further postal job opportunities, but
5  the Unions argue that the courts should look beyond the PES to the entire 1970
6  Postal Reorganization Act in applying the zone-of-interests test. The Unions argue
7  that, because one of the purposes of the labor-management provisions of the PRA
8  was to stabilize labor-management relations within the Postal Service, and because
9  the PES is the "linchpin" of the Postal Service, employment opportunities of postal
10 workers are arguably within the zone of interests covered by the PES. The Unions
11 rely upon our opinion in *Clarke v. Securities Industry Assn.*, 479 U.S. 388 (1987),
12 to support this contention.

13 *Clarke* is the most recent in a series of cases in which we have held that competitors
14 of regulated entities have standing to challenge regulations. In *Clarke,* we said that
15 "we are not limited to considering the statute under which respondents sued, but
16 may consider any provision that helps us to understand Congress' overall purposes
17 in the National Bank Act." 479 U.S., at 401. This statement, like all others in our
18 opinions, must be taken in the context in which it was made. In the next paragraph
19 of the opinion, the Court pointed out that 12 U.S.C. § 36, which the plaintiffs in
20 that case claimed had been misinterpreted by the Comptroller, was itself "a limited
21 exception to the otherwise applicable requirement of [12 U.S.C.] § 81," limiting the
22 places at which a national bank could transact business to its headquarters and any
23 "branches" permitted by § 36. Thus, the zone-of-interests test was to be applied
24 not merely in the light of § 36, which was the basis of the plaintiffs' claim on the
25 merits, but also in the light of § 81, to which § 36 was an exception.

26 The situation in the present case is quite different. The only relationship between
27 the PES, upon which the Unions rely for their claim on the merits, and the labor-
28 management provisions of the PRA, upon which the Unions rely for their standing,
29 is that both were included in the general codification of postal statutes embraced
30 in the PRA. * * *To adopt the unions' contention would require us to hold that the
31 "relevant statute" in this case is the PRA, with all of its various provisions united
32 only by the fact that they deal with the Postal Service. But to accept this level of
33 generality in defining the "relevant statute" could deprive the zone-of-interests test
34 of virtually all meaning.

35 Unlike the two sections of the National Bank Act discussed in *Clarke, supra,* none
36 of the provisions of the PES has any integral relationship with the labor-
37 management provisions of the PRA. * * *

38 * * * The Court of Appeals referred to the PES as the "linchpin" of the Postal
39 Service, which it may well be; but it stretches the zone-of-interests test too far to

1   say that, because of that fact, those whom a different part of the PRA was designed
2   to benefit may challenge a violation of the PES.

3   It would be a substantial extension of our holdings in *Clarke, supra, Data*
4   *Processing, supra,* and *Investment Co. Institute, supra,* to allow the Unions in this
5   case to leapfrog from their asserted protection under the labor-management
6   provisions of the PRA to their claim on the merits under the PES. We decline to
7   make that extension, and hold that the Unions do not have standing to challenge
8   the Postal Service's suspension of the PES to permit private couriers to engage in
9   international remailing. We therefore do not reach the merits of the Unions' claim
10  that the suspension was not in the public interest. The judgment of the Court of
11  Appeals is

12  *Reversed.*

13  JUSTICE STEVENS, with whom JUSTICE MARSHALL and JUSTICE
14  BLACKMUN join, concurring in the judgment.

15  There is no ambiguity in the text of 39 U.S.C. § 410(a). That section of the Postal
16  Reorganization Act provides that the judicial review provisions of the
17  Administrative Procedure Act (APA) do not apply to the exercise of the powers of
18  the Postal Service. It is therefore not only unnecessary, but also unwise, for the
19  Court to issue an opinion on the entirely hypothetical question whether, if the APA
20  did authorize judicial review of actions of the Postal Service, its employees would
21  have standing to invoke such review to challenge a regulation that may curtail their
22  job opportunities. I therefore do not join the opinion discussing this hypothetical
23  standing question.

24  Nor do I consider it necessary to decide whether this objection to judicial review
25  may be waived by the Government, because it is surely a matter that we may notice
26  on our own motion. Faithful adherence to the doctrine of judicial restraint provides
27  a fully adequate justification for deciding this case on the best and narrowest
28  ground available. I would do so. Accordingly, relying solely on 39 U.S.C. § 410(a),
29  I concur in the Court's judgment that the Unions' challenge must be dismissed.

30

31  ## 2. Article III Standing Doctrine

32  Article III of the Constitution gives federal courts jurisdiction over "cases" and
33  "controversies." But what makes something a case or controversy, within the
34  meaning of the Constitution? One requirement, according to the Supreme Court,
35  is that the parties before the court have something meaningful at stake. The
36  Supreme Court's constitutional standing cases seek to define what that is.

1    Constitutional standing requirements apply in all cases, but in most litigation, the
2    requirements are so clearly met that the issue is never even discussed, in part
3    because, ordinarily, only those with a concrete, personal interest in a case will go
4    to the enormous trouble and expense of litigating it. But matters can be different
5    in administrative law, where agency decisions often reflect public policy choices
6    with broad—and diffuse—impacts. For many decades, organizations have brought
7    litigation in "the public interest," as they understand it, subjecting those choices to
8    scrutiny. But does the Constitution impose limits on this kind of litigation? The
9    Supreme Court spelled out the constitutional requirements in the controversial
10   *Lujan v. Defenders of Wildlife* decision. The *FEC v. Akins* case addresses
11   constitutional as well as non-constitutional standing.

12

## Lujan v. Defenders of Wildlife

14   504 U.S. 555 (1992)

15   June 12, 1992

16   JUSTICE SCALIA delivered the opinion of the Court with respect to Parts I, II, III-
17   A, and IV; and an opinion with respect to Part III-B, in which THE CHIEF
18   JUSTICE, JUSTICE WHITE, and JUSTICE THOMAS join.

19   This case involves a challenge to a rule promulgated by the Secretary of the Interior
20   interpreting § 7 of the Endangered Species Act of 1973 (ESA), 87 Stat. 892, as
21   amended, 16 U.S.C. § 1536, in such fashion as to render it applicable only to actions
22   within the United States or on the high seas. The preliminary issue, and the only
23   one we reach, is whether respondents here, plaintiffs below, have standing to seek
24   judicial review of the rule.

25                                       I

26   The ESA seeks to protect species of animals against threats to their continuing
27   existence caused by man. The ESA instructs the Secretary of the Interior to
28   promulgate by regulation a list of those species which are either endangered or
29   threatened under enumerated criteria, and to define the critical habitat of these
30   species. Section 7(a)(2) of the Act then provides, in pertinent part:

31      "Each Federal agency shall, in consultation with and with the assistance of
32      the Secretary [of the Interior], insure that any action authorized, funded,
33      or carried out by such agency . . . is not likely to jeopardize the continued
34      existence of any endangered species or threatened species or result in the
35      destruction or adverse modification of habitat of such species which is
36      determined by the Secretary, after consultation as appropriate with
37      affected States, to be critical."

1    16 U.S.C. § 1536(a)(2).

2    In 1978, the Fish and Wildlife Service (FWS) and the National Marine Fisheries
3    Service (NMFS), on behalf of the Secretary of the Interior and the Secretary of
4    Commerce respectively, promulgated a joint regulation stating that the obligations
5    imposed by § 7(a)(2) extend to actions taken in foreign nations. The next year,
6    however, the Interior Department began to reexamine its position. A revised joint
7    regulation, reinterpreting § 7(a)(2) to require consultation only for actions taken
8    in the United States or on the high seas, was proposed in 1983 and promulgated in
9    1986.

10   Shortly thereafter, respondents, organizations dedicated to wildlife conservation
11   and other environmental causes, filed this action against the Secretary of the
12   Interior, seeking a declaratory judgment that the new regulation is in error as to
13   the geographic scope of § 7(a)(2) and an injunction requiring the Secretary to
14   promulgate a new regulation restoring the initial interpretation. The District Court
15   granted the Secretary's motion to dismiss for lack of standing. The Court of Appeals
16   for the Eighth Circuit reversed by a divided vote. On remand, the Secretary moved
17   for summary judgment on the standing issue, and respondents moved for
18   summary judgment on the merits. The District Court denied the Secretary's
19   motion, on the ground that the Eighth Circuit had already determined the standing
20   question in this case; it granted respondents' merits motion, and ordered the
21   Secretary to publish a revised regulation. The Eighth Circuit affirmed. We granted
22   certiorari.

23                                             II

24   Though some of its elements express merely prudential considerations that are
25   part of judicial self-government, the core component of standing is an essential
26   and unchanging part of the case-or-controversy requirement of Article III. See,
27   *e.g., Allen v. Wright,* 468 U.S. 737, 751 (1984). Over the years, our cases have
28   established that the irreducible constitutional minimum of standing contains three
29   elements. First, the plaintiff must have suffered an "injury in fact" -an invasion of
30   a legally protected interest which is (a) concrete and particularized, see *id.,* at
31   756; *Warth v. Seldin,* 422 U.S. 490, 508 (1975); *Sierra Club v. Morton,* 405 U.S.
32   727, 740-741, n. 16 (1972);[1] 1 and (b) "actual or imminent, not 'conjectural' or
33   'hypothetical,'"" *Whitmore, supra,* at 155 (quoting *Los Angeles v. Lyons,* 461 U.S.
34   95,102 (1983)). Second, there must be a causal connection between the injury and
35   the conduct complained of-the injury has to be "fairly . . . trace[able] to the
36   challenged action of the defendant, and not . . . thee] result [of] the independent

---

[1] By particularized, we mean that the injury must affect the plaintiff in a personal
and individual way.

724

1  action of some third party not before the court." *Simon v. Eastern Ky. Welfare*
2  *Rights Organization,* 426 U.S. 26, 41-42 (1976). Third, it must be "likely," as
3  opposed to merely "speculative," that the injury will be "redressed by a favorable
4  decision." *Id.,* at 38, 43.

5  The party invoking federal jurisdiction bears the burden of establishing these
6  elements. Since they are not mere pleading requirements but rather an
7  indispensable part of the plaintiff's case, each element must be supported in the
8  same way as any other matter on which the plaintiff bears the burden of proof,
9  i. *e.,* with the manner and degree of evidence required at the successive stages of
10  the litigation. , At the pleading stage, general factual allegations of injury resulting
11  from the defendant's conduct may suffice, for on a motion to dismiss we
12  "presum[e] that general allegations embrace those specific facts that are necessary
13  to support the claim." *National Wildlife Federation, supra,* at 889. In response to
14  a summary judgment motion, however, the plaintiff can no longer rest on such
15  "mere allegations," but must "set forth" by affidavit or other evidence "specific
16  facts," Fed. Rule Civ. Proc. 56(e), which for purposes of the summary judgment
17  motion will be taken to be true. And at the final stage, those facts (if controverted)
18  must be "supported adequately by the evidence adduced at trial." *Gladstone,*
19  *Realtors v. Village of Bellwood,* 441 U.S. 91, 115, n.31.

20  When the suit is one challenging the legality of government action or inaction, the
21  nature and extent of facts that must be averred (at the summary judgment stage)
22  or proved (at the trial stage) in order to establish standing depends considerably
23  upon whether the plaintiff is himself an object of the action (or forgone action) at
24  issue. If he is, there is ordinarily little question that the action or inaction has
25  caused him injury, and that a judgment preventing or requiring the action will
26  redress it. When, however, as in this case, a plaintiff's asserted injury arises from
27  the government's allegedly unlawful regulation (or lack of regulation) of *someone*
28  *else,* much more is needed. In that circumstance, causation and redressability
29  ordinarily hinge on the response of the regulated (or regulable) third party to the
30  government action or inaction-and perhaps on the response of others as well. The
31  existence of one or more of the essential elements of standing "depends on the
32  unfettered choices made by independent actors not before the courts and whose
33  exercise of broad and legitimate discretion the courts cannot presume either to
34  control or to predict," *ASARCO Inc. v. Kadish,* 490 U.S. 605, 615 (1989) (opinion
35  of KENNEDY, J.); see also *Simon, supra,* at 41-42; and it becomes the burden of
36  the plaintiff to adduce facts showing that those choices have been or will be made
37  in such manner as to produce causation and permit redressability of injury. Thus,
38  when the plaintiff is not himself the object of the government action or inaction he
39  challenges, standing is not precluded, but it is ordinarily "substantially more
40  difficult" to establish.

1     *Allen, supra,* at 758; *Simon, supra,* at 44-45; *Warth, supra,* at 505.

2                         III

3     We think the Court of Appeals failed to apply the foregoing principles in denying
4     the Secretary's motion for summary judgment. Respondents had not made the
5     requisite demonstration of (at least) injury and redressability.

6                         A

7     Respondents' claim to injury is that the lack of consultation with respect to certain
8     funded activities abroad "increas[es] the rate of extinction of endangered and
9     threatened species." Of course, the desire to use or observe an animal species, even
10    for purely esthetic purposes, is undeniably a cognizable interest for purpose of
11    standing. See, *e. g., Sierra Club v. Morton,* 405 U.S., at 734. "But the 'injury in fact'
12    test requires more than an injury to a cognizable interest. It requires that the party
13    seeking review be himself among the injured." *Id.,* at 734-735. To survive the
14    Secretary's summary judgment motion, respondents had to submit affidavits or
15    other evidence showing, through specific facts, not only that listed species were in
16    fact being threatened by funded activities abroad, but also that one or more of
17    respondents' members would thereby be "directly" affected apart from their"
18    'special interest' in the] subject." *Id.,* at 735, 739. See generally *Hunt v.*
19    *Washington State Apple Advertising Comm'n,* 432 U.S. 333, 343 (1977).

20    With respect to this aspect of the case, the Court of Appeals focused on the
21    affidavits of two Defenders' members Joyce Kelly and Amy Skilbred. Ms. Kelly
22    stated that she traveled to Egypt in 1986 and "observed the traditional habitat of
23    the endangered nile crocodile there and intend[s] to do so again, and hope[s] to
24    observe the crocodile directly," and that she "will suffer harm in fact as the result
25    of [the] American . . .role . . . in overseeing the rehabilitation of the Aswan High
26    Dam on the Nile . . . and [in] develop[ing] . . . Egypt's . . . Master Water Plan." Ms.
27    Skilbred averred that she traveled to Sri Lanka in 1981 and "observed the] habitat"
28    of "endangered species such as the Asian elephant and the leopard" at what is now
29    the site of the Mahaweli project funded by the Agency for International
30    Development (AID), although she "was unable to see any of the endangered
31    species"; "this development project," she continued, "will seriously reduce
32    endangered, threatened, and endemic species habitat including areas that I visited
33    . . . [, which] may severely shorten the future of these species"; that threat, she
34    concluded, harmed her because she "intend[s] to return to Sri Lanka in the future
35    and hope[s] to be more fortunate in spotting at least the endangered elephant and
36    leopard." When Ms. Skilbred was asked at a subsequent deposition if and when she
37    had any plans to return to Sri Lanka, she reiterated that "I intend to go back to Sri
38    Lanka," but confessed that she had no current plans:

1      "I don't know [when]. There is a civil war going on right now. I don't know.

2      Not next year, I will say. In the future."

3 We shall assume for the sake of argument that these affidavits contain facts

4 showing that certain agency-funded projects threaten listed species-though that is

5 questionable. They plainly contain no facts, however, showing how damage to the

6 species will produce "imminent" injury to Mses. Kelly and Skilbred. That the

7 women "had visited" the areas of the projects before the projects commenced

8 proves nothing. "'Past exposure to illegal conduct does not in itself show a present

9 case or controversy regarding injunctive relief . . . if unaccompanied by any

10 continuing, present adverse effects.'" *Lyons*, 461 U.S., at 102 (quoting *O'Shea v.*

11 *Littleton*, 414 U.S. 488, 495-496 (1974)). And the affiants' profession of an

12 "inten[t]" to return to the places they had visited before-where they will

13 presumably, this time, be deprived of the opportunity to observe animals of the

14 endangered species-is simply not enough. Such "some day" intentions-without any

15 description of concrete plans, or indeed even any specification of *when* the some

16 day will be-do not support a finding of the "actual or imminent" injury that our

17 cases require.

18 Besides relying upon the Kelly and Skilbred affidavits, respondents propose a

19 series of novel standing theories. The first, inelegantly styled "ecosystem nexus,"

20 proposes that any person who uses *any part* of a "contiguous ecosystem" adversely

21 affected by a funded activity has standing even if the activity is located a great

22 distance away. This approach, as the Court of Appeals correctly observed, is

23 inconsistent with our opinion in *National Wildlife Federation,* which held that a

24 plaintiff claiming injury from environmental damage must use the area affected by

25 the challenged activity and not an area roughly "in the vicinity" of it. It makes no

26 difference that the general-purpose section of the ESA states that the Act was

27 intended in part "to provide a means whereby the ecosystems upon which

28 endangered species and threatened species depend may be conserved," 16 U.S. C.

29 § 1531(b). To say that the Act protects ecosystems is not to say that the Act creates

30 (if it were possible) rights of action in persons who have not been injured in fact,

31 that is, persons who use portions of an ecosystem not perceptibly affected by the

32 unlawful action in question.

33 Respondents' other theories are called, alas, the "animal nexus" approach, whereby

34 anyone who has an interest in studying or seeing the endangered animals

35 anywhere on the globe has standing; and the "vocational nexus" approach, under

36 which anyone with a professional interest in such animals can sue. Under these

37 theories, anyone who goes to see Asian elephants in the Bronx Zoo, and anyone

38 who is a keeper of Asian elephants in the Bronx Zoo, has standing to sue because

39 the Director of the Agency for International Development (AID) did not consult

40 with the Secretary regarding the AID-funded project in Sri Lanka. This is beyond

1    all reason. Standing is not "an ingenious academic exercise in the
2    conceivable," *United States v. Students Challenging Regulatory Agency*
3    *Procedures (SCRAP),* 412 U.S. 669, 688 (1973), but as we have said requires, at the
4    summary judgment stage, a factual showing of perceptible harm. It is clear that the
5    person who observes or works with a particular animal threatened by a federal
6    decision is facing perceptible harm, since the very subject of his interest will no
7    longer exist. It is even plausible-though it goes to the outermost limit of
8    plausibility-to think that a person who observes or works with animals of a
9    particular species in the very area of the world where that species is threatened by
10    a federal decision is facing such harm, since some animals that might have been
11    the subject of his interest will no longer exist, see *Japan Whaling Assn. v.*
12    *American Cetacean Society,* 478 U.S. 221, 231, n. 4 (1986). It goes beyond the
13    limit, however, and into pure speculation and fantasy, to say that anyone who
14    observes or works with an endangered species, anywhere in the world, is
15    appreciably harmed by a single project affecting some portion of that species with
16    which he has no more specific connection.

17                                             B

18    Besides failing to show injury, respondents failed to demonstrate redressability.
19    Instead of attacking the separate decisions to fund particular projects allegedly
20    causing them harm, respondents chose to challenge a more generalized level of
21    Government action (rules regarding consultation), the invalidation of which would
22    affect all overseas projects. This programmatic approach has obvious practical
23    advantages, but also obvious difficulties insofar as proof of causation or
24    redressability is concerned. As we have said in another context, "suits challenging,
25    not specifically identifiable Government violations of law, but the particular
26    programs agencies establish to carry out their legal obligations . . . [are], even when
27    premised on allegations of several instances of violations of law, . . . rarely if ever
28    appropriate for federal court adjudication." *Allen,* 468 U.S., at 759-760.

29    The most obvious problem in the present case is redressability. Since the agencies
30    funding the projects were not parties to the case, the District Court could accord
31    relief only against the Secretary: He could be ordered to revise his regulation to
32    require consultation for foreign projects. But this would not remedy respondents'
33    alleged injury unless the funding agencies were bound by the Secretary's
34    regulation, which is very much an open question. Whereas in other contexts the
35    ESA is quite explicit as to the Secretary's controlling authority, see, *e. g.,* 16 U.S.C.
36    § 1533(a)(1) ("The Secretary shall" promulgate regulations determining
37    endangered species); § 1535(d)(1) ("The Secretary is authorized to provide
38    financial assistance to any State"), with respect to consultation the initiative, and
39    hence arguably the initial responsibility for determining statutory necessity, lies
40    with the agencies, see § 1536(a)(2) (*"Each Federal agency shall,* in consultation

1   with and with the assistance of the Secretary, insure that any" funded action is not
2   likely to jeopardize endangered or threatened species) (emphasis added). When
3   the Secretary promulgated the regulation at issue here, he thought it was binding
4   on the agencies, see 51 Fed. Reg. 19928 (1986). The Solicitor General, however, has
5   repudiated that position here, and the agencies themselves apparently deny the
6   Secretary's authority. * * * Respondents assert that this legal uncertainty did not
7   affect redressability (and hence standing) because the District Court itself could
8   resolve the issue of the Secretary's authority as a necessary part of its standing
9   inquiry. Assuming that it is appropriate to resolve an issue of law such as this in
10  connection with a threshold standing inquiry, resolution by the District Court
11  would not have remedied respondents' alleged injury anyway, because it would not
12  have been binding upon the agencies. They were not parties to the suit, and there
13  is no reason they should be obliged to honor an incidental legal determination the
14  suit produced.

15  The Court of Appeals tried to finesse this problem by simply proclaiming that "[w]e
16  are satisfied that an injunction requiring the Secretary to publish [respondents'
17  desired] regulatio[n] . . . would result in consultation." We do not know what would
18  justify that confidence, particularly when the Justice Department (presumably
19  after consultation with the agencies) has taken the position that the regulation is
20  not binding.

21                                      * * *

22  A further impediment to redressability is the fact that the agencies generally supply
23  only a fraction of the funding for a foreign project. AID, for example, has provided
24  less than 10% of the funding for the Mahaweli project. Respondents have produced
25  nothing to indicate that the projects they have named will either be suspended, or
26  do less harm to listed species, if that fraction is eliminated. As in *Simon*, 426 U.S.,
27  at 43-44, it is entirely conjectural whether the nonagency activity that affects
28  respondents will be altered or affected by the agency activity they seek to achieve.
29  There is no standing.

30                                       IV

31  The Court of Appeals found that respondents had standing for an additional
32  reason: because they had suffered a "procedural injury." The so-called "citizen-
33  suit" provision of the ESA provides, in pertinent part, that "any person may
34  commence a civil suit on his own behalf (A) to enjoin any person, including the
35  United States and any other governmental instrumentality or agency . . . who is
36  alleged to be in violation of any provision of this chapter." 16 U.S.C. § 1540(g). The
37  court held that, because § 7(a)(2) requires interagency consultation, the citizen-
38  suit provision creates a "procedural righ[t]" to consultation in all "persons"-so
39  that *anyone* can file suit in federal court to challenge the Secretary's (or

presumably any other official's) failure to follow the assertedly correct consultative procedure, notwithstanding his or her inability to allege any discrete injury flowing from that failure. To understand the remarkable nature of this holding one must be clear about what it does *not* rest upon: This is not a case where plaintiffs are seeking to enforce a procedural requirement the disregard of which could impair a separate concrete interest of theirs *(e. g.,* the procedural requirement for a hearing prior to denial of their license application, or the procedural requirement for an environmental impact statement before a federal facility is constructed next door to them).Nor is it simply a case where concrete injury has been suffered by many persons, as in mass fraud or mass tort situations. Nor, finally, is it the unusual case in which Congress has created a concrete private interest in the outcome of a suit against a private party for the Government's benefit, by providing a cash bounty for the victorious plaintiff. Rather, the court held that the injury-in-fact requirement had been satisfied by congressional conferral upon *all* persons of an abstract, selfcontained, noninstrumental "right" to have the Executive observe the procedures required by law. We reject this view.

We have consistently held that a plaintiff raising only a generally available grievance about government-claiming only harm to his and every citizen's interest in proper application of the Constitution and laws, and seeking relief that no more directly and tangibly benefits him than it does the public at large-does not state an Article III case or controversy. * * *

* * *

"It is an established principle," we said, "that to entitle a private individual to invoke the judicial power to determine the validity of executive or legislative action he must show that he has sustained or is immediately in danger of sustaining a direct injury as the result of that action and it is not sufficient that he has merely a general interest common to all members of the public." 302 U.S., at 634. * * *

We hold that respondents lack standing to bring this action and that the Court of Appeals erred in denying the summary judgment motion filed by the United States. The opinion of the Court of Appeals is hereby reversed, and the cause is remanded for proceedings consistent with this opinion.

It is so ordered.

JUSTICE KENNEDY, with whom JUSTICE SOUTER joins, concurring in part and concurring in the judgment.

* * *

1    I agree with the Court's conclusion in Part III-A that, on the record before us,
2    respondents have failed to demonstrate that they themselves are "among the
3    injured." *Sierra Club v. Morton*, 405 U.S. 727, 735 (1972). This component of the
4    standing inquiry is not satisfied unless "[p]laintiffs . . . demonstrate a 'personal
5    stake in the outcome.' . . . Abstract injury is not enough. The plaintiff must show
6    that he 'has sustained or is immediately in danger of sustaining some direct injury'
7    as the result of the challenged official conduct and the injury or threat of injury
8    must be both 'real and immediate,' not 'conjectural' or 'hypothetical.'" *Los Angeles*
9    *v. Lyons*, 461 U.S. 95, 101-102 (1983) (citations omitted).

10    While it may seem trivial to require that Mses. Kelly and Skilbred acquire airline
11    tickets to the project sites or announce a date certain upon which they will return,
12    this is not a case where it is reasonable to assume that the affiants will be using the
13    sites on a regular basis, nor do the affiants claim to have visited the sites since the
14    projects commenced. With respect to the Court's discussion of respondents'
15    "ecosystem nexus," "animal nexus," and "vocational nexus" theories, I agree that
16    on this record respondents' showing is insufficient to establish standing on any of
17    these bases. I am not willing to foreclose the possibility, however, that in different
18    circumstances a nexus theory similar to those proffered here might support a claim
19    to standing.

20    In light of the conclusion that respondents have not demonstrated a concrete
21    injury here sufficient to support standing under our precedents, I would not reach
22    the issue of redressability that is discussed by the plurality in Part III-B.

23                               \* \* \*

24    JUSTICE STEVENS, concurring in the judgment.

25    Because I am not persuaded that Congress intended the consultation requirement
26    in § 7(a)(2) of the Endangered Species Act of 1973 (ESA), 16 U. S. C. § 1536(a)(2),
27    to apply to activities in foreign countries, I concur in the judgment of reversal. I do
28    not, however, agree with the Court's conclusion that respondents lack standing
29    because the threatened injury to their interest in protecting the environment and
30    studying endangered species is not "imminent." Nor do I agree with the plurality's
31    additional conclusion that respondents' injury is not "redressable" in this
32    litigation.

33                                  I

34    In my opinion a person who has visited the critical habitat of an endangered
35    species has a professional interest in preserving the species and its habitat, and
36    intends to revisit them in the future has standing to challenge agency action that
37    threatens their destruction. Congress has found that a wide variety of endangered
38    species of fish, wildlife, and plants are of "aesthetic, ecological, educational,

historical, recreational, and scientific value to the Nation and its people." 16 U.S.
C. § 1531(a)(3). Given that finding, we have no license to demean the importance
of the interest that particular individuals may have in observing any species or its
habitat, whether those individuals are motivated by esthetic enjoyment, an interest
in professional research, or an economic interest in preservation of the species.
Indeed, this Court has often held that injuries to such interests are sufficient to
confer standing, and the Court reiterates that holding today. The Court
nevertheless concludes that respondents have not suffered "injury in fact" because
they have not shown that the harm to the endangered species will produce
"imminent" injury to them. I disagree. An injury to an individual's interest in
studying or enjoying a species and its natural habitat occurs when someone
(whether it be the Government or a private party) takes action that harms that
species and habitat. In my judgment, therefore, the "imminence" of such an injury
should be measured by the timing and likelihood of the threatened environmental
harm, rather than - as the Court seems to suggest - by the time that might elapse
between the present and the time when the individuals would visit the area if no
such injury should occur.

To understand why this approach is correct and consistent with our precedent, it
is necessary to consider the purpose of the standing doctrine. Concerned about
"the proper and properly limited-role of the courts in a democratic society," we
have long held that "Art. III judicial power exists only to redress or otherwise to
protect against injury to the complaining party." *Warth v. Seldin,* 422 U.S. 490,
498-499 (1975). The plaintiff must have a "personal stake in the outcome"
sufficient to "assure that concrete adverseness which sharpens the presentation of
issues upon which the court so largely depends for illumination of difficult . . .
questions."

*Baker v. Carr,* 369 U.S. 186, 204 (1962). * * * Consequently, we have denied
standing to plaintiffs whose likelihood of suffering any concrete adverse effect from
the challenged action was speculative. See, *e. g., Whitmore v. Arkansas,* 495 U.S.
149, 158-159 (1990); *Los Angeles v. Lyons,* 461 U.S. 95, 105 (1983); *O'Shea,* 414
U.S., at 497. In this case, however, the likelihood that respondents will be injured
by the destruction of the endangered species is not speculative. If respondents are
genuinely interested in the preservation of the endangered species and intend to
study or observe these animals in the future, their injury will occur as soon as the
animals are destroyed. Thus, the only potential source of "speculation" in this case
is whether respondents' intent to study or observe the animals is genuine. In my
view, Joyce Kelly and Amy Skilbred have introduced sufficient evidence to negate
petitioner's contention that their claims of injury are "speculative" or "conjectural."
* * *

* * *

732

1    JUSTICE BLACKMUN, with whom JUSTICE O'CONNOR joins, dissenting.

2    I part company with the Court in this case in two respects.

3    First, I believe that respondents have raised genuine issues of fact-sufficient to
4    survive summary judgment-both as to injury and as to redressability. Second, I
5    question the Court's breadth of language in rejecting standing for "procedural"
6    injuries. I fear the Court seeks to impose fresh limitations on the constitutional
7    authority of Congress to allow citizen suits in the federal courts for injuries deemed
8    "procedural" in nature. I dissent.

9                                             I

10                                          * * *

11                                           A

12    To survive petitioner's motion for summary judgment on standing, respondents
13    need not prove that they are actually or imminently harmed. They need show only
14    a "genuine issue" of material fact as to standing. Fed. Rule Civ. Proc. 56(c). This is
15    not a heavy burden. A "genuine issue" exists so long as "the evidence is such that a
16    reasonable   jury   could   return   a   verdict   for   the   nonmoving   party
17    [respondents]." *Anderson v. Liberty Lobby, Inc.,* 477 U.S. 242, 248 (1986). This
18    Court's "function is not [it]self to weigh the evidence and determine the truth of
19    the matter but to determine whether there is a genuine issue for trial." *Id.,* at 249.

20    The Court never mentions the "genuine issue" standard. Rather, the Court refers
21    to the type of evidence it feels respondents failed to produce, namely, "affidavits or
22    other evidence showing, through specific facts" the existence of injury. The Court
23    thereby confuses respondents' evidentiary burden (i. *e.,* affidavits asserting
24    "specific facts") in withstanding a summary judgment motion under Rule 56(e)
25    with the standard of proof (i. *e.,* the existence of a "genuine issue" of "material
26    fact") under Rule 56(c).

27    Were the Court to apply the proper standard for summary judgment, I believe it
28    would conclude that the sworn affidavits and deposition testimony of Joyce Kelly
29    and Amy Skilbred advance sufficient facts to create a genuine issue for trial
30    concerning whether one or both would be imminently harmed by the Aswan and
31    Mahaweli projects. In the first instance, as the Court itself concedes, the affidavits
32    contained facts making it at least "questionable" (and therefore within the province
33    of the factfinder) that certain agency funded projects threaten listed species. The
34    only remaining issue, then, is whether Kelly and Skilbred have shown that they
35    personally would suffer imminent harm.

36    I think a reasonable finder of fact could conclude from the information in the
37    affidavits and deposition testimony that either Kelly or Skilbred will soon return to

1    the project sites, thereby satisfying the "actual or imminent" injury standard. The
2    Court dismisses Kelly's and Skilbred's general statements that they intended to
3    revisit the project sites as "simply not enough." But those statements did not stand
4    alone. A reasonable finder of fact could conclude, based not only upon their
5    statements of intent to return, but upon their past visits to the project sites, as well
6    as their professional backgrounds, that it was likely that Kelly and Skilbred would
7    make a return trip to the project areas. Contrary to the Court's contention that
8    Kelly's and Skilbred's past visits "prov[e] nothing," the fact of their past visits could
9    demonstrate to a reasonable factfinder that Kelly and Skilbred have the requisite
10   resources and personal interest in the preservation of the species endangered by
11   the Aswan and Mahaweli projects to make good on their intention to return again.
12   Similarly, Kelly's and Skilbred's professional backgrounds in wildlife preservation,
13   also make it likely-at least far more likely than for the average citizen-that they
14   would choose to visit these areas of the world where species are vanishing.

15   By requiring a "description of concrete plans" or "specification of *when* the some
16   day [for a return visit] will be," the Court, in my view, demands what is likely an
17   empty formality. No substantial barriers prevent Kelly or Skilbred from simply
18   purchasing plane tickets to return to the Aswan and Mahaweli projects. This case
19   differs from other cases in which the imminence of harm turned largely on the
20   affirmative actions of third parties beyond a plaintiff's control. * * *

21   I fear the Court's demand for detailed descriptions of future conduct will do little
22   to weed out those who are genuinely harmed from those who are not. More likely,
23   it will resurrect a code-pleading formalism in federal court summary judgment
24   practice, as federal courts, newly doubting their jurisdiction, will demand more
25   and more particularized showings of future harm. Just to survive summary
26   judgment, for example, a property owner claiming a decline in the value of his
27   property from governmental action might have to specify the exact date he intends
28   to sell his property and show that there is a market for the property, lest it be
29   surmised he might not sell again. A nurse turned down for a job on grounds of her
30   race had better be prepared to show on what date she was prepared to start work,
31   that she had arranged daycare for her child, and that she would not have accepted
32   work at another hospital instead. And a Federal Tort Claims Act plaintiff alleging
33   loss of consortium should make sure to furnish this Court with a "description of
34   concrete plans" for her nightly schedule of attempted activities.

35   The Court also rejects respondents' claim of vocational or professional injury. The
36   Court says that it is "beyond all reason" that a zoo "keeper" of Asian elephants
37   would have standing to contest his Government's participation in the eradication
38   of all the Asian elephants in another part of the world. I am unable to see how the
39   distant location of the destruction *necessarily* (for purposes of ruling at summary
40   judgment) mitigates the harm to the elephant keeper. If there is no more access to

734

a future supply of the animal that sustains a keeper's livelihood, surely there is harm.

I have difficulty imagining this Court applying its rigid principles of geographic formalism anywhere outside the context of environmental claims. As I understand it, environmental plaintiffs are under no special constitutional standing disabilities. Like other plaintiffs, they need show only that the action they challenge has injured them, without necessarily showing they happened to be physically near the location of the alleged wrong. The Court's decision today should not be interpreted "to foreclose the possibility . . . that in different circumstances a nexus theory similar to those proffered here might support a claim to standing." (KENNEDY, J., concurring in part and concurring in judgment).

## B

\* \* \*

I find myself unable to agree with the plurality's analysis of redressability, based as it is on its invitation of executive lawlessness, ignorance of principles of collateral estoppel, unfounded assumptions about causation, and erroneous conclusions about what the record does not say. In my view, respondents have satisfactorily shown a genuine issue of fact as to whether their injury would likely be redressed by a decision in their favor.

## II

The Court concludes that any "procedural injury" suffered by respondents is insufficient to confer standing. It rejects the view that the "injury-in-fact requirement [is] satisfied by congressional conferral upon *all* persons of an abstract, selfcontained, noninstrumental 'right' to have the Executive observe the procedures required by law." *Ante,* at 573. Whatever the Court might mean with that very broad language, it cannot be saying that "procedural injuries" *as a class* are necessarily insufficient for purposes of Article III standing.

Most governmental conduct can be classified as "procedural." Many injuries caused by governmental conduct, therefore, are categorizable at some level of generality as "procedural" injuries. Yet, these injuries are not categorically beyond the pale of redress by the federal courts. \* \* \*

The Court expresses concern that allowing judicial enforcement of "agencies' observance of a particular, statutorily prescribed procedure" would "transfer from the President to the courts the Chief Executive's most important constitutional duty, to 'take Care that the Laws be faithfully executed,' Art. II, § 3." . In fact, the principal effect of foreclosing judicial enforcement of such procedures is to transfer

1 power into the hands of the Executive at the expense-not of the courts-but of
2 Congress, from which that power originates and emanates.

3 * * *

4 III

5 In conclusion, I cannot join the Court on what amounts to a slash-and-burn
6 expedition through the law of environmental standing. In my view, "[t]he very
7 essence of civil liberty certainly consists in the right of every individual to claim the
8 protection of the laws, whenever he receives an injury." *Marbury v. Madison*, 5
9 U.S. 137, 163 (1803). I dissent.

10

11 **Federal Election Commission v. Akins**

12 524 U.S. 11 (1998)

13 June 1, 1998

14 JUSTICE BREYER delivered the opinion of the Court.

15 The Federal Election Commission (FEC) has determined that the American Israel
16 Public Affairs Committee (AIPAC) is not a "political committee" as defined by the
17 Federal Election Campaign Act of 1971 (FECA or Act), 86 Stat. 11, as amended, 2
18 U.S.C. § 431(4), and, for that reason, the FEC has refused to require AIPAC to make
19 disclosures regarding its membership, contributions, and expenditures that FECA
20 would otherwise require. We hold that respondents, a group of voters, have
21 standing to challenge the Commission's determination in court, and we remand
22 this case for further proceedings.

23 I

24 In light of our disposition of this case, we believe it necessary to describe its
25 procedural background in some detail. As commonly understood, the FECA seeks
26 to remedy any actual or perceived corruption of the political process in several
27 important ways. The Act imposes limits upon the amounts that individuals,
28 corporations, "political committees" (including political action committees), and
29 political parties can contribute to a candidate for federal political office. §§ 441a(a),
30 441a(b), 441b. The Act also imposes limits on the amount these individuals or
31 entities can spend in coordination with a candidate. (It treats these expenditures
32 as "contributions to" a candidate for purposes of the Act.) § 441a(a)(7)(B)(i). As
33 originally written, the Act set limits upon the total amount that a candidate could
34 spend of his own money, and upon the amounts that other individuals,
35 corporations, and "political committees" could spend independent of a candidate-
36 though the Court found that certain of these last-mentioned limitations violated

736

1    the First Amendment. *Buckley v. Valeo,* 424 U.S. 1, 39-59 (1976) *(per curiam);*
2    *Federal Election Comm'n v. National Conservative Political Action Comm.,* 470
3    U.S. 480, 497 (1985); cf. *Colorado Republican Federal Campaign Comm. v.*
4    *Federal Election Comm'n,* 518 U.S. 604, 613-619 (1996) (opinion of BREYER, J.).

5    This case concerns requirements in the Act that extend beyond these better-known
6    contribution and expenditure limitations. In particular, the Act imposes extensive
7    recordkeeping and disclosure requirements upon groups that fall within the Act's
8    definition of a "political committee." Those groups must register with the FEC,
9    appoint a treasurer, keep names and addresses of contributors, track the amount
10   and purpose of disbursements, and file complex FEC reports that include lists of
11   donors giving in excess of $200 per year (often, these donors may be the group's
12   members), contributions, expenditures, and any other disbursements irrespective
13   of their purposes. §§ 432-434.

14                               \* \* \*

15    This case arises out of an effort by respondents, a group of voters with views often
16   opposed to those of AIPAC, to persuade the FEC to treat AIPAC as a "political
17   committee." Respondents filed a complaint with the FEC, stating that AIPAC had
18   made more than $1,000 in qualifying "expenditures" per year, and thereby became
19   a "political committee." They added that AIPAC had violated the FEC provisions
20   requiring "political committee[s]" to register and to make public the information
21   about members, contributions, and expenditures to which we have just
22   referred. *Id.,* at 2, 9-17. Respondents also claimed that AIPAC had violated § 441b
23   of FECA, which prohibits corporate campaign "contribution[sJ" and
24   "expenditure[sJ." They asked the FEC to find that AIPAC had violated the Act, and,
25   among other things, to order AIPAC to make public the information that FECA
26   demands of a "political committee."

27    AIPAC asked the FEC to dismiss the complaint. AIPAC described itself as an issue-
28   oriented organization that seeks to maintain friendship and promote goodwill
29   between the United States and Israel. \* \* \*

30                               \* \* \*

31    The FEC \* \* \* held that AIPAC was not subject to the disclosure requirements \* \* \*
32   . In the FEC's view, the Act's definition of "political committee" includes only those
33   organizations that have as a "major purpose" the nomination or election of
34   candidates. AIPAC, it added, was fundamentally an issue-oriented lobbying
35   organization, not a campaign-related organization, and hence AIPAC fell outside
36   the definition of a "political committee" regardless. The FEC consequently
37   dismissed respondents' complaint.

1 Respondents filed a petition in Federal District Court seeking review of the FEC's
2 determination dismissing their complaint. The District Court granted summary
3 judgment for the FEC, and a divided panel of the Court of Appeals affirmed. The
4 en banc Court of Appeals reversed, however, on the ground that the FEC's "major
5 purpose" test improperly interpreted the Act's definition of a "political
6 committee." We granted the FEC's petition for certiorari, which contained the
7 following two questions:

8 "1. Whether respondents had standing to challenge the Federal Election
9 Commission's decision not to bring an enforcement action in this case.

10 "2. Whether an organization that spends more than $1,000 on
11 contributions or coordinated expenditures in a calendar year, but is neither
12 controlled by a candidate nor has its major purpose the nomination or
13 election of candidates, is a 'political committee' within the meaning of the
14 [Act]."

15 We shall answer the first of these questions, but not the second.

16 <center>II</center>

17 The Solicitor General argues that respondents lack standing to challenge the FEC's
18 decision not to proceed against AIPAC. He claims that they have failed to satisfy
19 the "prudential" standing requirements upon which this Court has insisted.
20 See, *e.g., National Credit Union Admin. v. First Nat. Bank & Trust Co.,* 522 U.S.
21 479, 488 (1998) *(NCUA); Association of Data Processing Service Organizations,*
22 *Inc. v. Camp,* 397 U.S. 150, 153 (1970) *(Data Processing).* He adds that
23 respondents have not shown that they "suffe[r] injury in fact," that their injury is
24 "fairly traceable" to the FEC's decision, or that a judicial decision in their favor
25 would "redres[s]" the injury. *E.g., Bennett v. Spear,* 520 U.S. 154, 162 (1997)
26 (internal quotation marks omitted); *Lujan v. Defenders of Wildlife,* 504 U.S. 555,
27 560-561 (1992). In his view, respondents' District Court petition consequently
28 failed to meet Article Ill's demand for a "case" or "controversy."

29 We do not agree with the FEC's "prudential standing" claim. Congress has
30 specifically provided in FECA that "[a]ny person who believes a violation of this
31 Act . . . has occurred, may file a complaint with the Commission." § 437g(a)(1). It
32 has added that "[a]ny party aggrieved by an order of the Commission dismissing a
33 complaint filed by such party . . . may file a petition" in district court seeking review
34 of that dismissal. § 437g(a)(8)(A). History associates the word "aggrieved" with a
35 congressional intent to cast the standing net broadly—beyond the common-law
36 interests and substantive statutory rights upon which "prudential" standing
37 traditionally rested. *Scripps-Howard Radio, Inc. v. FCC,* 316 U.S. 4 (1942); *FCC v.*
38 *Sanders Brothers Radio Station,* 309 U.S. 470 (1940); *Office of Communication*
39 *of the United Church of Christ v. FCC,* 359 F.2d 994 (CADC 1966) (Burger,
738

J.); *Associated Industries of New York State v. Ickes,* 134 F.2d 694 (CA2 1943) (Frank, J.). Cf. Administrative Procedure Act, 5 U.S. C. § 702 (stating that those "suffering legal wrong" or "adversely affected or aggrieved . . . within the meaning of a relevant statute" may seek judicial review of agency action).

Moreover, prudential standing is satisfied when the injury asserted by a plaintiff" 'arguably [falls] within the zone of interests to be protected or regulated by the statute . . . in question.'" *NCUA, supra,* at 488 (quoting *Data Processing, supra,* at 153). The injury of which respondents complain—their failure to obtain relevant information—is injury of a kind that FECA seeks to address. *Buckley, supra,* at 6667 ("political committees" must disclose contributors and disbursements to help voters understand who provides which candidates with financial support). We have found nothing in the Act that suggests Congress intended to exclude voters from the benefits of these provisions, or otherwise to restrict standing, say, to political parties, candidates, or their committees.

Given the language of the statute and the nature of the injury, we conclude that Congress, intending to protect voters such as respondents from suffering the kind of injury here at issue, intended to authorize this kind of suit. Consequently, respondents satisfy "prudential" standing requirements. Cf. *Raines v. Byrd,* 521 U.S. 811, 820, n. 3 (1997) (explicit grant of authority to bring suit "eliminates any prudential standing limitations and significantly lessens the risk of unwanted conflict with the Legislative Branch").

Nor do we agree with the FEC or the dissent that Congress lacks the constitutional power to authorize federal courts to adjudicate this lawsuit. Article III, of course, limits Congress' grant of judicial power to "cases" or "controversies." That limitation means that respondents must show, among other things, an "injury in fact" –a requirement that helps assure that courts will not "pass upon . . . abstract, intellectual problems," but adjudicate "concrete, living contestes] between adversaries." *Coleman v. Miller,* 307 U.S. 433, 460 (1939) (FRANKFURTER, J., dissenting); see also *Bennett, supra,* at 167; *Lujan, supra,* at 560-561. In our view, respondents here have suffered a genuine "injury in fact."

The "injury in fact" that respondents have suffered consists of their inability to obtain information—lists of AIPAC donors (who are, according to AIPAC, its members), and campaign-related contributions and expenditures—that, on respondents' view of the law, the statute requires that AIPAC make public. There is no reason to doubt their claim that the information would help them (and others to whom they would communicate it) to evaluate candidates for public office, especially candidates who received assistance from AIPAC, and to evaluate the role that AIPAC's financial assistance might play in a specific election. Respondents' injury consequently seems concrete and particular. Indeed, this Court has previously held that a plaintiff suffers an "injury in fact" when the plaintiff fails to

1  obtain information which must be publicly disclosed pursuant to a statute. *Public*
2  *Citizen v. Department of Justice,* 491 U.S. 440, 449 (1989) (failure to obtain
3  information subject to disclosure under Federal Advisory Committee Act
4  "constitutes a sufficiently distinct injury to provide standing to sue"). See
5  also *Havens Realty Corp. v. Coleman,* 455 U.S. 363, 373-374 (1982) (deprivation
6  of information about housing availability constitutes "specific injury" permitting
7  standing).

8                                           * * *

9  The FEC's strongest argument is its contention that this lawsuit involves only a
10 "generalized grievance." (Indeed, if *Richardson* is relevant at all, it is because of its
11 broad discussion of *this* matter, see *id.,* at 176-178, not its basic rationale.) The
12 FEC points out that respondents' asserted harm (their failure to obtain
13 information) is one which is "'shared in substantially equal measure by all or a
14 large class of citizens.'" Brief for Petitioner 28 (quoting *Warth v. Seldin,* 422 U.S.
15 490, 499 (1975)). This Court, the FEC adds, has often said that "generalized
16 grievance[s]" are not the kinds of harms that confer standing. Brief for Petitioner
17 28; see also *Lujan,* 504 U.S., at 573-574; *Allen v. Wright,* 468 U.S. 737, 755-756
18 (1984); *Valley Forge Christian College v. Americans United for Separation of*
19 *Church and State, Inc.,* 454 U.S. 464, 475-479 (1982); *Richardson, supra,* at 176-
20 178; *Frothingham v. Mellon,* decided with *Massachusetts v. Mellon,* 262 U.S. 447,
21 487 (1923); *Ex parte Levitt,* 302 U.S. 633, 634 (1937) *(per curiam).* Whether
22 styled as a constitutional or prudential limit on standing, the Court has sometimes
23 determined that where large numbers of Americans suffer alike, the political
24 process, rather than the judicial process, may provide the more appropriate
25 remedy for a widely shared grievance. *Warth, supra,* at 500; *Schlesinger v.*
26 *Reservists Comm. to Stop the War,* 418 U.S. 208, 222 (1974); *Richardson,* 418
27 U.S., at 179; *id.,* at 188-189 (Powell, J., concurring); see also *Flast, supra,* at 131
28 (Harlan, J., dissenting).

29 The kind of judicial language to which the FEC points, however, invariably appears
30 in cases where the harm at issue is not only widely shared, but is also of an abstract
31 and indefinite nature—for example, harm to the "common concern for obedience
32 to law." *L. Singer & Sons v. Union Pacific R. Co.,* 311 U.S. 295, 303 (1940); see
33 also *Allen, supra,* at 754; *Schlesinger, supra,* at 217. Cf. *Lujan, supra,* at 572-578
34 (injury to interest in seeing that certain procedures are followed not normally
35 sufficient by itself to confer standing); *Frothingham, supra,* at 488 (party may not
36 merely assert that "he suffers in some indefinite way in common with people
37 generally"); *Perkins v. Lukens Steel Co.,* 310 U.S. 113, 125 (1940) (plaintiffs lack
38 standing because they have failed to show injury to "a particular right of their own,
39 as distinguished from the public's interest in the administration of the law"). The
40 abstract nature of the harm—for example, injury to the interest in seeing that the

1   law is obeyed—deprives the case of the concrete specificity that characterized those
2   controversies which were "the traditional concern of the courts at
3   Westminster," *Coleman,* 307 U.S., at 460 (Frankfurter, J., dissenting); and which
4   today prevents a plaintiff from obtaining what would, in effect, amount to an
5   advisory opinion. Cf. *Aetna Life Ins. Co. v. Haworth, 300* U.S. 227, 240-241
6   (1937).

7   Often the fact that an interest is abstract and the fact that it is widely shared go
8   hand in hand. But their association is not invariable, and where a harm is concrete,
9   though widely shared, the Court has found "injury in fact." See *Public Citizen,* 491
10   U.S., at 449-450 ("The fact that other citizens or groups of citizens might make the
11   same complaint after unsuccessfully demanding disclosure . . . does not lessen
12   [their] asserted injury"). Thus the fact that a political forum may be more readily
13   available where an injury is widely shared (while counseling against, say,
14   interpreting a statute as conferring standing) does not, by itself, automatically
15   disqualify an interest for Article III purposes. Such an interest, where sufficiently
16   concrete, may count as an "injury in fact." This conclusion seems particularly
17   obvious where (to use a hypothetical example) large numbers of individuals suffer
18   the same common-law injury (say, a widespread mass tort), or where large
19   numbers of voters suffer interference with voting rights conferred by law.
20   Cf. *Lujan, supra,* at 572; *Shaw v. Hunt,* 517 U.S. 899, 905 (1996). We conclude
21   that, similarly, the informational injury at issue here, directly related to voting, the
22   most basic of political rights, is sufficiently concrete and specific such that the fact
23   that it is widely shared does not deprive Congress of constitutional power to
24   authorize its vindication in the federal courts.

25   Respondents have also satisfied the remaining two constitutional standing
26   requirements. The harm asserted is "fairly traceable" to the FEC's decision about
27   which respondents complain. Of course, as the FEC points out, Brief for Petitioner
28   29-31, it is possible that even had the FEC agreed with respondents' view of the
29   law, it would still have decided in the exercise of its discretion not to require AIPAC
30   to produce the information. Cf. App. to Pet. for Cert. 98a (deciding to exercise
31   prosecutorial discretion, see *Heckler v. Chaney,* 470 U.S. 821 (1985), and "take no
32   further action" on § 441b allegation against AIPAC). But that fact does not destroy
33   Article III "causation," for we cannot know that the FEC would have exercised its
34   prosecutorial discretion in this way. Agencies often have discretion about whether
35   or not to take a particular action. Yet those adversely affected by a discretionary
36   agency decision generally have standing to complain that the agency based its
37   decision upon an improper legal ground. See, *e. g., Abbott Laboratories v.*
38   *Gardner,* 387 U.S. 136, 140 (1967) (discussing presumption of reviewability of
39   agency action); *Citizens to Preserve Overton Park, Inc. v. Volpe,* 401 U.S. 402, 410
40   (1971). If a reviewing court agrees that the agency misinterpreted the law, it will set
41   aside the agency's action and remand the case—even though the agency (like a new

1   jury after a mistrial) might later, in the exercise of its lawful discretion, reach the
2   same result for a different reason. *SEC* v. *Chenery Corp.,* 318 U.S. 80 (1943). Thus
3   respondents' "injury in fact" is "fairly traceable" to the FEC's decision not to issue
4   its complaint, even though the FEC might reach the same result exercising its
5   discretionary powers lawfully. For similar reasons, the courts in this case can
6   "redress" respondents' "injury in fact."

7   Finally, the FEC argues that we should deny respondents standing because this
8   case involves an agency's decision not to undertake an enforcement action—an
9   area generally not subject to judicial review. Brief for Petitioner 23, 29.
10  In *Heckler,* this Court noted that agency enforcement decisions "ha[ve]
11  traditionally been 'committed to agency discretion,'" and concluded that Congress
12  did not intend to alter that tradition in enacting the APA. 470 U.S., at 832; cf. 5
13  U.S.C. § 701(a) (courts will not review agency actions where "statutes preclude
14  judicial review," or where the "agency action is committed to agency discretion by
15  law"). We deal here with a statute that explicitly indicates the contrary.

16  In sum, respondents, as voters, have satisfied both prudential and constitutional
17  standing requirements. They may bring this petition for a declaration that the
18  FEC's dismissal of their complaint was unlawful. See 2 U.S.C. § 437 g(a)(8) (A).

19                                        III

20                                       * * *

21  For these reasons, the judgment of the Court of Appeals is vacated, and the case is
22  remanded for further proceedings consistent with this opinion.

23  It is so ordered.

24  JUSTICE SCALIA, with whom JUSTICE O'CONNOR and JUSTICE THOMAS join,
25  dissenting.

26  The provision of law at issue in this case is an extraordinary one, conferring upon
27  a private person the ability to bring an Executive agency into court to compel its
28  enforcement of the law against a third party. Despite its liberality, the
29  Administrative Procedure Act does not allow such suits, since enforcement action
30  is traditionally deemed "committed to agency discretion by law." 5 U.S.C. §
31  701(a)(2); *Heckler v. Chaney,* 470 U.S. 821, 827-835 (1985). If provisions such as
32  the present one were commonplace, the role of the Executive Branch in our system
33  of separated and equilibrated powers would be greatly reduced, and that of the
34  Judiciary greatly expanded.

35  Because this provision is so extraordinary, we should be particularly careful not to
36  expand it beyond its fair meaning. In my view the Court's opinion does that.
37  Indeed, it expands the meaning beyond what the Constitution permits.

1    I

2    It is clear that the Federal Election Campaign Act of 1971 (FECA or Act) does not
3    intend that *all* persons filing complaints with the Federal Election Commission
4    have the right to seek judicial review of the rejection of their complaints. This is
5    evident from the fact that the Act permits a complaint to be filed by
6    "[a]ny *person* who believes a violation of this Act . . . has occurred," 2 U.S.C. §
7    437g(a)(1) (emphasis added), but accords a right to judicial relief only to
8    "[a]ny *party aggrieved by* an order of the Commission dismissing a complaint
9    filed by such party," § 437 g(a)(8)(A) (emphasis added). The interpretation that
10   the Court gives the latter provision deprives it of almost all its limiting
11   force. *Any* voter can sue to compel the agency to require registration of an entity
12   as a political committee, even though the "aggrievement" consists of nothing more
13   than the deprivation of access to information whose public availability would have
14   been one of the consequences of registration.

15   This seems to me too much of a stretch. It should be borne in mind that the agency
16   action complained of here is not the refusal to make available information in its
17   possession that the Act requires to be disclosed. A person demanding provision of
18   information that the law requires the agency to furnish—one demanding
19   compliance with the Freedom of Information Act or the Federal Advisory
20   Committee Act, for example—can reasonably be described as being "aggrieved" by
21   the agency's refusal to provide it. What the respondents complain of in this suit,
22   however, is not the refusal to provide information, but the refusal (for an allegedly
23   improper reason) to commence an agency enforcement action against a third
24   person. That refusal *itself* plainly does not render respondents "aggrieved" within
25   the meaning of the Act, for in that case there would have been no reason for the
26   Act to differentiate between "person" in subsection (a)(1) and "party aggrieved" in
27   subsection (a)(8). Respondents claim that each of them is elevated to the special
28   status of a "party aggrieved" by the fact that the requested enforcement action (if
29   it was successful) would have had the effect, among others, of placing certain
30   information in the agency's possession, where respondents, along with everyone
31   else in the world, would have had access to it. It seems to me most unlikely that the
32   failure to produce that *effect—both* a secondary consequence of what respondents
33   immediately seek, *and* a consequence that affects respondents no more and with
34   no greater particularity than it affects virtually the entire population—would have
35   been meant to set apart each respondent as a "party aggrieved" (as opposed to just
36   a rejected complainant) within the meaning of the statute.

37   This conclusion is strengthened by the fact that this citizen-suit provision was
38   enacted two years after this Court's decision in *United States v. Richardson,* 418
39   U.S. 166 (1974), which, as I shall discuss at greater length below, gave Congress
40   every reason to believe that a voter's interest in information helpful to his exercise

743

of the franchise was *constitutionally inadequate* to confer standing. *Richardson* had said that a plaintiff's complaint that the Government was unlawfully depriving him of information he needed to "properly fulfill his obligations as a member of the electorate in voting" was "surely the kind of a generalized grievance" that does not state an Article III case or controversy. *Id.,* at 176.

\* \* \*

## II

In *Richardson,* we dismissed for lack of standing a suit whose "aggrievement" was precisely the "aggrievement" respondents assert here: the Government's unlawful refusal to place information within the public domain. The only difference, in fact, is that the aggrievement there was more direct, since the Government already had the information within its possession, whereas here respondents seek enforcement action that will bring information within the Government's possession and *then* require the information to be made public. The plaintiff in *Richardson* challenged the Government's failure to disclose the expenditures of the Central Intelligence Agency (CIA), in alleged violation of the constitutional requirement, Art. I, § 9, cl. 7, that "a regular Statement and Account of the Receipts and Expenditures of all public Money shall be published from time to time." We held that such a claim was a nonjusticiable "generalized grievance" because "the impact on [plaintiff] is plainly undifferentiated and common to all members of the public." 418 U.S., at 176-177 (internal quotation marks and citations omitted).

It was alleged in *Richardson* that the Government had denied a right conferred by the Constitution, whereas respondents here assert a right conferred by statute— but of course "there is absolutely no basis for making the Article III inquiry turn on the source of the asserted right." *Lujan v. Defenders of Wildlife,* 504 U.S. 555, 576 (1992). The Court today distinguishes *Richardson* on a different basis—a basis that reduces it from a landmark constitutional holding to a curio. According to the Court," *Richardson* focused upon taxpayer standing, . . . not voter standing." *Ante,* at 22. In addition to being a silly distinction, given the weighty governmental purpose underlying the "generalized grievance" prohibition—viz., to avoid "something in the nature of an Athenian democracy or a New England town meeting to oversee the conduct of the National Government by means of lawsuits in federal courts," 418 U.S., at 179, this is also a distinction that the Court in *Richardson* went out of its way explicitly to eliminate. \* \* \*

\* \* \*

The Court's opinion asserts that our language disapproving generalized grievances "invariably appears in cases where the harm at issue is not only widely shared, but is also of an abstract and indefinite nature." *Ante,* at 23. "Often," the Court says,

1   "the fact that an interest is abstract and the fact that it is widely shared go hand in
2   hand. But their association is not invariable, and where a harm is concrete, though
3   widely shared, the Court has found 'injury in fact.'" *Ante,* at 24. If that is so—if
4   concrete generalized grievances (like concrete particularized grievances) are OK,
5   and abstract generalized grievances (like abstract particularized grievances) are
6   bad—one must wonder why we ever *developed* the superfluous distinction
7   between generalized and particularized grievances at all. But of course the Court is
8   wrong to think that generalized grievances have only concerned us when they are
9   abstract. * * *

10  What is noticeably lacking in the Court's discussion of our generalized-grievance
11  jurisprudence is all reference to two words that have figured in it prominently:
12  "particularized" and "undifferentiated." See *Richardson, supra,* at 177; *Lujan,* 504
13  U.S., at 560, and n. 1. "Particularized" means that "the injury must affect the
14  plaintiff in a personal and individual way." *Id.,* at 560, n. 1. If the effect is
15  "undifferentiated and common to all members of the public," *Richardson,*
16  *supra,* at 177 (internal quotation marks and citations omitted), the plaintiff has a
17  "generalized grievance" that must be pursued by political, rather than judicial,
18  means. These terms explain why it is a gross oversimplification to reduce the
19  concept of a generalized grievance to nothing more than "the fact that [the
20  grievance] is widely shared," *ante,* at 25, thereby enabling the concept to be
21  dismissed as a standing principle by such examples as "large numbers of
22  individuals suffer[ing] the same common-law injury (say, a widespread mass tort),
23  or . . . large numbers of voters suffer[ing] interference with voting rights conferred
24  by law," *ante,* at 24. The exemplified injuries are widely shared, to be sure, but each
25  individual suffers a particularized and differentiated harm. One tort victim suffers
26  a burnt leg, another a burnt arm—or even if both suffer burnt arms they
27  are *different* arms. One voter suffers the deprivation of *his* franchise, another the
28  deprivation of *hers.* With the generalized grievance, on the other hand, the injury
29  or deprivation is not only widely shared but it is *undifferentiated.* The harm caused
30  to Mr. Richardson by the alleged disregard of the Statement-of-Accounts Clause
31  was precisely the same as the harm caused to everyone else: unavailability of a
32  description of CIA expenditures. Just as the (more indirect) harm caused to Mr.
33  Akins by the allegedly unlawful failure to enforce FECA is precisely the same as the
34  harm caused to everyone else: unavailability of a description of AIPAC's activities.

35  The Constitution's line of demarcation between the Executive power and the
36  judicial power presupposes a common understanding of the type of interest needed
37  to sustain a "case or controversy" against the Executive in the courts. A system in
38  which the citizenry at large could sue to compel Executive compliance with the law
39  would be a system in which the courts, rather than the President, are given the
40  primary responsibility to "take Care that the Laws be faithfully executed," Art. II,
41  § 3. We do not have such a system because the common understanding of the

interest necessary to sustain suit has included the requirement, affirmed in *Richardson,* that the complained-of injury be particularized and differentiated, rather than common to all the electorate. When the Executive can be directed by the courts, at the instance of any voter, to remedy a deprivation that affects the entire electorate in precisely the same way—and particularly when that deprivation (here, the unavailability of information) is one inseverable part of a larger enforcement scheme—there has occurred a shift of political responsibility to a branch designed not to protect the public at large but to protect individual rights. "To permit Congress to convert the undifferentiated public interest in executive officers' compliance with the law into an 'individual right' vindicable in the courts is to permit Congress to transfer from the President to the courts the Chief Executive's most important constitutional duty . . . ." *Lujan, supra,* at 577. If today's decision is correct, it is within the power of Congress to authorize any interested person to manage (through the courts) the Executive's enforcement of any law that includes a requirement for the filing and public availability of a piece of paper.

This is not the system we have had, and is not the system we should desire.

Because this statute should not be interpreted to confer upon the entire electorate the power to invoke judicial direction of prosecutions, and because if it is so interpreted the statute unconstitutionally transfers from the Executive to the courts the responsibility to "take Care that the Laws be faithfully executed," Art. II, § 3, I respectfully dissent.

## F. Primary Jurisdiction

The doctrine of primary jurisdiction is a judicial abstention doctrine. Courts invoke primary jurisdiction—rather rarely—to stay judicial proceedings on matters that also fall within the jurisdiction of an agency to permit the agency to act on them. The Supreme Court has had little to say about primary jurisdiction doctrine in recent years, and the circuit courts differ on its scope of application. *Compare Arsberry v. Illinois,* 244 F.3d 558, 563 (7th Cir. 2001) (holding the doctrine applies "only when, in a suit involving a regulated firm but not brought under the regulatory statute itself, an issue arises that is within the exclusive original jurisdiction of the regulatory agency") *and S. Utah Wilderness Alliance v. Bureau of Land Mgmt.,* 425 F.3d 735, 750 (10th Cir. 2005) (finding primary jurisdiction available more broadly where Congress has placed an issue within the "special competence" of an agency).

If *Darby v. Cisneros* established that courts lack the power to deny review on exhaustion grounds in cases governed by the APA, should courts nonetheless retain the power to stay review in APA cases on primary jurisdiction grounds?

## United States v. Western Pacific Railroad Co.

352 U.S. 59 (1956)

December 3, 1956

Mr. Justice HARLAN delivered the opinion of the Court.

The three respondent railroads each sued in the Court of Claims to recover from the United States as shipper the difference between the tariff rates actually paid and those allegedly due on 211 Army shipments of steel aerial bomb cases filled with napalm gel. Approximately 200 of the shipments were made over the lines of respondents Bangor and Seaboard in 1944; the remainder were carried by respondent Western Pacific in 1948 and 1950.

Napalm gel is gasoline which has been thickened by the addition of aluminum soap powder. The mixture is inflammable but not self-igniting. In a completed incendiary bomb the napalm gel is ignited by white phosphorus contained in a burster charge, which in turn is fired by a fuse. These shipments, however, involved only the steel casings and the napalm gel; burster and fuse had not yet been added.

The carriers billed the Government at the high first-class rates established in Item 1820 of Consolidated Freight Classification No. 17 for "incendiary bombs." Pursuant to § 322 of the Transportation Act of 1942, the Government paid the bills of the Bangor and the Seaboard as presented; on post-audit, however, the General Accounting Office made deductions against these respondents' subsequent bills on other shipments, on the ground that the shipments in question should have been carried at the lower, fifth-class, rate applicable to gasoline in steel drums. The bills of the Western Pacific were initially paid at the lower rate. Respondents thereupon brought the present suits to recover the difference between the bills as rendered and as paid in the case of the Western Pacific, and the amount of the deductions in the other two cases.

The Government defended on three grounds: (1) that Item 1820 was inapplicable because absence of burster and fuse deprived these bombs of the essential characteristics of "incendiary bombs," and hence no additional sums were due; (2) that if this tariff item was held to govern, the tariff would be unreasonable as applied to these shipments, and that as to this issue the court proceedings should be suspended and the matter referred to the Interstate Commerce Commission;

1 and (3) that in any event the Bangor and Seaboard were estopped from charging
2 the "1820" rate.

3 The Court of Claims, relying on its earlier decision in *Union Pacific R. Co. v. United*
4 *States*, 111 F.Supp. 266, entered summary judgment for respondents, two judges
5 dissenting. It held that the shipments in question were "incendiary bombs" within
6 the meaning of Item 1820 of the tariff and thus entitled to the higher rate. In
7 addition, while seemingly recognizing the Government's right to have the defense
8 of unreasonableness determined by the Interstate Commerce Commission, the
9 court ruled that the running of the two-year period of limitations provided by §
10 16(3) of the Interstate Commerce Act cut off the right of referral to the
11 Commission. Lastly, the court overruled the defense of estoppel as to the
12 respondents Bangor and Seaboard. Because of the importance of these questions
13 in the administration of the Interstate Commerce Act, and alleged conflict among
14 the lower courts on the issue of limitations, we granted certiorari.

15 I.

16 We are met at the outset with the question of whether the Court of Claims properly
17 applied the doctrine of primary jurisdiction in this case; that is, whether it correctly
18 allocated the issues in the suit between the jurisdiction of the Interstate Commerce
19 Commission and that of the court. In the view of the court below, the case
20 presented two entirely separate questions. One was the question of the
21 construction of the tariff—whether Item 1820 was applicable to these shipments.
22 The second was the question of the reasonableness of that tariff, if so applied. The
23 Court of Claims assumed, as it had in the Union Pacific case, supra, that the first
24 of these—whether the "1820" rate applied—was a matter simply of tariff
25 construction and thus properly within the initial cognizance of the court. The
26 second—the reasonableness of the tariff as applied to these shipments—it seemed
27 to regard as being within the initial competence of the Interstate Commerce
28 Commission. Before this Court neither side has questioned the validity of the lower
29 court's views in these respects. Nevertheless, because we regard the maintenance
30 of a proper relationship between the courts and the Commission in matters
31 affecting transportation policy to be of continuing public concern, we have been
32 constrained to inquire into this aspect of the decision. We have concluded that in
33 the circumstances here presented the question of tariff construction, as well as that
34 of the reasonableness of the tariff as applied, was within the exclusive primary
35 jurisdiction of the Interstate Commerce Commission.

36 The doctrine of primary jurisdiction, like the rule requiring exhaustion of
37 administrative remedies, is concerned with promoting proper relationships
38 between the courts and administrative agencies charged with particular regulatory
39 duties. "Exhaustion" applies where a claim is cognizable in the first instance by an
40 administrative agency alone; judicial interference is withheld until the

1   administrative process has run its course. "Primary jurisdiction," on the other
2   hand, applies where a claim is originally cognizable in the courts, and comes into
3   play whenever enforcement of the claim requires the resolution of issues which,
4   under a regulatory scheme, have been placed within the special competence of an
5   administrative body; in such a case the judicial process is suspended pending
6   referral of such issues to the administrative body for its views.

7   No fixed formula exists for applying the doctrine of primary jurisdiction. In every
8   case the question is whether the reasons for the existence of the doctrine are
9   present and whether the purposes it serves will be aided by its application in the
10   particular litigation. These reasons and purposes have often been given expression
11   by this Court. In the earlier cases emphasis was laid on the desirable uniformity
12   which would obtain if initially a specialized agency passed on certain types of
13   administrative questions. *See Texas & Pacific R. Co. v. Abilene Cotton Oil Co.*, 204
14   U.S. 426 (1907). More recently the expert and specialized knowledge of the
15   agencies involved has been particularly stressed. *See Far East Conference v.*
16   *United States*, 342 U.S. 570 (1952). The two factors are part of the same principle,

17   "now firmly established, that in cases raising issues of fact not within the
18   conventional experience of judges or cases requiring the exercise of administrative
19   discretion, agencies created by Congress for regulating the subject matter should
20   not be passed over. This is so even though the facts after they have been appraised
21   by specialized competence serve as a premise for legal consequences to be
22   judicially defined. Uniformity and consistency in the regulation of business
23   entrusted to a particular agency are secured, and the limited functions of review by
24   the judiciary are more rationally exercised, by preliminary resort for ascertaining
25   and interpreting the circumstances underlying legal issues to agencies that are
26   better equipped than courts by specialization, by insight gained through
27   experience, and by more flexible procedure." *Id.* at 574-75.

28   The doctrine of primary jurisdiction thus does "more than prescribe the mere
29   procedural timetable of the lawsuit. It is a doctrine allocating the law-making
30   power over certain aspects" of commercial relations. "It transfers from court to
31   agency the power to determine" some of the incidents of such relations.[8]

32   Thus the first question presented is whether effectuation of the statutory purposes
33   of the Interstate Commerce Act requires that the Interstate Commerce
34   Commission should first pass on the construction of the tariff in dispute here; this,
35   in turn, depends on whether the question raises issues of transportation policy

---

[8] Jaffe, *Primary Jurisdiction Reconsidered*, 102 Univ.Pa.L.Rev. 577, 583–584
(1954).

1 which ought to be considered by the Commission in the interests of a uniform and
2 expert administration of the regulatory scheme laid down by that Act. Decision is
3 governed by two earlier cases in this Court. In *Texas & Pacific R. Co. v. American*
4 *Tie & Timber Co.*, 234 U.S. 138 (1914), a shipper attempted to ship oak railroad ties
5 under a tariff for "lumber." The carrier rejected them, urging that such ties were
6 not lumber. In a damage action expert testimony was received on the question.
7 This Court, however, held that the Interstate Commerce Commission alone could
8 resolve the question. The effect of the holding is clear: the courts must not only
9 refrain from making tariffs, but, under certain circumstances, must decline to
10 construe them as well. A particularization of such circumstances emerged in *Great*
11 *Northern R. Co. v. Merchants Elevator Co.*, 259 U.S. 285 (1922). There the Court
12 held that where the question is simply one of construction the courts may pass on
13 it as an issue "solely of law." But where words in a tariff are used in a peculiar or
14 technical sense, and where extrinsic evidence is necessary to determine their
15 meaning or proper application, so that "the inquiry is essentially one of fact and of
16 discretion in technical matters," then the issue of tariff application must first go to
17 the Commission. The reason is plainly set forth: such a "determination is reached
18 ordinarily upon voluminous and conflicting evidence, for the adequate
19 appreciation of which acquaintance with many intricate facts of transportation is
20 indispensable, and such acquaintance is commonly to be found only in a body of
21 experts." *Id.* at 291. We must therefore decide whether a determination of the
22 meaning of the term "incendiary bomb" in Item 1820 involves factors "the
23 adequate appreciation of which" presupposes an "acquaintance with many
24 intricate facts of transportation." We conclude that it does.

25 A tariff is not an abstraction. It embodies an analysis of the costs incurred in the
26 transportation of a certain article and a decision as to how much should, therefore,
27 be charged for the carriage of that article in order to produce a fair and reasonable
28 return. Complex and technical cost-allocation and accounting problems must be
29 solved in setting the tariff initially. In the case of "incendiary bombs," since it is
30 expensive to take the elaborate safety precautions necessary to carry such items in
31 safety, evidently there must have been calculation of the costs of handling,
32 supervising and insuring an inherently dangerous cargo. In other words, there
33 were obviously commercial reasons why a higher tariff was set for incendiary
34 bombs than for, say, lumber. It therefore follows that the decision whether a
35 certain item was intended to be covered by the tariff for incendiary bombs involves
36 an intimate knowledge of these very reasons themselves. Whether steel casings
37 filled with napalm gel are incendiary bombs is, in this context, more than simply a
38 question of reading the tariff language or applying abstract "rules" of construction.
39 For the basic issue is how far the reasons justifying a high rate for the carriage of
40 extra-hazardous objects were applicable to the instant shipment. Do the factors
41 which make for high costs and therefore high rates on incendiary bombs also call
42 for a high rate on steel casings filled with napalm gel? To answer that question

1   there must be close familiarity with these factors. Such familiarity is possessed not
2   by the courts but by the agency which had the exclusive power to pass on the rate
3   in the first instance. And, on the other hand, to decide the question of the scope of
4   this tariff without consideration of the factors and purposes underlying the
5   terminology employed would make the process of adjudication little more than an
6   exercise in semantics.

7   The main thrust of the Government's argument on the construction question went
8   to the fact that the shipments here involved were not as hazardous as contemplated
9   by the term "incendiary bomb" as used in the tariff, and that therefore the tariff
10  should not be construed to cover them. Similarly, the dissenting judges below
11  emphasized the absence from the shipments of the commercial factors which call
12  for a high rate on incendiary bombs: "If the reason for the high freight rate is the
13  incendiary quality of the freight, and if the freight does not have the incendiary
14  quality, the reason for the high rate vanishes and the rate should vanish with it."
15  131 F.Supp. at 921. The difficulty with this line of argument is that we do not know
16  whether the "incendiary quality of the freight" was in fact the reason for the high
17  rate, still less whether that was the only reason and how much weight should be
18  assigned to it. Courts which do not make rates cannot know with exactitude the
19  factors which go into the rate-making process. And for the court here to undertake
20  to fix the limits of the tariff's application without knowledge of such factors, and
21  the extent to which they are present or absent in the particular case, is tantamount
22  to engaging in judicial guesswork. It was the Commission and not the court which
23  originally determined why incendiaries should be transported at a high rate. It is
24  thus the Commission which should determine whether shipments of napalm gel
25  bombs, minus bursters and fuses, meet those requirements; that is, whether the
26  factors making for certain costs and thus a certain rate on incendiaries are present
27  in the carriage of such incompleted bombs.

28  This conclusion is fortified by the artificiality of the distinction between the issues
29  of tariff construction and of the reasonableness of the tariff as applied, the latter
30  being recognized by all to be one for the Interstate Commerce Commission. For the
31  Government's thesis on the issue of reasonableness is not that the rate on
32  incendiary bombs is, in general, too high. It argues only that the rate "as applied"
33  to these particular shipments is too high—*i.e.*, that since the expenses which have
34  to be met in shipping incendiaries have not been incurred in this case, the carriers
35  will be making an unreasonable profit on these shipments. This seems to us to be
36  but another way of saying that the wrong tariff was applied. In both instances the
37  issue is whether the factors which call for a high rate on incendiary bomb
38  shipments are present in a shipment of bomb casings full of napalm gel but lacking
39  bursters and fuses. And the mere fact that the issue is phrased in one instance as a
40  matter of tariff construction and in the other as a matter of reasonableness should
41  not be determinative on the jurisdictional issue. To hold otherwise would make the

doctrine of primary jurisdiction an abstraction to be called into operation at the whim of the pleader.

* * *

We hold, therefore, that both the issues of tariff construction and the reasonableness of the tariff as applied were initially matters for the Commission's determination.

### III.

The judgment below must be reversed and the case remanded to the Court of Claims for further proceedings not inconsistent with this opinion. It is so ordered.

Reversed and remanded.

Mr. Justice DOUGLAS dissents from a reference of these matters to the Interstate Commerce Commission, since he is of the view that the principles of *Great Northern R. Co. v. Merchants Elevator Co.*, 259 U.S. 285 (1922), are applicable here.

Mr. Justice REED and Mr. Justice BRENNAN took no part in the consideration or decision of this case.


# G. Exhaustion

Exhaustion: a fitting topic for the end of the course, yes?

Before the enactment of the APA, judges developed an exhaustion doctrine for administrative law. The core idea is that litigants in administrative law matters should exhaust administrative remedies before seeking relief from court. The *Bethlehem Shipbuilding* case shows the doctrine in action. In *Darby*, the Supreme Court ruled that the exhaustion requirement does not apply to cases governed by the APA. The doctrine continues to apply as a matter of judicial discretion in administrative law cases not governed by the APA (such as, for instance, litigation in the federal prison system; see *McCarthy v. Madigan*, 503 U.S. 140 (1992)).


## Myers v. Bethlehem Shipbuilding Corp.

303 U.S. 41 (1938)

January 31, 1938

MR. JUSTICE BRANDEIS delivered the opinion of the Court.

752

1    The question for decision is whether a federal District Court has equity jurisdiction
2    to enjoin the National Labor Relations Board from holding a hearing upon a
3    complaint filed by it against an employer alleged to be engaged in unfair labor
4    practices prohibited by National Labor Relations Act. The Circuit Court of Appeals
5    for the First Circuit held in these cases that the District Court possesses such
6    jurisdiction, and granted preliminary injunctions. Every other Circuit Court of
7    Appeals in which the question has arisen has held the contrary. Because of the
8    importance of the questions presented, the conflict in the lower courts and alleged
9    conflict with our own decisions, we granted these writs of certiorari.

10   The declared purpose of the National Labor Relations Act is to diminish the causes
11   of labor disputes burdening and obstructing interstate and foreign commerce, and
12   its provisions are applicable only to such commerce. In order to protect it, the act
13   seeks to promote collective bargaining; confers upon employees engaged in such
14   commerce the right to form, and join in, labor organizations; defines acts of an
15   employer which shall be deemed unfair labor practice, and confers upon the Board
16   certain limited powers with a view to preventing such practices. If a charge is made
17   to the Board that a person "has engaged in or is engaging in any . . . unfair labor
18   practice," and it appears that a proceeding in respect thereto should be instituted,
19   a complaint stating the charge is to be filed, and a hearing is to be held thereon
20   upon notice to the person complained of.

21   The Industrial Union of Marine and Shipbuilding Workers of America, Local No.
22   5, made to the Board a charge that the Bethlehem Shipbuilding Corporation,
23   Limited, was engaging in unfair labor practices at its plant in Quincy, Mass., for
24   the production, sale, and distribution of boats, ships, and marine equipment. Upon
25   that charge, the Board filed, on April 13, 1936, a complaint which alleged, among
26   other things, that the company dominates and interferes in the manner described
27   "with a labor organization known as Plan of Representation of Employees in Plants
28   of the Bethlehem Shipbuilding Corporation, Ltd.;" that such action leads to strikes
29   interfering with interstate commerce, and that

30       "the aforesaid acts of respondent constitute unfair labor practices affecting
31       commerce, within the meaning of Section 8, subdivisions (1) and (2) and
32       Section 2, subdivisions (6) and (7) of said [National Labor Relations] Act."

33                                        * * *

34   The Board duly notified the corporation that a hearing on the complaint would be
35   held on April 27, 1936, at Boston, Massachusetts, in accordance with rules and
36   regulations of the Board, a copy of which was annexed to the notice, and that the
37   corporation "will have the right to appear, in person or otherwise, and give
38   testimony." On that day, the corporation filed, in the federal court for
39   Massachusetts, the bill in equity, herein numbered 181, against A. Howard Myers,

1    acting regional director for the First Region, National Labor Relations Board,
2    Edmund J. Blake, its regional attorney for the First Region, and Daniel M. Lyons,
3    trial examiner, to enjoin them from holding

> 4    "a hearing for the purpose of determining whether or not the plaintiff has
> 5    engaged at its Fore River Plant in any so-called unfair labor practices under
> 6    the National Labor Relations Act, and from having any proceedings or
> 7    taking any action whatsoever at any time or times with respect thereto."

8    There were prayers for a restraining order, an interlocutory injunction, and a
9    permanent injunction, and also a prayer that the court declare that the National
10   Labor Relations Act and "defendants' actions and proposed actions thereunder"
11   violate the Federal Constitution.

12   On May 4, 1936, another bill in equity, herein numbered 182, against the same
13   defendants, seeking, on largely the same allegations of fact, substantially the same
14   relief was brought in the same court by Charles MacKenzie, James E. Manning,
15   and Thomas E. Barker, employees of the Bethlehem Corporation and officers of
16   the so-called Plan of Representation at the Fore River Plant.

17   Upon the filing of each bill, the District Court issued a restraining order and an
18   order of notice to show cause why a preliminary injunction should not issue. In
19   each case, the defendants filed a motion to dismiss the bill of complaint, and also
20   a return to the order to show cause. The cases were heard together. In each, the
21   District Court issued the preliminary injunction, and the decrees therefor are still
22   in effect. They were affirmed by the Circuit Court of Appeals for the First Circuit
23   on February 12, 1937. * * *

24   The two cases present, in the main, the same questions. In discussing them,
25   reference will be made, in the first instance, only to the suit brought by the
26   corporation.

27   We are of opinion that the District Court was without power to enjoin the Board
28   from holding the hearings.

29   *First.* There is no claim by the corporation that the statutory provisions and the
30   rules of procedure prescribed for such hearings are illegal, or that the corporation
31   was not accorded ample opportunity to answer the complaint of the Board, or that
32   opportunity to introduce evidence on the allegations made will be denied. The
33   claim is that the provisions of the act are not applicable to the corporation's
34   business at the Fore River Plant because the operations conducted there are not
35   carried on, and the products manufactured are not sold, in interstate or foreign
36   commerce; that therefore the corporation's relations with its employees at the
37   plant cannot burden or interfere with such commerce; that hearings would, at best,
38   be futile, and that the holding of them would result in irreparable damage to the

754

1 corporation not only by reason of their direct cost and the loss of time of its officials
2 and employees, but also because the hearings would cause serious impairment of
3 the goodwill and harmonious relations existing between the corporation and its
4 employees, and thus seriously impair the efficiency of its operations.

5 *Second.* The District Court is without jurisdiction to enjoin hearings because the
6 power "to prevent any person from engaging in any unfair practice affecting
7 commerce" has been vested by Congress in the Board and the Circuit Court of
8 Appeals, and Congress has declared:

9 "This power shall be exclusive, and shall not be affected by any other means
10 of adjustment or prevention that has been or may be established by
11 agreement, code, law, or otherwise.

12 The grant of that exclusive power is constitutional because the act provided for
13 appropriate procedure before the Board and, in the review by the Circuit Court of
14 Appeals, an adequate opportunity to secure judicial protection against possible
15 illegal action on the part of the Board. No power to enforce an order is conferred
16 upon the Board. To secure enforcement, the Board must apply to a Circuit Court
17 of Appeals for its affirmance. And, until the Board's order has been affirmed by the
18 appropriate Circuit Court of Appeals, no penalty accrues for disobeying it. The
19 independent right to apply to a Circuit Court of Appeals to have an order set aside
20 is conferred upon any party aggrieved by the proceeding before the Board. The
21 Board is even without power to enforce obedience to its subpoena to testify or to
22 produce written evidence. To enforce obedience, it must apply to a District Court,
23 and to such an application, appropriate defense may be made.

24 As was said in *Labor Board v. Jones & Laughlin Steel Corp.*, 301 U.S. 1, 301 U.S.
25 46-47, the procedural provisions

26 "do not offend against the constitutional requirements governing the
27 creation and action of administrative bodies. The act establishes standards
28 to which the Board must conform. There must be complaint, notice and
29 hearing. The Board must receive evidence and make findings. The findings
30 as to the facts are to be conclusive, but only if supported by evidence. The
31 order of the Board is subject to review by the designated court, and only
32 when sustained by the court may the order be enforced. Upon that review,
33 all questions of the jurisdiction of the Board and the regularity of its
34 proceedings, all questions of constitutional right or statutory authority, are
35 open to examination by the court. We construe the procedural provisions
36 as affording adequate opportunity to secure judicial protection against
37 arbitrary action in accordance with the well settled rules applicable to
38 administrative agencies set up by Congress to aid in the enforcement of
39 valid legislation."

1  It is true that the Board has jurisdiction only if the complaint concerns interstate
2  or foreign commerce. Unless the Board finds that it does, the complaint must be
3  dismissed. And, if it finds that interstate or foreign commerce is involved, but the
4  Circuit Court of Appeals concludes that such finding was without adequate
5  evidence to support it, or otherwise contrary to law, the Board's petition to enforce
6  it will be dismissed, or the employer's petition to have it set aside will be granted.
7  Since the procedure before the Board is appropriate, and the judicial review so
8  provided is adequate, Congress had power to vest exclusive jurisdiction in the
9  Board and the Circuit Court of Appeals. *Anniston Manufacturing Co. v. Davis,* 301
10 U.S. 337, 301 U.S. 343-346.

11 *Third.* The corporation contends that, since it denies that interstate or foreign
12 commerce is involved and claims that a hearing would subject it to irreparable
13 damage, rights guaranteed by the Federal Constitution will be denied unless it be
14 held that the District Court has jurisdiction to enjoin the holding of a hearing by
15 the Board. So to hold would, as the government insists, in effect substitute the
16 District Court for the Board as the tribunal to hear and determine what Congress
17 declared the Board exclusively should hear and determine in the first instance. The
18 contention is at war with the long settled rule of judicial administration that no one
19 is entitled to judicial relief for a supposed or threatened injury until the prescribed
20 administrative remedy has been exhausted.[9] That rule has been repeatedly acted
21 on in cases where, as here, the contention is made that the administrative body
22 lacked power over the subject matter.

23 Obviously, the rules requiring exhaustion of the administrative remedy cannot be
24 circumvented by asserting that the charge on which the complaint rests is
25 groundless and that the mere holding of the prescribed administrative hearing
26 would result in irreparable damage. Lawsuits also often prove to have been
27 groundless, but no way has been discovered of relieving a defendant from the
28 necessity of a trial to establish the fact.

29 *Fourth.* The Circuit Court of Appeals should have reversed the decrees for a
30 preliminary injunction. It is true that, ordinarily, the decree of a District Court
31 granting or denying a preliminary injunction will not be disturbed on appeal. But
32 that rule of practice has no application where, as here, there was an insuperable

---

[9] The rule has been most frequently applied in equity where relief by injunction
was sought. But because the rule is one of judicial administration—not merely a
rule governing the exercise of discretion—it is applicable to proceedings at law, as
well as suits in equity. *Compare First National Bank of Fargo v. Board of County
Comm'rs,* 264 U.S. 450, 455 (1924); *Anniston Mfg. Co. v. Davis,* 301 U.S. 337, 343
(1937).

1  objection to the maintenance of the suit in point of jurisdiction, and where it clearly
2  appears that the decree was the result of an improvident exercise of judicial
3  discretion. Since the constitutionality of the act has been determined by our
4  decision in *Labor Board v. Jones & Laughlin Steel Corp.*, 301 U.S. 1, and the defect
5  in the bill is incapable of remedy by amendment, its dismissal should be directed.

6  * * *

7  *Decrees for preliminary injunction reversed, with direction to dismiss the bills.*

8  MR. JUSTICE CARDOZO took no part in the consideration or decision of this case.

9

10 **Darby v. Cisneros**

11 509 U.S. 137

12 June 21, 1993

13 JUSTICE BLACKMUN delivered the opinion of the Court.*

14 This case presents the question whether federal courts have the authority to
15 require that a plaintiff exhaust available administrative remedies before seeking
16 judicial review under the Administrative Procedure Act (APA), 5 U.S.C. § 701 *et
17 seq.*, where neither the statute nor agency rules specifically mandate exhaustion as
18 a prerequisite to judicial review. At issue is the relationship between the judicially
19 created doctrine of exhaustion of administrative remedies and the statutory
20 requirements of § 10(c) of the APA.

21  I

22 Petitioner R. Gordon Darby is a self-employed South Carolina real estate developer
23 who specializes in the development and management of multifamily rental
24 projects. In the early 1980's, he began working with Lonnie Garvin, Jr., a mortgage
25 banker, who had developed a plan to enable multifamily developers to obtain
26 single-family mortgage insurance from respondent Department of Housing and
27 Urban Development (HUD). Respondent Secretary of HUD (Secretary) is
28 authorized to provide single-family mortgage insurance under §203(b) of the
29 National Housing Act, 48 Stat. 1249, as amended, 12 U.S.C. § 1709(b). Although
30 HUD also provides mortgage insurance for multi-family projects under § 207 of
31 the National Housing Act, 12 U.S.C. § 1713, the greater degree of oversight and

---

* THE CHIEF JUSTICE, JUSTICE SCALIA, and JUSTICE THOMAS join all but
Part III of this opinion.

control over such projects makes it less attractive for investors than the single-family mortgage insurance option.

The principal advantage of Garvin's plan was that it promised to avoid HUD's "Rule of Seven." This rule prevented rental properties from receiving single-family mortgage insurance if the mortgagor already had financial interests in seven or more similar rental properties in the same project or subdivision. See 24 CFR § 203.42(a) (1992). Under Garvin's plan, a person seeking financing would use straw purchasers as mortgage insurance applicants. Once the loans were closed, the straw purchasers would transfer title back to the development company. Because no single purchaser at the time of purchase would own more than seven rental properties within the same project, the Rule of Seven appeared not to be violated. HUD employees in South Carolina apparently assured Garvin that his plan was lawful and that he thereby would avoid the limitation of the Rule of Seven.

Darby obtained financing for three separate multiunit projects, and, through Garvin's plan, Darby obtained single-family mortgage insurance from HUD. Although Darby successfully rented the units, a combination of low rents, falling interest rates, and a generally depressed rental market forced him into default in 1988. HUD became responsible for the payment of over $6.6 million in insurance claims.

HUD had become suspicious of Garvin's financing plan as far back as 1983. In 1986, HUD initiated an audit but concluded that neither Darby nor Garvin had done anything wrong or misled HUD personnel. Nevertheless, in June 1989, HUD issued a limited denial of participation (LDP) that prohibited petitioners for one year from participating in any program in South Carolina administered by respondent Assistant Secretary of Housing. Two months later, the Assistant Secretary notified petitioners that HUD was also proposing to debar them from further participation in all HUD procurement contracts and in any nonprocurement transaction with any federal agency. See 24 CFR § 24.200 (1992).

Petitioners' appeals of the LDP and of the proposed debarment were consolidated, and an Administrative Law Judge (ALJ) conducted a hearing on the consolidated appeals in December 1989. The judge issued an "Initial Decision and Order" in April 1990, finding that the financing method used by petitioners was "a sham which improperly circumvented the Rule of Seven." The ALJ concluded, however, that most of the relevant facts had been disclosed to local HUD employees, that petitioners lacked criminal intent, and that Darby himself "genuinely cooperated with HUD to try [to] work out his financial dilemma and avoid foreclosure." In light of these mitigating factors, the ALJ concluded that an indefinite debarment would be punitive and that it would serve no legitimate purpose; good cause existed, however, to debar petitioners for a period of 18 months.

1     Under HUD regulations,

2        "The hearing officer's determination shall be final unless, pursuant to 24
3        CFR part 26, the Secretary or the Secretary's designee, within 30 days of
4        receipt of a request decides as a matter of discretion to review the finding
5        of the hearing officer. The 30 day period for deciding whether to review a
6        determination may be extended upon written notice of such extension by
7        the Secretary or his designee. Any party may request such a review in
8        writing within 15 days of receipt of the hearing officer's determination." 24
9        CFR § 24.314(c) (1992).

10    Neither petitioners nor respondents sought further administrative review of the
11    ALJ's "Initial Decision and Order."

12    On May 31, 1990, petitioners filed suit in the United States District Court for the
13    District of South Carolina. They sought an injunction and a declaration that the
14    administrative sanctions were imposed for purposes of punishment, in violation of
15    HUD's own debarment regulations, and therefore were "not in accordance with
16    law" within the meaning of § 10(e)(B)(1) of the APA, 5 U.S.C. § 706(2)(A).

17    Respondents moved to dismiss the complaint on the ground that petitioners, by
18    forgoing the option to seek review by the Secretary, had failed to exhaust
19    administrative remedies. The District Court denied respondents'motion to
20    dismiss, reasoning that the administrative remedy was inadequate and that resort
21    to that remedy would have been futile. In a subsequent opinion, the District Court
22    granted petitioners'motion for summary judgment, concluding that the
23    "imposition of debarment in this case encroached too heavily on the punitive side
24    of the line, and for those reasons was an abuse of discretion and not in accordance
25    with the law."

26    The Court of Appeals for the Fourth Circuit reversed. It recognized that neither the
27    National Housing Act nor HUD regulations expressly mandate exhaustion of
28    administrative remedies prior to filing suit. The court concluded, however, that the
29    District Court had erred in denying respondents'motion to dismiss, because there
30    was no evidence to suggest that further review would have been futile or that the
31    Secretary would have abused his discretion by indefinitely extending the time
32    limitations for review.

33               * * *

34               II

35    Section 10(c) of the APA bears the caption "Actions reviewable." It provides in its
36    first two sentences that judicial review is available for "final agency action for
37    which there is no other adequate remedy in a court," and that "preliminary,

1  procedural, or intermediate agency action ... is subject to review on the review of
2  the final agency action." The last sentence of § 10(c) reads:

3  "Except as otherwise expressly required by statute, agency action otherwise final is
4  final for the purposes of this section whether or not there has been presented or
5  determined an application for a declaratory order, for any form of reconsideration
6  [see n. 1, *supra],* or, unless the agency otherwise requires by rule and provides that
7  the action meanwhile is inoperative, for an appeal to superior agency authority."
8  80 Stat. 392-393, 5 U.S.C. §704.

9  Petitioners argue that this provision means that a litigant seeking judicial review
10 of a final agency action under the APA need not exhaust available administrative
11 remedies unless such exhaustion is expressly required by statute or agency rule.
12 According to petitioners, since § 10(c) contains an explicit exhaustion provision,
13 federal courts are not free to require further exhaustion as a matter of judicial
14 discretion.

15 Respondents contend that § 10(c) is concerned solely with timing, that is, when
16 agency actions become "final," and that Congress had no intention to interfere with
17 the courts' ability to impose conditions on the timing of their exercise of
18 jurisdiction to review final agency actions. Respondents concede that
19 petitioners' claim is "final" under § 10(c), for neither the National Housing Act nor
20 applicable HUD regulations require that a litigant pursue further administrative
21 appeals prior to seeking judicial review. However, even though nothing in § 10(c)
22 precludes judicial review of petitioners' claim, respondents argue that federal
23 courts remain free under the APA to impose appropriate exhaustion
24 requirements.[9]

25 We have recognized that the judicial doctrine of exhaustion of administrative
26 remedies is conceptually distinct from the doctrine of finality:

27 "[T]he finality requirement is concerned with whether the initial decisionmaker
28 has arrived at a definitive position on the issue that inflicts an actual, concrete
29 injury; the exhaustion requirement generally refers to administrative and judicial
30 procedures by which an injured party may seek review of an adverse decision and
31 obtain a remedy if the decision is found to be unlawful or otherwise

---

[9]  Respondents also have argued that under HUD regulations,
petitioners' debarment remains "inoperative" pending review by the Secretary. See
48 Fed. Reg. 43304 (1983). But this fact alone is insufficient under § 10(c) to
mandate exhaustion prior to judicial review, for the agency also must require such
exhaustion by rule. Respondents concede that HUD imposes no such exhaustion
requirement. Brief for Respondents 31.

inappropriate." *Williamson County Regional Planning Comm'n v. Hamilton Bank of Johnson City,* 473 U.S. 172, 193 (1985).

Whether courts are free to impose an exhaustion requirement as a matter of judicial discretion depends, at least in part, on whether Congress has provided otherwise, for "[o]f 'paramount importance'to any exhaustion inquiry is congressional intent," *McCarthy v. Madigan,* 503 U.S. 140, 144 (1992), quoting *Patsy v. Board of Regents of Florida,* 457 U.S. 496, 501 (1982). We therefore must consider whether § 10(c), by providing the conditions under which agency action becomes "final for the purposes of" judicial review, limits the authority of courts to impose additional exhaustion requirements as a prerequisite to judicial review.

It perhaps is surprising that it has taken over 45 years since the passage of the APA for this Court definitively to address this question. Professor Davis noted in 1958 that § 10(c) had been almost completely ignored in judicial opinions, see 3 K. Davis, Administrative Law Treatise § 20.08, p. 101 (1958); he reiterated that observation 25 years later, noting that the "provision is relevant in hundreds of cases and is customarily overlooked." 4 K. Davis, Administrative Law Treatise § 26.12, pp. 468-469 (2d ed. 1983). Only a handful of opinions in the Courts of Appeals have considered the effect of § 10(c) on the general exhaustion doctrine.

This Court has had occasion, however, to consider § 10(c) in other contexts. For example, in *ICC v. Locomotive Engineers,* 482 U.S. 270 (1987), we recognized that the plain language of § 10(c), which provides that an agency action is final "whether or not there has been presented or determined an application" for any form of reconsideration, could be read to suggest that the agency action is final regardless whether a motion for reconsideration has been filed. We noted, however, that § 10(c) "has long been construed by this and other courts merely to relieve parties from the *requirement* of petitioning for rehearing before seeking judicial review (unless, of course, specifically required to do so by statute), but not to prevent petitions for reconsideration that are actually filed from rendering the orders under reconsideration non-final" (emphasis in original). *Id.,* at 284-285.

In *Bowen v. Massachusetts,* 487 U.S. 879 (1988), we were concerned with whether relief available in the Claims Court was an "adequate remedy in a court" so as to preclude review in Federal District Court of a final agency action under the first sentence of § 10(c). We concluded that "although the primary thrust of [§ 10(c)] was to codify the exhaustion requirement," *id.,* at 903, Congress intended by that provision simply to avoid duplicating previously established special statutory procedures for review of agency actions.

While some dicta in these cases might be claimed to lend support to respondents' interpretation of § 10(c), the text of the APA leaves little doubt that petitioners are

1    correct. Under § 10(a) of the APA, "[a] person suffering legal wrong because of
2    agency action, or adversely affected or aggrieved by agency action within the
3    meaning of a relevant statute, *is entitled to judicial review thereof*" 5 U.S.C. § 702
4    (emphasis added). Although § 10(a) provides the general right to judicial review of
5    agency actions under the APA, § 10(c) establishes when such review is available.
6    When an aggrieved party has exhausted all administrative remedies expressly
7    prescribed by statute or agency rule, the agency action is "final for the purposes of
8    this section" and therefore "subject to judicial review" under the first sentence.
9    While federal courts may be free to apply, where appropriate, other prudential
10   doctrines of judicial administration to limit the scope and timing of judicial review,
11   § 10(c), by its very terms, has limited the availability of the doctrine of exhaustion
12   of administrative remedies to that which the statute or rule clearly mandates.

13   The last sentence of § 10(c) refers explicitly to "any form of reconsideration" and
14   "an appeal to superior agency authority." Congress clearly was concerned with
15   making the exhaustion requirement unambiguous so that aggrieved parties would
16   know precisely what administrative steps were required before judicial review
17   would be available. If courts were able to impose additional exhaustion
18   requirements beyond those provided by Congress or the agency, the last sentence
19   of § 10(c) would make no sense. To adopt respondents'reading would transform §
20   10(c) from a provision designed to "'remove obstacles to judicial review of agency
21   action,'" *Bowen* v. *Massachusetts,* 487 U.S., at 904, quoting *Shaughnessy* v.
22   *Pedreiro,* 349 U.S. 48, 51 (1955), into a trap for unwary litigants. Section 10(c)
23   explicitly requires exhaustion of all intra-agency appeals mandated either by
24   statute or by agency rule; it would be inconsistent with the plain language of § 10(c)
25   for courts to require litigants to exhaust optional appeals as well.

26                                      III

27   Recourse to the legislative history of § 10(c) is unnecessary in light of the plain
28   meaning of the statutory text. Nevertheless, we consider that history briefly
29   because both sides have spent much of their time arguing about its implications.
30   In its report on the APA, the Senate Judiciary Committee explained that the last
31   sentence of § 10(c) was "designed to implement the provisions of section 8(a)."
32   Section 8(a), now codified, as amended, as 5 U.S.C. § 557(b), provides, unless the
33   agency requires otherwise, that an initial decision made by a hearing officer
34   "becomes the decision of the agency without further proceedings unless there is an
35   appeal to, or review on motion of, the agency within time provided by rule." The
36   Judiciary Committee explained:

37   "[A]n agency may permit an examiner to make the initial decision in a case, which
38   becomes the agency's decision in the absence of an appeal to or review by the
39   agency. If there is such review or appeal, the examiner's initial decision becomes
40   inoperative until the agency determines the matter. For that reason this subsection

1   [§ 10(c)] permits an agency also to require by rule that, if any party is not satisfied
2   with the initial decision of a subordinate hearing officer, the party must first appeal
3   to the agency (the decision meanwhile being inoperative) before resorting to the
4   courts. In no case may appeal to 'superior agency authority' be required by rule
5   unless the administrative decision meanwhile is inoperative, because otherwise the
6   effect of such a requirement would be to subject the party to the agency action and
7   to repetitious administrative process without recourse. There is a fundamental
8   inconsistency in requiring a person to continue 'exhausting' administrative
9   processes after administrative action has become, and while it remains, effective."
10  S. Rep. No. 752, 79th Cong., 1st Sess., 27 (1945); Administrative Procedure Act:
11  Legislative History 1944-1946, S. Doc. No. 248, 79th Cong., 2d Sess., 213 (1946)
12  (hereinafter Leg. Hist.).

13                                    * * *

14  The purpose of § 10(c) was to permit agencies to require an appeal to "superior
15  agency authority" before an examiner's initial decision became final. This was
16  necessary because, under § 8(a), initial decisions could become final agency
17  decisions in the absence of an agency appeal. See 5 U.S.C. § 557(b). Agencies may
18  avoid the finality of an initial decision, first, by adopting a rule that an agency
19  appeal be taken before judicial review is available, and, second, by providing that
20  the initial decision would be "inoperative" pending appeal. Otherwise, the initial
21  decision becomes final and the aggrieved party is entitled to judicial review.

22                                    * * *

23                                     IV

24  We noted just last Term in a non-APA case that "appropriate deference to
25  Congress' power to prescribe the basic procedural scheme under which a claim may
26  be heard in a federal court requires fashioning of exhaustion principles in a manner
27  consistent   with   congressional   intent   and   any   applicable   statutory
28  scheme." *McCarthy v. Madigan*, 503 U.S., at 144.

29  Appropriate deference in this case requires the recognition that, with respect to
30  actions brought under the AP A, Congress effectively codified the doctrine of
31  exhaustion of administrative remedies in § 10(c). Of course, the exhaustion
32  doctrine continues to apply as a matter of judicial discretion in cases not governed
33  by the APA. But where the APA applies, an appeal to "superior agency authority"
34  is a prerequisite to judicial review *only* when expressly required by statute or when
35  an agency rule requires appeal before review and the administrative action is made
36  inoperative pending that review. Courts are not free to impose an exhaustion
37  requirement as a rule of judicial administration where the agency action has
38  already become "final" under § 1O(c).

## EXHAUSTION

1 The judgment of the Court of Appeals is reversed, and the case is remanded for
2 further proceedings consistent with this opinion.

3   It is so ordered.

# APPENDIX

## A. Selected Constitutional Provisions

### Article I

### Section 1.

All legislative powers herein granted shall be vested in a Congress of the United States, which shall consist of a Senate and House of Representatives.

### Section 7.

All bills for raising revenue shall originate in the House of Representatives; but the Senate may propose or concur with amendments as on other Bills.

Every bill which shall have passed the House of Representatives and the Senate, shall, before it become a law, be presented to the President of the United States; if he approve he shall sign it, but if not he shall return it, with his objections to that House in which it shall have originated, who shall enter the objections at large on their journal, and proceed to reconsider it. If after such reconsideration two thirds of that House shall agree to pass the bill, it shall be sent, together with the objections, to the other House, by which it shall likewise be reconsidered, and if approved by two thirds of that House, it shall become a law. But in all such cases the votes of both Houses shall be determined by yeas and nays, and the names of the persons voting for and against the bill shall be entered on the journal of each House respectively. If any bill shall not be returned by the President within ten days (Sundays excepted) after it shall have been presented to him, the same shall be a law, in like manner as if he had signed it, unless the Congress by their adjournment prevent its return, in which case it shall not be a law.

Every order, resolution, or vote to which the concurrence of the Senate and House of Representatives may be necessary (except on a question of adjournment) shall be presented to the President of the United States; and before the same shall take effect, shall be approved by him, or being disapproved by him, shall be repassed by two thirds of the Senate and House of Representatives, according to the rules and limitations prescribed in the case of a bill.

### Section 8.

The Congress shall have power to lay and collect taxes, duties, imposts and excises, to pay the debts and provide for the common defense and general welfare of the United States; but all duties, imposts and excises shall be uniform throughout the United States;

# SELECTED CONSTITUTIONAL PROVISIONS

1   To borrow money on the credit of the United States;

2   To regulate commerce with foreign nations, and among the several states, and with
3   the Indian tribes;

4   To establish a uniform rule of naturalization, and uniform laws on the subject of
5   bankruptcies throughout the United States;

6   To coin money, regulate the value thereof, and of foreign coin, and fix the standard
7   of weights and measures;

8   To provide for the punishment of counterfeiting the securities and current coin of
9   the United States;

10   To establish post offices and post roads;

11   To promote the progress of science and useful arts, by securing for limited times
12   to authors and inventors the exclusive right to their respective writings and
13   discoveries;

14   To constitute tribunals inferior to the Supreme Court;

15   To define and punish piracies and felonies committed on the high seas, and
16   offenses against the law of nations;

17   To declare war, grant letters of marque and reprisal, and make rules concerning
18   captures on land and water;

19   To raise and support armies, but no appropriation of money to that use shall be for
20   a longer term than two years;

21   To provide and maintain a navy;

22   To make rules for the government and regulation of the land and naval forces;

23   To provide for calling forth the militia to execute the laws of the union, suppress
24   insurrections and repel invasions;

25   To provide for organizing, arming, and disciplining, the militia, and for governing
26   such part of them as may be employed in the service of the United States, reserving
27   to the states respectively, the appointment of the officers, and the authority of
28   training the militia according to the discipline prescribed by Congress;

29   To exercise exclusive legislation in all cases whatsoever, over such District (not
30   exceeding ten miles square) as may, by cession of particular states, and the
31   acceptance of Congress, become the seat of the government of the United States,
32   and to exercise like authority over all places purchased by the consent of the

766

1 legislature of the state in which the same shall be, for the erection of forts,
2 magazines, arsenals, dockyards, and other needful buildings;—And

3 To make all laws which shall be necessary and proper for carrying into execution
4 the foregoing powers, and all other powers vested by this Constitution in the
5 government of the United States, or in any department or officer thereof.

## Article II

6

### Section 1.

7

8 The executive power shall be vested in a President of the United States of America.
9 He shall hold his office during the term of four years, and, together with the Vice
10 President, chosen for the same term, be elected, as follows:

11 * * *

12 Before he enter on the execution of his office, he shall take the following oath or
13 affirmation:—"I do solemnly swear (or affirm) that I will faithfully execute the
14 office of President of the United States, and will to the best of my ability, preserve,
15 protect and defend the Constitution of the United States."

### Section 2.

16

17 The President shall be commander in chief of the Army and Navy of the United
18 States, and of the militia of the several states, when called into the actual service of
19 the United States; he may require the opinion, in writing, of the principal officer in
20 each of the executive departments, upon any subject relating to the duties of their
21 respective offices, and he shall have power to grant reprieves and pardons for
22 offenses against the United States, except in cases of impeachment.

23 He shall have power, by and with the advice and consent of the Senate, to make
24 treaties, provided two thirds of the Senators present concur; and he shall
25 nominate, and by and with the advice and consent of the Senate, shall appoint
26 ambassadors, other public ministers and consuls, judges of the Supreme Court,
27 and all other officers of the United States, whose appointments are not herein
28 otherwise provided for, and which shall be established by law: but the Congress
29 may by law vest the appointment of such inferior officers, as they think proper, in
30 the President alone, in the courts of law, or in the heads of departments.

31 The President shall have power to fill up all vacancies that may happen during the
32 recess of the Senate, by granting commissions which shall expire at the end of their
33 next session.

### Section 3.

34

He shall from time to time give to the Congress information of the state of the union, and recommend to their consideration such measures as he shall judge necessary and expedient; he may, on extraordinary occasions, convene both Houses, or either of them, and in case of disagreement between them, with respect to the time of adjournment, he may adjourn them to such time as he shall think proper; he shall receive ambassadors and other public ministers; he shall take care that the laws be faithfully executed, and shall commission all the officers of the United States.

## Section 4.

The President, Vice President and all civil officers of the United States, shall be removed from office on impeachment for, and conviction of, treason, bribery, or other high crimes and misdemeanors.

## Article III

## Section 1.

The judicial power of the United States, shall be vested in one Supreme Court, and in such inferior courts as the Congress may from time to time ordain and establish. The judges, both of the supreme and inferior courts, shall hold their offices during good behaviour, and shall, at stated times, receive for their services, a compensation, which shall not be diminished during their continuance in office.

## Section 2.

The judicial power shall extend to all cases, in law and equity, arising under this Constitution, the laws of the United States, and treaties made, or which shall be made, under their authority;—to all cases affecting ambassadors, other public ministers and consuls;—to all cases of admiralty and maritime jurisdiction;—to controversies to which the United States shall be a party;—to controversies between two or more states;—between a state and citizens of another state;—between citizens of different states;—between citizens of the same state claiming lands under grants of different states, and between a state, or the citizens thereof, and foreign states, citizens or subjects.

In all cases affecting ambassadors, other public ministers and consuls, and those in which a state shall be party, the Supreme Court shall have original jurisdiction. In all the other cases before mentioned, the Supreme Court shall have appellate jurisdiction, both as to law and fact, with such exceptions, and under such regulations as the Congress shall make.

The trial of all crimes, except in cases of impeachment, shall be by jury; and such trial shall be held in the state where the said crimes shall have been committed;

but when not committed within any state, the trial shall be at such place or places as the Congress may by law have directed.

## Amendment V

No person shall be held to answer for a capital, or otherwise infamous crime, unless on a presentment or indictment of a grand jury, except in cases arising in the land or naval forces, or in the militia, when in actual service in time of war or public danger; nor shall any person be subject for the same offense to be twice put in jeopardy of life or limb; nor shall be compelled in any criminal case to be a witness against himself, nor be deprived of life, liberty, or property, without due process of law; nor shall private property be taken for public use, without just compensation.

## Amendment XIV

## Section 1.

All persons born or naturalized in the United States, and subject to the jurisdiction thereof, are citizens of the United States and of the state wherein they reside. No state shall make or enforce any law which shall abridge the privileges or immunities of citizens of the United States; nor shall any state deprive any person of life, liberty, or property, without due process of law; nor deny to any person within its jurisdiction the equal protection of the laws.

\* \* \*

# B. Selected Administrative Procedure Act Provisions

## 5 U.S. Code § 551. Definitions

For the purpose of this subchapter—

    (1) "agency" means each authority of the Government of the United States, whether or not it is within or subject to review by another agency, but does not include—

    (A) the Congress;

    (B) the courts of the United States;

    (C) the governments of the territories or possessions of the United States;

    (D) the government of the District of Columbia;

    or except as to the requirements of section 552 of this title—

| | | |
|---|---|---|
| 1 | (E) | agencies composed of representatives of the parties or of |
| 2 | | representatives of organizations of the parties to the disputes |
| 3 | | determined by them; |

| | | |
|---|---|---|
| 4 | (F) | courts martial and military commissions; |

| | | |
|---|---|---|
| 5 | (G) | military authority exercised in the field in time of war or in occupied |
| 6 | | territory; or |

| | | |
|---|---|---|
| 7 | (H) | functions conferred by sections 1738, 1739, 1743, and 1744 of title 12; |
| 8 | | subchapter II of chapter 471 of title 49; or sections 1884, 1891–1902, |
| 9 | | and former section 1641(b)(2), of title 50, appendix; |

| | | |
|---|---|---|
| 10 | (2) | "person" includes an individual, partnership, corporation, association, or |
| 11 | | public or private organization other than an agency; |

| | | |
|---|---|---|
| 12 | (3) | "party" includes a person or agency named or admitted as a party, or |
| 13 | | properly seeking and entitled as of right to be admitted as a party, in an |
| 14 | | agency proceeding, and a person or agency admitted by an agency as a |
| 15 | | party for limited purposes; |

| | | |
|---|---|---|
| 16 | (4) | "rule" means the whole or a part of an agency statement of general or |
| 17 | | particular applicability and future effect designed to implement, |
| 18 | | interpret, or prescribe law or policy or describing the organization, |
| 19 | | procedure, or practice requirements of an agency and includes the |
| 20 | | approval or prescription for the future of rates, wages, corporate or |
| 21 | | financial structures or reorganizations thereof, prices, facilities, |
| 22 | | appliances, services or allowances therefor or of valuations, costs, or |
| 23 | | accounting, or practices bearing on any of the foregoing; |

| | | |
|---|---|---|
| 24 | (5) | "rule making" means agency process for formulating, amending, or |
| 25 | | repealing a rule; |

| | | |
|---|---|---|
| 26 | (6) | "order" means the whole or a part of a final disposition, whether |
| 27 | | affirmative, negative, injunctive, or declaratory in form, of an agency in a |
| 28 | | matter other than rule making but including licensing; |

| | | |
|---|---|---|
| 29 | (7) | "adjudication" means agency process for the formulation of an order; |

| | | |
|---|---|---|
| 30 | (8) | "license" includes the whole or a part of an agency permit, certificate, |
| 31 | | approval, registration, charter, membership, statutory exemption or |
| 32 | | other form of permission; |

| | | |
|---|---|---|
| 33 | (9) | "licensing" includes agency process respecting the grant, renewal, denial, |
| 34 | | revocation, suspension, annulment, withdrawal, limitation, amendment, |
| 35 | | modification, or conditioning of a license; |

1     (10)  "sanction" includes the whole or a part of an agency—

2        (A)  prohibition, requirement, limitation, or other condition affecting the
3             freedom of a person;

4        (B)  withholding of relief;

5        (C)  imposition of penalty or fine;

6        (D)  destruction, taking, seizure, or withholding of property;

7        (E)  assessment of damages, reimbursement, restitution, compensation,
8             costs, charges, or fees;

9        (F)  requirement, revocation, or suspension of a license; or

10       (G)  taking other compulsory or restrictive action;

11     (11)  "relief" includes the whole or a part of an agency—

12        (A)  grant of money, assistance, license, authority, exemption, exception,
13             privilege, or remedy;

14        (B)  recognition of a claim, right, immunity, privilege, exemption, or
15             exception; or

16        (C)  taking of other action on the application or petition of, and beneficial
17             to, a person;

18     (12)  "agency proceeding" means an agency process as defined by paragraphs
19         (5), (7), and (9) of this section;

20     (13)  "agency action" includes the whole or a part of an agency rule, order,
21         license, sanction, relief, or the equivalent or denial thereof, or failure to
22         act; and

23     (14)  "*ex parte* communication" means an oral or written communication not
24         on the public record with respect to which reasonable prior notice to all
25         parties is not given, but it shall not include requests for status reports on
26         any matter or proceeding covered by this subchapter.

27  **5 U.S. Code § 553. Rule making**

28     (a)  This section applies, according to the provisions thereof, except to the
29        extent that there is involved—

30     (1)  a military or foreign affairs function of the United States; or

(2)    a matter relating to agency management or personnel or to public property, loans, grants, benefits, or contracts.

(b)    General notice of proposed rule making shall be published in the Federal Register, unless persons subject thereto are named and either personally served or otherwise have actual notice thereof in accordance with law. The notice shall include—

    (1)    a statement of the time, place, and nature of public rule making proceedings;

    (2)    reference to the legal authority under which the rule is proposed; and

    (3)    either the terms or substance of the proposed rule or a description of the subjects and issues involved.

Except when notice or hearing is required by statute, this subsection does not apply—

    (A)    to interpretative rules, general statements of policy, or rules of agency organization, procedure, or practice; or

    (B)    when the agency for good cause finds (and incorporates the finding and a brief statement of reasons therefor in the rules issued) that notice and public procedure thereon are impracticable, unnecessary, or contrary to the public interest.

(c)    After notice required by this section, the agency shall give interested persons an opportunity to participate in the rule making through submission of written data, views, or arguments with or without opportunity for oral presentation. After consideration of the relevant matter presented, the agency shall incorporate in the rules adopted a concise general statement of their basis and purpose. When rules are required by statute to be made on the record after opportunity for an agency hearing, sections 556 and 557 of this title apply instead of this subsection.

(d)    The required publication or service of a substantive rule shall be made not less than 30 days before its effective date, except—

    (1)    a substantive rule which grants or recognizes an exemption or relieves a restriction;

    (2)    interpretative rules and statements of policy; or

    (3)    as otherwise provided by the agency for good cause found and published with the rule.

(e)  Each agency shall give an interested person the right to petition for the issuance, amendment, or repeal of a rule.

## 5 U.S. Code § 554. Adjudications

(a) This section applies, according to the provisions thereof, in every case of adjudication required by statute to be determined on the record after opportunity for an agency hearing, except to the extent that there is involved—

(1)  a matter subject to a subsequent trial of the law and the facts de novo in a court;

(2)  the selection or tenure of an employee, except a [1] administrative law judge appointed under section 3105 of this title;

(3)  proceedings in which decisions rest solely on inspections, tests, or elections;

(4)  the conduct of military or foreign affairs functions;

(5)  cases in which an agency is acting as an agent for a court; or

(6)  the certification of worker representatives.

(b)  Persons entitled to notice of an agency hearing shall be timely informed of—

(1)  the time, place, and nature of the hearing;

(2)  the legal authority and jurisdiction under which the hearing is to be held; and

(3)  the matters of fact and law asserted.

When private persons are the moving parties, other parties to the proceeding shall give prompt notice of issues controverted in fact or law; and in other instances agencies may by rule require responsive pleading. In fixing the time and place for hearings, due regard shall be had for the convenience and necessity of the parties or their representatives.

(c)  The agency shall give all interested parties opportunity for—

(1)  the submission and consideration of facts, arguments, offers of settlement, or proposals of adjustment when time, the nature of the proceeding, and the public interest permit; and

(2)  to the extent that the parties are unable so to determine a controversy by consent, hearing and decision on notice and in accordance with sections 556 and 557 of this title.

(d)  The employee who presides at the reception of evidence pursuant to section 556 of this title shall make the recommended decision or initial decision required by section 557 of this title, unless he becomes unavailable to the agency. Except to the extent required for the disposition of *ex parte* matters as authorized by law, such an employee may not—

(1)  consult a person or party on a fact in issue, unless on notice and opportunity for all parties to participate; or

(2)  be responsible to or subject to the supervision or direction of an employee or agent engaged in the performance of investigative or prosecuting functions for an agency.

An employee or agent engaged in the performance of investigative or prosecuting functions for an agency in a case may not, in that or a factually related case, participate or advise in the decision, recommended decision, or agency review pursuant to section 557 of this title, except as witness or counsel in public proceedings. This subsection does not apply—

(A)  in determining applications for initial licenses;

(B)  to proceedings involving the validity or application of rates, facilities, or practices of public utilities or carriers; or

(C)  to the agency or a member or members of the body comprising the agency.

(e)  The agency, with like effect as in the case of other orders, and in its sound discretion, may issue a declaratoryorder to terminate a controversy or remove uncertainty.

## 5 U.S. Code § 555. Ancillary matters

(a)  This section applies, according to the provisions thereof, except as otherwise provided by this subchapter.

(b)  A person compelled to appear in person before an agency or representative thereof is entitled to be accompanied, represented, and advised by counsel or, if permitted by the agency, by other qualified representative. A party is entitled to appear in person or by or with counsel or other duly qualified representative in an agency proceeding. So far as the orderly conduct of public business permits, an interested person may appear before an agency or its responsible employees for the presentation, adjustment, or determination of an issue, request, or controversy in a proceeding, whether interlocutory, summary, or otherwise, or in connection with anagency function. With due regard for the convenience and necessity of the parties or their representatives and within a reasonable time, each agency shall proceed to conclude a matter presented to it. This subsection does not grant or deny a person who is not a lawyer the right to appear for or represent others before an agency or in an agency proceeding.

(c) Process, requirement of a report, inspection, or other investigative act or demand may not be issued, made, or enforced except as authorized by law. A person compelled to submit data or evidence is entitled to retain or, on payment of lawfully prescribed costs, procure a copy or transcript thereof, except that in a nonpublic investigatory proceeding the witness may for good cause be limited to inspection of the official transcript of his testimony.

(d) Agency subpenas authorized by law shall be issued to a party on request and, when required by rules of procedure, on a statement or showing of general relevance and reasonable scope of the evidence sought. On contest, the court shall sustain the subpena or similar process or demand to the extent that it is found to be in accordance with law. In a proceeding for enforcement, the court shall issue an order requiring the appearance of the witness or the production of the evidence or data within a reasonable time under penalty of punishment for contempt in case of contumacious failure to comply.

(e) Prompt notice shall be given of the denial in whole or in part of a written application, petition, or other request of an interested person made in connection with any agency proceeding. Except in affirming a prior denial or when the denial is self-explanatory, the notice shall be accompanied by a brief statement of the grounds for denial.

## 5 U.S. Code § 556. Hearings; presiding employees; powers and duties; burden of proof; evidence; record as basis of decision

(a) This section applies, according to the provisions thereof, to hearings required by section 553 or 554 of this title to be conducted in accordance with this section.

(b) There shall preside at the taking of evidence—

(1) the agency;

(2) one or more members of the body which comprises the agency; or

(3)    one or more administrative law judges appointed under section 3105 of this title.

This subchapter does not supersede the conduct of specified classes of proceedings, in whole or in part, by or before boards or other employees specially provided for by or designated under statute. The functions of presiding employees and of employees participating in decisions in accordance with section 557 of this titleshall be conducted in an impartial manner. A presiding or participating employee may at any time disqualify himself. On the filing in good faith of a timely and sufficient affidavit of personal bias or other disqualification of a presiding or participating employee, the agency shall determine the matter as a part of the record and decision in the case.

(c)    Subject to published rules of the agency and within its powers, employees presiding at hearings may—

(1)    administer oaths and affirmations;

(2)    issue subpenas authorized by law;

(3)    rule on offers of proof and receive relevant evidence;

(4)    take depositions or have depositions taken when the ends of justice would be served;

(5)    regulate the course of the hearing;

(6)    hold conferences for the settlement or simplification of the issues by consent of the parties or by the use of alternative means of dispute resolution as provided in subchapter IV of this chapter;

(7)    inform the parties as to the availability of one or more alternative means of dispute resolution, and encourage use of such methods;

(8)    require the attendance at any conference held pursuant to paragraph (6) of at least one representative of each party who has authority to negotiate concerning resolution of issues in controversy;

(9)    dispose of procedural requests or similar matters;

(10)    make or recommend decisions in accordance with section 557 of this title; and

(11)    take other action authorized by agency rule consistent with this subchapter.

(d) Except as otherwise provided by statute, the proponent of a rule or order has the burden of proof. Any oral or documentary evidence may be received, but the agency as a matter of policy shall provide for the exclusion of irrelevant, immaterial, or unduly repetitious evidence. A sanction may not be imposed or rule or order issued except on consideration of the whole record or those parts thereof cited by a party and supported by and in accordance with the reliable, probative, and substantial evidence. The agency may, to the extent consistent with the interests of justice and the policy of the underlying statutes administered by the agency, consider a violation of section 557(d) of this title sufficient grounds for a decision adverse to a party who has knowingly committed such violation or knowingly caused such violation to occur. A party is entitled to present his case or defense by oral or documentary evidence, to submit rebuttal evidence, and to conduct such cross-examination as may be required for a full and true disclosure of the facts. In rule making or determining claims for money or benefits or applications for initial licenses an agency may, when a party will not be prejudiced thereby, adopt procedures for the submission of all or part of the evidence in written form.

(e) The transcript of testimony and exhibits, together with all papers and requests filed in the proceeding, constitutes the exclusive record for decision in accordance with section 557 of this title and, on payment of lawfully prescribed costs, shall be made available to the parties. When an agency decision rests on official notice of a material fact not appearing in the evidence in the record, a party is entitled, on timely request, to an opportunity to show the contrary.

## 5 U.S. Code § 557. Initial decisions; conclusiveness; review by agency; submissions by parties; contents of decisions; record

(a) This section applies, according to the provisions thereof, when a hearing is required to be conducted in accordance with section 556 of this title.

(b) When the agency did not preside at the reception of the evidence, the presiding employee or, in cases not subject to section 554(d) of this title, an employee qualified to preside at hearings pursuant to section 556 of this title, shall initially decide the case unless the agency requires, either in specific cases or by general rule, the entire record to be certified to it for decision. When the presiding employee makes an initial decision, that decision then becomes the decision of the agency without further proceedings unless there is an appeal to, or review on motion of, the agency within time provided by rule. On appeal from or review of the initial decision, the agency has all the powers which it would have in making the initial decision except as it may limit the issues on notice or by rule. When the agency makes the decision without having presided at the reception of the evidence, the presiding employee or an employee qualified to preside at hearings pursuant to section 556 of this title shall first recommend a decision, except that in rule making or determining applications for initial licenses—

(1) instead thereof the agency may issue a tentative decision or one of its responsible employees may recommend a decision; or

(2) this procedure may be omitted in a case in which the agency finds on the record that due and timely execution of its functions imperatively and unavoidably so requires.

(c) Before a recommended, initial, or tentative decision, or a decision on agency review of the decision of subordinate employees, the parties are entitled to a reasonable opportunity to submit for the consideration of the employees participating in the decisions—

(1) proposed findings and conclusions; or

(2) exceptions to the decisions or recommended decisions of subordinate employees or to tentative agency decisions; and

(3) supporting reasons for the exceptions or proposed findings or conclusions.

The record shall show the ruling on each finding, conclusion, or exception presented. All decisions, including initial, recommended, and tentative decisions, are a part of the record and shall include a statement of—

(A) findings and conclusions, and the reasons or basis therefor, on all the material issues of fact, law, or discretion presented on the record; and

(B) the appropriate rule, order, sanction, relief, or denial thereof.

(d)(1) In any agency proceeding which is subject to subsection (a) of this section, except to the extent required for the disposition of *ex parte* matters as authorized by law—

(A) no interested person outside the agency shall make or knowingly cause to be made to any member of the body comprising the agency, administrative law judge, or other employee who is or may reasonably be expected to be involved in the decisional process of the proceeding, an *ex parte* communication relevant to the merits of the proceeding;

(B) no member of the body comprising the agency, administrative law judge, or other employee who is or may reasonably be expected to be involved in the decisional process of the proceeding, shall make or knowingly cause to be made to any interested person outside the agency an *ex parte* communicationrelevant to the merits of the proceeding;

(C) a member of the body comprising the agency, administrative law judge, or other employee who is or may reasonably be expected to be involved in the decisional process of such proceeding who receives, or who makes or knowingly causes to be made, a communication prohibited by this subsection shall place on the public record of the proceeding:

   (i) all such written communications;

   (ii) memoranda stating the substance of all such oral communications; and

   (iii) all written responses, and memoranda stating the substance of all oral responses, to the materials described in clauses (i) and (ii) of this subparagraph;

(D) upon receipt of a communication knowingly made or knowingly caused to be made by a party in violation of this subsection, the agency, administrative law judge, or other employee presiding at the hearing may, to the extent consistent with the interests of justice and the policy of the underlying statutes, require the party to show cause why his claim or interest in the proceeding should not be dismissed, denied, disregarded, or otherwise adversely affected on account of such violation; and

(E) the prohibitions of this subsection shall apply beginning at such time as the agency may designate, but in no case shall they begin to apply later than the time at which a proceeding is noticed for hearing unless the person responsible for the communication has knowledge that it will be noticed, in which case the prohibitions shall apply beginning at the time of his acquisition of such knowledge.

(2) This subsection does not constitute authority to withhold information from Congress.

## 5 U.S. Code § 558. Imposition of sanctions; determination of applications for licenses; suspension, revocation, and expiration of licenses

(a) This section applies, according to the provisions thereof, to the exercise of a power or authority.

(b)    A sanction may not be imposed or a substantive rule or order issued except within jurisdiction delegated to theagency and as authorized by law.

(c)    When application is made for a license required by law, the agency, with due regard for the rights and privileges of all the interested parties or adversely affected persons and within a reasonable time, shall set and complete proceedings required to be conducted in accordance with sections 556 and 557 of this title or other proceedings required by law and shall make its decision. Except in cases of willfulness or those in which public health, interest, or safety requires otherwise, the withdrawal, suspension, revocation, or annulment of a license is lawful only if, before the institution of agency proceedings therefor, the licensee has been given—

    (1)    notice by the agency in writing of the facts or conduct which may warrant the action; and

    (2)    opportunity to demonstrate or achieve compliance with all lawful requirements.

    When the licensee has made timely and sufficient application for a renewal or a new license in accordance with agency rules, a license with reference to an activity of a continuing nature does not expire until the application has been finally determined by the agency.

## 5 U.S. Code § 559. Effect on other laws; effect of subsequent statute

This subchapter, chapter 7, and sections 1305, 3105, 3344, 4301(2) (E), 5372, and 7521 of this title, and the provisions of section 5335(a)(B) of this title that relate to administrative law judges, do not limit or repeal additional requirements imposed by statute or otherwise recognized by law. Except as otherwise required by law, requirements or privileges relating to evidence or procedure apply equally to agencies and persons. Each agency is granted the authority necessary to comply with the requirements of this subchapter through the issuance of rules or otherwise. Subsequent statute may not be held to supersede or modify this subchapter, chapter 7, sections 1305, 3105, 3344, 4301(2)(E), 5372, or 7521 of this title, or the provisions of section 5335(a)    (B) of this title that relate to administrative law judges, except to the extent that it does so expressly.

## 5 U.S. Code § 701. Application; definitions

(a)    This chapter applies, according to the provisions thereof, except to the extent that—

    (1)    statutes preclude judicial review; or

1   (2)   agency action is committed to agency discretion by law.

2   (b)   For the purpose of this chapter—

3   (1)   "agency" means each authority of the Government of the United States,
4          whether or not it is within or subject to review by another agency, but
5          does not include—

6   (A)   the Congress;

7   (B)   the courts of the United States;

8   (C)   the governments of the territories or possessions of the United States;

9   (D)   the government of the District of Columbia;

10  (E)   agencies composed of representatives of the parties or of
11        representatives of organizations of the parties to the disputes
12        determined by them;

13  (F)   courts martial and military commissions;

14  (G)   military authority exercised in the field in time of war or in occupied
15        territory; or

16  (H)   functions conferred by sections 1738, 1739, 1743, and 1744 of title 12;
17        subchapter II of chapter 471 of title 49; or sections 1884, 1891–1902,
18        and former section 1641(b)(2), of title 50, appendix;  and

19  (2)   "person", "rule", "order", "license", "sanction", "relief", and "agency
20        action" have the meanings given them by section 551 of this title.

21  ## 5 U.S. Code § 702. Right of review

22  A person suffering legal wrong because of agency action, or adversely affected or
23  aggrieved by agency action within the meaning of a relevant statute, is entitled to
24  judicial review thereof. An action in a court of the United States seekingrelief other
25  than money damages and stating a claim that an agency or an officer or employee
26  thereof acted or failed to act in an official capacity or under color of legal authority
27  shall not be dismissed nor relief therein be denied on the ground that it is against
28  the United States or that the United States is an indispensable party. The United
29  States may be named as a defendant in any such action, and a judgment or decree
30  may be entered against the United States: Provided, That any mandatory or
31  injunctive decree shall specify the Federal officer or officers (by name or by title),
32  and their successors in office, personally responsible for compliance. Nothing
33  herein (1) affects other limitations on judicial review or the power or duty of the
34  court to dismiss any action or deny relief on any other appropriate legal or

1    equitable ground; or (2) confers authority to grant relief if any other statute that
2    grants consent to suit expressly or impliedly forbids the relief which is sought.

## 5 U.S. Code § 703. Form and venue of proceeding

The form of proceeding for judicial review is the special statutory review
proceeding relevant to the subject matter in a court specified by statute or, in the
absence or inadequacy thereof, any applicable form of legal action, including
actions for declaratory judgments or writs of prohibitory or mandatory injunction
or habeas corpus, in a court of competent jurisdiction. If no special statutory
review proceeding is applicable, the action for judicial review may be brought
against the United States, the agency by its official title, or the appropriate officer.
Except to the extent that prior, adequate, and exclusive opportunity for judicial
review is provided by law, agency action is subject to judicial review in civil or
criminal proceedings for judicial enforcement.

## 5 U.S. Code § 704. Actions reviewable

Agency action made reviewable by statute and final agency action for which there
is no other adequate remedy in a court are subject to judicial review. A preliminary,
procedural, or intermediate agency action or ruling not directly reviewable is
subject to review on the review of the final agency action. Except as otherwise
expressly required by statute, agency action otherwise final is final for the purposes
of this section whether or not there has been presented or determined an
application for a declaratory order, for any form of reconsideration, or, unless the
agency otherwise requires by rule and provides that the action meanwhile is
inoperative, for an appeal to superior agency authority.

## 5 U.S. Code § 705. Relief pending review

When an agency finds that justice so requires, it may postpone the effective date of
action taken by it, pending judicial review. On such conditions as may be required
and to the extent necessary to prevent irreparable injury, the reviewing court,
including the court to which a case may be taken on appeal from or on application
for certiorari or other writ to a reviewing court, may issue all necessary and
appropriate process to postpone the effective date of an agency action or to
preserve status or rights pending conclusion of the review proceedings.

## 5 U.S. Code § 706. Scope of review

To the extent necessary to decision and when presented, the reviewing court shall
decide all relevant questions of law, interpret constitutional and statutory
provisions, and determine the meaning or applicability of the terms of an agency
action. The reviewing court shall—

1      (1)    compel agency action unlawfully withheld or unreasonably delayed; and

2      (2)    hold unlawful and set aside agency action, findings, and conclusions
3             found to be—

4        (A)    arbitrary, capricious, an abuse of discretion, or otherwise not in
5              accordance with law;

6        (B)    contrary to constitutional right, power, privilege, or immunity;

7        (C)    in excess of statutory jurisdiction, authority, or limitations, or short of
8              statutory right;

9        (D)    without observance of procedure required by law;

10       (E)    unsupported by substantial evidence in a case subject to sections 556
11             and 557 of this title or otherwise reviewed on the record of an agency
12             hearing provided by statute; or

13       (F)    unwarranted by the facts to the extent that the facts are subject to trial
14             de novo by the reviewing court.

15          In making the foregoing determinations, the court shall review the
16          whole record or those parts of it cited by a party, and due account shall
17          be taken of the rule of prejudicial error.

18

19

20

Made in United States
North Haven, CT
03 January 2024

46962462R00435